the Unofficial Guide® to Walt Disney World® 2010

The importance of arriving early. Fantasyland at 9 a.m. . . .

at 11 a.m. . . .

and at 1 p.m. . . .

Attractions with FASTPASS display both the traditional standby wait time and the time at which a FASTPASS obtained now will be valid.

A typical FASTPASS kiosk. Insert your park ticket face-up in the top slot. Your FASTPASS is printed and dropped in the bottom bin.

Stroller-rental locations are clearly marked and found at the front of each theme park.

Single- and double-wide strollers compared

Portion sizes at Disney restaurants are large, even by American standards. A regular Disney hamburger is about 30% bigger than a regular McDonald's hamburger.

(left) If you are flying to Orlando, the check-in desk for Disney's Magical Express bus service is located on the airport's car-rental floor.
(right) One of Disney's Magical Express buses

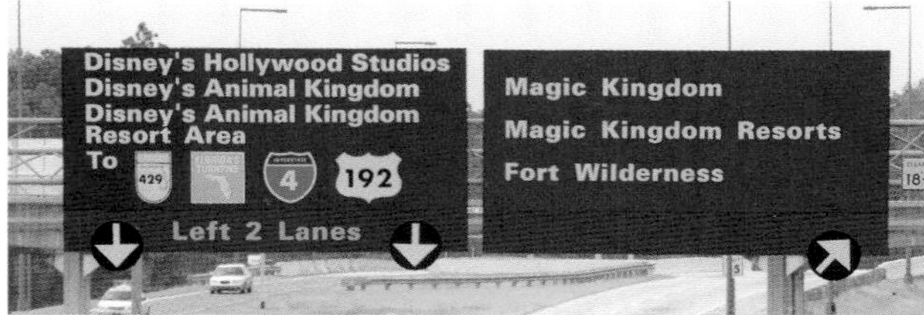

Disney's purple road signs provide directions to theme parks and hotels. If driving to your resort it is important to remember to which resort area it belongs.

The Transportation and Ticket Center offers monorail and ferry access to the Magic Kingdom.

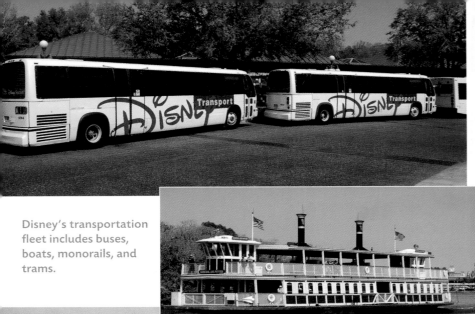

Disney's transportation fleet includes buses, boats, monorails, and trams.

Disney's value resorts are colorfully themed buildings designed to accommodate several thousand guests. All doors open to exterior hallways.

Value-resort pools are built to handle a large number of guests.

All value resorts have a food court similar to something you'd see at a local mall.

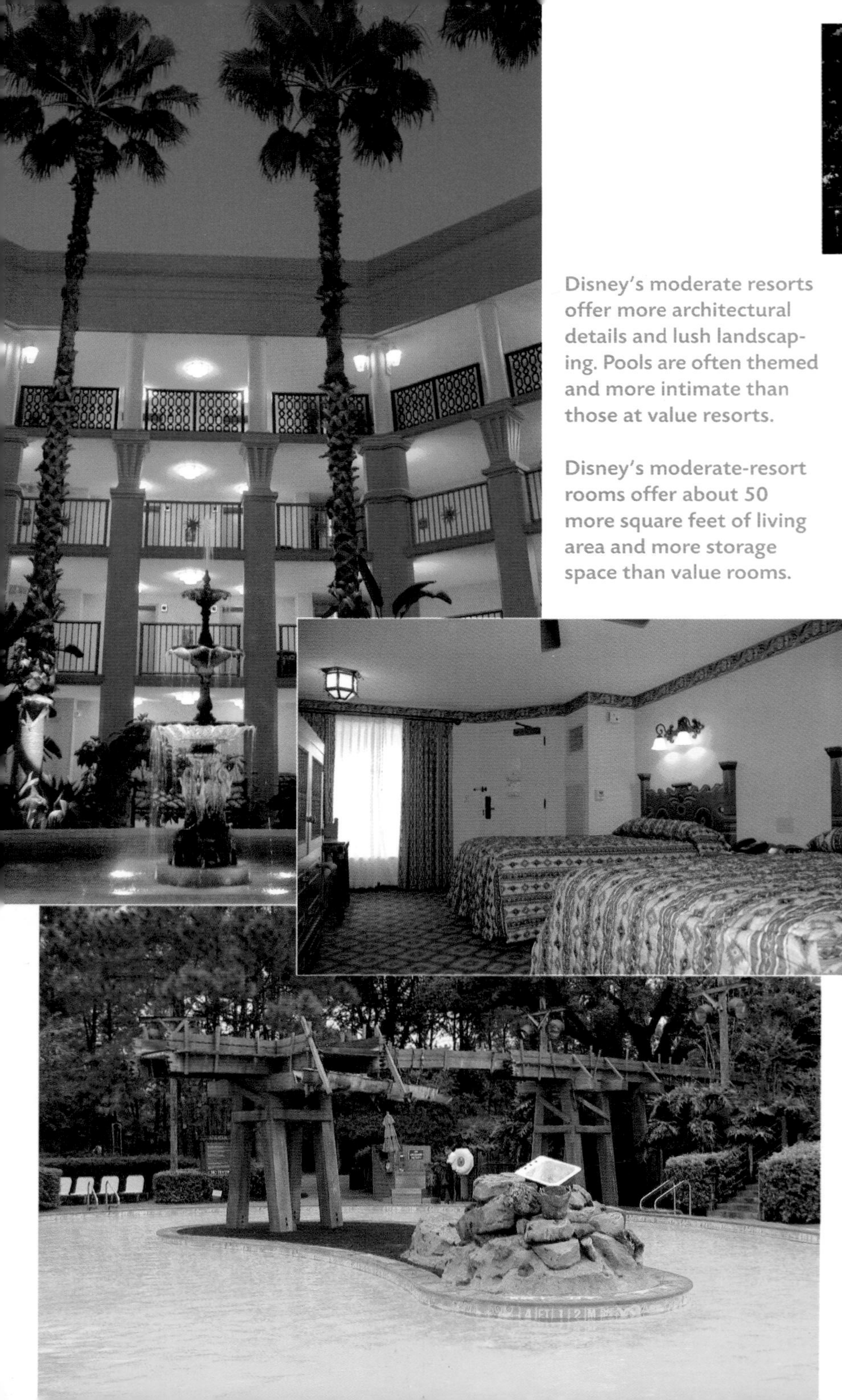

Disney's moderate resorts offer more architectural details and lush landscaping. Pools are often themed and more intimate than those at value resorts.

Disney's moderate-resort rooms offer about 50 more square feet of living area and more storage space than value rooms.

Disney's deluxe resorts are the best-themed hotels you'll find. Lobby areas continue the theme, with many creating dramatic interior spaces.

The Grand Floridian's pool is the size of a small lake, but landscaping and architecture keep it from appearing out of scale.

The Contemporary Resort's rooms are the best on Disney property, with the bathrooms being particularly well designed.

MONGALA MILLIE

(clockwise from top right) Electric icicles decorate Cinderella Castle during Christmas.

Fantasyland's Mad Tea Party—Does any adult look happy?

Taking a spin on Tomorrowland's Astro Orbiter.

Adventureland's Jungle Cruise begins another journey.

Airplane meets water tower at Toontown's Barnstormer, a child-friendly roller coaster.

(clockwise from top right)

Think your commute to work is bad? Jumping between trucks at the *Lights! Motors! Action! Extreme Stunt Show*.

The Osborne Family Spectacle of Lights is either a warning or an inspiration to Christmas decoration do-it-yourselfers.

Recently renovated, Spaceship Earth remains one of Disney World's most popular attractions.

Epcot's *IllumiNations* is arguably Walt Disney World's best nighttime fireworks show.

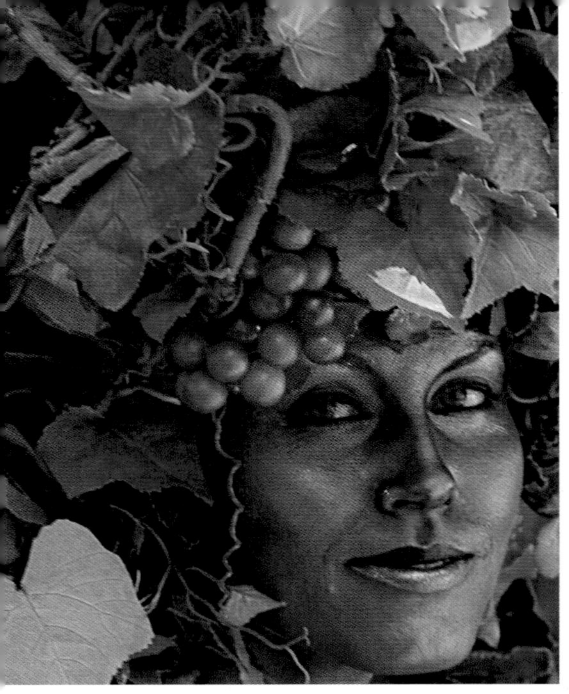

(left) Keep an eye out for the performer DeVine hanging around the lush walkway between Asia and Africa.

(right) Getting soaked on Asia's Kali River Rapids

(lower right) The Tree of Life's elaborately detailed animal carvings

A sample of animals from the Kilimanjaro Safaris. Etiquette note: it's apparently impolite to yell "Them's good eatin'!" at any point in the ride.

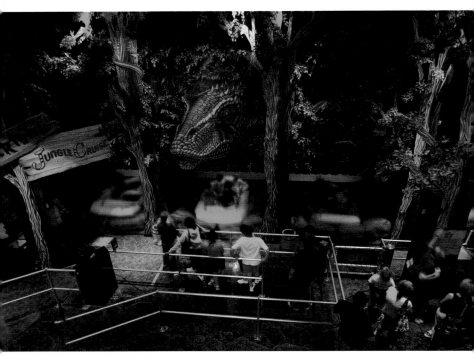

DisneyQuest offers five floors of virtual-reality and motion-simulator attractions in an indoor setting.

Oversize plastic sculpture abounds outside the LEGO Imagination Center at Downtown Disney.

THE *unofficial* GUIDE® TO Walt Disney World®

2010

ALSO AVAILABLE FROM JOHN WILEY & SONS, INC.:

Beyond Disney: The Unofficial Guide to Universal, SeaWorld, and the Best of Central Florida

Mini-Mickey: The Pocket-Sized Unofficial Guide to Walt Disney World

The Unofficial Guide Color Companion to Walt Disney World

The Unofficial Guide to California with Kids

The Unofficial Guide to Chicago

The Unofficial Guide to Cruises

The Unofficial Guide to Disneyland

The Unofficial Guide to Disneyland Paris *(John Wiley & Sons UK)*

The Unofficial Guide to Hawaii

The Unofficial Guide to Las Vegas

The Unofficial Guide to Maui

The Unofficial Guide to Mexico's Best Beach Resorts

The Unofficial Guide to New Orleans

The Unofficial Guide to New York City

The Unofficial Guide to Paris

The Unofficial Guide to San Francisco

The Unofficial Guide to Walt Disney World for Grown-Ups

The Unofficial Guide to Washington, D.C.

THE *unofficial* GUIDE® TO Walt Disney World®

2010

BOB SEHLINGER *with* LEN TESTA

(Walt Disney World® is officially known as Walt Disney World® Resort.)

WILEY

Please note that prices fluctuate in the course of time and that travel information changes under the impact of many factors that influence the travel industry. We therefore suggest that you write or call ahead for confirmation when making your travel plans. Every effort has been made to ensure the accuracy of information throughout this book, and the contents of this publication are believed to be correct at the time of printing. Nevertheless, the publishers cannot accept responsibility for errors or omissions, for changes in details given in this guide, or for the consequences of any reliance on the information provided by the same. Assessments of attractions and so forth are based upon the authors' own experiences; therefore, descriptions given in this guide necessarily contain an element of subjective opinion, which may not reflect the publisher's opinion or dictate a reader's own experience on another occasion. Readers are invited to write the publisher with ideas, comments, and suggestions for future editions.

Published by:
John Wiley & Sons, Inc.
111 River Street
Hoboken, NJ 07030-5774

Produced by Menasha Ridge Press

Cover design by Michael J. Freeland

Interior design by Vertigo Design

For information on our other products and services or to obtain technical support, please contact our Customer Care Department within the United States at 800-762-2974, outside the United States at 317-572-3993, or by fax at 317-572-4002.

John Wiley & Sons, Inc., also publishes its books in a variety of electronic formats. Some content that appears in print may not be available in electronic formats.

ISBN 978-0-470-46026-9

Manufactured in the United States of America

5 4 3 2

CONTENTS

LIST *of* MAPS

INTRODUCTION

WHY "UNOFFICIAL"?

DECLARATION OF INDEPENDENCE

THE AUTHORS AND RESEARCHERS of this guide specifically and categorically declare that they are and always have been totally independent of the Walt Disney Company, Inc.; of Disneyland, Inc.; of Walt Disney World, Inc.; and of any and all other members of the Disney corporate family not listed.

The material in this guide originated with the authors and researchers and has not been reviewed, edited, or approved by the Walt Disney Company, Inc.; Disneyland, Inc.; or Walt Disney World, Inc.

This guidebook represents the first comprehensive *critical* appraisal of Walt Disney World. Its purpose is to provide the reader with the information necessary to tour Walt Disney World with the greatest efficiency and economy and with the least hassle.

In this guide, we represent and serve you. If a restaurant serves bad food, or a gift item is overpriced, or a ride isn't worth the wait, we say so, and in the process we hope to make your visit more fun and rewarding.

DANCE TO THE MUSIC

A DANCE HAS A BEGINNING and an end. But when you're dancing, you're not concerned about getting to the end or where on the dance floor you might wind up. In other words, you're totally in the moment. That's the way you should be on your Walt Disney World vacation.

You may feel a bit of pressure concerning your vacation. Vacations, after all, are very special events, and expensive ones to boot. So you work hard to make your vacation the best that it can be. Planning and organizing are essential to a successful Walt Disney World vacation, but if they become your focus, you won't be able to hear the music and enjoy the dance.

So think of us as your dancing coach. We'll teach you the steps to the dance in advance so that when you're on vacation and the music plays, you will dance with effortless grace and ease.

THE IMPORTANCE OF BEING GOOFY

ONE EVENING NOT LONG AGO, a confidential meeting took place at a nondescript community center. . . .

"Hi, I'm George. I want to welcome all of you to our Tuesday Substance Problems Anonymous meeting. I see some new faces. Please know that you're among friends and that we're all here to help and support each other."

One of those new faces stood out from the others like a sore thumb—or, rather, a *green* thumb.

"You, sir," George intoned, "would you like to introduce yourself and tell us why you're here?"

"Hi, I'm Peter, and my whole life is in turmoil."

"What substance is causing you problems, Peter?"

"This is really hard for me, George. I've never talked about this before, but I'm hooked on pixie dust."

One of the regulars broke in. "Dude, you must have that confused with something else. Oops, sorry, forgot to introduce myself. I'm Jack."

"No, Jack, it's pixie dust," Peter replied. "I don't know what it is chemically, but I can't function without it."

"Like, what happens when you use it?" Jack queried.

"Hmm, let me think. . . . the last time I used it, I flew around the moon three times."

"No, that's the other stuff for sure, dude. One time I took it and flew to Venus, Neptune, *and* Detroit!"

"Jack, I'm not saying you don't know your stuff, but I don't think we're talking about the same thing."

"Well, where do you buy this pixie dust?"

"From a tiny little woman. And I don't buy it—she gives it to me."

"Wow, that's totally amazing, dude!"

A new voice spoke up. "Hi, I'm Morris. Peter, does your, um, *outfit* have anything to do with your problem? Or are you in a play or something?"

"No, I'm not in a play. Actually, this is my work uniform."

"A green jumpsuit, green tights, and a green hat with a feather in it?"

"Well, I get some funny looks at Red Lobster and down at the bowling alley, but I've gotten used to it. Here's the worst part, though—my employer, who makes me wear this getup, also requires that I use pixie dust on the job."

"Oh, that's not good. What exactly do you do at work, Peter?"

"Well, I've got a long commute, but once I get there I fight pirates and rescue lost boys."

"Um, all righty, then . . . where exactly is this place?"

"If you're flying, head for the second star to the right and keep straight on till morning."

"Hi, I'm Doris," chimed in another member of the group. "Your story really resonates with me, Peter. I used to work at a dry cleaners where everyone was lit up all the time. I couldn't get clean—no pun intended—till I ditched the job. Wherever you work, you've *gotta* get out of there."

"Where would I go? My skills are sort of specialized."

Another member said: "Hi, I'm Earl, and I'm in advertising. With those spiffy duds, you'd be perfect for a branding campaign I'm putting together for a peanut butter company. Whatcha think?"

"Well, Earl, you know, besides the pixie-dust thing, I've been fighting this same guy in a red overcoat for 50 years. Maybe a change would do me good. Can I get back to you by the end of the week?"

"*Fifty years*? You don't look a day over 14, kid. Sounds like you've got a lot of growing up to do."

"Don't I wish!"

And so it goes. . . .

What really makes writing about Walt Disney World fun is that the Disney people take everything so seriously. Day to day, they debate momentous decisions with far-ranging consequences: Will Goofy look swishy in a silver cape? Have we gone too far with the Little Mermaid's cleavage? At a time when the nation is concerned about the drug problem, should we have a dwarf named Dopey?

Unofficially, we think having a sense of humor is important. This guidebook has one, and it's probably necessary that you do, too—not to use this book, but to have the most fun possible at Walt Disney World. Think of the *Unofficial Guide* as a private trainer to help get your sense of humor in shape. It will help you understand the importance of being Goofy.

HONEY, I BLEW UP THE BOOK!

THE FIRST EDITION OF *The Unofficial Guide to Walt Disney World* was fewer than 200 pages, a mere shadow of its current size. Since that edition, Disney World has grown tremendously, adding Disney's Hollywood Studios and Animal Kingdom theme parks, the Downtown Disney and Disney's BoardWalk shopping and entertainment venues, swimming parks Typhoon Lagoon and Blizzard Beach, new attractions in all the parks, about 27,000 new hotel rooms, and the Wide World of Sports complex. The *Unofficial Guide* has grown to match this expansion (and, truth be told, the author has put on a little weight himself).

A mom from Streator, Illinois, was amazed by the size of the *Unofficial Guide,* writing not unsympathetically:

> *It had been ten years since we have been to WDW and I was shocked by how the size of your book grew. After going, it's surprising that it is so small.*

We have no idea where it will all end. In 30 years we may be selling an alphabetized, 26-volume edition, handsomely packaged in an imitation-oak bookcase. In the meantime, we offer a qualified apology for the bulk of this edition. We know it may be too heavy to carry comfortably without the assistance of a handcart or Sherpa, but we defend the inclusion of all the information presented. Not every diner uses ketchup, A.1. sauce, or Tabasco, but it's nice to have all three on the table.

Concerning *Unofficial Guide* content, a mom from Vallejo, California, requests that we include a map of the Orlando airport.

Other reader ideas for new content included these suggestions:

I think your guide should have a list of attractions that provide (1) seats, (2) air-conditioning, and (3) at least 15 minutes off your feet.

I feel your Unofficial Guide *should include a claustrophobia rating for each attraction.*

I think a great idea would be to have a sturdier pull-out part, maybe a little separate booklet that would list full-service and counter-service restaurants in back of the touring plans.

I wish you would discuss restrooms more in the next edition. I found myself constantly searching for one.

We think you need a rating system regarding water [i.e., how wet you can expect to get on specific attractions]. *EW = Extreme Water; SW = Some Water; M = Mist.*

I'd like to see a more adult version of the one-day touring plan for the Magic Kingdom—one that does not include Fantasyland, the Country Bears, or Tom Sawyer's Island. Title this plan "I hate those damn bears!"

These comments are representative in that many of you would like more detailed coverage of one thing or another. Believe me, we've debated adding an airport map, as well as hundreds of other things, but haven't done so. Why? Because we don't have an infinite number of pages with which to work, and we felt other information was more important. You'd be amazed by the wealth of worthwhile material that doesn't make the cut. What if we put it all in? Well, the book would look more at home in your hayloft than on your bookshelf.

FOR THOSE WHO DESIRE ADDITIONAL INFORMATION

AS THOROUGH AS WE TRY TO MAKE *The Unofficial Guide to Walt Disney World,* there isn't sufficient space for all the tips and information that may be important and useful to certain readers. Thus, we've developed four additional Disney World guides, each designed to work in conjunction with this book. All provide information tailored to specific visitors. Although some tips from the "Big Book" (such as arriving early at the theme parks) are echoed or elaborated on in the other guides, most of the information is unique. In addition to *The Unofficial Guide to Walt Disney World,* these titles are available:

Beyond Disney: The Unofficial Guide to Universal, SeaWorld, and the Best of Central Florida, by Bob Sehlinger and Grant Rafter with Katie Brandon

Mini-Mickey: The Pocket-Sized Unofficial Guide to Walt Disney World, by Bob Sehlinger

The Unofficial Guide to Walt Disney World with Kids, by Bob Sehlinger and Liliane J. Opsomer with Len Testa

The Unofficial Guide to Walt Disney World without Kids, by Eve Zibart and Len Testa

Mini-Mickey is a portable *CliffsNotes*-style version of *The Unofficial Guide to Walt Disney World.* It distills information from this comprehensive guide to help short-stay or last-minute visitors decide quickly how to plan their limited hours at Disney World. *The Unofficial Guide to Walt Disney World without Kids* helps adults traveling without children make the most of their Disney vacation, while *The Unofficial Guide to Walt Disney World with Kids* presents planning and touring tips for a family vacation, along with more than 20 special touring plans for families that are not published anywhere else. Finally, *Beyond Disney* is a guide to non-Disney attractions, restaurants, outdoor recreation, and nightlife in Orlando and Central Florida. All these guides are available from John Wiley & Sons and at most bookstores.

THE DEATH OF SPONTANEITY

ONE OF OUR ALL-TIME FAVORITE LETTERS came from a man in Chapel Hill, North Carolina:

> *Your book reads like the operations plan for an amphibious landing: Go here, do this, proceed to Step 15. You must think that everyone is a hyperactive, type-A theme-park commando. What happened to the satisfaction of self-discovery or the joy of spontaneity? Next you will be telling us when to empty our bladders.*

As it happens, *Unofficial Guide* researchers are a pretty existential crew. We are big on self-discovery if the activity is walking in the woods or watching birds. Some of us are able to improvise jazz, and others can whip up a mean pot of chili without a recipe. When it comes to Disney World, however, we all agree that you need either a good plan or a frontal lobotomy. The operational definition of self-discovery and spontaneity at Walt Disney World is the "pleasure" of heat prostration and the "joy" of standing in line.

Let's face it: Walt Disney World is not a very existential place. In many ways it's the quintessential system, the ultimate in mass-produced entertainment, the most planned and programmed environment anywhere.

We aren't saying that you can't have a great time at Walt Disney World. What we *are* saying is that you need a plan. You don't have to be compulsive or inflexible; just think about what you want to do before you go. Don't delude yourself by rationalizing that the information in this guide is only for the pathological and the super-organized. Ask not for whom the tome tells, Bubba—it tells for thee.

A WORD TO OUR READERS ABOUT ANNUAL REVISIONS

SOME WHO PURCHASE EACH NEW EDITION of the *Unofficial Guide* chastise us for retaining examples, comments, and descriptions from previous editions. This letter from a Grand Rapids, Michigan, reader is typical:

> *Your guidebook still has the same little example stories. When I got my* [new] *book I expected a true update and new stuff, not the same-old, same-old!*

First, the *Unofficial Guide* is a reference work. Though we're pleased that some users read the guide from cover to cover and that

some find it entertaining, our objective is to provide information that will enable you to have the best possible Walt Disney World vacation.

Each year during our revision research, we check every theme park, water park, attraction, hotel, restaurant, nightspot, shop, and entertainment offering. While there are many changes (some attributable to Disney World's growth), much remains the same from year to year. When we profile and critique an attraction, we try to provide the reader with the most insightful, relevant, and useful information, written in the clearest possible language. If an attraction doesn't change, it makes little sense to risk clarity for the sake of freshening the prose. Disney World guests who try the Mad Tea Party, Peter Pan's Flight, or the *Country Bear Jamboree* today, for example, experience substantially the same presentation as guests who visited Disney World in 2005, 1990, or 1986. Moreover, according to our patron surveys (several thousand each year), today's guests respond to these attractions in the same way as prior-year patrons.

The bottom line: we believe our readers are better served if we devote our time to what's changing and new as opposed to what

remains the same. The success or failure of the *Unofficial Guide* is determined not by the writing style but by the accuracy of the information and, ultimately, whether you have a positive experience at Walt Disney World. Every change we make (or don't make) is evaluated in this context.

CORRECTIONS, UPDATES, AND BREAKING NEWS

CORRECTIONS AND UPDATES can be found online at the *Unofficial Guide* Web site, **TouringPlans.com.** Also available on the site are custom touring plans, trip planning and organizing tools, research reports, and breaking Walt Disney World news.

WE'VE GOT ATTITUDE

SOME READERS DISAGREE about our attitude toward Disney. A woman from Golden, Colorado, lambasts us:

I read your book cover to cover and felt you were way too hard on Disney. It's disappointing when you're all enthused about going [to Walt Disney World] *to be slammed with all these criticisms.*

A reader from Little Rock, Arkansas, takes us to task for the opposite prejudice:

Your book was quite complimentary of Disney, perhaps too complimentary. Maybe the free trips you travel writers get at Disney World are chipping away at your objectivity.

And from a Williamsport, Pennsylvania, mother of three:

Reading your book irritated me before we went [to Walt Disney World] *because of all the warnings and cautions. I guess I'm used to having guidebooks pump me up about where I'm going. But once I arrived, I found I was fully prepared and we had a great time. In retrospect, I have to admit you were right on the money. What I regarded as you being negative was just a good dose of reality.*

Finally, a reader from Phoenixville, Pennsylvania, prefers no opinions at all, writing:

While each person has the right to his or her own opinion, I did not purchase the book for an opinion.

For the record, we've always paid our own way at Walt Disney World: hotels, admissions, meals, the works. We don't dislike Disney, and we don't have an ax to grind. We're positive by nature and much prefer to praise than to criticize. Personally, we have enjoyed the Disney parks immensely over the years, both experiencing them and writing about them. Disney, however, as with all corporations (and all people), is better at some things than others. Because our readers shell out big bucks to go to Walt Disney World, we believe they have the right to know in advance what's good and what's not. For those who think we're overly positive, please understand that the *Unofficial Guide* is a guidebook, not an exposé. Our aim is for you to enjoy your visit. To that end, we report fairly and objectively. When readers disagree with our opinions, we, in the interest of fairness, publish their viewpoints alongside ours. To the best of our knowledge, the *Unofficial Guides* are the only travel guides in print that do this.

unofficial **TIP**
Check out experienced Disney World visitors' opinions of the parks in this book, and apply them to your own travel circumstances.

THE SUM OF ALL FEARS

EVERY WRITER WHO EXPRESSES an opinion is accustomed to readers who strongly agree or disagree: it comes with the territory. Extremely troubling, however, is the possibility that our efforts to be objective have frightened some readers away from Walt Disney World or made others apprehensive.

A mom from Avon, Ohio, was just such a person, writing:

After reading parts of the Unofficial Guide, *I seriously reconsidered going to WDW at all. We've been to other theme parks before, and I felt that WDW required too much planning. It actually stressed me out to read your guide (at first), because it seemed that WDW had too many pitfalls—too many things to plan for that could go wrong, too many horrible outcomes (like waiting for hours in scorching heat with kids), etc. My friend convinced me it wouldn't be that bad, however, so I kept on with planning the trip.*

We certainly understand the reader's feelings, but the key point was that, though apprehensive, she stayed the course. Here's what she said after returning home:

Let me tell you, your guide and touring plans were DEAD-ON accurate! We didn't wait more than 10 or 15 minutes for almost every attraction in two days!

For the record, if you enjoy theme parks, Disney World is as good as it gets, absolute nirvana. If you arrive without knowing a thing about the place and make every possible mistake, chances are about 90% that you'll have a wonderful vacation anyway. In the end, guidebooks don't make or break great destinations. Rather, they are simply tools to help you enhance your experience and get the most for your money.

As wonderful as Walt Disney World is, however, it's a complex destination. Even so, it isn't nearly as challenging or difficult as New York, San Francisco, Paris, Acapulco, or any other large city or destination. And, happily, there are numerous ways to save money, minimize hassle, and make the most of your time. That's what this guide is about: giving you a heads-up regarding potential problems and opportunities. Unfortunately, some *Unofficial Guide* readers add up the warnings and critical advice and conclude that Walt Disney World is too intimidating, too expensive, or too much work. They lose track of the wonder of Disney World and focus instead on what might go wrong.

Our philosophy is that knowledge is power (and time and money, too). You're free to follow our advice or not at your discretion. But you can't exercise that discretion if we fail to present the issues.

With or without a guidebook, you'll have a great time at Walt Disney World. If you let us, we'll help you smooth the potential bumps. We're certain we can help you turn a great vacation into an absolutely superb one. Either way, once there, you'll get the feel of the place and quickly reach a comfort level that will allay your apprehensions and allow you to have a great experience.

TOO MANY COOKS IN THE KITCHEN?

WE RECEIVED THIS QUERY from a Manchester, Vermont, reader, and feel it deserves a serious response:

I read a review on the Internet criticizing the Unofficial Guide *because it was "written by a team of researchers." The reviewer doesn't say why he thinks the team approach is inferior, but the inference is along the lines of "too many cooks spoil the soup." Why do you use the team approach?*

> *unofficial* **TIP**
> **Researching and writing this book as a team results in a more objective guidebook for you.**

There are several reasons. Foremost is that the team approach enables us to undertake much more sophisticated and extensive research. Collecting waiting-time data for our touring-plan software (see page 75), for example, requires that more than a dozen researchers visit the Disney parks for several days at four or more different times of year. Another project, monitoring the Disney transportation system, requires riding and timing every bus, boat, and monorail route, a task that takes four researchers almost a week to complete. In covering lodging, the *Unofficial Guide* reviews, rates, and ranks about 250 Disney World–area hotels, more than four times as many as other guidebooks. On any research trip, we have one or two teams of hotel inspectors checking hotels all day long.

No other guides do this, nor can they, because the scope of the research and processing of data require time, experience, and resources beyond the capabilities of a single author or even several coauthors. An entire organization collects and compiles the information for the *Unofficial Guide,* an organization guided by individuals with extensive training and experience in research design as well as data collection and analysis. Known and respected in both the travel industry and academe, *Unofficial Guide* research has been recognized by *USA Today,* the BBC, the *New York Times,* the *Dallas Morning News,* the Travel Channel, and CNN, as well as by numerous academic journals.

Not all *Unofficial Guide* research relates to the parks and resorts. We also conduct extensive research on you, the reader. From the concept up, you see, *Unofficial Guides* are different from other guidebooks. Other guides are researched and developed by individual authors or coauthors, usually travel writers. Thus, everything is filtered through the lens of those authors' tastes, preferences, and opinions. Publishers of these guides hope the information the author presents is compatible with the needs of the reader, but if it is, the compatibility is largely accidental. In *Unofficial Guides,* by contrast, it's your tastes, preferences, and opinions that dictate the content of the guides. In other words, we start with the needs of our readers, identified through exhaustive research, and build a book that meets those needs.

Another reason for using a team approach is to minimize author bias. As discussed earlier, a single author incorporates his or her own tastes and opinions in his work. Our researchers, by contrast, include individuals ranging in age from 12 to 70 and sometimes, for special assignments, children as young as 8. Thus the opinions and advice in the *Unofficial Guide* are informed by the perspectives of a diverse group of researchers, a process that, we believe, achieves the highest level of objectivity.

A final reason for the team approach is the need for expertise in specific areas. No individual author can possibly be qualified to write about every topic in the vast range of important subjects that make up a good guide to Walt Disney World. Thus, our chapter on Walt Disney World with Kids (Part Six) was developed in consultation with three nationally respected child psychologists and an advisory group of parents. Similarly, we have professional culinary experts dedicated to the task of rating restaurants. Our golf coverage, likewise, is handled by pro-golf writer Larry Olmsted, and our database and touring-plan program are developed and managed by the programmer and software developer Len Testa. When you cover shopping, you want a local who lives to shop and knows where to find every back-counter deal within

50 miles. Guess what? We've got her! In a nutshell, there are more of us so that we can do more for you. I (Bob) put the fruits of our research into words, but behind me is an organization unequaled in travel publishing.

THE *UNOFFICIAL* TEAM

SO WHO ARE THESE FOLKS? Allow me to introduce them all, except for our dining critic, who shall remain anonymous:

BOB SEHLINGER Author and executive publisher

LEN TESTA Coauthor, touring-plans software developer, data-collection director, and **TouringPlans.com** Webmaster

FRED HAZELTON Statistician

KRISTEN HELMSTETTER Survey collator

KAREN TURNBOW, PhD Child psychologist

JIM HILL Disney historian

RICHARD MACKO, GAIL MOONEY Photographers

PAM BRANDON Shopping guru

LARRY OLMSTED Golf expert

STEVE JONES Cartographer

HENRY WORK Web developer

TAMI KNIGHT Cartoonist

MARIE HILLIN, STEVE MILLBURG, DARCIE VANCE Research editors

Data Collectors
Rob Sutton, supervisor
Chantale Brazeau
Kai Brückerhoff
Kenny Cottrell
Guy Garguilo
Lillian Macko
Richard Macko
Cliff Myers
Robert Pederson
Julie Saunders
Linda Sutton
Christine Testa
Mais Testa
Darcie Vance
Rich Vosburgh
Kelly Whitman

Hotel Inspectors
Sarah Biggs
Joshua Carver
Holly Cross
Jenn Gorman
Ritchey Halphen
Kristen Helmstetter
Myra E. Merkle
Megan Parks

Contributing Writers
Megan Parks
Sue Pisaturo
Grant Rafter
Darcie Vance
Mary Waring
Deb Wills

Editorial and Production
Molly B. Merkle, editorial and production manager
Ritchey Halphen, managing editor
Annie Long, typesetter-compositor
Elizabeth Hilligoss, editorial intern
Ann Cassar, indexer

Thanks to Joe Meyer at InvestOmatics for his dependable programming assistance with the touring-plan software. Thanks as well to Brent Clements, who worked like a horse on the trip planner for our Web site. Geoff Allen supplied the brainpower behind our online hotel-rate analysis. *Muchas gracias* to Bill O. and the folks at **www.kayak.com** for walking us through their fabulous search interface, and to Richard Mercer and Jol A. Silversmith for their careful proofreading.

THE HOW AND THE WHY OF IT

A DAYTON, OHIO, READER offers this comment:

> *I used several guides preparing for our* [Disney World] *trip. One of them dumped on the* Unofficial Guide *for referring to Dumbo as a "cycle ride." Though my kids are totally infatuated with Dumbo, I found your section about how the various types of rides work to be both interesting and useful. Dumbo's charm and appeal doesn't change the fact that it's a cycle ride. Get a life!*

Most guidebooks do a reasonably good job with what and where. *Unofficial Guides* add the how and why. Describing attractions or hotels or restaurants (the what) at a given destination (the where) is the foundation of other travel guidebooks. We know from our research, however, that our readers like to know how things work. Take hotels, for example. In the *Unofficial Guide,* we not only provide hotel choices (rated and ranked, of course) but also explain the economic and operational logic of the lodging industry (the why) and offer instructions (the how) that enable the reader to take advantage of opportunities for hotel discounts, room upgrades, and the like. In this and all our *Unofficial Guides,* whether we're discussing cruise ships, theme parks, ski resorts, casinos, or golf courses, we reveal the travel industry's inner workings and demonstrate how to use such insight in selecting and purchasing travel and for planning itineraries. For the reader, knowledge is power, which translates into informed decisions and confidence.

Most guides give the reader a plate of fish to choose from. An *Unofficial Guide* additionally says which fish are best. More important, however, an *Unofficial Guide* teaches the reader how to fish. Anyone who has read the hotel chapter in any *Unofficial Guide* can use the information to book a great room at a bargain price anywhere in the world.

THE *UNOFFICIAL GUIDE* PUBLISHING YEAR

WE RECEIVE MANY QUERIES asking when the next edition of the *Unofficial Guide* will be available. Usually our new editions are in stores by late August or early September. Thus, the 2011 edition will be on the shelves in August or September 2010.

LETTERS AND COMMENTS FROM READERS

MANY WHO USE *The Unofficial Guide to Walt Disney World* write us to comment or share their own strategies for visiting Disney World. We appreciate all such input, both positive and critical, and encourage our readers to continue writing. Their comments and observations are frequently incorporated into revised editions of the *Unofficial Guide* and have contributed immeasurably to its improvement. If you write us or return our reader-survey form, rest assured that we won't release your name and address to any mailing-list companies, direct-mail advertisers, or other third party. Unless you instruct us otherwise, we'll assume that you don't object to being quoted in the *Unofficial Guide.*

Reader Questionnaire and Restaurant Survey

At the back of this guide is a questionnaire you can use to express opinions about your Walt Disney World visit. The questionnaire allows every member of your party, regardless of age, to tell us what he or she thinks. Use the separate restaurant survey to describe your Disney World dining experiences. Clip the questionnaire and restaurant survey and mail them to: Reader Survey, The *Unofficial Guide* Series, P.O. Box 43673, Birmingham, AL 35243. For your convenience, an electronic version of the questionnaire and survey can be found online at **TouringPlans.com.**

unofficial **TIP**
If you're up for having your comments quoted in the guide, please be sure to tell us your hometown.

How to Contact the Authors

Bob Sehlinger and Len Testa
The Unofficial Guide to Walt Disney World
P.O. Box 43673
Birmingham, AL 35243
unofficialguides@menasharidge.com

When you write, put your address on both your letter and envelope; the two sometimes get separated. It's also a good idea to include your phone number. If you e-mail us, please tell us where you're from. Remember, as travel writers, we're often out of the office for long periods of time, so forgive us if our response is slow. *Unofficial Guide* e-mail isn't forwarded to us when we're traveling, but we'll respond as soon as possible after we return.

WALT DISNEY WORLD: *An* OVERVIEW

IF YOU'RE CHOOSING A U.S. TOURIST DESTINATION, the question is not whether to visit Walt Disney World, but how to see its best offerings with some economy of time, effort, and finances.

WHAT WALT DISNEY WORLD ENCOMPASSES

WALT DISNEY WORLD COMPRISES 43 square miles, an area twice as large as Manhattan or roughly the size of Boston. Situated strategically in this vast expanse are the **Magic Kingdom, Epcot, Disney's Hollywood Studios,** and **Animal Kingdom** theme parks; two swimming theme parks; two nighttime-entertainment areas; a sports complex; five golf courses, 34 hotels, and a campground; more than 100 restaurants; four interconnected lakes; a shopping complex; eight convention venues; a nature preserve; and a transportation system consisting of four-lane highways, elevated monorails, and a network of canals.

Walt Disney World has more than 50,000 employees, or "cast members," making it the largest single-site employer in the United States. Keeping the costumes of those cast members clean requires the equivalent of 16,000 loads of laundry a day and the dry-cleaning of 30,000 garments daily. Mickey Mouse alone has 175 different sets of duds, ranging from a scuba wet suit to a tux. (Minnie tops him with more than 200 outfits.) Each year, Disney restaurants serve 10 million burgers, 7 million hot dogs, 50 million Cokes, 9 million pounds of French fries, and 150 tons of popcorn. In the state of Florida, only Miami and Jacksonville have bus systems larger than Disney World's. The Disney monorail trains have logged mileage equal to more than 30 round-trips to the moon.

DISNEY-SPEAK POCKET TRANSLATOR

ALTHOUGH IT MAY COME AS A SURPRISE to many, Walt Disney World has its own somewhat peculiar language. See the following chart for some terms you are likely to bump into:

DISNEY-SPEAK	ENGLISH DEFINITION
Adventure	Ride
Attraction	Ride or theater show
Attraction host	Ride operator
Audience	Crowd
Backstage	Behind the scenes, out of view of customers
Bull pen	Queuing area
Cast member	Employee
Character	Disney character impersonated by an employee
Costume	Work attire or uniform
Dark ride	Indoor ride
Day guest	Any customer not staying at a Disney resort
Face character	A character who does not wear a head-covering costume (Snow White, Cinderella, Jasmine, and the like)
General public	Same as day guest
Greeter	Employee positioned at an attraction entrance
Guest	Customer
Hidden Mickeys	Frontal silhouette of Mickey's head worked subtly into the design of buildings, railings, vehicles, golf greens, attractions, and just about anything else
In rehearsal	Operating, though not officially open
Lead	Foreman or manager, the person in charge of an attraction
On stage	In full view of customers
Preshow	Entertainment at an attraction prior to the feature presentation
Resort guest	A customer staying at a Disney resort
Role	An employee's job
Security host	Security guard
Soft opening	Opening a park or attraction before its stated opening date
Transitional experience	An element of the queuing area and/or preshow that provides a story line or information essential to understanding the attraction

THE MAJOR THEME PARKS

The Magic Kingdom

When people think of Walt Disney World, most think of the Magic Kingdom, opened in 1971. It consists of the adventures, rides, and shows featuring the Disney cartoon characters, and Cinderella Castle. It's only one element of Disney World, but it remains the heart.

The Magic Kingdom is subdivided into seven "lands," six of which are arranged around a central hub. First encountered is **Main Street, U.S.A.,** which connects the Magic Kingdom entrance with the hub. Clockwise around the hub are **Adventureland, Frontierland, Liberty Square, Fantasyland,** and **Tomorrowland. Mickey's Toontown Fair,** the first new land added since the Magic Kingdom opened, is situated along the Walt Disney World Railroad on three acres between Fantasyland and Tomorrowland. Access is through Fantasyland or Tomorrowland or via the railroad. Main Street and the other six lands will be detailed later. Four hotels (**Bay Lake Tower** and the **Contemporary, Polynesian,** and **Grand Floridian** resorts) are near the Magic Kingdom and directly connected to it by monorail and boat. Two other hotels, **Shades of Green** and **Disney's Wilderness Lodge Resort and Villas,** are nearby but aren't served by the monorail.

Epcot

Opened in October 1982, Epcot is twice as big as the Magic Kingdom and comparable in scope. It has two major areas: **Future World** consists of pavilions concerning human creativity and technological advancement; **World Showcase,** arranged around a 40-acre lagoon, presents the architectural, social, and cultural heritages of almost a dozen nations, each country represented by replicas of famous landmarks and settings familiar to world travelers. Epcot is more educational than the Magic Kingdom and has been characterized as a permanent World's Fair.

The Epcot resort hotels—**Disney's Beach Club Resort and Villas, Disney's Yacht Club, Disney's BoardWalk Inn and Villas Resort,** the **Walt Disney World Swan,** and the **Walt Disney World Dolphin**—are within a 5- to 15-minute walk of the International Gateway (back-door) entrance to the theme park. The hotels are also linked to Epcot and Disney's Hollywood Studios by canal. Epcot is connected to the Magic Kingdom and its hotels by monorail.

Disney's Hollywood Studios

Opened in 1989 and about the size of the Magic Kingdom, Disney's Hollywood Studios has two areas. The first is a theme park focused on the past, present, and future of the motion-picture and television industries. This section contains movie-theme rides and shows and covers about half of the complex. Park highlights include a re-creation of Hollywood and Sunset boulevards from Hollywood's Golden Age, stunt demonstrations, a children's play area, shows on sound effects, and four high-tech rides.

The second area, formerly a working motion-picture and television production facility, encompasses soundstages, a back lot of streets and sets, and support services. Public access is limited to tours that take visitors behind the scenes for crash courses on Disney animation and moviemaking, including (on occasion) the opportunity to witness the shooting of a film, television show, or commercial.

Disney's Hollywood Studios is connected to other Walt Disney World areas by highway and canal but not by monorail. Guests can park in the Studios' pay parking lot or commute by bus. Guests at Epcot resort hotels can reach the Studios by boat or on foot.

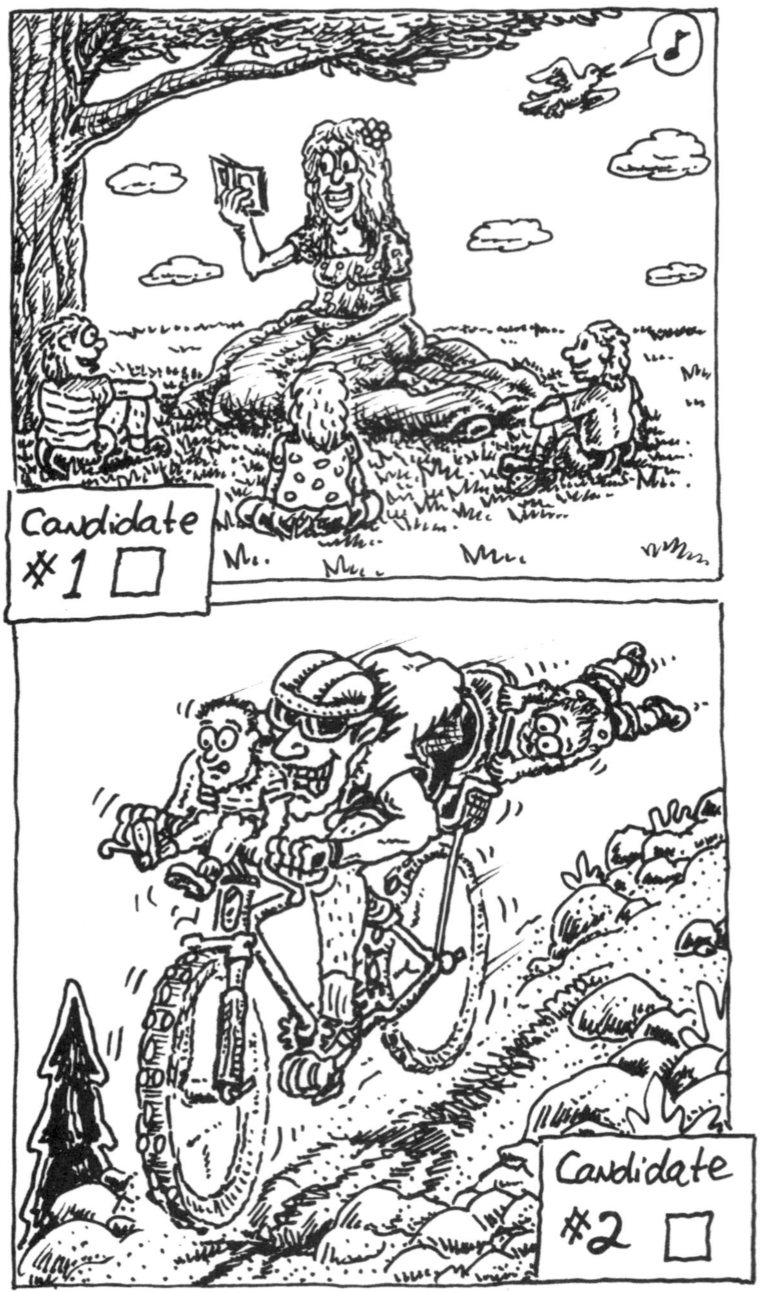

SURVEY: ***Which author do you prefer to write your guidebooks? (Guess which one you got?)***

Disney's Animal Kingdom

About five times the size of the Magic Kingdom, Animal Kingdom combines zoological exhibits with rides, shows, and live entertainment. The park is arranged somewhat like the Magic Kingdom, in a hub-and-spoke configuration. A lush tropical rain forest serves as Main Street, funneling visitors to **Discovery Island,** the park's hub. Dominated by the park's central icon, the 14-story-tall, hand-carved Tree of Life, Discovery Island offers services, shopping, and dining. From there, guests can access the themed areas: **Africa, Asia, DinoLand U.S.A.,** and **Camp Minnie-Mickey.** Discovery Island, Africa, Camp Minnie-Mickey, and DinoLand U.S.A. opened in 1998, followed by Asia in 1999. Africa, the largest themed area, at 100 acres, features free-roaming herds in a re-creation of the Serengeti Plain. Guests tour in open-air safari vehicles.

Animal Kingdom has its own pay parking lot and is connected to other Disney World destinations by the Disney bus system. Although there are no hotels within Animal Kingdom proper, the **All-Star Resorts, Animal Kingdom Lodge,** and **Coronado Springs Resort** are all nearby.

THE WATER PARKS

DISNEY WORLD HAS TWO MAJOR water parks: **Typhoon Lagoon** and **Blizzard Beach.** Opened in 1989, Typhoon Lagoon is distinguished by a wave pool capable of making six-foot waves. Blizzard Beach is newer, having opened in 1995, and it features more slides. Both parks are beautifully landscaped, and great attention is paid to atmosphere and aesthetics. Typhoon Lagoon and Blizzard Beach have their own adjacent parking lots and can be reached via Disney bus.

OTHER WALT DISNEY WORLD VENUES

Downtown Disney (Downtown Disney Marketplace and Disney's West Side)

Downtown Disney is a large shopping, dining, and entertainment complex encompassing the **Downtown Disney Marketplace** on the east and **Disney's West Side** on the west. Downtown Disney Marketplace contains the world's largest Disney-character merchandise store, upscale resort-wear and specialty shops, and several restaurants, including the tacky-but-popular **Rainforest Cafe** and its equally tacky cousin, **T-REX.** Disney's West Side, which opened in 1997, combines nightlife, shopping, dining, and entertainment. The **House of Blues** serves Cajun-Creole dishes in its restaurant and electric blues in its music hall. **Bongos Cuban Cafe,** a nightclub and cafe created by Gloria Estefan and her husband, Emilio, offers Cuban rhythms and flavors. **Wolfgang Puck Cafe,** sandwiched among pricey boutiques, is the West Side's prestige eatery. For entertainment, you'll find a 24-screen cinema; a permanent showplace for the extraordinary 70-person cast of **Cirque du Soleil's *La Nouba;*** and **DisneyQuest,** an interactive virtual reality and electronic games venue. Access Downtown Disney via Disney buses from most Disney World locations.

Disney's BoardWalk

Located near Epcot, Disney's BoardWalk is an idealized replication of an East Coast 1930s waterfront resort. Open all day, BoardWalk features upscale restaurants, shops and galleries, a brewpub, and an ESPN sports bar. In the evening, a nightclub with dueling pianos and a DJ dance club join the lineup. There is no admission fee for BoardWalk, but some individual clubs levy cover charges at night. In addition to the public facilities are a 372-room deluxe hotel and a 532-unit time-share development. BoardWalk is within walking distance of the Epcot resorts and Epcot's International Gateway. Boat transportation is available from Disney's Hollywood Studios; buses serve other Disney World locations.

unofficial **TIP**
If you crave a little nightlife but don't want to leave Disney property, check out these other Disney venues.

ESPN Wide World of Sports Complex

The 220-acre Wide World of Sports is a state-of-the-art competition and training facility consisting of a 9,500-seat ballpark, two field houses, and venues for baseball, softball, tennis, track and field, beach volleyball, and 27 other sports. The spring-training home of

"No, no, really, it's OK. It's just not what I expected."

the Atlanta Braves, the complex also hosts a mind-boggling calendar of professional and amateur competitions. Disney World guests are welcome as paying spectators but can't use the facilities unless they're participating in a scheduled competition.

Disney Cruise Line

In 1998, the Walt Disney Company launched (literally) its own cruise line with the 2,400-passenger ***Disney Magic.*** Its sister ship, the ***Disney Wonder,*** first sailed in 1999. Cruises depart from Port Canaveral, Florida (about a 90-minute drive from Walt Disney World), on 3-, 4-, and 7-day itineraries. Caribbean and Bahamian cruises include a day at Castaway Cay, Disney's private island. Cruises can be packaged with a stay at Disney World. Although the cruises are family oriented, extensive children's programs and elaborate child-care facilities allow parents plenty of opportunity for time away from the kids. For more on the Disney Cruise Line, see Part Five (page 292).

South Orlando and Walt Disney World Area

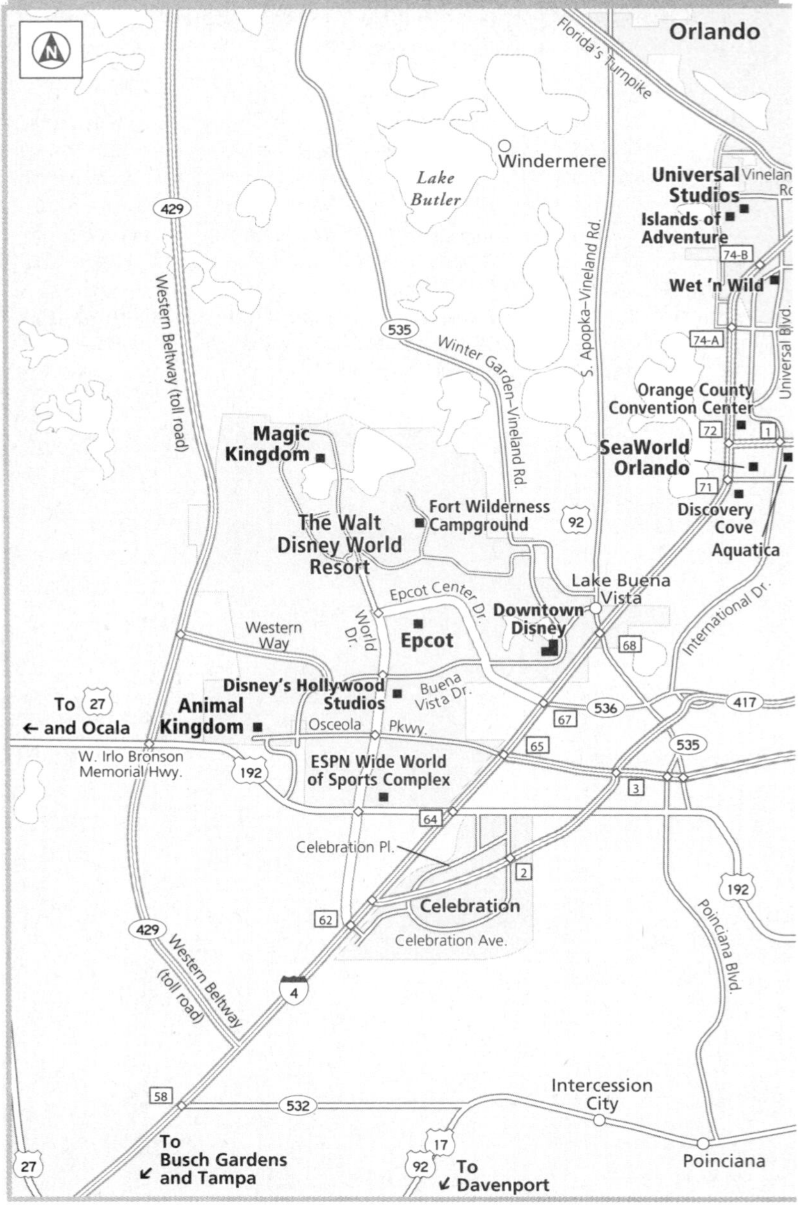

Orlando
Florida's Turnpike
Windermere
Lake Butler
Universal Studios
Vineland Rd.
Islands of Adventure
74-B
Wet 'n Wild
429
Western Beltway (toll road)
S. Apopka–Vineland Rd.
535
Winter Garden–Vineland Rd.
74-A
Universal Blvd.
Orange County Convention Center
72
1
Magic Kingdom
SeaWorld Orlando
71
Fort Wilderness Campground
92
Discovery Cove
The Walt Disney World Resort
Aquatica
Lake Buena Vista
Epcot Center Dr.
Downtown Disney
International Dr.
Western Way
World Dr.
Epcot
68
Disney's Hollywood Studios
Buena Vista Dr.
536
417
To 27 and Ocala
Animal Kingdom
Osceola Pkwy.
67
65
535
W. Irlo Bronson Memorial Hwy.
192
ESPN Wide World of Sports Complex
3
64
Celebration Pl.
2
192
Celebration
Poinciana Blvd.
62
429
Celebration Ave.
Western Beltway (toll road)
4
Intercession City
58
532
To Busch Gardens and Tampa
17
92
To Davenport
27
Poinciana

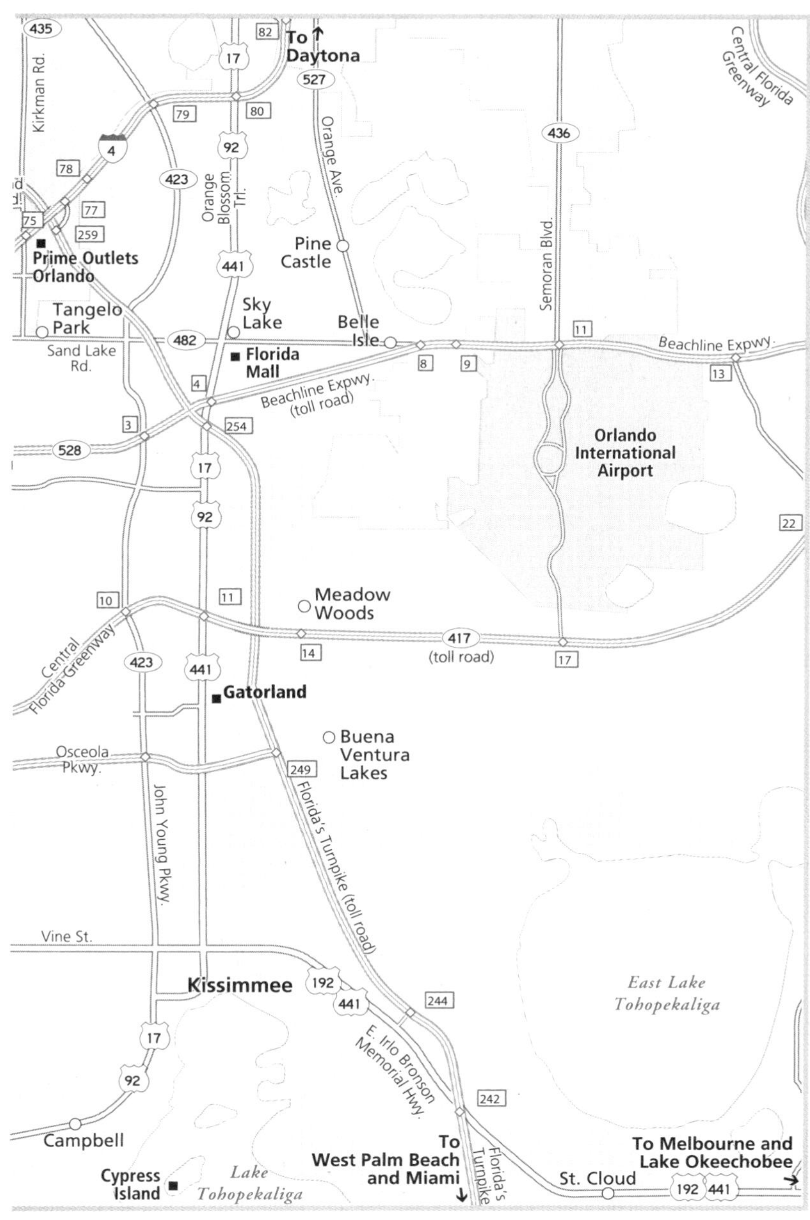

To Daytona
Kirkman Rd.
Central Florida Greenway
Orange Blossom Trl.
Orange Ave.
Semoran Blvd.
Pine Castle
Prime Outlets Orlando
Tangelo Park
Sky Lake
Belle Isle
Sand Lake Rd.
Florida Mall
Beachline Expwy.
Beachline Expwy. (toll road)
Orlando International Airport
Meadow Woods
(toll road)
Central Florida Greenway
Gatorland
Buena Ventura Lakes
Osceola Pkwy.
John Young Pkwy.
Florida's Turnpike (toll road)
Vine St.
Kissimmee
E. Irlo Bronson Memorial Hwy.
East Lake Tohopekaliga
Campbell
To West Palm Beach and Miami
Florida's Turnpike
To Melbourne and Lake Okeechobee
St. Cloud
Cypress Island
Lake Tohopekaliga

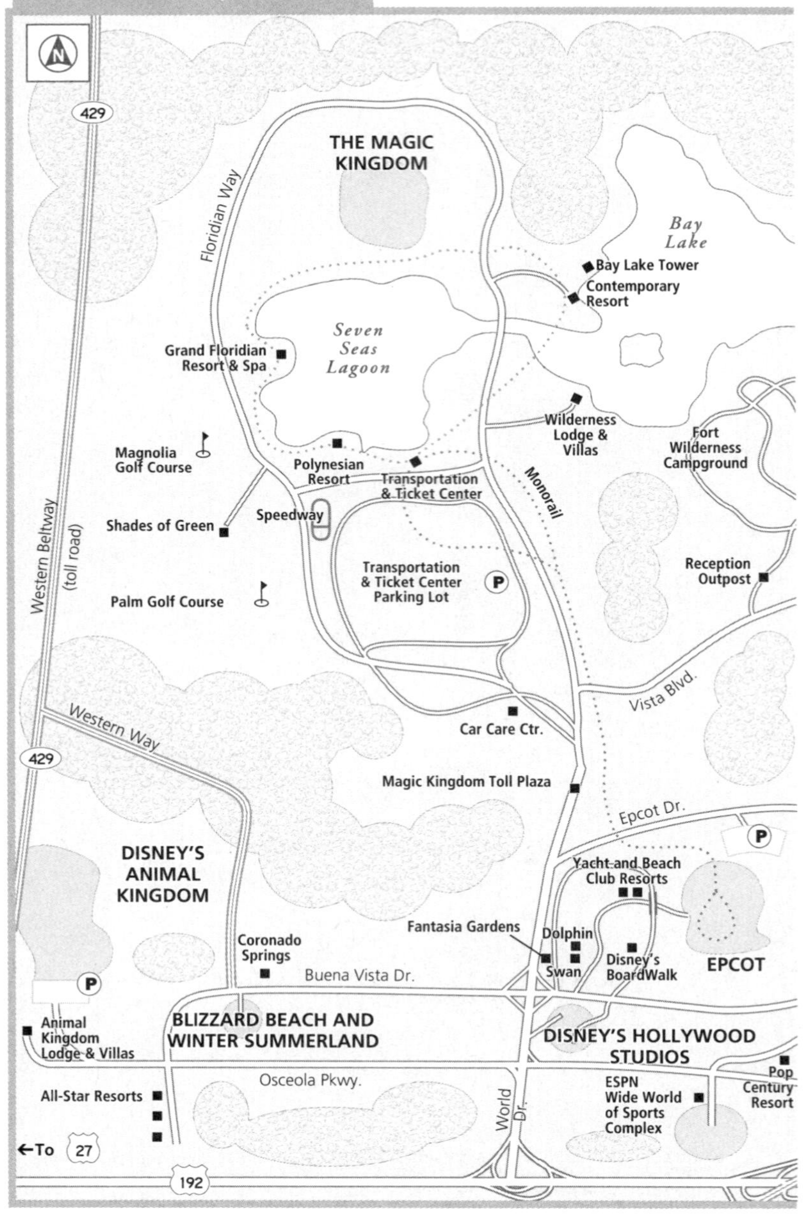

Walt Disney World
429
THE MAGIC KINGDOM
Floridian Way
Bay Lake
Bay Lake Tower
Contemporary Resort
Seven Seas Lagoon
Grand Floridian Resort & Spa
Wilderness Lodge & Villas
Fort Wilderness Campground
Magnolia Golf Course
Polynesian Resort
Transportation & Ticket Center
Monorail
Speedway
Shades of Green
Western Beltway (toll road)
Transportation & Ticket Center Parking Lot
P
Reception Outpost
Palm Golf Course
Vista Blvd.
Western Way
Car Care Ctr.
429
Magic Kingdom Toll Plaza
Epcot Dr.
P
DISNEY'S ANIMAL KINGDOM
Yacht and Beach Club Resorts
Fantasia Gardens
Dolphin
Coronado Springs
Swan
Disney's BoardWalk
EPCOT
Buena Vista Dr.
P
Animal Kingdom Lodge & Villas
BLIZZARD BEACH AND WINTER SUMMERLAND
DISNEY'S HOLLYWOOD STUDIOS
Pop Century Resort
Osceola Pkwy.
All-Star Resorts
ESPN Wide World of Sports Complex
World Dr.
←To 27
192

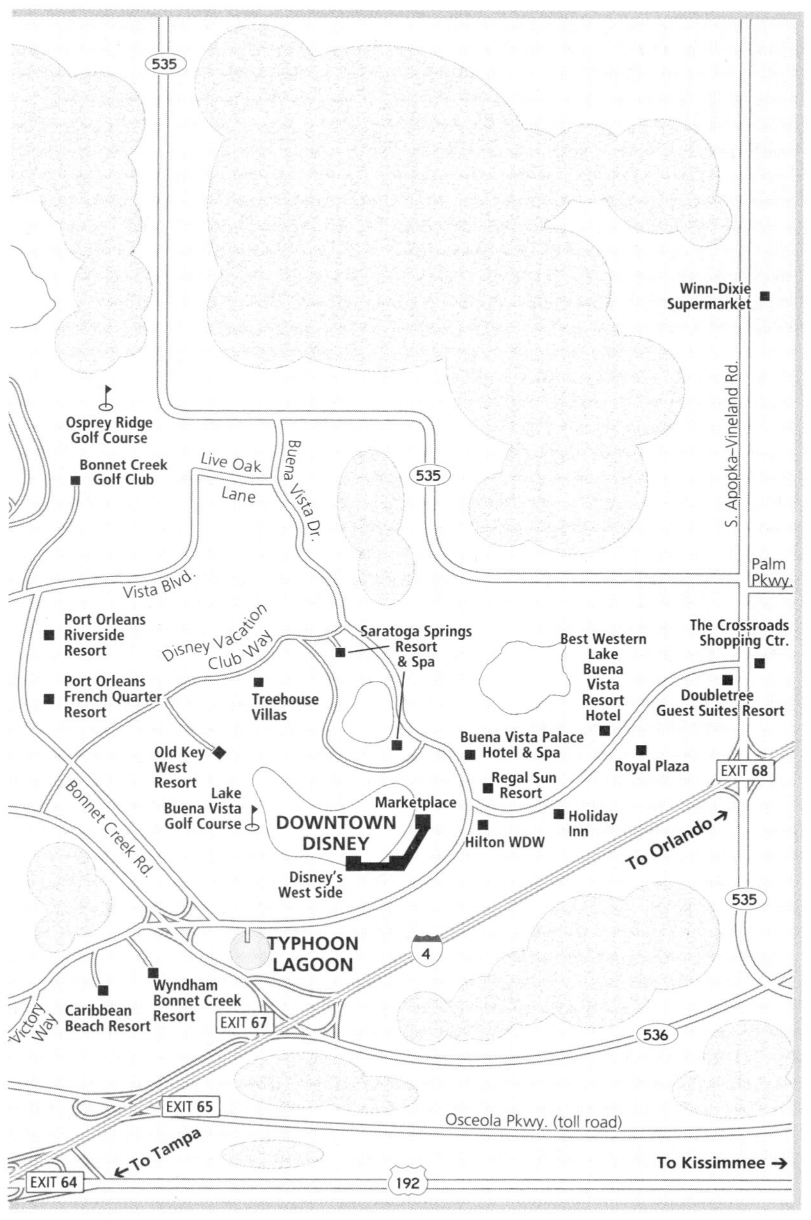
535
Winn-Dixie Supermarket
S. Apopka–Vineland Rd.
Osprey Ridge Golf Course
Bonnet Creek Golf Club
Live Oak Lane
Buena Vista Dr.
535
Palm Pkwy.
Vista Blvd.
Port Orleans Riverside Resort
Disney Vacation Club Way
Saratoga Springs Resort & Spa
Best Western Lake Buena Vista Resort Hotel
The Crossroads Shopping Ctr.
Port Orleans French Quarter Resort
Treehouse Villas
Doubletree Guest Suites Resort
Buena Vista Palace Hotel & Spa
Royal Plaza
EXIT 68
Old Key West Resort
Regal Sun Resort
Lake Buena Vista Golf Course
Marketplace
Holiday Inn
Bonnet Creek Rd.
DOWNTOWN DISNEY
Hilton WDW
To Orlando
Disney's West Side
535
TYPHOON LAGOON
4
Wyndham Bonnet Creek Resort
Caribbean Beach Resort
Victory Way
EXIT 67
536
EXIT 65
Osceola Pkwy. (toll road)
To Tampa
To Kissimmee
EXIT 64
192

PART ONE

PLANNING *before* YOU LEAVE HOME

Visiting Walt Disney World is a bit like childbirth—you never really believe what people tell you, but once you have been through it yourself, you know exactly what they were saying!

—Hilary Wolfe, a mother and *Unofficial Guide* reader from Swansea, Wales

GATHERING INFORMATION

IN ADDITION TO THIS GUIDE, we recommend that you obtain the following:

1. **THE WALT DISNEY TRAVEL COMPANY FLORIDA VACATIONS BROCHURE AND DVD** These cover Walt Disney World in its entirety, list rates for all Disney resort hotels and campgrounds, and describe Disney World package vacations. They're available from most travel agents, by calling the Walt Disney Travel Company at ☎ 407-828-8101 or 407-934-7639, or by visiting **www.disneyworld.com.** Be prepared to hold. When you get a representative, ask for the DVD vacation planner.
2. **THE DISNEY CRUISE LINE BROCHURE AND DVD** This brochure provides details on vacation packages that combine a cruise on the Disney Cruise Line with a stay at Disney World. Disney Cruise Line also offers a free DVD that tells all you need to know about Disney cruises and then some. To obtain a copy, call ☎ 800-951-3532 or order at **www.disneycruise.com.**
3. ***THE UNOFFICIAL GUIDE TO WALT DISNEY WORLD* WEB SITE** Our Web site, **TouringPlans.com,** offers a free online trip organizer, more than 100 different touring plans, and updates on changes at Walt Disney World, among other features. The site is described more fully later in this chapter.
4. **ORLANDO MAGICARD** If you're considering lodging outside Disney World or if you think you might patronize out-of-the-World attractions and restaurants, obtain an Orlando Magicard, a Vacation Planner, and the *Orlando Official Vacation Guide* (all free) from the Orlando Visitors Center. The Magicard entitles you to discounts for hotels, restaurants, ground transportation, shopping malls, dinner theaters, and non-Disney

theme parks and attractions. The Orlando Magicard can be conveniently downloaded for printing at **www.orlandoinfo.com/magicard.** To order the accommodations guide, call ☎ 800-643-9492. For additional information and materials, call ☎ 407-363-5872 weekdays during business hours, or go to **www.visitorlando.com.**

5. ***FLORIDA ROOMSAVER GUIDE*** Another good source of discounts on lodging, restaurants, and attractions statewide is *Florida RoomSaver,* published by Exit Information Guide. The guide is free, but you pay $3 for handling ($5 if shipped to Canada). Call ☎ 352-371-3948, Monday through Friday, 8 a.m. to 5 p.m. EST, or go to **www.travelerdiscount guide.com** and order online. To order by mail, write to 4205 NW Sixth Street, Gainesville, FL 32609. Similar guides to other states are available at the same number. You can also print hotel coupons and reserve rooms free at the **www.roomsaver.com** Web site.
6. **"CHOOSE KISSIMMEE" GUIDE** This full-color visitors guide is one of the most complete resources available and is of particular interest to those who intend to lodge outside of Disney World, featuring ads for hotels, rental houses, time-shares, and condominiums as well as a directory of attractions, restaurants, special events, and other useful info. For a copy, call the Kissimmee Convention and Visitors Bureau at ☎ 800-327-9159 or 407-944-2400, or view it online at **www.floridakiss.com.**
7. ***GUIDEBOOK FOR GUESTS WITH DISABILITIES*** Each park's edition of this publication is available online at the Disney World Web site (**www.disneyworld.com**).

unofficial **TIP**
Request information as far in advance as possible, and allow four weeks for delivery. Follow up if you haven't received your materials within six weeks.

PASSPORTER GUIDES

A PERFECT COMPANION to the *Unofficial Guide* is *PassPorter's Walt Disney World 2009 Planner and Organizer* ($22.95). In addition to being a fine guidebook, the spiral-bound organizer offers all the bells and whistles of a desk organizer, including pockets for tickets, coupons, and receipts, as well as blank daily-itinerary forms. A super resource for anyone with special needs is *PassPorter's Open Mouse for Walt Disney World and the Disney Cruise Line* ($22.95) by Deb Wills and Debra Martin Koma. The 436-page book covers everything from ADHD to asthma. Both books are available from PassPorter Travel Press at ☎ 877-929-3273 or **www.passporter.com.**

WALT DISNEY WORLD ON THE WEB

SEARCHING THE INTERNET for Disney information is like navigating an immense maze for a very small piece of cheese: there's a lot of information available, but you may have to wade through list after list until you find the Internet addresses you want and need.

Many individuals maintain elaborate Disney-related Web sites and chat groups, which can provide both correct and incorrect information, depending on who's chatting.

Recommended Web Sites

Unofficial Guide coauthor Len Testa has combed the Web looking for the best Disney sites. Turn the page for his picks.

BEST OFFICIAL THEME-PARK SITE We're not sure if it's some sort of make-work program for underemployed Web designers, but the official **Walt Disney World Web site** (**www.disneyworld.com** or **disneyworld .disney.go.com**) recently underwent its third major overhaul in four years. While it still has room for improvement, it gets our nod as the best official park Web site over the official sites for Universal Studios (**www.universalorlando.com**) and SeaWorld (**www.seaworld.com**). All three sites contain information on ticket options, park hours, height requirements for attractions, disabled-guest access, and the like, but Disney's site is the most comprehensive and best organized. On the minus side, however, the site remains bogged down by multimedia gimmickry that causes pages to load slower than Space Mountain's standby line in July. (Maybe they're just conditioning you?)

BEST OFFICIAL MOM'S SITE Who knew? Walt Disney World has a Mom's Panel composed of 15 moms and one red herring—er, one dad—all chosen from among 10,000-plus applicants. The panelists have a Web site, **www.disneyworldmoms.com,** where they offer tips, discuss how to plan a Disney World vacation, and answer questions about how that guy got into the henhouse. The moms are unpaid and are free to speak their minds. One mom actually went from fan to cast member when Disney recruited her to head the panel.

BEST GENERAL UNOFFICIAL WALT DISNEY WORLD WEB SITE Deb Wills's **AllEars.net** is the first Web site we recommend to friends who are interested in making a trip to Disney World. It contains information on virtually every hotel, restaurant, and activity in the World. Want to know what a room at a Disney resort looks like before you book one? This site has photos—sometimes for each floor of a resort. The site is updated several times per week and includes menus from Disney restaurants, ticketing information, maps, and such.

TOURINGPLANS.COM The Web companion to this guide is chock-full of useful features. For instance, we've written 140 Disney-theme-park touring plans in addition to those in this book, featuring variations for holidays, seniors, Extra Magic Hours, and those who like to sleep in. If our plans aren't quite what you're looking for, TouringPlans .com lets you to create your own, either from scratch or by using one of ours as a template (we'll automatically include restaurant information, hidden Mickeys, attraction trivia, park hours, and weather forecasts), and share them with family and friends. As of this writing, around 30,000 reader-contributed plans are available free of charge.

To help you select the best resort for your family, we've also uploaded thousands of photos and dozens of online videos covering every inch of every Disney resort plus many off-site accommodations.

One of the most popular parts of the site is our crowd calendar, which shows crowd projections for each theme park for every day of the year. Look up the dates of your Walt Disney World visit, and the calendar will not only show the projected wait times for each day but will also indicate for each day which theme park will be the least crowded.

In early 2010, TouringPlans.com will begin providing continuous real-time updates on wait times at the Walt Disney World parks.

Important Walt Disney World Addresses

Compliments, Complaints, and Suggestions
Walt Disney World Guest Communications
P. O. Box 10040
Lake Buena Vista, FL 32830-0040

Convention and Banquet Information
Walt Disney World Resort South
P.O. Box 10000
Lake Buena Vista, FL 32830-1000

Merchandise Mail Order (Guest Service Mail Order)
P.O. Box 10070
Lake Buena Vista, FL 32830-0070

Walt Disney World Central Reservations
P.O. Box 10100
Lake Buena Vista, FL 32830-0100

Walt Disney World Educational Programs
P.O. Box 10000
Lake Buena Vista, FL 32830-1000

Walt Disney World Info/Guest Letters/Letters to Mickey Mouse
P.O. Box 10040
Lake Buena Vista, FL 32830-0040

Walt Disney World Ticket Mail Order
P.O. Box 10140
Lake Buena Vista, FL 32830-0140

Using a combination of our in-park researchers and updates sent in by readers, this new feature will allow you to see all current wait and FASTPASS-distribution times at every attraction in all four parks, as well as our estimated wait times for these attractions for the next couple of hours in advance. If you've got a Web-enabled cell phone, you'll be able to see instantly where the shortest lines are at any time of day. And as long as you've got that smart phone handy while visiting the World, we and your fellow *Unofficial Guide* readers would love it if you could report on the wait times you see while you're there. Go to **m.TouringPlans.com,** log in to your user account, and click the button labeled "+Time" in the upper right corner to help everyone out.

Another feature of the site is a comprehensive free online trip planner that allows you to keep track of all your trip details, including packing checklists, flight information, ground transportation, lodging, budgets, and daily activities in each of the parks. Best of all, you can share trip details with family, friends, and others. When it's time for your trip, you can print the organizer's pages in any of three different sizes: the pocket size is handy for on-the-go types interested in traveling as light as possible; a standard size fits many off-the-shelf binders as well as the *PassPorter* organizer guides; and the large format is a notebook-sized page for folks who prefer more room. Free refills and blank templates for all formats are also available. The online organizer also includes pages for Disneyland.

If you develop software for mobile devices, note that virtually all information on TouringPlans.com—including attraction, resort, and wait-time data, as well as complete touring plans—is available by API using XML over HTTP. E-mail **len@touringplans.com** for details.

Much of our Web content, including the online trip planner and the Least Expensive Ticket Calculator described on page 49, is completely free for anyone to use. The online crowd calendar is also free to owners of the latest editions of this guide, *Mini-Mickey: The Pocket-Sized Unofficial Guide to Walt Disney World, The Unofficial Guide to Walt Disney World with Kids,* and *The Unofficial Guide to Walt Disney World without Kids.* Access to part of the site, most notably the additional touring plans and in-park wait times, requires a small subscription fee of around $10 (current-book owners get 50% off). This nominal charge helps keep us online and costs roughly the same as a sandwich and drink at Flame Tree Barbecue in the Animal Kingdom. Plus, TouringPlans.com offers a 45-day money-back guarantee—something we don't think Flame Tree can match.

BEST MONEY-SAVING SITE Mary Waring's **MouseSavers.com** is the kind of site for which the Web was invented. It keeps an updated list of discounts and reservation codes for use at Disney resorts. The codes are separated into categories such as "For the general public" and "For residents of certain states." Anyone who calls Disney's central reservations office (☎ 407-W-DISNEY) can use a current code and get the discounted rate. Savings can be considerable—up to 40% in many cases. The site also displays discounts for AAA members and Disney Annual Pass holders, making it easier to determine whether those options make financial sense for your trip. Two often-overlooked site features are the discount codes for rental cars and non-Disney hotels in the area.

BEST WALT DISNEY WORLD PREVIEW SITE If you want to prepare your children for the attractions, or if you just want to see what a particular attraction is like, visit **YouTube** (**www.youtube.com**). Enter the name of the desired attraction in the search bar at the top of the page, and several videos should come up. Videos of indoor ("dark") rides are usually inferior to those of outdoor rides due to poor lighting, but even the videos of indoor rides generally provide a good sense of what the attraction is about.

OTHER SITES No matter where you travel, do a Web search with the city name and the word *coupon*—for example, "Orlando coupon." You'll be surprised how many deals for discounts come up (avoid deals connected to time-shares and coupons that are valid only if you buy something first). Also, at **www.squaremouth.com,** you'll find an independent travel-insurance agency with a Web program that lets you compare more than 100 insurance options from a multitude of companies.

BEST DISNEY DISCUSSION BOARDS The best online discussions of all things Disney can be found at **www.disboards.com.** With tens of thousands of members and millions of posts, these discussion boards are the most active and popular on the Web. For boards that feel more

WDW Phone Numbers

General Information	☎ 407-824-4321
General Information for the Hearing Impaired (TTY)	☎ 407-827-5141
Accommodations/Reservations	☎ 407-W-DISNEY or 407-824-8000
All-Star Movies Resort	☎ 407-939-7000
All-Star Music Resort	☎ 407-939-6000
All-Star Sports Resort	☎ 407-939-5000
AMC Theatres Pleasure Island 24	☎ 407-298-4488 or 888-262-4386
Animal Kingdom Lodge and Villas (Jambo House and Kidani Village)	☎ 407-938-3000
Beach Club Resort	☎ 407-934-8000
Blizzard Beach Information	☎ 407-560-3400
BoardWalk Inn Resort	☎ 407-939-5100
Caribbean Beach Resort	☎ 407-934-3400
Celebration Realty Office	☎ 407-566-4663
Centra Care	☎ 407-200-2273
Formosa Gardens	☎ 407-397-7032
Kissimmee	☎ 407-390-1888
Lake Buena Vista	☎ 407-934-2273
Vineland	☎ 407-351-6682
Cirque du Soleil	☎ 407-939-7600
Contemporary Resort–Bay Lake Tower	☎ 407-824-1000
Convention Information	☎ 407-828-3200
Coronado Springs Resort	☎ 407-939-1000
Dining Advance Reservations	☎ 407-WDW-DINE (939-3463)
Disabled Guests Special Requests	☎ 407-939-7807
Disney Professional Seminars	☎ 407-824-7997
DisneyQuest	☎ 407-828-4600
Downtown Disney Information	☎ 407-828-3058
ESPN Wide World of Sports Complex	☎ 407-939-4263
Fantasia Gardens Miniature Golf	☎ 407-939-7529
Fort Wilderness Campground	☎ 407-824-2900
Golf Reservations and Information	☎ 407-WDW-GOLF (939-4653)
Grand Floridian Resort & Spa	☎ 407-824-3000
Group Camping	☎ 407-939-7807 (press 4)
Guided-tour Information	☎ 407-WDW-TOUR (939-8687)
Guided VIP Solo Tours	☎ 407-560-4033

WDW Phone Numbers (continued)

House of Blues Tickets and Information	☎ 407-934-2583
Lost and Found for articles lost:	
Today at Animal Kingdom	☎ 407-938-2785
Today at Disney's Hollywood Studios	☎ 407-560-3720
Today at Epcot	☎ 407-560-7500
Today at Magic Kingdom	☎ 407-824-4521
Today at Universal Orlando	☎ 407-224-4244
Today at Islands of Adventure	☎ 407-224-4245
Yesterday or before *(all Disney parks)*	☎ 407-824-4245
Merchandise Guest Services	☎ 407-363-6200
Ocala Chamber of Commerce	☎ 352-629-8051
Old Key West Resort	☎ 407-827-7700
Outdoor Recreation Reservations and Information	☎ 407-WDW-PLAY (939-7529)
Polynesian Resort	☎ 407-824-2000
Pop Century Resort	☎ 407-938-4000
Port Orleans Resort	☎ 407-934-6000
Resort Dining	☎ 407-WDW-DINE (939-3463)

familiar than your neighborhood bar, try **disneyecho.emuck.com.** Disney visitors from the United Kingdom can say "cheerio" to one another whilst online at **www.wdisneyw.com/forums,** where tips on transatlantic-airfare discounts, visa requirements, American customs, and more can be found.

BEST INTERNET RADIO STATION We thought our couple-hundred-hour collection of theme-park digital audio was complete until we found **www.mouseworldradio.com.** Several different radio stations are available (some free, others for a small fee), playing everything from attraction ride scores and hotel background music to old sound clips from Disney-resort TV ads. What makes Mouse World Radio special is that the tracks match what the Disney parks are playing at the time of day you're listening. So every morning at 8 a.m., you'll hear essentially the same music that's currently playing at the Magic Kingdom before it opens, and every night at 9 p.m. you'll hear *IllumiNations* just as if you were at Epcot. An added bonus: several stations contain lyric-free Disney background music, suitable for listening at work.

BEST PODCAST FOR DISNEY NEWS *Unofficial Guide* coauthor Len Testa cohosts three weekly podcasts (on Monday, Wednesday, and Friday) on all things related to Disney World. Free subscriptions are available through iTunes. These shows consistently rank among the top iTunes travel podcasts, drawing more than 20,000 listeners per

Saratoga Springs Resort & Spa–Treehouse Villas	☎ 407-827-1100
Security	
Routine	☎ 407-560-7959
Urgent	☎ 407-560-1990
Shades of Green Resort	☎ 407-824-3400
Telecommunication for the Deaf Reservations	☎ 407-939-7670
Tennis Reservations/Lessons	☎ 407-621-1991
Walt Disney Travel Company	☎ 407-828-3232
Walt Disney World Dolphin	☎ 407-934-4000
Walt Disney World Speedway	☎ 407-939-0130
Walt Disney World Swan	☎ 407-934-3000
Walt Disney World Ticket Inquiries	☎ 407-566-4985
Weather Information	☎ 407-827-4545
Wilderness Lodge and Villas Resort	☎ 407-824-3200
Winter Summerland Miniature Golf	☎ 407-560-3000
Wrecker Service	☎ 407-824-0976
Yacht Club Resort	☎ 407-934-7000

show. Len's podcast has covered topics from the best resorts and restaurants for small children to touring plans that show how Kevin Bacon is linked to every attraction in the Magic Kingdom. Noted for its spontaneity (read: lack of preparation) and what Disney geeks consider humor, the show assumes that everyone listening must be doing so as part of some court-mandated community service. Drop the hosts a line and they'll put in a good word with your parole officer. Visit **www.wdwtoday.com** for more details.

BEST DISNEY BLOG John Frost's unofficial Disney blog (**www.thedisneyblog.com**) is witty, concise, and updated continually. Topics cover everything in the Disney universe, from theme parks and movies to the latest rumors. Best of all, you'll find links to other Disney-related sites on the Web to continue your addiction, er, planning.

BEST SITE FOR BREAKING NEWS AND RUMORS We try to check **www.wdwmagic.com** every few days for the latest news and gossip on Disney World. The site also features pages dedicated to major rides, parades, and shows in each park, including audio and video. The calendar of events has traditionally been a good place to check park hours, Extra Magic Hours, and the like; some readers, however, report that maintenance and accuracy have taken a slight hit recently.

BEST THEME-PARK-INSIDER SITE If *The E! True Hollywood Story* ever did an episode on theme-park development, the result would be something like **www.jimhillmedia.com.** Well researched and supplied with limitless insider information, Jim Hill's columns guide you through the internal squabbles, shareholder revolts, budget compromises, and outside competition that have made (and that still make) Walt Disney World what it is.

BEST TRIVIA SITES Lou Mongello's excellent *Walt Disney World Trivia Book* has an equally good online companion; check it out on iTunes and at **www.wdwradio.com.** You'll find message boards, Disney theme-park news, and more. Lou hosts live Net chats at his site, usually on Tuesdays. Lou also hosts the *WDW Radio Show* podcast, where his name functions as an all-purpose greeting ("Mongello, everyone!") and invective ("Oh, Mongello!") to his fans.

At long last, fans of Steve Barrett's *Hidden Mickeys* book now have an online destination where they can keep updated on the latest tri-circle sightings at **www.hiddenmickeysguide.com.** Steve also writes the *Hassle-Free Walt Disney World Vacation* guidebook, chock-full of touring plans and Disney advice that he's developed for family and friends over the years. Aside from the *Unofficial Guide,* Steve's probably got the most thorough and thoughtful touring advice around.

BEST ONLINE TOUR Disney has teamed up with Google to present a 3-D virtual walk-through of the Orlando theme parks and resorts via Google Earth. While you can't yet go inside the attractions, you do get an unparalleled simulation of the park experience. Visit **www.disneyworld.com/3dparks** and hope for the day they're able to pipe the smell of the Main Street Bakery to your desktop.

BEST ORLANDO WEATHER INFORMATION Printable 15-day forecasts for the Orlando area are available from **www.accuweather.com**. The site is especially useful in winter and spring, when temperatures can vary dramatically. During summer, the ultraviolet-index forecasts will help you choose between a tube of sunscreen and a keg of it.

BEST SAFETY SITE All children younger than age 6 must be properly restrained when traveling by car in Florida. Check **www.flhsmv.gov/fhp/cps** to learn about state child-restraint requirements.

BEST WEB SITE FOR ORLANDO TRAFFIC, ROADWORK, AND CONSTRUCTION INFORMATION Visit **www.expresswayauthority.com** for the latest information on roadwork in the Orlando and Orange County areas. The site also contains detailed maps, directions, and toll-rate information for the most popular tourist destinations.

BEST DRIVING DIRECTIONS The printable directions available at **www.mapquest.com** are accurate and efficient. We especially like the feature that allows you to get driving directions for the return drive with the click of a button.

There are hundreds of other Disney sites, as well as sites that rate and contrast thrill rides in theme parks in the United States and all over the world. Start with the sites listed previously and follow the links.

Information about Disney World is also available at public libraries, travel agencies, and AAA; also see "Important Walt Disney World Addresses" on page 27.

WHEN *to* GO *to* WALT DISNEY WORLD

Why do they call it tourist season if we can't shoot them?

—Palatka, Florida, outdoorsman

SELECTING THE TIME OF YEAR FOR YOUR VISIT

WALT DISNEY WORLD IS BUSIEST Christmas Day through New Year's Day. Also extremely busy are Thanksgiving weekend, the week of Presidents' Day, the first full week of November, spring break for colleges, and the two weeks around Easter. On just a single day in these peak times, as many as 92,000 people have toured the Magic Kingdom! This level of attendance isn't typical—only those who simply cannot go at any other time should tackle the parks at their peak

unofficial **TIP**
You can't pick a less crowded time to visit Walt Disney World than the period between Thanksgiving and Christmas.

The least busy time is the week after Thanksgiving until the week before Christmas. Next slowest are the second full week of November through the weekend preceding Thanksgiving, September (after Labor Day) and October, January 4 through the first week of February (except the Martin Luther King holiday weekend), and the week after Easter through early June. Late February, March, and early April are dicey. Crowds ebb and flow according to spring-break schedules and the timing of Presidents' Day weekend. Though crowds have grown in September and October as a result of promotions aimed at locals and the international market, these months continue to be good for weekday touring at the Magic Kingdom, Disney's Hollywood Studios, and Animal Kingdom, and for weekend visits to Epcot.

The Downside of Off-season Touring

Though we strongly recommend going to Disney World in the fall, winter, or spring, there are a few trade-offs. The parks often open late and close early during off-season. When they open as late as 9 a.m., everyone arrives at about the same time. A late opening coupled with an early closing drastically reduces touring hours. Even when crowds are small, it's difficult to see big parks such as the Magic Kingdom between 9 a.m. and 6 p.m. Early closing (before 8 p.m.) also usually means no evening parades or fireworks. And because these are slow times, some rides and attractions may be closed. Finally, central Florida temperatures fluctuate wildly during late fall, winter, and early spring; daytime highs in the 40s and 50s aren't uncommon.

Given the choice, however, smaller crowds, bargain prices, and stress-free touring are worth risking cold weather or closed attractions. Touring in fall and other "off" periods is so much easier that our research team, at the risk of being blasphemous, would advise taking children out of school for a Disney World visit.

Most readers who have tried Disney World at various times agree. A gentleman from Ottawa, Ontario, who toured in early December, writes:

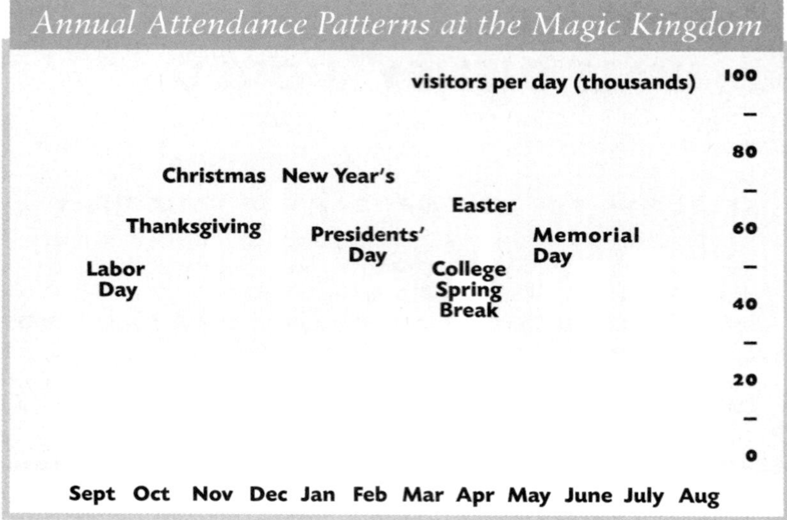

unofficial **TIP**
In our opinion, the risk of encountering colder weather and closed attractions during an off-season visit to Walt Disney World is worth it.

It was the most enjoyable trip [to Walt Disney World] *I have ever had, and I can't imagine going* [back] *to Disney World when it is crowded. Even without the crowds, we were still very tired by afternoon. We will never go again at any other time.*

A father of two from Reynoldsburg, Ohio, offers this opinion:

> *Taking your kids out of school. Is it worth it? Yes! It used to be true that missing a week of school would place your child so far behind it could take months for him/her to regain that lost week. Not so today. With advance preparations and informing the teachers months before our departure, this was no problem. With less than an hour of homework after dinner, our kids went back to school with assignments completed and no makeup work. But it was all those other hours with no lines and no heat that were the real payoff.*

There is another side to this story, and we have received some well-considered letters from parents and teachers who don't think taking kids out of school is such a hot idea. From a father in Fairfax, Virginia:

> *My wife and I are disappointed that you seem to be encouraging families to take their children out of school to avoid the crowds at WDW during the summer months. My wife is an eighth-grade science teacher of chemistry and physics. She has parents pull their children, some honor-roll students, out of school for vacations, only to discover when they return that the students are unable to comprehend the material. Parental suspicions* [about] *the quality of their children's education should be raised when children go to school for six hours a day yet supposedly can complete this same instruction with "less than an hour of homework" each night.*

Likewise, a teacher from Louisville, Kentucky, didn't mince words:

> *Teachers absolutely hate it when a kid misses school for a week, because (a) parents expect a neat little educational packet to take with them as if every minute can be planned—not practicable; (b) when the kid returns he is going to be behind, and it is difficult to make up classroom instruction.*
>
> *If a parent bothers to ask my opinion, I tell them bluntly it's their choice. If the student's grades go down, they have to accept that as part of their family decision. I have a student out this entire week, skiing in Colorado. There's no way she can make up some of the class activities (and that's exactly what I told her mom).*

A Martinez, California, teacher offers this compelling analogy:

> *There are a precious 180 days for us as teachers to instruct our students, and there are 185 days during the year for Disney World. I have seen countless students during my 14 years of teaching struggle to catch up the rest of the year due to a week of vacation during critical instructional periods.*
>
> *The analogy I use with my students' parents is that it is like walking out of a movie after watching the first five minutes, then returning for the last five minutes and trying to figure out what happened. That is what the students experience when they leave at the beginning of units of study to go to Disney World and return a week later.*

unofficial **TIP**
Instead of taking the kids out of school, consider scheduling your Disney World trip immediately following the last week of school in the spring or during the week prior to school starting in the fall. The crowds will be well below summer peak. Obviously, this strategy will require some advance planning and organization, but the payoff is well worth the effort.

BE UNCONVENTIONAL The Orange County Convention Center in Orlando hosts some of the largest conventions and trade shows in the world. Rooms anywhere near Walt Disney World are hard to find when there's a big convention, and as this Toronto, Ontario, reader points out, are also expensive:

> *If saving money on accommodations is an important part of your trip, be sure to check rates on the Net* before *you settle on a date. Trade shows at the Orange County Convention Center can host over 100,000 attendees, with most of them staying one to a room. This drives rates on even average properties to two or three times* [normal] *rates. Since all large conventions are scheduled over one year out, these spikes in room rates should be visible up to 12 months prior.*

You can check the convention schedule at the Orlando Orange County Convention Center for the next seven months at **www.occc.net/global/calendar.**

DON'T FORGET AUGUST Kids go back to school pretty early in Florida (and in a lot of other places, too). This makes mid- to late August a good time to visit Walt Disney World for families who can't vacation during the off-season. A New Jersey mother of two school-age children spells it out:

> *The end of August is the PERFECT* [reader's emphasis] *time to go (just watch out for hurricanes, it's the season). There were virtually no wait times, 20 minutes at the most.*

TOP TEN AMERICAN THEME PARKS

THEME PARK	ANNUAL ATTENDANCE	AVERAGE DAILY ATTENDANCE
Magic Kingdom	16.2 million	44,384
Disneyland	14.6 million	40,000
Epcot	9.9 million	27,123
Disney's Hollywood Studios	8.7 million	23,836
Animal Kingdom	8.2 million	22,466
Universal Studios Orlando	6.1 million	15,172
Islands of Adventure	5.8 million	15,890
Disney's California Adventure	5.8 million	15,890
SeaWorld	5.6 million	15,310
Universal Studios Hollywood	4.7 million	12,877

Source: *Amusement Business* magazine

A mom from Rapid City, South Dakota, agrees:

School starts very early in Florida, so our mid-August visit was great for crowds, but not for heat.

And from a family from Roxbury, New Jersey:

I recommend the last two weeks of August for anyone traveling there during the summer. We have visited twice during this time of year and have had great success touring the parks.

HIGH-LOW, HIGH-LOW, IT'S OFF TO DISNEY WE GO Though we recommend off-season touring, we realize that it's not possible for many families. We want to make it clear, therefore, that you can have a wonderful experience regardless of when you go. Our advice, irrespective of season, is to arrive early at the parks and avoid the crowds by using one of our touring plans. If attendance is light, kick back and forget the touring plans.

WE'VE GOT WEATHER! Long before Walt Disney World, tourists visited Florida year-round to enjoy the temperate tropical and subtropical climates. The best weather months generally are October, November, March, and April. Fall is usually dry, whereas spring is wetter. December, January, and February vary, with average highs of 72°F to 73°F intermixed with highs in the 50°F-to-65°F range. May is hot but tolerable. June, July, August, and September are the warmest months. Rain is possible anytime, usually in the form of scattered thunderstorms. An entire day of rain is unusual. (see chart next page)

CROWD CONDITIONS AND THE BEST AND WORST PARKS TO VISIT FOR EACH DAY OF THE YEAR Each year we receive more than 1,000 e-mails and letters inquiring about crowd conditions on specific dates throughout the year. Readers also want to know which park is best to visit on each day of their stay. To make things easier for you (and us!), on our Web site, **TouringPlans.com,** we provide a calendar covering all of 2010. For each date, we offer a crowd-level index based on a scale of 1 to 10, with 1 being least crowded and 10 being most crowded. Our calendar takes into account all holidays, special events, and more, as described below. The

Walt Disney World Climate

	Jan	Feb	Mar	Apr	May	Jun	Jul	Aug	Sep	Oct	Nov	Dec
Average Daily Low (F°)	49°	50°	55°	60°	66°	71°	73°	73°	73°	65°	57°	51°
Average Daily High (F°)	72°	73°	78°	84°	88°	91°	92°	92°	90°	84°	78°	73°
Average Daily Temperature (F°)	61°	62°	67°	72°	77°	81°	82°	82°	82°	75°	68°	62°
Average Daily-humidity Percentages	74	71	71	69	72	77	79	80	80	77	76	76
Average Rainfall per Month (Inches)	2.1	0.8	3.2	2.2	3.9	7.4	7.8	6.3	5.6	2.8	1.8	1.9
Number of Days of Rain per Month	6	7	8	6	9	14	17	16	14	9	6	6

same calendar lists the best and worst park(s) to visit in terms of crowd conditions on any given day. All you have to do is look up the days of your intended visit on the calendar.

HOW WE DETERMINE CROWD LEVELS AND BEST DAYS A number of factors contribute to the models we use to predict both crowd levels and the best days to visit each theme park.

Data we use to predict crowd levels:

- Historical park hours from the same time period in previous years
- Disney's special-events calendar (for example, Grad Nights and Mickey's Not-So-Scary Halloween Party)
- Legal holidays in the United States
- Public-school schedules (including spring-break schedules for the 50 largest public-school districts east of the Mississippi, plus Massachusetts and Connecticut)
- Weekly historical occupancy rates for Orlando-area hotels
- Central Florida tourism demographics

Historical park hours include the actual operating hours for all of the past five years. Special events include everything from official Disney-sanctioned events such as Grad Nights and Super Soap Weekend to such independent events as Gay Days. Our hotel data contains weekly occupancy rates for seven different areas within the Orlando market, including the key Disney-area hotels located in Lake Buena Vista, in the greater International Drive area, in Kissimmee, and along US 192 (Irlo Bronson Memorial Highway). Our central-Florida tourism demographics cover everything from where Orlando visitors come from and how long they stay, to how many people make up each party and which theme parks they visit.

Data we use to determine the best days for each park:

- Actual wait-time statistics gathered in the parks

- Our own surveys of Disney guests' touring habits
- Disney's Extra Magic Hours schedule
- Special events calendars
- U.S. legal holidays
- Outside sources (such as the U.S. Department of Transportation and *Consumer Reports*)

SOME EXCEPTIONS You'll occasionally see a particular recommendation in the calendar that contradicts general advice given in this guide. As an example, the *Unofficial Guide* recommends, as a rule of thumb, to avoid any park on its Extra Magic Hour days. But we recommend Epcot on the Tuesday before Christmas, even though Tuesday is typically Epcot's morning Extra Magic Hour day. Why? Because Epcot is the best park to be in when crowds are large, as they are around Christmas. The effect of additional crowds from Epcot's morning Extra Magic Hours pales in comparison to the effect of holiday crowds in the other parks, especially the Magic Kingdom. In this case, Epcot is not so much a "good" choice as it is the proverbial lesser evil.

Likewise, we'll occasionally recommend the Magic Kingdom on a Thursday or Monday, especially during the slower months, even if there's a special event like Mickey's Not-So-Scary Halloween Party scheduled there. This is because we're trying to recommend each park at least once in any seven-day period so that families taking a week-long vacation can be sure to visit each park on at least one day. When all the other rules used don't fulfill this requirement, we're forced to make another of those lesser evil recommendations.

EXTRA MAGIC HOURS

EXTRA MAGIC HOURS is a perk for families staying at a Walt Disney World resort, including the Swan, Dolphin, and Shades of Green, and the Hilton in the Downtown Disney resort area. On selected days of the week, Disney-resort guests will be able to enter a Disney theme park one hour earlier, or stay in a selected theme park up to three hours later than the official park-operating hours. Theme park visitors not staying at a Disney resort may stay in the park for Extra Magic Hour evenings, but cannot experience any rides, attractions, or shows. In other words, they can shop and eat.

Because Extra Magic Hours figure so prominently in our Crowd-level Calendar calculations, and because Disney is constantly rearranging the Extra Magic Hours schedule for each theme park, we have been forced to withdraw the calendar from the guidebook. Fortunately we can make daily changes to our Crowd-level Calendar on our Web site, **TouringPlans.com,** and thus keep the calendar totally updated for you.

unofficial **TIP**
You'll need to have a Park Hopper option on your admission ticket to take advantage of the Extra Magic Hours at more than one theme park on the same day.

We should also mention that the swimming theme parks, Typhoon Lagoon and Blizzard Beach, also offer Extra Magic Hours.

WHAT'S REQUIRED? A valid admission ticket is required to enter the park, and you must show your Disney Resort ID when entering. For evening Extra Magic Hours, show your Disney Resort ID if you want to experience any of the rides or attractions, or just show up at the park turnstiles at any time after evening Extra Magic Hours begin.

unofficial **TIP**
Extra Magic Hours draw more Disney-resort guests to the host park, which results in longer lines than you would otherwise experience.

WHEN ARE EXTRA MAGIC HOURS OFFERED? The regular Extra Magic Hours schedule is subject to constant change, especially during holidays and other periods of peak attendance. Gone are the days when you could be certain which park was running Extra Magic Hours.

You can phone Walt Disney World Information at ☎ 407-824-4321 or 407-939-6244 (press 0 for a live representative), check the parks calendars at **www.disneyworld.com,** or visit **www.wdwmagic.com/calendar.htm** for the dates of your visit (see our caveat on page 31, though). The same information, plus tips for avoiding crowds, is available at our Web site.

We seriously hope that Disney will adopt a permanent schedule, but if it does not, use the information available from Walt Disney World Information, the official Web site, or WDWMagic.com to discover any schedule changes that might affect you. To avoid the most crowded park, simply steer clear of the one(s) offering Extra Magic Hours, or access **TouringPlans.com** for guidance.

WHAT DO EXTRA MAGIC HOURS MEAN TO YOU? Crowds are likely to be larger when the theme parks host an Extra Magic Hours session. If you're not staying at a Disney resort, the *Unofficial Guide* suggests avoiding the park hosting Extra Magic Hours, if at all possible.

If you're staying at a Disney resort, there are a couple of strategies you can employ to cut down on your wait in lines. One strategy is to avoid the park hosting Extra Magic Hours entirely, if possible.

If you can be at the park when it opens, a second strategy would be to visit the park offering a morning Extra Magic Hours session until lunchtime, then visit another, less-crowded park in the afternoon. This strategy would allow you to take advantage of smaller morning crowds to visit the headliner attractions in one park, then take a slower, more relaxed tour of another park in the afternoon. For example, you might visit the Magic Kingdom Thursday morning, seeing as much of Tomorrowland or Fantasyland as possible during Extra Magic Hours, then visit the rest of the park until lunch. Before the Magic Kingdom crowds peaked in the early afternoon, you'd leave for Epcot and spend the rest of the day there.

unofficial **TIP**
Whatever edge resort guests gain by taking advantage of early entry is offset by horrendous crowds later in the day. During busier times of year, regardless of your hotel, avoid any park on the day it's scheduled for early entry.

Consider two things if choosing between morning or evening Extra Magic Hours sessions: first, whether your family functions better getting up early or staying up late, and second, the time at which the parks close to day guests. If you can handle those early mornings, you'll find shorter lines during morning Extra Magic Hours. Evening Extra Magic Hours are most useful when the crowds are low and the parks close relatively early to the general public, so your family doesn't have to stay up past midnight to take advantage of the perk.

EARLY ENTRY (AKA MORNING EXTRA MAGIC HOURS)

THE EARLY-ENTRY PROGRAM APPLIES to the Magic Kingdom, Epcot, Animal Kingdom, Disney's Hollywood Studios, Blizzard Beach, and Typhoon Lagoon Water Park. Several days of the week, Disney-resort guests are invited to enter a designated theme park one hour before the general public. During the early-entry hour, guests can enjoy attractions opened early just for them.

How Early Entry Affects Attendance at the Theme Parks

Early entry strongly affects attendance at the theme parks, especially during busier times of year. Vast numbers of Disney-resort guests tour whichever park is designated for early entry. If the Magic Kingdom is tapped for early entry on Thursday, for example, it'll be more crowded that day, while Epcot, Animal Kingdom, and Disney's Hollywood Studios will be less crowded. Epcot, Animal Kingdom, and Disney's Hollywood Studios will be more crowded when those parks are slated for early entry.

TYPICAL EXTRA MAGIC HOURS SCHEDULE ***(frequently varies)***

Morning

MONDAY	TUESDAY	WEDNESDAY	THURSDAY	FRIDAY	SATURDAY	SUNDAY
Animal Kingdom	Epcot	–	Magic Kingdom	–	DHS	–

Evening

MONDAY	TUESDAY	WEDNESDAY	THURSDAY	FRIDAY	SATURDAY	SUNDAY
DHS	–	Animal Kingdom	–	Epcot	–	Magic Kingdom

During holiday periods and summer, when Disney hotels are full, early entry makes a tremendous difference in crowds at the designated park. The program funnels so many people into the early-entry park that it fills by about 10 a.m. and is practically gridlocked by noon.

If you elect to use your early-entry privileges, be among the first early entrants. A mother of three from Lee Summit, Missouri, writes:

> *Our first full day at WDW, we went to the Magic Kingdom on an early-entry day for resort guests. We were there at 7:30 a.m. and were able to walk onto all the rides in Fantasyland with no wait. At 8:45 a.m. we positioned ourselves at the Adventureland rope and ran toward Splash Mountain when the rope dropped. We were able to ride Splash Mountain with no wait (switching off), and then Big Thunder with about a 15-minute wait (switching off). We then went straight to the Jungle Cruise and the wait was already 30 minutes, so we skipped it. The park became incredibly crowded as the day progressed, and we were all exhausted from getting up so early to get there for early entry.*

We left the park around noon. After that day, I resolved to avoid early-entry days and instead be at a non-early-entry park about a half hour before official opening time. This worked much better for us.

This note from a North Bend, Washington, dad emphasizes the importance of arriving at the beginning of the early-entry period.

We only used early entry once—to [Disney's Hollywood Studios]. *We got there 20 minutes after early entry opened, and the wait for Tower of Terror was already one-and-a-half hours long* [without FASTPASS]. *We skipped it.*

A Dallas mother of two had a similar experience:

The crowds were generally OK, but we did not follow your advice to avoid the morning Extra Magic Hours park. We went to the Magic Kingdom and it was wall-to-wall people, even at opening. . . . EVERYBODY from EVERY DISNEY HOTEL was there, it seemed. We started to go to Animal Kingdom for Extra Magic Hours one morning, got to the bus stop, then changed our plans and went to [Disney's Hollywood Studios]. *It was nearly empty, and we completed our tour in almost half a day. . . . The morning Extra Magic Hours weren't a big deal the first year because the crowds were so light, but this year we learned the hard way.*

A Louisville, Kentucky, family concurs:

We attended all of the morning EMHs that week, looking at the crowd levels projected by the Unofficial Guide *and thinking that EMHs would be lightly attended. Big mistake. The headline attractions at each park (Space Mountain, Soarin', Expedition Everest, and Tower of Terror) had long lines almost from the beginning. We got much more accomplished in the mornings at parks that weren't holding morning EMHs. No more EMHs for us.*

A woman from Ann Arbor, Michigan, who is clearly working overtime trying to figure all this stuff out, says:

We are starting to think that reverse–reverse psychology might work: Disney opens one park earlier for all their guests, so all the guests go to that park, but then everyone buys your book in which you tell them not to go to that park because all Disney guests are there, so no one goes to that park; therefore we can go to that park because people think it is going to be packed and they avoid it. What do you think?

Early Entry and Park Hopping

An alternative strategy for Disney-resort guests is to take advantage of early entry, but only until the designated park gets crowded. At that time, move to another park. This plan works particularly well at the Magic Kingdom for families with young children who love the attractions in Fantasyland. However, it will take you about an hour to commute to the second park of the day. If, for example, you depart the Magic Kingdom for the Disney's Hollywood Studios at 10 a.m., you'll find the Studios pretty crowded when you arrive at about 11 a.m. Keeping these and other considerations in mind, here are some guidelines:

1. Use the early-entry–park-hopping strategy during the less busy times of year when the parks close early. You'll get a jump on the general public and add an hour to what, in the off-season, is an already short touring day.
2. Use the early-entry–park-hopping strategy to complete touring a second park that you've already visited on a previous day, or specifically to see live entertainment in the second park.

A Providence, Rhode Island, reader found early admission an advantage:

> *During the off-season, the early admission was great. Only on Saturday did the crowd get so large that there were lines and bottlenecks. The mother behind me at Dumbo told me that they had waited three hours to ride Dumbo during their last visit to WDW. She took advantage of early admission to let her kid ride three times in a row with no waiting.*

Never hop to Animal Kingdom—it is almost always the first park to close each evening, so arriving later than 2 p.m. for the handful of remaining hours is not generally a good use of time, plus it will be too crowded by the time you arrive.

On any day except the park's Extra Magic Hours days, hopping to Epcot is usually good. Epcot is able to handle large crowds better than any other Disney park, minimizing the effects of a midday arrival. Also, World Showcase has a large selection of interesting dining options, making it a good choice for evening touring.

Don't hop to the park with early entry (Extra Magic Hours). The idea is to avoid crowds, not join them.

Limit your hopping to two parks per day. Hopping to a third park in one day would result in more time spent commuting than saved by avoiding crowds.

Nighttime Version of Extra Magic Hours

The nighttime Extra Magic Hours program allows Disney-resort guests to enjoy a different theme park on specified nights for up to three hours after it closes to the general public. Guests pay no additional charge to participate but must show their resort IDs at each ride or attraction they wish to experience. You can also show up at the turnstiles at any point after evening Extra Magic Hours have started. Note that if you've been in another park that day, you'll need the Park Hopping feature on your admission ticket to enter.

Evening Extra Magic Hours now approach morning Extra Magic Hours in terms of crowd levels. A mom from Fairhaven, Massachusetts, doesn't mince words:

> *I say steer clear of a park that is open late. There are only a few attractions open and tons of people trying to get on them. It was a nightmare trying to get around!*

A New Hampshire reader agrees:

> *I do think you should put in big, bold letters to avoid EMH days at parks. I know they're on the Web sites and they're mentioned in the*

book, but that was the biggest thing we noticed. Epcot the day after Memorial Day was worse than the Magic Kingdom on the same day, just because it was an EMH night.

And a Parma, Ohio, family of four chimes in with this:

There are two important things for everyone to know: never go to the park offering early admission for resort guests, and never go to the Magic Kingdom when the late-night Extra Magic Hours are offered. The only unmanageable crowds we encountered were on Friday night during Extra Magic Hours. Instead, we typically arrived at a non-early-entry park at 8:45 a.m. and always stayed ahead of the crowds. We never stayed in a park past 3 p.m., always returning to our resort for a quick refresher before hopping to another park in the evening.

From a Fredericton, New Brunswick, dad:

Don't bother with evening Extra Magic Hours unless they start at 11 p.m. or later. We found the park was PACKED and the crowds didn't ease up till about an hour before closing. Wait times for the big-ticket rides were over an hour, and it was difficult to make your way from one part of the park to another.

Animal Kingdom, with its shorter operating hours, is somewhat problematic, especially for evening Extra Magic Hours, as a Sydney, Australia, couple explains:

Animal Kingdom was an amazing place to visit—we were there for the Extra Magic Hours but were disappointed that most of the attractions close early, so there seems to be little point in having extended hours. Disney really needs to advertise this fact so that patrons will not miss out on most [Animal Kingdom] *attractions by coming for the evening.*

Another disadvantage to evening Extra Magic Hours at Animal Kingdom is the animals' bedtimes—most hit the hay at dusk.

More attractions operate during the extended evening period than during the early-entry hour in the morning. Certain fast-food and full-service restaurants remain open as well. The program is presumably in response to perks extended to Universal Orlando hotel guests that allow them to go to the front of the line at any Universal attraction. Disney has thus far maintained a level playing field, rejecting programs that extend line-breaking privileges to resort guests.

SUMMER AND HOLIDAYS

A READER FROM COLUMBUS, OHIO, once observed, "The main thing I learned from your book is not to go during the summer or at holiday times. Once you know that, you don't need a guidebook."

While we might argue with the reader's conclusion, we agree that avoiding summer and holidays is a wise strategy. That said, we also understand that many folks have no choice concerning the time of year they visit Disney World. Much of this book, in fact, is dedicated to making sure those readers who visit during busier times enjoy their experience. Sure, off-season touring is preferable, but, armed with knowledge and some strategy, you can have a great time whenever you visit.

To put things in perspective, early summer (up to about June 15) and late summer (after August 15) aren't nearly as crowded as the intervening period. And even midsummer crowds pale in comparison to the hordes during holiday periods. If you visit in midsummer or during a holiday, the first thing you need to know is that the theme parks' guest capacity is not infinite. In fact, once a park reaches capacity, only Disney-resort guests arriving via the Disney transportation system are allowed to enter. If you aren't a Disney resort guest, you may find yourself in a situation similar to this Boise, Idaho, dad's:

unofficial **TIP**
If it's not your first trip to Walt Disney World and you must go during a crowded holiday weekend, you may have just as much fun enjoying Disney's fantastic array of shows, parades, fireworks, and more as you would riding the rides.

This is the worst of it. The Magic Kingdom and [Disney's Hollywood Studios] *were so full they closed the parks. For three days we could not enter those parks, so we were forced to go to Epcot and use up two days of our four-day pass. We decided to pay for another night at our hotel to see if the crowds would let up, but no luck. All we could do was just drive around Orlando and sightsee.*

We hasten to point out that this reader would have had no difficulty gaining admission to the parks of his choice had he committed to being at the turnstiles 35 to 60 minutes before official opening time.

Packed-parks Compensation Plan

The thought of teeming throngs jockeying for position in endless lines under the baking Fourth of July sun is enough to wilt the will and ears of the most ardent Mouseketeer. Disney, however, feeling bad about those long lines and challenging touring conditions on packed holidays, compensates patrons with a no-less-than-incredible array of first-rate live entertainment and events.

Shows, parades, concerts, and pageantry continue throughout the day. In the evening, so much is going on that you have to make tough choices. Concerts, parades, light shows, laser shows, fireworks, and dance productions occur almost continually. No question about it: you can go to Walt Disney World on the Fourth of July (or any crowded extended-hours day), never get on a ride, and still have a good time. Admittedly, the situation isn't ideal for a first-timer who wants to experience the attractions, but for anyone else it's a great party.

Disney provides colorful decorations for most holidays, plus special parades and live entertainment for Christmas, New Year's, Easter, and Fourth of July, among others. Regarding Christmas, we advise visiting in early December when you can enjoy the decorations and festivities without the crowds. If you must tour during the holidays and New Year's, skip the Magic Kingdom; consider visiting Epcot or Disney's Hollywood Studios instead.

If you visit on a nonholiday midsummer day, arrive at the turnstile 30 minutes before the stated opening on a non-early-entry day. If you visit during a major holiday period, arrive 60 minutes before. Hit your favorite rides early using one of our touring plans, then go back to your hotel for lunch, a swim, and perhaps a nap. If you're interested in the special parades and shows, return to the park in late afternoon or early evening. Assume that unless you use FASTPASS, early morning will be the only time you can experience the attractions without long waits. Finally, don't wait until the last minute in the evening to leave the park. The exodus at closing is truly mind-boggling.

Epcot is usually the least crowded park during holiday periods. Expect the other parks to be mobbed. To save time in the morning, buy your admission in advance. Also, consider bringing your own stroller or wheelchair instead of renting one of Disney's. If you're touring Epcot or the Magic Kingdom and plan to spend the day, try exiting the park for lunch at a nearby resort hotel. Above all, bring your sense of humor, and pay attention to your group's morale. Bail out when touring is more work than fun.

THE DISNEY CALENDAR

WALT DISNEY WORLD MARATHON Usually held the second weekend after New Year's, the marathon pulls in about 20,000 runners and their families, enough people to affect crowd conditions in the parks. It also disrupts vehicular and pedestrian traffic throughout Disney World. The event expanded to four days in 2009 with the addition of kids' races and a health-and-fitness expo.

MICKEY'S PIRATE AND PRINCESS PARTY This bash takes place in the Magic Kingdom on select evenings from mid-January to early June, and mid-August to early September. The special-ticket event that begins following park closing features a pirate-and-princess-themed fireworks show and parade, and a "quest" for beads and candy. Kids are encouraged to come dressed as their favorite pirate or princess. **Note:** *All 2009 parties have been canceled; call ☎ 407-939-2469 or visit* **www.disneyworld.com** *for information as it becomes available.*

BLACK HISTORY MONTH Black History Month is celebrated throughout Walt Disney World in February with displays, artisans, storytellers, and entertainers. There is no extra charge for the activities, and the celebration's effect on crowd levels is negligible.

ATLANTA BRAVES SPRING TRAINING The Braves hold spring training and play a number of exhibition games at ESPN Wide World of Sports Complex from mid-February through March. You can obtain the exhibition schedule and purchase tickets by calling TicketMaster at ☎ 800-745-3000 or Wide World of Sports at 407-839-3900, or by visiting **www.ticketmaster.com.** You can watch the training sessions at no charge when you buy general admission to Wide World of Sports ($12.75 adults, $10 kids ages 3 to 9).

EPCOT INTERNATIONAL FLOWER & GARDEN FESTIVAL Held annually from mid-March to early June. Expert horticulturists showcase exotic floral displays, share gardening tips, and demonstrate techniques for planting, cultivating, and pest control. The 20 million blooms from some 1,200 species will make your eyes pop, and, best of all, the event doesn't seem to affect crowd levels at Epcot.

GAY DAYS Since 1991, gay, lesbian, bisexual, and transgendered (GLBT) people from around the world have converged on and around the World in early June for a week of events centered around the theme parks. Today, Gay Days attracts more than 135,000 GLBT visitors and their families and friends. Universal Studios, SeaWorld, and Busch Gardens also participate. For additional information, visit **www.gaydays.com.**

TOM JOYNER FAMILY REUNION Radio personality Tom Joyner hosts an extremely popular party at Walt Disney World. Usually held during Labor Day weekend, the Reunion typically features live musical performances, comedy acts, and family-oriented discussions. For more information, visit **www.blackamericaweb.com.**

NIGHT OF JOY This is a Christian-music festival staged at Disney's Hollywood Studios, usually on the second weekend in September. About 16 nationally known acts perform concerts on Friday and Saturday evenings after the park has closed. Cost with tax is $49.95 for one night and $84.95 for both nights. Tickets sold on the day of the event (if available) go for $54.95 with tax. For information or to purchase tickets, call ☎ 407-W-DISNEY or visit **www.tinyurl.com/night-of-joy.**

EPCOT INTERNATIONAL FOOD & WINE FESTIVAL From late September through mid-November, about 30 nations trot out their most famous cuisine, wine, and entertainment. Held in the World Showcase, the celebration includes demonstrations, wine seminars, tastings, and opportunities to see some of the world's top chefs. Although many activities are included in Epcot admission, the best workshops and tastings are by reservation only and cost extra. Call ☎ 407-WDW-DINE well in advance for more information. Crowd conditions at Epcot are affected only slightly.

MICKEY'S NOT-SO-SCARY HALLOWEEN PARTY Held each year two dozen or so nights before Halloween, plus Halloween night, the party runs from 7 p.m. to midnight at the Magic Kingdom. The event includes trick-or-treating in costume, parades, live music, storytelling, and a fireworks show. Aimed primarily at younger children, the party is happy and upbeat rather than spooky and scary. Admission (plus tax) is about $52 for adults and $46 for kids ages 3 to 9 if purchased in advance; tickets at the gate (assuming they're available) run $59 for adults and $53 for children; admission on October 31 is $64 for adults and $58 for kids. For reservations and details, call ☎ 407-W-DISNEY. Teens and young adults looking for a Halloween happening should check out parties at Disney's Hollywood Studios, Universal CityWalk, and the Universal theme parks.

A woman from Nokomis, Florida, reports that crowds were the only scary thing at the Not-So-Scary Halloween Party:

> *I've been to Mickey's Not-So-Scary Halloween Party twice, and both times it has been an overcrowded nightmare! Don't even bother to try and ride anything.*

Another reader chose a date well in advance of Halloween and had a totally different experience:

> *We did Mickey's Not-So-Scary Halloween Party. Yeah, advance tickets cost about $40 each, but we ended up with about six pounds of candy and there were virtually no lines at any ride. It was worth it.*

A mother from Kissimmee, Florida, writes:

> *For me, the festive nature of the* [Not-So-Scary Halloween] *Party makes up for the crowds. I love seeing all the kids and characters.*

The partying and entertainment are what make Disney Halloween and Christmas events special. These celebrations aren't a good choice if your primary agenda is to experience the attractions.

MOUSEFEST Usually held in mid-December, MouseFest is a meeting of hundreds of Disney theme-park fans, unofficial Disney Web site owners, and guidebook authors (including us). Dozens of activities are offered, from trivia contests to guided walks through the theme parks. Visit **www.mousefest.org** for more details. **Note:** *The organizers of MouseFest report that the event will not be held in 2009. No decision regarding 2010 has been made.*

CHRISTMAS AND NEW YEAR'S AT THE THEME PARKS Don't expect to see all the attractions in a single day of touring at any park. Skip the Magic Kingdom, if possible, if you tour the week between Christmas and New Year's. We love the Magic Kingdom. Really. But that love is tempered by the fact that women will have to wait up to 20 minutes to use the restrooms during this week.

unofficial **TIP**
Remember: During major holiday periods such as Christmas, many of the festive extras at Disney World can be enjoyed in the weeks before the actual week in which the holiday occurs.

Epcot, on the other hand, is at its best during the holidays. Touring in the evening will reward you with stunning displays of holiday decorations and slightly smaller crowds than during the day. Exceptional live entertainment abounds, too. The U.S. Pavilion, for example, has two choral groups performing holiday favorites during this week.

Disney's Hollywood Studios is also a good choice for evening touring. Crowds will be larger than normal, but the decorations make up for it. One must-see is the Osborne Family Spectacle of Dancing Lights, featuring a staggering 5 million Christmas lights.

MICKEY'S VERY MERRY CHRISTMAS PARTY This event is staged 7 p.m. to midnight (after regular hours) on several evenings in November and December. Advance tickets cost about $52 for adults and $46 for kids ages 3 to 9; tickets at the gate run about $59 and $53, respectively (tax is not included). For dates and prices, call ☎ 407-W-DISNEY. Included in the cost is the use of all attractions during party hours, holiday-themed stage shows featuring Disney characters, cookies and hot chocolate, performances of Mickey's Once Upon a Christmastime Parade, carolers, "a magical snowfall on Main Street," white lights on Cinderella Castle, and fireworks.

A reader from Pineville, Louisiana, tried the Very Merry Christmas Party and found the guest list too large for her liking:

> *Another thing I will not do again is go to the Very Merry Christmas Party. We went in early December to avoid crowds and were taken by surprise to find wall-to-wall people. They offered some great shows, but we could not get to them. The parade at 9 p.m. and the fireworks at 10 p.m., then fighting our way back to the parking lot, was all we could muster.*

PART TWO

MAKING *the* MOST *of* YOUR TIME *and* MONEY

ALLOCATING MONEY

Did Walt really intend for it to be so expensive that the average family couldn't afford it?

—*Unofficial Guide* reader from Amarillo, Texas

EVEN IF YOU STOP AT DISNEY WORLD for only an afternoon, be prepared to drop a bundle. In Part Three, we'll show you how to save money on lodging, and in Part Ten, you'll find tips for economizing on meals. This section will give some sense of what admission will cost, as well as which admission option will best meet your needs.

DISNEY AND THE RECESSION

THESE ARE DIFFICULT TIMES, and many of you will likely forgo or cut short a Walt Disney World vacation. For those of you who can afford one, however, there will be bargains galore. Throughout most of 2009, for example, Disney is promoting a "Buy 4, Get 3 Free" package offering the last three nights of a week-long stay at no charge. The package also includes a week's worth of theme-park admissions. Also look for discounts or "sweeteners" (such as free dining) on other Walt Disney World packages. Numerous Disney deals can be found at **www.disneyworld.com;** click on "Special Offers" on the home page at top right, just under "My Disney Vacation."

> *unofficial* **TIP**
> **The money you can save makes researching Disney's dizzying array of ticket options worthwhile.**

In the Orlando area, hotels, especially non-Disney hotels, are flogging discounts of all sorts. PFK Hospitality Research forecasts that demand for hotel rooms in general will fall sharply, while supply will increase by almost 3%. Leisure markets such as Orlando will feel the pinch most, so those are the places where you'll see the real deals.

WALT DISNEY WORLD ADMISSION OPTIONS

IN AN EFFORT TO ACCOMMODATE various vacation needs, Disney offers a number of different admission options. These range from the basic "One Day, One Park" ticket, good for a single entry into one Disney theme park, to the top-of-the-line Premium Annual Pass, good for 365 days of admission into every Disney theme or water park, plus DisneyQuest.

The sheer number of ticket options available makes it difficult and, yes, daunting to sort out which option represents the least expensive way to see and do everything you want. An average family staying for a week at an off-World hotel and planning a couple of activities outside the theme parks has about a dozen different ticket options to consider. To complicate matters, comparing options requires detailed knowledge of the myriad perks included with specific admissions. Finding the optimum admission, or combination of admissions, however, could save the average family a nice little bundle. Many families, we suspect, become overwhelmed trying to sort out the different options, and simply purchase a more expensive ticket with features they will probably not use. Adding to the frustration, Disney's reservation agents are trained to avoid answering subjective questions about which ticket option is "best."

HELP IS ON THE WAY!

TO SIMPLIFY THINGS, we tried to define guidelines to help you choose the best ticket options for your vacation. Eight hours into this project, we sounded like a theme-park version of *Forrest Gump*. Remember that scene where Bubba rattles off 7,000 different ways to prepare shrimp? Well, that was kinda like us, babbling about tickets. Even saying some of the ticket names ("Adult Internet-only Seven-day Base Ticket with Park Hopper Option") made us sound like our local Starbucks barista, only not as perky.

After a day or so, we realized that coming up with a handful of general guidelines was an impossible task, so we wrote a computer program to figure it out. You can use it to determine the best ticket options for you by visiting our Web site, **TouringPlans.com.** The program takes into account discounts for Florida residents as well as members of the military. Just answer a few simple questions relating to the theme parks you intend to visit and whether you intend to stay at a Disney or non-Disney hotel. The program then identifies your four least expensive ticket options.

unofficial **TIP**
Try **TouringPlans.com** before your trip to Walt Disney World—it's free and considers almost all of the different ticket options.

The program will also make recommendations for considerations other than price. For example, Annual Passes, although they might cost more, make sense in certain circumstances because Disney often offers substantial resort discounts and other deals to Annual Pass holders. Those resort discounts, especially during off-season times, can more than offset a small incremental charge for the Annual Pass.

MAGIC YOUR WAY

IN 2005, WALT DISNEY WORLD pretty much chucked its entire panoply of admission options and introduced a completely new array of theme-park tickets in a program called Magic Your Way. The new scheme applies to both one-day and multiday passports and begins with a Base Ticket. Features that were previously bundled with certain tickets, such as the ability to visit more than one park per day ("park hopping"), or the inclusion of admission to Disney's minor venues (Typhoon Lagoon,

WDW Theme-park Ticket Options

	1-day	2-day	3-day	4-day	5-day
BASE TICKET AGE 10 AND UP					
	$84.14	$166.14	$233.24	$239.63	$242.82
	–	($83.07/day)	($77.75day)	($59.91/day)	($48.56/day)
BASE TICKET AGES 3–9					
	$72.42	$141.65	$199.16	$204.48	$207.68
	–	($70.82/day)	($66.39/day)	($51.12/day)	($41.54/day)

Base Ticket admits guest to one theme park each day of use. Park choices are Magic Kingdom, Epcot, Disney's Hollywood Studios, or Disney's Animal Kingdom.

	1-day	2-day	3-day	4-day	5-day
FOR PARK HOPPER, ADD:					
	$55.38	$55.38	$55.38	$55.38	$55.38
	–	($27.69/day)	($18.46/day)	($13.85/day)	($11.08/day)

Park Hopper option entitles guest to visit more than one theme park on each day of use. Park choices are any combination of Magic Kingdom, Epcot, Disney's Hollywood Studios, or Disney's Animal Kingdom on each day of use.

	1-day	2-day	3-day	4-day	5-day
FOR WATER PARK FUN AND MORE, ADD:					
	$55.38	$55.38	$55.38	$55.38	$55.38
	2 visits	2 visits	3 visits	4 visits	5 visits

Water Park Fun and More option entitles guest to a specified number of visits (between 2 and 10) to a choice of entertainment and recreation venues. Choices are Disney's Blizzard Beach water park, Disney's Typhoon Lagoon water park, DisneyQuest, Oak Trail Golf Course, or ESPN Wide World of Sports Complex.

	1-day	2-day	3-day	4-day	5-day
FOR NO EXPIRATION, ADD:					
	N/A	$19.17	$25.56	$55.38	$77.75
	–	($9.59/day)	($8.52/day)	($13.85/day)	($15.55/day)

No Expiration means unused admissions on a ticket have no expiration date. All tickets expire 14 days after first use unless No Expiration is purchased.

Blizzard Beach, DisneyQuest, and the like), are now available as individual add-ons to the Base Ticket.

As before, there is a volume discount. The more days of admission you purchase, the lower the cost per day. For example, if you buy an adult Five-day Base Ticket for $242.82 (taxes included), each day will cost $48.56, compared with $84.14 a day for a one-day pass. Base Tickets can be purchased from one to up to ten days and admit you to exactly one theme park per day.

Under the old system, unused days on multiday passes were good indefinitely. Now passes expire 14 days from the first day of use. If, say, you purchase a Four-day Base Ticket on June 1 and use it that day for admission to the Magic Kingdom, you'll be able to visit a single Disney theme park on any of your three remaining days between June 2 and June 15. After that, the ticket expires and any unused days will be lost. Through another

unofficial **TIP**
Unlike Disney's previous multiday tickets, Base Tickets can't be used to visit more than one park per day.

(Note: *All ticket prices include 6.5% sales tax)*

6-day	7-day	8-day	9-day	10-day
BASE TICKET AGE 10 AND UP				
$246.02 ($41.00/day)	$249.21 ($35.60/day)	$252.41 ($31.55/day)	$255.60 ($28.46/day)	$258.80 ($25.88/day)
BASE TICKET AGES 3–9				
$210.87 ($35.15/day)	$214.07 ($30.58/day)	$217.26 ($27.16/day)	$220.46 ($24.50/day)	$223.65 ($22.37/day)
FOR PARK HOPPER, ADD:				
$55.38 ($9.23/day)	$55.38 ($7.91/day)	$55.38 ($6.92/day)	$55.38 ($6.15/day)	$55.38 ($5.54/day)
FOR WATER PARK FUN AND MORE, ADD:				
$55.38 6 visits	$55.38 7 visits	$55.38 8 visits	$55.38 9 visits	$55.38 10 visits
FOR NO EXPIRATION, ADD:				
$89.46 ($14.91/day)	$122.48 ($17.50/day)	$161.88 ($20.24/day)	$184.57 ($21.06/day)	$222.59 ($22.26/day)

Note: Check **TouringPlans.com** for the latest ticket prices, which are subject to change after this guide goes to press.

add-on, however, you can avoid the 14-day expiration and make your ticket valid forever. More on that later.

BASE-TICKET ADD-ON OPTIONS

NAVIGATING THE MAGIC YOUR WAY PROGRAM is like ordering dinner in an upscale restaurant where all menu selections are à la carte: many choices, mostly expensive, virtually all of which require some thought.

Three add-on options are offered with the Magic Your Way Base Ticket, each at an additional cost:

PARK HOPPER Adding this feature to your Base Ticket allows you to visit more than one theme park per day. The cost is $55.38 (including tax) on top of the price of any Base Ticket. It's an exorbitant price for one or two days, but it becomes more affordable the longer your stay. As an add-on to a Seven-day Base Ticket, the flat fee above would work out to $7.91 per day for park-hopping privileges. If you want to visit the Magic Kingdom in the morning and dine at Epcot in the evening, this is the feature to request.

NO EXPIRATION Adding this option to your ticket means that unused admissions to the major theme parks and the swimming parks, as well as other minor venues, never expire. If you added this option to a Ten-day Base Ticket and used only four days this year, the remaining six days could be used for admission at any date in the future. The No Expiration option ranges from $19.17 with tax for a two-day ticket to $222.59 for a Ten-day Base Ticket. This option is not available on one-day tickets.

WATER PARK FUN AND MORE (WPFAM) This option gives you a single admission to one of Disney's water parks (Blizzard Beach and Typhoon Lagoon), DisneyQuest, Oak Trail Golf Course, or the ESPN Wide World of Sports Complex. The cost is a flat $55.38 (including tax). Except for the one-day WPFAM ticket, which gives you two admissions, the number of admissions equals the number of days on your base ticket. If you buy an Eight-day Base Ticket, for example, and add the WPFAM option, you get eight WPFAM admissions. What you *can't* do is, say, buy a Ten-day Base Ticket with only three admissions or a Three-day Base Ticket with four admissions. You can, however, skip WPFAM entirely and buy an individual admission to any of these minor parks. This last option is almost always the best deal if you want to visit only one of the venues above.

The foregoing add-ons are available for purchase in any combination (except for the No Expiration add-on on one-day tickets). If you buy a Base Ticket and then decide later on that you want one or more of the options, you can upgrade the Base Ticket to add the feature(s) you desire.

Annual Passes

An Annual Pass provides unlimited use of the major theme parks for one year; a Premium Annual Pass also provides unlimited use of the minor parks. Annual Pass holders also get perks, including free parking and seasonal offers such as room-rate discounts at Disney resorts. The Annual Pass is not valid for special events, such as admission to Mickey's Very Merry Christmas Party. Tax included, Annual Passes run $520.79 for adults and $460.08 for children ages 3 to 9. A Premium Annual Pass, at $659.24 for adults and $581.49 for children ages 3 to 9, provides unlimited admission to Blizzard Beach, Typhoon Lagoon, DisneyQuest, and Oak Trail Golf Course, in addition to the four major theme parks. In addition to Annual Passes, Florida residents are eligible for discounts on one-day theme-park Base Tickets (about 10%) as well as on various add-on options.

Florida-resident Passes

Disney offers several special admission options to Florida residents. The Florida Resident Annual Pass ($393 adults, $346 children ages 3 to 9) and the Florida Resident Premium Annual Pass ($521 adults, $449 children ages 3 to 9) both offer unlimited admission and park-hopping privileges to the four major theme parks. The Florida Resident Premium Annual Pass also provides unlimited admission to Blizzard Beach, Typhoon Lagoon, DisneyQuest, and Oak Trail Golf Course, in addition to the four major theme parks. AAA offers some nice discounts on these passes. And the Florida Resident Seasonal Pass

($265 adults, $234 children ages 3 to 9) provides unlimited admission to the four major theme parks except on select blackout dates.

One final note: it doesn't cost as much to renew an Annual Pass as it does to buy it in the first place. When you renew any Annual Pass, you get an 8%-to-9% savings from the cost of the original pass.

DIZ SPIN

ACCORDING TO DISNEY PRESS RELEASES, Magic Your Way is the hottest thing since barbecue sauce on pig. Former Walt Disney World President Al Weiss announced at the program's debut, "People want things customized to fit their individual needs. And now Walt Disney World guests will have that same ability to customize their dream vacation, creating the ticket that is just right for them." A similar release gushes, "Because Magic Your Way tickets offer savings that increase with the length of stay, a weeklong Walt Disney World vacation becomes even more affordable."

Well, let's see. For starters, Walt Disney World multiday admissions have always incorporated a volume discount: the more days of admission you purchase, the lower the cost per day. So there's nothing new there. And it's always been possible, though confusing, to customize your vacation using one or more of the dizzying 180 different admission options available before Magic Your Way.

The main difference between Magic Your Way and the previous admissions program is that Magic Your Way is an à la carte system. À la carte systems can work for or against you. If you go to a restaurant where everything is à la carte, and all you want is a bowl of soup and a glass of wine, you'll be able to order and pay for just those items. If, however, you want appetizer, soup, salad, main course, dessert, and drinks, the à la carte prices will eat you alive.

Before Magic Your Way, you could buy an adult Four-day Park Hopper Pass with tax included for $233. Unused days on the pass were good forever, and you could flit from park to park like Tinker Bell on a scavenger hunt. With the new program, you start with a Four-day Base Ticket costing $239.63, including tax. Then, to obtain the features of the old Four-day Park Hopper Pass, you'd purchase à la carte the Park Hopper feature ($55.38) and the No Expiration option (also $55.38). Adding it all up, you'd pay $350.39 for the same pass that was available before for $233. That's a 50% price hike. Now consider this: Disney is expected to raise its admission prices again in 2009 and 2010.

The new Magic Your Way ticket prices represent an increase of anywhere from 29% to 68%, with children's tickets falling toward the upper end of that range, as the chart on the next page shows (all prices include 6.5% tax).

In an era of ever-shrinking margins, we understand that Disney needs to continually find ways to increase profits, especially with the theme parks constituting a large share of Disney's operating revenue. When things go south for corporate Disney, it's always the theme parks and we, the guests, who are burdened with making up the shortfall.

To put the increases in perspective, Disney's price hikes have far outpaced those in almost every other sector of the U.S. economy. For example, the price of a One-day, One-park ticket has jumped more than

TICKET	BEFORE MAGIC YOUR WAY	MAGIC YOUR WAY	INCREASE
One-day, One-park (Adult)	$58.31	$84.14	44%
One-day, One-park (Child)	$46.60	$72.42	55%
Three-day, One-park (Adult)	$164.28	$233.24	42%
Three-day, One-park (Child)	$129.13	$199.16	54%
Four-day Park Hopper (Adult)	$233.24	$295.01	26%
Four-day Park Hopper (Child)	$187.44	$259.86	39%
Five-day Park Hopper Plus (Adult, five WPFAM admissions)	$300.34	$353.58	18%
Five-day Park Hopper Plus (Child, five WPFAM admissions)	$240.70	$318.44	32%
Annual Pass (Adult)	$403.95	$520.79	29%

44%, and the price of a child's Four-day Park Hopper has increased 39%. In comparison, the hourly wage of the average American worker has risen only 14%, and consumer prices have increased only 9% during the same period.

Disney seems to be employing an "all the market can bear" pricing strategy that has become substantially more aggressive in the past few years. We think they'll probably continue to boost prices aggressively until there's an angry backlash and attendance starts to decline. If this happens, Disney will lose more in hotel, food-and-beverage, and retail revenue than it will gain from higher admission prices.

Disney is hoping that guests will regard the increases in admission prices as relatively minor compared with the cost of the WDW vacation overall. No matter how you shake it up, however, the runaway price hikes leave a bad taste in your mouth. Walt Disney World was not conceived as an exclusive playground for the rich.

A CLOUD IS JUST A CLOUD

THIS SECTION WAS FORMERLY TITLED "Every Cloud Has a Polyester Lining." In it we explained the few ways that Magic Your Way could save you money. Well, forget that—almost all good deals have gone the way of the dinosaur. The only exception is for folks who do not intend to park-hop and will require four or more days' admission, all to be used during a single vacation. If this describes your situation, you can realize some significant economies of scale. As you can see from our admissions chart, the more days you buy, the more you save: The cost of an adult Ten-day Base Ticket ($258.80) is only $25.56 more than the cost of an adult Three-day Base Ticket ($233.24). If you buy the ten-day ticket, you can whittle your admission cost per day, tax included, down to $25.88 for adults and $22.37 for children. So what's changed for everybody else?

Consider that most guests only need four or five days' admission; the most cost-effective strategy would seem to be to buy a Ten-day Base Ticket plus the No Expiration option so you could roll over any unused admission days to a subsequent trip. When Disney first rolled out Magic Your Way, the No Expiration option actually was pretty reasonable.

Well, they couldn't let *that* continue, could they?

unofficial **TIP**
Magic Your Way offers significant incentives for taking a longer vacation or buying more days of admission.

As of this writing, Disney has increased the cost of the No Expiration option by 86% from the time Magic Their, oops, *Your* Way (a joke any way you look at it) was introduced. If you buy an adult Ten-day Base Ticket for $258.80 plus No Expiration for $222.59, you'll pay $481.39 including tax, or $48.14 a day—a savings of less than 50¢ a day compared with simply buying a Five-day Base Ticket each time you visit Walt Disney World. While it is true that admission prices might go up before you visit again, in which case No Expiration would be to your benefit, it's equally true that you might misplace the tickets you bought in the previous scenario, or that you might have some better use for the $222.59 you shelled out on top of your ticket purchase.

BIG BROTHER IS WATCHING

ALL MAGIC YOUR WAY TICKETS are personalized, with the ticket holder's name and biometric information stored on the ticket. This doesn't mean, however, that you have to provide a DNA sample when you plunk down your cash. Recording the biometric information requires a quick and painless measurement of one finger from your right hand, taken the first time you use the ticket. It's been used without incident for a number of years on Disney's Annual Pass.

unofficial **TIP**
In our estimation, considering the time value of money, buying the No Expiration option is pretty much a sucker play.

The advantages of the bio scan are not altogether clear, though it's doubtless intended to prevent the original purchaser of the pass from selling unused days to a third party. If you're purchasing admission for your entire family and are worried about the difficulty in keeping everyone's tickets, we're told that Disney's computer system will link every family member's data to every ticket, allowing anyone to enter with anyone else's ticket. We've confirmed this by having a platoon of *Unofficial Guide* researchers (including men, women, and children) swap passes with each other; all were admitted.

This new scanning process is so cumbersome, that it has taken guests more than 30 minutes to enter some parks during peak periods, and sometimes more than an hour. In response to this, Disney frequently turns off the scanning process entirely (usually at Animal Kingdom).

HOW TO GET THE MOST FROM MAGIC YOUR WAY

FIRST, HAVE A REALISTIC IDEA of what you want out of your vacation. As with anything, it doesn't make sense to pay for options you won't use. A seven-day theme-park ticket with seven WPFAM admissions might seem like a wonderful idea when you're snowbound and planning your trip in February. But actually trying to visit all those parks in a week in July might end up feeling more like Navy SEAL training. If you're going to make only one visit to a water park, DisneyQuest, or ESPN Wide World of Sports, you're almost always better off purchasing that admission separately rather than in the WPFAM option. If you plan to visit two or more WPFAM venues, you're better off buying the add-on.

Next, think carefully about paying for the No Expiration option. An inside source reports that fewer than one in ten admission tickets with rollover days are ever reused at a Disney theme park. The rest are misplaced, discarded, or forgotten. Unless you are absolutely certain you'll be returning to Walt Disney World within the next year or two and have identified a safe place to keep those unused tickets, we don't think the additional cost is worth the risk. (We've lost a few of these passes ourselves.)

WHERE TO PURCHASE MAGIC YOUR WAY TICKETS

YOU CAN BUY YOUR ADMISSION PASSES on arrival at Walt Disney World or purchase them in advance. Admission passes are available at Walt Disney World resorts and theme parks. Passes are also available at some non-Disney hotels and Orlando-area shopping centers, as well as through independent ticket brokers. Because Disney admission prices are not discounted in the greater Walt Disney World–Orlando area, the only reason for you to purchase from an independent broker is convenience. Offers of free or heavily discounted tickets abound, but they generally require you to attend a time-share sales presentation.

Magic Your Way tickets are available at Disney Stores and at **www.disneyworld.com** for the same prices listed in the chart on pages 50 and 51.

If you're trying to keep your costs to an absolute minimum, consider using an online ticket wholesaler, such as **Undercover Tourist, Kissimmee Guest Services, Maple Leaf Tickets,** or the **Official Ticket Center,** especially for trips with five or more days in the theme parks. All tickets sold are brand-new, and the savings can range from $7 to more than $25, depending on the ticket and options chosen. We've spoken with representatives from each company, and they're very well versed in the pros and cons of the various tickets and options. If the new options don't make sense for your specific vacation plans, the reps will tell you so.

All four companies offer discounts on tickets for almost all central-Florida attractions, including Disney, Universal, SeaWorld, and Cirque du Soleil. Discounts for the major theme parks are about 6% to 8.5%. Tickets for other attractions are more deeply discounted. **Undercover Tourist** (U.S.: ☎ 800-846-1302, Monday through Friday, 9 a.m. to 4 p.m. EST; U.K.: ☎ 0800 081-1702, Monday through Friday, 2 p.m. to 9 p.m. GMT; worldwide: ☎ +1 386 239-8624; fax +1 386 252-3469; **www.undercovertourist.com**) offers free delivery and has a sweetheart relationship with **MouseSavers.com.** If you subscribe to the MouseSavers e-newsletter, you can access Undercover Tourist through a special "secret" link that provides additional savings on top of the normal discount. **Kissimmee Guest Services** (215 Celebration Place, Suite 500, in Celebration; ☎ 877-273-5636; U.K.: ☎ 0208 432-4024; **www.kgstickets.com**) offers a lowest-price guarantee and $10 delivery to any Orlando-area hotel. The **Official Ticket Center** (215 Celebration Place, Suite 190, Kissimmee; ☎ 877-406-4836; **www.theofficialticketcenter.com**) offers FedEx shipping for a flat $12-to-$18 fee or $12 for delivery to Orlando-area hotels; it's of course free if you pick up at

unofficial **TIP**
If you order tickets in advance of your trip, be sure to allow enough time for the tickets to be mailed to your home.

their office. **Maple Leaf Tickets** (4647 West Irlo Bronson Highway [US 192], Kissimmee; ☎ 407-396-0300 local and international, 800-841-2837 toll-free, fax 407-396-4127, **www.mapleleaftickets.com**) offers the same deal on pickup at their store and for $6.95 delivery to Orlando-area hotels; U.S. Priority Mail service is a flat $6.95 per order.

You can also save money on Disney World tickets just by planning ahead and watching the calendar, as this mom from Broomfield, Colorado, explains:

> *If you are planning a trip well in advance, purchase your passes before the end of the year. Our travel agent recommended this because Disney usually increases their prices in the new year. So we purchased our tickets for June back in December and sure enough, I found the price of a pass had increased $20 per person. That's an $80* [savings] *for our family.*

Finally, if all this is too confusing, our Web site will help you navigate all of the new options and find the least expensive ticket options for your vacation. Visit **TouringPlans.com** for more details.

FOR ADDITIONAL INFORMATION ON PASSES

IF YOU HAVE A QUESTION OR CONCERN regarding admissions that can be addressed only through a person-to-person conversation, call **Disney Ticket Inquiries** at ☎ 407-566-4985, or e-mail **wdw.ticket .inquiries@disneyworld.com.** If you call, be aware that you may spend a considerable time on hold; if you e-mail, be aware that it can take up to three days to get a response. If you just need routine information, call ☎ 407-824-4321 for recorded info. If the recorded information does not answer your question, return to the main menu and press 0 to reach a live Disney representative. Information is also available at **www.disneyworld.com.**

WHERE THE REAL DEALS ARE

BOTH GREAT THEME PARKS, **Universal Studios** and Universal's **Islands of Adventure** routinely offer admission discounts and specials. At one time, for example, you could score a free two-day, two-park park-hopping ticket for the kids (ages 3 to 9) for every adult two-day, two-park ticket you bought online at **www.universalorlando.com.** For a family of four—say, Mom, Dad, and two kids under age 10—the total cost to visit both Universal parks was $213, including tax. For the same family to spend two days at Disney parks with park-hopping privileges during the same period, it cost a whopping $737, tax included.

FREE TICKETS AND THE TIME-SHARE GAME

IF YOU'VE EVER DRIVEN IN FLORIDA, you've certainly noticed huge billboards advertising free or deeply discounted admission passes to Orlando-area theme parks. Most Florida visitors intuit that there's a catch, but some who know there's a catch figure they can beat the system. Specifically, they think they can politely sit through a sales presentation, usually for a time-share condominium, then say "No thanks" and walk away with a pot of freebies. Sounds easy? Think again. Consider the story of Jim from Texas, traveling with his wife and their four children (ages 1, 2, 11, and 14):

On our way down south, we kept seeing these signs: "Florida Vacations for Less! 50% off Hotels! Discount Tickets!" We thought, "What the heck? Let's see what they've got."

Upon inquiring, they were indeed offered a discounted hotel room and theme-park tickets, but Jim balked at the prospect of enduring a time-share sales pitch. They moved on.

Later, driving down Florida's Turnpike and still pondering the task of getting tickets for the Universal theme parks, Jim and family saw more signs hawking the same kinds of discounts. Deciding to try again, they were offered an amazing deal: tickets at nearly half price, plus a two-bedroom suite hotel with Jacuzzi and all the trimmings for only $100 a night. The catch, of course, was that they'd have to listen to a 90-minute sales presentation on time-shares at the end of their vacation.

"I hate those presentations," says Jim. "Still, I felt compelled." Jim explained his dislike of high-pressure pitches to the salespeople, but they assured him, "It's not like that. They'll serve you breakfast and show you around. That's all. No pressure at all. Very nice people."

After three days of theme-park touring, the day arrived for the scheduled time-share presentation. "We sat down with a very nice gentleman, richly dressed, and not intimidating at all," notes Jim. The couple had their 1-year-old with them, while the older children watched the 2-year-old back at the hotel room. "We sat down, made some cordial introductions, and made our way into the buffet line for free eggs and sausage."

After breakfast, their salesman shared various aspects of his personal life, including stories about his family, past athletic achievements, and work habits. The salesman claimed that he successfully closes more than half of his deals, and he showed them a certificate he got recently. He went on to say that everyone was going to want to stay in our time-share because everyone wants to go to Orlando; he explained that the company had resorts all over the world, and they're all wonderful places like this one.

"It was looking like a really good deal," says Jim. "The baby started getting fussy after about the first two hours," of what was supposed to last 90 minutes, "but the salesman was being so pleasant and interesting. He explained all about how if we wanted a vacation home, we'd have to spend $500,000 and then find people to stay there when we weren't there. Then there's upkeep and taxes, and isn't this hotel better? And you can trade with anyone and stay in Alaska or Israel or Peru or California, no problems, only $129 for a whole week, you build equity . . . isn't this better? And if you tell someone else about it and they buy one, you get a cash bonus, and there's this lady that's retiring early and sending her kids through college on referrals, it's so easy."

"Now let me show you around our property on this nice little golf cart," said the salesman. Jim and his wife and child rode around, walked around, and looked the place over. They were impressed, as it was a beautiful property with many amenities. Then it was time for the close. They were ushered into a room full of tables where other vacationers were sitting with their respective salespeople and talking about their deals. Finally, the price for the time-share is revealed: $25,000.

"There's no way," recalls Jim. The salesman wanted a $4,900 down payment that very day, plus $450 a month for ten years. "I tried to work these numbers out, and near as I can tell that's [an excessive] interest rate." Jim was right. The interest rate for such a deal would be 24.99% annually, not including closing costs. "So I told him no way," Jim concluded. "There is no way we can squeeze that kind of money out of our budget. Forget it."

The salesman looked hurt, but he told them to wait while he consulted his manager. The manager appeared and said she had one time-share available for only $8,800. "What a break!" thought Jim. "How lucky can you get? Over half off! Unfortunately, we didn't travel to Florida planning to make a real-estate purchase, so we didn't have either the $250 down payment nor the $150 a month in our budget." Of course, they were told that a decision had to be made that day, right then.

Another manager appears, and Jim and his wife explain that though it sounds good, they need to think it over, and perhaps they can come back with the down payment. "OK," she says. "We'll just keep this offer open until next time. So, just give me $250 now, plus $50 a month, and next January you can stay here and buy the time-share. No? How about this, you give me just $50 now, then $100 the next month, then $200 the next month. . . ."

The no-pressure, 90-minute presentation turned into a high-pressure, full-court-press sales pitch that stretched over three hours. With the baby crying and irritable and concern over the other kids rising, Jim and his wife felt like "a hamburger on the grill." Jim's wife had finally had enough, so she said they had to go—they had to check on the kids, and they couldn't decide this immediately. The message finally got through. "The second manager grabbed the paper away from us, wrote 'Refused offer. Refused to come back' on the bottom, and told each of us to sign it." They were told that they could never come back again, and both swore they'd never try, though they still picked up their theme-park tickets.

There is no way of knowing how representative Jim's experience is of time-share pitches in general, but it's a sobering example of what you might be walking into. Among other things, the psychological methodology of the sales presentation is very interesting. It started very socially with a shared meal, followed by the salesman sharing aspects of his personal life. These tactics help lower the prospects' defenses by shifting the tenor of the encounter from a business meeting to a relaxed, social gathering. With the sharing of his personal life, the salesman invited reciprocal intimacy on the part of the Texas couple. This is calculated not only to lessen resistance, but also to establish a relationship wherein the couple cares about the salesman. If the salesman is successful in establishing this connection, it makes it more difficult to say no to the offer when the time comes.

Notice that the presentation, including the meal, is drawn out over several hours. At two hours and counting, the salesman was still extolling the virtues of the time-share. He had not even gotten to the site inspection, much less any discussion of price and terms. The strategy here is twofold: First, as researchers have proven, customers who invest a lot of time in a purchase decision are less likely to walk away. Second, occupying so much of the salesman's time, in addition to accepting his extended hospitality, made the couple feel obligated to him.

The salesman buttresses his main presentation and dazzles the prospective buyers with ancillary deals, specifically the discussion of referrals and how one lady had sent her kids to college with money she had earned referring prospects. This tactic distracts the couple from the real proposition on the table, makes the deal appear more affordable, and, in regard to referrals, puts the prospective buyers and the salesman on the same team. As a referral source, in other words, the buyers are hypothetically joining forces with the salesman to sell time-shares. If the salesman can get the couple to actually picture doing this, they'll abandon some of the inhibitions inherent in the naturally adversarial relationship of buyer and seller.

The salesman laid a lot of track in preparation for divulging the price and terms and closing the sale. Because Jim doesn't mention being offered any alternative financing, and because of the mortgage holder's legal obligation to disclose the Annual Percentage Rate (APR) of interest in the event the deal goes forward, it's probable that the opening price quote and terms were a setup. In other words, if the deal proceeded based on the price and terms initially offered, any marginally sane person would (as did the husband) figure out that the interest rate was sky-high. If they didn't work it out on their own, they'd certainly have it shoved in their faces when the mortgage holder disclosed the APR as required by law. Either way, the opening offer is set up to create a deal breaker. This, in turn, cues the little act where the manager miraculously arrives on the scene with the deal of the century.

This is the real offer, the one that the entire manipulative, carefully stage-managed drama has been leading up to. Expressed differently, the candy is dangled in front of the prospects, and by then, they want it. Suddenly it's yanked out of reach because the initial deal is out of the question. At this point, the prospects are disappointed, deflated, and emotionally wrung out. But wait, because their salesman has become so fond of them, he intervenes on their behalf, and the manager swoops onstage offering the candy at a fraction of the original price. Disappointment turns to elation, and the prospects jump hungrily on the candy. At least that's how it's scripted. For the Texas couple, an intuitive sense that something was fishy, reinforced by a fussy baby, saved the day.

The appearance of the third manager on the scene gives the impression that the time-share sellers are really bending over backward to work with the couple. This applies additional pressure—and it makes the prospects feel even more obligated to respond positively. If the Texas couple had continued to vacillate, there's no telling how many managers might have turned up. Because the prospects dug in their heels, however, the sellers played their last remaining cards: anger and guilt. Grabbing the offer document and demanding that the couple sign a written "refused offer" statement communicated to the prospects that they had wasted everyone's time, had abused the salesman's friendship, and had spurned management's (supposed) good-faith efforts to accommodate them in every respect. The icing on the guilt cake was the implicit message that the couple must be pretty stupid, worthless, or both to walk away from such an extraordinary opportunity.

There is nothing intrinsically wrong with the time-share concept, and a number of reputable firms have diversified into this area of real estate. If you're interested in a time-share, do your homework before leaving on your vacation. Identify the sellers, check out their reputations, and make appointments to visit the properties that interest you. You might not get the deal of the century, but few discounts are worth the physical and psychological torture chamber of a boiler-room sales pitch.

THE BRITISH ARE COMING!

IN THE UNITED KINGDOM, DISNEY offers advance-purchase tickets not available in the United States. The Five-day Premium Ticket costs £206 for adults and £186 for children. It provides unlimited admission as well as park-hopping privileges to the major theme parks, and five admissions to the minor venues. The Seven-day Premium Ticket runs the same as the five-day pass and provides the same features except that it includes seven admissions to the venues. Both expire 14 days from the date of first use.

Ultimate Tickets are priced at £216 for adults and £196 for children for 14-day passes, and £236 and £216 for 21-day passes. The Ultimate Tickets provide unlimited admission to both major and minor parks along with park-hopping privileges to the major parks. The 14-day Ultimate Ticket expires 14 days after first use, and the 21-day Ultimate Ticket expires 21 days after first use. For additional information see **www.disneyworld.co.uk,** or call ☎ 0870-242-4900.

MORE DISCOUNTS ON ADMISSIONS

Admission Discounts Available to Certain Groups and Individuals

AAA MEMBERS Members can buy passes for a discount of 3% to 5%.

DISNEY VACATION CLUB Members receive a $100 to $125 discount on Annual Passes.

DISNEY CORPORATE SPONSORS If you work for a Disney World corporate sponsor, you might be eligible for discounted admissions or preferential treatment at the parks. Ask your employee-benefits office.

MILITARY, DEPARTMENT OF DEFENSE, CIVIL SERVICE Active-duty and retired military, Department of Defense (DOD) civilian employees, some civil service employees, and dependents of these groups can buy Disney multiday admissions at a 9%-to-10% discount. At most military and DOD installations, the passes are available from the Morale, Welfare, and Recreation office. Civil service employees should contact their personnel office to see if they're eligible and for instructions on how and where to purchase tickets. Military personnel can buy a discounted admission for nonmilitary guests as long as the military member accompanies the nonmilitary member. If a group seeks the discount, at least half must be eligible for the military discount.

Special Passes

Walt Disney World offers a number of special and situational passes that are not known to the general public and are not sold at any Disney World ticket booth. The best information we've found on these passes is available on the Internet at **MouseSavers.com.**

PARTIALLY USED PASSES PURCHASED BEFORE JANUARY 2005

READERS ASK IF THEY CAN USE remaining admissions on four- through seven-day passes brought home by relatives before January 2005. Whoever bought the pass agreed that "the pass must be used by the same person for all days." Since most passes sold in recent years do not bear the buyer's photograph or signature—or even the buyer's name—guests have generally had no difficulty gaining admission with a partially used pass acquired from a friend or relative. This makes the pass perfectly, though illegally, transferable.

unofficial **TIP**
What to do with the kid's pass you bought long before your 6-foot-tall teenager hit puberty? Go to Guest Services and ask to have it changed into a regular-admission pass for the number of days left on the ticket. If you're lucky, they'll do so without asking you to pay the price difference, but if not, you're still better off paying the difference and using the pass instead of wasting whatever value is left on it.

Lately, black-market ticket sellers have gotten bolder. While it's true that most theme-park tickets offered at a deep discount involve suffering a time-share pitch, there's now an active market in unused admissions on multiday passes. Most of this activity is on US 192 in stores with signs reading "We Buy Unused Days on Park Passes" or similar language. Savings on "pre-owned" passes may be more than 50%, and salespersons claim that buying and reselling passes is legal. Disney has yet to challenge these operations. We advise buying only new passes from a legitimate source. The modern plastic pass must be computer-scanned to ascertain the number of days left on it. When you purchase a partially used card from a stranger, you can't verify how many, if any, unused days remain.

HOW MUCH DOES IT COST PER DAY?

A TYPICAL DAY WOULD COST $567.64, excluding lodging and transportation, for a family of four—Mom, Dad, 12-year-old Tim, and 8-year-old Sandy—driving their own car and staying outside the World. They plan to stay a week, so they buy Five-day Base Tickets with Park Hopper Option. Here's a breakdown:

While ticket prices account for a big part of any year's price increases, the largest price hikes lately have been at Disney's sit-down restaurants. Our typical dinner at Italy—two shared appetizers, median-priced entrees for the adults, a child's dinner, and two shared desserts—has increased by 47% in the past year and a half.

A Birmingham, Alabama, mom of two begs to differ with our budget recommendation at top right for souvenirs:

> *Sorry, but Uncle Bob is totally out of touch when he says "you won't have to buy souvenirs every day."* [In my experience,] *you'll head home with several sets of character ears; enough dress-up costumes to outfit the neighborhood; and countless pins, toys, and knickknacks.*

ALLOCATING TIME

DURING DISNEY WORLD'S FIRST DECADE, a family with a week's vacation could enjoy the Magic Kingdom and the now-closed River

HOW MUCH DOES A DAY COST?

Breakfast for four at Denny's with tax and tip	$30.36
Epcot parking fee (free for passholders and resort guests)	$12.00
One day's admission on a 5-day Base Ticket with Park Hopper Option	
Dad: Adult 5-day with tax = $298.20 divided by five (days)	$59.64
Mom: Adult 5-day with tax = $298.20 divided by five (days)	$59.64
Tim: Adult 5-day with tax = $298.20 divided by five (days)	$59.64
Sandy: Child 5-day with tax = $263.06 divided by five (days)	$52.61
Morning break (soda or coffee)	$11.90
Fast-food lunch (sandwich or burger, fries, soda), no tip	$38.00
Afternoon break (soda and popcorn)	$22.00
Dinner at Italy (no alcoholic beverages) with tax and tip	$182.85
Souvenirs (Mickey T-shirts for Tim and Sandy) with tax*	$39.00
One-day total (without lodging or transportation)	**$567.64**

**Cheer up—you won't have to buy souvenirs every day.*

Country and still have several days left for the beach or other area attractions. Since Epcot opened in 1982, however, Disney World has steadily been enlarging to monopolize the family's entire vacation. Today, with the addition of Blizzard Beach, Typhoon Lagoon, Disney's Hollywood Studios, Animal Kingdom, and Downtown Disney, you should allocate six days for a whirlwind tour (seven to ten if you insist on a little relaxation during your vacation). If you don't have six or more days or think you might want to venture outside the World, be prepared to make some hard choices.

The theme parks and water parks are huge and require a lot of walking and, sometimes, a lot of waiting in lines. Approach Disney World the same way you would an eight-course Italian dinner: with plenty of time between courses. Don't cram too much into too little time.

WHICH PARK TO SEE FIRST?

THIS QUESTION IS LESS ACADEMIC than it appears, especially if your party includes children or teenagers. Children who see the Magic Kingdom first expect the same type of entertainment at the other parks. At Epcot, they're often disappointed by the educational orientation and serious tone (many adults react the same way). Disney's Hollywood Studios offers some wild action, but the general presentation is educational and more adult. Though most children enjoy zoos, animals can't be programmed to entertain. Thus, children may not find Animal Kingdom as exciting as the Magic Kingdom or DHS.

First-time visitors should see Epcot first; you'll be able to enjoy it without having been preconditioned to think of Disney entertainment as solely fantasy or adventure.

See Animal Kingdom second. Like Epcot, it's educational, but its live animals provide a change of pace.

Next, see Disney's Hollywood Studios, which helps all ages transition from the educational Epcot and Animal Kingdom to the fanciful Magic Kingdom. Also, because DHS is smaller, you won't walk as much or stay as long.

Save the Magic Kingdom for last.

The foregoing advice notwithstanding, we know that most readers make a beeline for the Magic Kingdom, mostly for the reason that this North Carolina reader asserts:

> *Although you recommend sort of a reverse order for park* [visitation], *ending up at the Magic Kingdom last, I disagree. We went to the Magic Kingdom first, which* is *Disney World for many of us.*

OPERATING HOURS

DISNEY RUNS A DOZEN OR MORE SCHEDULES each year. Call ☎ 407-824-4321 for the exact hours before you arrive. Off-season, parks may be open as few as eight hours (9 a.m. to 5 p.m.). At busy times (particularly holidays), they may operate from 8 a.m. until 2 a.m.

OFFICIAL OPENING VERSUS REAL OPENING

WHEN YOU CALL, you're given "official hours." Sometimes, parks open earlier. If the official hours are 9 a.m. to 9 p.m., for example, Main Street in the Magic Kingdom might open at 8:30 a.m., and the remainder of the park at 9 a.m.

Disney surveys local hotel reservations, estimates how many visitors to expect on a given day, and opens the theme parks early to avoid bottlenecks at parking facilities and ticket windows and to absorb crowds as they arrive.

Rides and attractions shut down at approximately the official closing time. Main Street in the Magic Kingdom remains open 30 minutes to an hour after the rest of the park has closed.

THE VACATION THAT FIGHTS BACK

VISITING DISNEY WORLD REQUIRES levels of industry and stamina more often associated with running marathons. A mother from Middletown, New York, spells it out:

> *A vacation at WDW is not a vacation in the usual sense—sleeping late, total relaxation, leisurely meals, etc. It is a vacation that's frankly exhausting, but definitely worth doing. WDW is a magical place, where the visitor feels welcomed from the minute they arrive at their accommodations to the last second before boarding the shuttle bus back to the airport.*

A British gentleman, thinking we exaggerated about the walking required, measured his outings using a pedometer. His discovery:

> *I decided to wear a pedometer for our recent visit to WDW. Our visits to the theme parks were spread over five days, during which my wife and I (ages 51 and 55) walked a total of 68 miles for an average of 13 miles per day!*

A Cranleigh, U.K., mum reminds us that a chain is only as strong as its weakest link:

> *The touring plans really helped over President's Day weekend, but the family rebelled on day five and insisted on two lie-ins.*

The point is, at Walt Disney World less is more. Take the World in small doses, with plenty of swimming, napping, reading, and relaxing in between. If you don't see everything, guess what? You can come back!

Also, you can prepare. An Ohio reader discovered this secret too late:

I fly a desk for a living and don't get near enough walking or standing exercise to prepare myself for the rigors of the World. My wife and I have determined that before we go to Disney World again, we will be able to walk at least five miles without a rest or feeling any pain the next day. After pounding the pavement for hours on end, we were so exhausted that we had no choice but to spend two of our vacation days just recovering from the previous day's walking.

Hitting the Wall

As you plan your time at Disney World, consider your physical limitations. It's exhausting to rise at dawn and run around a theme park for 8 to 12 hours day after day. Sooner or later (usually sooner), you hit the wall. Every Disney World vacation itinerary should include days when you don't go to a theme park and days when you sleep in and take the morning off. Plan these to follow unusually long and arduous days, particularly those when you stay in the parks to see the evening parades or fireworks. Keep telling yourself that you'll enjoy your vacation more if you're rested.

A Suwanee, Georgia, reader makes this suggestion:

The one area that I think you can expand on in your book is preparing people for the overall pace that this type of vacation warrants. My initial plan for the family entailed a day at MK, one day each at Epcot, Animal Kingdom, [Disney's Hollywood Studios], *Universal Studios, and Islands of Adventure, one down day, and a leftover day for a second visit to something we hadn't finished. By day two, I became acutely aware that there was no way we would be able to keep up that pace.*

A mom from La Grange, Illinois, sidestepped our advice to stay rested:

As I was planning, I was very sure we would not be taking a swim/nap break in the middle of the day. No way! On the very first day of touring (at the Magic Kingdom), my 7-year-old said (at 9:30 a.m.—after only two hours at the park), "I'm hot—when can we go back to the hotel and swim?" Needless to say, we took that little break every day.

A Lexington, Massachusetts, mother of a 5-year-old had this to say:

We followed your advice to take an afternoon break religiously, and it made all the difference in the world to everyone's mood.

A Tolland, Connecticut, family altered their touring for an "easy day":

There is so much to do and see at WDW, we inevitably push the kids, and then pay the price. One day, when they were tired, we went to [Disney's Hollywood Studios] *and only did shows. Since most of the day was seated, the kids got time to rest and weren't too cranky.*

A Narberth, Pennsylvania, mom changed their dinnertime:

We found that getting up as early as we did, it was important to make early dinner reservations—6:30 p.m. at the latest. The one time we tried to eat at 8 p.m., our younger son fell asleep at the table and could not be awakened.

THE PRACTICALITY OF RETURNING TO YOUR HOTEL FOR REST

MANY READERS WRITE ABOUT the practicality of departing the theme park for a nap and swim at the hotel. A dad from Sequim, Washington, made this request:

I would like to see nearness to the parks emphasized in your accommodation guide, taking traffic and hotel access into account. We tried going back to the hotel for midday breaks, but it was too time-consuming. By the time you got to the car, negotiated traffic, rested, and reversed the process to get back to the park, it took two to three hours for a short rest and was not worth it!

First, in response to the reader's request, we now publish a chart in Part Three, Accommodations, that provides the commuting times to each of the Disney theme parks from virtually every hotel within 20 miles of Walt Disney World. But to address the larger issue, we think the reader was overly anxious about the time away from the parks. Two to three hours really won't cut it. Had he resigned himself to a four- to five-hour break, his family would have stayed rested and relaxed.

Here's the scoop: At Animal Kingdom, Disney's Hollywood Studios, and Epcot, you can get to your car in the parking lot in about 15 to 20 minutes. From the Magic Kingdom, it will take you 30 to 35 minutes. Obviously, if you're at the farthest point from the park entrance when you decide to return to the hotel, or you barely miss a parking-lot tram, it will take longer. But from most places in the parks, the previous times are correct. Once in your car, you'll be able to commute to most US 192 hotels, all Disney World hotels, all Lake Buena Vista hotels, and most hotels along the Interstate 4 corridor and southbound International Drive ("I-Drive") in 20 minutes or less. It will take about the same time to reach hotels on I-Drive north of Sand Lake Road and in the Universal Orlando area.

So, for most people, the one-way commute will average 30 minutes. But here's what you get for your time: a less-expensive lunch at a restaurant of your choosing; a swim; and a one-and-a-half- to two-hour nap. If you add up the times, you'll be away from the parks about four to five hours, counting the commute. If you want, eat dinner outside the World before returning. Clearly, this won't work during times of year when the parks close early, but these aren't times when most families go to Disney World. If you visit when the parks close early, you'll see more attractions in less time, owing to reduced attendance, and you will be able to leave the parks earlier and take your break in the late

unofficial **TIP**
If energy and/or spirits are running low in your group, take a long break from the parks back at your hotel, a nap, a meal, a movie, or a swim.

afternoon or early evening. Not ideal, but neither are the crowds and heat of summer.

A corollary to this discussion is what you do the next day. If you're getting a three- to five-hour break each day and not keeping late hours, you'll be fine. If you forgo the break, you'll need to alternate full days with very easy, sleep-late days in order to recharge your batteries. If you do neither, you'll say hello to the wall by your third day.

ARRIVAL- AND DEPARTURE-DAY BLUES: WHAT TO DO WHEN YOU HAVE ONLY HALF A DAY

ON ARRIVAL AND DEPARTURE DAYS, you probably will have only part of a day for touring or other recreational pursuits. It's a common problem: you roll into the World about 1 p.m., excited and ready to go, but where?

The first question: do you feel comfortable blowing an expensive day's admission to the parks when you have less than a full day to tour? Certainly, your arrival time and the parks' closing times are considerations, but so is the touring disadvantage you suffer by not being there when a park opens. FASTPASS, a reservation system for popular attractions (see page 88), provides some relief from long afternoon lines, but it isn't available for every attraction, nor is there an unlimited supply of passes.

Opting for a Partial Day at the Theme Parks

If you decide to splurge and burn a pass on a half day or less, refer to our *Unofficial Guide* Crowd-level Calendar at **TouringPlans.com.**

One option, if you can reach the park by 1 p.m. and stay until closing (5 to 8 p.m., depending on season), is Animal Kingdom, which requires the least time to tour. Because guests who arrive at opening frequently complete their tour by about 2 p.m., crowds thin in late afternoon. As a bonus, FASTPASS is offered for the most popular attractions. If you arrive much after 1 p.m., however, the daily allocation of FASTPASSes, especially for Kilimanjaro Safaris or Expedition Everest, might be exhausted. And Animal Kingdom closes earlier than the other parks.

Whenever you arrive at a theme park (including Universal parks) after 10 a.m., go to higher-capacity attractions where waiting time is relatively brief even during the most crowded part of the day. In Disney parks, you can also cut your time in line by using FASTPASS. Another time-saver at Soarin' and Test Track in Epcot, at Expedition Everest in Animal Kingdom, Rock 'n' Roller Coaster and *Toy Story* Mania! in Disney's Hollywood Studios, and at several Universal Studios and Islands of Adventure attractions is the "singles line," a separate line for individuals who are alone or don't mind riding alone. The objective is to fill odd spaces left by groups that don't quite fill the entire ride vehicle. Because there aren't many singles and most groups are unwilling to split up, singles lines are usually much shorter than regular lines.

Disney parks are better for partial-day touring than Universal parks because Disney parks generally operate more high-capacity attractions than Universal does. However, the Universal Express program has more perks than Disney's equivalent FASTPASS (if you're staying at a Universal resort). This means that those who use Universal Express may tour more efficiently than a similar guest at Disney. Even so, nothing is guaranteed. We like the Universal parks and admire their cutting-edge technology, but the best way to see them is to be there at opening and follow our touring plans.

Our Touring-plan Companions (in the back of this book) list attractions in each Disney park that require the least waiting during the most crowded part of the day. Although the queues for these attractions may seem humongous, they move quickly. Also check out parades, stage shows, and other live entertainment. Popular attractions generally stay packed until an hour or so before closing; however, they often require little waiting during evening parades, fireworks, or, in the case of Disney's Hollywood Studios, *Fantasmic!*

Alternatives to the Theme Parks on Arrival Day

Before you head out for fun on arrival day, you must check in, unpack, and buy admissions, and you probably will detour to the grocery or convenience store to buy snacks, drinks, and breakfast food. At all Disney resorts and many non-Disney hotels, you cannot occupy your room until after 3 p.m.; however, many properties will check you in, sell you tickets, and store your luggage before that hour.

The least expensive way to spend your arrival day is to check in, unpack, do your chores, and relax at your hotel swimming pool. (Be careful not to get sunburned.)

Other daytime options include a trip to a local water park. Because the Disney water parks are so crowded (during summer you need to be on hand for opening, just as you do at the other Disney parks), we recommend **Wet 'n Wild** (**www.wetnwildorlando.com**) on International Drive, which is generally less crowded than Disney's water parks but more expensive. What's great about Wet 'n Wild is that it stays open late in summer. Any water park that stays open past 5 p.m. is worth a look, because crowds at all parks clear out substantially after 4 p.m. If the park is open late and you get hungry, you'll find ample fast food. No matter which water park you choose, slather on waterproof sunscreen. (For details on water parks, see Part Sixteen.)

If you want something drier, we heartily recommend **Gatorland,** a quirky attraction on US 441 near Kissimmee (about 20 minutes from Walt Disney World). Gatorland, a slice of pre-Disney Florida, is exceptionally interesting and well managed. It's perfect for a half-day outing, provided you like alligators, snakes, and lizards. For information, call Gatorland at ☎ 800-393-JAWS, or check its Web site, **www.gatorland.com.**

unofficial **TIP**
You may want to forgo a half-day at the Disney parks for other area attractions that are smaller and require less visiting time—or to just unpack and gear up for your first full Disney day.

If none of the above fires your boiler, consider miniature golf (expensive in the World; more reasonable outside it) or **DisneyQuest,** Disney's venue featuring interactive games and simulator technology. Alas, like the Disney parks, DisneyQuest is expensive and doesn't handle crowds particularly well. It's at Disney's West Side. Late mornings and early afternoons are the best times to go.

In the Evening

Dinner provides a great opportunity to plan the next day's activities. If you're hungry for entertainment, too, try a dinner show or take in a show after dinner. If you go the show route, we recommend Cirque du Soleil's *La Nouba* at Disney's West Side. Cirque is expensive, but we think it's the single best thing in all of Walt Disney World. Disney also offers some dinner shows, of which the *Hoop-Dee-Doo Musical Revue* is our pick of the litter. Both Cirque and *Hoop-Dee-Doo* are extremely popular; make reservations far in advance. A dozen or so non-Disney dinner shows are advertised in visitor magazines available at any non-Disney hotel.

If you're not up for Cirque or a dinner show, consider **CityWalk,** Universal's nighttime-entertainment complex. Other options include **Jellyrolls,** a dueling-pianos club at Disney's BoardWalk, and **Raglan Road,** an Irish pub with live music and good food at Downtown Disney. All are best appreciated by adults—energetic adults, at that.

Departure Days

Departure days don't seem to cause as much consternation as arrival days. If you want to visit a theme park on your departure day, get up early and be there when it opens. If you have a lot of time, check out and store your luggage with the bell desk or in your car. Or, if you can arrange a late checkout, you might want to return to your hotel for a shower and change of clothes before departing. Some hotels are quite lenient regarding late checkouts; others assess a charge.

OPTIMUM TOURING SITUATION

WE DON'T BELIEVE THERE'S ONE IDEAL ITINERARY. Tastes, energy levels, and perspectives on what constitutes entertainment and relaxation vary. This said, here are some considerations for developing your ideal itinerary.

Optimum touring at Disney World requires a good itinerary, at least six days on-site (excluding travel time), and a fair amount of money. It also requires a prodigious appetite for Disney entertainment. The essence of optimum touring is to see the attractions in a series of shorter, less-exhausting visits during cooler, less-crowded times of day, with plenty of rest and relaxation between excursions.

Because optimum touring calls for leaving and returning to the theme parks on most days, it makes sense to stay in a Disney resort hotel or a non-Disney hotel no more than 12 minutes away. Disney-resort guests have freer use of the bus, boat, and monorail systems and more choices for babysitting and children's programs. Sound good? It is, but be prepared to pay.

If you visit during busy times, you need to get up early to beat the crowds. Short lines and stress-free touring are incompatible with sleeping in. If you want to sleep late and enjoy your touring, visit Disney World when attendance is lighter.

THE CARDINAL RULES FOR SUCCESSFUL TOURING

MANY VISITORS DON'T HAVE SIX DAYS to devote to Disney. Some are en route to other destinations or may wish to sample additional central Florida attractions. For these visitors, efficient touring is a must.

Even the most time-effective touring plan won't allow you to comprehensively cover two or more major theme parks in one day. Plan to allocate an entire day to each park (an exception to this is when the parks close at different times, allowing you to tour one park until closing, then proceed to another).

One-day Touring

A comprehensive one-day tour of the Magic Kingdom, Animal Kingdom, Epcot, or Disney's Hollywood Studios is possible but requires knowledge of the park, good planning, good navigation, and plenty of energy and endurance. One-day touring leaves little time for sit-down meals, prolonged browsing in shops, or lengthy breaks. One-day touring can be fun and rewarding, but allocating two days per park, especially for the Magic Kingdom and Epcot, is preferable.

unofficial **TIP**
If your schedule permits only one day of touring, concentrate on one theme park and save the others for another visit.

Successfully touring the Magic Kingdom, Animal Kingdom, Epcot, or Disney's Hollywood Studios hinges on three rules:

1. Determine in Advance What You Really Want to See

Which rides and attractions appeal most to you? Which ones would you like to experience if you have time left? What are you willing to forgo?

To help you set your touring priorities, we describe the theme parks and every attraction in detail in this book. In each description, we include the authors' evaluation of the attraction and the opinions of Disney World guests expressed as star ratings. Five stars is the highest rating.

Finally, because attractions range from midway-type rides and horse-drawn trolleys to high-tech extravaganzas, we have developed a hierarchy of categories to pinpoint an attraction's magnitude:

SUPER-HEADLINERS The best attractions the theme park has to offer. Mind-boggling in size, scope, and imagination. Represent the cutting edge of attraction technology and design.

HEADLINERS Multimillion-dollar, full-scale, themed adventures and theater presentations. Modern in technology and design and employing a full range of special effects.

MAJOR ATTRACTIONS More modestly themed adventures, but ones that incorporate state-of-the-art technologies. Or larger-scale attractions of older design.

MINOR ATTRACTIONS Midway-type rides, small "dark" rides (cars on a track, zigzagging through the dark), small theater presentations, transportation rides, and elaborate walk-through attractions.

DIVERSIONS Exhibits, both passive and interactive. Includes playgrounds, video arcades, and street theater.

Though not every attraction fits neatly into these descriptions, the categories provide a comparison of attraction size and scope. Remember that bigger and more elaborate doesn't always mean better. Peter Pan's Flight, a minor attraction in the Magic Kingdom, continues to be one of the park's most beloved rides. Likewise, for many young children, no attraction, regardless of size, surpasses Dumbo.

2. Arrive Early! Arrive Early! Arrive Early!

This is the single most important key to efficient touring and avoiding long lines. First thing in the morning, there are no lines and fewer people. The same four rides you experience in one hour in early morning can take as long as three hours after 10:30 a.m. Eat breakfast before you arrive; don't waste prime touring time sitting in a restaurant.

The earlier a park opens, the greater your advantage. This is because most vacationers won't rise early and get to a park before it opens. Fewer people are willing to make an 8 a.m. opening than a 9 a.m. opening. On those rare occasions when a park opens at 10 a.m., almost everyone arrives at the same time, so it's almost impossible to beat the crowd. If you visit during midsummer, arrive at the turnstile 30 to 40 minutes before opening. During holiday periods, arrive 45 to 60 minutes early.

Many readers share their experiences about getting to the parks before opening. From a 13-year-old girl from Bloomington, Indiana:

> *Please stress this to your readers: If you want to ride anything with a short wait, you HAVE to get up in the morning! If this is a sacrifice you aren't willing to make, reconsider a Disney World vacation. Most people say they will then be exhausted, but if* [you] *take a break at the hot part of the day, you'll be fine.*

From a Cincinnati mom:

> *Arriving early made a tremendous difference. I'll admit that at 6:15 in the morning when I was dragging our children out of bed to go to the Magic Kingdom, I thought we'd lost our minds. But we had so much fun that morning, riding rides with no waiting in line. It was worth the early arrival.*

An Austin, Texas, couple waxes enthusiastic:

> *I am telling everyone about your book. It saved my girlfriend and me hours and hours of waiting in line (during spring break, no less!) We were first in line for the parks every morning, and boy, was it worth it.*

A Strafford, England, mum opines:

> *The single best words of advice I would give anyone planning to visit the World is to GET UP EARLY. We were the first at the parks—the* very *first, 11 days out of 14—and while hanging out at the turnstiles an hour before rope drop is reasonably dull, it is worth it for the payoff of short lines for the rest of the day. To exemplify: one day we rode* Toy Story *Mania! three times as walk-ons, picking up FASTPASSes after ride number one* [to use] *later. The lines that day were at 100 minutes* [a half hour] *after park opening. I'm from the U.K., but I think you U.S. guys would call it a no-brainer!*

Most touring plans are compromised if you're not on hand for park opening, as this mom from Port Talbot, Wales, attests:

> *After arriving shortly after 9 a.m. at Universal's Islands of Adventure, we were disappointed to discover a wait of 50 minutes for our first ride in the plan, the Incredible Hulk Coaster. All other rides in the plan had long waits as well, so we didn't get to ride much in that park.*

A family of five from Great Falls, Virginia, weighs in:

> *The* Unofficial Guide *allowed us to have a wonderful trip, even during the spring break–Easter holiday. We followed the touring plans every day in every park. The plans and the timely use of FASTPASS worked flawlessly. The basic theory of survival is "EE"—Everything Early. We had a light breakfast in our room so we could get to the parks 40 minutes before opening.*

Finally, from a Galesburg, Illinois, dad:

> *It is a big deal to get to the parks at the rope drop (that's an intense experience). We got a lot done then. We would get FASTPASSes for the first ride, then ride it right away using the regular line. It allowed us to get* Toy Story *Mania! and Expedition Everest at least twice each day.*

If getting the kids up earlier than usual makes for rough sailing, don't despair: you'll have a great time no matter when you get to the park. Many families with young children have found that it's better to accept the relative inefficiencies of arriving at the park a bit late than to jar the children out of their routine. In our guide especially for families, *The Unofficial Guide to Walt Disney World with Kids,* we provide a number of special touring plans (including touring plans for sleepyheads) that we don't have room for in this guide.

3. Avoid Bottlenecks

Helping you avoid bottlenecks is what the *Unofficial Guide* is about. Bottlenecks are caused by crowd concentrations and/or faulty crowd management. Avoiding bottlenecks involves being able to predict where, when, and why they occur. Concentrations of hungry people create bottlenecks at restaurants during lunch and dinner; concentrations of people moving toward the exit near closing time create bottlenecks in gift shops en route; concentrations of visitors at new and popular rides, and at rides slow to load and unload, create bottlenecks and long lines.

We provide touring plans for the Magic Kingdom, Animal Kingdom, Epcot, and Disney's Hollywood Studios to help you avoid bottlenecks. We also provide detailed information on all rides and performances, enabling you to estimate how long you may have to wait in line and allowing you to compare rides for their crowd capacity.

All touring plans are in the back of this book, immediately following the indexes. Plans for the Magic Kingdom begin on page 815, Epcot on page 822, Animal Kingdom on page 829, and Disney's Hollywood Studios on page 831. We also include one-day touring plans for Universal Studios Florida on page 833 and Universal's Islands of Adventure on page 835.

WHAT'S A QUEUE?

ALTHOUGH IT'S NOT COMMONLY USED in the United States, *queue* (pronounced "cue") is the universal English word for a line, such as one in which you wait to cash a check at the bank or to board a ride at a theme park. There's a mathematical area of specialization within the field of operations research called queuing theory, which studies and models how lines work. Because the *Unofficial Guide* draws heavily on this discipline, we use some of its terminology. In addition to the noun, the verb "to queue" means to get in line, and a "queuing area" is a waiting area that accommodates a line. When guests decline to join a queue because they perceive the wait to be too long, they are said to "balk."

OF UTMOST IMPORTANCE: READ THIS!

IN ANALYZING READER SURVEYS, we were astonished by the percentage of readers who *do not* use our touring plans. Scientifically tested and proven, these plans can save you four entire hours or more of waiting in line. Did you get that? *Four hours!* Four fewer hours of standing, four hours freed up to do something fun. Our groundbreaking research that created the touring plans has been the subject of front-page articles in the *Dallas Morning News* and the *New York Times* and has been cited in numerous scholarly journals. So the question is, why would you *not* use them?

We get a ton of reader mail—98% of it positive—commenting on our touring plans. First, from a family of four from West Chester, Pennsylvania:

> *This book and your touring plans, without a doubt, made the trip. We followed the adult one-day plans almost to the letter. Probably the longest line we stood in was maybe 30 minutes max during one of the [busiest] times of the year. The key was getting to the parks 30 minutes or so before opening. The plans also saved arguing over what to do next. We simply followed the guide. We are believers!*

A family from Waynesville, Ohio, visited Walt Disney World at one of the most crowded times of year:

> *We picked spring break week (week before Easter) to go and knew we had to have a game plan or it would be a terrible experience. I ordered two guides and used only one! The touring plans were a lifesaver, with the crowd levels being at 10 for almost the whole week. We planned our days according to your park recommendations and followed the plans. We were successful in EVERY park* [reader's emphasis].

From a New Albany, New York, reader:

> [I had] *only one full day in Disney, and I used the One-day Touring Plan for Adults for the Magic Kingdom. I was shocked by how well it worked. I even took about a three-hour break to go to Downtown Disney (via the Contemporary), and I was still able to do everything on the plan. Incredible.*

A mom from Danville, Pennsylvania, had to overcome a doubting spouse:

> *My husband thought the touring plans were a product of an overly obsessive-compulsive mind. He laughed at me for wanting to use them, but he finally conceded on Christmas Eve at the Magic Kingdom. He wasn't laughing anymore by noon, when we had already ridden all of the rides with really long lines!*

An Ohio family felt the wind in their sails:

> *The whole time we were in the Magic Kingdom, following the touring plan, it seemed that we were traveling in front of a hurricane—we'd wait ten minutes or so for an attraction (or less—sometimes we just*

walked right on), but when we got out and started moving on to the next one, we could see the line building for what we just did. My friend and I just laughed the whole time—and followed the touring plan to the letter!

A fellow Buckeye, from Cleveland, comments:

Some of your readers have complained about "the death of spontaneity" in following your touring plans. I say, who cares about spontaneity when you have such overwhelming success at a place as complex as WDW? I mean, we did everything there, and we didn't have to wait to do it. There's really not much more you can ask for. When you go to a museum or some such place and take a guided tour, there's no spontaneity in that, but you come away feeling very satisfied that you got to see and do everything that is available. Following the Guide *and the touring plans is just like that—it's like a guided tour without the human guide. And we were completely satisfied and happy with our Disney experience. I'll take that over spontaneity any day!*

An exclamation-point-happy woman from Baton Rouge, Louisiana, has this to say:

The touring plans were amazing! It was my husband's first trip to Disney, and he is officially spoiled! He has no idea what it is like to wait in a long line! He never will either, because we will always use the touring plans from now on!

A mother of three from Perry, Georgia, scored a personal best with the help of the plans:

I can't believe the difference the plans made! I've read every tip and time-saver, stayed away from Extra Magic Hours parks, and tried going at lower crowd times, but I've always found myself frustrated, dazed, and stuck in the crowds. This was our fifth and shortest stay, but we were able to tour everything we wanted—never even came close in the past. I'm spreading the touring-plans message to all of my friends.

A somewhat irritated Washington, West Virginia, wife weighs in with this:

I saw several people with the Unofficial Guide *and had to ask if the plans really work. They all said that they do. Unfortunately, my husband had his own plans . . . which didn't include following anyone else's.*

Finally, from a mom with two school-age children from Murrieta, California:

Wow! The Unofficial Guide *touring plans were fantastic. Our longest waits were in the mornings, waiting for the parks to open each day. Seriously, we didn't have a single ride that we had to wait a long time for. I didn't time it, but I'd guess 10 minutes was our average wait. Maelstrom was about 20 to 25 minutes, and that was our longest line of the whole week. Unbelievable for July at WDW! It was amazing. We did have to hustle in the mornings, but it was SO worth it! I can't imagine what all those poor people without your book did. Well, yes I can—I think we saw them arguing over a park map as we passed by.*

TOURING PLANS: WHAT THEY ARE AND HOW THEY WORK

See More, Do More, Wait Less

From the first edition of the *Unofficial Guide*, minimizing our readers' wait in lines has been a top priority. We know from our research and that of others that theme-park patrons measure overall satisfaction based on the number of attractions they're able to experience during a visit: the more attractions, the better. Thus, we developed and offered our readers field-tested touring plans that allow them to experience as many attractions as possible with the least amount of waiting in line.

Our touring plans have always been based on theme-park traffic flow, attraction capacity, the maximum time a guest is willing to wait (called a "balking constraint"), walking distance between attractions, and waiting-time data collected at specific intervals throughout the day and at various times of year. The plans derived from a combinatorial model (for anyone who cares) that married the well-known assignment problem of linear programming with queuing (waiting-line) theory. The model approximated the most time-efficient sequence in which to visit the attractions of a specific park. After we created a preliminary touring plan from the model, we field-tested it in the park, using a test group (who followed our plan) and a control group (who didn't have our plan and who toured according to their own best judgment).

The two groups were compared, and the results were amazing. On days of heavy attendance, the groups touring without our plans spent an average of three and a half hours more in line and experienced 37% fewer attractions than did those who used our touring plans.

Over the years, this research has been recognized by both the travel industry and academe, having been cited by such diverse sources as the *New York Times, USA Today, Travel Weekly, Bottom Line, Money, Operations Research Forum,* CBS News, Fox News, the BBC, the Travel Channel, and the *Dallas Morning News,* among others.

John Henry and the Nail-driving Machine

As sophisticated as our model may sound, we recognized that it was cumbersome and slow, and that it didn't approximate the "perfect" touring plan as closely as we desired. Moreover, advances in computer technology and science, specifically in the field of genetic algorithms, demonstrated that it wouldn't be long before a model, or program, was created that would leave ours in the dust.

Do you remember the story of John Henry, the fastest nail driver on the railroad? One day a man appeared with a machine he claimed could drive spikes faster than any man. John Henry challenged the machine to a race, which he won, but which killed him in the process. We felt a bit like John Henry. We were still very good at what we did but knew with absolute certainty that sooner or later we'd have to confront the touring-plan version of a nail-driving machine.

Our response was to build our own nail-driving machine. We teamed up during the mid-1990s with Len Testa, a scientist and programmer who was working in the field of evolutionary algorithms and who, coincidentally, was a theme-park junkie. Marrying our many years of collecting Walt Disney World observations and data to Len's vision and programming expertise, we developed a state-of-the-art program for creating nearly perfect touring plans.

Several university professors, many of them leaders in their fields, have contributed research or ideas to the new software program. Findings from early versions of the software have been published in peer-reviewed academic journals. The most recent versions of the program are protected through pending patent applications. Special thanks go to Albert C. Esterline, PhD, of North Carolina A&T State University and Gerry V. Dozier, PhD, of Auburn University. Credit is also due to Nikolaos Sahinidis, PhD, as well as his graduate students at the University of Illinois at Urbana-Champaign, who have contributed a number of exceptionally helpful studies. Chryssi Malandraki, PhD, of United Parcel Service and Robert Dial, PhD, of the Volpe National Transportation System Center have likewise provided assistance and encouragement over the years.

unofficial **TIP**
The facts and figures in our books come from years of data collection and analysis by expert statisticians, programmers, field researchers, and lifelong Disney enthusiasts.

It has been a process of evolution and refinement, but in each year of its development, the new program came closer to beating the results of our long-lived model. In 2002 at field trials during the busy spring-break period, the new program beat the best touring plan generated by the traditional *Unofficial* model by 90 minutes at the Magic Kingdom. This was in addition to the three hours saved by the earlier model. Getting there, however, wasn't easy.

The Challenge

One factor that makes creating effective touring plans difficult is that there are many ways to see the same attractions. For example, if we want to visit Space Mountain, Pirates of the Caribbean, and Splash Mountain as soon as the Magic Kingdom opens, there are six ways to do so:

1. First ride Space Mountain, then Pirates of the Caribbean, then Splash Mountain.
2. First ride Space Mountain, then Splash Mountain, then Pirates of the Caribbean.
3. First ride Splash Mountain, then Space Mountain, then Pirates of the Caribbean.
4. First ride Splash Mountain, then Pirates of the Caribbean, then Space Mountain.
5. First ride Pirates of the Caribbean, then Splash Mountain, then Space Mountain.
6. First ride Pirates of the Caribbean, then Space Mountain, then Splash Mountain.

Some of these combinations make better touring plans than others. Because the queue for Space Mountain increases rapidly, it's best to ride this particular attraction first thing in the morning. For similar reasons, it would be better to ride Splash Mountain before Pirates. In this example, touring plan number 2 would probably save us the most time standing in line. Touring plan 5 would probably result in the most waiting in line.

As we add attractions to our list, the number of possible touring plans grows rapidly. Adding a fourth attraction would result in 24 possible touring plans, since there are four possible variations for each of the 6 plans listed previously. In general, the number of possible touring plans for n attractions is $n \cdot (n-1) \cdot (n-2) \ldots \cdot 1$. (Don't let the mathematical notation throw you. If we plug real numbers in, it's quite simple.) For five attractions, as an example, there are $5 \times 4 \times 3 \times 2 \times 1$ possible touring plans. If you don't have a calculator handy, that adds up to 120 potential plans. For six attractions, there are $6 \times 5 \times 4 \times 3 \times 2 \times 1$, or 720 possible plans. A list of ten attractions has more than 3 million possible plans. The 21 attractions in the Magic Kingdom One-day Touring Plan for Adults have a staggering 51,090,942,171,709,440,000 possible touring plans. That's over 51 billion billion combinations, or roughly six times as many as the estimated number of grains of sand on Earth. Adding in complexities such as FASTPASS, parades, meals, and breaks further increases the combinations.

Scientists have been working on similar problems for years. Companies that deliver packages, for example, plan each driver's route to minimize the distance driven, saving time and fuel. In fact, finding ways to visit many places with minimal effort is such a common problem that it has its own nickname: the traveling-salesman problem.

For more than a small number of attractions, the number of possible touring plans is so large it would take a very long time for even a powerful computer to find the single best plan. A number of proposed techniques give very good, but not necessarily exact, solutions to the traveling-salesman problem in a reasonable amount of time.

The *Unofficial Guide* Touring Plan program contains two algorithms that allow it to quickly analyze tens of millions of possible plans in a very short time. (An algorithm is to a computer what a recipe is to a chef. Just as a chef takes specific steps to make a cake, a computer takes specific steps to process information. Those steps, when grouped, form an algorithm.) The program can analyze FASTPASS distribution patterns at all attractions, for example, and suggest the best times and attractions to use FASTPASS. The software can also schedule rest breaks throughout the day. If you're going to eat lunch in the park, the software can suggest restaurants near where you'll be at lunchtime that will minimize the time you spend looking for food. Numerous other features are available, many of which we'll discuss in the next section, "Custom Touring Plans."

The program, however, is only part of what's needed to create a good touring plan. Good data is also important. For more than six years, we've been collecting data in the theme parks at every conceivable time of year. At each park, researchers recorded the estimated wait at every attraction, show, FASTPASS booth, and restaurant, every 30 minutes, from park opening to closing. On a typical day at the Magic Kingdom, for example, each researcher walked about 18 miles and collected around 500 pieces of data. One of several research routes would start researchers at the Swiss Family Treehouse in Adventureland. After collecting data on all of Adventureland, they would continue to the attractions and restaurants in Frontierland. After that came Liberty Square, then finally half of Fantasyland, before they returned to Swiss Family Treehouse for an eight-minute break before starting the next round of data collection. A platoon of additional volunteers collected data in the other half of the park.

So how good are the new touring plans in the *Unofficial Guide*? Our computer program typically gets within about 2% of the optimal touring plan and finds an optimal plan for most straightforward situations around 70% of the time. To put this in perspective, if the hypothetical "perfect" Adult One-day Touring Plan took about 10 hours to complete, the *Unofficial* touring plan would take about 10 hours and 12 minutes. Since it would take about 30 years for a really powerful computer to find that "perfect" plan, the extra 12 minutes is a reasonable trade-off.

In the 2003 edition of this guidebook, we noted the possibility of using our touring-plan software to see all of the 40-plus attractions in the Magic Kingdom in one day. We dubbed this the Ultimate Magic Kingdom Touring Plan and offered it free to anyone up for the challenge. Several people have completed this plan since that time, and many others have come close. The current record-holders are the *Unofficial Guide*'s own Fred Hazelton and Henry Work, who experienced 55 attractions in 11 hours and 38 minutes on December 14, 2009. Their average wait in line was less than 2 minutes per attraction. This surpassed the record of Drs. Yvette Bendeck and Edward Waller of Houston, who experienced 50 attractions in 12 hours and 48 minutes in October 2007. Drop us a line if you're interested in the challenge; we think it's possible to knock another 15 minutes off the record, and it's become routine for most challengers to experience more than 40 attractions on any attempt throughout the year. Note that this touring plan isn't intended for families, first-time visitors, or anyone simply wanting a nice day in the Magic Kingdom. Rather, it's like running a marathon.

Custom Touring Plans

The *Unofficial Guide* Touring Plan program allows us to offer readers customized touring plans to all Disney parks. *The best touring plans our program can produce are the ones published in this guide.* Most of the plans, however, require that you be on hand when the park opens. If you are able to meet this requirement, you won't need a custom touring plan. If you want to sleep in, arrive at the park at 11 a.m. instead of at park opening, or commence touring at 3 p.m., a customized plan will guarantee the least time waiting in line given your arrival time.

In response to readers urging us to create additional touring plans, we've posted on our Web site, **TouringPlans.com,** more than 110 of the most requested custom plans. These are one- and two-day touring plans that cover all four Walt Disney World theme parks and a whole array of special situations: plans for senior citizens, Disney Cruise guests, holiday touring, and much more. While the plans in this guide emphasize efficient touring and seeing as much as possible, the Web site's touring plans offer rather laid-back itineraries allowing guests to tour in a more relaxed fashion. By making the plans available online, we're able to reflect changes in park operating hours, parade times and showtimes, and closing of attractions for maintenance.

Further, our Web site allows you to create your own free custom touring plan based on your favorite attractions, restaurants, and shows. Simply choose the things you want to do, the order in which you want to do them, and your travel dates. We'll display your plan along with the park hours, parade times and showtimes, attraction trivia, hidden Mickeys, and more.

Allow us to underscore that the most efficient touring plans are those included in this guide. They allow you to see more attractions with less waiting because they require you to be on hand when the parks open. If you can't get the kids up and out early, or if you want to take a morning off, or if you prefer attractions different from those included in our touring plans, a custom plan is a good option for you.

OVERVIEW OF THE TOURING PLANS

OUR TOURING PLANS ARE STEP-BY-STEP guides for seeing as much as possible with a minimum of standing in line. They're designed to help you avoid crowds and bottlenecks on days of moderate-to-heavy attendance. On days when attendance is lighter (see "Selecting the Time of Year for Your Visit," page 33), the plans will save time, but they won't be as critical to successful touring.

What You Can Realistically Expect from the Touring Plans

Though we present one-day touring plans for each theme park, be aware that the Magic Kingdom and Epcot have more attractions than you can reasonably expect to see in one day. Because the *two-day plans* for the Magic Kingdom and Epcot are the most comprehensive, efficient, and relaxing, we strongly recommend them over the one-day plans. However, if you must cram your visit into a single day, the one-day plans will allow you to see as much as is humanly possible. Although Disney's Hollywood Studios has grown considerably since its 1989 debut, seeing everything in one day is no problem. Likewise, Animal Kingdom is a one-day outing.

Variables That Will Affect the Success of the Touring Plans

The plans' success will be affected by how quickly you move from ride to ride; when and how many refreshment and restroom breaks you take; when, where, and how you eat meals; and your ability (or lack thereof) to find your way around. Smaller groups almost always move faster than larger groups, and parties of adults generally cover more ground than families with young children. Switching off (page 339), also known as baby swapping or child swapping, among other things, inhibits families with little ones from moving expeditiously among attractions. Plus, some children simply cannot conform to the plans' "early to rise" conditions.

unofficial **TIP**
Because park hours can change without notice, the best time to request your custom plan is two to four weeks before leaving home.

A mom from Nutley, New Jersey, writes:

> [Although] *the touring plans all advise getting to parks at opening, we just couldn't burn the candle at both ends. Our kids (10, 7, and 4) would not go to sleep early and couldn't be up at dawn and still stay sane. It worked well for us to let them sleep a little later, go out, and*

bring breakfast back to the room while they slept, and still get a relatively early start by not spending time on eating breakfast out. We managed to avoid long lines with an occasional early morning, and hitting popular attractions during parades, mealtimes, and late evenings.

And a family from Centerville, Ohio, says:

The toughest thing about your touring plans was getting the rest of the family to stay with them, at least to some degree. Getting them to pass by attractions in order to hit something across the park was no easy task (sometimes impossible).

If you have young children in your party, be prepared for character encounters. The appearance of a Disney character usually stops a touring plan in its tracks. While some characters stroll the parks, it's equally common that they assemble in a specific venue (such as the Hall of Fame at Mickey's Toontown Fair) where families queue up for photos and autographs. Meeting characters, posing for photos, and collecting autographs can burn hours of touring time. If your kids collect character autographs, you need to anticipate these interruptions and negotiate some understanding with your children about when you will follow the plan and when you will collect autographs. Our advice is to go with the flow or set aside a specific morning or afternoon for photos and autographs. Note that queues for autographs, especially in Toontown at the Magic Kingdom and Camp Minnie-Mickey at Animal Kingdom, are sometimes as long as the queues for major attractions. The only time-efficient way to collect autographs is to line up at the character-greeting areas first thing in the morning. This is also the best time to experience the popular attractions, so you may have tough choices to make.

While we realize that following the plans isn't always easy, we nevertheless recommend continuous, expeditious touring until around noon. After noon, breaks and diversions won't affect the plans significantly.

Some variables that can profoundly affect the plans are beyond your control. Chief among these are the manner and timing of bringing a particular ride to capacity. For example, Big Thunder Mountain Railroad, a roller coaster in the Magic Kingdom, has five trains. On a given morning, it may begin operation with two of the five, then add the other three when needed. If the waiting line builds rapidly before operators go to full capacity, you could have a long wait, even in early morning.

Another variable relates to the time you arrive for a theater performance. You'll wait from the time you arrive until the end of the presentation in progress. Thus, if a show is 15 minutes long and you arrive one minute after it has begun, your wait will be 14 minutes. Conversely, if you arrive as the show is wrapping up, your wait will be only a minute or two.

Flexibility

The attractions included in the touring plans are the most popular ones as determined by more than 25,000 reader surveys. Even so, *your* favorite attractions might be different. Fortunately, the touring plans are flexible. If a plan calls for an attraction you don't wish to experience, simply skip it and move on to the next one. You can also substitute similar attractions in the same area of the park. If a plan calls for, say, riding Dumbo and you're not interested but you would enjoy the Mad Tea Party (which is not on the plan), then go ahead and substitute it for Dumbo. As long as the substitution is a similar attraction—substituting a show for a ride won't work—and is pretty close to the attraction called for in the touring plan, you won't compromise the plan's overall effectiveness.

A family of four from South Slocan, British Columbia, found they could easily tailor the touring plans to meet their needs:

> *We amended your touring plans by taking out the attractions we didn't want to do and just doing the remainder in order. It worked great, and by arriving before the parks opened we got to see everything we wanted, with virtually no waits! The best advice by far was "get there early"!*

Likewise, a Jacksonville, Florida, family modified our touring plans to meet their needs:

> *We used a combination of the Two-day Touring Plan for Parents with Small Children and the Two-day Touring Plan for Adults. We were able to get on almost everything with a 10-minute wait or less. Our longest wait was on our second day for the Jungle Cruise, but the wait was still only 20 minutes. We were just amazed at how well the plan worked! Not only will I be recommending this to all my friends with kids but will use it when we visit again in December. Thank you!*

What to Do if You Lose the Thread

Anything from a blister to a broken attraction can throw off a touring plan. If unforeseen events interrupt a plan:

1. Skip one step on the plan for every 20 minutes' delay. If, for example, you lose your billfold and spend an hour finding it, skip three steps and pick up from there.
2. Forget the plan and organize the remainder of your day using the Recommended Attraction Visitation Times clip-out lists at the back of this guide. These timetables summarize the best times to visit each attraction.

A multigenerational family from Aurora, Ohio, wonders how to know if you're on track or not, writing:

> *It seemed like the touring plans were very time-dependent, yet there were no specific times attached to the plan outside of the early morning. On more than one day, I often had to guess as to whether we were "on track." Having small children and a grandparent in our group, we couldn't move at a fast pace.*

Honestly, there *is* no objective measurement for being on track. Each family's or touring group's experience will differ to some degree. Whether your group is large or small, fast or slow, the sequence of attractions in the touring plans will allow you to enjoy the greatest number of attractions in least possible time. Two quickly moving adults will probably take in more attractions in a specific time period than will a large group consisting of children, parents, and grandparents. However, given the characteristics of the respective groups, each will maximize its touring time and experience as many attractions as possible.

What to Expect When You Arrive at the Parks

Because most touring plans are based on being present when the theme park opens, you need to know about opening procedures. Disney transportation to the parks begins an hour and a half to two hours before official opening. The parking lots open at around the same time.

Each park has an entrance plaza outside the turnstiles. Usually, you're held there until 30 minutes before the official opening time, when you're admitted. What happens next depends on the season and the day's crowds.

1. **LOW SEASON** At slower times, you will usually be confined outside the turnstiles or in a small section of the park until the official opening time. At the Magic Kingdom you might be admitted to Main Street, U.S.A.; at Animal Kingdom, to The Oasis and sometimes to Discovery Island; at Epcot, to the fountain area around Spaceship Earth; and at Disney's Hollywood Studios, to Hollywood Boulevard. Rope barriers supervised by Disney cast members keep you there until the "rope drop," when the barrier is removed and the park and its attractions are opened at the official start time.
2. **HIGH-ATTENDANCE DAYS** When large crowds are expected, you will usually be admitted through the turnstiles up to 30 minutes before official opening, and the entire park will be operating.
3. **VARIATIONS** Sometimes Disney will run a variation of those two procedures. In this, you'll be permitted through the turnstiles and find that one or several specific attractions are open early. At Epcot, Spaceship Earth and sometimes Test Track or Soarin' will be operating. At Animal Kingdom, you may find Kilimanjaro Safaris and *It's Tough to Be a Bug!* running early. At Disney's Hollywood Studios, look for Tower of Terror, *Toy Story* Mania!, and/or Rock 'n' Roller Coaster. The Magic Kingdom almost never runs a variation. Instead, you'll usually encounter number 1, or occasionally 2.
4. **A WORD ABOUT THE ROPE DROP** For many years at all four parks, Disney cast members would dive for cover when the rope was dropped as thousands of adrenaline-crazed guests stampeded to the parks' most popular attractions. This practice occasioned the legendary Space Mountain Morning Mini-Marathon and the Splash Mountain Rapid Rampage at the Magic Kingdom, the Tower of Terror Trot at Disney's Hollywood Studios, and the Safari Sprint at Animal Kingdom, among others. Each morning, a throng would crowd the rope barriers, waiting to sprint to their favorite ride. It was each person for himself—parents against offspring, brother against sister, coeds against truck drivers, nuns against beauticians. There was nothing to do but tie up your Reeboks and get ready to run.

This ritual insanity no longer exists—at least not in the tumultuous versions of years past. Disney has increased the number of cast members supervising the rope drop in order to suppress the melee. In some cases, the rope isn't even "dropped." Instead, it's walked back: cast members lead you with the rope at a fast walk toward the attraction you're straining to reach, forcing you (and everyone else) to maintain their pace. Not until they near the attraction do cast members step aside. A New Jersey mom described it thus:

> *You are no longer allowed to sprint to these* [attractions] *because of people being trampled. Now there is a phalanx of cast members lined up at the rope who instruct you in friendly but no uncertain terms that when the rope drops they will lead you to the rides at a fast walk. However, you are not allowed to pass them. (No one ever said what would happen if you did pass.) To my surprise, everyone followed the rules and we were splish-splashing within five minutes after 9 a.m.*

You never know with Disney. The current rope-drop procedure may be abandoned, and the traditional insanity allowed to resume. But we don't think so.

So here's the straight poop. If Disney persists in walking the rope back, the only way you can gain an advantage is to arrive early enough to be up front near the rope. Be alert, though; cast members sometimes step out of the way after about 50 yards. If this happens, fire up the afterburners and speed the remaining distance to your destination.

Touring-plan Clip-out Pocket Versions

For your convenience, we've prepared clip-out copies of all touring plans. These pocket versions combine touring-plan itineraries with maps and directions. Select the plan appropriate for your party, and get familiar with it. Then clip the pocket version from the back of this guide and carry it with you as a quick reference at the theme park.

Will the Plans Continue to Work Once the Secret Is Out?

Yes! First, all the plans require that a patron be there when a park opens. Many Disney World patrons simply won't get up early while on vacation. Second, less than 1% of any day's attendance has been exposed to the plans—too few to affect results. Last, most groups tailor the plans, skipping rides or shows according to taste.

How Frequently Are the Touring Plans Revised?

Because Disney is always adding new attractions and changing operations, we revise the plans every year. Most complaints we receive come from readers using out-of-date editions of the *Unofficial Guide*. Be prepared, however, for surprises. Opening procedures and showtimes may change, for example, and you can't predict when an attraction might break down.

Tour Groups from Hell

We have discovered that tour groups of up to 200 people sometimes use our plans. A woman from Memphis, Tennessee, writes:

> *When we arrived at The Land* [pavilion at Epcot], *a tour guide was holding your book and shouting into a bullhorn, "Step 7—proceed to Journey into Imagination!" With this, about 65 Japanese tourists in red T-shirts ran out the door.*

Unless your party is as large as the Japanese group, this development shouldn't alarm you. Because tour groups are big, they move slowly and have to stop to collect stragglers. The tour guide also has to accommodate the unpredictability of five dozen or so bladders. In short, you should have no problem passing a group after the initial encounter.

"Bouncing Around"

Many readers object to crisscrossing a theme park as our touring plans sometimes require. A lady from Decatur, Georgia, said she "got dizzy from all the bouncing around." We empathize, but here's the rub, park by park.

In the Magic Kingdom, the most popular attractions are positioned across the park from one another. This is no accident. It's a method of more equally distributing guests throughout the park. If you want to experience the most popular attractions in one day without long waits, you can arrive before the park fills and see those attractions first (requires crisscrossing the park), or you can enjoy the main attractions on one side of the park first, then try the most popular attractions on the other side during the hour or so before closing, when crowds presumably have thinned. Using FASTPASS lessens the time you wait in line but tends to increase the bouncing around because you must visit the same attraction twice: once to obtain your FASTPASS and again to use it.

The best way to minimize "bouncing around" at the Magic Kingdom is to use the Magic Kingdom Two-day Touring Plan, which spreads the more popular attractions over two mornings and works beautifully even when the park closes at 8 p.m. or earlier.

Disney's Hollywood Studios is configured in a way that precludes an orderly approach to touring, or to a clockwise or counterclockwise rotation. Orderly touring is further confounded by live entertainment that prompts guests to interrupt their touring to head for whichever theater is about to crank up. At the Studios, therefore, you're stuck with "bouncing around" whether you use our plan or not. In our opinion, when it comes to Disney parks, it's best to have a plan.

unofficial **TIP**
We've revised the Epcot plans to eliminate most of the "bouncing around" and have added instructions to minimize walking.

Animal Kingdom is arranged in a spoke-and-hub configuration like the Magic Kingdom, simplifying crisscrossing the park. Even so, the only way to catch various shows is to stop what you're doing and troop across the park to the next performance.

Touring Plans and the Obsessive-compulsive Reader

We suggest you follow the touring plans religiously, especially in the mornings, if you're visiting during busy times. The consequence of touring spontaneity in peak season is hours of standing in line. During quieter times, there's no need to be compulsive about following the plans.

A mom in Atlanta suggests:

> *Emphasize perhaps not following* [the touring plans] *in off-season. There is no reason to crisscross the park when there are no lines.*

A mother in Minneapolis advises:

> *Please let your readers know to stop along the way to various attractions to appreciate what else may be going on around them. We encountered many families using the* Unofficial Guide [who] *became too serious about getting from one place to the next, missing the fun in between.*

What can we say? It's a lesser-of-two-evils situation. If you visit

Walt Disney World at a busy time, you can either rise early and hustle around, or you can sleep in and see less.

When using the plans, however, relax and always be prepared for surprises and setbacks. When your type-A brain does cartwheels, reflect on the advice of a woman from Trappe, Pennsylvania:

> *You cannot emphasize enough the dangers of using your touring plans that were printed in the back of the book, especially if the person using them has a compulsive personality. I planned for this trip for two years and researched it by use of guidebooks, computer programs, videotapes, and information received from WDW. I had a two-page itinerary for our one-week trip in addition to your touring plans of the theme parks. On night three of our trip, I ended up taking an unscheduled trip to the emergency room of Sand Lake Hospital in Lake Buena Vista. When the doctor asked what seemed to be the problem, I responded with "I don't know, but I can't stop shaking, and I can't stay here very long because I have to get up in a couple hours to go to* [Disney's Hollywood Studios] *according to my itinerary." Diagnosis: an anxiety attack caused by my excessive itinerary. He gave me a shot of something, and I slept through the first four attractions the next morning. This was our third trip to WDW (not including one trip to Disneyland); on all previous trips I used only the Steve Birnbaum book, and I suffered no ill effects. I am not saying your book was not good—it was excellent! However, it should come with a warning label for people with compulsive personalities.*

Lastly, from an Omaha, Nebraska, couple:

> *We created our own 4.25-by-5.5 guidebook for our trip that included a number of pages from the TouringPlans.com Web site. This was the first page:*

The Type A Spouse's Bill of Rights

1. *We will not see everything in one vacation, and any attempt to do so may be met with blunt trauma.*
2. *Len Testa will not be vacationing with us. His plans don't schedule time for benches. Ours may.*
3. *We may deviate from the touring plans at some point. Really.*
4. *Even if it is not on the Disney dining plan, a funnel cake or other snack may be purchased without a grouchy face from the nonpurchasing spouse.*
5. *Sometimes, sitting by the pool may sound more fun than going to a park, show, or other scheduled event. On this vacation, that will be fine.*
6. *"But I thought we were going to . . ." is a phrase that must be stricken from the discussion of any plans that had not been previously discussed as a couple.*
7. *Other items may be added as circumstances dictate at the parks.*

> *It was a much happier vacation with these generally understood principles in writing.*

Touring-plan Rejection

Some folks don't respond well to the regimentation of a touring plan. If you encounter this problem with someone in your party, roll with the punches as this Maryland couple did:

The rest of the group was not receptive to the use of the touring plans. I think they all thought I was being a little too regimented about planning this vacation. Rather than argue, I left the touring plans behind as we ventured off for the parks. You can guess the outcome. We took our camcorder with us and watched the movies when we returned home. About every five minutes or so there is a shot of us all gathered around a park map trying to decide what to do next.

Finally, as a Connecticut woman alleges, the plans are incompatible with some readers' bladders and personalities:

I want to know if next year when you write those "day" schedules you could schedule bathroom breaks in there, too. You expect us to be at a certain ride at a certain time and with no stops in between. In one of the letters in your book, a guy writes, "You expect everyone to be theme-park commandos." When I read that, I thought there is a man who really knows what a problem the schedules are if you are a laid-back, slow-moving, careful detail noticer. What were you thinking when you made these schedules?

Touring Plans for Low-attendance Days

We receive a number of letters each year similar to this one from Lebanon, New Jersey:

The guide always assumed there would be large crowds. We had no lines. An alternate tour for low-traffic days would be helpful.

If attendance is low, you don't need a touring plan. Just go where your taste and instinct direct, and glory in the hassle-free touring. Having said that, however, there are attractions in each park that bottleneck even if attendance is low. These are Space Mountain, Splash Mountain, Dumbo, The Many Adventures of Winnie the Pooh, and Peter Pan's Flight in the Magic Kingdom; Test Track, Soarin', and Mission: Space at Epcot; Kilimanjaro Safaris and Expedition Everest at Animal Kingdom; and Rock 'n' Roller Coaster, *The Twilight Zone* Tower of Terror, and *Toy Story* Mania! at Disney's Hollywood Studios. All are FASTPASS attractions. Experience them immediately after the parks open, or use FASTPASS. Remember that crowd size is relative and that large crowds can gather at certain attractions even during less-busy times. We recommend following a touring plan through the first five or six steps. If you're pretty much walking onto every attraction, feel free to scrap the remainder of the plan.

A Clamor for Additional Touring Plans

We're inundated by letters urging us to create additional plans. These include a plan for ninth- and tenth-graders, a plan for rainy days, a seniors' plan, a plan for folks who sleep late, a plan omitting rides that "bump, jerk, and clonk," a plan for gardening enthusiasts, a plan for kids who are afraid of skeletons, and a plan for single women.

The plans in this book are flexible. Adapt them to your preferences. If you don't like rides that bump and jerk, skip those when they come up in a plan. If you want to sleep in and go to the park at noon, use the afternoon part of a plan. If you're a ninth-grader and want to ride Space

Mountain three times in a row, do it. Will it decrease the plans' effectiveness? Sure, but they were created only to help you have fun. It's your day.

Although we believe, as stated previously, that the touring plans in this guide can be modified to fit the needs of any Walt Disney World guest, we have nevertheless responded to your urging by creating more than 110 touring plans designed for special situations. These plans, available on our Web site, **TouringPlans.com,** cover scenarios we just don't have space for in this book. All four Walt Disney World theme parks are covered, with one- and two-day plans available for senior citizens, holiday touring, Disney Cruise Line guests, and much more. While the touring plans in this book emphasize efficient touring and are the best available for that purpose, the focus of the Web site's touring plans is to offer plans that address specific individual needs as well as unusual situations. For parents who aren't certain their small children are up to all the walking, for example, we have an alternate version of a two-day Magic Kingdom touring plan that cuts down on backtracking around the park. You won't see everything as fast as you would if you used the plans in the guide, but you won't get as tired either. We also have one- and two-day "late arrival" touring plans that address the needs of those who can't get an early start or who just want to sleep in. Most online touring plans contain detailed, step-by-step descriptions of your entire visit to each theme park, along with a one-page, easy-to-carry summary of each plan. Free sample touring plans are available at **www.touringplans.com/ak_sample.html.**

And for those using the plans in this guide or the specialized plans on TouringPlans.com, the Web site provides updated information on park operating hours, parade times and showtimes, and attractions closed for maintenance.

EXTRA MAGIC HOURS AND THE TOURING PLANS

IF YOU'RE A DISNEY RESORT GUEST and use your morning Extra Magic Hours privileges, complete your early-entry touring before the general public is admitted, and position yourself to follow the touring plan. When the public is admitted, the park will suddenly swarm. A Wilmington, Delaware, mother advises:

> *The early-entry times went like clockwork. We were finishing up the Great Movie Ride when* [Disney's Hollywood Studios] *opened* [to the public], *and* [we] *had to wait in line quite a while for* Voyage of the Little Mermaid, *which sort of screwed up everything thereafter. Early-opening attractions should be finished up well before regular opening time so you can be at the plan's first stop as early as possible.*

In the Magic Kingdom, early-entry attractions currently operate in Adventureland, Fantasyland, Liberty Square, and Tomorrowland. At Epcot, they're in the Future World section. At Disney's Hollywood Studios, they're dispersed. Practically speaking, see any attractions on the plan that are open for early entry, crossing them off as you do. If you finish all early-entry attractions and have time left before the general public is admitted, sample early-entry attractions not included in the plan. Stop touring about ten minutes before the public is admitted, and position yourself for the first attraction on the plan that *wasn't* open for early entry. During early entry in the Magic Kingdom, for example, you can almost always experience Peter Pan's Flight and It's a Small World in Fantasyland, plus Space Mountain and *Stitch's Great Escape* in Tomorrowland. As official opening nears, go to the boundary between Fantasyland and Liberty Square and be ready to blitz Splash and Big Thunder mountains according to the touring plan when the rest of the park opens.

Evening Extra Magic Hours, when a designated park remains open for Disney-resort guests three hours beyond normal closing time, have less effect on the touring plans than early entry in the morning. Parks are almost never scheduled for both early entry and evening Extra Magic Hours on the same day. Thus a park offering evening Extra Magic Hours will enjoy a fairly normal morning and early afternoon. It's not until late afternoon, when park hoppers coming from the other theme parks descend, that the late-closing park will become especially crowded. By that time, you'll be well toward the end of your touring plan.

FASTPASS

IN 1999 DISNEY LAUNCHED a system for moderating the wait at popular attractions. Called FASTPASS, it was originally tried at Animal Kingdom, then expanded to attractions at the other parks.

Here's how it works. Your handout park map and signage at attractions will tell you which attractions are included. Attractions operating FASTPASS will have a regular line and a FASTPASS line. A sign at the entrance will say how long the wait is in the regular line. If the wait is acceptable to you, hop in line. If it seems too long, insert your park admission pass into a FASTPASS machine and receive an appointment time (for later in the day) to return and ride. When you return at the designated time, you enter the FASTPASS line and proceed directly to the attraction's preshow or boarding area. Interestingly, this procedure was pioneered by Universal Studios Hollywood years ago and had been virtually ignored by theme parks since (Universal now has a reworked variation called Universal Express). The system works well, however, and can save a lot of waiting time. There's no extra charge to use FASTPASS.

FASTPASS is evolving, and attractions continue to be added and deleted from the lineup. Changes aside, here's an example of how to use FASTPASS. Say you have only one day to tour the Magic Kingdom. You arrive early and ride Space Mountain and Buzz Lightyear with minimal waits. Then you cross the park to Splash Mountain and find a substantial line. Because Splash Mountain is a FASTPASS attraction, you can insert your admission pass into the machine and receive an appointment to come back and ride, thus avoiding a long wait.

The effort to accommodate FASTPASS holders makes anyone in the regular line feel second class. And a telling indication of their status is that they're called "standby guests." Indeed, we watched people in regular lines despondently stand by and stand by, while dozens and sometimes hundreds of FASTPASS holders were ushered into the boarding area ahead of them. Disney is sending a message here: FASTPASS is heaven; anything else is limbo at best and probably purgatory. In any event, you'll think you've been in hell if you're stuck in the regular line during the hot, crowded part of the day.

Readers regularly send standby-line horror stories. Here's one from a Pequea, Pennsylvania, family:

> *We, a group of four 12-year-olds and five adults, decided to ride Test Track when we arrived at Epcot at 11:00 a.m. FASTPASSes were being issued for* [late that night] *and the singles line was not open yet, so we decided to brave the 120-minute wait (at MK and* [Disney's Hollywood Studios] *many waits ended up being less than the posted time). What a disaster! Once inside the building, the FASTPASS and singles line (which opened when we were very near the building) sped ahead while the standby line barely moved. After 3 hours and 20 minutes, we finally made it to the car! One man who was in the FASTPASS line said that he counted a 12:1 ratio between FASTPASSers and standby people being let into the* [boarding] *area. Disney needs to seriously reconsider their boarding policy!*

FASTPASS doesn't eliminate the need to arrive early at a theme park. Because each park offers a limited number of FASTPASS attractions, you still need an early start if you want to see as much as possible in one day. Plus, there's a limited supply of FASTPASSes available for each attraction on any day. If you don't arrive until midafternoon, you might find that no more FASTPASSes are available. FASTPASS does make it possible to see more with less waiting, and it's a great benefit to those who like to sleep late or who choose an afternoon or evening at the parks on their arrival day. It also allows you to postpone wet rides, such as Kali River Rapids at Animal Kingdom or Splash Mountain at the Magic Kingdom, until a warmer time of day.

Understanding the FASTPASS System

The purpose of FASTPASS is to reduce the wait for designated attractions by distributing guests at those attractions throughout the day. This is accomplished by providing an incentive (a shorter wait) for guests willing to postpone experiencing the attraction until later in the day. The system also, in effect, imposes a penalty (standby status) on those who don't use it. However, spreading out guest arrivals sometimes also decreases the wait for standby guests.

When you insert your admission pass into a FASTPASS time clock, the machine spits out a slip of paper about two-thirds the size of a credit card—small enough to fit in your wallet but also small enough to lose easily. Printed on it is the attraction's name and a time window, for example 1:15 to 2:15 p.m., during which you can return to ride.

Returning to Ride

At both Walt Disney World and Disneyland in California, the return-window expiration time is ignored as a matter of policy, though Disney keeps this something of a secret. In other words, a FASTPASS is good from the beginning of the return window until closing time. In the unlikely event that a cast member doesn't let you reenter an attraction because your FASTPASSes have expired, hold on to them if possible and try again 15 to 30 minutes later. Another cast member will probably be staffing the return line by that time, and he or she will more than likely allow you to reenter. A frequent exception to this practice is Soarin' at Epcot, where cast members are strict about enforcing the return window.

A Selkirk, New York, family share their experiences using expired FASTPASSes:

> *At Toy Story Mania! at Hollywood Studios, the FASTPASSes ran out almost immediately, and the standby line jumped to 90 minutes within 20 minutes of the rope drop. We actually got FASTPASSes and then came back another day and used them. We used old FASTPASSes a number of times with no problems, except the last two days we were there, when we got turned away at Dinosaur and Soarin' with old FASTPASSes. All in all, though, ignoring the return time really enhanced our touring.*

When you report back, you'll enter a line marked "FASTPASS Return" that routes you more or less directly to the boarding or preshow area. Each person in your party must have his own FASTPASS and be ready to show it at the entrance of the FASTPASS return line. Before you enter the boarding area or theater, another cast member will collect your FASTPASS.

unofficial **TIP**
FASTPASS works remarkably well, mainly because FASTPASS holders get amazingly preferential treatment.

Cast members are instructed to minimize waits for FASTPASS holders. Thus, if the FASTPASS return line is suddenly inundated (something that occurs by chance), cast members intervene to reduce the FASTPASS line. As many as 25 FASTPASS holders will be admitted for each standby guest until the FASTPASS line is reduced to an acceptable length. Although FASTPASS usually eliminates 85% or more of the wait you would experience in the regular line, you can still expect a short wait, usually less than 15 minutes and frequently less than 10 minutes.

Obtaining a FASTPASS

You can ordinarily obtain a FASTPASS anytime after a park opens (some attractions are a little tardy getting their FASTPASS system up), but the FASTPASS return lines don't usually begin operating until 35 to 90 minutes after opening.

Whenever you obtain a FASTPASS, you can be assured of a period of time between when you receive your FASTPASS and when you report back. The interval can be as short as 15 minutes or as long as three to seven hours, depending on park attendance and the attraction's popularity and hourly capacity. Generally, the earlier in the day you obtain a FASTPASS, the shorter the interval before your return window. If the park opens at 9 a.m. and you obtain a FASTPASS for Splash Mountain at 9:25 a.m., your appointment for returning to ride would be 10 to 11 a.m. or 10:10 to 11:10 a.m. The exact time will be determined by how many other guests have obtained FASTPASSes before you.

To more effectively distribute guests over the day, FASTPASS machines bump the one-hour return period back a few minutes for a set number of passes issued (usually about 6% of the attraction's hourly capacity). For example, when Splash Mountain opens at 9 a.m., the first 125 people to obtain a FASTPASS will get a 9:40-to-10:40-a.m. return window. The next 125 guests are issued FASTPASSes with a 9:45-to-10:45-a.m. window. And so it goes, with the time window dropping back five minutes for every 125 guests. The fewer guests who obtain

FASTPASSes for an attraction, the shorter the interval between receipt of your pass and the return window. Conversely, the more guests issued FASTPASSes, the longer the interval. If an attraction is exceptionally popular and/or its hourly capacity is relatively small, the return window might be pushed back to park closing time. When this happens the FASTPASS machines shut down and a sign is posted saying all FASTPASSes are gone for the day. It's not unusual, for example, for Test Track at Epcot or Winnie the Pooh at the Magic Kingdom to have distributed all available FASTPASSes by 1 p.m.

unofficial **TIP**
Each person in your party must have his or her own FASTPASS.

Rides routinely exhaust their daily FASTPASS supply, but shows almost never do. FASTPASS machines at theaters try to balance attendance at each show so that the audience for any given performance is divided about evenly between standby and FASTPASS guests. Consequently, standby guests for shows aren't discriminated against to the degree experienced by standby guests for rides. In practice, FASTPASS diminishes the wait for standby guests. With few exceptions, the standby line at theater attractions requires less waiting than using FASTPASS.

WHEN TO USE FASTPASS Except as discussed on the next page, there's no reason to use FASTPASS during the first 30 to 40 minutes a park is open. Lines for most attractions are manageable during this period, and this is the only time of day when FASTPASS attractions exclusively serve those in the regular line.

Using FASTPASS requires two trips to the same attraction: one to obtain the pass and another to use it. You must invest time to obtain the pass, then interrupt your touring later to backtrack in order to use it. The additional time, effort, and touring modification are justified only if you can save more than 30 minutes. Don't forget: even the FASTPASS line requires some waiting.

Nine attractions build lines so quickly in the morning that failing to queue up within the first six or so minutes of operation will all but guarantee a long wait: Mission: Space, Soarin', and Test Track at Epcot); Expedition Everest and Kilimanjaro Safaris at Animal Kingdom); Space Mountain at the Magic Kingdom); and Rock 'n' Roller Coaster, *Toy Story* Mania!, and *The Twilight Zone* Tower of Terror at Disney's Hollywood Studios). With these, you should race directly to the attractions when the park opens or obtain a FASTPASS.

Another four FASTPASS attractions—Splash Mountain, Winnie the Pooh, Peter Pan's Flight, and Jungle Cruise in the Magic Kingdom—develop long queues within 30 to 50 minutes of park opening. If you can make your way to them before the wait becomes intolerable, lucky you. Otherwise, your options are FASTPASS or a long time waiting in line.

In case you're wondering how FASTPASS waits compare with waits in the standby line, here's what we observed at Space Mountain during spring break on a day when the park opened at 9 a.m. From 9 to 10 a.m., both sides of Space Mountain served standby guests (there are two identical roller coasters in the Space Mountain building). At 10 a.m. the entire right side was cleared and became dedicated to FASTPASS. At 10:45 a.m., the posted standby wait time was 45 minutes; for FASTPASS, only 10 minutes. At 1:45 p.m., the posted standby wait time was 60 minutes,

unofficial **TIP**
Regardless of the time of day, if your wait in the regular line at a FASTPASS attraction is 25–30 minutes or less, join the regular line.

with 10 minutes for FASTPASS. These observations document the benefit of FASTPASS and, interestingly, also reveal shorter waits in the regular line than those observed at the same time of day before the advent of FASTPASS.

FASTPASS RULES Disney allows you to obtain a second FASTPASS at a time printed on the bottom of your most recent FASTPASS, usually two hours or less from the time the first was issued. The lesson here is to check the posted return time before obtaining a FASTPASS, as a father of two from Cranston, Rhode Island, advises:

> *Always check on the sign above the FASTPASS machines to see the* [return] *time that you will receive. We made the mistake of not looking at the time before we got our FASTPASSes for Space Mountain. The time we received was not for two hours and was at a time when we could not ride because of lunch reservations. So we couldn't take advantage of FASTPASS at Space Mountain and couldn't get any other FASTPASSes until after lunch.*

If the return time is hours away, forgo FASTPASS. Especially in the Magic Kingdom, there will be other FASTPASS attractions where the return time is only an hour or so away.

At a number of attractions, the time gap between issuance and return can be three to seven hours. If you think you might want to use FASTPASS on the following attractions, obtain it before 11 a.m.:

FASTPASS ODDITIES AND EXCEPTIONS Generally, you can obtain a second FASTPASS when you enter your return window, at the time printed at the bottom of the FASTPASS, or two hours after the time of issue, whichever is first. An exception is *The Twilight Zone* Tower of Terror at Disney's Hollywood Studios, where you're eligible to get a second FASTPASS after one hour.

A more interesting exception concerns the *Lights! Motors! Action! Extreme Stunt Show* at Disney's Hollywood Studios. When you obtain a FASTPASS here, the pass states that you can acquire another FASTPASS at any other FASTPASS attraction in just five minutes. We aren't sure whether this is an experiment or a glitch in the system, or if it will last, but it's potentially a big time-saver for those in the know.

TRICKS OF THE TRADE It's possible to acquire a second FASTPASS before using the first one (and sooner than two hours after getting it). Let's say you obtain a FASTPASS to Kilimanjaro Safaris at Animal Kingdom with a return time of 10:15 to 11:15 a.m. Any time after your FASTPASS window begins, you can obtain another FASTPASS, say for Kali River Rapids. This is possible because the FASTPASS computer monitors only the distribution of passes, ignoring whether or when a FASTPASS is used.

When obtaining FASTPASSes, it's quicker and more considerate if one person obtains passes for your entire party. This means entrusting one individual with your valuable park-admission passes and your FASTPASSes, so choose wisely.

MAGIC KINGDOM	DHS	EPCOT	ANIMAL KINGDOM
Winnie the Pooh	Rock 'n' Roller Coaster	Soarin'	Expedition Everest
Peter Pan's Flight	*Indiana Jones**	Mission: Space	
Space Mountain	*Lights! Motors! Action!**	Test Track	
Splash Mountain	*Toy Story* Mania!		
Buzz Lightyear			

**Available seasonally*

Obtain FASTPASSes for all members of your party, including those who are too short, too young, or simply not interested in riding, as this family of four recommends:

> *Utilize the FASTPASSes of people in your group who don't want to ride. Our 6-year-old didn't want to ride anything rough. All four of us got FASTPASSes for each ride.* [When] *the 6-year-old didn't want to ride, my husband and I took turns riding with the 12-year-old. It was our version of the FASTPASS child swap, and the 12-year-old got double rides.*

FASTPASS Guidelines

- Don't mess with FASTPASS unless it can save you 30 minutes or more.
- If you arrive after a park opens, obtain a FASTPASS for your preferred FASTPASS attraction first thing.
- Do not obtain a FASTPASS for a theater attraction until you have experienced all the FASTPASS rides on your itinerary. (Using FASTPASS at theater attractions usually requires more time than using the standby line.)
- Check the FASTPASS return time before obtaining a FASTPASS.
- Obtain FASTPASSes for Winnie the Pooh, Peter Pan's Flight, Space Mountain, and Splash Mountain at the Magic Kingdom; Mission: Space, Soarin', and Test Track at Epcot; Expedition Everest at Animal Kingdom; and Rock 'n' Roller Coaster and *Toy Story* Mania! at Disney's Hollywood Studios as early in the day as possible.
- Try to obtain FASTPASSes for rides not mentioned in the preceding tip by 1 p.m.
- Don't depend on FASTPASSes being available after 2 p.m. during busier times.
- Make sure everyone in your party has his or her own FASTPASS.
- You can obtain a second FASTPASS at the time printed at the bottom of your first FASTPASS.

UNDERSTANDING WALT DISNEY WORLD ATTRACTIONS

DISNEY WORLD'S PRIMARY APPEAL IS IN ITS rides and shows. Understanding how these are engineered to accommodate guests is interesting and invaluable to developing an efficient itinerary.

All attractions, regardless of location, are affected by two elements: capacity and popularity. Capacity is how many guests the attraction can serve at one time—in an hour or in a day. Popularity shows how well visitors like an attraction. Capacity can be adjusted at some attractions. It's possible, for example, to add trams at the Disney's Hollywood Studios Backlot Tour or put extra boats on the Magic Kingdom's Jungle Cruise. Generally, however, capacity remains relatively fixed.

Designers try to match capacity and popularity as closely as possible. A high-capacity ride that isn't popular is a failure. Lots of money, space, and equipment have been poured into the attraction, yet there are empty seats. Journey into Imagination, a ride in Epcot, fits this profile.

It's extremely unusual for a new attraction not to measure up, but it's fairly common for an older ride to lose appeal. The Magic Kingdom's *Enchanted Tiki Room,* for example, played to half-capacity audiences until its 1998 renovation.

Some attractions, such as Space Mountain at the Magic Kingdom, have sustained great appeal years beyond their debut, while others declined in popularity after a few years. Most attractions, however, work through the honeymoon, then settle down to handle the level of demand for which they were designed. When this happens, there are enough interested guests during peak hours to fill almost every seat, but not so many that long lines develop.

Sometimes Disney correctly estimates an attraction's popularity but fouls the equation by mixing in a third variable such as location. Spaceship Earth, the ride inside the geosphere at Epcot, is a good example. Placing the ride squarely in the path of every person entering the park assures that it will be inundated during morning when the park is filling. On the flip side, *The American Adventure,* at the opposite end of Epcot, has huge capacity but plays to a partially filled theater until midafternoon, when guests finally reach that part of the park.

unofficial **TIP**
Generally, attractions are immensely popular when they're new, and thus have longer lines.

If demand is high and capacity is low, large lines materialize. Dumbo the Flying Elephant in the Magic Kingdom has the smallest capacity of almost any Disney World attraction, yet it is probably the most popular ride among young children. The result of this mismatch is that children and parents often suffer long, long waits for a one-and-a-half-minute ride. Dumbo is a simple yet visually appealing midway ride. Its capacity is limited by the very characteristics that make it popular.

Capacity design is predicated on averages: the average number of people in the park, the normal distribution of traffic to specific areas, and the average number of staff needed to operate the ride. On a holiday weekend, when all the averages are exceeded, all but a few attractions operate at maximum capacity, and even then they are overwhelmed by the huge crowds. On days of low attendance in the fall, capacity is often not even approximated, and guests can ride without having to wait.

Only the Magic Kingdom and Animal Kingdom offer low-capacity midway rides and spook-house "dark" rides. They range from state-of-the-art to antiquated. This diversity makes efficient touring of the Magic Kingdom much more challenging. If guests don't understand the capacity–popularity relationship and don't plan accordingly, they might spend most of the day in line.

unofficial **TIP**
The Magic Kingdom offers the greatest variety in capacity and popularity, with vastly differing rides and shows.

Although Epcot, Animal Kingdom, and Disney's Hollywood Studios have fewer rides and shows than the Magic Kingdom, almost all their attractions are major features on par with the Magic Kingdom's Pirates of the Caribbean and The Haunted Mansion in scope, detail, imagination, and spectacle. All but one or two Epcot, Animal Kingdom, and DHS rides are fast-loading, and most have large capacities. Because Epcot, Animal Kingdom, and DHS attractions are generally well engineered and efficient, lines may appear longer than those in the Magic Kingdom but usually move more quickly. There are no midway rides at Epcot or DHS, and fewer attractions are intended for children.

In the Magic Kingdom, crowds are more a function of the popularity and engineering of individual attractions. At Epcot and Animal Kingdom, traffic flow and crowding are more affected by park layout. For touring efficiency, it's important to understand how Magic Kingdom rides and shows operate. At Epcot and Animal Kingdom, this knowledge is less important.

Crowds at Disney's Hollywood Studios were larger than anticipated when the park opened. Disney has added attractions, making a touring plan essential. Likewise, Animal Kingdom is operating with only five of its six originally planned themed areas open. Lack of capacity plus the allure of a newer roller coaster translates into lengthy queues.

To develop an efficient touring plan, it's necessary to understand how rides and shows are designed and function. We'll examine both.

CUTTING YOUR TIME IN LINE BY UNDERSTANDING THE RIDES

WALT DISNEY WORLD HAS MANY TYPES OF RIDES. Some, such as The Great Movie Ride at Disney's Hollywood Studios, can carry more than 3,000 people an hour. At the other extreme, Dumbo the Flying Elephant can handle only around 400 people an hour. Most rides fall somewhere in between. Many factors figure into how long you'll wait to experience a ride: its popularity; how it loads and unloads; how many persons can ride at once; how many units (cars, rockets, boats, flying elephants, and the like) are in service at a time; and how many cast members are available to operate the ride. Let's take the factors one by one.

1. How Popular Is the Ride?

Newer rides such as Expedition Everest at Animal Kingdom and *Toy Story* Mania! at Disney's Hollywood Studios attract a lot of people, as do such longtime favorites as the Magic Kingdom's Jungle Cruise. If a ride is popular, you need to know how it operates in order to determine the best time to ride. But a ride need not be especially popular to generate long lines; in some cases, such lines are due not to a ride's popularity but to poor traffic engineering. This is the case at the Mad Tea Party and Cinderella's Golden Carousel (among others) in Fantasyland. Both rides serve only a small percentage of any day's attendance at the Magic Kingdom, yet because they take so long to load and unload, long lines form regardless.

2. How Does the Ride Load and Unload?

Some rides never stop. They are like conveyor belts that go around and around. These are "continuous loaders." The Magic Kingdom's Haunted Mansion and Epcot's Spaceship Earth are continuous loaders. The number of people that can be moved through in an hour depends on how many cars—"doom buggies" or whatever—are on the conveyor. The Haunted Mansion and Spaceship Earth have lots of cars on the conveyor, and each consequently can move more than 2,000 people an hour.

Other rides are "interval loaders." Cars are unloaded, loaded, and dispatched at set intervals (sometimes controlled manually, sometimes by computer). Space Mountain in Tomorrowland is an interval loader. It has two tracks (the ride has been duplicated in the same facility). Each track can run as many as 14 space capsules, released at 36-, 26-, or 21-second intervals. (The bigger the crowd, the shorter the interval.)

In one kind of interval loader, empty cars, as in Space Mountain's space capsules, return to where they reload. In a second kind, such as Splash Mountain, one group of riders enters the vehicle while the previous group departs. Rides of the latter type are referred to as "in and out" interval loaders. As a boat docks, those who have just completed their ride exit to the left; at almost the same time, those waiting to ride enter the boat from the right. The reloaded boat is released to the dispatch point a few yards down the line, where it is launched according to the interval being used.

Interval loaders of both types can be very efficient people-movers if (1) the dispatch (launch) interval is relatively short and (2) the ride can accommodate many vehicles at one time. Since many boats can float through Pirates of the Caribbean at one time, and since the dispatch interval is short, almost 3,000 people can see this attraction each hour.

The least efficient rides, in terms of traffic engineering, are "cycle rides," also called "stop and go" rides. On cycle rides, those waiting to ride exchange places with those who have just ridden. Unlike in-and-out interval rides, cycle rides shut down during loading and unloading. While one boat is loading and unloading in It's a Small World (an interval loader), many other boats are advancing through the ride. But when Dumbo the Flying Elephant touches down, the whole ride is at a standstill until the next flight launches (ditto Cinderella's Golden Carousel).

In cycle rides, the time in motion is "ride time." The time the ride idles while loading and unloading is "load time." Load time plus ride time equals "cycle time," or the time from the start of one run of the ride until the start of the next. The only cycle rides in Disney World are in the Magic Kingdom and Animal Kingdom.

3. How Many Persons Can Ride at One Time?

This figure expresses "system capacity," or the number of people who can ride at one time. The greater the carrying capacity of a ride (all other things being equal), the more visitors it can accommodate per hour. Some rides can add extra units (cars, boats, and such) as crowds build, to increase capacity; others, such as the Astro Orbiter in Tomorrowland, have a fixed capacity (it's impossible to add more rockets).

4. How Many Units Are in Service at a Given Time?

Unit is our term for the vehicle in which you ride. At the Mad Tea Party the unit is a teacup, at Peter Pan's Flight a pirate ship. On some rides (mostly cycle rides), the number of units operating at one time is fixed. There are always 16 flying elephants at Dumbo and 90 horses on Cinderella's Golden Carousel. There is no way to increase the capacity of such rides by adding units. On a busy day, the only way to carry more people each hour on a fixed-unit cycle ride is to shorten the loading time or decrease the ride time. The bottom line: on a busy day for a cycle ride, you'll wait longer and possibly be rewarded with a shorter ride. This is why we steer you away from cycle rides unless you're willing to ride them early in the morning or late at night. These are the cycle rides:

MAGIC KINGDOM Dumbo the Flying Elephant, Cinderella's Golden Carousel, Mad Tea Party, The Magic Carpets of Aladdin, Astro Orbiter, Goofy's Barnstormer

ANIMAL KINGDOM TriceraTop Spin

Many other rides throughout Disney World can increase their capacity by adding units as crowds build. For example, if attendance is light, Big Thunder Mountain Railroad in Frontierland can start the day by running only one of its five mine trains from one of two available loading platforms. If lines build, the other platform is opened and more mine trains are placed into operation. At capacity, the five trains can carry about 2,400 persons an hour. Likewise, Star Tours at Disney's Hollywood Studios can increase its capacity by using all its simulators, and the Maelstrom boat ride at Epcot can add more Viking ships. Sometimes a long queue will disappear almost instantly when new units are brought online. When an interval loader places more units into operation, it usually shortens the dispatch intervals, allowing more units to be dispatched more often.

5. How Many Cast Members Are Available to Operate the Ride?

Adding cast members to a ride can allow more units to operate or additional loading or holding areas to open. In the Magic Kingdom, Pirates of the Caribbean and It's a Small World can run two waiting lines and loading zones. The Haunted Mansion has a one-and-a-half-minute preshow staged in a "stretch room." On busy days, a second stretch room can be activated, permitting a more continuous flow of visitors to the actual loading area.

Additional staff makes a world of difference to some cycle rides. Often, the Mad Tea Party has only one attendant. This person alone must clear visitors from the ride just completed, admit and seat visitors for the upcoming ride, check that each teacup is secured, return to the control panel, issue instructions to the riders, and finally activate the ride (whew!). A second attendant divides these responsibilities and cuts loading time by 25% to 50%.

CUTTING YOUR TIME IN LINE BY UNDERSTANDING THE SHOWS

MANY FEATURED ATTRACTIONS AT DISNEY WORLD are theater presentations. While they aren't as complex as rides, understanding them from a traffic-engineering standpoint may save you touring time.

How Walt Disney World Theaters Work

Most theater attractions operate in three phases:

1. Guests are in the theater viewing the presentation.
2. Guests who have passed through the turnstile wait in a holding area or lobby. They will be admitted to the theater as soon as the show in progress concludes. Several attractions offer a preshow in their lobby to entertain guests until they're admitted to the main show. Examples include *Enchanted Tiki Room* and *Stitch's Great Escape* in

the Magic Kingdom; *Honey, I Shrunk the Audience* at Epcot; and *Sounds Dangerous* and *Muppet-Vision 3-D* at Disney's Hollywood Studios.

3. A line waits outside. Guests in line enter the lobby when there is room, and will ultimately move into the theater.

Theater capacity, the presentation's popularity, and park attendance determine how long lines will be at a theater attraction. Except for holidays and other days of heavy attendance, and excluding two particularly popular shows (see below), the longest wait for a show usually doesn't exceed the length of one performance. As almost all theater attractions run continuously, stopping only long enough for the previous audience to leave and the waiting audience to enter, a performance will be in progress when you arrive. *O Canada!* at Epcot's Canada Pavilion lasts 18 minutes; your longest wait under normal circumstances is about 18 minutes if you arrive just after the show has begun.

All theaters (except a few amphitheater productions) are very strict about access. You can't enter during a performance. This means you will always have at least a short wait. Most theaters hold a lot of people. When a new audience is admitted, any outside line will usually disappear. Exceptions are *Honey, I Shrunk the Audience* in the Imagination! Pavilion at Epcot and *Voyage of the Little Mermaid* at Disney's Hollywood Studios. Because these shows are so popular, you may have to wait through more than one show before you're admitted (unless you go early in the morning or after 4:30 p.m.).

A WORD ABOUT DISNEY THRILL RIDES

READERS OF ALL AGES SHOULD ATTEMPT TO BE open-minded about Disney "thrill rides." In comparison with those at other theme parks, the Disney attractions are quite tame, with more emphasis on sights, atmosphere, and special effects than on the motion, speed, or feel of the ride. While we suggest you take Disney's pre-ride warnings seriously, we can tell you that guests of all ages report enjoying rides such as Tower of Terror, Big Thunder Mountain, and Splash Mountain.

A Washington reader sums up the situation well:

> *Our boys and I are used to imagining typical amusement park rides when it comes to roller coasters. So, when we thought of Big Thunder Mountain and Space Mountain, what came to mind was gigantic hills, upside-down loops, huge vertical drops, etc. I actually hate roller coasters, especially the unpleasant sensation of a long drop, and I have never taken a ride that loops you upside down.*
>
> *In fact, the Disney* [thrill rides] *are all tame in comparison. There are never any long and steep hills (except Splash Mountain, and it is there for anyone to see, so you have informed consent going on the ride). I was able to build up courage to go on all of them, and the more I rode them, the more I enjoyed them—the less you tense up expecting a big, long drop, the more you enjoy the special effects and even swinging around curves, which is really the primary motion challenge of Disney roller coasters.*

Seniors who experience Disney thrills generally enjoy the smoother rides like Splash Mountain, Big Thunder Mountain, and Tower of

Terror and tend to dislike more jerky attractions. This letter from a Gig Harbor, Washington, woman is typical:

> *I am a senior woman of small stature and good health. I am writing my comments on Space Mountain, Splash Mountain, Big Thunder Mountain, and Star Tours. My experience* [is that] *all of the rides, with the exception of Star Tours, were wonderful rides. Star Tours is too jerky and fast, the music is too loud, and I found it to be unacceptable.*

Notwithstanding this letter, most comments we receive from seniors about Star Tours are positive. The Rock 'n' Roller Coaster and Expedition Everest, however, are a different story. Both are serious coasters that share more in common with Revenge of the Mummy at Universal Studios than they do with Space Mountain or Big Thunder Mountain.

Mission: Space, a high-tech simulation ride at Epcot, is a toss-up (pun intended). It absolutely has the potential to make you sick. Disney, however, tinkered with it throughout its first year of operation to minimize the likelihood of motion sickness without compromising the thrill. The ride vehicles are constructed with an easy-clean design that allows cast members to quickly hose down any mess that occurs. But don't worry: Disney is as interested in avoiding this unpleasant exercise as you are in keeping your cookies right where they belong. A no-spin version, launched in 2006, is less likely to launch your lunch.

THE WONDERFUL, THE WILD, AND THE WUSSY: CENTRAL FLORIDA ROLLER COASTERS

IF YOU EVER GO TO A PARTY where guests are discussing Immelmanns, batwings, heartline rolls, dive loops, rollovers, lift hills, and LIM launchers, don't mistake the guests for fighter pilots. Incredibly, you will be among the intelligentsia of roller-coaster aficionados. This growing population, along with millions of other not-quite-so-fanatical coaster lovers, is united in the belief that roller coasters are—or ought to be—the heart of every theme park.

Though Disney pioneered the concept of super-coasters with the **Matterhorn Bobsleds** at Disneyland in 1959, it took them 16 years to add another roller coaster, **Space Mountain** at Walt Disney World, to their repertoire. In relatively quick succession followed Space Mountain at Disneyland and **Big Thunder Mountain Railroad** at both Disneyland's and Walt Disney World's Magic Kingdoms. Irrespective of the Mountains' popularity, Disney didn't build another coaster in the United States for almost 20 years. In the interim, coasters enjoyed a technical revolution that included aircraft-carrier-type launching devices and previously unimaginable loops, corkscrews, vertical drops, and train speeds. Through all this, Disney sat on the sidelines. After all, Disney parks didn't offer "rides" but, rather, "adventure experiences" in which the sensation of the ride itself was always secondary to story lines and visuals. Competition, however, has long been Disney's alarm clock, and when archrival Universal announced plans for its Islands of Adventure theme park, featuring an entire arsenal of thrill rides, Disney went to work.

unofficial **TIP**
Warning: Mission: Space can make you sick to your stomach.

The upshot was a banner year in 1999 for central-Florida coasters, with the **Incredible Hulk, Dueling Dragons: Fire,** and **Dueling**

Dragons: Ice opening at Universal Studios' Islands of Adventure, the **Rock 'n' Roller Coaster** coming online at the Disney's Hollywood Studios, and **Gwazi,** a wooden coaster, premiering at Busch Gardens Tampa. Close on their heels in early 2000 was **Kraken** at SeaWorld. All six of the new arrivals were serious thrill rides, making Space and Big Thunder mountains look like cupcakes and wienie buns. All the new coasters featured inversions, corkscrews, and rollovers except Gwazi. Best of all for coaster lovers, none of the players were content to rest on their laurels. Universal Studios came back with **Revenge of the Mummy** in 2004, followed by **SheiKra** at Busch Gardens in 2005 and the awe-inspiring **Expedition Everest** at Animal Kingdom in 2006.

The spring and summer of 2009 witnessed the unveiling of two new coasters: **Manta** at SeaWorld Orlando and **Hollywood Rip Ride Rockit** at Universal Studios. Manta is an inverted flying steel coaster on which riders are suspended under the tracks, prone and facedown, from a carriage shaped like a giant manta ray. After a first drop of 113 feet, the coaster zooms through a pretzel loop, a 360-degree inline roll, and two corkscrews. Manta reaches a height of 140 feet and speeds of more than 55 miles per hour.

Like Manta, Hollywood Rip Ride Rockit at Universal Studios is a steel coaster, only here you sit as opposed to being suspended. The first hill is a 16-second *vertical* climb, followed by a 65-mph plunge. Technologically advanced, the coaster boasts three maneuvers that have never been seen before. Like the Rock 'n' Roller Coaster at Disney's Hollywood Studios, the coaster features a musical soundtrack; however, guests get to choose the genre of music they want to hear as they ride: classic rock, country, disco, pop, or rap.

Today there are 13 big-time roller coasters in central Florida, 15 if you want to include the measurably tamer Space Mountain and Big Thunder Mountain rides. The Incredible Hulk, Rock 'n' Roller Coaster, and Revenge of the Mummy feature accelerated launch systems in which the train is hurled as opposed to ratcheted up the first hill; Rock 'n' Roller Coaster and Revenge of the Mummy are indoor coasters augmented by mind-blowing visuals, special effects, and soundtracks. Expedition Everest is the most fully realized attraction of the 13, with a story line, astounding attention to detail, and a track that plunges in and out of the largest (albeit man-made) mountain in Florida. Expedition Everest shares with Revenge of the Mummy the distinction of constantly surprising you and catching you off-guard. Kraken and Expedition Everest are the longest of the lot, their tracks exceeding 4,000 feet in length. **Montu** at Busch Gardens, along with Dueling Dragons: Fire and Ice at Universal, are inverted coasters, meaning that the track is overhead and your feet dangle.

Having ridden all the coasters until we could no longer walk straight, we rank them as follows. Note that the new coasters, Manta and Hollywood Rip Ride Rockit, described previously and in Part Fifteen, had just opened at press time. Both will be integrated into the rankings in the next edition of the *Unofficial Guide,* and you can

Central Florida Roller Coasters

COASTER	HOST PARK	CENTRAL FLORIDA RANK	INTERNATIONAL RANK	TYPE
Manta	SeaWorld	N/A	N/A	Steel/Inverted
Hollywood Rip Ride Rockit	Universal Studios	N/A	N/A	Steel/Sit-down
Expedition Everest	Animal Kingdom	1	82	Steel/Sit-down
Dueling Dragons: Fire	Universal IOA	2	19	Steel/Inverted
Montu	Busch Gardens	3	15	Steel/Inverted
Incredible Hulk	Universal IOA	4	32	Steel/Sit-down
Kumba	Busch Gardens	5	18	Steel/Sit-down
Dueling Dragons: Ice	Universal IOA	6	26	Steel/Inverted
Kraken	SeaWorld	7	22	Steel/Sit-down
SheiKra	Busch Gardens	8	11	Steel/Sit-down
Rock 'n' Roller Coaster	DHS	9	112	Steel/Sit-down
Gwazi	Busch Gardens	10	77*	Wood/Sit-down
Revenge of the Mummy	Universal Studios	11	52	Steel/Sit-down
Space Mountain	Magic Kingdom	12	144	Steel/Sit-down
Big Thunder Mountain	Magic Kingdom	13	183	Steel/Sit-down

Wooden roller-coaster poll,* **www.bestrollercoasterpoll.com

assume they will almost certainly rank in the top six. (For a glossary of roller-coaster terminology, see **www.ultimaterollercoaster.com/coasters/glossary.**)

1. EXPEDITION EVEREST, ANIMAL KINGDOM This coaster offers such a complete package, with something to dazzle each of the senses, that it overcomes its lack of loops and inversions. The segment on Expedition Everest where the train corkscrews downward in the dark may be the most unusual in roller-coaster annals. Though you begin the segment in reverse, you soon succumb to an almost disembodied and dreamlike state of drifting in a void, with an exhilarating sense of speed but with no certain sense of direction. "Are we still going backwards?" my companion screamed, totally lost in the whirl of motion. When you can see, there's plenty to look at. The mountain, with its caverns, cliffs, and crags, is a work of art; then there's that pesky yeti who menaces you throughout the ride. And for those of you who hate rough coasters, Expedition Everest is oh-so-smooth. Die-hard coaster junkies, who are often ill-tempered unless they're upside down and shaken like a ketchup bottle, give short shrift to the great ride Expedition Everest provides.

2. DUELING DRAGONS: FIRE, UNIVERSAL'S ISLANDS OF ADVENTURE This ranking was disputed within our research group, with several of us placing Montu at Busch Gardens second. Dueling Dragons has two trains, Fire and Ice, that are launched simultaneously. Their tracks are intertwined, making it seem on several occasions that the two trains will collide (they actually come within one foot of each other!). Though Fire and Ice share the same lift hill, their respective layouts are different,

LENGTH (FEET)	HEIGHT (FEET)	INVERSIONS	SPEED (MPH)	RIDE TIME	RIDE FEEL
3,359	140	4	56	2:35	Very smooth
3,800	167	2	65	2:30	Very smooth
4,424	112	0	50	3:45	Very smooth
3,200	125	5	60	2:25	Very smooth
3,983	150	7	60	3:00	Smooth
3,700	110	7	67	2:15	Smooth
3,978	143	7	60	2:54	Slightly rough
3,200	115	5	55	2:25	Very smooth
4,177	149	7	65	2:02	Smooth
3,188	200	1	70	3:00	Very smooth
3,403	80	3	57	1:22	Very smooth
3,400	90	0	50	2:30	Very rough
2,200	60	0	40	4:00	Very smooth
3,196	90	0	27	2:35	Rough
2,780	45	0	36	3:30	Smooth

and Fire offers the superior ride. The action is unrelenting yet very smooth, with a 115-foot drop, five inversions, and speeds of 60 mph. Because this is an inverted coaster, your feet dangle throughout.

3. MONTU, BUSCH GARDENS Montu is a little longer than Dueling Dragons: Fire and features seven inversions—including loops of 104 and 60 feet and a 0-g roll—on a layout distinguished by its very tight turns. With an initial drop of 128 feet, Montu posts top speeds of 60 mph and pulls 3.8 g's. Also inverted, Montu is intense and exhilarating but less visually interesting than and not as smooth as Fire. Like some of our researchers, the CoasterFanatics.com and Internet Best Roller Coaster (**www.ushsho.com/bestrollercoasterpoll.htm**) polls rank Montu ahead of Dueling Dragons: Fire.

4. THE INCREDIBLE HULK, UNIVERSAL'S ISLANDS OF ADVENTURE Hulk doesn't have any weak points. A tire-propelled launch system takes you from 0 to 40 mph in two seconds up the first hill, hurling you into a twisting dive of 105 feet. From there it's two loops, two flat-spin corkscrews, a cobra roll, and a plunge through a 150-foot-long tunnel to the end. You hit speeds of 67 mph and pull as many as 4 g's. Unequivocally, the Hulk has the best start of any roller coaster in central Florida. The ride, however, is not quite as smooth as Fire's, and it's not inverted like Fire and Montu, which is why we've ranked it fourth instead of second or third.

5. KUMBA, BUSCH GARDENS With a track of almost 4,000 feet, seven inversions, a 135-foot first drop, g-forces of 3.8, a top speed of 60 mph, and a very tight layout, Kumba can hold its own with any coaster.

Features include a 114-foot-tall vertical loop, two rolls, and interlocking corkscrews, among others. We find Kumba a little rough, but sitting toward the back of the train mitigates the problem somewhat.

6. DUELING DRAGONS: ICE, UNIVERSAL'S ISLANDS OF ADVENTURE Ice is Fire's slightly less evil twin, with speeds of 55 mph and a first drop of 95 feet, compared with Fire's 60 mph and 115 feet. So too Ice's design elements are different, though both coasters hit you with five inversions bundled in a mix of rolls, corkscrews, and a loop. Like Fire, Ice is an inverted coaster.

7. KRAKEN, SEAWORLD Based on ancient myth, the Kraken was a ferocious sea monster kept caged by Poseidon, Greek god of the sea. Much of Kraken's track is over water, and there are a number of sweeping dives into subterranean caverns. A very fast coaster, Kraken hits speeds of 65 mph with one drop of 144 feet, and it boasts loops, rolls, and corkscrews for a total of seven inversions. Though not inverted, the cars are open-sided and floorless.

8. SHEIKRA, BUSCH GARDENS While the higher-rated coasters do a lot of things well, SheiKra is pretty much one-dimensional—it drops like a rock straight down (a sheikra is an African hawk known for diving vertically on its prey). That's right: a no-slope, 90-degree free fall. After scaling the 200-foot lift hill, the coaster descends over the lip of the first drop and brakes to a stop. There you're suspended, dangling for a few anxious moments until the train is released. On the way down, you hit speeds of 70 mph—a very high speed for roller coasters—and enjoy the best airtime of any Florida coaster. (Airtime is the sensation of floating when your body is forced up from the seat bottom, creating air between the seat and your body. The phenomenon is most commonly experienced on a drop or while cresting hills.) Following a loop, the drill is repeated on a second, more modest drop. The cars on SheiKra are the widest we've seen, seating eight people across in each of three rows. Accordingly, the track is very wide. This width, among other things, makes for a plodding, uninspiring ride except during the two big drops. More compelling is the view of downtown Tampa from the top of the lift hill.

9. ROCK 'N' ROLLER COASTER, DISNEY'S HOLLYWOOD STUDIOS This wasn't a unanimous ranking either. The Rock 'n' Roller Coaster only reaches a height of 80 feet, lasts only a minute and 22 seconds, and incorporates just a couple of design elements, but that 0-to-57 mph launch in two seconds is totally sweet. Rock 'n' Roller Coaster is a dark ride (that is, it's indoors) and the story is that you're on your way to an Aerosmith concert in Hollywood in a big stretch limousine. Speakers in each car blast a soundtrack of the group's hits synchronized with the myriad visuals that erupt out of the gloom. The ride is smooth. Not the biggest or baddest coaster in the realm, but like Expedition Everest, it'll put a big grin on your face every time.

10. GWAZI, BUSCH GARDENS Holy Toledo! As the only traditional wooden roller coaster in the 13 rides ranked, Gwazi at first looked like a snore, with no inversions, corkscrews, loops, barrel rolls, or any of the other stuff that had been rearranging our innards. *Wrong!* This coaster serves up an unbelievably wild ride that seems literally out of control most of the time. Teeth-rattlingly rough, with much side-to-side lurching, Gwazi reaches a top speed of 50 mph but feels twice that fast. In the best wooden-coaster tradition, riders attempt to hold their arms in the air, but on Gwazi it's impossible. The track is hard to read, and the way the train shifts and banks surprises you constantly. Like Dueling Dragons at Islands of Adventure, Gwazi is a racing coaster (a dual-track roller coaster whose trains leave the station at the same moment and race each other through the circuit) with two trains, Lion/Yellow and Tiger/Blue. Of the two, Tiger/Blue gives you the biggest bang for your buck.

11. REVENGE OF THE MUMMY, UNIVERSAL STUDIOS If we were ranking attractions as opposed to roller coasters, this one would rank much higher. Revenge of the Mummy is a super-headliner hybrid and, in Disney parlance, a full-blown "adventure experience," of which its coaster dimension is only one aspect. A complete description of the attraction can be found on page 684; for the moment, however, we can tell you that Revenge of the Mummy is a dark ride full of tricks and surprises, and in roller-coaster mode only for about a third of the ride. The ride is wild enough, but the visuals and special effects are among the best you'll find.

12. SPACE MOUNTAIN, MAGIC KINGDOM When you strip away the theme of this beloved Disney favorite (renovated in 2009), you're left with a souped-up version of the Wild Mouse, a midway staple with sharp turns and small, steep drops that runs with two- or four-passenger cars instead of trains. But when you put a Wild Mouse in the dark—where you can't anticipate the turns and drops—it's like feeding the mouse steroid-laced cheese. With Space Mountain, Disney turned a dinky coaster with no inversions and a top speed of 27 mph into a fairly robust attraction that set the standard for Disney thrill rides until the debut of *The Twilight Zone* Tower of Terror. Space Mountain may bring up the rear of our ranking, but in the hearts of many theme-park guests, it remains number one.

13. BIG THUNDER MOUNTAIN RAILROAD, MAGIC KINGDOM With its runaway-mine-train story line, Big Thunder is long on great visuals but ranks as a very innocuous roller coaster. Though many riders consider it jerky and rough, it's a Rolls-Royce compared with the likes of Gwazi and Kumba at Busch Gardens. Unlike on Gwazi, it's not only possible but easy to ride with your arms in the air. Though a steel coaster, Big Thunder offers no inversions and a top speed of only 36 mph. Then again, the higher-ranked coasters don't offer falling boulders, flash floods, possums, buzzards, and dinosaur bones.

"UNHERALDED TREASURES" TOURING

UNHERALDED TREASURES ARE special features found in all of the Disney theme parks and add texture, context, beauty, depth, and subtlety to your visit. Generally speaking, Unheralded Treasures are nice surprises that should be accorded a little time. They are the proverbial Disney roses you should stop and smell. Mike Scopa, *Unofficial Guide* friend and writer for **AllEars.net,** knows them all. His list follows.

THE MAGIC KINGDOM

TREASURE Roy Disney Statue
LOCATION Magic Kingdom Town Square

In the center of the town square near the flagpole is a statue of Roy Disney sitting on a bench. Few guests are aware of this tribute to Walt Disney's brother, whose contribution to the success of the Disney Company rivaled Walt's. Roy was somewhat unheralded, as is his statue. Take an opportunity to sit next to Roy and have your picture taken with the lesser-known Disney.

TREASURE Animated Mural **LOCATION** Disneyana Building

When you enter the Magic Kingdom from underneath the train station, to your right is the building where Tony's Town Square Restaurant resides. The far right side of that building used to be home to an attraction known as *The Walt Disney Story,* which featured a film on Walt Disney's life and showed how Walt and Mickey first got started, as well as Walt's work in television and his eventual leap into the world of theme-park entertainment.

Although the attraction has been moved, something essential has remained. Prior to the showing of the movie, guests were treated to a brief introduction by the attraction's cast-member host. The cast member delivered this introduction in front of a wall upon which were drawn all the major animated characters from Walt Disney animation. New characters were added to the mural as they emerged. That mural is still there. To see the mural, walk down the hallway lined with vintage WDW photos. At the end of the hallway, turn to your left to view this masterpiece.

EPCOT

TREASURE Leapfrog Fountains **LOCATION** Future World

To the left of *Honey, I Shrunk the Audience* are Future World's Leapfrog Fountains. They offer guests a unique look at how water can appear to "leap" from fountain to fountain. On a warm day, you can sit and enjoy the amused guests, especially children, reveling at the unusual fountains and catching a welcome shower. Plus, they're a joy to watch.

TREASURE Miniature Train **LOCATION** World Showcase, Germany

Many guests may not realize that between Germany and Italy is an area that contains a miniature train display (often called the railway garden), complete with trains, buildings, and miniature people. The detail of this display, including the landscaping, is a wonder to behold. Look for the full-scale train light that draws guests' attention to the display at night.

TREASURE Japan Pavilion Garden **LOCATION** World Showcase, Japan

Epcot's World Showcase has many gardens to explore. However, the garden at the Japan Pavilion is extra-special because almost all its plants and flowers are native to that country. Great care was taken to accurately represent Japanese horticulture. Of all the World Showcase gardens, this one is by far the best-kept secret.

ANIMAL KINGDOM

TREASURE Discovery Island Trails **LOCATION** Base of the Tree of Life

If you walk around the base of the Tree of Life, you'll find many extraordinary animal figures carved into this structure. Look for the owl, the scorpion, the gorilla, and especially the six-foot rabbit.

TREASURE DeVine **LOCATION** Asia

If you're lucky when walking through Asia, you may see DeVine, a cast member whom you'd swear is a walking vine. DeVine is often found up against a building and moves ever so slightly, if at all. The talent of this cast member brings smiles to guests, especially children. How do you know it's not a regular plant? Look for her eyes.

TREASURE Talking Palm Tree **LOCATION** Turnstile Area

Just before you approach Animal Kingdom turnstile area, you may notice a very mobile palm tree conversing with guests, especially children. This treasure introduces young guests to the environment they are about to enter. The fascination on the faces of the children as this tree talks to them is priceless. The adults can have fun trying to figure out how the tree works.

DISNEY'S HOLLYWOOD STUDIOS

TREASURE *Indiana Jones* Set
LOCATION Next to the Indiana Jones Outpost

As you walk past the 50's Prime Time Cafe and the Indiana Jones Outpost, you will see, tucked away in a corner, a display of props used in the movie *Indiana Jones and the Last Crusade.* You'll recognize the vehicles (especially that famous tank). Unless you happen to attend the *Indiana Jones Epic Stunt Spectacular* and exit to the left, you might never know this exhibit is here.

TREASURE Cement Footprints

LOCATION The Great Movie Ride Plaza

The plaza in front of The Great Movie Ride contains cement blocks that have hand- and shoe-prints of famous celebrities. Not every block "made" by celebrities is displayed; they are often rotated, with special consideration given to celebrities currently getting a lot of press. Prints made by celebrities who have passed away also get special attention.

TREASURE Academy of Television Arts and Sciences Hall of Fame Busts

LOCATION Between ABC Theater and *Sounds Dangerous*

This relatively small alcove contains marble busts of some of the most influential people in television history. The attraction is not listed on the official guide map, making it easy to miss. It offers guests a place to sit and reflect on some of the greatest TV entertainers of all time.

PART THREE

ACCOMMODATIONS

The BASIC CONSIDERATIONS

LOCATING A SUITABLE HOTEL OR CONDO is critical to planning any Walt Disney World vacation. The basic question is whether to stay inside the World. Luxury lodging can be found both in and out of Disney World. Budget lodging is another story. In the World, hotel-room rates range from about $82 to more than $900 per night during high season. Outside, rooms are as low as $35 a night.

Beyond affordability is convenience. We've lodged both in and out of Disney World, and there's special magic and peace of mind associated with staying inside the World. "I feel more a part of everything and less like a visitor," one guest writes.

There's no real hardship in staying outside Disney World and driving or taking a hotel shuttle to the theme parks. Meals can be less expensive, and rooming outside the World makes you more receptive to other Orlando-area attractions and eating spots. **Universal Studios** and Universal's **Islands of Adventure, Kennedy Space Center Visitor Complex, SeaWorld,** and **Gatorland** are well worth your attention.

Because Disney World is so large, some off-property hotels are closer in time and distance to many of the theme parks than are some Disney resorts. Check our chart on pages 406 and 407, which lists commuting times from both Disney and non-Disney hotels. Lodging prices are subject to change, but our researchers lodged in an excellent (though not plush) motel surrounded by beautiful orange groves for half the cost of staying in the least expensive Disney hotel. Our one-way commute to the Magic Kingdom or Epcot parking lots was 17 minutes.

If you have young children, read Part Six, Walt Disney World with Kids, before choosing lodging. Similarly, seniors, couples on a honeymoon or romantic holiday, and disabled guests should read the applicable sections of Part Seven, Special Tips for Special People, before booking.

unofficial **TIP**
Request a renovated room at your hotel—these can be much nicer than the older rooms.

THE TAX MAN COMETH

SALES AND LODGING TAXES can add a chunk of change to the cost of your hotel room.

Cumulative tax in Orange County is 12.5% and in adjacent Osceola County, 13%. Lake Buena Vista, the Universal Studios area, International Drive, and all the Disney resorts except the All-Star Resorts are in Orange County.

ABOUT HOTEL RENOVATIONS

WE INSPECT SEVERAL HUNDRED HOTELS in the Disney World area to compile the *Unofficial Guide*'s list of lodging choices. Each year we call each hotel to verify contact information and inquire about renovations or refurbishments. If a hotel has been renovated or has refurbished its guest rooms, we reinspect it, along with any new hotels, for the next edition of the *Guide*. Hotels reporting no improvements are rechecked every two years.

Most hotels more than five years old, both in and out of the World, refurbish 10% to 20% of their guest rooms each year. This incremental approach minimizes disruption but makes your room assignment a crap shoot.

You might luck into a newly renovated room or be assigned a threadbare one. Disney resorts won't guarantee specific rooms but will note your request for a recently refurbished room and will try to accommodate you. Non-Disney hotels will often guarantee an updated room when you book.

BENEFITS OF STAYING IN THE WORLD

DISNEY RESORT HOTEL AND CAMPGROUND GUESTS have privileges and amenities unavailable to those staying outside the World. Though some of these perks are advertising gimmicks, others are real and potentially valuable.

Here are the benefits and what they mean:

1. CONVENIENCE If you don't have a car, commuting to the parks is easy via the Disney Transportation System. This is especially advantageous if you stay in a hotel connected by monorail or boat service. If you have a car, however, dozens of hotels outside Disney World are within five to ten minutes of theme-park parking lots.

2. EXTRA MAGIC HOURS AT THE THEME PARKS Disney World lodging guests (excluding guests at the independent hotels of the Downtown Disney Resort Area, except the Hilton) are invited to enter a designated park one hour earlier than the general public each day or to enjoy a designated theme park for up to three hours after it closes to the general public in the evening. Disney guests are also offered specials on admission, including discount tickets to the water parks. These benefits are subject to change without notice.

unofficial **TIP**
Power shoppers, rejoice: If you're staying on Disney property, you can charge theme-park and Downtown Disney purchases to your hotel room.

Early entry can be quite valuable if you know how to use it. It can also land you in gridlock. (See our detailed discussion of early entry, starting on page 40.)

3. BABYSITTING AND CHILD-CARE OPTIONS Disney hotel and campground guests have several options for babysitting, child care, and children's programs. Disney's Polynesian and Grand Floridian hotels, connected by the monorail, as well as several other Disney hotels, offer "clubs," themed child-care centers where potty-trained children ages 3 to 12 can stay while the adults go out.

Though somewhat expensive, the clubs are highly regarded by children and parents. On the negative side, they're open only in the evening, and not all Disney hotels have them. If you're staying at a Disney hotel without a club, you're better off using a private in-room babysitting service (see page 358). In-room babysitting is also available at hotels outside Disney World.

4. DISNEY'S MAGICAL EXPRESS SERVICE If you arrive in Orlando by commercial airliner, Disney will collect your checked baggage and send it via bus directly to your Walt Disney World resort, allowing you to bypass baggage claim. There's also a bus waiting to transport you to your hotel. This complimentary service still has kinks to work out, and your bus may stop at other Disney resorts before you're deposited at your hotel, but you can't beat the price.

When it's time to go home, you can check your baggage and receive your boarding pass at the front desk of your Disney resort. This service is available to all Disney-resort guests, even those who don't use the Magical Express service (folks who have rental cars, for example). Resort check-in counters are open from 5 a.m. until 1 p.m., and you must check in no later than three hours before your flight. Participating airlines are **AirTran, Alaska, American, Continental, Delta, JetBlue, Northwest, United,** and **US Airways.** At press time, **Southwest Airlines** had begun participating on a trial basis but served only guests staying at Pop Century Resort.

5. PRIORITY THEME-PARK ADMISSIONS On days of unusually heavy attendance, Disney may restrict admission into the theme parks for all customers. When deciding whom to admit into the parks, priority is given to guests staying at Disney resorts. In practice, no guest is turned away until a park's parking lot is full. When this happens, that park will be packed to gridlock. Under such conditions, you would exhibit the common sense of an amoeba to exercise your priority-admission privilege.

6. CHILDREN SHARING A ROOM WITH THEIR PARENTS There's no extra charge per night for children younger than 18 sharing a room with their parents. Many hotels outside Disney World also offer this.

7. FREE PARKING Disney-resort guests with cars pay nothing to park in theme-park lots. This saves $12 per day.

8. RECREATIONAL PRIVILEGES Disney guests get preferential treatment for tee times at the golf courses.

unofficial **TIP 3**
Occasionally, cast members reserve the right to turn away even resort guests if a given theme park gets so crowded that safety becomes a concern.

STAYING IN OR OUT OF THE WORLD: WEIGHING THE PROS AND CONS

1. COST If cost is a primary consideration, you'll lodge much less expensively outside Disney World. Our ratings of hotel quality, cost, and commuting times to the theme parks (pages 406 and 407) compare hotels both in and out of the World.

A Canfield, Ohio, woman ponders whether Disney resorts live up to the expense:

> *We chose to stay at a Disney resort this time, and I don't know that the cost was worth it. We spent very little time at the resort. The only plus was the Disney transportation—they would drop you off just steps from the entrance* [of the theme parks]. *In contrast, when we've stayed off-grounds, transportation to and from the parks was random, and you were dropped off in the middle of the parking lots.*

2. EASE OF ACCESS Even if you stay in Disney World, you're dependent on some mode of transportation. It may be less stressful to use the Disney transportation system, but with the single exception of commuting to the Magic Kingdom, the fastest, most efficient, and most flexible way to get around is usually a car. If you're at Epcot, for example, and want to take the kids back to Disney's Contemporary Resort for a nap, forget the monorail. You'll get back much faster by car.

A reader from Raynham, Massachusetts, who stayed at the Caribbean Beach Resort writes:

> *Even though the resort is on the Disney bus line, I recommend renting a car if it fits one's budget. The buses do not go directly to many destinations, and often you have to switch* [buses]. *Getting a* [bus] *seat in the morning is no problem* [because] *they allow standing. Getting a bus back to the hotel after a hard day can mean a long wait in line.*

Since the economy took a nosedive in the first quarter of 2009, we've noticed a marked increase in reader complaints about problems with the Disney Transportation System. These comments from a College Station, Texas, reader put the point plainly:

> *I remember from staying on-property in years past that each hotel had its own shuttle bus to each park. However, during our* [most recent] *stay we stopped at multiple hotels many times between our hotel and the parks, making staying on-property for the transportation a moot point. We also encountered 40-minute waits for buses and boats that docked at our hotel* [Wilderness Lodge], *and they were so crowded no one could get on (and this in the off-season). We stayed off-site the previous two visits and would most likely go back to that plan, since Disney transportation no longer seems to be an advantage.*

Although it's only for the use and benefit of Disney guests, the Disney Transportation System is nonetheless public, and users must expect inconveniences: conveyances that arrive and depart on their schedule, not yours; the occasional need to transfer; multiple stops; time lost loading and unloading passengers; and, generally, the challenge of understanding and using a large, complex transportation network.

If you plan to have a car, consider this: Disney World is so large that some destinations within the World can be reached more quickly from off-property hotels than from Disney hotels. For example, guests at lodgings on US 192 (near the so-called Walt Disney World main entrance) are closer to Disney's Hollywood Studios, Animal Kingdom, and Blizzard Beach water park than guests at many hotels inside Disney World.

A Kentucky dad overruled his family about staying at a Disney resort and is glad he did:

> *My wife read in another guidebook that it can take two hours to commute to the parks if you stay outside Walt Disney World. What nonsense! I guess it could take two hours if you stayed in Tampa, but from our hotel on [US] 192 we could commute to any of the parks except the Magic Kingdom and have at least one ride under our belt in about an hour. We found out later that the writer of the other guidebook is a writer for* Disney Magazine.

For commuting times from specific non-Disney hotels, see our Hotel Information Chart on pages 268–285.

3. YOUNG CHILDREN Although the hassle of commuting to most non-World hotels is only slightly (if at all) greater than that of commuting to Disney hotels, a definite peace of mind results from staying in the World. Regardless of where you stay, make sure you get your young children back to the hotel for a nap each day.

4. SPLITTING UP If you're in a party that will probably split up to tour (as frequently happens in families with teens or children of widely varying ages), staying in the World offers more transportation options and, thus, more independence. Mom and Dad can take the car and return to the hotel for a relaxed dinner and early bedtime while the teens remain in the park for evening parades and fireworks.

5. FEEDING THE ARMY OF THE POTOMAC If you have a large crew that chows down like cattle on a finishing lot, you may do better staying outside the World, where food is far less expensive.

6. VISITING OTHER ORLANDO-AREA ATTRACTIONS If you will be visiting SeaWorld, Kennedy Space Center Visitor Complex, Universal Orlando, or other area attractions, it may be more convenient to stay outside the World.

The DISNEY RESORTS

DISNEY RESORTS 101

BEFORE YOU MAKE ANY DECISIONS, understand these basics regarding Disney resorts.

1. RESORT CLASSIFICATIONS Disney loves to categorize, so it's not surprising that they've developed a hierarchy of resort classifications. **Deluxe resorts** are Disney's top-of-the-line hotels. **Disney Deluxe Villa (DDV) resorts** (also known as Disney Vacation Club resorts) offer suites, some with full kitchens. These resorts equal or surpass Deluxe resorts in quality; several are attached to Deluxe resorts. (Be aware that all Disney resorts except DDV resorts levy a nightly surcharge for every additional adult in a room beyond the standard two.) **Moderate resorts** are a step down in guest-room quality, amenities, and cost. Anchoring the bottom of the list are **Value resorts,** with the smallest rooms, most limited amenities, and lowest rates of any Disney-owned hotels. Finally, there's the **Fort Wilderness Resort & Campground,** which offers both campsites and fully equipped cabins.

2. MAKING RESERVATIONS Whether you book through Disney, a travel agent, online, with a tour operator, or through an organization like AAA, you will frequently save by booking the room exclusive of any vacation package. This is called a *room-only reservation*. Though later in this chapter we'll scrutinize the advantages and disadvantages of buying a package, we'll tell you now that Disney World packages at list price rarely save you money (though sometimes they're worthwhile for the convenience and peace of mind). It should be mentioned, however, that in response to the recession, Disney has done a lot more package discounting than room-only discounting, and that some of the package discounts have been very deep.

unofficial **TIP**
Understand that Disney Reservations Center and Walt Disney Travel Company representatives don't have detailed personal knowledge of resorts.

In dealing with Disney for rooms only, call the Disney Reservations Center (DRC) at ☎ 407-W-DISNEY. Because of some administrative and operational consolidation, reservationists at the DRC are now trained to sell only Walt Disney Travel Company packages. Even if you insist that you want only a room, they'll try to bundle it with some small extra, like a miniature-golf pass, so that your purchase can be counted as a "basic" package. This seems innocuous enough, and you might even appreciate the mini-golf passes, but classifying your reservation as a package allows Disney to apply numerous restrictions and cancellation policies that you won't be saddled with if you buy a room only. In regard to cancellation policies, however, be aware that there are trade-offs. If you book a package and cancel within two weeks of arrival, you lose your $200 deposit. If you book only a room and cancel within five days of arrival, you lose your deposit of one night's room charge, which can easily be more than $200 if you stay at a Deluxe resort or DDV resort. Also, Disney dining plans cannot be booked with a room-only reservation.

When you call, tell the agent what you want in terms of lodging and obtain a room-only rate quote. Then tell the agent what you're looking for in terms of admissions. When you've pinned down your room and lodging costs, ask the agent if he or she can offer any packages that beat the à la carte prices. But don't be swayed by little sweeteners included in a package unless they have real value for you. If the first agent you speak to isn't accommodating, hang up and call back. There are a couple hundred agents, some more helpful than others.

If you need specific information, call the resort directly, ask for the front desk, and pose your question before phoning the DRC. If your desired dates aren't available, keep calling back or check online at **www.disneyworld.com.** Something might open up.

3. A MOST CONFUSING VIEW Rates at Disney hotels vary from season to season (see the next section) and from room to room according to view. Further, each Disney resort has its own seasonal calendar. Seasons such

unofficial **TIP**
Avoid calling the DRC between 11 a.m. and 3 p.m.—this is their busiest time of day.

as "regular," "value," "peak," and "holiday" vary depending on the resort instead of that tired old January-to-December calendar the rest of us use. But confusing as Disney seasons are, they're logic personified compared to the panoply of guest-room views the resorts offer. Depending on the resort, you can choose standard views, water views, pool views, lagoon views, garden views, or savanna views, among others. "Standard view," the most ambiguous category, crops up at about three-fourths of Disney resorts. It's usually interpreted as a view that doesn't fit any other view classification the hotel offers. At Animal Kingdom Lodge, for example, you have savanna views, water views, and standard views. Savanna views overlook the replicated African savanna, water views overlook the swimming pool, and standard views offer stunning vistas of other stuff . . . whatever it might be.

With a standard view, however, you can at least pinpoint what you *won't* be seeing. Every resort defines water views differently. According to a manager at the Grand Floridian Resort & Spa, for example, a water view is a direct, unobstructed frontal view of Seven Seas Lagoon. Views of swimming pools or sideways views of the lagoon don't count. If the Grand Floridian sells you a water-view room, by George, you're going to see some water.

Zip over to the Yacht Club Resort, another Deluxe property, and the definition of "water view" is completely different. Like the Grand Floridian, the Yacht Club is on a lake, but booking a water-view room doesn't guarantee you'll see the lake. At the Yacht Club, anything wet counts, whether it's in front of you or so far to the side you have to crane your neck. If somehow you can glimpse the lake, a creek, or a swimming pool, you have a water view.

unofficial **TIP**
If you book a king room at a Moderate resort, you can request a water-view room at no extra charge (this isn't guaranteed, though).

Our favorite water views are at the Contemporary Resort's Garden Building, which extends out toward Bay Lake to the south of the giant A-frame. Rooms in this three-story structure afford some of the best lake vistas in Walt Disney World. Many rooms are so near the water, in fact, you could spit a prune seed into the lake from your window. And their category? Garden views.

We could go on and on, but pinning Disney down on precisely what will be outside your window is the point. In our discussion of individual resorts later in this chapter, we'll tell you which rooms have the good views.

4. HOW TO GET THE ROOM YOU WANT Disney will not guarantee a specific room when you book but will post your request on your reservation record. Our experience indicates that making a request by room number confuses the Disney reservationists; as a result, they're unsure where to place you if the room you've asked for is unavailable. To increase your odds of getting the room you want, tell the reservationist exactly what characteristics and amenities you desire—for example: "I'd like a room with a balcony on the second or third floor of the

Contemporary Resort's Garden Building with an unobstructed view of the lake." (It is no longer necessary to ask for a nonsmoking room at a Disney resort, as all rooms were designated smoke-free in 2007.)

Be direct and politely assertive when speaking to the Disney agent. Port Orleans Resort, for example, offers either standard or water-view rooms . . . but "water view" could mean a view of the river or a swimming pool. If you want to overlook the river, say so; likewise, if you want a pool view, speak up. Similarly, state clearly such preferences as a particular floor, a corner room, a room near restaurants, a room away from elevators and ice machines, or a room with a certain type of balcony. If you have a laundry list of preferences, type it in order of importance, and e-mail, fax, or mail it to the DRC. Include your contact information and reservation confirmation number.

unofficial **TIP**
Disney will guarantee connecting rooms if your party includes more children than adults.

It will be the resort that actually assigns your room. Call back in a few days to make sure your preferences were posted to your record.

We'll provide info needed for each resort to frame your requests, including a resort layout map and our recommendations for specific rooms or buildings. We'll use "to" to indicate a range of rooms. Thus, "rooms 2230 to 2260" refers to the 31 rooms within that range. Sometimes we'll specify even- or odd-numbered rooms within a range, for example, "odd-numbered rooms 631 to 639." In this case we're referring to rooms 631, 633, 635, 637, and 639, eliminating intervening even-numbered rooms. For brevity, we may refer to "rooms 1511, -22, -31, and -40." In this instance, "15" is a numerical prefix that applies to all the rooms listed. The actual room numbers are 1511, 1522, 1531, and 1540.

HOW TO GET DISCOUNTS ON LODGING

THERE ARE SO MANY GUEST ROOMS in and around Disney World that competition is brisk, and everyone, including Disney, wheels and deals to fill them. This has led to a more flexible discount policy for Disney hotels. Here are tips for getting price breaks:

1. SEASONAL SAVINGS Save from $15 to $50 per night on a Disney hotel room by visiting during the slower times of year. However, Disney uses so many adjectives (regular, holiday, peak, value, and the like) to describe its seasonal calendar that it's hard to keep up. Plus, the dates for each "season" vary among resorts. If you're set on staying at a Disney resort, order a copy of the Walt Disney Travel Company Florida Vacations video/DVD brochure, described on page 24.

Disney seasonal dates aren't sequential like spring, summer, fall, and winter. That would be way too simple. For any specific resort, there are often two or more seasonal changes in a month. To add to this complexity, Disney also varies the price of its hotel rooms with the day of the week, charging more for the same room on Friday and Saturday nights. The increased rates typically apply only during busier times of the year, such as holidays, and range from $10 to $20 per room per night.

unofficial **TIP**
Three to four days before you arrive, call the resort front desk. Call late in the evening when they're not so busy, and reconfirm the requests that by now should be appearing in their computers.

2. ASK ABOUT SPECIALS When you talk to Disney reservationists, ask specifically about specials. For example, "What special rates or discounts are available at Disney hotels during the time of our visit?" Being specific and assertive paid off for a Warren, New Jersey, dad:

> *Your tip on asking Disney employees about discounts was invaluable. They will not volunteer this information, but by asking we saved almost $500 on our hotel room using a AAA discount.*

Another New Jersey reader takes a high-calorie approach:

> *My husband and I begin planning each WDW vacation the same way: call the famous 407-W-DISNEY number and speak to someone with a ridiculous name (this time it was Flower and Buffy). I present my vacation plan to the operator, which* [consists of] *my specific date, WDW resort, and ticket choice. She quotes me a price; I thank her for her help and hang up. I call again and present my EXACT same plan to a new operator, who quotes me a totally DIFFERENT price! I repeat the phone process again and obtain ANOTHER price for the same plan. After three years, my husband and I feel like we're playing "Spin the Wheel to Get a Price for the WDW Vacation." Now, instead of getting disgusted, we make it a night of calling with coffee and dessert. Whichever quoted price is the lowest of the night, we book it. Why can't Disney just make it ONE SET PRICE?*

3. "TRADE-UP" OR "UPSELL" RATES If you request a room at a Disney Value resort and none is available, you may be offered a discounted room in the next category up (Moderate resorts, in this example). Similarly, if you ask for a room in a Moderate resort and none is available, Disney will usually offer a deal for Home-Away-from-Home rooms or a Deluxe resort. You can angle for a trade-up rate by asking for a resort category that's more likely to be sold out.

4. KNOW THE SECRET CODE The folks at **MouseSavers.com** maintain an updated list of discounts and reservation codes for Disney resorts. The codes are separated into categories such as "for anyone," "for residents of certain states," and "for Annual Pass holders." For example, the site once listed code CVZ, published in an ad in some Spanish-language newspapers and magazines, offering a rate of $65 per night for Disney's All-Star Resorts from April 22 to August 8. Anyone calling the Disney Reservations Center at ☎ 407-W-DISNEY can use a current code and get the discounted rate.

Be aware that Disney targets people with PIN codes in e-mails and direct mailings. PIN-code discounts are offered to specific individuals and are correlated with a given person's name and address. When you try to make a reservation using the PIN, Disney will verify that the street or e-mail address to which the code was sent is yours.

MouseSavers.com has a great historical list of when discounts were released and what they encompassed at **www.mousesavers.com/historicalwdwdiscounts.html.** There's no guarantee that Disney will repeat discounts from previous years, but the list is a great guideline when planning your vacation.

To get your name in the Disney system, call the Disney Reservation Center at ☎ 407-824-8000 and request that written info or the free trip-planning DVD/video be sent to you. If you've been to Walt Disney World previously, your name and address will of course already be on record, but you won't be as likely to receive a PIN-code offer as you would by calling and requesting to be sent information. On the Web, go to the official site, **www.waltdisneyworld.com** and sign up to automatically be sent offers and news at your e-mail address. You might also consider getting a **Disney Rewards Visa card,** which entitles you to around two days' advance notice when a discount is released (visit **disney.go.com/visa** for details).

unofficial **TIP**
To enhance your chances of receiving a PIN-code offer, you need to get your name and street or e-mail address into the Disney system.

Two other sites, **www.allears.net** and **www.wdwinfo.com,** have discount codes we've used to get up to 50% off rack rates at the Swan and Dolphin.

5. INTERNET SELLERS Online travel sellers Expedia (**www.expedia.com**), Travelocity (**www.travelocity.com**), and One Travel (**www.onetravel.com**) discount Disney hotels. Most breaks are in the 7%-to-25% range, but they can go as deep as 40%. See our expanded discussion of hotel shopping on the Internet, starting on page 235.

6. WALT DISNEY WORLD WEB SITE Particularly with the recession upon us, Disney has become more aggressive about offering deals on its Web site. Go to **www.disneyworld.com** and and look for "Magical Holidays Packages and Offers" to the right of the "Quote Your Trip" box. Click on whatever special is listed, even if you aren't interested. This will bring up a new screen. About halfway down you'll find "See all of our great special offers." Click here and all available specials will come up. You can also click on "Special Offers" in the bar just below the banner at the top of the page. You must click on the specific special to get the discounts: if you click on "Reservations and Tickets," you'll be charged the full rack rate with no mention of available discounts. You must cancel reservations for rooms sold at a discount 46 days before arrival if you want a full refund. Reservations booked through "Reservations and Tickets" may be canceled six days before arrival. Before booking rooms on Disney's or any Web site, click on "Terms and Conditions" and read the fine print.

7. ANNUAL PASS–HOLDER DISCOUNTS Annual Pass holders are eligible for discounts on dining, shopping, parking, and lodging. With the help of **MouseSavers.com,** we analyzed every Annual Pass resort discount available at every resort, every day, from 2005 through mid-2009. Recent average discounts were $18 per night for Value resorts, $34 for moderates, and $98 for Deluxe resorts, including tax. At those rates, a stay of only three nights at a Deluxe resort would save you $32 more than the same stay without the discount, even after accounting for the higher cost of the Annual Pass versus a base three-day Magic Your Way ticket. If you're staying at a Moderate resort, you're likely better off with an Annual Pass if you're staying at least 8 nights, and at least 13 nights at a Value resort.

Those break-evens are for the average discount, but in a worst-case scenario, the minimum discount adds about two nights to the number of nights you'd need to stay for the Annual Pass to save you money.

The number of discounted rooms available to pass holders is limited, and the rooms often are offered only on short notice. Discounts are generally not available from the third week of December through New Year's Day, and occasionally not during other peak seasons.

8. RENTING DISNEY VACATION CLUB POINTS The Disney Vacation Club (DVC) is Disney's time-share-condominium program. DVC resorts (aka Disney Deluxe Villa resorts) at Walt Disney World include Bay Lake Tower at the Contemporary Resort, Old Key West, Saratoga Springs Resort & Spa, Treehouse Villas at Saratoga Springs, the Beach Club Villas, the Villas at Wilderness Lodge, Animal Kingdom Villas, and the BoardWalk Villas. Each resort offers studios and one- and two-bedroom villas (some resorts also offer three-bedroom villas). All accommodations are roomy and luxurious. The studios are equipped with wet bars and fridges, and the villas come with full kitchens. Most accommodations have patios or balconies.

DVC members receive a number of "points" annually that they use to pay for their Disney accommodations. Sometimes members elect to "rent" (sell) their points instead of using them in a given year. Though Disney is not involved in the transaction, it allows DVC members to make these points available to the general public. The going rental rate is usually in the range of $10 per point. A studio for a week at the BoardWalk Villas would run you $2,303 plus tax for regular season if you booked through the Disney Reservation Center. The same studio costs the DVC member 123 points for a week. If you rented his points at $10 per point, the BoardWalk Villas Studio would cost you $1,230, that is, more than $1,000 less.

When you rent points, you deal with the selling DVC member and pay him or her directly. The DVC member makes a reservation in your name and pays Disney the requisite number of points. Arrangements vary widely, but some trust is required from both parties. Usually your reservation is documented by a confirmation sent from Disney to the owner, and then passed along to you. Though the deal you cut is strictly up to you and the owner, you should always insist on receiving the aforementioned confirmation before making more than a one-night deposit.

Disboards, **www.disboards.com,** the popular Disney discussion boards site, has a specific board that deals with DVC rentals, and the unofficial discount Web site **MouseSavers.com** has a page with tips on renting DVC points: see **www.mousesavers.com/disneyresorts.html#rentpoints.**

9. TRAVEL AGENTS are active players and particularly good sources of information on limited-time programs and discounts. We believe a good travel agent is the best friend a traveler can have. And though we at the *Unofficial Guide* know a thing or two about the travel industry, we always give our agent a chance to beat any deal we find. If she can't beat it, we let her book it anyway if it's commissionable. We nurture a relationship that gives her plenty of incentive to roll up her sleeves and work on our behalf.

As you might expect, there are travel agents and agencies that specialize, sometimes exclusively, in selling Walt Disney World. These agents have spent an incredible amount of time at the resort, and they have also completed extensive Disney-education programs. They are usually the most Disney-knowledgeable agents in the travel industry. Most of these specialists and their agencies display the "Earmarked" logo stating that they are Authorized Disney Vacation Planners.

These Disney specialists are so good we use them ourselves. The needs of our research team are many, and our schedules are complicated. When we work with an Authorized Disney Vacation Planner, we know we're dealing with someone who knows Disney inside and out, including where to find the deals and how to use all tricks of the trade that keep our research budget under control. Simply stated, they save us time and money, sometimes lots of both.

The best of the best include **Sue Pisaturo,** whom we've used many times and who contributes to this guide (**sue@wdwvacations.com**); **Lynne Amodeo** (**lynnetravel@verizon.net**); **Karen Nunn** (**karen.nunn@gmail.com**); and **Sue Ellen Soto-Rios** (**disneytravelagent@gmail.com**). There are good Disney specialists throughout the country, however, if you prefer to work with someone close to home.

10. ORGANIZATIONS AND AUTO CLUBS Disney has developed time-limited programs with some auto clubs and organizations. Recently, for example, AAA members were offered 10% to 20% savings on Disney hotels, preferred parking at the theme parks, and discounts on Disney package vacations, including packages with dining. Such deals come and go, but the market suggests there will be more. If you're a member of AARP, AAA, or any travel or auto club, ask whether the group has a program before shopping elsewhere.

11. ROOM UPGRADES Sometimes a room upgrade is as good as a discount. If you're visiting Disney World during a slower time, book the least expensive room your discounts will allow. Checking in, ask very politely about being upgraded to a "water view" or "pool view" room. A fair percentage of the time, you'll get one at no additional charge. Understand, however, that a room upgrade should be considered a favor. Hotels are under no obligation to upgrade you, so if your request is not met, accept the decision graciously. Also, note that suites (such as the All-Star Family Suites) are exempt from discount offers.

12. MILITARY DISCOUNTS The Shades of Green Armed Forces Recreation Center, near the Grand Floridian Resort & Spa, offers luxury accommodations at rates based on a service member's rank, as well as attraction tickets to the theme parks. For rates and other information, see **www.shadesofgreen.org** or call ☎ 888-593-2242.

13. YEAR-ROUND DISCOUNTS AT THE SWAN AND DOLPHIN RESORTS Government workers, teachers, nurses, military, and Entertainment Club members can save on their rooms at the Dolphin or the Swan (when space is available, of course). Call ☎ 800-227-1500.

CHOOSING A WALT DISNEY WORLD HOTEL

IF YOU WANT TO STAY IN THE WORLD but don't know which hotel to choose, consider these factors:

1. COST Consider your budget. Hotel rooms start at about $82 a night at the All-Star and Pop Century resorts during Value Season and top out near $1,030 at the Grand Floridian Resort & Spa during Holiday Season. Suites, of course, are more expensive than standard rooms.

BoardWalk Villas, Wilderness Lodge Villas, Old Key West Resort, Animal Kingdom Villas, Saratoga Springs Resort & Spa, and Beach Club Villas offer condo-type accommodations with one-, two-, and (at Saratoga Springs, BoardWalk Villas, and Old Key West) three-bedroom units with kitchens, living rooms, VCRs, and washers and dryers. Prices range from $269 per night for a studio suite at Animal Kingdom Villas to more than $2,000 per night for a three-bedroom villa at BoardWalk Villas. Fully equipped cabins at Fort Wilderness Resort & Campground cost $265 to $410 per night. A limited number of suites are available at the more expensive Disney resorts, but they don't have kitchens.

For any extra adults in a room (more than two), here is the nightly surcharge for each extra adult:

Value resorts, *including suites:* $10 per night plus tax

Moderate resorts: $15 per night plus tax

Deluxe resorts: $25 per night plus tax

Fort Wilderness cabins: $5 per night plus tax

Disney Deluxe Villa resorts: No charge for extra adults

Also at Disney World are the seven hotels of the Downtown Disney Resort Area (DDRA). Accommodations range from fairly luxurious to Holiday Inn quality. Though not typically good candidates for bargains, these hotels surprised us with some great deals during 2008. While the DDRA is technically part of Disney World, staying there is like visiting a colony rather than the motherland. Free parking at theme parks isn't offered—nor is early entry, with one exception, the Hilton—and hotels operate their own buses rather than use Disney transportation. For more information on DDRA properties, see page 203.

WHAT IT COSTS TO STAY IN THE DOWNTOWN DISNEY RESORT AREA	
Best Western Lake Buena Vista Resort Hotel	$104–$250
Buena Vista Palace Hotel & Spa	$179–$1,009
Doubletree Guest Suites	$82–$505
Hilton Walt Disney World	$95–$329
Holiday Inn at Walt Disney World *(closed for renovation at press time)*	N/A
Regal Sun Resort	$77–$399
Royal Plaza	$109–$249

2. LOCATION Once you determine your budget, think about what you want to do at Disney World. Will you go to all four theme parks or concentrate on one or two?

If you will have a car, your Disney hotel's location isn't especially important unless you plan to spend most of your time at the Magic Kingdom. (Disney transportation is always more efficient than your car in this case because it bypasses the Transportation and Ticket Center,

COSTS PER NIGHT OF DISNEY-RESORT HOTEL ROOMS	
All-Star Resorts	$82–$160
All-Star Music Resort Family Suites	$184–$327
Animal Kingdom Lodge	$240–$555
Animal Kingdom Villas (Jambo House and Kidani Village)	$269–$2,215
Bay Lake Tower	$375–$2,430
Beach Club Resort	$335–$770
Beach Club Villas	$335–$1,175
BoardWalk Inn	$335–$825
BoardWalk Villas	$335–$2,215
Caribbean Beach Resort	$149–$274
Contemporary Resort	$280–$835
Coronado Springs Resort	$149–$249
Dolphin (Sheraton)	$229–$519
Fort Wilderness Resort & Campground (cabins)	$265–$410
Grand Floridian Resort & Spa	$399–$1,040
Old Key West Resort	$295–$1,690
Polynesian Resort	$335–$900
Pop Century Resort	$82–$160
Port Orleans Resort	$149–$249
Saratoga Springs Resort & Spa	$295–$1,690
Swan (Westin)	$260–$405
Treehouse Villas	$545–$900
Wilderness Lodge	$240–$770
Wilderness Lodge Villas	$325–$1,155
Yacht Club Resort	$335–$760

the World's transportation hub, and deposits you at the theme-park entrance.) If you haven't decided whether you want a car for your Disney vacation, see "How to Travel around the World" (page 393).

Most convenient to the Magic Kingdom are the three resorts linked by monorail: the Grand Floridian, Contemporary–Bay Lake Tower, and Polynesian. Commuting to the Magic Kingdom via monorail is quick and simple, allowing visitors to return to their hotel for a nap, swim, or meal.

The Contemporary Resort–Bay Lake Tower, in addition to being on the monorail, is only a 10- to 15-minute walk to the Magic Kingdom. Guests reach Epcot by monorail but must transfer at the Transportation and Ticket Center. Buses connect the resort complex to Disney's Hollywood Studios and Animal Kingdom. No transfer is required, but the bus makes several stops before reaching either destination.

The Polynesian Resort is served by the Magic Kingdom monorail and is an easy walk from the transportation center. At the center, you can catch an express monorail to Epcot. This makes the Polynesian the only Disney resort with direct monorail access to both Epcot and the Magic Kingdom. To minimize your walk to the transportation center, request a room in the Rapa Nui, Tahiti, or Tokelau guest buildings.

The Wilderness Lodge Resort and Villas, along with Fort Wilderness Resort & Campground, are linked to the Magic Kingdom by boat, and to everywhere else in the World by somewhat convoluted bus service.

Most convenient to Epcot and Disney's Hollywood Studios are the BoardWalk Inn, BoardWalk Villas, Yacht and Beach Club Resorts, Beach Club Villas, the Swan, and the Dolphin. Though all are within easy walking distance of Epcot's International Gateway, boat service is also available. Vessels also connect Epcot hotels to DHS. Epcot hotels are best for guests planning to spend most of their time at Epcot or DHS.

Centrally located are Caribbean Beach and Disney's Pop Century resorts. Along Bonnet Creek, Old Key West and Port Orleans resorts also offer a central location.

Though they're not centrally located, the All-Star, Coronado Springs, and Animal Kingdom Lodge and Villas resorts have very good bus service to all Disney World destinations and are closest to Animal Kingdom. Wilderness Lodge and Villas and Fort Wilderness Resort & Campground have the most convoluted transportation service.

unofficial **TIP**
If you plan to use Disney transportation to visit all four major parks and one or both of the water parks, book a centrally located resort that has good transportation connections. The Epcot resorts and the Polynesian, Caribbean Beach, Pop Century, and Port Orleans resorts fill the bill. Old Key West Resort is centrally located but offers only limited bus service between noon and 6 p.m.

If you plan to play golf, book Old Key West Resort or the Saratoga Springs Resort & Spa, both built around golf courses. The military-only Shades of Green resort is adjacent to two courses. Near but not on a golf course are the Grand Floridian, Polynesian, and Port Orleans resorts. For boating and water sports, try the Polynesian, Contemporary, or Grand Floridian resorts, the Fort Wilderness Resort & Campground, or the Wilderness Lodge and Villas. The lodge and campground are also great for hikers, bikers, and joggers.

3. ROOM QUALITY Few Disney guests spend much time in their hotel rooms, though these rooms are among the best designed and most well appointed anywhere. Plus, they're meticulously maintained. At the top of the line are the luxurious rooms of the Contemporary, Grand Floridian, and Polynesian resorts; bringing up the rear are the small rooms of the Pop Century Resort. But even these economy rooms are sparkling clean and quite livable.

The chart at right shows how Disney hotels (along with the Swan and Dolphin, which are Westin and Sheraton hotels) stack up for quality.

4. THE SIZE OF YOUR GROUP Larger families and groups may be interested in how many persons a Disney resort room can accommodate, but only Lilliputians would be comfortable in a room filled to capacity. Groups requiring two or more guest rooms should consider condo or villa accommodations in or out of the World. The most cost-efficient

HOTEL	ROOM-QUALITY RATING
1. Bay Lake Tower	93
2. Contemporary Resort	93
3. Grand Floridian Resort & Spa	93
4. Polynesian Resort	92
5. Animal Kingdom Villas	91
6. Shades of Green	91
7. Swan	91
8. Treehouse Villas (studios)	91
9. Beach Club Resort	90
10. Beach Club Villas (studios)	90
11. BoardWalk Villas (studios)	90
12. Saratoga Springs Resort & Spa (studios)	90
13. Wilderness Lodge Villas (studios)	90
14. Old Key West Resort (studios)	90
15. Dolphin	87
17. Animal Kingdom Lodge	89
18. BoardWalk Inn	89
19. Yacht Club Resort	89
20. Fort Wilderness Cabins	86
21. Wilderness Lodge	86
22. Port Orleans French Quarter	84
23. Coronado Springs Resort	83
24. Port Orleans Riverside	83
25. Caribbean Beach Resort	80
26. All-Star Resorts	73
27. Pop Century Resort	71

Disney lodgings for groups of five or six persons are the cabins at Fort Wilderness Resort & Campground. They sleep six adults plus a child or toddler in a crib. If your party includes more than six people, you'll need either two hotel rooms, a suite, or a condo. The Disney room-layout schematics on the following pages show the rooms' relative sizes and configurations, along with the maximum number of persons per room (see pages 125–128).

5. THEME All Disney hotels are themed. Each is designed to make you feel you're in a special place or period of history.

Some resorts carry off their themes better than others, and some themes are more exciting. The Wilderness Lodge and Villas, for example, is extraordinary, reminiscent of a grand national-park lodge from the early 20th century. The lobby opens eight stories to a timbered ceiling supported by giant columns of bundled logs. One look eases you into

HOTEL	THEME
All-Star Resorts	Sports, music, and movies
Animal Kingdom Lodge and Villas	African game preserve
Bay Lake Tower	Upscale, ultramodern urban hotel
Beach Club Resort and Villas	New England beach club of the 1870s
BoardWalk Inn	East Coast boardwalk hotel of the early 1900s
BoardWalk Villas	East Coast beach cottage of the early 1900s
Caribbean Beach Resort	Caribbean islands
Contemporary Resort	Future as perceived by past, present generations
Coronado Springs Resort	Northern Mexico and the American Southwest
Dolphin	Modern Florida resort
Grand Floridian Resort & Spa	Turn-of-the-20th-century luxury hotel
Old Key West Resort	Key West
Polynesian Resort	Hawaii–South Sea islands
Pop Century Resort	Icons from various decades of the 20th century
Port Orleans French Quarter Resort	Turn-of-the-19th-century New Orleans
Port Orleans Riverside Resort	Antebellum Louisiana plantation, bayou
Saratoga Springs Resort & Spa	Upstate New York 1880s Victorian lakeside retreat
Swan	Modern Florida resort
Treehouse Villas	Rustic vacation homes with modern amenities
Wilderness Lodge and Villas	National park grand lodge of the early 1900s in the American Northwest
Yacht Club Resort	New England seashore hotel of the 1880s

the Northwest-wilderness theme. The lodge is a great choice for couples and seniors and is heaven for children.

Animal Kingdom Lodge and Villas replicates grand safari lodges of Kenya and Tanzania and overlooks its own African game preserve. By far the most exotic Disney resort, it's made to order for couples on romantic getaways and for families with children. The Polynesian, likewise dramatic, conveys the feeling of the Pacific Islands. It's great for romantics and families. Many waterfront rooms offer a perfect view of Cinderella Castle and the Magic Kingdom fireworks across Seven Seas Lagoon.

Grandeur, nostalgia, and privilege are central to the Grand Floridian and Yacht and Beach Club Resorts and the BoardWalk Inn and Villas. Although modeled after Eastern seaboard seaside hotels of different eras, the resorts are similar. Saratoga Springs Resort & Spa, supposedly representative of an upstate New York country retreat, looks like what you'd get if you crossed the Beach Club with the Wilderness Lodge. For all the resorts inspired by northeastern resorts, thematic distinctions are subtle and lost on many guests.

The Port Orleans French Quarter Resort lacks the mystery and sultriness of the real New Orleans French Quarter but captures enough of its

Continued on page 128

DELUXE RESORTS ROOM DIAGRAMS

Contemporary Resort

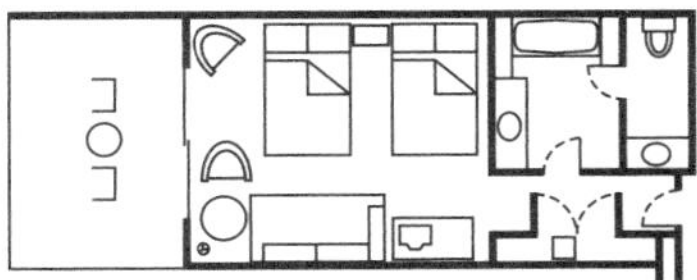

Typical Room, 394 Square Feet
Rooms accommodate 5 guests, plus 1 child under age 3 in a crib.

Polynesian Resort

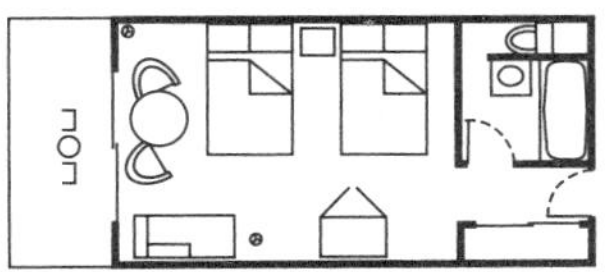

Typical Room, 415 Square Feet
Rooms accommodate 5 guests, plus 1 child under age 3 in a crib.

Grand Floridian Resort & Spa

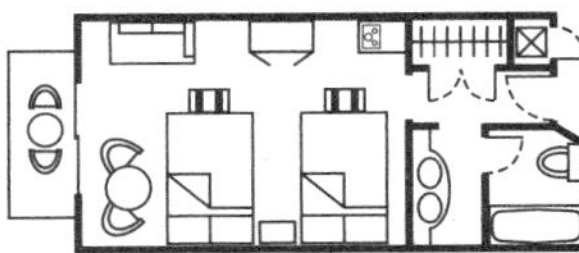

Typical Room, 440 Square Feet
Rooms accommodate 5 guests, plus 1 child under age 3 in a crib.

BoardWalk Inn

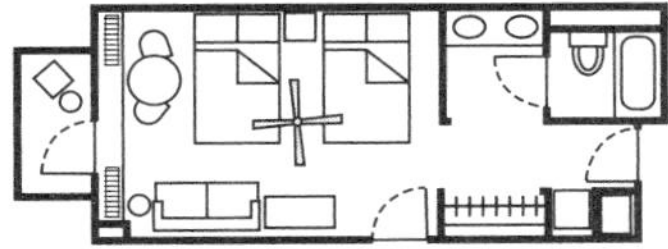

Typical Room, 371 Square Feet
Rooms accommodate 4 guests, plus 1 child under age 3 in a crib.

Beach Club Resort

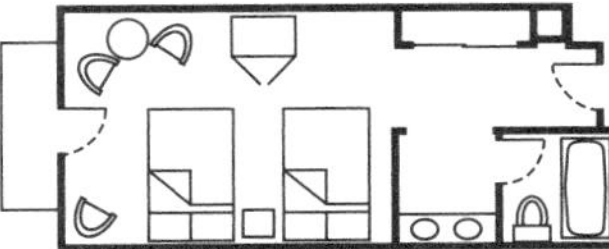

Typical Room, 381 Square Feet
Rooms accommodate 5 guests, plus 1 child under age 3 in a crib.

Yacht Club Resort

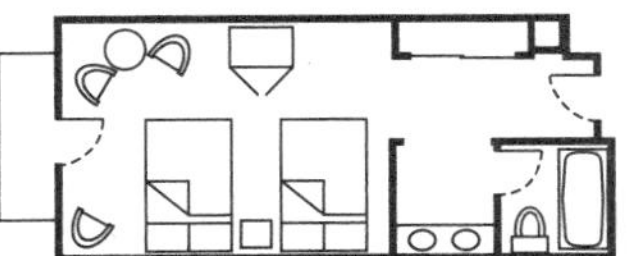

Typical Room, 381 Square Feet
Rooms accommodate 5 guests, plus 1 child under age 3 in a crib.

Wilderness Lodge

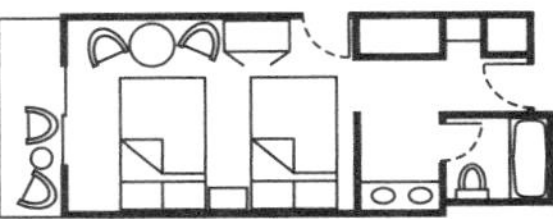

Typical Room, 344 Square Feet
Rooms accommodate 4 guests, plus 1 child under age 3 in a crib.

Animal Kingdom Lodge

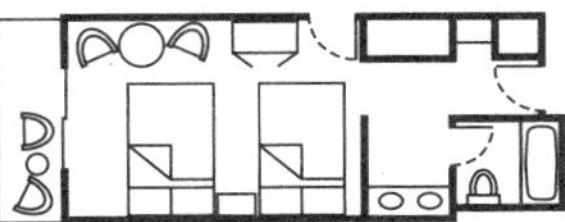

Typical Room, 344 Square Feet
Rooms accommodate 2 to 5 guests, plus 1 child under age 3 in a crib.

DISNEY DELUXE VILLA RESORTS ROOM DIAGRAMS

Old Key West Resort

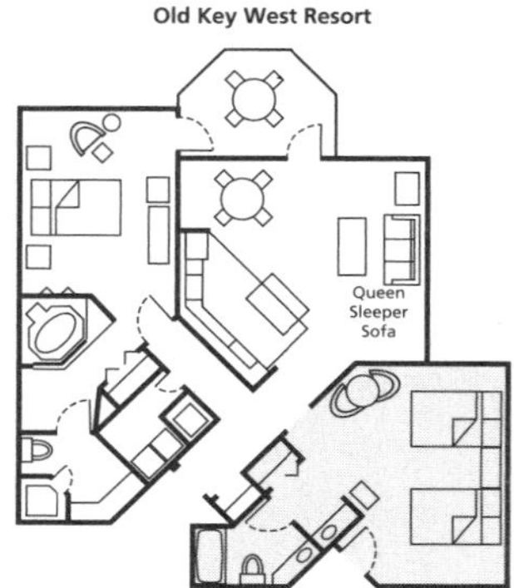

Studio (gray)—376 square feet
One Bedroom—942 square feet
Two Bedroom—1,333 square feet
Grand Villa—2,202 square feet

Disney's BoardWalk Villas

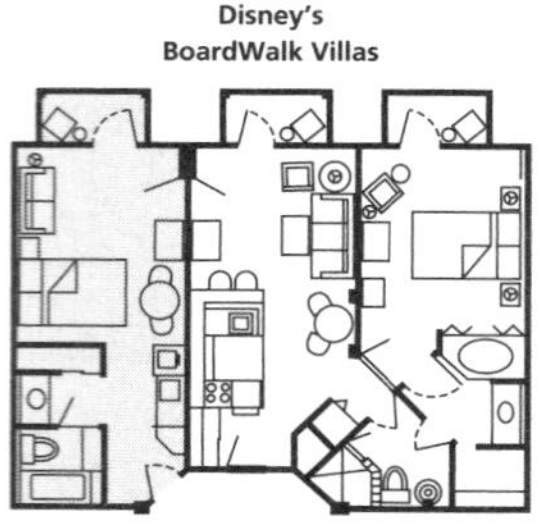

Studio (gray)—412 square feet
One Bedroom—814 square feet
Two Bedroom—1,236 square feet
Grand Villa—2,491 square feet

Bay Lake Tower

Studio (gray)—TK square feet
One Bedroom—TK square feet
Two Bedroom—TK square feet
Grand Villa—TK square feet

Animal Kingdom Villas (Jambo House and Kidani Village)

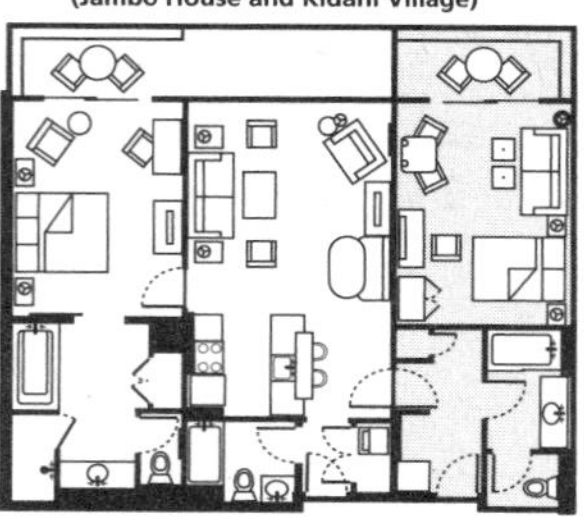

Studio (gray)—316–365 square feet (Jambo House), 366 square feet (Kidani Village)
One Bedroom—629–710 square feet (Jambo House), 807 square feet (Kidani Village)
Two Bedroom—945–1,075 square feet (Jambo House), 1,173 square feet (Kidani Village)
Grand Villa—2,349 square feet (Jambo House), 2,201 square feet (Kidani Village)

Treehouse Villas

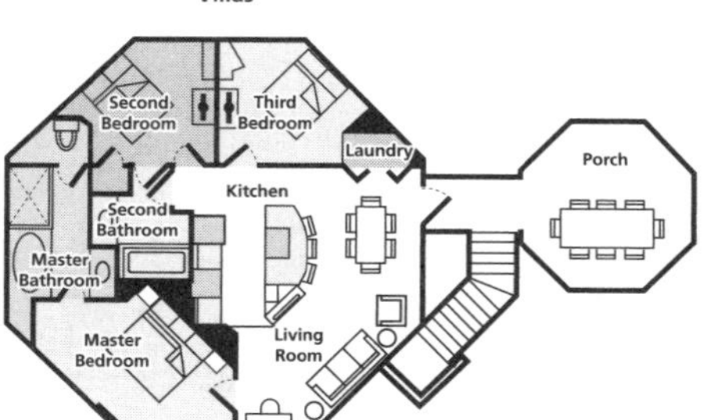

Standard Plan
Three Bedrooms—1,074 square fee

DDV guest-occupancy limits: studios and one-bedroom Villas, 4 persons; two-bedroom villas, 8 persons; three-bedroom Grand Villas, 12 persons. Note: *To all these limits you may add 1 child under age 3 in a crib.*

DISNEY DELUXE VILLA RESORTS ROOM DIAGRAMS (CONTINUED)

Villas at Disney's Wilderness Lodge

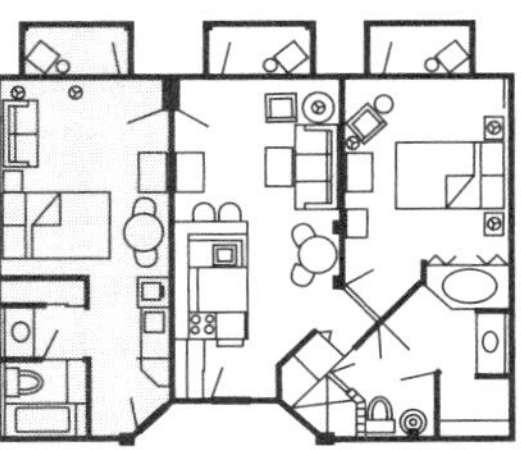

Studio (gray)—356 square feet
One Bedroom—727 square feet
Two Bedroom—1,080 square feet
Grand Villa—2,202 square feet

Saratoga Springs Resort & Spa

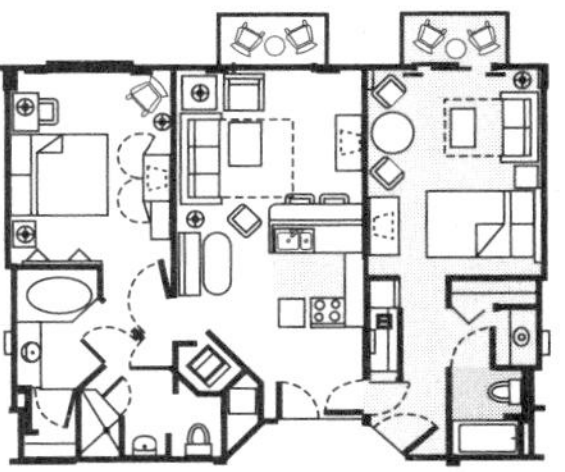

Studio (gray)—355 square feet
One Bedroom—714 square feet
Two Bedroom—1,075 square feet
Grand Villa—2,113 square feet

Disney's Beach Club Villas

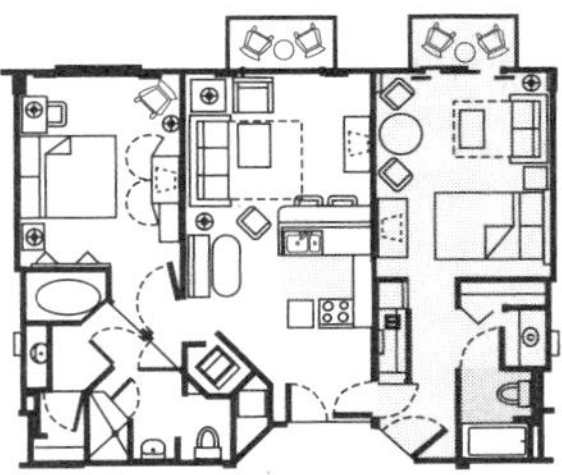

Studio (gray)—356 square feet
One Bedroom—726 square feet
Two Bedroom—1,083 square feet

MODERATE RESORTS ROOM DIAGRAMS

Coronado Springs Resort

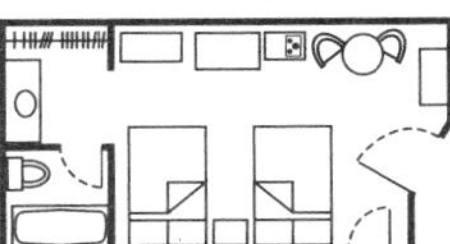

Typical Room, 314 square feet
Rooms accommodate 4 guests, plus 1 child under age 3 in a crib.

Port Orleans French Quarter Resort

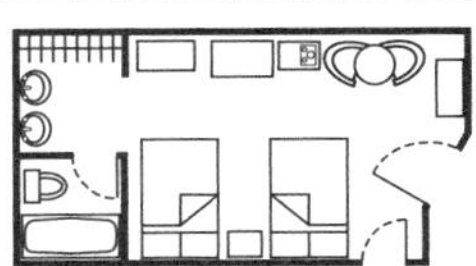

Typical Room, 314 square feet
Rooms accommodate 4 guests, plus 1 child under age 3 in a crib.

Caribbean Beach Resort

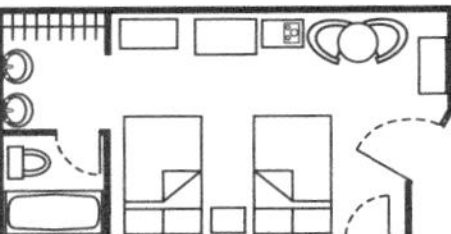

Typical Room, 314 square feet
Rooms accommodate 4 guests, plus 1 child under age 3 in a crib.

Port Orleans Resort Riverside

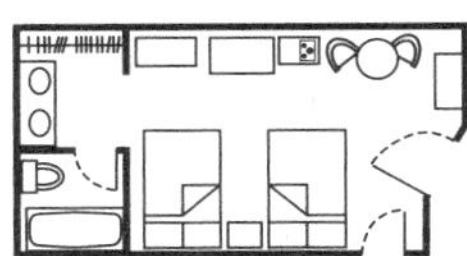

Typical Room, 314 square feet
Rooms accommodate 4 guests, plus 1 child under age 3 in a crib. Alligator Bayou has trundle bed for extra child (54" long) at no extra charge.

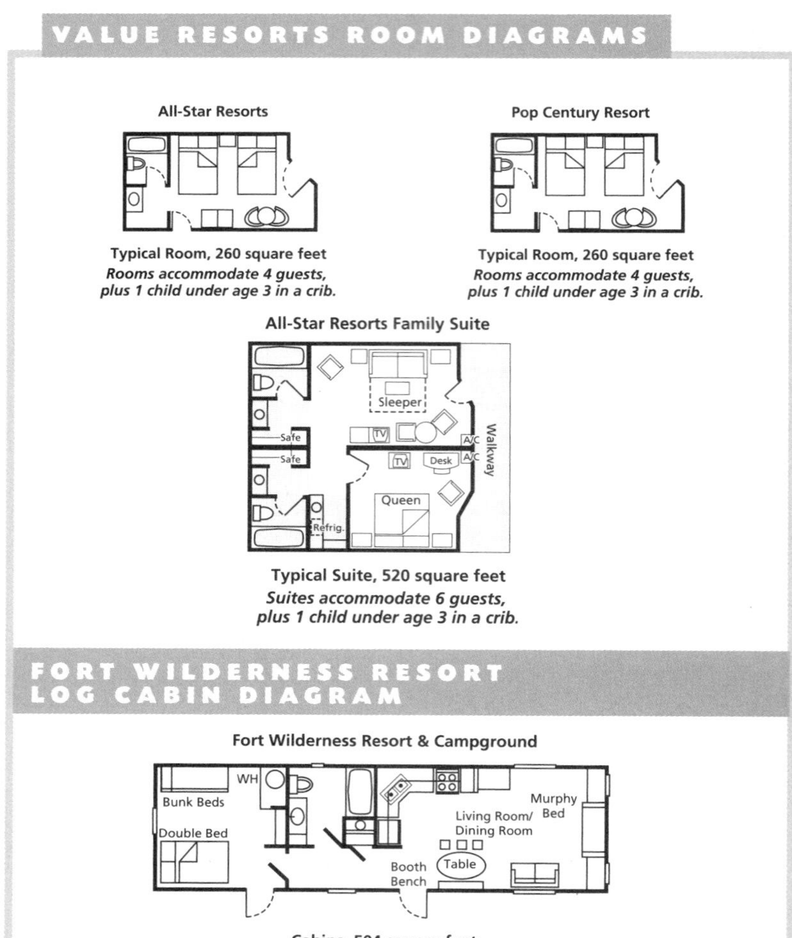

Cabins, 504 square feet
Cabins accommodate 6 guests, plus 1 child under age 3 in a crib.

Continued from page 124

architectural essence to carry off the theme. Port Orleans Riverside Resort likewise succeeds with its plantation and bayou setting. Old Key West Resort gets the architecture right, but cloning Key West on such a large scale totally glosses over Key West's idiosyncratic, patchwork personality. The Caribbean Beach Resort's theme is much more effective at night, thanks to creative lighting. By day, it looks like a Miami condo development.

Coronado Springs Resort offers several styles of Mexican and southwestern American architecture. Though the lake setting is lovely and the resort is attractive and inviting, the theme (with the exception of the main swimming area) isn't especially stimulating—more like a Scottsdale, Arizona, country club than a Disney resort. The resort will be adding "Club Level" (concierge) rooms in 2009.

The All-Star Resorts comprise 30 three-story, *T*-shaped hotels with almost 6,000 guest rooms. There are 15 themed areas: 5 celebrate sports (surfing, basketball, tennis, football, and baseball), 5 recall Hollywood movies, and 5 have musical motifs. The resort's design, with entrances shaped like giant Dalmatians, Coke cups, footballs, and the like, is pretty adolescent, sacrificing grace and beauty for energy and novelty. Guest rooms are small, with decor reminiscent of a teenage boy's bedroom. Despite the theme, there are no sports, music, or movies at All-Star Resorts. The Pop Century Resort is pretty much a clone of All-Star Resorts, only this time the giant icons symbolize decades of the 20th century (Big Wheels, 45-rpm records, silhouettes of people doing period dances, and such), and period memorabilia decorate the rooms.

Pretense aside, the Contemporary, Swan, and Dolphin are essentially themeless though architecturally interesting. The original Contemporary Resort is a 15-story A-frame building with monorails running through the middle. Views from guest rooms here and in the brand-new Bay Lake Tower are among the best at Disney World. Swan and Dolphin are massive yet whimsical. Designed by Michael Graves, they're excellent examples of "entertainment architecture." The two resorts' guest rooms, originally avant-garde bordering on garish, have been totally redesigned. Although still visually interesting, they're now more restful and easier on the eye.

6. DINING The best resorts for dining quality and selection are the Epcot resorts: Swan, Dolphin, Yacht and Beach Club Resorts, Beach Club Villas, and BoardWalk Inn and Villas. Each has good restaurants and is within easy walking distance of the others (and of the 12 ethnic restaurants in Epcot's World Showcase section). If you stay at an Epcot resort, you have 21 of Disney World's finest restaurants within a 5- to 12-minute walk.

The only other place in Disney World where restaurants and hotels are similarly concentrated is in the Downtown Disney Resort Area. In addition to restaurants in the hotels themselves, the Hilton, Holiday Inn at Walt Disney World, Regal Sun Resort, and Buena Vista Palace Hotel & Spa, as well as Disney's Saratoga Springs Resort & Spa, are within walking distance of restaurants in Downtown Disney.

Guests at the Contemporary, Polynesian, and Grand Floridian can eat in their hotels, or they can commute to restaurants in the Magic Kingdom (not recommended) or in other monorail-linked hotels. Riding the monorail to another hotel or to the Magic Kingdom takes about ten minutes each way, plus waiting for the train.

All the other Disney resorts are somewhat isolated. This means you're stuck dining at your hotel unless (1) you have a car and can go anywhere or (2) you're content to eat at the theme parks or Downtown Disney.

Here's the deal. Disney transportation works fine for commuting from hotels to theme parks and Downtown Disney, but it's hopeless for getting from one hotel to another. If you're staying at Port Orleans and want to dine at the Swan, forget it. It can take you up to an hour and a half each way by bus. You could take a bus to the Magic Kingdom and catch a train to one of the monorail-served hotels for dinner. That would take "only" 45 minutes each way. When all is said and done, your best strategy for commuting from hotel to hotel by road is to pony up for a cab.

Of the more-isolated resorts, Wilderness Lodge and Villas and Animal Kingdom Lodge and Villas serve the best food. Coronado Springs, Port Orleans, Old Key West, and Caribbean Beach resorts each have a full-service restaurant, a food court, and in-room pizza delivery. None of the isolated resorts, however, offer enough variety for the average person to be happy eating in his/her hotel every day. The Pop Century Resort and All-Star Resorts (Disney's most isolated hotel) have more than 8,500 guest rooms but no full-service restaurants. There are three food courts, but you have to get to them before 11 p.m.

7. AMENITIES AND RECREATION Disney resorts offer a staggering variety of amenities and recreational opportunities (see charts at right and following). All provide elaborate swimming pools, themed shops, restaurants or food courts, bars or lounges, and access to five Disney golf courses. The more you pay for your lodging, the more amenities and opportunities are at your disposal. The Grand Floridian, Animal Kingdom Lodge and Villas, Yacht and Beach Club Resorts, Swan, and Dolphin, for example, offer concierge floors.

For swimming and sunning, the Contemporary–Bay Lake Tower, Polynesian, Wilderness Lodge and Villas, and Grand Floridian offer both pools and white-sand nonswimming beaches on Bay Lake or Seven Seas Lagoon. The Caribbean Beach Resort and the Yacht and Beach Club also provide both pools and nonswimming beaches. Though lacking a lakefront beach, Saratoga Springs Resort & Spa, Animal Kingdom Lodge and Villas, Port Orleans and Coronado Springs resorts, and the BoardWalk Inn and Villas have exceptionally creative pools. Here's how we ranked and rated swimming facilities at each Disney resort:

Bay Lake and the Seven Seas Lagoon are the best venues for boating. Resorts fronting these lakes are the Contemporary–Bay Lake Tower, Polynesian, Wilderness Lodge and Villas, Grand Floridian, and Fort Wilderness Resort & Campground. Though on smaller bodies of water, Caribbean Beach, Old Key West, Port Orleans, Coronado Springs, Saratoga Springs Resort & Spa, and Yacht and Beach Club resorts also rent watercraft.

Most convenient for golf are Shades of Green, Saratoga Springs, Old Key West, Contemporary, Polynesian, Grand Floridian, and Port Orleans. Tennis is available at the resorts indicated with bullets (•) in the top chart on page 132. Disney resorts with fitness and weight-training facilities are rated and ranked in the bottom chart on page 132 (resorts not listed don't have such facilities).

While there are many places to bike or jog at Disney World (including golf-cart paths), the best biking and jogging are at Fort Wilderness Resort & Campground and the adjacent Wilderness Lodge and Villas. Caribbean Beach Resort offers a lovely hiking,

Disney Resort Amenities

RESORT	SUITES	CONCIERGE	NUMBER OF ROOMS	ROOM SERVICE	BROADBAND-INTERNET CONNECTIVITY
All-Star Resorts	•	–	5,664	–	•
Animal Kingdom Lodge	•	•	972	•	•
Animal Kingdom Villas	•	–	458	•	•
Bay Lake Tower	•	–	295	•	•
Beach Club Villas	•	–	282	•	•
BoardWalk Inn	•	•	372	•	•
BoardWalk Villas	•	–	532	•	•
Caribbean Beach Resort	–	–	2,112	–	•
Contemporary Resort	•	•	655	•	•
Coronado Springs Resort	•	•	1,921	–	•
Dolphin	•	•	1,509	•	•
Fort Wilderness Resort	–	–	409	–	•
Grand Floridian Resort & Spa	•	•	867	•	•
Old Key West Resort	•	–	761	–	•
Polynesian Resort	•	•	853	•	•
Pop Century Resort	–	–	2,880	–	•
Port Orleans Resort	–	–	3,056	–	•
Saratoga Springs Resort & Spa	•	–	840	–	•
Shades of Green	–	•	586	•	•
Swan	•	•	758	•	•
Treehouse Villas	•	–	60	–	•
Wilderness Lodge and Villas	•	•	864	•	•
Yacht and Beach Club Resorts	•	•	1,197	•	•

biking, and jogging trail around the lake. Also good for biking and jogging is the area along Bonnet Creek extending through Port Orleans and Old Key West toward Downtown Disney. Epcot resorts offer a lakefront promenade and bike path, as well as a roadside walkway suitable for jogging.

On-site child-care programs are offered at the Animal Kingdom Lodge and Villas, Dolphin, Grand Floridian Resort & Spa, Hilton WDW, Polynesian, Swan, Wilderness Lodge and Villas, and Yacht Club and Beach Club resorts. All other resorts offer in-room babysitting (see page 360 for details).

8. NIGHTLIFE The boardwalk at BoardWalk Inn and Villas has an upscale dance club (albeit one that has never lived up to its potential), a club with dueling pianos and sing-alongs, a brew pub, and a sports bar. BoardWalk clubs are within easy walking distance of all Epcot resorts. Most non-Disney hotels in the Downtown Disney Resort

unofficial **TIP**
The best lounges are Mizner's Lounge at the Grand Floridian Resort & Spa, Kimonos at the Swan, and the California Grill Lounge on the 15th floor of the Contemporary Resort.

Disney Resort Recreation

	FITNESS CENTER	WATER SPORTS	MARINA	BEACH	TENNIS	BIKING
All-Star Resorts	–	–	–	–	–	–
Animal Kingdom Lodge and Villas	•	–	–	–	•*	–
Bay Lake Tower	•	•	•	•	–	–
Beach Club Resort and Villas	•	•	•	•	•	–
BoardWalk Inn	•	•	•	–	•	•
BoardWalk Villas	•	•	•	–	•	•
Caribbean Beach Resort	–	•	•	•	–	•
Contemporary Resort	•	•	•	•	–	–
Coronado Springs Resort	•	•	•	–	–	–
Dolphin	•	•	•	•	•	–
Fort Wilderness Resort	–	•	•	•	•	•
Grand Floridian Resort & Spa	•	•	•	•	•	–
Old Key West Resort	•	•	•	–	•	•
Polynesian Resort	–	•	•	•	–	–
Pop Century Resort	–	–	–	–	–	–
Port Orleans Resort	–	•	•	–	–	•
Saratoga Springs Resort & Spa–Treehouse Villas	•	–	–	–	•	•
Shades of Green	•	–	–	–	•	•
Swan	•	–	–	•	•	–
Wilderness Lodge and Villas	•	•	•	•	–	•
Yacht and Beach Club Resorts	•	•	•	•	•	–

***Kidani Village only**

HOTEL	FITNESS-CENTER RATING
1. Saratoga Springs Resort & Spa–Treehouse Villas	★★★★★
2. Grand Floridian Resort & Spa	★★★★½
3. Bay Lake Tower	★★★★½
4. Animal Kingdom Lodge and Villas	★★★★
5. BoardWalk Inn and Villas	★★★★
6. Yacht and Beach Club Resorts	★★★★ (shared facility)
7. Contemporary Resort	★★★½
8. Coronado Springs Resort	★★★½
9. Wilderness Lodge and Villas	★★★½
10. Dolphin	★★★
11. Swan	★★★
12. Old Key West Resort	★½

HOTEL	POOL RATING
1. Yacht and Beach Club Resorts and Villas	★★★★★ (shared complex)
2. Animal Kingdom Villas (Kidani Village)	★★★★½
3. Port Orleans Resort	★★★★½
4. Saratoga Springs Resort & Spa–Treehouse Villas	★★★★½
5. Wilderness Lodge and Villas	★★★★½
6. Animal Kingdom Lodge and Villas (Jambo House)	★★★★
7. Bay Lake Tower	★★★★
8. Coronado Springs Resort	★★★★
9. Dolphin	★★★★
10. Polynesian Resort	★★★★
11. Swan	★★★★
12. Contemporary Resort	★★★½
13. BoardWalk Inn and Villas	★★★½
14. Grand Floridian Resort & Spa	★★★½
15. All-Star Resorts	★★★
16. Caribbean Beach Resort	★★★
17. Fort Wilderness Resort & Campground	★★★
18. Old Key West Resort	★★★
19. Pop Century Resort	★★★
20. Shades of Green	★★★

Area, as well as Saratoga Springs Resort & Spa, are within walking distance of Downtown Disney nightspots. Nightlife at other Disney resorts is limited to lounges that stay open late.

At the California Grill Lounge, you can relax over dinner and watch the fireworks at the nearby Magic Kingdom.

RESEARCHING WALT DISNEY WORLD HOTELS

THE *UNOFFICIAL GUIDE* HOTEL TEAM inspects thousands of hotel rooms each year throughout North America and stays abreast of current trends and issues in the lodging industry. One such issue is the list of frequent complaints hotel guests make regarding their rooms. Over the past few years, the most common complaints include excessive noise, uncomfortable beds, poor lighting, outdated furnishings, high phone charges, and substandard towels. Because these complaints are ongoing concerns, the hotel team undertook a complete reevaluation of every Walt Disney World resort (including the **Swan** and **Dolphin**) in each of these areas. Findings for the new Animal Kingdom Villas–Kidani Village, Bay Lake Tower, and Treehouse Villas at Saratoga Springs Resort & Spa will be included in future editions of this guide.

Disney Hotels: Complaints and Comparisons

	SOUND	LIGHTING	PILLOWS	OVERALL
All-Star Movies	D	D	B	C-
All-Star Music	A	D	C	C+
All-Star Sports	A	D	B	B
Animal Kingdom Lodge and Villas (Jambo House)	F	A	B	C+
Beach Club Resort	B	D	B	C+
BoardWalk Inn	B	F	B	C
BoardWalk Villas	B	D	B	C+
Caribbean Beach Resort	B	C	B	B
Contemporary Resort	D	A	A	B+
Coronado Springs Resort **(studios)**	B	B	B	B+
Dolphin	A	D	A	B+
Fort Wilderness Resort **(cabins)**	C	D	D	D
Grand Floridian Resort & Spa	F	A	D	C-
Old Key West Resort	A	D	C	C+
Polynesian Resort	F	A	B	C+
Pop Century Resort	B	F	B	C
Port Orleans French Quarter	B	C	D	C
Port Orleans Riverside	A	C	D	C+
Saratoga Springs Resort & Spa	B	C	C	C+
Swan	A	F	A	B
Yacht Club	B	F	B	C
Wilderness Lodge	D	A	A	B+
Wilderness Lodge Villas	F	A	A	B

In the Lab with Dr. Fluffy

Our tests included everything from the quality of the bed linens to the age of the mattresses to the fluffiness (loft) of the pillows. While evaluation criteria for linens and mattresses are fairly well known, we couldn't find any standard test to measure pillow fluffiness. A search of *Consumer Reports*' Web site failed to find anything, and fear of another restraining order kept us from making all the phone calls to the magazine that we wanted. So we had to invent our own.

The method we came up with is based on measuring how far a half-filled gallon jug of water sank into the middle of a pillow. (Two quarts of water weigh between one-third and one-half as much as a typical human head, according to most estimates. Also, a gallon jug is easy to find, and no one thinks twice if you bring one into a hotel lobby. Not so with a replica of a human head, trust us.)

Key to this experiment was determining the proper range of support a good pillow should provide. A test bottle that sank too deep into a pillow would indicate not enough support; on the other hand, a bottle that sank very little might indicate an experience akin to sleeping on a brick. We therefore evaluated a wide range of pillows prior to the test to establish the proper range of support.

The best pillows are found at the non-Disney-owned **Swan** and **Dolphin** resorts. It's probably no coincidence that these are the only hotels using pillows made with goose feathers and down; all of the Disney-owned resorts use either polyester fill or foam. Other good pillows were found at Disney's **Wilderness Lodge** and **Wilderness Lodge Villas.** The pillows at the **Grand Floridian, Port Orleans Riverside,** and **Fort Wilderness Cabins** did poorly in our tests.

Mattresses at all the Walt Disney World resorts come from brand-name manufacturers such as Sealy and Simmons. Value and Moderate resorts typically have either two full-size mattresses or one king; Deluxe resorts have two queen beds (about 20% larger than a full) or one king. One notable exception is the Swan, which uses the aptly named Heavenly Bed mattresses. Throughout the resorts, almost all the mattresses we inspected were less than two years old, and about half were less than a year old. The oldest mattress we found on Disney property—in service for eight years—was at Disney's Fort Wilderness Cabins. (Outside Disney, we've seen 17-year-old mattresses still in use.)

Disney's Value and Moderate resorts use the same brand of 180-thread-count sheets for their bed linens. Disney's Deluxe and DDV resorts (except the Contemporary) and the independent Swan and Dolphin resorts all use 250-thread-count sheets.

Pipe Down Out There!

Noisy rooms rank near the top of hotel guests' complaints every year. A well-designed room blocks both the noise coming from an adjacent room's television and from the swimming pool across the resort. Based on our initial tests of both interior and exterior soundproofing, and for reasons outlined on the next page, we believe that a room's exterior door is the critical component in keeping sound out.

Illustration: Chris Eliopoulos

Our test equipment consisted of a digital sound meter, a portable CD player, and a copy of The Who's greatest hits. We first calibrated the volume of the CD player until Roger Daltrey's ear-piercing wail in "Baba O'Riley" reached 70 decibels on the sound meter. Next, we took the CD player outside the room and placed the meter on top of the pillow of the bed closest to the exterior door. We replayed "Baba O'Riley" and recorded the decibel reading on the sound meter. For good measure, we also recorded the sound level in the room with and without the A/C running, and around the resort in general.

With the tests completed, we were surprised that the six worst results came from Deluxe resorts, with the **Grand Floridian, Wilderness**

Lodge Villas, and the **Polynesian** making up the bottom three. Six hotels earned top marks in our test: **All-Star Music, All-Star Sports,** the **Dolphin, Old Key West, Port Orleans Riverside,** and the **Swan.** In addition to the Deluxe resorts mentioned previously, **Animal Kingdom Lodge** and **Wilderness Lodge** were near the bottom of the list.

Overall, Value and Moderate resorts did much better than Deluxe resorts when it came to blocking out exterior noise, with Disney's All-Star Music and All-Star Sports (both Value resorts) being the overall winners. That certainly runs counter to what consumers would expect, so we set about trying to find an explanation. Like any good detective, we looked for an economic motive first.

The explanation turns out to be fairly simple, and it does come down to money—Disney's money. At Disney's Value and Moderate resorts (and, notably, Disney's Vacation Club resorts), each room's exterior door opens onto the great outdoors, just as the average home's exterior door opens to the outside world. These exterior doors must have extensive weather stripping to keep out wind and rain. Also, exterior-facing walls tend to be thicker and better insulated than interior walls, as these measures reduce Disney's costs to heat and cool the rooms. Such walls also work really well at blocking noise.

In contrast, Deluxe rooms typically have doors that open onto an interior hallway that Disney is already paying to heat and cool. Thus, there's little economic incentive for Disney to put the same materials into the outward-facing doors and walls of some Deluxe resorts, since the temperature range outside the room is relatively constant and there's no need to keep rain or wind out. (In fact, many Deluxe resorts have a small gap of one- to three-quarters of an inch at the bottom of their doors to aid in getting fresh air *into* the rooms.) Unfortunately, this permits more sound to enter. Finally, the interior hallways themselves can function as giant echo chambers, allowing sounds to bounce off the walls back and forth, up and down the hallway. Not so at the other resorts, where many sounds bounce off an exterior wall and out into space.

Room soundproofing, however, is only half of the story. The other half, as any good real estate agent knows, is location; despite the resort's relatively good performance, a pool-view room at All-Star Sports is likely to pick up a lot more noise than an upper-floor corner room at the Grand Floridian, because the former faces a heavily used public space. So our next task was to determine the amount of external noise affecting every single room at the Walt Disney World Resort.

We assigned *Unofficial Guide* researcher Rich Vosburgh to the task, as he seemed the one least likely to go insane from it. Using a combination of resort maps, aerial photography, and a whole lot of old-fashioned legwork, Rich created an "External Noise Potential" metric for each hotel room on Disney property, taking into account factors including the floor level, pedestrian traffic, proximity to public spaces, and number of nearby hotel rooms. Finally, the research team revisited every building in every resort to verify our rankings. For the most part, we were spot on. But there were a couple of surprises that we're sure we would have overlooked had we not reviewed every single room. For example, the southwest-facing rooms in buildings 7 and 8 of Disney's All-Star Music resort are situated well away from most public spaces in the resort and overlook the extreme end of a parking lot. There's not a lot of pedestrian traffic around, and the rooms themselves tested well for soundproofing—hey, these should be some quiet rooms, right? Well, when we visited the resort, we discovered that this particular section of parking lot, because it was away from most guest rooms, is where Disney decides to warm up its diesel buses in the morning before servicing the three All-Star Resorts. At 6 a.m., the area around these buildings sounded like Daytona International Speedway on race day.

Our research indicates that quiet rooms can be found in almost any resort. For readers who put peace and quiet at the top of their list, we've listed the ten quietest spots among all WDW resorts in the chart below.

QUIETEST ROOMS IN WALT DISNEY WORLD

All-Star Music **Buildings 5 and 6, rooms facing west; building 4, rooms facing northwest**

All-Star Sports **Building 3, rooms facing west; building 2, rooms facing north**

Beach Club **Easternmost buildings, rooms facing east**

Beach Club Villas **Southernmost wings, rooms facing north-northwest**

BoardWalk Inn **All rooms facing courtyard, just east of main lobby**

Caribbean Beach **Trinidad South, buildings 35 and 38, rooms facing lake; Barbados, buildings 11 and 12, facing south**

Port Orleans Riverside **Alligator Bayou, buildings 26 and 28, rooms facing east; Acadian House, north wings, rooms facing west**

Port Orleans French Quarter **Building 1, rooms facing water; building 7, north wing, rooms facing water; building 6, north wing, rooms facing water**

Wilderness Lodge **Northernmost wing, rooms facing northwest (woods)**

Wilderness Lodge Villas **Southernmost building, water-view rooms facing east**

Let There Be Light

As with noise, poor lighting generally ranks near the top of hotel guests' complaints. Of particular concern is the lighting in the bathroom and grooming area, the head of the bed (for reading), and the desk or table area (for working). In fact, lighting here is so important that professional associations publish standards listing the minimum amount of lighting needed for each area. Our evaluations incorporate the standards and recommendations of the Illuminating Engineering Society of North America (IESNA), a leading institution for lighting research, technology, and its applications.

Our test equipment was an industrial-grade digital light meter, able to detect a wide range of light levels. In addition to testing the lighting at the grooming, desk, and bed areas, we also tested the bath/shower area, the armchair or sitting area (if the room had one), and the overall light level in the room. The results were weighted to emphasize the quality of light in the grooming, desk, and bed areas.

The rooms with the best lighting were found at Disney's newly renovated **Contemporary** and **Polynesian** resorts, the **Wilderness Lodge**

and Villas, Animal Kingdom Lodge, and the **Grand Floridian,** all Deluxe resorts. **Coronado Springs** was the highest-scoring Moderate resort. No Value resort posted acceptable scores in lighting.

New rooms at the Polynesian exceeded the IESNA's minimum recommendations in every area, and the Contemporary's new rooms exceeded the recommendations in all except the armchair reading area. Disney seems to be giving special attention to room lighting when doing its latest round of resort rehabs, and it's paying off.

Outside the Contemporary and Polynesian, the **Caribbean Beach** and **Grand Floridian** scored high with their grooming-and-bath-area lighting, while the **Wilderness Lodge Villas** and **Coronado Springs** had the best lighting in the desk/work area, with Coronado Springs using a specially designed ceiling lamp to ensure bright work surfaces; and **Wilderness Lodge** and **Port Orleans Riverside** had the best bed lighting. The three worst scores were recorded at the **Swan, Pop Century,** and **Yacht Club** resorts. How bad is the lighting? Rooms this dim are usually accompanied by Barry White music when you're trying to put the moves on your sweetie.

Check-in and Checkout

Disney introduced a free online check-in service in 2009. Up to ten days before you arrive, you can log on to **www.mydisneyreservation.com** to complete the check-in process, make room requests, and note events such as birthdays and anniversaries you're celebrating during your trip. Provide a credit-card number and your arrival and departure times, and Disney will send you an e-mail confirmation that your check-in is complete. When you arrive at your resort, you'll bypass the regular check-in desk and head for another desk reserved for those who've already done so online. While the service is still new, early reviews have been positive.

If you're unable to check in online prior to your trip, then check-in processing is another area of guest service where you'd expect the more highfalutin resorts to shine, but our research shows that the Value resorts are by far the most efficient. The best of the best is the **Pop Century Resort,** where it's rare to wait in line for more than a couple of minutes. The Pop Century has the largest registration desk as well as the most agents manning it. What's more, a front-desk supervisor paces the registration lobby, directing guests and ensuring minimum waits. Even when a Magical Express bus deposits 45 people at one time, they are quickly processed. Almost as good is check-in efficiency at the Value **All-Star Resorts.**

Deluxe resorts have smaller front desks and fewer agents, but then guests generally arrive in smaller numbers than at the Value and Moderate resorts. A line of four or five waiting guests is not unusual, but the wait is usually less than 15 minutes. The arrival of a busload of guests can overwhelm the front desk of Deluxe resorts, but this is the exception rather than the rule. The least efficient of the Deluxe resorts' front desks is that of the **Polynesian Resort.**

By far the longest registration lines occur at the Moderate resorts, with the **Caribbean Beach Resort** being the worst of the worst.

If your room is not available when you arrive, Disney will either give you a phone number to call to check on the room or will offer to call or send a text message to your cell phone when it's ready.

Checking out is a snap at all Disney resorts. Your bill will be prepared and affixed to your doorknob or slipped under your door the night before you leave. If everything is in order, you have only to pack up and depart. If there's a problem with your bill, however, you'll have to resolve it at the front desk, where the previous order of most efficient to least efficient is a good gauge of the probable hassle you're in for.

UNOFFICIAL GUIDE READERS SPEAK OUT

MANY READERS SHARE WITH US their experiences and criticisms regarding Disney hotels. Some copy us on letters of complaint sent to Disney. If you've written or copied us about a bad experience, you might be surprised that we haven't quoted your letter. Any business can have a bad day, even a Disney hotel, and a single incident might not be indicative of the hotel's general level of quality and service. In our experience, if a problem is endemic the same complaint will usually surface in a number of letters. But even with our voluminous reader mail, your comments often paint a mixed picture. For instance, for every letter we get that's critical of Disney's Grand Floridian Resort & Spa, it's not unusual for us to receive another letter telling us it's the best place the reader ever stayed.

WOULD YOU RECOMMEND THIS HOTEL TO A FRIEND?

RESORT NAME	DEFINITELY (+/– SINCE 2008)	RESORT NAME	DEFINITELY (+/– SINCE 2008)
Wilderness Lodge Villas	91% (+5%)	All-Star Sports	68% (+1%)
Beach Club Villas	91% (+5%)	All-Star Music	65% (–15%)
Grand Floridian Resort	87% (+14%)	Saratoga Springs Resort	65% (–8%)
Fort Wilderness Cabins	87% (+3%)	Contemporary Resort	64% (+21%)
Beach Club Resort	86% (+6%)	Yacht Club Resort	64% (–22%)
Animal Kingdom Lodge*	80% (–2%)	Coronado Springs Resort	64% (+15%)
Shades of Green	80% (–1%)	Caribbean Beach Resort	63% (same)
BoardWalk Inn	78% (+11%)	Old Key West Resort	63% (–25%)
Polynesian Resort	76% (–14%)	All-Star Movies	60% (–3%)
Pop Century Resort	71% (+5%)	Swan	57% (–32%)
Port Orleans Riverside	71% (same)	BoardWalk Villas	56% (–38%)
Wilderness Lodge	71% (–12%)	Dolphin	50% (–19%)
Port Orleans French Qtr.	70% (–21%)		
Average for WDW hotels	**71% (–7%)**	**Average for off-site hotels**	**69% (+13%)**

**Animal Kingdom Lodge and Jambo House Villas*

We tend to hear more often from readers when things go badly than when things go well. Whether your experience was positive or negative, we encourage you to share it with us. The more comments we receive, the more accurate and complete a picture we can provide.

WOULD YOU STAY AT THIS HOTEL AGAIN?

RESORT NAME	YES (+/– SINCE 2008)	RESORT NAME	YES (+/– SINCE 2008)
Wilderness Lodge Villas	100% (same)	All-Star Movies	88% (+10%)
Beach Club Villas	100% (same)	Port Orleans Riverside	87% (–4%)
Fort Wilderness Cabins	100% (same)	Caribbean Beach Resort	87% (+13%)
BoardWalk Inn	100% (+32%)	Beach Club Resort	86% (–14%)
Dolphin	100% (same)	Swan	86% (–14%)
All-Star Music	96% (same)	All-Star Sports	86% (–5%)
Shades of Green	93% (–7%)	Yacht Club Resort	83% (–3%)
Pop Century Resort	93% (+1%)	Wilderness Lodge	82% (–8%)
Port Orleans French Qtr.	92% (–4%)	Coronado Springs Resort	82% (+5%)
Animal Kingdom Lodge*	89% (+1%)	Old Key West Resort	81% (–19%)
Grand Floridian Resort	89% (+9%)	Contemporary Resort	80% (–6%)
Polynesian Resort	89% (–6%)	Saratoga Springs Resort	77% (–14%)
BoardWalk Villas	89% (–11%)		
Average for WDW hotels	**89% (–2%)**	**Average for off-site hotels**	**89% (+11%)**

**Animal Kingdom Lodge and Jambo House Villas*

READERS' 2009 DISNEY RESORT REPORT CARD

EACH YEAR, SEVERAL THOUSAND READERS mail or e-mail us their responses to the survey at the end of this guide. The Reader Report Card documents their opinions of the Disney resorts as well as the Swan, the Dolphin, and Shades of Green. Findings for the new Animal Kingdom Villas–Kidani Village, Bay Lake Tower, and Treehouse Villas at Saratoga Springs Resort & Spa will be included in future editions.

Room Quality reflects readers' level of satisfaction with their rooms, while **Check-in Efficiency** rates the speed and ease of check-in. **Quietness of Room** measures how well, in the guests' perception, their rooms are insulated from external noise. **Shuttle Service** rates Disney bus, boat, and/or monorail service to and from the hotels. **Pool Facilities** reflects reader satisfaction with the resorts' swimming pools. **Hotel Staff** measures the friendliness and helpfulness of the resort's employees, and **Food Court** rates counter-service dining facilities and value at the resort.

In the 2009 edition of the survey, readers indicated much less satisfaction with Disney resorts than in years past. In each report-card category, the number of hotels scoring lower than last year exceeded the number of those scoring higher by large margins (16 to 1 for overall ratings). Most Disney resorts lost the equivalent of about half a letter grade in each category, and for the first time in our survey, no Disney hotel earned an overall A rating from readers. In particular, dissatisfaction with Disney's on-site resort dining has reached crisis levels, with the overall average dropping to a D+.

More worrisome for Disney management might be that readers now rate the average off-site hotel about the same as the average Disney resort, and vacation homes as substantially better. In fact, had vacation homes been a separate category, they would have earned the

Readers' Disney Resort Report Card

RESORT	ROOM QUALITY	CHECK-IN EFFICIENCY	QUIETNESS OF ROOM	SHUTTLE SERVICE	POOL	HOTEL STAFF	DINING	OVERALL RATING
All-Star Movies	C	B	B	C+	B	B	C	C+
All-Star Music	C+	B+	B	C	B	B	D+	C+
All-Star Sports	C	B	C+	C+	C+	B	C–	C+
Animal Kingdom Lodge & Villas*	B	B	B	C–	B	A–	C	B
Beach Club Resort	B	A–	C	B–	A	B	D+	B
Beach Club Villas	B	B	A–	B	A	A–	C	B
BoardWalk Inn	B–	A–	B–	B–	B	B+	C	B
BoardWalk Villas	A–	B–	A	C	A	B–	C	B
Caribbean Beach Resort	C+	B–	B+	C	B	B	C	B–
Contemporary Resort	B	B	C	B	B	B	D	B–
Coronado Springs Resort	C+	B	B	B	A	B	D+	B–
Dolphin	B	B–	A–	B	B–	B+	C+	B–
Fort Wilderness Cabins	B	B	A–	B	C	B	C	B
Grand Floridian Resort	B+	A	B+	A–	B+	A	C–	B+
Old Key West Resort	B	B	B	C–	B	B–	D–	C+
Polynesian Resort	B	B	C	B	B	B	C–	B–
Pop Century Resort	C	B+	C	C	B	B	C	C+
Port Orleans French Quarter	C+	B+	B	C	B	B	C	B
Port Orleans Riverside	C+	B–	A–	C	B	B	C+	B–
Saratoga Springs Resort	B	B+	A–	D	B	B	D	B–
Shades of Green	B	B+	B	C+	B	B–	D–	B–
Swan	B	B	C	B–	C	B	D	C
Wilderness Lodge	B–	B	B–	C	B	B	C	B–
Wilderness Lodge Villas	B	B	A	B	C	B+	C	B
Yacht Club Resort	C+	B	C+	D	B	C+	C–	C+
Average for WDW hotels	**B**	**B**	**B**	**C+**	**B**	**B**	**D+**	**B**
Average for all off-site hotels	**B**	**B**	**A**	**D**	**B–**	**C+**	**C**	**B**

**Jambo House only*

only overall A in the report card, ranked first in response to the question "Would you recommend this hotel to a friend?", and tied for first in response to the question "Would you stay at this hotel again?"

Indeed, the only category keeping the average off-site property from rating higher than the average Disney property is poor shuttle service to the parks. (Some plucky young entrepreneur just might find an opportunity there.) The one bright spot for Disney's resorts in this year's survey was the **BoardWalk Inn,** which improved to a solid B rating overall on the strength of improved Hotel Staff and Check-in Efficiency ratings.

In 2009 we continued asking questions designed to further gauge readers' overall satisfaction with their hotels. The most important of these questions are "Would you recommend this hotel to a friend?" and "Would you stay at this hotel again?" Used widely in the service industry, these questions serve as a simple way to measure a customer's overall opinion of a product. Used with our detailed survey questions, these two new questions allow us to identify the specific criteria that determine satisfaction at a particular resort.

Putting It All Together: Reader Picks for Best and Worst Resorts

For the second year in a row, **Wilderness Lodge Villas** appears near the top of the results for every satisfaction question we asked; **Coronado Springs Resort,** while improved, appears near the bottom. In addition, readers ranked the **Beach Club Villas, Fort Wilderness Cabins, Animal Kingdom Lodge,** and **BoardWalk Inn** as better than average across all three surveys. All are considered Deluxe properties except the Moderate Fort Wilderness Cabins. Among other Moderates, the **Port Orleans French Quarter** and **Port Orleans Riverside** resorts fare well overall. The highest-rated Value property is the **Pop Century Resort.**

Resorts at the bottom of our survey results tend to have multiple problems identified by readers. For example, the Contemporary Resort's overall B– rating is not that much lower than average, but problems with room soundproofing and on-site dining seem to be dragging down its "Would you recommend to a friend?" and "Would you stay here again?" numbers, signifying that these issues are enough to prevent readers from doing either.

Finally, readers tended to be tougher this year than the *Unofficial Guide* hotel inspectors when it came to ratings. But remember that readers are rating one guest room during a specific visit, while the *Unofficial Guide* inspectors provide a comparative rating of more than 250 Disney and non-Disney hotels in and around Walt Disney World. For our ratings, see "How the Hotels Compare" on pages 262–267.

WALT DISNEY WORLD HOTEL PROFILES

FOR THOSE OF YOU WHO'VE PLOWED through the foregoing and remain undecided, here are our profiles of each Disney resort. For both exterior and interior photos of the Walt Disney World resorts, check out our Web site, **TouringPlans.com.**

THE MAGIC KINGDOM RESORTS

Disney's Grand Floridian Resort & Spa

GRAND FLORIDIAN RESORT & SPA

STRENGTHS	WEAKNESSES
On Magic Kingdom monorail	Somewhat formal
Ferry service to Magic Kingdom	Cavernous, impersonal lobby
Excellent guest rooms	Overly large physical layout
Children's programs, character meals	Children don't get theme
Excellent children's pool	Only one on-site restaurant suitable for younger children
Beach	Imposing, rather formal public areas
Recreational options	Distant guest self-parking
Restaurant selection via monorail	
Child-care facility on-site	

Disney World's flagship hotel is inspired by Florida's grand Victorian seaside resorts from the turn of the last century. A complex of four- and five-story white frame buildings, the Grand Floridian integrates verandas, intricate latticework, dormers, and turrets beneath a red shingle roof to capture the most memorable elements of 19th-century ocean-resort architecture. A five-story domed lobby encircled by enameled balustrades and overhung by crystal chandeliers establishes the resort's understated opulence. Covering 40 acres along the Seven Seas Lagoon, the Grand Floridian offers lovely pools, white-sand beaches, and a multifaceted marina.

The 867 guest rooms, with wood trim and soft goods (curtains, linens, towels, and the like) in beachy tones, are luxurious yet warm and inviting rather than stuffy or overly feminine. Armoires, marble-topped sinks, and ceiling fans amplify the Victorian theme. The typical room is 440 square feet (dormer rooms are smaller), large by any standard, and furnished with two queen beds, a daybed, a reading chair, and a table with two side chairs. Many rooms have a balcony.

With a high ratio of staff to guests, service is outstanding. The resort has several full-service restaurants, and others are a short monorail ride away. The hotel is connected directly to the Magic Kingdom by monorail and to other Disney World destinations by bus. Walking time to the monorail and bus-loading areas from the most remote guest rooms is about seven to ten minutes.

Most reader comments concerning the Grand Floridian are positive. First, from a Durham, North Carolina, mother of two preschoolers:

> *The Grand Floridian pool with the waterslide was a big hit with our kids. They also loved taking the boat across the lagoon to return from the Magic Kingdom. The resort's location and transportation services were unbeatable.*

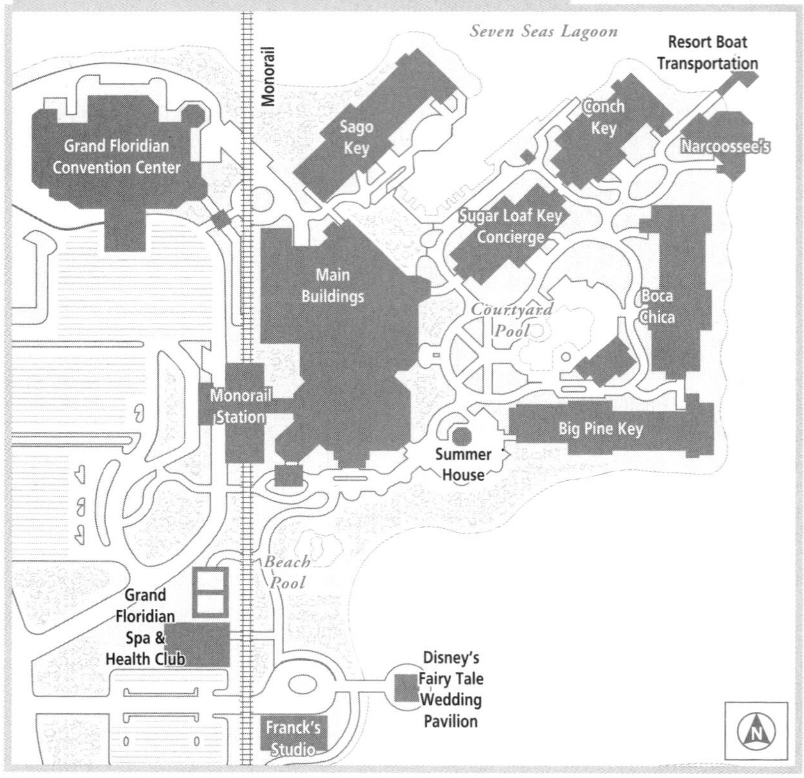

A College Station, Texas, dad weighs in with this:

At the Grand Floridian, the only noise we heard outside our room was toilets flushing and doors closing. We had a view of the Magic Kingdom, which was fabulous, and the housekeeping staff was great. I also enjoyed having real plants in the room.

Finally from a Yorktown, Virginia, couple:

The service and "mousekeeping" at the Grand Floridian were exceptional. Next time we go to WDW, we'll definitely stay there again.

GOOD (AND NOT-SO-GOOD) ROOMS AT THE GRAND FLORIDIAN The resort is spread over a peninsula jutting into Seven Seas Lagoon. In addition to the main building, there are five dispersed, rectangular buildings also hosting guests. Most rooms have a balcony, and most balconies are enclosed by a rail that affords good visibility. Rooms just beneath the roof in each building (dormer rooms) have smaller, inset, solidly enclosed balconies that limit visibility when you're seated. Most dormer rooms, however, have vaulted ceilings and a coziness that compensates for the less desirable balconies.

If you want to be near the bus and monorail stations, most of the restaurants, and shopping, ask for a room in the main building (all concierge rooms). The best rooms are 4322 to 4329 and 4422 to 4429, which have full balconies and overlook the lagoon in the direction of the beach and the Polynesian Resort. Other excellent main-building rooms are 4401 to 4409, with full balconies overlooking the marina and an unobstructed view of Cinderella Castle across the lagoon.

Of the five lodges, three (Conch Key, Boca Chica, and Big Pine Key) have one long side facing the lagoon and the other facing inner courtyards and swimming pools. At Conch Key, full-balcony rooms 7228 to 7231, 7328 to 7331, and 7425 to 7431 offer vistas across the lagoon to the Magic Kingdom and castle. Less expensive rooms in the same building that offer good views are 72-, 73-, and 7411, -13, -15, -17, -19, and -21, and 72-, 73-, and 7412 and -14. (Grand Floridian room numbers are coded. Take room 7213: 7 is the building number, 2 is the floor, and 13 is the room number.) In Boca Chica and Big Pine Key, ask for a lagoon-view room on the first, second, or third floor. Many garden-view rooms in Big Pine Key, and a few in Boca Chica, have views obstructed by a poolside building. These are the worst views from any Grand Floridian room.

The two remaining buildings, Sugar Loaf Key (concierge only) and Sago Key, face each other across the marina. The opposite side of Sugar Loaf Key faces a courtyard, while the other side of Sago Key faces a finger of the lagoon and a forested area. All these views are pleasant but not in the same league as those from the rooms listed above. Exceptions are end rooms in Sago Key (rooms 5139, 5144, 5145, 5242 to 5245, 5342 to 5345) that have a view of the lagoon and Cinderella Castle.

Disney's Polynesian Resort

POLYNESIAN RESORT

STRENGTHS	WEAKNESSES
Relaxed and casual ambience	Overly large and confusing layout
Ferry service to Magic Kingdom	Walkways exposed to rain
Romantic atmosphere	Noise from nearby motor speedway
Exotic theme that children love	Front-desk inefficiency
On Magic Kingdom monorail	
Epcot monorail within walking distance	
Transportation and Ticket Center adjoins resort	
Newly redecorated rooms, among nicest at WDW	
Child care, children's programs, and character meals	
Beach and marina	
Excellent swimming complex	
Recreational options	

South Pacific tropics are re-created at this Deluxe resort. The Polynesian consists of 11 two- and three-story Hawaiian "longhouses" situated around the four-story Great Ceremonial House. Buildings at the Polynesian feature wood tones, with exposed-beam roofs and tribal-inspired geometric inlays in the cornices. The Great Ceremonial House contains

Polynesian Resort

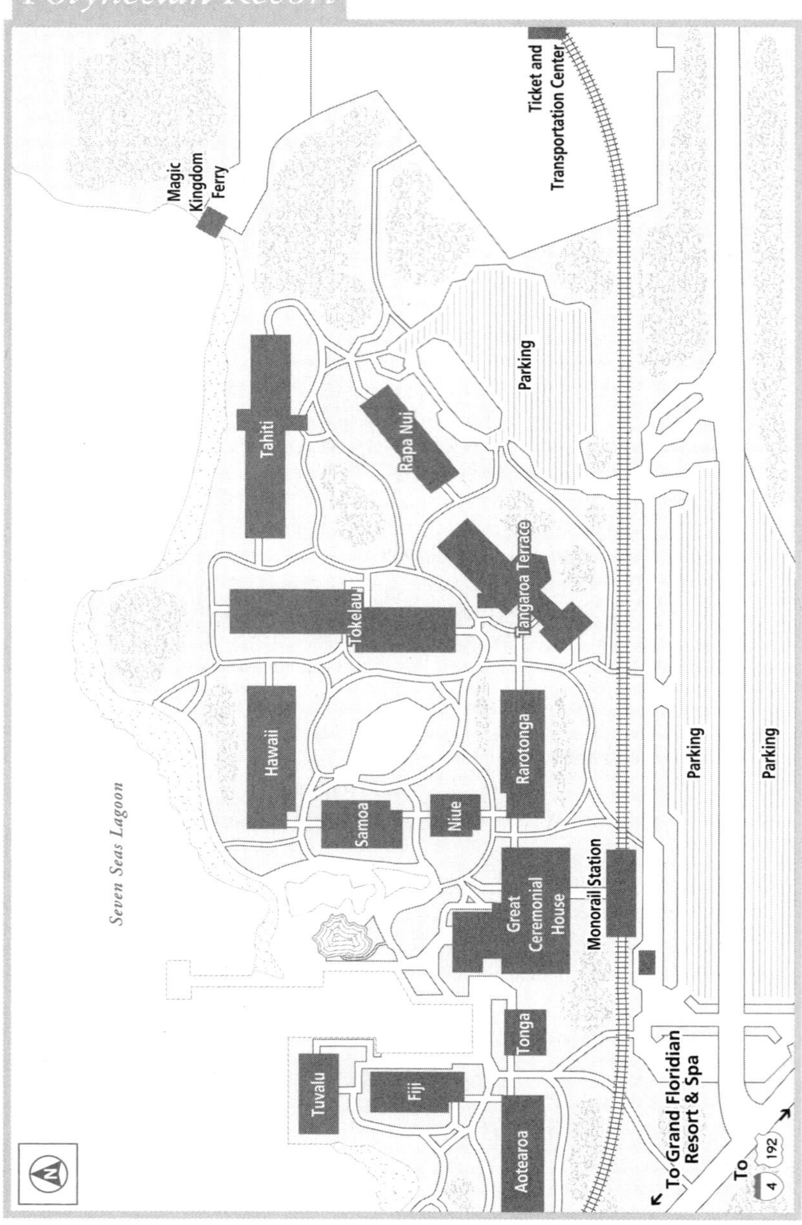

restaurants, shops, and a rain-forest atrium lobby with a rocky waterfall and more than 70 species of tropical plants. Spread across 39 acres along Seven Seas Lagoon, the resort has three white-sand beaches, some with volleyball courts. Its pool complex was completely redesigned in 2001. The Polynesian does not have an on-site fitness center, but its guests are welcome at the Grand Floridian's facility a short quarter-mile walk or two-minute monorail ride away. Landscaping is superb, with periodic refurbishment, so garden-view rooms are generally a cut above garden- or standard-view rooms at other resorts.

Many of the Polynesian's 853 guest rooms offer lagoon views, and many have balconies. Slightly more than half of the Polynesian's rooms measure 415 square feet, a bit more than average for Disney's Deluxe rooms. Of the rest, about 40% (in Tokelau, Rapa Nui, and Tahiti) measure 476 square feet—among the largest standard rooms on Disney property. Most contain two queen-size beds; each has a daybed, a dresser, a table, and one or two chairs. Batik-design bedspreads and curtains continue the island theme and add visual interest.

Although the Polynesian is one of Disney's oldest resorts, periodic refurbishments keep it well maintained. A two-year rehab completed in 2007 brought in new carpet, paint, and soft goods in all rooms. Also added are in-room high-speed Internet access, flat-panel televisions, new furniture and beds, and built-in closets. Plus, Disney seems to be updating the television and closet designs in its Deluxe resorts, and the results are quite good. Each dresser includes two horizontal shelves above and below the TV for extra storage capacity—a big improvement in both form and function over previous designs. Similarly, the new closets are spacious, light, and eminently functional. A nice touch on most of the new furniture and woodwork is the addition of textured surfaces (some of them carved). Lighting throughout the rooms, including the desk/work areas and beds, has been greatly improved and is among the best on Disney property.

Bathrooms are well designed, albeit somewhat small. Shelves above and below sinks allow plenty of storage. Outward-curving shower rods were installed during refurbishment, adding substantial elbowroom to the shower without increasing its size. The idea is such pure genius that you're apt to go looking for one of these shower rods when you get home. (We did!) New light fixtures in the bathrooms have brought a tremendous improvement in usability.

Easily accessible by monorail are full-service restaurants at the Grand Floridian and Contemporary resorts, as well as restaurants in the Magic Kingdom. The Polynesian has a monorail station on-site and is within easy walking distance of the Transportation and Ticket Center. Bus service is available to other Disney destinations. Walking time to the bus- and monorail-loading areas from the most remote rooms is 8 to 11 minutes.

Some readers would not stay anywhere else, as these readers attest. First from a Harrisburg, North Carolina, family of four:

> *The Polynesian Resort was perfect. Would recommend to anyone! Feel like you are in the tropics, not central Florida. Disney Transportation from there was fast, efficient, and easy to use. Monorail perfect for Epcot, Magic Kingdom, Contemporary, and Grand Floridian. Also has direct boat to Magic Kingdom with one stop at Grand Floridian. Buses very convenient.*

And a family from Summerville, South Carolina, agrees, writing:

Polynesian was WONDERFUL. We were in the Tahiti building and could walk to the Transportation and Ticket Center to get on the buses to [Disney's Hollywood Studios] *and Animal Kingdom without getting on the monorail. From now on, we will ONLY stay at the Polynesian. Well worth the extra $. Even had* [a] *fridge in* [the] *room and got* [a] *microwave for free just for asking. Pools were only okay, as they were so crowded midday that there wasn't one empty chair.*

From a Shreveport, Louisiana, mom with three younger children:

We loved our stay at the Polynesian. We were given a room in Fiji overlooking the marina, and it had a lovely view. The room was very quiet, as was the entire resort, in spite of our visiting in late May.

A family of four from Portsmouth, New Hampshire, has this to say:

Loved the Polynesian. Room was clean, and "mousekeeping" was always done before noon. The pool was fun, and having the monorail in the hotel made getting to the Magic Kingdom and Epcot very easy. The bus service to the other parks did seem rather slow, though—we waited 20 to 25 minutes for buses on at least three occasions, and while returning from [Disney's Hollywood Studios] *we just gave up and took a cab.*

From a Cambria, California, mother of three:

Polynesian was great except for the low, low water pressure of the shower. The room was spacious, with two queens and a daybed, but I really wanted a great hot shower after being at the parks all day, and that didn't happen.

A Holliston, Massachusetts, reader advises:

For people who stay at the Polynesian: take your shower in the evening or at night. Early-morning showers were cold, and the water never fully warmed up. Also, the heated pool does not feel heated on cool days.

A family of four from Ashburn, Virginia, found the guest-room soundproofing somewhat lacking:

Quiet factor: Polynesian is borderline-unacceptable. You have to hope your neighbors are not noisy. It's good when the air-conditioning fan is on, but you can't set it to stay on.

Likewise from a Maryland family of four:

Connecting rooms at the Polynesian were noisy. We took towels from the pool and stuffed them under the door to deaden the noise coming from the other room.

GOOD (AND NOT-SO-GOOD) ROOMS AT THE POLYNESIAN RESORT The Polynesian's 11 guest-room buildings, called longhouses, are spread over a long strip of land bordered by the monorail on one side and Seven Seas Lagoon on the other. All the buildings, except for the more recently added Tahiti, Rapa Nui, and Tokelau, were part of the original hotel, which opened with the Magic Kingdom in 1971.

All buildings feature first-floor patios and third-floor balconies. The older buildings, comprising more than half the resort's rooms, have fake balconies on their second floors. (The newer buildings offer full balconies on both the second and third floors, and patios on the first.) A small number of patios in the first-floor rooms have views blocked by mature vegetation, but these patios provide more room than do the balconies on the third floor. If view is important and you're staying in one of the eight older longhouses, ask for a third-floor room.

Within the Great Ceremonial House are most restaurants and shops, as well as the resort lobby, guest services, and bus and monorail stations. Longhouses most convenient to the Great Ceremonial House (Fiji, Tonga suites, Rarotonga, Niue, and Samoa) offer views of the swimming complex, a small marina, or inner gardens. There are no lagoon views except for oblique views from the upper floors of Fiji and Samoa, Aotearoa, and Tokelau, and a tunnel view from Tonga (suites only). Samoa, however, by virtue of its proximity to the main swimming complex, is a good choice for families who plan to spend time at the pool. If your children are under age 8, request a first-floor room on the Nanea Volcano Pool side of Samoa.

You can specifically request a lagoon- or Magic Kingdom–view room at the Polynesian, if you're willing to pay extra. The best of these rooms are on the second and third floors in Tahiti, the third floor in Tuvalu, and, if you're staying in a concierge room, the first and third floors in Hawaii.

There are some quirks in the way Disney categorizes room views at the Polynesian, however, and it's possible to get a view of the castle and fireworks while staying in a garden-view room. Those on the second and third floors in Tokelau (rooms X901 to X913 and X939 to X948) have the best chance of getting sideways views of the castle and fireworks. First-floor rooms (1901 to 1913 and 1939 to 1948) may have landscaping blocking some of the Magic Kingdom view, but the patio provides more room to move to find a better spot, too.

In addition to second-floor rooms in the older buildings (the buildings with fake balconies), also avoid the monorail-side rooms in Rarotonga and the parking-lot side of Rapa Nui. Garden-view rooms in Aotearoa are especially nice, but the monorail, though quiet, runs within spitting distance.

If you plan to spend a lot of time at Epcot, Tahiti and Rapa Nui are within easy walking distance of the Transportation and Ticket Center (TTC) and the Epcot monorail. Even if you're going to the Magic Kingdom, it's a shorter walk from Tahiti and Rapa Nui to the TTC and Magic Kingdom monorail than to the monorail station at the Great Ceremonial House. Tuvalu, Fiji, and Aotearoa are the most distant accommodations from the Polynesian's bus stop. For large strollers or wheelchair access, take the ferry to the Magic Kingdom.

The Polynesian's theme and meticulous landscaping have inspired a legion of fans over the years, including a couple of *Unofficial Guide* researchers who honeymooned there. To see what they're talking about, visit Steve "Tikiman" Seifert's homage to this lush, tropical resort online at **www.tikimanpages.com.**

Disney's Wilderness Lodge and Villas

WILDERNESS LODGE AND VILLAS

STRENGTHS	WEAKNESSES
Magnificently rendered theme	No character meals
The favorite resort of children	Must take boat or bus to get to off-site dining options
Romantic setting, architecture	
Good on-site dining	
Great views from guest rooms	
Extensive recreational options	
Elaborate swimming complex	
Health and fitness center	
Child-care facility on-site	
Convenient self-parking	

This Deluxe resort is inspired by national-park lodges of the early 20th century. The Wilderness Lodge and Villas ranks with Animal Kingdom Lodge as one of the most impressively themed and meticulously detailed Disney resorts. Situated on the shore of Bay Lake, the lodge consists of an eight-story central building flanked by two seven-story guest wings and a wing of studio and one- and two-bedroom condominiums. The hotel features exposed timber columns, log-cabin-style facades, and dormer windows. The grounds are landscaped with evergreen pines and pampas grass. The lobby boasts an 87-foot-tall stone fireplace and two 55-foot Pacific Northwest totem poles. Timber pillars, giant tepee chandeliers, and stone-, wood-, and marble-inlaid floors accentuate the lobby's rustic luxury. Although the resort isn't on vast acreage, it does have a beach and a delightful pool modeled on a mountain stream complete with waterfall and geyser.

The lodge's 864 rooms have darkly stained Mission-style furniture accented by primary colors in the soft goods. The Native American–patterned bedspreads, animal-motif armoires, and faux-calfskin fixtures create a sort of log-cabin coziness. Typical rooms have two queen-size beds, and some have one queen bed and bunk beds. All rooms have a table and chairs and a vanity outside the bathroom. Most rooms have balconies. Guest rooms were refurbished in 2006 with new wall coverings, carpeting, and fixtures.

Part of the Disney Vacation Club time-share program, the adjoining Wilderness Lodge Villas are studio and one- and two-bedroom units in a freestanding building to the right of the lodge. Studios offer kitchenettes; one- and two-bedroom villas come with full kitchens. The lodge's rustic decor extends to the villas, which can be booked by non-DVC members as space allows. The villas share restaurants, pools, and other amenities with Wilderness Lodge.

Service at Wilderness Lodge and Villas is excellent. There are two full-service restaurants, with several more a boat ride away. The resort is connected to the Magic Kingdom by boat and to other Disney

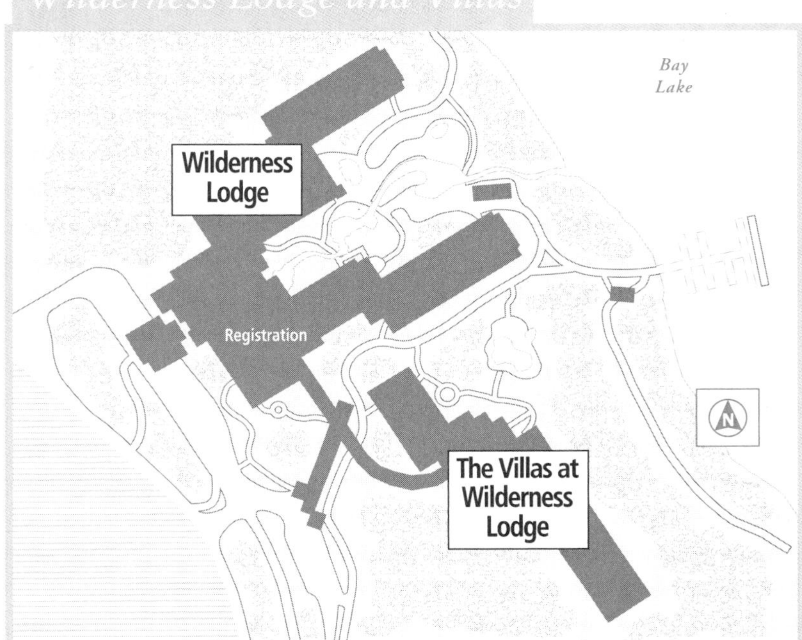

parks by bus. Walking time to bus- and boat-loading areas from the most remote rooms is about five to eight minutes.

A three-generation family from Clifton, Virginia, is high on the Wilderness Lodge, writing:

> *I LOVE going to the Wilderness Lodge and can't recommend it enough to guests. The theming is fabulous, and they're really welcoming to kids. While others might go to Disney for other reasons, if you're looking to go with little kids or because you're a kid at heart, it's worth a visit!*

Two adult couples from Fort Smith, Arkansas, think the Wilderness Lodge is great, with one reservation (pardon the pun):

> *The ambience of the lodge makes up for a lot of the transportation problems, but there has been a real downturn in my opinion in the efficacy of the bus transportation.*

An Atlanta mom also comments on transportation:

> *The only complaint we had was that the Wilderness Lodge bus is shared by the Fort Wilderness Campground. Stopping at both resorts made some of our bus rides extremely long.*

GOOD (AND NOT-SO-GOOD) ROOMS AT WILDERNESS LODGE AND VILLAS
The lodge is shaped like a very blocky *V*. The main entrance and lobby are at the closed end of the *V*. Next are middle wings that connect

the lobby to the parallel end sections, which extend to the open part of the *V*. The *V*'s open end flanks pools and gardens and overlooks Bay Lake directly or obliquely. Avoid rooms on the fourth, fifth, and sixth floors numbered 70 to 99; these overlook the main lobby and pick up every whoop, holler, and shout from the boisterous Whispering Canyon restaurant downstairs. The noise makes it difficult to get to sleep before Whispering Canyon closes, usually at 10 p.m.

The better rooms are on floors 4, 5, and 6 toward the *V*'s open end. On the very end of the *V*, odd- and even-numbered rooms 4000 to 4003, 4166 to 4169, 5000 to 5003, 5166 to 5169, 6000 to 6003, and 6166 to 6169 offer a direct frontal view of the lake. Toward the end of the *V* on the parallel wings, but facing inward, odd-numbered rooms 4005 to 4023, 4147 to 4165, 5005 to 5023, 5147 to 5165, 6005 to 6023, and 6147 to 6165 face the courtyard, but with excellent oblique lake views. Even-numbered rooms 5004 to 5030 and 6004 to 6030 front a woodland northwest of the lodge, and beyond the woodland, the Magic Kingdom. Odd-numbered rooms 5035 to 5041, 5123 to 29, 6035 to 6041, and 6123 to 6129, on the lake end of the parallel middle wings, offer a direct but distant view of the lake, with pools and gardens in the foreground. Rooms looking southeast face the Wilderness Lodge Villas, a garden area, and woods. The map suggests that these rooms offer a lake view, but the trees block the line of sight.

There are only a handful of rooms at the lodge that overlook parking lots, service areas, and such. The rooms listed above afford the most desirable views, but if you can't score one of them, you're pretty much assured of a woodland view or a room fronting the faux rocks and creek in the *V*'s inner courtyard. Concierge rooms on the seventh floor aren't recommended. Only those facing the Magic Kingdom have nice views, and even those have a service area in the foreground. Almost all rooms at the lodge have balconies.

Except for a few rooms overlooking the pool, rooms at Wilderness Villas offer woodland views. The best are odd-numbered rooms 2531 to 2563 and 3531 to 3563, which open to the northeast, or lakeside, of the resort (though you can't see the lake). Rooms on the opposite side of the same wing offer similar views, but with some roads and parking lots visible, and with traffic noise.

Disney's Contemporary Resort and Bay Lake Tower

This Deluxe resort on Bay Lake is the least themed of the Disney-owned properties. The Contemporary is unique in that its A-frame design permits the Magic Kingdom monorail to pass through the structure's cavernous atrium. The only real source of color in the atrium is a 90-foot mosaic depicting Native American children and nature. The off-white central tower is augmented by a three-story Garden Building fronting Bay Lake to the south and by Bay Lake Tower, a new 16-story DDV development, to the north.

Standard rooms in the A-frame afford fantastic views of Bay Lake or the Magic Kingdom, and all have balconies. At 394 square feet each, they're only slightly smaller than equivalent rooms at the

CONTEMPORARY RESORT

STRENGTHS	WEAKNESS
On Magic Kingdom monorail	Sterility of theme and decor in public areas
Ten-minute walk to Magic Kingdom	
Interesting A-frame architecture	
Nicest guest rooms at WDW	
Great views of the Magic Kingdom or Bay Lake	
Children's programs, character meals	
Excellent children's pool	
Marina	
Recreational options, including super games arcade	
Restaurant selection via monorail	
Child-care facility on-site	

Grand Floridian. The Contemporary completed a total renovation of its rooms in 2007.

The renovated rooms are quite stunning and, in our opinion, the nicest of any Disney resort. Perhaps for the first time since the early 1970s, the room decor lives up to the resort's name. Amenities include wall-mounted flat-screen plasma TVs, built-in closets, new soft goods, and high-speed Internet access (including Wi-Fi). Wood accents, in a warm red tone, are a welcome relief from the beige that dominated so many hotel palettes over the past decade. Orange and yellow accent pieces add just the right splash of color. The flat-screen TV is surrounded by a modern interpretation of the traditional family hearth: two expansive curved shelves (perfect for storing small items) serve as the hearth's mantle, while a colorful tiled display underneath simulates the fireplace. Functional, attractive, and clever, it's the furniture equivalent of George Clooney.

A lot of thought went into the bathroom design, too. You enter the bath through a sliding pocket door instead of a traditional hinged model. The pocket door provides plenty of room and makes it easy to move around inside. It's such a great idea, we're surprised that other hotels haven't adopted it. The curved shower-curtain rod (also found in the Polynesian's renovated bathrooms) is inspired. Combined with the pocket door, the bathroom feels much bigger than it is. Another thoughtful touch: a small motion sensor detects when you're up and moving at night, and turns on a dimmed bathroom light to help you find your way.

Bathroom sinks have an avant-garde flat-bottom design. If you can name a single Belgian architect or you own shoes made in Scandinavia, you'll probably love them; other folks think they look like lab equipment. When brushing your teeth, spit directly over the drain; otherwise, the toothpaste glob doesn't move. One minor gripe: you have to scoot around one of the sinks to get in the shower. (We're sure George Clooney has his quirks, too.)

Contemporary Resort

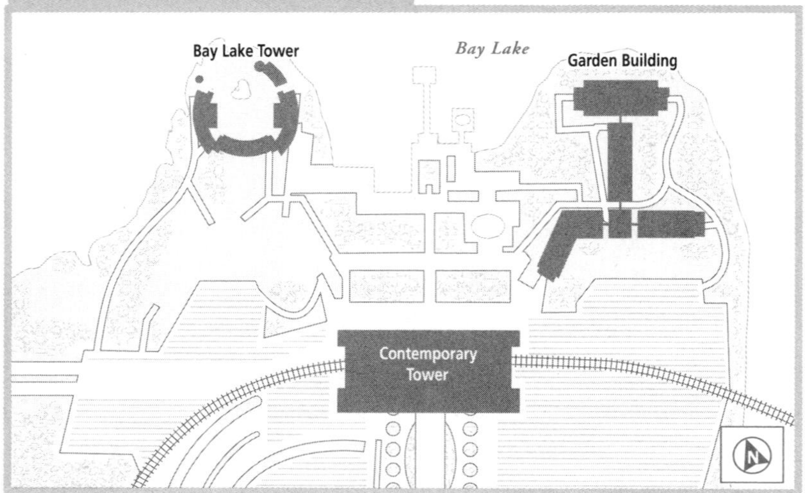

The work area is vastly improved, with ample surface space provided by an *L*-shaped, glass-topped desk; it looks high-tech, but rounded corners perfectly soften the piece. An Internet-connected PC is included. Lighting in the new rooms is superb, with top scores in the bathroom grooming, reading, and work areas. Small, stylish overhead lights are more than ample for reading in bed, assuming you're not exhausted.

The renovations belatedly extend to the bedding, upgrading the old 180-thread count sheets for 250. Down-filled pillows replace Disney's ubiquitous polyester-filled. Sadly, the air-conditioning system was not included in the upgrade, and it's a little noisier than most. If you like to sleep with a bit of white noise in the background, however, you'll be in heaven.

The resort's restaurants have undergone a series of changes culminating in the 2008 opening of The Wave, a 220-seat "health-conscious 21st century" restaurant on the first floor. What does "health-conscious" mean in Disney-speak? You can still get bacon for breakfast, but the coffee it comes with is certified organic and bird-friendly (whatever that means). The Contempo Café, acounter-service restaurant in the lobby, serves upscale sandwiches, salads, and flatbread pizzas throughout the day.

The pool has slides and waterfalls, and the resort has around a half-dozen shops. The Contemporary is within easy walking distance of the Magic Kingdom; monorail transportation is available to both the Magic Kingdom and Epcot. Other destinations can be accessed by bus or boat. Walking time to transportation loading areas from the most remote rooms is six to nine minutes.

While we think the Contemporary is fabulous, an Eden, New

York, couple could've used a little more peace and quiet in their newly renovated room:

We thought the Internet-connected PC was a great feature and used it quite a bit at first, until at 6:13 a.m. the first morning the computer turned itself on with a great bit of noise and fanfare alerting us that we had messages, which were basically ads for various Disney events and resort features. We turned it off only to have it wake back up with more messages ten minutes later. I finally unplugged it from the wall. (Ugh!) The worst part of the Contemporary, though, was the blaring M-I-C-K-E-Y from Chef Mickey's just below our room—the noise started promptly at 8 a.m. and repeated every 30 minutes. Not fun when you're on vacation and want to sleep in.

GOOD (AND NOT-SO-GOOD) ROOMS AT THE CONTEMPORARY RESORT There are two guest-room buildings at the Contemporary: the A-frame tower and the Garden Building. Rooms in the A-frame overlook either Bay Lake and the marina and swimming complex on one side, or the parking lot with Seven Seas Lagoon and the Magic Kingdom in the background on the other. Each guest room has a balcony furnished with two chairs and a table. If you stay on the Magic Kingdom side, ask for a room on the ninth floor or higher. The parking lot and connecting roads are less distracting (and noisy) there. On the Bay Lake side, the view is fine from all floors, though higher floors are preferable.

In the Garden Building, all ground-floor rooms have patios. Only end rooms on the second and third floors facing Bay Lake have full balconies. All other rooms have balconies only a foot deep—fine for standing at the rail but not wide enough to sit outdoors. The Garden Building is a fair walk from the restaurants, shops, front desk, guest services, and monorail station in the A-frame. This isolation, however, is a plus when it comes to the scenery and tranquility offered by some guest rooms.

There's a lot of boat traffic in the lake and canal alongside the Garden Building. Nearest the lake and quietest are rooms 6116 to 6123, 6216 to 6223, and 6316 to 6323. At the water's edge but noisier are rooms 6107 to 6115, 6207 to 6215, and 6307 to 6315. Flanking the canal connecting Bay Lake and Seven Seas Lagoon are rooms 5128 to 5143, 5228 to 5251, and 5328 to 5351. All these have nice canal and lake views, but they're subjected to a lot of noise from passing watercraft.

The Garden Building also has rooms facing the marina, pool, and playground; these work well for families with young children. The view isn't comparable to views from the rooms previously listed, but ground-floor rooms 5110 to 5125 provide easy access to the pool.

In addition to offering some of the most scenic and tranquil guest rooms in Disney World, the Garden Building likewise contains some of the most undesirable ones. Avoid rooms ending with numbers 52 through 70—almost all of these look directly onto a parking lot.

BAY LAKE TOWER Opened in 2009, Bay Lake Tower is a 16-story, 295-unit DDV resort featuring studios and one-, two-, and three-bedroom villas, as well as two-story, three-bedroom Grand Villas with spectacular views of the Magic Kingdom. Laid out in a semicircle, Bay Lake Tower is connected to the Contemporary Resort by an elevated, covered walkway and shares the Contemporary's monorail service.

Rooms at Bay Lake Tower are well appointed, with flat-panel TVs, DVD players, minifridges, microwaves, and coffeemakers. Brightly colored accessories and paintings complement a neutral gray color scheme. Wood tables and granite countertops add a natural touch to the surroundings. Each room features a private balcony or patio.

Studios sleep up to four people and include one queen-size and one full-size bed. Larger rooms have substantially more amenities. One-bedroom villas have two bathrooms; a full kitchen with dishwasher, full-size refrigerator, silverware, plates, and glasses; and a laundry room with washer and dryer. The master bedroom features another flat-screen TV, a king-size bed, and a connected bathroom with glass shower and whirlpool tub. Other sleeping accommodations include a queen-size sofa bed and sleeper chair in the living room.

Two-bedroom villas sleep nine and include all of the kitchen amenities found in a one-bedroom, plus an extra bathroom. One of the baths is attached to a second bedroom with two queen beds. As with the one-bedrooms, a sofa bed and sleeper chair in the living room provide extra places to snooze, though they're best suited to small children (or folks whose backs don't yet cause them problems). Bathrooms in the two-bedroom villas are laid out a bit better than those in the one-bedrooms, with more room to move about. One odd feature in these (also found at other DVC resorts) is a folding door separating the tub from the master bedroom. Nevertheless, we think the two-bedroom villas are the best of Bay Lake Tower's standard offerings.

The two-story Grand Villas sleep 12 and include four bathrooms, the same master-bedroom layout, and two bedrooms with two queen beds apiece. An upstairs seating area overlooking the main floor provides a sleeper sofa and chair. These rooms have two-story windows offering unparalleled views of the Magic Kingdom—and unparalleled prices to match.

Bay Lake Tower has its own pool and pool bar but shares dining, transportation, and recreational activities with the Contemporary Resort.

Shades of Green

This Deluxe resort is owned and operated by the U.S. Armed Forces and is available only to U.S. military personnel (including members of the National Guard and reserves, retired military, and employees of the U.S. Public Health Service and the Department of Defense). Shades of Green consists of one three-story building nestled among three golf courses. Tastefully nondescript, Shades of Green is at the same time pure peace and quiet. There's no beach or lake, but there are several pools, including one shaped like Mickey's head. Surrounding golf courses are open to all Disney guests.

At 455 square feet each, the 586 guest rooms at Shades of Green are larger than those at the Grand Floridian. They're luxuriously decorated in an English-countryside theme, with light-oak furniture, dust ruffles, and soft colors. Most rooms have two queen-size beds, a

SHADES OF GREEN

STRENGTHS	WEAKNESSES
Large guest rooms	No interesting theme
Informality	Limited on-site dining
Quiet setting	Limited bus service
Views of golf course from guest rooms	
Convenient self-parking	
Swimming complex, fitness center	
Video arcade	
Game room with pool tables	
Ice-cream shop	

daybed, and a table and four chairs, as well as a television in an armoire. All rooms have a patio or balcony.

According to a serviceman from Fort Worth, Texas, Shades of Green is the way to go:

> *Shades of Green is the best-kept secret in Disney. It is actually a* [military] *resort in the Disney complex with all the benefits of being a Disney resort. It was a great deal, and military members usually look for the best deals. When my wife and I stayed there in May, we paid $58 a night* [rates range from $96 to $141 depending on rank]. *That is not per person. That was the total price. . . . The rooms were huge. It had two double beds and a lot of room to spare. They also had VCRs in the rooms and a movie-vending machine on the second floor. Shades of Green is right across the street from the Polynesian Resort. It is about a 10- to 15-minute walk to the Transportation and Ticket Center. The hotel does have shuttle buses that take you to the TTC (about a two-minute ride). Our overall stay at Shades of Green was wonderful.*

But a Wilmington, North Carolina, family had a somewhat different experience:

> *We were in the older section of Shades of Green this time, and it was like being at a different, far inferior hotel altogether.* [There was] *NO soundproofing; it felt like the crying kids next door were in our room. The room was far more run-down as well, although still very clean. I guess if we'd never stayed in the new building it might have been fine, but I will always book far enough ahead to get* [the new building] *from now on.*

Even though the resort isn't operated by Disney, service is comparable to that at Disney Deluxe properties. Transportation to all theme parks is by bus, with a transfer required to almost all destinations. Walking time to the bus-loading area from the most remote rooms is about five minutes. The resort is immensely popular; make reservations seven months in advance.

Shades of Green completed a major expansion in 2004. The project added 299 guest rooms, 10 suites, a multilevel parking structure, an Italian restaurant, and a new family-style restaurant. You don't have to worry much about bad rooms at Shades of Green. Except for a small

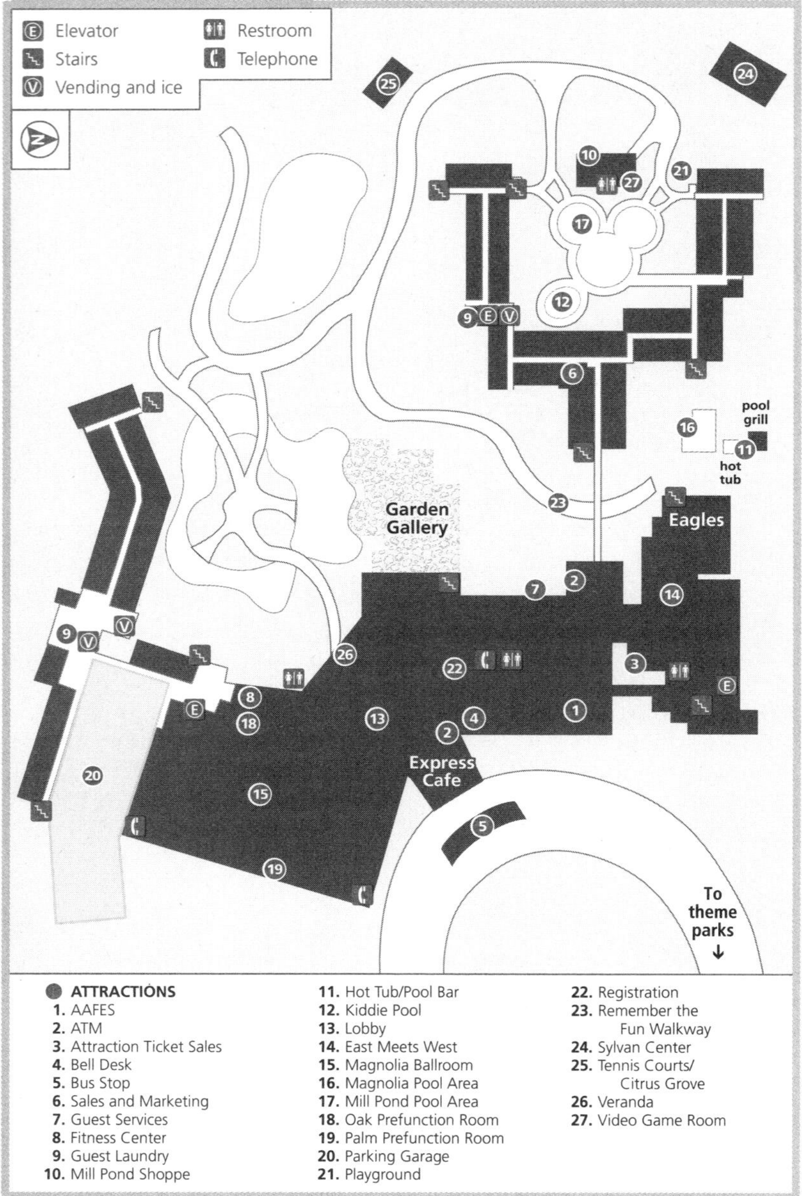

percentage that overlook the entrance road and parking lot, most offer views of the golf courses that surround the hotel, or the swimming area. When you book your reservation, make your preference known. Shades of Green has its own Web site at **www.shadesofgreen.org.**

THE EPCOT RESORTS

THE EPCOT RESORTS ARE ARRAYED around Crescent Lake between Epcot and the Disney's Hollywood Studios (but closer to Epcot). Both theme parks are accessible by boat and on foot. No Epcot resort offers transportation to Epcot's main entrance. As a Greenville, South Carolina, mom reports, this can be a problem:

> *I would like to point out one inconvenience of staying in the Epcot-area resorts. The only transportation to Epcot is by boat or foot. There is no bus available to take you to the front gates of Epcot. We had to walk through the International Gateway and all the way to the front of Epcot to ride Future World attractions. And if we finished Epcot at the end of the day near the front entrance, the only way back home was a long hike through Future World and the International Gateway.*

A reader from Emporia, Kansas, did not let the transportation problem get her down:

> *We had no transportation to the front gate of Epcot for arrival before opening. So we decided to do the early entry at Magic Kingdom (7 a.m.), take in one popular attraction, and then catch the* [monorail] *to Epcot. Worked like a charm. We were at Epcot by 8:20 a.m.*

Disney's Yacht Club and Beach Club Resorts and Villas

YACHT CLUB AND BEACH CLUB RESORTS AND VILLAS

STRENGTHS	WEAKNESSES
Nautical/New England theme	No transportation to Epcot main entrance except by taxi
Attractive guest rooms	No convenient counter-service food
Good on-site dining	Poor room-to-hall soundproofing
Kids' programs, character meals	
Excellent selection of nearby off-site dining	
Boat service to Disney's Hollywood Studios and Epcot	
Ten-minute walk to rear entrance of Epcot	
Ten-minute walk to BoardWalk	
Fifteen-minute walk to Disney's Hollywood Studios	
Best resort swimming complex at WDW	
Health and fitness center	
Convenient self-parking	
View from waterside guest rooms	
Child-care facility on-site	

These adjoining five-story Deluxe resorts are similarly themed. Both have clapboard facades with whitewashed-wood trim. The Yacht Club is painted a subdued gray, while the Beach Club is painted a brighter blue. The Yacht Club has a nautical theme with model ships and antique navigational instruments in public areas. The Beach Club is embellished with beach scenes in foam green and white. Both resorts have themed lobbies, with a giant globe in the Yacht Club's

Disney's Yacht Club and Beach Club Resorts and Villas

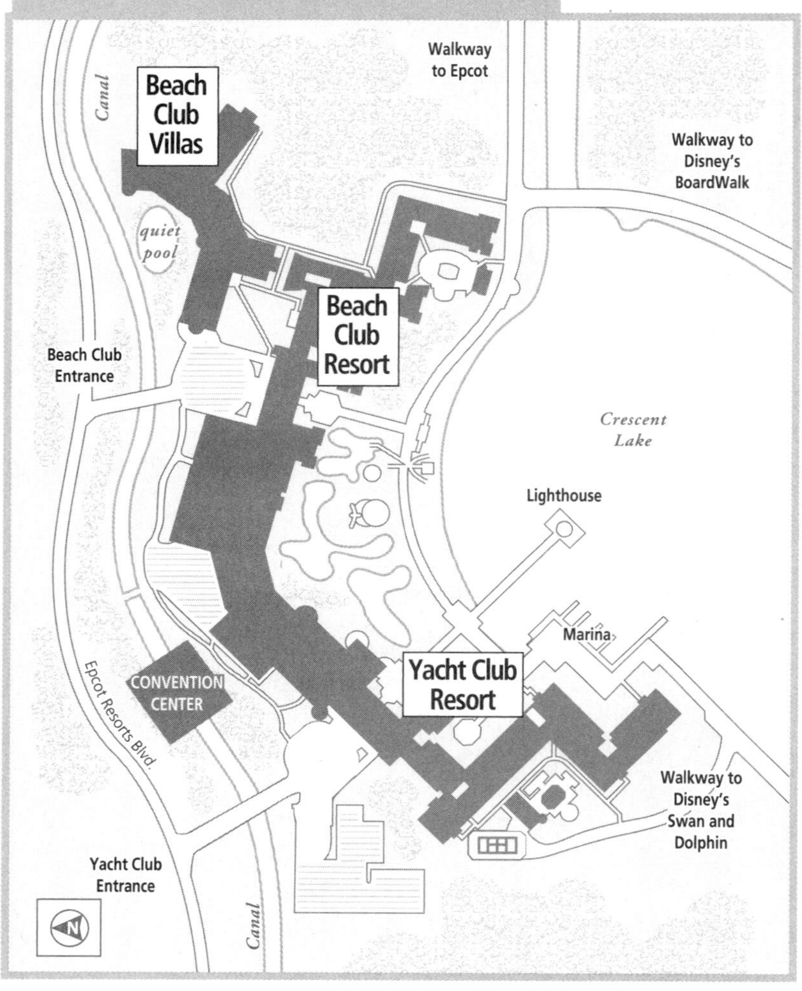

and sea-horse fixtures in the Beach Club's. The resorts face 25-acre Crescent Lake and share an elaborate swimming complex.

There are 621 guest rooms at the Yacht Club, 576 guest rooms at the Beach Club, and 282 studio and one- and two-bedroom villas at the Beach Club Villas, part of the Disney Vacation Club time-share program. Most of the hotel rooms are 381 square feet and have two queen-size beds, a daybed, and a table and two chairs. Like the Grand Floridian's, rooms have a lot of drawer space. Yacht Club rooms are decorated in navy blue and white; Beach Club offers soft green and blue tones. Some rooms have balconies.

The Beach Club Villas evoke seaside Victorian cottages. Studio accommodations offer kitchenettes; one- and two-bedroom villas have full kitchens. Subject to availability, villas are open to the public as well as to Vacation Club (time-share) members. The villas share restaurants, pools, and other amenities with the Yacht and Beach Club Resorts. A small business center serves guests' work needs for both the Yacht and Beach Clubs and Beach Club Villas.

As Disney Deluxe resorts, the Yacht Club and Beach Club provide excellent service. They offer nine restaurants and lounges and are within walking distance of Epcot and Disney's BoardWalk. Transportation to other destinations is by bus or boat. Walking time to the transportation loading areas from the most remote rooms is seven minutes.

Although the Yacht and Beach Club resorts are arrayed along Crescent Lake opposite Disney's BoardWalk, a relatively small percentage of guest rooms actually overlook the lake. Many additional rooms have an oblique view of the lake but face a courtyard or garden. To complicate matters, the resorts don't differentiate between a room with a lake view and one overlooking a swimming pool, pond, or canal. All are considered water views. We receive letters each year from readers complaining that their "water view" was a distant, sidelong peek at a swimming pool. Such disappointments might explain why many readers give the resorts a mediocre C in value.

The Beach Club consists of a long main building with several wings protruding toward Crescent Lake. Looking at the resort from Crescent Lake, the Beach Club adjoins the Yacht on the left and spreads toward Epcot on the right. The main building and the various wings range from three to five stories. Most rooms have balconies, or on the ground floor, patios. Balconies are either big enough for a couple of chairs, or about six inches deep (stand at the rail or sit in a chair inside the room). Top-floor rooms often have enclosed balconies inset into the roof. Unless you're standing, visibility is somewhat limited from these dormer balconies.

We receive a lot of mail about the Yacht Club and Beach Club resorts, most of it positive. First, these remarks from an Ashburn, Virginia, family of four:

Stay at the Beach Club for a touch of elegance without the Grand Floridian prices; the pool complex; and walking to Epcot and the BoardWalk.

From a Wayland, Massachusetts, mother of two:

This was the first time we stayed at the Beach Club, and for us the amazing pool complex was worth the extra money. Several nights we climbed up to the top of the waterslide as the sun was setting, and it was an incredible sight—truly a memorable experience!

A 13-year-old from Long Island, New York, had this to say:

The Beach Club Resort was great because you could enjoy the pool and surroundings by day, then head off to the parks by night—in the hot summertime, this is the best itinerary!

This mom from Brownsville, Texas, however, has some issues with the Beach Club:

The room doors at the Beach Club do not fit very snugly, so any noise from the hall was practically broadcast into our room. The room was close to the elevators, so it sounded like everyone in the hotel was stampeding past our door in the morning. I like the Beach Club very much, but if we go back I'll ask for a more remote room way at the end of the hall.

From a Norman, Oklahoma, mom who visited during the summer:

[Beach Club] *hotel was great, but swimming facilities close at 8 p.m., leaving nothing to do in the evening if you choose not to tour a park at night. For $400+ a day, you'd think the swimming pool would be open at least until sunset!*

GOOD (AND NOT-SO-GOOD) ROOMS AT THE BEACH CLUB RESORT The Beach Club's better views are from rooms with full balconies, and from those that overlook the lake. Other good rooms include those facing woods, with Epcot in the background. The latter are the resort's quietest, most peaceful rooms, in terms of both noise and scenery. They're also nearest to Epcot's International Gateway entrance if you're walking, but farthest from the resort's main pool area, lobby, and restaurants. Of the remaining rooms, most face courtyards, with some of these providing oblique views of the lake, and others overlooking parking lots and the resort's front entrance.

Here are our recommendations for good Beach Club rooms. All room numbers are four digits, with the first digit specifying the floor and the remaining three digits the room number.

Water-view rooms with full balconies facing the lake Odd-numbered rooms: 2641 to 2647, 3501 to 3511, 3683 to 3691, 3725 to 3795, 5607 to 5623, 5683 to 5691, 5725 to 5795. (The Beach Club will charge you for a water-view room if there's so much as a birdbath in sight. If you're going to pay the price, get a real water view.)

Standard-view rooms with full balconies facing the woods and Epcot Even-numbered rooms 3512 to 3536, 4578 to 4598.

GOOD (AND NOT-SO-GOOD) ROOMS AT THE YACHT CLUB RESORT When you look at the Yacht Club from Crescent Lake, the resort is connected to the Beach Club on the right and angles toward the Dolphin hotel on the left. All Yacht Club rooms offer full balconies or, on the ground floor, patios. Rooms with the best views are as follows (the higher the last three digits in the room number, the closer to lobby, main pool area, and restaurants):

Rooms with full balconies directly facing the lake with Disney's BoardWalk in the background Odd-numbered rooms 2003 to 2009, 3003 to 3009, 3057 to 3065, 3161 and 3163, 3201 to 3209, 4057 to 4065, 4161 and 4163, 4201 to 4209, 5161 and 5163, 5201 and 5241.

Rooms directly facing the lake with Epcot in the background Odd-numbered rooms 2011 to 2025, 2067 to 2081, 3011 to 3025, 3067 to 3081, 4067 to 4081, 5171 to 5185.

Some other rooms face the BoardWalk or Epcot across Crescent Lake, but they're inferior to the rooms listed above.

Avoid standard-view rooms at either resort except for rooms 3512 to 3536 and 4578 to 4598 at the Beach Club; these overlook a dense pine thicket. In addition to offering a nice vista for a standard-view rate, these are the closest rooms to Epcot available at any resort on Crescent Lake.

Disney's Beach Club Villas

The Beach Club Villas is a DDV property supposedly inspired by the grand Atlantic seaside homes of the early 20th century. We'll bet the villas don't resemble any seaside home you ever saw. Thematically, there's little to differentiate the Beach Club Villas from the Yacht and Beach Club Resorts, or from the parts of the BoardWalk Inn and Villas that don't front the BoardWalk.

Configured roughly in the shape of a fat *Y* or slingshot, the Beach Club Villas are away from the lake adjoining the front of the Beach Club Resort. Arrayed in connected four- and five-story taffy-blue sections topped with cupolas, the villas are festooned with white woodwork and slat-railed balconies. The effect is clean, breezy, and evocative, though we're not certain of what. Accommodations include studios, with a kitchenette, one queen bed, and a sofa sleeper; and one- and two-bedroom villas with full kitchens. The rooms are a bit small but attractively furnished in pastels with New England–style summer-home furniture. Patterned carpets and seashore-themed art complete the package.

We don't like the Beach Villas as well as the Wilderness Lodge Villas (more visually interesting) or the villas of Old Key West (roomier, more luxurious, more private). Beach Club Villas has its own modest pool but otherwise shares the restaurants, facilities, and transportation options of the adjoining Yacht and Beach Club Resorts. The Beach Club Villas' strengths and weaknesses include all of those listed for the Yacht Club and Beach Club Resorts. Additional strengths at the villas include laundry and kitchen facilities in the one- and two-bedroom units, and self-parking directly adjacent to the building. The villas' one additional weakness is that they offer no lake view.

GOOD (AND NOT-SO-GOOD) ROOMS AT THE BEACH CLUB VILLAS Though the studios and villas are attractive and livable, the location of the Beach Club Villas, between parking lots, roads, and canals, leaves much to be desired. Rooms facing the pool offer a limited view of a small canal but are subject to traffic noise. Ditto the rooms on the northeast side, but they don't face the pool. Only southeast-facing rooms provide both a scenic landscape (woods) and relative relief from traffic noise. The nearby road is only two-lane, and traffic noise probably won't bother you if you're indoors with the balcony door closed, but for the bucks you shell out to stay at the villas, you can find nicer, quieter accommodations elsewhere on Disney property. If you elect to stay at the Beach Club Villas, go for odd-numbered rooms 229 to 251, 329 to 351, 429 to 451, and 529 to 551.

Disney's BoardWalk Inn and BoardWalk Villas

On Crescent Lake across from the Yacht and Beach Club Resorts, the BoardWalk Inn is another of the Walt Disney World Deluxe resorts. The complex is a detailed replica of an early-20th-century Atlantic coast boardwalk. Facades of hotels, diners, and shops create an inviting and exciting waterfront skyline. In reality, the BoardWalk Inn and Villas are a single integrated structure behind the facades. Restaurants and

BOARDWALK INN AND VILLAS RESORT

STRENGTHS	WEAKNESSES
Lively seaside and amusement-pier theme	No restaurants within easy walking distance suitable for young children
Newly refurbished guest rooms	No restaurants in hotel
Ten-minute walk to Epcot rear entrance	Limited children's activities and no character meals
Fifteen-minute walk to Disney's Hollywood Studios	No transportation to Epcot main entrance
Boat service to Disney's Hollywood Studios and Epcot	Distant guest self-parking
Well-themed swimming complex	
Three-minute walk to BoardWalk midway and nightlife	
Good selection of off-site dining within walking distance	
Health and fitness center	
Good views from waterside guest rooms	

shops occupy the boardwalk level, while accommodations rise up to six stories above. Painted bright red and yellow along with weathered pastel greens and blues, the BoardWalk resorts are the only Disney hotels that use neon signage as architectural detail. The complex shares one pool having an old-fashioned amusement-park theme. Refurbished in 2008, the BoardWalk Inn's 372 Deluxe rooms measure 371 square feet each. Most contain two queen-size beds with hardwood headboards, an unpholstered sleeper sofa, a cherry desk and chair, an iPod-capable alarm clock, and ceiling fans. Decor includes yellow-and-white-striped wallpaper and striped green curtains. Closet space exceeds that in other Disney Deluxe rooms. Most rooms have balconies.

The 532 BoardWalk Villas are decorated in warmer tones and primary colors, with bright tiles in the kitchens and bathrooms. Villas range from 412 to 2,491 square feet (studio through three-bedroom), and sleep 4 to 12 people. Many villas have full kitchens, laundry rooms, and whirlpool tubs. The villas tend to be more expensive than similar accommodations at other Disney resorts—you pay for the address.

The inn and villas are well staffed and offer excellent service. They are also home to some of Disney World's finest restaurants and shops. The complex is within walking distance of Epcot and is connected to other destinations by bus and boat. Walking time to transportation loading areas from the most remote rooms is five to six minutes.

Reader comments about the BoardWalk Inn and Villas include the following. From an Iowa City, Iowa, family:

> *We were surprised that so relatively few rooms at the BoardWalk Inn have interesting views. We were in a group staying there before a Disney cruise, and the one couple who actually had a view of the boardwalk said it was noisy.*

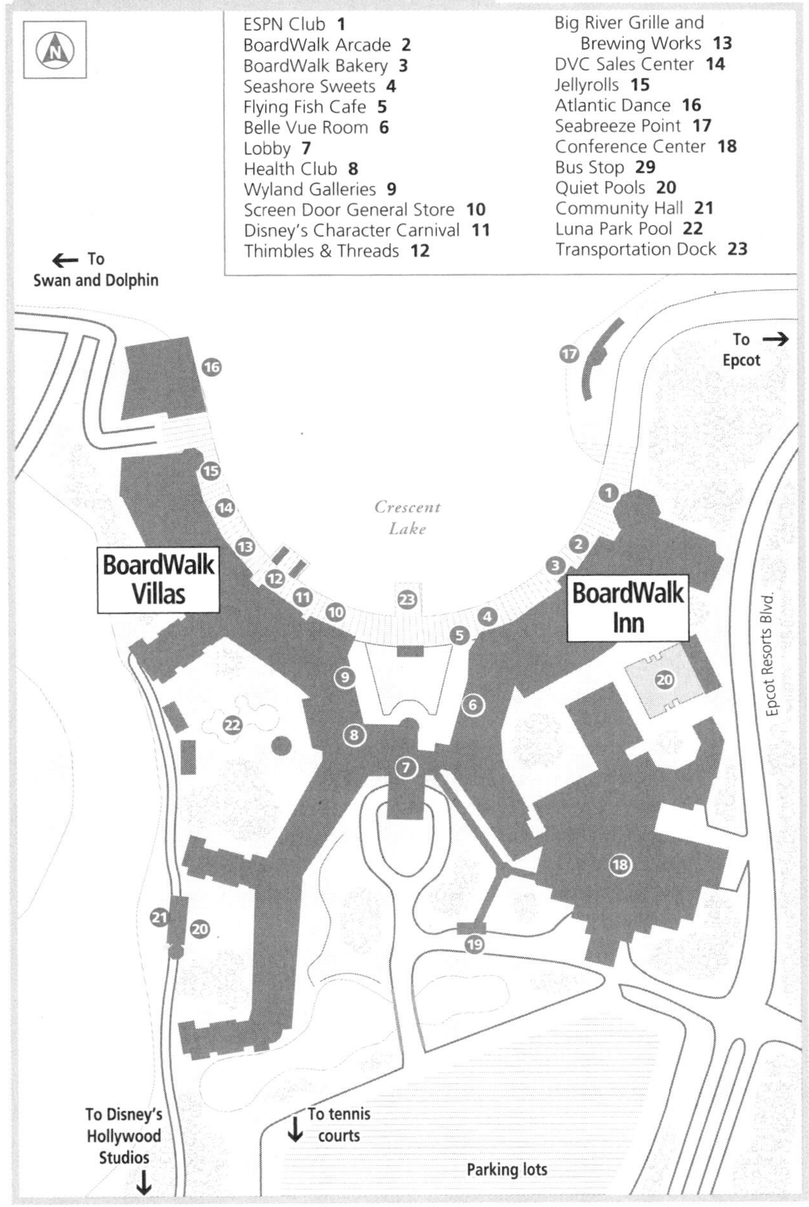
BoardWalk Inn and Villas
ESPN Club 1
BoardWalk Arcade 2
BoardWalk Bakery 3
Seashore Sweets 4
Flying Fish Cafe 5
Belle Vue Room 6
Lobby 7
Health Club 8
Wyland Galleries 9
Screen Door General Store 10
Disney's Character Carnival 11
Thimbles & Threads 12
Big River Grille and Brewing Works 13
DVC Sales Center 14
Jellyrolls 15
Atlantic Dance 16
Seabreeze Point 17
Conference Center 18
Bus Stop 29
Quiet Pools 20
Community Hall 21
Luna Park Pool 22
Transportation Dock 23
To Swan and Dolphin
To Epcot
Crescent Lake
BoardWalk Villas
BoardWalk Inn
Epcot Resorts Blvd.
To Disney's Hollywood Studios
To tennis courts
Parking lots

A number of readers have complained about the bus service at the BoardWalk Inn. This comment is typical:

Regarding the BoardWalk, the transportation by bus (Animal Kingdom and Magic Kingdom) was the worst. We waited at least 40 minutes every time and almost missed a dinner reservation (for which we left 1½ hours early). I also did not like having multiple stops.

GOOD (AND NOT-SO-GOOD) ROOMS AT THE BOARDWALK INN AND VILLAS The complex comprises several wings that radiate from the lobby complex, roughly in the shape of a giant H. Crescent Lake and the Promenade (pedestrian boardwalk) are to the north, the entrance is to the south, and the canal that runs to Disney's Hollywood Studios is to the west. At the BoardWalk, the "water" part of "water view" can mean Crescent Lake, the canal, or a small pool. There are two concierge floors for those wanting extra service.

Most rooms at the inn and villas have a balcony or patio, though balconies on the standard upper-floor rooms alternate between large and medium. The BoardWalk Inn and Villas each share about half the frontage on the Promenade, which overlooks Crescent Lake. The Promenade's clubs, stores, and attractions are spread about equally between the two sections, leading to similar levels of noise and commotion. However, the inn side is closer to Epcot and the nearby access road; this provides better views of Epcot fireworks and easier access to that park, but it also means more road noise.

Otherwise, the inn is actually less noisy than the more expensive villas; there's one tranquil, enclosed courtyard, and another half-enclosed area with a quiet pool (where BoardWalk's Garden Suites are located). There are many rooms to avoid at the inn, starting with rooms overlooking access roads and parking lots, and rooms looking down on the unattractive roof of the adjacent conference center. And although the aforementioned quiet rooms face courtyards, the views are pretty hohum. When you get right down to it, the only rooms with decent views are those fronting the Promenade and lake, specifically, odd-numbered rooms 3213 to 3255 and 4213 to 4255. We're told by Disney insiders that most of these rooms are reserved more than ten months in advance, so snagging one requires advance planning and a lot of luck. As for the others, you're more likely to get a better view at the far less expensive Port Orleans, Caribbean Beach, or Coronado Springs resorts.

The villas are somewhat better. Most overlook a canal to the west with the Swan resort and its access road and parking lots on the far side. Worse are the rooms that front BoardWalk's entrance and car lots. As at the inn, the villas offer only a handful of rooms with good views. Odd-numbered rooms 3001 to 3033, 4001 to 4033, and 5001 to 5033 afford dynamic views of the Promenade and Crescent Lake, with Epcot in the background. They're a little noisy if you open your balcony door but otherwise offer a glimpse of one of Disney World's more happening places. Unless you bag one of these rooms, however, you'll spend a bundle for a very average (or worse) view.

Promenade-facing villa rooms have noise issues identical to their inn counterparts. The midsection of the canal-facing villas look out on Luna Park Pool, a carnival-themed family-pool complex that gets extremely noisy during the day. Some of the quieter villas are away from the Promenade with views of the canal and a partially enclosed quiet pool. Noise is practically nonexistent; the only downside is that the rooms are relatively distant from the Promenade and Epcot. Rooms on the opposite side of this wing are almost as quiet, but they face BoardWalk's parking lot and thus are less desirable.

The Swan and the Dolphin

THE SWAN AND THE DOLPHIN

STRENGTHS	WEAKNESSES
Exotic architecture	Confusing layout
Extremely nice guest rooms	No transportation to Epcot main entrance
Good on-site and nearby dining	Self-parking distant, requires daily fee
Health and fitness center	Resorts do not qualify for Disney's Magical Express service
Excellent beach, swimming complex	
Best WDW resort for business travelers	
Business center	
Child-care facilities on-site	
Children's programs, character meals	
Varied recreational offerings	
View from guest rooms	
Ten-minute walk to BoardWalk nightlife	
Boat service to Disney's Hollywood Studios and Epcot	
Participates in Extra Magic Hours program	

Although these resorts are inside the World and Disney handles their reservations, they're owned by Sheraton (Dolphin) and Westin (Swan) and can be booked directly through their parent companies, too. The resorts face each other on either side of an inlet of Crescent Lake. The Dolphin is a 27-story triangular turquoise building. On its roof are two 56-foot-tall fish balanced with their tails in the air. The Swan has a 12-story main building flanked by two seven-story towers. Two 47-foot-tall swans adorn its roof, staring incredulously at the fish across the way. The Swan and the Dolphin have been described as bizarre and stylistically disjointed. At the very least, they're eclectic in their theming. Disney says you'll step into a "fantasy world." We think the experience is more akin to Art Deco gone haywire. The giant swans look swanlike, but the Dolphin's fish are more like catfish from outer space. The atmosphere at these properties could be described as adventurous or confusing, depending on how much you value the work of a good interior decorator.

The Dolphin's restyled lobby is the more ornate, featuring a rotunda with spokelike corridors branching off to shops, restaurants, and other public areas. At the other end of the spectrum, the Swan's lobby is so small that it seems an afterthought. Both resorts feature art of wildly different styles and eras (from Matisse to Roy Lichtenstein). The Dol-

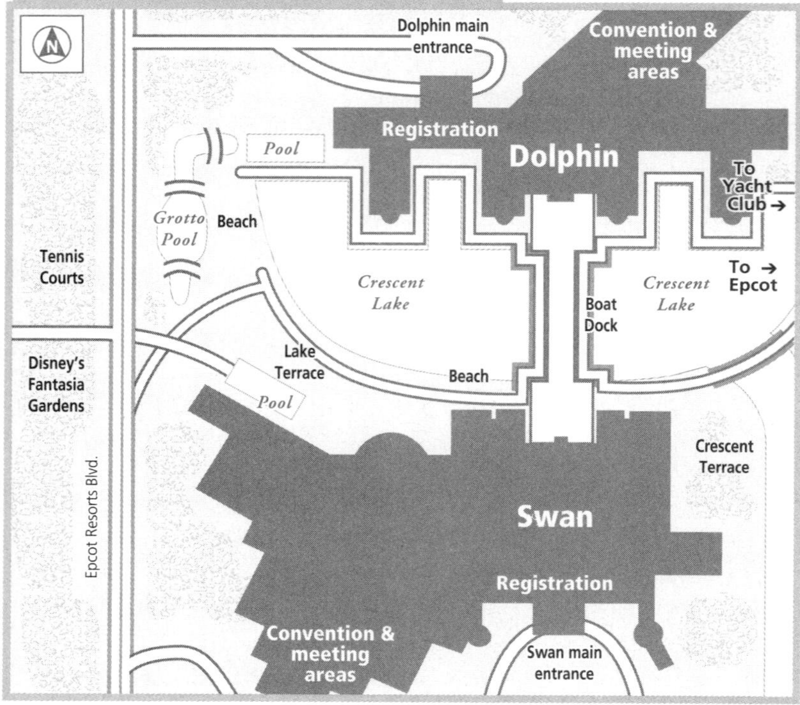

phin's Grotto pool is shaped like a seashell and has a waterfall, while the Swan's pool is a conventional rectangle.

The Dolphin's rooms underwent a complete redesign in 2004 and 2005; soft goods and televisions are being updated as of press time. Where garish decor had characterized (some say branded) the hotel's rooms for years, the current design incorporates light-colored woods, floral earth-tone carpeting, and pastel-blue draperies. The plush "Heavenly Beds" are buttressed by oversize wood headboards adorned with abstract murals. A sleek, contemporary dresser-desk combo and a reading chair complete the furnishings. Some rooms have balconies.

The Swan's guest rooms were redecorated in 2003 and 2004; soft goods and televisions were updated in 2008. The once eye-poppingly bold colors have given way to restful earth-tone pastels and handsome Scandinavian-modern blond bedsteads and dressers. The rooms have great light for reading, in or out of bed. A huge, round mirror framed in blond wood hangs above the dresser. The bath, though small for a Disney World hotel, is elegantly appointed.

Because the Swan and the Dolphin aren't run by Disney, service is less sugar-coated than at other Disney resorts. The two hotels collectively house more than a dozen restaurants and lounges and are within easy walking distance of Epcot and the BoardWalk. They're also connected to other destinations by bus and boat. Walking time from the most remote rooms to the transportation loading areas is seven to nine minutes.

Reader comments about the Swan and Dolphin touch on the same several themes. The following remarks from an El Paso, Texas, reader are representative:

> *I had heard the Swan and Dolphin were pretty much convention hotels, but since I was able to score a really great deal through MouseSavers.com, we gave the Swan a try. There were a lot of businesspeople, but there were a lot of families, too. The swimming-pool setup was super, and our room was beautiful and had a great view looking toward Epcot. Taking the two hotels together, the restaurant selection was the best I've seen in or out of the World. On the downside, both hotels are really spread out, and it was quite a hike from self-parking to the entrance of the Swan.*

GOOD (AND NOT-SO-GOOD) ROOMS AT THE SWAN AND THE DOLPHIN

These sprawling hotels are configured very differently, and their irregular shapes mean it's easier to discuss groups of rooms in relation to exterior landmarks and compass directions rather than by room numbers. When speaking with a Disney reservationist, use our tips to ask for a particular view or area.

THE SWAN East-facing rooms offer prime views, particularly in the upper half of the seven-story wing above the Il Mulino restaurant. From this vantage point, guests overlook a canal and the BoardWalk, with Epcot in the distance. *IllumiNations* fireworks enliven the view nightly. Balcony rooms are available on floors five, six, and seven. However, rooms in the wing nearest the hotel's main section have the southern portion of their view obscured by the building's easternmost portion, which juts east beyond the seven-story wing. There are some east-facing rooms on that portion of the main section, sans balconies. Lofty palm trees obscure the view from east-facing rooms below the fourth floor. The best rooms with an Epcot view are 626 and 726.

North-facing rooms afford views of the Dolphin and (generally) of the courtyard. Exceptions are the north-facing rooms on the easternmost portion of the main section, which look across Crescent Terrace to the BoardWalk. These afford angled views of Epcot and are buffered by palms on the lowest three floors. The few north-facing rooms at the end of the Swan's two eight-story wings directly overlook Crescent Lake. However, the bulk of north-facing rooms are in the main section and overlook the courtyard, with greenery, fountains, and an indoor cafe in its center. Courtyard-facing rooms are subject to noise from below, though never much.

Above the eighth floor, north-facing rooms in the main section overlook roofs of the shorter wings. In these rooms, height enhances the vista from your window, but only near the center of the hotel is the view not seriously marred by rooftops below.

North-facing main-section rooms have a more direct view of the Dolphin across the lake than the courtyard-facing rooms in either eight-story wing. However, most wing rooms can view the lake at an angle. Those on the northern edge of the western wing also view the BoardWalk at an angle.

Most courtyard-facing rooms have balconies; 224 rooms are so equipped, and these balconies offer panoramic 180-degree views. Of course, from most rooms at the Swan, part of any 180-degree view will include another section of the hotel.

The Swan's worst views are from west-facing rooms above the fourth floor, which overlook the unsightly roof of the hotel's western wing. The northernmost rooms in the wing directly above Kimonos restaurant are an exception to this, as their balconies overlook the pool and the beach on Crescent Lake's western shore. Rooms 680 to 691 offer nice pool views.

Above the Swan's main entrance, south-facing rooms overlook the parking lot, with forest and Disney's Hollywood Studios in the distance. However, the canal is also visible to the east. These rooms lack balconies.

THE DOLPHIN Consisting of a central A-frame with large wings jutting off each side and four smaller arms extending from the rear of the building, the Dolphin is attached to a large conference center, which means that the majority of guests are ostensibly there on business. The same amenities found at Disney Deluxe resorts are found at the Dolphin. All parks are accessible from a shuttle stop or a boat dock between the Dolphin and the Swan.

If you want a room with easy access to shopping, dining, and transport to and from the parks, almost any Dolphin room will do. The shuttle (outside the main entrance) and the boat dock are equidistant from the main front and rear exits. Restaurants and shopping are primarily on the first and third floors. If you would also like a view of something other than parking-lot asphalt, your choices narrow considerably. Rooms in the Dolphin with pleasant views are in the four arms on the rear of the building. Rooms on all the arms sport balconies from the first through fourth floors, then offer balconies or windows alternately on floors five through nine.

One of the Dolphin's best views overlooks the Grotto pool on the far west side of the building. A man-made beach with a small waterfall is visible from rooms at the very end of the large west wing. None of these rooms has a balcony, but that might be a blessing, since the pool comes with canned tiki music and a bar. A better bet would be to ask for a room on the far west side of the first rear arm. These outer rooms have balconies and are more removed from the pool. Rooms on the inner, west part of that arm overlook a bladderwort-encrusted reflecting pool; these aren't recommended. Nor are the facing rooms on the next arm.

Between the second and third arms looms the monstrous Dolphin fountain, and the better choices here are on the top two floors. There, from arm two you can see the BoardWalk (including any nighttime fireworks), and from arm three the Grotto pool. Otherwise, you may find you have a view of massive, green-concrete fish scales. The noise from the water is loud, and the fountain geysers continuously. Depending upon your personality, this is either soothing or maddening.

Arm three and arm four are situated around a reflecting pool. A concern for rooms in this area is that the ferry toots its horn every time it approaches and departs the dock. Its path runs right by these rooms, and the horn blows just as it passes. The first time that happens, it's quaint. By the 117th, your hair will be coming out in clumps.

The Crescent Lake side of arm four, and the small jut of the large Dolphin wing perpendicular to it, offer arguably the best views. You have an unobstructed view of the lake and Epcot fireworks, a fine BoardWalk view for people-watching, and, from higher floors, a view of the beach at Beach Club. There's ferry noise, but these rooms still have the most going for them. The best of the best in this arm are rooms 8015, 7015, 5015, 4015, and 3015. Balcony rooms at the Dolphin generally run $30 a day more than rooms without balconies.

Disney's Caribbean Beach Resort

CARIBBEAN BEACH RESORT

STRENGTHS	WEAKNESSES
Attractive Caribbean theme	Large, confusing layout
Children's play areas	Long lines to check in
Convenient self-parking	Lackluster on-site dining
Walking, jogging, biking	No easily accessible off-site dining
Lakefront setting	No character meals
	Extreme distance of many guest rooms from dining and services
	Occasionally poor bus service

The Caribbean Beach Resort occupies 200 acres surrounding a 45-acre lake called Barefoot Bay. This midpriced resort, modeled after resorts in the Caribbean, consists of the registration area ("Custom House") and five two-story "villages" named after Caribbean islands. Each village has its own pool, laundry room, and beach. The Caribbean motif is maintained with red-tile roofs, widow's walks, and wooden railed porches. The atmosphere is cheerful, with buildings painted blue, lime green, and sherbet orange. In addition to the five village pools, the resort's main swimming pool is themed as an old Spanish fort, complete with slides and water cannons.

Most of the 2,112 guest rooms are 314 square feet and contain two double beds and a table and two chairs. Some are decorated with bright tropical colors, while others are decorated with neutral beach tones. All are outfitted with the same light-oak furniture. Rooms don't have balconies, but the access passageways are external and have railings. Many of the rooms are being refurbished and rethemed to include characters from Disney/Pixar's *Finding Nemo*. In addition, rooms in Trinidad South have recently been rethemed to a *Pirates of the Caribbean* motif. These rooms cost about $25 more than comparable ones elsewhere in the resort.

One of the most centrally located resorts, the Caribbean Beach offers transportation to all Disney World destinations by bus. Though

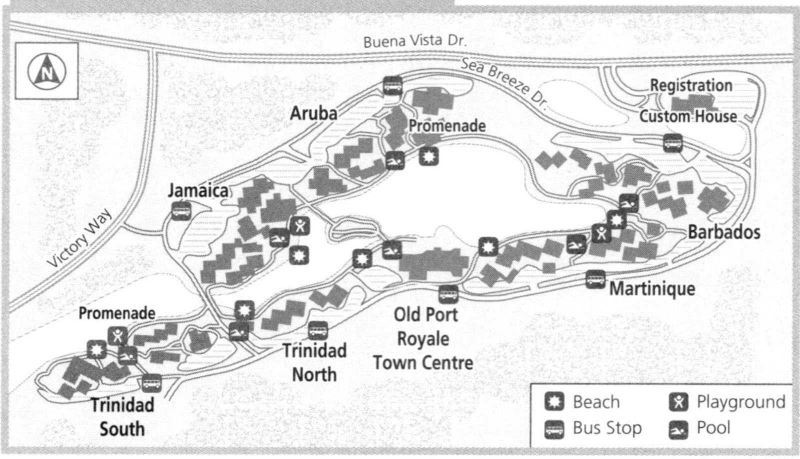

it has one full-service restaurant and a food court, food service is woefully inadequate for a resort of this size. Walking time to the transportation loading area from the most remote rooms is seven to ten minutes, so guests should seriously consider having a car.

Despite these limitations, many readers love the Caribbean Beach, including this family from Westford, Massachusetts:

> *We loved the Caribbean Beach* [Resort]. *We thought the courtyard was lovely, and at night after the kids went to sleep we would sit out on the benches, and it was peaceful and beautiful. After dinner we would walk over to the beach; the kids would play in the sand and on the playground, and we could sit in chairs and hammocks. We went to the big pool in the afternoon and the kids loved it. It was really a wonderful place for families.*

Four wild and crazy guys from Wooster, Ohio, chimed in with this:

> *We think CBR is really underrated. We've had nothing but great experiences there on our stays.*

A Philadelphia dad with two tots in tow liked the Caribbean:

> *The Caribbean Beach Resort was beautiful. Our island (Barbados) was very quiet and relaxing on the courtyard/garden side, but the walk to the bus stop with a child was a bit of a haul. The bus service was also slower than in my past experiences.*

From a Randolph, Massachusetts, family of three:

> *The* Unofficial Guide *really helped us with the decision to stay at Caribbean Beach, and we were pleasantly surprised. Despite the vastness of the resort, everything is relatively close by. The food court, although smaller than other resorts', was outstanding, as was the pool area at Old Port Royale. It was so quiet and serene.*

A family of four from Gretna, Louisiana, disagrees that "everything is relatively close by," writing:

Trinidad South was wonderfully quiet, but our room felt cramped. Would have been much more comfortable if Disney had used fitted bottom sheets or sheet straps so sheets would have stayed on the bed. Extremely annoying every night to wake up because sheets have bunched up beneath one. Also, too far around resort for convenience. To main desk to solve key problems—45-minute round-trip by shuttle. To food court—40 minutes, plus 3-minute walk in rain to and from bus stop.

From a Ridgeway, Virginia, mother of one:

The Caribbean Beach Resort was great—especially the housekeeping staff, who creatively rearranged my daughter's toys every day. Made coming back to the room much more fun. My only complaint with CBR was the inefficiency of checkout—although express checkout was available, someone had to be present to have luggage moved from the room to the main house for transport via Magical Express. We had scheduled a late-afternoon flight on our last day so we could all spend one last morning in the park—I missed most of it because I had to go and sit with the luggage. I was not happy AT ALL.

A mom from Fenton, Michigan, gives the Caribbean high marks except for bus service:

We loved [the] *Caribbean Beach Resort for the most part, but we recommend renting a car and/or paying for a preferred room location—especially if you are going in the hotter months or are impatient. The buses just take way too long with all the stops, and we thought it* [was] *a long hike to the food court* [and] *pools in the heat. Otherwise, it's a great resort. We thought the food court, pools, and landscaping were great.*

A dad from Medina, Ohio, agrees:

After staying at the Caribbean Beach Resort for eight nights, my party and I found out many things that I did not remember when I stayed at the resort eight years ago. For a resort of this size, the transportation is inadequate. Supposedly a bus comes every 20 minutes, but the actual time is every 25 to 30 minutes. The staff for this place is undersized and overwhelmed.

GOOD (AND NOT-SO-GOOD) ROOMS AT THE CARIBBEAN BEACH RESORT The resort's grounds are quite pleasant. Landscaping—lots of ferns and palm trees—is verdant, especially in the courtyards. The six "islands," or groups of buildings clustered around Barefoot Bay, are identical. The two-story motel-style structures are arranged in various ways to face courtyards, pools, the bay, and so forth. The setup is similar to Disney's Coronado Springs Resort in nearly every way but theme.

In general, corner rooms at Caribbean Beach Resort are preferable since they have more windows. Standard-view rooms face either the parking lots or courtyards, and the usual broad interpretation of water views is in play here. Beyond that, your main choices will revolve around your preference for proximity to (or distance from) the Custom House, pools, parking lots, or beaches on Barefoot Bay. Each island has direct access to at least one beach, playground, bus stop, and parking lot.

The island of Barbados is nearest the Custom House, but its central location guarantees that it also experiences the most foot traffic and road noise. It also shares its only beach and playground with Martinique, which probably is the best area for families. (Martinique has access to two beaches, is adjacent to the main pool and playground at the Old Port Royale Town Centre, and yet is removed enough from the Custom House to offer a little serenity for parents.) The islands of Aruba and Jamaica are similar in character to Martinique, but each has only one beach, and guests must cross a footbridge to reach Old Port Royale center. Trinidad North comprises three buildings, and its thin layout means that noise penetrates its courtyard from surrounding roads and from rambunctious kids at Old Port Royale next door. The quietest island is Trinidad South, which is most remote from resort facilities. It has its own playground and beach, and the beach has a bonus—the view across Barefoot Bay is of wild, undeveloped Florida forest, a rarity on Disney property.

After you've sorted out your convenience and location priorities, think about the view. Avoid the standard-view rooms; all look onto a parking lot, road, or tiny garden. Water views at the Caribbean overlook swimming pools or Barefoot Bay. Pool views are less than enchanting, and there's lots of noise and activity around the pools. Bay views are the pick of the litter at the Caribbean. Such rooms in Barbados, Martinique, Trinidad North, and Trinidad South catch the afternoon sun. Bay-view rooms in Aruba and Jamaica catch the morning sun. Because we like the sun at our back in the evening, we always go for rooms 4245 to 4252 in Jamaica or rooms 5253 to 5264 and 5541 to 5548 in Aruba. If you don't mind the sun in your eyes during cocktail time, rooms 2245 to 2256 and 2413 to 2416 in Martinique, 1246 to 1248 in Barbados, and all lake-facing second-story rooms in buildings 35, 38, and 39 in Trinidad South are good bets. We're not crazy about any room in Trinidad North. Be aware that the aging air-conditioning units for individual buildings are pretty loud. One room with an especially nice bay view (2525 in Martinique) is nonetheless not recommended because of its proximity to a clunky air-conditioner.

THE BONNET CREEK RESORTS

Saratoga Springs Resort & Spa–Treehouse Villas

This DDV resort features a theme wordily described by Disney as recalling an "1880s, Victorian, upstate New York lakeside retreat" amid "pastoral landscapes, formal gardens, bubbling springs, and natural surroundings." Saratoga Springs comprises 840 studio and one-, two-, and three-bedroom villas across the lake from Downtown Disney. Housed in 12 buildings, most accommodations are of recent vintage, while the fitness center, check-in building, and spa are retooled vestiges of the erstwhile Disney Institute. An adjacent 60-unit DDV complex, Treehouse Villas at Saratoga Springs Resort & Spa, opened in 2009.

The fitness center is by far the best at Walt Disney World, and in 2007 the spa was named one of the top five resort spas in North America and

SARATOGA SPRINGS RESORT & SPA

STRENGTHS	WEAKNESSES
Extremely nice studio rooms and villas	Traffic congestion at resort's southeast exit
Lushly landscaped setting	Small living areas in villas
Best fitness center at Walt Disney World	Distance of some accommodations from dining and services
Convenient self-parking	Limited dining options
Close to Downtown Disney	No character meals
Best spa at Walt Disney World	Most distant of all Disney resorts from the theme parks
Golf on-property	Theme and atmosphere not very kid-friendly
Hiking, jogging, water recreation	
Excellent themed swimming complex	

the Caribbean by readers of *Condé Nast Traveler* magazine. Surrounded on three sides by golf courses, Saratoga Springs is the only Disney-owned resort that affords direct access to the links (the military-only Shades of Green also provides golf on-property).

The main pool is the resort's focal point. Called High Rock Springs, it tumbles over boulders into a clear, free-form heated pool. The area offers a waterslide that winds among the rocks, two whirlpool spas, and an interactive wet-play area for children. Two quiet pools serve villas far from the main pool. Other recreational features include tennis courts, playgrounds, and paths for jogging, walking, and biking. Disney buses provide transportation to the theme parks. Downtown Disney is accessible by boat, or from some accommodations by foot.

Furnishings and soft goods in the villas and studios are less whimsical and a little more upscale and masculine than in other Disney resorts. Chairs, sofas, and tables are quite substantial, perhaps a little too large for the rooms they inhabit. The overall effect, however, is sophisticated and restful. A Gulf Shores, Alabama, family, however, takes a slight exception to the restful part, writing:

> *Saratoga Springs Resort was beautiful, comfortable, and exactly what we needed for our family of five. It was VERY quiet . . . except for the toilets. When you flushed, it sounded like the space shuttle launching. I was always afraid of what might get sucked down in there from the surrounding room!*

A father of three from Temecula, California, was also sold on Saratoga Springs:

> *We really liked Saratoga Springs. There was so much to do there for the kids between the pool and the community hall that they wanted to skip the parks one day, so we just spent the day at the resort.*

A couple from Peru, Indiana, takes a more critical tack:

> *Saratoga Springs is our least favorite resort. We did not enjoy the theming, and unless you have a car, getting around by the bus system is a real hassle. The food court is very small for the size of*

resort, and the food is expensive for what you get. We were very surprised by the menu items at the food court, which were nothing close to basic foods. Also, the checkout process was very slow, and our room seemed smaller than comparable rooms at BoardWalk [Villas] *and Old Key West. Overall, our stay at Saratoga did not give*

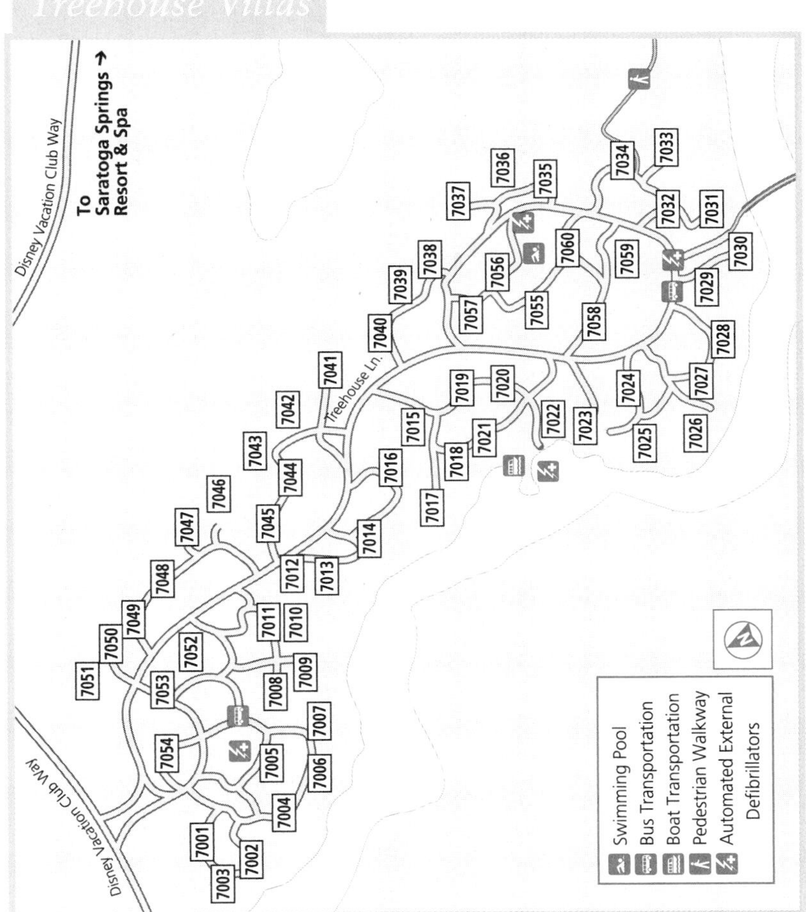

us that Disney feeling we usually experience while staying at other WDW resorts, but rather the feeling we normally get when we stay off-property—like staying at a high-priced apartment complex.

A Cartersville, Georgia, reader echoes the previous complaint about bus service:

No matter what time we attempted to leave a park for Saratoga Springs, there were no buses. Forty-five minutes was the norm. The cab business is booming, which is a shame. We loved Saratoga Springs, but why pay the premium when we ended up driving or taking cabs so as not to waste two to three hours per day?

GOOD (AND NOT-SO-GOOD) ROOMS AT SARATOGA SPRINGS RESORT & SPA
This resort's sprawling size puts some of its best rooms very far away from the main lobby, restaurants, and shops. If you don't have a car, the

best rooms are those in The Springs, numbered 3101 to 3436 and 3501 to 3836. Ask for a room toward the northeast side of these buildings (away from the lobby), as the southwest rooms border a well-traveled road. Avoid rooms 4101 through 4436 in building 14; a pedestrian walkway runs behind the patios of this building and gets a lot of use early in the morning from guests headed to breakfast.

If you've got a car or you don't mind a couple of extra furlongs' walk to the lobby, rooms 1101 to 1436 and 2501 to 2836 in Congress Park offer quietness, a view of Downtown Disney, and a relatively short walk to the bus stop. Also good are rooms 4501 to 4826, 6101 to 6436, and 6501 to 6836 in The Paddock. Avoid rooms on the northeast side of the 5101-to-5435 building of The Paddock, as well as the northwest side of the 5501-to-5836 building; these border a swimming pool and bus stop.

In addition to being quiet, rooms 1101 to 1436 of Congress Park and rooms 6101 to 6436 and 6501 to 6836 of The Paddock afford the closest walks to Downtown Disney shops, restaurants, and entertainment.

TREEHOUSE VILLAS AT SARATOGA SPRINGS RESORT & SPA Opened in 2009, this complex of 60 three-bedroom villas lies between Old Key West and the Grandstand section of Saratoga Springs proper, with a separate entrance off Disney Vacation Club Way. The treehouses are bordered by Saratoga Springs' golf course to the northeast and a waterway to the southwest that feeds into Village Lake.

True to their name, the villas stand on stilts ten feet off the ground (ramps provide wheelchair access) and are surrounded by a densely wooded landscape. Each villa is an eight-sided structure with three bedrooms and two full bathrooms in approximately 1,074 square feet—about the same size as two-bedroom villas at the Wilderness Lodge, Beach Club, and Saratoga Springs but smaller than those at Animal Kingdom, BoardWalk, and Old Key West.

Each villa holds nine people, one more than comparably sized rooms at the other DDV resorts. The master and second bedrooms have queen beds, and the third bedroom has bunk beds. A sofa bed and sleeper chair in the living room round out the mattress lineup. As with other sleeper sofas and chairs, we think these are more appropriate for kids than adults.

Because of their size, the treehouses cost about the same as a two-bedroom villa elsewhere at Saratoga Springs. If you don't mind a bit less wiggle room per person, the extra bedroom might be a good value.

The interior of each villa is decorated with natural materials, such as stone floors in the kitchen, granite countertops, and stained wood furniture. End tables, picture frames, and bunk beds are made from rustic logs. Bathrooms, outfitted in modern tile, have showers and tubs plus a decent amount of counter space.

Because of its location, Treehouse Villas has few amenities of its own: each villa has a large wooden deck with charcoal grill, and all villas share a small central pool with spa. A walking path connects the complex to the main Saratoga Springs grounds, and Treehouse Villas guests can use all of the facilities at Saratoga Springs. Two dedicated bus stops serve the villas.

Treehouses 7024 to 7034 and 7058 to 7060 are closest to one of the villas' two dedicated bus stops and the walkway to Saratoga Springs; 7026 through 7033 also have water views. Treehouses 7001 through 7011 and 7052 through 7054 are closest to the other bus stop. Finally, treehouses 7035 through 7037, 7055, 7056, and 7060 surround the pool.

Disney's Old Key West Resort

OLD KEY WEST RESORT

STRENGTHS	WEAKNESSES
Extremely nice studios and villas	Large, confusing layout
Full kitchens in villas	Substandard bus service
Quiet, lushly landscaped setting	Limited on-site dining
Convenient self-parking	No easily accessible off-site dining
Small, private swimming pools	Extreme distance of many guest rooms from dining and services
Recreation options	
Boat service to Downtown Disney	No character meals

This was the first DDV property. Although the resort is a time-share property, units not being used by owners are rented on a nightly basis. Old Key West is a large aggregation of two- to three-story buildings modeled after Caribbean residences and guesthouses of the Florida Keys. Set subdivision-style around a golf course and along Bonnet Creek, the buildings are arranged in small, neighborhood-like clusters. They feature pastel facades, white trim, and shuttered windows. The registration area is in Conch Flats Community Hall, along with a full-service restaurant, modest fitness center, marina, and sundries shop. Each cluster of accommodations has a quiet pool; a larger pool is at the community hall. (A new waterslide in the shape of a giant sandcastle has been installed at the main pool.)

This resort offers some of the roomiest accommodations at Walt Disney World. Studios are 376 square feet; one-bedroom villas, 942; and two-bedroom villas, 1,333. Studios contain two queen-size beds, a table and two chairs, and an extra vanity outside the bathroom. One-bedroom villas have a king-size bed in the master bedroom, a queen-size sleeper sofa in the living room, a laundry room, and a full kitchen. Two-bedroom villas feature a king-size bed in the master bedroom and two queen beds in the second bedroom. All villas have enough closet space to contain your entire wardrobe. Studios and villas are tastefully decorated with wicker and upholstered furniture and peach and light-green color schemes. Each villa has a private balcony that opens onto a delightfully landscaped private courtyard.

Transportation to other Disney World destinations is by bus. Walking time to transportation loading areas from the most remote rooms is about six minutes.

An Erie, Pennsylvania, reader thinks Old Key West is Walt Disney World's most well-kept secret:

> *We've been coming to WDW for 14 years and have stayed at all the* [DDV] *resorts except the new one at Animal Kingdom* [Lodge]. *Old*

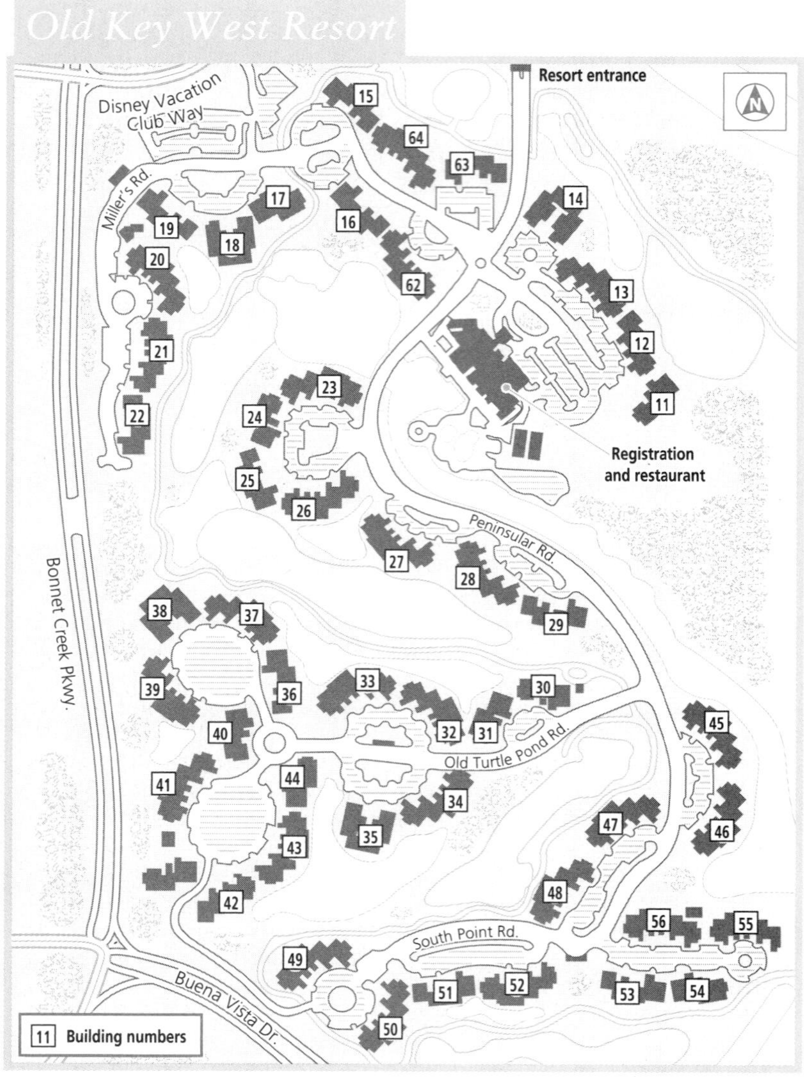

Key West has the most spacious rooms and villas and the easiest access to your car (right outside your door!). It's in a great location and built around a gorgeous golf course. There are a number of small, almost private pools, so you don't have to go to the main pool to swim. You don't hear much about Old Key West, but if you go there you won't want to stay anywhere else.

GOOD (AND NOT-SO-GOOD) ROOMS AT OLD KEY WEST RESORT Old Key West is huge, with 56 three-story villa buildings. Each contains a mix of studio and multiroom villas. Views are nice from almost all villas. To enhance the view, all multiroom villas and some studios have a large balcony furnished with a table and chairs. Though nice vistas are easy to come by, quiet is more elusive. Because the resort is bordered by busy Bonnet Creek Parkway and even busier Buena Vista Drive, the best villas are those as far from the highway noise as possible. For quiet isolation and a lovely river view, ask for building 46 or 45, in that order. For a lake and golf-course view away from road noise but closest to restaurants, recreation, the marina, the main swimming complex, and shopping, ask for building 13. Nearby buildings 12 and 11 are likewise quiet and convenient but offer primarily golf-course views. Next-best choices are buildings 32 and 34. Building 32 looks onto a lake with the golf course in the background, while 34 faces the golf course with tennis courts to the left and a lake to the right. None of the buildings recommended is more than a two- to five-minute walk to the nearest bus stop or pool. Avoid buildings 19 to 22, 38 and 39, 41 and 42, and 49 to 51.

Ground-floor villas make lugging in suitcases and groceries less taxing. Though the top floor requires a three-story climb, views from on high are superior. The top floor also ensures that you'll have no noisy neighbors clomping above you.

Disney's Port Orleans Resort

PORT ORLEANS RESORT

STRENGTHS	WEAKNESSES
Creative swimming areas	Large, confusing layout
Nice guest rooms, especially in French Quarter	Extreme distance of many guest rooms from dining and services
Beautiful landscaping and grounds	Insufficient on-site dining
Pleasant setting along Bonnet Creek	No easily accessible off-site dining
Food courts	No character meals
Convenient self-parking	Congested bus loading areas
Children's play areas	
Varied recreational offerings	
Boat service to Downtown Disney	

In 2001 the Port Orleans and Dixie Landings Resorts were merged. The combined Moderate resort, called Port Orleans, is divided into two sections. The smaller, southern part that previously was Port Orleans is now called the French Quarter. The larger section encompassing the former Dixie Landings is labeled Riverside.

PORT ORLEANS FRENCH QUARTER RESORT The 1,008-room French Quarter section is a sanitized Disney version of New Orleans's Vieux Carré. Consisting of seven three-story guest-room buildings next to the Sassagoula River, the resort suggests what New Orleans would look like if its buildings were painted every year and garbage collectors never went on strike. There are prim pink-and-blue guest buildings with wrought-iron filigree, shuttered windows, and old-fashioned iron lampposts. In keeping with the Crescent City theme, the French Quarter is landscaped with magnolia trees and overgrown vines. The centrally

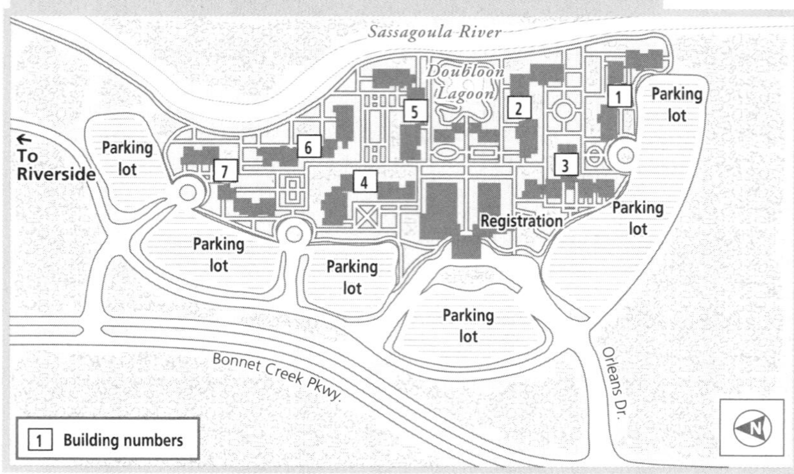

located "Mint" contains the registration area and food court and is a reproduction of a turn-of-the-19th-century building where Mississippi Delta farmers sold their harvests. The registration desk features a vibrant Mardi Gras mural and old-fashioned bank-teller windows. The section's "Doubloon Lagoon" surrounds a colorful fiberglass creation depicting Neptune riding a sea serpent.

French Quarter rooms measure 314 square feet. Most contain two double beds, a table and two chairs, a dresser/credenza, and a vanity outside the bathroom. All rooms were refurbished from bow to stern in 2005, resulting in the most attractive and tasteful rooms of any of the Disney Moderate resorts. With their cherry headboards, Mardi Gras–pastel bedspreads, cherry-wood credenzas with oak inlays, and dark-blue floral carpet, the rooms rival those of several Deluxe resorts. No rooms have balconies, but ornamental, iron-railed accessways on each floor provide a good (though less private) substitute.

There's a food court but no full-service restaurant. The closest full-service eatery is in the adjacent Riverside section of the resort, about a 15-plus-minute walk. The commute to restaurants in other hotels may be 40 to 60 minutes each way. The Disney bus system links the French Quarter to all Disney World destinations. Walking time to bus-loading areas from the most remote French Quarter rooms is seven to ten minutes.

Most readers really like Port Orleans French Quarter. This comment from a Lincoln, Nebraska, family is typical:

> *Port Orleans French Quarter is a real gem. The pool is exceptional for kids, and you can also use the very good pool at Riverside, which is an added bonus. They already have life jackets there for kids and good laundry facilities; shuttle service to parks was pretty good.*

A dad from Danbury, Connecticut, says the secret is out:

[Port Orleans] *French Quarter used to be our little secret. Thanks to greater word of mouth on the Internet, it was much more crowded this trip, which affected the pool, food court, and bus service. The* [food at the] *food court was much improved and was really quite good. We also enjoyed Boatwright's at the Port Orleans Riverside. Very relaxed dining compared to other on-property restaurants, and the new menu was very good.*

This from a mother of two hungry teens:

Port Orleans French Quarter was beautiful! It was very quiet. We had two adults and two teenagers in our room, and we had plenty of room for everyone. We had a refrigerator, which was very handy because we ate breakfast in our room and kept sodas and cold meat and cheese on hand.

A Milford, Connecticut, mom experienced transportation problems:

We had a wonderful time at Disney, but I do wish Port Orleans [French Quarter] *and Riverside didn't share a bus route. After the French Quarter bus stop, there are four stops at Riverside. You always got a seat, but sometimes it took upwards of an hour to get to the parks after waiting for the bus, then stopping at all four Riverside depots.*

One Philadelphia Gen Xer wasn't exactly flushed with joy about his Port Orleans stay:

The in-room toilets seem to be powered by jet thrusters. We were woken up far too many times in the night when someone in a neighboring room would flush.

GOOD (AND NOT-SO-GOOD) ROOMS AT THE PORT ORLEANS FRENCH QUARTER RESORT Seven guest-room buildings flank the pool and Guest Services building and bus stop. The best views are from rooms directly facing the river and natural pine forest on the opposite bank. Wings of buildings 1, 2, 5, 6, and 7 flank the river and provide the best river views in either the French Quarter or Riverside sections of Port Orleans. River-view rooms in buildings 1, 6, and 7 are a long walk from French Quarter public facilities, but they're the most tranquil. Families with children should request river-view rooms in buildings 2 and 5, nearest the swimming complex. Make sure the reservationist understands that you are requesting a room with a river view, not just a water view. All river-view rooms are also water-view rooms, but not vice versa.

Following are the best river-view rooms in each building:

Building 1	Rooms 1127 to 1132, 1227 to 1232, 1327 to 1332
Building 2	Rooms 2127 to 2132, 2227 to 2232, 2327 to 2332
Building 5	Rooms 5117 to 5122, 5217 to 5222, 5317 to 5322
Building 6	Rooms 6123 to 6126, 6223 to 6226, 6323 to 6326, 6133 to 6140, 6233 to 6240, 6333 to 6340, 6141 to 6148, 6241 to 6248, 6341 to 6348
Building 7	Rooms 7141 to 7148, 7241 to 7248, 7341 to 7348

Standard-view rooms look onto a courtyard or a parking lot. There are no private balconies, but you can bring a lawn chair and sit on the exterior accessway. You'll have to make way for fellow guests coming and going to their rooms, but most of the time you'll be undisturbed.

PORT ORLEANS RIVERSIDE RESORT Riverside draws on the lifestyle and architecture of Mississippi River communities in antebellum Louisiana. Spread along the Sassagoula River, which encircles "Ol' Man Island" (the section's main swimming area), Riverside is subdivided into two more themed areas: the "mansion" area, which features plantation-style architecture, and the "bayou" area, with tin-roofed rustic (imitation) wooden buildings. Mansions are three stories tall, while bayou guesthouses are a story shorter. The river-life theme is augmented by groves of azalea and juniper. Riverside's food court houses a working cotton press powered by a 32-foot waterwheel.

Each of Riverside's 2,048 rooms is 314 square feet. Most provide two double beds, a table and two chairs, and two pedestal sinks outside the bathroom. Rooms in the Alligator Bayou section of Riverside feature brass bathroom fixtures, hickory-branch bedposts, trundle beds, and quilted bedspreads. Rooms in the plantation-themed Magnolia Bend section of Riverside are more conventional, with light yellow walls, dark wood furnishings, and teal carpets with dark-blue floral patterns. Room refurbishment is under way throughout Riverside, but the look will be substantially the same as before.

Many readers have written asking us to emphasize that, aside from the differences in guest rooms described above, all the rooms are the more or less the same regardless of the facade of your building. In other words, if your building looks like a mansion, that doesn't mean your guest room will look like it belongs in one.

Riverside has one full-service restaurant and a food court. The restaurant is a 15-minute walk from many of the guest buildings. The Disney bus system links the resort to all Disney World destinations. The commute to restaurants in other hotels may be 40 to 60 minutes each way. Walking time from the most remote rooms to the transportation loading areas is ten minutes.

A multigenerational family from Little Rock, Arkansas, shares the following:

We loved Port Orleans. The cast members were very friendly and helpful—much more so than at the Polynesian. The grounds were absolutely beautiful. The rooms were also very quiet as opposed to the Polynesian's. The only downside about this resort is the shuttle service: it was standing-room-only much of the time, and this was the off-season—we wonder how bad it would be in July! However, we liked the resort so much, we can't wait to stay there again.

From a Des Moines, Iowa, mom:

We are going back to Port Orleans Riverside—it was amazing. I would put it up against the Polynesian any day of the week, having stayed there two times before. I got all my room requests met at Port Orleans, and the building was in a great location!

Finally, from a New York City reader who doesn't think the atmosphere there lives up to its promise:

Port Orleans Riverside Resort

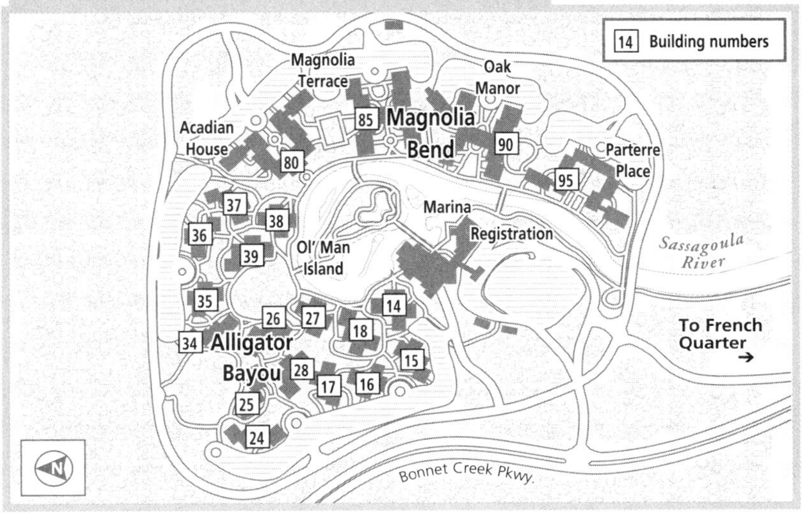

Although the Riverside section (formerly Dixie Landings) is modeled after mansions of the Old South, this will have no bearing on one's stay. The outside decor of each building is simply a "shell" that is irrelevant to your guest room. In other words, there are no interior public areas of these buildings that provide the feeling that you are staying inside a Southern mansion. In fact, there is little or no decor inside your guest room that corresponds to this theme either. (Believe it or not, the official Disney guidebook actually suggests this property as a "romantic" alternative for those who cannot afford the Grand Floridian. Talk about an exaggeration!)

GOOD (AND NOT-SO-GOOD) ROOMS AT THE PORT ORLEANS RIVERSIDE RESORT Riverside is so large that we use bicycles whenever we work there. All told, there are 20 guest-room buildings (not counting flanking wings on two buildings). Divided into two sections, Alligator Bayou and Magnolia Bend, the resort is arrayed around two pine groves and a watercourse that Disney calls the Sassagoula River. Magnolia Bend consists of four three-story, grand-plantation-style complexes named Acadian House, Magnolia Terrace, Oak Manor, and Parterre Place. Though Magnolia Bend is on the river, only about 15% of the guest rooms have an unobstructed view of the water. The vast majority of rooms overlook a courtyard or parking lot. Trees and other vegetation block the view of many rooms actually facing the river. The best views in Magnolia Bend are from the third-floor river side of Acadian House (building 80), which overlooks the river and Ol' Man Island.

To the south are Magnolia Terrace (building 85) and Oak Manor (building 90), each in an H shape. In them, only second- and third-floor rooms on the very top of the H (facing the river) have an unobstructed water view. Ask for rooms 9416, 9417, 9039, 9042, and 9239 to 9242.

Both *H*-shaped buildings, however, are nearer the front desk, restaurant, lounge, and shopping complex than is Acadian House. Continuing south, Parterre Place (building 95) has a number of rooms overlooking the river, but they also overlook the parking lot on the far shore. In general, with the few exceptions described above, if you really want a nice river view, opt for Port Orleans French Quarter downriver.

Alligator Bayou, the other part of Port Orleans Riverside, forms an arch around the resort's northern half. Sixteen smaller, two-story guest-room buildings, set among pine groves and abundant gardens, offer a cozy, tranquil alternative to the more-imposing structures of the Magnolia Bend section of Riverside and Port Orleans French Quarter. If you want a river view, ask for a second-story water-view room in building 27 or 38. Building 14 also offers some river-view rooms and is convenient to shops, the front desk, and the restaurant, but it's in a noisy, high-traffic area. A good compromise building for families is building 18. It's insulated from traffic and noise by landscaping, yet is next to a satellite swimming pool and within an easy walk of the Guest Services building.

Disney's Port Orleans Riverside map shows two lakes north of the river bend, suggesting additional water views in Alligator Bayou. But these are dried-up lakes now forested with pine. This area, however, is richly landscaped to complement the "pine islands," and though out of sight of water, it offers the most peaceful and serene accommodations in the Port Orleans resort. In this area, we recommend buildings 26, 25, and 39, in that order. Note that these buildings are somewhat distant from the resort's central facilities, and there's no adjacent parking. In Alligator Bayou, avoid buildings 15, 16, 17, and 24, all of which are subject to traffic noise from nearby Bonnet Creek Parkway.

Remember: All Port Orleans guest buildings have exterior corridors. When you look out your window, a safety rail will be in the foreground, and other guests will periodically walk past.

THE ANIMAL KINGDOM RESORTS

Animal Kingdom Lodge and Villas

In the far southwest corner of the World and adjacent to Animal Kingdom theme park, Animal Kingdom Lodge opened in 2001. Designed by Peter Dominick of Wilderness Lodge fame, Animal Kingdom Lodge fuses African tribal architecture with the exotic, rugged style of grand East African national-park lodges. Five-story, thatched-roof guest-room wings fan out from a vast central rotunda housing the lobby and featuring a huge mud fireplace. Public areas and about half of the rooms offer panoramic views of a private 33-acre plain, punctuated with streams and elevated *kopje* (rock outcroppings) and populated with some 200 free-roaming animals and 130 birds. Most of the 972 guest rooms measure 344 square feet and boast hand-carved furnishings and richly colored soft goods. Almost all have full balconies.

In 2007, in the first of two phases, Disney converted 134 rooms of the original hotel into DDV accommodations. Disney opened part of the second phase, called Kidani Village, in the spring of 2009, and the remaining portion in late 2009. To avoid the confusion of having to

ANIMAL KINGDOM LODGE AND VILLAS

STRENGTHS	WEAKNESSES
Exotic theme	Remote location
Uniquely appointed guest rooms	
Most rooms have private balconies	
Views of savanna and animals from guest rooms	
Themed swimming area	
Excellent on-site dining, including a buffet	
On-site nature programs and storytelling	
Health and fitness center	
Child-care center on-site	
Proximity to non-Disney restaurants on US 192	

differentiate two separate DDV buildings with "Animal Kingdom Villas" in their names, Disney has christened the units in the original hotel—as well as the building itself—as Jambo House. Thus, if you're staying in a DDV unit at Animal Kingdom Lodge you're at Jambo House, and if you're staying in the new building you're at Kidani Village. The entire complex, classified by Disney as a Deluxe resort, is called Animal Kingdom Lodge and Villas.

Animal Kingdom Lodge–Jambo House offers fine dining in a casual setting at Jiko—The Cooking Place. Twin wood-burning ovens are the focal point of the restaurant, which serves meals inspired by the myriad cuisines of Africa. Boma, the family restaurant, serves a buffet with food prepared in an exhibition kitchen featuring a wood-burning grill and rotisserie. Tables are under thatched roofs. Mara, a quick-service restaurant with extended hours, and Victoria Falls, a delightful mezzanine lounge overlooking Boma, round out the hotel's food-and-beverage service. Other amenities include an elaborate swimming area and a village marketplace. A kids' program called Bush Camp is available on Saturday only, from 1 to 4 p.m. Children ages 6 to 14 can explore African culture through games and crafts. Cost is $70 per child; reservations must be made using a credit card.

Consisting of a separate freestanding building shaped like a backwards 3, Kidani Village comprises 324 units, a dedicated savanna, a new pool, and Sanaa, a sit-down restaurant combining Indian and African cuisines. Other features include a fitness center, an arcade, a gift shop, and tennis, shuffleboard, and basketball courts. Kidani Village is connected to the original hotel by a half-mile walking trail; DDV guests at either resort can use the facilities at both buildings.

Both Jambo House and Kidani Village have studios and one-, two, and three-bedroom villas. Most rooms at Kidani Village are larger, however, and the difference is anywhere from 50 square feet for a studio to more than 200 square feet for a two-bedroom unit. (The three-bedroom Grand Villas at Jambo House, 148 square feet larger

Animal Kingdom Lodge and Villas

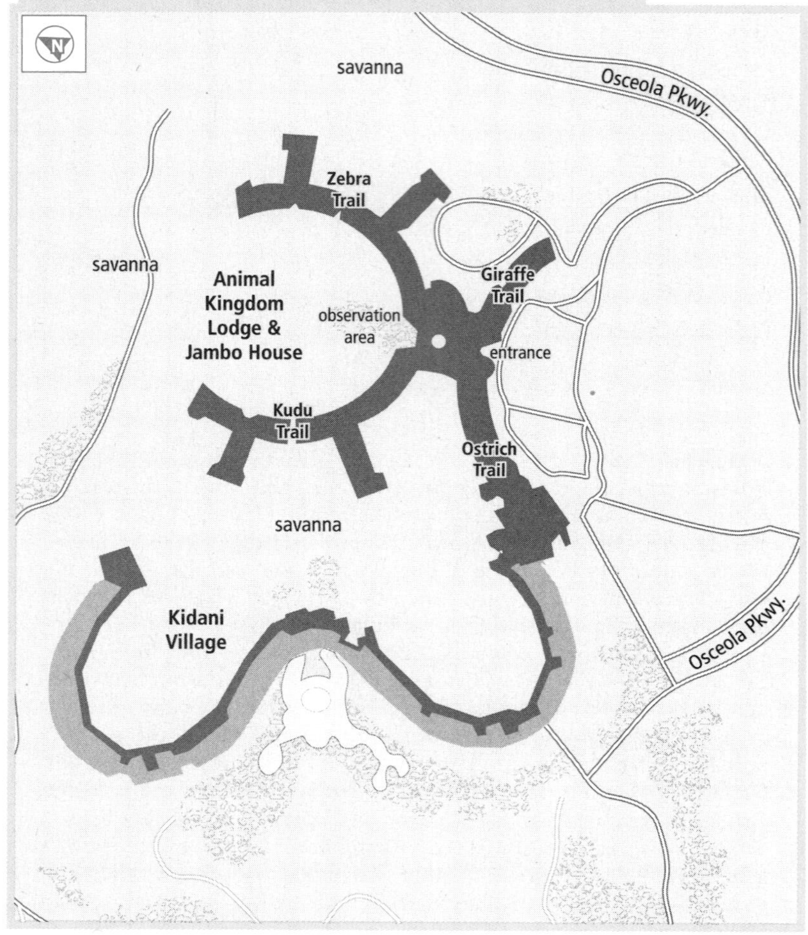

than those in Kidani Village, are the exception.) Because of the difference in area, one-bedroom units in Kidani Village can accommodate up to five people and two-bedroom units can hold up to nine—one more each than corresponding units at Jambo House, through the inclusion of a sleeper chair in the living room.

Animal Kingdom Lodge and Villas is connected to the rest of Disney World by bus, but because of the resort's remote location, you should seriously consider having a car if you stay there.

A family of four from Lincoln, England, gives Animal Kingdom Lodge a mixed, though mostly positive, review:

> *We had a fab holiday, but we would not recommend people paying the extra money to have a savanna room. The animals are scarce, and you don't really spend much time in your room. If you want to*

see the animals, there are plenty of free viewing areas. The pool and the kids' club were fantastic and the hotel stunning. We visited Boma, but my children found the food very different and spicy. The food court was fine, although we wished they'd change the menu as after two weeks you are fed up of the same choices.

From an Owensboro, Kentucky, family:

We had Kilimanjaro Club (concierge-level) privileges at Animal Kingdom Lodge and found them to be a great value. We were willing to pay up to get a savanna-view room, and club level wasn't much more expensive than that. They had a wonderful Continental breakfast in the mornings, snacks all day, and hot hors d'oeuvres in the evening that we ate for our evening meal before going back out. The timing of the food fits well with your suggestions of going to the parks until midday, escaping the crowds at your hotel in the afternoon, and returning to the parks in the evening.

Finally, from a Chandler, Arizona, couple:

Specifically wanted to stay at Animal Kingdom Lodge. We weren't disappointed! Fantastic resort. We loved sitting on our balcony in the afternoon and watching the animals. Found the transportation to be easy and convenient from this location as well.

GOOD (AND NOT-SO-GOOD) ROOMS AT ANIMAL KINGDOM LODGE AND VILLAS A glance at the resort map tells you where the best rooms and villas are. Kudu Trail and Zebra Trail, two wings branching from the rear of Jambo House, form a semicircle around the central wildlife savanna. Along each wing are seven five-story buildings, with accommodations on floors two through five. Five buildings on each wing form the semicircle, while the remaining two building jut away from the center. The best rooms—on floors three and four, facing into the circle—are high enough to survey the entire savanna yet low enough to let you appreciate the ground-level detail of this amazing wildlife exhibit; plus, these rooms offer the easiest access to the the lobby and restaurants. Second-floor rooms really can't take in the panorama, and fifth-floor rooms are a little too high for intimate views of the animals. Most of the fourth-floor rooms in Jambo House are reserved for concierge guests, and the fifth and sixth floors house the DDV units.

Most rooms in the outward-jutting buildings, as well as rooms facing away from the interior, also survey a savanna, but one not as compelling as that of the inner circle. On the Zebra Trail, the first two buildings plus the first jutting building provide savanna views on one side and look onto the swimming complex on the other.

Less attractive still are two smaller wings, Ostrich Trail and Giraffe Trail, branching from either side of the lodge near the main entrance. Some rooms in Ostrich Trail, on the left, overlook a small savanna. Rooms on the opposite side of the same buildings overlook the front entrance. Least desirable is Giraffe Trail, extending from the right side of the lobby. Rooms in this wing overlook either the pool (water view) or the resort entrance (standard view).

The best views in Kidani Village are the north-facing rooms near the bottom and middle of the backwards 3. These overlook the savanna next to the lodge's Kudu Trail rooms and beyond into undeveloped woods. West- and south-facing rooms in the bottom half of the Kidani building overlook the parking lot, while west-facing rooms in the top half have either pool or savanna views.

Disney's Coronado Springs Resort

CORONADO SPRINGS RESORT

STRENGTHS	WEAKNESSES
Nice guest rooms	Insufficient on-site dining
Good view from waterside guest rooms	Extreme distance of many guest rooms from dining and services
Food court	No character meals
Themed swimming area with waterslides	Low-flow showerheads make rinsing off take longer
Fitness center	
Business center	
Convenient self-parking	

Coronado Springs Resort, near Animal Kingdom, is Disney's only midpriced convention property. Inspired by northern Mexico and the American Southwest, the resort is divided into three separately themed areas. The two- and three-story Ranchos call to mind southwestern cattle ranches, while the two- and three-story Cabanas are modeled after Mexican beach resorts. The multistoried Casitas embody elements of Spanish architecture found in Mexico's great cities. The lobby, part of the Casitas, features a mosaic ceiling and tiled floor. The vast resort surrounds a 15-acre lake, and there are three small pools as well as one large swimming complex. The main pool features a reproduction of a Mayan steppe pyramid with a waterfall cascading down its side.

Most of the resort's 1,921 guest rooms measure 314 square feet and contain two double beds, a table and chairs, and a vanity outside the bathroom. Rooms are decorated with sunset colors and feature hand-painted Mexican wall hangings. All have coffeemakers. No room has its own balcony.

Perhaps because it's geared to conventions, getting work done at Coronado Springs is easier than at any other Disney Moderate resort. A specially designed light fixture above the desk holds a halogen bulb and provides excellent illumination of the work area. Wireless Internet access is available in many public spaces throughout the resort, and the business-center staff is friendly and knowledgeable.

Coronado Springs offers one full-service restaurant as well as Disney World's most interesting food court. Unfortunately, there's not nearly enough food service for a resort this large and remote. If you book Coronado Springs, we suggest you have a car to expand your dining options. The resort is connected to other Disney destinations by bus only. Walking time from the most remote rooms to the bus stop is eight to ten minutes.

Coronado Springs Resort

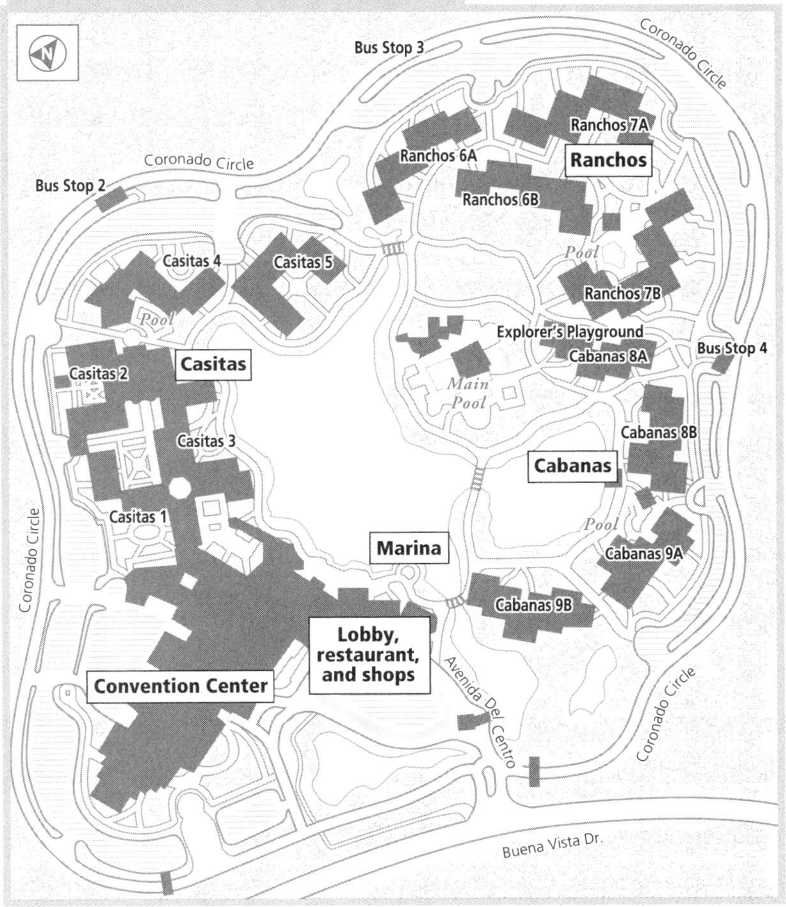

Disney is adding concierge facilities to the resort. Club Level rooms will cost an additional $106 to $126 per night depending on the season.

Reader opinions concerning Coronado Springs are split. A mother and daughter from Kalamazoo, Michigan, write:

> *Coronado Springs is my new favorite Moderate resort—the bus transportation is the best I've seen at any Disney resort, including deluxes. The choices at Pepper Market were excellent, and the resort never seemed crowded, even though it was fully booked.*

But a family from Cumming, Georgia, had a different experience:

> *We stayed two nights at the Coronado Springs Resort, which I would not recommend to anyone. It was more comparable to Pop*

Century than Port Orleans Riverside. The convention center really interferes with a family vacation—everyone we met there was working and wanted to talk about work while we were trying to get away from work! There was no luggage assistance available, and bus service was slow. We will not stay there again.

A mom from St. Catharines, Ontario, says, "Enough walking already!"

This resort was far too big. It was a ten-minute walk to get to the main pool and a ten-minute walk in a different direction to get to the food court. After walking all day at the parks, you don't want to walk that much!

A family from Indianapolis had no complaints about the swimming pools:

The pool at Coronado Springs was excellent—the kids loved the slide! Clean, well attended by lifeguards, not too crowded. Also utilized smaller pool close to our room—was good for kids to relax prior to bedtime.

A longtime reader from Horsham, Pennsylvania, shares this:

I was really disappointed at the rating for Coronado Springs Resort. When I stayed there last summer, I thought it was great. The theme and atmosphere were exceptional. The rooms were very clean, comfortable, and quiet, which is very important to almost every family. The food court was great, and the pool was the best I have ever seen at a resort. Also right by the pool was a great counter-service food court that was great for lunch out by the pool. Lastly, it had beautiful lake set in the middle of the resort that you could take a boat out on or ride a bike around. I would definitely recommend this Moderate resort to anybody. I was very pleased with my stay there.

As a convention hotel, Coronado Springs is peculiar. Unlike most convention hotels, where everything is centrally located with guest rooms in close proximity, rooms at this resort are spread around a huge lake. If you're assigned a room on the opposite side of the lake from the meeting area (and restaurants!), plan on an 11- to 15-minute hike every time you leave your room. If your organization books Coronado Springs for a meeting, consider having your meals catered. The hotel's restaurants simply don't have the capacity during a large convention to accommodate the breakfast rush or to serve a quick lunch between sessions.

GOOD (AND NOT-SO-GOOD) ROOMS AT CORONADO SPRINGS RESORT Coronado Springs encircles a large man-made lake called Lago Dorado. In addition to the main building (El Centro), which contains shopping venues, restaurants, and a conference center, there are three communities of accommodations, each different in appearance and layout. Moving clockwise around the lake, the Casitas are near the lobby, restaurants, shops, and convention center. Standard-view rooms face parking lots or a courtyard. Water-view rooms cover pools, lake, birdbaths, and so on. For a good view of Lago Dorado, try to book one of these rooms:

3220 to 3287 (except 3224, 3230, 3260, 3261, 3265 to 3267, and 3274)
3320 to 3387 (except 3324, 3330, 3360, 3361, 3365 to 3367, and 3374)
3420 to 3487 (except 3424, 3430, 3460, 3461, 3465 to 3467, and 3474)
4230 to 4266
5200 to 5213, 5223 to 5263 (except 5250)
5300 to 5313, 5323 to 5363 (except 5350)
5400 to 5413, 5423 to 5463 (except 5450)

Next in our rotation are the Ranchos, set back from the lake. The desert theme translates to plenty of cactus and gravel, not much water or shade, and almost no good views. Though near the main swimming facility, Ranchos are a hike from everything else. The following rooms afford the best views:

6103, 6203, 6303, 6225, 6226, 6325, 6326, 6245, 6246 (water views);
6600 to 6604, 6610 (water views); 6750 to 6760 (woods views)

Next are the Cabanas, which offer some very nice lake views. Cabana 9B is our favorite, near restaurants and the convention center, and only a moderate walk to the main pool. Rooms with the best views are 9500 to 9507, 9600 to 9611, and 9650 to 9657, with lake views, and 4640 to 4647 and 9640 to 9647, with a view of a small lagoon. Rooms that overlook the lake are subject to some generally tolerable traffic noise.

Other lake-view rooms we recommend include:

8120, 8121, 8124 to 8126, 8128 to 8131, and 8140 to 8147
8500 to 8511, 8550 to 8553, 8571, and 8573
8600 to 8611, 8650 to 8653, 8671, and 8673
9108 to 9110, 9150 to 9153, 9170 to 9173, 9203 to 9210, 9250 to 9253, and 9270 to 9273

As at Port Orleans and the Caribbean Beach Resort, external railed walkways to guest rooms double as balconies. Because there's not a lot of traffic along them, you can pull a chair from your room onto the walkway and enjoy the view. We always bring lawn chairs expressly for "balcony" use when we stay at Coronado Springs.

Disney's All-Star Sports, All-Star Music, and All-Star Movies Resorts

ALL-STAR RESORTS

STRENGTHS	WEAKNESSES
Super-kid-friendly theme	Remote location
Low (for Disney) rates	Small guest rooms (except family suites)
Large swimming pools	No full-service dining
Food courts	Large, confusing layout
Convenient self-parking	Congested bus-loading areas
Close to McDonald's	No character meals
	Limited recreation options

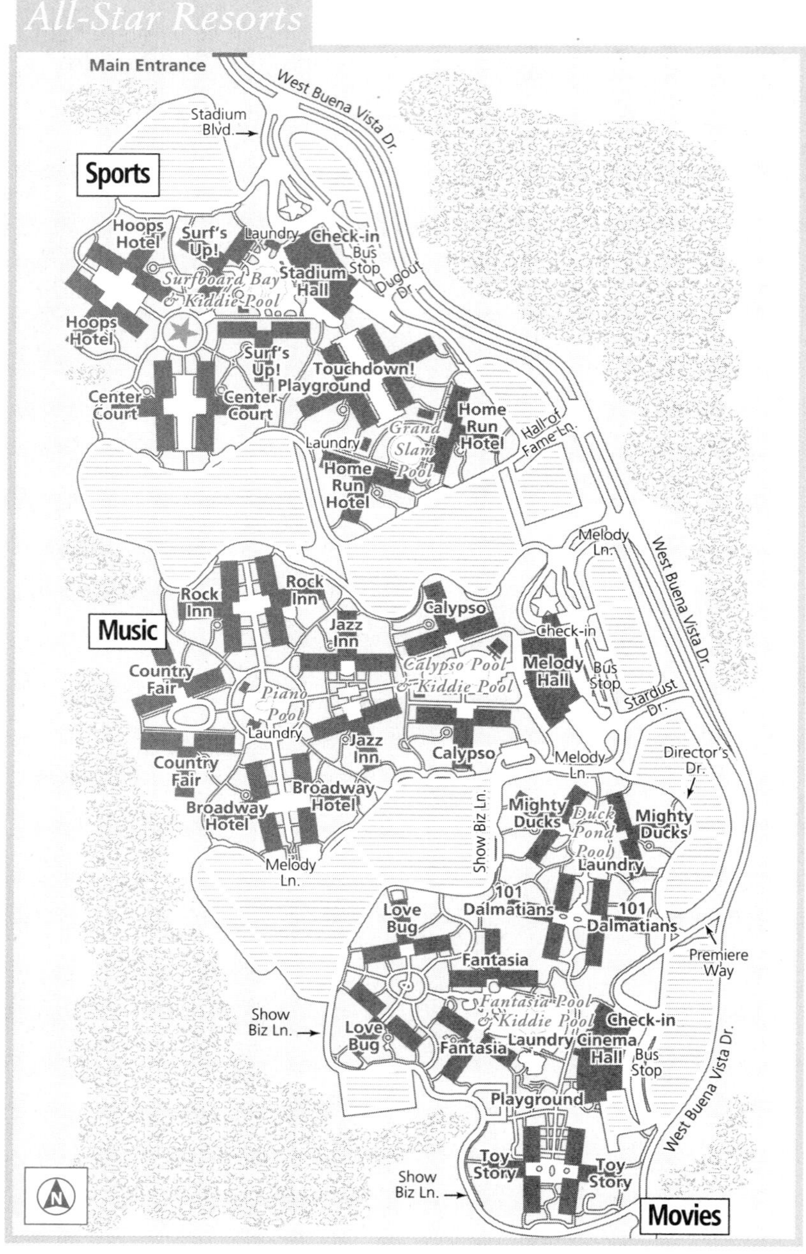

Disney's version of a budget resort features three distinct themes executed in the same hyperbolic style. Spread over a vast expanse, the resorts comprise 30 three-story motel-style guest-room buildings. Although the three resorts are neighbors, each has its own lobby, food court, and registration area. The All-Star Sports Resort features huge sports icons: bright football helmets, tennis rackets, and baseball bats—all taller than the buildings they adorn. Similarly, the All-Star Music Resort features 40-foot guitars, maracas, and saxophones, while the All-Star Movies Resort showcases giant popcorn boxes and icons from Disney films. Lobbies of all are loud (in both decibels and brightness) and cartoonish, with checkerboard walls and photographs of famous athletes, musicians, or film stars. There's even a photo of Mickey Mouse with Alice Cooper. Each resort has two main pools; Music's are shaped like musical instruments (the Piano Pool and the guitar-shaped Calypso Pool), and one of Movies' is star-shaped. All six pools feature plastic replicas of Disney characters, some shooting water pistols.

At 260 square feet, guest rooms at the All-Star Resorts are very small. They're so small that a family of four attempting to stay in one room might redefine "family values" by week's end. Each room has two double beds or one king bed, a separate vanity area, and a table and chairs. The bedspreads feature athletes, movie stars, or musicians; the light fixtures are star shaped. No rooms have balconies.

If you're planning to save for a Disney vacation, you may want to save enough for a bigger room at another resort if space is an important consideration. Also, the All-Stars are the noisiest Disney resorts, though guest rooms are well soundproofed and quiet.

To the rejoicing of parents everywhere, Disney has opened 192 family suites at its All-Star Music Resort. Located in the Jazz and Calypso buildings, these suites measure roughly 520 square feet, slightly larger than the cabins at Fort Wilderness. Each suite, formed from the combination of two formerly separate rooms, includes a kitchenette with mini-refrigerator, microwave, and coffeemaker. Sleeping accommodations include a queen bed in the bedroom, plus a pullout sleeper sofa and two chairs that convert to beds in the family room. We're not sure we'd let adult friends (ones we want to keep, anyway) on the sofa bed or those chair beds, but they're probably fine for children. A hefty door separates the two rooms.

The suites also feature flat-screen televisions in each room, plus two bathrooms—one more than the Fort Wilderness cabins. The suites cost anywhere from 25% to 40% less than the cabins, but they don't have the kitchen space or appliances to prepare anything more than rudimentary meals. If you're trying to save money by eating in your room, the cabins are your best bet. If you just want a little extra space and somewhere to nuke your Pop-Tarts in the morning, go with the All-Star suites.

Reader comments concerning the family suites have been generally positive, though measured. First, a Verona, Kentucky, mother of three:

> *We stayed at an All-Star Music family suite. We have a 15-year-old, a 7-year-old, a 5-year-old, and a 2-year-old. The room was great, but it didn't accommodate us because we needed a "grown-up" room so we could relax after the little kids went to bed. People might want to book two individual rooms instead.*

A mother of three from Clementon, New Jersey, is more enthusiastic:

We tried out the family suites at All-Star Music and loved them! Finally, parents can sleep in a queen bed and have their own room at Disney without breaking the bank. If you don't cook on vacation, the suites work out better than a Fort Wilderness cabin.

With a low staff-to-guest ratio, service is not the greatest. Also, there are no full-service restaurants, and the bus ride from the remote All-Stars to a full-service restaurant at another resort is about 45 minutes each way. There is, however, a McDonald's about a quarter mile away. Bus service to the theme and water parks is pretty efficient. Walking time to the bus stop from the most remote guest rooms is about eight minutes.

We receive a lot of letters commenting on the All-Star Resorts. The following are representative:

From a family group of 13 from East Greenbush, New York:

The All-Star Resorts are perfectly family-oriented. Some nice touches that were not mentioned in your guide—a small amphitheater set up in the lobby to occupy the kids while you check in, and soft sidewalk material surrounding the kiddie pool, which is only about ten inches deep. And the playground has two separate jungle gyms—one for older kids and one for younger kids.

Regardless of your personal preference, if you are going to stay at an All-Star Resort, stay at Sports. The sole reason is that the shuttle buses pick up and drop off at the All-Star Resorts in this order: Sports, Music, Movies. That little difference can mean a lot when traveling with kids or with a group.

An Orland Park, Illinois, family had a tough time with their All-Star neighbors, copying us on a letter to Disney:

I am not a person who usually complains, but I had to write and tell you how extremely disappointed I was with the accommodations we had at the All-Star Sports. I was expecting that a Disney resort would be geared toward families. Boy, was I mistaken! What we mostly had staying with us were young teenagers who were extremely loud and foul-mouthed. We could hardly get any rest. We had groups of people outside our room partying on the football field one night until midnight before someone finally closed them down. Then in the morning (one time as early as 6:30 a.m.), we had cheerleaders practicing right outside our door, shouting their cheers.

A Canadian family had a similar experience:

The guide did not prepare us for the large groups of students who take over the resorts. They are very noisy and very pushy when it comes to getting on buses. Our scariest experience was when we tried getting on a bus and got mobbed by about 100 students. We didn't know if our children would come out alive from the experience. We don't think we would go back to the All-Star Resorts for this reason (they offer packages to student groups). Also, the motel does not want to hear your complaints at all.

From a Massachusetts family of four:

I would never recommend the All-Star for a family. It was like dormitory living. Our room was about one mile from the bus stop, and the room was tiny. I'm in the hotel business, and it was one of the smallest I've been in. You needed to step into the bathroom, shut the door, then step around the toilet that blocked half the tub.

But a Baltimore family had a very positive experience:

We decided early on that we'd rather spend more money on food than lodging. We love to eat and figured that we wouldn't spend that much time in the room, so we picked the All-Star Movies Resort. We were pleasantly surprised. Yes, the rooms are small. But the overall magic there is amazing. The lobby played Disney movies, which is perfect if you get up early and the buses aren't running yet. There are great photo ops everywhere (Donald and Daisy were awesome). It's heaven for fans of Fantasia 2000. *Customer service was impeccable. Everyone seems to bust on the food court, which—let's face it—is crap . . . except for the refrigerator cases, where you can buy fresh-tasting (albeit expensive) fruit, water, healthy snacks, and great chicken-salad sandwiches. Further, despite forewarnings of loud children, we were in the Love Bug building and found it very quiet. The express-checkout service was also a godsend.*

From a 20-something woman from Georgetown, Texas:

We stayed at the All-Star Movies Resort, which was great for us. The room was small, but it was just my sister and me, so we did fine. It didn't have a lot of amenities, but we probably wouldn't have taken advantage of them anyway. The food court was very convenient.

From a North Adams, Massachusetts, dad:

We opted for the [All-Star Music] *Family Suite this trip and were really pleased. The biggest advantage was the two full bathrooms. We were thinking about going to the Fort Wilderness Resort and renting a cabin (for the full kitchen and homey atmosphere), but between having a meal plan and then realizing that there would be two bathrooms in the Family Suite, we decided on that. It was about $300 less expensive* [than Fort Wilderness] *as well.*

From a Skokie, Illinois, family of five:

We found the All-Star Music Family Suite to be very roomy for the six of us. Our teenagers and preteen were quite comfortable on the pull-out sofa, chair, and ottoman. Having the two bathrooms was a must, and the kitchen area was great; lots of shelf space for the food we had delivered from GardenGrocer (they are excellent, by the way) [see page 421]. *Our only complaint about the resort is that from 7:30 a.m. until midnight there is always music playing—it can get annoying to always have that beat going in the background. I did ask them to turn it down once, but that didn't work. The rooms are soundproofed but not enough; had to use earplugs. Also, the housekeeping was terrible. Could not get them to leave regular coffee and enough towels without calling several times. The bus service was very good, though; the*

Music Resort often had its own bus and did not make stops at the other All-Star Resorts. Overall, it was a good experience.

From a young Washington, D.C., couple:

Many rooms at All-Star Movies are closer to All-Star Music for food and shuttle pickups. Knowing this gives you twice as many options for shuttle-bus return trips from the parks.

A mom from Scotch Plains, New Jersey:

I felt the book did not do justice to the All-Star Resorts. Because of the book, my expectations were very *low, but the resort was very good. Although it* [doesn't offer] *four- or five-star hotel service (front desk, housekeeping, etc.), it was excellent and the hotel staff knowledgeable and friendly.*

GOOD (AND NOT-SO-GOOD) ROOMS AT THE ALL-STAR RESORTS Though the layouts of All-Star Resorts' Movies, Music, and Sports sections are different, the buildings are identical three-story, three-winged structures. The *T*-shaped buildings are further grouped into pairs, generally facing each other, and share a common subtheme. For example, there's a *Toy Story* pair in the Movies section. In addition to being named by theme, such as *Fantasia,* buildings are numbered 1 to 10 in each section. Rooms are accessed via a motel-style outdoor walkway, but each building has an elevator.

Parking is plentiful, all in sprawling lots buffering the three sections. A room near a parking lot means easier loading and unloading but also unsightly views of the lot during your stay. The resort offers a luggage service, but it often takes up to an hour for your bags to arrive.

The sure way to avoid a parking-lot vista is to request a room facing a courtyard or pool. The trade-off is noise. The sound of cars starting in the parking lot are no match for shrieking children or hooting teenagers in the pool. But don't count on a good view of the pool, even if your room faces it directly. The buildings' themed facade decorations are placed on their widest face—the top of the *T*—which is also the side facing the pool or courtyard. In some cases, as with the surfboards in the sports section, these significantly obstruct the view from nearby rooms. Floodlights are trained on these facades and if you step out of your room at night to view the action below, looking down may result in temporary blindness.

The sort of traveler you are should dictate the room you request at All-Star Resorts. If you choose the resort because you'd rather spend time and money at the parks, opt to be near the bus stop, your link to the rest of the World. Note that buses leave from the central public buildings of each section, which are near the larger, noisier pools. If you're planning to return to your room for an afternoon nap, request a room farther from the pools. Also consider an upper-story room to minimize foot traffic past your door. On the other hand, if you choose All-Star for its kid-friendly aspects, consider roosting near the action. A bottom-floor room provides easy pool access, and a room looking out on a courtyard or pool allows you to keep an eye on children playing outside.

For travelers without young children (infants excluded), the best bets for privacy and quiet are buildings that overlook the forest behind the resort, buildings 2 to 4 in All-Star Sports and 4 to 7 in All-Star Music. Interior-facing rooms in these buildings (and their partners) also fill the bill, since they overlook courtyards farthest from the large pools. The courtyards vary with theme but are generally only mildly amusing.

If you're traveling with children, opt for a section and building with a theme that appeals to your kids. Often, that will be a film—movies are the lifeblood of the Disney empire—but it might be a sport. If you're staying in Home Run Hotel, don't forget the ball and gloves to maximize the experience (just keep games of catch away from the pool). Older elementary- and middle-school children probably will want to spend hotel time in or near the bigger pools or arcades in nearby halls. Periodically, cadres of teenagers—too cool for their younger siblings—effectively commandeer the smaller secondary pools. Playgrounds are tucked behind building 9 in All-Star Music and behind building 6 in All-Star Sports. Rooms facing these are ideal for families with children too young or timid for the often-chaotic larger pools. In All-Star Movies, the playground is nearer to the food court than to any rooms.

The following tip from a former All-Star Resorts cast member from Fayetteville, Georgia, illustrates just how big these resorts are:

Please tell your readers that rooms at the far end of the Mighty Ducks building of All-Star Movies are closer to All-Star Music food court, pool, and buses than to All-Star Movies' own facilities. Follow the walkway from the Ducks building north to All-Star Music's Melody Hall.

The same reader also mentioned that All-Star Sports guests are usually the first to be picked up on the Disney bus route, even when the same bus services all three All-Star Resorts. During busier times of the year, Sports passengers can completely fill the first bus dispatched, resulting in longer waits at the other All-Star Resorts. Each All-Star Resort generally has its own separate bus for the return trip.

Disney's Pop Century Resort

POP CENTURY RESORT

STRENGTHS	WEAKNESSES
Kid-friendly theme	Small guest rooms
Low (for Disney) rates	No full-service dining
Large swimming pools	Large, confusing layout
Food courts	No character meals
Convenient self-parking	Limited recreation options
Fast check-in	

Located on Victory Way near the ESPN Wide World of Sports Complex, Pop Century is the newest Disney Value resort. It's to be completed in phases, but the first section, scheduled to open in December 2001, was actually opened in early 2004. The second phase, which would complete the planned 5,760 guest rooms, is still in limbo.

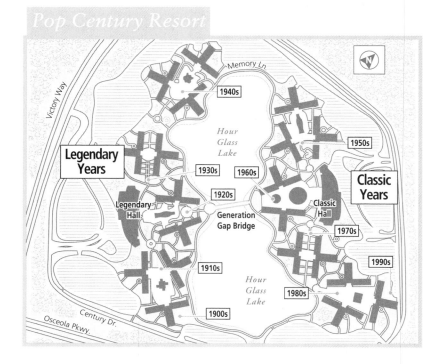

Pop Century Resort

Pop Century is an economy resort; rooms run about $80 to $140 per night. In terms of layout, architecture, and facilities, Pop Century is almost a clone of the All-Star Resorts (that is, four-story, motel-style buildings built around a central pool, food court, and registration area). Decorative touches make the difference. Where the All-Star Resorts display larger-than-life icons from sports, music, and movies, Pop Century draws its icons from decades of the 20th century. Look for such oddities as building-sized Big Wheels, Hula-Hoops, and the like, punctuated by silhouettes of people dancing the decade's fad dance.

The public areas at Pop Century are marginally more sophisticated than the ones at the All-Star Resorts, with 20th-century period furniture and decor rolled up in a saccharine, those-were-the-days theme. Food courts, bars, playgrounds, pools, and so on emulate the All-Star Resorts model in size and location. A Pop Century departure from the All-Star precedent has merchandise retailers thrown in with the fast-food concessions in a combination dining-and-shopping area. This apparently is what happens when a giant corporation tries to combine selling pizza with hawking Goofy hats. (You just know the word *synergy* was used like cheap cologne in those design meetings.) As at the All-Star Resorts, there is no full-service restaurant. The resort is connected to the rest of Walt Disney World by bus, but because of the limited dining options, we recommend having a car.

Guest rooms at Pop Century are small at 260 square feet. The decor is upbeat, with print bedspreads and wall art depicting pop memorabilia from decades past. Light-finish wood-inlaid furniture and dark, patterned carpet provide an upscale touch, but these are not rooms you'd want to spend a lot of time in. Bathrooms are tiny, and counter space is a scarce commodity. Worst of all, we've received many complaints from readers to the effect that the soundproofing between rooms is inadequate. A lake separating the resort's two halves offers water views not available at the All-Star Resorts.

A reader from Dublin, Georgia, thinks we're underrating the Pop Century Resort:

> *I am a Disney fanatic from Georgia. I have stayed in all the resort hotels except BoardWalk and can't believe you don't like Pop Century. It is now my favorite. (1) It is far superior to the All-Stars but the same price. (2) There is a lake at a Value resort and a view of fireworks. (3) The courtyards have Twister games, neat pools, and a Goofy "surprise fountain" for little children. (4) The memorabilia is interesting to us over 18 years old. (5) I love the gift shop, food court, and bar combo. (6) There are frozen Cokes in the refillable-mug section. (7) Bus transportation is better than anywhere else, including Grand Floridian! (8)You can rent surrey bikes. (9) The rooms have real soap instead of the All-Stars' yucky, globby stuff. (10) The layout is more convenient to the food court. (11) I never hear construction noise, and the noise from neighbors is not worse than anywhere else. (12) Where else do the* [cast members] *do the shag to oldies? Also, the shrimp lo mein is the best bargain and among the best food anywhere.*

Don't know what it is about Pop Century fans, but they seem to have a propensity for making lists—take this Waukee, Iowa, family:

> *We loved Pop Century Resort; it was perfect for our family: (1) It was cheap enough that we had plenty of money left over for other fun things at Disney. (2) The shrimp lo mein was one of the most awesome fast-food items we've had at Disney. (3) Although the rooms are a little small and the lighting isn't the best, the resort is affordable enough that without tax two rooms at the Pop Century are in the same price range as one room at other resorts. (4) It's not far from any park at Disney, nor from Downtown Disney. (5) The combo food court–shopping area really works: my grandparents (seniors ages 66 and 64) can eat breakfast in the food court while my brother, sister, parents, and I shop. (6) Food is actually pretty affordable for Disney. (7) Great pools that are not too far from our rooms; plus, there's lots of room so that parents and grandparents can watch the kids swim. (8) You can request a room on the first floor, near the parking lot. They were really accommodating when we explained that I had to have a rather heavy oxygen tank brought to our room, so it would be easier on us to stay on the first floor. (9) Check-in takes probably the least amount of time that I have ever seen at a Disney resort. (We've stayed at Port Orleans French Quarter, Port Orleans Bayou, Caribbean Beach Resort, All-Star Movies, and a hotel outside the World.)*

A young couple from Montreal gives Pop Century a thumbs-up:

> *We stayed at the Pop Century Resort and we absolutely loved it! We don't have children yet, but we became kids ourselves when we saw*

the huge icons representing Disney's characters, like Lady and the Tramp. The food court was great; we always had many choices, at decent prices, especially for breakfast: waffles, pancakes, buns, eggs, fruits. . . . I also found many gifts for my family at the resort's store, which had a large selection of WDW souvenirs.

A group of four adults from Tigard, Oregon, offers this:

We stayed at the Pop Century Resort, and while the rooms were small and noisy, the A/C worked well and the bus transportation was fantastic. We never waited longer than ten minutes for a bus.

But a mom from St. Louis gave the Pop Century a mixed review:

The Pop Century hotel was nice but very crowded. Also, the room was noisy. We stayed in the 1990s complex and could hear loud noise coming from the pool until midnight each night we stayed. Overall, the food court was very good, stocked with lots of different food options. The dining area was clean, with lots of room and vibrant colors. Bus service was great; we rarely waited for a bus to the parks at all. Even despite the loud noises at night, I would stay at the Pop Century again because of the charming decor and fun atmosphere, the convenient large food court, [and] *great bus service to the theme parks. You cannot beat the value.*

From a Kentucky mom of three:

We stayed at All-Star Movies two years ago and had a much better experience than at Pop Century. Even though the rooms are the same size, I think they used even less soundproofing for the Pop Century rooms.

A dad from Ajax, Ontario, offers this:

I was pleased with Pop overall, but the smaller room (compared to, say, Port Orleans or Coronado) makes a BIG difference—particularly if you have children.

A multigenerational family from Chambersburg, Pennsylvania, liked Pop Century, with one exception:

Because we were traveling with our grandson, we thought staying at Pop Century would be a fun place for him, with the larger-than-life icons and bright colors. I thought the resort was a good value and comfortable, and the rooms were large enough. I had heard that the soundproofing wasn't very good, but I didn't think it was too bad. The pools were great. The worst thing about the trip was the food court—crowds and rude guests were the problems. After a hot day and crowds in the parks, you came back to grab something to eat and found yourself being jostled by the crowd. And the crowds made it impossible for the cast members to keep the tables and drink area anywhere near clean.

A dad from Tonawanda, New York, agrees about the dining:

The Pop Century food court after park closing is an absolute zoo. If you can, avoid eating a late counter-service dinner here and get one in the parks.

Likewise, from a Kentucky family of four:

The Pop Century food court seemed to run out of ice early in the evening, and they'd shut down drink dispensers early. There were still lots of people up late coming back from the parks, and it created huge bottlenecks for drinks.

A Granite Falls, North Carolina, couple isn't sweating the small stuff, though:

On this trip, we stayed at Pop Century, which gets a lot of criticism at certain planning Web sites. This was our third stay there, and while it is small and not as comfortable as the Polynesian (or any other Deluxe hotel), it provides us with a clean place to sleep at night and transportation to the parks, and the price allows us to visit WDW every year!

This comment from a Springfield, Massachusetts, family of four:

Pop Century Resort was outstanding! We stayed in the 1950s building with an Epcot view. This had to be the best-value room in all of Walt Disney World. For the off-season AAA discount rate of $64.99 per night, we were able to watch the IllumiNations *fireworks from our hotel room with Spaceship Earth in the background!*

And, finally, a reader named Melanie (who didn't mention where she was from) had the following experience:

We decided to stay at the Pop Century. I called them directly to ask a few questions so I would be prepared when I called Disney reservations. I told the person who answered that I had heard the hotel was noisy. She said, "The hotel is not noisy, just the kids who stay here." HA!

GOOD (AND NOT-SO-GOOD) ROOMS AT THE POP CENTURY RESORT Guest rooms don't have private patios or balconies. If you bring a lawn chair, however, you can sit on the railed walkway that serves as the guest-room access corridor on each floor. The best rooms for both view and convenience are the lake-view rooms in buildings 4 and 5, representing the 1960s. These rooms are subject to highway noise from Victory Way and Osceola Parkway across the lake. If work resumes on the other half of Pop Century, these rooms will also contend with the sights and noise of construction. A safer short-term bet, though with a less compelling view, would be east-facing rooms in the same building, that is, rooms facing the registration and food-court building. Next-best choices would be the east-facing rooms of building 3 in the 1950s, and of building 6 in the 1970s. Avoid south-facing rooms in 1980s building 7 and 1990s building 8. Both are echo chambers for noise from nearby Osceola Parkway.

INDEPENDENT HOTELS OF THE DOWNTOWN DISNEY RESORT AREA

THE SEVEN HOTELS OF THE DOWNTOWN DISNEY RESORT AREA (DDRA) were created in the days when Disney had far fewer of its own resorts. The hotels—the Holiday Inn at Walt Disney World, Doubletree Guest Suites, Regal Sun Resort, Hilton, Royal Plaza, Best Western Lake Buena Vista Resort Hotel, and Buena Vista Palace Hotel & Spa—

AMENITIES AT DOWNTOWN DISNEY RESORT AREA HOTELS

NAME	CHILDREN'S PROGRAMS	DINING	KID-FRIENDLY	POOL(S)	RECREATION
Best Western LBV Resort	–	★★½	★★★	★★½	★★
Buena Vista Palace	★★★★	★★★★	★★★½	★★★½	★★★★
Doubletree Guest Suites	–	★★	★★★	★★½	★★½
Hilton WDW	–	★★½	★★½	★★★	★★½
Holiday Inn at WDW	*N/A for all—hotel is being extensively refurbished.*				
Regal Sun Resort	★★½	★★½	★★★	★★★	★★★
Royal Plaza	★★½	★★	★★½	★★½	★★★

are chain-style hotels with minimal or nonexistent theming, though the Buena Vista Palace, especially, is pretty upscale. All were hit hard by the tourism slump in recent years, and several of the larger properties shifted their focus to convention and business travelers. Now that Disney has trouble filling its own massive inventory of rooms, DDRA properties are struggling to refurbish or re-create themselves while clinging tenaciously to the Disney World connection.

The main advantage to staying in the DDRA is being in Disney World and proximal to Downtown Disney. Guests at the Hilton, Regal Sun Resort, Buena Vista Palace, and Holiday Inn at Walt Disney World are an easy 5- to 15-minute walk from Disney Marketplace on the east side of Downtown Disney. Guests at the Royal Plaza, Best Western Lake Buena Vista Resort Hotel, or Doubletree Guest Suites are about ten minutes farther by foot. Disney transportation can be accessed at Downtown Disney, though the Disney buses take a notoriously long time to leave due to the number of stops throughout the shopping and entertainment complex. Although all DDRA hotels offer shuttle buses to the theme parks, the service is provided by private contractors and is somewhat inferior to Disney Transportation in frequency of service, number of buses, and hours of operation. Get firm details in advance about shuttle service from any DDRA hotel you're considering. All these hotels are easily accessible by car and are only marginally farther from the Disney parks than several of the Disney resorts (and DDRA hotels are quite close to Typhoon Lagoon water park).

All DDRA hotels try to appeal to families, even the business and meeting hotels. Some have pool complexes that rival those at any Disney resort, whereas others offer a food court or all-suite rooms. A few sponsor Disney character meals and organized children's activities; all have counters for buying Disney tickets, and most have Disney gift shops. In addition, we've seen some real room deals in the DDRA, especially off-season. To help you decide if the DDRA is right for you, here are descriptions. Also take a peek at the combined Web site for the DDRA hotels at **www.downtowndisneyhotels.com.** Finally, check the comparative chart on the previous page.

Best Western Lake Buena Vista Resort Hotel ★★★★

THE 18-STORY, 325-ROOM Best Western Lake Buena Vista completed a substantial renovation in 2003 of all guest rooms and public areas. The improvements help compensate for its offering fewer of the extras common to most other DDRA properties. A breakfast buffet and dinner service of American fare are available in the Trader's Island Grill, while the Parakeet Café offers sandwiches and snacks. The poolside Flamingo Cove Lounge provides its own menu of pub standards as well as alcoholic refreshment. The pool is small though pleasantly landscaped, and there's a kiddie pool. Also offered are a fitness room, game room, and playground. Although there are no organized children's programs, the resort can arrange for child care.

2000 Hotel Plaza Boulevard
☎ 407-828-2424 or 800-348-3765
www.lakebuenavistaresorthotel.com

Buena Vista Palace Hotel & Spa ★★★★

THOUGH IT HAS NO DISNEYESQUE THEME, the sprawling Buena Vista Palace (family-hotel profile on page 250) can compete with Disney's best resorts as far as the number and variety of amenities. Plus, it's larger and it offers a bit more of everything than most other Downtown Disney resorts. The Buena Vista Palace's 1,014 rooms and suites are spread over 27 acres and four towers, and the spa and fitness center is one of the most comprehensive on Disney World property (60 spa services and treatments, including private outdoor whirlpools). Dining options abound, including the Outback Restaurant (not affiliated with the chain of the same name), specializing in steaks and seafood; Watercress Café (breakfast buffet, plus American fare); and a poolside snack bar. The Watercress Café also hosts a Disney character brunch each Sunday. Visit the Lobby Lounge for cocktails and conversation. The wet set will enjoy three tropical-themed pools, a whirlpool, and a sauna. Two lighted tennis courts, jogging trails, a white-sand volleyball court, and an arcade and playground round out the recreational offerings.

1900 Buena Vista Drive
☎ 407-827-2727
www.buenavistapalace.com

We've stayed in both the main building and tower rooms and found each to be clean, spacious, and full of amenities. Rooms are quiet, with ample lighting, and the bedding is above average. Bath and grooming areas are better than most. Balconies are smallish but have pretty views of the landscaping and the Downtown Disney area. The only complaint we have is that the check-in area is too small, limiting the staff's ability to handle more than a few people at once. If possible, check in during off-hours to avoid long waits.

Regular room prices start at around $180—comparable to prices at a Disney Moderate resort—and we've found Internet-only rates here for as little as $99 per night, making the hotel one of the best bargains in Orlando. (Rates do not include a $17-per-night resort fee.) Overall, the Buena Vista Palace is certainly one of the top couple of hotels in the Downtown Disney area.

Doubletree Guest Suites ★★★½

THIS GIANT WHITE BUNKER of a hotel is the only all-suite establishment on Disney World property. What Doubletree Guest Suites lacks in atmosphere and creative attributes, it makes up for in convenience and comfort. Located within walking distance of Downtown Disney, the 229 suites are spacious for a family, although the decor is startling, with no apparent theme. No rooms have balconies, though ground floors offer patios.

2305 Hotel Plaza Boulevard
☎ 407-934-1000
www.doubletreeguestsuites.com

Amenities include a safe, hair dryer, refrigerator, microwave, coffeepot, fold-out bed, two TVs (bedroom and living room), and even a black-and-white TV-radio in the bathroom.

Children will enjoy the kids' check-in desk and complimentary chocolate-chip cookie and small playground. The heated pool, children's pool, and whirlpool spa are moderate in size, and traffic noise from I-4 can faintly be heard from the pool deck. The tiny fitness center (more like a fitness closet), pool table, four tennis courts, and outdoor bar are adjacent to the pool. High-speed Internet and a business center in the lobby (includes fax, printer, two computers, and copier) are convenient for those on working holidays. The Market (open 7 a.m. to 11 p.m.) offers groceries, drinks, ice cream, and sundaes for those late-night munchies; Evergreen Cafe, a new eco-friendly restaurant, serves breakfast, lunch, and dinner. Babysitting service is available.

Hilton Walt Disney World ★★★★

1751 Hotel Plaza Boulevard
☎ 407-827-4000
www.hilton-wdwv.com

THIS UPSCALE HILTON is the nicest hotel in the Downtown Disney Resort Area, challenged only by the Buena Vista Palace. It's also the only DDRA hotel offering Disney's Extra Magic Hours program to its guests. Rooms are a cut above others in the DDRA. Dining on-site includes the Covington Mill Restaurant, offering American sandwiches and pasta; Andiamo, an Italian bistro; and Benihana, a Japanese steak house and sushi bar. Covington Mill hosts a Disney character breakfast on Sundays. The two pools are matched with a children's "spray pool" and a 24-hour fitness center. An exercise room and game room are available, as is a 24-hour market. Babysitting is available, but there are no organized children's programs. (See page 251 for family-hotel profile.)

A Denver family of five found the Hilton's shuttle service lacking:

Transportation from the Hilton, provided by a company called Mears, was unreliable. They did a better job of getting guests back to the hotel from the park than getting them to the park from the hotel. Shuttles from the hotel were randomly timed and went repeatedly to the same parks—skipping others and leaving guests to wait for up to an hour.

Regal Sun Resort ★★★½

1850 Hotel Plaza Boulevard
☎ 407-828-4444
or 800-624-4109
www.regalsunresort.com

LOCATED ACROSS FROM DOWNTOWN DISNEY and formerly known as the Grosvenor, the Regal Sun has recently reopened following an extensive refurbishment. The first noticeable improvement is the lobby, now made bright and airy. Check-in service is friendly, but we've had reports of minor issues, which we think are attributable to the staff still getting the hang of a new computer system. The rooms are larger than most and renovated as well, with new furniture and bedding along with in-room refrigerators. Pool-facing rooms in the hotel's wings have exterior hallways that overlook the pool and center courtyard; these hallways can be noisy during summer months. Elevators are available, but they're unusually slow—it's probably faster to walk to the second and third floors, assuming you're up for the exercise.

Royal Plaza ★★★★ (tower rooms); ★★★ (garden rooms)

THE ROYAL PLAZA REOPENED IN 2006 after an extensive renovation, motivated in part by damage sustained during the 2004 hurricane season. The old generic decor has been replaced with stylish, muted blues in standard rooms and vibrant yellows, rich reds, and warm wood tones in the hotel's tower rooms. Bathroom space in the standard rooms is on the smaller side, while tower rooms have more than enough elbowroom. Each room has a small sitting area, a desk, and high-speed Internet access. New soft goods, including towels, curtains, and pillow-top mattresses, are upgrades from previous versions.

1905 Hotel Plaza Boulevard
☎ 407-828-2828 or 800-248-7890
www.royalplaza.com

The Giraffe Café serves American breakfast, lunch, and dinner; the attached Giraffe Lounge is the main hotel bar, though Sips is open seasonally poolside. The pool itself is comfortable and pleasant, though not flashy or particularly kid-oriented. Four lighted tennis courts and an exercise room are available.

Service at the Royal Plaza is very good, with many of the original employees having returned after the two-year renovation. We've thrown a number of unique situations at this staff over the years, all handled with the grace and aplomb of seasoned professionals. The Royal Plaza's main competition in the Downtown Disney area seems to be the Buena Vista Palace (see page 205), which offers slightly larger rooms of similar quality and more amenities, frequently at lower rates. Because of this, establishing the right price for its rooms is going to be crucial for the Royal Plaza over the next year or so. You'd choose the Royal Plaza if the cost were comparable and you had even the slightest feeling that you might need help from the hotel staff during your trip. Discounts are often available at **MouseSavers.com.**

On the first and second floors, ask for rooms X49 to X64. Tower rooms X02 to X07, 14, 16, and 17 are also good. The other rooms on the first two levels are subject to more foot traffic, noise from public spaces, and guests entering and leaving the main building. While they'll have less traffic, tower rooms not listed above can pick up noise from the elevators and ice machines on each floor.

CAMPING AT WALT DISNEY WORLD

FORT WILDERNESS RESORT & CAMPGROUND is a spacious area for tent and RV camping. Fully equipped, air-conditioned prefabricated log cabins are also available for rent.

Tent/Pop-Up campsites provide water, electricity, and cable TV and run from $43 to $73 depending on season. **Preferred Hook-Up** campsites for tents and RVs have all of the above plus sewer connections and run from $57 to $91 per night. **Full Hook-Up** campsites accommodate large RVs and run from $62 to $96 per night. **Premium** campsites add an extra-large concrete parking pad and run from $72 to $106 a night.

All sites are level and provide picnic tables, waste containers, grills, and high-speed Internet (additional fee). No fires are permitted except in the grills. Pets are permitted in some Premium, Full Hook-Up, and Preferred loops.

Fort Wilderness Resort & Campground

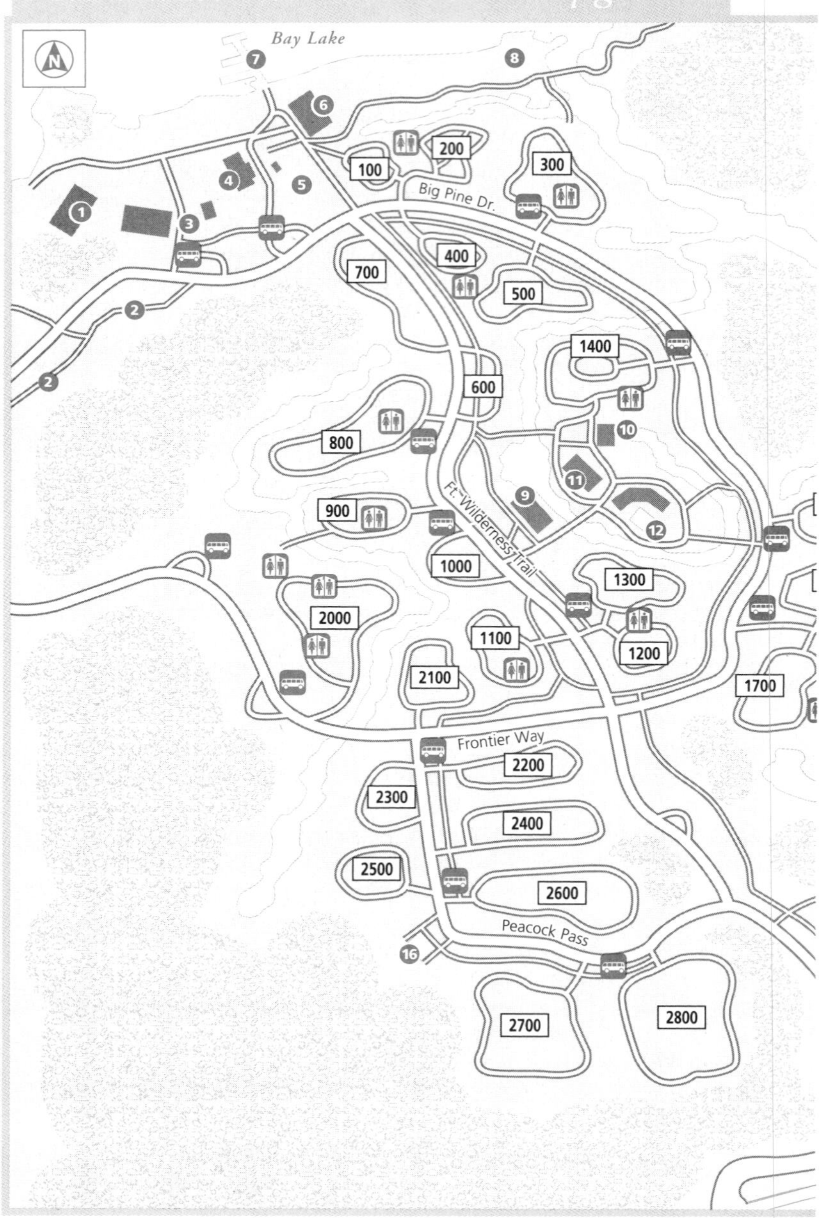

Bay Lake

Big Pine Dr.

Ft. Wilderness Trail

Frontier Way

Peacock Pass

100 200 300 400 500 600 700 800 900 1000 1100 1200 1300 1400 1700 2000 2100 2200 2300 2400 2500 2600 2700 2800

1 2 3 4 5 6 7 8 9 10 11 12 16

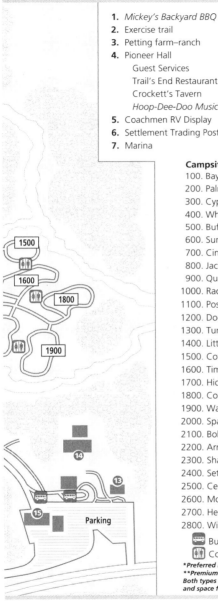

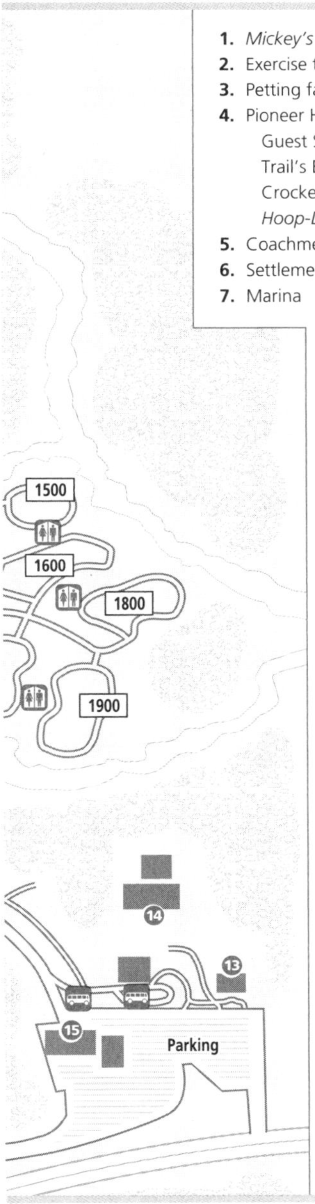

1. *Mickey's Backyard BBQ*
2. Exercise trail
3. Petting farm–ranch
4. Pioneer Hall
   Guest Services
   Trail's End Restaurant
   Crockett's Tavern
   Hoop-Dee-Doo Musical Revue
5. Coachmen RV Display
6. Settlement Trading Post
7. Marina
8. Nature trail
9. Meadow Trading Post
10. Campfire program
11. Bike barn
12. Meadow, pool, and tennis courts
13. Kennel
14. Trail ride
15. Reception Outpost
16. Peacock Pass Pool

Campsite Loops

100. Bay Tree Lake*
200. Palmetto Path*
300. Cypress Knee Circle*
400. Whispering Pine Way**
500. Buffalo Bend**
600. Sunny Sage Way**
700. Cinnamon Fern Way**
800. Jack Rabbit Run**
900. Quail Trail**
1000. Raccoon Lane**
1100. Possum Path**
1200. Dogwood Drive**
1300. Tumblewood Turn**
1400. Little Bear Path and Big Bear Path**
1500. Cottonwood Curl*
1600. Timber Trail*
1700. Hickory Hollow*
1800. Conestoga Trail*
1900. Wagon Wheel Way*
2000. Spanish Moss Lane
2100. Bobcat Bend
2200. Arrowhead Way
2300. Shawnee Bend
2400. Settler's Bend
2500. Cedar Circle
2600. Moccasin Trail
2700. Heron Hollow
2800. Willow Way

Bus stop

Comfort station–laundry facility

***Preferred Hook-Up campsites**
****Premium campsites**
Both types of sites have power, water, sewer, cable TV, and space for large RVs.

FORT WILDERNESS RESORT & CAMPGROUND

STRENGTHS	WEAKNESSES
Informality	Isolated location
Children's play areas	Complicated bus service
Best recreational options at WDW	Confusing campground layout
Special day and evening programs	Lack of privacy
Campsite amenities	Very limited on-site dining options
Shower and toilet facilities	Limited automobile traffic
Hoop-Dee-Doo Musical Revue show	Crowding at beaches and pools
Convenient self-parking	Small baths in cabins
Off-site dining via boat at Magic Kingdom	Extreme distance to store and restaurant facilities from many campsites

Campsites are arranged on loops accessible from one of three main roads. There are 28 loops, with loops 100 to 2000 for tent and RV campers, and loops 2100 to 2800 offering cabins at $265 to $410 per night. RV sites are roomy by eastern-U.S. standards, with the Premium and Full Hook-Up campsites able to accommodate RVs more than 45 feet long, but tent campers will probably feel a bit cramped. (Note that tent stakes cannot be put into the concrete at the Premium sites.) On any given day, 90% or more of campers are RV-ers.

Fort Wilderness Resort & Campground arguably offers the most recreational facilities and activities of any Disney resort. Among them are two video arcades; nightly campfire programs; Disney movies; a dinner theater; two swimming pools; a beach; walking paths; bike, boat, canoe, golf-cart, and water-ski rentals; a petting zoo; horseback riding; hay rides; fishing; and tennis, basketball, and volleyball courts. There are two convenience stores, a restaurant, and a tavern. Comfort stations with toilets, showers, pay phones, ice machine, and laundry facilities are within walking distance of all campsites.

Access to the Magic Kingdom is by boat from Fort Wilderness Landing, and to Epcot by bus with a transfer at the Transportation and Ticket Center (TTC) to the Epcot monorail. An alternate route to the Magic Kingdom is by internal bus to the TTC, then by monorail or ferry to the park. Transportation to all other Disney destinations is by bus. Motor traffic within the campground is permitted only when entering or exiting. Get around within the campground by bus, golf cart, or bike, the latter two available for rent.

For tent and RV campers, there's a fairly stark trade-off between sites convenient to pools, restaurant, trading posts, and other amenities, and those that are most scenic, shady, and quiet. RV-ers who prefer to be near guest services, the marina, the beach, and the restaurant and tavern should go for loops 100, 200, 700, and 400 (in that order). Loops near the campground's secondary facility area with pool, trading post, bike and golf-cart rentals, and campfire program are 1400, 1300, 600, 1000, and 1500, in order of preference. If you're looking for a tranquil, scenic setting among mature trees, we recommend loops

1800, 1900, 1700, and 1600, in that order, and the backside sites on the 700 loop. The best loop of all, and the only one to offer both a lovely setting and proximity to key amenities, is loop 300. The best loops for tents and pop-up campers are loops 1500 and 2000, with 1500 being nearest a pool, convenience store, and the campfire program.

With the exception of loops 1800 and 1900, avoid sites within 40 yards of the loop entrance. These sites are almost always flanked by one of the main traffic arteries within Fort Wilderness. Further, sites on the outside of the loop are almost always preferable to those in the center of the loop. RV-ers should be forewarned that all sites are back-ins and that although most sites will accommodate large rigs, the loop access roads are pretty tight and narrow.

Rental cabins offer a double bed and two bunk beds in the only bedroom, augmented by a Murphy bed (pulls down from the wall) in the living room. There's one rather small bathroom with shower and tub.

The prefab log cabins (classified as Moderate resorts in the Disney hirearchy) are warm and homey, but the stem-to-stern interior wood paneling and smallish windows make for pretty dark accommodations at night. Neither the lighting fixtures provided nor the wattage of their bulbs are up to the job of lighting the cabins once the sun goes down.

All cabins offer air-conditioning, color televisions with VCRs, fully equipped kitchens, and dining tables. Housekeeping is provided daily. Most readers are crazy about the cabins. Some representative comments follow.

A Wappingers Falls, New York, family writes:

We stayed at Fort Wilderness in a cabin because

- *We wanted a separate bedroom area.*
- *We wanted a kitchen.*
- *Our kids are very lively and the cabins were apart from each other so we wouldn't disturb other guests.*
- *We thought the kids might meet other children to play with.*

The cabins worked out just right for us. Although the kids did not meet any other children to play with, they had a ball chasing the little lizards and frogs, kicking around pinecones, sitting on the deck to eat ice pops, and sleeping in bunk beds. We went to the campfire twice (we brought our own marshmallows and sticks). Our cabin was a short walk to our bus stop and two "blocks" away from the pool and laundry. I loved the dishwasher, the generous storage space, the extra towels, the air-conditioning, and the daily cleaning service. There was no canned music or fake bird calls in the trees, just peace and quiet.

This Massachusetts mother of two preschoolers needed more storage space:

We liked Fort Wilderness a lot, but the cabins need a full-sized dresser. It was a pain having to live out of two suitcases all week.

From a Downers Grove, Illinois, family of five:

While we all enjoyed the cabins and resort, we spent a LOT of time waiting for buses and ferries, more than we remember waiting a few years ago. They've recently made some changes to the bus routes, and while we liked having a stop at the Meadow area, there was always a long wait for a purple bus to take us back to the cabin when returning from the parks (from both depots). They need a separate bus route just for the cabins, since many of the campers have cars and/or golf carts, an expense we didn't want after spending so much for the cabin. This factor may make us consider a different resort/villa for our next trip unless the bus system for the cabins is improved.

A Rochester, New York, dad agrees:

If you're staying at Fort Wildnerness Cabins, we would highly recommend getting a golf cart. There is a lot going on at the campground itself, and the bus system can be cumbersome. Also, our 3-year-old wasn't always up for the walk—just getting from our cabin to the main loop was a lot for her.

A mother of two from Albuquerque, New Mexico, offers this:

Regarding Fort Wilderness: We stayed in a cabin and liked having all the space and the full kitchen. I was very disappointed in the pools, restaurant, and service, however. I had expected a Disney-resort pool, and instead there were only two relatively small concrete holes in the ground. The pool nearest our cabin (still a quarter mile away!) never even had a lifeguard. I had hoped to be able to send the kids to the pool without us when we needed some adult time to ourselves, but with the distance and lack of lifeguards, there was no way to do that.

The restaurant (one mile away) was good, but it was an all-you-can-eat-buffet with adult prices for ages 10 and over at about $25. I'm unwilling to pay $25 for my 10-year-old daughter to eat one chicken wing and Jell-O very often. We only ate there once. I guess they figured that if you had a kitchen or were camping, you were committed to cooking every meal. It would have been nice after a tiring day to get a light meal or salad.

Though the cabins are especially popular, RV and tent campers love Fort Wilderness, too. First from a Marietta, Georgia, multigenerational family:

I do wish you would stress more the advantages of using Fort Wilderness. With sites for any size/type of camper/tent, it is FAR more affordable than any hotel inside the park. Additionally, you could theoretically (although not likely) prepare all of your own meals. We usually had breakfast, packed snacks, and returned for lunch and dinner every day. We were able to decrease our food budget and devote it to a character lunch and tea at the Grand Floridian. Additionally, Fort Wilderness provides a place for kids to ride bikes, two 24-hour pools, nightly movies, sing-alongs, s'mores roasts, and direct access to the Magic Kingdom. Honestly, the "comfort stations" are nicer than the bathrooms you see on the HGTV shows. If you want to see the fireworks any night you're not in the park, make your way to the beach for a terrific view. It's an affordable alternative in a nonaffordable "world."

A mother of two from Mechanicsville, Virginia, puts Fort Wilderness on a pedestal as well:

The quality of camping at Fort Wilderness is second to none! The sites are level, the activities great! This is one of the few ways that a family on a fixed income can enjoy a true WDW vacation. Even those who don't own a camper can make the investment in simple camping equipment (that can be used repeatedly) and enjoy a week at the World for as low as $41 per day for lodging, not to mention the savings on dining. When staying here, you can bring your own food. You can pack sandwiches for the parks and barbecue at dinner. Every site has a charcoal grill.

Now, the most important thing—the family time. This is the only resort where you are encouraged to go outside and play! Your kids are not stuck in a hotel room, at the pool, or at an arcade. You can bike, swim, visit two arcades, hike the nature trail, ride a horse, rent a boat, play volleyball, go to the beach, attend a free character sing-along and marshmallow roast followed by a classic Disney movie that many younger families never knew existed (we were introduced to Snowball Express *and* Robin Hood*), enjoy multiple playgrounds, play tennis, rent a golf cart, walk around at night to see the festively decorated campsites (many Disney-themed), take a romantic carriage ride, take your first pony ride, find the armadillo that lives next to the bathrooms in the 1300 loop, and see a wild turkey. Don't forget the fishing or the great view of the fireworks from the beach or the up-close water light parade. It may not be for everyone, but for a family who thinks they can't afford the Disney experience, this is a GREAT option. With all of this stuff, much of it free or very affordable, who needs the parks? We visited last June and never set foot in a park.*

Bus service at Fort Wilderness leaves a lot to be desired, so much in fact that we wouldn't stay there unless we had our own car. To go anywhere you first have to catch an internal bus that makes many, many stops. If your destination is outside Fort Wilderness, you then have to transfer to a second bus. To complicate things, buses serving destinations outside the campground depart from two locations, the Reception Outpost and Pioneer Hall. This means that you have to keep track of which destinations each transfer center serves.

Finally, if you rent a cabin or camp in a tent or RV, particularly in fall or spring, keep abreast of local weather conditions. This is not the place to be in a tornado.

A number of independent campgrounds are within 30 miles of Walt Disney World. Here are the closest:

Kissimmee-Orlando KOA ☎ 407-396-2400; **www.kissorlandokoa.com.** 96 licensed sites; approximately six miles to Walt Disney World US 192 (Maingate) entrance.

Sherwood Forest RV Resort ☎ 800-548-9981; **www.mhcrv.com.** 531 licensed sites; approximately four miles to Walt Disney World US 192 (Maingate) entrance.

Tropical Palms Encore SuperPark and Cottages ☎ 407-396-4595; **www.tropicalpalmsrv.com.** 441 licensed sites; approximately 2.5 miles to Walt Disney World US 192 (Maingate) entrance.

Disney Lodging for Less

Mary Waring, *Webmaster at* **MouseSavers.com** *(see page 28), knows more about Disney hotel packages than anyone on the planet. Here are her money-saving suggestions.*

BOOK "ROOM-ONLY." It's frequently a better deal to book a room-only reservation instead of buying a vacation package. Disney likes to sell vacation packages because they're easy and profitable. When you buy a package, you're typically paying a premium for convenience. You can often save money by putting together your own package. It's not hard: just book room-only at a resort and buy passes, meals, and extras separately.

Disney now prices its standard packages at the same rates as if you had purchased individual components separately at full price. However, what Disney doesn't tell you is that components can usually be purchased separately at a discount—and those discounts are not reflected in the brochure prices of Disney's packages. (Sometimes you can get special-offer packages that do include discounts; see below.)

Keep in mind that Disney's packages often include extras you are unlikely to use. Also, packages require a $200 deposit and full payment 45 days in advance; plus, they have stringent change and cancellation policies. Generally, booking room-only requires a deposit of one night's room rate with the remainder due at check-in. Your reservation can be changed or canceled for any reason until five days before check-in.

Whether you decide to book a Disney vacation package or create your own, there are a number of ways to save:

- ***Use discount codes to reduce your room-only rate.*** Disney uses these codes to push unsold rooms at certain times of year. (In the past two years, however, these codes have become scarcer.) Check a Web site like **MouseSavers.com** to learn about codes that may be available for your vacation dates. Some codes are available to anyone, while others are just for Florida residents, Annual Pass holders, and so on.

  Discount codes aren't always available for every hotel or every date, and they typically don't appear until two to six months in advance. The good news is that you can usually apply a code to an existing room-only reservation. Simply call the Disney Reservations

HOW *to* EVALUATE *a* WALT DISNEY WORLD TRAVEL PACKAGE

HUNDREDS OF WALT DISNEY WORLD PACKAGE VACATIONS are offered each year. Some are created by the Walt Disney Travel Company, others by airline touring companies, independent travel agents, and wholesalers. Almost all include lodging at or near Disney World

Center at ☎ 407-W-DISNEY (or contact a Disney-savvy travel agent) and ask whether any rooms are available at your preferred hotel for your preferred dates using the code.

- ***Use discount codes to reduce your vacation package rate.*** Disney occasionally offers packages that include resort discounts or value-added features such as a free dining plan. For those who like the convenience of packages, these offers are well worth seeking out.

  You'll need to present a discount code to get the special package rates. Check a Web site like **MouseSavers.com** to get more information.

  As with room-discount codes, package-discount codes aren't available for every hotel or every date, and they typically don't appear until two to six months in advance. You can usually apply a code to an existing package reservation. Again, call the Disney Reservations Center at ☎ 407-W-DISNEY (or contact a Disney-savvy travel agent) and ask whether any rooms are available at your preferred hotel for your preferred dates using the package code.
- ***Be flexible.*** Buying a room or package with a discount code is a little like shopping for clothes at a discount store: if you wear size XX-small or XXXX-large, or you like green when everyone else is wearing pink, you're a lot more likely to score a bargain. Likewise, resort discounts are available only when Disney has excess rooms. You're more likely to get a discount during less-popular times (such as value season) and at larger or less-popular resorts. Animal Kingdom Lodge and Old Key West seem to have discounted rooms available more often than the other resorts do.
- ***Be persistent.*** This is the most important tip. Disney allots a certain number of rooms to each discount; reportedly this averages 100 rooms per night per code. Once the discounted rooms are gone, you won't get that rate unless someone cancels. Fortunately, people change and cancel reservations all the time. If you can't get your preferred dates or hotel with one discount code, try another one (if available) or keep calling back first thing in the morning to check for cancellations—the system resets overnight, and any reservations with unpaid deposits are automatically released for resale.

plus theme-park admissions. Packages offered by airlines include air transportation.

Prices vary seasonally; mid-March through Easter, summer, and holiday periods are the most expensive. Off-season, forget packages: there are plenty of empty rooms, and you can negotiate great discounts, especially at non-Disney properties. Similarly, airfares and rental cars are cheaper off-peak.

unofficial **TIP**
If you consider a non-Disney hotel, check its quality as reported in independent travel references such as the *Unofficial Guides,* AAA directories, Mobil guides, or *Frommer's* guides.

Almost all package ads are headlined "5 Days at Walt Disney World from $645" (or such). The key word is *from:* the rock-bottom price includes the least desirable hotels; if you want better or more-convenient digs, you'll pay more—often much more.

Packages offer a wide selection of hotels. Some, like the Disney resorts, are very dependable. Others run the gamut of quality.

Checking two or three independent sources is best. Also, before you book, ask how old the hotel is and when the guest rooms were last refurbished. Locate the hotel on a map to verify its proximity to Disney World. If you won't have a car, make sure that the hotel has an adequate shuttle service.

Packages with non-Disney lodging are much less expensive. But guests at Disney-owned properties get Extra Magic Hours privileges, free parking, and access to the Disney transportation system. These privileges (except Extra Magic Hours for Hilton guests) don't apply to guests at the independent hotels of the Downtown Disney Resort Area (Buena Vista Palace Hotel & Spa, Regal Sun Resort, Doubletree Guest Suites Resort, Hilton, Holiday Inn at Walt Disney World, Royal Plaza, and Best Western Lake Buena Vista Resort Hotel).

Packages should be a win–win proposition for both buyer and seller. The buyer makes only one phone call and deals with one salesperson to set up the whole vacation (transportation, rental car, admissions, lodging, meals, and even golf and tennis). The seller, likewise, deals with the buyer only once. Some packagers also buy airfares in bulk on contract, not unlike a broker playing the commodities market. By buying a large number of airfares in advance, the packager saves significantly over posted fares. The practice is also applied to hotel rooms. Because selling packages is efficient and the packager often can buy package components in bulk at discount, the seller's savings in operating expenses are sometimes passed on to the buyer, making the package not only convenient but also an exceptional value.

In practice, however, the seller may realize all the economies and pass on no savings. Packages sometimes are loaded with extras that cost the packager almost nothing but run the package's price sky-high. Savings passed on to customers are still somewhere in Fantasyland.

Choose a package that includes features you're sure to use. You'll pay for all of them whether you use them or not. If price is more important than convenience, call around to see what the package would cost if you booked its components on your own. If the package price is less than the à la carte cost, the package is a good deal. If costs are about equal, the package probably is worth it for the convenience. Much of the time, however, you'll find you save significantly by buying the components individually.

WALT DISNEY TRAVEL COMPANY MAGIC YOUR WAY PACKAGES

DISNEY'S MAGIC YOUR WAY travel-package program mirrors the admission-ticket program of the same name. Here's how it works: You begin with a base package room and tickets. Tickets can be customized to match the number of days you intend to tour the theme parks, and range in length from one to ten days. As with theme-park admissions, the package program offers strong financial incentives to book a longer stay. "The longer you play, the less you pay per day," is the way Disney puts it, borrowing a page from Sam Walton's concept of the universe. A one-day adult base ticket (with tax) costs $79.88, whereas if you buy a seven-day ticket, the average cost per day drops to $34.69. You can purchase options to add on to your base tickets, such as hopping between theme parks; visiting water parks, DisneyQuest, or ESPN Wide World of Sports; and buying your way out of an expiration date for any unused ticket features.

With Magic Your Way packages, you can avoid paying for features you don't intend to use. No longer must you purchase a package with theme-park tickets for your entire length of stay. With Magic Your Way you can choose to purchase as many days of admission as you intend to use. On a one-week vacation, for example, you might want to spend only five days in the Disney parks, saving a day each for Universal Studios and SeaWorld. With Magic Your Way you can buy only five days of admission on a seven-day package. Likewise, if you do not normally park-hop, you can now purchase multiday admissions that do not include the park-hopping feature. If you don't use all your admissions, you can opt for the No Expiration add-on, and the unused days will be good forever. Best of all, you can buy the various add-ons at any time during your vacation.

Before we deluge you with a boxcar of options and add-ons, let's define the basic components of Disney's Magic Your Way package:

- One or more nights of accommodations at your choice of any Disney resort. Rates vary with lodging choice: the Grand Floridian is the most expensive, the All-Star and Pop Century the least expensive.
- Magic Your Way Base Ticket for the number of days you tour the theme parks.
- Unlimited use of the Disney transportation system.
- Free theme-park parking.
- Official Walt Disney Travel Company luggage tag (one per person).

Magic Your Way Dining Plans

Disney offers dining plans to accompany its Magic Your Way ticket system. They're available to all Disney-resort guests except those staying at the Swan, the Dolphin, the hotels of the Downtown Disney Resort Area, and Shades of Green, none of which are Disney-owned or -operated. Guests must also purchase a Magic Your Way package, have Annual Passes, or be members of the Disney Vacation Club (DVC) to participate in the plan. Except for DVC members, a three-night minimum stay is typically also required. Overall cost is determined by the number of nights you stay at a Disney resort.

As a family of five from Waldron, Michigan, learned, you must purchase a Disney package vacation to be eligible for a dining plan:

> *We read through the* Unofficial Guide *and noticed that it said not to book a package during slow season. We were overwhelmed with the decisions that we had to make, so we booked the resort first, then*

the tickets, and then we wanted the dining plan. Well, they wouldn't add the dining plan on because we had already booked everything. I talked with other families who have been to Disney, and not once did anybody mention that we needed to book everything all at once.

MAGIC YOUR WAY PLUS DINING PLAN Introduced in 2005, this dining plan provides, for each member of your group, for each night of your stay, one counter-service meal, one full-service meal, and one snack at participating Disney dining locations and restaurants, including room service at some Disney resorts (type "Disney Dining Plan Locations 2010" into your favorite Internet search engine to find sites with the entire list). For guests age 10 and up, the price is $39.99 per night; for guests ages 3 to 9, the price is $10.99 per night, tax included. Children younger than age 3 eat free from an adult's plate.

The counter-service meal includes a main course (sandwich, dinner salad, pizza, or the like), dessert, and nonalcoholic drink, or a complete combo meal (a main course and a side dish—think burger and fries), dessert, and nonalcoholic drink, including tax. The full-service sit-down meals include a main course, dessert, a nonalcoholic drink, and tax. If you're dining at a buffet, the full-service meal includes the buffet, a nonalcoholic drink, and tax. The snack includes items normally sold from carts or small stands throughout the parks and resorts: ice cream, popcorn, soft drinks, fruit, chips, apple juice, and the like.

For instance, if you're staying for three nights, each member of your party will be credited with three counter-service meals, three full-service meals, and three snacks. All those meals will be put into an individual "meal account" for each person in your group. Meals in your account can be used on any combination of days, so you're not required to eat every meal every day. Thus, you can skip a full-service meal one day and have two on another day.

Disney's top-of-the-line restaurants (dubbed "Disney Signature" restaurants in the plan), along with all the dinner shows, count as two full-service meals. If you dine at one of these locations, two full-service meals will be deducted from your account for each person dining.

In addition to the preceding, the dining plan comes with several other important rules:

- Everyone staying in the same resort room must participate in the plan.
- Children ages 3 to 9 must order from the kids' menu, if one is available. This rule is occasionally not enforced at Disney's counter-service restaurants, enabling older children to order from the regular (adult) menu.
- In-room minibars and refillable mugs are not included in the plan.
- A full-service meal can be breakfast, lunch, or dinner. The greatest savings occur when you use your full-service meal allocations for dinner.
- The meal plan expires at midnight **on the day you check out** of the Disney resort. **Unused meals are nonrefundable.**
- The dining plan is occasionally unavailable when using certain room-only discounts.

QUICK SERVICE DINING PLAN This new plan includes meals, snacks, and nonalcoholic drinks at most counter-service eateries in Walt Disney World. The cost is $29.99 per day for guests age 10 and up, $8.99 per day for kids ages 3 to 9. The plan includes two counter-service meals and two snacks per day, plus one refillable drink mug per person, per package (eligible for refills only at counter-service locations only in your Disney resort), and 30 minutes of play at a Disney-resort arcade. The economics of the plan are difficult to justify unless you're drinking gallons of soda or coffee to offset Disney's inflated prices.

MAGIC YOUR WAY DELUXE DINING PLAN Another new plan, this one offers a choice of full-service or counter-service meals for three meals a day at any participating restaurant. In addition to the three meals a day, the plan also includes two snacks per day and a refillable drink mug. The Deluxe Plan costs $69.99 for adults and $19.99 for children for each night of your stay. Cranking it up another notch, there are even more extravagant dining plans associated with Magic Your Way Premium and Platinum packages, both described a little later.

In addition to food, all the plans include deal sweeteners such as a free round of miniature golf, a certificate for a 5-by-10-inch print from Disney's PhotoPass, a sort of two-for-one certificate for use of Sea Raycers watercraft, a "commemorative" luggage tag, and such.

Disney ceaselessly tinkers with the dining plans' rules, meal definitions, and participating restaurants. For example, it's possible (though not documented) to exchange a sit-down-meal credit for a counter-service meal, although doing this even once can negate any savings you get from using a plan in the first place.

THINGS TO CONSIDER WHEN EVALUATING THE PLUS DINING PLAN If you prefer to always eat at counter-service restaurants, you'll be better off with the Quick Service plan. Other poor candidates for the Plus plan include finicky eaters, light eaters, families who can't agree on restaurants, and those who can't get reservations at their first- or second-choice sit-down restaurants.

When the dining plan was first introduced, it included an appetizer and gratuity for each full-service meal, making it a pretty good deal for many families; by our estimate, savings of up to 13% per person per day were possible in some of Disney's best restaurants. As a result, the dining plan was one of the most requested of Disney's package add-ons.

Alas, with the initial success of the plan, Disney saw an opportunity to make more money. In 2008, Disney eliminated the appetizer and gratuity from the plan, increasing the cost of a full-service meal by at least 15% to 18% for the gratuity alone, and an additional 15% to 20% per appetizer per person. (To be fair, many appetizers are

unofficial **TIP**
The Plus dining plan costs $39.99/day for adults and $10.99/day for kids ages 3–9. Combining two of your table-service options, you can eat one meal higher on the hog at Disney's more upscale eateries. Maximizing the value of the dining plan requires research and planning, but the money you can save is worth the time and effort. The average counter-service meal runs $8–$10 for an adult, and the price of the more expensive dishes at many Disney restaurants can total more than the daily cost of the Plus plan.

large enough to share.) Some of the pricier entrees were modified or eliminated from menus.

These changes should make every family reconsider the economics of the dining plan. Our research indicates that the plan still saves the typical family around $4 to $7 per person per day, assuming the family uses every meal credit. But skipping a single full-service meal during a visit of five or fewer days can mean the difference between saving and losing money. In our experience, having a scheduled sit-down meal for every day of a weeklong vacation can be mentally exhausting, especially for kids and teens. One option might be to schedule a meal at a Disney Signature restaurant, which requires two full-service credits, and have no scheduled sit-down meal on another night in the middle of your trip, allowing everyone to decide on the spot whether they're up for something formal.

Many of the most popular restaurants are fully booked as soon as their reservation window opens, so book your restaurants as soon as possible, typically 90 to 180 days before you visit. Then decide whether the dining plan makes economic sense. For more on Advance Reservations—the term is Disney-speak (hence the capital letters) and not exactly what it implies—see Part Ten.

If you're making reservations at restaurants in Disney hotels other than your own, a car allows you to easily access all the participating restaurants. When you use the Disney transportation system, dining at the various Disney-resort restaurants can be a logistical nightmare. Those without a car may want to weigh the immediate services of a taxi (typically at $10 to $12 each way across Disney property) versus a 45- to 60-minute trip on Disney transportation each way.

For an in-depth discussion of the various plans, including number-crunching (with algebra, even!), visit **Touring Plans.com** (click "Dining" on the home page, then "Disney Dining Plan").

Readers who tried the Disney dining plan had varying experiences. A mother of two from Marshalltown, Iowa, volunteered the following:

> *The dining plan is great in theory, but it had way too much food and used too much valuable park time for the table-service meals. We won't use it again.*

From a Minnesota family of three:

> *We purchased the basic Disney Dining Plan, and I my wife and I were almost overwhelmed by the amount of food we received. I skipped a counter-service meal one day, which allowed my son to use* [the meal credit] *for breakfast from the resort food court the next day.*

A St. Louis family of three comments:

> *We purchased the dining plan and would* never *do it again. Far too expensive, far too much food, and then you have to tip on top of the expense. Additionally, table-service meals were hard to use for us, reservations hard to obtain. Much easier to purchase what you want, where and when you want. (Intended to use a counter-service meal at*

McDonald's at Epcot for 12-year-old. Found out you had to get the large [nine-piece] *nuggets, the large fries, a large drink, and a McFlurry in order to use the counter-service meal. Most adults I know wouldn't eat that much food, let alone a 12-year-old!) Food is a "gotcha" at Disney, but the dining plan proved to be a poor choice for us.*

A Toronto family says gratuities add up:

Families should be warned that tips in Disney table-service restaurants can add up quickly in a week. The tip for our party of five at Le Cellier alone was $45.

A father of two from Danbury, Connecticut, however, gave the plan a thumbs-up.

We had the dining plan, so all of our meals were on the property. We were pleasantly surprised at both the service and quality of food. The entertainment during the meals, especially at the 50's Prime Time Cafe and Whispering Canyon, really added to the meals.

A Belmont, Massachusetts, dad likes the Quick Service Dining Plan:

If you intend to eat Disney food, the counter-service meal plan is a good option. We didn't want the full plan because the restaurants seemed overpriced, and the necessity of reservations months in advance seemed crazy and a bar to flexibility. You get two counter-service meals (entree/combo, dessert, drink) and two snacks (food item or drink) per person per as part of the plan, and even though kids' meals are cheaper, there is no distinction when you order—kids can order (more-expensive) adult meals.

But a reader from The Woodlands, Texas, laments that the plan has altered the focus of her vacation:

For me, the Disney Dining Plan has taken a lot of the fun out of going to Disney World.. No longer are we free to enjoy the parks and fit in meals as a secondary matter. Now, dining for each day must be planned months in advance unless one is to eat just hot dogs, pizza, and other walk-up items. As heretical as it may sound, I'm actually less *inclined to go to WDW now. I want to have fun. I don't want to be locked into a tight schedule, always worrying about where we need to be when it's time to eat. I don't want to eat when I'm not hungry just because I have a reservation somewhere. Eating has become the primary consideration at WDW, not the parks and entertainment.*

Along similar lines, a Bethany, Connecticut, dad adds this:

We took the dining plan and were disappointed. It was a lot of work to coordinate. We made travel plans six weeks prior to departure and were unable to procure reservations in our favorite restaurants (or they were at inconvenient times—9:50 p.m. at Boma). I would have canceled the meal plan but was told I'd also have to cancel the entire reservation, which would have entailed risking the airfare (airline package deal). I heard similar complaints from other patrons in the park. Fortunately, your guidebook gave us alternate places to eat. Unless you go at a very low-attendance time or make reservations three months out, I recommend against the dining plan.

A Midland Park, New Jersey, family of four says ditto:

With so many people now using the dining plan, it seems that if you were to book a last-minute trip or miss one of your reservations, you might not be able to get a table-service meal at all—reservations were hard to come by, even though I called two months before our trip!

A mom from Orland Park, Illinois, comments on the difficulty of getting Advance Reservations:

I purchased the dining plan for this trip and must say I will never do that again. It's impossible to get table reservations anywhere good—the [restaurants] *that are available are available for a reason. We found ourselves taking whatever was open and were unhappy with every sit-down meal we had, except for lunch at Liberty Tree Tavern. I do not enjoy planning my day exclusively around eating at a certain restaurant at a certain time, but that is what you must do six months in advance if you want to eat at a good sit-down restaurant in Disney. That is ridiculous.*

As this reader from San Jose, California, explains, guests who are not on the dining plan need to know how the plan has affected obtaining Advance Reservations:

The Disney Dining Plan has almost eliminated any chance of spontaneity when visiting any of the sit-down restaurants. When planning 90 days out for the off-season, I was told by the Disney rep to make all my priority-seating reservations then because the restaurants are booked by people on the dining plan. In fact, I was told that most of the sit-down restaurants don't even take walk-ins anymore. Sure enough, even though I was well over 90 days away from my vacation, a lot of my restaurant choices were unavailable. I had to rearrange my entire schedule to fit the open slots at the restaurants I didn't want to miss.

Pesky Technicalities and Administrative Problems

Readers report experiencing a host of problems with both understanding and using the Disney Dining Plan. A dad from Tonawanda, New York, opines:

The dining plan is great, but unfortunately, not enough guests actually read the literature about it and become confused, leading to long, slow lines at some counter-service locations.

A family of four from Mount Pleasant, South Carolina, observes:

The impact of the Disney Dining Plan was amazing. It created longer lines at the registers because they were programmed to ring up each thing individually, or so it seemed. For instance, for a Mickey Meal, the checkout guy had to push buttons for chicken nuggets, applesauce, milk, and fries—not just one button for the entire meal. It took the guy about seven minutes to figure it and process us. Meanwhile, people stood there gazing up at the menu trying to figure out how they could fit their meals into their dining plans. It was incredibly frustrating for those of us who paid with cash and had no interest in the overpriced plan. One mother did say that with her three boys, she was spending more time in the restaurants eating than on the rides, so hey—maybe it isn't such a bad thing after all!

A woman from Atco, New Jersey, warns:

The Disney Dining Plan does not always work for snacks, even though vendors have signs posted stating they accept the card. We were told many times, "Oh, the machine isn't working today."

An Atlanta reader has this to say:

The downside to our stay was [using credits] *at the fast-food counter at Coronado Springs. I thought I was prepared. . . . NOT! Servers didn't seem to know what was included as a snack or what comprised a meal with the dining plan. It was a very frustrating experience. We spent the majority of our* [credits] *at the parks or other resorts.*

Many families purchase the dining plan without understanding how limited the menu choices are for kids age 9 and under. First from a West Chester, Ohio, mom:

We had only one complaint in our six days there, and that was with the Disney Dining Plan. All three of our girls are under 9 and had to choose "Kid's Picks" wherever offered. We did not come across any offerings like hamburgers, hot dogs, or pizza the whole time we were there. My kids couldn't even get pizza at Pizzafari in Animal Kingdom! They were so sick of mac and cheese and chicken nuggets after day two that going out to eat wasn't that exciting for them. We were given a hard time by food-service workers when we asked about substituting something different, and we were turned down 50% of the time. On our last day, a sympathetic employee told us we could get any counter-service food we wanted and just not tell the cashier that it was for a child (apparently, for counter service, Disney doesn't keep track of whether it is for an adult or child). It did work for us on that last day, but I wish we would have known that sooner. Hope this info will help some families with young kids.

A Pittsburgh mother of three recounts a similar experience:

I have one negative comment about the Disney Dining Plan. For adults, it was great. The problem was with the kids' meals: there was no variety at all at the table-service or counter-service restaurants. My two kids were actually sick of eating macaroni and cheese and chicken fingers. The amount of food they get is also very small—OK for my 4-year-old but not for my 9-year-old, who ended up eating off my plate; otherwise, I would have had to buy something extra to fill him up. Plus, we went to a pizza place in Animal Kingdom park, and there was NO pizza on the [dining plan's] *kids' menu.* No pizza at a pizza place?

From a family of five:

We had the dining plan and wish we had gone to the cafeteria and asked for details on exactly what a meal consisted of. For instance, for breakfast you could have an omelet or waffle and drink, or you could have a pastry, a piece of fruit, and two bottled drinks. The kids' meals were adequate, but you'd be in trouble if your child didn't like chicken nuggets.

From a Midwestern reader:

We could almost relate our dining experience to that of a person who receives food stamps—very restricted and always at the mercy of someone else for food selection. We spent close to $1,000 on food and were extremely frustrated with the entire experience. I would prefer to be able to eat whatever I want rather than be restricted to certain food items at certain places.

From a Wisconsin father of two:

On the last day of our visit, we were still learning about acceptable substitutions. For example, at breakfast you can have two drinks (coffee and OJ). You can also do this for lunch, but you have to give up your dessert. In the 90-degree heat, I would have gladly given up my fattening dessert to have a bottle of cold water to bring along.

The dining plan left a family of five from Nashville, Tennessee, similarly dazed and confused:

What was annoying was the inconsistency. You can get a 16-ounce chocolate milk on the kids' plan, but only 8 ounces of white milk at many places. At the Earl of Sandwich, you can get 16 ounces of either kind. A pint of milk would count as a snack (price $1.52), but they wouldn't count a quart of milk (price $1.79) because it wasn't a single serving. However, in Animal Kingdom, my husband bought a water-bottle holder (price $3.75) and used a snack credit. The kids choices' were limited as well, maybe one or two per restaurant.

Readers also report difficulties in keeping their accounts straight. A Saskatoon, Saskatchewan, father of three says you have to watch vendors like a hawk:

We had a problem with a vendor who charged us meal service for each of the ice-cream bars we purchased. This became evident at our final sit-down meal, when we didn't have any meal vouchers left. Check the receipts after every purchase! *You could save yourself a lot of hassles.*

A Havre de Grace, Maryland, mom had a similar experience:

I did want to tell you that we used the dining plan and found it to be not at all user-friendly. There was a lot of confusion on how many meals were on which card, and each place charged differently. It was very frustrating to use. Anyone else using this plan should make sure they put the correct number of meals on the correct cards.

A mom from Shawnee, Kansas, found the dining plan too complex on the restaurants' end:

A comment on Disney Dining—a great savings for us, but it seems like it was tough on the servers at the restaurants. It always took FOREVER for everything to be settled. They just seemed to really dislike dealing with the plan.

Reader Tips for Getting the Most Out of the Plan

A mom from Radford, Virginia, shares this tip:

Warn people to eat lunch early if they have dinner reservations before 7 p.m. Disney does not skimp on food—if you eat a late lunch (where, by the way, they feed you the same ungodly amount of food), you WILL NOT be hungry for dinner. Also, depending on where you go, different Disney employees give you different answers on what counts as a snack. One employee told us anything under $5, and another one said anything under $3. Hint: Use the snacks as your breakfast once you get in the park—we did this the last two days and it worked out great!

A mom from Overland Park, Kansas, has children with dietary restrictions:

Our children are allergic to dairy products, and I found the staff were pretty willing to provide a nondairy dessert option so the kids didn't feel left out.

A mom from Brick, New Jersey, found that the dining plan streamlined her touring:

We truly enjoyed our Disney trip, and this time we purchased the Dining Plan. This was great for the kids because we did a character-dining experience every day. This helped us in the parks because we didn't have to wait in line to see the characters. Instead, we got all of our autographs during our meals.

From a Missouri family of four:

Regarding dining, we found the Dining Plan worthwhile but probably not a fantastic bargain. I felt pressure to spend all of our credits—we went crazy our last day there! It was particularly hard to spend the kids' counter-service credits. We would not have been likely to order many desserts, but they come with the meals—leaving the cost of the desserts off, we probably didn't save much money.

Magic Your Way Premium Package

With the Magic Your Way Premium Package you get lodging; Magic Your Way Premium tickets with Park Hopping and Plus Pack features; breakfast, lunch, and dinner, including character meals and dinner shows; unlimited golf, tennis, fishing excursions, and water sports; select theme-park tours; Cirque du Soleil show tickets; unlimited use of child-care facilities—everything you can think of except for alcoholic beverages. (*Note:* The length of the Magic Your Way Premium Package must equal the total number of nights you stay at a Disney resort, plus one day. Package length cannot be customized to fit your touring plans.)

Disney, needless to say, has built a nice profit into every component of the Magic Your Way Premium Package. If you don't use all features of

unofficial **TIP**
For all Magic Your Way plans, everyone in the room must be on the same package and ticket options. All tickets must be used within 14 days of first use, unless the No Expiration option is purchased.

the plan and did not purchase the No Expiration option on your tickets, Disney makes out even better.

PLATINUM PACKAGE REPRISE The favorite of high rollers who want to prepay for everything they might desire while at Walt Disney World, the Platinum Package gets you lodging; tickets; breakfast, lunch, and dinner in full-service restaurants; unlimited golf, tennis, boating, and recreation; unlimited dinner shows and character breakfasts; primo Cirque du Soleil seats; private in-room child care; unlimited use of child-care facilities; personalized itinerary planning; dinner at Victoria & Albert's restaurant; a spa treatment; a fireworks cruise; admission to select tours; reserved seating for *Fantasmic!*; and (here's the kicker) nightly turndown service! Everything you can think of, in other words, except alcoholic beverages. Per diem prices for the Platinum Package are $209 for adults and $144 for kids in addition to the cost of a standard Magic Your Way package—but anyone who buys this package doesn't give a Goofy fart what the prices are anyway.

NUMBER CRUNCHING

COMPARING A MAGIC YOUR WAY PACKAGE with purchasing the package components separately is a breeze.

1. Pick a Disney resort and decide how many nights you want to stay.
2. Next, work out a rough plan of what you want to do and see so you can determine the admission passes you'll require.
3. When you're ready, call the Disney Reservations Center (DRC) at ☎ 407-W-DISNEY and price a Magic Your Way package with tax for your selected resort and dates. The package will include both admissions and lodging. It's also a good idea to get a quote from a Disney-savvy travel agent (see pages 118 and 119).
4. Now, to calculate the costs of buying your accommodations and admission passes separately, call the DRC a second time. This time, price a room-only rate for the same resort and dates. Be sure to ask about the availability of any special deals. While you're still on the line, obtain the prices, with tax, for the admissions you require. If you're not sure which of the various admission options will best serve you, consult our free Admissions Option analyzer at **TouringPlans.com.**
5. Add the room-only rates and the admission prices. Compare this sum to the DRC quote for the Magic Your Way package.
6. Check for deals and discounts for packages, room-only rates, and admission.

When you upgrade to a Magic Your Way Premium Package, you load the plan with so many features that it's extremely difficult to price them individually. For a rough comparison, price the plan of your choice using the previous steps. To complete the picture, work up a dining budget, excluding alcohol. Add your estimated dining costs to the room-only quote and admissions quote, and compare this to the price of the plan.

THROW ME A LINE!

IF YOU BUY A PACKAGE FROM DISNEY, don't expect reservationists to offer suggestions or help you sort out your options. Generally, they respond only to your specific questions, ducking queries that require an opinion. A reader from North Riverside, Illinois, complains:

> *I have received various pieces of literature from WDW, and it is very confusing to figure out everything. My wife made two telephone calls, and the representatives from WDW were very courteous. However, they only answered the questions posed and were not eager to give advice on what might be most cost-effective.* [The] *WDW reps would not say if we would be better off doing one thing over the other. I feel a person could spend eight hours on the phone with WDW reps and not have any more input than you get from reading the literature.*

If you can't get the information you need from Disney, contact a good travel agent. Chances are the agent can help you weigh your options.

PACKAGES FROM A DIFFERENT PERSPECTIVE

WE'VE ALWAYS EVALUATED PACKAGES from a dollars-and-cents point of view, paying scant attention to other consideration such as time, economy, and convenience. A reader from Westchester County, New York, finally got our attention, writing:

> *I fully understand your position not to recommend the* [Premium] *plans in your guide, because they are not a good buy by financial comparison. However, when one books six rooms, as I have, with guests ages 4 through 59, including a wife, grandchildren, children, sons- and daughters-in-law, and a nanny, the thought of trying to find out what way each family segment would like to go and then arranging for it on a daily basis is a scary scenario. With the Premium Plan, they can go where they want, eat where they want, and Gramps and his roommate don't have the hassle.*

A Mobile, Alabama, couple, also enthusiastic about the Premium Plan, offers these thoughts:

> *Our last trip was for our honeymoon, and we purchased the Premium Magic Your Way Plan. We really enjoyed most of the restaurants we ate at, and we loved being able to order anything we wanted from the menus, but I wouldn't recommend this plan to anyone who is impatient or whose goal is to see the parks. While we had plenty of time to see and do the things we wanted to do, if we had been there for a week or less I probably would have been frustrated with how much time it took to eat three table-service meals a day, once you calculate the secondary time expense of traveling to the restaurant (which may or may not be in the park you're in at the moment). There was one time in particular where we finished eating lunch and basically had to go check in for dinner almost immediately! But if a person has plenty of time, the Premium Plan can be fun, and the Cirque du Soleil tickets were a big bonus—we loved the show!*

Purchasing Room-only Plus Passes versus a Package

*Sue Pisaturo of Small World Vacations (**www.smallworldvacations.com**), a travel agency that specializes in Disney, also thinks there is more involved in a package-purchase decision than money.*

Should you purchase a Walt Disney World package, or buy all the components of the package separately? There's no single answer to this confusing question.

A Walt Disney World package can be compared to a store-bought prepackaged kids' meal, the kind with the little compartments filled with meat, cheese, crackers, drink, and dessert: you just grab the package and go. It's easy, and if it's on sale, why bother doing it yourself? If it's not on sale, it still may be worth the extra money for convenience.

Purchasing the components of your vacation separately is like buying each of the meal's ingredients, cutting them up into neat piles and packaging the lunch yourself. Is it worth the extra time and effort to do it this way? Will you save money if you do it this way?

You have two budgets to balance when you plan your Disney World vacation: time and money. Satisfying both is your ultimate goal. Research and planning are paramount to realizing your Disney vacation dreams. Create your theme-park touring plan prior to making a final decision with regard to the number of days and options on your theme-park passes. Create your dining itinerary (along with advance dining reservations, if possible) to determine if Disney's dining plan can save you some money.

HOTELS *outside* WALT DISNEY WORLD

SELECTING AND BOOKING A HOTEL OUTSIDE WALT DISNEY WORLD

LODGING COSTS OUTSIDE DISNEY WORLD vary incredibly. If you shop around, you can find a clean motel with a pool within 5 to 20 minutes of the World for as low as $40 a night. Because of hot competition, discounts abound, particularly for AAA and AARP members.

There are three primary out-of-the-World areas to consider:

1. INTERNATIONAL DRIVE AREA This area, about 15 to 25 minutes northeast of the World, parallels Interstate 4 on its eastern side and offers a wide selection of hotels and restaurants. Prices range from $56 to $400 per night. The chief drawbacks of this area are its terribly congested roads, countless traffic signals, and inadequate access to westbound I-4. While International's biggest bottleneck is its intersection with Sand Lake Road, the mile between Kirkman and Sand Lake roads is almost always gridlocked. We provide tips for avoiding this traffic in Part Eight (see "Sneak Routes," page 397).

Regarding traffic on International Drive (known locally as I-Drive), these comments are representative. From a Seattle mom:

> *After spending half our trip sitting in traffic on International Drive, those Disney hotels didn't sound so expensive after all.*

A convention-goer from Islip, New York, weighed in with this:

> *When I visited Disney World with my family last summer, we wasted huge chunks of time in traffic on International Drive. Our hotel was*

> *in the section between the big McDonald's* [at Sand Lake Drive] *and Wet 'n Wild* [at Universal Boulevard]. *There are practically no left-turn lanes in this section, so anyone turning left can hold up traffic for a long time. Recently, I returned to Orlando for a trade show and stayed at a hotel on International Drive near the convention center. This section was much saner and far less congested. It's also closer to Disney World.*

Traffic aside, a man from Ottawa, Ontario, sings the praises of his I-Drive experience:

> *International Drive is the place to stay when going to Disney. Your single-paragraph description of this location failed to point out that* [there are] *several discount stores, boutiques, restaurants, mini-putts, and other entertainment facilities, all within walking distance of remarkably inexpensive accommodations and a short drive away from WDW. Many of the chain motels and hotels are located in this area, and the local merchants have created a mini-resort to cater to the tourists. It is the ideal place to unwind after a hard day visiting WDW. I have recommended this location for years and have never heard anything but raves about the wisdom of this advice.*

I-Drive hotels are listed in the *Orlando Official Accommodations Guide* published by the Orlando–Orange County Convention and Visitors Bureau. For a copy, call ☎ 800-255-5786 or 407-363-5872, or see **www.orlandoinfo.com.**

2. LAKE BUENA VISTA AND THE I-4 CORRIDOR A number of hotels are along FL 535 and west of I-4 between Disney World and I-4's intersection with Florida's Turnpike. They're easily reached from the interstate and are near many restaurants, including those on International Drive. The *Orlando Official Accommodations Guide* lists most of them. For some traffic-avoidance tips, see "The I-4 Blues" (page 382) in Part Eight, Arriving and Getting Around.

3. US 192/IRLO BRONSON MEMORIAL HIGHWAY This is the highway to Kissimmee to the south of Disney World. In addition to large, full-service hotels, there are many small, privately owned motels that are often a good value. Several dozen properties on US 192 are nearer Disney parks than are more expensive hotels inside the World. The number and variety of restaurants on US 192 has increased markedly, compensating for the area's primary shortcoming. Locally, US 192 is called Irlo Bronson Memorial Highway. The section to the west of I-4 and the Disney "Maingate" is designated Irlo Bronson Memorial Highway West, while the section from I-4 running southeast toward Kissimmee is Irlo Bronson Highway East.

A senior citizen from Brookfield, Connecticut, was pleased with lodging in the US 192–Kissimmee area:

> *We were amazed to find that from our cheaper and superior accommodations in Kissimmee it took only five minutes longer to reach the park turnstiles than it did from the Disney accommodations.*

Continued on page 234

Hotel Concentrations around Walt Disney World

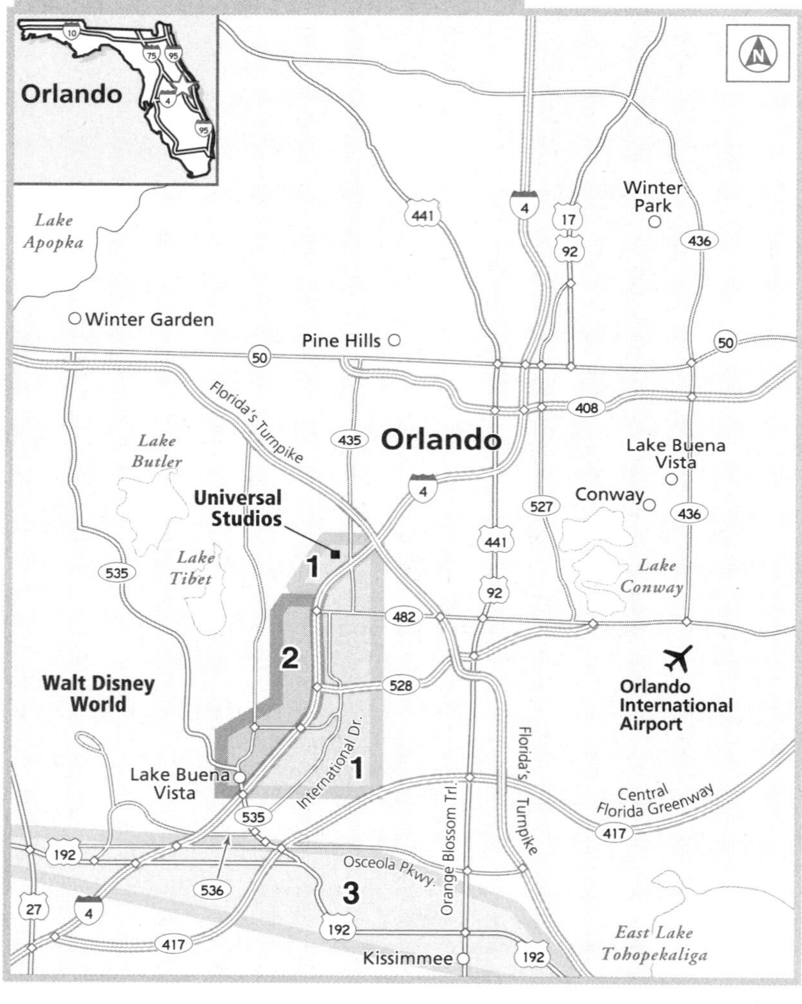

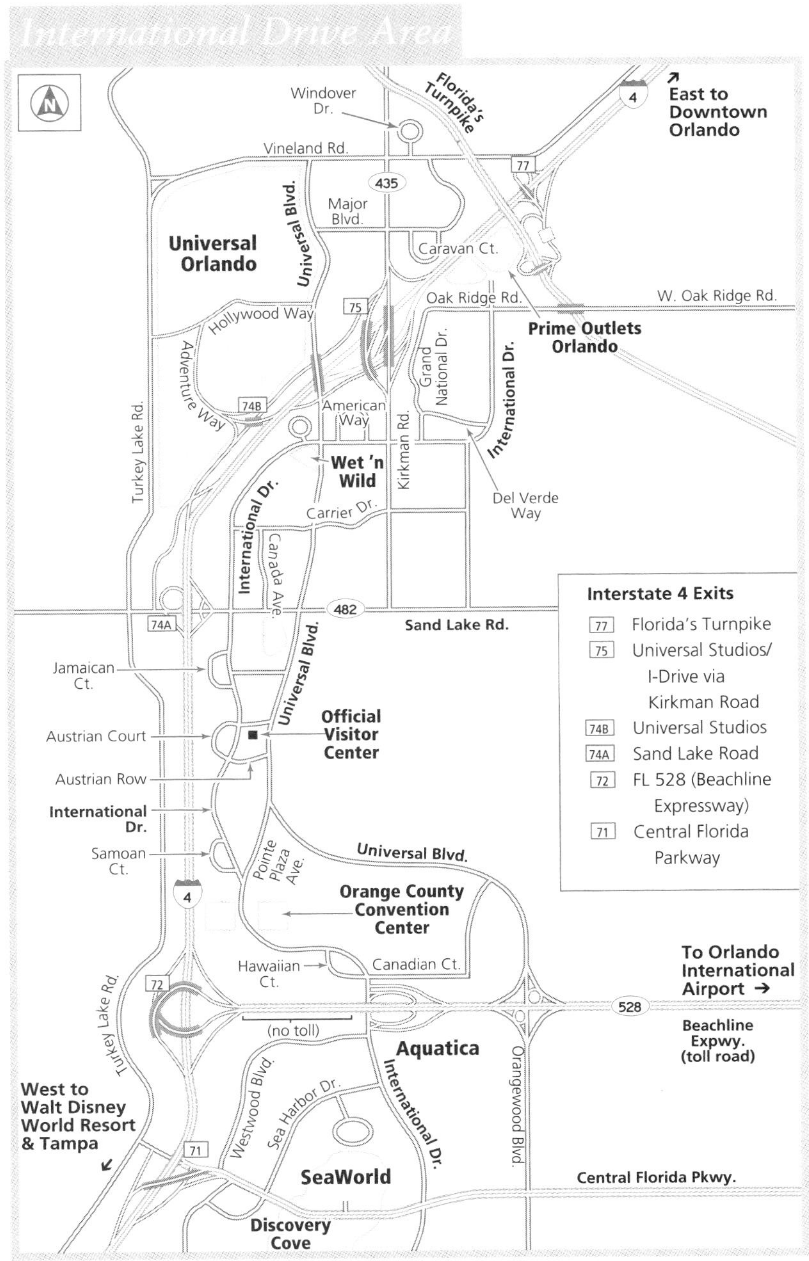
International Drive Area
N
Windover Dr.
Florida's Turnpike
4
East to Downtown Orlando
Vineland Rd.
77
435
Major Blvd.
Universal Blvd.
Universal Orlando
Caravan Ct.
Oak Ridge Rd.
W. Oak Ridge Rd.
75
Hollywood Way
Prime Outlets Orlando
Adventure Way
Grand National Dr.
International Dr.
74B
American Way
Kirkman Rd.
Turkey Lake Rd.
Wet 'n Wild
Del Verde Way
International Dr.
Carrier Dr.
Canada Ave.
482
Sand Lake Rd.
74A
Universal Blvd.
Jamaican Ct.
Austrian Court
Official Visitor Center
Austrian Row
International Dr.
Samoan Ct.
Universal Blvd.
Pointe Plaza Ave.
4
Orange County Convention Center
Hawaiian Ct.
Canadian Ct.
To Orlando International Airport →
72
528
Turkey Lake Rd.
(no toll)
Aquatica
Beachline Expwy. (toll road)
Westwood Blvd.
Sea Harbor Dr.
International Dr.
Orangewood Blvd.
West to Walt Disney World Resort & Tampa
71
SeaWorld
Central Florida Pkwy.
Discovery Cove
Interstate 4 Exits
77 Florida's Turnpike
75 Universal Studios/ I-Drive via Kirkman Road
74B Universal Studios
74A Sand Lake Road
72 FL 528 (Beachline Expressway)
71 Central Florida Parkway

Lake Buena Vista Resort Area and the I-4 Corridor

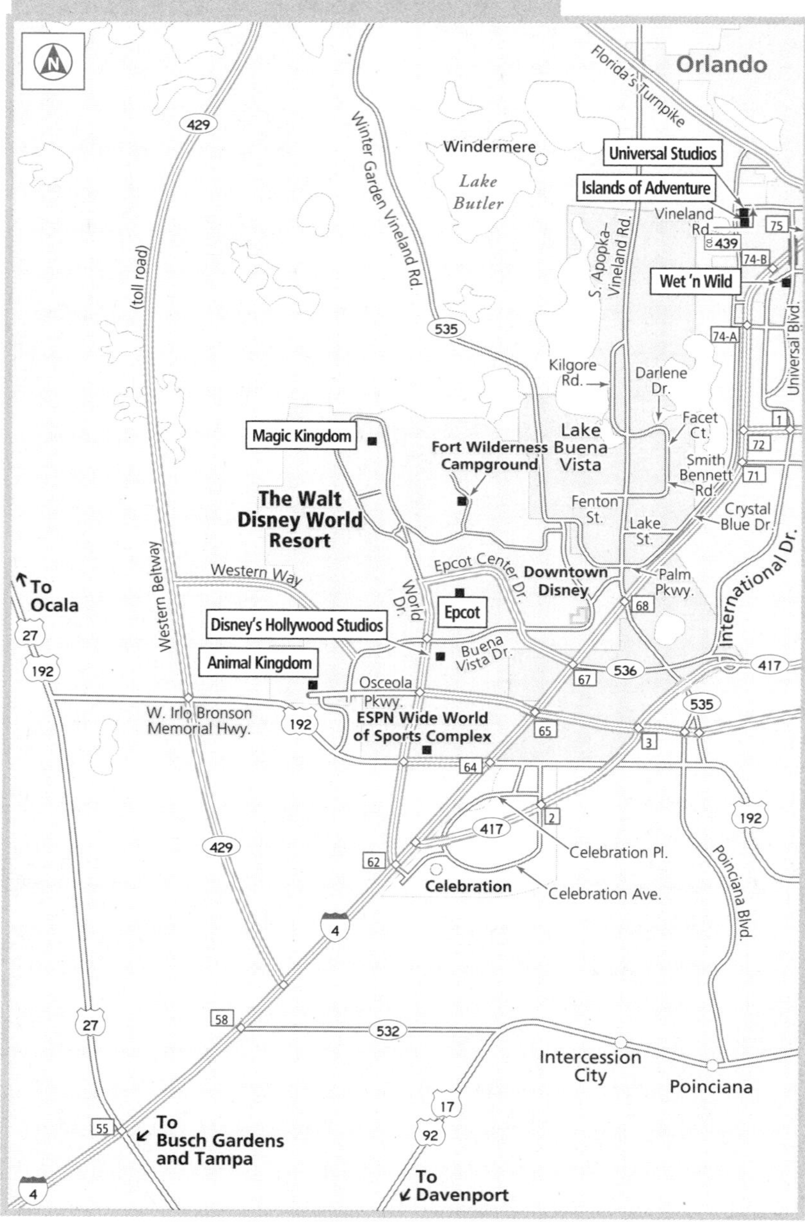

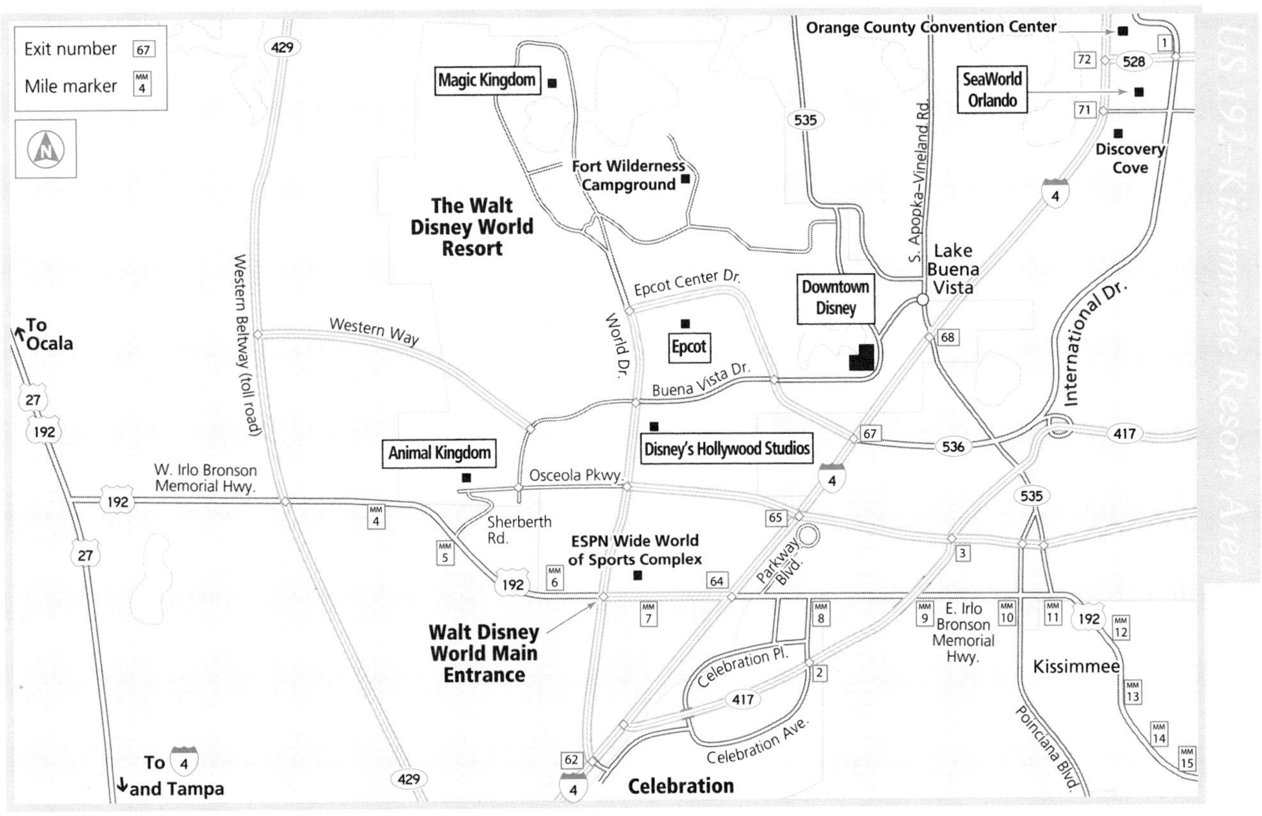
US 192–Kissimmee Resort Area
Exit number
Mile marker
Magic Kingdom
Fort Wilderness Campground
The Walt Disney World Resort
Orange County Convention Center
SeaWorld Orlando
Discovery Cove
S. Apopka–Vineland Rd.
Lake Buena Vista
International Dr.
Downtown Disney
Epcot Center Dr.
Epcot
World Dr.
Buena Vista Dr.
Western Way
Western Beltway (toll road)
To Ocala
Animal Kingdom
Disney's Hollywood Studios
Osceola Pkwy.
W. Irlo Bronson Memorial Hwy.
Sherberth Rd.
ESPN Wide World of Sports Complex
Parkway Blvd.
E. Irlo Bronson Memorial Hwy.
Kissimmee
Walt Disney World Main Entrance
Celebration Pl.
Celebration Ave.
Poinciana Blvd.
Celebration
To 4 and Tampa

Continued from page 229

Hotels on US 192 and in Kissimmee are listed in the "Choose Kissimmee" visitors guide. Order a copy by calling ☎ 800-327-9159, or view it online **www.floridakiss.com.**

DRIVING TIME TO THE PARKS FOR VISITORS LODGING OUTSIDE WALT DISNEY WORLD

OUR HOTEL INFORMATION CHART on pages 268–285 shows the commuting time to the Disney theme parks from each hotel listed. Those commuting times represent an average of several test runs. Your actual time may be shorter or longer depending on traffic, road construction (if any), and delays at traffic signals.

The commuting times in "How the Hotels Compare" show conclusively that distance from the theme parks is not necessarily the dominant factor in determining commuting times. Among those we list, the hotels on Major Boulevard opposite the Kirkman Road entrance to Universal Orlando, for example, are the most distant (in miles) from the Disney parks. But because they're only one traffic signal from easy access to I-4, commuting time to the parks is significantly less than for many closer hotels.

Note that times in the chart differ from those in "Door-to-Door Commuting Times" in Part Eight. The door-to-door chart in Part Eight compares using the Disney Transportation System and driving your own car *inside* Walt Disney World. These times include actual transportation time plus tram, monorail, or other connections required to get from the parking lots to the entrance turnstiles. The hotel chart's commuting times, by contrast, represent only the driving time to and from the parks, with no consideration of getting to and from the parking lot to the turnstiles.

Add to the commuting times in our "How the Hotels Compare" chart a few minutes for paying your parking fee and parking. Once you park at the Transportation and Ticket Center (Magic Kingdom parking lot), it takes 20 to 30 minutes more to reach the Magic Kingdom via monorail or ferry. To reach Epcot from its parking lot, add 7 to 10 minutes. At Disney's Hollywood Studios and Animal Kingdom, the lot-to-gate transit is 5 to 10 minutes. If you haven't purchased your theme-park admission in advance, tack on another 10 to 20 minutes.

GETTING A GOOD DEAL ON A ROOM OUTSIDE WALT DISNEY WORLD

HOTEL DEVELOPMENT AT WALT DISNEY WORLD has sharpened competition among lodgings throughout the Walt Disney World–Orlando–Kissimmee area. Hotels outside the World struggle to fill their rooms, and the recession has only made things worse. Unable to compete with Disney resorts for convenience or perks, off-World hotels lure patrons with bargain rates. In high season, during holiday periods, and during large conventions at the Orange County Convention Center, even the most modest property is sold out.

Here are strategies for getting a good deal on a room outside Walt Disney World. The list may refer to travel-market players unfamiliar to you, but many tips we provide for Disney World deals work equally well almost anyplace you need a hotel. Once you understand these strategies, you'll be able to routinely obtain rooms for the lowest possible rates.

1. ORLANDO MAGICARD Orlando Magicard is a discount program sponsored by the Orlando–Orange County Convention and Visitors Bureau. Cardholders are eligible for discounts of 12% to 50% at about 50 hotels. The Magicard is also good for discounts at some area attractions and a dinner theater. Valid for up to six persons, the card isn't available for larger groups or conventions.

To obtain a free Magicard and a list of participating hotels and attractions, call ☎ 800-643-9492 or 407-363-5872. On the Web, go to **www.orlandoinfo.com/magicard;** the Magicard and accompanying brochure can be printed from a personal computer. If you miss getting one before you leave home, obtain one at the Convention and Visitors Bureau Information Center at 8723 International Drive. When you call for your Magicard, also request the *Orlando Official Vacation Guide.*

2. EXIT INFORMATION GUIDE Exit Information Guide (EIG) publishes a book of coupons for discounts at hotels statewide. It's free in many restaurants and motels on main highways leading to Florida. Because most travelers make reservations before leaving home, picking up the book en route doesn't help much. If you call and use a credit card, EIG will send the guide first class for $3 ($5 U.S. for Canadian delivery). Contact Exit Information Guide at 4205 NW Sixth Street, Gainesville, FL 32609; ☎ 352-371-3948 or 800-332-3948; **www.travelerdiscountguide.com.**

3. HOTEL SHOPPING ON THE INTERNET Hotels use the Internet to fill rooms during slow periods and to advertise limited-time specials. Hotels also use more-traditional communication avenues, such as promoting specials through travel agents. If you enjoy cybershopping, have at it, but hotel shopping on the Internet isn't as quick or convenient as handing the task to your travel agent. When we bump into a great deal on the Web, we call our agent. Often she can beat the deal or improve on it (perhaps with an upgrade). A good agent working with a savvy, helpful client can work wonders.

See the chart on the next page for Web sites we've found most dependable for discounts on Disney-area hotels.

The secret to shopping on the Internet is, well, shopping. When we're really looking for a deal, we check all the sites listed in the chart. Flexibility on dates and location are helpful, and we always give our travel agent the opportunity to beat any deal we find.

We recommend choosing a hotel based on location, room quality, price, commuting time to the parks (all summarized in the chart on pages 268–285), plus any features important to you. Next, check each of the applicable sites that follow. You'll be able to ferret out the best Internet deal in about 30 minutes. Then call the hotel to see if you can save more by booking directly. Start by asking the hotel for specials. If their response doesn't beat the Internet deal, tell them what you've found and ask if they can do better.

OUR FAVORITE ONLINE HOTEL RESOURCES

www.mousesavers.com Best site for hotels in Disney World.

www.dreamsunlimitedtravel.com Excellent for both Disney and non-Disney hotels.

www.2000orlando-florida.com Comprehensive hotel site.

www.valuetrips.com Specializes in budget accommodations.

www.travelocity.com Multidestination travel superstore.

www.roomsaver.com Provides discount coupons for hotels.

www.floridakiss.com Primarily US 192–Kissimmee area hotels.

www.orlandoinfo.com Good info; not user-friendly for booking.

www.orlandovacation.com Great rates for condos and home rentals.

www.expedia.com Largest of the multidestination travel sites.

www.hotels.com Largest Internet hotel-booking service; many other sites link to this site and its subsidiary, **www.hoteldiscounts.com.**

SO WHO OFFERS THE BEST DEALS ON THE NET? *Unofficial Guide* statistician Fred Hazelton analyzed more than 81 million rate quotes from Internet sellers, individual and chain-hotel Web sites, and hotel reservations departments for 350 Disney and Orlando-area hotels. The idea was to determine which sellers had the best deals most (or a high percentage) of the time.

We picked the sellers in the chart on the next page based on how often a given seller's rate was lower than all its competitors. For example, a success rate of 70% means the seller beat all competitors who market the same hotels 70% of the time. The numbers can be tricky, though. A seller that offers hotels not sold by others is obviously going to have the best deals on those properties most of the time, and consequently score high. Conversely, a seller that lists a large number of hotels also sold by many competitors will offer the best price a lower percentage of the time.

We collected rates from most of Web sites with rates for hotels in and around the Orlando-Kissimmee area; we also obtained rates from hotel front desks and hotel Web sites. When we compared the rates from all sellers, we found that the rates offered **www.hotels.com** and **www.skoosh.com** beat out all others about half of the time. Skoosh, however, offers a much smaller selection of hotels than biggies like Expedia and Travelocity. The best of the large Web sites (and best overall) was **www.hotels.com,** with a 27% success rate. Although it doesn't have the best rates frequently, **www.octopustravel.com** offers substantial savings when it does. Also note that hotel front desks and hotel Web sites offered the lowest rate about two-thirds of the time (65% and 60%, respectively). The Web site **MouseSavers.com,** which specializes in discount codes for hotels, is not listed because the site doesn't actually sell rooms. To use the codes, you quote the relevant code to an actual seller—the Walt Disney Travel Company, for example.

One thing we noticed when getting rates from all the different sellers is that no one seller offered the best rate all the time. Rankings are ordered from top to bottom, best to worst.

During our research on hotel rates we noticed that there is a period where the rates are almost always at their lowest. It happens between 45 and 60 days before the date of arrival. We collected more than 108 million rate quotes, covering all possible dates of arrival and starting at 300 days before the date of arrival. As the date gets closer we record the changes in the price and see that the lowest available price for a hotel room occurs in that 45- to 60-day window about 80% of the time. This means that no matter when you book your hotel room, you should always check to see if a lower rate is available about 60 days before your date of arrival. We checked this result with experts in the hotel industry and discovered that hotel companies typically discuss their occupancy rates about 45 to 60 days in the future. So if a hotel is experiencing lower-than-expected occupancy rates, it is most likely to adjust its prices around the 60-day mark.

While Expedia is often able to offer better deals on some larger properties (for example, Hilton and Doubletree), some Disney-centric travel sites, such as **www.dreamsunlimitedtravel.com** and **MouseSavers .com,** form special relationships with specific hotels that can result in unusually juicy discounts. Because the megasites like Orbitz, Expedia, and **www.hotels.com** have neither the time nor inclination to nurture such relationships, they can't obtain these sweetheart deals. At the Buena Vista Suites, for example, Dreams Unlimited's rate was more than 10% lower than Hotels.com's already discounted rate.

The chart below summarizes how much you can expect to save on average from each of the Internet sellers listed previously. (Only those for which we have a minimum of 1,000 observations are included.)

Method 1: Average percentage by which the seller beats its nearest competitor.

Method 2: Average percentage by which the seller beats the highest rate advertised.

Other tools in the hotel-hunting arsenal are **Travelaxe.com, Kayak.com,** and the *Unofficial Guide*'s own Web site, **TouringPlans.com.** Travelaxe

SELLER	%AGE OF DAYS ON WHICH SELLER HAS LOWER RATE	AVERAGE SAVINGS (METHOD 1)	AVERAGE SAVINGS (METHOD 2)
www.hotels.com	27%	8%	9%
www.skoosh.com	20%	5%	7%
www.orbitz.com	17%	3%	10%
www.worldres.com	14%	2%	15%
www.hotelclub.com	11%	8%	9%
wwwtravelworm.com	3%	1%	7%
www.octupustravel.com	2%	11%	17%
www.hotelkingdom.com	2%	6%	9%
www.expedia.com	2%	2%	2%
ALL OTHERS	2%	4%	5%

and Kayak are hotel search engines that look at hotelier Web sites to find the cheapest rate for more than 200 Disney-area hotels. Travelaxe does this through free software you can download to your PC (it won't run on Macs), while Kayak is a traditional Web site with no download needed. Both sites offer filters such as price, quality rating, and proximity to a specific location (Walt Disney World, SeaWorld, the convention center, airport, and so on) to allow you to narrow your search. Both sites also scan for the best rates in cities throughout the United States.

TouringPlans.com uses both Travelaxe and Kayak to tell you which Web site has the best rate for most of the hotels covered in this book up to 300 days in advance, with prices updated nightly. These nightly rates are added to our database of more than 108 million hotel quotes covering the Walt Disney World area since 2005. We use this massive archive of historical prices to predict, for any given hotel and Web site, whether the rate you're quoted today is likely to go up, down, or stay the same over the next week. That lets you know whether you should lock in at that price or whether you'd be better off biding your time. And how do you know whether a rate is good? TouringPlans.com does something we've not seen on any other Web site: It tells you the highest, lowest, and average price paid over the past 90 days for the same room and length of stay. By giving you historical context around the rate you're quoted, you'll easily be able to determine whether it's a fantastic deal, just average, or not worth considering.

4. IF YOU MAKE YOUR OWN RESERVATION Always call the hotel in question, not the chain's national toll-free number. Often, reservationists at the toll-free number are unaware of local specials. Always ask about specials before you inquire about corporate rates. Don't hesitate to bargain, but do it before you check in. If you're buying a hotel's weekend package and want to extend your stay, for example, you can often obtain at least the corporate rate for the extra days.

CONDOMINIUMS AND VACATION HOMES

VACATION HOMES ARE FREESTANDING, while condominiums are essentially one- to three-bedroom accommodations in a larger building housing a number of similar units. Because condos tend to be part of large developments (frequently time-shares), amenities such as swimming pools, playgrounds, game arcades, and fitness centers often rival those found in the best hotels. Generally speaking, condo developments do not have restaurants, lounges, or spas. In a condo, if something goes wrong, there will be someone on hand to fix the problem. Vacation homes rented from a property-management company likewise will have someone to come to the rescue, though responsiveness tends to vary vastly from company to company. If you rent directly from an owner, correcting problems is often more difficult, particularly when the owner doesn't live in the same area as the rental home.

In a vacation home, all the amenities are contained in the home (though in planned developments there may be community amenities available as well). Depending on the specific home, you might find a small swimming pool, hot tub, two-car garage, family room, game room, and even a home theater. Features found in both condos and vacation homes include full kitchens, laundry rooms, TVs, DVD players/VCRs, and frequently stereos. Interestingly, though almost all freestanding vacation homes have private pools, very few have backyards. This means that, except for swimming, the kids are pretty much relegated to playing in the house.

Time-share condos are clones when it come to furniture and decor, but single-owner condos and vacation homes are furnished and decorated in a style that reflects the taste of the owner. Vacation homes, usually one- to two-story houses located in a subdivision, very rarely afford interesting views (though some overlook lakes or natural areas), while condos, especially the high-rise variety, sometimes offer exceptional ones.

The Price Is Nice

The best deals in lodging in the Walt Disney World area are vacation homes and single-owner condos. Prices range from about $65 a night for two-bedroom condos and townhomes to $200 to $500 a night for three- to seven-bedroom vacation homes. Forgetting about taxes to keep the comparison simple, let's compare renting a vacation home to staying at one of Disney's Value resorts. A family of two parents, two teens, and two grandparents would need three hotel rooms at Disney's Pop Century Resort. At the lowest rate obtainable, that would run you $82 per night, per room, or $246 total. Rooms are 260 square feet each, so you'd have a total of 780 square feet. Each room has a private bath and a television.

Renting at the same time of year from **All Star Vacation Homes** (no relation to Disney's All-Star Resorts), you can stay at a 2,053-square-foot, four-bedroom, three-bath vacation home with a private pool three miles from Walt Disney World for $219—a savings of $27 per night over the Disney Value-resort rate. With four bedrooms, each of the teens can have his or her own room. Further, for the dates we checked, All Star Vacation Homes was running a special in which they threw in a free rental car with a one-week home rental.

But that's not all—the home comes with the following features and amenities: a big-screen TV with PlayStation, DVD player, and VCR (assorted games and DVDs available for complimentary checkout at the rental office); a CD player; a heatable private pool; five additional TVs (one in each bedroom and one in the family room); a fully equipped kitchen; a two-car garage; a hot tub; a laundry room with full-size washer and dryer; a fully furnished private patio; and a child-safety fence.

The home is in a community with a 24-hour gated entrance. Available at the community center are a large swimming pool; a whirlpool; tennis, volleyball, and half-court basketball courts; a children's playground; a gym and exercise room; a convenience store; and a 58-seat cinema.

One thing we like about All Star Vacation Homes is that its Web site (**www.allstarvacationhomes.com**) offers detailed information, including a dozen or more photos of each specific home. When you book, the home you've been looking at is the actual one you're reserving. (If you want to see how the home previously described is furnished, for instance,

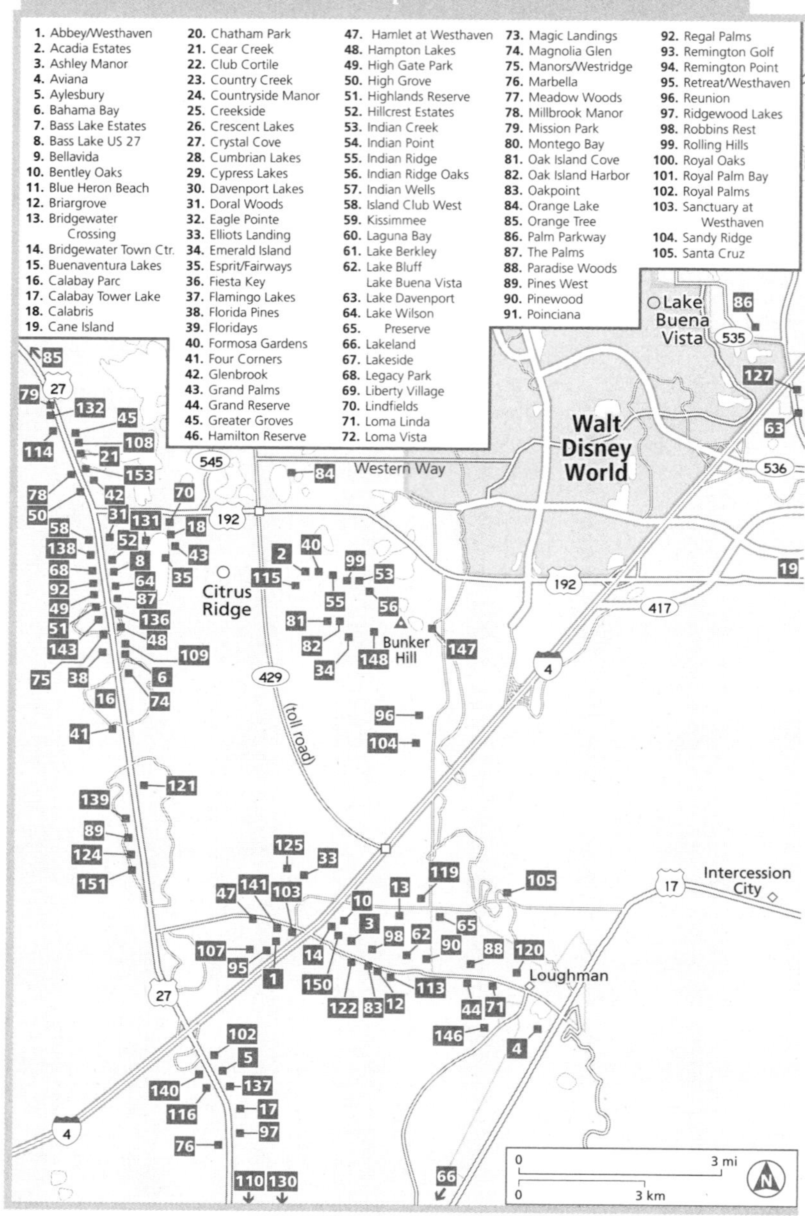
Rental-home Developments near WDW
1. Abbey/Westhaven
2. Acadia Estates
3. Ashley Manor
4. Aviana
5. Aylesbury
6. Bahama Bay
7. Bass Lake Estates
8. Bass Lake US 27
9. Bellavida
10. Bentley Oaks
11. Blue Heron Beach
12. Briargrove
13. Bridgewater Crossing
14. Bridgewater Town Ctr.
15. Buenaventura Lakes
16. Calabay Parc
17. Calabay Tower Lake
18. Calabris
19. Cane Island
20. Chatham Park
21. Cear Creek
22. Club Cortile
23. Country Creek
24. Countryside Manor
25. Creekside
26. Crescent Lakes
27. Crystal Cove
28. Cumbrian Lakes
29. Cypress Lakes
30. Davenport Lakes
31. Doral Woods
32. Eagle Pointe
33. Elliots Landing
34. Emerald Island
35. Esprit/Fairways
36. Fiesta Key
37. Flamingo Lakes
38. Florida Pines
39. Floridays
40. Formosa Gardens
41. Four Corners
42. Glenbrook
43. Grand Palms
44. Grand Reserve
45. Greater Groves
46. Hamilton Reserve
47. Hamlet at Westhaven
48. Hampton Lakes
49. High Gate Park
50. High Grove
51. Highlands Reserve
52. Hillcrest Estates
53. Indian Creek
54. Indian Point
55. Indian Ridge
56. Indian Ridge Oaks
57. Indian Wells
58. Island Club West
59. Kissimmee
60. Laguna Bay
61. Lake Berkley
62. Lake Bluff
Lake Buena Vista
63. Lake Davenport
64. Lake Wilson
65. Preserve
66. Lakeland
67. Lakeside
68. Legacy Park
69. Liberty Village
70. Lindfields
71. Loma Linda
72. Loma Vista
73. Magic Landings
74. Magnolia Glen
75. Manors/Westridge
76. Marbella
77. Meadow Woods
78. Millbrook Manor
79. Mission Park
80. Montego Bay
81. Oak Island Cove
82. Oak Island Harbor
83. Oakpoint
84. Orange Lake
85. Orange Tree
86. Palm Parkway
87. The Palms
88. Paradise Woods
89. Pines West
90. Pinewood
91. Poinciana
92. Regal Palms
93. Remington Golf
94. Remington Point
95. Retreat/Westhaven
96. Reunion
97. Ridgewood Lakes
98. Robbins Rest
99. Rolling Hills
100. Royal Oaks
101. Royal Palm Bay
102. Royal Palms
103. Sanctuary at Westhaven
104. Sandy Ridge
105. Santa Cruz
Lake Buena Vista
Walt Disney World
Western Way
Citrus Ridge
Bunker Hill
(toll road)
Intercession City
Loughman
0 3 mi
0 3 km
N

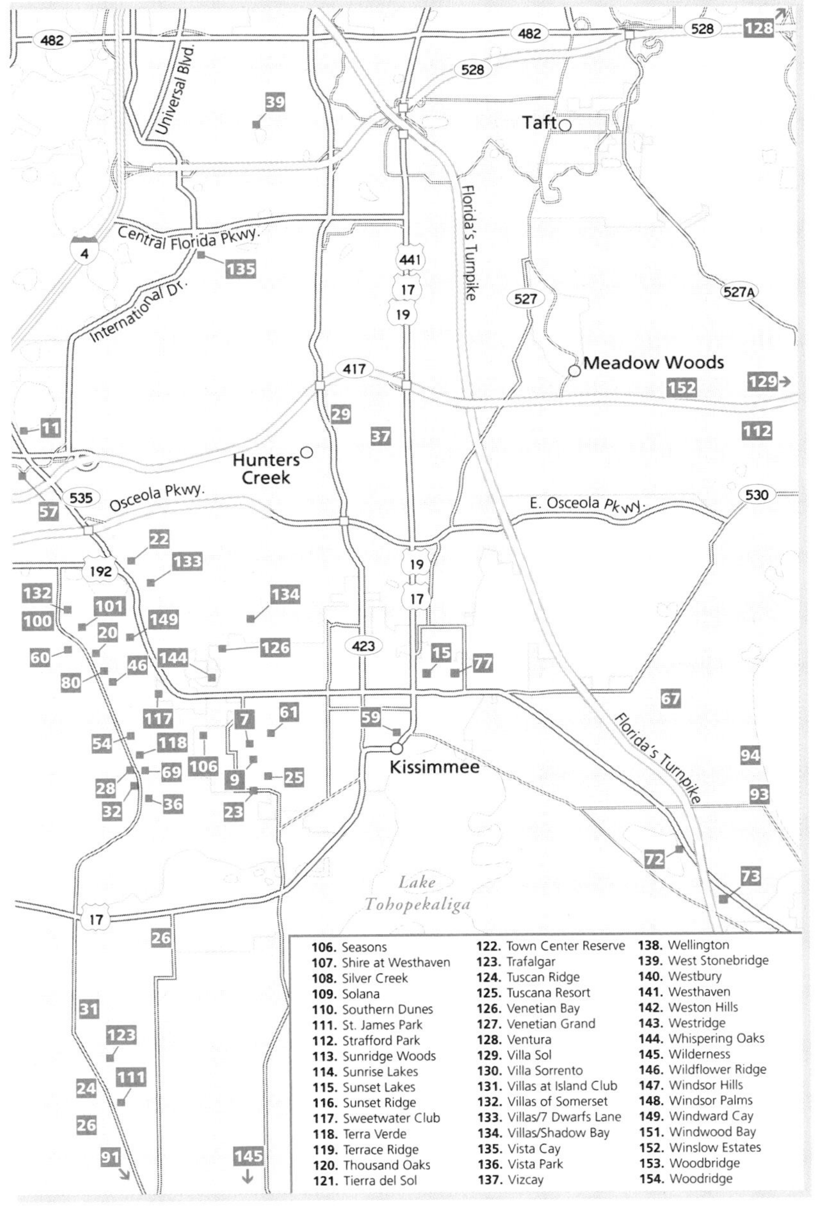
482
Universal Blvd.
39
482
528
528
128
Taft
Florida's Turnpike
Central Florida Pkwy.
4
135
International Dr.
441
17
19
527
527A
Meadow Woods
152
129
417
29
37
112
11
Hunters Creek
535
Osceola Pkwy.
57
E. Osceola Pkwy.
530
22
133
192
19
17
132
100
101
149
134
20
60
126
423
15
77
144
46
80
117
7
61
59
67
54
118
106
69
Kissimmee
Florida's Turnpike
94
28
9
25
93
32
36
23
72
73
Lake Tohopekaliga
17
26
31
123
111
24
26
91
145
106. Seasons
107. Shire at Westhaven
108. Silver Creek
109. Solana
110. Southern Dunes
111. St. James Park
112. Strafford Park
113. Sunridge Woods
114. Sunrise Lakes
115. Sunset Lakes
116. Sunset Ridge
117. Sweetwater Club
118. Terra Verde
119. Terrace Ridge
120. Thousand Oaks
121. Tierra del Sol
122. Town Center Reserve
123. Trafalgar
124. Tuscan Ridge
125. Tuscana Resort
126. Venetian Bay
127. Venetian Grand
128. Ventura
129. Villa Sol
130. Villa Sorrento
131. Villas at Island Club
132. Villas of Somerset
133. Villas/7 Dwarfs Lane
134. Villas/Shadow Bay
135. Vista Cay
136. Vista Park
137. Vizcay
138. Wellington
139. West Stonebridge
140. Westbury
141. Westhaven
142. Weston Hills
143. Westridge
144. Whispering Oaks
145. Wilderness
146. Wildflower Ridge
147. Windsor Hills
148. Windsor Palms
149. Windward Cay
151. Windwood Bay
152. Winslow Estates
153. Woodbridge
154. Woodridge

go to the home page and enter the property code **2-8144 SP-WP** in the search box at the top right. Choose the first link in the search results; on the next page, scroll down until you see the home with the property code above. Click the link for photos and a floor plan.)

On the other hand, some vacation-home companies, like rental-car agencies, don't assign you a specific home until the day you arrive. These companies provide photos of a "typical home" instead of making information available on each of the individual homes in their inventory. In this case, you have to take the company's word that the typical home pictured is representative and that the home you'll be assigned will be just as nice.

How the Vacation-home Market Works

In the Orlando–Walt Disney World area, there are almost 19,000 rental homes, including stand-alone homes, single-owner condos (that is, not time-shares), and townhomes. The same area has about 112,000 hotel rooms. Almost all the rental homes are owned by individuals who occupy them for at least a week or two each year; the rest of the year, the owners make the homes available for rent. Some owners deal directly with renters, while others enlist the assistance of a property-management company.

Incredibly, about 700 property-management companies operate in the Orlando–Walt Disney World market. Most of these are mom-and-pop outfits that manage an inventory of ten homes or less (probably fewer than 70 companies oversee more than 100 rental homes).

Homeowners pay these companies to maintain and promote their properties and handle all rental transactions. Some homes are made available to wholesalers, vacation packagers, and travel agents in deals negotiated either directly by the owners or by property-management companies on the owners' behalf. A wholesaler or vacation packager will occasionally drop its rates to sell slow-moving inventory, but more commonly the cost to renters is higher than when dealing directly with owners or management companies: because most wholesalers and packagers sell their inventory through travel agents, both the wholesaler/packager's markup and the travel agent's commission are passed along to the renter. These costs are in addition to the owner's cut and/or the fee for the property manager.

Along similar lines, logic may suggest that the lowest rate of all can be obtained by dealing directly with owners, thus eliminating middlemen. Although this is sometimes true, it's more often the case that property-management companies offer the best rates. With their marketing expertise and larger customer base, these companies can produce a higher occupancy rate than can the owners themselves. What's more, management companies, or at least the larger ones, can achieve economies of scale not available to owners in regard to maintenance, cleaning, linens, even acquiring furniture and appliances (if a house is not already furnished). The combination of higher occupancy rates and economies of scale adds up to a win–win situation for owners, management companies, and renters alike.

Location, Location, Location

The best vacation home is one that is within easy commuting distance of the theme parks. If you plan to spend some time at SeaWorld and the Universal parks, you'll want something just to the northeast of Walt Disney World (between the World and Orlando). If you plan to spend most of your time in the World, the best selection of vacation homes is along US 192 to the south of the park.

Walt Disney World is located mostly in Orange County but has a small southern tip that dips into Osceola County, which, along with Polk County to the west of the World, is where most vacation homes and single-owner condos and town houses are located. Zoning laws in Orange County (which also includes most of Orlando, Universal Studios, SeaWorld, Lake Buena Vista, and the International Drive area) used to prohibit short-term rentals of homes and single-owner condos, but in recent years the county has loosened its zoning restrictions in a few predominantly tourist-oriented areas. So far, practically all of the vacation-rental homes in Orange County are in the **Floridays** and **Vista Cay** developments.

By our reckoning, about half the rental homes in Osceola County and all the rental homes in Polk County are too far away from Walt Disney World for commuting to be practical. That said, an entrance to Walt Disney World off the FL 429 four-lane toll road halves the commute from many of the vacation-home developments arrayed around the intersection of US 192 and US 27. FL 429 runs north–south from I-4 south of Walt Disney World to Florida's Turnpike. You might be able to save a few bucks by staying farther out, but the most desirable homes to be found are in Vista Cay and in developments no more than four miles from Disney World's main entrance on US 192 (Irlo Bronson Memorial Highway), in Osceola County.

To get the most from a vacation home, you need to be close enough to commute in 20 minutes or less to your Walt Disney World destination. This will allow for naps, quiet time, swimming, and dollar-saving meals you prepare yourself. Though traffic and road conditions are as important as the distance from a vacation home to your Disney destination, we recommend a home no farther than 5 miles away in areas northeast of Walt Disney World and no farther than 4.5 miles away in areas south of the park. Bear in mind that rental companies calculate distance from the vacation home to the absolute nearest square inch of Disney property, so in most instances you can expect to commute another three or more miles within Walt Disney World to reach your ultimate destination.

Shopping for a Vacation Home

The only practical way to shop for a rental home is on the Web. This makes it relatively easy to compare different properties and rental companies; on the downside, there are so many owners, rental companies, and individual homes to choose from that you could research yourself into a stupor. There are three main types of Web sites in the home-rental game: those for property-management companies, which showcase a given company's homes and are set up for direct bookings;

individual owner sites; and third-party listings sites, which advertise properties available through different owners and sometimes management companies as well. Sites in the last category will usually refer prospective renters to an owner's or management company's site for reservations.

We've found that most property-management sites are not very well designed and will test your patience to the max. You can practically click yourself into old age trying to see all the homes available or figure out where on earth they're located. Nearly all claim to be "just minutes from Disney." (By that reasoning, we should list our homes; they're also just minutes from Disney . . . 570 minutes, to be exact!)

Many Web sites list homes according to towns (such as Auburndale, Clermont, Davenport, Haines City, and Winter Garden) or real-estate developments (including Eagle Point, Formosa Gardens, Indian Ridge, and Wyndham Palms) in the general Disney area, none of which you're likely to be familiar with. The information that counts is the distance of a vacation home or condo from Walt Disney World; for that you often must look for something like "four miles from Disney" embedded in the home's description. If you visit a site that lists homes by towns or real estate developments, begin by looking at our map on the following pages that shows where all these places are in relation to Walt Disney World. Otherwise, you should shop elsewhere.

The best Web sites provide the following:

- Numerous photos and in-depth descriptions of individual homes to make comparisons quick and easy
- Overview maps or text descriptions that reflect how distant specific homes or developments are from Walt Disney World
- The ability to book the specific individual rental home of your choice on the site
- A easy-to-find telephone number for non-Internet bookings and questions

The best sites are also easy to navigate, they let you see what you're interested in without your having to log in or divulge any personal information, and they list memberships in such organizations as the Better Business Bureau and the Central Florida Vacation Rental Managers Association (log on to **www.cfvrma.org** for the association's code of ethics).

Recommended Web Sites

After checking out dozens upon dozens of sites, here are the ones we recommend. All of them meet the criteria listed above. If you're stunned that there are so few of them, well, so were we. (For the record, we elected not to list some sites that met our criteria but whose homes are too far away from Walt Disney World.)

All Star Vacation Homes (**www.allstarvacationhomes.com**) is easily the best of the management-company sites, with easily accessible photos and plenty of details about featured homes. All the company's rental properties are within either four miles of Walt Disney World or three miles of Universal Studios.

Orlando's Finest Vacation Homes (**www.orlandosfinest.com**) represents both homeowners and vacation-home-management companies. Offering a broad inventory, the Orlando's Finest Web site features photos and information on individual homes. Although the info is not as detailed as that offered by the All Star Vacation Homes site, friendly Disney Rents sales agents can fill in the blanks.

The Web site for the **Orlando–Orange County Convention and Visitors Bureau** (**www.orlandoinfo.com**) is the place to go if you're interested in renting a condominium at one of the many time-share developments (click on "Places to Stay" at the site's home page). You can call the developments directly, but going through this Web site allows you to bypass sales departments and escape their high-pressure invitations to sit through sales presentations (see "Free Tickets and the Time-share Game" (page 57) for a worst-case scenario. The site also lists hotels and vacation homes.

Vacation Rental by Owner (**www.vrbo.com**) is a nationwide vacation-homes listings service that puts prospective renters in direct contact with owners. The site is straightforward and always lists a large number of rental properties in Celebration, Disney's planned community situated about eight to ten minutes from the theme parks. Two similar listings services with good Web sites are **Vacation Rentals 411** (**www.vacationrentals411.com**) and **Last Minute Villas** (**www.lastminutevillas.net**).

Making Contact

Once you've found a vacation home you like, check around the Web site for a Frequently Asked Questions (FAQ) page. If there's not a FAQ page, here are some of the things you'll want to check out on the phone with the owner or rental company.

1. How close is the property to Walt Disney World?
2. Is the home or condominium that I see on the Internet the one that I'll get?
3. Is the property part of a time-share development?
4. Are there any specials or discounts available?
5. Is everything included in the rental price, or are there additional charges? What about taxes?
6. How old is the home or condo I'm interested in? Has it been refurbished recently?
7. What is the view from the property?
8. Is the property near any noisy roads?
9. What is your smoking policy?
10. Are pets allowed? This consideration is as important to those who want to avoid pets as to those who want to bring them.
11. Is the pool heated?
12. Is there a fenced backyard where children can play?
13. How many people can be seated at the main dining table?
14. Is there a separate dedicated telephone at the property?

15. Is high-speed Internet access available?
16. Are linens and towels provided?
17. How far are the nearest supermarket and drugstore?
18. Are child-care services available?
19. Are there restaurants nearby?
20. Is transportation to the parks provided?
21. Will we need a car?
22. What is required to make a reservation?
23. What is your change/cancellation policy?
24. When is checkout time?
25. What will we be responsible for when we check out?
26. How will we receive our confirmation and arrival instructions?
27. What are your office hours?
28. What are the directions to your office?
29. What if we arrive after your office has closed?
30. Whom do we contact if something breaks or otherwise goes wrong during our stay?
31. How long have you been in business?
32. Are you licensed by the state of Florida?
33. Do you belong to the Better Business Bureau and/or the Central Florida Vacation Rental Managers Association?

We frequently receive letters from readers extolling the virtues of renting a condo or vacation home. This endorsement by a family from Ellington, Connecticut, is typical:

> *Our choice to stay outside Disney was based on cost and sanity. We've found over the last couple of years that our children can't share the same bed. We have also gotten tired of having to turn off the lights at 8 p.m. and lie quietly in the dark waiting for our children to fall asleep. With this in mind, we needed a condo/suite layout. Anything in Disney offering this option* [BoardWalk Villas, Beach Club Villas, Old Key West, and the like] *was going to cost $400 to $500 a night. This was not built into our Disney budget. We decided on the Sheraton Vistana Resort. We had a two-bedroom villa with full kitchen, living room, three TVs, and washer/dryer. I packed for half the trip and did laundry almost every night. The facilities offered a daily children's program and several pools, kiddie pools, and "playscapes." Located on FL 535, we had a five- to ten-minute drive to most attractions, including SeaWorld, Disney, and Universal.*

A St. Joe, Indiana, family also had a good experience, writing:

> *We rented a home in Kissimmee this time, and we'll never stay in a hotel at WDW again. It was by far the nicest, most relaxing time we've ever had down there. Our rental home was within 10 to 15 minutes of all the Disney parks, and 25 minutes from SeaWorld. We had three bedrooms, two baths, and an in-ground pool in a screened enclosure out back. We paid $90 per night for the whole shootin' match. We did spring for the pool heating, $25 per night extra* [in

February]. *We used AAA Dream Homes Rental Company and they did a great job by us. They provided us with detailed info before we went down so we would know what we needed to bring.*

From a New Jersey family of five:

I cannot stress enough how important it is if you have a large family (more than two kids) to rent a house for your stay! We had visited WDW several times in the past by ourselves when we were newlyweds. Fast-forward to ten years later, when we took our three kids, ages 6 years, 4 years, and 20 months. We stayed at Windsor Hills Resort, which I booked through **www.globalresorthomes.com.** *I was able to see all the homes and check availability when I was reserving the house. This development is one and a half miles from the Disney Maingate. It took us about ten minutes to drive there in the a.m., and we had no traffic issues at all. We had a brand-new four-bedroom, four-bathroom house with our own pool. It was professionally decorated and just stunning! All for $215 a night! This was in October, but rates never climb above $300 even in the high season. We loved getting away from the hubbub of Disney and relaxing back at the house in "our" pool.*

AAA Dream Homes (**www.1dreamhomes.com**) has a good reputation for customer service but does not have photos of or information about the homes in its inventory online, citing lack of room.

THE BEST HOTELS FOR FAMILIES OUTSIDE WALT DISNEY WORLD

WHAT MAKES A SUPER FAMILY HOTEL? Roomy accommodations, in-room fridge, great pool, complimentary breakfast, child-care options, and programs for kids are a few of the things the *Unofficial Guide* hotel team researched in selecting the top hotels for families from among hundreds of properties in the Disney World area. Some of our picks are expensive, others are more reasonable, and some are a bargain. Regardless of price, be assured that these hotels understand a family's needs.

Though all the following hotels offer some type of shuttle to the theme parks, some offer very limited service. Call the hotel before you book and ask what the shuttle schedule will be when you visit. Since families, like individuals, have different wants and needs, we haven't ranked the following properties here; they're listed by zone and alphabetically.

INTERNATIONAL DRIVE AREA

Doubletree Castle Hotel ★★★½

Rate per night $100–$240. **Pool** ★★★. **Fridge in room** Yes. **Shuttle to parks** Yes (Disney, Universal, and SeaWorld; additional fee). **Maximum number of occupants per room** 4. **Special comments** For an additional fee ($13.95 adults, $6.95 kids), up to 4 people receive a full breakfast; 2 signature chocolate-chip cookies come with every room. Pets are welcome for a $100 fee.

8629 International Drive
Orlando
☎ 407-345-1511 or
800-952-2785
www.doubletreecastle.com

YOU CAN'T MISS THIS ONE; it's the only castle on I-Drive. Inside you'll find royal colors (purple dominates), opulent fixtures, European art, Renaissance music, and a mystic Castle Creature at the door. The 216 guest rooms also receive the royal treatment in decor, though some guests may find them gaudy. All, however, are fairly large and well equipped with TV with PlayStation, fridge, three phones, coffeemaker, iron and board, hair dryer, and safe. The Castle Café off the lobby serves full or Continental breakfast. For lunch or dinner, you might walk next door to Vito's Chop House (dinner only) or Café Tu Tu Tango (an *Unofficial* favorite). The heated circular pool is five feet deep and features a fountain in the center, a poolside bar, and a whirlpool. There's no separate kiddie pool. Other amenities include a fitness center, arcade, gift shop, lounge, valet laundry service and facilities, and guest services desk with park passes for sale and babysitting recommendations. Security feature: elevators require an electronic key card.

Hard Rock Hotel ★★★★½

Rate per night $244–$689. **Pool** ★★★★. **Fridge in room** Available, $15 per day. **Shuttle to parks** Yes (Universal, SeaWorld, Discovery Cove, and Wet 'n Wild). **Maximum number of occupants per room** 4. **Special comments** Microwaves available for $15 per day.

5800 Universal Boulevard
Orlando
☎ 407-503-2000
www.hardrockhotel
orlando.com

LOCATED ON UNIVERSAL PROPERTY, the 650-room Hard Rock Hotel is nirvana for any kid older than eight, especially those interested in music. Architecture is California Mission–style, and rock memorabilia is displayed throughout. If you plan to spend at least a few days at Universal parks, this is an excellent upscale option. Guests receive theme-park privileges such as all-day access to the Universal Express line-breaking program, as well as delivery of packages to their rooms and priority seating at select Universal restaurants. The music-filled pool area has a white-sand beach, a 260-foot waterslide, a 12,000-square-foot pool, an underwater audio system, and an ultrahip pool bar. You'll also find five restaurants and lounges, including the Palm Restaurant, a chic lounge, fitness center, and Hard Rock merchandise store. Guest rooms are ultrahip, too, with cutting-edge contemporary decor, a CD sound system, TV with pay-per-view movies and video games, coffeemaker, iron and board, robes, hair dryer, and two phones. A supervised activity center, Camp Lil' Rock, serves kids ages 4 to 14. Pet-friendly rooms are available.

International Plaza Resort & Spa ★★★½ (tower rooms); ★★★ (garden rooms)

Rate per night $89–$179. **Pools** ★★★½. **Fridge in room** Yes. **Shuttle to parks** Yes. **Maximum number of occupants per room** 4. **Special comments** A good option if you're visiting SeaWorld.

10100 International Drive
Orlando
☎ 407-352-1100 or
800-327-0363
www.intlplazaresort.com

SET ON 28 ACRES, the International Plaza Resort offers plenty of room for kids to roam. And with three heated pools, two kiddie pools, a small playground, an arcade, and a free mini-golf course (very mini), this resort offers ample kid-friendly diversions. The main pool is especially pleasant, with fountains, lush landscaping, and a poolside bar. Other amenities and services include fitness center, spa, gift shop, guest services desk, and lounge. Book a room in the tower if possible, even though it's away from the kiddie pools and playground. Tower rooms, renovated in 2008, are a bit larger and more upscale than low-rise rooms. Each of the 1,100 rooms includes a fridge, coffeemaker, TV, iron and board, hair dryer, and safe. The hotel has one restaurant and a deli with a Pizza Hut. If your family loves SeaWorld, you're in luck: Shamu and friends are within walking distance.

Loews Portofino Bay Hotel ★★★★½

Rate per night $269–$714. **Pools** ★★★★. **Fridge in room** Minibar; fridge available for $15 per day. **Shuttle to parks** Yes (Universal, SeaWorld, Discovery Cove, and Wet 'n Wild). **Maximum number of occupants per room** 4. **Special comments** Character dinner on Friday.

5601 Universal Boulevard
Orlando
☎ 407-503-1000 or
888-273-1311
www.loewshotels.com/
hotels/orlando_portofino_bay

LOCATED IN UNIVERSAL ORLANDO, the 750-room Portofino Bay Hotel is themed like an Italian Riviera village. Guests receive theme-park privileges such as all-day access to the Universal Express line-breaking program, as well as delivery of packages to their room and priority seating at select Universal restaurants. The rooms are ultraluxurious, with Italian furnishings, opulent baths, and soothing neutral hues. Standard guest-room amenities include minibar, coffeemaker, iron and board, hair dryer, safe, umbrella, and TV with pay-per-view movies. Microwaves are available ($15 per day). Camp Portofino offers supervised activities (movies, video games, crafts, and such) for children ages 4 to 14. The cost is $14 per hour, per child; hours vary. Trattoria del Porto restaurant offers a character dinner from 6:30 until 9:30 p.m. on Friday, with characters such as Scooby Doo and Woody Woodpecker in attendance. The cost is $29.95 for adults, $12.95 for 12 and younger. Portofino has four other Italian restaurants (each with a children's menu), an Italian bakery (also serves gelato), and two bars. Three elaborate pools, gardens, jogging trails, pet-friendly rooms, and a spa and fitness center round out major amenities. If you have the bank account to pay for it and plan to spend time at Universal, you can't go wrong here.

Nickelodeon Family Suites by Holiday Inn ★★★½

Rate per night $144–$680. **Pools** ★★★★. **Fridge in room** Yes. **Shuttle to parks** Yes. **Maximum number of occupants per room** 7. **Special comments** Daily character breakfast; resort fee of $25/night.

14500 Continental Gateway
Orlando
☎ 407-387-5437 or
877-NICK-111
www.nickhotel.com

SPONGEBOB SQUAREPANTS, EAT YOUR HEART OUT. This revamped resort is as kid-friendly as they come. Decked out in all themes Nickelodeon, the hotel is sure to please any fan of TV shows the likes of *Rugrats, Jimmy Neutron: Boy Genius,* and *The Fairly OddParents,* to name a few. Nickelodeon characters from the channel's many shows hang out in the resort's lobby and mall area, greeting kids while parents check in. Guests can choose from among 777 one-, two-, and three-bedroom KidSuites executed in a number of different themes—all very brightly and creatively decorated. All suites include kitchenettes or full kitchens; also standard are a microwave, fridge, coffeemaker, TV, iron and board, two hair dryers, and a safe. KidSuites feature a semiprivate kids' bedroom with bunk beds, pull-out sleeper bed, 36-inch TV and DVD player, PlayStation 2 (you can rent games for a small fee at the hotel's video arcade), CD/cassette player, and activity table. The master bedroom offers ample storage space that the kids' bedroom lacks. Additional amenities include a high-tech video arcade, Studio Nick—a game-show studio that hosts six game shows a night for the entertainment of a live studio audience, a buffet (kids 5 and younger eat free with a paying adult), a food court offering Pizza Hut and A&W Root Beer, the full-service Nicktoons Cafe (offers character breakfasts), a convenience store, a lounge, a gift shop, a fitness center, a washer and dryer in each courtyard, and a guest-activities desk (buy Disney tickets and get recommendations on babysitting). Not to be missed—don't worry, your kids won't let you—are the resort's two pools, Oasis and Lagoon. Oasis features a water park complete with water cannons, rope ladders, geysers, and dump buckets, as well as two hot tubs for adults (with a view of the rest of the pool to keep an eye on little ones) and a smaller play area for younger kids. Kids will love the huge, zero-depth-entry Lagoon Pool, replete with 400-gallon dump bucket, plus nearby basketball court and nine-hole mini-golf course. Pool activities for kids are scheduled several times a day, seasonally; some games feature the infamous green slime. "Dive-in" movies, family-friendly films shown on a giant screen on the deck, are in the works. Whatever you do, avoid letting your kids catch you saying the phrase "I don't know" while you're here—trust us.

Rosen Shingle Creek ★★★★

Rate per night $149–$309. **Pools** ★★★★. **Fridge in room** Yes. **Shuttle to parks** Yes (Universal, Wet 'n Wild, Discovery Cove, Aquatica, and SeaWorld only). **Maximum number of occupants per room** 4.

9939 Universal Boulevard
Orlando
☎ 407-996-9939
or 866-996-9939
www.rosenshinglecreek.com

BEAUTIFUL ROOMS (east-facing ones have great views) and excellent restaurants distinguish this mostly meeting- and convention-oriented resort. The pools are large and lovely and include a lap pool, a family pool, and a kiddie wading pool. There's an 18-hole golf course on-site as well as a superior spa, an adequate fitness center, even a horseshoe pitch. The Swamp provides both activities and child care. Though a state-of-the-art video arcade will gobble up your kids' pocket change, the real kicker, especially for the 8 years-and-up crowd, is a natural area encompassing lily ponds, grassy wetlands, Shingle Creek, and an adjacent cypress swamp. Running through the area is a nature trail complete with signs to help you identify wildlife. Great blue herons, wood storks, coots, egrets, mallard ducks, anhingas, and ospreys are common, as are sliders (turtles), chameleons, and skinks (lizards). Oh yeah, there are alligators and snakes, too—real ones, but that's part of the fun. If you stay at Shingle Creek and plan to visit the theme parks, you'll want a car. Shuttle service is limited, departing and picking up at rather inconvenient times and stopping at three other hotels before delivering you to your destination.

LAKE BUENA VISTA AND I-4 CORRIDOR

Buena Vista Palace Hotel & Spa ★★★★

Rate per night $179–$1,009. **Pools** ★★★½. **Fridge in room** Yes. **Shuttle to parks** Yes (Disney only). **Maximum number of occupants per room** 4. **Special comments** Sunday character breakfast available.

1900 Buena Vista Drive
Lake Buena Vista
☎ 407-827-2727 or
866-397-6516
www.buenavistapalace.com

IN THE DOWNTOWN DISNEY RESORT AREA, the Buena Vista Palace is upscale and convenient. Surrounded by a man-made lake and plenty of palms, the spacious pool area contains three heated pools, the largest of which is partially covered (nice for when you need a little shade); a whirlpool and sauna; a basketball court; and a sand volleyball court. Plus, a pool concierge will fetch your favorite magazine or fruity drink. On Sunday, the Watercress Café hosts a character breakfast ($26 for adults and $15 for children). The 897 guest rooms are posh and spacious; each comes with a desk, coffeemaker, hair dryer, cable TV with pay-per-view movies, iron and board, and minibar. There are also 117 suites. In-room babysitting is available through the All about Kids and Sitters Solutions services. One lighted tennis court, a European-style spa offering 60 services, a fitness center, an arcade, a playground, and a beauty salon round out amenities. Two restaurants and a mini-market are on-site. And if you aren't wiped out after time in the parks, consider dropping by the Lobby Lounge or the full-menu sports bar for a nightcap. *Note:* All these amenities and services come at a price—a $17-per-night resort fee will be added to your bill.

Hilton Walt Disney World ★★★★

Rate per night $95–$329. **Pools** ★★★½. **Fridge in room** Minibar. **Shuttle to parks** Yes (Disney theme and water parks only). **Maximum number of occupants per room** 4. **Special comments** Sunday character breakfast and Disney Extra Magic Hours program.

1751 Hotel Plaza Boulevard
Lake Buena Vista
☎ 407-827-4000 or
800-782-4414
www.hilton-wdwv.com

THE HILTON OCCUPIES 23 ACRES in the Downtown Disney Resort Area. Since it's an official Walt Disney World hotel, guests can take advantage of the Disney Extra Magic Hours program, which allows entry to a selected Disney park one hour before official opening and late stays to a selected park up to three hours after official close. The Hilton's 814 guest rooms and suites are spacious, luxurious, and tasteful. Decorated in earth tones, all standard rooms have marble baths, iron and board, hair dryer, two phones, desk, minibar, coffeemaker, and cable TV with pay-per-view movies and video games. One big plus family amenity is the character breakfast, offered from 8:30 to 11 a.m. on Sunday. (Reservations aren't accepted.) Food is served buffet-style, and five characters attend (only two are present at a time). Other important family amenities include babysitting services; an arcade and pool table; and two beautifully landscaped heated swimming pools, as well as a kiddie pool. Adults and older children can relax in the fitness center after a long day touring. Seven restaurants, including Benihana, add to the hotel's convenience.

Holiday Inn SunSpree Resort ★★★

Rate per night $90–$160. **Pool** ★★★. **Fridge in room** Yes. **Shuttle to parks** Yes (Disney only). **Maximum number of occupants per room** 4–6. **Special comments** The first hotel in the world to offer KidSuites; resort fee of $5.95/night entitles guests to numerous perks, including use of fitness center and daily fountain drinks for kids.

13351 FL 535
Lake Buena Vista
☎ 407-239-4500 or
800-366-6299
www.holidayinn
sunspree.com

PUT ON YOUR SUNGLASSES. You'll know you're here when the hot pink, bright blue, green, and yellow exterior comes into view. Inside, kids have their own check-in counter, where they'll receive a free goody bag. But the big lure is KidSuites, 405-square-foot rooms with a separate children's area. Themes include a tree house, jail, space capsule, and fort, among others. The kids' area sleeps three to four children in two sets of bunk beds or one bunk bed and a twin. The separate adult area has its own TV, safe, hair dryer, and mini-kitchenette with fridge, microwave, sink, and coffeemaker. Standard guest rooms offer these adult amenities. Other kid-friendly amenities include free bedtime tuck-in by a member of the KidSuite Gang (reservations required); the tiny Castle Movie Theater, which shows movies all day every day and presents clown and magic shows and karaoke nightly; a playground; an arcade with video games and air hockey, among its many games; a basketball court; and Camp Holiday, a supervised program for ages 4 to 12 ($5 per hour, per child). Hours vary, so call ahead. Held in Max's Magic Castle, Camp Holiday might include movies and cartoons, bingo, face painting, and karaoke. Also offered are a large, free-form pool complete with kiddie pool and two whirlpools, and a fitness center. Max's Cafe serves breakfast and dinner buffets and offers an à la carte menu for dinner. There's also a mini-mart. Another perk: kids age 12 and younger eat free from a special menu when dining with one paying adult (maximum four kids per adult). Finally, pets weighing 30 pounds or less are welcome (for an additional $40 nonrefundable fee).

Hyatt Regency Grand Cypress ★★★★½

Rate per night $229–$409. **Pool** ★★★★★. **Fridge in room** Minibar; fridge available on request. **Shuttle to parks** Yes. **Maximum number of occupants per room** 4. **Special comments** Wow, what a pool!

1 Grand Cypress Boulevard
Lake Buena Vista
☎ 407-239-1234 or
888-591-1234
grandcypress.hyatt.com

THERE ARE MYRIAD REASONS to stay at this 1,500-acre resort, but the pool ranks as number one. The 800,000-gallon tropical paradise has a 45-foot waterslide, waterfalls, caves and grottos, and a suspension bridge. Your kids may never want to leave the pool to visit the theme parks. The Hyatt also is a golfer's paradise. With a 45-hole championship Jack Nicklaus–designed course, an 18-hole course, a 9-hole pitch-and-putt course, and a golf academy, there's something for golfers of all abilities. Other recreational perks include a racquet facility with hard and clay courts, a private lake with beach, a fitness center, and miles of trails for biking, walking, jogging, and horseback riding. The 683 standard guest rooms are 360 square feet and have a Florida ambience, with green and reddish hues, touches of rattan, and private balconies. Amenities include minibar, iron and board, safe, hair dryer, ceiling fan, and cable TV with pay-per-view movies and video games. Suite and villa accommodations offer even more amenities. Camp Hyatt provides supervised programs for kids ages 5 to 12; a child-care center is available. Six restaurants offer dining options. Four lounges provide nighttime entertainment. If outdoor recreation is high on your family's list, Hyatt is an excellent high-end choice.

Marriott Village at Lake Buena Vista ★★★

Rate per night $99–$305. **Pools** ★★★. **Fridge in room** Yes. **Shuttle to parks** Yes (Disney, Universal, SeaWorld, and Wet 'n Wild). **Maximum number of occupants per room** 4. **Special comments** Free Continental breakfast at Fairfield Inn and SpringHill Suites.

8623 Vineland Avenue
Orlando
☎ 407-938-9001 or
877-682-8552
www.marriottvillage.com

THIS GATED HOTEL COMMUNITY INCLUDES a 388-room Fairfield Inn, a 400-suite SpringHill Suites, and a 312-room Courtyard. Whatever your budget, you'll find a room here to fit it. If you need a bit more space, book SpringHill Suites; if you're looking for value, try the Fairfield Inn; if you need limited business amenities, reserve at the Courtyard. Amenities at all three properties include fridge, cable TV with PlayStation (for an extra fee), iron and board, and hair dryer. Additionally, all SpringHill suites have microwaves, and all Courtyard rooms feature Web TV. Cribs and rollaway beds are available at no extra charge at all locations. Swimming pools at all three hotels are attractive and medium-sized, featuring children's interactive splash zones and whirlpools; in addition, each property has its own fitness center. The incredibly convenient Village Marketplace food court includes Pizza Hut, Village Grill, Village Coffee House, along with a 24-hour convenience store. The Bahama Breeze, Fish Bones, and Golden Corral full-service restaurants are within walking distance. Other services and amenities include a Disney planning station and ticket sales, an arcade, and a Hertz car-rental desk. Shoppers will find the Orlando Premium Outlets adjacent. You'll get plenty of bang for your buck at Marriott Village.

Sheraton Safari Hotel & Suites ★★★★

Rate per night $109–$279. **Pool** ★★★. **Fridge in room** Safari suites only. **Shuttle to parks** Yes (Disney free; other parks for a fee). **Maximum number of occupants per room** 4–6. **Special comments** Cool python waterslide. Dogs allowed.

12205 South Apopka–Vineland Road
Orlando
☎ 407-239-0444 or
800-423-3297
www.sheratonsafari.com

THE SAFARI THEME IS NICELY EXECUTED throughout the property—from the lobby dotted with African artifacts and native decor to the 79-foot python waterslide dominating the pool. The 393 guest rooms and 90 safari suites sport African-inspired art and tasteful animal-print soft goods in brown, beige, and jewel tones. Amenities include cable TV with PlayStation, coffeemaker, iron and board, hair dryer, and safe. Suites are a good option for families since they provide added space with a separate sitting room and a kitchenette with a fridge, microwave, and sink. The first thing your kids will probably want to do is take a turn on the python waterslide. It's pretty impressive, but as one *Unofficial Guide* researcher pointed out, it's somewhat of a letdown: the python doesn't actually spit you out of its mouth. Instead you're deposited below its chin. Other on-site amenities include a restaurant (children's menu available), lounge, arcade, and fitness center.

Sheraton Vistana Resort ★★★★

Rate per night $149–$289. **Pools** ★★★½. **Fridge in room** Yes. **Shuttle to parks** Yes (Disney). **Maximum number of occupants per room** 8. **Special comments** Though time-shares, the villas are rented nightly as well.

8800 Vistana Centre Drive
Orlando
☎ 866-208-0003 or
407-239-3100
www.sheraton.com

THE SHERATON VISTANA IS DECEPTIVELY LARGE, stretching across both sides of Vistana Center Drive. Because Sheraton's emphasis is on selling the time-shares, the rental angle is little known. But families should consider it; the Vistana is one of Orlando's best off-Disney properties. If you want a serene retreat from your days in the theme parks, this is an excellent base. The spacious villas come in one-bedroom, two-bedroom, and two-bedroom-with-lock-off models. All are decorated in beachy pastels, but the emphasis is on the profusion of amenities. Each villa has a full kitchen (including fridge/freezer, microwave, oven/range, dishwasher, toaster, and coffee-maker, with an option to prestock with groceries), clothes washer and dryer, TVs in the living room and each bedroom (one with DVD player), stereo with CD player, separate dining area, and private patio or balcony in most. Grounds offer seven swimming pools (four with bars), four play-grounds, two restaurants, game rooms, fitness centers, a mini-golf course, sports equipment rental (including bikes), and courts for basketball, volley-ball, tennis, and shuffleboard. A mind-boggling array of activities for kids (and adults) ranges from crafts to games and sports tournaments. Of special note: Vistana is highly secure, with locked gates bordering all guest areas, so children can have the run of the place without parents worrying about them wandering off.

US 192 AREA

Comfort Suites Maingate ★★★½

Rate per night $70–$200. **Pool** ★★★. **Fridge in room** Yes. **Shuttle to parks** Yes (Disney, Universal, and SeaWorld). **Maximum number of occupants per room** 6. **Special comments** Complimentary Continental breakfast daily.

7888 West Irlo Bronson
Memorial Highway
Kissimmee
☎ 407-390-9888 or
888-390-9888
www.comfortsuites
kissimmee.com

THIS PROPERTY HAS 150 SPACIOUS one-room suites, each with double sofa bed, microwave, fridge, coffee-maker, TV, hair dryer, and safe. The suites aren't lavish, but they are clean and contemporary, with muted deep-purple and beige tones. Extra bathroom counter space is especially convenient for larger families. The heated pool is large and has plenty of lounge chairs and moderate landscaping. A kiddie pool, whirlpool, and poolside bar complete the courtyard. Other amenities include an arcade and a gift shop. But Maingate's big plus is its location next door to a shopping center with about everything a family could need. There, you'll find nine dining options, including Outback Steakhouse, Dairy Queen, Subway, T.G.I. Friday's, and Chinese and Italian eateries; a Winn-Dixie supermarket; one-hour film developing; a hair salon; a bank; a dry cleaner; a tourist information center with park passes for sale; and a Centra Care walk-in clinic, among other services. All this a short walk from your room.

Gaylord Palms Resort ★★★★½

Rate per night $199–$379. **Pool** ★★★★. **Fridge in room** Yes. **Shuttle to parks** Yes. **Maximum number of occupants per room** 4. **Special comments** Probably the closest you'll get off-World to Disney-level extravagance. Resort fee of $15/day.

6000 West Osceola Parkway
Kissimmee
☎ 407-586-0000
www.gaylordpalms.com

THIS DECIDEDLY UPSCALE RESORT has a colossal convention facility and strongly caters to business clientele but still is a nice (if pricey) family resort. Hotel wings are defined by the three themed, glass-roofed atriums they overlook. Key West's design is reminiscent of island life in the Florida Keys; Everglades is an overgrown spectacle of shabby swamp chic, complete with piped-in cricket noise and a robotic alligator; and the immense, central St. Augustine harks back to Spanish Colonial Florida. Lagoons, streams, and waterfalls cut through and connect all three, and walkways and bridges abound. Rooms reflect the colors of their respective areas, though there's no particular connection in decor (St. Augustine atrium-view rooms are the most opulent, but they're not Spanish). A fourth wing, Emerald Bay Tower, overlooks the Emerald Plaza shopping and dining area of the St. Augustine atrium. These rooms are the nicest and the most expensive, and they're mostly used by convention-goers. Though rooms have fridges and stereos with CD (as well as other high-end perks, like high-speed Internet access), the rooms themselves really work better as retreats for adults rather than kids. However, children will enjoy wandering the themed areas, playing in the family pool (with water-squirting octopus), or participating in La Petite Academy Kids Station, which organizes games and activities for kids ages 3 to 14.

Orange Lake Resort & Country Club ★★★★½

Rate per night $125–$275 (2-bedroom summer rate). **Pools** ★★★★. **Fridge in room** Yes. **Shuttle to parks** Yes (fee varies depending on destination). **Maximum number of occupants per room** Varies. **Special comments** This is a time-share property, but if you rent directly through the resort (as opposed to the sales office), you can avoid time-share sales pitches.

8505 West Irlo Bronson Memorial Highway
Kissimmee
☎ 800-877-6522 or 407-239-0000
www.orangelake.com

YOU COULD SPEND YOUR ENTIRE VACATION never leaving this property, located about six to ten minutes from the Disney theme parks. From its ten pools and two mini–water parks to its 40-plus holes of golf, Orange Lake offers an extensive menu of amenities and recreational opportunities. If you tire of lazing by the pool, try waterskiing, wakeboarding, tubing, fishing, or other activities on the 80-acre lake. There's also a live alligator show, exercise programs, organized competitive sports and games, arts-and-crafts sessions, and miniature golf. Activities don't end when the sun goes down. Karaoke, live music, a Hawaiian luau, and movies at the resort cinema are some of the evening options.

The more than 2,000 units are tastefully decorated and comfortably furnished, ranging from suites and studios to three-bedroom villas, all containing fully equipped kitchens. If you'd rather not cook on vacation, try one of the seven restaurants scattered across the resort: two cafes, three grills, one pizzeria, and a fast-food eatery. If you need help with (or a break from) the kids, babysitters are available to come to your villa, accompany your family on excursions, or take your children to attractions for you.

Radisson Resort Orlando Celebration ★★★★

Rate per night $89–$149. **Pool** ★★★★½. **Fridge in room** Yes. **Shuttle to parks** Yes (Disney, Universal, and SeaWorld). **Maximum number of occupants**

per room 4. **Special comments** $10/day resort fee; kids age 10 and younger eat free with a paying adult at Mandolin's restaurant.

2900 Parkway Boulevard
Kissimmee
☎ 407-396-7000 or
800-634-4774
www.radisson.com

THE POOL ALONE IS WORTH A STAY HERE, but the Radisson Resort gets high marks in all areas. The free-form pool is huge, with a waterfall and waterslide surrounded by palms and flowering plants, plus a smaller heated pool, two whirlpools, and a kiddie pool. Other outdoor amenities include two lighted tennis courts, sand volleyball, a playground, and jogging areas. Kids can also blow off steam at the arcade, while adults might visit the fitness center. Rooms are elegant, featuring Italian furnishings and marble baths. They're of above-average size and include a minibar, coffeemaker, TV, iron and board, hair dryer, and safe. Dining options include Mandolin's for breakfast and dinner buffets, and a 1950s-style diner serving burgers, sandwiches, shakes, and Pizza Hut pizza, among other fare. A sports lounge with an 11-by-6-foot TV offers nighttime entertainment. Guest services can help with tours, park passes, car rental, and babysitting. While there are no children's programs per se, there are plenty of activities such as board games and coloring.

Wyndham Bonnet Creek Resort ★★★★

Rate per night $134–$628. **Pool** ★★★★. **Fridge in room** Yes. **Shuttle to parks** Yes. **Maximum number of occupants per room** 4 plus child in crib. **Special comments** A non-Disney suite hotel within Walt Disney World.

9560 Via Encinas
Lake Buena Vista
☎ 407-238-3500
www.wyndham
bonnetcreek.com

WYNDHAM BONNET CREEK RESORT is a condo hotel on the south side of Buena Vista Drive, about a quarter mile east of Disney's Caribbean Resort. The property has an interesting history: When Walt Disney began secretly buying up real estate in the 1960s under the names of numerous front companies, the land on which this resort stands was the last holdout and was never sold to Disney, though the company tried repeatedly to acquire it through the years. (The owners reportedly took issue with the way Disney went about acquiring land and preferred to see the site languish undeveloped.) The 70-acre site was ultimately bought by Marriott, which put up a Fairfield Inn time-share development in 2004. The Wyndham is part of a luxury-hotel complex on the same site that will eventually include a 500-room Waldorf-Astoria and a 1,000-room Hilton. The development is surrounded on three sides by Disney property and on one side by I-4.

The Bonnet Creek Resort offers upscale, family-friendly accommodations: one- and two-bedroom condos with fully equipped kitchens, washer-dryers, jetted tubs, and balconies. Activities and amenities on-site include two outdoor swimming pools, a "lazy river" float stream, a children's activities program, a game room, a playground, and miniature golf. There is free scheduled transportation to all the Disney parks. One-bedroom units are equipped with a king bed in the bedroom and a sleeper sofa in the living area; two-bedroom condos have two double beds in the second bedroom and an additional bath.

HOTELS *and* MOTELS: *Rated and Ranked*

IN THIS SECTION, WE COMPARE HOTELS in three main areas outside Walt Disney World (see next page) with those inside the World.

In addition to Disney properties, we rate hotels in the three lodging areas defined earlier in this chapter. There are additional hotels at the intersection of US 27 and Interstate 4, on US 441 (Orange Blossom Trail), and in downtown Orlando. Most of these require more than 30 minutes of commuting to Disney World and thus are not rated. We also haven't rated lodging east of Siesta Lago Drive on US 192.

WHAT'S IN A ROOM?

EXCEPT FOR CLEANLINESS, state of repair, and decor, travelers pay little attention to hotel rooms. There is, of course, a clear standard of quality and luxury that differentiates Motel 6 from Holiday Inn, Holiday Inn from Marriott, and so on. Many guests, however, fail to appreciate that some rooms are better engineered than others. Making the room usable to its occupants is an art that combines both form and function.

Decor and taste are important. No one wants to stay in a room that's dated, garish, or ugly. But beyond decor, how "livable" is the room? In Orlando, for example, we've seen some beautifully appointed rooms that aren't well designed for human habitation. The next time you stay in a hotel, note your room's details and design elements. Even more than decor, these are the things that will make you feel comfortable and at home.

ROOM RATINGS

TO EVALUATE PROPERTIES FOR THEIR QUALITY, tastefulness, state of repair, cleanliness, and size of their standard rooms, we have grouped the hotels and motels into classifications denoted by stars—the overall star rating. Star ratings in this guide apply only to Orlando-area properties and don't necessarily correspond to ratings awarded by *Frommer's*, Mobil, AAA, or other travel critics. Because stars have little relevance when awarded in the absence of recognized standards of comparison, we have tied our ratings to expected levels of quality established by specific American hotel corporations.

OVERALL STAR RATINGS

★★★★★	Superior rooms	Tasteful and luxurious by any standard
★★★★	Extremely nice rooms	What you would expect at a Hyatt Regency or Marriott
★★★	Nice rooms	Holiday Inn or comparable quality
★★	Adequate rooms	Clean, comfortable, and functional without frills—like a Motel 6
★	Super-budget	These exist but are not included in our coverage

Overall star ratings apply only to room quality and describe the property's standard accommodations. For most hotels, a standard accommodation is a room with one king bed or two queen beds. In an all-suite property, the standard accommodation is either a studio or one-bedroom suite. In addition to standard accommodations, many hotels offer luxury rooms and special suites, which aren't rated in this guide. Star ratings for rooms are assigned without regard to whether a property has restaurant(s), recreational facilities, entertainment, or other extras.

In addition to stars (which delineate broad categories), we use a numerical rating system—the room-quality rating. Our scale is 0 to 100, with 100 being the best possible rating and zero (0) the worst. Numerical ratings show the difference we perceive between one property and another. For instance, rooms at both the Country Inn & Suites Calypso Cay and the Comfort Suites Maingate are rated three and a half stars (★★★½). In the supplemental numerical ratings, the Country Inn & Suites Calypso Cay is an 82 and the Comfort Suites Maingate a 76. This means that within the three-and-a-half-star category, the Country Inn & Suites Calypso Cay has slightly nicer rooms than the Comfort Suites Maingate.

The location column identifies the area around Walt Disney World where you'll find a particular property. The designation **WDW** means the property is inside Walt Disney World. A **1** means it's on or near International Drive. Properties on or near US 192 (aka Irlo Bronson Memorial Highway, Vine Street, and Space Coast Parkway) are indicated by a **3.** All others are marked with **2** and for the most part are along the FL 535 and the I-4 corridor, though some are in nearby locations that don't meet any other criteria.

LODGING AREAS

WDW	Walt Disney World
1	International Drive
2	I-4 Corridor
3	US 192 (Irlo Bronson Memorial Highway)

Names of properties along US 192 also designate location (for example, Holiday Inn Maingate West). The consensus in Orlando seems to be that the main entrance to Disney World is the broad interstate-type road that runs off US 192. This is called the **Maingate.** Properties along US 192 call themselves Maingate East or West to differentiate their positions along the highway. So, driving southeast from Clermont or Florida's Turnpike, the properties before you reach the Maingate turnoff are called Maingate West, while the properties after you pass the Maingate turnoff are called Maingate East.

Cost estimates are based on the hotel's published rack rates for standard rooms. Each **$** represents $50. Thus a cost symbol of **$$$** means that a room (or suite) at that hotel will be about $150 a night.

We've focused on room quality and excluded consideration of location, services, recreation, or amenities. In some instances, a one- or two-room suite is available for the same price or less than that of a single standard hotel room.

If you've used an earlier edition of this guide, you'll notice that new properties have been added and many ratings and rankings have changed, some because of room renovation or improved maintenance or housekeeping. Failure to maintain rooms or lax housekeeping can bring down ratings.

Before you shop for a hotel, consider this letter from a man in Hot Springs, Arkansas:

> *We canceled our room reservations to follow the advice in your book and reserved a hotel highly ranked by the* Unofficial Guide. *We wanted inexpensive, but clean and cheerful. We got inexpensive, but* [also] *dirty, grim, and depressing. I really felt disappointed in your advice and the room. It was the pits. That was the one real piece of information I needed from your book! The room spoiled the holiday for me aside from our touring.*

This letter was as unsettling to us as the bad room was to our reader. Our integrity as travel journalists is based on the quality of the information we provide. When rechecking the hotel our reader disliked, we found our rating was representative, but he had been assigned one of a small number of threadbare rooms scheduled for renovation.

Note that some chains use the same guest-room photo in promotional literature for all its hotels and that the room in a specific property may not resemble the photo. When you or your travel agent calls, ask how old the property is and when the guest room you're being assigned was last renovated. If you are assigned a room inferior to expectations, demand to be moved.

unofficial **TIP**
The key to avoiding disappointment is to snoop in advance. Ask how old the hotel is and when its guest rooms were last renovated.

A WORD ABOUT TOLL-FREE TELEPHONE NUMBERS

AS WE'VE REPEATED SEVERAL TIMES IN THIS CHAPTER, it's essential to communicate with the hotel directly when shopping for deals and stating your room preferences. Most toll-free numbers are routed directly to a hotel chain's central reservations office, and the customer-service agents there typically have little or no knowledge of the individual hotels in the chain or of any specials those hotels may be offering. In the following charts, therefore, we list the toll-free number only if it connects directly to the hotel in question; otherwise, we provide the hotel's local phone number. Disney hotels, which must be booked through Disney Central Reservations (DCR), are a notable exception. After you've made your reservation, however, it's a good idea to call the hotel directly about two weeks before arrival to make sure the reservation is in order. Direct phone numbers for the Disney resorts are listed in Part One of this guide.

THE 30 BEST HOTEL VALUES

LET'S LOOK AT THE BEST COMBINATIONS of quality and value in a room. Rankings are made without consideration for location or the availability of restaurant(s), recreational facilities, entertainment, and/or amenities.

A reader recently wrote to complain that he had booked one of our top-ranked rooms in terms of value and had been very disappointed in the room. We noticed that the room the reader occupied had a quality rating of ★★½. Remember that the list of top deals is intended to give you some sense of value received for dollars spent. A ★★½ room at $40 may have the same value as a ★★★★ room at $115, but that doesn't mean the rooms will be of comparable quality. Regardless of whether it's a good deal, a ★★½ room is still a ★★½ room.

For example, the Magic Castle Inn and Suites is a clean, reasonably comfortable motel with an exceptionally friendly staff, within 15 minutes of every Disney theme park. During one Christmas season they had available basic rooms for around $54 per night when every other hotel within 20 miles of Walt Disney World was charging $150. The catch? They're located right next door to a place that gives helicopter tours of Orlando . . . all day long. You won't notice a thing if you don't plan on midday breaks, but our midafternoon naps were filled with visions of *M*A*S*H* and *Apocalypse Now.* We'd still stay there again, but our wives have different opinions.

The Top 30 Best Deals

HOTEL	LOCATION	OVERALL QUALITY RATING	ROOM-QUALITY RATING	COST ($ = $50)
1. Rodeway Inn Maingate	3	★★½	59	$–
2. Ramada Maingate West	3	★★★	65	$–
3. Orlando Vista Hotel	2	★★★★	83	$+
4. Legacy Grand Hotel and Suites	3	★★★	65	$–
5. Extended Stay Deluxe Convention Center	1	★★★★	84	$+
6. Monumental Hotel	1	★★★★½	94	$$–
7. Doubletree Universal	1	★★★★	89	$$–
8. Holiday Inn Maingate East	3	★★★★½	90	$$–
9. Howard Johnson Inn Maingate East	3	★★½	59	$–
10. Inn Nova	3	★★½	64	$–
11. Super 8 East	3	★★★	70	$
12. Celebrity Resorts Lake Buena Vista	2	★★★★	85	$$–
13. Hawthorn Suites Orlando at SeaWorld	1	★★★½	80	$+
14. Champions World Resort	3	★★★	66	$
15. Omni Orlando Resort at ChampionsGate	2	★★★★★	96	$$+
16. Liki Tiki Village	3	★★★★½	90	$$
17. Four Points by Sheraton Orlando Studio City	1	★★★★½	90	$$
18. Seralago Hotel	3	★★★	71	$+
19. Super 8 Kissimmee	3	★★½	60	$–
20. Celebrity Resorts Orlando	3	★★★½	80	$$–
21. Polynesian Isles Resort (Phase 1)	3	★★★★	83	$$–
22. Westgate Inn	3	★★½	59	$–
23. Continental Plaza Kissimmee Hotel	3	★★½	60	$–
24. La Quinta Inn I-Drive	1	★★★	73	$+
25. Motel 6 I-Drive	1	★★½	61	$–
26. Econo Lodge Inn & Suites	1	★★½	62	$
27. Extended Stay America Convention Center	1	★★★	72	$+
28. Hyatt Place	1	★★★★	84	$$
29. Imperial Swan Hotel	1	★★½	61	$
30. Ramada Inn Convention Center	1	★★★	65	$+

How the Hotels Compare

HOTEL	LOCATION	OVERALL QUALITY RATING	ROOM-QUALITY RATING	COST ($ = $50)
Omni Orlando Resort at ChampionsGate	2	★★★★★	96	$$+
Animal Kingdom Lodge **(Kidani Village)**	WDW	★★★★½	95	$$$$$$$$–
Bay Lake Tower at Contemporary Resort	WDW	★★★★½	95	$$$$$$$$–
Quality Suites Royal Parc Suites	3	★★★★½	95	$$$–
Monumental Hotel	1	★★★★½	94	$$–
Ritz-Carlton Orlando, Grande Lakes	1	★★★★½	94	$$$$
Contemporary Resort	WDW	★★★★½	93	$$$$$+
Grand Floridian Resort	WDW	★★★★½	93	$$$$$$$$$–
Hard Rock Hotel	1	★★★★½	93	$$$$–
JW Marriott Grande Lakes	1	★★★★½	93	$$$$–
Orange Lake Country Club	3	★★★★½	93	$$$$–
Westgate Vacation Villas **(town center)**	3	★★★★½	93	$$$$+
Loews Portofino Bay Hotel	1	★★★★½	92	$$$$+
Marriott's Grande Vista	1	★★★★½	92	$$$$–
Polynesian Resort	WDW	★★★★½	92	$$$$$$$$
Sheraton Vistana Resort	2	★★★★½	92	$$$$+
Westgate Lakes	2	★★★★½	92	$$$+
Animal Kingdom Villas **(Jambo House)**	WDW	★★★★½	91	$$$$$$$$–
Shades of Green	WDW	★★★★½	91	$$$–
Vacation Village at Parkway	3	★★★★½	91	$$$–
Beach Club Resort	WDW	★★★★½	90	$$$$$$$+
Beach Club Villas	WDW	★★★★½	90	$$$$$$$+
BoardWalk Villas	WDW	★★★★½	90	$$$$$$$+
Celebration Hotel	WDW	★★★★½	90	$$$$–
Dolphin	WDW	★★★★½	90	$$$$+
Four Points by Sheraton Orlando Studio City	1	★★★★½	90	$$
Gaylord Palms Resort	3	★★★★½	90	$$$$–
Holiday Inn Maingate East	3	★★★★½	90	$$–
Hyatt Regency Grand Cypress	2	★★★★½	90	$$$+
Liki Tiki Village	3	★★★★½	90	$$
Loews Royal Pacific Resort at Universal Orlando	1	★★★★½	90	$$$
Marriott's Harbour Lake	1	★★★★½	90	$$$$$
Old Key West Resort	WDW	★★★★½	90	$$$$$$+
Peabody Orlando	1	★★★★½	90	$$$$$$$–
Rosen Centre Hotel	1	★★★★½	90	$$$$
Saratoga Springs Resort & Spa	WDW	★★★★½	90	$$$$$$+
Swan	WDW	★★★★½	90	$$$$$–
Treehouse Villas at Saratoga Springs Resort & Spa	WDW	★★★★½	90	$$$$$$$$–

HOTEL	LOCATION	OVERALL QUALITY RATING	ROOM-QUALITY RATING	COST ($ = $50)
Westgate Vacation Villas **(villas)**	3	★★★★½	90	$$$–
Wilderness Lodge Villas	WDW	★★★★½	90	$$$$$$$+
Animal Kingdom Lodge	WDW	★★★★	89	$$$$$$–
BoardWalk Inn	WDW	★★★★	89	$$$$$$$+
Doubletree Universal	1	★★★★	89	$$–
Hilton Grand Vacations Club SeaWorld	1	★★★★	89	$$$–
Marriott Orlando World Center Resort	2	★★★★	89	$$$+
Renaissance Orlando Hotel at SeaWorld	1	★★★★	89	$$$$$$$$$–
Rosen Plaza Hotel	1	★★★★	89	$$$$–
Yacht Club Resort	WDW	★★★★	89	$$$$$$$+
Caribe Royale Orlando Resort Suites	3	★★★★	88	$$$–
Hilton Grand Vacations Club	2	★★★★	88	$$$–
Rosen Shingle Creek	1	★★★★	88	$$$$+
Wyndham Bonnet Creek Resort	WDW	★★★★	88	$$$+
Hawthorn Suites Lake Buena Vista	2	★★★★	87	$$+
Hilton Walt Disney World	WDW	★★★★	87	$$$$+
Mystic Dunes Resort	3	★★★★	87	$$$$$$+
Royal Plaza **(tower)**	WDW	★★★★	87	$$$+
Westin Imagine Orlando	1	★★★★	87	$$$$+
Wyndham Cypress Palms	3	★★★★	87	$$$
Doubletree Guest Suites	WDW	★★★★	86	$$+
Fort Wilderness Resort **(cabins)**	WDW	★★★★	86	$$$$$$
Marriott Cypress Harbour Villas	1	★★★★	86	$$$$$+
Marriott Imperial Palm Villas	1	★★★★	86	$$$$$$$–
Radisson Resort Orlando Celebration	3	★★★★	86	$$$–
Wilderness Lodge	WDW	★★★★	86	$$$$$$–
Best Western Lake Buena Vista Resort Hotel	WDW	★★★★	85	$$+
Celebrity Resorts Lake Buena Vista	2	★★★★	85	$$–
Marriott Residence Inn Orlando SeaWorld/International Center	1	★★★★	85	$$$–
Extended Stay Deluxe Convention Center	1	★★★★	84	$+
Hyatt Place	1	★★★★	84	$$
Port Orleans Resort **(French Quarter)**	WDW	★★★★	84	$$$+
Star Island Resort	3	★★★★	84	$$+
Buena Vista Suites	3	★★★★	83	$$+
Coronado Springs Resort	WDW	★★★★	83	$$$
Extended Stay Deluxe Lake Buena Vista	2	★★★★	83	$$$–
Orlando Vista Hotel	2	★★★★	83	$+
Polynesian Isles Resort **(Phase 1)**	3	★★★★	83	$$–

How the Hotels Compare (continued)

HOTEL	LOCATION	OVERALL QUALITY RATING	ROOM-QUALITY RATING	COST ($ = $50)
Port Orleans Resort (Riverside)	WDW	★★★★	83	$$$+
Sheraton Safari Hotel & Suites	2	★★★★	83	$$$–
Wyndham Orlando	1	★★★★	83	$$+
Country Inn & Suites Calypso Cay	3	★★★½	82	$$–
Courtyard Orlando Lake Buena Vista at Vista Centre	2	★★★½	82	$$–
Courtyard Orlando LBV in Marriott Village	2	★★★½	82	$$–
Doubletree Castle Hotel	1	★★★½	82	$$$$–
Hawthorn Suites Universal	1	★★★½	82	$$+
Hilton Garden Inn at SeaWorld International Center	1	★★★½	82	$$$–
Hilton Garden Inn Orlando	1	★★★½	82	$$+
Nickelodeon Family Suites by Holiday Inn	1	★★★½	82	$$$$$–
Parkway International Resort	3	★★★½	82	$$+
Radisson Hotel Lake Buena Vista	2	★★★½	82	$$+
Embassy Suites Resort Lake Buena Vista	2	★★★½	81	$$$+
Homewood Suites I-Drive	1	★★★½	81	$$$+
Westgate Vacation Villas (tower)	3	★★★½	81	$$$
Buena Vista Palace Hotel & Spa	WDW	★★★½	80	$$$–
Caribbean Beach Resort	WDW	★★★½	80	$$$+
Celebrity Resorts Orlando	3	★★★½	80	$$–
Embassy Suites Plaza I-Drive	1	★★★½	80	$$$+
Hawthorn Suites Orlando at SeaWorld	1	★★★½	80	$+
Holiday Inn Express Lake Buena Vista	2	★★★½	80	$$
Residence Inn Orlando Convention Center	1	★★★½	80	$$$–
Saratoga Resort Villas	3	★★★½	80	$$$$
SpringHill Suites Orlando Convention Center	1	★★★½	80	$$+
Holiday Inn SunSpree Resort	2	★★★½	79	$$
Country Inn & Suites Lake Buena Vista (rooms)	2	★★★½	78	$$
Country Inn & Suites Lake Buena Vista (suites)	2	★★★½	78	$$+
Radisson Resort Worldgate	3	★★★½	77	$$–
Comfort Suites Maingate	3	★★★½	76	$$$–
Courtyard Orlando I-Drive/ Convention Center	1	★★★½	76	$$+
Grand Lake Resort	3	★★★½	76	$$+
Hampton Inn Lake Buena Vista	2	★★★½	76	$$$–
Palms Hotel & Villas by Lexington	3	★★★½	76	$$–
Embassy Suites Orlando I-Drive	1	★★★	75	$$$

HOTEL	LOCATION	OVERALL QUALITY RATING	ROOM-QUALITY RATING	COST ($ = $50)
Extended Stay America Universal	1	★★★	75	$+
Extended Stay Deluxe Orlando Universal	1	★★★	75	$$–
Fairfield Inn & Suites Orlando LBV in Marriott Village	2	★★★	75	$$+
Holiday Inn Universal Studios	1	★★★	75	$+
International Plaza Resort & Spa (garden)	1	★★★	75	$$–
International Plaza Resort & Spa (tower)	1	★★★	75	$$$–
Regal Sun Resort	WDW	★★★	75	$$$
Residence Inn Lake Buena Vista	2	★★★	75	$$+
Residence Inn Orlando I-Drive	1	★★★	75	$$$–
Staybridge Suites Hotel	1	★★★	75	$$$+
Comfort Suites Orlando	2	★★★	74	$$–
Galleria Palms Maingate	3	★★★	74	$+
Hampton Inn Convention Center	1	★★★	74	$$$–
Holiday Inn Hotel & Suites Convention Center	1	★★★	74	$+
Quality Suites Lake Buena Vista	2	★★★	74	$$+
Fairfield Inn & Suites Orlando Near Universal Resort	1	★★★	73	$$+
Holiday Inn Orlando International Drive Hotel	1	★★★	73	$$+
All-Star Resorts	WDW	★★★	73	$$+
La Quinta Inn I-Drive	1	★★★	73	$+
Extended Stay America Convention Center	1	★★★	72	$+
Ramada Inn I-Drive Orlando	1	★★★	72	$+
Staybridge Suites Lake Buena Vista	2	★★★	72	$$$–
Pop Century Resort	WDW	★★★	71	$$
Ramada Gateway (tower)	3	★★★	71	$$–
Royal Plaza (garden)	WDW	★★★	71	$$$
Seralago Hotel	3	★★★	71	$+
SpringHill Suites Orlando LBV in Marriott Village	2	★★★	71	$$+
Holiday Inn Express Summerbay Resort	3	★★★	70	$$–
Super 8 East	3	★★★	70	$
Monumental MovieLand Hotel	1	★★★	68	$+
Westgate Palace	1	★★★	68	$$$$
Best Western Lakeside	3	★★★	67	$+
Enclave Suites	1	★★★	67	$$$–
Hampton Inn Universal	1	★★★	67	$$+
Hotel Universal	1	★★★	67	$$
Champions World Resort	3	★★★	66	$

How the Hotels Compare (continued)

HOTEL	LOCATION	OVERALL QUALITY RATING	ROOM-QUALITY RATING	COST ($ = $50)
Comfort Inn Universal Studios Area	1	★★★	66	$+
Comfort Suites Universal	1	★★★	66	$$–
Quality Inn & Suites Eastgate	3	★★★	66	$+
Destiny Palms Maingate West	3	★★★	65	$+
Legacy Grand Hotel and Suites	3	★★★	65	$–
Ramada Inn Convention Center	1	★★★	65	$+
Ramada Maingate West	3	★★★	65	$–
Best Western Kissimmee	3	★★½	64	$$–
Clarion Inn & Suites at I-Drive/ Convention Center	1	★★½	64	$$
Comfort Inn Lake Buena Vista	2	★★½	64	$+
Hampton Inn Kirkman	1	★★½	64	$$+
Inn Nova	3	★★½	64	$–
Ramada Gateway **(garden)**	3	★★½	64	$$–
Silver Lake Resort	3	★★½	64	$$
Baymont Inn & Suites	1	★★½	63	$+
Best Western Universal Inn	1	★★½	63	$$–
Country Inn & Suites I-Drive	1	★★½	63	$$–
Inn at Summer Bay	3	★★½	63	$$$$
La Quinta Universal	1	★★½	63	$+
Orlando Metropolitan Express	1	★★½	63	$+
Days Inn West Kissimmee	3	★★½	62	$
Econo Lodge Inn & Suites	1	★★½	62	$
Days Inn I-Drive North	1	★★½	61	$
Imperial Swan Hotel	1	★★½	61	$
Motel 6 I-Drive	1	★★½	61	$–
Suites at Old Town	3	★★½	61	$+
Clarion Maingate	3	★★½	60	$$–
Comfort Inn I-Drive	1	★★½	60	$+
Continental Plaza Kissimmee Hotel	3	★★½	60	$–
Days Inn Convention Center	1	★★½	60	$+
Days Inn Universal Studios	1	★★½	60	$
Quality Inn Plaza	1	★★½	60	$$+
Royal Celebration	3	★★½	60	$+
Super 8 Kissimmee	3	★★½	60	$–
Howard Johnson Inn Maingate East	3	★★½	59	$–

HOTEL	LOCATION	OVERALL QUALITY RATING	ROOM-QUALITY RATING	COST ($ = $50)
Howard Johnson Inn Orlando	1	★★½	59	$+
Rodeway Inn Maingate	3	★★½	59	$–
Westgate Inn	3	★★½	59	$–
Extended Stay Deluxe Convention Center/Pointe Orlando	1	★★½	58	$$
Red Roof Inn Convention Center	1	★★½	58	$$+
Super 8 Lakeside	3	★★½	58	$
Travelodge Suites East Gate Orange	3	★★½	58	$+
HomeSuiteHome Eastgate	3	★★½	57	$$$+
Knights Inn Maingate	3	★★	55	$–
Masters Inn Kissimmee	3	★★	55	$–
Masters Inn Maingate West	3	★★	55	$–
Golden Link Motel	3	★★	54	$–
Sleep Inn Convention Center	1	★★	54	$+
Sun Inn & Suites	3	★★	53	$–
Knights Inn	3	★★	52	$–
Motel 6 Maingate West	3	★★	52	$–
Quality Suites Universal	1	★★	52	$$–
Central Motel	3	★★	51	$–
Days Hotel Maingate	3	★★	51	$+
Key Motel	3	★★	51	$
Rodeway Inn I-Drive	1	★★	51	$+
Super 8 Universal	1	★★	51	$
Travelodge I-Drive Orlando	1	★★	51	$+
Fun Spots Hotel at Fountain Park	3	★★	50	$
Howard Johnson Lake Front Park	3	★★	50	$+
La Quinta Inn I-Drive North	1	★★	50	$+
Magic Castle Inn & Suites	3	★★	50	$–
Masters Inn I-Drive	1	★★	50	$+
Quality Inn I-Drive	1	★★	50	$+
HomeSuiteHome Nikki Bird Maingate	3	★★	48	$$$
Monte Carlo	3	★★	48	$–
Motel 6 Maingate East	3	★★	47	$–
Orlando Continental Plaza Hotel	1	★★	47	$
Red Roof Inn Kissimmee	3	★★	47	$

Hotel Information Chart

All-Star Resorts ★★★
Walt Disney World
1701–1901 W. Buena Vista Dr.
Orlando 32830
☎ 407-934-7639
www.disneyworld.com

LOCATION **WDW**
ROOM RATING **73**
COST ($ = $50) **$$+**
COMMUTING TIMES TO PARKS (in minutes)
MAGIC KINGDOM **6:15**
EPCOT **5:45**
ANIMAL KINGDOM **4:15**
DHS **5:15**

Animal Kingdom Lodge ★★★★
Walt Disney World
2901 Osceola Pkwy.
Bay Lake, FL 32830
☎ 407-938-3000
FAX 407-938-4799
www.disneyworld.com

LOCATION **WDW**
ROOM RATING **89**
COST ($ = $50) **$$$$$$–**
COMMUTING TIMES TO PARKS (in minutes)
MAGIC KINGDOM **8:15**
EPCOT **6:15**
ANIMAL KINGDOM **2:15**
DHS **6:00**

Animal Kingdom Lodge (Kidani Village) ★★★★½
Walt Disney World
2901 Osceola Pkwy.
Bay Lake, FL 32830
☎ 407-938-3000
FAX 407-938-4799
www.disneyworld.com

LOCATION **WDW**
ROOM RATING **95**
COST ($ = $50) **$$$$$$$$–**
COMMUTING TIMES TO PARKS (in minutes)
MAGIC KINGDOM **8:15**
EPCOT **6:15**
ANIMAL KINGDOM **2:15**
DHS **6:00**

Beach Club Resort ★★★★½
Walt Disney World
1800 Epcot Resorts Blvd.
Lake Buena Vista, FL 32830
☎ 407-934-8000
FAX 407-934-3850
www.disneyworld.com

LOCATION **WDW**
ROOM RATING **90**
COST ($ = $50) **$$$$$$$+**
COMMUTING TIMES TO PARKS (in minutes)
MAGIC KINGDOM **7:15**
EPCOT **5:15**
ANIMAL KINGDOM **6:45**
DHS **4:00**

Beach Club Villas ★★★★½
Walt Disney World
1900 Epcot Resorts Blvd.
Lake Buena Vista, FL 32830
☎ 407-934-2175
FAX 407-934-3850
www.disneyworld.com

LOCATION **WDW**
ROOM RATING **90**
COST ($ = $50) **$$$$$$$+**
COMMUTING TIMES TO PARKS (in minutes)
MAGIC KINGDOM **7:15**
EPCOT **5:15**
ANIMAL KINGDOM **6:45**
DHS **4:00**

Best Western Kissimmee ★★½
5196 W. Irlo Bronson Mem. Hwy.
Kissimmee, FL 34746
☎ 407-787-3555
FAX 407-787-0700
www.bestwestern.com

LOCATION **US 192**
ROOM RATING **64**
COST ($ = $50) **$$–**
COMMUTING TIMES TO PARKS (in minutes)
MAGIC KINGDOM **14:30**
EPCOT **14:00**
ANIMAL KINGDOM **12:30**
DHS **15:30**

BoardWalk Inn ★★★★
Walt Disney World
2101 Epcot Resorts Blvd.
Orlando, FL 32830
☎ 407-939-5100
FAX 407-939-5150
www.disneyworld.com

LOCATION **WDW**
ROOM RATING **89**
COST ($ = $50) **$$$$$$$+**
COMMUTING TIMES TO PARKS (in minutes)
MAGIC KINGDOM **7:15**
EPCOT **5:30**
ANIMAL KINGDOM **7:00**
DHS **3:00**

BoardWalk Villas ★★★★½
Walt Disney World
2101 Epcot Resorts Blvd.
Orlando, FL 32830
☎ 407-939-5100
FAX 407-939-5150
www.disneyworld.com

LOCATION **WDW**
ROOM RATING **90**
COST ($ = $50) **$$$$$$$+**
COMMUTING TIMES TO PARKS (in minutes)
MAGIC KINGDOM **7:15**
EPCOT **5:30**
ANIMAL KINGDOM **7:00**
DHS **3:00**

Buena Vista Palace Hotel & Spa ★★★★
Walt Disney World
1900 Buena Vista Dr.
Lake Buena Vista, FL 32830
☎ 407-827-2727
FAX 407-827-3136
www.buenavistapalace.com

LOCATION **WDW**
ROOM RATING **80**
COST ($ = $50) **$$$–**
COMMUTING TIMES TO PARKS (in minutes)
MAGIC KINGDOM **16:00**
EPCOT **11:15**
ANIMAL KINGDOM **15:15**
DHS **13:00**

DHS **8:15**

Celebration Hotel ★★★★½
700 Bloom St.
Celebration, FL 34747
☎ 407-566-6000
FAX 407-566-1844
www.celebrationhotel.com

LOCATION **WDW**
ROOM RATING **90**
COST ($ = $50) **$$$$–**
COMMUTING TIMES TO PARKS (in minutes)
MAGIC KINGDOM **13:30**
EPCOT **13:00**
ANIMAL KINGDOM **13:00**
DHS **12:30**

Celebrity Resorts Lake Buena Vista ★★★★
8451 Palm Pkwy.
Lake Buena Vista, FL 32836
☎ 866-507-1428
FAX 407-238-0255
www.celebrityresorts.com

LOCATION **I-4 Corridor**
ROOM RATING **85**
COST ($ = $50) **$$–**
COMMUTING TIMES TO PARKS (in minutes)
MAGIC KINGDOM **13:15**
EPCOT **8:30**
ANIMAL KINGDOM **11:30**
DHS **11:00**

Celebrity Resorts Orlando ★★★½
2800 N. Poinciana Blvd.
Orlando, FL 34746
☎ 866-507-1428
FAX 407-997-5998
www.celebrityresorts.com

LOCATION **US 192**
ROOM RATING **80**
COST ($ = $50) **$$–**
COMMUTING TIMES TO PARKS (in minutes)
MAGIC KINGDOM **16:30**
EPCOT **16:15**
ANIMAL KINGDOM **14:30**

Animal Kingdom Villas (Jambo Village) ★★★★½
Walt Disney World
2901 Osceola Pkwy.
Bay Lake, FL 32830
☎ 407-938-3000
FAX 407-938-4799
www.disneyworld.com

LOCATION WDW
ROOM RATING 91
COST ($ = $50) $$$$$$$$–
COMMUTING TIMES TO PARKS (in minutes)
MAGIC KINGDOM 8:15
EPCOT 6:15
ANIMAL KINGDOM 2:15
DHS 6:00

Bay Lake Tower at Contemporary Resort ★★★★½
Walt Disney World
4600 N. World Dr.
Bay Lake, FL 32830
☎ 407-824-1000
FAX 407-824-3539
www.disneyworld.com

LOCATION WDW
ROOM RATING 95
COST ($ = $50) $$$$$$$$–
COMMUTING TIMES TO PARKS (in minutes)
MAGIC KINGDOM on monorail
EPCOT 11:00
ANIMAL KINGDOM 17:15
DHS 14:15

Baymont Inn & Suites ★★½
7531 Canada Ave.
Orlando, FL 32819
☎ 407-226-9887
FAX 407-226-9877
www.baymontinns.com

LOCATION I-Drive
ROOM RATING 63
COST ($ = $50) $+
COMMUTING TIMES TO PARKS (in minutes)
MAGIC KINGDOM 20:15
EPCOT 15:45
ANIMAL KINGDOM 18:45
DHS 18:15

DHS 13:00

Best Western Lake Buena Vista Resort Hotel ★★★★
2000 Hotel Plaza Blvd.
Lake Buena Vista, FL 32830
☎ 407-828-2424
FAX 407-827-6390
www.lakebuenavistaresorthotel.com

LOCATION WDW
ROOM RATING 85
COST ($ = $50) $$+
COMMUTING TIMES TO PARKS (in minutes)
MAGIC KINGDOM 16:00
EPCOT 11:15
ANIMAL KINGDOM 15:15

DHS 13:00

Best Western Lakeside ★★★
7769 W. Irlo Bronson Mem. Hwy.
Kissimmee, FL 34747
☎ 407-396-2222
FAX 407-396-7087
www.bestwesternflorida.com

LOCATION US 192
ROOM RATING 67
COST ($ = $50) $+
COMMUTING TIMES TO PARKS (in minutes)
MAGIC KINGDOM 9:15
EPCOT 8:30
ANIMAL KINGDOM 6:30

DHS 8:30

Best Western Universal Inn ★★½
5618 Vineland Rd.
Orlando, FL 32819
☎ 407-226-9119
FAX 407-370-2448
www.bestwestern.com

LOCATION I-Drive
ROOM RATING 63
COST ($ = $50) $$–
COMMUTING TIMES TO PARKS (in minutes)
MAGIC KINGDOM 17:30
EPCOT 13:00
ANIMAL KINGDOM 16:00

Buena Vista Suites ★★★★
8203 World Center Dr.
Orlando, FL 32821
☎ 407-239-8588
FAX 407-239-1401
www.bvsuites.com

LOCATION US 192
ROOM RATING 83
COST ($ = $50) $$+
COMMUTING TIMES TO PARKS (in minutes)
MAGIC KINGDOM 9:15
EPCOT 4:30
ANIMAL KINGDOM 7:30
DHS 8:15

Caribbean Beach Resort ★★★½
Walt Disney World
900 Cayman Way
Lake Buena Vista, FL 32830
☎ 407-934-3400
FAX 407-934-3288
www.disneyworld.com

LOCATION WDW
ROOM RATING 80
COST ($ = $50) $$$+
COMMUTING TIMES TO PARKS (in minutes)
MAGIC KINGDOM 8:00
EPCOT 6:00
ANIMAL KINGDOM 7:15
DHS 4:15

Caribe Royale Orlando Resort Suites ★★★★
8101 World Center Dr.
Orlando, FL 32821
☎ 407-238-8000
FAX 407-238-8050
www.cariberesorts.com

LOCATION US 192
ROOM RATING 88
COST ($ = $50) $$$–
COMMUTING TIMES TO PARKS (in minutes)
MAGIC KINGDOM 9:15
EPCOT 4:45
ANIMAL KINGDOM 7:45

DHS 15:30

Central Motel ★★
4698 W. Irlo Bronson Mem. Hwy.
Kissimmee, FL 34748
☎ 407-396-2333
FAX 407-997-5998

LOCATION US 192
ROOM RATING 51
COST ($ = $50) $–
COMMUTING TIMES TO PARKS (in minutes)
MAGIC KINGDOM 18:15
EPCOT 17:45
ANIMAL KINGDOM 16:15

DHS 16:45

Champions World Resort ★★★
8660 W. Irlo Bronson Mem. Hwy.
Kissimmee, FL 34747
☎ 407-396-4500
FAX 407-396-0305
www.championsworldresort.com

LOCATION US 192
ROOM RATING 66
COST ($ = $50) $
COMMUTING TIMES TO PARKS (in minutes)
MAGIC KINGDOM 13:45
EPCOT 13:45
ANIMAL KINGDOM 10:45

DHS 13:00

Clarion Inn & Suites at I-Drive/ Convention Center ★★½
9956 Hawaiian Ct.
Orlando, FL 32819
☎ 407-351-5100
FAX 407-352-7188
www.hojo.com

LOCATION I-Drive
ROOM RATING 64
COST ($ = $50) $$
COMMUTING TIMES TO PARKS (in minutes)
MAGIC KINGDOM 19:30
EPCOT 14:15
ANIMAL KINGDOM 17:15

Hotel Information Chart (continued)

DHS 16:45
Clarion Maingate ★★½
7675 W. Irlo Bronson Mem. Hwy.
Kissimmee, FL 34747
☎ 407-396-4000
FAX 407-396-0714
www.clarionhotelmaingate.com

LOCATION **US 192**
ROOM RATING **60**
COST ($ = $50) **$$–**
COMMUTING TIMES TO PARKS (in minutes)
MAGIC KINGDOM **8:30**
EPCOT **8:00**
ANIMAL KINGDOM **5:30**

DHS 7:30
Comfort Inn I-Drive ★★½
8134 International Dr.
Orlando, FL 32819
☎ 407-313-4000
FAX 407-313-4001
www.comfortinn.com

LOCATION **I-Drive**
ROOM RATING **60**
COST ($ = $50) **$+**
COMMUTING TIMES TO PARKS (in minutes)
MAGIC KINGDOM **20:00**
EPCOT **15:30**
ANIMAL KINGDOM **18:30**

DHS 18:00
Comfort Inn Lake Buena Vista ★★½
8442 Palm Pkwy.
Lake Buena Vista, FL 32836
☎ 407-239-7300
FAX 407-996-1475
www.comfortinn.com

LOCATION **I-4 Corridor**
ROOM RATING **64**
COST ($ = $50) **$+**
COMMUTING TIMES TO PARKS (in minutes)
MAGIC KINGDOM **13:15**
EPCOT **8:30**
ANIMAL KINGDOM **11:30**

DHS 18:30
Comfort Suites Universal ★★★
5617 Major Blvd.
Orlando, FL 32819
☎ 407-363-1967
FAX 407-363-6873
www.choicehotels.com

LOCATION **I-Drive**
ROOM RATING **66**
COST ($ = $50) **$$–**
COMMUTING TIMES TO PARKS (in minutes)
MAGIC KINGDOM **17:45**
EPCOT **13:15**
ANIMAL KINGDOM **16:15**

DHS 15:15
Contemporary Resort ★★★★½
Walt Disney World
4600 N. World Dr.
Bay Lake, FL 32830
☎ 407-934-7639
FAX 407-824-3539
www.disneyworld.com

LOCATION **WDW**
ROOM RATING **93**
COST ($ = $50) **$$$$$+**
COMMUTING TIMES TO PARKS (in minutes)
MAGIC KINGDOM **on monorail**
EPCOT **11:00**
ANIMAL KINGDOM **17:15**

DHS 14:15
Continental Plaza Kissimmee Hotel ★★½
7785 W. Irlo Bronson Mem. Hwy.
Kissimmee, FL 34747
☎ 407-396-1828
FAX 407-396-1305

LOCATION **US 192**
ROOM RATING **60**
COST ($ = $50) **$–**
COMMUTING TIMES TO PARKS (in minutes)
MAGIC KINGDOM **9:15**
EPCOT **8:45**
ANIMAL KINGDOM **6:30**

DHS 18:45
Country Inn & Suites Lake Buena Vista (rooms) ★★★½
12191 S. Apopka–Vineland Rd.
Lake Buena Vista, FL 32836
☎ 407-239-1115
FAX 407-239-8882
www.countryinns.com

LOCATION **I-4 Corridor**
ROOM RATING **78**
COST ($ = $50) **$$**
COMMUTING TIMES TO PARKS (in minutes)
MAGIC KINGDOM **14:00**
EPCOT **9:15**
ANIMAL KINGDOM **12:15**

DHS 11:45
Country Inn & Suites Lake Buena Vista (suites) ★★★½
12191 S. Apopka–Vineland Rd.
Lake Buena Vista, FL 32836
☎ 407-239-1115
FAX 407-239-8882
www.countryinns.com

LOCATION **I-4 Corridor**
ROOM RATING **78**
COST ($ = $50) **$$+**
COMMUTING TIMES TO PARKS (in minutes)
MAGIC KINGDOM **14:00**
EPCOT **9:15**
ANIMAL KINGDOM **12:15**

DHS 11:45
Courtyard Orlando I-Drive/ Convention Center ★★★½
8600 Austrian Ct.
Orlando, FL 32819
☎ 407-351-2244
FAX 407-351-3306
www.tinyurl.com/courtyardidrive

LOCATION **I-Drive**
ROOM RATING **76**
COST ($ = $50) **$$+**
COMMUTING TIMES TO PARKS (in minutes)
MAGIC KINGDOM **21:45**
EPCOT **17:00**
ANIMAL KINGDOM **20:00**

DHS 7:45
Days Inn Convention Center ★★½
9990 International Dr.
Orlando, FL 32819
☎ 407-352-8700
FAX 407-363-3965
www.daysinnorlandohotel.com

LOCATION **I-Drive**
ROOM RATING **60**
COST ($ = $50) **$+**
COMMUTING TIMES TO PARKS (in minutes)
MAGIC KINGDOM **18:45**
EPCOT **14:00**
ANIMAL KINGDOM **17:00**

DHS 16:30
Days Inn I-Drive North ★★½
5858 International Dr.
Orlando, FL 32819
☎ 407-351-4410
FAX 407-351-2481
www.daysinn.com

LOCATION **I-Drive**
ROOM RATING **61**
COST ($ = $50) **$**
COMMUTING TIMES TO PARKS (in minutes)
MAGIC KINGDOM **20:30**
EPCOT **16:00**
ANIMAL KINGDOM **19:00**

DHS 18:30
Days Inn Universal Studios ★★½
5827 Caravan Ct.
Orlando, FL 32819
☎ 407-351-3800
FAX 407-363-2793
www.daysinn.com

LOCATION **I-Drive**
ROOM RATING **60**
COST ($ = $50) **$**
COMMUTING TIMES TO PARKS (in minutes)
MAGIC KINGDOM **18:45**
EPCOT **14:00**
ANIMAL KINGDOM **17:00**

DHS 11:00
Comfort Inn Universal Studios Area ★★★
6101 Sand Lake Rd.
Orlando, FL 32919
☎ 407-363-7886
FAX 407-345-0670
www.comfortinn.com

LOCATION I-Drive
ROOM RATING 66
COST ($ = $50) $+
COMMUTING TIMES TO PARKS (in minutes)
MAGIC KINGDOM 22:15
EPCOT 17:30
ANIMAL KINGDOM 20:30

DHS 20:00
Comfort Suites Maingate ★★★½
7888 W. Irlo Bronson Mem. Hwy.
Kissimmee, FL 34747
☎ 407-390-9888
FAX 407-390-0981
www.comfortsuiteskissimmee.com

LOCATION US 192
ROOM RATING 76
COST ($ = $50) $$$–
COMMUTING TIMES TO PARKS (in minutes)
MAGIC KINGDOM 10:00
EPCOT 9:15
ANIMAL KINGDOM 7:00

DHS 9:00
Comfort Suites Orlando ★★★
9350 Turkey Lake Rd.
Orlando, FL 32819
☎ 407-351-5050
FAX 407-363-7953
www.comfortsuitesorlando.com

LOCATION I-4 Corridor
ROOM RATING 74
COST ($ = $50) $$–
COMMUTING TIMES TO PARKS (in minutes)
MAGIC KINGDOM 20:45
EPCOT 16:00
ANIMAL KINGDOM 19:00

DHS 8:30
Coronado Springs Resort ★★★★
Walt Disney World
1000 West Buena Vista Dr.
Orlando, FL 32830
☎ 407-939-1000
FAX 407-939-1001
www.disneyworld.com

LOCATION WDW
ROOM RATING 83
COST ($ = $50) $$$
COMMUTING TIMES TO PARKS (in minutes)
MAGIC KINGDOM 5:30
EPCOT 4:00
ANIMAL KINGDOM 4:45

DHS 4:45
Country Inn & Suites Calypso Cay ★★★½
5001 Calypso Cay Way
Kissimmee, FL 34746
☎ 407-997-1400
FAX 407-997-1401
www.countryinns.com

LOCATION US 192
ROOM RATING 82
COST ($ = $50) $$–
COMMUTING TIMES TO PARKS (in minutes)
MAGIC KINGDOM 13:30
EPCOT 13:00
ANIMAL KINGDOM 11:30

DHS 12:30
Country Inn & Suites I-Drive ★★½
7701 Universal Blvd.
Orlando, FL 32819
☎ 407-313-4200
FAX 407-313-4201
www.countryinns.com

LOCATION I-Drive
ROOM RATING 63
COST ($ = $50) $$–
COMMUTING TIMES TO PARKS (in minutes)
MAGIC KINGDOM 21:00
EPCOT 16:15
ANIMAL KINGDOM 19:15

DHS 19:30
Courtyard Orlando Lake Buena Vista at Vista Centre ★★★½
8501 Palm Pkwy.
Lake Buena Vista, FL 32836
☎ 407-239-6900
FAX 407-239-1287
www.tinyurl.com/courtyardlbv

LOCATION I-4 Corridor
ROOM RATING 82
COST ($ = $50) $$–
COMMUTING TIMES TO PARKS (in minutes)
MAGIC KINGDOM 13:15
EPCOT 8:30
ANIMAL KINGDOM 11:30

DHS 11:00
Courtyard Orlando LBV in Marriott Village ★★★
8623 Vineland Ave.
Orlando, FL 32821
☎ 407-938-9001
FAX 407-938-9002
www.marriottvillage.com

LOCATION I-4 Corridor
ROOM RATING 82
COST ($ = $50) $$–
COMMUTING TIMES TO PARKS (in minutes)
MAGIC KINGDOM 12:00
EPCOT 7:15
ANIMAL KINGDOM 10:15

DHS 9:45
Days Hotel Maingate ★★
7601 Black Lake Rd.
Kissimmee, FL 34747
☎ 407-396-1100
FAX 407-396-0689
www.legacygrand.com

LOCATION US 192
ROOM RATING 51
COST ($ = $50) $+
COMMUTING TIMES TO PARKS (in minutes)
MAGIC KINGDOM 8:30
EPCOT 8:15
ANIMAL KINGDOM 5:30

DHS 16:30
Days Inn West Kissimmee ★★½
9240 W. Irlo Bronson Mem. Hwy.
Kissimmee, FL 34711
☎ 863-424-6099
FAX 863-424-5779
www.daysinn.com

LOCATION US 192
ROOM RATING 62
COST ($ = $50) $
COMMUTING TIMES TO PARKS (in minutes)
MAGIC KINGDOM 14:00
EPCOT 13:15
ANIMAL KINGDOM 11:00

DHS 13:00
Destiny Palms Maingate West ★★★
8536 W. Irlo Bronson Mem. Hwy.
Kissimmee, FL 34747
☎ 407-396-1600
FAX 407-396-1971

LOCATION US 192
ROOM RATING 65
COST ($ = $50) $+
COMMUTING TIMES TO PARKS (in minutes)
MAGIC KINGDOM 13:45
EPCOT 13:15
ANIMAL KINGDOM 11:00

DHS 13:00
Dolphin ★★★★½
Walt Disney World
1500 Epcot Resorts Blvd.
Lake Buena Vista, FL 32830
☎ 407-934-4000
FAX 407-934-4884
www.swandolphin.com

LOCATION WDW
ROOM RATING 90
COST ($ = $50) $$$$+
COMMUTING TIMES TO PARKS (in minutes)
MAGIC KINGDOM 6:45
EPCOT 5:00
ANIMAL KINGDOM 6:15

Hotel Information Chart (continued)

DHS 4:00

Doubletree Castle Hotel ★★★½
8629 International Dr.
Orlando, FL 32819
☎ 407-345-1511
FAX 407-248-8181
www.doubletreecastle.com

LOCATION I-Drive
ROOM RATING 82
COST ($ = $50) $$$$–
COMMUTING TIMES TO PARKS (in minutes)
MAGIC KINGDOM 22:30
EPCOT 17:45
ANIMAL KINGDOM 20:45

DHS 20:15

Doubletree Guest Suites ★★★★
2305 Hotel Plaza Blvd.
Lake Buena Vista, FL 32830
☎ 407-934-1000
FAX 407-934-1015
www.doubletreeguestsuites.com

LOCATION WDW
ROOM RATING 86
COST ($ = $50) $$+
COMMUTING TIMES TO PARKS (in minutes)
MAGIC KINGDOM 13:00
EPCOT 8:30
ANIMAL KINGDOM 12:30

DHS 10:00

Doubletree Universal ★★★★
5780 Major Blvd.
Orlando, FL 32819
☎ 407-351-1000
FAX 407-363-0106
www.doubletree.com

LOCATION I-Drive
ROOM RATING 89
COST ($ = $50) $$–
COMMUTING TIMES TO PARKS (in minutes)
MAGIC KINGDOM 19:00
EPCOT 14:15
ANIMAL KINGDOM 17:15

Embassy Suites Resort Lake Buena Vista ★★★½
8100 Lake Ave.
Orlando, FL 32836
☎ 407-239-1144
FAX 407-239-1718
www.embassysuiteslbv.com

LOCATION I-4 Corridor
ROOM RATING 81
COST ($ = $50) $$$+
COMMUTING TIMES TO PARKS (in minutes)
MAGIC KINGDOM 12:45
EPCOT 8:00
ANIMAL KINGDOM 11:00
DHS 10:30

Enclave Suites ★★★
6165 Carrier Dr.
Orlando, FL 32819
☎ 407-351-1155
FAX 407-351-2001
www.enclavesuites.com

LOCATION I-Drive
ROOM RATING 67
COST ($ = $50) $$$–
COMMUTING TIMES TO PARKS (in minutes)
MAGIC KINGDOM 20:45
EPCOT 16:15
ANIMAL KINGDOM 19:15
DHS 18:45

Extended Stay America Convention Center ★★★
6451 Westwood Blvd.
Orlando, FL 32821
☎ 407-352-3454
FAX 407-352-1708
www.extendedstayamerica.com

LOCATION I-Drive
ROOM RATING 72
COST ($ = $50) $+
COMMUTING TIMES TO PARKS (in minutes)
MAGIC KINGDOM 17:30
EPCOT 12:45
ANIMAL KINGDOM 15:45
DHS 15:30

Extended Stay Deluxe Lake Buena Vista ★★★★
8100 Palm Pkwy.
Orlando, FL 32836
☎ 407-239-4300
FAX 407-239-4446
www.extendedstaydeluxe.com

LOCATION I-4 Corridor
ROOM RATING 83
COST ($ = $50) $$$–
COMMUTING TIMES TO PARKS (in minutes)
MAGIC KINGDOM 13:45
EPCOT 9:00
ANIMAL KINGDOM 12:00
DHS 11:30

Extended Stay Deluxe Orlando Universal ★★★
5610 Vineland Rd.
Orlando, FL 32819
☎ 407-370-4428
FAX 407-370-9456
www.extendedstaydeluxe.com

LOCATION I-Drive
ROOM RATING 75
COST ($ = $50) $$–
COMMUTING TIMES TO PARKS (in minutes)
MAGIC KINGDOM 18:00
EPCOT 14:15
ANIMAL KINGDOM 18:00
DHS 16:00

Fairfield Inn & Suites Orlando LBV in Marriott Village ★★★
8615 Vineland Ave.
Orlando, FL 32821
☎ 407-938-9001
FAX 407-938-9002
www.marriottvillage.com

LOCATION I-4 Corridor
ROOM RATING 75
COST ($ = $50) $$+
COMMUTING TIMES TO PARKS (in minutes)
MAGIC KINGDOM 12:00
EPCOT 7:15
ANIMAL KINGDOM 10:15
DHS 9:45

Fun Spots Hotel at Fountain Park ★★
5150 W. Irlo Bronson Mem. Hwy.
Kissimmee, FL 34746
☎ 407-396-1111
FAX 407-396-1607
www.funspotshotels.com/fountainpark

LOCATION US 192
ROOM RATING 50
COST ($ = $50) $
COMMUTING TIMES TO PARKS (in minutes)
MAGIC KINGDOM 15:45
EPCOT 15:15
ANIMAL KINGDOM 13:45
DHS 15:00

Galleria Palms Maingate ★★★
3000 Maingate Lane
Kissimmee, FL 34747
☎ 407-396-6300
FAX 407-396-8989
www.galleriapalmsorlando.com

LOCATION US 192
ROOM RATING 74
COST ($ = $50) $+
COMMUTING TIMES TO PARKS (in minutes)
MAGIC KINGDOM 8:15
EPCOT 7:30
ANIMAL KINGDOM 5:15
DHS 7:15

Gaylord Palms Resort ★★★★½
6000 Osceola Pkwy.
Kissimmee, FL 34746
☎ 407-586-0000
FAX 407-586-1999
www.gaylordpalms.com

LOCATION US 192
ROOM RATING 90
COST ($ = $50) $$$$–
COMMUTING TIMES TO PARKS (in minutes)
MAGIC KINGDOM 9:00
EPCOT 8:45
ANIMAL KINGDOM 7:00
DHS 8:15

DHS 16:45

Econo Lodge Inn & Suites ★★½
8738 International Dr.
Orlando, FL 32819
☎ 407-345-8195
FAX 407-351-9766
www.econolodge.com

LOCATION I-Drive
ROOM RATING 62
COST ($ = $50) $
COMMUTING TIMES TO PARKS (in minutes)
MAGIC KINGDOM 22:00
EPCOT 17:15
ANIMAL KINGDOM 20:15

DHS 19:45

Embassy Suites Orlando I-Drive ★★★
8978 International Dr.
Orlando, FL 32819
☎ 407-352-1400
FAX 407-363-1120
www.embassysuitesorlando.com

LOCATION I-Drive
ROOM RATING 75
COST ($ = $50) $$$
COMMUTING TIMES TO PARKS (in minutes)
MAGIC KINGDOM 22:00
EPCOT 17:15
ANIMAL KINGDOM 20:15

DHS 19:45

Embassy Suites Plaza I-Drive ★★★½
8250 Jamaican Ct.
Orlando, FL 32819
☎ 407-345-8250
FAX 407-352-1463
www.orlandoembassysuites.com

LOCATION I-Drive
ROOM RATING 80
COST ($ = $50) $$$+
COMMUTING TIMES TO PARKS (in minutes)
MAGIC KINGDOM 20:15
EPCOT 15:30
ANIMAL KINGDOM 18:30

DHS 15:30

Extended Stay America Universal ★★★
5620 Major Blvd.
Orlando, FL 32819
☎ 407-351-1788
FAX 407-351-7899
www.extendedstayamerica.com

LOCATION I-Drive
ROOM RATING 75
COST ($ = $50) $+
COMMUTING TIMES TO PARKS (in minutes)
MAGIC KINGDOM 18:00
EPCOT 14:15
ANIMAL KINGDOM 18:00

DHS 16:00

Extended Stay Deluxe Convention Center ★★★★
6443 Westwood Blvd.
Orlando, FL 32821
☎ 407-351-1982
FAX 407-351-1719
www.extendedstaydeluxe.com

LOCATION I-Drive
ROOM RATING 84
COST ($ = $50) $+
COMMUTING TIMES TO PARKS (in minutes)
MAGIC KINGDOM 17:30
EPCOT 12:45
ANIMAL KINGDOM 15:45

DHS 15:30

Extended Stay Deluxe Convention Center/Pointe Orlando ★★½
8750 Universal Blvd.
Orlando, FL 32819
☎ 407-903-1500
FAX 407-903-1555
www.extendedstaydeluxe.com

LOCATION I-Drive
ROOM RATING 58
COST ($ = $50) $$
COMMUTING TIMES TO PARKS (in minutes)
MAGIC KINGDOM 17:45
EPCOT 13:00
ANIMAL KINGDOM 17:00

Fairfield Inn & Suites Orlando Near Universal Resort ★★★
5614 Vineland Rd.
Orlando, FL 32819
☎ 407-581-5600
FAX 407-581-5601
www.tinyurl.com/fairfielduniversal

LOCATION I-Drive
ROOM RATING 73
COST ($ = $50) $$+
COMMUTING TIMES TO PARKS (in minutes)
MAGIC KINGDOM 17:30
EPCOT 12:45
ANIMAL KINGDOM 15:45
DHS 15:15

Fort Wilderness Resort (cabins) ★★★★
Walt Disney World
4510 N. Fort Wilderness Trl.
Lake Buena Vista, FL 32830
☎ 407-824-2900
FAX 407-824-3508
www.disneyworld.com

LOCATION WDW
ROOM RATING 86
COST ($ = $50) $$$$$$
COMMUTING TIMES TO PARKS (in minutes)
MAGIC KINGDOM 13:15
EPCOT 8:30
ANIMAL KINGDOM 20:00
DHS 14:00

Four Points by Sheraton Orlando Studio City ★★★★½
5905 International Dr.
Orlando, FL 32819
☎ 407-351-2100
FAX 407-345-5249
www.sheraton.com

LOCATION I-Drive
ROOM RATING 90
COST ($ = $50) $$
COMMUTING TIMES TO PARKS (in minutes)
MAGIC KINGDOM 20:30
EPCOT 15:45
ANIMAL KINGDOM 18:45
DHS 18:15

Golden Link Motel ★★
4914 W. Irlo Bronson Mem. Hwy.
Kissimmee, FL 34746
☎ 407-396-0555
FAX 407-396-6531
www.goldenlinkmotel.com

LOCATION US 192
ROOM RATING 54
COST ($ = $50) $–
COMMUTING TIMES TO PARKS (in minutes)
MAGIC KINGDOM 16:15
EPCOT 16:00
ANIMAL KINGDOM 14:15
DHS 15:45

Grand Floridian Resort ★★★★½
Walt Disney World
4401 Floridian Way
Lake Buena Vista, FL 32830
☎ 407-824-3000
FAX 407-824-3136
www.disneyworld.com

LOCATION WDW
ROOM RATING 93
COST ($ = $50) $$$$$$$$$–
COMMUTING TIMES TO PARKS (in minutes)
MAGIC KINGDOM on monorail
EPCOT 4:45
ANIMAL KINGDOM 11:45
DHS 6:45

Grand Lake Resort ★★★½
7770 W. Irlo Bronson Mem. Hwy.
Kissimmee, FL 34747
☎ 407-396-3000
FAX 407-396-1822
www.dailymanagementresorts.com

LOCATION US 192
ROOM RATING 76
COST ($ = $50) $$+
COMMUTING TIMES TO PARKS (in minutes)
MAGIC KINGDOM 9:15
EPCOT 8:30
ANIMAL KINGDOM 6:15
DHS 8:30

Hotel Information Chart (continued)

Hampton Inn Convention Center ★★★
8900 Universal Blvd.
Orlando, FL 32819
☎ 407-354-4447
FAX 407-354-3031
www.hamptoninn.com

LOCATION	I-Drive
ROOM RATING	74
COST ($ = $50)	$$$–
COMMUTING TIMES TO PARKS (in minutes)	
MAGIC KINGDOM	21:30
EPCOT	17:00
ANIMAL KINGDOM	20:00

DHS 19:30

Hampton Inn Kirkman ★★½
7110 South Kirkman Rd.
Orlando, FL 32819
☎ 407-345-1112
FAX 407-352-6591
www.hamptoninn.com

LOCATION	I-Drive
ROOM RATING	64
COST ($ = $50)	$$+
COMMUTING TIMES TO PARKS (in minutes)	
MAGIC KINGDOM	21:15
EPCOT	16:45
ANIMAL KINGDOM	19:45

DHS 19:15

Hampton Inn Lake Buena Vista ★★★½
8150 Palm Pkwy.
Orlando, FL 32836
☎ 407-465-8150
FAX 407-465-0150
www.hamptoninn.com

LOCATION	I-4 Corridor
ROOM RATING	76
COST ($ = $50)	$$$–
COMMUTING TIMES TO PARKS (in minutes)	
MAGIC KINGDOM	12:45
EPCOT	8:00
ANIMAL KINGDOM	11:00

DHS 18:00

Hawthorn Suites Orlando at SeaWorld ★★★½
6435 Westwood Blvd.
Orlando, FL 32821
☎ 407-351-6600
FAX 407-351-1977
www.hawthornsuitesorlando.com

LOCATION	I-Drive
ROOM RATING	80
COST ($ = $50)	$+
COMMUTING TIMES TO PARKS (in minutes)	
MAGIC KINGDOM	17:30
EPCOT	12:45
ANIMAL KINGDOM	15:45

DHS 15:30

Hawthorn Suites Universal ★★★½
7601 Canada Ave.
Orlando, FL 32819
☎ 407-581-2151
FAX 407-581-2152
www.hawthornsuitesuniversal.com

LOCATION	I-Drive
ROOM RATING	82
COST ($ = $50)	$$+
COMMUTING TIMES TO PARKS (in minutes)	
MAGIC KINGDOM	20:15
EPCOT	15:45
ANIMAL KINGDOM	18:45

DHS 19:15

Hilton Garden Inn at SeaWorld International Center ★★★½
6850 Westwood Blvd.
Orlando, FL 32821
☎ 407-354-1500
FAX 407-354-1528
www.tinyurl.com/hgiseaworld

LOCATION	I-Drive
ROOM RATING	82
COST ($ = $50)	$$$–
COMMUTING TIMES TO PARKS (in minutes)	
MAGIC KINGDOM	15:30
EPCOT	11:00
ANIMAL KINGDOM	14:00

DHS 15:30

Hilton Walt Disney World ★★★★
1751 Hotel Plaza Blvd.
Orlando, FL 32830
☎ 407-827-4000
FAX 407-827-3890
www.hilton-wdwv.com

LOCATION	WDW
ROOM RATING	87
COST ($ = $50)	$$$$+
COMMUTING TIMES TO PARKS (in minutes)	
MAGIC KINGDOM	15:15
EPCOT	10:30
ANIMAL KINGDOM	14:30

DHS 12:15

Holiday Inn Express Lake Buena Vista ★★★½
8686 Palm Pkwy.
Orlando, FL 32836
☎ 407-239-8400
FAX 407-239-8025
www.holidayinn.com

LOCATION	I-4 Corridor
ROOM RATING	80
COST ($ = $50)	$$
COMMUTING TIMES TO PARKS (in minutes)	
MAGIC KINGDOM	14:15
EPCOT	9:45
ANIMAL KINGDOM	12:45

DHS 12:15

Holiday Inn Express Summerbay Resort ★★★
105 Summer Bay Blvd.
Clermont, FL 34711
☎ 407-239-8315
FAX 407-239-8297
www.hiexpress.com

LOCATION	US 192
ROOM RATING	70
COST ($ = $50)	$$–
COMMUTING TIMES TO PARKS (in minutes)	
MAGIC KINGDOM	14:00
EPCOT	9:15
ANIMAL KINGDOM	11:30

DHS 19:15

Holiday Inn SunSpree Resort ★★★
13351 FL 535
Orlando, FL 32821
☎ 407-239-4500
FAX 407-239-8463
www.holidayinnsunspree.com

LOCATION	I-4 Corridor
ROOM RATING	79
COST ($ = $50)	$$
COMMUTING TIMES TO PARKS (in minutes)	
MAGIC KINGDOM	10:45
EPCOT	6:00
ANIMAL KINGDOM	9:00

DHS 8:30

Holiday Inn Universal Studios ★★★
5905 Kirkman Rd.
Orlando, FL 32819
☎ 407-351-3333
FAX 407-351-3577
www.holidayinn.com

LOCATION	I-Drive
ROOM RATING	75
COST ($ = $50)	$+
COMMUTING TIMES TO PARKS (in minutes)	
MAGIC KINGDOM	19:00
EPCOT	14:15
ANIMAL KINGDOM	17:15

DHS 16:45

HomeSuiteHome Eastgate ★★½
5565 W. Irlo Bronson Mem. Hwy.
Kissimmee, FL 34746
☎ 407-396-0707
FAX 407-396-6644
www.homesuitehome.com

LOCATION	US 192
ROOM RATING	57
COST ($ = $50)	$$$+
COMMUTING TIMES TO PARKS (in minutes)	
MAGIC KINGDOM	13:30
EPCOT	13:15
ANIMAL KINGDOM	11:30
DHS	12:15

DHS 10:30
Hampton Inn Universal ★★★
5621 Windhover Dr.
Orlando, FL 32819
☎ 407-351-6716
FAX 407-363-1711
www.hamptoninn.com

LOCATION I-Drive
ROOM RATING 67
COST ($ = $50) $$+
COMMUTING TIMES TO PARKS (in minutes)
MAGIC KINGDOM 19:00
EPCOT 14:15
ANIMAL KINGDOM 17:15

DHS 16:45
Hard Rock Hotel ★★★★½
5800 Universal Blvd.
Orlando, FL 32819
☎ 407-503-2000
FAX 407-503-2010
www.hardrockhotelorlando.com

LOCATION I-Drive
ROOM RATING 93
COST ($ = $50) $$$$–
COMMUTING TIMES TO PARKS (in minutes)
MAGIC KINGDOM 21:45
EPCOT 17:00
ANIMAL KINGDOM 20:00

DHS 19:30
Hawthorn Suites Lake Buena Vista ★★★★
8303 Palm Pkwy.
Orlando, FL 32836
☎ 407-597-5000
FAX 407-597-6000
www.hawthorn.com

LOCATION I-4 Corridor
ROOM RATING 87
COST ($ = $50) $$+
COMMUTING TIMES TO PARKS (in minutes)
MAGIC KINGDOM 20:15
EPCOT 15:30
ANIMAL KINGDOM 18:30

DHS 13:30
Hilton Garden Inn Orlando ★★★½
5877 American Way
Orlando, FL 32819
☎ 407-363-9332
FAX 407-363-9335
www.hiltongardenorlando.com

LOCATION I-Drive
ROOM RATING 82
COST ($ = $50) $$+
COMMUTING TIMES TO PARKS (in minutes)
MAGIC KINGDOM 21:15
EPCOT 16:30
ANIMAL KINGDOM 19:30

DHS 19:00
Hilton Grand Vacations Club ★★★★
8122 Arrezzo Way
Orlando, FL 32821
☎ 800-448-2736
FAX 407-465-2600
www.hiltongrandvacations.com

LOCATION I-4 Corridor
ROOM RATING 88
COST ($ = $50) $$$–
COMMUTING TIMES TO PARKS (in minutes)
MAGIC KINGDOM 16:15
EPCOT 14:00
ANIMAL KINGDOM 17:00

DHS 16:30
Hilton Grand Vacations Club SeaWorld ★★★★
6924 Grand Vacations Way
Orlando, FL 32821
☎ 407-239-0100
FAX 407-239-0200
www.hilton.com

LOCATION I-Drive
ROOM RATING 89
COST ($ = $50) $$$–
COMMUTING TIMES TO PARKS (in minutes)
MAGIC KINGDOM 17:00
EPCOT 12:30
ANIMAL KINGDOM 16:30

DHS 13:15
Holiday Inn Hotel & Suites Convention Center ★★★
8214 Universal Blvd.
Orlando, FL 32819
☎ 407-581-9001
FAX 407-581-9002
www.holidayinn.com

LOCATION I-Drive
ROOM RATING 74
COST ($ = $50) $+
COMMUTING TIMES TO PARKS (in minutes)
MAGIC KINGDOM 23:00
EPCOT 18:15
ANIMAL KINGDOM 21:15

DHS 20:45
Holiday Inn Maingate East ★★★★½
5711 W. Irlo Bronson Mem. Hwy.
Kissimmee, FL 34746
☎ 407-396-4222
FAX 407-396-0570
www.holidayinn.com

LOCATION US 192
ROOM RATING 90
COST ($ = $50) $$–
COMMUTING TIMES TO PARKS (in minutes)
MAGIC KINGDOM 12:15
EPCOT 12:00
ANIMAL KINGDOM 10:15

DHS 11:30
Holiday Inn Orlando International Drive Hotel ★★★
6515 International Dr.
Orlando, FL 32819
☎ 407-351-3500
FAX 407-351-5727
www.tinyurl.com/holidayinnidrive

LOCATION I-Drive
ROOM RATING 73
COST ($ = $50) $$+
COMMUTING TIMES TO PARKS (in minutes)
MAGIC KINGDOM 21:15
EPCOT 16:45
ANIMAL KINGDOM 19:45

HomeSuiteHome Nikki Bird Maingate ★★
7300 W. Irlo Bronson Mem. Hwy.
Kissimmee, FL 34747
☎ 407-396-7300
FAX 407-396-7555
www.homesuitehome.com

LOCATION US 192
ROOM RATING 48
COST ($ = $50) $$$
COMMUTING TIMES TO PARKS (in minutes)
MAGIC KINGDOM 8:15
EPCOT 8:00
ANIMAL KINGDOM 5:00
DHS 7:45

Homewood Suites I-Drive ★★★½
8745 International Dr.
Orlando, FL 32819
☎ 407-248-2232
FAX 407-248-6552
www.homewoodsuitesorlando.com

LOCATION I-Drive
ROOM RATING 81
COST ($ = $50) $$$+
COMMUTING TIMES TO PARKS (in minutes)
MAGIC KINGDOM 21:45
EPCOT 17:00
ANIMAL KINGDOM 20:00
DHS 19:30

The Hotel Universal ★★★
7299 Universal Dr.
Orlando, FL 32819
☎ 407-351-5009
FAX 407-352-7277
www.clarionuniversal.com

LOCATION I-Drive
ROOM RATING 67
COST ($ = $50) $$
COMMUTING TIMES TO PARKS (in minutes)
MAGIC KINGDOM 20:30
EPCOT 15:45
ANIMAL KINGDOM 18:45
DHS 18:30

Hotel Information Chart (continued)

Howard Johnson Inn Maingate East ★★½
6051 W. Irlo Bronson Mem. Hwy.
Kissimmee, FL 34747
☎ 407-396-1748
FAX 407-396-4835
www.hojo.com

LOCATION	US 192
ROOM RATING	59
COST ($ = $50)	$–
COMMUTING TIMES TO PARKS (in minutes)	
MAGIC KINGDOM	11:15
EPCOT	11:00
ANIMAL KINGDOM	8:15
DHS	10:30

Howard Johnson Inn Orlando ★★½
6603 International Dr.
Orlando, FL 32819
☎ 407-351-2900
FAX 407-351-1327
www.hojo.com

LOCATION	I-Drive
ROOM RATING	59
COST ($ = $50)	$+
COMMUTING TIMES TO PARKS (in minutes)	
MAGIC KINGDOM	21:00
EPCOT	16:30
ANIMAL KINGDOM	19:30
DHS	19:00

Howard Johnson Lake Front Park ★★
4836 W. Irlo Bronson Mem. Hwy.
Kissimmee, FL 34746
☎ 407-396-4762
FAX 407-396-4866
www.hojo.com

LOCATION	US 192
ROOM RATING	50
COST ($ = $50)	$+
COMMUTING TIMES TO PARKS (in minutes)	
MAGIC KINGDOM	16:30
EPCOT	16:15
ANIMAL KINGDOM	14:30
DHS	15:45

The Inn at Summer Bay ★★½
9400 W. Irlo Bronson Mem. Hwy.
Clermont, FL 34711
☎ 863-420-8282
FAX 352-241-2268
www.summerbayresort.com

LOCATION	US 192
ROOM RATING	63
COST ($ = $50)	$$$$
COMMUTING TIMES TO PARKS (in minutes)	
MAGIC KINGDOM	14:15
EPCOT	13:45
ANIMAL KINGDOM	11:15
DHS	13:30

Inn Nova ★★½
9330 W. Irlo Bronson Mem. Hwy.
Clermont, FL 34714
☎ 863-424-8420
FAX 863-424-9670
www.magnusonhotels.com

LOCATION	US 192
ROOM RATING	64
COST ($ = $50)	$–
COMMUTING TIMES TO PARKS (in minutes)	
MAGIC KINGDOM	14:00
EPCOT	13:15
ANIMAL KINGDOM	11:00
DHS	13:00

International Plaza Resort & Spa (garden) ★★★
10100 International Dr.
Orlando, FL 32821
☎ 407-352-1100
FAX 407-354-4700
www.intlplazaresort.com

LOCATION	I-Drive
ROOM RATING	75
COST ($ = $50)	$$–
COMMUTING TIMES TO PARKS (in minutes)	
MAGIC KINGDOM	17:45
EPCOT	13:00
ANIMAL KINGDOM	16:00
DHS	15:30

Knights Inn ★★
2880 Poinciana Blvd.
Kissimmee, FL 34746
☎ 407-396-8186
FAX 407-396-8569
www.knightsinn.com

LOCATION	US 192
ROOM RATING	52
COST ($ = $50)	$–
COMMUTING TIMES TO PARKS (in minutes)	
MAGIC KINGDOM	15:45
EPCOT	15:30
ANIMAL KINGDOM	13:45
DHS	15:00

Knights Inn Maingate ★★
7475 W. Irlo Bronson Mem. Hwy.
Kissimmee, FL 34746
☎ 407-396-4200
FAX 407-396-8838
www.knightsinn.com

LOCATION	US 192
ROOM RATING	55
COST ($ = $50)	$–
COMMUTING TIMES TO PARKS (in minutes)	
MAGIC KINGDOM	8:15
EPCOT	7:45
ANIMAL KINGDOM	5:45
DHS	7:30

La Quinta Inn I-Drive ★★★
8300 Jamaican Ct.
Orlando, FL 32819
☎ 407-351-1660
FAX 407-351-9264
www.lq.com

LOCATION	I-Drive
ROOM RATING	73
COST ($ = $50)	$+
COMMUTING TIMES TO PARKS (in minutes)	
MAGIC KINGDOM	21:45
EPCOT	17:15
ANIMAL KINGDOM	20:15
DHS	19:45

Liki Tiki Village ★★★★½
17777 Bali Blvd.
Winter Garden, FL 34787
☎ 407-856-7190
FAX 407-239-5092
www.likitiki.com

LOCATION	US 192
ROOM RATING	90
COST ($ = $50)	$$
COMMUTING TIMES TO PARKS (in minutes)	
MAGIC KINGDOM	9:00
EPCOT	8:45
ANIMAL KINGDOM	5:15
DHS	8:15

Loews Portofino Bay Hotel ★★★★½
5601 Universal Blvd.
Orlando, FL 32819
☎ 407-503-1000
FAX 407-224-7118
www.tinyurl.com/portofinobay

LOCATION	I-Drive
ROOM RATING	92
COST ($ = $50)	$$$$+
COMMUTING TIMES TO PARKS (in minutes)	
MAGIC KINGDOM	21:45
EPCOT	17:15
ANIMAL KINGDOM	20:15
DHS	19:45

Loews Royal Pacific Resort at Universal Orlando ★★★★½
6300 Hollywood Way
Orlando, FL 32819
☎ 407-503-3000
FAX 407-503-3010
www.tinyurl.com/royalpacific

LOCATION	I-Drive
ROOM RATING	90
COST ($ = $50)	$$$
COMMUTING TIMES TO PARKS (in minutes)	
MAGIC KINGDOM	20:00
EPCOT	15:15
ANIMAL KINGDOM	18:15
DHS	17:45

Hyatt Place ★★★★
5895 Caravan Ct.
Orlando, FL 32819
☎ 407-351-0627
FAX 407-351-3317
www.hyatt.com

LOCATION	I-Drive
ROOM RATING	84
COST ($ = $50)	$$
COMMUTING TIMES TO PARKS (in minutes)	
MAGIC KINGDOM	19:00
EPCOT	14:15
ANIMAL KINGDOM	17:45
DHS	16:45

Hyatt Regency Grand Cypress ★★★★½
1 Grand Cypress Blvd.
Orlando, FL 32836
☎ 407-239-1234
FAX 407-239-3800
grandcypress.hyatt.com

LOCATION	I-4 Corridor
ROOM RATING	90
COST ($ = $50)	$$$+
COMMUTING TIMES TO PARKS (in minutes)	
MAGIC KINGDOM	13:30
EPCOT	8:45
ANIMAL KINGDOM	11:45
DHS	11:15

Imperial Swan Hotel ★★½
7050 South Kirkman Rd.
Orlando, FL 32819
☎ 407-351-2000
FAX 407-363-1835
www.imperialswanhotel.com

LOCATION	I-Drive
ROOM RATING	61
COST ($ = $50)	$
COMMUTING TIMES TO PARKS (in minutes)	
MAGIC KINGDOM	22:00
EPCOT	16:30
ANIMAL KINGDOM	19:30
DHS	19:00

International Plaza Resort & Spa (tower) ★★★½
10100 International Dr.
Orlando, FL 32821
☎ 407-352-1100
FAX 407-354-4700
www.intlplazaresort.com

LOCATION	I-Drive
ROOM RATING	75
COST ($ = $50)	$$$–
COMMUTING TIMES TO PARKS (in minutes)	
MAGIC KINGDOM	17:45
EPCOT	13:00
ANIMAL KINGDOM	16:00
DHS	15:35

JW Marriott Grande Lakes ★★★★½
4040 Central Florida Pkwy.
Orlando, FL 32837
☎ 407-206-2300
FAX 407-206-2301
jw-marriott.grandelakes.com

LOCATION	I-Drive
ROOM RATING	93
COST ($ = $50)	$$$$–
COMMUTING TIMES TO PARKS (in minutes)	
MAGIC KINGDOM	23:00
EPCOT	18:15
ANIMAL KINGDOM	21:30
DHS	20:45

Key Motel ★★
4810 W. Irlo Bronson Mem. Hwy.
Kissimmee, FL 34746
☎ 407-396-6200
FAX 407-396-6987

LOCATION	US 192
ROOM RATING	51
COST ($ = $50)	$
COMMUTING TIMES TO PARKS (in minutes)	
MAGIC KINGDOM	16:30
EPCOT	16:15
ANIMAL KINGDOM	14:30
DHS	15:45

La Quinta Inn I-Drive North ★★
5825 International Dr.
Orlando, FL 32819
☎ 407-351-4100
FAX 407-996-4599
www.lq.com

LOCATION	I-Drive
ROOM RATING	50
COST ($ = $50)	$+
COMMUTING TIMES TO PARKS (in minutes)	
MAGIC KINGDOM	20:30
EPCOT	16:00
ANIMAL KINGDOM	19:00
DHS	18:30

La Quinta Universal ★★½
5621 Major Blvd.
Orlando, FL 32819
☎ 407-313-3100
FAX 407-313-3131
www.lq.com

LOCATION	I-Drive
ROOM RATING	63
COST ($ = $50)	$+
COMMUTING TIMES TO PARKS (in minutes)	
MAGIC KINGDOM	18:00
EPCOT	13:15
ANIMAL KINGDOM	16:15
DHS	16:00

Legacy Grand Hotel and Suites ★★★
5245 W. Irlo Bronson Mem. Hwy.
Kissimmee, FL 34746
☎ 407-396-7700
FAX 407-396-0293
www.legacygrand.com

LOCATION	US 192
ROOM RATING	65
COST ($ = $50)	$–
COMMUTING TIMES TO PARKS (in minutes)	
MAGIC KINGDOM	15:45
EPCOT	15:30
ANIMAL KINGDOM	13:45
DHS	15:15

Magic Castle Inn & Suites ★★
5055 W. Irlo Bronson Mem. Hwy.
Kissimmee, FL 34746
☎ 407-396-2212
FAX 407-396-0253
www.themagiccastleinn.com

LOCATION	US 192
ROOM RATING	50
COST ($ = $50)	$–
COMMUTING TIMES TO PARKS (in minutes)	
MAGIC KINGDOM	14:15
EPCOT	13:45
ANIMAL KINGDOM	12:15
DHS	13:30

Marriott Cypress Harbour Villas ★★★★
11251 Harbour Villa Rd.
Orlando, FL 32821
☎ 407-238-1300
FAX 407-238-1083
www.tinyurl.com/cypressharbourvillas

LOCATION	I-Drive
ROOM RATING	86
COST ($ = $50)	$$$$$+
COMMUTING TIMES TO PARKS (in minutes)	
MAGIC KINGDOM	17:45
EPCOT	13:15
ANIMAL KINGDOM	17:45
DHS	16:15

Marriott Imperial Palm Villas ★★★★
8404 Vacation Way
Orlando, FL 32821
☎ 407-238-6200
FAX 407-238-6247
www.tinyurl.com/imperialpalmvillas

LOCATION	I-Drive
ROOM RATING	86
COST ($ = $50)	$$$$$$$–
COMMUTING TIMES TO PARKS (in minutes)	
MAGIC KINGDOM	9:45
EPCOT	5:00
ANIMAL KINGDOM	8:00

Hotel Information Chart (continued)

DHS 7:30
Marriott Orlando World Center Resort ★★★★
8701 World Center Dr.
Orlando, FL 32821
☎ 407-239-4200
FAX 407-238-8777
www.marriottworldcenter.com
LOCATION I-4 Corridor
ROOM RATING 89
COST ($ = $50) $$$+
COMMUTING TIMES TO PARKS (in minutes)
MAGIC KINGDOM 9:45
EPCOT 5:00
ANIMAL KINGDOM 8:00

DHS 7:30
Marriott Residence Inn Orlando SeaWorld/International Center ★★★★
11000 Westwood Blvd.
Orlando, FL 32821
☎ 407-313-3600
FAX 407-313-3611
www.tinyurl.com/residenceinn seaworld
LOCATION I-Drive
ROOM RATING 85
COST ($ = $50) $$$–
COMMUTING TIMES TO PARKS (in minutes)
MAGIC KINGDOM 15:45
EPCOT 11:15
ANIMAL KINGDOM 14:15

DHS 13:45
Marriott's Grande Vista ★★★★½
5925 Avenida Vista
Orlando, FL 32821
☎ 407-238-7676
FAX 407-238-0900
www.tinyurl.com/marriotts grandevista
LOCATION I-Drive
ROOM RATING 92
COST ($ = $50) $$$$–
COMMUTING TIMES TO PARKS (in minutes)
MAGIC KINGDOM 15:00
EPCOT 12:45
ANIMAL KINGDOM 15:45

DHS 13:00
Masters Inn Maingate West ★★
2945 Entry Point Blvd.
Kissimmee, FL 34747
☎ 407-396-7743
FAX 407-396-6307
www.mastersinn.com
LOCATION US 192
ROOM RATING 55
COST ($ = $50) $–
COMMUTING TIMES TO PARKS (in minutes)
MAGIC KINGDOM 8:30
EPCOT 8:30
ANIMAL KINGDOM 6:45

DHS 7:45
Monte Carlo ★★
4733 W. Irlo Bronson Mem. Hwy.
Kissimmee, FL 34746
☎ 407-396-4700
LOCATION US 192
ROOM RATING 48
COST ($ = $50) $–
COMMUTING TIMES TO PARKS (in minutes)
MAGIC KINGDOM 18:30
EPCOT 18:15
ANIMAL KINGDOM 16:30

DHS 17:45
Monumental Hotel ★★★★½
12120 International Dr.
Orlando, FL 32821
☎ 407-239-1222
FAX 407-239-1190
www.monumentalhotelorlando.com
LOCATION I-Drive
ROOM RATING 94
COST ($ = $50) $$–
COMMUTING TIMES TO PARKS (in minutes)
MAGIC KINGDOM 14:45
EPCOT 10:00
ANIMAL KINGDOM 13:00

DHS 11:45
Motel 6 Maingate West ★★
7455 W. Irlo Bronson Mem. Hwy.
Kissimmee, FL 34747
☎ 407-396-6422
FAX 407-396-0720
www.motel6.com
LOCATION US 192
ROOM RATING 52
COST ($ = $50) $–
COMMUTING TIMES TO PARKS (in minutes)
MAGIC KINGDOM 7:15
EPCOT 6:45
ANIMAL KINGDOM 4:45

DHS 6:30
Mystic Dunes Resort ★★★★
7900 Mystic Dunes Lane
Kissimmee, FL 34747
☎ 407-396-1311
www.mystic-dunes-resort.com
LOCATION US 192
ROOM RATING 87
COST ($ = $50) $$$$$$+
COMMUTING TIMES TO PARKS (in minutes)
MAGIC KINGDOM 10:45
EPCOT 10:30
ANIMAL KINGDOM 7:45

DHS 10:00
Nickelodeon Family Suites by Holiday Inn ★★★½
14500 Continental Gateway
Orlando, FL 32821
☎ 407-387-5437
FAX 407-387-1490
www.nickhotel.com
LOCATION I-Drive
ROOM RATING 82
COST ($ = $50) $$$$$–
COMMUTING TIMES TO PARKS (in minutes)
MAGIC KINGDOM 9:45
EPCOT 5:00
ANIMAL KINGDOM 8:00

Orlando Continental Plaza Hotel ★★
6825 Visitors Cir.
Orlando, FL 32819
☎ 407-352-8211
FAX 407-370-3485
www.orlandocontinentalplaza hotel.com
LOCATION I-Drive
ROOM RATING 47
COST ($ = $50) $
COMMUTING TIMES TO PARKS (in minutes)
MAGIC KINGDOM 20:30
EPCOT 15:45
ANIMAL KINGDOM 18:45
DHS 18:30

Orlando Metropolitan Express ★★½
6323 International Dr.
Orlando, FL 32819
☎ 407-351-4430
FAX 407-345-0742
www.orlandometropolitan express.com
LOCATION I-Drive
ROOM RATING 63
COST ($ = $50) $+
COMMUTING TIMES TO PARKS (in minutes)
MAGIC KINGDOM 20:45
EPCOT 16:00
ANIMAL KINGDOM 19:00
DHS 18:30

Orlando Vista Hotel ★★★★
12490 S. Apopka–Vineland Rd.
Orlando, FL 32836
☎ 407-239-4646
FAX 407-239-8469
www.orlandovistahotel.com
LOCATION I-4 Corridor
ROOM RATING 83
COST ($ = $50) $+
COMMUTING TIMES TO PARKS (in minutes)
MAGIC KINGDOM 13:00
EPCOT 8:30
ANIMAL KINGDOM 11:30
DHS 11:00

DHS 15:15
Marriott's Harbour Lake ★★★★½
7102 Grand Horizons Blvd.
Orlando, FL 32821
☎ 407-465-6100
FAX 407-465-6267
www.tinyurl.com/harbourlake

LOCATION	I-Drive
ROOM RATING	90
COST ($ = $50)	$$$$$
COMMUTING TIMES TO PARKS (in minutes)	
MAGIC KINGDOM	18:00
EPCOT	13:30
ANIMAL KINGDOM	18:00

DHS 16:30
Masters Inn I-Drive ★★
8222 Jamaican Ct.
Orlando, FL 32819
☎ 407-345-1172
FAX 407-352-2801
www.mastersinn.com

LOCATION	I-Drive
ROOM RATING	50
COST ($ = $50)	$+
COMMUTING TIMES TO PARKS (in minutes)	
MAGIC KINGDOM	8:30
EPCOT	8:15
ANIMAL KINGDOM	11:15

DHS 10:45
Masters Inn Kissimmee ★★
5367 W. Irlo Bronson Mem. Hwy.
Kissimmee, FL 34746
☎ 407-396-4020
FAX 407-396-5450
www.mastersinn.com

LOCATION	US 192
ROOM RATING	55
COST ($ = $50)	$–
COMMUTING TIMES TO PARKS (in minutes)	
MAGIC KINGDOM	13:45
EPCOT	13:30
ANIMAL KINGDOM	11:45

DHS 12:30
Monumental MovieLand Hotel ★★★
6233 International Dr.
Orlando, FL 32819
☎ 800-327-2114
www.monumentalmovieland hotel.com

LOCATION	I-Drive
ROOM RATING	68
COST ($ = $50)	$+
COMMUTING TIMES TO PARKS (in minutes)	
MAGIC KINGDOM	20:30
EPCOT	15:45
ANIMAL KINGDOM	18:45

DHS 18:15
Motel 6 I-Drive ★★½
5909 American Way
Orlando, FL 32819
☎ 407-351-6500
FAX 407-352-5481
www.motel6.com

LOCATION	I-Drive
ROOM RATING	61
COST ($ = $50)	$–
COMMUTING TIMES TO PARKS (in minutes)	
MAGIC KINGDOM	20:15
EPCOT	16:00
ANIMAL KINGDOM	19:00

DHS 18:30
Motel 6 Maingate East ★★
5731 W. Irlo Bronson Mem. Hwy.
Kissimmee, FL 34747
☎ 407-396-6333
FAX 407-396-7715
www.motel6.com

LOCATION	US 192
ROOM RATING	47
COST ($ = $50)	$–
COMMUTING TIMES TO PARKS (in minutes)	
MAGIC KINGDOM	12:30
EPCOT	12:00
ANIMAL KINGDOM	10:30

DHS 7:30
Old Key West Resort ★★★★½
Walt Disney World
1510 North Cove Rd.
Lake Buena Vista, FL 32830
☎ 407-827-7700
FAX 407-827-7710
www.disneyworld.com

LOCATION	WDW
ROOM RATING	90
COST ($ = $50)	$$$$$$+
COMMUTING TIMES TO PARKS (in minutes)	
MAGIC KINGDOM	10:45
EPCOT	6:00
ANIMAL KINGDOM	14:30

DHS 10:30
Omni Orlando Resort at ChampionsGate ★★★★★
1500 Masters Blvd.
ChampionsGate, FL 33896
☎ 407-390-6664
FAX 407-390-0600
www.omnihotels.com

LOCATION	I-4 Corridor
ROOM RATING	96
COST ($ = $50)	$$+
COMMUTING TIMES TO PARKS (in minutes)	
MAGIC KINGDOM	15:30
EPCOT	15:00
ANIMAL KINGDOM	15:00

DHS 14:30
Orange Lake Resort & Country Club ★★★★½
8505 W. Irlo Bronson Mem. Hwy.
Kissimmee, FL 34747
☎ 407-239-0000
FAX 407-239-1039
www.orangelake.com

LOCATION	US 192
ROOM RATING	93
COST ($ = $50)	$$$$–
COMMUTING TIMES TO PARKS (in minutes)	
MAGIC KINGDOM	8:45
EPCOT	8:30
ANIMAL KINGDOM	5:30

DHS 11:00
Palms Hotel & Villas by Lexington ★★★½
3100 Pkwy. Blvd.
Kissimmee, FL 34747
☎ 407-396-2229
FAX 407-396-4833
www.thepalmshotelandvillas.com

LOCATION	US 192
ROOM RATING	76
COST ($ = $50)	$$–
COMMUTING TIMES TO PARKS (in minutes)	
MAGIC KINGDOM	8:30
EPCOT	8:15
ANIMAL KINGDOM	6:30

DHS 7:45
Parkway International Resort ★★★½
6200 Safari Trail
Kissimmee, FL 34746
☎ 407-396-6600
FAX 407-396-6165
www.islandone.com

LOCATION	US 192
ROOM RATING	82
COST ($ = $50)	$$+
COMMUTING TIMES TO PARKS (in minutes)	
MAGIC KINGDOM	8:30
EPCOT	8:15
ANIMAL KINGDOM	6:15

DHS 7:45
Peabody Orlando ★★★★½
9801 International Dr.
Orlando, FL 32819
☎ 407-352-4000
FAX 407-321-3501
www.peabodyorlando.com

LOCATION	I-Drive
ROOM RATING	90
COST ($ = $50)	$$$$$$$–
COMMUTING TIMES TO PARKS (in minutes)	
MAGIC KINGDOM	19:30
EPCOT	15:15
ANIMAL KINGDOM	18:15

Hotel Information Chart (continued)

DHS 17:45

Polynesian Isles Resort (Phase 1) ★★★★
3045 Polynesian Isles Blvd.
Kissimmee, FL 34746
☎ 407-396-1622
FAX 407-396-1744
www.sunterra.com

LOCATION	US 192
ROOM RATING	83
COST ($ = $50)	$$–
COMMUTING TIMES TO PARKS (in minutes)	
MAGIC KINGDOM	14:30
EPCOT	14:15
ANIMAL KINGDOM	12:30

DHS 14:00

Polynesian Resort ★★★★½
Walt Disney World
1600 Seven Seas Dr.
Lake Buena Vista, FL 32830
☎ 407-824-2000
FAX 407-824-3174
www.disneyworld.com

LOCATION	WDW
ROOM RATING	92
COST ($ = $50)	$$$$$$$$
COMMUTING TIMES TO PARKS (in minutes)	
MAGIC KINGDOM	12:00
EPCOT	8:00
ANIMAL KINGDOM	16:15

DHS 12:30

Pop Century Resort ★★★
Walt Disney World
1050 Century Dr.
Orlando, FL 32830
☎ 407-938-4000
FAX 407-938-4040
www.disneyworld.com

LOCATION	WDW
ROOM RATING	71
COST ($ = $50)	$$
COMMUTING TIMES TO PARKS (in minutes)	
MAGIC KINGDOM	8:30
EPCOT	6:30
ANIMAL KINGDOM	6:15
DHS	5:00

DHS 14:45

Quality Inn I-Drive ★★
7600 International Dr.
Orlando, FL 32819
☎ 407-996-1600
FAX 407-996-1477
www.qualityinn.com

LOCATION	I-Drive
ROOM RATING	50
COST ($ = $50)	$+
COMMUTING TIMES TO PARKS (in minutes)	
MAGIC KINGDOM	19:45
EPCOT	15:00
ANIMAL KINGDOM	18:00

DHS 17:30

Quality Inn Plaza ★★½
9000 International Dr.
Orlando, FL 32819
☎ 407-996-8585
FAX 407-996-1476
www.qualityinn.com

LOCATION	I-Drive
ROOM RATING	60
COST ($ = $50)	$$+
COMMUTING TIMES TO PARKS (in minutes)	
MAGIC KINGDOM	22:15
EPCOT	17:30
ANIMAL KINGDOM	20:30

DHS 20:00

Quality Suites Lake Buena Vista ★★★
8200 Palm Pkwy.
Orlando, FL 32836
☎ 407-465-8200
FAX 407-465-0200
www.qualitysuiteslbv.com

LOCATION	I-4 Corridor
ROOM RATING	74
COST ($ = $50)	$$+
COMMUTING TIMES TO PARKS (in minutes)	
MAGIC KINGDOM	13:45
EPCOT	9:15
ANIMAL KINGDOM	12:15

Radisson Resort Orlando Celebration ★★★★
2900 Pkwy. Blvd.
Kissimmee, FL 34747
☎ 407-396-7000
FAX 407-396-6792
www.radisson.com

LOCATION	US 192
ROOM RATING	86
COST ($ = $50)	$$$–
COMMUTING TIMES TO PARKS (in minutes)	
MAGIC KINGDOM	8:30
EPCOT	8:00
ANIMAL KINGDOM	6:30
DHS	7:45

Radisson Resort Worldgate ★★★½
3011 Maingate Lane
Kissimmee, FL 34747
☎ 407-396-1400
FAX 407-396-0660
www.radisson.com

LOCATION	US 192
ROOM RATING	77
COST ($ = $50)	$$–
COMMUTING TIMES TO PARKS (in minutes)	
MAGIC KINGDOM	8:15
EPCOT	7:45
ANIMAL KINGDOM	5:45
DHS	7:45

Ramada Gateway (garden) ★★½
7470 W. Irlo Bronson Mem. Hwy.
Kissimmee, FL 34747
☎ 407-396-4400
FAX 407-396-4320
www.ramada.com

LOCATION	US 192
ROOM RATING	64
COST ($ = $50)	$$–
COMMUTING TIMES TO PARKS (in minutes)	
MAGIC KINGDOM	8:15
EPCOT	8:00
ANIMAL KINGDOM	6:00
DHS	7:45

Ramada Maingate West ★★★
7491 W. Irlo Bronson Mem. Hwy.
Kissimmee, FL 34747
☎ 407-396-6000
FAX 407-396-7393
www.ramada.com

LOCATION	US 192
ROOM RATING	65
COST ($ = $50)	$–
COMMUTING TIMES TO PARKS (in minutes)	
MAGIC KINGDOM	8:15
EPCOT	7:30
ANIMAL KINGDOM	5:00
DHS	7:15

Red Roof Inn Convention Center ★★½
9922 Hawaiian Ct.
Orlando, FL 32801
☎ 407-352-1507
FAX 407-352-5550
www.redroof.com

LOCATION	I-Drive
ROOM RATING	58
COST ($ = $50)	$$+
COMMUTING TIMES TO PARKS (in minutes)	
MAGIC KINGDOM	19:00
EPCOT	14:15
ANIMAL KINGDOM	17:15
DHS	16:45

Red Roof Inn Kissimmee ★★
4970 Kyng's Heath Rd.
Kissimmee, FL 34746
☎ 407-396-0065
FAX 407-396-0245
www.redroof.com

LOCATION	US 192
ROOM RATING	47
COST ($ = $50)	$
COMMUTING TIMES TO PARKS (in minutes)	
MAGIC KINGDOM	16:45
EPCOT	16:15
ANIMAL KINGDOM	14:45
DHS	16:00

Port Orleans Resort (French Quarter) ★★★★
Walt Disney World
2201 Orleans Dr.
Lake Buena Vista, FL 32830
☎ 407-934-5000
FAX 407-934-5353
www.disneyworld.com

LOCATION WDW
ROOM RATING 84
COST ($ = $50) $$$+
COMMUTING TIMES TO PARKS (in minutes)
MAGIC KINGDOM 12:00
EPCOT 8:00
ANIMAL KINGDOM 16:15
DHS 12:30

Port Orleans Resort (Riverside) ★★★★
Walt Disney World
1251 Riverside Dr.
Lake Buena Vista, FL 32830
☎ 407-934-6000
FAX 407-934-5777
www.disneyworld.com

LOCATION WDW
ROOM RATING 83
COST ($ = $50) $$$+
COMMUTING TIMES TO PARKS (in minutes)
MAGIC KINGDOM 12:00
EPCOT 8:00
ANIMAL KINGDOM 16:15
DHS 12:30

Quality Inn & Suites Eastgate ★★★
4960 W. Irlo Bronson Mem. Hwy.
Kissimmee, FL 34746
☎ 407-396-1376
FAX 407-396-0716
www.qualityinn.com

LOCATION US 192
ROOM RATING 66
COST ($ = $50) $+
COMMUTING TIMES TO PARKS (in minutes)
MAGIC KINGDOM 15:45
EPCOT 15:30
ANIMAL KINGDOM 13:45
DHS 11:45

Quality Suites Royal Parc Suites ★★★★½
5876 W. Irlo Bronson Mem. Hwy.
Kissimmee, FL 34746
☎ 407-396-8040
FAX 407-396-6766
www.qualityinn.com

LOCATION US 192
ROOM RATING 95
COST ($ = $50) $$$–
COMMUTING TIMES TO PARKS (in minutes)
MAGIC KINGDOM 11:15
EPCOT 11:00
ANIMAL KINGDOM 9:15
DHS 10:30

Quality Suites Universal ★★
7400 Canada Ave.
Orlando, FL 32819
☎ 407-363-0332
FAX 407-264-7977
www.qualityinn.com

LOCATION I-Drive
ROOM RATING 52
COST ($ = $50) $$–
COMMUTING TIMES TO PARKS (in minutes)
MAGIC KINGDOM 20:30
EPCOT 15:45
ANIMAL KINGDOM 18:45
DHS 18:15

Radisson Hotel Lake Buena Vista ★★★½
12799 Apopka–Vineland Rd.
Orlando, FL 32836
☎ 407-597-3400
www.radisson.com

LOCATION I-4 Corridor
ROOM RATING 82
COST ($ = $50) $$+
COMMUTING TIMES TO PARKS (in minutes)
MAGIC KINGDOM 13:45
EPCOT 9:00
ANIMAL KINGDOM 12:00
DHS 11:30

Ramada Gateway (tower) ★★★
7470 W. Irlo Bronson Mem. Hwy.
Kissimmee, FL 34747
☎ 407-396-4400
FAX 407-396-4320
www.ramada.com

LOCATION US 192
ROOM RATING 71
COST ($ = $50) $$–
COMMUTING TIMES TO PARKS (in minutes)
MAGIC KINGDOM 8:15
EPCOT 8:00
ANIMAL KINGDOM 6:00
DHS 7:45

Ramada Inn Convention Center ★★★
8342 Jamaican Ct.
Orlando, FL 32819
☎ 407-363-1944
FAX 407-363-4844
www.ramada.com

LOCATION I-Drive
ROOM RATING 65
COST ($ = $50) $+
COMMUTING TIMES TO PARKS (in minutes)
MAGIC KINGDOM 20:15
EPCOT 15:30
ANIMAL KINGDOM 18:30
DHS 18:00

Ramada Inn I-Drive Orlando ★★★
6500 International Dr.
Orlando, FL 32819
☎ 407-345-5340
FAX 407-345-0976
www.ramada.com

LOCATION I-Drive
ROOM RATING 72
COST ($ = $50) $+
COMMUTING TIMES TO PARKS (in minutes)
MAGIC KINGDOM 21:30
EPCOT 16:45
ANIMAL KINGDOM 19:45
DHS 19:15

Regal Sun Resort ★★★
1850 Hotel Plaza Blvd.
Lake Buena Vista, FL 32830
☎ 407-828-4444
FAX 407-828-8192
www.regalsunresort.com

LOCATION WDW
ROOM RATING 75
COST ($ = $50) $$$
COMMUTING TIMES TO PARKS (in minutes)
MAGIC KINGDOM 15:15
EPCOT 10:45
ANIMAL KINGDOM 14:45
DHS 12:15

Renaissance Orlando Hotel at SeaWorld ★★★★
6677 Sea Harbor Dr.
Orlando, FL 32821
☎ 407-351-5555
FAX 407-351-9991
www.tinyurl.com/renorlandoseaworld

LOCATION I-Drive
ROOM RATING 89
COST ($ = $50) $$$$$$$$$–
COMMUTING TIMES TO PARKS (in minutes)
MAGIC KINGDOM 16:45
EPCOT 12:15
ANIMAL KINGDOM 15:15
DHS 14:45

Residence Inn Lake Buena Vista ★★★
11450 Marbella Palms Ct.
Orlando, FL 32836
☎ 407-465-0075
FAX 407-465-0050
www.tinyurl.com/residenceinnlbv

LOCATION I-4 Corridor
ROOM RATING 75
COST ($ = $50) $$+
COMMUTING TIMES TO PARKS (in minutes)
MAGIC KINGDOM 15:40
EPCOT 11:00
ANIMAL KINGDOM 14:00
DHS 13:30

Hotel Information Chart (continued)

Residence Inn Orlando Convention Center ★★★½
8800 Universal Blvd.
Orlando, FL 32819
☎ 407-226-0288
FAX 407-226-9979
www.tinyurl.com/resinnconventioncenter

LOCATION I-Drive
ROOM RATING 80
COST ($ = $50) $$$–
COMMUTING TIMES TO PARKS (in minutes)
MAGIC KINGDOM 22:00
EPCOT 17:30
ANIMAL KINGDOM 20:30
DHS 20:00

Residence Inn Orlando I-Drive ★★★
7975 Canada Ave.
Orlando, FL 32819
☎ 407-345-0117
FAX 407-352-2689
www.tinyurl.com/residenceinnidrive

LOCATION I-Drive
ROOM RATING 75
COST ($ = $50) $$$–
COMMUTING TIMES TO PARKS (in minutes)
MAGIC KINGDOM 20:00
EPCOT 15:15
ANIMAL KINGDOM 18:15
DHS 17:45

Ritz-Carlton Orlando, Grande Lakes ★★★★½
4012 Central Florida Pkwy.
Orlando, FL 32837
☎ 407-206-2400
FAX 407-206-2401
www.grandlakes.com

LOCATION I-Drive
ROOM RATING 94
COST ($ = $50) $$$$
COMMUTING TIMES TO PARKS (in minutes)
MAGIC KINGDOM 23:00
EPCOT 18:15
ANIMAL KINGDOM 21:30
DHS 20:45

Rosen Plaza Hotel ★★★★
9700 International Dr.
Orlando, FL 32819
☎ 407-996-9700
FAX 407-354-5774
www.rosenplaza.com

LOCATION I-Drive
ROOM RATING 89
COST ($ = $50) $$$$–
COMMUTING TIMES TO PARKS (in minutes)
MAGIC KINGDOM 20:45
EPCOT 16:15
ANIMAL KINGDOM 19:15
DHS 18:45

Rosen Shingle Creek ★★★★
9939 Universal Blvd.
Orlando, FL 32819
☎ 407-996-9939
FAX 407-996-9938
www.rosenshinglecreek.com

LOCATION I-Drive
ROOM RATING 88
COST ($ = $50) $$$$+
COMMUTING TIMES TO PARKS (in minutes)
MAGIC KINGDOM 21:00
EPCOT 16:15
ANIMAL KINGDOM 19:30
DHS 18:45

Royal Celebration ★★½
4944 W. Irlo Bronson Mem. Hwy.
Kissimmee, FL 34746
☎ 407-396-4455
FAX 407-997-2435
www.royalcelebrationorlando.com

LOCATION US 192
ROOM RATING 60
COST ($ = $50) $+
COMMUTING TIMES TO PARKS (in minutes)
MAGIC KINGDOM 15:45
EPCOT 15:30
ANIMAL KINGDOM 13:45
DHS 15:00

Saratoga Springs Resort & Spa ★★★★½
Walt Disney World
1960 Broadway
Lake Buena Vista, FL 32830
☎ 407-827-1100
FAX 407-827-1151
www.disneyworld.com

LOCATION WDW
ROOM RATING 90
COST ($ = $50) $$$$$$+
COMMUTING TIMES TO PARKS (in minutes)
MAGIC KINGDOM 14:45
EPCOT 8:45
ANIMAL KINGDOM 18:15
DHS 14:30

Seralago Hotel ★★★
5678 W. Irlo Bronson Mem. Hwy.
Kissimmee, FL 34746
☎ 407-396-4488
FAX 407-396-8915
www.seralagohotel.com

LOCATION US 192
ROOM RATING 71
COST ($ = $50) $+
COMMUTING TIMES TO PARKS (in minutes)
MAGIC KINGDOM 12:15
EPCOT 12:00
ANIMAL KINGDOM 10:15
DHS 11:30

Shades of Green ★★★★½
Walt Disney World
1950 West Magnolia Palm Dr.
Lake Buena Vista, FL 32830
☎ 407-824-3400
FAX 407-824-3665
www.shadesofgreen.org

LOCATION WDW
ROOM RATING 91
COST ($ = $50) $$$–
COMMUTING TIMES TO PARKS (in minutes)
MAGIC KINGDOM 3:30
EPCOT 4:45
ANIMAL KINGDOM 9:30
DHS 7:30

Sleep Inn Convention Center ★★
6301 Westwood Blvd.
Orlando, FL 32821
☎ 407-313-4100
FAX 407-313-4101
www.orlandosleepinn.com

LOCATION I-Drive
ROOM RATING 54
COST ($ = $50) $+
COMMUTING TIMES TO PARKS (in minutes)
MAGIC KINGDOM 17:45
EPCOT 13:00
ANIMAL KINGDOM 16:00
DHS 15:30

SpringHill Suites Orlando Convention Center ★★★½
8840 Universal Blvd.
Orlando, FL 32819
☎ 407-345-9073
FAX 407-345-9075
www.tinyurl.com/shsconventioncenter

LOCATION I-Drive
ROOM RATING 80
COST ($ = $50) $$+
COMMUTING TIMES TO PARKS (in minutes)
MAGIC KINGDOM 22:30
EPCOT 17:50
ANIMAL KINGDOM 20:45
DHS 20:20

SpringHill Suites Orlando LBV in Marriott Village ★★★
8601 Vineland Ave.
Orlando, FL 32821
☎ 407-938-9001
FAX 407-938-4995
www.marriottvillage.com

LOCATION I-4 Corridor
ROOM RATING 71
COST ($ = $50) $$+
COMMUTING TIMES TO PARKS (in minutes)
MAGIC KINGDOM 12:00
EPCOT 7:15
ANIMAL KINGDOM 10:15

Rodeway Inn I-Drive ★★
6327 International Dr.
Orlando, FL 32819
☎ 407-996-4444
FAX 407-996-5806
www.rodewayinnorlando.com

LOCATION I-Drive
ROOM RATING 51
COST ($ = $50) $+
COMMUTING TIMES TO PARKS (in minutes)
MAGIC KINGDOM 21:00
EPCOT 16:15
ANIMAL KINGDOM 19:15
DHS 18:45

Rodeway Inn Maingate ★★½
5995 W. Irlo Bronson Mem. Hwy.
Kissimmee, FL 34747
☎ 407-396-4300
FAX 407-589-1240
www.choicehotels.com

LOCATION US 192
ROOM RATING 59
COST ($ = $50) $–
COMMUTING TIMES TO PARKS (in minutes)
MAGIC KINGDOM 11:15
EPCOT 11:00
ANIMAL KINGDOM 9:15
DHS 10:30

Rosen Centre Hotel ★★★★½
9840 International Dr.
Orlando, FL 32819
☎ 407-996-9840
FAX 407-996-2659
www.rosencentre.com

LOCATION I-Drive
ROOM RATING 90
COST ($ = $50) $$$$
COMMUTING TIMES TO PARKS (in minutes)
MAGIC KINGDOM 19:45
EPCOT 15:15
ANIMAL KINGDOM 18:15
DHS 17:45

Royal Plaza (garden) ★★★
1905 Hotel Plaza Blvd.
Lake Buena Vista, FL 32830
☎ 407-828-2828
FAX 407-827-6338
www.royalplaza.com

LOCATION WDW
ROOM RATING 71
COST ($ = $50) $$$
COMMUTING TIMES TO PARKS (in minutes)
MAGIC KINGDOM 15:45
EPCOT 11:00
ANIMAL KINGDOM 15:00
DHS 12:45

Royal Plaza (tower) ★★★★
1905 Hotel Plaza Blvd.
Lake Buena Vista, FL 32830
☎ 407-828-2828
FAX 407-827-6338
www.royalplaza.com

LOCATION WDW
ROOM RATING 87
COST ($ = $50) $$$+
COMMUTING TIMES TO PARKS (in minutes)
MAGIC KINGDOM 15:45
EPCOT 11:00
ANIMAL KINGDOM 15:00
DHS 12:45

Saratoga Resort Villas ★★★½
4787 W. Irlo Bronson Mem. Hwy.
Kissimmee, FL 34746
☎ 407-397-0555
FAX 407-397-0553
www.saratogaresortvillas.com

LOCATION US 192
ROOM RATING 80
COST ($ = $50) $$$$
COMMUTING TIMES TO PARKS (in minutes)
MAGIC KINGDOM 18:15
EPCOT 17:45
ANIMAL KINGDOM 16:15
DHS 17:30

DHS 6:15

Sheraton Safari Hotel & Suites ★★★★
12205 South Apopka–Vineland Rd.
Orlando, FL 32836
☎ 407-239-0444
FAX 407-239-1778
www.sheratonsafari.com

LOCATION I-4 Corridor
ROOM RATING 83
COST ($ = $50) $$$–
COMMUTING TIMES TO PARKS (in minutes)
MAGIC KINGDOM 13:45
EPCOT 9:00
ANIMAL KINGDOM 12:00

DHS 11:30

Sheraton Vistana Resort ★★★★
8800 Vistana Centre Dr.
Orlando, FL 32821
☎ 407-239-3100
FAX 407-239-3111
www.sheraton.com

LOCATION I-4 Corridor
ROOM RATING 92
COST ($ = $50) $$$$+
COMMUTING TIMES TO PARKS (in minutes)
MAGIC KINGDOM 11:15
EPCOT 6:30
ANIMAL KINGDOM 9:30

DHS 9:00

Silver Lake Resort ★★½
7751 Black Lake Rd.
Kissimmee, FL 34747
☎ 407-397-2828
FAX 407-589-8410
www.silverlakeresort.com

LOCATION US 192
ROOM RATING 64
COST ($ = $50) $$
COMMUTING TIMES TO PARKS (in minutes)
MAGIC KINGDOM 8:15
EPCOT 8:00
ANIMAL KINGDOM 4:30

DHS 9:45

Star Island Resort ★★★★
5000 Ave. of the Stars
Kissimmee, FL 34746
☎ 407-997-8000
FAX 407-997-5252
www.star-island.com

LOCATION US 192
ROOM RATING 84
COST ($ = $50) $$+
COMMUTING TIMES TO PARKS (in minutes)
MAGIC KINGDOM 15:45
EPCOT 15:15
ANIMAL KINGDOM 14:15

DHS 13:30

Staybridge Suites Hotel ★★★
8480 International Dr.
Orlando, FL 32819
☎ 407-352-2400
FAX 407-352-4631
www.staybridge.com

LOCATION I-Drive
ROOM RATING 75
COST ($ = $50) $$$+
COMMUTING TIMES TO PARKS (in minutes)
MAGIC KINGDOM 21:15
EPCOT 16:30
ANIMAL KINGDOM 19:30

DHS 19:00

Staybridge Suites Lake Buena Vista ★★★
8751 SuiteSide Dr.
Orlando, FL 32836
☎ 407-238-0777
FAX 407-238-2640
www.staybridge.com

LOCATION I-4 Corridor
ROOM RATING 72
COST ($ = $50) $$$–
COMMUTING TIMES TO PARKS (in minutes)
MAGIC KINGDOM 14:15
EPCOT 9:30
ANIMAL KINGDOM 12:30

Hotel Information Chart (continued)

DHS 12:00

Suites at Old Town ★★½
5820 W. Irlo Bronson Mem. Hwy.
Kissimmee, FL 34746
☎ 407-396-7900
FAX 407-396-0940
www.suitesatoldtown.com

LOCATION US 192
ROOM RATING 61
COST ($ = $50) $+
COMMUTING TIMES TO PARKS (in minutes)
MAGIC KINGDOM 11:15
EPCOT 11:00
ANIMAL KINGDOM 9:15

DHS 10:30

Sun Inn & Suites ★★
5020 W. Irlo Bronson Mem. Hwy.
Kissimmee, FL 34746
☎ 407-396-2673
FAX 407-396-0878
www.suninnandsuitesorlando.com

LOCATION US 192
ROOM RATING 53
COST ($ = $50) $–
COMMUTING TIMES TO PARKS (in minutes)
MAGIC KINGDOM 16:00
EPCOT 15:45
ANIMAL KINGDOM 14:00

DHS 15:15

Super 8 East ★★★
5875 W. Irlo Bronson Mem. Hwy.
Kissimmee, FL 34746
☎ 407-396-8883
FAX 407-396-8907
www.super8.com

LOCATION US 192
ROOM RATING 70
COST ($ = $50) $
COMMUTING TIMES TO PARKS (in minutes)
MAGIC KINGDOM 11:45
EPCOT 11:15
ANIMAL KINGDOM 9:45

Swan ★★★★½
Walt Disney World
1500 Epcot Resorts Blvd.
Lake Buena Vista, FL 32830
☎ 407-934-3000
FAX 407-934-4499
www.swandolphin.com

LOCATION WDW
ROOM RATING 90
COST ($ = $50) $$$$$–
COMMUTING TIMES TO PARKS (in minutes)
MAGIC KINGDOM 6:30
EPCOT 4:45
ANIMAL KINGDOM 6:15
DHS 4:00

Travelodge I-Drive Orlando ★★
5859 American Way
Orlando, FL 32819
☎ 407-345-8880
FAX 407-363-9366
www.travelodge.com

LOCATION I-Drive
ROOM RATING 51
COST ($ = $50) $+
COMMUTING TIMES TO PARKS (in minutes)
MAGIC KINGDOM 21:15
EPCOT 16:30
ANIMAL KINGDOM 19:30
DHS 19:00

Travelodge Suites East Gate Orange ★★½
5399 W. Irlo Bronson Mem. Hwy.
Kissimmee, FL 34746
☎ 407-396-7666
FAX 407-396-0696
www.travelodge.com

LOCATION US 192
ROOM RATING 58
COST ($ = $50) $+
COMMUTING TIMES TO PARKS (in minutes)
MAGIC KINGDOM 13:30
EPCOT 13:15
ANIMAL KINGDOM 11:45
DHS 12:45

Westgate Lakes ★★★★½
10000 Turkey Lake Rd.
Orlando, FL 32819
☎ 407-345-0000
FAX 407-370-3445
www.westgateresorts.com

LOCATION I-4 Corridor
ROOM RATING 92
COST ($ = $50) $$$+
COMMUTING TIMES TO PARKS (in minutes)
MAGIC KINGDOM 17:30
EPCOT 14:30
ANIMAL KINGDOM 19:15
DHS 18:00

Westgate Palace ★★★
6145 Carrier Dr.
Orlando, FL 32819
☎ 407-996-6000
FAX 407-355-2979
www.westgateresorts.com

LOCATION I-Drive
ROOM RATING 68
COST ($ = $50) $$$$
COMMUTING TIMES TO PARKS (in minutes)
MAGIC KINGDOM 20:45
EPCOT 16:15
ANIMAL KINGDOM 19:15
DHS 18:45

Westgate Vacation Villas (tower) ★★★½
2770 Old Lake Wilson Rd.
Kissimmee, FL 34747
☎ 407-239-0510
FAX 407-396-6517
www.westgateresorts.com

LOCATION US 192
ROOM RATING 81
COST ($ = $50) $$$
COMMUTING TIMES TO PARKS (in minutes)
MAGIC KINGDOM 8:45
EPCOT 8:30
ANIMAL KINGDOM 5:45
DHS 8:00

Wilderness Lodge ★★★★
Walt Disney World
901 W. Timberline Dr.
Orlando, FL 32830
☎ 407-824-3200
FAX 407-824-3232
www.disneyworld.com

LOCATION WDW
ROOM RATING 86
COST ($ = $50) $$$$$$–
COMMUTING TIMES TO PARKS (in minutes)
MAGIC KINGDOM n/a
EPCOT 10:00
ANIMAL KINGDOM 15:15
DHS 13:30

Wilderness Lodge Villas ★★★★½
Walt Disney World
901 W. Timberline Dr.
Orlando, FL 32830
☎ 407-824-3200
FAX 407-824-3232
www.disneyworld.com

LOCATION WDW
ROOM RATING 90
COST ($ = $50) $$$$$$$+
COMMUTING TIMES TO PARKS (in minutes)
MAGIC KINGDOM n/a
EPCOT 10:00
ANIMAL KINGDOM 15:15
DHS 13:30

Wyndham Bonnet Creek Resort ★★★★
9560 Via Encinas
Lake Buena Vista, FL 32830
☎ 407-238-3500
FAX 407-238-3167
www.wyndhambonnetcreek.com

LOCATION WDW
ROOM RATING 88
COST ($ = $50) $$$+
COMMUTING TIMES TO PARKS (in minutes)
MAGIC KINGDOM 8:00
EPCOT 6:00
ANIMAL KINGDOM 7:15
DHS 4:15

DHS 11:00

Super 8 Kissimmee ★★½
1815 W. Vine St.
Kissimmee, FL 34741
☎ 407-847-6121
FAX 407-847-0728
www.super8.com

LOCATION US 192
ROOM RATING 60
COST ($ = $50) $–
COMMUTING TIMES TO PARKS (in minutes)
MAGIC KINGDOM 8:30
EPCOT 8:00
ANIMAL KINGDOM 5:45

DHS 7:45

Super 8 Lakeside ★★½
4880 W. Irlo Bronson Mem. Hwy.
Kissimmee, FL 34746
☎ 407-396-1144
FAX 407-396-4389
www.super8.com

LOCATION US 192
ROOM RATING 58
COST ($ = $50) $
COMMUTING TIMES TO PARKS (in minutes)
MAGIC KINGDOM 16:30
EPCOT 16:00
ANIMAL KINGDOM 14:30

DHS 15:45

Super 8 Universal ★★
5900 American Way
Orlando, FL 32819
☎ 407-352-8383
FAX 407-352-3496
www.super8.com

LOCATION I-Drive
ROOM RATING 51
COST ($ = $50) $
COMMUTING TIMES TO PARKS (in minutes)
MAGIC KINGDOM 21:15
EPCOT 16:30
ANIMAL KINGDOM 19:30

DHS 12:45

Treehouse Villas at Saratoga Springs Resort & Spa ★★★★½
Walt Disney World
1960 Broadway
Lake Buena Vista, FL 32830
☎ 407-827-1100
FAX 407-827-1151
www.disneyworld.com

LOCATION WDW
ROOM RATING 90
COST ($ = $50) $$$$$$$$–
COMMUTING TIMES TO PARKS (in minutes)
MAGIC KINGDOM 12:45
EPCOT 7:15
ANIMAL KINGDOM 16:45

DHS 12:30

Vacation Village at Parkway ★★★★½
2949 Arabian Nights Blvd.
Kissimmee, FL 34747
☎ 407-396-9086
FAX 407-390-7247
www.dailymanagementresorts.com

LOCATION US 192
ROOM RATING 91
COST ($ = $50) $$$–
COMMUTING TIMES TO PARKS (in minutes)
MAGIC KINGDOM 8:30
EPCOT 8:15
ANIMAL KINGDOM 6:45

DHS 7:45

Westgate Inn ★★½
9200 W. Irlo Bronson Mem. Hwy.
Kissimmee, FL 34714
☎ 863-424-2621
FAX 863-424-4630
www.westgateinnorlando.com

LOCATION US 192
ROOM RATING 59
COST ($ = $50) $–
COMMUTING TIMES TO PARKS (in minutes)
MAGIC KINGDOM 13:45
EPCOT 13:15
ANIMAL KINGDOM 10:45

Westgate Vacation Villas (town center) ★★★★½
2770 Old Lake Wilson Rd.
Kissimmee, FL 34747
☎ 407-239-0510
FAX 407-396-6517
www.westgateresorts.com

LOCATION US 192
ROOM RATING 93
COST ($ = $50) $$$$+
COMMUTING TIMES TO PARKS (in minutes)
MAGIC KINGDOM 8:45
EPCOT 8:30
ANIMAL KINGDOM 5:45
DHS 8:00

Westgate Vacation Villas (villas) ★★★★½
2770 Old Lake Wilson Rd.
Kissimmee, FL 34747
☎ 407-239-0510
FAX 407-396-6517
www.westgateresorts.com

LOCATION US 192
ROOM RATING 90
COST ($ = $50) $$$–
COMMUTING TIMES TO PARKS (in minutes)
MAGIC KINGDOM 8:45
EPCOT 8:30
ANIMAL KINGDOM 5:45
DHS 8:00

Westin Imagine Orlando ★★★★
9501 Universal Blvd.
Orlando, FL 32819
☎ 407-233-2200
www.westin.com

LOCATION I-Drive
ROOM RATING 87
COST ($ = $50) $$$$+
COMMUTING TIMES TO PARKS (in minutes)
MAGIC KINGDOM 19:45
EPCOT 15:00
ANIMAL KINGDOM 18:15
DHS 17:30

Wyndham Cypress Palms ★★★★
5324 Fairfield Lake Dr.
Kissimmee, FL, FL 34746
☎ 407-397-1600
FAX 407-377-9167
www.wyndhamvacationresorts.com

LOCATION US 192
ROOM RATING 87
COST ($ = $50) $$$
COMMUTING TIMES TO PARKS (in minutes)
MAGIC KINGDOM 15:15
EPCOT 15:00
ANIMAL KINGDOM 14:45
DHS 14:45

Wyndham Orlando ★★★★
8001 International Dr.
Orlando, FL, FL 32819
☎ 407-351-2420
FAX 407-345-5611
www.wyndhamorlandohotels.com

LOCATION I-Drive
ROOM RATING 83
COST ($ = $50) $$+
COMMUTING TIMES TO PARKS (in minutes)
MAGIC KINGDOM 19:45
EPCOT 15:00
ANIMAL KINGDOM 18:15
DHS 17:30

Yacht Club Resort ★★★★
Walt Disney World
1700 Epcot Resorts Blvd.
Orlando, FL, FL 32830
☎ 407-934-7000
FAX 407-934-3450
www.disneyworld.com

LOCATION WDW
ROOM RATING 89
COST ($ = $50) $$$$$$$+
COMMUTING TIMES TO PARKS (in minutes)
MAGIC KINGDOM 7:15
EPCOT 5:15
ANIMAL KINGDOM 6:45
DHS 4:00

PART FOUR

SERENITY NOW! *A Look at Disney-area Spas*

YOU'VE JUST SUGGESTED ANOTHER EARLY-MORNING theme-park mini-marathon to your spouse, and from her barely audible murmur you realize she's debating which relative should get the kids when she stands trial for killing you.

We've all been there. Fortunately, Orlando is awash in spas ready to rub, wrap, and restore your loved one to domestic tranquility.

Be forewarned that the cost of a basic one-hour massage is well over $100 before tip at most of these places. Even midpriced hotels seem eager to tack "Resort and Spa" onto their names to get a cut of that action, regardless of whether they actually know how to run either. In an effort to get you the most inner peace for your money, we sent the *Unofficial Guide* research team to evaluate eight Walt Disney World–area spas.

At each resort, our team had a standard massage, a basic facial, and a manicure–pedicure combination. Each service was scheduled during a different week to ensure that one person's bad day didn't mar the whole evaluation. Also, we used the same small group of researchers throughout the tests to ensure the most consistent comparisons of what is admittedly a somewhat subjective experience.

We rated each spa on a scale of one (poor) to five (excellent) in four areas. **Customer service** includes our interactions with the spa staff on everything from scheduling appointments and the massage, facial, or nail work, to follow-up questions after the visit. **Facilities** rates the amenities, functionality, and decor of the locker rooms, waiting areas, and equipment used before and after the services. **Amenities** rates secondary spa offerings such as food and snacks, pools, fitness centers, and the like. Finally, **sales pressure** indicates how hard the spa staff pushes you to buy its products after your treatment.

unofficial **TIP**
When you pay, check whether a gratuity has already been added to your bill. Most spas we visited (but not Disney's) automatically tack on a tip of 18%–20%.

The **Ritz-Carlton Orlando, Grande Lakes** spa earned the top spot in our evaluations, with Disney's **Saratoga Springs Resort & Spa** finishing second. The Ritz-Carlton is so good, we recommend it despite its 20-minute distance from Disney property. Perhaps a surprise, the best resort on Disney property seems to be the **Saratoga Springs Resort & Spa,** which earned better marks than the more well-known **Grand Floridian Resort & Spa.**

A fabulous money-saving idea is to find out if the spa you're interested in offers a day pass. These inexpensive (around $10 to $20) tickets typically allow use of the spa's fitness center, pool, sauna, steam room, and showers for an entire day. Complimentary fresh fruit and tea are usually included. Disney spas only offer passes to Disney-resort guests, but the other spas we checked will accommodate anyone regardless of whether they are staying at that resort.

ORLANDO SPAS RATED AND RANKED

SPA	OVERALL RATING
1. The Ritz-Carlton Orlando, Grande Lakes	★★★★★
2. Disney's Saratoga Springs Resort & Spa	★★★★
3. Buena Vista Palace Hotel & Spa	★★★★
4. Mandara Spa at Portofino Bay Hotel	★★★½
5. Canyon Ranch SpaClub	★★★½
6. **Tie between** Disney's Grand Floridian Resort & Spa **and** Mandara Spa at the Walt Disney World Dolphin	★★★½
7. The Spa at Marriott Orlando World Center Resort	★★½

SPA PROFILES

Buena Vista Palace Hotel & Spa ★★★★

1900 Buena Vista Drive, Lake Buena Vista, FL 32830; ☎ 407-827-3200; www.buenavistapalace.com

Customer service ★★★★★. **Facilities** ★★★½. **Amenities** ★★★★. **Sales pressure** Low. **Price range** $25–$185 spa services; $20–$115 nail services; 15% discount for Florida residents.

COMMENTS Plush, swallow-you-whole robes are the first of the pleasures awaiting guests at the Spa at Buena Vista Palace Hotel & Spa (formerly the Wyndham Palace Hotel & Spa).

Locker rooms offer two small, private changing rooms and a posh, nicely lit vanity area. Treatment rooms are small and nondescript, but clean. Separate waiting rooms are provided for men and women. On the downside, the facilities are older and in need of updating. Treatments were top-notch; staff encouraged the use of the sauna, steam room, and other facilities, and took time to explain the benefits of each. All services were performed with care and professionalism.

Water was from a cooler, and no fruit or other snacks were offered during our visits. Sales pressure after our visits was low, with no attempt to sell any of the oils, lotions, robes, or WD-40 (joke!) applied to our bodies. A tip was included in the service, so read the receipt before adding a gratuity. Children's treatments (for kids ages 11 to 16) are available, ranging from $25 to $65, but the money's better spent on you and your sanity.

Canyon Ranch SpaClub ★★★½

Gaylord Palms Resort and Convention Center, 6000 West Osceola Parkway, Kissimmee, FL 34746; ☎ 407-586-4772; www.gaylordhotels.com/gaylordpalms/spa

Customer service ★★★. **Facilities** ★★★★½. **Amenities** ★★★★. **Sales pressure** Medium. **Price range** $65–$250 spa services; $40–$85 nail services; 10% discount for Florida residents Monday–Friday.

COMMENTS We've sent three different researchers to the Canyon Ranch over the past two years. Our first experience was a nightmare, but the last two visits have been fabulous. When everything goes right, the Canyon Ranch is better that any spa in Orlando except the Ritz-Carlton. You're greeted warmly as soon as you walk in, treatment rooms are clean and soothing, and the robes and slippers are luxurious. The unisex changing areas have fresh fruit, water and hot tea, and soft music playing in the background, but note that the main waiting area is coed. Unlike those at many spas, facial treatments include a neck, shoulder, arm, and foot massage. The salon area offers hair, nail, and waxing services.

Unfortunately, the Canyon Ranch's customer service failed us the one time we had a problem. One of our researchers underwent a disastrous eyebrow waxing that left her with burns and redness, but neither the therapist nor management was responsive when we brought this to their attention. It took more phone calls days later to receive a small discount on our treatment and a grudging apology. It'll take many more consistently good visits before we consider this a one-time mistake.

Disney's Grand Floridian Resort & Spa ★★★½

4111 North Floridian Way, Lake Buena Vista, FL 32830; ☎ 407-824-2332; www.relaxedyet.com

Customer service ★★★½. **Facilities** ★★½. **Amenities** ★★★. **Sales pressure** Medium. **Price range** $55–$300 spa services; $55–$110 nail services; 10% off for Disney Annual Pass holders, Disney Vacation Club members, and guests with military ID. Children's services available at reduced cost.

COMMENTS Operated by Niki Bryan Spas, the spa at Walt Disney World's flagship resort is in a separate building between the resort and the wedding pavilion, along the walking path to Disney's Polynesian Resort.

As Disney's oldest spa, the Grand Floridian has not upgraded its facilities to the level of luxury found at other high-end spas. Robes and lockers are self-serve, and the only private place to change is in the bathroom stalls. All but one nail-drying machine was broken during two of our visits several weeks apart, and much of the other equipment seems to be showing its age. On a positive note, some of the best conversations we had with other guests happened in the Grand Floridian's lounge.

Our researchers had mixed feelings about the Grand Floridian. One thought it felt like a "high-school locker room," while another praised the friendly service she received despite arriving for her appointment on the wrong day. We did get some pressure at checkout to buy products used during several of our treatments. If you're staying on Disney property, try the Saratoga Springs Resort & Spa instead.

Disney's Saratoga Springs Resort & Spa ★★★★

1490-A Disney Vacation Club Way, Lake Buena Vista, FL 32830; ☎ 407-827-4455; www.relaxedyet.com

Customer service ★★★★. **Facilities** ★★★★. **Amenities** ★★★★. **Sales pressure** Low. **Price range** $55–$300 spa services; $55–$110 nail services; 10% off for Disney Annual Pass holders, Disney Vacation Club members, and guests with military ID.

COMMENTS Also operated by Niki Bryan Spas, the spa at this Disney Deluxe Villa resort is a cut above the spa at the Grand Floridian. This is likely due to the newness of this location, with Saratoga Springs Resort having opened its first phase in May 2004.

Decorated in soothing shades of green, with a beach-themed waiting room, this multilevel spa is the real thing. Locker rooms, sauna, and fitness center are on the first floor, while the treatment rooms are a private elevator ride away on the second. Overall, the spa is more spacious than the Grand Floridian's, with the exception of similar small treatment rooms. They also have an ultracool machine that extracts all of the water from your bathing suit, if you decide to wear one! Our only complaint: during busier times of year, attendants don't always provide tours of the facilities, leaving you to figure out how to navigate the lockers and changing areas.

A wide variety of Niki Bryan Spa products are available for purchase during checkout, yet sales pressure was lower than that at the Grand Floridian.

Mandara Spa at Walt Disney World Dolphin ★★★½

Walt Disney World Dolphin, 1500 Epcot Resorts Boulevard, Orlando, FL 32830; ☎ 407-934-4772; www.mandaraspa.com

Customer service ★★★★★. **Facilities** ★★★. **Amenities** ★★★. **Sales pressure** High. **Price range** $75–$300 spa services; $30–$160 hair and nail services; $75–$200 spa and nail services for ages 13–17; 15% discount for Disney Annual Pass holders.

COMMENTS Although the Mandaras at the Dolphin and the Portofino Bay Hotel share an Asian theme, everything is dialed down a notch at the Dolphin spa, starting with the waiting areas, of which there are two: the Meditation room, stocked with teas, water, and fruit; and the Consultation room, which is so close to the treatment rooms that voices occasionally disrupt the experience of clients receiving treatment.

Gone are the comfy sofas and chairs found at its sister spa—at the Dolphin, it's standing room only. And with its two waiting rooms, we were surprised that both are coed, mixing robe-clad men and women.

The treatment rooms, though pleasant, are also not on par with the Portofino Mandara's. Instead of silk-draped ceilings, an Asian-inspired wall hanging decorates one wall. Trappings aside, the Dolphin's spa also lacks a sauna, offering patrons only a coed steam room.

The one important asset that both Mandara Spas have in common is exceptional treatments—including tooth whitening—delivered by skilled staff. The Dolphin's employees seemed to be the most talkative of any we encountered.

Mandara Spa at Portofino Bay Hotel ★★★½

Universal Studios, 5601 Universal Boulevard, Orlando, FL 32819; ☎ 407-503-1244; www.mandaraspa.com

Customer service ★★★★★. **Facilities** ★★★★½. **Amenities** ★★★. **Sales pressure** Medium. **Price range** $75–$420 spa services; $35–$155 hair and nail services; $25–$100 spa and nail services for ages 13–17; 10–20% discount for Universal Annual Pass holders.

COMMENTS As mentioned previously, the Universal Studios Mandara has an edge over its sister spa in Walt Disney World. Both locations are well themed with Eastern influences, such as Buddha statues and silk drapes or wall hangings, but the Portofino location has some pluses, such as blankets offered while waiting.

The Portofino Bay Mandara Spa has a soothing, unmistakably Asian theme. Waiting areas are decorated in comfortable earth tones; treatment rooms feature silk-draped ceilings. Changing and bathroom areas are spacious and clean, but they also include less-than-subtle advertisements for products sold on premises.

The emphasis on tranquility extends to the stellar spa services, which included complimentary self-heating oil for our massages. Male and female patrons enjoy separate steam and sauna facilities. The Portofino's sand-bottom pool is conveniently located near the entrance to the spa, as are nail services. The fitness center is on the other side of the glass wall, however, so you may feel a bit like that doggie in the window . . . especially if you're wearing only a robe and a smile.

The Ritz-Carlton Orlando, Grande Lakes ★★★★★

4012 Central Florida Parkway, Orlando, FL 32837; ☎ 407-393-4200; www.ritzcarlton.com/en/properties/orlando/spa

Customer service ★★★★★. **Facilities** ★★★★★. **Amenities** ★★★★★. **Sales pressure** Low–medium. **Price range** $75–$350 spa services; $35–$120 nail services; 15% discount for Florida residents Monday–Thursday.

COMMENTS You'll enter the Ritz asking yourself whether you can afford the spa. You'll leave wondering why you're not staying at the hotel. So good are the services and facilities that you won't even mind the commute from Walt Disney World property.

The spa is housed in a separate three-story building behind the main hotel. Guests are given a full tour when they arrive, showing them where each amenity is located. Every level is tastefully and elegantly decorated, including locker rooms, treatment rooms, and waiting rooms. Both unisex and coed waiting areas are available.

Spa-goers also have the use of a separate Jacuzzi, sauna and steam rooms, and an outside lap pool where an attendant supplies complimentary towels, water, and sunscreen. All the equipment we used and observed was in working order during our visits. The only criticism our researchers had during any of our treatments was that the Ritz's atmosphere might seem too formal to some folks. But there's no doubt that it's luxurious and professional.

The Ritz was one of the few spas that offered a variety of massage oils, and the only one that adjusted the massage table's headrest to ensure our comfort. Sales pressure after the treatments was fairly low; no one followed us around as we browsed the spa store.

The Spa at Orlando World Center Marriott Resort ★★½

8701 World Center Drive, Orlando, FL 32821; ☎ 407-238-8705; www.marriottworldcenter.com

Customer service ★★★★. **Facilities** ★★. **Amenities** ★★★. **Sales pressure** High. **Price range** $53–$230 spa services; $30–$110 nail services.

COMMENTS Located in a small, separate building at the back of a sprawling hotel complex, The Spa at Marriott Orlando World Center Resort requires a hike from your room, or a really good set of directions if you're coming by car.

The women's locker room has no private changing areas; however, the bathroom stalls are big enough to make do. Spa-goers have the use of steam rooms and fitness facilities. Women should know that once they're in their spa robes, they're directed to a coed quiet room to await treatments. (On our visit, the spa was rife with male bonding.)

A staffer pressured us insistently to buy expensive oils and lotions after our treatments. Worse yet, the nail-drying equipment was either broken or nonexistent when we visited for our manicure: after shelling out $35 (plus tip), we were told to sit in the quiet room and blow on our nails to dry them.

PART FIVE

THE DISNEY CRUISE LINE

The MOUSE *at* SEA

THE WALT DISNEY COMPANY HAS BEEN in the cruise business with two almost identical ships, the ***Disney Wonder*** and the ***Disney Magic,*** since 1998. Cruises leave Port Canaveral, Florida (about an hour from the Orlando airport), and visit Nassau in the Bahamas and Castaway Cay, Disney's private Bahamian island, on three- and four-day itineraries. Seven-day itineraries in the Eastern Caribbean include calls at St. Maarten and St. Thomas, U.S. Virgin Islands, plus Castaway Cay. Western Caribbean itineraries are offered on alternate weeks; the ports include Key West, Florida; Grand Cayman Island; Cozumel, Mexico; and Castaway Cay. In the summer of 2008, the *Disney Magic* was based in Los Angeles and offered a seven-night itinerary to the Mexican Riviera.

unofficial **TIP**
All Disney East Coast cruise itineraries can be bundled with a stay at Walt Disney World.

From April to mid-September of 2010, the *Disney Magic* will offer cruises in Europe on the Mediterranean, North, and Baltic seas. Northern European itineraries, originating from Dover, England, will run 12 nights and call on Oslo, Norway; Copenhagen, Denmark: Warnemünde (Berlin), Germany; St. Petersburg, Russia; Tallinn, Estonia, or Helsinki, Finland; and Stockholm, Sweden.

Ten- and eleven-night cruises depart from Barcelona, Spain, and make port at Valletta, Malta; Tunis, Tunisia; Civitavecchia (near Rome) and La Spezia, Italy; Ajaccio, Corsica; and Villefranche, France (near Monte Carlo, Cannes, and Nice). Seven- and eight-night cruises originating in Barcelona or Dover call on Gibraltar; Cadiz, Spain; and Lisbon, Portugal. The European itineraries are as well conceived and interesting as Disney Cruise Line's Bahamian and Caribbean itineraries are unimaginative and prosaic (more about that later).

The European itineraries are bracketed on either end of the season by 14-night repositioning cruises. The latter aren't particularly compelling, but they're a good value if you enjoy being at sea.

At the outset, Disney put together a team of respected cruise-industry veterans, dozens of the world's best-known ship designers, and Disney's own unrivaled creative talent. Together, they created the Disney

Disney Cruise Line Standard Features

Officers American and international

Staff Cabin and dining, multinational; cruise, American

Dining Three themed family restaurants with "rotation" dining; alternative adults-only restaurant; indoor/outdoor cafe for breakfast, lunch, snacks, and buffet dinner for children; pool bar/grill for burgers, pizza, and sandwiches; ice-cream bar

Special diets On request at the time of booking; health-conscious cuisine program

Room service 24 hours

Dress code Casual by day; casual and informal in the evenings

Cabin amenities Direct-dial telephone with voice mail; tub and shower; TV; safe; hair dryer; mini-fridge

Electrical outlets 110 A/C

Wheelchair access Yes

Smoking Only in designated areas

Disney-suggested tipping Dining-room server: $3–$4 per night. Assistant server: $3 per night. Dining-room head server: 3- and 4-night cruise, $3 and $4; 7-night cruise, $7; 10-night cruise, $8. Stateroom host: $4 per night. Dining manager and room service: your discretion. A 15% service charge is added automatically to bar bills.

Credit cards For cruise payment and on-board charges, all major credit cards.

ships, recognizing that every detail would be critical to the line's success. Their task was to design a product that makes every adult and child on board feel that the vacation is intended for him or her.

The first surprise is the ships' appearance. They're simultaneously classic and innovative. Exteriors are traditional, reminiscent of great ocean liners of the past, but even in that you'll find a Disney twist or two. Inside, they're up-to-the-minute technologically, and full of novel ideas for dining, entertainment, and cabin design. Disney's exclusive cruise terminal at Port Canaveral is integral to the overall strategy, which aims to make even embarkation and debarkation enjoyable. Likewise, Disney's private island, Castaway Cay, was chosen in order to avoid the hassle of tendering. As for dining, each evening you dine in a different restaurant with a different motif, but your waiters and dining companions move with you.

Disney's plan has been to create a "seamless vacation package" by combining a stay at Disney World with a cruise. Cruise passengers are met at the airport by Disney staff and transported to Port Canaveral in easily identifiable Disney Cruise Line buses. During the hour-long ride, passengers watch a video preview of the cruise. To smooth embarkation, check-in is streamlined. When your cruise is packaged with a Disney World stay, you check in once. The key that unlocks your hotel room opens the door to your cruise cabin.

The company targets first-time cruisers, counting on Disney's reputation for quality, service, and entertainment to dispel noncruisers' doubts about cruise vacations. Much time and effort has been spent to ensure that the ships appeal to adults—with or without children—as much as to children and families. Adults are catered to in myriad ways and presented with an extensive menu of adult-oriented activities. For example, the ships have an adults-only alternative restaurant, swimming pool, and nightclub; entertainment ranges from family musicals to adults-only variety performances. Meanwhile, almost from sunrise to midnight, children are offered equally varied programs. Because all programs are offered à la carte, families can choose how much time to spend together or pursuing separate interests.

The children's programs are excellent. In fact, they're rated the best in the cruise industry in *The Unofficial Guide to Cruises,* by Kay Showker and Bob Sehlinger. Thus, it's no surprise that many parents see their kids only at breakfast and dinner. But while adults can easily get a breather from children, it's tougher to escape Disney's syrupy, wholesome, cuter-than-a-billion–Beanie Babies entertainment, which permeates every cruise. In other words, to enjoy a Disney cruise, you'd better love Disney.

THE FUTURE IS NOW

IN 2007, DISNEY CRUISE LINE PLACED ORDERS for two new 4,000-passenger ships with the Meyer Werft shipyard in Papenburg, Germany. When the vessels launch in 2011 and 2012, they will more than double the line's passenger capacity. The new ships will sport the same black hulls as the *Disney Wonder*'s and *Disney Magic*'s and, like the two ships in service, will draw their inspiration from the classic transoceanic liners of the 1930s. In addition to carrying more passengers, the new ships will be two decks taller than the *Wonder* and *Magic*. Our suggested names for the liners included the *Walter E. Disney* and the *Roy O. Disney;* the *Chip* and the *Dale;* and the *Beavis* and the *Butt-head* (cartoon characters rule when it comes to anything Disney). Ultimately, Disney has named them the *Disney Dream,* coming online in 2011, and the *Disney Fantasy,* due to debut in 2012.

Disney itineraries in the Mediterranean have been very successful, so the line is expected to dedicate one of the new ships to that body of water during the warm-weather months and reposition it to the Caribbean for the rest of the year. The other ship, or one of the current ships, is expected to operate Mexican Riviera and possibly Alaskan itineraries out of Los Angeles. Two ships are expected to continue serving the Caribbean market.

Go Forth and Be Goofy: The Itineraries

Disney Cruise Line offers three- and four-night cruises to the Bahamas as well as seven-night cruises to the Eastern and Western Caribbean.

Bahamian cruises can be purchased separately or as part of week-long packages that also include three or four days at Walt Disney World. You get your Disney hotel, theme park admissions, the cruise, and transportation (called transfers) from the airport to Walt Disney World, and to the ship.

In 2010, Disney Cruise Line will additionally offer ten five-night Bahamian cruises. Half follow the same itinerary as the four-night cruise but with a second day at Castaway Cay; the other half will add a stop at Key West. For more information, see **www.disneycruise.com.**

2009 EAST COAST ITINERARY

	SEVEN-NIGHT EASTERN CARIBBEAN	SEVEN-NIGHT WESTERN CARIBBEAN
Saturday	Port Canaveral	Port Canaveral
Sunday	At sea	Key West
Monday	At sea	At sea
Tuesday	St. Maarten	Grand Cayman
Wednesday	St. Thomas/St. John	Cozumel
Thursday	At sea	At sea
Friday	Castaway Cay	Castaway Cay
Saturday	Port Canaveral	Port Canaveral

	FOUR-NIGHT BAHAMIAN CRUISE*	THREE-NIGHT BAHAMIAN CRUISE	
Sunday	Port Canaveral	Thursday	Port Canaveral
Monday	Nassau	Friday	Nassau
Tuesday	Castaway Cay	Saturday	Castaway Cay
Wednesday	At sea	Sunday	Port Canaveral
Thursday	Port Canaveral		

To Boldly Go Where Everyone Has Gone Before

To say that Disney's Bahamian and Caribbean ports of call are trite is an understatement. The cruises ply the same waters on pretty much the same itineraries as every other ship. On any given day, you'll see other megaliners disgorging thousands of vacationers onto once-sleepy little islands, now reincarnated as giant sprawling malls dedicated entirely to cruise-ship passengers. Our perspective here is more green than jaded, incidentally—the cruise industry has taken a terrible toll on the culture and lifestyle of the Caribbean.

The three- and four-night Bahamian cruises offer an easy introduction to cruising, but the ports of call are lackluster. **Nassau,** aside from some lovely beaches, just isn't very interesting. Adjacent (via a bridge) **Paradise Island** offers a huge, upscale casino, but you probably didn't take a Disney cruise because you were hot to play blackjack. Then, of course, there's the obligatory "native market." The third "port," **Castaway Cay,** is Disney's own private island, where you can sunbathe, swim, and enjoy a barbecue. There are also some well-conceived organized programs for children. While Disney's done a good job with the island, there isn't much to see or explore, though your choices of how to explore (hike, snorkel, kayak, bike) are plentiful. You'll love it if you're a sun worshiper or water puppy; most others get their fill in an hour or two. Clearly, on the three- and four-night itineraries, the ship itself is the main attraction.

On the seven-night Western Caribbean itinerary, **Key West** is a lot of fun, especially if you've never been, but the ship sails at 7:30 p.m., just about the time the town is waking up. **Grand Cayman** is a real snore except for the shore excursion, during which you swim and snorkel with stingrays. **Cozumel** is the best port of call on the itinerary, with a world-famous scuba and snorkeling reef, Mayan ruins at Parador Turístico de San Gervasio, and excursions to more-celebrated Mayan ruins on the mainland. (In 2009, Disney substituted Nassau, Bahamas, for Cozumel because of the flu epidemic that originated in Mexico.) The last port is Castaway Cay.

Of all Disney cruises offered, the seven-night Eastern Caribbean itinerary is the pick of the litter. The first port of call is **St. Maarten,** the smallest island in the world ever to have been partitioned between two different nations, shared by the French and the Dutch in a spirit of neighborly goodwill for almost 350 years. **St. Thomas** and **St. John** in the U.S. Virgin Islands are the most beautiful, varied, and interesting ports of call in Disney's Caribbean–Bahamian mix, though they lack the mystique of being in a foreign country. Once again, Castaway Cay completes the itinerary.

The SHIPS

DISNEY MAGIC AND *DISNEY WONDER* are modern cruise ships with sleek lines, twin smokestacks, and nautical styling that calls to mind classic ocean liners, but with instantly recognizable Disney signatures. The colors—black, white, red, and yellow—and the famous face-and-ears silhouette on the stacks are clearly those of Mickey Mouse. Look closely, and you'll see that *Magic*'s stern ornamentation is a 15-foot Goofy (Donald Duck on *Wonder*) swinging upside down from a boatswain's chair, "painting" the stern.

Interiors combine nautical themes with Art Deco inspiration. Disney images are everywhere, from Mickey's profile in the wrought-iron balustrades to the bronze statue of Helmsman Mickey at the center of the three-deck Grand Atrium. Disney art is on every wall and in every stairwell and corridor. A grand staircase sweeps from the atrium lobby to shops selling Disney Cruise Line–themed clothing, collectibles, jewelry, sundries, and more. (The shops are always full of eager buyers; some observers speculate that the cruise line will derive as much revenue here as other lines do from their casinos, which Disney ships don't have.)

The ships have two lower decks with cabins, three decks with dining rooms and show rooms, then three upper decks of cabins. Two sports and sun decks offer separate pools and facilities for families, and for adults without children. Signs point toward lounges and facilities, and all elevators are clearly marked forward, aft, or amidships.

unofficial **TIP**
If you want to see the sea on your Disney cruise, book a cabin with a private veranda.

Our main complaint concerning the ships' design is that outdoor public areas focus inward toward the pools instead of seaward, as if Disney wants you to forget you're on a cruise liner. There's no public place where you can curl up in the shade and watch the ocean (at least not without a Plexiglas wall between you and it).

Another predictable but nonetheless irritating design characteristic is the extensive childproofing. There's enough Plexiglas on the *Magic* and *Wonder* to build a subdivision of see-through homes. On the pool decks (Deck 9) especially, it feels as if the ships are hermetically sealed.

CABINS

CABINS AND SUITES ARE SPACIOUS, with wood paneling throughout. About three-fourths are outside; almost half of those have private verandas. The 12 cabin categories range from standard to deluxe, deluxe with veranda, family suite, one- and two-bedroom suites, and royal suite. Passengers who spend three or four days at a Disney resort are assigned a cabin in a comparable category.

Cabin design reveals Disney's finely tuned sense of the needs of families and children and offers a cruise-industry first: a split bathroom with a bathtub and shower combo and sink in one room, and toilet, sink, and vanity in another. This configuration, found in all but standard inside cabins, allows any family member to use the bathroom without monopolizing it. All bathrooms have tub and shower, except disabled rooms (shower only).

Decor includes unusual features such as bureaus designed to look like steamer trunks. Cabins also have a direct-dial telephone with voice mail, TV, hair dryer, and mini-fridge. In some higher-priced cabins (Category 7 or above), pull-down Murphy beds allow for additional daytime floor space. Storage is generous, with deep drawers and large closets.

Each ship has 256 inside cabins and 621 outside cabins. There are 8 one-bedroom suites and 80 family cabins. Of the outside cabins, 384 have private verandas. Fourteen cabins are wheelchair-accessible. Cabins in Categories 1 through 4 accommodate four or more guests. Cabins in Categories 7 and 12 accommodate three. Cabins in other categories typically accommodate four guests, in some cases three.

A Maylene, Alabama, reader offers this useful information:

> *A big difference between Walt Disney World and Disney Cruise Line is that when it comes to room capacity, infants are counted just like adults. So while a family of five can stay at a value resort (four adults on the double beds and an infant in a crib), that same family of five must either book a Category 4 (or above) cabin or book a pair of lower-category cabins.*
>
> *Another question that keeps cropping up on the Disney message boards over and over is the question of children and cabins with a veranda. The two things parents need to know to put their minds at ease are that the railings are guarded by Plexiglas and that the veranda door has a two-part locking mechanism, with one of the mechanisms located six feet off the floor. Even many adults have problems trying to figure out how to operate these doors. The only way a child is going overboard is if an adult leaves a veranda door open and the child uses a piece of veranda furniture to climb over the railing.*

SERVICES *and* AMENITIES

PASSENGERS LAVISHLY PRAISE Disney cast members. They're among the most accommodating you'll ever encounter in travel, and they try hard to smooth your way from boarding to departure. *Unofficial Guides* cruise writer Kay Showker reports, "More than once when I stopped to get my bearings, a Disney cast member was there within seconds to help me."

You'll receive a *Disney Magic Passport,* a purse-sized booklet covering about everything you need to know for your cruise. Daily in your cabin, you'll receive "Your Personal Navigator," listing entertainment and activities, with options for teens, children, adults, and families, as well as information on shore excursions.

DINING

DINING IS DISNEY'S MOST INNOVATIVE AREA. Ships have three family restaurants, plus an adults-only alternative restaurant. Each night, passengers move to a different family restaurant, each with a different theme and menu. Their table companions and waitstaff move with them. In each restaurant, tableware, linens, menu covers, and waiters' uniforms fit the theme.

On *Magic,* **Lumière's,** named for the candlestick character in *Beauty and the Beast,* is a handsome Art Deco venue serving continental cuisine. A mural depicts *Beauty and the Beast.* (The equivalent restaurant on *Wonder* is **Triton's,** themed after *The Little Mermaid.*)

Parrot Cay dishes up Caribbean-accented food in a colorful, fun, tropical setting that reminds Disney veterans of the *Enchanted Tiki Room.* Parrot Cay is the most popular of the three restaurants for breakfast. Children particularly enjoy the decor and festivity, but the food, although adequate, is a notch below that of the other restaurants.

Animator's Palate reflects the creative genius of Disney animation and is the ships' dining pièce de résistance. Diners are given the impression that they have entered a black-and-white sketchbook. As the meal progresses, sketches on the walls are transformed through lighting, video, and fiber optics into a full-color extravaganza. Waiters change their costumes from black-and-white to color. Conversation is often difficult, and the entertainment, though creative, is the ultimate in Disney cute (and totally inescapable). Children love it, but adults may find it overwhelming.

Palo, the casual Italian restaurant named for the pole that gondoliers use to navigate Venetian canals, is the intimate adults-only eatery. It's the best on board and has its own kitchen. The sophisticated semicircular room has soft lighting, Venetian glass, inlaid wood, and a backlit bar. Northern Italian cuisine is featured. Food and presentation are excellent. More than two dozen wines are available by the glass for $4.75 to $25. There's a $15-per-person cover charge, but no signs in the restaurant, on the menu, or in the ship's literature alert you to the fact. Service is attentive but leisurely, though it may just seem that way in comparison to the staccato pace in the other restaurants. On days at sea, Palo also serves a Champagne brunch, once again with the $15 surcharge. On weeklong cruises, a high tea is offered for no additional charge.

Palo is exceedingly popular. Make reservations at **www.disneycruise.com** at least 75 days before your sail date (see page 303). If you forget, make reservations as soon as you board. The restaurant usually fills every night, but some very late or very early seatings sometimes become available after the ship sails. Palo is so superior to the other dining options on board that we check in there every day to see if anything is available. By so doing on one seven-day cruise, we were able to eat at Palo three times.

There are two seatings for dinner at Lumière's (Triton's), Animator's Palate, and Parrot Cay. If your children are age 12 or younger and you plan to dine as a family, we recommend the early seating. If your kids are involved in programs where they dine with other children, go with your preference. All three restaurants offer special meals if your picky eaters can't find something they like on the menu.

On a three-day cruise, your normal rotation will have you dine one night each at Lumière's (Triton's), Animator's Palate, and Parrot Cay. If you book Palo (adults only), you'll skip the restaurant designated for that night on your rotation. Thus, you should choose your Palo night carefully.

We view Parrot Cay as the most expendable in the rotation, and if you miss it for dinner, you can try it at lunch or breakfast. On a four-day cruise, one restaurant will pop up twice on your rotation.

Shortly after boarding, you're given the opportunity to make Palo reservations (taken in the restaurant) and/or change your restaurant rotation. We believe one night each at Animator's Palate or Parrot Cay is enough. If your rotation calls for you to repeat a night in either, book Palo or substitute a second night at Lumière's (Triton's).

unofficial **TIP**
If you want to eat at all restaurants, including Palo, reserve Palo for the night you're scheduled to repeat one of the basic three.

Wondering how to feed your children if you dine at Palo? You have several options: make a late reservation for Palo, then keep your children company (but don't eat) while they dine at the regularly assigned restaurant (this works only if you eat at the first seating); enroll your children in a program where they'll eat with other kids; or take your children to **Pluto's Dog House** (poolside on Deck 9) for hot dogs and burgers.

BUFFET AND FAST FOOD Other dining options include **Topsiders** on *Magic* (**Beach Blanket Buffet** on *Wonder*), an indoor/outdoor cafe with a free soda fountain serving breakfast, lunch, snacks, and a buffet dinner for children; **Pluto's Dog House,** a pool bar and grill for hamburgers, hot dogs, and sandwiches; **Goofy's Galley,** which offers fresh fruit, panini sandwiches, wraps, and salads; **Pinocchio's Pizzeria;** an ice-cream and frozen-yogurt bar; and 24-hour room service. Topsiders is the weakest; it's OK for breakfast but long on bulk and short on flavor for lunch. Pizza, dogs, burgers, yogurt, and ice cream are good.

FACILITIES AND ENTERTAINMENT

NIGHTLY ENTERTAINMENT IS UNLIKE any other cruise line's. The 977-seat Walt Disney Theater stages a different show nightly, with talented actors, singers, and dancers. These family productions are on par with Disney parks' entertainment rather than Broadway and will probably appeal more to children than adults. Longer cruises present a welcome variety show and an end-of-cruise farewell show in addition to the following productions.

The **Pirates in the Caribbean** party on both ships transforms passengers into pirates for the evening and treats them to a special dinner. The meal is followed by a deck party with Disney characters dressed in pirate garb. The mood of the party changes as Captain Hook, Mr. Smee, and a gang of "bad" pirates take over the party. In the end Captain Mickey saves the day.

The Golden Mickeys is an Academy Awards–style tribute to the music and characters of Disney films over the decades.

On the *Wonder, Disney Dreams* has about every Disney character and song ever heard and offers a thin plot wherein Peter Pan visits a girl who dreams of Disney's characters. As a variation on the dream theme, *Disney Magic* has a show in which Mickey and the other characters help a boy achieve his dream of becoming a seafaring captain. It's pure schmaltz, but audiences give it a standing ovation. At the late show, many kids doze off before the curtain falls.

Twice Charmed: An Original Twist on the Cinderella Story demonstrates that "living happily ever after" is not all it's cracked up to be. Beginning where the original story ended, the musical—offered only on the *Disney Magic*—introduces a wicked Fairy Godfather who sends the mean stepmother back in time to break Cinderella's glass slipper and thus destroy her chances of marrying the prince. It's a weird Disney version of *Back to the Future,* except that the stepmother doesn't travel in a DeLorean. The show fields a cast of 21 performers in Disney's largest seagoing production to date. The third show on the *Disney Wonder* is *Toy Story—The Musical,* which tunefully chronicles the evolving relationship of Buzz Lightyear and Woody as they transform from jealous adversaries to best friends. On seven-night cruises, a *Welcome Aboard Variety Show,* magic show, and *Magical Farewell* are added.

First-run movies and classic Disney films are shown daily in the **Buena Vista Theater,** a 268-seat venue with full screen and Dolby sound and under the stars on Deck 5 on a jumbo 24- by 14-foot LED screen.

Studio Sea, modeled after a television- or film-production set, is a family-oriented nightclub offering dance music, cabaret acts, passenger game shows, karaoke, and multimedia entertainment. The Art Deco **Promenade Lounge** offers a haven for reading and relaxing by day, and enjoying cocktails and piano music by night. **Cove Cafe** is a quiet, secluded venue for reading over a designer coffee. *Magic* features **Beat Street,** an adult-oriented evening-entertainment district with shops and three themed nightclubs: **Rockin' Bar D,** with live bands playing rock and roll, Top 40, and country music; **Diversions,** a sports pub offering group sing-alongs and karaoke in what Disney calls "a cross between a golf clubhouse and a local neighborhood bar" (running on empty in the theme department, eh?); and **Sessions,** a casual place to enjoy easy-listening music and jazz. On *Wonder,* Beat Street is replaced with the **Route 66** club complex: **Wavebands** features live bands playing pop and oldies, and **Cadillac Lounge** is the place for quiet music.

unofficial **TIP**
Disney ships have no casinos or libraries.

CHILDREN'S PROGRAMS

PLAYROOMS AND OTHER KIDS' FACILITIES occupy more than 15,000 square feet of each ship. Age-specific programs are among the most extensive in cruising. They include challenging interactive activities and play areas supervised by trained counselors. Age groups are 3 to 7, 8 to 12, and teens. Babysitting (ages 12 weeks to 3 years) is provided in the **Flounder's Reef** nursery; hours vary according to the cruise itinerary. Cost is $6 per child per hour, $5 per hour for each additional child. Make reservations for Flounder's Reef at **www.disney cruise.com** at least 75 days before your sail date (see page 303). If you forget, make reservations as soon as you board.

The **Oceaneer's Adventure** program encompasses **Oceaneer's Club** (ages 3 to 7), themed to resemble Captain Hook's pirate ship, with plenty of activity space; and **Oceaneer's Lab** (ages 8 to 12), with video games, computers, lab equipment, and an area for listening to CDs. On the *Disney Magic,* kids can enjoy a computer simulator, complete with a replica of the *Magic*'s bridge, that allows them to see what it's like to steer the ship in and out of various ports of call. Kids wear ID bracelets, and parents receive pagers for staying in touch with them. Both parents and children give youth programs high marks. Children in the drop-off program eat dinner at Topsiders. As with babysitting, you can register your children in advance for the programs described at the Disney Cruise Line Web site.

Aloft (*Wonder*) and **The Stack** (*Magic*) are teen areas with a coffee-bar theme, featuring a game arcade, videos, and a CD-listening lounge. Located in a nonfunctioning smokestack on the top deck, the venues allow teens to rock out in arguably the most isolated part of the ship (chaperoned, of course). There are also organized activities, including nighttime volleyball. Activities are supervised in a way that makes participants feel unfettered. For example, other than counselors, no adults are allowed in The Stack/Aloft.

SPORTS, FITNESS, AND BEAUTY

OF THREE TOP-DECK POOLS, one has a Mickey Mouse motif and waterslide and is intended for families; the second, a little less elaborate, is also set aside for families; the third is adults only. Unique to the *Disney Wonder* is a Toddler Splash Zone on Deck 9 that is designed for children who are not fully toilet trained and wear swim diapers. (As you might expect, the Toddler Splash Zone stays pretty much in cleanup mode.) At night the pool area can be a stage for deck parties and dancing.

The 8,500-square-foot, ocean-view **Vista Spa and Salon** above the bridge offers Cybex exercise equipment, an aerobics room, exercise instruction, a thermal-bath area, saunas, and steam rooms. A qualified fitness director supervises. The spa, run by British-based Steiner, offers pricey beauty treatments plus a sales pitch for Steiner products. Passengers in concierge-level suites can have a private massage in their suite or veranda (50 minutes for about $109; prices vary). Spa reservations can be made in advance at **www.disney cruise.com.**

The Sports Deck has a paddle tennis court, table tennis, basketball court, and shuffleboard. The full promenade deck lures walkers and joggers.

CASTAWAY CAY

EACH CRUISE INCLUDES A DAY AT CASTAWAY CAY, Disney's 1,000-acre private island. The island's environment and beauty have been preserved, with white-sand beaches surrounded by emerald water. A pier allows access without tendering. A four-car open tram (like those at Disney parks) links the ship to **Scuttle's Cove** family beach. The tram runs every five minutes; you could walk the quarter-mile to the beach, but it's inadvisable in the blistering heat. (Bring sunblock and wear a hat.) Strollers are available, as are rental floats, bikes, kayaks, and snorkel gear. Lounge chairs under pastel umbrellas are plentiful, and hammocks swing under the palms, but there's very little shade otherwise.

Disney Imagineers have created shops, restrooms, and pavilions that give the impression they've been there for years. A supervised children's area includes a "dig" at a half-buried whale skeleton. Water sports are offered in a protected lagoon. One snorkeling course is near shore; the other, farther out, requires more endurance. On the distant course, snorkelers see fish they identify from a waterproof card provided with rental equipment; lifeguards watch all snorkelers. A shore excursion provides guests with the opportunity to swim with live stingrays in a private lagoon. The cruise line has planted several "shipwrecks." On one, in about ten feet of water, snorkelers see Mickey Mouse riding the ship's bow. Rental equipment costs $25 for adults and $10 for children ages 5 to 9. The *Flying Dutchman*, the ghost ship from Disney's *Pirates of the Caribbean: Dead Man's Chest*, resides at Castaway Cay. An elaborate prop from the hit film, the *Flying Dutchman* is 175 feet long, with ragged sails and a barnacle-encrusted bow. Nature trails and bike paths are available. The main beach offers kids' activities, live Bahamian music, and shops. **Cookie's Bar-B-Cue** serves a buffet lunch of burgers, ribs, hot dogs, baked beans, slaw, corn on the cob, fruit, and potato chips. A teen beach offers swimming, snorkeling, kayaking, volleyball, tetherball, soccer, basketball, ping pong, pool, and more.

A second tram connects to **Serenity Bay,** the adult beach on the island's opposite side. A bar serves drinks, and passengers can enjoy a massage in one of the private cabanas opening on the sea. Passengers must be back aboard by 5 p.m. Many cruisers say they would've liked more time on the island.

DISNEY CRUISE LINE *and the* RECESSION

TODAY'S ECONOMIC DOLDRUMS have hit the cruise industry hard, and although the Disney Cruise Line has fared better than most, it's having to work very hard to fill its berths. Throughout the industry, demand has declined and capacity, with the introduction of a number of new ships, has gone up. Disney Cruise Line offers a distinctive product and has a loyal client base. With other lines heavily discounting their cruises, however, the deals are often so good (especially on lines that have good children's programs, like Princess, Royal Caribbean, and Norwegian) that Disney is forced to struggle mightily to hang on to its market share. When you can buy, say, a weeklong Alaska cruise on another line for less than a four-day Disney cruise to Nassau and Castaway Cay, it strains the loyalty of even the most ardent Mouseketeer. Disney, therefore, has been discounting and offering "Kids Sail Free" specials for children who share a cabin with their parents.

unofficial **TIP**
Search engine **www.kayak.com** is a great resource for uncovering cruise bargains.

To sum it up: cruises are unequivocally the best deal in travel right now and for the immediate future. Deals abound. Check Web sites like **www.cruisecritic.com, www.cruisemates.com,** and **www.lastminutetravel.com,** as well as **www.disneycruise.com,** for the latest discounts.

If you prefer to buy directly from Disney, here's how to get in touch:

Disney Cruise Line
210 Celebration Place, Suite 400
Celebration, FL 34747-4600
☎ 800-951-6499 or 800-951-3532; fax 407-566-7739
www.disneycruise.com

Disney Cruise Line offers a free planning DVD that tells all you need to know about Disney cruises and then some. To obtain a copy call ☎ 888-DCL-2500, or order online at **www.disneycruise.com.**

CRUISE–WDW PACKAGES

DISNEY OFFERS PACKAGE VACATIONS that combine a three- or four-day Bahamas cruise with three or four days at Walt Disney World. Regarding the Disney World part of the package, an Ithaca, New York, mom registers this complaint:

> *If you are cruising also, you do not get to use the last day of your ticket in the World due to the 11 a.m. bus departure to the terminal. They should offer packages with fewer days.*

ADVANCE RESERVATIONS FOR SHORE EXCURSIONS, SPA, PALO, AND CHILDREN'S PROGRAMS

DISNEY CRUISE LINE OFFERS SHORE EXCURSIONS at each port of call on all of its itineraries. These excursions can be previewed and booked at the Disney Cruise Line Web site. On the home page, click "Ports of Call" in the red bar at the upper left; then click on the port you're interested in.

unofficial **TIP**
Disney releases bookable activities on a rolling basis, with only a limited number for Concierge and Castaway Club guests in the beginning; they release more as the 75-day mark approaches. So if you can't get an excursion at the 105- or 90-day mark, try again 75 days before you sail.

When you can reserve depends on the accommodations you book. Here's the deal:

Concierge guests (Categories 1, 2, and 3) *paid in full* can book shore excursions, spa treatments, children's programs, and meals at Palo 105 days before their sail date.

Castaway Club guests (guests who have sailed on a previous Disney cruise) paid in full can reserve the previous 90 days before their sail date.

All other guests paid in full can reserve the previous 75 days before their sail date.

A FEW TIPS

1. If you opt for a week that includes the cruise and a Disney World stay, go first to Disney World. Cruising at the end of your vacation will ensure you arrive home rested.
2. At least 75 days before you sail and as soon as your booking is paid in full, reserve meals at Palo, spa treatments, children's programs, babysitting, and any shore excursions you can't do without at **www.disneycruise.com.**
3. Board the ship as early as possible. Check your dining rotation, and change it if desired. If you didn't reserve Palo, spa treatments, children's programs, or babysitting, do it now.
4. Disney requests that gentlemen wear jackets (no ties required) in the evening at Palo and Lumière's (Triton's).
5. If you have purchased a Land/Sea package, complete and return your cruise forms at the hotel. Your shoreside room key card will allow you to bypass lines at the cruise terminal and board the ship directly. Cruise-only passengers may encounter a wait at check-in.
6. All cabins have a mini-fridge; bring your own snacks and beverages.
7. The Sessions (Cadillac Lounge) piano bar is one of the most relaxing and beautiful lounges we've seen on any cruise ship. Make a before- or after-dinner drink there part of your routine. It's on Deck 3, forward.
8. Don't miss the kids' programs.

PART SIX

WALT DISNEY WORLD *with* KIDS

The ECSTASY *and the* AGONY

SO OVERWHELMING IS THE DISNEY MEDIA and advertising presence that any child who watches TV or shops with Mom is likely to get revved up about going to Walt Disney World. Parents, if anything, are even more susceptible. Almost all parents brighten at the prospect of guiding their children through this special place. But the reality of taking a young child (particularly during the summer) can be closer to the agony than to the ecstasy.

A Dayton, Ohio, mother took her 5-year-old to Disney World in July:

> *I felt so happy and excited before we went. I guess it was all worth it, but when I look back I think I should have had my head examined. The first day we went to* [the Magic Kingdom] *it was packed. By 11 in the morning, we had walked so far and stood in so many lines that we were all exhausted. Kristy cried about going on anything that looked or even sounded scary and was frightened by all of the Disney characters (they are so big!) except Minnie and Snow White.*
>
> *We got hungry about the same time as everyone else, but the lines for food were too long and my husband said we would have to wait. By 1 in the afternoon we were just plugging along, not seeing anything we were really interested in, but picking rides because the lines were short, or because whatever it was was air-conditioned. . . . At around 2:30, we finally got something to eat, but by then we were so hot and tired that it felt like we had worked in the yard all day. Kristy insisted on being carried, and we had 50 fights about not going on rides where the lines were too long. At the end, we were so P.O.'d and uncomfortable that we weren't having any fun. Mostly by this time, we were just trying to get our money's worth.*

Before you stiffen in denial, let us assure you that this family's experience is not unusual. Most young children are as picky about rides as they are about what they eat, and more than half of all preschoolers are intimidated by the Disney characters. Few humans (of any age) are mentally or physically equipped to march all day in a throng of 50,000 people in the hot Florida sun. And would you be surprised to learn that almost 60% of preschoolers said the thing they liked best about their Disney vacation was the hotel swimming pool?

But even somewhat older kids will surprise you, as this Windsor, Ontario, mom relates:

> *On day three, as we pursued our "Around the World in 80 Minutes" through the World Showcase,* [our] *two girls suddenly stopped in their tracks between Italy and Germany. They looked around for a minute, and we asked what was wrong, thinking they might need a bathroom visit. Turns out they'd finally seen something other than characters that appealed to them. "Could we just run around on that grass over there for a few minutes?" they wanted to know. "We won't take too long."*
>
> *So away they went to chase each other on the grass for ten minutes, and now, ten years later,* that *is what they remember about the trip. Ever since, we've tried to include time in each trip plan to "run around on that grass over there," wherever "there" might be.*

REALITY TESTING: WHOSE DREAM IS IT?

REMEMBER WHEN YOU WERE LITTLE and you got that nifty electric train for Christmas, the one Dad wouldn't let you play with? Did you wonder who the train was really for? Ask yourself a similar question about your vacation to Walt Disney World. Whose dream are you trying to make come true: yours or your child's?

unofficial **TIP**
When considering a trip to Walt Disney World, think about whether your kids are old enough to enjoy what can be a very fun, but taxing, trip.

Young children read their parents' emotions. When you ask, "Honey, how would you like to go to Disney World?" your child will respond more to your smile and enthusiasm than to any notion of what Disney World is all about. The younger the child, the more this holds true. From many preschoolers, you could elicit the same excitement by asking, "Sweetie, how would you like to go to Cambodia on a dogsled?"

So, is your happy fantasy of introducing your child to Disney magic a pipe dream? Not necessarily, but you have to be practical and open to reality testing. For example, would you increase the probability of a successful visit by waiting a year or two? Is your child adventuresome enough to sample the variety of Disney World? Will your child have sufficient endurance and patience to cope with long lines and large crowds?

RECOMMENDATIONS FOR MAKING THE DREAM COME TRUE

WHEN YOU'RE PLANNING A DISNEY WORLD VACATION with young children, consider:

AGE Although Disney World's color and festivity excite all children and specific attractions delight toddlers and preschoolers, Disney entertainment is generally oriented to older children and adults. Children should be a fairly mature 7 years old to *appreciate* the Magic Kingdom and Animal Kingdom, a year or two older to get much out of Epcot or Disney's Hollywood Studios.

Readers continually debate how old a child should be or the ideal age to go to Disney World. A Waldwick, New Jersey, mother reports:

My kids, not in the least shy or clingy, were frightened of many attractions. I thought my 6-year-old was the "perfect age" but quickly realized this was not the case. Disney makes even the most simple, child-friendly story into a major theatrical production, to the point where my kids couldn't associate their beloved movies with the attraction in front of them.

A Rockaway, New Jersey, mom writes:

You were absolutely right about young kids; I found myself re-reading your section "The Ecstasy and the Agony." Unfortunately, our experience was pure agony, with the exception of our hotel pool. It was the one and only thing our kids wanted to do. I planned this trip and saved for over a year and cried all week at the disappointment that our kids just wanted to swim.

A dad from Columbus, Ohio, felt like he was in a maternity ward:

We were shocked to see so many newborns as well. I could have sworn that one woman gave birth at the bus stop, her baby was so small.

A Dallas dad says:

I must echo the thoughts of readers about parents who bring infants and toddlers to WDW. Are these people nuts? They should find a better way to waste their hard-earned vacation dollars. These children (and therefore their parents) cannot ride any of the best rides and won't remember the ones they do ride five minutes after they get off. It is tough enough walking these huge parks without pushing around one or more children in a stroller. My advice to these parents is to go to a nice beach, rest, let the kids play in the sand, spend less money, and come back in a few years. Disney World will still be there.

But a Cleveland mother takes exception:

The best advice for parents with young kids is to remember for whom you are there and if possible accommodate the kids' need to do things again and again. I think you underestimate Disney's appeal to young children. Since we've gotten home, my 4-year-old has said "I don't want to live in Cleveland, I want to live at Disney World!" at least five times a day.

A New York City mom had a great vacation—but not exactly the one she'd been expecting:

Unfortunately, I was unprepared for traveling with a 2½-year-old. All the indoor rides were deemed too dark and scary, and all she wanted to do was see the characters (which I though she'd be petrified of!). We had a great trip once I threw all my maps and plans out the window and just went with the flow! Also, three nights was not enough to have a leisurely trip. We were running around way too much. We all would have appreciated more pool time. It was a great trip overall, but I would definitely warn people to think twice before bringing a toddler. It is one exhausting trip!

An Iowa City, Iowa, mother of three administers some tough love:

Get over it! In my opinion, people think too much about the age thing. If taking your 3-year-old to Disney World would make you happy, that's all that counts. End of story. It doesn't matter if the trip is really for you or your child—it's all good. You shouldn't have to jump through a bunch of hoops to give yourself permission to go.

A Lawrenceville, Georgia, mother of two toddlers advises maintaining the children's normal schedule:

The first day, we tried your suggestion about an early start; so we woke the children (ages 4 and 2) and hurried them to get going. BAD IDEA with toddlers. This put them off schedule for naps and meals the rest of the day. It is best to let young ones stay on their regular schedule and see Disney at their own pace.

Finally, an Alabama woman encourages parents to be more open-minded about taking toddlers to Disney World:

Parents of toddlers, don't be afraid to bring your little ones! Ours absolutely loved it, and we have priceless photos and videos of our little ones and their grandparents with Mickey and the gang. For all those people in your book who complained about our little sweethearts crying, sorry, but we found your character-hogging, cursing, ill-mannered, cutting-in-line, screaming-in-our-ears-on-the-roller-coasters teens and preteens much more obnoxious.

unofficial **TIP**
Coupled with a sense of humor and a little preparedness on your part, our touring plans and tips for families ensure a super experience at any time of year.

WHEN TO VISIT Avoid the hot, crowded summer months, especially if you have preschoolers. Go in October, November (except Thanksgiving), early December, January, February, or May. If you have children of varied ages and they're good students, take the older ones out of school and visit during the cooler, less congested off-season. Arrange special assignments relating to educational aspects of Disney World. If your children can't afford to miss school, take your vacation as soon as the school year ends. Alternatively, try late August before school starts. Please understand that you don't have to visit during one of the more ideal times of year to have a great vacation.

A Peterborough, England, dad agrees:

We visited WDW at the end of August, and we expected that the crowds would be almost unbearable. However, we were surprised to find that since most local schools were back in session, we could walk on most headliner rides up until late afternoon, and even then there was only a short wait—some rides at Universal Studios didn't even open until 11 a.m. because we were visiting on a low-attendance day! We would recommend that more people go at this time of year, especially those people whose children don't return to school until later.

BUILD NAPS AND REST INTO YOUR ITINERARY The parks are huge: don't try to see everything in one day. Tour in early morning and return to your hotel around 11:30 a.m. for lunch, a swim, and a nap. Even during off-season, when crowds are smaller and the temperature is more pleasant, the major parks' size will exhaust most children younger than age 8 by lunchtime. Return to the park in late afternoon or early evening and continue touring. A family from Texas underlines the importance of naps and rest:

> *Despite not following any of your "tours," we did follow the theme of visiting a specific park in the morning, leaving midafternoon for either a nap back at the room or a trip to the* [hotel] *pool, and then returning to one of the parks in the evening. On the few occasions when we skipped your advice, I was muttering to myself by dinner. I can't tell you* what *I was muttering. . . .*

Regarding naps, this mom doesn't mince words:

> *For parents of small kids: take the book's advice and get out of the park and take the nap, take the nap, TAKE THE NAP! Never in my life have I seen so many parents screaming at, ridiculing, or slapping their kids. (What a vacation!) WDW is overwhelming for kids and adults. Even though the rental strollers recline for sleeping, we noticed that most of the toddlers and preschoolers didn't give up and sleep until 5 p.m., several hours after the fun had worn off, and right about the time their parents wanted them to be awake and polite in a restaurant.*

From a Hamburg, New York, mother of a toddler:

> *Since we were traveling with our 2-year-old, we went to the parks when they opened every morning (usually by 9 a.m.), then followed the advice to return to our hotel for an afternoon nap. If we began lunch in the park by 11:30, our son was down for his nap by 1. This was the best decision we made. We all stayed rested, since one of us would nap in the room and the other would swim or shop during our son's nap. After napping, we were all refreshed and ready to head back to the park. Our son stayed in good spirits throughout the ten-day trip, while his 4-year-old and 7-year-old cousins, who did not take a break during the day, were exhausted and whiny for half of the vacation. I was worried that ten days would be too long for a 2-year-old, but going at this pace allowed us to thoroughly cover all of the parks without stress.*

And finally, from an Alice, Texas, mother of two school-age children:

> *Probably the most important tip your guide gave us was going to the hotel to swim and regroup during the day. The parks became unbearable by noon—and so did my husband and boys. The hotel was an oasis that calmed our nerves and refreshed our hearts! After about three hours of playtime, we headed out to a different park for dinner and a cool evening of fun.*

If you plan to return to your hotel at midday and want your room made up, let housekeeping know.

> *unofficial* **TIP**
> **If you must rent a car to make returning to your hotel practicable, do it.**

WHERE TO STAY The time and hassle involved in commuting to and from the theme parks will be less if your hotel is close by. This doesn't necessarily mean you have to lodge inside Disney World. Because the World is so geographically dispersed, many off-property hotels are closer to the parks than some Disney resorts (see our chart on pages 406 and 407 showing commuting times from Disney and non-Disney hotels). Regardless of where you stay, it's imperative that you take young children out of the parks each day for a few hours of rest. Neglecting to relax can ruin the day—or the vacation—for everyone.

If you have young children, book a hotel that is located within a 20-minute driving distance from the theme parks. It's true that you can revive somewhat by retreating to a Disney hotel for lunch or by finding a quiet restaurant in the parks, but there's no substitute for returning to the comfort of your hotel. Regardless of what you've heard, children too large to sleep in a stroller won't relax unless you take them back to your hotel.

Thousands of new rooms have been built in and near Disney World, many of them affordable. With planning, you should have no difficulty finding lodging to meet your requirements.

If you're traveling with children 12 years old and younger and want to stay in the World, we recommend the Polynesian, Grand Floridian, or Wilderness Lodge and Villas Resorts (in that order), if they fit your budget. For less expensive rooms, try the Port Orleans Resort. Bargain lodging is available at the All-Star and Pop Century resorts. In addition to standard hotel rooms, the All-Star Resorts offer two-room family suites that can sleep as many as six and provide modest kitchens. Log cabins at Fort Wilderness Campground are also a good bet. Outside the World, check our top hotels for families, starting on page 247.

unofficial **TIP**
The way to protect your considerable investment in your Disney vacation is to stay happy and have a good time. You don't have to meet a quota for experiencing attractions. *Do what you want.*

BE IN TOUCH WITH YOUR FEELINGS When you or your children get tired and irritable, call time-out. Trust your instincts. What would feel best? Another ride, an ice-cream break, or going back to the room for a nap?

LEAST COMMON DENOMINATORS Somebody is going to run out of steam first, and when he or she does, the whole family will be affected. Sometimes a snack break will revive the flagging member. Sometimes, however, it's better to return to your hotel. Pushing the tired or discontented beyond their capacity will spoil the day for them—and you. Energy levels vary. Be prepared to respond to members of your group who poop out. *Hint:* "We've driven a thousand miles to take you to Walt Disney World and now you're ruining everything!" is not an appropriate response.

BUILDING ENDURANCE Though most children are active, their normal play usually doesn't condition them for the exertion required to tour a Disney park. Start family walks four to six weeks before your trip to get in shape. A mother from Wesconsville, Pennsylvania, reports:

> *We had our 6-year-old begin walking with us a bit every day one month before leaving—when we arrived* [at Walt Disney World], *her little legs could carry her, and she had a lot of stamina.*

A father of two from Albion, Minnesota, had this to say:

> *My wife walked with my son to school every day when it was nice. His stamina was outstanding.*

SETTING LIMITS AND MAKING PLANS Avoid arguments and disappointment by establishing guidelines for each day, and getting everybody committed. Include the following:

1. Wake-up time and breakfast plans
2. When to depart for the park
3. What to take with you
4. A policy for splitting the group or for staying together
5. What to do if the group gets separated or someone is lost
6. How long you intend to tour in the morning and what you want to see, including plans in the event an attraction is closed or too crowded
7. A policy on what you can afford for snacks
8. A time for returning to the hotel to rest
9. When you will return to the park and how late you will stay
10. Dinner plans
11. A policy for buying souvenirs, including who pays: Mom and Dad or the kids
12. Bedtimes

BE FLEXIBLE Any day at Disney World includes surprises; be prepared to adjust your plan. Listen to your intuition.

WHAT KIDS WANT According to research by Yesawich, Pepperdine, Brown, and Russell, 71% of children between the ages of 6 and 17 say they need a vacation because school and homework get them down. The chart below shows what kids want and don't want when taking a vacation. Kids surveyed have a lot in common about what they want, less so concerning what they don't want. The "don't wants" in the chart are the four most common.

WHAT DO KIDS WANT?	
To go swimming/have pool time	80%
To eat in restaurants	78%
To stay at a hotel or resort	76%
To visit a theme park	76%
To stay up late	73%
WHAT DO KIDS NOT WANT?	
To get up early	52%
To ride in a car	36%
To play golf	34%
To go to a museum	31%

MAINTAINING SOME SEMBLANCE OF ORDER AND DISCIPLINE OK, OK, wipe that smirk off your face. Order and discipline on the road may seem like an oxymoron to you, but you won't be hooting when your 5-year-old launches a tantrum in the middle of Fantasyland. Your willingness to give this subject serious consideration before you leave home may well be the most important element of your pre-trip preparation.

Discipline and maintaining order are more difficult when traveling than at home because everyone is, as a Boston mom put it, "in and out"—in strange surroundings and out of the normal routine. For children, it's hard to contain excitement and anticipation that pop to the surface in the form of fidgety hyperactivity, nervous energy, and sometimes, acting out. Confinement in a car, plane, or hotel room only exacerbates the situation, and kids often tend to be louder than normal, more aggressive with siblings, and much more inclined to push the envelope of parental patience. Once you're in the theme parks, it doesn't get much better. There's more elbowroom, but there are also overstimulation, crowds, heat, and miles of walking. All this, coupled with marginal or inadequate rest, can lead to a meltdown in the most harmonious of families.

Sound parenting and standards of discipline practiced at home, applied consistently, will suffice to handle most situations on vacation. Still, it's instructive to study the hand you are dealt when traveling. For starters, aside from being jazzed and ablaze with adrenaline, your kids may believe that rules followed at home are somehow suspended when traveling. Parents reinforce this misguided intuition by being inordinately lenient in the interest of maintaining peace in the family. While some of your home protocols (like cleaning your plate and going to bed at a set time) might be relaxed to good effect on vacation, differing from your normal approach to discipline can precipitate major misunderstanding and possibly disaster.

Children, not unexpectedly, are likely to believe that a vacation (especially a vacation to Walt Disney World) is intended expressly for them. This reinforces their focus on their own needs and largely erases any consideration of yours. Such a mind-set dramatically increases their sense of hurt and disappointment when you correct them or deny them something they want. An incident that would hardly elicit a pouty lip at home could well escalate to tears or defiance when traveling. It's important before you depart on your trip, therefore, to discuss your vacation needs with your children, and to explore their wants and expectations as well.

unofficial **TIP**
Just because they're on vacation doesn't mean you should let the kids monopolize your trip—maintain some of your everyday rules, and you'll all have a better time together.

The stakes are high for everyone on a vacation—for you because of the cost in time and dollars, but also because your vacation represents a rare opportunity for rejuvenation and renewal. The stakes are high for your children too. Children tend to romanticize travel, building anticipation to an almost unbearable level. Discussing the trip in advance can ground expectations to a certain extent, but a child's imagination will, in the end, trump reality every time. The good news is that you can take advantage of your children's emotional state to establish preset rules and conditions for their conduct while on vacation. Because your children want what's being offered *sooooo* badly, they will be unusually accepting and conscientious regarding whatever rules are agreed upon.

According to *Unofficial Guide* child psychologist Karen Turnbow, PhD, successful response to (or avoidance of) behavioral problems on the road begins with a clear-cut disciplinary policy at home. Both at home and on vacation the approach should be the same, and should be based on the following key concepts:

1. LET EXPECTATIONS BE KNOWN Discuss what you expect from your children, but don't try to cover every imaginable situation (that's what lawyers are for—just kidding). Cover expectations regarding compliance with parental directives, treatment of siblings, resolution of disputes, schedules (including morning wake-up and bedtimes), courtesy and manners, staying together, and who pays for what.

2. EXPLAIN THE CONSEQUENCES OF NONCOMPLIANCE Detail very clearly and firmly the consequence of not meeting expectations. This should be very straightforward and unambiguous: "If you do X (or don't do X), this is what will happen."

3. WARNING You're dealing with excited, expectant children, not machines, so it's important to issue a warning before meting out discipline. It's critical to understand that we're talking about one unequivocal warning rather than multiple warnings or nagging. These last undermine your credibility and make your expectations appear relative or less than serious. Multiple warnings or nagging also effectively pass control of the situation from you to your child (who sometimes may continue acting out as an attention-getting strategy).

4. FOLLOW THROUGH If you say you're going to do something, do it. Period. Children must understand that you are absolutely serious and committed.

5. CONSISTENCY Inconsistency makes discipline a random event in the eyes of your children. Random discipline encourages random behavior, which translates to a nearly total loss of parental control. Long term, both at home and on the road, your response to a given situation or transgression must be perfectly predictable. Structure and repetition, essential for a child to learn, cannot be achieved in the absence of consistency.

Although the previous methods are the five biggies, there are several corollary concepts and techniques worthy of consideration.

Understand that whining, tantrums, defiance, sibling friction, and even holding up the group are ways in which children communicate with parents. Frequently the object or precipitant of a situation has little or no relation to the unacceptable behavior. A fit may on the surface appear to be about the ice cream you refused to buy little Robby, but there's almost always something deeper, a subtext that is closer to the truth (this is why ill behavior often persists after you give in to a child's demands). As often as not, the real cause is a need for attention. This need is so powerful in some children that they will subject themselves to certain punishment and parental displeasure to garner the attention they crave, even if it is negative.

To get at the root cause of the behavior in question requires both active listening and empowering your child with a "feeling vocabulary." Active listening is a concept that's been around a long time. It involves being alert not only to what a child says,

unofficial **TIP**
Teaching your kids to tell you clearly what they want or need will help make the trip more enjoyable for everyone.

but also to the context in which it is said, to the words used and possible subtext, to the child's emotional state and body language, and even to what's not said. Sounds complicated, but it's basically being attentive to the larger picture and, more to the point, being aware that there is a larger picture.

Helping your child develop a feeling vocabulary consists of teaching your child to use words to describe what's going on. The idea is to teach the child to articulate what's really troubling him, to be able to identify and express emotions and mood states in language. Of course, learning to express feelings is a lifelong learning experience, but it's much less dependent on innate sensitivity than being provided the tools for expression and being encouraged to use them.

It all begins with convincing your child that you're willing to listen attentively and take what he's saying seriously. By listening to your child, you help him transcend the topical by reframing the conversation to address the underlying emotional state(s). That his brother hit him may have precipitated the mood state, but the act is topical and of secondary importance. What you want is for your child to be able to communicate how that makes him feel, and to get in touch with those emotions. When you reduce an incident (hitting) to the emotions triggered (anger, hurt, rejection), you have the foundation for helping him develop constructive coping strategies. Being in touch with one's feelings and developing constructive coping strategies are essential to emotional well-being, and they also have a positive effect on behavior. A child who can tell his mother why he is distressed is a child who has discovered a coping strategy far more effective (not to mention easier for all concerned) than a tantrum.

Children are almost never too young to begin learning a feeling vocabulary. And helping your child to be in touch with—and to communicate—his or her emotions will stimulate you to focus on your feelings and mood states in a similar way. In the end, with persistence and effort, the whole family will achieve a vastly improved ability to communicate.

Until you get the active listening and feeling vocabulary going, be careful not to become part of the problem. There's a whole laundry list of adult responses to bad behavior that only make things worse. Hitting, swatting, yelling, name-calling, insulting, belittling, using sarcasm, pleading, nagging, and inducing guilt (as in "We've spent thousands of dollars to bring you to Disney World and now you're spoiling the trip for everyone!") figure prominently on the list.

Responding to a child appropriately in a disciplinary situation requires thought and preparation. Following are things to keep in mind, and techniques to try, when your world blows up while waiting in line for Dumbo.

1. BE THE ADULT It's well understood that children can push their parents' buttons faster and more skillfully than just about anyone or anything else. They've got your number, know precisely how to elicit a response, and are not reluctant to go for the jugular. Fortunately (or unfortunately), you're the adult, and to deal with a situation effectively, you've got to act like one. If your kids get you ranting and caterwauling, you effectively abdicate your adult status. Worse, you suggest by way of example that being out of control is an acceptable expression of hurt or anger. No matter what happens, repeat the mantra, "I am the adult in this relationship."

2. FREEZE THE ACTION Being the adult and maintaining control almost always translates to freezing the action, to borrow a sports term. Instead of responding in knee-jerk fashion (that is, at a maturity level closer to your child's than yours), freeze the action by disengaging. Wherever you are or whatever the family is doing, stop in place and concentrate on one thing, and one thing only: getting all involved calmed down. Practically speaking this usually means initiating a time-out. It's essential that you take this action immediately. Grabbing your child by the arm or collar and dragging him toward the car or hotel room only escalates the turmoil by prolonging the confrontation and by adding a coercive physical dimension to an already volatile emotional event. For the sake of everyone involved, including the people around you (as when a toddler throws a tantrum in church), it's essential to retreat to a more private place. Choose the first place available. Firmly sit the child down and refrain from talking to him until you've both cooled off. This might take a little time, but the investment is worthwhile. Truncating the process is like trying to get on your feet too soon after surgery.

3. ISOLATE THE CHILD You'll be able to deal with the situation more effectively and expeditiously if the child is isolated with one parent. Dispatch the uninvolved members of your party for a snack break or have them go on with the activity or itinerary without you (if possible) and arrange to rendezvous later at an agreed time and place. In addition to letting the others get on with their day, isolating the offending child with one parent relieves him of the pressure of being the group's focus of attention and object of anger. Equally important, isolation frees you from the scrutiny and expectations of the others in regard to how to handle the situation.

4. REVIEW THE SITUATION WITH THE CHILD If, as discussed on page 313, you've made your expectations clear, stated the consequences of failing to meet those expectations, and administered a warning, review the situation with the child and follow through with the discipline warranted. If, as often occurs, things are not so black-and-white, encourage the child to communicate his feelings. Try to uncover what occasioned the acting out. Lectures and accusatory language don't work well here, nor do threats. Dr. Turnbow suggests that a better approach (after the child is calm) is to ask, "What can we do to make this a better day for you?"

5. FREQUENT TANTRUMS OR ACTING OUT The preceding four points relate to dealing with an incident as opposed to a chronic condition. If a child frequently acts out or throws tantrums, you'll need to employ a somewhat different strategy.

Tantrums are cyclical events evolved from learned behavior. A child learns that he can get your undivided attention by acting out. When you respond, whether by scolding, admonishing, threatening, or negotiating, your response further draws you into the cycle and prolongs the behavior. When you accede to the child's demands, you reinforce the effectiveness of the tantrum and raise the cost of capitulation next time around. When a child thus succeeds in monopolizing your attention, he effectively becomes the person in charge.

To break this cycle, you must disengage from the child. The object is to demonstrate that the cause-and-effect relationship (that is, tantrum elicits parental attention) is no longer operative. This can be accomplished by refusing to interact with the child as long as the untoward behavior continues. Tell the child that you're unwilling to discuss his problem until he calms down. You can ignore the behavior, remove yourself from the child's presence (or vice versa), or isolate the child with a time-out. It's important to disengage quickly and decisively with no discussion or negotiation.

Most children don't pick the family vacation as the time to start throwing tantrums. The behavior will be evident before you leave home, and home is the best place to deal with it. Be forewarned, however, that bad habits die hard, and that a child accustomed to getting attention by throwing tantrums will not simply give up after a single instance of disengagement. More likely, the child will at first escalate the intensity and length of his tantrums. By your consistent refusal over several weeks (or even months) to respond to his behavior, however, he will finally adjust to the new paradigm.

Children are cunning as well as observant. Many understand that a tantrum in public is embarrassing to you and that you're more likely to cave in than you would at home. Once again, consistency is the key, along with a bit of anticipation. When traveling, it's not necessary to retreat to the privacy of a hotel room to isolate your child. You can carve out space for a time-out almost anywhere: on a theme-park bench, in a park, in your car, in a restroom, even on a sidewalk.

You can often spot the warning signs of an impending tantrum and head it off by talking to the child before he reaches an explosive emotional pitch. And don't forget that tantrums are about getting attention. Giving your child attention when things are on an even keel often preempts acting out.

6. SALVAGE OPERATIONS Who knows what evil lurks in the hearts of children? What's for sure is that they are full of surprises, and sometimes the surprises are not good. If your sweet child manages to pull a stunt of mammoth proportions, what do you do? This happened to an Ohio couple, resulting in the offending kid pretty much being grounded for life. Fortunately there were no injuries or lives lost, but the parents had to determine what to do for the remainder of the vacation. For starters, they split up the group. One parent escorted the offending child back to the hotel, where he was effectively confined to his guest room for the duration. That evening, the parents arranged for in-room sitters for the rest of the stay. Expensive? You bet, but better than watching your whole vacation go down the tubes.

A family at Walt Disney World's Magic Kingdom theme park had a similar experience, although the offense was of a more modest order of magnitude. Because it was their last day of vacation, they elected to place the misbehaver in time-out, in the theme park, for the rest of the day. One parent monitored the culprit while the other parent and the siblings enjoyed the attractions. At agreed times the parents would switch places. Once again, not ideal, but preferable to stopping the vacation.

Parenting Advice: Readers Weigh In

Though the foregoing section was developed by top child psychologists, it rubs some readers the wrong way. Take this teacher from Corryton, Tennessee:

> *The one thing I don't like is the section on how to make your kids behave. As a preschool teacher, I can honestly say that people who need this advice won't take it anyway—so why bother?*

But a North Carolina psychiatrist disagrees:

> *The section of the* Unofficial Guide *dealing with child behavioral issues while traveling is one of the most concise and well-articulated presentations on this subject that I have encountered anywhere. I recommend it to many of my patients who are contemplating traveling with their children.*

A New Hampshire father of two had this to say:

> *Your advice on touring with children was fabulous. Your book gave us confidence to do the parks without being deer caught in the headlights.*

ABOUT THE *UNOFFICIAL GUIDE* TOURING PLANS

PARENTS WHO USE OUR TOURING PLANS are often frustrated by interruptions and delays caused by their young children. Here's what to expect:

1. CHARACTER ENCOUNTERS CAN WREAK HAVOC WITH THE TOURING PLANS. Many children will stop in their tracks whenever they see a Disney character. Attempting to haul your child away before he has satisfied his curiosity is likely to cause anything from whining to full-scale revolt. Either go with the flow or specify a morning or afternoon for photos and autographs. Be aware that queues for autographs, especially in Toontown at the Magic Kingdom and Camp Minnie-Mickey at Animal Kingdom, are as long as the queues for major attractions.

2. OUR TOURING PLANS CALL FOR VISITING ATTRACTIONS IN A SEQUENCE, OFTEN SKIPPING ATTRACTIONS ALONG THE WAY. Children don't like to skip anything! If something catches their eye, they want to see it that moment. Some can be persuaded to skip attractions if parents explain their plans in advance. Other kids flip out at skipping something, particularly in Fantasyland. A mom from Charleston, South Carolina, writes:

> *We did not have too much trouble following the touring plans at* [Disney's Hollywood Studios] *and at Epcot. The Magic Kingdom plan, on the other hand, turned out to be a train wreck. The main problem with the plan is that it starts in Fantasyland. When we were on Dumbo, my 5-year-old saw eight dozen other things in Fantasyland she wanted to see. The long and the short is that after Dumbo, there was no getting her out of there.*

A mother of two from Burlington, Vermont, adds:

> *I found out that my kids were very curious about the castle because we had read* Cinderella *at home. Whenever I wanted to leave Fantasyland, I would just say, "Let's go to the castle and see if Cinderella is there." Once we got as far as the front door to the castle, it was no problem going out to the* [central] *hub and then to another land.*

3. CHILDREN HAVE AN INSTINCT FOR FINDING RESTROOMS. We have seen adults with maps search interminably for a restroom. Young children, however, including those who can't read, will head for the nearest restroom with the certainty of a homing pigeon. You can be sure your children will ferret out (and want to use) every restroom in the park.

4. IF YOU'RE USING A STROLLER, YOU WON'T BE ABLE TO TAKE IT INTO ATTRACTIONS OR ONTO RIDES. This includes rides such as the Walt Disney World Railroad that are included in the touring plans as in-park transportation.

5. YOU PROBABLY WON'T FINISH THE TOURING PLAN. Varying hours of operation, crowds, your group's size, your children's ages, and your stamina will all affect how much of the plan you'll complete. Tailor your expectations to this reality, or you'll be frustrated as this mother of two from Nazareth, Pennsylvania, was:

> *We do not understand how anyone could fit everything you have on your plans into the time allotted while attending to small children. We found that long lines, potty stops, diaper changes, stroller searches, and autograph breaks ate huge chunks of time. And we were there during the off-season.*

While our touring plans allow you to make the most of your time at the parks, it's impossible to define what "most" will be. It differs from family to family. If you have two young children, you probably won't see as much as two adults will. If you have four children, you probably won't see as much as a couple with only two children.

STUFF TO THINK ABOUT

OVERHEATING, SUNBURN, AND DEHYDRATION These are the most common problems of younger children at Disney World. Carry and use sunscreen. Apply it on children in strollers, even if the stroller has a canopy. To avoid overheating, stop for rest regularly—say, in the shade, or in a restaurant or at a show with air-conditioning.

unofficial **TIP**
Keep little ones well covered in sunscreen and hydrated with fluids. Don't count on hydrating young children with soft drinks and stops at water fountains. Carry plastic bottles of water. Squeeze bottles with caps are sold in all major parks for about $3. Remember: Excited kids may not tell you when they're thirsty or hot.

BLISTERS AND SORE FEET All guests should wear comfortable, broken-in shoes and socks that wick away perspiration, like SmartWool socks. If you or your children are susceptible to blisters, bring along some precut moleskin and Johnson & Johnson blister bandages. They offer excellent protection, stick great, and won't sweat off. When you feel a "hot spot," stop, air out your foot, and place a moleskin bandage over the area before a blister forms. Moleskin is available at all drugstores. Preschoolers may not say they're developing a blister until it's too late, so inspect their feet two or more times a day. For an expanded discussion about keeping your feet happy, see page 415.

FIRST AID Each major theme park has a first-aid center. In the Magic Kingdom, it's at the end of Main Street to your left, between Casey's Corner and The Crystal Palace. At Epcot, it's on the World Showcase side of Odyssey Center. At Disney's Hollywood Studios, it's in the Guest Relations Building inside the main entrance. At Animal Kingdom, it's in Discovery Island, on your left just before you cross the bridge to Africa. And in all four parks, First Aid and the Baby Care Center are right next to each other. If you or your children have a medical problem, go to a first-aid center. They're friendlier than most doctor's offices and are accustomed to treating everything from paper cuts to allergic reactions.

CHILDREN ON MEDICATION Some parents of hyperactive children on medication discontinue or decrease the child's dosage at the end of the school year. If you have such a child, be aware that Disney World might overstimulate him or her. Consult your physician before altering your child's medication regimen.

SUNGLASSES If your younger children wear sunglasses, put a strap or string on the frames so the glasses will stay on during rides and can hang from the child's neck while indoors. This works for adults too.

THINGS YOU FORGOT OR THINGS YOU RAN OUT OF Rain gear, diapers, diaper pins, formula, film, painkillers, topical sunburn treatments, and other sundries are sold at all major theme parks and at Typhoon Lagoon, Blizzard Beach, and Downtown Disney. Rain gear is a bargain, but most other items are high. Ask for goods you don't see displayed.

INFANTS AND TODDLERS AT THE THEME PARKS The major parks have centralized facilities for infant and toddler care. Everything necessary for changing diapers, preparing formulas, and warming bottles and food is available. Supplies are for sale (two diapers plus ointment are $3.50, for example), and there are rockers and special chairs for nursing mothers. At the Magic Kingdom, the Baby Center is next to The Crystal Palace at the end of Main Street. At Epcot, Baby Services is near the Odyssey Center, right of the Test Track in Future World. At Disney's Hollywood Studios, Baby Care is in the Guest Relations Building left of the entrance. At Animal Kingdom, Baby Changing/ Nursing is in Discovery Island in the park's center. Dads are welcome at the centers and can use most services. In addition, many men's restrooms in the major parks have changing tables.

A mom from New Berlin, Wisconsin, offers this tip for families with babies on formula:

> *A note to families with infants: we got hot water from the food vendors at WDW and mixed the formula as we went. It eliminated keeping bottles cold and then warming them up.*

Infants and toddlers are allowed in any attraction that doesn't have minimum height or age restrictions. But as a Minneapolis mother reports, some attractions are better for babies than others:

> *Theater and boat rides are easier for babies (ours was almost a year old, not yet walking). Rides where there's a bar that comes down are doable, but harder. Peter Pan was our first encounter with this type* [of ride], *and we had barely gotten situated when I realized he might fall out of my grasp. The standing auditorium films are too intense; the noise level is deafening, and the images inescapable. You don't have a rating system for babies, and I don't expect to see one, but I thought you might want to know what our baby thought (based on his reactions).* [At the Magic Kingdom:] *Jungle Cruise—didn't get into it. Pirates—slept through it. Riverboat—while at Aunt Polly's, the horn made him cry. Aunt Polly's—ate while watching the birds in relative quiet. Small World—wide-eyed, took it all in. Peter Pan—couldn't really sit on the seat. A bit dangerous. He didn't get into it. WDW RR—liked the motion and scenery.* Tiki Room—*loved it. Danced, clapped, sang along. At Epcot:* Honey, I Shrunk the Audience—*we skipped due to recommendation of Disney worker that it got too loud and adults screamed throughout. Journey into Imagination—loved it. Tried to catch things with his hands. Bounced up and down, chortled. The Land—watchful, quiet during presentation. Gran Fiesta Tour—loved it.*

The same mom also advises:

> *We used a baby sling on our trip and thought it was great when standing in lines—much better than a stroller, which you have to park before getting in line (and navigate through crowds). The only really great place I found to nurse in MK was a hidden bench in the shade in Adventureland between the freezee stand (next to* Tiki Room*) and the small shops. It is impractical to go to the baby station every time, so a nursing mom had better be comfortable about nursing in very public situations.*

If you think you might try nursing during a theater attraction, be advised that most shows run about 17 to 20 minutes. Exceptions are *The Hall of Presidents* at the Magic Kingdom and *The American Adventure* at Epcot, which run 23 and 29 minutes, respectively.

STROLLERS

THE GOOD NEWS: STROLLERS ARE AVAILABLE for rent at all four theme parks and the Downtown Disney area (single stroller, $15 per day with no deposit, $13 per day for the entire stay; double stroller, $31 per day with no deposit, $27 per day for the entire stay; stroller rentals at Downtown Disney require a $100 credit-card deposit; double strollers not available at Downtown Disney). Strollers are welcome at Blizzard Beach and Typhoon Lagoon, but no rentals are available. With multi-day rentals, you can skip the rental line entirely—just head over to the stroller-handout area, show your receipt, and you'll be wheeling out of there in no time. Even better, Disney has replaced the ancient blue clunkers at Epcot and the Magic Kingdom with brand-new models. If you rent a stroller at the Magic Kingdom and decide to go to Epcot, Animal Kingdom, or Disney's Hollywood Studios, turn in your Magic Kingdom stroller and present your receipt at the next park. You'll be issued another stroller at no additional charge.

You can pay in advance for stroller rentals—this allows you to bypass the "paying" line and head straight for the "pickup" line. Disney-resort guests can pay in advance at their resort's gift shop. Save receipts! Obtain strollers at the Magic Kingdom entrance, to the left of Epcot's Entrance Plaza and at Epcot's International Gateway, and at Oscar's Super Service just inside the entrance of Disney's Hollywood Studios. At Animal Kingdom, they're to the right just inside the entrance. Rental at all parks is fast and efficient, and returning the stroller is a breeze. You can ditch your rental stroller anywhere in the park when you're ready to leave.

Readers inform us that there is a lively "gray market" for strollers at the parks. Families who arrive late look for families who are heading for the exit and "buy" their stroller at a bargain price. A mom from Chester, New Hampshire, ever vigilant for a bargain, reports:

> *We "bought" strollers for $3 when we saw people returning them. Also, we "sold" our strollers for $3 when leaving.*

Strollers are a must for infants and toddlers, but we have seen many sharp parents renting strollers for somewhat older children (up to age 5 or so). The stroller spares parents from having to carry children when they sag and provides a convenient place to tote water and snacks.

A family from Tulsa, Oklahoma, recommends springing for a double stroller:

> *We rent a double for baggage room or in case the older child gets tired of walking.*

But a New Lenox, Illinois, family advocates not leaving anyone out!

> *If your kids are 8 or under, RENT STROLLERS* [reader's emphasis] *for all of them! An 8-year-old* will *fit in a stroller, and you can fit up to four kids in two doubles. We tried this the first time we visited Disney ten years ago, when my oldest was 6. My husband suggested getting a stroller for him and the two "babies" (ages 4 and 3). I thought he was nuts but didn't want to argue, and it turned out to be the best idea ever. We plowed through crowds, and the kids didn't get nearly as tired since they could be seated whenever they wanted. It was also a great place to stow heavy gear like video cameras. The Disney strollers are extremely sturdy and can take a lot of abuse—try it!*

Dean, a kindred spirit of the foregoing reader, made the best use of a stroller that we've heard to date:

When my wife was pregnant with our third [child], *she was very sick and spent almost all of her second trimester in the hospital. When she finally started feeling better and was released from the hospital, we promptly planned a quick trip to WDW in October 2004 to celebrate (that's a testament to our family's addiction to Disney). During this trip her health and energy held up most of the time, but sometimes she would get really fatigued. Once while at the MK, fatigue set in and we were still deep in the park near Mickey's Toontown. We decided to get creative. Out came the older two kids and in went Mom (my wife) into the double stroller. My daughter (then 4) barely fit on the end, held on by my wife. My son (then 7) stood on the edge and held on the side like a fireman. We got a lot of funny looks from people as I pushed them all around the park that afternoon (some looks of approval from other moms and admiration from some husbands), but we proved that 2½ kids PLUS Mom can fit in a double stroller. With the challenging summer we had, we were just glad to be at our favorite place on earth.*

If you go to your hotel for a break and intend to return to the park, leave your rental stroller by an attraction near the park entrance, marking it with something personal like a bandanna. When you return, your stroller will be waiting.

Rental strollers are too large for all infants and many toddlers. If you plan to rent a stroller for your infant or toddler, bring pillows, cushions, or rolled towels to buttress him in.

Bringing your own stroller is permitted. However, only collapsible strollers are allowed on monorails, parking-lot trams, and buses. Your stroller is unlikely to be stolen, but mark it with your name.

Having her own stroller was indispensable to a Mechanicsville, Virginia, mother of two toddlers:

How I was going to manage to get the kids from the parking lot to the park was a big worry for me before I made the trip. I didn't read anywhere that it was possible to walk to the entrance of the parks instead of taking the tram, so I wasn't sure I could do it.

I found that for me personally, since I have two kids aged 1 and 2, it was easier to walk to the entrance of the park from the parking lot with the kids in [my own] *stroller than to take the kids out of the stroller, fold the stroller (while trying to control the two kids and associated gear), load the stroller and the kids onto the tram, etc. . . . No matter where I was parked, I could always just walk to the entrance. . . . it sometimes took a while, but it was easier for me.*

A Secaucus, New Jersey, mom weighed all the considerations in exemplary type-A fashion:

If your child is under age 2, bring your own stroller. Three reasons to bring your own: First, you have all the way from your car to the TTC [Transportation and Ticket Center] *to the monorail (or ferry) to the stroller rental without a stroller, but with your child, diaper bag, and own self and stuff in tow. Not half as bad as doing it in reverse when leaving, when you're exhausted and have added to your luggage with purchases and the toddler who might have walked in wants to be carried out. Second, the WDW stroller is simply too large for most children under age 2 to be comfortable without significant padding. The seat is so low that the child is forced to keep their legs straight out in front of them. Third, despite being sooo big, there is NO PLACE to store anything. The body of the stroller is so low, there is no underneath storage for the diaper bag. There is a small net bag on the back of the carriage, but it seems designed to hold, at most, a small purse. If you hang a diaper bag by its straps from the handle, the stroller will tip backwards very, very easily. And you can't balance it on the top or the canopy won't stay open. It amazed me that the Disney folks did not provide ample space for all the souvenirs they want you to buy!*

Now, if your child is past needing a diaper bag, the WDW strollers seem like a pretty good deal. You won't need the storage space, and they do maneuver very well. They seem especially good for children who no longer need a stroller at home (ages 4 to 6) but who won't make it walking all day.

If your child is between ages 2 and 3, it's a toss-up. If you're a type-A mom, like me, who carries extra clothes, snacks, toys, enough diapers for three days, along with a pocketbook and extra-jackets-for-everyone-just-in-case, you've probably found a stroller that suits your needs, and will be miserable with the WDW kind. If you're a type-B "we can get everything else we need at the park; I'll just throw a diaper in my back pocket" mom, you'll probably be tickled with the WDW strollers. Also consider your toddler's personality. Will his familiar stroller add a level of comfort to a pretty intense experience? Or will he enjoy the novelty of the new wheels?

An Oklahoma mom, however, reports a bad experience with bringing her own stroller:

The first time we took our kids, we had a large stroller (big mistake). It is so much easier to rent one in the park. The large [personally owned] *strollers are nearly impossible to get on the buses and are a hassle at the airport. I remember feeling dread when a bus pulled up that was even semifull of people. People look at you like you have a cage full of live chickens when you drag heavy strollers onto the bus.*

DISPOSABLE STROLLERS If you want to avoid stroller rental fees and can get by with a very basic collapsible stroller, Walmart sells one for about ten bucks. When you're ready to go home, just chuck it—er, or maybe not. Readers Jason and Jennifer (no hometown given) chastised us thusly:

There is nothing [in the guide] *but good advice—except for the recommendation to go to Walmart and buy a "disposable" stroller. Our society is already too inclined to throw away usable items without your encouragement! Why not suggest something better, like donating it?*

Point taken.

STROLLER-RENTAL OPTIONS Orlando Stroller Rentals (☎ 800-281-0884; **www.orlandostrollerrentals.com**) offers folding strollers that are more comfortable and of higher quality than Disney's all-plastic models. Run by a local wife-and-husband team, OSR will drop your

unofficial **TIP**
When you enter a show or board a ride, you must park your stroller, usually in an open area. Bring a cloth or towel to dry it if it rains before you return.

stroller off at your hotel before you arrive and pick it up there when you're done. If you think you'll need a stroller while walking around your resort or getting to the theme parks, this might be your best option. Single-stroller rates are competitive with Disney's, and double-stroller rates are far less expensive after four or five days. We've evaluated both models and were impressed with the quality.

STROLLER WARS Sometimes strollers disappear while you're enjoying a ride or show. Disney staff will often rearrange strollers parked outside an attraction. This may be done to tidy up or to clear a walkway. Don't assume that your stroller is stolen because it isn't where you left it. It may be neatly arranged a few feet away—or perhaps more than a few feet away, as this Skokie, Illinois, dad reports:

> *The stroller* [reorganizations] *while you're on rides are a bit unnerving. More than once, our stroller was moved out of visible distance from the original spot. On one occasion, it was moved to a completely different stroller-parking area near another ride, and no sign or cast member was around to advise where. We had to track [a cast member] down, and she had to call in to find out where it had been moved. Be prepared for this.*

Sometimes, however, strollers are taken by mistake or ripped off by people not wanting to spend time replacing one that's missing. Don't be alarmed if yours disappears. You won't have to buy it, and you'll be issued a new one. In the Magic Kingdom, replacements are available at Tinker Bell's Treasures in Fantasyland and at the main rental facility near the park entrance. At Epcot, get replacements at the Entrance Plaza rental headquarters and at the International Gateway (in World Showcase between the United Kingdom and France pavilions). Strollers at Disney's Hollywood Studios can be replaced at the Animation Courtyard Shops next to *Voyage of the Little Mermaid*. In Animal Kingdom, they're available at Garden Gate Gifts and Mombasa Marketplace.

While replacing a stroller is no big deal, it's inconvenient. A Minnesota family complained that their stroller was taken six times in one day at Epcot and five times in a day at Disney's Hollywood Studios. Even with free replacements, larceny on this scale represents a lot of wasted time. Through our own experiments and readers' suggestions, we've developed a technique for hanging on to a rented stroller: affix something personal (but expendable) to the handle. Evidently, most strollers are pirated by mistake (they all look alike) or because it's easier to swipe someone else's than to replace one that has disappeared. Because most stroller "theft" results from confusion or laziness, the average pram-pincher will hesitate to haul off a stroller containing another person's property. We tried several items and concluded that a bright, inexpensive scarf or bandanna tied to the handle works well as identification. A sock partially

unofficial **TIP**
Beware of stroller stealers. With so many identical strollers, it's easy to grab the wrong one. Mark yours with a bandanna or some other easily identifiable flag.

stuffed with rags or paper works even better (the weirder and more personal the object, the greater the deterrent). Best might be an Ann Arbor, Michigan, mother's strategy:

> *We used a variation on your stroller-identification theme. We tied a clear plastic bag with a diaper in it on the stroller. Jon even poured a little root beer on the diaper for effect. Needless to say, no one took our stroller, and it was easy to identify.*

STROLLERS AS LETHAL WEAPONS A father of one from Purcellville, Virginia, complains about some inconsiderate parents:

> *The biggest problem is surviving the migrating herds of strollers. The drivers of these contraptions appear to believe they have the right-of-way in all situations and use the strollers as battering rams. . . . I know they will not be banned from the parks, but how about putting speed governors on these things?*

You'd be surprised at how many people are injured by strollers pushed by parents who are driving aggressively, in a hurry, or in the ozone. Given the number of strollers, pedestrians, and tight spaces, mishaps are inevitable on both sides. A simple apology and a smile are usually the best remediation.

unofficial **TIP**
We suggest that children younger than 8 years be color coded by dressing them in purple T-shirts or equally distinctive clothes.

LOST CHILDREN

ALTHOUGH IT'S AMAZINGLY EASY TO LOSE a child (or two) in the theme parks, it usually isn't a serious problem: Disney employees are schooled in handling the situation. If you lose a child in the Magic Kingdom, report it to a Disney employee, and then check at the Baby Center and at City Hall, where lost-children "logs" are kept. At Epcot, report the loss, then check at Baby Services near the Odyssey Center. At Disney's Hollywood Studios, report the loss at the Guest Relations Building at the entrance end of Hollywood Boulevard. At Animal Kingdom, go to the Baby Center in Discovery Island. Paging isn't used, but in an emergency, an "all-points bulletin" can be issued throughout the park(s) via internal communications. If a Disney employee encounters a lost child, he or she will take the child immediately to the park's Guest Relations center or Baby Care center.

Sew a label into each child's shirt that states his or her name, your name, the name of your hotel, and if you have one, your cell phone number. Accomplish the same thing by writing the information on a strip of masking tape. Security professionals suggest the information be printed in small letters and the tape be affixed to the outside of the child's shirt, five inches below the armpit. Also, name tags can be obtained at the major theme parks.

A Kingston, Washington, reader recommends recording vital info for each child on a plastic key tag or luggage tag and affixing it to the child's shoe. This reader also snaps a photo of the kids each morning to document what they're wearing. A mother from Rockville, Maryland, reported a strategy one step short of a brand or tattoo:

Traveling with a 3-year-old, I was very anxious about losing him. I wrote my cell-phone number on his leg with a permanent marker, and felt much more confident that he'd get back to me quickly if he became lost.

One way to better keep track of your family is to buy each person a "Disney uniform"—in this case, the same brightly and distinctively colored T-shirt. A Yuma, Arizona, family tried this with great success:

We tried the family plan of all of us getting the same shirts (bright red) so that we could easily spot each other in case of separation (VERY easy to do). It was a lifesaver when our 18-month-old decided to get out of the stroller and wander off. As I've heard before, Dumbo seems to draw them in, and lo and behold, guess where we found him (still dragging his leash but with a nice cast member following him)? No matter what precautions you may try, it seems there are always those opportunities [to lose a child], *but the recognizable shirts helped tremendously.*

Finally, from a Swindon, England, mum:

In case they got lost, I photo'd my 7-year-old twins every morning so we had a picture of what they were wearing. They wore wristbands with our cell-phone numbers on them. I made one adult responsible for each twin for the morning so that no one assumed someone else was holding their hand; then we switched after lunch. We also taught them if they got lost to shout our first names, not just "Mum" or "Dad."

HOW KIDS GET LOST

CHILDREN GET SEPARATED FROM THEIR PARENTS every day at Disney parks under remarkably similar (and predictable) circumstances:

1. PREOCCUPIED SOLO PARENT The party's only adult is preoccupied with something like buying refreshments, loading the camera, or using the restroom. Junior is there one second and gone the next.

2. THE HIDDEN EXIT Sometimes parents wait on the sidelines while two or more young children experience a ride together. Parents expect the kids to exit in one place and the youngsters pop out elsewhere. Exits from some attractions are distant from entrances. Know exactly where your children will emerge before letting them ride by themselves.

3. AFTER THE SHOW At the end of many shows and rides, a Disney staffer announces, "Check for personal belongings and take small children by the hand." When dozens, if not hundreds, of people leave an attraction simultaneously, it's easy for parents to lose their children unless they have direct contact.

4. RESTROOM PROBLEMS Mom tells 6-year-old Tommy, "I'll be sitting on this bench when you come out of the restroom." Three possibilities: One, Tommy exits through a different door and becomes disoriented (Mom may not know there is another door). Two, Mom decides she also will use the restroom, and Tommy emerges to find her gone. Three, Mom pokes around in a shop while keeping an eye on the bench but misses Tommy when he comes out.

If you can't be with your child in the restroom, make sure there's only one exit. The restroom on a passageway between Frontierland and Adventureland in the Magic Kingdom is the all-time worst for disorienting visitors. Children and adults alike have walked in from the Adventureland side and walked out on the Frontierland side (and vice versa). Adults realize quickly that something is wrong. Children, however, sometimes fail to recognize the problem.

Designate a distinctive meeting spot and give clear instructions: "I'll meet you by this flagpole. If you get out first, stay right here." Have your child repeat the directions back to you. When children are too young to leave alone, sometimes you have to think outside the box, as our Rockville, Maryland, mom (quoted previously on page 326) did:

> *It was very scary for me at times, being alone with children that had just turned 1 and 2. I'm reminded of the time on the trip when I couldn't fit the double stroller into the bathroom. I was at Epcot inside one of the buildings and I had to leave my kids with a WDW employee outside of the restroom because the stroller just wouldn't fit inside with me. Thinking about the incident now makes me laugh. The good news is that I found that most WDW bathrooms can accommodate a front-and-back double stroller inside the handicapped stall* [with you].

5. PARADES There are many parades and shows at which the audience stands. Children tend to jockey for a better view. By moving a little this way and that, the child quickly puts distance between you and him before either of you notices.

6. MASS MOVEMENTS Be on guard when huge crowds disperse after fireworks or a parade, or at park closing. With 20,000 to 40,000 people at once in an area, it's very easy to get separated from a child or others in your party. Use extra caution after the evening parade and fireworks in the Magic Kingdom, *Fantasmic!* at the Disney's Hollywood Studios, and *IllumiNations* at Epcot. Families should plan where to meet if they get separated.

7. CHARACTER GREETINGS When the Disney characters appear, children can slip out of sight. (See "Then Some Confusion Happened," page 344.)

8. GETTING LOST AT ANIMAL KINGDOM It's especially easy to lose a child in Animal Kingdom, particularly at the Oasis entryway, on the Maharaja Jungle Trek, and on the Pangani Forest Exploration Trail. Mom and Dad will stop to observe an animal. Junior stays close for a minute or so, and then, losing patience, wanders to the exhibit's other side or to a different exhibit.

Especially in the multipath Oasis, finding a lost child can be maddening, as a Safety Harbor, Florida, mother describes:

> *Manny wandered off in the paths that lead to the jungle village while we were looking at a bird. It reminded me of losing somebody in the supermarket when you run back and forth looking down each*

aisle but can't find the person you're looking for because they are running around too. I was nutso before we even got to the first ride.

A mother from Flint, Michigan, came up with yet another way to lose a kid: abandonment.

From the minute we hit the park it was gripe, whine, pout, cry, beg, scream, pick, pester, and aggravate. When he went to the restroom for the ninth time before 11 a.m., I thought, I'M OUTTA HERE. . . . let the little snothead walk back to Flint. Unfortunately, I was brought up Catholic with lots of guilt, so I didn't follow through.

DISNEY, KIDS, *and* SCARY STUFF

DISNEY RIDES AND SHOWS ARE ADVENTURES, and they focus on themes of all adventures: good and evil, death, beauty and ugliness, fellowship and enmity. As you sample the attractions at Walt Disney World, you will transcend the spinning and bouncing of midway rides to thought-provoking and emotionally powerful entertainment. All the endings are happy, but the adventures' impact, given Disney's gift for special effects, often intimidates and occasionally frightens young children.

unofficial **TIP**
Monsters and special effects at Disney's Hollywood Studios are more real and sinister than those in the other parks.

There are attractions with menacing witches, burning towns, and ghouls popping out of their graves, all done with humor, provided you're old enough to understand the joke. And bones. There are bones everywhere: human bones, cattle bones, dinosaur bones, even whole skeletons. There's a stack of skulls at the headhunters' camp on the Jungle Cruise, a platoon of skeletons sailing ghost ships in Pirates of the Caribbean, and an assemblage of skulls and skeletons in The Haunted Mansion. Skulls, skeletons, and bones punctuate Snow White's Scary Adventures, Peter Pan's Flight, and Big Thunder Mountain Railroad. Animal Kingdom has an entire playground composed exclusively of giant bones and skeletons.

If your child has difficulty coping with the witch in Snow White's Scary Adventures, think twice about exposing him at the Studios to machine-gun battles, earthquakes, and the creature from *Alien* in The Great Movie Ride.

One reader tells of taking his preschool children on Star Tours:

We took a 4-year-old and a 5-year-old, and they had the [poop] *scared out of them at Star Tours. We did this first thing, and it took hours of Tom Sawyer Island and Small World to get back to normal. Our kids were the youngest by far in Star Tours. I assume other adults had more sense.*

Preschoolers should start with Dumbo and work up to the Jungle Cruise in late morning, after being revved up and before getting hungry, thirsty, or tired. Pirates of the Caribbean is out for preschoolers. You get the idea.

You can reliably predict that Disney World will, at one time or another, send a young child into system overload. Be sensitive, alert, and prepared for almost anything, even behavior that is out of character for your child. Most children take Disney's macabre trappings in stride, and others are easily comforted by an arm around the shoulder or a squeeze of the hand. Parents who know that their children tend to become upset should take it slow and easy, sampling benign adventures like the Jungle Cruise, gauging reactions, and discussing with the children how they felt about what they saw.

Sometimes young children will rise above their anxiety in an effort to please their parents or siblings. This doesn't necessarily indicate a mastery of fear, much less enjoyment. If children leave a ride in apparently good shape, ask if they would like to go on it again (not necessarily now, but sometime). The response usually will indicate how much they actually enjoyed the experience.

Evaluating a child's capacity to handle the visual and tactile effects of Disney World requires patience, understanding, and experimentation. Each of us has our own demons. If a child balks at or is frightened by a ride, respond constructively. Let your children know that lots of people, adults and children, are scared by what they see and feel. Help them understand that it's OK if they get frightened and that their fear doesn't lessen your love or respect. Take pains not to compound the discomfort by making a child feel inadequate; try not to undermine self-esteem, impugn courage, or ridicule. Most of all, don't induce guilt by suggesting the child's trepidation might be ruining the family's fun. It's also sometimes necessary to restrain older siblings' taunting.

A reader from New York City expresses strong feelings about pressuring children:

> *As a psychologist who works with children, I felt ethically torn (and nearly filed a report!) watching parents force their children to go on rides they didn't want to ride (especially the Tower of Terror and Dinosaur). The Disney staff were more than willing to organize a parental swap to save these children from such abuse!*

A visit to Disney World is more than an outing or an adventure for a young child. It's a testing experience, a sort of controlled rite of passage. If you help your little one work through the challenges, the time can be immeasurably rewarding and a bonding experience for you both.

THE FRIGHT FACTOR

WHILE EACH YOUNGSTER IS DIFFERENT, following are seven attraction elements that alone or combined could push a child's buttons and indicate that a certain attraction isn't age appropriate for that child:

1. NAME OF THE ATTRACTION Young children will naturally be apprehensive about something called The Haunted Mansion or Tower of Terror.

2. VISUAL IMPACT OF THE ATTRACTION FROM OUTSIDE Splash Mountain, the Tower of Terror, and Big Thunder Mountain Railroad look scary enough to give adults second thoughts, and they terrify many young children.

3. VISUAL IMPACT OF THE INDOOR-QUEUING AREA Pirates of the Caribbean's caves and dungeons and The Haunted Mansion's "stretch rooms" can frighten children.

Continued on page 332

Small-child Fright-potential Chart

This is a quick reference to identify attractions to be wary of, and why. The chart represents a generalization, and all kids are different. It relates specifically to kids ages 3 to 7. On average, children at the younger end of the range are more likely to be frightened than children in their sixth or seventh year.

Magic Kingdom

MAIN STREET, U.S.A.

Main Street Vehicles Not frightening in any respect.

Walt Disney World Railroad Not frightening in any respect.

ADVENTURELAND

Enchanted Tiki Room A thunderstorm, loud volume level, and simulated explosions frighten some preschoolers.

Jungle Cruise Moderately intense, some macabre sights. A good test attraction for little ones.

Pirates of the Caribbean Slightly intimidating queuing area; intense boat ride with gruesome (though humorously presented) sights and a short, unexpected slide down a flume.

The Magic Carpets of Aladdin Much like Dumbo. A favorite of young children.

Swiss Family Treehouse May not be suitable for kids who are afraid of heights.

FRONTIERLAND

Big Thunder Mountain Railroad Visually intimidating from outside, with moderately intense visual effects. The roller coaster is wild enough to frighten many adults, particularly seniors. Switching-off option provided (see page 339).

Country Bear Jamboree Not frightening in any respect.

Frontierland Shootin' Arcade Not frightening in any respect.

Splash Mountain Visually intimidating from outside, with moderately intense visual effects. The ride, culminating in a 52-foot plunge down a steep chute, is somewhat hair-raising for all ages. Switching-off option provided (see page 339).

Tom Sawyer Island Some very young children are intimidated by dark walk-through tunnels that can be easily avoided.

LIBERTY SQUARE

The Hall of Presidents Not frightening, but boring for young ones.

The Haunted Mansion Name raises anxiety, as do sounds and sights of waiting area. Intense attraction with humorously presented macabre sights. The ride itself is gentle.

Liberty Belle Riverboat Not frightening in any respect.

FANTASYLAND

Cinderella's Golden Carousel Not frightening in any respect.

Dumbo the Flying Elephant A tame midway ride; a great favorite of most young children.

It's a Small World Not frightening in any respect.

Mad Tea Party Midway-type ride can induce motion sickness in all ages.

The Many Adventures of Winnie the Pooh Frightens a small percentage of preschoolers.

Peter Pan's Flight Not frightening in any respect.

Snow White's Scary Adventures Moderately intense spook-house-genre attraction with some grim characters. Absolutely terrifies many preschoolers.

MICKEY'S TOONTOWN FAIR

All attractions except roller coaster Not frightening in any respect.

The Barnstormer at Goofy's Wiseacres Farm *(children's roller coaster)* May frighten some preschoolers.

TOMORROWLAND

Astro Orbiter Visually intimidating from the waiting area, but the ride is relatively tame.

Buzz Lightyear's Space Ranger Spin Dark ride with cartoonlike aliens may frighten some preschoolers.

Monsters, Inc. Laugh Floor May frighten a small percentage of preschoolers.

Space Mountain Very intense roller coaster in the dark; the Magic Kingdom's wildest ride and a scary roller coaster by any standard. Switching-off option provided (see page 339).

Stitch's Great Escape! Very intense. May frighten children age 9 and younger. Switching-off option provided (see page 339).

Tomorrowland Speedway Noise of waiting area slightly intimidates preschoolers; otherwise, not frightening.

Tomorrowland Transit Authority Not frightening in any respect.

Walt Disney's Carousel of Progress Not frightening in any respect.

Epcot

FUTURE WORLD

Innoventions East and West Not frightening in any respect.

Journey into Imagination—*Honey, I Shrunk the Audience* Extremely intense visual effects and loudness frighten many young children.

Journey into Imagination with Figment Loud noises and unexpected flashing lights startle younger children.

The Land—*Circle of Life* Theater Not frightening in any respect.

The Land—Living with the Land Not frightening in any respect.

The Land—Soarin' May frighten children age 7 and younger. Really a very mellow ride.

Mission: Space Extremely intense space-simulation ride that has been known to frighten guests of all ages. Preshow may also frighten some children. Switching-off option provided (see page 339).

The Seas—The Seas with Nemo & Friends Very sweet but may frighten some toddlers.

The Seas—Sea Base Alpha Exhibits Not frightening in any respect.

The Seas—*Turtle Talk with Crush* Not frightening in any respect.

Spaceship Earth Dark, imposing presentation intimidates a few preschoolers.

Test Track Intense thrill ride may frighten any age. Switching-off option provided (see page 339).

Small-child Fright-potential Chart (cont'd)

Epcot (continued)

FUTURE WORLD (CONTINUED)

Universe of Energy Dinosaur segment frightens some preschoolers; visually intense, with some intimidating effects.

WORLD SHOWCASE

The American Adventure Not frightening in any respect.

Canada–*O Canada!* Not frightening in any respect, but audience must stand.

China–*Reflections of China* Not frightening in any respect.

France–*Impressions de France* Not frightening in any respect.

Germany Not frightening in any respect.

Italy Not frightening in any respect.

Japan Not frightening in any respect.

Mexico–Gran Fiesta Tour Not frightening in any respect.

Morocco Not frightening in any respect.

Norway–Maelstrom Visually intense in parts. Ride ends with a plunge down a 20-foot flume. A few preschoolers are frightened.

United Kingdom Not frightening in any respect.

Disney's Hollywood Studios

The American Idol Experience At times, the singing may frighten anyone.

Backstage Walking Tours Not frightening in any respect.

Disney's Hollywood Studios Backlot Tour Sedate and nonintimidating except for Catastrophe Canyon, where an earthquake and a flash flood are simulated. Prepare younger children for this part of the tour.

Fantasmic! Terrifies some preschoolers.

The Great Movie Ride Intense in parts, with very realistic special effects and some visually intimidating sights. Frightens many preschoolers.

Honey, I Shrunk the Kids Movie Set Adventure Not scary (though oversized).

Indiana Jones Epic Stunt Spectacular An intense show with powerful special effects, including explosions, but young children generally handle it well.

Jim Henson's Muppet-Vision 3-D Intense and loud, but not frightening.

Lights! Motors! Action! Extreme Stunt Show Super stunt spectacular; intense with loud noises and explosions, but not threatening in any way.

The Magic of Disney Animation Not frightening in any respect.

Playhouse Disney: Live on Stage Not frightening in any respect.

Continued from page 329

4. INTENSITY OF THE ATTRACTION Some attractions are overwhelming, inundating the senses with sights, sounds, movement, and even smell. Epcot's *Honey, I Shrunk the Audience,* for example, combines loud sounds, lasers, lights, and 3-D cinematography to create a total sensory experience. For some preschoolers, this is two or three senses too many.

Rock 'n' Roller Coaster The wildest coaster at Walt Disney World. May frighten guests of any age. Switching-off option provided (see page 339).

Sounds Dangerous Noises in the dark frighten children as old as 8.

Star Tours Extremely intense visually for all ages. Switching-off option provided (see page 339).

***Toy Story* Mania!** Dark ride may frighten some preschoolers.

***The Twilight Zone* Tower of Terror** Visually intimidating to young children; contains intense and realistic special effects. The plummeting elevator at the ride's end frightens many adults as well as kids. Switching-off option provided (see page 339).

Voyage of the Little Mermaid Not frightening in any respect.

Walt Disney: One Man's Dream Not frightening in any respect.

Animal Kingdom

The Boneyard Not frightening in any respect.

Dinosaur High-tech thrill ride rattles riders of all ages. Switching-off option provided (see page 339).

Expedition Everest Frightening to guests of all ages.

Festival of the Lion King A bit loud, but otherwise not frightening in any respect.

Finding Nemo: The Musical Not frightening in any respect, but loud.

Flights of Wonder Swooping birds alarm a few small children.

It's Tough to Be a Bug! Very intense and loud with special effects that startle viewers of all ages and potentially terrify young children.

Kali River Rapids Potentially frightening and certainly wet for guests of all ages. Switching-off option provided (see page 339).

Kilimanjaro Safaris A "collapsing" bridge and the proximity of real animals make a few young children anxious.

Maharaja Jungle Trek Some children may balk at the bat exhibit.

The Oasis Not frightening in any respect.

Pangani Forest Exploration Trail Not frightening in any respect.

Primeval Whirl A beginner roller coaster. Most children age 7 and older will take it in stride.

Rafiki's Planet Watch Not frightening in any respect.

TriceraTop Spin A midway-type ride that will frighten only a small percentage of younger children.

Wildlife Express Train Not frightening in any respect.

5. VISUAL IMPACT OF THE ATTRACTION Sights in various attractions range from falling boulders to lurking buzzards, from grazing dinosaurs to waltzing ghosts. What one child calmly absorbs may scare the bejeepers out of another the same age.

6. DARK Many Disney World attractions operate indoors in the dark. For some children, this triggers fear. A child who gets frightened on one dark ride (Snow White's Scary Adventures, for example) may be unwilling to try other indoor rides.

7. THE TACTILE EXPERIENCE OF THE RIDE Some rides are wild enough to cause motion sickness, wrench backs, and discombobulate guests of any age.

As a footnote to the preceding, be aware that gaining the courage and confidence in regard to the attractions is not necessarily an upwardly linear process. A dad from Maryland explains:

As a 4-year-old, my daughter absolutely adored The Haunted Mansion. At 5 she was scared to death on it! At 6 she was fine again. Just because a child loves a ride at one age does not mean that he or she will love it on the next trip. The terror curve can go in either direction. (And then back again.)

A BIT OF PREPARATION

WE RECEIVE MANY TIPS FROM PARENTS telling how they prepared their young children for the Disney experience. A common strategy is to acquaint children with the characters and stories behind the attractions by reading Disney books and watching Disney videos at home. A more direct approach is to watch Walt Disney World travel videos that show the attractions. Of the latter, a father from Arlington, Virginia, reports:

My kids both loved The Haunted Mansion, with appropriate preparation. We rented a tape before going so they could see it, and then I told them it was all "Mickey Mouse Magic" and that Mickey was just "joking you," to put it in their terms, and that there weren't any real ghosts, and that Mickey wouldn't let anyone actually get hurt.

A Lexington, Kentucky, mom reports:

We watched every ride and show on YouTube before going so my timid 7-year-old daughter would be prepared ahead of time, and we cut out all the ones that looked too scary to her. She still did not like, and cried at, Honey, I Shrunk the Audience *and also disliked* It's Tough to Be a Bug! [Ellen's] Energy Adventure *made her tense up, but she loved, loved, loved Kali River Rapids.*

A Gloucester, Massachusetts, mom solved the problem on the spot:

The 3½-year-old liked It's a Small World [but] *was afraid of The Haunted Mansion. We just pulled his hat over his face and quietly talked to him while we enjoyed* [the ride].

If your video store doesn't rent Disney travel videos, you can order the free **Walt Disney World Vacation Planning Kit** and video/DVD by calling Disney reservations at ☎ 407-824-8000. Ignore all prompts, and the phone system will assume you're on a rotary phone and patch you through to a live person. This video/DVD isn't as comprehensive as travelogues you might rent, but it's adequate for giving your kids a sense of what they'll see. You can also ask for information on lodging, restaurants, etc. Allow at least one month for delivery. You can also log on to **disneyworld.disney.go.com/wdw/myVacation** and click on "Vacation Planning Kit" to order online or view. *Note:* Because Disney is in a cost-containment fit, it's possible that the video/DVD may be discontinued.

Not everything at Disney World is covered in the video/DVD, but you can find most of what's missing at **YouTube** (see previous page).

ATTRACTIONS THAT EAT ADULTS

YOU MAY SPEND SO MUCH ENERGY worrying about Junior that you forget to take care of yourself. If the motion of a ride is potentially disturbing, persons of any age may be affected. The attractions below can cause motion sickness or other problems for older kids and adults:

POTENTIALLY PROBLEMATIC ATTRACTIONS FOR GROWN-UPS

MAGIC KINGDOM	Fantasyland: **Mad Tea Party**
	Frontierland: **Big Thunder Mountain Railroad**
	Frontierland: **Splash Mountain**
	Tomorrowland: **Space Mountain**
EPCOT	Future World: **Mission Space**
	Future World: **Test Track**
DISNEY'S HOLLYWOOD STUDIOS	**Rock 'n' Roller Coaster**
	Star Tours
	***The Twilight Zone* Tower of Terror**
ANIMAL KINGDOM	**Dinosaur**
	Expedition Everest
	Kali River Rapids

A WORD ABOUT HEIGHT REQUIREMENTS

A NUMBER OF ATTRACTIONS REQUIRE children to meet minimum height and age requirements. If you have children too short or too young to ride, you have several options, including switching off (see page 339). Although the alternatives may resolve some practical and logistical issues, your smaller children may nonetheless be resentful of their older (or taller) siblings who qualify to ride. A mom from Virginia writes of such a situation:

> *You mention height requirements for rides but not the intense sibling jealousy this can generate. Frontierland was a real problem in that respect. Our very petite 5-year-old, to her outrage, was stuck hanging around while our 8-year-old went on Splash Mountain and* [Big] *Thunder Mountain with* [her] *grandma and granddad, and the nearby alternatives weren't helpful (too long a line for rafts to Tom Sawyer Island, etc.). If we had thought ahead, we would have left the younger kid back in Mickey's Toontown fair with one of the grown-ups for another roller-coaster ride or two and then met up later. . . . The best areas had a playground or other quick attractions for short people near the rides with height requirements, like The Boneyard near the Dinosaur ride at Animal Kingdom.*

The reader makes a point, though splitting the group and meeting later can be more complicated than she imagines. If you split up, ask the Disney attendant (called a greeter) at the entrance to the attraction(s) with height requirements how long the wait is. If you tack five minutes for riding onto the anticipated wait and add five or so minutes to exit and reach the meeting point, you'll have a sense of how

Attraction and Ride Restrictions

MAGIC KINGDOM	
The Barnstormer at Goofy's Wiseacres Farm	35" minimum height
Big Thunder Mountain Railroad	40" minimum height
Mickey's Toontown Fair playground attractions	40" maximum height
Space Mountain	44" minimum height
Splash Mountain	40" minimum height
Stitch's Great Escape!	40" minimum height
Tomorrowland Speedway	54" minimum height (to drive unassisted)
EPCOT	
Mission: Space	44" minimum height
Soarin'	40" minimum height
Test Track	40" minimum height
DISNEY'S HOLLYWOOD STUDIOS	
Honey, I Shrunk the Kids Movie Set Adventure	4 years minimum age
Rock 'n' Roller Coaster	48" minimum height
Star Tours	40" minimum height
The Twilight Zone Tower of Terror	40" minimum height
ANIMAL KINGDOM	
Dinosaur	40" minimum height
Expedition Everest	44" minimum height
Kali River Rapids	38" minimum height

long the younger kids (and their supervising adult) will have to do other stuff. Our guess is that even with a long line for the rafts, the reader would have had sufficient time to take her daughter to Tom Sawyer Island while the sibs rode Splash Mountain and Big Thunder Mountain with the grandparents. For sure, she had time to tour the Swiss Family Treehouse in adjacent Adventureland. (For more info, see the chart above.)

WAITING-LINE STRATEGIES *for* ADULTS *with* YOUNG CHILDREN

CHILDREN HOLD UP BETTER through the day if you limit the time they spend in lines. Arriving early and using our touring plans greatly reduce waiting. Here are other ways to reduce stress for children:

1. LINE GAMES Anticipate that children will get restless in line, and plan activities to reduce the stress and boredom. In the morning, have waiting

ANIMAL KINGDOM *(CONTINUED)*	
Primeval Whirl	48" minimum height
BLIZZARD BEACH WATER PARK	
Chair Lift	32" minimum height
Downhill Double Dipper slide	48" minimum height
Slush Gusher slide	48" minimum height
Summit Plummet slide	48" minimum height
T-Bar (in Ski Patrol Training Camp)	48" maximum height
Tike's Peak children's area	48" maximum height
TYPHOON LAGOON WATER PARK	
Bay Slides	60" minimum height
Crush 'n' Gusher	48" minimum height
Humunga Kowabunga slide	48" minimum height
Ketchakiddee Creek children's area	48" maximum height
Mayday Falls raft ride	48" minimum height
Shark Reef saltwater reef swim	10 years minimum age unless accompanied by an adult
Wave Pool	Adult supervision required
DISNEYQUEST	
Buzz Lightyear's AstroBlasters	51" minimum height
CyberSpace Mountain	51" minimum height
Mighty Ducks Pinball Slam	48" minimum height

children discuss what they want to see and do during the day. Later, watch for and count Disney characters or play simple games such as 20 Questions. Lines move continuously; games requiring pen and paper are impractical. Waiting in the holding area of a theater attraction is a different story. Here, tic-tac-toe, hangman, drawing, and coloring make the time fly.

A Springfield, Ohio, mom reports on an unexpected but welcome assist from her brother:

I have a bachelor brother who joined my 5-, 7-, and 9-year-olds and me for vacation. Pat surprised all of us with a bunch of plastic animal noses he had in his hip pack. When the kids got restless or cranky in line, he'd turn away and pull out a pig nose or a parrot nose or something. When he turned back around with the nose on, the kids would majorly crack up. The other people in line thought he was nuts, but he restored my kids' good humor more times than I can count.

2. LAST-MINUTE ENTRY If an attraction can accommodate many people at once, standing in line is often unnecessary. The Magic Kingdom's

ATTRACTIONS YOU CAN USUALLY ENTER AT THE LAST MINUTE

Magic Kingdom	
Liberty Square	*The Hall of Presidents*
	Liberty Belle Riverboat
Tomorrowland	*Walt Disney's Carousel of Progress*
Epcot	
Future World	*The Circle of Life* (except during mealtimes)
World Showcase	*The American Adventure*
	O Canada!
	Reflections of China
Disney's Hollywood Studios	Backlot Tour
	Sounds Dangerous
Animal Kingdom	*Flights of Wonder*

Liberty Belle Riverboat is an example. The boat holds about 450 people, usually more guests than are waiting in line. Instead of standing in a crowd, grab a snack and sit in the shade until the boat arrives and loading is under way. When the line is almost gone, join it.

At large-capacity theaters like the one for Epcot's *The American Adventure,* ask the greeter how long it will be until guests are admitted for the next show. If it's 15 minutes or more, take a toilet break or get a snack, returning a few minutes before showtime. Food and drink aren't allowed in the attraction; be sure you have time to finish your snack before entering.

3. THE HAIL-MARY PASS Certain lines (see chart below) are configured to allow you and your smaller children to pass under the rail to join your partner just before entry or boarding. This technique allows children and one adult to rest, snack, cool off, or potty while another adult or older sibling stands in line. Other guests are understanding about this

ATTRACTIONS WHERE YOU CAN USUALLY COMPLETE A HAIL-MARY PASS

Magic Kingdom	
Adventureland	Swiss Family Treehouse
Frontierland	*Country Bear Jamboree*
Fantasyland	Cinderella's Golden Carousel
	Dumbo the Flying Elephant
	Mad Tea Party
	Peter Pan's Flight
	Snow White's Scary Adventures
Epcot	
Future World	Living with the Land
	Spaceship Earth
Disney's Hollywood Studios	*Indiana Jones Epic Stunt Spectacular*
	Sounds Dangerous
Animal Kingdom	
DinoLand U.S.A.	TriceraTop Spin

strategy when used for young children. Expect opposition, however, if you try to pass older children or more than one adult under the rail.

4. SWITCHING OFF (AKA THE BABY SWAP) Several attractions have minimum height and/or age requirements. Some couples with children too small or too young forgo these attractions, while others take turns riding. Missing some of Disney's best rides is an unnecessary sacrifice, and waiting in line twice for the same ride is a tremendous waste of time.

ATTRACTIONS WHERE SWITCHING OFF IS COMMON

Magic Kingdom
Big Thunder Mountain Railroad
Space Mountain
Splash Mountain

Epcot
Mission: Space
Test Track

Disney's Hollywood Studios
Rock 'n' Roller Coaster
Star Tours
The Twilight Zone Tower of Terror

Animal Kingdom
Dinosaur
Expedition Everest
Kali River Rapids
Primeval Whirl

Instead, take advantage of the "switching off" option, also called the Baby Swap. To switch off, there must be at least two adults. Adults and children wait in line together. When you reach a cast member, say you want to switch off. The cast member will allow everyone, including young children, to enter the attraction. When you reach the loading area, one adult rides while the other stays with the kids. Then the riding adult disembarks and takes charge of the children while the other adult rides. A third adult in the party can ride twice, once with each switching-off adult, so that the switching-off adults don't have to ride alone.

On most FASTPASS attractions, Disney handles switching off somewhat differently. When you tell the cast member that you want to switch off, he or she will issue you a special "rider exchange" FASTPASS good for three people. One parent and the nonriding child (or children) will at that point be asked to leave the line. When those riding reunite with the waiting adult, the waiting adult and two other persons from the party can ride using the special FASTPASS. This system eliminates confusion and congestion at the boarding area while sparing the nonriding adult and child the tedium and physical exertion of waiting in line.

Attractions where switching off is practiced are oriented to more-mature guests. Sometimes it takes a lot of courage for a child just to move through the queue holding Dad's hand. In the boarding area, many children suddenly fear abandonment when one parent leaves to ride. Prepare your children for switching off, or you might have an emotional crisis on your hands. A mom from Edison, New Jersey, writes:

> *Once my son came to understand that the switch-off would not leave him abandoned, he did not seem to mind. I would recommend to your readers that they practice the switch-off on some dry runs at home, so that their child is not concerned that he will be left behind. At the very least, the procedure could be explained in advance so that the little ones know what to expect.*

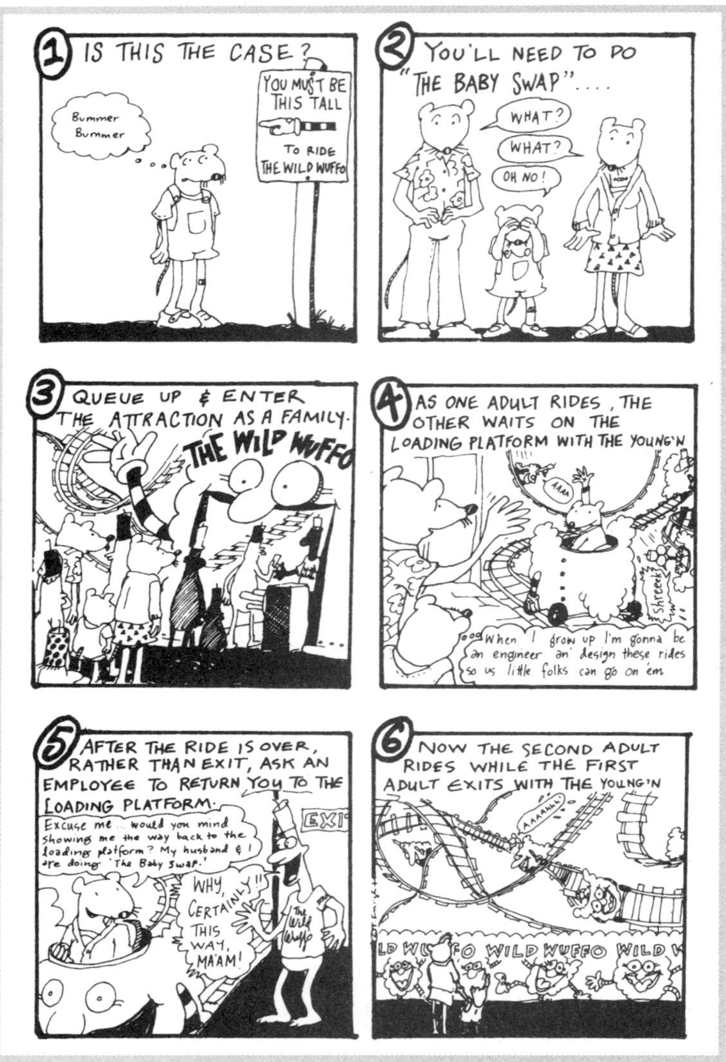

An Ada, Michigan, mother discovered that the switching-off procedure varies among attractions. She says:

> *Parents need to tell the very first attendant they come to that they would like to switch off. Each attraction has a different procedure for this. Tell every other attendant too because they forget quickly.*

An Elkhart, Indiana, mom who missed notifying the first cast member (greeter) had the following experience:

> *We had tried to do the swap on The Haunted Mansion. My 5-year-old son did not want to ride, so we told him that one of us would stay with him while the others rode. We did not have an opportunity to talk to a cast member during the* [wait in] *line. When I checked at*

the boarding area, they said that once you are on the conveyor belt, you MUST ride. My son was so angry that we had "tricked" him that he brought it up over and over during the next few days.

5. HOW TO RIDE TWICE IN A ROW WITHOUT WAITING Many young children like to ride a favorite attraction two or more times in succession. Riding the second time often gives them a feeling of mastery and accomplishment. Unfortunately, even in early morning, repeat rides can eat time. If you ride Dumbo as soon as the Magic Kingdom opens, for instance, you will wait only a minute or two for your first ride. When you return for your second, the wait will be about 12 to 15 minutes. For a third, count on 20 minutes or longer.

The best way to get your child on the ride twice (or more) without blowing your morning is to use the "Chuck Bubba Relay" (named in honor of a Kentucky reader):

a. Mom and little Bubba enter the waiting line.
b. Dad lets a specific number of people go in front of him (24 at Dumbo), then gets in line.
c. As soon as the ride stops, Mom exits with Bubba and passes him to Dad to ride the second time.
d. If everybody is really getting into this, Mom can hop in line again, at least 24 people behind Dad.

The Chuck Bubba Relay won't work on every ride, because waiting areas are configured differently (that is, it's impossible in some cases to exit the ride and make the pass). For those rides where the relay works, here are how many people to count off:

MAGIC KINGDOM

Mad Tea Party 53	Snow White's Scary Adventures 52
Dumbo the Flying Elephant 24	Cinderella's Golden Carousel 75
Peter Pan's Flight 64	The Magic Carpets of Aladdin 48

ANIMAL KINGDOM TriceraTop Spin 56

If you're the relay's second adult, you'll reach a place in line where it's easiest to make the handoff. This may be where those exiting the ride pass closest to those waiting to board. You'll know it when you see it. If you reach it and the first parent hasn't arrived with Bubba, let those behind you pass until Bubba shows up.

6. LAST-MINUTE COLD FEET If your young child gets cold feet just before boarding a ride where there's no age or height requirement, you usually can arrange a switch-off with the loading attendant. This is a common occurrence after experiencing Pirates of the Caribbean's dungeon waiting area.

No law says you have to ride. If you reach the boarding area and someone is unhappy, tell an attendant you've changed your mind, and you'll be shown the way out.

An apparent exception to this rule was reported by an Elkhart, Indiana, mother of a 7-year-old girl:

While in an extremely long wait for the Tower of Terror, my 7-year-old daughter needed URGENTLY to use the restroom. We were within sight of the loading area and knew we couldn't go back the way we came. We "excuse me'd" our way to the loading area, telling the people we were passing that we had a nonrider coming through. When I asked the attendant how to exit without riding, we were told that there was no other way out. Even when we told them that she was afraid that she was going to pee her pants on the ride, they still said the only way out was to ride. She did ride (since they told her she had no choice) and, amazingly, did not pee her pants. As soon as we were off the ride, we ran for the restroom.

The reader's experience underscores the importance of emptying one's bladder before getting in a long queue.

7. THROW YOURSELF ON THE GRENADE, MILDRED! For conscientious parents who are determined to sacrifice themselves on behalf of their children, we provide a Magic Kingdom One-day Touring Plan called the Dumbo-or-Die-in-a-Day Touring Plan for Parents with Small Children. This plan (see page 818) will ensure that you run yourself ragged. Designed to help you forfeit everything of personal interest for your children's pleasure, the plan guarantees you will go home battered and exhausted, with extraordinary stories of devotion and perseverance. By the way, it really works. Anyone under age 8 will love it.

The DISNEY CHARACTERS

THE LARGE AND FRIENDLY COSTUMED versions of Mickey, Minnie, Donald, Goofy, and others—known as Disney characters—provide a link between Disney animated films and the theme parks. To people emotionally invested, the characters in Disney films are as real as next-door neighbors, never mind that they're drawings on plastic. In recent years, theme-park personifications of the characters also have become real to us. It's not a person in a mouse costume; it's Mickey himself. Similarly, meeting Goofy or Snow White is an encounter with a celebrity, a memory to be treasured.

> *unofficial* **TIP**
> **Don't underestimate your child's excitement at meeting the Disney characters—but also be aware that very small children may find the large costumed characters a little frightening.**

While Disney animated-film characters number in the hundreds, only about 250 have been brought to life in costume. Of these, fewer than a fifth are "greeters" (characters who mix with patrons); the others perform in shows or parades. Originally confined to the Magic Kingdom, characters are now found in all major theme parks and Disney hotels.

CHARACTER WATCHING Watching characters has become a pastime. Families once were content to meet a character occasionally. They now pursue them relentlessly, armed with autograph books and cameras. Because some characters are only rarely seen, character watching has become character collecting. (To cash in on character collecting, Disney sells autograph books throughout the World.) Mickey, Minnie, and Goofy are a snap to bag; they seem to be everywhere. But some characters, like Tinker Bell and Jiminy Cricket, seldom come out, and quite a few appear only in parades or stage shows. Other characters appear only in a location consistent with their starring role. Cinderella, predictably, reigns at Cinderella Castle in Fantasyland, while Br'er Fox and Br'er Bear frolic in Frontierland near Splash Mountain.

A Brooklyn dad complains that character collecting has gotten out of hand:

> *Whoever started the practice of collecting autographs from the characters should be subjected to water torture! We went to WDW 11 years ago with an 8-year-old and an 11-year-old. We would bump into characters, take pictures, and that was it. After a while, our children noticed that some of the other children were getting autographs. We managed to avoid joining in during our first day at the Magic Kingdom and our first day at Epcot, but by day three our children were collecting autographs. But it did not get too out of hand, since it was limited to accidental character meeting.*
>
> *This year, when we took our youngest child (who is now 8 years old), he had already seen his siblings' collection and was determined to outdo them. However, rather than random meetings, the characters are now available practically all day long at different locations, according to a printed schedule, which our son was old enough to read. We spent more time standing in line for autographs than we did for the most popular rides!*

A family from Birmingham, Alabama, found some benefit in their children's pursuit of characters:

> *We had no idea we would be caught up in this madness, but after my daughters grabbed your guidebook to get Pocahontas to sign it (we had no blank paper), we quickly bought a Disney autograph book and gave*

in. It was actually the highlight of their trip, and my son even got into the act by helping get places in line for his sisters. They LOVED looking for characters (I think it has all been planned by Kodak to sell film). The possibility of seeing a new character revived my 7-year-old's energy on many occasions. It was an amazing, totally unexpected part of our visit.

PREPARING YOUR CHILDREN TO MEET THE CHARACTERS Almost all characters are quite large, and several, like Br'er Bear, are huge! Small children don't expect this, and preschoolers especially can be intimidated.

Discuss the characters with your children before you go. On first encounter, don't thrust your child at the character. Allow the little one to deal with this big thing from whatever distance feels safe. If two adults are present, one should stay near the youngster while the other approaches the character and demonstrates that it's safe and friendly. Some kids warm to the characters immediately; some never do. Most take a little time and several encounters.

There are two kinds of characters: "furs,"or those whose costumes include face-covering headpieces (including animal characters and such humanlike characters as Captain Hook), and "face characters," those for whom no mask or headpiece is necessary. These include Mary Poppins, Ariel, Jasmine, Aladdin, Cinderella, Belle, Snow White, Esmeralda, and Prince Charming.

Only face characters speak. Because cast members couldn't possibly imitate the furs' distinctive cinema voices, Disney has determined that it's more effective to keep such characters silent. Lack of speech notwithstanding, headpiece characters are warm and responsive, and they communicate effectively with gestures. Tell children in advance that these characters don't talk.

Some character costumes are cumbersome and give cast members very poor visibility. (Eyeholes frequently are in the mouth of the costume or even on the neck or chest.) Children who approach the character from the back or side may not be noticed, even if the child touches the character. It's possible in this situation for the character to accidentally step on the child or knock him down. A child should approach a character from the front, but occasionally not even this works. Duck characters (Donald, Daisy, Uncle Scrooge), for example, have to peer around their bills. If a character appears to be ignoring your child, pick up your child and hold her in front of the character until the character responds.

It's OK for your child to touch, pat, or hug the character. Understanding the unpredictability of children, the character will keep his feet still, particularly refraining from moving backward or sideways. Most characters will pose for pictures or sign autographs. Costumes make it difficult for characters to wield a normal pen. If your child collects autographs, carry a pen the width of a Magic Marker.

THE BIG HURT Many children expect to meet Mickey the minute they enter the park and are disappointed if they don't. If your children can't enjoy things until they see Mickey, ask a cast member where to find him. If the cast member doesn't know, he or she can phone to learn exactly where characters are.

"THEN SOME CONFUSION HAPPENED" Children sometimes become lost at character encounters. Usually, there's a lot of activity around a character, with both adults and children touching it or posing for pictures. Most commonly, Mom and Dad stay in the crowd while Junior approaches the character. In the excitement and with the character moving around, Junior heads in the wrong direction to look for Mom and Dad. In the words of a Salt Lake City mom: "Milo was shaking hands with Dopey one minute, then some confusion happened and [Milo] was gone."

Families with several young children, and parents who are busy with cameras, can lose a youngster in a heartbeat. We recommend that parents with preschoolers stay with them when they meet characters, stepping back only to take a quick picture.

unofficial **TIP**
If you're using a touring plan and get interrupted, simply skip one step in the plan for every 15 minutes you're delayed, and continue on. Really, it's no big deal.

CHARACTER HOGS While we're on the subject of cameras, give other families a chance. Especially if you're shooting video, consider the perspective of this Houston mom:

> *One of the worst parts to deal with are the people with movie cameras who take about three minutes filming their child with Mickey, asking everyone else to move. A 35-millimeter camera takes about two seconds.*

PLANNUS INTERRUPTUS An admittedly type-A mom from eastern Tennessee was done in by (who else?) Chicken Little:

> *Please caution overplanning parents like me that character meet-and-greets can wreak havoc with the best-laid plans! We were at* [Disney's Hollywood Studios] *on my husband's birthday, and our 5-year-old just couldn't pass up Chicken Little and Abbey at the entrance, and Daisy Duck at the Magic Hat. Well, now we were off schedule, and there was no line at the Great Movie Ride beside us, so we rode that. Now we were drifting further and further from the plan. By afternoon, it seems all the adult shows hubby wanted to see were at EXACTLY the same times as the* Little Mermaid *and* Playhouse Disney *shows! As daughter and I dissolved into tears at midday, I realized two things: (1) DO NOT go full-tilt touring for more than two days without a day off in between; and (2) if you have an* Unofficial Guide *touring plan, STICK TO IT! THEY WORK!* [reader's emphasis].

MEETING CHARACTERS FOR FREE

YOU CAN SEE DISNEY CHARACTERS IN LIVE SHOWS at all the theme parks and in parades at the Magic Kingdom and Disney's Hollywood Studios. Your daily entertainment schedule lists times. If you want to meet characters, get autographs, and take photos, consult the park map or the handout *Times Guide* sometimes provided with it. If there's a particular character you're itching to meet, ask any cast member to call the character hotline and ask if the character is out and about, and if so, where.

Disney has several initiatives intended to satisfy its guests' inexhaustible desire to meet characters. Most important, Disney assigned Mickey and a number of other characters to all-day duty in Mickey's Toontown Fair in the Magic Kingdom and

unofficial **TIP**
To find out where any character is or will be appearing, call ☎ 407-824-2222.

Camp Minnie-Mickey in Animal Kingdom. While making the characters more available has taken the guesswork out of finding them, it has robbed encounters of much of their spontaneity. To address this problem, especially at the Magic Kingdom, Disney has put a throng of characters back on the street. At park opening, there are enough characters on hand to satisfy any child's desires. If you line up at one of the permanent character-greeting venues, be aware that lines for face characters move *m-u-c-h* more slowly than do those for nonspeaking characters. Because face characters are allowed to talk, they often engage children in lengthy conversations, much to the dismay of families still in the queue.

AT THE MAGIC KINGDOM Characters are encountered more frequently here than anywhere else in Walt Disney World. A character almost always will be next to City Hall on Main Street, and there will usually be one or more in Town Square or near the railroad station.

Characters appear in all of the lands but are most plentiful in Fantasyland and Mickey's Toontown Fair. At Mickey's Toontown Fair, you can meet Mickey privately in his Judge's Tent. Characters actually work shifts at the Toontown Hall of Fame next to Mickey's Country House. Here, you can line up to meet two or three different assortments of characters. Each assortment has its own greeting area and its own line. One group, variously labeled Mickey's Pals, Toon Pals, or some such, includes characters such as Daisy Duck, Pluto, and Goofy. The other two assortments are almost always dedicated to Disney's princesses and fairies. The Fairy lineup features Tinker Bell and her friends, while the Princess crew includes Snow White, Belle, Cinderella, Jasmine, the Fairy Godmother, yadda-yadda-yadda. In Fantasyland, Cinderella regularly greets diners at Cinderella's Royal Table in the castle, and Ariel holds court in her grotto. Nearby, check out the Fantasyland Character Festival by the lagoon opposite Dumbo. Also look for characters in the central hub, by Splash Mountain in Frontierland, and by the *Carousel of Progress* in Tomorrowland.

unofficial **TIP**
If it's rainy, look for characters on the veranda of Tony's Town Square Restaurant or in the Town Square Exposition Hall next to Tony's.

Characters are featured in afternoon and evening parades and also play a major role in Castle Forecourt shows (at the castle entrance on the central-hub side). Find performance times for shows and parades in the daily entertainment schedule (*Times Guide*). Characters sometimes stay to mingle after shows.

AT EPCOT Disney at first didn't think characters would fit the more serious, educational style of Epcot. Later, characters were imported to blunt criticism that Epcot lacked warmth and humor. To integrate them thematically, new and often bizarre costumes were created, but are rarely worn these days. Goofy was seen roaming Future World in a metallic silver cape reminiscent of Buck Rogers. Mickey greeted guests at The American Adventure dressed like Ben Franklin.

Today, characters are plentiful at Epcot and usually appear in their normal garb. In Future World, one or more characters, including Mickey, Minnie, Pluto, Goofy, and Chip 'n' Dale can be found from opening until early evening at the Epcot Character Spot in Innoventions West (waits of an hour or more are not uncommon). In the World Showcase, most pavilions host a character or two. Donald trots his stuff in Mexico, while Mulan and Mushu greet guests in China. Princess Aurora, Belle, and the Beast hang out in France, and Snow White and Dopey are regulars in Germany, as are Jasmine, Aladdin, and the Genie in Morocco. Pooh and friends, Alice in Wonderland, and Mary Poppins appear in the United Kingdom, and the *Brother Bear* characters lurk around Canada. In addition, character shows are performed daily at the America Gardens Theatre in World Showcase. Check the daily entertainment schedule (*Times Guide*) for times.

Because Epcot is a more adult park than the Magic Kingdom, characters are often easier to meet. A father from Effingham, Illinois, writes:

> *Trying to get autographs and pictures with Disney characters in the Magic Kingdom was a nightmare. Every character we saw was mobbed by kids and adults. Our kids had no chance. But at Epcot and* [Disney's Hollywood Studios], *things were much better. We got autographs, pictures, and more involvement. Our kids danced with several characters and received a lot of personal attention.*

AT DISNEY'S HOLLYWOOD STUDIOS Characters are likely to turn up anywhere at the Studios but are most frequently found inside the Animation Building, along Pixar Place (leading to the soundstages), by Al's Toy Barn, at Star Tours, and on Streets of America. The main meet-and-greet area, however, is at the giant sorcerer's hat at the end of Hollywood Boulevard, where up to four characters hold court from 9 a.m. until about 1 p.m. Characters are also prominent in shows, with *Voyage of the Little Mermaid* running almost continuously and an abbreviated version of *Beauty and the Beast* performed several times daily at the Theater of the Stars. Check the daily entertainment schedule (*Times Guide*) for showtimes.

AT ANIMAL KINGDOM Camp Minnie-Mickey in Animal Kingdom is designed specifically for meeting characters. Meet Mickey, Minnie, Goofy, and Donald on designated character-greeting "trails." Elsewhere in the park, Pooh, Eeyore, Tigger, and Piglet appear at the river landing opposite Flame Tree Barbecue, and you might encounter a character or two at Rafiki's Planet Watch. Also at Camp Minnie-Mickey is a stage show featuring characters from *The Lion King*.

unofficial **TIP**
Even with Advance Reservations, expect to wait 10–20 minutes to be seated.

CHARACTER DINING

FRATERNIZING WITH CHARACTERS has become so popular that Disney offers character breakfasts, brunches, lunches, and dinners where families can dine in the presence of Mickey, Minnie, Goofy, and other costumed versions of animated celebrities. Aside from grabbing customers from Denny's and Hardee's, character meals provide a controlled setting in which young children can warm to the characters. All

Character-meal Hit Parade

	1. CINDERELLA'S ROYAL TABLE	2. AKERSHUS ROYAL BANQUET HALL	3. CHEF MICKEY'S
LOCATION	Magic Kingdom	Epcot	Contemporary
MEALS SERVED	Breakfast, lunch, dinner	Breakfast, lunch, dinner	Breakfast, dinner
CHARACTERS	Cinderella, Snow White, Belle, Jasmine (breakfast and lunch), Fairy Godmother, Suzy, and Perla (dinner)	4–6 characters chosen from Belle, Mulan, Snow White, Sleeping Beauty, Ariel, Alice, Mary Poppins, Jasmine, Pocahontas	*Breakfast:* Minnie, Mickey, Chip, Pluto, Goofy *Dinner:* Mickey, Minnie, Donald, Pluto, Goofy
SERVED	Daily	Daily	Daily
SETTING	★★★★★	★★★★	★★★
TYPE OF SERVICE	Fixed menu	Family-style and menu (all you care to eat)	Buffet
FOOD VARIETY AND QUALITY	★★★	★★★½	★★★ (breakfast) ★★★½ (dinner)
NOISE LEVEL	Quiet	Quiet	Loud
CHARACTER-TO-GUEST RATIO	1:26	1:54	1:56

	7. TUSKER HOUSE RESTAURANT	8. CAPE MAY CAFE	9. 'OHANA
LOCATION	Animal Kingdom	Beach Club	Polynesian Resort
MEAL SERVED	Breakfast	Breakfast	Breakfast
CHARACTERS	Donald, Daisy, Mickey, Goofy	Goofy, Chip, Dale, Pluto, Minnie	Lilo and Stitch, Mickey, Pluto
SERVED	Daily	Daily	Daily
SETTING	★★★	★★★	★★
TYPE OF SERVICE	Buffet	Buffet	Family-style
FOOD VARIETY AND QUALITY	★★★	★★½	★★½
NOISE LEVEL	Very loud	Moderate	Moderate
CHARACTER-TO-GUEST RATIO	1:112	1:67	1:57

meals are attended by several characters. Adult prices apply to persons age 10 or older, children's prices to kids ages 3 to 9. Children younger than age 3 eat free. For more information on character dining, call ☎ 407-WDW-DINE (939-3463).

Because character dining is very popular, you should arrange Advance Reservations as early as possible by calling ☎ 407-WDW-DINE. Advance Reservations aren't reservations, per se, only a commitment to seat you ahead of walk-in patrons at the scheduled date and time.

At very popular character meals like the breakfast at Cinderella's Royal Table, you are required to make a for-real reservation and guarantee it with a for-real deposit.

CHARACTER DINING: WHAT TO EXPECT

CHARACTER MEALS ARE BUSTLING AFFAIRS held in hotels' or theme parks' largest full-service restaurants. Character breakfasts offer a fixed menu served individually, family-style, or on a buffet.

4. THE CRYSTAL PALACE

LOCATION	Magic Kingdom
MEALS SERVED	Breakfast, lunch, dinner
CHARACTERS	Pooh, Tigger, Piglet, Eeyore
SERVED	Daily
SETTING	★★★
TYPE OF SERVICE	Buffet
FOOD VARIETY AND QUALITY	★★½ (breakfast) ★★★ (lunch and dinner)
NOISE LEVEL	Very loud
CHARACTER-TO-GUEST RATIO	1:67 (breakfast) 1:89 (lunch and dinner)

5. 1900 PARK FARE

LOCATION	Grand Floridian
MEALS SERVED	Breakfast, dinner
CHARACTERS	*Breakfast:* Mary Poppins, Alice, Mad Hatter *Dinner:* Cinderella, Prince Charming, Lady Tremaine, the two stepsisters
SERVED	Daily
SETTING	★★★
TYPE OF SERVICE	Buffet
FOOD VARIETY AND QUALITY	★★★ (breakfast) ★★★½ (dinner)
NOISE LEVEL	Moderate
CHARACTER-TO-GUEST RATIO	1:54 (breakfast) 1:44 (dinner)

6. THE GARDEN GRILL RESTAURANT

LOCATION	Epcot
MEALS SERVED	Dinner
CHARACTERS	Mickey, Chip 'n' Dale, Pluto
SERVED	Daily
SETTING	★★★★½
TYPE OF SERVICE	Family-style
FOOD VARIETY AND QUALITY	★★★½
NOISE LEVEL	Very quiet
CHARACTER-TO-GUEST RATIO	1:46

10. HOLLYWOOD & VINE

LOCATION	Disney's Hollywood Studios
MEALS SERVED	Breakfast, lunch
CHARACTERS	JoJo, Goliath, June, Leo
SERVED	Daily
SETTING	★★½
TYPE OF SERVICE	Buffet
FOOD VARIETY AND QUALITY	★★★
NOISE LEVEL	Moderate
CHARACTER-TO-GUEST RATIO	1:71

11 . GARDEN GROVE

LOCATION	Swan
MEAL SERVED	Dinner
CHARACTERS	Goofy and Pluto or Rafiki and Timon
SERVED	Saturday and Sunday
SETTING	★★★
TYPE OF SERVICE	Buffet/Menu
FOOD VARIETY AND QUALITY	★★★½
NOISE LEVEL	Moderate
CHARACTER-TO-GUEST RATIO	1:198

The typical breakfast includes scrambled eggs; bacon, sausage, and ham; hash browns; waffles or French toast; biscuits, rolls, or pastries; and fruit. With family-style service, the meal is served in large skillets or platters at your table. Seconds (or thirds) are free. Buffets offer much the same fare, but you fetch it yourself.

Character dinners range from a set menu served family-style to buffets or ordering off the menu. The character breakfast at Cinderella's Royal Table, for example, is served family-style and consists of typical breakfast fare such as scrambled eggs, bacon and sausage, and danish pastries. Character dinner buffets, such as those at 1900 Park Fare at the Grand Floridian and Chef Mickey's at the Contemporary Resort, offer separate adults' and children's serving lines. Typically, the children's buffet includes hamburgers, hot dogs, pizza, fish sticks, chicken nuggets, macaroni and cheese, and peanut-butter-and-jelly sandwiches. Selections at the adult buffet usually include prime rib or other carved meat, baked or broiled Florida seafood, pasta, chicken, an ethnic dish or two, vegetables, potatoes, and salad.

At all meals, characters circulate around the room while you eat. During your meal, each of the three to five characters present will visit your table, arriving one at a time to cuddle the kids (and sometimes the adults), pose for photos, and sign autographs. Keep autograph books (with pens) and loaded cameras handy. For the best photos, adults should sit across the table from their children. Seat the children where characters can easily reach them. If a table is against a wall, for example, adults should sit with their backs to the wall and children on the aisle.

Theresa Brown posted this great tip for getting the best photos on the independent Disney Web site **AllEars.net:**

> *We did several character meals. At first, we would only use our cameras to take pictures of our children with the characters after they had signed the autograph books and were posing with them. But after the second meal, we started snapping away as soon as the characters approached our table. We are so glad we did this, because we captured a very funny sequence of events while at 1900 Park Fare at the Grand Floridian. These candid shots tell a funny story showing the playful interaction between my sons and the characters. After that, we started snapping away at all of the character meals, and now that we're back, we see that the candid shots usually gave us better pictures than the posed ones! Of course, you want the posed pictures, but the candid ones just might end up being your favorite memories of the meals!*

At some larger restaurants, including 'Ohana at the Polynesian Resort and Chef Mickey's at the Contemporary, character meals involve impromptu parades of characters and children around the room, group singing, napkin waving, and other organized madness.

Servers don't rush you to leave after you've eaten—you can stay as long as you wish to enjoy the characters. Remember, however, that lots of eager kids and adults are waiting not so patiently to be admitted.

WHEN TO GO

ATTENDING A CHARACTER BREAKFAST usually prevents you from arriving at the theme parks in time for opening. Because early morning is best for touring and you don't want to burn daylight lingering over breakfast, we suggest:

1. Go to a character dinner or lunch instead of breakfast; it won't conflict with your touring schedule.
2. Substitute a late character breakfast for lunch. Have a light breakfast early from room service or your cooler to tide you over. Then tour the theme park for an hour or two before breaking off around 10:15 a.m. to go to the character breakfast. Make a big brunch of your character breakfast and skip lunch. You should be fueled until dinner.
3. Go on your arrival or departure day. The day you arrive and check in is usually good for a character dinner. Settle at your hotel, swim, then dine with the characters. This strategy has the added benefit of exposing your children to the characters before chance encounters

at the parks. Some children, moreover, won't settle down to enjoy the parks until they have seen Mickey. Departure day also is good for a character meal. Schedule a character breakfast on your check-out day before you head for the airport or begin your drive home.

4. Go on a rest day. If you plan to stay five or more days, you'll probably take a day or half day from touring to rest or do something else. These are perfect days for a character meal.

HOW TO CHOOSE A CHARACTER MEAL

MANY READERS ASK FOR ADVICE about character meals. This question from a Waterloo, Iowa, mom is typical:

Are all character breakfasts pretty much the same or are some better than others? How should I go about choosing one?

In fact, some *are* better, sometimes much better. When we evaluate character meals, we look for:

1. THE CHARACTERS The meals offer a diverse assortment of characters. Select a meal that features your kids' favorites. Check out our Character-meal Hit Parade chart (see previous pages) to see which characters are assigned to each meal. With the exception of 1900 Park Fare at the Grand Floridian, most restaurants stick with the same characters. Even so, check the lineup when you call to make Advance Reservations.

A mom from Michigan offers this report:

Our character meal at 1900 Park Fare was a DISASTER! Please warn other readers with younger children that if they make Advance Reservations and the characters are villains, they may want to rethink their options. We went for my daughter's 5th birthday, and she was scared to death. The Queen of Hearts chased her sobbing and screaming down the hallway. Most young children we saw at the dinner were very frightened. Captain Hook and Prince John were laid-back, but Governor Ratcliffe [from *Pocahontas*] *and the Queen were amazingly rude and intimidating.*

The villains have abdicated 1900 Park Fare in favor of more benign characters, but you never know where they might show up next. Moral? Call before making Advance Reservations and ask which characters you'll be dining with.

2. ATTENTION FROM THE CHARACTERS At all character meals, characters circulate among guests, hugging children, posing for pictures, and signing autographs. How much time a character spends with you and your children depends primarily on the ratio of characters to guests. The more characters and fewer guests, the better. Because many character-meal venues never fill to capacity, the character-to-guest ratios in our Character-meal Hit Parade chart have been adjusted to reflect an average attendance. Even so, there's quite a range. The best ratio is at Cinderella's Royal Table, where there is approximately 1 character to every 26 guests.

unofficial **TIP**
Many kids take special delight in meeting the "face characters," such as Jasmine, Aladdin, and Cinderella, who can speak to them and engage them in a way that the mute animal characters can't.

The worst ratio is at the Swan resort's Garden Grove. Here, there's only 1 character for every 198 guests. In practical terms, this means your family will get about eight times as much attention from characters at Cinderella's Royal Table as from those at Garden Grove.

A Jerseyville, Illinois, mom gives the face characters high marks:

> *Our 7-year-old daughter wanted to have dinner with Sleeping Beauty, so we scheduled a character dinner with the princesses in the Norway Pavilion. The princesses were so accessible and took their time with our child, answering questions and smiling for pictures. We would definitely recommend that to every parent. In fact, our daughter told us she "had the best day of her life," and parents want to hear that from their child.*

An Indiana mother of two relates the importance of keeping tabs on the characters:

> *For character meals, take note of which characters are there when you arrive, and mentally check them off as they visit your table. If the last one or two seem slow to arrive, seek out the "character manager" (they wear black jackets with a big Mickey hand on the back) and let him or her know ASAP. We took our daughters to the princess dinner in Norway, and Ariel—the one princess our girls really wanted to see—never showed up at our table. Just by chance the character manager happened to walk past, and when I told her Ariel had not yet come by, she said that Ariel had already left (yet all the other princesses were still mingling) and would not be returning for over an hour! This delayed our evening's plan, as we then had to wait around for Ariel's return.*

3. THE SETTING Some character meals are in exotic settings. For others, moving the event to an elementary-school cafeteria would be an improvement. Our chart rates each meal's setting with the familiar scale of zero (worst) to five (best) stars. Two restaurants, Cinderella's Royal Table in the Magic Kingdom and The Garden Grill Restaurant in the Land Pavilion at Epcot, deserve special mention. Cinderella's Royal Table is on the first and second floors of Cinderella Castle in Fantasyland, offering guests a look inside the castle. The Garden Grill is a revolving restaurant overlooking several scenes from the Living with the Land boat ride. Also at Epcot, the popular Princesses Character Breakfast is held in the castlelike Akershus Royal Banquet Hall. Though Chef Mickey's at the Contemporary Resort is rather sterile in appearance, it affords a great view of the monorail running through the hotel. Themes and settings of the remaining character-meal venues, while apparent to adults, will be lost on most children.

4. THE FOOD Although some food served at character meals is quite good, most is average (palatable but nothing to get excited about). In variety, consistency, and quality, restaurants generally do a better job with breakfast than with lunch or dinner (if served). Some restaurants offer a buffet, while others opt for "one-skillet" family-style service, in which all hot items are served from the same pot or skillet. To help you sort it out, we rate the food at each character meal in our chart using the five-star scale.

The same Texas mom quoted on the previous page also notes:

The family-style meals are much better for character dining. At the buffet, you're scared to leave your table in case you miss a character or other action.

5. THE PROGRAM Some larger restaurants stage modest performances where the characters dance, head a parade around the room, or lead songs and cheers. For some guests, these activities give the meal a celebratory air; for others, they turn what was already mayhem into absolute chaos. Either way, the antics consume time the characters could spend with families at their table.

6. NOISE If you want to eat in peace, character meals are a bad choice. That said, some are much noisier than others. Our chart gives you an idea of what to expect.

7. WHICH MEAL? Although breakfasts seem to be most popular, character lunches and dinners are usually more practical because they don't interfere with early-morning touring. During hot weather, a character lunch can be heavenly.

8. COST Dinners cost more than lunches and lunches more than breakfasts. Prices for meals (except those at Cinderella Castle) vary only about $4 from the least expensive to the most expensive restaurant. Breakfasts run $19 to $34 for adults and $11 to $23 for kids ages 3 to 9. For character lunches, expect to pay $21 to $36 for adults and $12 to $24 for kids. Dinners are $27 to $41 for adults and $18 to $26 for children. Little ones ages 2 years and younger eat free. The meals at the high end of the price range are at Cinderella's Royal Table in the Magic Kingdom and Akershus Royal Banquet Hall at Epcot. The reasons for the sky-high prices: (1) Cinderella's Royal Table is small but in great demand and (2) the prices at Cinderella's and Akershus include a set of photos of your group taken by a Disney photographer. Whereas photos at other venues are optional, at Cindy's and Akershus you don't have a say in the matter.

BOOSTING SALES OF MEMENTOS AND SOUVENIRS Usually when Disney sees a horse carrying moneybags, it rides the beast until it drops. Disney's latest scheme of bundling photos in the price of character meals at Cinderella's Royal Table extends to Akershus Royal Banquet Hall at Epcot. Adding photos of your group taken by a Disney photographer is Disney's justification for raising the price of the character meals by about 60%. Disney insists that you're getting the photos at a bargain price. This is well and good if you're in the market, but if buying photos was not in your plans, well, they gotcha. It's a matter of some conjecture how far Disney will run with this idea. Maybe next year the price will be $200 and include fanciful medieval costumes for your entire party (charges for the changing room and locker to store your street clothes not included).

9. ADVANCE RESERVATIONS Disney makes Advance Reservations for character meals 180 days before you wish to dine (Disney-resort guests can reserve 10 additional days in advance). Advance Reservations for most character meals are easy to obtain even if you call only a couple of weeks before you leave home. Breakfast and lunch at Cinderella's Royal Table are another story. To eat at Cinderella's during summer, holidays, and other peak times, you'll need our strategy (see below), as well as help from Congress and the Pope.

10. CHECKING IT TWICE Disney occasionally shuffles the characters and theme of a character meal. If your little one's heart is set on Pooh and Piglet, getting Hook and Mr. Smee is just a waste of time and money. Reconfirm all character-meal Advance Reservations three weeks or so before you leave home by calling ☎ 407-WDW-DINE.

11. "FRIENDS" For some venues, Disney has stopped specifying characters scheduled for a particular meal. Instead, they say it's a given character "and friends"—for example, "Pooh and friends," meaning Eeyore, Piglet, and Tigger, or some combination thereof, or "Mickey and friends" with some assortment chosen among Minnie, Goofy, Pluto, Donald, Daisy, Chip, and Dale.

12. THE BUM'S RUSH Most character meals are leisurely affairs, and you can usually stay as long as you want. An exception is Cinderella's Royal Table at the Magic Kingdom. Because Cindy's is in such high demand, the restaurant does everything short of pre-chewing your food to move you through, as this European mother of a 5-year-old can attest:

We dined a lot, did three character meals and a few signature restaurants, and every meal was awesome except for lunch with Cinderella in the castle. While I'd often read it wouldn't be a rushed affair, it was exactly that. We had barely sat down when the appetizers were thrown on our table, the princesses each spent just a few seconds with our daughter—almost no interaction—and the side dishes were cold. We were out of there within 40 minutes and felt very stressed. Considering the price for the meal, I cannot recommend it.

GETTING AN ADVANCE RESERVATION AT CINDERELLA'S ROYAL TABLE

CINDERELLA'S ROYAL TABLE, in Cinderella Castle in the Magic Kingdom, hosts the immensely popular character breakfast starring Cinderella and various and sundry other Disney princesses. Admittedly, the toughest character-meal ticket at Disney World is an Advance Reservation for this venue. Why? Cinderella's Royal Table is Disney's tiniest character-meal restaurant, accommodating only about 130 diners at a time. During the busiest times of year, demand so outdistances supply for this event that some Walt Disney World visitors find themselves going to unbelievable lengths to secure an Advance Reservation.

This frustrated reader from Golden, Colorado, complains:

I don't know what you have to do to get an Advance Reservation for Cinderella's Royal Table in the castle. I called Disney Dining every morning at 7 a.m., which was 5 a.m. where I live! It was like calling in to one of those radio shows where the first person to call wins a prize. Every time I finally got through, all the tables were gone. I am soooo *frustrated and mad I could spit.*

On the upside, after decades of guests complaining and beating their chests over their inability to get a table, Disney offers a lunch and dinner with the same cast of characters. These additions, along with rising prices, have made tables at Cinderella's breakfast relatively easier to get—but only during the off-season. If you're visiting Walt Disney World during summer, around a major holiday, or the like, read on.

The only way to get a table is to obtain an Advance Reservation through Disney reservations. Your best chance of getting that reservation is to call ☎ 407-WDW-DINE at 7 a.m. Eastern time, exactly 180 days before the day you want to eat at Cinderella's. (*Note:* If you're looking to reserve during a slower time of year, our research has found that you can book 80 to 85 days out; see page 435.) If you live in California and have to get up at 4 a.m. Pacific time to call, Disney couldn't give a mouse's patoot. There's no limit to the number of hoops they can make their patrons jump through if demand exceeds supply.

Here's how it works: It's 6:50 a.m. Eastern time, and all the Disney dining reservationists are warming up their computers to begin filling available seats at 7 a.m. As the clock strikes seven, Disney dining is blasted with an avalanche of calls, all trying to make Advance Reservations for most of the popular restaurants and character meals. There are more than 100 reservationists on duty, and most Advance Reservations can be assigned in two minutes or less. Thus, the coveted seats at the best restaurants go quickly, selling out as early as 7:02 a.m. on many days.

To be among the fortunate few who score an Advance Reservation during peak times, try the following: First, call on the correct morning. Use a calendar and count backward exactly 180 days from (but not including) the day you wish to dine. (The computer doesn't understand months, so you can't, for example, call on January 1 to make an Advance Reservation for July 1 because that's more than 180 days.) If you want to eat on May 1, for example, begin your 180-day *backward* count on April 30. If you count correctly, you'll find that the correct morning to call is November 2. If you don't feel like counting days, call ☎ 407-WDW-DINE and the Disney folks will calculate it for you. Call them during the afternoon, when they're less busy, about 185 days before your trip. Let them know when you'd like your Advance Reservation, and they'll tell you the morning to call.

To get a table, you must dial at almost exactly 7 a.m. Eastern time. Disney does not calibrate its clock with the correct time as determined by the U.S. Naval Observatory or the National Institute of Standards and Technology, but we conducted synchronizing tests and determined that Disney reservation-system clocks are accurate to within one to three seconds. Several Internet sites will give you the exact time. Our favorite is **www.atomictime.net,** which offers the exact time in displays that show hours, minutes, and seconds. Once the Atomic Time home page is up, click on "HTML multizone continuous" and look for the Eastern Time Zone. Using this site or your local Time of Day number from the phone directory, synchronize your watch *to the second*. About 18 to 20 seconds before 7 a.m., dial ☎ 407-WDW-DINE, waiting to dial the final *E* in *DINE* until 7 seconds before the hour.

Hang up and redial until your call is answered. When it is, you will hear one of two recorded messages:

1. "Disney World Resort. Our office is currently closed. . . . " If you get this message, hang up the instant you hear the words "Our office" and hit redial.

OR

2. You'll get a recording with a number of voice prompts. Say "reservations" as soon as possible, then "no" to indicate that you're not seeking reservations for Victoria & Albert's.

Your call will be answered momentarily by a Disney Reservations Center (DRC) agent. Don't get nervous if you're on hold for a bit. The worst thing you can do now is hang up and try again.

As soon as a live DRC agent comes on the line, interrupt immediately and say, "I need Cindy's breakfast [lunch], for May 1, for four people, any available time" (substituting your own breakfast or lunch dates, of course). Don't engage in "good mornings" or other pleasantries. Time is of the essence. You can apologize later to the DRC agent for your momentary rudeness if you feel the need to do so, but she already knows what's going on. Don't try to pick a specific time. Even two seconds to ask for a specific time will seriously diminish your chances of getting an Advance Reservation.

If the atomic-clock thing seems too complicated (not to mention anal), start dialing ☎ 407-WDW-DINE about 50 seconds before 7 a.m. If the reservation center isn't open yet, you'll get a recorded message saying so. When this happens, hang up and call back immediately. If you have a redial button on your phone, use it to speed the dialing process. Continue hanging up and redialing as fast as you can until you get the recording with the prompts. This recording verifies that your call has been placed in the service queue in the order in which it was received. If you were among the first to get through, a reservationist will normally pick up in 3 to 20 seconds. What happens next depends on how many others got through ahead of you, but chances are good that you'll be able to get an Advance Reservation. Bear in mind that while you're talking, other agents are confirming Advance Reservations for other guests, so you want the transaction to go down as fast as possible. Flexibility on your part counts. It's much harder to get a seating for a large group, so give some thought to breaking your group into numbers that can be accommodated at tables for four.

All Advance Reservations for Cinderella's Royal Table character meals require complete prepayment with a credit card at the time of the booking. The name on the booking can't be changed after the Advance Reservation is made. Advance Reservations may be canceled with the deposit refunded in full by calling ☎ 407-WDW-DINE at least 24 hours before the seating time.

While many readers have been successful using our strategies, some have not:

> [Regarding] *reservations for breakfast at Cinderella Castle, I did exactly what you suggested, five days in a row, and was unable to get*

through to an actual person until after 7:15 each day (although I was connected and put on hold at exactly 7 a.m. each time). Of course, by then, all reservations were gone.

On most days, a couple hundred calls slam Disney's automated call-queuing system within milliseconds of one another. With this call volume, a 20th of a second or less can make the difference between getting a table and not getting one. As it happens, there are variables beyond your control. When you hit the first digit of a long-distance number, your phone system leaps into action. As you continue entering digits, your phone system is already searching for the best path to the number you're calling. According to federal regulation, a phone system must connect the call to the target number within 20 seconds of your entering the last digit. In practice, most systems make the connection much faster, but your system could be pokey. How fast your call is connected, therefore, depends on your local phone system's connection speed, and even this varies according to traffic volume and available routing paths for individual calls. Distance counts too, though we're talking milliseconds. Thus, it takes just a bit longer for a call to reach Disney World from Chicago than from Atlanta, and longer yet if you're calling from San Francisco.

So, if you're having trouble getting an Advance Reservation at Cinderella's Royal Table (or any other popular restaurant) using the strategies outlined earlier, here are our suggestions. Make a test call to ☎ 407-WDW-DINE at 7 a.m. EST a couple of days before you call in earnest. Using a stopwatch or the stopwatch function on your watch, time the interval between entering the last digit of the number and when the phone starts to ring. This exercise will provide a rough approximation of the call connection speed at that time from your area, taking into account both speed of service and distance. For most of you, the connection interval will be very short. Some of you, however, might discover that your problem in getting through is because of slow service. Either way, factor in the connection interval in timing your call to Disney. Phone traffic is heavier on weekdays than weekends, so if you plan to call reservations on a weekday, conduct your test on a weekday. Finally, don't use a cell phone to make the call. The connection time will usually be slower and certainly less predictable.

This is one of the most widely used sections in this guidebook, but we're amazed that anyone would go to this much trouble to eat with Cinderella. Atomic clocks, split-second timing, test calls . . . *ye gods!*

As a postscript, we've found it's often easier to get through to reservations if you call on Saturday or Sunday. Presumably, folks don't mind calling at the break of dawn if they're up getting ready for work but object to interrupting their beauty rest on weekends.

IF YOU CAN'T GET AN ADVANCE RESERVATION If you insist on a meal at Cinderella's but can't get an Advance Reservation, go to the restaurant on the day you wish to dine and try for a table as a walk-in. This is a long shot, though it's possible during the least busy times of year. There's also a fair shot at success on cold or rainy days, when there's an above-average probability of no-shows. If you try to walk in, your chances are best during the last hour of serving.

Landing an Advance Reservation for dinner is somewhat easier, but the price is a whopping $43 for adults and $27 for children ages 3 to 9. As at breakfast and lunch, five photos of your group are included in the price (like it or not), but you also receive an unframed matted lithograph that Disney claims is worth $30. If you're unable to lock up a table for breakfast or lunch, a dinner reservation will at least get your children inside the castle.

A Snellville, Georgia, mom recalls:

> *We ate* [dinner] *at Cinderella Castle to fulfill my longtime dream. The menu was very limited and expensive. For three people, no appetizers or dessert, the bill was $100.*

And no booze, either—alcohol isn't served in the Magic Kingdom.

THE CINDERELLA ALTERNATIVE A Rochester, Michigan, mother of two toddlers suggests a less stressful way to dine with Cinderella:

> *We went to the Cinderella character dinner at 1900 Park Fare. Once we did this, I stopped trying to get a last-minute reservation at Cinderella's Royal Table. My daughter loved the dinner. The decor of the restaurant was elegant and befitting Cinderella. I think you should emphasize that this is a more easily obtained alternative to Cinderella's Royal Table. It wasn't easy to get, but I was able to get a reservation only about two months in advance instead of the 180-days-and-atomic-clock routine that the Royal Table requires. Maybe someday we'll do the Royal Table, but this time my daughter was delighted with the dinner at 1900 Park Fare.*

OTHER CHARACTER EVENTS

A CAMPFIRE AND SING-ALONG ARE HELD NIGHTLY (times vary with the season) near the Meadow Trading Post and Bike Barn at Fort Wilderness Resort & Campground. Chip 'n' Dale lead the songs, and a Disney film is shown. The program is free and open to resort guests (☎ 407-824-2900). Another character encounter at Fort Wilderness is ***Mickey's Backyard BBQ,*** held seasonally on Thursday and Saturday. See page 772 for details.

BABYSITTING

CHILD-CARE CENTERS Child care isn't available inside the theme parks, but three Magic Kingdom resorts connected by monorail or boat (Polynesian, Grand Floridian, and Wilderness Lodge and Villas), four Epcot resorts (the Yacht Club and Beach Club resorts, the Swan, and the Dolphin), and Animal Kingdom Lodge, along with the Hilton at Walt Disney World, have child-care centers for potty-trained children older than age 3 (see chart on page 360). Services vary, but children generally can be left between 4:30 p.m. and midnight. Milk and cookies and blankets and pillows are provided at all centers, and dinner is provided at most. Play is supervised but not organized, and toys, videos, and games are plentiful. Guests at any Disney resort or campground may use the services.

Babysitting Services

	KID'S NITE OUT	ALL ABOUT KIDS	FAIRY GODMOTHERS
Phone / Web	☎ 407-828-0920 or 800-696-8105 www.kidsniteout.com	☎ 407-812-9300 or 800-728-6506 www.all-about-kids.com	☎ 407-277-3724 or 407-275-7326
HOTELS SERVED	All WDW and Orlando-area hotels	All WDW hotels and many outside the WDW area	All WDW hotels and those in the general WDW area
SITTERS	Men and women	Men and women	Mothers, grandmothers, women college students
MINIMUM CHARGES	4 hours	4 hours	4 hours
BASE HOURLY RATES	1 child, $16 2 children, $18.50 3 children, $21 4 children, $23.50	1 child, $13 2 children, $15 3 children, $17 4 children, $19	1 child, $16 2 children, $16 3 children, $16 4 children, $18
EXTRA CHARGES	Transportation fee, $10; starting before 6:30 a.m. or after 9 p.m., +$2 per hour; additional fee for holidays	Transportation fee, $12; starting before 7 a.m. or after 9 p.m., +$2 per hour	Transportation fee, $14; starting after 10 p.m., +$2 per hour
CANCELLATION DEADLINE	24 hours before service when reservation is made	More than 24 hours before service to avoid cancellation charge ($50 when 6–24 hours' notice is given)	3 hours before service
FORM OF PAYMENT	AE, D, MC, V; gratuity in cash	Cash or traveler's checks for actual payment; gratuity in cash; credit card to hold reservation	Cash or traveler's checks for actual payment; gratuity in cash
THINGS SITTERS WON'T DO	Transport children in private vehicle, take children swimming, give baths	Transport children	Transport children, give baths. Swimming is at sitter's discretion.

The most elaborate of the child-care centers (variously called "clubs" or "camps") is **Never Land Club** at the Polynesian Resort. The rate for ages 4 to 12 is $11 per hour, per child.

All the clubs accept reservations (some six months in advance!) with a credit-card guarantee. Call the club directly, or reserve through Disney central reservations at ☎ 407-WDW-DINE. Most clubs require a 24-hour cancellation notice and levy a hefty penalty of two hours' time or $22 per call for no-shows. A limited number of walk-ins are usually accepted on a first-come, first-served basis.

unofficial **TIP**
Child-care clubs close at or before midnight. If you intend to stay out late, in-room babysitting is your best bet.

If you're staying in a Disney resort that doesn't offer a child-care club and you *don't* have a car, you're better off using in-room babysitting. Trying to take your child to a club in another hotel by Disney bus requires a 50- to 90-minute trip each way. By the time you've deposited your little one, it will almost be time to pick him or her up again.

IN-ROOM BABYSITTING Three companies provide in-room sitting in Walt Disney World and surrounding areas, including the International Drive–Orange County Convention Center area, the Universal Orlando area, and the Lake Buena Vista area. They are **Kid's Nite Out** (run by the KinderCare chain), **All About Kids,** and **Fairy Godmothers** (no kidding). Kid's Nite Out also serves hotels in the greater Orlando area, including downtown. All three provide sitters older than age 18 who are insured,

CHILD-CARE CLUBS*

HOTEL	NAME OF PROGRAM	AGES	PHONE
Animal Kingdom Lodge	**Simba's Cubhouse**	4–12	☎ 407-938-4785
Dolphin	**Camp Dolphin**	4–12	☎ 407-934-4241
Grand Floridian Resort & Spa	**Mouseketeer Club**	4–12	☎ 407-824-2985
Hilton WDW	**All About Kids**	4–12	☎ 407-812-9300
Polynesian Resort	**Never Land Club**	4–12	☎ 407-824-1639
Swan	**Camp Dolphin**	4–12	☎ 407-934-4241
Yacht and Beach Club Resorts	**Sandcastle Club**	4–12	☎ 407-934-3750
Wilderness Lodge and Villas	**Cub's Den**	4–12	☎ 407-824-1083

Child-care clubs operate afternoons and evenings. Before 4 p.m., call the hotels rather than the numbers listed above. All programs require reservations.

bonded, and trained in CPR. Some sitters have advanced medical and first-aid training and/or education credentials. All sitters are screened, reference checked, and police checked. In addition to caring for your children in your guest room, the sitters will, if you direct (and pay), take your children to the theme parks or other venues. Many sitters arrive loaded with books and games. All three services offer bilingual sitters.

SPECIAL PROGRAMS *for* CHILDREN

SEVERAL CHILDREN'S PROGRAMS ARE AVAILABLE at Walt Disney World parks and resorts. While all are undoubtedly fun, we find them somewhat lacking in educational focus.

DISNEY'S PIRATE ADVENTURE Children ages 4 to 12 get to don bandannas, hoist the Jolly Roger, and set out on a boat trip to search for buried treasure by following a map. At the final port of call, the kids find the treasure (doubloons, beads, and rubber bugs!) and wolf down PB&J sandwiches. The treasure is split among the kids. The adventure costs $32 per child and is offered at Port Orleans (Bayou Pirate Adventure), the Grand Floridian (Pirate Adventure), the Yacht Club (Albatross Cruise), and the Caribbean Resort (Caribbean Pirate Adventure). Though the setting is different at each resort, the program is largely the same. The Grand Floridian runs the excursion every day except Sunday; the other resorts offer the program three days a week. Call ☎ 407-WDW-PLAY for days offered and other information. Boys and girls alike really love this outing—many report it as the highlight of their vacation. Parents cannot accompany kids on the outing.

DISNEY'S THE MAGIC BEHIND OUR STEAM TRAINS Kids must be age 10 or older for this three-hour tour, presented every Monday, Thursday, and Saturday. At the 7:30 a.m. start time, join the crew of the Walt Disney World Railroad as they prepare their steam locomotives for the day. Cost is $45 per person plus a valid Magic Kingdom admission. Call ☎ 407-WDW-TOUR for information and reservations.

MAGIC KINGDOM FAMILY MAGIC TOUR This is a two-and-a-half-hour guided tour of the Magic Kingdom for the entire family. Even children in strollers (no younger than age 3) are welcome. The tour combines information about the Magic Kingdom with the gathering of clues that ultimately lead the group to a character greeting at the tour's end. Definitely not for the self-conscious, the tour involves skipping, hopping, and walking sideways as you progress from land to land. There's usually a marginal plot such as saving Wendy from Captain Hook, in which case the character at the end of the tour is Wendy. You get the idea. The tour departs daily at 10 a.m. The cost is $30 per person plus a valid Magic Kingdom admission. The maximum group size is 16 persons. Reservations can be made up to one year in advance by calling ☎ 407-WDW-TOUR.

MY DISNEY GIRL'S PERFECTLY PRINCESS TEA PARTY It takes a princely sum to cover the tab on this Grand Floridian soiree, hosted by Rose Petal, "an enchanted rose who delights in storytelling and sing-alongs." Your little princess gets dressed up in her favorite regal attire and sips tea with Princess Aurora. Girls receive an 18-inch My Disney Girl doll dressed in a matching Princess Aurora gown plus accessories. Other loot includes a ribbon tiara, silver link bracelet, fresh rose, scrapbook set, and "Best Friend" certificate. A luncheon is served as well. The cost is $250 (plus tax, including gratuity) for one adult and one child ages 3 to 11; add an additional adult for $85 and additional child for $165 (plus tax). ***Note:* This event is not covered by the Disney Dining Plan.** The tea party is held every Sunday, Monday, and Wednesday through Friday from 10:30 a.m. to noon. Call ☎ 407-939-6397 for reservations and information.

A St. Louis father who sprang for the tea party reports:

> *I made this reservation based on the fabulous description at the WDW Web site. My 4-year-old daughter was greeted enthusiastically, and rose petals were sprinkled on her head when she entered the gorgeous tea room. The event is hosted by Rose Petal, who is an excellent entertainer, though not a* [traditional] *Disney character (I noticed many of the girls asking who she was). Aurora herself does make an appearance, but she doesn't spend any more time with the girls than at any other character meal. She stops by each table, gives each girl a fresh rose, and takes time to sign an autograph and pose for a photo. However, with the exception of the rose, this is consistent with all other character meals we attended. The food was scarce and average at best. We did have a slice of delicious cake—good thing since we were both starving. My daughter received many gifts during the tea; she was thrilled to find the bracelet that fell out of her napkin when Rose Petal asked her to wave it. We ended the day with a princess parade (of girls at the tea) through the Grand Floridian that ended with each girl being deemed a true princess. While overall it was a fun event, I prefer lunch at the castle with a lower price, better food, and the opportunity to meet multiple Disney characters/princesses.*

WONDERLAND TEA PARTY Although the name of this enchanting soiree is enough to make most boys break out in hives, it is nevertheless available at the Grand Floridian on Monday through Friday afternoons at 1:30 p.m. for $40 per child (ages 4 to 12). The program consists of making (and eating) cupcakes and having lunch and tea with characters from Alice in Wonderland. Reservations can be made by calling ☎ 407-WDW-DINE 180 days in advance.

BIRTHDAYS *and* SPECIAL OCCASIONS

IF SOMEONE IN YOUR FAMILY CELEBRATES A BIRTHDAY while you're at Disney World, don't keep it a secret. A Lombard, Illinois, mom put the word out and was glad she did:

> *My daughter was turning 5 while we were there, and I asked about special things that could be done. Our hotel asked me who her favorite character was and did the rest. We came back to our room on her birthday and there were helium balloons, a card, and a Cinderella 5 x 7 photo autographed in ink! When we entered the Magic Kingdom, we received an "It's My Birthday Today" pin (FREE!), and at the restaurant she got a huge cupcake with whipped cream, sprinkles, and a candle. IT PAYS TO ASK!*

During 2009 only, Walt Disney World is offering free birthday admission to one theme park; register online at **disneybirthday.delivery.net.** Adults need to present a valid driver's license, state ID card, or U.S. passport; kids need to show an original birth certificate or a certified copy.

If you need a last-minute birthday cake, try **Goofy's Candy Co.** at Downtown Disney (☎ 407-828-3104).

PART SEVEN

SPECIAL TIPS *for* SPECIAL PEOPLE

WALT DISNEY WORLD *for* SINGLES

DISNEY WORLD IS GREAT FOR SINGLES. It's safe, clean, and low-pressure. Safety and comfort are unsurpassed, especially for women traveling alone. Parking lots are well lit and constantly patrolled.

If you're looking for a place to relax without being hit on, Disney World is perfect. Bars, lounges, and nightclubs are the most laid-back and friendly you're likely to find. Between the BoardWalk and Downtown Disney, nightlife abounds; virtually every type of entertainment is available at a reasonable price. If you overimbibe and are a Disney resort guest, Disney buses will return you safely to your hotel.

See "Tips for Going Solo" on the following pages for more ways to enjoy Disney World on your own.

WALT DISNEY WORLD *for* COUPLES

SO MANY COUPLES MARRY OR HONEYMOON in the World that a department was created to tend to their needs. Disney's Fairy Tale Weddings & Honeymoons offers a range of wedding venues and services, plus honeymoon packages.

WEDDINGS

DISNEY'S INTIMATE WEDDING (maximum 18 or fewer guests, plus bride and groom) includes a cake and Champagne toast for the couple and four guests, a personalized wedding Web site, a Disney wedding certificate, a photographer, an Annual Pass for the bride and groom, and a wedding album. Packages require a four-night stay at a Disney-owned and -operated resort; some ceremony locations have a limit of ten guests. The cost starts at about $4,500; prices also include a musician, cake, bouquet, limousine ride, and wedding coordinator. If you invite more than 18 guests, you must buy one of Disney's customized wedding packages,

Tips for Going Solo

Single *can mean traveling alone as well as unmarried, and being by yourself doesn't mean you can't have a great time at Disney World. Deb Wills, Webmaster of the Walt Disney World Information Guide* (**www.allears.net**), *offers this advice.*

Some people say visiting Disney World by yourself can't possibly be fun. They couldn't be more wrong! You can have a very magical time exploring the World on your own. Whether you're in Orlando on business and visiting the parks to kill time, or you came to get away from it all, visiting the parks by yourself need not be lonely. It affords you the opportunity to see and do what you want, when you want. For those of you who are hesitating—***just do it***! You'll be glad you did. Here are ways to maximize your experience when alone at WDW.

- The tendency might be to plan your days full of activity. I suggest the opposite: don't plan much at all. Keep your schedule as open as you can. One of the best parts about traveling solo is that you can be your own boss. Sleep in, have leisurely morning coffee on the balcony, relax by the pool . . . or not. If you'd rather get up and go early, who's to stop you?
- Put some spontaneity into your day. If you're taking Disney transportation, get on the first park bus that arrives.
- Get on the resort monorail (not the Express!) at the Magic Kingdom, and visit each of the resorts it stops at. Each resort has its own theme and character, with lots to see and explore. The resorts are especially beautiful during the holidays, when all the decorations are in place.
- Did you know that you can walk through the queues and view the preshows of the thrill rides even if you don't intend to ride? Wander through at your own pace; then tell the cast member prior to boarding that you don't wish to ride, and you'll be shown to a nearby exit. This way you don't have to miss, for example, the very detailed queue of Expedition Everest with its hundreds of unique artifacts.
- If you *do* want to experience the thrill rides, take advantage of the single-rider lines for the Rock 'n' Roller Coaster, Expedition Everest, and Test Track. They can cut your wait time significantly.
- One of my favorite things to do when I'm traveling solo is play photographer. If you encounter folks taking photos of each other, ask if they would

unofficial **TIP**
It takes big bucks to marry at Disney World.

which start at $10,000 (Monday through Thursday) and $15,000 (Friday, Saturday, or Sunday), not including taxes and gratuities.

You can choose from one of the following locations for your ceremony: Disney's Wedding Pavilion at the Grand Floridian, Sea Breeze Point at Disney's BoardWalk Resort, the Wedding Gazebo at Disney's Yacht Club Resort, Sunset Pointe at Disney's Polynesian Resort, or Sunrise Terrace at Disney's Wilderness Lodge.

If you're short on friends, you can rent Disney characters by the half hour to attend your wedding reception. Volume discounts are available: characters cost $800 for one, $1,200 for two, $1,600 for like to be in one photo, then offer to snap the picture. This is a great way to make friends.

- Get your favorite Disney snack, find a bench, and people-watch. You'll be amazed at what you see: the honeymooning couple wearing bride-and-groom mouse ears, toddlers giving Mickey and the characters their first hugs, grandparents smiling indulgently as the grandchildren smear ice cream all over their faces. If you're missing the smiles of your own children, buy a couple of balloons and give them away. You'll help make the kids near you very, very happy.
- Learn how some of the magic is created. Take a behind-the-scenes tour (see descriptions in Part Fourteen) or one of the deluxe hotel tours.
- Visit Animal Kingdom Lodge and relax at an animal-viewing area. Find an animal keeper; they'll gladly discuss care of the wild animals at the resort.
- Don't hesitate to strike up conversations with cast members or guests in line with you. Foreign cast members in Epcot's World Showcase are happy to share stories about their homelands.
- With no one pulling to go to Space Mountain, get a snack, or go to the bathroom, you can enjoy a leisurely shop around the World. Some stores (Arribas Brothers in Downtown Disney, and Mitsukoshi Department Store in the Japan section of World Showcase) have really neat displays and exhibits.
- Go to that restaurant you've always wanted to try but your picky eater has always declined. You don't have to order a full meal; try several appetizers or, better yet, just dessert.
- You don't want the folks at home to think you've forgotten them, so go to Innoventions in Epcot to e-mail a photo of yourself to your family.
- Use common sense about your personal security. I feel very comfortable and safe traveling alone at Disney World and have done so many times, but I still don't do things I wouldn't do at home (like announce to anyone listening that I'm traveling solo). If you aren't comfortable walking to your room alone, ask at the front desk for a security escort. Use extra caution in the parking lots at night, just as you would at home.

three, and so on. If character prices sound steep, be comforted that they don't eat or drink.

One of the more improbable services available is bachelor parties (☎ 407-828-3400 for information). What goes on at a Disney bachelor party? Stag cartoons?

To marry in the World, you need a marriage license. They're $93.50 at any Florida county courthouse (cash, traveler's checks, or money orders accepted). There's no waiting period; your license is issued when you apply. If you're a Florida resident, however, you must wait three days after obtaining the license to marry unless you have completed a four-hour premarital course. The ceremony must occur within 60 days. Blood tests aren't required, but you must present ID (driver's license, passport, or birth certificate plus Social Security number). If you were widowed or divorced within 300 days of the wedding, you must produce a certified copy of the deceased spouse's death certificate or your divorce decree. For more information, call the wedding consultant at ☎ 321-939-4610 or 877-566-0969, or visit **www.disneyweddings.com.**

HONEYMOONS AND VOWS RENEWALS

HONEYMOON PACKAGES ARE ADAPTATIONS of regular Walt Disney Travel Company vacations. No special rooms are included unless you upgrade. Honeymoon features vary with the package purchased. Rates are $1,300 to $5,700; vows-renewal packages are $4,500 to $2s5,000. For more information, contact Disney's Fairy Tale Weddings & Honeymoons, P.O. Box 10000, Lake Buena Vista, FL 32830-1000; ☎ 800-370-6009; **www.disneyweddings.com.**

An Easton, Pennsylvania, couple enjoyed the reception they received and offer advice on how to make it even warmer:

> *We found that everyone, guests and cast members, bent over backwards for us when they learned it was our honeymoon. I highly recommend buying the bride-and-groom mouse ears and wearing them everywhere. I know most men will be hesitant, as was my husband, but once you see what you get, you'll wear them gladly.*

ROMANTIC GETAWAYS

DISNEY WORLD IS A FAVORITE GETAWAY FOR COUPLES, but not all Disney hotels are equally romantic. Some are too family-oriented; others swarm with convention-goers. For romantic (though expensive) lodging, we recommend Animal Kingdom Lodge and Villas, Bay Lake Tower at the Contemporary Resort, the Polynesian Resort, Wilderness Lodge and Villas, the Grand Floridian, BoardWalk Inn and Villas, and the Yacht Club and Beach Club resorts.

The Alligator Bayou section at Port Orleans Riverside, a moderate Disney resort, also has secluded rooms. In Part Three, Accommodations, we provide recommendations for the best rooms in each Disney resort, taking into consideration view, quiet, and convenience.

WALT DISNEY WORLD *"At Large"*

YOU'VE JUST SPENT A SMALL FORTUNE for your vacation to Walt Disney World. If you're a person of size, the last thing you want to worry about now is whether you'll have trouble fitting in the ride vehicles. Fortunately, Walt Disney World realizes that its guests come in all shapes and sizes and is quite accommodating. Deb Wills and Debra Martin Koma, authors of *PassPorter's Open Mouse for Walt Disney World and the Disney Cruise Line: Easy Access Vacations for Travelers with Extra Challenges,* offer these suggestions.

- As you wander around the World, you'll find that the newer theme parks are more "size-friendly." Certain turnstiles in the Magic Kingdom are very narrow (such as the ones at the Hall of Presidents and *Country Bear Jamboree*), but you don't have to go through these. Simply ask the cast member to let you enter through the wheelchair entrance.

- Remember that you will be on your feet for hours at a time. Be sure to wear comfortable, broken-in shoes. Pay attention to your feet: if you feel a blister starting, take care of it quickly. (Note that each park has a first-aid station where you can find bandages and other needs. For more on blister prevention, see page 415.)
- If you're prone to chafing, consider bringing a commercial antifriction product (such as Bodyglide) that is designed to control or eliminate rubbing. You can find this and similar products at most pharmacies and sporting-goods stores.
- Know before you go! Not all attractions have the same types of vehicles or seating. Some have bench seats, while others have individual seats; some have overhead harnesses, while others have seat belts or lap bars. Learn what type of seating or vehicle each attraction has before you go so you know what to expect. Check out **www.allears.net** for the details. If the attraction has a seat belt, pull it all the way out before you sit down to make it easier to strap yourself in. Note that some attractions even have seat-belt extenders—ask a cast member about these.
- Several attractions (Expedition Everest and Test Track, for example) offer a sample ride vehicle for you to try out before you get in line. These are usually discreetly located out of view of the general public; ask a cast member for the location.
- Front seats (such as those in the Rock 'n' Roller Coaster and Test Track) often have more legroom.
- In restaurants, look for chairs without arms. If you don't see any, the host or hostess should be able to provide one for you.
- Request a resort hotel room with a king-size bed. Everyone needs a good night's sleep, especially after touring the parks all day. It may cost a bit more, but it will be more than worth it!

WALT DISNEY WORLD *for* EXPECTANT MOTHERS

IT'S SAID THAT A GOOD SHEPHERD will lay down his life for his sheep. Heaven knows we have tried to be good shepherds for you. While researching this guide, we have spun in teacups and been jostled in simulators until we turned green. We have baked in the sun, flapped in the wind, and been drenched in the rain. But we have failed expectant mothers. Try as they might, the authors have never become pregnant. Consequently, the *Unofficial Guide* has never included firsthand information for mothers-to-be. Then to the rescue came Debbie Grubbs, a Colorado reader in her fifth month of pregnancy. She fearlessly waddled all over Disney World, compiling observations and tips for expectant moms. Here are her conclusions:

> *Generally speaking, pregnant women can experience more attractions than not at Walt Disney World. Therefore, I will outline only those rides that are prohibited to pregnant women and the reasons why. There were several rides that I just knew I could ride even*

though they were restricted, so I sent my husband and friends to ride first and they reported why they thought I could or could not ride.

Magic Kingdom

Splash Mountain is restricted obviously due to the drop, or so I thought. It turns out that the seat configuration in the "logs" has more to do with it than the drop. The seats are made so that your knees are higher than your rear, causing compression on the abdomen (when it is this large). This is potentially harmful to the baby. As always, better safe than sorry.

Big Thunder Mountain Railroad is restricted for obvious reasons as well. It's just not a good idea to ride roller coasters when you're pregnant.

Mad Tea Party may be OK if you don't spin the cups. We didn't ride this one because my doctor advised me not to ride things with centrifugal [or centripetal] *force. Dumbo and the Astro Orbiter in Tomorrowland are OK, but the Mad Tea Party is too fast if you spin the cups.*

Space Mountain is one of my favorite rides, but a roller coaster nonetheless.

Tomorrowland Speedway is not recommended due to the amount of rear-ending that always occurs from overzealous younger drivers.

Epcot

Mission: Space and Test Track are restricted, as are all simulator rides. They are too rough and jerky, much like a roller coaster. [Non-moving seats are available in some simulation attractions—ask a cast member.] *Soarin' is fine.*

Disney's Hollywood Studios

Tower of Terror is restricted for the drop alone, and Star Tours is restricted because it is a simulator. Although not as rough as Mission: Space, Star Tours is still a no-no. The Rock 'n' Roller Coaster is clearly off-limits.

There might be some question about the Backlot Tour due to Catastrophe Canyon, where there is a simulated earthquake. It is very tame compared to Disaster! *at Universal Studios. I rode with no problems.*

Animal Kingdom

Dinosaur is very jerky and should be avoided. Same for Primeval Whirl. Kali River Rapids is a toss-up—it's somewhat bouncy and very wet.

We think Debbie would've avoided Expedition Everest, too.

Water Parks

All of the slides are off-limits. Pregnant women can, however, do Shark Reef at Typhoon Lagoon with an extra-large wet-suit vest. The wave pools and floating creeks are great for getting the weight off your feet.

A mother of three from Bethesda, Maryland, adds:

First, anyone who is pregnant should go to their local golf shop and buy one of those canes that has a seat attached to it. They are lightweight and easy to carry. Without a seat, I would have been gone. Second, a pregnant woman must come with some type of support or a BellyBra.

Valerie from Little Rock, Arkansas, who visited the World when she was seven months pregnant, describes her experiences:

We went in March when it was cool, which helped me a lot. I was never overheated. We also did not use Disney-resort transportation. I found it very nice to have my personal space at the end of the day. We did the parks in four days, though, which I do not recommend to others.

We found that there were some great benefits to my condition, my husband's favorite being the FASTPASS! We were able to get two FASTPASSes at a time for rides I couldn't go on. He got two passes for Expedition Everest and rode once at the beginning of the day and once at the end. I was also allowed to walk the whole way with him so neither of us had to wait alone. Once he boarded the ride, I was guided to the "chicken door" and met him at the end. I got to see the hidden halls of Disney, which was kind of fun. I was also able to do several rides. Soarin' is one of my favorites, and pregnant women are allowed. Same with Pirates of the Caribbean and all the Fantasyland rides. It didn't seem like I was missing much. The only ride I thought I would be able to do and couldn't was Kilimanjaro Safaris in Animal Kingdom, because it was so bumpy.

There were seats everywhere for me, so I was never stuck on my feet. Other guests were always nice and would let me have their seat. And I only had one person touch my belly the whole trip! I had so much fun, but I don't suggest this trip if you are having a difficult pregnancy—mine was easy and I had no problems. Also, I walked a lot before the trip to prepare, and I saw women way less pregnant than me miserable and in wheelchairs because they weren't physically fit.

Finally, from an expecting Virginia reader:

At eight months pregnant during our visit, I had no trouble squeezing my belly into anything that I wanted to ride—and I'm 5'10" and overweight to boot. My husband, who is about the same size, was also very comfortable on all of the rides.

MORE TIPS FOR MOMS

IN ADDITION TO DEBBIE'S TIPS, here are a few of ours:

1. Go over your Disney-vacation plans with your obstetrician before your trip.
2. Be prepared for a lot of walking. Get in shape by walking at home, gradually building endurance and distance.
3. Get as much rest as you need, even if you have to sacrifice some time at the theme parks. Try to nap each afternoon.
4. Eat properly. Drink plenty of water throughout the day, especially in warmer months.
5. Use in-park transportation whenever available to cut down on walking.
6. Stay in the World if possible. This will make it easier to return to your hotel for rest.

WALT DISNEY WORLD *for* SENIORS

SENIOR CITIZENS' PROBLEMS AND CONCERNS are common to Disney visitors of all ages. Older guests do, however, get into predicaments caused by touring with younger people. Pressured by their grandchildren to endure a frantic pace, many seniors concentrate on surviving Disney World rather than enjoying it. Seniors must either set the pace or dispatch the young folks to tour on their own.

An older reader in Alabaster, Alabama, writes:

> *Being a senior is not for wussies. At Disney World particularly, it requires courage and pluck. Things that used to be easy take a lot of effort, and sometimes your brain has to wait for your body to catch up. Half the time, your grandchildren treat you like a crumbling ruin and then turn around and trick you into getting on a roller coaster in the dark. What you need to tell seniors is that they have to be alert and not trust anyone. Not their children or even the Disney people, and especially not their grandchildren. When your grandchildren want you to go on a ride, don't follow along blindly like a lamb to the slaughter. Make sure you know what the ride is all about. Stand your ground and do not waffle. He who hesitates is launched!*

unofficial **TIP**
Because seniors are varied and willing, there are few attractions we suggest that they avoid.

Most seniors we interview enjoy Disney World much more when they tour with folks their own age. If, however, you're considering visiting Disney World with your grandchildren, we recommend making an orientation visit without them first. If you know firsthand what to expect, the easier it'll be to establish limits, maintain control, and set a comfortable pace later on.

If you're *determined* to take the grandkids, read carefully the sections of this book that discuss family touring. (*Hint:* The Dumbo-or-Die-in-a-Day Touring Plan has been known to bring grown-ups of all ages to their knees.)

Personal taste is more important than age. We hate to see mature visitors pass an exceptional attraction like Splash Mountain because it's a so-called thrill ride. Splash Mountain is a full-blown adventure that gets its appeal more from music and visual effects than from the thrill of the ride. Because you must choose among attractions that might interest you, we provide facts to help you make informed decisions.

GETTING AROUND

MANY SENIORS LIKE TO WALK, but a seven-hour visit to a theme park includes four to eight miles on foot. If you aren't up to that, let someone push you in a rented wheelchair (theme parks: $12 per day with no deposit, $10 per day for multiday rentals; Downtown Disney: $100 rental deposit required). The theme parks also offer fun-to-drive electric carts (electric convenience vehicles, or ECVs) for $50 per day, with a $20 refundable deposit. Don't let your pride keep you from having a good time. Sure, you could march ten miles if you had to—*but you don't have to!*

Your wheelchair-rental deposit slip is good for a replacement wheelchair in any park during the same day. You can rent a chair at the Magic Kingdom in the morning, return it, go to Epcot, present your deposit slip, and get another chair at no additional charge.

TIMING YOUR VISIT

RETIREES SHOULD MAKE THE MOST of their flexible schedules and go to Disney World in fall or spring (excluding holiday weeks), when the weather is nicest and crowds are thinnest. Crowds are also sparse from late January through early February, but the weather can be unpredictable. If you visit in winter, take coats and sweaters, plus warm-weather clothing. Be prepared for anything from near-freezing rain to afternoons in the 80s.

LODGING

IF YOU CAN AFFORD IT, STAY IN DISNEY WORLD. Rooms are among the Orlando-Kissimmee area's nicest, and transportation is always available to any Disney destination at no additional cost.

Disney hotels reserve rooms closer to restaurants and transportation for guests of any age who can't tolerate much walking. They also provide golf carts to pick up and deliver guests at their rooms. Service can vary dramatically depending on the time of day and the number of guests requesting carts. At check-in time (around 3 p.m.), for example, the wait for a ride can be as long as 40 minutes.

Here are five reasons to consider staying in Disney World:

1. The quality of the properties is consistently above average.
2. Buses run only hourly or so for "outside" hotels. Disney buses run about every 20 minutes. Staying in the World guarantees transportation when you need it. On the flip side, the buses that serve out-of-the-World areas usually operate on a fixed schedule so you know exactly what time to be at the loading point.
3. Boarding pets overnight at the kennels is available only to Disney-resort guests.
4. You get free parking in major theme parks' lots.
5. You get preferential tee times on resort golf courses.

All Disney hotels are spread out. It's easy to avoid most stairs, but it's often a long hike to your room from parking lots, bus stops, or public areas. Seniors intending to spend more time at Epcot and Disney's Hollywood Studios than at the Magic Kingdom or Animal Kingdom should consider the Yacht Club and Beach Club resorts, the Swan, the Dolphin, or BoardWalk Inn and Villas.

The Contemporary Resort and the adjacent Bay Lake Tower are good choices for seniors who want to be on the monorail system. So are the Grand Floridian and Polynesian resorts, though they cover many acres, necessitating a lot of walking. For a restful, rustic feeling, choose the Wilderness Lodge and Villas. If you want a kitchen and the comforts of home, book Old Key West Resort, the Beach Club Villas, Animal Kingdom Villas, or BoardWalk Villas. If you enjoy watching birds and animals, try Animal Kingdom Lodge and Villas. Try Saratoga Springs for golf.

RV-ers will find pleasant surroundings at Disney's Fort Wilderness Resort & Campground. There also are several KOA campgrounds within 20 minutes of Disney World. None offers the wilderness setting or amenities that Disney does, but they cost less.

TRANSPORTATION

ROADS IN DISNEY WORLD CAN BE DAUNTING. Armed with a moderate sense of direction and above-average sense of humor, however, even the most timid driver can get around.

If you drive, parking isn't a problem. Lots are served by trams linking the parking area and the theme park's entrance. Parking for the disabled is available adjacent to each park's entrance. Pay-booth attendants will provide a dashboard ticket and direct you to the reserved spaces. Disney requires that you be recognized officially as disabled to use this parking, but temporarily disabled or injured persons also are permitted access.

SENIOR DINING

EAT BREAKFAST AT YOUR HOTEL RESTAURANT or save money by having juice and rolls in your room. Carry snacks in a fanny pack supplemented by fruit, fruit juice, and soft drinks purchased from vendors. Make Advance Reservations for lunch before noon to avoid the crowds. Follow with an early dinner and be out of the restaurants, ready for evening touring and fireworks, long before the main crowd even thinks about dinner.

We recommend seniors fit dining and rest into each day. Plan lunch as a break. Sit back, relax, and enjoy. Then return to your hotel for a nap or swim during the hot, crowded hours of the day.

BEHIND-THE-SCENES TOURS

EVERY SENIOR SHOULD TAKE AT LEAST ONE behind-the-scenes tour, most of which are at Epcot. They offer an in-depth look at Walt Disney World operations. If you don't have time for these lengthy tours, the shorter **Behind the Seeds** tour at the Land Pavilion in Epcot is a must-see. **Backstage Magic** visits behind-the-scenes locations at several theme parks, while **Keys to the Kingdom** provides a glimpse of the Magic Kingdom's history and hidden operations. Ranging from one to seven hours long and $10 to $199 per person, all tours require a lot of walking and standing. (For more information on these, see Part Fourteen, Behind the Scenes at Walt Disney World.)

WALT DISNEY WORLD *for* GUESTS *with* DISABILITIES

DISNEY WORLD IS SO ATTUNED TO GUESTS with physical challenges that unscrupulous people have been known to fake a disability in order to take unfair advantage. If you have a disability, even a restricted diet, Disney World is prepared to meet your needs.

Valuable information for trip planning is available at **www.disney world.com.** Each major theme park offers a free booklet describing disabled services and facilities. Disney people are somewhat resistant to mailing you the booklets, but if you're polite and persistent, they can be persuaded. The same information is on the Web site; click on "Guests with Disabilities" on the home page, at bottom right. Or get a booklet at wheelchair-rental locations in the parks. Another great resource is *PassPorter's Open Mouse for Walt Disney World and the Disney Cruise Line* ($22.95) by Deb Wills and Debra Martin Koma. The 436-page book covers everything from ADHD to motion sensitivity to allergies and asthma. The book is available from PassPorter Travel Press at ☎ 877-929-3273 or **www.passporter.com.**

For specific requests, such those for special accommodations at hotels or on the Disney Transportation System, call ☎ 407-939-7807 (voice) or 407-939-7670 (TTY). When the recorded menu comes up, press "1" on your touch-tone phone. Limit questions and requests to those regarding disabled services and accommodations (address other questions to ☎ 407-824-4321). If you'll be staying at a Disney resort, let the reservation agent know of any special needs when you book your room.

The following equipment, services, and facilities are available at Disney hotels, though not all hotels offer all items:

Wheelchairs
Bed and bathroom rails
Wide bath doors
Roll-in showers
Shower benches
Handheld showerheads
Accessible vanities
Rubber bed-pads
Lower beds
Refrigerators
Knock and phone alerts
Closed-captioned televisions
TTYs
Strobe-light smoke detectors
Double peepholes in doors
Braille on signs and elevators
Portable commodes

Service animals are welcome in all Disney resorts.

Much of the Disney Transportation System is disabled-accessible. Monorails can be accessed by ramp or elevator, and all bus routes are served by vehicles with wheelchair lifts, though unusually wide or long wheelchairs (or motorized chairs) may not fit the lift. Watercraft accommodations for wheelchairs are iffier. If you plan to stay at Wilderness Lodge and Villas, Fort Wilderness Campground, or an Epcot resort, call ☎ 407-939-7807 (voice) or 407-939-7670 (tty) for the latest information on watercraft accessibility.

Food and merchandise locations at theme parks, Downtown Disney, and hotels are generally accessible, but some fast-food queues and shop aisles are too narrow for wheelchairs. At these locations, ask a cast member or member of your party for assistance.

Disabled guests and their families give Disney high marks for accessibility and sensitivity. An Arlington, Virginia, woman writes:

> *Before the trip, I thought of Disney as a sort of corporate monster that successfully accessed my pocketbook through my innocent and*

trusting children with its diabolical marketing expertise. I also considered a Disney vacation pretty ersatz. . . . However, I must say that Disney is dynamite in its treatment of handicapped vacationers, and this perspective has turned me into a fan. My mom has mobility problems that got a lot worse between the time my dad made reservations and the time we arrived, and she was worried about getting around. Disney supplied a free wheelchair, and every bus had kneeling steps for wheelchair users. The disabled brochures for each park were incredibly informative about access for each attraction, and the hosts sprang into action when they saw us coming.

VISITORS WITH SPECIAL NEEDS

WHOLLY OR PARTIALLY NONAMBULATORY guests may rent wheelchairs. Most rides, shows, attractions, restrooms, and restaurants accommodate the nonambulatory disabled. If you're in a park and need assistance, go to Guest Relations.

A limited number of electric carts or ECVs (electric convenience vehicles) are available for rent. Easy to drive, they give nonambulatory guests tremendous freedom and mobility. For some reason, vehicles at the Magic Kingdom go much faster than those at other parks.

All Disney lots have close-in parking for disabled visitors. Request directions when you pay your parking fee. All monorails and most rides, shows, restrooms, and restaurants accommodate wheelchairs.

unofficial **TIP**
Park maps issued to each guest on admission are coded to show which attractions accommodate wheelchairs.

Wheelchairs rent for $10 with no deposit required; ECVs are $45 per day with a $20 refundable deposit. Rentals are available at the major theme parks and Downtown Disney. A very limited number of wheelchairs are available at no charge at both Blizzard Beach and Typhoon Lagoon water parks. A refundable deposit of $10 is required. The rental deposit at Downtown Disney is $100.

Even if an attraction doesn't accommodate wheelchairs, nonambulatory guests may ride if they can transfer from their wheelchair to the ride's vehicle. Disney staff, however, aren't trained or permitted to assist with transfers. Guests must be able to board the ride unassisted or have a member of their party assist them. Either way, members of the nonambulatory guest's party will be permitted to ride with him or her.

Because the waiting areas of most attractions won't accommodate wheelchairs, nonambulatory guests and their parties should request boarding instructions as soon as they arrive at an attraction. Almost always, the entire group will be allowed to board without a lengthy wait. A reader from New Orleans who traveled to Disney World with a nonambulatory friend writes:

I went with a very dear friend of mine who is paraplegic and confined to a wheelchair. It was his first trip to WDW, and I knew that it was a handicap-friendly place, but we were still a little apprehensive about how much we would be able to do. The official pamphlet distributed by the WDW staff is helpful, but it implies limitations, such as stating that one must be able to navigate (that is, walk) the catwalks of Space

Mountain in case of emergency. After reading this, Brian and I thought that we would end up walking around the MK looking at the rides, not riding them. The reality is, nonambulatory visitors are able to do much more—one only has to ask the cast members what is really allowed. Of course, I'm sure the WDW publication is written to cover liability purposes; also, Brian is a very active person who is able to transfer from his wheelchair without too much difficulty, so we were able to ride almost everything we wanted! We both had a terrific time. The only ride that it seems we should have been able to ride but couldn't was Pirates of the Caribbean, and [this was] *only because the railings at the loading site are just a few inches too close together for a wheelchair to pass through. Anyway, my point is that it may be encouraging to disabled readers of the* Unofficial Guide *to know that options are available; of course, with the caveat that it depends on the individual's mobility. I would recommend to anyone to not avoid a ride—ask first.*

DIETARY RESTRICTIONS Visitors with dietary restrictions can find assistance at Guest Relations in the parks. For Disney World restaurants outside the parks, call a day ahead for assistance.

SIGHT- AND/OR HEARING-IMPAIRED GUESTS Guest Relations at the parks provides free cassette tapes and portable tape players to sight-impaired guests ($25 refundable deposit). At the same locations, TDDs are available for hearing-impaired guests. Many pay phones in the major parks are equipped with amplifying headsets. See your Disney map for locations.

Braille guide maps are available from Guest Relations at all parks ($25 refundable deposit). Some rides provide closed-captioning; many theater attractions provide reflective captioning.

Disney provides sign-language interpretations of live shows at the theme parks on certain designated days of the week:

Animal Kingdom: Saturdays
Disney's Hollywood Studios: Sundays and Wednesdays
Epcot: Tuesdays and Fridays
Magic Kingdom: Mondays and Thursdays

Get confirmation of the interpreted-performance schedule a minimum of a week in advance by calling Disney World information at ☎ 407-824-4321 (voice) or 407-827-5141 (TTY). You'll be contacted before your visit with a show schedule that lists the names, dates, and times of the interpreted performances.

NONAPPARENT DISABILITIES We receive many letters from readers whose traveling companion or child requires special assistance but who, unlike a person in a wheelchair, is not visibly disabled. Autism, for example, makes it very difficult or impossible for someone with the disorder to wait in line for more than a few minutes or in queues surrounded by a crowd.

A trip to Disney World can be nonetheless positive and rewarding for guests with autism and similar conditions. And while any Disney vacation requires planning, a little extra effort to accommodate the affected person will pay large dividends.

THE GUEST ASSISTANCE CARD Visitors with nonapparent disabilities, whether temporary or permanent, should obtain a Guest Assistance Card (GAC), a pass that explains to cast members any special accommodation a guest may need. To request the card, go to the Guest Relations area inside any Disney theme park or just outside the park's gates. If you are requesting the GAC for someone else (your child, for example), he or she must be with you when you make the request.

Having a specific diagnosis doesn't qualify or disqualify someone for a GAC. Rather, the card is issued based on a person's needs—people with the same diagnosis can have very different needs. Also, you don't need a doctor's letter to request a GAC: according to the Americans with Disabilities Act, you cannot be required to provide proof of a disability.

To figure out what those needs are, think about the sorts of things that happen in a day at Disney World and how the following situations, among others, would affect you or someone else with a nonapparent disability:

- Do you have a relative who needs a quiet place to wait or a place away from other people as much as possible? If so, a GAC might help, although not all attractions offer such accommodations.
- Does your ambulatory child need to wait in line in a stroller? Some kids might, either because they can't or won't walk in line or because they need a safe haven where they're not so close to other people. A GAC lets you bring the stroller into lines just as you would a wheelchair. In this case, you will be issued a red strap, which you will put around the stroller's handle and show to the first cast member you encounter at each attraction. *Note:* If you or someone else in your party uses a wheelchair or ECV, you do not need a GAC unless you have needs other than access to entrances, lines, and boarding areas.
- Do you take medication or do you have a condition that may cause problems with being in the sun or heat? If so, a GAC might help, although most lines are shaded and many are indoors.
- Do you, despite being able to walk, need extra time getting into/out of ride vehicles where rides have moving walkways? If so, a GAC might help by letting you board/disembark at designated wheelchair spots.

Guest Services can add different stamps to a GAC to tell cast members at attractions what assistance the guest requires. You don't need to remember or ask for these specific stamps; just be ready to explain your needs.

unofficial **TIP**
If you encounter a cast member who is unfamiliar with the Guest Assistance Card, just ask for a manager and explain your situation.

The GAC usually covers up to six people (five plus the person with a disability). However, the person whose name is on the card must be present when you use it.

GACs are available at any of the theme parks but not at Downtown Disney or Disney resorts. A card issued at one park is good at all parks and is usually valid for your whole vacation, but theme-park GACs are not valid at the water parks. If you obtained a GAC on a previous trip to Walt Disney World, you cannot reuse it. Also, a GAC cannot be obtained in advance of your visit.

Having a GAC doesn't mean that you can go to the front of a line (that privilege is extended only to seriously ill children who are visiting Disney World courtesy of the Make-A-Wish Foundation or similar organizations). Rather, the card is designed to provide "more convenient entrance" into attractions. Note that GACs are not valid at restaurants or character-greeting areas.

To use the GAC, simply show it to the first cast member you see at the attraction. Keep in mind, though, that even with the same attraction, the GAC is not always handled the same way each time. Exactly what happens depends on how busy the attraction is, how many other people with special needs are there at the time, and staffing.

More Tips for Visitors with Special Needs

Families have sent us their hotel, restaurant, and transportation tips. For example, a quiet hotel room can often help the affected individual unwind after a day in the parks. (See page 137 for the quietest rooms in each of the Disney resorts.)

Schedule breaks. A midday nap or dip in the pool may relax frazzled members of your group.

Consider using a town-car service from the Orlando airport to your hotel. Shuttle and bus services usually drop guests at several hotels, and it's common for the trip to take two or more hours. In contrast, most town-car services will drive you directly to your destination; our recommendations are listed on page 384.

If you'd like a meal with Disney characters, our section on character dining in Part Six (see page 347) will help you choose a suitable experience. For example, Cinderella's Gala Feast at the Grand Floridian is a boisterous affair that may overwhelm any child.

Whenever possible, obtain Advance Reservations (page 431) for meals, and consider asking for a table near an exit or window.

To save time, consider taking a taxi between Disney resorts.

Sensory-defensive children may enjoy the "deep pressure" sensation of the sandy beaches or whirlpools at some Disney resorts. The wave pool at Typhoon Lagoon also gets high marks from readers.

Pin trading with Disney cast members (see page 747) offers a great opportunity for children to work on social and communication skills.

We're grateful to the many families with autistic children who have shared their Disney experiences with us. Special thanks goes to the Cartwright family of Fond du Lac, Wisconsin.

FRIENDS OF BILL W.

A LINTHICUM, MARYLAND, MOM suggested this:

> *We went on this vacation with a recovering alcoholic. He was able to attend daily 3 to 4 p.m. meetings that were held just outside the park in one of the hotels. It would be helpful if you mentioned that there are meetings available for Alcoholics Anonymous. Disney does not sponsor them. This is a very sensitive issue for many who are too afraid to ask for fear of public ridicule. The person in our group took a cab from the resort the first time and never had to after that. There are regulars in the meetings who will pick up anyone from their resorts* [who] *needs a ride.*

GUESTS WHO DON'T SPEAK ENGLISH

DISNEY HAS DEVELOPED A WIRELESS DEVICE called **Ears to the World** that provides synchronized narration in French, German, Japanese, Portuguese, or Spanish for more than 15 attractions in the major theme parks. The wireless, lightweight headsets provide real-time translation, allowing guests with limited fluency in English to understand the story lines of the designated attractions. The device is available for a $100 refundable deposit at Guest Relations in all parks.

PART EIGHT

ARRIVING *and* GETTING AROUND

GETTING THERE

unofficial **TIP**
Warning! I-4 is an east–west highway but takes a north–south drop through the Orlando-Kissimmee area. This change in direction complicates getting oriented in and around Disney World. Logic suggests that highways branching off I-4 should run north and south, but most run east and west here.

DIRECTIONS

YOU CAN DRIVE TO ANY WALT DISNEY WORLD destination via World Drive off US 192; via Epcot Drive off Interstate 4, which connects Daytona and Tampa; or from the Hartzog Road/Walt Disney World interchange off FL 429, aka the Western Beltway (see all maps in this chapter).

FROM INTERSTATE 10 Take I-10 east across Florida to I-75 southbound. Exit onto Florida's Turnpike. Take FL 429 (toll) southbound off the turnpike. Exit FL 429 at the Hartzog Road/Walt Disney World interchange in the direction of Walt Disney World, and follow the signs to your Disney destination. (This is a revised route based on the 2007 opening of a new western entrance to Walt Disney World. It's much faster than staying on the Turnpike to I-4.) Also use these directions to reach hotels along US 192, the Irlo Bronson Memorial Highway.

FROM INTERSTATE 75 SOUTHBOUND Exit I-75 southbound onto Florida's Turnpike. Continue south, exiting on FL 429 (toll) southbound. Exit at the Hartzog Road/Walt Disney World interchange in the direction of Walt Disney World. Follow the signs to your Disney destination. Also use these directions to reach hotels along US 192, the Irlo Bronson Memorial Highway.

FROM INTERSTATE 95 SOUTHBOUND Follow I-95 south to I-4. Go west on I-4 through Orlando. Take Exit 67, marked Epcot/Downtown Disney, and follow the signs.

FROM DAYTONA, SANFORD INTERNATIONAL AIRPORT (FSB), OR ORLANDO Head west on I-4 through Orlando. Take Exit 67, marked Epcot/Downtown Disney, and follow the signs.

FROM THE ORLANDO INTERNATIONAL AIRPORT (MCO) There are two routes from the airport to Walt Disney World (see the South Orlando

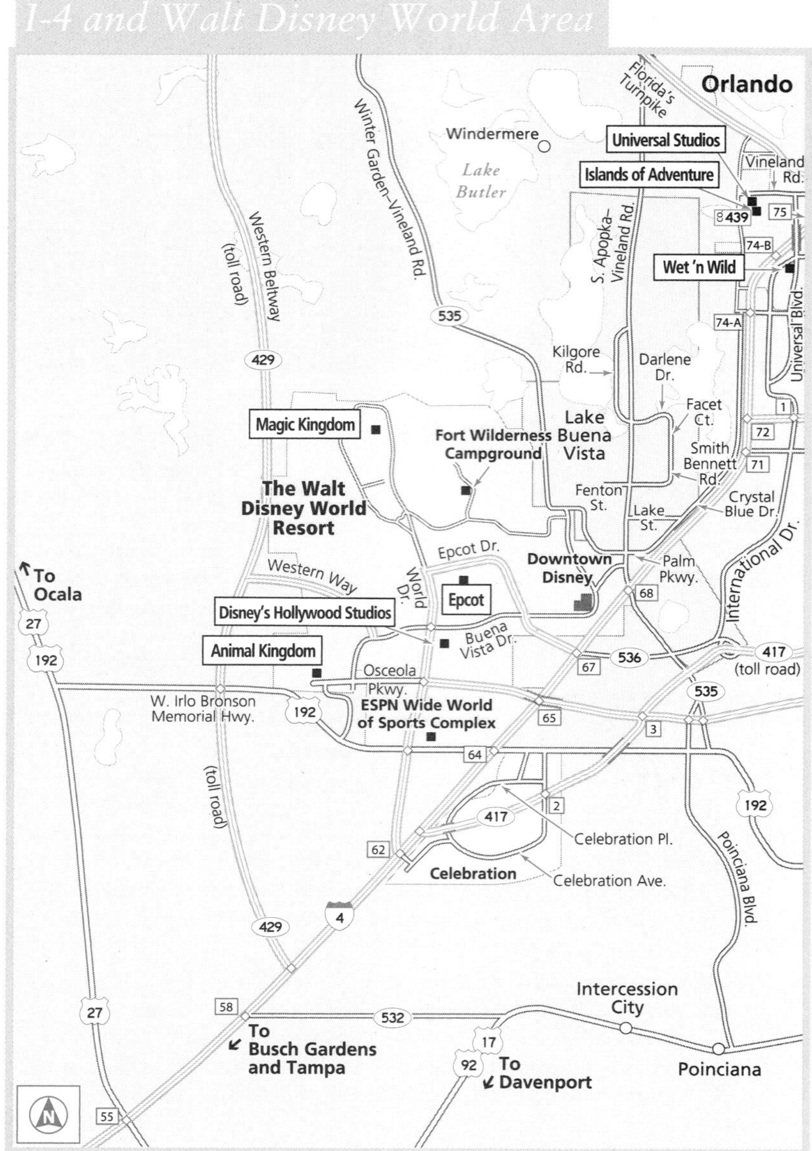

and Walt Disney World Area map on pages 20 and 21). Both routes take almost exactly the same time to drive except during rush-hour traffic when Route One via FL 417 is far less congested than Route Two via the Beachline Expressway. Also, Route One eliminates the need to drive on I-4, which is always very congested.

Route One: Drive southwest on Central Florida Greenway (FL 417), a toll road. Take Exit 6 toward FL 535. FL 536 will cross I-4 and become

Epcot Drive. From here, follow signs to your Walt Disney World destination. If you are going to a hotel on US 192 (Irlo Bronson Memorial Highway), follow the same route until you reach I-4. Take I-4 west toward Tampa. Take the first US 192 exit if your hotel is on West Irlo Bronson, or the second exit if your hotel is on East Irlo Bronson. If your hotel is in Lake Buena Vista, take Exit 6 onto FL 536 as described previously, then turn right on FL 535 to the Lake Buena Vista area.

unofficial **TIP**
If you take either of the routes described, you'll need money for tolls. Some exits are unmanned and require exact change, so be sure you have at least $2 in quarters. Also, be forewarned that the manned toll booths do not take bills larger than $10 and likewise do not accept credit cards.

Route Two: Take FL 528 (Beachline Expressway toll road) west for about 12 miles to the intersection with I-4. Go west on I-4 to Exit 67, marked Epcot/Downtown Disney, and follow the signs to your Walt Disney World destination. This is also the route to take if your hotel is on International Drive or Universal Boulevard, near Universal Studios, near SeaWorld, or near the Orange County Convention Center. For these destinations, take I-4 east toward Orlando.

FROM MIAMI, FORT LAUDERDALE, AND SOUTHEASTERN FLORIDA Head north on Florida's Turnpike to I-4 westbound. Take Exit 67, marked Epcot/Downtown Disney, and follow the signs.

FROM TAMPA AND SOUTHWESTERN FLORIDA Take I-75 northbound to I-4. Go east on I-4, take Exit 64 onto US 192 west, and follow the signs.

Walt Disney World Exits off I-4

East to west (direction of Orlando to Tampa), four I-4 exits serve Disney World.

EXIT 68 (marked FL 535/Lake Buena Vista) primarily serves the Downtown Disney Resort Area and Downtown Disney, including Downtown Disney Marketplace and Disney's West Side. It also serves non-Disney hotels with a Lake Buena Vista address. This exit puts you on a road with lots of traffic signals. Avoid it unless you're headed to one of the preceding destinations.

EXIT 67 (marked Epcot/Downtown Disney) delivers you to a four-lane expressway into the heart of Disney World. It's the fastest and most convenient way for westbound travelers to access almost all Disney destinations except Animal Kingdom and ESPN Wide World of Sports.

EXIT 65 (marked Osceola Parkway) is the best exit for westbound travelers to access Animal Kingdom, Animal Kingdom Lodge, Pop Century Resort, All Star Resorts, and ESPN Wide World of Sports.

EXIT 64 (marked US 192/Magic Kingdom) is the best route for eastbound travelers to all Disney destinations.

EXIT 62 (marked Disney World/Celebration) is the first Disney exit you'll encounter if you're headed eastbound. This four-lane, controlled-access highway connects to the so-called Maingate of Walt Disney World. Accessing Walt Disney World via the next exit, Exit 64, also routes you through the main entrance.

THE I-4 BLUES

OVER MANY YEARS OF COVERING WALT DISNEY WORLD, we've watched I-4 turn from a modern interstate highway into a parking lot. Although the greatest congestion is between the Universal Florida–International Drive area and downtown Orlando, the section to the southwest serving the tourist areas is becoming a real slog as well. Adding to the problem are construction projects both on the highway itself and at the interchanges. If you are commuting to Walt Disney World from the Universal Florida–International Drive area in particular, try to avoid I-4 during rush hours. If you're going to the airport from the Walt Disney World, Lake Buena Vista, or US 192 areas, use FL 417 rather than the Beachline Expressway. If you're considering a hotel on or near International Drive, try to find one toward the southern end of I-Drive. If the I-4 traffic becomes intolerable, it's pretty easy to commute from the Universal Florida–International Drive area to Walt Disney World via Turkey Lake Road, connecting to Palm Parkway on the northwest side of I-4, or on the southernmost section of I-Drive, connecting to FL 536 on the southeast side of the interstate.

SANFORD INTERNATIONAL AIRPORT

A SHORT DISTANCE NORTHEAST OF ORLANDO is Sanford International Airport (SFB). Small, convenient, and easily accessible, it's totally low-hassle compared with the huge Orlando International Airport (MCO) and its block-long security-checkpoint lines.

The primary domestic carrier serving Sanford International is **Allegiant Air** (☎ 702-505-8888; **www.allegiantair.com**), with service from large and small airports throughout the eastern United States. Scheduled domestic charter flights are operated by **Direct Air** (☎ 877-432-3473; **www.visitdirectair.com**).

If you're coming from Europe, **Icelandair** (☎ 800-223-5500; **www.icelandair.com**) offers flights via Reykjavík, Iceland, from Amsterdam, the Netherlands; Copenhagen, Denmark; Frankfurt, Germany; Glasgow, Scotland; Helsinki, Finland; London-Heathrow; Oslo, Norway; Paris; and Stockholm, Sweden. A third carrier, **flyglobespan** (**www.flyglobespan.com;** ☎ 800-663-8614; U.K.: ☎ 0781 271 9000), provides service from Belfast, Northern Ireland, and Glasgow.

A reader from Roanoke, Virginia, uses Sanford International frequently, writing:

> *The 45-minute drive to WDW is more than made up for by avoiding the chaos at Orlando International, and it is stress-free.*

SECURITY AT ORLANDO INTERNATIONAL AIRPORT

THIS AIRPORT HANDLES about 34 million passengers a year. It's not unusual to see lines from the checkpoints snaking out of the terminal and into the main shopping corridor and food court. Airport officials sometimes actually shut down moving sidewalks to use them for more queuing space. A number of passengers have reported missing their flights even when they arrived at the airport 90 minutes before departure. System improvements made in 2007 alleviated some, but by no means all, of the congestion. Most waits to clear security just before we went to press were 22 minutes on average, compared with as many as 45 minutes before the improvements. Even so, there are substantial fluctuations.

unofficial **TIP**
We recommend arriving at Orlando International Airport from 90 minutes to 2 hours before your scheduled departure.

A couple from Martinsburg, West Virginia, thought they were playing it safe and still had a close call:

> *Thank you for the good advice about the security lines at Orlando International. Even in October they were long, but the line at the JetBlue counter was actually longer. We arrived at the airport two hours before our flight and got to the gate just ten minutes before boarding began.*

GETTING TO WALT DISNEY WORLD FROM THE AIRPORT

YOU HAVE FOUR OPTIONS for getting from Orlando International to Disney World:

1. TAXI Taxis carry four to eight passengers (depending on vehicle type). Rates vary according to distance. If your hotel is in the World, your fare will be about $52, plus tip. For the US 192 Maingate area, it will be about $48. To International Drive or downtown Orlando, expect to pay about $32.

2. SHUTTLE SERVICE **Mears Transportation Group** (☎ 407-423-5566; **www.mearstransportation.com**) provides your transportation if your vacation package includes airport transfers. But nonpackage travelers also can use the service. The shuttles collect passengers until they fill a van (or bus). They're then dispatched. Mears charges *per-person* rates (children under age 3 ride free). One-way and round-trip services are available.

FROM THE AIRPORT TO:	ONE-WAY ADULT/CHILD	ROUND-TRIP ADULT/CHILD
International Drive	$18/$14	$29/$23
Downtown Orlando	$17/$14	$28/$22
Walt Disney World–Lake Buena Vista	$20/$16	$33/$26
US 192 Maingate Area	$20/$16	$33/$26

You might have to wait at the airport until a vehicle fills. Once under way, the shuttle will probably stop several times to discharge passengers before reaching your hotel. Obviously, it takes less time to fill a van than a bus, and less time to deliver and unload those passengers.

From your hotel to the airport, you're likely to ride in a van (unless you're part of a tour group, for which Mears might send a bus). Because shuttles make several pickups, they ask you to leave much earlier than you would depart if you were taking a cab or returning a rental car.

3. TOWN-CAR SERVICE Like a taxi, town-car service will transport you directly from the airport to your hotel. The driver will usually be waiting for you in your airline's baggage-claim area. If saving time and hassle is worth the money, book a town car.

Each town-car service we surveyed offers large, well-appointed late-model sedans, such as the Lincoln Town Car series, or limousines. These hold four adults or two adults and three children comfortably. To reserve a child's car seat, call ahead. Trunks easily hold golf bags.

Tiffany Towncar Service (☎ 888-838-2161 or 407-370-2196; **www.tiffanytowncars.com**) provides a prompt, clean ride. The round-trip fee to a Disney or non-Disney resort is $109 plus tip; one-way is about $60. Tiffany offers a free stop at a Publix supermarket en route to your hotel. Also, check Tiffany's Web site for a coupon worth $5 off a round-trip (valid with online reservations only).

Quicksilver Tours & Transportation (☎ 888-GO-TO-WDW or 407-299-1434; **www.quicksilver-tours.com**) offers ten-person limos and vans in addition to town cars. Rates for a round-trip range from $110 to $120 depending on location. Like Tiffany, Quicksilver throws in a stop at the supermarket en route.

4. RENTAL CARS Short- and long-term rentals are available. Most companies allow drop-off at certain hotels or subsidiary locations in the Disney area if you don't want the vehicle for your entire stay. Likewise, any time during your stay, you can pick up a car at those hotels and locations. Check **MouseSavers.com** for rental-car discount codes.

The preferred routes to Walt Disney World, Universal Orlando, SeaWorld, International Drive, and US 192 (all involve toll roads. Some roads require exact change to enter or exit via automated gates, and manned toll booths will not accept any denomination bill higher than a $20 bill. So before you leave the airport, make sure you're armed with a dollar in quarters and some lower-denomination currency.

DOLLARS AND SENSE Which option is the best deal depends on how many people are in your party and how much you value your time. If you're traveling solo or have only two in your party and you're pretty sure you won't need a rental car, the shuttle is your least expensive bet. A cab for two makes sense if you want to get to your hotel faster than the shuttle can arrange. The cab will cost about $36 to $52, including tip. That's $18 to $26 per person. The shuttle will cost $16 each, saving $4 per person. You must decide whether the cab's timeliness and convenience are worth the extra bucks. A one-day car rental costs $40 to $70, plus you have to take time to complete the paperwork, get the vehicle, and fill the tank before you return it. The more people in your group, the more economical the cab becomes over the shuttle. Likewise with the rental car, though the cab will get you there faster.

DISNEY'S MAGICAL EXPRESS

DISNEY'S MAGICAL EXPRESS is a free bus service running between Orlando International Airport and most Walt Disney World hotels. Guests with confirmed reservations at most Disney-owned and -operated resorts are eligible, even if their stays have been booked independently of the Walt Disney Travel Company. (The exceptions are guests staying at the Swan, Dolphin, Shades of Green, or any of the independently owned hotels in the Downtown Disney Resort Area.) In addition to transportation, Magical Express provides free luggage-delivery service between your airline and your Disney hotel room, except for flights arriving after 10 p.m., when you'll need to pick up your suitcases from baggage claim.

About two weeks prior to your departure date, you should receive a document booklet containing your reservation confirmation, transportation vouchers, and special Magical Express luggage tags. Put a tag on any piece of luggage you plan to check with the airline. At the airport, check your bags as you normally would. If all goes well, you'll be reunited with your luggage at your Disney-resort hotel room. International travelers must first claim their bags to go through customs and then recheck them; Disney will take over from there.

When you arrive at the terminal, follow the signs to the Magical Express Welcome Center. Here, you'll begin acclimating yourself to Disney regimentation. In other words, you'll wait in your first lines. In front of the queuing area for the Welcome Center, a Disney greeter will ask one or two adults from your party to join the line for initial processing. The rest of your group will sprawl on the floor (there is no seating) and wait for you. This is done in an effort not to jam up the queuing area (which holds only about 300 people) with children and "nonessential" adults. Fortunately, the Welcome Center is adequately staffed, and the line moves quickly. On a weekday, you'll be whisked through in less than ten minutes; on weekends, especially during crunch time (between 9 a.m. and 5:30 p.m.), it may take upwards of 30 minutes. It's not unusual on a Saturday or Sunday for 10,000 or more guests to move through the Magical Express system.

When you reach the Welcome Center counter, present your document booklet. After your Disney-resort reservation is verified, the transportation vouchers in your booklet will be validated. If you accidentally packed your document booklet in your checked baggage, you'll have to ride to Walt Disney World in the back of a stakebed truck carrying goats and free-range chickens (we're kidding; just trying to see if you're paying attention). Actually, if for some reason you can't put your hands on your document booklet, a cast member at the Welcome Center will find your reservation on his computer, reenter all of your information, and get you set up with vouchers for the bus. Furthermore, if you have a Disney-resort reservation but you didn't sign up for or know about Magical Express in advance, you can sign up on the spot at the Welcome Center using the same process, but you'll have to handle your own luggage.

After collecting your family, proceed to the bus-queuing area, where you'll present your validated transportation vouchers to a cast member. This queuing area is much larger and can hold maybe 600 or 700 guests. After checking your vouchers, the cast member will direct you to one of five queues depending on your resort destination. Bus routes almost always serve more than one resort (thus, if you're going to the Old Key West Resort, you can expect the bus to also stop at the Port Orleans French Quarter, Port Orleans Riverside, and Saratoga Springs resorts). Each bus holds 55 people, and five buses can load at once. From our observations, you'll be accorded priority attention if you're staying at one of the deluxe resorts such as the Grand Floridian. Otherwise, a dispatcher controls where the buses are sent based on the number of people in the queue for each route. Buses load slowly—you can't chase people onto a bus as if you were herding mustangs into a canyon. Once you're under way, it takes about 30 minutes on average to reach the first hotel on the route.

On weekdays, you can expect to reach your hotel anywhere from 70 to 100 minutes from the time you arrived at the Welcome Center; on weekends between 9 a.m. and 5:30 p.m., you're looking at an hour and 45 minutes to three hours. In truth, Magical Express functions about as efficiently as possible. But because of certain constraints, such as the number of buses that can be loaded at the same time and uncontrollable variables like the number of arrivals that hit the system at once, Magical Express is subject to being overwhelmed. Remember, though, that with Magical Express you don't have to wait for your luggage at baggage claim. This amounts to about 20 minutes saved that you can net against the overall time it takes to reach your hotel via Magical Express.

Behind the scenes, Disney baggage handlers work with your airline to retrieve suitcases marked with those special tags. All tagged luggage is sent to an airport warehouse, where it's sorted by destination, then loaded onto a truck for delivery. At the resort, the luggage is matched to your reservation. If your room is ready, the luggage is brought up; otherwise it's held by the bellhops until you can check in.

In practice the logistical challenge of matching totes and tourists is proving to be a bit more than Disney bargained for, with lost and delayed baggage marring the service's reputation. A mother from Baton Rouge, Louisiana, was one of the unlucky ones:

> *We found out the true meaning of Disney Magical Express: they magically make your luggage disappear. They are still working on the reappear part of the trick. It took about four hours for us to get our luggage, which would not have been that bad, except the bellhop showed up at our door with our luggage at 1:30 a.m. After we traveled all day in hopes of getting an early start the next day, this did not start our trip off well. A word of advice to future travelers: get your own luggage at the airport!*

You can, as the reader suggests, claim your own luggage at baggage claim and bring it to the Magical Express Welcome Center. You'll have to deal with the hassle of dragging your bags around through the various queues, but you'll have the peace of mind of knowing that your luggage is aboard the same bus as you. As noted above, claiming your luggage yourself will add about 20 minutes to the Magical Express process. If you choose to do this, don't attach the Magical Express luggage tags until you reach the Welcome Center. One final word about luggage: never pack anything in your checked luggage that you might need in the first 24 hours after arriving. This is especially true for documents, medications, eyeglasses or contacts, cell-phone chargers, and, for obvious reasons, jewelry.

The night before your flight home, check in with your resort's Airline Check-in Desk to schedule your departure; buses typically leave three hours before your flight. You can check your baggage and receive your domestic flight boarding pass at the front desk of your Disney resort. This service is available to all Disney-resort guests, even those who have rental cars. Resort check-in counters are open from 5 a.m. until 1 p.m., and you must check in no later than three hours before your flight. Participating airlines are **AirTran, Alaska, American, Continental, Delta, JetBlue, Northwest, United,** and **US Airways.** At press time, **Southwest Airlines** had begun participating on a trial basis but served only guests staying at Pop Century Resort.

The following comments relating readers' experience with Disney's Magical Express are representative. First, from a Dallas businessman attending a meeting at Disney World:

> *Magical Express worked great in both directions. Bags were in my room within two hours (maybe arrived sooner—I was out at dinner). Departure was right after terrorist scare in U.K.—flight check-in at hotel desk was fast and professional, no problem at all, even though there were many more bags being checked than I'm sure was usual.*

A mother of three from LaPorte, Indiana, loved Magical Express:

> *Magical Express was perfect—worked like a dream! Barely waited, would definitely use again!*

From a Provo, Utah, dad:

> *Magical Express got us to the Port Orleans Riverside by about 10 a.m. The line to check in stretched across the entire lobby, and only three clerks were working. It took 90 minutes or more just to get through the line. This is because buses drop whole busloads of guests at once. Non–Magical Express guests are affected, too, if they try to check in just after a Magical Express bus has unloaded. No more equal distribution of* [guests] *joining the queue.*

Regarding the previous comment, always try to find a bus seat as close to a door as possible. When the bus reaches your resort, you'll be one of the first to get off and one of the first to reach the check-in desk.

A family of four from Janesville, Wisconsin, offers this report:

> *Our travel agent directed us to use Magical Express from the airport to the Wilderness Lodge. Our flight landed at 4:20 p.m., but we did not receive our luggage until 9:45 at night! They should warn guests that the bags take a secret side trip of their own.*

A Park City, Utah, reader votes yea:

> *I liked Magical Express and will use it again. I admit it's off-putting to be tossed in three different lines the minute you get off the plane, but the lines move pretty fast, so it's not as painful as it seems at first glance. Plus, you don't have to wait for your luggage at baggage claim.*

A family of four from Trussville, Alabama, almost missed their flight:

> *We were more than slightly miffed about the bus schedule from our hotel the day we departed. Our flight was at 2:20 p.m.; the hotel checked us in but wouldn't let us leave for the airport until 11:30 a.m. That bus was 5 minutes late and had to stop at another hotel*

Rent at the Airport or Off-site?

If you take a look at the taxes and other fees you're billed when you rent a car at an airport, you might wonder whether a better deal might be available off-site, where many of the extra charges don't apply. In cities such as Las Vegas, for example, rentals are often less expensive at some of the larger hotels, which generally have at least one full-service office of a national brand on-site. Our research team set out to determine whether similar deals existed in the Orlando market off airport property.

As in past years, we began by obtaining quotes from the Web sites of all the car-rental companies in the Orlando airport—for economy cars, midsize vehicles, and minivans—for Saturday-to-Saturday rentals during every month from June through December, including Thanksgiving and Christmas. We also got quotes for companies near the airport, at major hotels around International Drive, and on Disney property—more than 300 quotes in all. To get the very best prices, we also used car-rental discount codes available at **Mouse Savers.com.**

Although there are more than two dozen combinations of car-rental companies and locations around Walt Disney World, our research indicates that you need only look at three to find the best deals:

1. Start with **Dollar (www.dollar.com)** at the Orlando airport (MCO), using MouseSavers discount code **KISS2.** This Dollar location has the cheapest prices about two-thirds of the time.
2. Next, check prices at **Enterprise**'s airport location (**www.enterprise.com;** no discount code needed). It may be worth as much as $150 in savings to do

(Old Key West) for about 20 to 30 minutes. We got to the airport, but the bus had to go to Terminal A first, unload those passengers, and then go to Terminal B. After waiting in a HUGE security line, we had just 20 minutes to get to our gate. Not sure why we couldn't go to the airport when we wanted, but next time we will insist.

A family of five from Bethany, Connecticut, is decidedly upbeat:

Magical Express is definitely worth it. It makes the beginning of the vacation start as soon as you check those bags in!

RENTING A CAR

READERS PLANNING TO STAY IN THE WORLD ask frequently if they'll need a car. If your plans don't include restaurants, attractions, or destinations outside Disney World, then the answer is a very qualified no. But consider the thoughts of this reader from Snohomish, Washington:

We rented a car and were glad we did. It gave us more options, though we used the [Disney] *bus transportation quite extensively. With a car we could drive to the grocery store to restock our snack supply. It also came in handy for our night out. I shudder at how long it might have taken us to get from the Caribbean Beach to the Polynesian to leave our kids* [at the child-care facility], *then back to the Polynesian* [to get the kids], *and then back to the Caribbean Beach.*

so. Enterprise has had the cheapest rates for Thanksgiving and Christmas over the past couple of years.

3. If getting the absolute rock-bottom price is critical, check **National Car Rental**'s Walt Disney World Dolphin location (**www.nationalcarrental.com;** discount code **5000304**). During the July 4 and Columbus Day holidays, National's economy-car and minivan prices can be $180 less than the best airport prices. Even factoring in $100 for a round-trip cab ride, it's still the best deal around.

Except for certain holidays (see above), renting a car at the Orlando airport is always cheaper than renting at off-site locations. Most likely, competition among on-site agencies keeps prices at the airport low—it's difficult to charge significantly more than a competitor when that competitor is 20 feet away and smiling at your customers! Off-site rental locations, on the other hand, typically have little nearby competition, so they often can get away with charging higher rates.

For families, whatever markdowns may be available off-site may not be worth the cab fare and hassle of hauling kids and luggage back and forth. But if you're staying at a hotel with a rental office, it doesn't hurt to call and ask about specials for guests.

A St. Louis mom writes in after following our advice:

We reserved a car from Dollar weeks ago for our trip. After purchasing your book today, we found a promo code for a reduced rate. We tried it, and to our amazement we saved 60% of the price. Thank you!

A dad from Avon Lake, Ohio, adds:

It was unbelievable how often we used our rental car. Although we stayed at the Grand Floridian, we found the monorail convenient only for the Magic Kingdom. Of the six nights we stayed, we used our car five days.

A family from Lynn Haven, Florida, reports:

The transportation system (buses specifically) was a mess. Nothing like the efficient system they had when we visited four years ago. What has happened? It took us an hour and 45 minutes to get from the BoardWalk to Fort Wilderness by bus. Bus transportation was very bad the whole time. Boat transportation was just fine.

A Portland, Maine, family had a complaint about non-Disney transportation:

We stayed outside WDW and tried to commute on the bus furnished by our hotel. After two days, we gave up and rented a car.

PLAN TO RENT A CAR

1. If your hotel is outside Walt Disney World.
2. If your hotel is in the World and you want to dine someplace other than the theme parks and your hotel.

3. If you plan to return to your hotel for naps or swimming during the day.
4. If you plan to visit other area theme parks or water parks (including Disney's).

Renting a Car at Orlando International Airport

The airport has two terminals: A and B. Airlines serving Orlando are assigned to one or the other. Each terminal has three levels and a parking garage. Ticket counters are on Level Three. Baggage claim is on Level Two. Level One is where car-rental counters are, or, where you'll catch a courtesy vehicle to an off-site rental company location.

unofficial **TIP**
To save time in front of the computer, first check **www.dollar.com** or **www.thrifty.com** for rates; one of those sites always had the lowest price for every date we checked.

Orlando is the world's largest rental-car market. At last count, 25 companies competed for your business. Seven—**Alamo, Avis, Budget, Dollar, Enterprise, E-Z Rent-A-Car, L&M,** and **National**—have counters on Level One of both terminals. **Hertz, Payless, Thrifty,** and 15 other companies have locations near the airport and provide courtesy shuttles outside Level One at both terminals. Most shuttles run continuously; you don't have to call for pickup. We prefer using one of the six companies inside the airport because (1) you can complete your paperwork while you wait for your checked luggage to arrive at baggage claim and (2) it's a short walk to the garage to pick up your car (no shuttle needed).

COMPANY	PICKUP EFFICIENCY	CONDITION OF CAR	CLEANLINESS OF CAR	RETURN EFFICIENCY	SHUTTLE EFFICIENCY	OVERALL RATING
Alamo	82	88	90	92	N/A	88
Avis	78	88	84	92	N/A	84
Budget	70	86	90	84	N/A	82
Dollar	76	80	86	92	N/A	84
Enterprise	84	90	94	84	N/A	86
Hertz	64	80	84	84	78	78
L&M	94	74	88	96	N/A	90
National	88	92	92	96	N/A	92
Payless	86	94	94	84	86	86

If you rent from an on-site company, you'll return your car to the garage adjacent to the terminal where your airline is assigned. If you return your car to the wrong garage, you'll have to haul your luggage on foot from one side of the airport to the other in order to reach your check-in.

Most rental companies charge about $5 to $7 a gallon if they fill the tank. If you plan to drive extensively, prepay for a tank of gas so you can return the car empty. Alternatively, fill up near your hotel on your way back to the airport. If you're taking the FL 417 toll road, a reader from Redwood City, California, has discovered possibly the closest gas station to Orlando International:

> *When exiting FL 417 at the Airport/Boggy Creek exit, instead of turning left (north) to enter the airport, turn right (south) on Boggy Creek Road. About one mile south is a gas station that rivals the Hess WDW stations in price, but is way ahead in convenience. It also has some central-Florida ambience, as many times we have seen chickens wandering around the pumps. The station only takes ten extra minutes to get filled up and back to the airport car-rental return.*

How the Orlando Rental-car Companies Stack Up

Unofficial Guide readers provide lots of information about the quality of the car and service they receive from Orlando car-rental companies. Most folks are looking for:

1. Quick, courteous, and efficient processing on pickup.
2. A nice, well-maintained, late-model automobile.
3. A car that is clean and odor-free.
4. Quick, courteous, and efficient processing on return.
5. If applicable, an efficient shuttle between the rental agency and airport.

Most of our readers rent from Alamo, Avis, Budget, Dollar, Hertz, or National. On a scale of 0 (worst) to 100 (best), the table at left shows how they rate the Orlando operations of each company, based on the five points listed above. If you would like to participate in our rental-car survey, complete and return the form at the back of this book.

L&M, a lesser-known company, often offers to beat the rate you were quoted when you reserved with one of the majors. L&M's cars are new, in good condition, and at the airport. *Unofficial Guide* readers rank L&M processing among the highest. Before picking up the car you reserved elsewhere, stop by the L&M counter to comparison-shop. If you want to check L&M's rates and specials before you go, see **www.lmcarrental.net.**

If you rent a car, a 6%-to-7% sales tax, $2.05-per-day state surcharge, and 31¢-to-$1.45-per-day vehicle license recovery fee will be heaped onto your final bill. If you rent from an agency with airport facilities or shuttles, a 10% airport tax will be added. Remember: You can rent a car at your hotel on the day you actually need it.

unofficial **TIP**
The easiest way to avoid standing in line at a car-rental counter is to sign up for the company's "frequent renter" program before your trip. Most programs are free and allow you to skip long waits in line to receive your car. We've used the free membership programs of Dollar and Budget for years; Alamo, Avis, National, and Hertz have similar no-cost programs.

As a measure of how long you have to stand in line before you're assisted by a rental agent, we observed the number of people in line at each rental-car company's counter from 9:30 a.m. to 4:30 p.m., the period during which most people arrive. Observations were recorded at both Terminals A and B. L&M, a local company, almost never had a line. Customers were processed the moment they walked up. Budget, Avis, Dollar, and National averaged between two and six persons in line, with an average of three agents (four to five agents during the busiest times) working the counter. Alamo averaged a whopping 25 people in line, with three to six (average 4.4) agents. In processing customers, Dollar and Avis were fastest, at 5.1 minutes per renter. Alamo and National each required 6.5 minutes, and Budget and L&M came in last at just over 8 minutes.

The Insurance Thing

The following reader report is about an incident with Alamo, but we've encountered variations on this scenario all across the nation with a number of different car-rental companies.

> *Our family recently went on a trip to Walt Disney World and had a wonderful time that was marred only by our experience with Alamo Rent A Car. We reserved a car in advance and were quoted an estimated cost. Then, after arriving at the Orlando airport, we went to pick up our rental car. The Alamo desk clerk looked at our auto-insurance card and informed us quite clearly that our insurance would not cover collision damage to the car. Already quite tired following a very early morning and with two kids in tow who were anxious to get to Disney World, we agreed to the extra coverage.*
>
> *Later, after finding the time to read all the fine print, it became clear that we had paid a good amount of unnecessary* [insurance] *fees. The final cost for the car was double the original quote. Following the trip we spoke with our insurance company; their response concerning rental-car companies was, "Yes, of course we cover collisions." Perhaps had we been more seasoned travelers, we would have not allowed ourselves to be taken advantage of, but hopefully others can learn from our experience.*

The point here is not whether Alamo took advantage of the reader, but rather that anyone who rents a car should know what his or her auto insurance does and does not cover. If you have the slightest question about your coverage, call your insurance agent. For the record, it's very rare for an auto-insurance policy not to cover a vehicle rented and driven in the United States. A corollary discussion pertains to added coverage from your credit-card company if the rental fee is charged on the card. Usually, credit-card coverage picks up deductibles and some ancillary charges that your auto-insurance policy doesn't cover. The tune is the same, however: make sure you understand what is and isn't covered.

GETTING ORIENTED

A GOOD MAP

READERS FREQUENTLY COMPLAIN about signs and maps provided by Disney. While it's easy to find the major theme parks, locating other Disney destinations can be challenging. Many Disney-supplied maps are stylized and hard to read, while others provide incomplete information. The most easily obtained map is in the Walt Disney World "Your Handy Guide to All the Magic" guide. Available at any resort or theme-park Guest Relations office, the guide provides a reduced version of the Walt Disney World Property Map and Disney Transportation System information. The guide also covers dining, recreation, and shopping. Unfortunately, Disney isn't very good about updating its property map. New interstate and expressway interchanges take months or even years to show up, and as we were going to press, the huge new west entrance to Walt Disney World off FL 429 had yet to make an appearance. In fact, FL 429 itself isn't shown! The Disney map is fine for sorting out bus routes, but if you really need to navigate, the maps in this guide are much more current.

A very good map of the Orlando–Kissimmee–Disney World area is free at the **AAA Car Care Center** operated by Goodyear near the Magic Kingdom parking lot (see map on following pages).

FINDING YOUR WAY AROUND

WALT DISNEY WORLD IS LIKE ANY BIG CITY. It's easy to get lost. Signs for the theme parks are excellent, but finding a restaurant or hotel is often confusing. The easiest way to orient yourself is to think in terms of five major areas, or clusters (see map on following pages):

1. The first encompasses all hotels and theme parks around Seven Seas Lagoon. This includes the Magic Kingdom, hotels connected by the monorail, Shades of Green Resort, and two golf courses.
2. The second includes developments on and around Bay Lake: Wilderness Lodge and Villas, Fort Wilderness Campground, and two golf courses.
3. Cluster three contains Epcot, Disney's Hollywood Studios, Disney's BoardWalk, ESPN Wide World of Sports, Epcot resort hotels, Pop Century Resort, and Caribbean Beach Resort.
4. The fourth cluster encompasses Downtown Disney (including Downtown Disney Marketplace and Disney's West Side); Typhoon Lagoon; a golf course; the Downtown Disney Resort Area; and the Port Orleans, Saratoga Springs, and Old Key West resorts.
5. The fifth and newest cluster contains Animal Kingdom, Blizzard Beach, and the Disney All-Star, Coronado Springs, and Animal Kingdom Lodge and Villas resorts.

HOW *to* TRAVEL *around the* WORLD *(or The* Real *Mr. Toad's Wild Ride)*

TRYING TO COMMUTE AROUND WALT DISNEY WORLD can be frustrating. A Magic Kingdom street vendor, telling us how to get to Epcot, proposed, "You can take the ferry or the monorail to the Transportation and Ticket Center. Then you can get another monorail, or you can catch the bus, or you can take a tram out to your car and drive over there yourself." What he didn't say was that it would be easier to ride a mule than to take any conceivable combination from this transportation smorgasbord.

unofficial **TIP**
There's no simple way to travel around the World, but there are ways to make it easier. Just give yourself plenty of time.

TRANSPORTATION TRADE-OFFS FOR GUESTS: LODGING OUTSIDE WALT DISNEY WORLD

DAY GUESTS (THOSE STAYING OUTSIDE THE WORLD) can use the monorail, bus, and boat systems. Our most important advice for these guests is to park in the lot of the theme park (or other Disney destination) where they plan to finish their day. This is critical if you

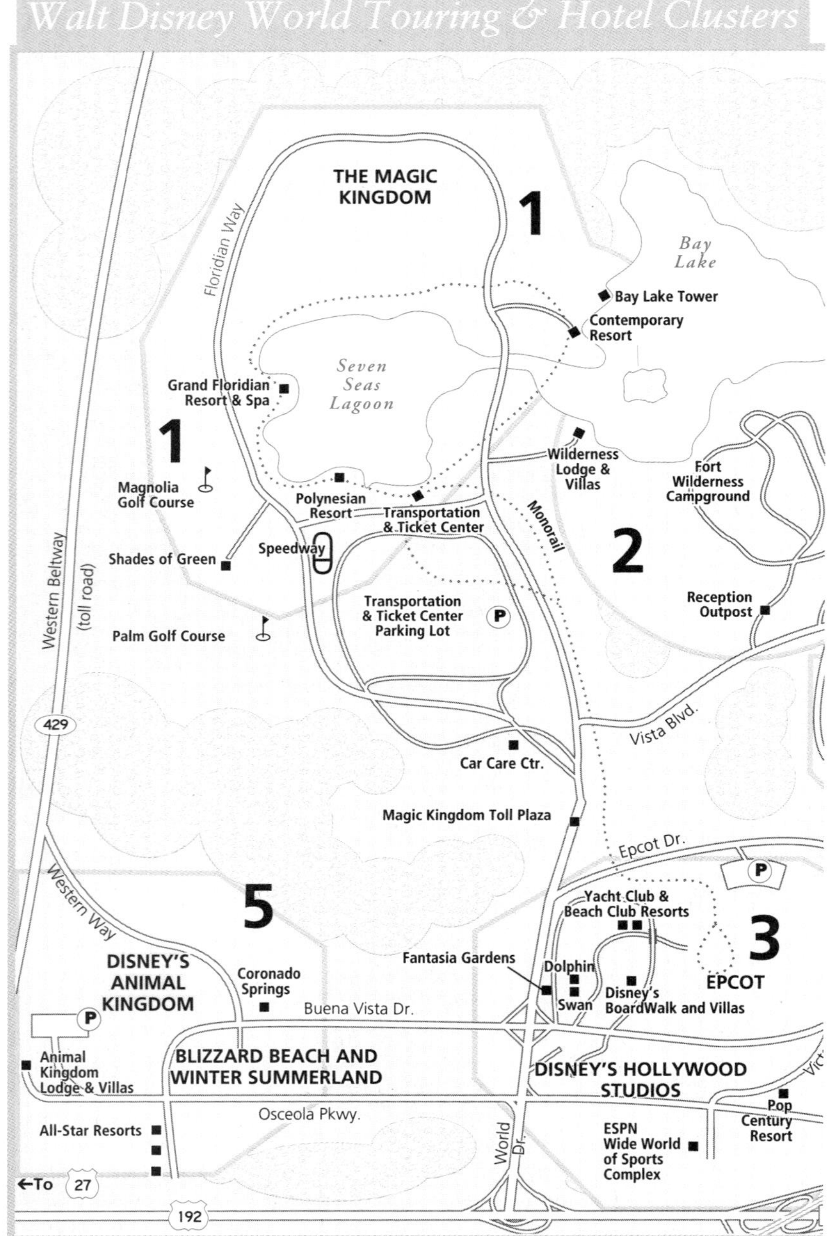
Walt Disney World Touring & Hotel Clusters
THE MAGIC KINGDOM
1
Bay Lake
Bay Lake Tower
Contemporary Resort
Floridian Way
Seven Seas Lagoon
Grand Floridian Resort & Spa
1
Magnolia Golf Course
Polynesian Resort
Transportation & Ticket Center
Wilderness Lodge & Villas
Fort Wilderness Campground
Monorail
2
Speedway
Shades of Green
Transportation & Ticket Center Parking Lot
P
Reception Outpost
Western Beltway
(toll road)
Palm Golf Course
429
Vista Blvd.
Car Care Ctr.
Magic Kingdom Toll Plaza
Epcot Dr.
P
Western Way
5
Yacht Club & Beach Club Resorts
3
Fantasia Gardens
Dolphin
Swan
Disney's BoardWalk and Villas
EPCOT
DISNEY'S ANIMAL KINGDOM
Coronado Springs
Buena Vista Dr.
P
Animal Kingdom Lodge & Villas
BLIZZARD BEACH AND WINTER SUMMERLAND
DISNEY'S HOLLYWOOD STUDIOS
Osceola Pkwy.
All-Star Resorts
World Dr.
ESPN Wide World of Sports Complex
Pop Century Resort
←To 27
192

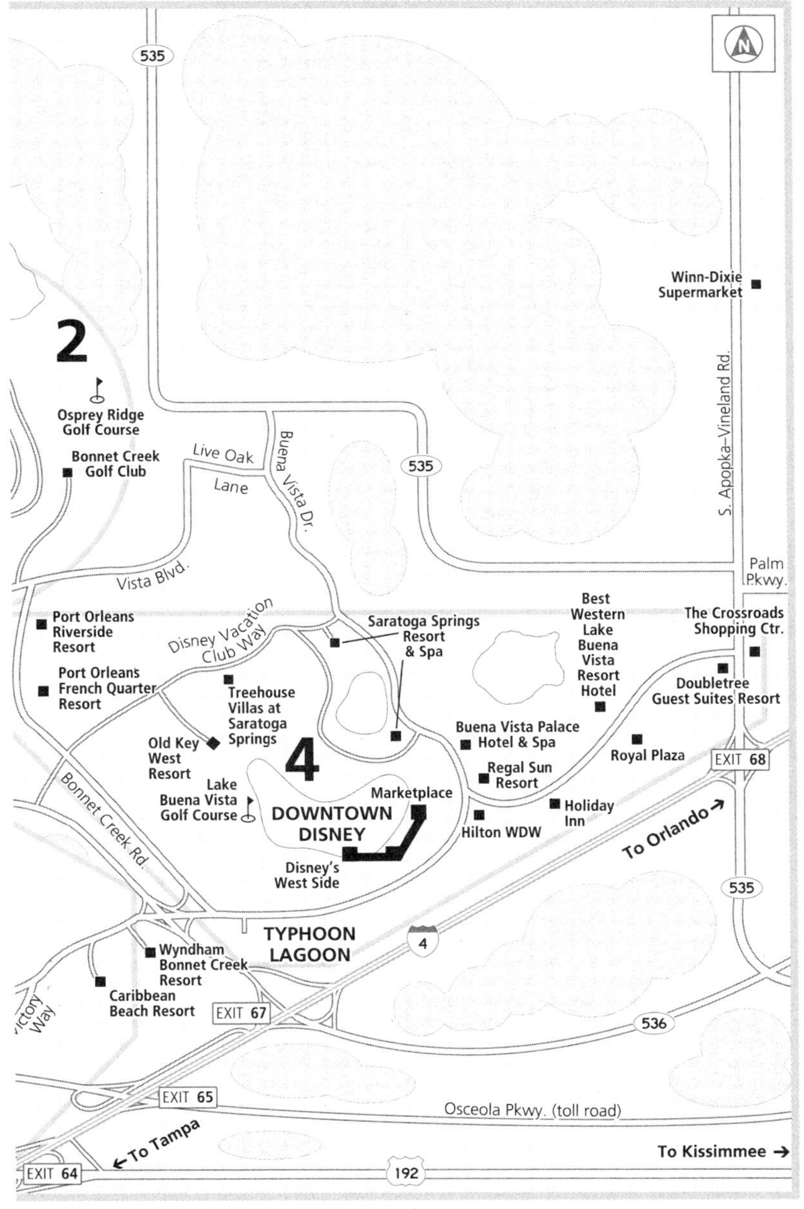
535
2
Osprey Ridge Golf Course
Bonnet Creek Golf Club
Live Oak Lane
Buena Vista Dr.
535
Winn-Dixie Supermarket
S. Apopka–Vineland Rd.
Palm Pkwy.
Vista Blvd.
Port Orleans Riverside Resort
Disney Vacation Club Way
Saratoga Springs Resort & Spa
Best Western Lake Buena Vista Resort Hotel
The Crossroads Shopping Ctr.
Doubletree Guest Suites Resort
Port Orleans French Quarter Resort
Treehouse Villas at Saratoga Springs
Old Key West Resort
4
Buena Vista Palace Hotel & Spa
Royal Plaza
EXIT 68
Regal Sun Resort
Bonnet Creek Rd.
Lake Buena Vista Golf Course
Marketplace
DOWNTOWN DISNEY
Holiday Inn
Hilton WDW
To Orlando
Disney's West Side
535
TYPHOON LAGOON
4
Wyndham Bonnet Creek Resort
Caribbean Beach Resort
Victory Way
EXIT 67
536
EXIT 65
Osceola Pkwy. (toll road)
To Tampa
To Kissimmee
EXIT 64
192

stay at a park until closing.

Moving Your Car from Lot to Lot on the Same Day

Once you've paid to park in any major theme-park lot ($12 per day), show your receipt and you'll be admitted into another park's lot on the same day without further charge. Annual Pass holders and Disney-resort guests park free in any theme-park lot.

ALL YOU NEED TO KNOW ABOUT DRIVING TO THE THEME PARKS

1. POSITIONING OF THE PARKING LOTS Animal Kingdom, Disney's Hollywood Studios, and Epcot parking lots are adjacent to each park's entrance. The Magic Kingdom lot is adjacent to the Transportation and Ticket Center (TTC). From the TTC, take a ferry or monorail to the park's entrance.

2. PAYING TO PARK Disney-resort guests and Annual Pass holders park free. All others pay. If you pay to park and you move your car during that day, show your receipt and you won't have to pay at the new lot.

3. FINDING YOUR CAR WHEN IT'S TIME TO DEPART Parking lots are huge. Jot down the section and row where you park. If you're driving a rental car, note the license-plate number.

4. GETTING FROM YOUR CAR TO THE PARK ENTRANCE Each lot provides trams to the park entrance or, at the Magic Kingdom, to the TTC. If you arrive early in the morning, it may be faster to walk to the entrance (or TTC) than to take the tram.

5. GETTING TO ANIMAL KINGDOM FOR PARK OPENING If you're staying on property and are planning to be at this theme park when it opens, take a Disney bus from your resort instead of driving. For some reason, Animal Kingdom's parking lot frequently opens 15 minutes before the park itself—which doesn't leave you enough time to park, hop on a tram, and pass through security before park opening.

6. HOW MUCH TIME TO ALLOT FOR PARKING AND GETTING TO THE PARK ENTRANCE At Epcot and Animal Kingdom, figure about 10 to 15 minutes to pay, park, and walk or ride to the entrance. At Disney's Hollywood Studios, allow 8 to 12 minutes; at the Magic Kingdom, 10 to 15 minutes to the TTC and another 20 to 30 to reach the park entrance via the monorail (most of which is waiting to board) or ferry (slower but usually less in demand). If you haven't purchased your theme-park admission in advance, tack on another 10 to 20 minutes before you actually enter the park.

7. COMMUTING FROM PARK TO PARK You can commute among the theme parks via Disney bus, or to and from the Magic Kingdom and Epcot by monorail. You also, of course, can commute in your own car. Using Disney transportation or your car, allow 45 to 60 minutes entrance to entrance one-way. If you plan to park-hop, leave your car in the lot of the park where you will finish the day.

8. LEAVING THE PARK AT THE END OF THE DAY If you stay at a park until closing, expect the parking-lot trams, monorails, and ferries to be mobbed. If the wait for the tram is unacceptable, walk to your car, or walk to the first stop on the tram route and wait there for a tram. When someone gets off, you can get on.

9. DINNER AND A QUICK EXIT One way to beat closing crowds at the Magic Kingdom is to arrange reservations for dinner at a restaurant in the Contemporary Resort. When you leave the Magic Kingdom for dinner, move your car from the TTC lot to the Contemporary lot. After dinner, walk (8 to 10 minutes) or take the monorail back to the Magic Kingdom. When the park closes and everyone else is fighting to board the monorail or ferry, you can stroll back to the Contemporary, claim your car, and get on your way. Use the same strategy at Epcot by arranging a reservation at an Epcot resort. When the park closes after *IllumiNations,* exit via the International Gateway and walk to the resort where you parked.

10. CAR TROUBLE All parking lots have security patrols. If you have a dead battery or minor automotive problem, the patrols will help you.

For more serious trouble, the **AAA Car Care Center** (☎ 407-824-0976), operated by Goodyear near the Magic Kingdom parking lot, will help. Prices for most services are comparable to those at home. The facility stays busy; expect to leave your car unless the fix is simple.

11. SCORING A GREAT PARKING PLACE If you arrive at a park after noon or move your car from park to park, there will be empty parking spaces near the entrance vacated by early guests who have left. Instead of following Disney signage or being directed by staff to a distant space, drive to the front and hunt a space, or use the approach of a Coopersburg, Pennsylvania, couple:

> *After leaving Epcot on our first day for a lunch break, we returned to find a fullish parking lot. We were unhappy because we had left a third-row parking spot. My husband told the attendant that we had left just an hour ago and that there were lots of spaces up front. Without a word of protest, he waved us to the front, and we got the same spot we had left!*

12. AAA PARKING If you purchase certain Walt Disney World vacation packages from AAA, you'll receive a special Diamond parking card. Show it at the parking-fee booth and you'll be directed to a reserved parking area (if capacity allows). Each park's AAA area is handled differently. Parking-lot cast members will instruct you as required.

GOOD FUZZ, BAD FUZZ

FOR AS LONG AS ANYONE CAN REMEMBER, Disney World security imposed little to no restraint on speeding drivers. In more than 20 years, we've received not one letter or e-mail from readers about being pulled over. However, we've been alerted to the increasing presence of Orange County law enforcement busting speeders on Disney World property. So for the lead-footed among you, there will be no more Fairy Godmother treatment, and the character with the flashing blue lights isn't Goofy.

SNEAK ROUTES

"SNEAK ROUTE" IS A WHITEWATER-PADDLING TERM for an easy way through tough rapids. Unfortunately, not all difficult rapids have a sneak route. For those that don't, there's only one way through: the hard way. As we research this guide, we're constantly looking for ways to avoid traffic snarls. For some roads and areas, there are no alternative routes. For others, we have discovered sneak routes.

THE LIGHTS OF DOWNTOWN DISNEY Although dozens of searchlights are ablaze at Downtown Disney after dark, what we're talking about here are the many multifunction traffic signals on Buena Vista Drive in front of Downtown Disney. For as long as we can remember, Walt Disney World has been miraculously free of traffic congestion, but no more. Buena Vista Drive near Downtown Disney is a traffic bottleneck of the first order. In the evening especially it can take more than 15 minutes to go less than half a mile. It wouldn't be so bad if only traffic to Downtown Disney was affected, but because Buena Vista Drive is one of Walt Disney World's most important traffic arteries, the traffic jam is on the order of a blocked coronary ventricle.

Most traffic entering and exiting Walt Disney World from the FL 535 entrance must run this traffic signal gauntlet, and so too must guests staying at the seven hotels of the Downtown Disney Resort Area and Disney's Saratoga Springs resort when traveling to Epcot, Disney's Hollywood Studios, the Magic Kingdom, Animal Kingdom, and Typhoon Lagoon. To avoid the bottlenecked area requires long but nearly traffic-free circumnavigation. Coming from the theme parks, you can bypass the mess by taking I-4 or alternatively by looping around on Bonnet Creek Road and Disney Vacation Club Way. Any way you look at it, though, it's a small (congested) world.

unofficial **TIP**
To locate your I-Drive hotel, check **www.iridetrolley.com**, or call ☎ 866-2-I-DRIVE and request the I-Ride Trolley Route Map. It will help you pinpoint your hotel within about 200 yards.

INTERNATIONAL DRIVE (I-DRIVE) By far the most difficult area to navigate without long traffic delays is International Drive. Most hotels on I-Drive are between Kirkman Road to the north and the Central Florida Parkway to the south. Between Kirkman Road and the Central Florida Parkway, three major roads cross I-Drive. From north to south on I-Drive (in the direction of Disney World), the first major crossroad is Universal Boulevard. Next south is Sand Lake Road (FL 482), pretty squarely in the middle of the hotel district. Then farther south, the Beachline Expressway (FL 528) connects I-4 and the airport.

I-Drive is a mess for a number of reasons: scarcity of left-turn lanes, long multidirectional traffic signals, and, most critically, very limited access to westbound I-4 (toward Disney). From the Orange County Convention Center south to the Beachline Expressway and Central Florida Parkway, getting on westbound I-4 is straightforward and easy. But in the stretch where the hotels are concentrated (from Kirkman Road to about a mile south of Sand Lake Road), the only way most visitors know to access I-4 westbound is to fight through the gridlock of the I-Drive–Sand Lake Road intersection en route to the I-4–Sand Lake Road interchange. A long, long traffic signal, a sea of motorists, and insufficient turn lanes make this absolutely grueling.

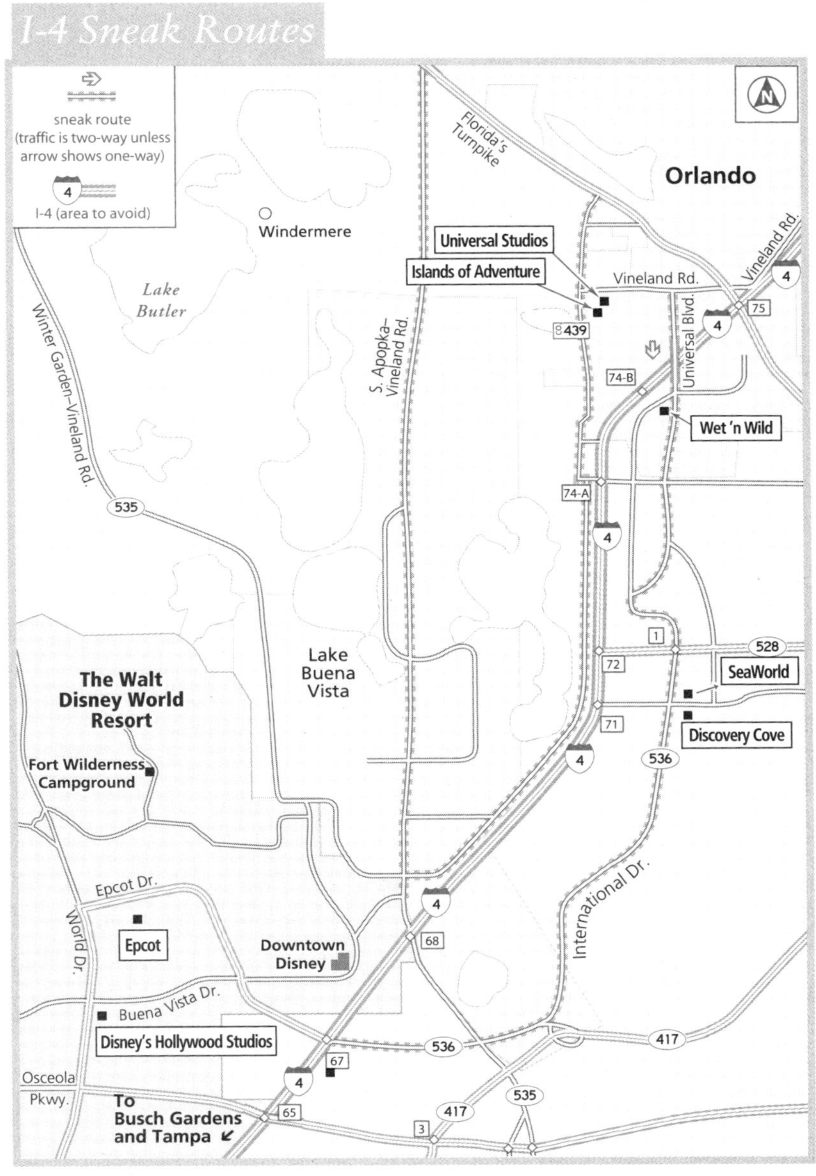

The object, therefore, is to access I-4 westbound without getting on Sand Lake Road. If your hotel is north of Sand Lake, access Kirkman Road by going north on I-Drive (in the opposite direction of the heaviest traffic) to the Kirkman Road intersection and turning left, or by cutting over to Kirkman via eastbound Carrier Drive. In either case, take Kirkman north over I-4, and at the first traffic signal (at the entrance to Universal Orlando), make a U-turn. This will put you

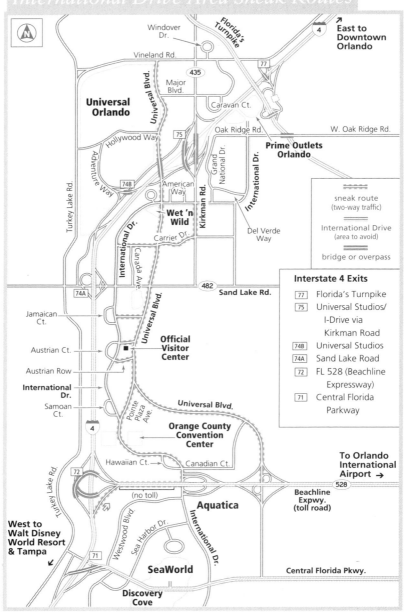

International Drive Area Sneak Routes

sneak route (two-way traffic)
International Drive (area to avoid)
bridge or overpass

Interstate 4 Exits

77	Florida's Turnpike
75	Universal Studios/ I-Drive via Kirkman Road
74B	Universal Studios
74A	Sand Lake Road
72	FL 528 (Beachline Expressway)
71	Central Florida Parkway

N
Windover Dr.
Florida's Turnpike
4
East to Downtown Orlando
Vineland Rd.
77
435
Major Blvd.
Universal Blvd.
Universal Orlando
Caravan Ct.
Oak Ridge Rd.
W. Oak Ridge Rd.
75
Hollywood Way
Prime Outlets Orlando
Grand National Dr.
International Dr.
Adventure Way
74B
American Way
Kirkman Rd.
Turkey Lake Rd.
Wet 'n Wild
Del Verde Way
International Dr.
Carrier Dr.
Canada Ave.
482
Sand Lake Rd.
74A
Universal Blvd.
Jamaican Ct.
Austrian Ct.
Official Visitor Center
Austrian Row
International Dr.
Samoan Ct.
Universal Blvd.
Pointe Plaza Ave.
4
Orange County Convention Center
Hawaiian Ct.
Canadian Ct.
To Orlando International Airport →
72
528
Turkey Lake Rd.
(no toll)
Aquatica
Beachline Expwy. (toll road)
Westwood Blvd.
Sea Harbor Dr.
International Dr.
West to Walt Disney World Resort & Tampa
71
SeaWorld
Central Florida Pkwy.
Discovery Cove

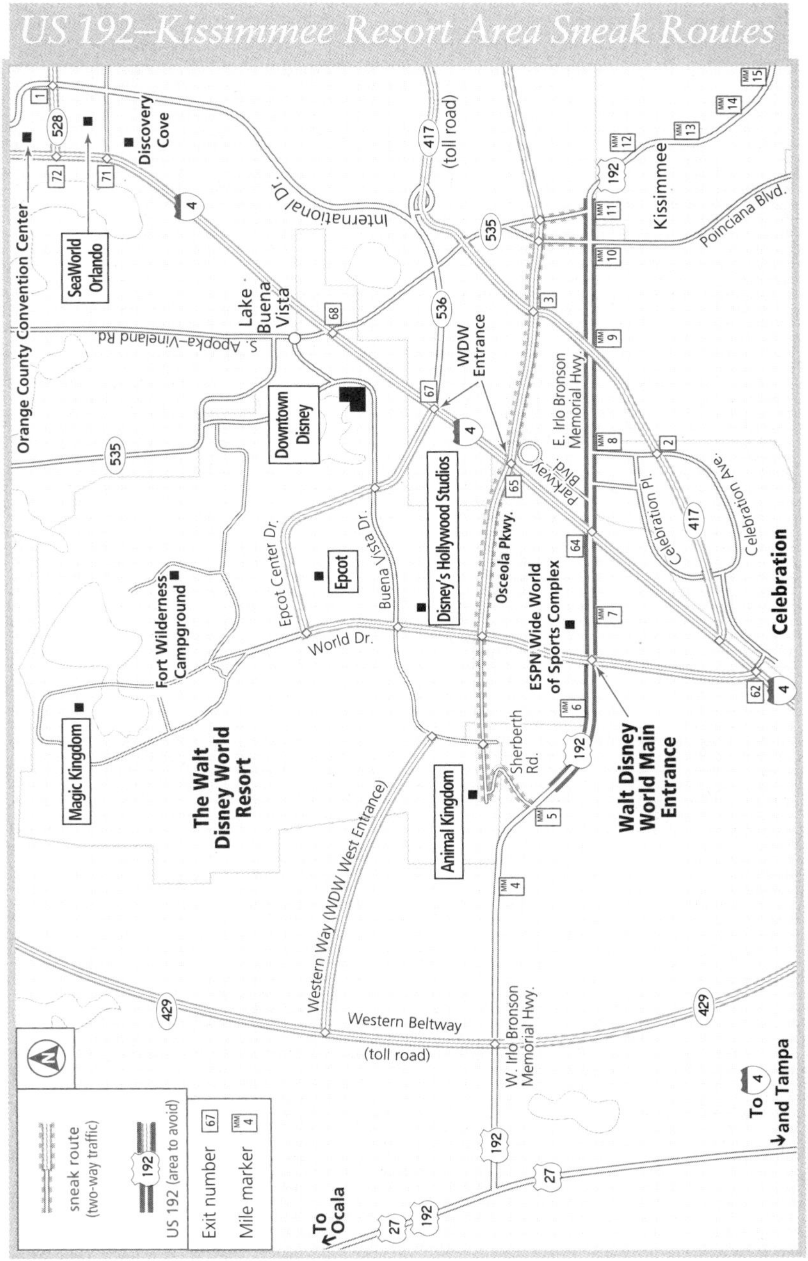

US 192–Kissimmee Resort Area Sneak Routes

Orange County Convention Center
SeaWorld Orlando
Discovery Cove
International Dr.
417 (toll road)
Lake Buena Vista
S. Apopka–Vineland Rd.
Downtown Disney
WDW Entrance
Kissimmee
Poinciana Blvd.
E. Irlo Bronson Memorial Hwy.
Parkway Blvd.
Celebration Pl.
Celebration Ave.
Celebration
Disney's Hollywood Studios
Osceola Pkwy.
ESPN Wide World of Sports Complex
Epcot
Epcot Center Dr.
Buena Vista Dr.
World Dr.
Fort Wilderness Campground
Magic Kingdom
The Walt Disney World Resort
Walt Disney World Main Entrance
Sherberth Rd.
Animal Kingdom
Western Way (WDW West Entrance)
Western Beltway (toll road)
W. Irlo Bronson Memorial Hwy.
To Ocala
To 4 and Tampa

sneak route (two-way traffic)
US 192 (area to avoid)
Exit number
Mile marker

directly onto an I-4 westbound ramp. A second way to access I-4 westbound from this section of I-Drive is to take Universal Boulevard (parallels I-Drive to the east) north. After you cross I-4 onto Universal property, stay left and follow the signs through two left turns to I-4. The signs are small, so stay alert.

If your hotel is south of Sand Lake Road but north of Austrian Court, cut over to Universal Boulevard, which parallels I-Drive to the east. Do this via Austrian Row. Turn right (south) on Universal Boulevard. Continue until you intersect the Beachline Expressway, and then take the Beachline west to I-4 (no toll).

US 192 (IRLO BRONSON MEMORIAL HIGHWAY) US 192, known locally as the Irlo Bronson Memorial Highway, runs east–west along the southern border of Disney World. From the Disney World entrance west on US 192 toward Clermont and east toward Kissimmee is a concentration of hotels. The highway was widened in 2001–02, and, though heavily used, it has ample turn lanes and traffic flows pretty well. The problem is the many long, multidirectional traffic signals. Even so, driving US 192 is easy compared with International Drive. Best of all, there are no godawful intersections like that of I-Drive and Sand Lake Road.

Conspicuous mile markers are posted along US 192. If you know which marker is closest to your hotel, navigation is a snap. The main entrance (Maingate) to Disney World is between mile markers 6 and 7, and almost all US 192 hotels and restaurants are between mile markers 4 and 15. If your hotel is between markers 5 and 10, no sneak routes are necessary. If it's between markers 1 and 5, save time by entering Disney property via Sherberth Road, which runs into Animal Kingdom and the west end of Osceola Parkway. This road existed before Animal Kingdom or Osceola Parkway, but there are absolutely no signs on US 192 indicating that Sherberth Road affords a shortcut into and out of Disney property. When you turn onto Sherberth from US 192, bear right almost immediately at the fork. Continue until you reach a major intersection with Disney signage. Turn right and then continue straight to Osceola Parkway and most of Disney World, or left to Animal Kingdom Lodge. To get to Animal Kingdom, turn right and look immediately for the turn lane that will take you into the theme park's parking lot. Osceola Parkway, a toll road, doesn't levy tolls until it crosses I-4 and leaves Disney property.

If your hotel is between markers 10 and 15, save time (but pay modest tolls) by taking Osceola Parkway west to Disney World. If your hotel is between markers 10 and 11, go north on Poinciana Boulevard to access Osceola Parkway. If your hotel is between markers 11 and 15, go north on FL 535. Turn west onto Osceola Parkway to reach Animal Kingdom and Disney's Hollywood Studios. For Epcot, the Magic Kingdom, and Downtown Disney, continue on FL 535 past the Osceola Parkway to the intersection with FL 536. Turn left on FL 536 and follow the signs to your Disney destination.

FL 535 (APOPKA–VINELAND ROAD) There are a number of hotels northeast and southwest of I-4 on FL 535 (Apopka–Vineland Road) and on streets connecting to it. Though many guests commute to the parks through Disney property via Hotel Plaza Drive to Downtown Disney and then via Buena Vista Drive, it's much easier to take I-4 west from FL 535 and enter the Disney property on Epcot Center Drive for Epcot and the Magic Kingdom; and on Osceola Parkway for Disney's Hollywood Studios and Animal Kingdom.

I-4 Construction at the I-4–US 192 interchange was completed in 2009, so many of the construction-related delays on I-4 have been eliminated. Nevertheless, expect heavy traffic and possible delays westbound on I-4 from 7 to about 9:30 a.m. Eastbound toward Orlando, expect heavy traffic from 4 to 7 p.m. If you want to avoid I-4 altogether, check out our I-4 sneak routes, detailed in the map on page 399.

TAKING A SHUTTLE BUS FROM YOUR OUT-OF-THE-WORLD HOTEL

MANY INDEPENDENT HOTELS and motels near Disney World provide trams and buses. They're fairly carefree, depositing you near theme-park entrances and saving you parking fees. The rub is that they might not get you there as early as you desire (a critical point if you take our touring advice) or be available when you wish to return to your lodging. Each service is different; check details before you make reservations.

Some shuttles go directly to Disney World, while others stop at other hotels en route. This can be a problem if your hotel is the second or third stop on the route. During periods of high demand, buses frequently fill up at the first stop, leaving little or no room for passengers at subsequent stops. Before booking, inquire how many hotels are on the route and the sequence of the stops. The different hotels are often so close together that you can easily walk to the first hotel on the route and board there. Similarly, if there's a large hotel nearby, it might have its own dedicated bus service that is more efficient. Use it instead of the service provided by your hotel. The majority of out-of-the-World shuttles work on a fixed schedule instead of arriving and departing somewhat randomly like the Disney buses. Knowing exactly when a bus will depart makes it easier to plan your day.

unofficial **TIP**
Warning: Most shuttles don't add vehicles at park-opening or -closing times. In the mornings, you may not get a seat.

At closing or during a hard rain, more people will be waiting for the shuttle than it can hold, and some will be left behind. Most shuttles return for stranded guests, but guests may wait 20 minutes to more than an hour for a ride.

If you're depending on shuttles, leave the park at least 45 minutes before closing. If you stay until closing and don't want to hassle with the shuttle, take a cab. Cab stands are near the Bus Information buildings at Animal Kingdom, Epcot, Disney's Hollywood Studios, and the TTC. If no cabs are on hand, Bus Information staff will call one. If you're leaving the Magic Kingdom at closing, it's easier to take the monorail to a hotel and hail a cab there rather than at the TTC taxi stand.

THE DISNEY TRANSPORTATION SYSTEM

THE DISNEY TRANSPORTATION SYSTEM (DTS) IS LARGE, diversified, and generally efficient, but it sometimes is overwhelmed, particularly at park-opening and -closing times. If you could be assured of getting on a bus, boat, or monorail at these critical times, we would advise you to leave your car at home. However, when huge crowds want to go somewhere at the same time, delays are unavoidable. In addition, some destinations are served directly, while many others require one or more transfers. Finally, it's sometimes difficult to figure how the buses, boats, and monorails interconnect.

Basically, Disney has a "hub and spoke" system. Hubs include the TTC, Downtown Disney, and all four major theme parks (from two hours before official opening time to two to three hours after closing). Although there are exceptions, there's direct service from Disney resorts to the major theme parks and Downtown Disney, and between parks.

If a hotel offers boat or monorail service, its bus service will be limited; you'll have to transfer at a hub for many destinations. If you're staying at a Magic Kingdom resort served by monorail (Polynesian, Contemporary–Bay Lake Tower, Grand Floridian), you'll be able to commute efficiently to the Magic Kingdom. If you want to visit Epcot, you must take the monorail to the TTC and transfer to the Epcot monorail. (Guests at the Polynesian can eliminate the transfer by walking 5 to 10 minutes to the TTC and catching the direct monorail to Epcot.)

unofficial **TIP**
If you want to go from resort to resort or almost anywhere else, you'll have to transfer at a hub.

If you're staying at an Epcot resort (Swan, Dolphin, Yacht Club and Beach Club resorts, BoardWalk Inn and Villas), you can walk or commute via boat to Epcot's International Gateway (backdoor) entrance. Although direct buses link Epcot resorts to the Magic Kingdom and Animal Kingdom, there's no direct bus to Epcot's main entrance or Disney's Hollywood Studios. To reach the Studios from Epcot resorts, you must take a boat or walk.

The Caribbean Beach, Pop Century, Saratoga Springs, Port Orleans, Coronado Springs, Old Key West, Animal Kingdom Lodge and Villas, and All-Star resorts offer direct buses to all theme parks. The rub is that guests sometimes must walk a long way to bus stops or endure more than a half-dozen additional pickups before actually heading for the park(s). Commuting in the morning from these resorts is generally easy, though you may have to ride standing. Returning in the evening, however, can be a different story. Shades of Green runs continuous shuttles from the resort to the TTC, where guests can transfer to their final destination.

Hotels of the Downtown Disney Resort Area (DDRA) (except the Hilton) terminated their guest-transportation contract with Disney some years ago and provide service through another carrier. The substitute, which we feel doesn't measure up, constitutes a real problem for guests at these hotels. Before booking a hotel in the DDRA, check the nature and frequency of shuttles.

Fort Wilderness guests must use campground buses to reach boat landings, or the Settlement Depot and Reception Outpost bus stops. From these points, guests can travel directly by boat to the Magic Kingdom or by bus to other destinations. Except for going to the Magic Kingdom, the best way for Fort Wilderness guests to commute is in their car.

Though readers who use the Disney bus system are generally satisfied customers, this Frankston, Texas, mom thinks there's need for improvement:

The only complaint I have about WDW is the bus system. I understand the wait is going to seem long at times. I understand that it is about as efficient as it can be given the sheer number of people they are moving at a time. I do not *understand making people pack in and stand on a moving bus. This does not seem at all safe to me, especially when traveling with children. I'm thinking Disney could buy bigger buses or add an extra bus or four into the rotation. We chose to wait on another bus rather than stand while holding all of our stuff and a tired toddler. There has got to be a better and safer way.*

The Disney Transportation System versus Driving Your Own Car

To help you assess your transportation options, we've developed a chart (see following pages) comparing the approximate commuting times from Disney resorts to various Walt Disney World destinations, using Disney transportation or your own car.

DISNEY TRANSPORTATION Times on the chart in the DTS columns represent an average-case and worst-case scenario. For example, if you want to go from the Caribbean Beach Resort to Epcot, the chart indicates the times as 34 (48). The first number, 34, indicates how many minutes your commute will take on an average day. It assumes that buses run every 13 minutes, there are no major delays, and everything else is as usual. It represents the average time we observed during our research of the transportation system. For the pessimists, the number in parentheses (48) indicates the worst-case scenario. (*Example:* The bus is pulling away as you arrive at the stop, and you must wait 13 minutes for the next one. When you finally board, the bus makes a number of additional stops before heading for Epcot. Once en route, the bus hits every red light.) When planning your transportation time, you'll do best to assume that your trip will take about the same time as the average in the chart (the first number). If you are running on a rigid schedule and you need to be sure of your arrival time, you can use the maximum time (the second number) to plan conservatively.

By far the biggest influence on your travel time between two points on the DTS is the amount of time you have to wait for your bus to arrive. Once you hop on your bus, the travel time is pretty consistent barring any unusual traffic problems; but your time waiting for the bus can vary greatly. Most cast members will tell you that buses run every 10 to 15 minutes—and, with the exceptions of Old Key West and Saratoga Springs (where buses often run every 45 to 50 minutes), they typically do. But they are also adjusted based on demand. We observed and timed over 250 bus routes: the intervals between buses arriving at a resort and those headed for the same destination ranged from 1 minute to 48 minutes!

The first number in the chart expresses the average transportation time, but our data shows that about 20% of the time your actual travel time will be less than half the average. So don't be surprised if your trip from Caribbean Beach Resort to Epcot takes only 15 minutes instead of the 34 (48) listed. Consider yourself lucky and enjoy the extra 19 minutes, doing something fun.

Door-to-door Commuting Times to and from the Disney Resorts and Parks

AVERAGE TIME (maximum time) IN MINUTES FROM	TO MAGIC KINGDOM		TO EPCOT		TO DHS	
	Your car	Disney system	Your car	Disney system	Your car	Disney system
ALL-STAR RESORTS	37 (47)	22 (32)	18 (23)	29 (40)	16 (20)	23 (33)
ANIMAL KINGDOM	37 (48)	49 (67)	16 (17)	26 (37)	16 (17)	24 (34)
ANIMAL KNG. LODGE & VILLAS	39 (50)	35 (50)	19 (21)	28 (39)	18 (19)	26 (37)
BEACH CLUB	36 (46)	22 (32)	16 (21)	17 (28*)	14 (18)	26 (37)
BLIZZARD BEACH	36 (46)	27 (38)	18 (23)	50 (69)	18 (22)	39 (54)
BOARDWALK INN & VILLAS	36 (46)	25 (35)	16 (21)	10 (21)	14 (18)	26 (37)
CARIBBEAN BEACH	37 (47)	30 (42)	18 (23)	34 (48)	15 (19)	23 (33)
CONTEMPORARY–BAY LAKE	–	11 (16)	21 (26)	20 (28)	23 (27)	29 (39)
CORONADO SPRINGS	37 (47)	22 (31)	18 (23)	19 (27)	16 (20)	18 (26)
DHS	36 (46)	24 (34)	19 (24)	24 (34)	–	–
DOLPHIN	35 (45)	19 (29)	15 (20)	23 (35*)	15 (19)	22 (32)
DOWNTOWN DISNEY#	38 (49)	46 (64)	20 (25)	45 (63)	17 (22)	56 (77)
D'TWN. DISNEY RESORT AREA	41 (51)	68 (90)	21 (26)	46 (61)	20 (24)	45 (60)
EPCOT	36 (46)	25 (36)	–	–	19 (23)	21 (30)
FORT WILDERNESS	37 (47)	16 (26)	18 (23)	48 (66)	19 (23)	39 (54)
GRAND FLORIDIAN	–	6 (7)	18 (23)	32 (44)	20 (24)	23 (33)
MAGIC KINGDOM	–	–	26 (39)	32 (44)	21 (29)	24 (34)
OLD KEY WEST	36 (46)	30 (42)	18 (23)	25 (36)	18 (22)	26 (37)
POLYNESIAN	–	10 (13)	17 (22)	37 (52**)	19 (23)	19 (29)
POP CENTURY RESORT	40 (51)	24 (34)	23 (28)	20 (31)	20 (24)	18 (28)
PORT ORLEANS FRENCH QTR.	37 (47)	22 (32)	19 (24)	25 (36)	19 (23)	24 (34)
PORT ORLEANS RIVERSIDE	38 (48)	22 (32)	20 (25)	23 (33)	20 (24)	24 (34)
SARATOGA SPRINGS	38 (48)	22 (32)	18 (23)	27 (38)	20 (24)	24 (34)
SHADES OF GREEN	28 (36)	34 (48)	18 (23)	32 (44)	20 (24)	20 (28)
SWAN	35 (45)	19 (29)	15 (20)	23 (35*)	15 (19)	22 (32)
TYPHOON LAGOON	37 (47)	40 (55)	18 (23)	50 (69)	15 (19)	62 (85)
TREEHOUSE VILLAS	37 (47)	26 (37)	18 (23)	26 (37)	19 (23)	25 (36)
WILDERNESS LODGE	–	19 (34)	20 (25)	32 (44)	22 (26)	37 (52)
YACHT CLUB	36 (46)	37 (47)	16 (21)	26 (34*)	14 (18)	26 (37)

†Driving time vs. time on DTS. Driving times include time in your car, stops to pay tolls, time to park, and transfers on Disney trams and monorails where applicable.

#Transportation between Downtown Disney and the parks requires transfers at a nearby resort.

In Your Car versus the Disney Transportation System[†]

TO ANIMAL KINGDOM		TO TYPHOON LAGOON		TO DOWNTOWN DISNEY		TO BLIZZARD BEACH	
Your car	Disney system	Your car	Disney system	Your car	Disney system	Your car	Disney system
11 (12)	22 (34)	12 (13)	17 (25)	13 (14)	27 (39)	6 (7)	25 (36)
–	–	17 (19)	45 (63)	19 (21)	42 (58)	10 (13)	21 (30)
9 (10)	11 (18)	19 (21)	44 (62)	22 (24)	41 (57)	11 (14)	27 (39)
17 (18)	25 (37)	9 (10)	29 (41)	10 (11)	22 (33)	12 (13)	28 (40)
10 (13)	27 (39)	13 (14)	60 (83)	14 (15)	61 (84)	–	–
17 (18)	27 (39)	9 (10)	30 (44)	10 (11)	24 (35)	12 (13)	28 (40)
17 (18)	32 (46)	6 (7)	26 (38)	7 (8)	30 (42)	12 (13)	40 (56)
20 (21)	26 (38)	17 (18)	27 (39)	16 (17)	37 (52)	15 (16)	42 (58)
11 (12)	19 (28)	12 (13)	17 (25)	13 (14)	27 (39)	6 (7)	24 (35)
16 (17)	21 (31)	8 (9)	57 (79)	9 (10)	58 (80)	11 (12)	36 (51)
16 (17)	24 (36)	10 (11)	33 (47)	11 (12)	27 (39)	11 (12)	19 (28)
19 (21)	39 (55)	6 (7)	16 (24)	–	–	14 (16)	36 (51)
21 (22)	49 (65)	9 (10)	6 (9)	6 (7)	–	16 (17)	46 (61)
16 (17)	34 (49)	12 (13)	30 (42)	13 (14)	40 (56)	11 (12)	31 (45)
24 (25)	42 (58)	10 (11)	37 (52)	11 (12)	45 (63)	19 (20)	42 (58)
18 (19)	24 (36)	15 (16)	39 (55)	16 (17)	49 (68)	13 (14)	30 (44)
17 (18)	46 (64)	23 (31)	39 (55)	27 (36)	49 (68)	12 (13)	41 (57)
19 (20)	30 (42)	8 (9)	22 (33)	9 (10)	23 (34)	14 (15)	35 (50)
17 (18)	20 (32)	14 (15)	44 (62)	15 (16)	54 (75)	12 (13)	32 (46)
14 (16)	20 (32)	12 (14)	36 (51)	15 (16)	27 (39)	10 (12)	37 (52)
19 (20)	28 (40)	9 (10)	23 (34)	10 (11)	30 (44)	14 (15)	42 (60)
20 (21)	28 (40)	10 (11)	22 (33)	11 (12)	27 (39)	15 (16)	35 (50)
21 (22)	28 (40)	9 (10)	24 (35)	6 (7)	18 (27)	16 (17)	34 (49)
18 (19)	23 (34)	15 (16)	39 (55)	18 (20)	49 (68)	13 (14)	30 (44)
16 (17)	24 (36)	10 (11)	33 (47)	11 (12)	27 (39)	11 (12)	19 (28)
17 (19)	42 (60)	–	–	6 (7)	16 (24)	13 (14)	42 (60)
20 (21)	29 (41)	9 (10)	23 (34)	8 (9)	21 (31)	15 (16)	35 (50)
20 (21)	37 (52)	17 (18)	32 (46)	18 (19)	52 (72)	15 (16)	40 (56)
17 (18)	29 (41)	9 (10)	30 (44)	10 (11)	24 (35)	12 (13)	28 (40)

*This hotel is within walking distance of Epcot; time given is for boat transportation to the International Gateway (Epcot's rear entrance).

**By foot to Transportation and Ticket Center and then by Epcot monorail

DRIVING YOUR OWN CAR The chart's "Your Car" column indicates the average-case and worst-case scenario for driving. To make these times directly comparable to DTS times, we added the time needed to get from your parked car to the park's entrance. While buses and monorails deposit guests at the park's entrance, those who drive must take a tram from their car to the gate or walk. At the Magic Kingdom, you must take a tram from the parking lot to the TTC, then catch a monorail or ferry to the entrance.

Disney Transportation System for Teenagers

If you're staying at Disney World and have teens in your party, familiarize yourself with the Disney bus system. Safe, clean, and operating until 1 a.m. (later from Downtown Disney) on most nights, buses are a great way for teens to get around.

Walt Disney World Bus Service

Disney buses have an illuminated panel above the windshield that flashes the bus's destination. Also, theme parks have designated waiting areas for each Disney destination. To catch the bus to the Caribbean Beach Resort from Disney's Hollywood Studios, for example, go to the bus stop and wait in the area marked TO THE CARIBBEAN BEACH RESORT. At the resorts, go to any bus stop and wait for the bus displaying your destination on the illuminated panel. Directions to Disney destinations are available when you check in or at your hotel's Guest Relations desk. Guest Relations also can answer questions about the transportation system.

Service from resorts to major theme parks is fairly direct. You may have intermediate stops, but you won't have to transfer. Service to the water parks and other Disney World hotels sometimes requires transfers.

The fastest way to commute among resorts by bus is to take a bus from your resort to one of the major theme parks and transfer there for your resort destination. This works, of course, only when the parks are open (actually, from two hours before opening until two to three hours after closing). If you're attempting to commute to another resort for a late dinner during the off-season, when parks close early, you'll have to transfer at Downtown Disney or the TTC. Disney, in its transportation instructions, somewhat disingenuously lists Downtown Disney as the transfer point for all resort-to-resort commuting, hoping that you'll stop and do a little shopping en route. If the theme-park buses are running, however, proceed to the theme park closest to your resort and transfer to the bus going to the resort where you'll be dining.

Bus service to the theme parks begins about 7 a.m. on days when the parks' official opening is 9 a.m. Generally, the buses run every 20 minutes. Buses to all four parks deliver you to the park entrance.

To be on hand for opening time (when official opening is 9 a.m.), catch direct buses to Epcot, Animal Kingdom, and Disney's Hollywood Studios between 7:30 and 8 a.m. Catch direct buses to the Magic Kingdom between 8 and 8:15 a.m. If you must transfer to reach your park, leave 15 to 20 minutes earlier. On days when official opening is 7 or 8 a.m., move up your departure time accordingly.

For your return bus trip in the evening, leave the park 40 minutes to an hour before closing to avoid the rush. If you're caught in the exodus, you may be inconvenienced, but you won't be stranded. Buses, boats, and monorails continue to operate for two hours after the parks close.

Is It the Recession?

Causality is often hard to determine in the mysterious Oz that controls the Disney Transportation System. However, a barrage of reader comments and complaints in the first half of 2009 suggests that cost-cutting measures have led to myriad problems in the system—and much inconvenience to guests.

A woman from Charlotte, North Carolina, offers this:

The bus service to the parks from Animal Kingdom Lodge was poor in the evenings. We had to wait an hour two times because there were so many people waiting. I think Animal Kingdom Lodge should use the chain system [i.e., create an organized queuing area] *like the Value resorts do to maintain the queue. Guests pushed their way to the front when others had clearly been waiting longer.*

From a Decatur, Georgia, reader:

I was really gung-ho about staying on-site and using the buses, but having done it, I would probably not do it again. The buses were just too crowded and unpleasant. Even staying at one of the closest resorts (by bus), we found it took about an hour each way by the time we walked to the bus stations, waited, and walked back to our rooms.

A Tacoma, Washington, reader comments:

Bus service overall: marginal. We may not stay on-property next time due to poor bus service; four years ago, buses were great. ???

From a Spartanburg, South Carolina, family of four:

We went to WDW in June 2006 and had a great experience with the buses. This time, bus service was deplorable. We often had to wait 30 to 60 minutes for a bus at our resort's bus depot. Clearly, not enough buses were running to accommodate people. We almost missed dinner reservations a few times because of slow bus service. It's ridiculous to have to leave the resort AT LEAST an hour before the reservation. . . . you have to spend half of your vacation at the bus depot!

A reader who stayed at Port Orleans reports:

The Disney Transportation System was, of course, wildly erratic, but we ended up with more luck than not. For every time we had to wait a half-hour at the bus stop, there were two or three times with no wait at all.

From a Torrington, Connecticut, couple:

Buses are totally efficient in the morning but fall apart in the afternoon. By afternoon the waits can get long, but then two or three buses to the same park will show up at nearly the same time. They get out of sequence, I guess.

A Laurel, Maryland, dad shared the following:

> *Bus service was frustrating. Some occasions we walked to the bus stop at the hotel and walked right on a bus; other occasions we waited while buses for other parks came and went. Sometimes a bus made many stops at* [Port Orleans] *Riverside resort; other times it went straight to the park. The bus service from the park to the hotel was worse, with two occasions where it took us over an hour from the time we got to the bus stop at the park until we arrived at our hotel.*

If you're planning on riding a bus from Port Orleans Riverside to a park around opening time, going to the West or North bus stop may be your best option. These are the first stops on the route, and the bus is sometimes full or or standing-room-only before it gets to all the stops.

From a Huntsville, Alabama, mother of three:

> *Best advice given was driving to the park instead of relying on the bus system.*

Finally, a family from Toms River, New Jersey, who stayed at the BoardWalk Inn reports:

> *The transportation by bus (Magic Kingdom and Animal Kingdom) was the worst. We waited at least 40 minutes every time and almost missed a dinner reservation (for which we left 1½ hours early). I also did not like having multiple stops.* [The BoardWalk Inn and Villas provide boat service to the other two parks.]

Not All Hubs Are Created Equal

All major theme parks, Downtown Disney, and the TTC are hubs on the bus system. If your route requires you to transfer at a hub, transfer at the closest park or the TTC, except at theme-park closing time. Avoid Downtown Disney as a transfer point. Because each bus makes multiple stops within Downtown Disney, it takes 16 to 25 minutes just to get out of the complex!

unofficial **TIP**
There are multiple stops at Downtown Disney, so never use it as a transfer point except as a last resort.

Downtown Disney Resort Area Bus Service

Although they're inside Disney World, hotels of Downtown Disney Resort Area provide their own bus service—one that many guests, including a family from Prospect, Connecticut, find inferior:

> *We were disappointed in the shuttle bus for the* [DDRA] *hotels. They do not run often enough, and there is no schedule.* [The b]*us at the parks picks up in* [the] *middle of busy parking lots. Treats you as second class* [compared] *to Disney-resort guests. Take a cab instead of waiting late at night to get back to* [your] *hotel. Costs only $9.*

Walt Disney World Monorail Service

Picture the monorail system as three loops. Loop A is an express route that runs counterclockwise connecting the Magic Kingdom with the

TTC. Loop B runs clockwise alongside Loop A, making all stops, with service to (in this order) the TTC, Polynesian Resort, Grand Floridian, Magic Kingdom, Contemporary Resort–Bay Lake Tower, and back to the TTC. The long Loop C dips southeast, connecting the TTC with Epcot. The hub for all loops is the TTC (where you usually park to visit the Magic Kingdom).

The monorail serving Magic Kingdom resorts usually starts an hour and a half before official opening. If you're staying at a Magic Kingdom resort and wish to be among the first in the Magic Kingdom when official opening is 9 a.m., board the monorail at these times:

From the Contemporary Resort–Bay Lake Tower	7:45–8 a.m.
From the Polynesian Resort	7:50–8:05 a.m.
From the Grand Floridian Beach Resort	8–8:10 a.m.

If you're a day guest, you'll be allowed on the monorail at the TTC between 8:15 and 8:30 a.m. when official opening is 9 a.m. If you want to board earlier, walk from the TTC to the Polynesian Resort and board there.

The monorail connecting Epcot and the TTC begins operating at 7:30 a.m. when Epcot's official opening is 9 a.m. To be at Epcot when it opens, catch the Epcot monorail at the TTC by 8:05 a.m.

unofficial **TIP**
Monorails usually run for 2 hours after closing. If a train is too crowded or you need transportation after the monorails have stopped, catch a bus. *Note:* As a safety measure, Disney no longer permits guests to ride in the front of a train.

While your Park Hopper pass suggests you can flit among parks, getting there is more complicated. For example, you can't go directly from the Magic Kingdom to Epcot. You must catch the express monorail (Loop A) to the TTC and transfer to the Loop C monorail to Epcot. If lines to board either monorail are short, you can usually reach Epcot in 30 to 40 minutes. But should you want to go to Epcot for dinner (as many do) and you're departing the Magic Kingdom in late afternoon, you may have to wait 30 minutes or longer to board the Loop A monorail. Adding this delay boosts your commute to 50 to 60 minutes.

PART NINE

BARE NECESSITIES

CREDIT CARDS *and* MONEY

CREDIT CARDS

AMERICAN EXPRESS, DINERS CLUB, DISCOVER, Japan Credit Bureau, MasterCard, and Visa are accepted throughout Walt Disney World.

BANKING SERVICES

BANK SERVICE AT THE THEME PARKS is limited to ATMs, which are marked on the park maps and are plentiful throughout Walt Disney World; most MasterCard and Visa cards are accepted. To use an American Express card, you must sign an agreement with Amex before your trip. If your credit card doesn't work in the ATMs, a teller at any **SunTrust Bank** full-service location will process your transaction (visit **www.suntrust.com** for Orlando and WDW-area branches).

A LICENSE TO PRINT MONEY

ONE OF DISNEY'S MORE SUBLIME PLOYS for separating you from your money is the printing and issuing of **Disney Dollars.** Available throughout Disney World in denominations of $1, $5, $10, and $50, each emblazoned with a Disney character, the colorful cash can be used for purchases in Disney World, Disneyland, and Disney Stores nationwide. Disney Dollars can also be exchanged one-for-one with U.S. currency, but only while you're in Disney World. Also, you need your sales receipt to exchange for U.S. dollars. Disney money is sometimes a perk (for which you're charged dollar-for-dollar) in Walt Disney Travel Company packages.

While Disney Dollars are one of Disney's better moneymakers. Some guests keep the money as souvenirs. Others forget to spend or exchange it before they leave the World, then fail to go to a Disney Store or to exchange it by mail. A Michigan family, however, found a way to make their Disney Dollars useful:

> *Your criticism of Disney Dollars is valid if people are dumb enough not to cash them in or use them in their local Disney Store. We used them. Since we had planned on going to Disney a year ahead of time,*

we asked people giving our children money for birthdays, Christmas, Tooth Fairy, etc., to give Disney Dollars instead. This forced both of our children (ages 5 and 7) to save the money for the trip.

VISITING MORE THAN ONE PARK IN A SINGLE DAY

IF YOU HAVE A PASS ALLOWING YOU to visit the Magic Kingdom, Animal Kingdom, Epcot, and Disney's Hollywood Studios in the same day, it will be validated with the date when you enter your first park. To enter another park, present your pass and have the fingertip of your index finger scanned by a biometric reader.

PROBLEMS *and* UNUSUAL SITUATIONS

ATTRACTIONS CLOSED FOR REPAIRS

FIND OUT IN ADVANCE WHAT RIDES AND ATTRACTIONS may be closed for maintenance or repair during your visit (check online at the WDW site or elsewhere). A mom from Dover, Massachusetts, laments:

> *We were disappointed to find Space Mountain, Swiss Family Treehouse, and the* Liberty Belle *Riverboat closed for repairs. We felt that a large chunk of the Magic Kingdom was not working, yet the tickets were still full price and expensive!*

A woman from Pasadena, California, adds:

> *Rides can close without warning. Our hotel even gave us a list of closed attractions. So, imagine our surprise when we get to the Magic Kingdom and find that Space Mountain is closed with no prior warning. Needless to say, we were disappointed.*

CAR TROUBLE

SECURITY PATROLS WILL HELP if you lock the keys in your parked car or find the battery dead. For more-serious problems, the closest repair facility is the **AAA Car Care Center** near the Magic Kingdom parking lot (☎ 407-824-0976).

The nearest off-World repair center is **Maingate Citgo** (US 192 west of Interstate 4; ☎ 407-396-2721). Disney security can help you find it. Farther away but highly recommended by one of our Orlando-area researchers is **Riker's Automotive & Tire** (5700 Central Florida Parkway, near SeaWorld; ☎ 407-238-9800; **www.rikersauto.com**). Says our source, "They do great work and are the only car place that has never tried to get extra money out of me 'cause I'm a woman and know nothing about cars. I love this place!"

GASOLINE

THERE ARE THREE FILLING STATIONS on Disney property. One station is adjacent to the AAA Car Care Center on the exit road from the Ticket and Transportation Center (Magic Kingdom) parking lot.

It's also convenient to the Shades of Green, Grand Floridian, and Polynesian resorts. Most centrally located is the station at the corner of Buena Vista Drive and Epcot Resorts Boulevard, near the BoardWalk Inn. A third station, also on Buena Vista Drive, is across from the former Pleasure Island site in Downtown Disney.

LOST AND FOUND

IF YOU LOSE (OR FIND) SOMETHING in the Magic Kingdom, go to City Hall. At Epcot, Lost and Found is in the Entrance Plaza. At Disney's Hollywood Studios, it's at Hollywood Boulevard Guest Relations, and at Animal Kingdom, it's at Guest Relations at the main entrance. If you discover your loss after you have left the park(s), call ☎ 407-824-4245 (for all parks). See page 30 for the number(s) to call if you're at the park(s) and discover your loss.

It's unusual for readers to send us tips about Lost and Found, but a mom from Indianapolis sent two!

> *Another one of our Disney experiences to learn from: hold on to your things on Space Mountain! My daughter lost her bag going over the first turn, and on an 80-minute wait-time day they had to shut the ride down to retrieve the bag! If you lose something on a ride and it has medication in it, Disney cast members will shut down a ride for 45 seconds to try and retrieve it. If they can't find it or it didn't contain meds, you have to come back to Lost and Found for it at the end of the day.*
>
> *You should tell people (especially families with teenagers!) that they should write down the serial numbers on their Park Hopper passes as soon as they get them. My 15-year-old daughter lost her pass one year, and with the serial number, cast members can look up when it was last used, giving you an idea of where it was lost. (We found ours in the hotel room, thankfully!)*

MEDICAL MATTERS

HEADACHE RELIEF Aspirin and other sundries are sold at the Emporium on Main Street in the Magic Kingdom (they're behind the counter; you must ask), at most retail shops in Epcot's Future World and World Showcase, and in Disney's Hollywood Studios and Animal Kingdom.

ILLNESSES REQUIRING MEDICAL ATTENTION A **Centra Care** walk-in clinic is at 12500 South Apopka–Vineland Road (☎ 407-934-CARE). It's open 8 a.m. to midnight weekdays and 8 a.m. to 8 p.m. weekends. Centra Care also operates a 24-hour physician-house-call service and runs a free shuttle (☎ 407-938-0650).

A North Carolina family of four had a good experience at **Buena Vista Urgent Care** (8216 World Center Drive, Suite D; ☎ 407-465-1110):

> *We started day one needing medical care for our son, who has asthma and had developed croup. We found great care two miles down FL 535 at Buena Vista Urgent Care. We waited 20 minutes, and then we were off to the parks. Please add them to your guide.*

EastCoast Medical Network (☎ 407-648-5252) has board-certified physicians available 24/7 for house calls to your hotel room. They offer in-room X-rays and IV therapy service as well as same-day dental and specialist appointments. They also rent medical equipment. Insurance receipts, insurance billing, and foreign-language interpretation are provided. Walk-in clinics are also available. You also can inquire about transportation arrangements.

DOCS (Doctors on Call Service; ☎ 407-399-DOCS; **www.doctorsoncallservice.com**) offers 24-hour house-call service. All DOCS physicians are certified by the American Board of Medical Specialties.

DENTAL EMERGENCIES Call **Celebration Dental Group** (☎ 407-566-2222).

PRESCRIPTION MEDICINE Two nearby pharmacies are **Walgreens Lake Buena Vista** (☎ 407-238-0600) and **Winn-Dixie Pharmacy Lake Buena Vista** (☎ 407-465-8606). **Turner Drugs** (☎ 407-828-8125) charges $5 to deliver a filled prescription to your hotel's front desk. The service is available to Disney and non-Disney hotels in Turner Drugs' area. The fee is charged to your hotel account.

SERGEANT BLISTERBLASTER'S GUIDE TO HAPPY FEET

1. ON YOUR FEET! Get up, La-Z-Boy rider: when you go to Walt Disney World, you'll have to walk a lot farther than to the refrigerator. You can log 5 to 12 miles a day at the parks, so now's the time to shape up them dogs. Start with short walks around the neighborhood. Increase your distance gradually until you can do six miles without CPR.

2. A-TEN-SHUN! During your training program, pay attention when those puppies growl. They'll give you a lot of information about your feet and the appropriateness of your shoes. Listen up! No walking in flip-flops, loafers, or sandals. Wear well-constructed, broken-in running or hiking shoes. If you feel a "hot spot," that means a blister is developing. The most common sites for blisters are heels, toes, and balls of the feet. If you develop a hot spot in the same place every time you walk (a clue!), cover it prophylactically with moleskin (in drugstores without prescription) before you set out. No, Sofa Bunny, I didn't tell you to wear condoms on your feet! *Prophylactically* means to anticipate the problem and treat it in advance. One more thing: keep your toenails cut short and straight across.

3. SOCK IT UP, TRAINEE! Good socks are as important as good shoes. When you walk, your feet sweat like a mule in a peat bog, and the moisture only increases friction. To minimize friction, wear a pair of socks, such as SmartWool or CoolMax, that wick perspiration away from your feet (SmartWool makes socks of varying thicknesses). To further combat moisture, dust your dogs with some antifungal talcum powder.

4. WHO DO YOU THINK YOU ARE, JOHN WAYNE? Don't be a hero. Take care of a foot problem the minute you notice it. Carry a small foot-emergency kit for your platoon. Include gauze, Betadine antibiotic ointment, moleskin or Johnson & Johnson blister bandages, scissors, a sewing needle or such (to drain blisters), and matches to sterilize the needle. Extra socks and talc are optional.

5. BITE THE BULLET! If you develop a hot spot, cover it ASAP with moleskin. Cut the material large enough to cover the skin surrounding the spot. If you develop a blister, air out and dry your foot. Next, drain the fluid, but don't remove the top skin. Clean the area with Betadine and place a Johnson & Johnson blister bandage over the blister. The bandages come in several sizes, including specially shaped ones for fingers and toes; they're also good for covering hot spots. If you don't have moleskin or blister bandages, don't cover the hot spot or blister with Band-Aids; they'll slip and wad up.

6. TAKE CARE OF YOUR PLATOON. If you have young, green troops in your outfit, they might not sound off when a hot spot develops. Stop several times a day and check their feet. If you forgot your emergency kit and a problem arises, call the Disney medics. They have all the stuff you need to keep your command in action.

OK, troops, prepare to move out. Hit the trail and move those feet: left, right, left!

RAIN

WEATHER BAD? Go to the parks anyway. Crowds are lighter, and most attractions and waiting areas are under cover. Showers, especially during warmer months, are short.

Ponchos are about $7; umbrellas, about $13. All ponchos sold at Disney World are made of clear plastic, so picking out somebody in your party on a rainy day can be tricky. Walmart sells an inexpensive green poncho that will make your family emerald beacons in a plastic-covered sea of humanity.

unofficial **TIP**
Rain gear is one of the few bargains at the parks. It isn't always displayed in shops, so you have to ask for it.

Some unusually heavy rain precipitated (no pun intended) dozens of reader suggestions for dealing with soggy days. The best came from this Memphis, Tennessee, mom:

1. Rain gear should include poncho and umbrella. Umbrellas make the rain much more bearable. When rain isn't beating down on your ponchoed head, it's easier to ignore.
2. Buy blue ponchos at Walgreens. We could keep track of each other much easier because we had blue ponchos instead of clear ones.
3. If you're using a stroller, bring a plastic sheet or extra poncho to protect it from rain. Ponchos will cover the Disney single rental strollers but not the double strollers. Carry a towel in a plastic bag to wipe off your stroller after experiencing an attraction during a rainfall.

HOW TO LODGE A COMPLAINT WITH DISNEY

COMPLAINING ABOUT A LEAKY FAUCET or not having enough towels is pretty straightforward, and you usually will find Disney folks highly responsive. However, a more global gripe, or one beyond an on-site manager's ability to resolve, is likely to founder in the labyrinth of Disney bureaucracy.

One of our readers' foremost gripes relates to Disney's unresponsiveness in fielding complaints. A Providence, Rhode Island, dad's remarks are typical:

It's all warm fuzzies and big smiles until you have a problem. Then everybody plays [hide-and-seek]. *The only thing you know for sure is that it's never the responsibility of the Disney person you are talking to.*

A Mobile, Alabama, mother echoes his comment:

I made call after call, with one [Disney] *person passing me on to the next, until finally I ran out of steam. Basically, I had to choose between getting my problem addressed, which was pretty much a full-time job, or going ahead with my vacation.*

A Portland, Maine, reader summed it up in quintessential New England style:

Lodging a complaint with Disney is like shouting at a brick.

Like most companies, Disney would rather hear from you when the message is good. Regarding complaints, Disney prefers to receive them in writing, but by the time you get home and draft a letter, it's often too late to correct the problem. And though Disney would have you believe that it's a touchy-feely outfit, it generally isn't a company that will make things right for you after the fact. You may receive a letter thanking you for writing and expressing regret without acknowledging responsibility (for example, "We're sorry you felt inconvenienced"—as if the perception somehow arose from your imagination). It's unlikely, though, that they'll offer to do anything remedial. That said, if you want to lodge a complaint, write to **Walt Disney World Guest Communications, P.O. Box 10040, Lake Buena Vista, FL 32830-0040.** If you're really steamed, try writing the following higher-ups:

Robert Iger, CEO
The Walt Disney Company
500 South Buena Vista Street
Burbank, CA 91521

James Rasulo, Chairman
Walt Disney Parks & Resorts
500 South Buena Vista Street
Burbank, CA 91521

Meg Crofton, President
The Walt Disney World Resort
P.O. Box 10040
Lake Buena Vista, FL 32830

If Disney doesn't respond, you can always go public by writing:

Letters to the Editor
Orlando Sentinel
633 North Orange Avenue
Orlando, FL 32801-1349
☎ 407-420-5000; fax 407-420-5286
insight@orlandosentinel.com

If you're at Disney World and really need to settle an issue, keep your resort general manager's feet to the fire until he hooks you up with the person who can solve it.

SERVICES

MESSAGES

MESSAGES LEFT AT CITY HALL in the Magic Kingdom, Guest Relations at Epcot, Hollywood Boulevard Guest Relations at Disney's Hollywood Studios, or Guest Relations at Animal Kingdom can be retrieved at any of the four.

PET CARE

PETS AREN'T ALLOWED IN THE MAJOR or minor theme parks. But never leave an animal in a hot car while you tour; Fido will croak. Kennels and holding facilities are provided for temporary care of pets. They're adjacent to the Transportation and Ticket Center (for Magic Kingdom guests), left of the Epcot entrance plaza, left of the Disney's Hollywood Studios entrance plaza, at the outer entrance to Animal Kingdom, and at Fort Wilderness Campground. If you insist, kennel staff will accept about any type of animal (except wildlife), though owners of exotic and/or potentially vicious pets must place them in their assigned cage. Small pets (such as mice, hamsters, birds, snakes, and turtles) must stay in their own escape-proof carrier. Large pets (walrus, hippos, buffalo, emu, etc.) must be scrubbed and brushed before being admitted to the kennel. (Just seeing if you're awake.)

Here are additional details you should know:

- When traveling with your pet in Florida, have proof of vaccination and immunization, including bordatella for dogs.
- It's against Orange County law to leave a pet in a closed vehicle.
- Disney has contracted with **Best Friends Pet Care** (**www.bestfriends petcare.com**) to run its kennels.
- Advance Reservations for animals are required.
- Kennels open 1 hour before the park opens and close 1 hour after it closes. Kennels, however, are staffed 24 hours a day.
- Disney-resort guests may board a pet overnight for $18 per pet, per night. Others pay $20 per pet, per night. Pet day care for all guests is $15 per day. Kennels aren't set up for multiday boarding. Rates include two walks a day at Magic Kingdom, Epcot, and Fort Wilderness kennels. For Animal Kingdom and Disney's Hollywood Studios kennels, you must walk your dog yourself at least twice a day. For animals other than dogs, rates are $15 overnight for day visitors, $13 overnight for Disney-resort guests, and $10 for day care.
- Guests leaving exotic pets should supply their food.
- Pets are allowed at a limited number of sites at Fort Wilderness Campground; $5 per day, per pet.

For more information on pet care, call ☎ 407-824-6568 (Magic Kingdom), 407-560-6229 (Epcot), 407-560-4282 (Disney's Hollywood Studios), 407-938-2100 (Animal Kingdom), and 407-824-2735 (Fort Wilderness Resort and Campground).

PHOTOPASS

IF THE IDEA OF LUGGING A CAMERA AROUND Walt Disney World makes you think "pack mule" more than "vacation," Disney's willing to take that burden off your back. A service called PhotoPass allows you to collect digital photos taken by Disney photographers around Walt Disney World's theme parks and water parks throughout your vacation. When your trip is complete, all your photos will be available for purchase at **www.disneyphotopass.com.** Here's how it works:

1. Find a PhotoPass photographer to take your first picture. Photographers can be found throughout the theme parks and water parks, including near park entrances, in restaurants (and character meals), and around iconic attractions such as Splash Mountain.
2. After snapping the picture, the photographer will hand you a small plastic card with a PhotoPass ID number on it. Keep this card for your entire trip—the ID number uniquely identifies you in the PhotoPass system. Present the card to any other photographer before you have more PhotoPass pictures taken, and all the photos will be linked to that one PhotoPass account.
3. Visit the Web site within 30 days of your trip and enter your ID number to view your photos. The Web site allows you to add decorative borders and short captions to your pictures, too, as well as share photos online.

Unofficial Guide readers have sent in mixed reviews about the PhotoPass system. Those who favor the service say that it helps them avoid carrying a camera at all times. But modern multi-megapixel digital cameras and smart phones fit comfortably in your pocket, and most can take short videos as well as photos. The biggest complaint about PhotoPass is the cost: $13 for one 5-by-7-inch photo (plus shipping), and $149 for a CD with all your photos (advance purchase discounts are sometimes available). An entry-level ten-megapixel digital camera plus memory card costs roughly the same price; what's more, online photo printers such as **www.snapfish.com** and **photos .walmart.com** offer prints for as little as 9¢ apiece for a 4-by-6 (Snapfish) or 58¢ for a 5-by-7 (Walmart).

EXCUSE ME, BUT WHERE CAN I FIND . . .

RELIGIOUS SERVICES IN THE WALT DISNEY WORLD AREA? A complete list can be found on the Web at **www.allears.net/btp/church.htm.**

SOMEPLACE TO PUT ALL THESE PACKAGES? Lockers are available on the ground floor of the Main Street railroad station in the Magic Kingdom, to the right of Spaceship Earth in Epcot, and on the Ticket and Transportation Center's east and west ends. At Disney's Hollywood Studios, lockers are to the right of the entrance at Oscar's Classical Car Souvenirs. Animal Kingdom lockers are to the left inside the entrance. Cost is $7 a day for small lockers and $9 a day for large lockers; prices include a $5 refundable deposit. Lockers at Blizzard Beach and Typhoon Lagoon cost $8 (small) and $10 (large), also with a $5 refundable deposit.

Package Pick-Up is available at each major theme park. Ask the salesperson to send your purchases to Package Pick-Up. When you leave the park, they'll be waiting for you. Epcot has two exits, thus two Package Pick-Ups; specify main entrance or International Gateway. If you're staying at a Disney resort, you can also have the packages delivered to your room. If you're leaving within 24 hours, however, take them with you or use the in-pack pick-up location.

CAMERAS AND FILM? Camera Centers at the major parks sell disposable cameras for about $12 ($19 with flash). Film is sold throughout the World. Developing is available at most Disney hotel gift shops and at Camera Centers. Film processing is no longer available in any theme park, but Disney will take your digital memory cards and transfer the contents to a CD while you're in the parks. The cost is around $13 for 120 images, and around $6.50 for an additional 120 images. Prints are around 75¢ each. You'll need to leave your digital media with Disney while they create the CD, typically around two to five hours, so make sure you've got extra media on hand.

A GROCERY STORE? **Gooding's Supermarket,** in the Crossroads Shopping Center, across FL 535 from the Disney World entrance, is a large designer grocery. While its location makes it undeniably convenient, its gourmet selections (cheese, wine, and such) aren't nearly as extensive as they used to be, and if you're just looking for staples, you'll find the prices higher than the Tower of Terror, and just as frightening. For down-to-earth prices, try **Publix** at the intersection of International Drive and US 192, or **Winn-Dixie** on Apopka–Vineland Road about a mile north of Crossroads Shopping Center.

unofficial **TIP**
Be aware that Package Pick-Up closes two hours before the park. Disney-resort guests can have their purchases delivered to their hotel's gift shop.

We compiled a list of common vacation grocery items and went shopping. No item purchased was on sale. Here's how prices at Gooding's, Publix, and Winn-Dixie compared:

ITEM	GOODING'S	PUBLIX	WINN-DIXIE
Dozen doughnuts (Krispy Kreme)	$4.99	$4.99	$4.99
Maxwell House coffee (13 oz.)	$5.39	$3.41	$3.49
Mr. Coffee coffee filters (100 count)	$3.99	$1.79	$2.09
One gallon of milk (store brand)	$5.49	$2.89	$3.99
Tropicana orange juice (64 oz.)	$2.49	$3.79	$3.69
Cheerios (8.9 oz.)	$5.99	$4.89	$5.29
Coca-Cola (dozen 12-oz. cans)	$5.99	$4.71	$4.89
Lay's Potato Chips (12.5 oz.)	$3.99	$3.99	$3.99
Sugar (2 lbs., store brand)	$1.99	$1.29	$1.59
Chips Ahoy cookies (1 lb.)	$3.39	$3.69	$3.79
Budweiser (6-pack of 12-oz. cans)	$6.99	$5.69	$6.49
Bananas (4 lbs.)	$3.96	$2.76	$2.76
Wonder white bread (20 oz.)	$2.49	$2.59	$2.59
Jif or Skippy creamy peanut butter (12 oz.)	$3.59	$1.99	$2.79
Welch's grape jelly (18 oz.)	$2.89	$1.99	$2.19
Oral-B Advantage toothbrush	$4.59	$3.69	$3.99
Hawaiian Tropic SPF 30 sunscreen (8 oz.)	$11.99	$7.99	$7.99
Kodak Gold 200 film (24 exposures)	$6.99	$4.39	$5.99
TOTAL	**$87.19**	**$66.53**	**$72.59**

GROCERY MARKETS THAT DELIVER? If you don't have a car or you don't want to take the time to go to the supermarket, **GardenGrocer** (**www.gardengrocer.com**) will shop for you and deliver your groceries. The best way to compile your order is on GardenGrocer's Web site before you leave home. It's simple, and the selection is huge. If there's something you want that's not on their list of available items, they'll try to find it for you. Delivery arrangements are per your instructions. If you're staying at a hotel, you can arrange for your groceries to be left with bell services. For the sake of order-fulfillment accuracy and customer service, GardenGrocer is primarily set up for online ordering. If you can't get online, though, you can order by phone (☎ 866-855-4350) or fax (321-284-1946). For orders of $200 or more, there's no delivery charge; for orders less than $200, the delivery charge is $12; a minimum order of $40 is required. Prices for individual items are pretty much the same as you'd pay at the supermarket.

We've had lots of positive reader feedback about GardenGrocer. The following comment from an Eagan, Minnesota, family is representative:

> *GardenGrocer was fabulous. I ordered our groceries online about one week before our arrival. I had a few questions, so I called and actually spoke with a human who was very helpful! Our flight got in about 7 p.m., and I called to let them know we were on our way. They arrived about 20 minutes after we did with everything we ordered. We were ready to hit the parks early the next morning!*

You can also order online at the **Gooding's** Web site (**www.goodings.com**); a $50 minimum order is required, and a $20 service charge applies.

WINE, BEER, AND LIQUOR? Wine and beer are sold in grocery stores. **Gooding's,** on FL 535, used to be well regarded by the *Unofficial* team, but these days their selections are disappointing (not to mention expensive). The best selection of wine, beer, and liquor is at the **ABC Store** less than a mile north of the Crossroads shopping center, on Apopka–Vineland Road.

PART TEN

DINING *in and around* WALT DISNEY WORLD

DINING *outside* WALT DISNEY WORLD

UNOFFICIAL GUIDE RESEARCHERS love good food and invest a fair amount of time scouting new places to eat. And because food at Walt Disney World is so expensive, we (like you) have an economic incentive for finding palatable meals outside the World. Alas, the area surrounding Disney World is not exactly a culinary nirvana. If you thrive on fast food and the fare at chain restaurants (Denny's, T.G.I. Friday's,

In or Out of the World for These Cuisines?

American Good selections both in and out of the World.

Barbecue Better out of the World.

Buffets A toss-up—Disney buffets are expensive, but they offer excellent quality and extensive selections. Off-World buffets aren't as upscale but are inexpensive.

Chinese Better out of the World.

Eastern European Passable, but not great, in or out of the World.

French Toss-up. Reasonably good but expensive both in and out of the World.

Italian Tie on quality; better value out of the World.

Japanese/sushi Teppan Edo in the Japan Pavilion at Epcot is tops for teppan (table grilling). For sushi and sashimi, try Tokyo Dining, also in Japan, or visit Kimonos at the Swan resort.

Mexican San Angel Inn at Epcot is good but expensive, with more-affordable fare at Mexico's casual waterfront eatery, Cantina de San Angel. For decent Tex-Mex, try Vallarta Mexican Grill outside the World.

Middle Eastern More choice and better value out of the World.

Seafood Toss-up.

Steak/prime rib Try Yachtsman Steakhouse at the Yacht Club Resort, Shula's Steak House at the Dolphin, or The Capital Grille on International Drive out of the World.

The Olive Garden, and the like), you'll be as happy as an alligator at a chicken farm. But if you're in the market for a superlative dining experience, you'll find the pickings outside the World of about the same quality as those inside, only less expensive. Plus, some ethnic cuisines aren't represented in Walt Disney World restaurants.

Among specialty restaurants both in and out of the World, location and price will determine your choice. There are, for example, some decent Italian restaurants in Walt Disney World as well as in adjoining tourist areas—which one you select depends on how much money you want to spend and how convenient the place is to reach. Our recommendations for specialty and ethnic fare served outside of Disney World are summarized in the table that starts on pages 424–426.

Better restaurants outside Walt Disney World cater primarily to adults and aren't as well equipped to deal with children. If, however, you are looking to escape children or want to eat in peace and quiet, you're more likely to find such an environment outside the World.

TAKE OUT EXPRESS

IF YOU'RE STAYING IN A HOTEL outside Disney World, **Take Out Express** (7111 Grand National Drive; ☎ 407-352-1170; **www.orlandotakeoutexpress.com**) will deliver a meal from your choice of more than 20 restaurants, including **T.G.I. Friday's, Toojay's Deli, Passage to India,** and **Peacock Garden.** The delivery charge is $4.99 per restaurant, with a minimum $15 order. Gratuity is added to the bill. Cash, traveler's checks, MasterCard, Visa, American Express, and Discover are accepted. Hours are 4:30 until 11 p.m.

DINING AT UNIVERSAL CITYWALK

UNIVERSAL ROLLED OUT ITS ANSWER to Downtown Disney with a vengeance in 1999. Like Downtown Disney, CityWalk is a combination of entertainment and dining with a focus on adults. Restaurant tastes run the gamut, from the elegant (**Emeril's Orlando**) to the basic (**NASCAR Sports Grille**)—or, if you prefer, from the sublime to the ridiculous. All the restaurants share one common trait: they are loud. But there is good food to be found inside some of them. Most of the eateries are partners with Universal's culinary team.

BOB MARLEY—A TRIBUTE TO FREEDOM ☎ 407-224-FOOD A medium-sized (and moderately loud) tribute to the reggae superstar.

BUBBA GUMP SHRIMP CO. ☎ 407-903-0044 This seafood eatery is part of an international chain inspired by the film *Forrest Gump.* Take a wild guess what the specialty here is.

EMERIL'S ORLANDO ☎ 407-224-2424 Chief among your dining options here, this is Emeril Lagasse's Florida version of his New Orleans restaurant. Lagasse is on hand from time to time, though he tends to stay in the kitchen. But even when he's not there, you're in for some good eating. The food is Louisiana-style with a creative flair.

HARD ROCK CAFE ☎ 407-224-FOOD Serves up so-so burgers, ribs, and other American fare. More remarkable is the extensive collection of music memorabilia, including a pink 1959 Cadillac revolving over

Where to Eat outside Walt Disney World

AMERICAN

Everglades Restaurant Rosen Centre, 9840 International Drive, Orlando; ☎ 407-996-2385; **www.evergladesrestaurant.com;** moderate to expensive. Seafood and steaks and unusual creations like gator chowder and buffalo tenderloin.

Hue* 629 East Central Boulevard, Orlando; ☎ 407-849-1800; **www.hue restaurant.com;** moderate to expensive. Chic hot spot in trendy Thornton Park, but the food is still star of the show—try the sea bass.

Luma on Park* 290 South Park Avenue, Winter Park; ☎ 407-599-4111; **www.lumaonpark.com;** moderate to expensive. New American cuisine in a cool dining room on Winter Park's trendy Park Avenue.

Plantation Room Celebration Hotel, 700 Bloom Street, Celebration; ☎ 407-566-6000; **www.celebrationhotel.com;** moderate to expensive. "New Florida" cuisine focusing on seafood and locally grown fruits and vegetables.

Seasons 52 7700 West Sand Lake Road, Orlando; ☎ 407-354-5212; **www .seasons52.com;** moderate to expensive. Delicious, creative New American food (and low in fat and calories). Solid wine list.

BARBECUE

Bubbalou's Bodacious Bar-B-Que 5818 Conroy Road, Orlando (near Universal Orlando); ☎ 407-423-1212; **www.bubbalous.com;** inexpensive. Tender, smoky barbecue; tomato-based "killer" sauce.

CARIBBEAN

Bahama Breeze 8849 International Drive, Orlando; ☎ 407-248-2499; **www .bahamabreeze.com;** moderate. A creative and tasty version of Caribbean cuisine from the owners of the Olive Garden and Red Lobster chains.

CHINESE

Ming Court 9188 International Drive, Orlando; ☎ 407-351-9988; **www .ming-court.com;** moderate to expensive. Wok-fired dishes, sushi.

CUBAN/SPANISH

Columbia 649 Front Street, Celebration; ☎ 407-566-1505; **www.columbia restaurant.com;** moderate. Authentic Cuban and Spanish creations, including paella and the famous 1905 Salad.

Havana's Cafe 3628 West Vine Street, Orlando; ☎ 407-201-7957; **www .havanascaferestaurant.com;** inexpensive. No-frills traditional Cuban eats; excellent seafood.

EASTERN EUROPEAN

Chef Hans Cafe* 3716 Howell Branch Road, Winter Park; ☎ 407-657-2230; **www.chefhanscafe.com;** moderate. Family-run cafe with authentic and delicious dishes. Don't leave without having a slice (or five) of the apple strudel.

ETHIOPIAN

Nile Ethiopian Restaurant 7040 International Drive, Orlando; ☎ 407-354-0026; **www.nile07.com;** moderate. Small space in a strip mall; authentic stews and delicious vegetarian dishes.

**20 minutes or more from Walt Disney World*

FRENCH

Le Coq au Vin* 4800 South Orange Avenue, Orlando; ☎ 407-851-6980; **www.lecoqauvinrestaurant.com;** moderate to expensive. Country French cuisine in a relaxed atmosphere. Reservations suggested.

INDIAN

Passage to India 5532 International Drive, Orlando; ☎ 407-351-3456; **www.passagetoindiarestaurant-orlando.com;** moderate. A lot of locals brave International Drive just to dine here.

Tabla Bar and Grill 5827 Caravan Court, Orlando; ☎ 407-248-9400; **www.tablabar.com;** moderate. Near the entrance to Universal Orlando, this family-owned restaurant offers authentic, innovative dishes.

ITALIAN

Bice Loews Portofino Bay Hotel, Universal Orlando Resort, 5601 Universal Boulevard, Orlando; ☎ 407-503-1415; **www.biceorlando.com;** expensive. Authentic Italian; great wines.

Vinito Tuscan Tavern 4971 International Drive, Orlando; ☎ 407-354-0404; **www.vinitousa.com;** moderate. Authentic Italian at the Prime Outlets shopping center.

JAPANESE/SUSHI

Amura 7786 West Sand Lake Road, Orlando; ☎ 407-370-0007; **www.amura.com;** moderate. A favorite sushi bar for locals. The tempura is popular, too.

Hanamizuki 8255 International Drive, Orlando; ☎ 407-363-7200; **www.hanamizuki.us;** moderate to expensive. Usually filled with Japanese visitors; pricey but very authentic.

Nagoya Sushi 7600 Dr. Phillips Boulevard, in the very rear of The Marketplace at Dr. Phillips; ☎ 407-248-8558; **www.nagoyasushi.com;** moderate. A small, intimate restaurant with great sushi and an extensive menu.

MEXICAN

Chevys Fresh Mex 12547 State Road 535, Lake Buena Vista; ☎ 407-827-1052; **www.chevys.com;** inexpensive to moderate. Conveniently located across from the FL 535 entrance to WDW.

Don Pablo's 8717 International Drive, Orlando; ☎ 407-354-1345; **www.donpablos.com;** inexpensive. Good food but can be a bit noisy.

Moe's Southwest Grill 7541-D West Sand Lake Road, Orlando; ☎ 407-264-9903; **www.moesorland.com;** inexpensive. Dependable southwestern fare.

Vallarta Mexican Grill 12167 South Apopka–Vineland Road, Orlando; ☎ 407-238-5300; inexpensive. Family-owned restaurant serving freshly prepared Mexican dishes. Full bar.

NEW WORLD

Norman's 4012 Central Florida Parkway, in the Ritz-Carlton Orlando; ☎ 407-393-4333; **www.normans.com;** expensive. Norman Van Aken, patron of New World cuisine, offers a menu that changes often—but you'll always find his sinfully delicious conch chowder. World-class wine menu.

Where to Eat outside WDW (continued)

SEAFOOD

Bonefish Grill 7830 West Sand Lake Road, Orlando; ☎ 407-355-7707; **www.bonefishgrill.com;** moderate. Casual setting along busy Restaurant Row on Sand Lake Road. Choose your fish, and then choose a favorite sauce to accompany. Also steaks and chicken.

McCormick & Schmick's 4200 Conroy Road, Mall at Millenia, Orlando; ☎ 407-226-6515; **www.mccormickandschmicks.com;** expensive. Menu changes often based on freshness. Raw oysters are a big hit.

STEAK/PRIME RIB

The Capital Grille Pointe Orlando, 9101 International Drive, Orlando; ☎ 407-370-4392; **www.thecapitalgrille.com;** expensive. Dry-aged steaks, extensive wine list, and classic decor.

Charley's Steak House 6107 South Orange Blossom Trail, Orlando; ☎ 407-851-7130; **www.charleyssteakhouse.com;** moderate to expensive. Another location is just east of the Interstate 4 interchange on US 192.

Texas de Brazil 5259 International Dr., Orlando; ☎ 407-355-0355; **www.texasdebrazil.com;** expensive. All-you-care-to-eat in an upscale Brazilian-style *churrascuria.* Filet mignon, sausage, pork ribs, chicken, lamb, and more. Kids under age 6 free, ages 7 to 12 half price. Salad bar with more than 40 options.

Vito's Chop House 8633 International Drive, Orlando; ☎ 407-354-2467; **www.vitoschophouse.com;** moderate. Surprisingly upscale meat house with a taste of Tuscany.

THAI

Red Bamboo 6803 South Kirkman Road at International Drive, Orlando; ☎ 407-226-8997; **www.redbamboothai.com;** moderate. Housed in an unassuming strip-mall location and acclaimed by Orlando dining critics for its authentic Thai dishes. Delicious vegetarian options; impressive wine list. The *Unofficial* research team agrees that this is some of the best Thai food anywhere. Try the fried cheesecake for dessert.

the bar. It's the biggest such collection on display anywhere in the Hard Rock chain.

JIMMY BUFFETT'S MARGARITAVILLE ☎ 407-224-2155 A boisterous tribute to the head Parrothead. None of the food, including the cheeseburger, will make you think you're in paradise, but fans don't seem to care. The focal point is a volcano that erupts occasionally, spewing margarita mix instead of lava.

LATIN QUARTER ☎ 407-224-FOOD Simple Latin cuisine is served here—beans and rice, plantains, and flan. Most of the patrons come to dance and drink.

NASCAR SPORTS GRILLE ☎ 407-224-RACE A large and noisy tribute to all things motorized. You may find yourself sitting under a full-size race car that from time to time starts up and roars at a too-realistic sound level. The food? See all the logos for oil companies on the walls?

NBA CITY ☎ 407-363-5919 Serves decent theme-restaurant eats. The dining area looks like a miniature basketball arena, and TVs throughout play videos of famous basketball players and key moments in roundball history.

PASTAMORÉ ☎ 407-224-FOOD This is the requisite Italian restaurant. The decor is modern and stylish, and the food—with portions big enough to share—is better than average.

PAT O'BRIEN'S ☎ 407-224-2106, and **CityWalk's Rising Star** are mostly music venues that serve some food. Pat O'Brien's, behind a facade that looks remarkably similar to the New Orleans original, has the best bites (try the jambalaya).

BUFFETS AND MEAL DEALS OUTSIDE WALT DISNEY WORLD

BUFFETS, RESTAURANT SPECIALS, and discount dining abound in the area surrounding Walt Disney World, especially on US 192 (known locally as the Irlo Bronson Memorial Highway) and along International Drive. The local visitor magazines, distributed free at non-Disney hotels among other places, are packed with advertisements and discount coupons for seafood feasts, Chinese buffets, Indian buffets, breakfast buffets, and a host of combination specials for everything from lobster to barbecue. For a family trying to economize, some of the come-ons are mighty appealing. But are these places any good? Is the food fresh, tasty, and appealing? Are the restaurants clean and inviting? Armed with little more than a roll of Tums, the *Unofficial* research team tried all the eateries that advertise heavily in the free tourist magazines. Here's what we discovered.

CHINESE SUPER BUFFETS Whoa! Talk about an oxymoron. If you've ever tried preparing Chinese food, especially a stir-fry, you know that split-second timing is required to avoid overcooking. So it should come as no big surprise that Chinese dishes languishing on a buffet lose their freshness, texture, and flavor in a hurry.

For the past few editions of this guide, we were able to find several Chinese buffets that were a cut above the rest and that we felt comfortable recommending. Unfortunately, however, our endorsements seem to be the kiss of death: we return the next year to discover that quality has slipped precipitously. We attempted to find a new buffet to replace the ones we deleted from the guide, and we can tell you that wasn't fun work. At the end of the day, **Mei Asian Bistro** (8255 International Drive; ☎ 407-352-0881) is the only Chinese buffet we've elected to list. To call it a *super* buffet might be stretching things, but aside from a lackluster dessert selection, it's pretty good.

INDIAN BUFFETS Indian food works much better on a buffet than Chinese food; in fact, it actually improves as the flavors marry. In the Walt Disney World area, most Indian restaurants offer a buffet at lunch only—not too convenient if you plan on spending your day at the theme parks. If you're out shopping or taking a day off, here are some Indian buffets worth trying:

Aashirwad Indian Cuisine 5748 International Drive, at the corner of International Drive and Kirkman Road; ☎ 407-370-9830

Punjab Indian Restaurant 7451 International Drive; ☎ 407-352-7887

Spice Cafe 7536 Dr. Phillips Boulevard, in The Marketplace at Dr. Phillips, Sand Lake Road at Dr. Phillips Boulevard; ☎ 407-264-0205

BRAZILIAN BUFFETS A number of Brazilian buffets have sprung up along International Drive. The best of these is **Vittorio's** (5159 International Drive, near the outlet malls at the northern end of I-Drive; ☎ 407-352-1255; **www.vittoriosrestaurant.com**).

GENERAL BUFFETS **Bill Wong's** (5668 International Drive; ☎ 407-352-5373), offer fair value. The restaurant represents itself as a Chinese buffet but shores up its Asian selections with peel-and-eat shrimp, prime rib, and a nice selection of hot and cold vegetables.

SEAFOOD AND LOBSTER BUFFETS These affairs don't exactly fall under the category of inexpensive dining. The main draw (no pun intended) is all the lobster you can eat. The problem is that lobsters, like Chinese food, don't wear well on a steam table. After a few minutes on the buffet line, they make better tennis balls than dinner. If, however, there's someone in the kitchen who knows how to steam a lobster, and if you grab your lobster immediately after a fresh batch has been brought out, it will probably be fine. There are three lobster buffets on US 192 and another two on International Drive. Although all five do a reasonable job, we prefer **Boston Lobster Feast** (6071 West Irlo Bronson Memorial Highway; ☎ 407-396-2606; and 8731 International Drive, five blocks north of the Convention Center; ☎ 407-248-8606; **www.bostonlobsterfeast.com**). Both locations are distinguished by a vast variety of seafood in addition to the lobster. The International Drive location is cavernous and insanely noisy, which is why we prefer the Irlo Bronson location, where you can actually have a conversation over dinner. There's ample parking at the International Drive location, while parking places are in short supply at the Irlo Bronson restaurant. At about $33 for early birds (4 to 6 p.m.) and $38 after 6 p.m., dining is expensive at both locations.

SALAD BUFFETS The most popular of these in the Walt Disney World area is **Sweet Tomatoes** 6877 South Kirkman Road; ☎ 407-363-1616; 12561 South Apopka–Vineland Road; ☎ 407-938-9461; **www.sweettomatoes.com;**). During lunch and dinner, you can expect a line out the door, but fortunately one that moves fast. The buffet features prepared salads and an extensive array of ingredients to build your own. In addition to the rabbit food, Sweet Tomatoes offers a variety of soups, a modest pasta bar, a baked-potato bar, an assortment of fresh fruit, and ice-cream sundaes. Dinner runs $9.59 for adults, $4.69 for children ages 6 to 12, and $2.19 for children ages 3 to 5. Lunch is $8.19 for adults and the same prices as dinner for children (all prices are without tax).

BREAKFAST AND ENTREE BUFFETS Entree buffets are offered by most chain steak houses in the area, such as **Ponderosa, Sizzler,** and **Golden Corral.** Among them, they have 18 locations in the Walt Disney World area. All serve breakfast, lunch, and dinner. At lunch and dinner, you get the buffet when you buy an entree, usually a steak. Generally speaking, the buffets are less elaborate than a stand-alone buffet but considerably more varied than a salad bar. Breakfast service is a straightforward buffet (that is, there is no obligation to buy an entree). As for the food, it's chain-restaurant quality but decent all the same. Prices are a bargain, and you can get in and out at lightning speed—important at breakfast when you're trying to get to the theme parks early. Some locations offer lunch and dinner buffets at a set price without your having to buy an entree.

Though you can argue about which chain serves the best steak, Golden Corral wins the buffet contest hands down, with at least twice as many offerings as its three competitors. While buffets at Golden Corral and Ponderosa are pretty consistent from location to location, the buffets at the various Sizzlers vary a good deal. The pick of the Sizzlers is the one at 7602 West Irlo Bronson Memorial Highway (☎ 407-397-0997). In addition to the steak houses, area **Shoney's** also offer breakfast, lunch, and dinner buffets. Local freebie visitor magazines are full of discount coupons for all of the above.

MEAL DEALS Discount coupons are available for a wide range of restaurants, including some wonderful upscale-ethnic places such as **Ming Court** (Chinese; 9188 International Drive, Orlando; ☎ 407-351-9988; **www.ming-court.com**). Prime-rib specials can be found at **Cattle man's Steakhouse,** (8801 International Drive, a quarter-mile north of the convention center; ☎ 407-354-9888). Our favorite prime-rib joint is **Wild Jack's Steaks & BBQ** (7364 International Drive; ☎ 407-352-4407). The decor is strictly cowboy modern, but the beef is some of the best in town, and the price is right.

The best steak deal in the Disney World area is the $10.99, ten-ounce New York strip at the **Black Angus Steak House.** The beef is served with salad, a choice of vegetables or potato, and bread, and it's available at two locations convenient to Disney: 7516 West Irlo Bronson Memorial Highway, ☎ 407-390-4548; and 6231 International Drive, ☎ 407-354-3333. Another meat eater's delight is the Feast for Four at **Sonny's Real Pit Bar-B-Q,** a Florida chain that turns out good barbecue. For $37 per family of four, you get sliced pork and beef plus chicken, ribs, your choice of three sides (beans, slaw, fries) garlic bread or cornbread, and soft drinks or tea, all served family-style. The closest Sonny's location to the Walt Disney World and Universal tourist areas is at 7423 South Orange Blossom Trail in Orlando (☎ 407-859-7197); for a listing of other restaurants within a wider radius, visit **www.sonnysbbq.com.** No coupons are needed or available for Sonny's, but they are available for the other "meateries."

COUPONS Find discounts and twofer coupons for many of the restaurants mentioned in freebie visitor guides available at most hotels outside of Walt Disney World. The **Orlando–Orange County Official Visitors Center** (8723 International Drive; ☎ 407-363-5872; open daily, 8:30 a.m. to 6 p.m., except Christmas) offers a treasure trove of coupons and free visitor magazines. On the Internet, check out **www.couponsalacarte.com** and **www.orlandocoupons.com** for printable coupons.

DINING *in* WALT DISNEY WORLD

THIS SECTION AIMS TO HELP YOU find good food without going broke or tripping over one of the World's many culinary landmines. More than 100 restaurants operate within Walt Disney World, including about 75 full-service restaurants, 27 of which are inside the theme parks. Collectively, Disney restaurants offer exceptional variety, serving everything from Moroccan to Texas barbecue. Most restaurants are expensive, and many of them serve less-than-distinguished fare, but the culinary scene gets better every year.

GETTING IT RIGHT

ALTHOUGH WE WORK HARD to be fair, objective, and accurate, many readers, like this one from Coudersport, Pennsylvania, think we're too critical of Disney restaurants. He writes:

> *Everyone has to eat while* [at Walt Disney World], *so it benefits no one to be this critical. Lighten up a little bit and make your dining recommendations in the same spirit as the rest of the book.*

In a similar vein, a Charleston, West Virginia, woman came out swinging:

> *Get a life! It's crazy and unrealistic to be so snobbish about restaurants at a theme park. Considering the number of people Disney feeds each day, I think they do a darn good job. Also, you act so surprised that the food is expensive. Have you ever eaten at an airport? HELLO IN THERE? . . . Surprise, you're a captive! It's a theme park!*

And a mom from Erie, Pennsylvania, struck a practical note:

> *Most of the food* [at Walt Disney World] *is OK. If you pay attention to what other visitors say and what's in the guidebooks, you can avoid the yucky places. It's true that you pay more than you should, but it's more convenient* [to eat in Walt Disney World] *than to run around trying to find cheaper restaurants somewhere else. When it comes to Walt Disney World, who needs more running around?*

As you may infer from these reader comments, researching and reviewing restaurants is no straightforward endeavor—to the contrary, it is fraught with peril. We have read dining reviews by writers who turn up their noses at anything except four-star French restaurants. We've read reviews absolutely devoid of criticism, written by "experts" unwilling to risk offending the source of their free meals. Finally, we've seen reviews in dining guides that are wholly based on surveys submitted by diners whose credentials for evaluating fine dining are mysterious at best and questionable at least.

How, then, do we go about presenting the best possible dining coverage? At the *Unofficial Guide,* we begin with highly qualified culinary experts and then balance their opinions with those of our readers—which, by the way, don't always coincide. (Likewise, the coauthors' assessments don't always agree with those of our dining experts.)

In the spirit of democracy, we also encourage you to fill out the restaurant surveys in the back of this guide. If you want to share your dining experience in great depth, write to us at the address on page 13 or e-mail us at **unofficialguides@menasharidge.com.**

DISNEY DINING 101

(A DISCUSSION OF Disney dining plans start on page 217.)

IT'S THE ECONOMY, PLUTO

AS THE RECESSION AFFECTS the number of travelers visiting the World, Disney is scrambling furiously to make up for lost revenue. Unfortunately, this translates to higher and higher prices at Disney restaurants. Main-course prices at some restaurants have risen more than 35%; plus, Disney levies a "dining surcharge" during the summer and other busy times of year. Recently we dined at the new Wave restaurant at the Contemporary Resort and ordered a wine that retails for about $10.95. It was $9 a glass (!)—about a five-times markup. Believe us, if you rent a car and eat only dinner each day at non-Disney restaurants, you'll more than pay for the rental cost.

These comments from a Tennessee reader spell it out:

The first time we ate at Liberty Tree Tavern a few years ago, the cost was about $23 per person for each adult. This year, the cost would have been about $33 per person with the increased prices and the "holiday dining surcharge" they add during the summer months. This is a nearly 40% price increase over a period of three years for basically the same experience! We decided that turkey and mashed potatoes weren't worth the $33 and ended up eating elsewhere.

And from a New Orleans mom:

Disney keeps pushing prices up and up. For us, the sky is NOT the limit. We won't be back.

ADVANCE RESERVATIONS: WHAT'S IN A NAME

DISNEY TINKERS CEASELESSLY with its restaurant-reservations policy. In 1997, reservations were replaced with Priority Seating, a confusing system with a befuddling name that issued reservations that weren't really reservations. In 2005, after eight years, and just when we were beginning to understand what a Priority Seating was, Disney decided to change the name from Priority Seating to the rather redundant Advance Reservations. Indeed, the name is all that changed: When you call, your name and essential information are taken as if you were making an honest-to-goodness reservation. The Disney representative then tells you that you have Advance Reservations for the restaurant on the date and time you requested and usually explains that you'll be seated ahead of walk-ins—that is, those without Advance Reservations.

BEHIND THE SCENES AT ADVANCE RESERVATIONS

DISNEY RESTAURANTS OPERATE on what they call a "template system." Instead of scheduling Advance Reservations for actual tables, reservationists fill time slots. The number of time slots available is based on the average observed length of time that guests occupy a table at a particular restaurant, adjusted for seasonality.

Here's a rough example of how it works: Let's say the Coral Reef Restaurant at Epcot has 40 tables for four and 8 tables for six, and that the average length of time for a family to be seated, order, eat, pay, and depart is 40 minutes. Add 5 minutes to bus the table and set it up for the next guests, and the table is turning every 45 minutes. The restaurant provides Walt Disney World Dining (aka WDW-DINE) with a computer template of its capacity along with the average time the table is occupied. Thus, when WDW-DINE makes Advance Reservations for four people at 6:15 p.m., the system removes one table for four from overall capacity for 45 minutes. The template on the reservationist's computer indicates that the table will not be available for reassignment until 7 p.m. (45 minutes later). So it goes for all tables in the restaurant, each being subtracted from overall capacity for 45 minutes, then listed as available again, and then assigned to other guests and subtracted again, and so on, throughout the meal period. The WDW-DINE hotline tries to fill every time slot for every seat in the restaurant, or come as close to filling every slot as possible. No seats—repeat, none—are reserved for walk-ins.

Templates are filled differently depending on the season. During slower times of year, when Advance Reservations are easier to get, WDW-DINE will overbook a given restaurant for each time slot on the assumption that there will be lots of no-shows. During busy times of year, when Advance Reservations are harder to come by, there are few no-shows, so the restaurant is booked according to its actual capacity.

unofficial **TIP**
The no-show rate in January, a slow month, is about 33%, while in July it's less than 10%.

With Advance Reservations, your wait will usually be less than 20 minutes during peak hours, and often less than 10 minutes. If you walk in, especially during busier seasons, expect to wait 40 to 75 minutes.

GETTING YOUR ACT TOGETHER

IF YOU WANT TO PATRONIZE any of the Walt Disney World Resort full-service restaurants, buffets, character meals, or dinner shows, you should make Advance Reservations; on page 434 is a listing of how far ahead of time you can make them. You can now make Advance Reservations online (see page 434) as well as by calling ☎ 407-WDW-DINE.

For the most in-demand full-service restaurants, buffets, and character meals, you should make Advance Reservations 180 days ahead of time—although there are exceptions to the rule (see page 435).

If you fail to make Advance Reservations before you leave home, or if you want to make your dining decisions spontaneously, your chances of getting a table at the restaurants of your choice aren't the best, especially during the hours when most folks prefer to eat dinner.

If you visit Walt Disney World during a very busy time of year, it's to your advantage to make Advance Reservations before you leave home, as this Houston couple attests:

Make reservations if you plan on having table service. Even trying to walk in for full service at off-times was impossible.

Another reader warns of a sea change in Advance Reservations policy that practically eliminates same-day reservations and walk-ins:

While walking around the parks and resorts this weekend, I think literally every sit-down restaurant we passed had a sign out front saying something like, IN ORDER TO SERVE OUR GUESTS WITH DINING RESERVATIONS IN A TIMELY MANNER, WE ARE NOT ACCEPTING WALK-UP DINING REQUESTS AT THIS TIME. *I believe every World Showcase country had this sign, as did the Magic Kingdom, the Yacht and Beach Club, and Animal Kingdom Lodge's two sit-downs, all weekend, so I don't think this is a one-time thing. This may also explain why the World Showcase restaurants are going through refurbishments one by one—must be to add capacity.*

A dad from St. Paul, Minnesota, changed course, much to his and his family's satisfaction:

We had so much difficulty booking the Disney restaurants that we just threw up our hands and reread the part of the guide about places to eat outside of WDW. We ended up eating only one meal (a character breakfast) in a Disney restaurant. The rest of the time we followed your suggestions for non-Disney restaurants in the general area. I'm happy to report that we had some super meals and that the money we saved more than paid for our rental car.

Though securing Advance Reservations before you leave home is more important than ever, there's no need, except as stated previously, to call 90 to 180 days in advance. For most restaurants, calling 45 days in advance will get you the restaurants you desire. If you're visiting during an extremely busy time of year, try to call about 80 days out.

unofficial **TIP**
For Advance Reservations, make sure you bring your confirmation number to the restaurant.

If you poop out at the theme park and you don't feel like using your Advance Reservations that night, be aware that some restaurants have penalties for being a no-show and will charge you a cancellation fee. Note that you must pay in full at the time of booking for all meals at Cinderella's Royal Table, the *Hoop-Dee-Doo Musical Revue*, the *Spirit of Aloha Dinner Show*, and *Mickey's Backyard BBQ*. If you're a no-show, you lose the entire amount, so be sure to get the exact cancellation policy at the time you book your meal. Incidentally, if you're asked for a credit card to secure a seating, be aware that it's a *real* reservation as opposed to an Advance Reservation. Also be aware that if you're a no-show for a particular reservation, it will not affect any other Advance Reservations you may have made.

If you've lined up many Advance Reservations, it's a good idea to phone ☎ 407-WDW-DINE a few days before you arrive to make sure everything's in order. If you stay at a Disney resort, Guest Services can print out a summary of all your Advance Reservations.

unofficial **TIP**
Disney-resort guests can make Advance Reservations up to 10 additional days ahead of time.

Advance Reservations: The Official Line

You can make reservations up to 180 days in advance for:

Afternoon tea and children's programs **at the Grand Floridian Resort & Spa**

All Disney table-service restaurants and character-dining venues

Cirque du Soleil's *La Nouba* **at Downtown Disney**

Fantasmic! dinner package **at Disney's Hollywood Studios**

Hoop-Dee-Doo Musical Revue **at Fort Wilderness Resort**

Mickey's Backyard BBQ **at Fort Wilderness Resort**

Spirit of Aloha Dinner Show **at the Polynesian Resort**

Guests staying at Walt Disney World resorts—these do not include the Swan, the Dolphin, Shades of Green, or the hotels of the Downtown Disney Resort Area—can make Advance Reservations up to 10 additional days ahead, effectively giving them a maximum window of 190 days.

ADVANCE RESERVATIONS GO ONLINE

As of June 2009, you can make Advance Reservations at the Walt Disney World Web site. The service is open to everyone, regardless of whether you're lodging inside or outside of Disney World. Go to **disneyworld.disney.go.com/restaurants;** if you know which restaurant(s) you're interested in, it's easiest to search by alphabetical listing than by location. Click the blue "Sort By" bar just above the restaurant descriptions, and scroll down to the restaurant of your choice. Restaurants that accept Advanced Reservations have a yellow bar just below the restaurant photo that reads "Book a Reservation." Clicking the yellow bar takes you to the reservations page for that restaurant. You can search for reservations on a particular date or within a range of five days. If you want to retrieve or review your reservations online, you can register or, if you're already registered, log in. (*Note:* Some readers have reported Disney's online-reservations system opening at 6 a.m. Eastern time—one hour earlier than the phone-reservations system.

If you have an Advance Reservation for a theme-park restaurant at a time prior to opening, simply proceed to the turnstiles and inform a cast member, who will admit you to the park. If you fail to make Advance Reservations, most full-service theme-park restaurants will take walk-ins between 2:30 and 4:30 p.m.

DRESS

DRESS IS INFORMAL AT MOST THEME-PARK restaurants, but in 2005 Disney instituted a "business casual" dress code for some of its resort restaurants: khakis, dress slacks, jeans, or dress shorts with a collared shirt for men and jeans, skirts, or dress shorts with a blouse or sweater (or a dress) for women. Restaurants with this dress code are **Jiko—The Cooking Place** at Animal Kingdom Lodge and Villas, the **Flying Fish Cafe** at Disney's BoardWalk, the **California Grill** at the Contemporary Resort, **Bistro de Paris** at Epcot's France Pavilion, **Cítricos** and **Narcoossee's** at the Grand Floridian Resort & Spa, **Artist Point** at Wilderness Lodge, **Yachtsman Steakhouse** at the Yacht Club Resort, **bluezoo** and **Shula's Steak House** at the Dolphin, and **Il Mulino** at the Swan. **Victoria & Albert's** at the

Advance Reservations: The Unofficial *Scoop*

WHILE WALT DISNEY WORLD VISITOR NUMBERS haven't suffered that much in the current recession, Disney brass has noticed that people are likelier these days to book last-minute trips to Orlando. The *Unofficial Guide* staff began to notice this phenomenon as well in early 2009, when we began receiving e-mails asking for recommendations for good in-park sit-down restaurants that families could book within 30 days of their trip.

Using dozens of volunteers with free long-distance phone plans and access to the online Advance Dining Reservation system used by Disney travel agents, we began building profiles of each theme-park restaurant, showing how many days in advance (on average) that restaurant filled up for various meals. Our results are shown in the chart on the next page. All meals are dinner unless otherwise noted.

Not surprisingly, you'll need to book highly rated restaurants such as Canada's **Le Cellier** and the Magic Kingdom's **Crystal Palace** dinner buffet a full 180 days in advance. Interestingly, however, Epcot's **Coral Reef** restaurant also requires dining reservations about 180 days in advance—while it's no culinary hot spot, it is one of the few nonethnic sit-down restaurants in Epcot, it has relatively few tables, and it's the only dedicated seafood restaurant in any Walt Disney World park.

Surprisingly, and slightly farther down the list, the Magic Kingdom's three **Cinderella's Royal Table** meals generally need to be booked within one to three weeks of reserving a table, except during the busiest times of year (see page 354). Breakfast here has traditionally been the hottest ticket in the parks, but price increases and additional capacity at lunch and dinner have made tables somewhat easier to get.

It's possible to snag reservations at Germany's **Biergarten** buffet within three weeks of your trip, which is surprising because it's well regarded by both our dining reviewer and our readers. **Tutto Italia,** which was exceedingly difficult to get into back when it was L'Originale Alfredo di Roma, now requires less than a month of lead time to reserve.

Bringing up the rear are World Showcase's **Nine Dragons Restaurant** (China) and most of the sit-down restaurants at Animal Kingdom. Nine Dragons' placement is well deserved due to its overpriced, underwhelming food. Regarding Animal Kingdom's eateries, we think our findings don't have so much to do with these restaurants' quality as they do with the fact that people don't need to hang around until dinner to see the entire park.

Grand Floridian is the only Disney restaurant that requires men to wear a jacket to dinner.

SMOKING

WALT DISNEY WORLD RESTAURANTS adopted a nonsmoking policy several years ago, after Florida voters passed an amendment to the state's constitution that also prohibits smoking in restaurant lounges. (Freestanding bars—those that get less than 10% of their revenues from food sales—are exempt.)

unofficial **TIP**
Because smoking is banned at all restaurants and lounges on Walt Disney World property, diners who puff must feed their nicotine fix outdoors—and in the theme parks, that might also mean going to one of the designated smoking areas.

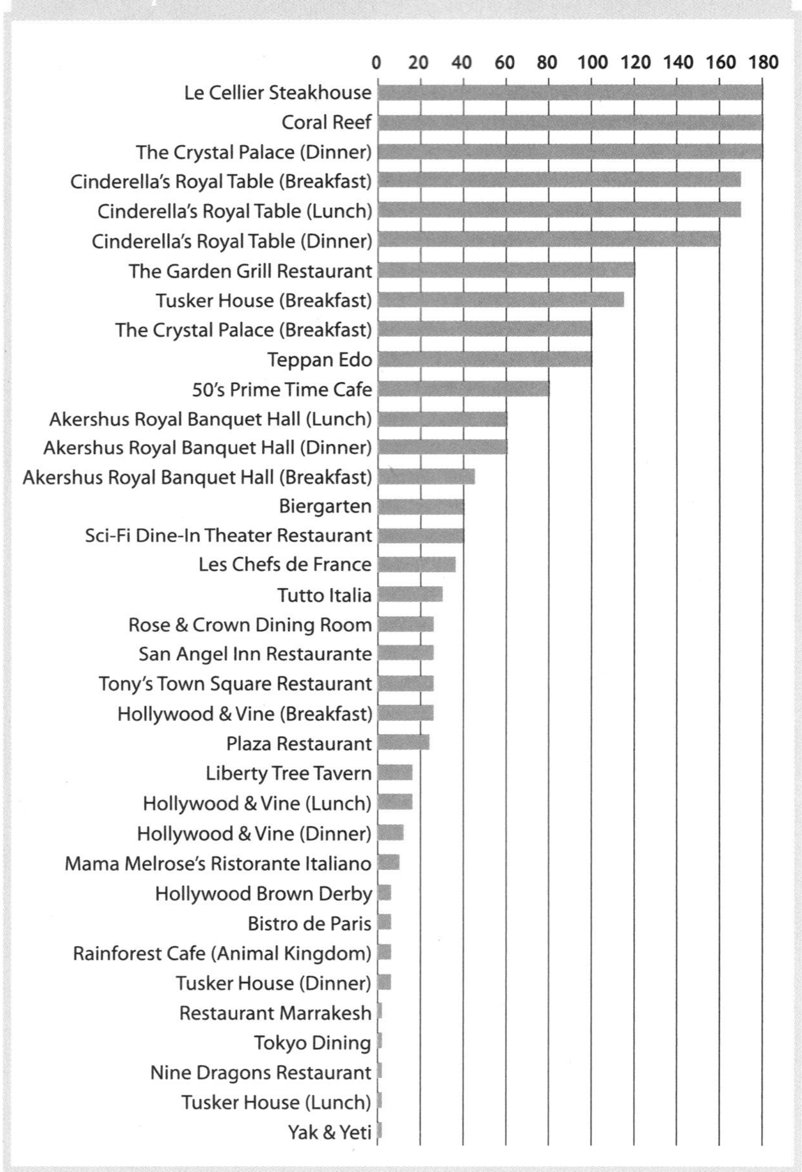

FOOD ALLERGIES AND SPECIAL REQUESTS

IF YOU HAVE FOOD ALLERGIES or observe some specific type of diet like eating kosher, make your needs known when you make your

Advance Reservations. Does it work? Well, a Phillipsburg, New Jersey, mom reports her family's experience:

> *My 6-year-old has many food allergies, and we often have to bring food with us to restaurants when we go out to eat. I was able to make reservations at the Disney restaurants in advance and indicate these allergies to the reservation clerk. When we arrived at the restaurants, the staff was already aware of my child's allergies and assigned our table a chef who double-checked the list of allergies with us. Each member of the waitstaff was also informed of the allergies. The chefs were very nice and made my son feel very special.*

A FEW CAVEATS

BEFORE YOU BEGIN EATING your way through the World, you need to know:

1. Theme-park restaurants rush their customers in order to make room for the next group of diners. Dining at high speed may appeal to a family with young, restless children, but for people wanting to relax, it's more like eating in a pressure chamber than fine dining.

   If you want to linger over your expensive meal, don't order your entire dinner at once. Order drinks. Study the menu while you sip, then order appetizers. Tell the waiter you need more time to decide among entrees. Order your main course only after appetizers have been served. Dawdle over coffee and dessert.
2. If you're dining in a theme park and cost is an issue, make lunch your main meal. Entrees are similar to those on the dinner menu, but prices are significantly lower.
3. Disney adds a surcharge of $4 per adult and $2 per child to certain popular restaurants during weeks of peak attendance, including Easter, Thanksgiving, and Christmas, and in 2009 every day from Memorial Day through July 4. The following restaurants participate in the gouging: **Akershus Royal Banquet Hall** (Princess Storybook Meals), **Boma** (breakfast and dinner), **Cape May Cafe** (breakfast and dinner buffet), **Captain's Grille** (breakfast buffet), **Chef Mickey's** (breakfast and dinner), **Cinderella's Royal Table, The Crystal Palace, The Garden Grill Restaurant, Hollywood & Vine** (Play 'n Dine character buffets), **1900 Park Fare** (breakfast and dinner), **'Ohana** (breakfast and dinner), **Trail's End Restaurant at Fort Wilderness,** and **Tusker House Restaurant.**

WALT DISNEY WORLD RESTAURANT CATEGORIES

IN GENERAL, FOOD AND BEVERAGE offerings at Walt Disney World are defined by service, price, and convenience:

FULL-SERVICE RESTAURANTS Full-service restaurants are in all Disney resorts (except the All-Star complex, Port Orleans French Quarter, and Pop Century) and all major theme parks, Downtown Disney Marketplace, and Disney's West Side. Disney operates most of the restaurants in the theme parks and its hotels, while contractors or franchisees operate the restaurants in hotels of the Downtown Disney Resort Area (DDRA), the Swan and Dolphin resorts, and some in Animal Kingdom, Epcot, Disney's BoardWalk, and Downtown Disney Marketplace–West Side. Advance Reservations (see page 431) are recommended for all full-service restaurants except those in the DDRA. The restaurants accept American Express, Carte Blanche, Diners Club, Japan Credit Bureau, MasterCard, and Visa.

BUFFETS AND FAMILY-STYLE RESTAURANTS Many of these have Disney characters in attendance, and most have a separate children's menu featuring dishes such as hot dogs, burgers, chicken nuggets, pizza, macaroni and cheese, and spaghetti and meatballs. In addition to the buffets, several restaurants serve a family-style, all-you-can-eat, fixed-price meal.

Advance Reservations arrangements are required for character buffets and recommended for all other buffets and family-style restaurants. Most major credit cards are accepted.

If you want to eat a lot but don't feel like standing in yet another line, then consider one of the all-you-can-eat family-style restaurants. These feature platters of food brought to your table in courses by a server. You can sample everything on the menu and eat as much as you like. You can even go back to a favorite appetizer after you finish the main course. The food tends to be a little better than what you'll find on a buffet line.

The table at right lists buffets and family-style restaurants (where you can belly up for bulk loading) at Walt Disney World.

FOOD COURTS Featuring a collection of counter-service eateries under one roof, food courts can be found at all Disney theme parks except Animal Kingdom and at the moderate (Coronado Springs, Caribbean Beach, Port Orleans) and value (All-Star and Pop Century) resorts. Advance Reservations are neither required nor available at these restaurants.

COUNTER SERVICE Counter-service fast food is available in all theme parks and at Downtown Disney Marketplace, Disney's BoardWalk, and Disney's West Side. The food compares in quality with Captain D's, McDonald's, or Taco Bell but is more expensive, though often served in larger portions.

FAST CASUAL Somewhere between burgers and formal dining are the establishments in Disney's new "fast casual" category, including three in the theme parks: **Tomorrowland Terrace Noodle Station** in the Magic Kingdom, **Sunshine Seasons Food Fair** in Epcot, and **Studio Catering Co.** in Disney's Hollywood Studios. Fast-casual restaurants feature menu choices a cut above what you'd normally see at a typical counter-service location. At Sunshine Seasons, for example, chefs will prepare grilled salmon on an open cooking surface while you watch, or you can choose from rotisserie chicken or pork, tasty noodle bowls, or large sandwiches made with artisanal breads. These locations all feature Asian or Mediterranean cuisine, something previously lacking inside the parks. Entrees cost about $2 more on average than traditional counter service, but the variety and food quality more than make up for the difference.

VENDOR FOOD Vendors abound at the theme parks, Downtown Disney Marketplace, Disney's West Side, and Disney's BoardWalk. Offerings include popcorn, ice-cream bars, churros (Mexican pastries), soft drinks, bottled water, and (in theme parks) fresh fruit. Prices include

Walt Disney World Buffets and Family-style Restaurants

LOCATION	RESTAURANT	CUISINE	MEALS SERVED	DISNEY CHARACTERS PRESENT
Animal Kingdom	Tusker House Restaurant	African (L, D) American (B, L, D)	B, L, D	Yes (B)
Animal Kingdom Lodge	Boma	African (D) American (B)	B, D	No
Beach Club Resort	Cape May Cafe	American (B, D)	B, D	Yes (B)
Contemporary Resort	Chef Mickey's	American	B, D	Yes
Coronado Springs	Maya Grill	American	B*, D	No
Disney's Hollywood Studios	Hollywood & Vine	American	B, L, D	Yes (B, L)
Dolphin	Fresh Mediterranean Market	Mediterranean, American	B*, L	No
Epcot	Akershus Royal Banquet Hall	American (B), Norwegian (L, D)	B, L, D	Yes (B, L)
Epcot	Biergarten	German	L, D	No
Epcot	The Garden Grill Restaurant	American	D	Yes
Fort Wilderness	*Hoop-Dee-Doo Musical Revue*	American	D	No
Fort Wilderness	*Mickey's Backyard BBQ*	American	D	Yes
Fort Wilderness	Trail's End Restaurant	American	B, L, D	No
Grand Floridian	1900 Park Fare	American	B, D	Yes
Magic Kingdom	Cinderella's Royal Table	American	B*, L, D	Yes
Magic Kingdom	The Crystal Palace	American	B, L, D	Yes
Magic Kingdom	Liberty Tree Tavern	American	L, D†	No
Polynesian Resort	'Ohana	Polynesian	B, D	Yes (B)
Polynesian Resort	*Spirit of Aloha Dinner Show*	American	D	No
Swan	Garden Grove	American	B‡, L‡, D	Yes**
Wilderness Lodge	Whispering Canyon Cafe	American	B, L, D	No
Yacht Club Resort	Captain's Grille	American	B*, L, D	No

* *Serves family-style meals only at breakfast.*

† *Serves family-style meals only at dinner.*

‡ *Serves family-style meals only at breakfast and lunch.*

** *Character-breakfast buffet served only on weekends.*

tax; many vendors are set up to accept credit cards, charges to your room at a Disney resort, and the Disney Dining Plan. Others take only cash (look for a sign near the cash register).

HARD CHOICES

DINING DECISIONS WILL DEFINITELY affect your Walt Disney World experience. If you're short on time and you want to see the theme parks, avoid full service. Ditto if you're short on funds. If you do want full service, arrange Advance Reservations—again, they won't actually reserve you a table, but they can minimize your wait.

Integrating Meals into the *Unofficial Guide* Touring Plans

Arrive before the park of your choice opens. Tour expeditiously, using your chosen plan (taking as few breaks as possible), until about 11 or 11:30 a.m. Once the park becomes crowded around midday, meals and other breaks won't affect the plan's efficiency. If you intend to stay in the park for evening parades, fireworks, or other events, eat dinner early enough to be finished in time for the festivities.

Character Dining

A number of restaurants, primarily those that serve all-you-can-eat buffets and family-style meals, offer character dining. At character meals, you pay a fixed price and dine in the presence of one to five Disney characters who circulate throughout the restaurant, hugging children (and sometimes adults), posing for photos, and signing autographs. Character breakfasts, lunches, and dinners are served at restaurants in and out of the theme parks. For an extensive discussion of character dining, see page 347 in Part Six, Walt Disney World with Kids.

FULL-SERVICE DINING FOR FAMILIES WITH YOUNG CHILDREN

DISNEY RESTAURANTS OFFER AN EXCELLENT (though expensive) opportunity to introduce young children to the variety and excitement of ethnic food. No matter how formal a restaurant appears, the staff is accustomed to fidgety, impatient, and often boisterous children. **Les Chefs de France** at Epcot, for instance, may be the nation's only French restaurant where most patrons wear shorts and T-shirts and at least two dozen young diners are attired in basic black . . . mouse ears.

Almost all Disney restaurants offer children's menus, and all have booster seats and high chairs. Servers understand how tough it may be for children to sit still for an extended period of time, and they'll supply little ones with crackers and rolls and serve your dinner much faster than in comparable restaurants elsewhere. Reader letters suggest that being served too quickly is much more common than having a long wait.

Good Walt Disney World Theme-park Restaurants for Children

In Epcot, preschoolers most enjoy the **Biergarten** in Germany, **San Angel Inn** in Mexico, and **Coral Reef** at the Seas Pavilion in Future World. The Biergarten combines a rollicking and noisy atmosphere with good basic food, including roast chicken; a German oompah band entertains, and children can often participate in Bavarian dancing. San Angel Inn is in the Mexican village marketplace. From the table, children can watch boats on the Gran Fiesta Tour drift beneath a smoking volcano. With a choice of chips, tacos, and other familiar items, picky kids usually have no difficulty finding something to eat. (Be aware, though, that the service here is sometimes glacially slow.) The Coral Reef, with tables beside windows looking into The Seas' aquarium, offers a satisfying mealtime diversion for all ages. If your children don't eat fish, Coral Reef also serves beef and chicken.

unofficial **TIP**
Disney Kids' Meals are now for ages 3–9; the cutoff used to be age 11.

The Biergarten offers reasonable value, plus good food. The Coral Reef and San Angel Inn are overpriced, though the food is palatable.

Cinderella's Royal Table in Cinderella Castle is the big draw in the Magic Kingdom. Interestingly, other Magic Kingdom full-service restaurants hold little appeal for children, but for the best combination of food and entertainment, we recommend booking a character meal at **The Crystal Palace.**

At Disney's Hollywood Studios, all ages enjoy the atmosphere and entertainment at **Hollywood & Vine,** the **Sci-Fi Dine-In Theater Restaurant,** and the **50's Prime Time Cafe.** Unfortunately, the Sci-Fi's food is close to dismal except for dessert, and the Prime Time's is uneven.

The three full-service restaurants at Animal Kingdom are **Tusker House Restaurant;** the **Rainforest Cafe,** a great favorite of children; and **Yak & Yeti.**

QUIET, ROMANTIC PLACES TO EAT

RESTAURANTS WITH GOOD FOOD *and* a couple-friendly ambience are rare in the theme parks. Only a handful of dining locales satisfy both requirements: the **Coral Reef,** the terrace at the **Rose & Crown,** and the upstairs tables at the France Pavilion's **Bistro de Paris,** all in Epcot; and the corner booths at **The Hollywood Brown Derby** in Disney's Hollywood Studios. Waterfront dining is available at **Fulton's Crab House** at Downtown Disney and **Narcoossee's** at the Grand Floridian.

unofficial **TIP**
The **California Grill** atop the Contemporary Resort has the best view at Walt Disney World. If window tables aren't available, ask to be served in the adjoining lounge.

Victoria & Albert's at the Grand Floridian is the World's showcase gourmet restaurant; expect to pay big bucks. Other good choices for couples include **Artist Point** at Wilderness Lodge, **Cítricos** at the Grand Floridian, **Shula's Steak House** at the Dolphin, **Jiko—The Cooking Place** at Animal Kingdom Lodge, and the **Flying Fish Cafe** at the BoardWalk.

Eating later in the evening and choosing a restaurant we've mentioned will improve your chances for intimate dining; nevertheless, children—well behaved or otherwise—are everywhere at Walt Disney World, and there's no way to escape them. These honeymooners from Slidell, Louisiana, write:

> *We made dinner reservations at some of the nicer Disney restaurants. We made sure to reserve past dinner hours, and we tried to*

stress that we were on our honeymoon. [In] *every restaurant we went to, we were seated next to large families. The kids were usually tired and cranky. It's very difficult to enjoy a romantic dinner when there are small children crawling around under your table. We looked around the restaurant and always noticed lots of childless couples. Our suggestion: seat couples without children together and families with kids elsewhere.*

A couple from Woodbridge, Virginia, adds:

We found it very difficult to find a quiet restaurant for dinner anywhere. We tried a restaurant that you recommended as quiet and pleasant. We even waited until 8:30 p.m. to eat, and we were still surrounded by out-of-control children. . . . The food was very good, but after a long day in the park, our nerves were shot.

FAST FOOD IN THE THEME PARKS

BECAUSE MOST MEALS DURING a Disney World vacation are consumed on the run while touring, we'll tackle counter-service and vendor foods first. Plentiful in all theme parks are hot dogs, hamburgers, chicken sandwiches, green salads, and pizza. They're augmented by special items that relate to the park's theme or the part of the park you're touring. In Epcot's Germany, for example, counter-service bratwurst and beer are sold. In Frontierland in the Magic Kingdom, vendors sell smoked turkey legs. Counter-service prices are fairly consistent from park to park. Expect to pay the same for your coffee or hot dog at Animal Kingdom as at Disney's Hollywood Studios.

Getting your act together in regard to counter-service restaurants in the parks is more a matter of courtesy than necessity. Rude guests rank fifth among reader complaints. A mother from Fort Wayne, Indiana, points out that indecision can be as maddening as outright discourtesy, especially when you're hungry:

Every fast-food restaurant has menu signs the size of billboards, but do you think anybody reads them? People waiting in line spend enough time in front of these signs to memorize them and still don't have a clue what they want when they finally get to the order taker. If by some miracle they've managed to choose between the hot dog and the hamburger, they then fiddle around another ten minutes deciding what size Coke to order. Tell your readers PULEEEZ get their orders together ahead of time!

A North Carolina reader offers a tip for counter-service food lines:

[Many] *counter-service registers serve two queues each, one to the left and one to the right of each register. People are not used to this and will instinctively line up in one queue per register, typically on the right side, leaving the left vacant. We had register operators wave us up to the front several times to start a left queue instead of waiting behind others on the right.*

Healthful Food at Walt Disney World

One of the most commendable developments in food service at Walt Disney World has been the introduction of healthier foods and

THE COST OF COUNTER-SERVICE FOOD

Bagel or muffin	$2.29
Brownie	$2.39
Cake or pie	$3.59
Cereal with milk	$3.09
Cheeseburger with fries	$6.59–$8.09
Chicken-breast sandwich (grilled)	$6.19 ($8.19 basket)
Children's meals	$4.99–$6.50
Chips	$1.29–$2.50
Cookies	$1.49–$2.75
Fish basket (fried) with fries	$7.09–$7.99
French fries	$2.49–$4.09
Fried-chicken strips with fries	$6.89–$8.25
Fruit (whole piece)	$1.00
Fruit cup/fruit salad	$3.39
Hot dogs	$4.79–$7.50 ($6.59 basket)
Ice-cream bars	$2.50--$3.75
Nachos with cheese	$7.95
PB&J sandwich	$4.99
Pizza	$5.79–$8.29
Popcorn	$3.09
Pretzel	$3.79–$4.29
Salad (entree)	$5.50–$8.75
Salad (side)	$2.99–$4.99
Smoked turkey leg	$6.59
Soup/chili	$2.59–$3.09
Sub/deli sandwich	$6.99–$9.19 (cold), $8.69 (hot)
Taco salad	$5.25–$7.39
Taco with yellow rice	$5.49 (veggie), $5.99 (beef)
Veggie burger (basket)	$6.79–$8.39

THE COST OF COUNTER-SERVICE DRINKS

Drinks	Small	Large
Beer (not available in the Magic Kingdom)	$5.00	$7.50
Bottled water	$1.50	$2.50
Cappuccino/espresso	$2.69	$3.69/$5.75 (double)
Coffee	$1.69	$1.89
Floats/milk shakes/sundaes	$3.69	$4.19
Fruit juice	$1.69	$2.39
Hot tea and cocoa	$1.89	
Milk	$1.29	$1.99
Soft drinks, iced tea, and lemonade	$2.09	$2.49

Refillable souvenir mugs cost $13.25 (free refills) at Disney resorts and water parks; mugs sold at Animal Kingdom cost $7.50 (refills $1).

snacks. People who have diabetes, vegetarians, weight-watchers, those requiring kosher meals, and the like should have no trouble finding something to eat. The same goes for anyone seeking wholesome, nutritious food. Health-conscious choices are available at most fast-food counters and even from vendors. All the major theme parks, for example, have fruit stands.

Walt Disney World for Java Junkies

We seem to get more reader complaints about Disney's coffee than any other adult food item. And those complaints are justified—virtually everywhere in the World, you're served a bitter blend of beans that would make Juan Valdez growl and spit.

If you're headed to the Magic Kingdom, however, leave 20 minutes earlier and stop by the **Kona Island Cafe Coffee Bar** at the Polynesian Resort for a cup of genuine Kona coffee. In Epcot, try the coffee and espresso in the back of the **Tangierine Cafe** at the Morocco Pavilion, or a press pot at **Bistro de Paris.** It's slim pickings at the Studios, whose ersatz "espresso bar" seems to serve the same stuff found everywhere else. At Animal Kingdom, head to the **Joffrey's Coffee & Tea Company** kiosk near Expedition Everest. Based in Tampa, Joffrey's imports and hand-roasts beans from five continents—they've won the Disney blind taste test for six years.

Starbucks is served at **Picabu** and **Fresh Mediterranean Market** at the Dolphin; the **Hilton Walt Disney World** in Downtown Disney imports a few gallons each morning in one of its shops. If you're staying near US 192 in Kissimmee, there's a **Krispy Kreme** doughnut shop at 5310 West Irlo Bronson Highway (US 192) and a **Dunkin' Donuts** about a block away on the other side of the road (5341 West Irlo Bronson). Both have good coffee.

All Disney Signature Restaurants offer coffee press pots, with an original blend for each dining room: the **Flying Fish Cafe** at the Board-Walk Inn and Villas; the **California Grill** at the Contemporary Resort; **Cítricos, Narcoossee's,** and **Victoria & Albert's** at the Grand Floridian Resort & Spa, **Artist Point** at the Wilderness Lodge; and Villas; and **Yachtsman Steakhouse** at the Yacht Club Resort.

Cutting Your Dining Time at the Theme Parks

Even if you confine your meals to vendor and counter-service fast food, you lose a lot of time getting food in the theme parks. At Walt Disney World, everything begins with a line and ends with a cash register. When it comes to fast food, *fast* may apply to the time you spend eating it, not the time invested in obtaining it.

Here are our suggestions for minimizing the time you spend hunting and gathering:

1. Eat breakfast before you arrive. Restaurants outside the World offer some outstanding breakfast specials. Plus, some hotels furnish small refrigerators in their guest rooms, or you can rent a fridge. If you can get by on cold cereal, rolls, fruit, and juice, having an in-room refrigerator will save a ton of time. If you can't get one, bring a cooler.
2. After a good breakfast, buy snacks from vendors in the parks as you tour,

or stuff some snacks in a fanny pack. This is very important if you're on a tight schedule and can't spend a lot of time waiting in line for food.

3. All theme-park restaurants are busiest between 11:30 a.m. and 2:15 p.m. for lunch and 6 and 9 p.m. for dinner. For shorter lines and faster service, don't eat during these hours, especially 12:30 to 1:30 p.m.
4. Many counter-service restaurants sell cold sandwiches. Buy a cold lunch (except for drinks) before 11:30 a.m., and carry it until you're ready to eat. Ditto for dinner. Bring small plastic bags in which to pack the food. Purchase drinks at the appropriate time from any convenient vendor.
5. Most fast-food eateries have more than one service window. Regardless of the time of day, check the lines at all windows before queuing. Sometimes a window that's staffed but out of the way will have a much shorter line or none at all. Note, however, that some windows may offer only certain items.
6. If you're short on time and the park closes early, stay until closing and eat dinner outside Disney World before returning to your hotel. If the park stays open late, eat dinner about 4 or 4:30 p.m. at the restaurant of your choice. You should miss the last wave of lunchers and sneak in just ahead of the dinner crowd.

Beyond Counter Service: Tips for Saving Money on Food

Though buying food from counter-service restaurants and vendors will save time and money (compared with full-service dining), additional strategies can bolster your budget and maintain your waistline. Here are some suggestions our readers have offered over the years:

1. Go to Disney World during a period of fasting and abstinence. You can save a fortune and save your soul at the same time!
2. Wear clothes that are slightly too small and make you feel like dieting (no spandex allowed!).
3. Whenever you're feeling hungry, ride the Mad Tea Party, Mission: Space, or other attractions that induce motion sickness.
4. Leave your cash and credit cards at your hotel. Buy food only with money that your children fish out of fountains and wishing wells.

Fortunately, readers have also volunteered more-feasible ideas for stretching food dollars. A family from Lee's Summit, Missouri, tells us:

> *Last year we requested a small refrigerator for our room and were given one for no charge. This year we were charged $5 a day* [now it's $10 a day at Disney's value resorts, free at moderates and deluxes] *for use of the fridge, but it was definitely worth it for us to be able to eat breakfast in the room to save time and money.*

An Ashburn, Virginia, dad also has a few cool thoughts about Disney fridges:

> *We were surprised at how small the fridge was and that it did not have a freezer compartment. We heard some people had purchased a fridge when they arrived in Florida, then packed it up in the box and took it home with them. We spent $80 for the eight days we were there, probably enough to have bought* [a refrigerator] *cheaper.*

A Missouri mom writes:

We arrived at WDW after some days on the beach south of Sarasota. We shopped there and arrived with our steel Coleman cooler well stocked with milk and sandwich fixings. I froze a block of ice in a milk bottle, and we replenished it daily with ice from the resort ice machine. I also froze small packages of deli-type meats for later in the week. We ate cereal, milk, and fruit each morning, with boxed juices. I also had a hot pot to boil water for instant coffee, oatmeal, and soup.

Each child had a belt bag of his own, which he filled from a special box of "goodies" each day. I made a great mystery of filling that box in the weeks before the trip. Some things were actual food, like packages of crackers and cheese, packets of peanuts and raisins. Some were worthless junk, like candy and gum. They grazed from their belt bags at will throughout the day, with no interference from Mom and Dad. Each also had a small, rectangular plastic water bottle that could hang on the belt. We filled these at water fountains before getting into lines and were the envy of many.

We left the park before noon, ate sandwiches, chips, and soda in the room, and napped. We purchased our evening meal in the park, at a counter-service eatery. We budgeted for both morning and evening snacks from a vendor but often did not need them. It made the occasional treat all the more special.

We interviewed one woman who brought a huge picnic for her family of five packed in a large diaper–baby paraphernalia bag. She stowed the bag in a locker under the Main Street Station and retrieved it when the family was hungry. A Pennsylvania family adds:

Despite the warning against bringing food into the park, we packed a double picnic lunch in a backpack and a small shoulder bag. Even with a small discount, it cost $195 for the seven of us to tour the park for a day, and I felt that spending another $150 or so on two meals was not in the cards. We froze juice boxes to keep the meat sandwiches cool and had extra of juice boxes and peanut-butter sandwiches for a late-afternoon snack. We took raisins and a pack of fig bars for sweets, but didn't carry any other cookies or andy to avoid a "sugar low" . . .

After 9/11 all packs, purses, diaper bags, and such are searched, but Walt Disney World security usually does not enforce the food ban, as this reader points out:

The food at the parks is much better than [the food I had on] *my first trip to Disney in 1994, but I prefer bringing my own lunch and water. The savings equate to a nice meal at a fancy restaurant at least once during our trip (Texas de Brazil!). I think Disney understands that a lot of families just can't afford to eat at those prices and hopefully will continue to turn a blind eye to bringing drinks and food into the park.*

A mom from Whiteland, Indiana, who purchases drinks in the parks, offers this suggestion:

One "must-take" item if you're traveling with younger kids is a supply of small paper or plastic cups to split drinks, which are both huge and expensive.

It's become a real trend for readers to bring a suitcase full of food and various necessities that are consumed during the vacation. For the trip home, the now-empty suitcase is used for souvenirs and other purchases. A mom from Newton, New Jersey, has the suitcase thing buttoned down:

> *The last time we flew from New Jersey to Disney with our two daughters, then 5 and 7, we had "The Suitcase." Knowing that we'd come back with much more than we flew down with, we packed this suitcase full of breakfast food and snacks as well as cheap things to keep them occupied during quiet times when we weren't at the parks. By packing bagels, doughnuts, individual boxes of cereal, breakfast bars, juice boxes, etc., we were able to grab a bite before we headed off to the parks. This saved us restaurant costs for breakfasts that were expensive and in the way of getting to the parks early. I had a bunch of snacks that could take the flight, like Pringles, popcorn, candy, and gum. A bunch of coloring books, puzzles, and art stuff from the dollar store gave them something to do quietly before bed or whenever we wanted a little peace. We ate the breakfast food and snacks, then threw out the cheap puzzles and stuff when we were ready to leave. "The Suitcase" was now ready to be filled with the souvenirs we were bringing back.*

A variation on the theme is to mail a box of stuff to your hotel. A Dodge City, Kansas, reader elaborates:

> *Here is a short [?] list of what we're sending this December: an ice cooler with wheels packed with an extra razor, mouthwash, Bengay, Bounce, laundry soap, extra disposable cameras, a small multi-tool, batteries, Crystal Light single-drink mixes, some small flashlights, Charmin, Gaviscon, Tylenol, Pepcid AC, Imodium AD, deodorants, and bug repellent. Most of these items were purchased at dollar or discount stores, so if they don't get used, they can be left behind without causing grief. As for the cooler itself, it will be sent back home in the original box and will hold many of our Disney purchases safely.*

We don't remember—did she mention a forklift? A blowtorch?

DISNEY DINING SUGGESTIONS

FOLLOWING ARE SUGGESTIONS for dining at each of the major theme parks. If you want to try a full-service restaurant at one of the theme parks, be aware that the restaurants continue to serve after the park's official closing time. We once showed up at The Hollywood Brown Derby just as Disney's Hollywood Studios closed at 8 p.m. We were seated almost immediately and enjoyed a leisurely dinner while the crowds cleared out.

unofficial **TIP**
Don't worry about dining late if you're depending on Disney transportation: buses, boats, and monorails run two to three hours after the parks close.

THE MAGIC KINGDOM

FOOD AT THE MAGIC KINGDOM has improved noticeably over the past several years. **The Crystal Palace** at the end of Main Street offers a good (albeit pricey) buffet chaperoned by Disney characters, while the **Liberty Tree Tavern** in Liberty Square features hearty family-style dining at dinner. **Cinderella's Royal Table,** a full-service restaurant on the second floor of the castle, delivers palatable meals in one of Walt Disney World's most distinctive (and popular) settings.

THE MAGIC KINGDOM

Author's Favorite Counter-service Restaurants

Cosmic Ray's (limited kosher items)	*Tomorrowland*
Pecos Bill Tall Tale Inn and Cafe	*Frontierland*

unofficial **TIP**
Kosher quick-service meals are available at **Cosmic Ray's** in the Magic Kingdom, as well as at **Pizzafari** in Animal Kingdom, **ABC Commissary** in Disney's Hollywood Studios, and **Liberty Inn** in Epcot.

Fast food at the Magic Kingdom is, well, fast food. It's more expensive, of course, than what you would pay at McDonald's, but what do you expect? It's like dining at an airport—you're a captive audience. On the positive side, portions are large, sometimes large enough for children to share. Overall, the variety of fast-food offerings provides a lot of choice, though the number of selections at any specific eatery remains quite limited. Check our mini-profiles of the park's counter-service restaurants before you queue up.

Our dining recommendations for a day at the Magic Kingdom:

1. Take the monorail to one of the hotels for lunch. The trip takes very little time, and because most guests have left the hotels for the parks, the resorts' restaurants are often uncrowded. The food is better than the Magic Kingdom's; the service is faster; the atmosphere is more relaxed; and beer, wine, and mixed drinks are available.
2. Full-service restaurants that accept Advance Reservations for lunch and/or dinner fill quickly in the summer and during holiday periods. To obtain Advance Reservations, call ☎ 407-939-3463 or hotfoot it to your chosen restaurant as soon as you enter the park. Advance Reservations are explained starting on page 431, and all Magic Kingdom full-service and counter-service restaurants are profiled later in this chapter.
3. Of the park's five full-service restaurants, **Liberty Tree Tavern** in Liberty Square is the best. **Tony's Town Square** on Main Street and **Cinderella's Royal Table** in the castle also serve decent food. Because children love Cinderella and everyone's curious about the castle, you need to make Advance Reservations before you leave home if you want to eat a meal at Cinderella's Royal Table (see page 354). Here, Advance Reservations for lunch and for dinner are easier to arrange than for breakfast.
4. A good rule at any full-service restaurant is to keep it simple. Order sandwiches or basic dishes (roast turkey and mashed potatoes, for example).

Here are some comments from readers about Magic Kingdom full-service and counter-service restaurants. First, regarding Cinderella's Royal Table character meals:

Our whole family did Cinderella's Royal Table for lunch. Our two little boys (ages 3 and 4) loved it even more than their 6-year-old sister. The boys loved all the princesses paying special attention to them since they were the only guys in the whole place. My 3-year-old left with his face covered in princess lipstick and even managed to propose to Cinderella—who sadly mentioned she was already married.

The food was OK—a lot of characters: Snow White, Cinderella, Belle, Sleeping Beauty, Fairy Godmother, Mary Poppins. The place was not that big, but the characters spent a lot of time at each table—so much time that we only got to meet Snow White and Belle. The boys were bored. Was not worth the trouble of getting the seating.

Mediocre it was not, and believe me, I've been subjected to plenty of mediocre food. Airport food is mediocre. Convention hall food is mediocre. Cafeteria food is mediocre. Cindy's Royal Table was not *in the same category. Our lunch was attractively served and very tasty (I had the pork for lunch). It greatly exceeded my expectations.*

The Crystal Palace gets consistently good reviews from readers. A sampling:

Great food, great service, good price. We went at 4:30, and the din from small children was loud. (We didn't care!)

The Crystal Palace is highly underrated. We feasted on vegetables, salmon, salads, and fruits. The kids were overjoyed with the characters. . . . great way to refill the batteries.

Of all the restaurants we visited, I can't rave enough about The Crystal Palace or Liberty Tree Tavern. The food at both places was great (you just can't beat The Crystal Palace's breakfast buffet!), the service was wonderful, and the characters were awesome.

As with the reader above, we also receive many positive comments regarding the Liberty Tree Tavern:

Liberty Tree Tavern—didn't expect much here but made a reservation based on your book. What a surprise. The food was great as well as the atmosphere.

Pecos Bill Tall Tale Inn and Cafe is a Magic Kingdom counter-service favorite among our readers:

If you're looking for heart-healthy meals, Pecos Bill Cafe has a great chicken wrap. Pecos Bill also has a pretty tasty hamburger with an outstanding fixin's bar (grilled onions and mushrooms, hot cheese, and chili) for those not looking for a heart-healthy menu.

EPCOT

SINCE THE BEGINNING, dining has been an integral component of Epcot's entertainment product. The importance of dining is reflected in the number of restaurants and their ability to serve consistently interesting and well-prepared meals. This is in stark contrast to the Magic Kingdom, where, until recently, food service was seemingly an afterthought, with quality and selection a distant runner-up to logistical efficiency.

For the most part, Epcot's restaurants have always served decent food, though the World Showcase restaurants have occasionally been timid about delivering honest representations of their host nations' cuisine. While these eateries have struggled with authenticity and have sometimes shied away from challenging the meat-and-potatoes sensibilities of the average tourist, they are bolder now, encouraged by America's exponentially expanding appreciation of ethnic dining. It's still true that the less adventuresome diner can still find sanitized and homogenized meals, but the same kitchens will serve up the real thing for anyone with a spark of curiosity and daring.

EPCOT
Author's Favorite Counter-service Restaurants

Kringla Bakeri og Kafé *Norway*	Sommerfest *Germany*
Sunshine Season Food Fair *The Land*	Yakitori House *Japan*

Many Epcot restaurants are overpriced, most conspicuously the **Coral Reef** (The Seas). Representing decent value with their combination of attractive ambience and well-prepared food are **Les Chefs de France** (France), **Biergarten** (Germany), and **Restaurant Marrakesh** (Morocco). Biergarten and Restaurant Marrakesh also feature live entertainment.

unofficial **TIP**
Epcot has 14 full-service restaurants: 2 in Future World and 12 in the World Showcase. With a couple of exceptions, these are among the best restaurants at Disney World, in or out of the theme parks. Epcot's full-service and counter-service restaurants are profiled later in this chapter.

While eating at Epcot can be a consummate hassle, an afternoon without Advance Reservations for dinner in World Showcase is like not having a date on the day of the prom. Each pavilion (except The American Adventure) has a beautifully seductive ethnic restaurant, offering the gastronomic delights of the world. To tour these exotic settings and not partake is almost beyond the limits of willpower. And while the fare in some World Showcase restaurants isn't always compelling, the overall experience is exhilarating. If you fail to dine in World Showcase, you'll miss one of Epcot's most delightful features.

If you want to sample the ethnic foods of World Showcase without eating in restaurants requiring Advance Reservations, we recommend these counter-service specialties:

France *Boulangerie Pâtisserie,* for French pastries

Germany *Sommerfest,* for bratwurst and Beck's beer

Japan *Yakitori House,* for noodle dishes, teriyaki, and tempura

Norway *Kringla Bakeri og Kafé,* for pastries, open-face sandwiches, and Carlsberg beer (our favorite)

United Kingdom *Rose & Crown Pub,* for Guinness, Harp, and Bass beers

Unofficial Guide readers have many diverse opinions of Epcot's full-service restaurants. Concerning the much-hyped Les Chefs de France:

> *Cafeteria food served on linen place mats. An expensive rip-off;* [food] *on par with Denny's.*

> *What a joke! Premade food that anyone can get* [where they live], *served by snotty little princesses.*

We were very disappointed by Les Chefs de France. We were served cold food—it might as well have been a defrosted frozen dinner. The mashed potatoes tasted like a powdered mix. The service was rushed, the food pedestrian—only the manner was haute.

And finally, from a United Kingdom reader, a detailed account of his experience:

We took dinner at the Les Chefs de France, expecting from previous experience a really classy meal, albeit expensive. The ambience was great—we could have been in Paris. The menu contained all the right items. But the entrees seriously disappointed. We tried sending one back because it arrived cold. The waiter took it away, stuck it under a hot lamp, and brought it back minutes later. The top was now hot, sure enough, but the underside was still lukewarm, and the gravy was gaining a skin. This is not how it is done in France—we should have received a fresh entree. Others in the party later admitted that their meals were not correctly heated. We also ordered a carafe of wine expecting European measures, but received only enough for three glasses. We had to order up another, so making the wine doubly expensive. Les Chefs de France needs to address its problems.

Though Les Chefs de France fares better with our *Unofficial Guide* restaurant reviewers and on our reader (thumbs-up/thumbs-down) survey, comments in our reader mail and e-mail have been pretty scathing. Negative feelings toward Les Chefs de France do not, incidentally, extend to Bistro de Paris, the other French restaurant, which is generally highly regarded by all.

unofficial **TIP**
If cost is an issue, make lunch your main meal. Entrees are similar to those on the dinner menu, but prices are significantly lower.

The Coral Reef Restaurant in the Seas Pavilion fared a bit better:

Food was good; however, service was poor and portions were small and overpriced. Music has added a lot of atmosphere.

You were dead on; we went this year, and it was fairly disastrous. I think my dinner was prepared under water.

We were surprised by how much everyone loved Coral Reef. We had great service, and the food was awesome. We had a booth directly in front of the tank and didn't even request it!

Tried Coral Reef for the first time, despite reviews. Waited 40 minutes beyond our reserved time, and the food was mediocre and pricey. Next time I'll cook a burger next to my daughter's goldfish bowl.

Restaurant Marrakesh likewise garnered mixed reviews:

Restaurant Marrakesh is overrated. It may be a walk on the wild side for someone from, say, Wichita, but I can find better and more exotic food at a dozen places in my neighborhood.

(For all you folks in Wichita who are wondering where this reader is from: Arlington, Virginia.) More comments:

It's worth eating here just to see the interior. Going to Epcot and passing this gem up is like going to Paris and skipping Notre Dame.

Full-service Restaurants in Epcot

FUTURE WORLD	
Coral Reef	The Seas
The Garden Grill Restaurant	The Land
WORLD SHOWCASE	
Akershus Royal Banquet Hall	Norway
Biergarten	Germany
Bistro de Paris	France
Le Cellier Steakhouse	Canada
Les Chefs de France	France
Nine Dragons Restaurant	China
Restaurant Marrakesh	Morocco
Rose & Crown Dining Room	United Kingdom
San Angel Inn	Mexico
Teppan Edo	Japan
Tokyo Dining	Japan
Tutto Italia	Italy

We spent a very memorable lunch at Restaurant Marrakesh. Our son (age 8) loved it when the belly dancer brought him to the floor to dance with her. The portions were very generous, and our waiter, Isaam, took time to speak with us about Moroccan family traditions.

Marrakesh—everything was Moroccan except the food. Not good at all. Very disappointed.

Le Cellier at the Canada Pavilion has risen from obscurity to become the most popular restaurant at Epcot:

Le Cellier and the Yachtsman Steakhouse were outstanding. At Le Cellier I didn't even need a knife to cut my steak.

You don't mention it in your book, but Le Cellier is one of the hardest restaurants for which to get [Advance Reservations] *(the dining rep confirmed this). It wasn't available any of the 10 days of my trip, and I called more than 90 days in advance. If your readers want to try this restaurant, they'll want to plan and call early.*

Akershus Royal Banquet Hall in the Norway Pavilion has become quite the favorite of character-dining enthusiasts:

I took my 4-year-old daughter and 4-year-old niece, and of course they were both obsessed with seeing the princesses. I wasn't able to afford or procure reservations for Cinderella's Royal Table, but I can't believe it could have been much better than Akershus. The girls got to see Belle, Ariel, Cinderella, Aurora, and Jasmine. Each princess came to the table one at a time, and the place was not overbooked, so you did not feel rushed. The lunch also included a professional photo of the girls with Belle, which we received at the table. The food was great, the dessert to die for, and the waitstaff extremely friendly and outgoing. The princesses were really engaged with the girls, and the best thing was that Ariel saw my daughter outside while she was leaving the restaurant. Ariel swooped down and planted a kiss on her cheek—my daughter wouldn't wash her cheek for the rest of the day!

And, finally, about the San Angel Inn:

Expensive, but where else can you drink Corona beer and dine under a moonlit sky at the base of a vaulted pyramid while serene boats drift by?

We love the view! The food was good, we enjoyed lunch there since the portions are generous, and the prices are a little lower. [Advance Reservations] *are definitely recommended.*

A popular adult pastime is to make a complete circuit of the World Showcase, sampling the exceptional beer native to each nation represented. Truth be told, the beer is great (Carlsberg beer in Norway is our favorite), but the price per brew makes the circumnavigation only a bit less expensive than an actual around-the-world tour, as this reader laments:

As a beer lover, I was looking forward to tasting beers from around the world. That was quickly put to a stop by the $7.25-per-cup cost . . .

ANIMAL KINGDOM

BECAUSE TOURING ANIMAL KINGDOM takes less than a day, crowds are heaviest from 9:30 a.m. until about 3:30 p.m. Expect a mob at lunch and thinner crowds at dinner. We recommend you tour early after a good breakfast, then eat a very late lunch or graze on vendor food. If you tour later in the day, eat lunch before you arrive, then enjoy dinner in or out of the theme park. Animal Kingdom full-service and counter-service restaurants are profiled later in this chapter.

unofficial **TIP**
Although grilled meats are available, don't expect a broad choice of exotic dishes in Animal Kingdom.

Animal Kingdom offers a lot of counter-service fast food but has converted **Tusker House** to a buffet-style restaurant and added **Yak & Yeti,** a table-service restaurant, in Asia. You'll find plenty of traditional Disney theme-park food—hot dogs, hamburgers, deli sandwiches, and the like—but even the fast food is a cut above the average Disney fare. Our two favorites: **Flame Tree Barbecue** in Discovery Island, with its waterfront dining pavilions, and **Yak & Yeti Local Food Cafe,** for casual Asian fare from egg rolls to crispy honey chicken. The sit-down Yak & Yeti also serves above-average food (especially the seafood and duck).

ANIMAL KINGDOM

Author's Favorite Counter-service Restaurant

Flame Tree Barbecue *Discovery Island*

The third full-service restaurant in Animal Kingdom, the **Rainforest Cafe,** has entrances both inside and outside the park (you don't have to purchase theme-park admission, in other words, to eat at the restaurant). Both Rainforest Cafes (the other is at Downtown Disney Marketplace) accept Advance Reservations.

DISNEY'S HOLLYWOOD STUDIOS

DINING AT DHS is more interesting than at the Magic Kingdom and less ethnic than at Epcot. The park has five restaurants where Advance Reservations are recommended: **The Hollywood Brown Derby, 50's Prime Time Cafe, Sci-Fi Dine-In Theater Restaurant, Mama Melrose's Ristorante Italiano,** and the **Hollywood & Vine** cafeteria. The upscale Brown Derby is by far the best restaurant at the Studios. For simple Italian food, including pizza, Mama Melrose's is fine; just don't expect anything fancy. At the Sci-Fi Dine-In, you eat in little cars at a simulated drive-in movie from the 1950s. Though you won't find a more entertaining restaurant in Walt Disney World, the food is quite disappointing. Somewhat better is the 50's Prime Time Cafe, where you sit in Mom's fabulous-'50s kitchen and scarf down meat loaf while watching clips of classic TV sitcoms. The 50's Prime Time Cafe is fun, and the food is a step up. The best way to experience either restaurant is to stop in for dessert or a drink between 2:30 and 4:30 p.m. Hollywood & Vine features singing and dancing characters from *Playhouse Disney* during breakfast and lunch. DHS full-service and counter-service restaurants are profiled later in this chapter.

DISNEY'S HOLLYWOOD STUDIOS

Author's Favorite Counter-service Restaurants

ABC Commissary *Backlot*

Backlot Express *Backlot*

Pizza Planet *Backlot*

Toluca Legs Turkey Co. *Sunset Boulevard*

We receive considerable mail from readers recounting their DHS dining experiences. A reader from Sumter, South Carolina, writes:

> *We had lunch at the Sci-Fi Dine-In. In the guide you gave it a terrible review, but I have always felt you guys are too hard on the Disney restaurants, so we went ahead and ate there. Well, on this one you were right on target! While the atmosphere was fun, and the clips were a hoot, the food was lousy . . . and expensive!*

A Mechanicsville, Virginia, family agrees:

> *You tried to warn us about the Sci-Fi Dine-In, but my 4-year-old was dying to eat there. The food was even worse than you said, and the cost—$9.50 for basic food!*

From an East Lansing, Michigan, woman who'd had it to here with togetherness:

> *I also disagree with your review of the Sci-Fi Dine-In. After a busy and hot day of touring, it is heaven to be in a dark, air-conditioned room, with no pressure to keep up conversation with the other members of your party, who you could no doubt use a break from after much time spent in line or waiting for the bus together.*

The 50's Prime Time Cafe is always a hot topic. First, from a Maryland reader:

> *50's Prime Time Cafe was a fun experience, but again, the food quality was at best mediocre. If my mom really did cook that way, I would have many times run away from home. Our reaction to the poor food quality pushed us quickly into the car and out of WDW. I never thought I would get down on my knees and kiss the sidewalk outside of a Perkins Pancake House.*

But a West Newton, Massachusetts, family loved the Prime Time:

> *50's Prime Time Cafe: we know you guys didn't rate it very well, but we decided to go against your recommendation and give it a shot. We're so glad we did! For the five of us (ages 16 to 20), this dining experience was a blast. Our waiter (and big brother for the meal), "Leroy," came and sat at our table and helped us set our places so we wouldn't get in trouble with "Mom." When one member of our party cursed, "Mom" arrived to punish him, making him clear the table onto her tray, which he did shamefully. Overall, the experience was a total kick that we talked about for the rest of the trip.*

Other Prime Time advocates had this to say:

> *Best meal in park, but you must get into character* [that is, go along with the role-playing] *to have fun.*

> *My teens' favorite restaurant was the 50's Prime Time Cafe. Our waitress gave them a ribbing about their elbows on the table, not pushing their chairs in, and just general grief. They were laughing so hard they had tears in their eyes. It was the only place where they wanted a picture with the restaurant staff.*

The Brown Derby was a favorite of a San Diego reader:

> *Delicious food, great selections, and an excellent end to an evening at the Studios.*

While yet another reader made a culinary find at Mama Melrose's Ristorante Italiano:

> *Great flatbread pizza! Our waiter was as slow as a snail, but the food was good.*

Other readers agreed about the slow-service part, not so much about the food:

> *At Mama Melrose's, we had reservations at 4:20 p.m. for dinner and a show package to see* Fantasmic! *The food was TERRIBLE and the service was even worse. A person in our party ordered the grilled salmon—it was burned to a crisp. We got no refills on our drinks, and at 5:50 we still had not gotten our dessert (and never did).*

If you arrive at Disney's Hollywood Studios without having arranged Advance Reservations for meals, do so at the Advance Reservations kiosk at the corner of Hollywood and Sunset boulevards or at the restaurants.

If you have no Advance Reservations and become hungry during meal times, try Pizza Planet (sometimes overlooked by the teeming hordes).

MORE READER COMMENTS ABOUT WALT DISNEY WORLD DINING

EATING IS A POPULAR TOPIC among *Unofficial Guide* readers. In addition to participating in our annual restaurant survey, many readers share their thoughts. The following comments are representative.

Here's a 13-year-old girl from Omaha, Nebraska, who doesn't get her knickers in a twist over one bad meal:

> *Honestly, when was the last time you came from Disney World and said, "Gosh, my vacation really sucked because I ate at a bad restaurant"? Disney World is Disney World, no matter what.*

A reader from Carbondale, Illinois, exhorts other readers to be adventuresome in their choice of restaurants:

> *Please advise your readers to try "different" restaurants at Epcot! We had a blast dining at Akershus and Marrakesh! The service was great; food was different but not weird. My husband is a picky eater, but even he was able to say that he tried Norwegian and Moroccan food at the end of our vacation! I feel like Marrakesh is not popular because people think the food is too ethnic. Well, it was ethnic enough, but not too hot or spicy, and the atmosphere was great. To me, it was the most themed restaurant—the inside SCREAMED Mediterranean, and the belly dancer was GREAT!*

Another Illinois reader, this one from Glendale, had a positive experience with Disney food, writing:

> *In general, we were pleasantly surprised. I expected it to be overpriced, generally bad, and certainly unhealthy. There were a lot of options, and almost all restaurants (including counter service) had generally good food and some healthy options. It is not the place to expect fine cuisine—and is certainly overpriced—but if you understand the parameters, you can eat quite well. One thing I appreciated was having a children's menu that did not consist only of hot dogs and fries. My children ate well, and we were able to get them a good variety of food, with plenty of fruits and vegetables.*

Another big thumbs-up from Terre Haute, Indiana, for the California Grill:

> *I had what might be the most memorable meal of my life at the California Grill. We left the kids with a sitter and went out for a romantic evening. You mentioned being seated at the counter overlooking the show kitchen, which I'm sure would be great, but for a romantic dinner, you can't beat the smaller dining room. We didn't know it existed, but we were led through the end of the main dining room through large glass doors to a table in the corner of a smaller room with only seven other tables. Away from the cacophony of the main dining room, this was a quiet haven with a spectacular view. We watched as a*

thunderstorm with all its lightning glory rolled toward and then over us. Afterward, we were awed by a stunning full rainbow. It was a nice treat for our tenth anniversary. The food was out of this world, and the service (by Judy) was impeccable.

But a Canadian mom raises a caution:

We ate dinner on our last night at the California Grill. It was beautiful and delicious, but it took three hours. This is not a great place to take your kids. We were there from 7 to 10 p.m., and it was just too much for them.

A family of five loved Whispering Canyon Cafe at the Wilderness Lodge:

Our best experience for dining was at the Whispering Canyon. My girls (ages 6, 10, and 11) thought the servers were great. They joked with each other, shouted, and laughed with the kids. Our waiter even sat down with our kids and helped my oldest "finish" her salad and showed my youngest how to eat whipped cream off her nose. Out of all the places we ate, this was my kids' (and Mom's and Dad's) favorite. Oh, and the food was pretty good too.

We've received consistent raves for Boma:

Please stop telling everyone how wonderful Boma is, because I love it so much there and I don't want everyone to know the secret as it is already difficult to get a table! Prime rib and Zebra Domes—yum!

I would recommend most heartily Boma at Animal Kingdom Lodge. It was worth having to take a taxi back to the Wilderness Lodge after a fantastic meal. The children (ages 6 and 9) enjoyed it as much as the adults (five of us from age 26 to 57). Great food, terrific atmosphere, and very decent prices.

We went as recommended to Boma (late reservation made by a cast member following three failed attempts to reserve before departure). Food was amazing, cooked to perfection, and really creative.

A Lombard, Illinois, mom underscores the need to make Advance Reservations ahead of time:

Please stress that if you want a "normal" dining hour at a specific restaurant, call them 90 or 60 days in advance—IT IS WORTH IT! One reservation I wanted to change about two weeks before our arrival date, and I had a choice of dinner times of either 7:45 or 9 p.m. (not feasible with little ones).

A Baltimore reader thinks we failed to give Wolfgang Puck his due:

Bob, you greatly underestimated the Wolfgang Puck Express in Marketplace. It's not five-star, but it is a great fast-food alternative. We got yummy gourmet pizzas and rotisserie chicken . . . but the best part was the beer barrels. We ended up eating there on two occasions.

I was apprehensive about the food, but our experiences were very good overall at both the full-service and counter-service restaurants. Face it, you don't go to Disney for the dinner bargains.

But a mom from New Richmond, Wisconsin, points out that service is important too:

The service at Wolfgang Puck Cafe was terrible. They had no booster seats for smaller children, and it took 30 minutes to get a high chair.

A family from Youngsville, Louisiana, got a leg up on other guests:

The best things we ate were the smoked turkey legs.

A mom from Aberdeen, South Dakota, writes:

When we want great food, we'll be on a different vacation. Who wants to waste fun time with the kids at a sit-down restaurant when you know the food will be mediocre anyway?

A woman from Verona, Wisconsin, offers this:

We think the character meals are underrated in all guidebooks. These meals are in pleasant settings and provide an easy, efficient way for little kids to interact with characters while providing adults with an opportunity to relax. For value and good food, we especially like the breakfasts. Yes, they're a little pricey, but you get more than food. Probably our favorite character meal is the one at The Garden Grill in Epcot. This year, they even gave us souvenir hats.

And a Seattle family of four found a new favorite restaurant:

The best meal we had at Walt Disney World was at Cítricos [at the Grand Floridian]. *The service was spectacular, and the food was prepared with a lot of zest and creativity. A wonderful meal.*

A Tallahassee, Florida, reader thinks we underrate Cítricos at the Grand Floridian:

How come you gave Cítricos only 3½ stars? We had the most amazing meal ever there! The service was the most outstanding I have ever received, and the food matched. My grandmother had some dietary restrictions; the chef came to our table to talk with her about what she could eat, then sent her out a side dish free of charge. They even let her order from the kids' menu even though she's way over the 9-year-old limit.

(For the record, Cítricos is one of the *Unofficial* team's favorite eateries. The food is indeed excellent, and it's one of the most quiet and sedate restaurants at Walt Disney World.)

A couple from Oxford, England, had a discount coupon and still didn't like Planet Hollywood:

We got $15 off at Planet Hollywood, but it was awful, so noisy with [loud] *music that children were covering their ears—it ruined the meal for us.*

A Pennsylvania Gen Y guy likes PH—and clearly knows how to deal with the loud music:

Planet Hollywood had the best (strongest) mixed drinks, and great ribs and ravioli.

A mother of three from Jamaica, New York, waited two hours and 40 minutes for a table at the Rainforest Cafe and still had a good time:

The Rainforest Cafe was an absolute delight. Our 6-year-old sat right next to a gorilla that ranted every few minutes, our 10-month-old loved the huge fish tanks, and they loved the food. Our wait for a table was two hours, so we went back to the hotel and returned two hours later. We still had to wait 40 minutes, but it was worth it. The gorilla room had more of a jungle feel than the elephant room.

But a Richardson, Texas, family had this to say:

A terrible dining experience. It was wild, wet, and loud, and the service was the worst in WDW.

A Charleroi, Pennsylvania, reader offered this report:

I walked in to find no host in sight, so I stood and stood. When the host came, she said the servers were on break and I would be seated in 15 minutes. I pointed out the three customers in a room of empty tables and asked why I was not allowed to sit to examine the menu. The host huffed and walked away. When she came back, she said she would seat me after she seated the customers behind me. I told her they were not even in the building while I was looking for her. I got a table right away—after an argument.

(We should note that most negative reader comments concerning the Rainforest Cafe pertain to the Downtown Disney location, not the Animal Kingdom location.)

On the topic of saving money, a Seattle woman offered the following advice:

For those wanting to save a few bucks, we definitely suggest eating outside WDW for as many meals as possible. We ate a large breakfast before leaving the hotel, had a fast-food lunch in the park and a snack later to hold us over, and then ate a good dinner outside the park. Several good restaurants in the area have excellent food at reasonable prices, notably Cafe Tu Tu Tango and Ming [Court], *both on International Drive. We also obtained the "Entertainment Book" for Orlando, which offers 50% off meals all over town.*

COUNTER-SERVICE RESTAURANT MINI-PROFILES

TO HELP YOU FIND palatable fast-service food that suits your taste, we've developed mini-profiles of Walt Disney World theme-park counter-service restaurants. The restaurants are listed alphabetically by theme park. They're rated for quality and portion size (self-explanatory), as well as for value. (The average thumbs-up rating for all Disney restaurants is 82%.) The value rating ranges from A to F as follows:

A	=	Exceptional value; a real bargain
B	=	Good value
C	=	Fair value; you get exactly what you pay for
D	=	Somewhat overpriced
F	=	Extremely overpriced

MAGIC KINGDOM

Casey's Corner

QUALITY Good VALUE B PORTION Medium LOCATION Main Street, U.S.A.
READER-SURVEY RESPONSES 88% 👍 12% 👎 DISNEY DINING PLAN Yes

Selections Quarter-pound hot dogs, fries, and brownies.
Comments A little pricey on the dogs and very crowded—keep walking.

Columbia Harbour House

QUALITY Fair VALUE C+ PORTION Medium LOCATION Liberty Square
READER-SURVEY RESPONSES 90% 👍 10% 👎 DISNEY DINING PLAN Yes

Selections Fried fish and chicken strips; hummus and tuna-salad sandwiches; child's plate with macaroni and cheese or garden chicken salad with grapes and child's beverage; New England clam chowder and vegetarian chili; coleslaw; chips; fries; garden salad; chocolate cake.
Comments No trans fats in the fried items, and the soups and sandwiches are a nice change from the usual pizza and burger fare. It's the quickest service within spitting distance of Fantasyland.

Cosmic Ray's Starlight Cafe

QUALITY Good VALUE B PORTION Large LOCATION Tomorrowland
READER-SURVEY RESPONSES 84% 👍 16% 👎 DISNEY DINING PLAN Yes

Selections There's something for everyone at this quick-service location: rotisserie chicken and ribs; turkey-bacon and vegetarian wraps; hot dogs; hamburgers, including veggie burgers; Caesar salad with chicken; chicken-noodle soup; chili; carrot cake and no-sugar-added brownies for dessert. Kosher choices include a burger, chicken strips, and corned beef on rye.
Comments Big place. Tables inside usually available. Out-of-this-world entertainment on stage. This is the place if everybody in your party is picky—you'll have plenty of options. Nice burger-fixin's bar. Cosmic Ray's was the first Disney counter-service restaurant to offer kosher food.

El Pirata y el Perico *(open seasonally)*

QUALITY Fair VALUE B PORTION Medium–large LOCATION Adventureland
READER-SURVEY RESPONSES 73% 👍 27% 👎 DISNEY DINING PLAN Yes

Selections Beef taco salad, vegetarian and beef tacos, quesadillas for kids.
Comments Large, shaded eating area. Open seasonally.

Golden Oak Outpost

QUALITY Good VALUE B+ PORTION Medium–large LOCATION Frontierland
READER-SURVEY RESPONSES TOO NEW TO RATE DISNEY DINING PLAN Yes

Selections Chicken nuggets, fried-chicken-breast sandwich, vegetarian flatbread wrap.
Comments All of the above are served with apple slices or French fries.

The Lunching Pad

QUALITY Good VALUE B– PORTION Medium LOCATION Tomorrowland
READER-SURVEY RESPONSES 76% 👍 24% 👎 DISNEY DINING PLAN Yes

Selections Smoked turkey legs, pretzels, frozen sodas.
Comments Smack in the middle of Tomorrowland, The Lunching Pad is a good place to grab a smoked turkey leg or cold drink.

Mrs. Potts' Cupboard

QUALITY Good **VALUE** B **PORTION** Medium **LOCATION** Fantasyland
READER-SURVEY RESPONSES 93% 👍 7% 👎 **DISNEY DINING PLAN** No

Selections Sundaes, including fudge brownie and strawberry shortcake; floats and shakes; cookies; drinks.

Comments An ice-cream stop. Good options and decent value.

Pecos Bill Tall Tale Inn and Cafe

QUALITY Good **VALUE** B **PORTION** Medium–large **LOCATION** Frontierland
READER-SURVEY RESPONSES 90% 👍 10% 👎 **DISNEY DINING PLAN** Yes

Selections Cheeseburgers, veggie burgers, chicken wraps, chicken salad, chili, child's plate with hamburger or salad with grilled chicken and child's beverage, fries and chili-cheese fries, peanut-butter-brownie mousse.

Comments Use the great fixin's station to garnish your burger. Combos come with fries or carrots.

The Pinocchio Village Haus

QUALITY Fair **VALUE** C **PORTION** Medium **LOCATION** Fantasyland
READER-SURVEY RESPONSES 77% 👍 23% 👎 **DISNEY DINING PLAN** Yes

Selections Personal pizzas, chicken nuggets, Caesar salad with chicken, Mediterranean salad, kids' meals of mac and cheese or PB&J, fries plain or with toppings.

Comments Almost always crowded, and with several cash registers open, the Village Haus is always filled with families taking a Fantasyland break. Consider Columbia Harbour House and Pecos Bill Tall Tale Inn and Cafe, both only a few minutes' walk away.

Scuttle's Landing

QUALITY Good **VALUE** B **PORTION** Medium **LOCATION** Fantasyland
READER-SURVEY RESPONSES 78% 👍 22% 👎 **DISNEY DINING PLAN** No

Selections Frozen Cokes, soft pretzels, and chips.

Comments Essentially a snack bar, but not a bad place to grab a drink.

Tomorrowland Terrace Noodle Station

QUALITY Good **VALUE** B **PORTION** Medium–large **LOCATION** Tomorrowland
READER-SURVEY RESPONSES 64% 👍 36% 👎 **DISNEY DINING PLAN** Yes

Selections Chicken or vegetable noodle bowl, fried-chicken nuggets, orange chicken with rice, beef and broccoli, Caesar salad, child's plate of chicken nuggets or beef and mac. Chocolate cake for dessert; beverage selections include iced green teas and hot teas.

Comments Good if you're looking for something beyond dogs and burgers.

EPCOT

Africa Coolpost

QUALITY Good **VALUE** B– **PORTION** Small **LOCATION** Between Germany and China
READER-SURVEY RESPONSES 89% 👍 11% 👎 **DISNEY DINING PLAN** Yes

Selections Hot dogs, ice cream (waffle cone); fresh fruit; frozen slushes (frozen soda); coffee or tea; draft Safari Amber beer ($6.25).

Comments Mainly prepackaged food for a quick drink or snack.

Boulangerie Pâtisserie

QUALITY Good **VALUE** B **PORTION** Small–medium **LOCATION** France
READER-SURVEY RESPONSES 92% 👍 8% 👎 **DISNEY DINING PLAN** Yes

Selections Coffee, croissants, pastries, chocolate mousse, sandwiches, baguettes, cheese plate, ham-and-cheese croissant, quiche.

Comments The French pastries are tempting at this tucked-away spot. A few shaded outside tables provide a place to relax and savor sweets.

Cantina de San Angel

QUALITY Fair–good **VALUE** C+ **PORTION** Medium **LOCATION** Mexico
READER-SURVEY RESPONSES 78% 👍 22% 👎 **DISNEY DINING PLAN** Yes

Selections Tacos; burritos; quesadillas; *ensalada mexicana;* nachos; churros; draft beer and frozen margaritas.

Comments Most meals are served with refried beans and salsa. Tables are outdoors. The margaritas pack a punch—sip slowly.

Crêpes des Chefs de France

QUALITY Good **VALUE** B+ **PORTION** Medium **LOCATION** France
READER-SURVEY RESPONSES 78% 👍 22% 👎 **DISNEY DINING PLAN** No

Selections Crêpes with chocolate, strawberry, or sugar; vanilla and chocolate ice cream; specialty beer (Kronenbourg 1664); espresso.

Comments Kiosk treats made while you watch.

Electric Umbrella Restaurant

QUALITY Fair–good **VALUE** B– **PORTION** Medium **LOCATION** Innoventions East
READER-SURVEY RESPONSES 79% 👍 21% 👎 **DISNEY DINING PLAN** Yes

Selections Burgers and chicken nuggets with fries; vegetable wrap; island chicken salad; grilled-chicken sandwich; child's plate with cheeseburger or turkey-and-cheese pinwheels; fruit cups; cookies; cheesecake.

Comments One of the busiest restaurants in Future World. There's more-interesting fast food in the World Showcase.

Fife and Drum Tavern

QUALITY Fair **VALUE** C **PORTION** Large **LOCATION** United States
READER-SURVEY RESPONSES 87% 👍 13% 👎 **DISNEY DINING PLAN** Yes

Selections Turkey legs, pretzels, ice cream, and smoothies.

Comments Better for a quick snack to tide you over than for an actual meal. Seating is available in and around the Liberty Inn, behind the Fife and Drum.

Kringla Bakeri og Kafé

QUALITY Good–excellent **VALUE** B **PORTION** Small–medium **LOCATION** Norway
READER-SURVEY RESPONSES 88% 👍 12% 👎 **DISNEY DINING PLAN** Yes

Selections Pastries; no-sugar-added chocolate mousse; *lefse* (traditional potato bread); cakes and cookies; rice cream; open-faced sandwiches (smoked ham, turkey, or salmon); green salad; fruit cup; sweet pretzels with raisins and almonds; imported beers (Carlsberg beer for $7.50).

Comments Pricey but good (try the rice cream). Shaded outdoor seating.

Liberty Inn

QUALITY Fair VALUE C PORTION Medium LOCATION United States
READER-SURVEY RESPONSES 75% 👍 25% 👎 DISNEY DINING PLAN Yes

Selections Bacon double cheeseburger; barbecued pork; hot dogs; veggie burgers; chicken nuggets; Caesar chicken salad; child's plate of grilled chicken over romaine lettuce, chicken nuggets with fries, or PB&J with applesauce.

Comments The menu offers more than dogs and burgers; kosher items also available. Still, World Showcase has more-inspired selections.

Lotus Blossom Cafe

QUALITY Fair VALUE C PORTION Medium LOCATION China
READER-SURVEY RESPONSES 59% 👍 41% 👎 DISNEY DINING PLAN Yes

Selections Egg rolls, pot stickers, veggie stir-fry, sesame chicken salad, shrimp fried rice, orange chicken with steamed rice, beef-noodle soup bowl.

Comments Middling, overpriced Chinese food.

Promenade Refreshments

QUALITY Fair VALUE C PORTION Large LOCATION Between World Showcase and Future World
READER-SURVEY RESPONSES 89% 👍 11% 👎 DISNEY DINING PLAN Yes

Selections Hot dogs, pretzels, chips, ice cream, and smoothies.

Comments Best for a quick snack, especially if you have a reservation at one of the World Showcase's full-service restaurants. Seating is limited to nonexistent, depending on whether cast members have put out tables and chairs—be prepared to walk and chew.

Refreshment Port

QUALITY Good VALUE B PORTION Medium LOCATION Between World Showcase and Future World
READER-SURVEY RESPONSES 98% 👍 2% 👎 DISNEY DINING PLAN Yes

Selections Chicken nuggets, fries, ice cream.

Comments Convenient place for a snack.

Rose & Crown Pub

QUALITY Good VALUE C PORTION Medium LOCATION United Kingdom
READER-SURVEY RESPONSES 94% 👍 6% 👎 DISNEY DINING PLAN Yes

Selections Fish-and-chips; turkey sandwich; Guinness, Harp, and Bass beers, as well as other spirits.

Comments The attractions here are the pub atmosphere and the draft beer. Note that the restaurant usually requires Advance Reservations while the pub does not. Outside the pub is Yorkshire County Fish Shop, which serves food to go. Also see the full-service restaurant profile for the Rose & Crown Dining Room later in this chapter.

Sommerfest

QUALITY Good VALUE B– PORTION Medium LOCATION Germany
READER-SURVEY RESPONSES 88% 👍 12% 👎 DISNEY DINING PLAN Yes

Selections Bratwurst and frankfurter sandwiches with kraut; soft pretzels; apple strudel; German wine and beer (Löwenbrau, Franziskaner Weissbier, and Spaten Optimator).

Comments Tucked in the entrance to the Biergarten restaurant, Sommerfest is hard to find from the street. Very limited seating. Not for picky eaters, but a good place to grab a cold brew and bratwurst.

Sunshine Seasons Food Fair

QUALITY Excellent **VALUE** A **PORTION** Medium **LOCATION** The Land
READER-SURVEY RESPONSES 93% 👍 7% 👎 **DISNEY DINING PLAN** Yes

Selections Comprises the following four areas: (1) wood-fired grills and rotisseries, with rotisserie chicken or pork chops and wood-grilled salmon with olive pesto sauce; (2) sandwich shop with made-to-order sandwiches like grilled-vegetable Cuban, Black Forest ham–salami grinder, and turkey and cheese on focaccia; (3) Asian shop, with noodle bowls and various stir-fry combos; (4) soup-and-salad shop, with soups made daily and unusual creations like seared tuna on mixed greens with sesame–rice wine vinaigrette.

Comments No fried food, no pizza, no burgers—everything is prepared fresh as you watch. Diverse choices are perfect for picky eaters.

Tangierine Cafe

QUALITY Good **VALUE** B **PORTION** Medium **LOCATION** Morocco
READER-SURVEY RESPONSES 88% 👍 12% 👎 **DISNEY DINING PLAN** Yes

Selections Chicken and lamb *shawarma;* hummus; tabbouleh; lentil salad; chicken and tabbouleh wraps; olives; child's meal of pizza, hamburger, or chicken tenders with carrot sticks and apple slices and small beverage; Moroccan wine and beer; baklava.

Comments You won't get the belly dancers who entertain inside the pavilion at Restaurant Marrakesh, but the food here is good, with an authentic flavor. The best seating is at the outdoor tables.

Yakitori House

QUALITY Excellent **VALUE** B **PORTION** Small–medium **LOCATION** Japan
READER-SURVEY RESPONSES 80% 👍 20% 👎 **DISNEY DINING PLAN** Yes

Selections Shogun combo meal with beef and chicken teriyaki, vegetables, and rice (adult and child versions); beef curry; vegetable tempura with shrimp and udon noodles; side salad; sushi; miso soup; green tea; sponge cake with ginger-flavored frosting; Kirin beer, sake, and plum wine.

Comments A great place for a light meal. Nice cultural detailing. Limited seating.

Yorkshire County Fish Shop

QUALITY Good **VALUE** B+ **PORTION** Medium **LOCATION** United Kingdom
READER-SURVEY RESPONSES 91% 👍 9% 👎 **DISNEY DINING PLAN** Yes

Selections Fish-and-chips, shortbread, Bass Ale draft.

Comments A convenient fast-food window attached to the Rose & Crown Pub (see profile on previous page). Outdoor seating overlooks the lagoon.

ANIMAL KINGDOM

Flame Tree Barbecue

QUALITY Good **VALUE** B– **PORTION** Large **LOCATION** Discovery Island
READER-SURVEY RESPONSES 90% 👍 10% 👎 **DISNEY DINING PLAN** Yes

Selections Half slab St. Louis–style ribs; smoked half chicken; smoked-beef and -pork sandwiches; crisp green salad with barbecued chicken; child's plate of baked chicken drumsticks or hot dog; French fries, coleslaw, onion rings; chocolate cake; Safari Amber beer, Bud Light, and wine.

Comments Queues very long at lunch time, but seating is ample and well shaded. One of our favorites for lunch. Try the covered gazebo overlooking the water.

Kusafiri Coffee Shop

QUALITY Good **VALUE** B **PORTION** Medium **LOCATION** Africa
READER-SURVEY RESPONSES Too new to rate **DISNEY DINING PLAN** No

Selections Fruit turnovers, Danish and other pastries, muffins, croissants, bagel with cream cheese, cookies, brownies, cake, fruit cup, yogurt, coffee, cocoa, juice

Comments A good early-morning sugar rush on the way to Kilimanjaro Safaris. Shares space with Tusker House; easy walk-up window.

Picnic in the Park

QUALITY Fair **VALUE** C **PORTION** Small–medium **LOCATION** Varies
READER-SURVEY RESPONSES Too new to rate **DISNEY DINING PLAN** Yes

Selections Sandwiches: grilled-chicken wraps, ham grinders, and turkey on focaccia; entrees: rotisserie chicken, and sliced ham. Sides: fruit salad, mac and cheese, pasta salad, mashed potatoes and gravy, potato wedges, tomatoes and cucumbers, coleslaw, and green beans. Desserts: fruit, cookies, brownies, and crisped-rice treats. (Curiously, cornbread is also classified as a dessert.) Bottled water is the only beverage choice.

Comments Introduced in 2009 and available only at Animal Kingdom, Picnic in the Park provides you with a ready-made bag of food that you can eat anywhere around the park. Here's how it works:

Before 1 p.m., stop by Guest Relations at the front of the park to place your order; after 1 p.m., head to Tusker House in Africa. Choose one of the two meal options available and specify a pickup time, allowing at least two hours between ordering and pickup. When your order is ready, pick it up at the Kusafiri Coffee Shop, in Africa next to Tusker House (entrees), or DinoBites, in DinoLand U.S.A. (sandwiches); then select a spot to eat and dig in. Utensils and condiments are included.

A sandwich option and an entree option are available. Both include sides, desserts, and small bottled waters. Meals can be sized to feed two to six people. If your party is smaller or larger than that range, you'll have to decide whether to share, order extras, or make other plans. Prices run from $25 plus tax for the three-person sandwich option to $57 plus tax for the rotisserie chicken or ham for six.

The food quality is decent, and it's fairly easy to find nice places to eat throughout the park. But while the entrees and desserts are large enough for adults, we've found the sides too small for moderately hungry adults and kids. Plus, the only beverage you get is a small bottle of water, and that's usually not enough on warm days. Finally, since you have to specify when you'll pick up the picnic, you've got to plan your day around the mealtime—just as if you'd made a sit-down dining reservation.

Pizzafari

QUALITY Fair **VALUE** B **PORTION** Medium **LOCATION** Discovery Island
READER-SURVEY RESPONSES 82% 👍 18% 👎 **DISNEY DINING PLAN** Yes

Selections Cheese and pepperoni personal pizzas; chicken Parmesan sandwich; grilled-chicken Caesar salad; breadsticks; Italian deli sandwich; child's mac and cheese or cheese pizza; apple pie; frozen strawberry lemonade; Safari Amber beer and wine.

Comments A favorite with children. Hectic at peak mealtimes. The pizza is pretty unimpressive—toppings resemble those on a cheap frozen pizza. Kosher menu is available.

Restaurantosaurus

QUALITY Good **VALUE** B+ **PORTION** Medium–large **LOCATION** DinoLand U.S.A.
READER-SURVEY RESPONSES 69% 👍 31% 👎 **DISNEY DINING PLAN** Yes

Selections Cheeseburgers; hot dogs; chicken nuggets; Mandarin chicken salad; veggie burger; fries; chocolate cake and carrot cake; coffee, tea, and cocoa; apple and orange juice; beer.

Comments Picky children might enjoy Restaurantosaurus. Topping bar available.

Royal Anandapur Tea Company

QUALITY Good **VALUE** B **PORTION** Medium **LOCATION** Asia
READER-SURVEY RESPONSES 86% 👍 14% 👎 **DISNEY DINING PLAN** No

Selections Wide variety of hot and iced teas; lattes; coffee, espresso, and cappuccino; pastries.

Comments Located halfway between Expedition Everest and Kali River Rapids, this is the kind of small, eclectic food stand unique to Animal Kingdom that you wish could be found at other parks. Offers about a dozen loose-leaf teas from Asia and Africa, many of which can be made either hot or iced. Pastries violate the "never eat anything larger than your head" rule, but everyone knows that doesn't apply when you're on vacation.

Tamu Tamu

QUALITY Good **VALUE** C **PORTION** Large **LOCATION** Africa
READER-SURVEY RESPONSES 63% 👍 37% 👎 **DISNEY DINING PLAN** No

Selections Milk shakes. During peak seasons, turkey sandwiches, tuna-salad sandwiches, and burgers on multigrain buns are on the menu at Tamu Tamu and neighboring Drinkwallah.

Comments Seating is behind building and could easily be overlooked.

Yak & Yeti Local Food Cafe

QUALITY Fair **VALUE** C **PORTION** Large **LOCATION** Asia
READER-SURVEY RESPONSES 83% 👍 17% 👎 **DISNEY DINING PLAN** Yes

Selections Crispy honey chicken with steamed rice, kung pao beef, lo mein, Asian salads. Kids' menu includes chicken bites with pork egg roll and mini-cheeseburgers with applesauce and carrots.

Comments The crispy honey chicken is the best choice—the beef and lo mein simply demonstrate how poorly those dishes fare sitting under a heat lamp until someone orders them. Adjacent to the table-service restaurant named Yak & Yeti (see full-service profile on page 511).

DISNEY'S HOLLYWOOD STUDIOS

ABC Commissary

QUALITY Fair **VALUE** B– **PORTION** Medium–large **LOCATION** Backlot
READER-SURVEY RESPONSES 61% 👍 39% 👎 **DISNEY DINING PLAN** Yes

Selections Asian salad; Cuban sandwich; chicken curry; cheeseburgers with apple slices or fries; fried fish with apple slices or fries; child's chicken nuggets, cheeseburger, or ham-and-cheese wrap; chocolate mousse; no-sugar-added strawberry parfait; wine and beer.

Comments Indoors, centrally located, air-conditioned, and usually not too crowded. Hard to find. Offers kosher food.

Backlot Express

QUALITY Fair **VALUE** C **PORTION** Medium–large **LOCATION** Backlot
READER-SURVEY RESPONSES 75% 👍 25% 👎 **DISNEY DINING PLAN** Yes

Selections Burgers with fries or carrot sticks, Southwest salad with chicken, grilled turkey and cheese, chicken nuggets, hot dogs, grilled-vegetable sandwich, desserts. For children, chicken nuggets or sloppy joe with vegetables. Soft drinks and beer.

Comments A big dining space that's often overlooked. Great burger-fixin's bar. Indoor and outdoor seating.

Catalina Eddie's

QUALITY Fair **VALUE** B **PORTION** Medium–large **LOCATION** Sunset Boulevard
READER-SURVEY RESPONSES 76% 👍 24% 👎 **DISNEY DINING PLAN** Yes

Selections Cheese and pepperoni pizzas, hot Italian deli sandwich, salads, carrot cake and chocolate fudge cake.

Comments Seldom crowded.

Min and Bill's Dockside Diner

QUALITY Fair **VALUE** C **PORTION** Small–medium **LOCATION** Echo Lake
READER-SURVEY RESPONSES 79% 👍 21% 👎 **DISNEY DINING PLAN** No

Selections Shakes and soft drinks; beer; chips and cookies; variety of pretzels, including spicy cheese-stuffed and apple-cinnamon.

Comments Limited outdoor seating.

Pizza Planet

QUALITY Good **VALUE** B+ **PORTION** Medium **LOCATION** Backlot
READER-SURVEY RESPONSES 74% 👍 26% 👎 **DISNEY DINING PLAN** Yes

Selections Cheese, pepperoni, and vegetarian pizzas; salads; cookies and crisped-rice treats.

Comments The place for pizza at the Studios. Fresh ingredients. Gets good marks from readers.

Rosie's All American Cafe

QUALITY Fair **VALUE** C **PORTION** Medium **LOCATION** Sunset Boulevard
READER-SURVEY RESPONSES 70% 👍 30% 👎 **DISNEY DINING PLAN** Yes

Selections Cheeseburgers; veggie burgers; chicken strips; soups; side salads; fries; child's cheeseburger or chicken nuggets with grapes, carrot sticks, or applesauce; apple pie and chocolate cake.

Comments Sandwiches are premade. Backlot Express is a better option for the same fare.

Starring Rolls Cafe

QUALITY Good **VALUE** B **PORTION** Small–medium **LOCATION** Sunset Boulevard
READER-SURVEY RESPONSES 87% 👍 13% 👎 **DISNEY DINING PLAN** Yes

Selections Deli sandwiches, salads, pastries, desserts, chocolates, coffee.
Comments Open for breakfast on some mornings. Slowest service of any counter-service eatery.

Studio Catering Co.

QUALITY Good **VALUE** B **PORTION** Small–medium **LOCATION** Backlot
READER-SURVEY RESPONSES 63% 👍 37% 👎 **DISNEY DINING PLAN** Yes

Selections Barbecued pulled pork, grilled chicken with rice and black beans, chili-cheese hot dog, chicken Caesar wrap, Greek salad.
Comments Good place for a break while your kids enjoy the *Honey, I Shrunk the Kids* playground. Shady outside seating.

Toluca Legs Turkey Co.

QUALITY Good **VALUE** B **PORTION** Medium–large **LOCATION** Sunset Boulevard
READER-SURVEY RESPONSES 80% 👍 20% 👎 **DISNEY DINING PLAN** Yes

Selections Smoked turkey legs; hot dogs; coffee, tea, hot chocolate, bottled soda, and beer.
Comments For fans of the giant turkey legs.

WALT DISNEY WORLD RESTAURANTS: *Rated and Ranked*

TO HELP YOU MAKE YOUR DINING CHOICES, we've developed profiles of full-service restaurants at Disney World. Each profile allows you to quickly check the restaurant's cuisine, location, star rating, cost range, quality rating, and value rating. Profiles are listed alphabetically by restaurant.

STAR RATING The star rating represents the entire dining experience: style, service, and ambience, in addition to the taste, presentation, and quality of the food. Five stars is the highest rating and indicates that the restaurant offers the best of everything. Four-star restaurants are above average, and three-star restaurants offer good, though not necessarily memorable, meals. Two-star restaurants serve mediocre fare, and one-star restaurants are below average. Our star ratings don't correspond to ratings awarded by AAA, Mobil, Zagat, or other restaurant reviewers.

COST RANGE The next rating tells how much a complete meal will cost. We include a main dish with vegetable or side dish and a choice of soup or salad. Appetizers, desserts, drinks, and tips aren't included. We've rated the cost as inexpensive, moderate, or expensive.

Inexpensive	$15 or less per person
Moderate	$15–$28 per person
Expensive	More than $28 per person

QUALITY RATING The food quality is rated on a scale of one to five stars, five being the best rating attainable. The quality rating is based on the taste, freshness of ingredients, preparation, presentation, and creativity of food served. There is no consideration of price. If you want the best food available and cost is not an issue, you need look no further than the quality ratings.

VALUE RATING If, on the other hand, you are looking for both quality and value, then you should check the value rating, expressed as stars.

★★★★★	Exceptional value, a real bargain
★★★★	Good value
★★★	Fair value, you get exactly what you pay for
★★	Somewhat overpriced
★	Significantly overpriced

PAYMENT All Disney restaurants accept American Express, Carte Blanche, Diners Club, Discover, JCB (Japan Credit Bureau), MasterCard, and Visa.

READERS' RESTAURANT-SURVEY RESPONSES

For each Disney World restaurant profiled, we include the results of last year's reader-survey responses. Results are expressed as a percentage of responding readers who liked the restaurant well enough to eat there again (thumbs up 👍), as opposed to the percentage of responding readers who had a bad experience and wouldn't go back (thumbs down 👎). (Readers tend to be less critical than our *Unofficial Guide* reviewers.) The average thumbs-up rating for all Disney restaurants is 82%. If you'd like to participate in the survey, complete and return the restaurant survey in the back of this book.

unofficial **TIP**
Spoodles at Disney's BoardWalk closes in summer 2009 and will be replaced in the fall with **Kouzzina,** a family-style eatery featuring celebrity chef Cat Cora's Mediterranean-style recipes.

In this year's survey, an impressive 16 sit-down restaurants merited reader-satisfaction ratings of 90% or greater. Topping the list with 96% approval were **Jiko—The Cooking Place** at Animal Kingdom Lodge and **Beaches and Cream** at the Beach Club Resort. Close behind were **Teppan Edo** at Epcot's Japan Pavilion and **Narcoossee's** at the Grand Floridian Resort & Spa, both at 95%. Hot on their heels were the **House of Blues** at Downtown Disney and the **California Grill** at the Contemporary Resort. Remember, though, that the survey reports overall reader satisfaction—the quality of the food is only one element among many that readers consider.

Walt Disney World Restaurants by Cuisine

CUISINE	LOCATION	OVERALL RATING	COST	QUALITY RATING	VALUE RATING
AFRICAN					
Jiko–The Cooking Place	Animal Kingdom Lodge	★★★★½	Exp	★★★★½	★★★½
Boma	Animal Kingdom Lodge	★★★★	Exp	★★★★	★★★★½
Tusker House Restaurant	Animal Kingdom	★½	Mod	★	★★
AMERICAN					
California Grill	Contemporary	★★★★½	Exp	★★★★½	★★★
The Hollywood Brown Derby	DHS	★★★★	Exp	★★★★	★★★
Artist Point	Wilderness Lodge	★★★½	Exp	★★★★	★★★
Cape May Cafe	Beach Club	★★★½	Mod	★★★½	★★★★
Whispering Canyon Cafe	Wilderness Lodge	★★★	Mod	★★★½	★★★★
Captain's Grille	Yacht Club	★★★	Mod	★★★½	★★★
The Crystal Palace	Magic Kingdom	★★★	Mod	★★★½	★★★
House of Blues	West Side	★★★	Mod	★★★½	★★★
50's Prime Time Cafe	DHS	★★★	Mod	★★★	★★★
The Garden Grill Restaurant	Epcot	★★★	Exp	★★★	★★★
Liberty Tree Tavern	Magic Kingdom	★★★	Mod	★★★	★★★
Planet Hollywood	West Side	★★★	Mod	★★	★★
Trail's End Restaurant	Fort Wilderness Resort	★★★	Mod	★★★	★★★
Cinderella's Royal Table	Magic Kingdom	★★★	Exp	★★★	★★
T-REX	Downtown Disney	★★★	Mod	★★	★★
The Wave	Contemporary	★★★	Mod	★★	★★
Chef Mickey's	Contemporary	★★½	Exp	★★★	★★★
ESPN Club	BoardWalk	★★½	Mod	★★★	★★★
ESPN Wide World of Sports Cafe	ESPN Wide World of Sports Complex	★★½	Mod	★★★	★★★
Hollywood & Vine	DHS	★★½	Mod	★★★	★★★
1900 Park Fare	Grand Floridian	★★½	Mod	★★★	★★★
Boatwrights Dining Hall	Port Orleans	★★½	Mod	★★★	★★
Grand Floridian Cafe	Grand Floridian	★★½	Mod	★★★	★★

CUISINE	LOCATION	OVERALL RATING	COST	QUALITY RATING	VALUE RATING
AMERICAN (CONTINUED)					
Sand Trap Bar & Grill	Osprey Ridge Golf Course	★★½	Mod	★★½	★★½
Beaches & Cream	Beach Club	★★½	Inexp	★★½	★★½
Rainforest Cafe	Downtown Disney and Animal Kingdom	★★½	Mod	★★	★★
Garden Grove	Swan	★★	Mod	★★★	★★
Olivia's Cafe	Old Key West	★★	Mod	★★½	★★
Wolfgang Puck Cafe	West Side	★★	Exp	★½	★½
Sci-Fi Dine-In Theater Restaurant	DHS	★★	Mod	★★½	★★
LakeView Restaurant	Regal Sun Resort	★★	Mod	★	★★★
Big River Grille & Brewing Works	BoardWalk	★★	Mod	★★	★★
The Fountain	Dolphin	★★	Mod	★★	★★
Plaza Restaurant	Magic Kingdom	★★	Mod	★★	★★
Turf Club Bar & Grill	Saratoga Springs	★★	Mod	★★	★★
Tusker House Restaurant	Animal Kingdom	★½	Mod	★	★★
Maya Grill	Coronado Springs	★	Exp	★	★
BUFFET					
Boma	Animal Kingdom Lodge	★★★★	Exp	★★★★	★★★★½
Cape May Cafe	Beach Club	★★★½	Mod	★★★½	★★★★
Akershus Royal Banquet Hall	Epcot	★★★½	Exp	★★★	★★★★
Biergarten	Epcot	★★★½	Exp	★★★	★★★★
The Crystal Palace	Magic Kingdom	★★★	Mod	★★★½	★★★
Trail's End Restaurant	Fort Wiklerness Resort	★★★	Mod	★★★	★★★
Chef Mickey's	Contemporary	★★½	Exp	★★★	★★★
Hollywood & Vine	DHS	★★½	Mod	★★★	★★★
1900 Park Fare	Grand Floridian	★★½	Mod	★★★	★★★
Garden Grove	Swan	★★	Mod	★★★	★★
Tusker House Restaurant	Animal Kingdom	★½	Mod	★	★★
CHINESE					
Nine Dragons Restaurant	Epcot	★★★	Mod	★★★	★★

WDW Restaurants by Cuisine (continued)

CUISINE	LOCATION	OVERALL RATING	COST	QUALITY RATING	VALUE RATING
CUBAN					
Bongos Cuban Cafe	West Side	★★	Mod	★★	★★
ENGLISH					
Rose & Crown Dining Room	Epcot	★★★	Mod	★★★½	★★
FRENCH					
Bistro de Paris	Epcot	★★★	Exp	★★★½	★★
Les Chefs de France	Epcot	★★★	Exp	★★★	★★★
GERMAN					
Biergarten	Epcot	★★★½	Exp	★★★	★★★★
GOURMET					
Victoria & Albert's	Grand Floridian	★★★★★	Exp	★★★★★	★★★★
INDIAN/AFRICAN					
Sanaa	Animal Kingdom Lodge	★★★★	Exp	★★★★	★★★★
IRISH					
Raglan Road Irish Pub & Restaurant	Downtown Disney	★★★★	Mod	★★★½	★★★
ITALIAN					
Andiamo Italian Bistro & Grille	Hilton	★★★	Exp	★★★	★★★
Il Mulino	Swan	★★★	Exp	★★★	★★
Portobello	Downtown Disney	★★★	Exp	★★★	★★
Mama Melrose's Ristorante Italiano	DHS	★★½	Mod	★★★	★★
Tony's Town Square Restaurant	Magic Kingdom	★★½	Mod	★★★	★★
Tutto Italia	Epcot	★★½	Exp	★★½	★★½
JAPANESE					
Kimonos	Swan	★★★★	Mod	★★★★½	★★★
Teppan Edo	Epcot	★★★½	Exp	★★★★	★★★
Tokyo Dining	Epcot	★★★	Mod	★★★★	★★★
Benihana	Hilton	★★★	Mod	★★★½	★★★

CUISINE	LOCATION	OVERALL RATING	COST	QUALITY RATING	VALUE RATING
GLOBAL					
Paradiso 37	Downtown Disney	★★★	Inexp	★★★	★★★
MEDITERRANEAN					
Cítricos	Grand Floridian	★★★½	Exp	★★★★½	★★★
Fresh Mediterranean Market	Dolphin	★★½	Mod	★★½	★★
MEXICAN					
San Angel Inn	Epcot	★★★	Exp	★★	★★
MOROCCAN					
Restaurant Marrakesh	Epcot	★★	Mod	★★½	★★
NORWEGIAN					
Akershus Royal Banquet Hall	Epcot	★★★½	Exp	★★★	★★★★
POLYNESIAN/PAN-ASIAN					
'Ohana	Polynesian	★★★	Mod	★★★½	★★★
Yak & Yeti	Animal Kingdom	★★★	Exp	★★★½	★★★
Kona Cafe	Polynesian	★★★	Mod	★★★	★★★★
SEAFOOD					
Flying Fish Cafe	BoardWalk	★★★★	Exp	★★★★	★★★
Artist Point	Wilderness Lodge	★★★½	Mod	★★★★	★★★
Narcoossee's	Grand Floridian	★★★½	Exp	★★★½	★★
bluezoo	Dolphin	★★★	Exp	★★★	★★
Fulton's Crab House	Downtown Disney	★★½	Exp	★★★½	★★
Cap'n Jack's Restaurant	Downtown Disney	★★½	Mod	★★	★★
Coral Reef	Epcot	★★½	Exp	★★	★★
Shutters at Old Port Royale	Caribbean Beach	★★	Mod	★★½	★★
STEAK					
Shula's Steak House	Dolphin	★★★★	Exp	★★★★	★★
Le Cellier Steakhouse	Epcot	★★★½	Exp	★★★½	★★★
Yachtsman Steakhouse	Yacht Club	★★★	Exp	★★★½	★★
The Outback	Buena Vista Palace	★★	Exp	★★★	★★
Shutters at Old Port Royale	Caribbean Beach	★★	Mod	★★½	★★

FULL-SERVICE RESTAURANT PROFILES

Akershus Royal Banquet Hall ★★★½

NORWEGIAN/BUFFET EXPENSIVE QUALITY ★★★ VALUE ★★★★
READER-SURVEY RESPONSES 81% 👍 19% 👎 DISNEY DINING PLAN YES

Norway, World Showcase, Epcot; ☎ 407-939-3463

Reservations Required; credit card required to reserve at breakfast and lunch. **Dining Plan credits** 1 per person, per meal. **When to go** Anytime. **Cost range** Breakfast $29 (child $18), lunch $31 (child $19), dinner $36 (child $20). **Service** ★★★★. **Friendliness** ★★★★. **Parking** Epcot lot. **Bar** Full service. **Wine selection** Good. **Dress** Casual. **Disabled access** Yes. **Customers** Theme-park guests. **Character breakfast** 8:30–10:30 a.m. **Character lunch** Daily, 11:20 a.m.–2:55 p.m. **Character dinner** Daily, 4:20–8:30 p.m.

SETTING AND ATMOSPHERE Home to Princess Storybook Meals for breakfast, lunch, and dinner—the characters are the focus rather than the food. Modeled on a 14th-century fortress, Akershus entertains its guests in a great banquet hall under A-framed ceilings and massive iron chandeliers.

HOUSE SPECIALTIES *Koldtbord* (cold buffet), braised pork shank, mustard-glazed salmon, traditional *kjottkake* (ground-beef-and-lamb patty).

OTHER RECOMMENDATIONS Cold Carlsberg beer on tap.

SUMMARY AND COMMENTS Akershus is an all-you-can-eat establishment. Start at the *koldtbord,* where there's a wonderful array of cheeses, meats, and salads; then order hot entrees from the kitchen (you may order more than one of these, but only one at a time). Service can sometimes be slow, but the cuisine is above average.

Andiamo Italian Bistro & Grille ★★★

ITALIAN EXPENSIVE QUALITY ★★★ VALUE ★★★
READER-SURVEY RESPONSES 63% 👍 37% 👎 DISNEY DINING PLAN NO

Hilton Walt Disney World, Downtown Disney Resort Area; ☎ 407-827-3838

Reservations Accepted. **When to go** Early evening. **Cost range** $16–$38. **Service** ★★★. **Friendliness** ★★★★. **Parking** Free valet and lot. **Bar** Full bar. **Wine selection** Good. **Dress** Casual. **Disabled access** Yes. **Customers** Hotel guests. **Dinner** Daily, 5:30–11 p.m.

SETTING AND ATMOSPHERE Casual Italian bistro and wine bar that's suitable for families (kids under age 5 eat free on weekdays).

HOUSE SPECIALTIES Fried calamari, mussels with spicy marinara, chicken marsala, filet mignon, butternut ravioli with sage, dried cranberries, walnuts, and shaved Parmesan over Swiss chard.

OTHER RECOMMENDATIONS Rigatoni Bolognese, broiled salmon with tomato relish, eggplant parmigiana.

SUMMARY AND COMMENTS Better-than-average Italian. Though this is not destination dining, vacationers at the Downtown Disney resorts can head here for a satisfying meal.

Artist Point ★★★½

AMERICAN **EXPENSIVE** **QUALITY** ★★★★ **VALUE** ★★★
READER-SURVEY RESPONSES 88% 👍 12% 👎 **DISNEY DINING PLAN** YES

Wilderness Lodge and Villas; ☎ 407-824-3200

Reservations Recommended. **Dining Plan credits** 2 per person, per meal. **When to go** Anytime. **Cost range** $20–$43 (child $6–$11). **Service** ★★★★★. **Friendliness** ★★★★★. **Parking** Hotel lot. **Bar** Full service. **Wine selection** All wines from Pacific Northwest. **Dress** Dressy casual. **Disabled access** Yes. **Customers** Hotel guests, locals. **Dinner** Daily, 5:30–9:30 p.m.

SETTING AND ATMOSPHERE Two-story-high paintings depict the landscape of the Pacific Northwest, and out the tall windows you'll see wildflowers, the lake, a waterfall off high rocks, and even an erupting geyser. Cast-iron chandeliers hold 12 lanterns with milk-glass panes; tables are made of heavy wood and engraved with animals native to the Northwest.

HOUSE SPECIALTIES Roasted cedar-plank salmon, braised Penn Cove mussels, smoky Portobello soup, berry cobbler.

OTHER RECOMMENDATIONS Wild-boar-tenderloin appetizer, braised buffalo short rib, pan-seared duck breast, scallops with wild-mushroom risotto.

SUMMARY AND COMMENTS The cavernous dining room can feel a little sterile, but the food and friendly service warm up the place. The cedar-plank salmon is a must-try, but the buffalo short rib runs a close second in today's fat- and carb-conscious world. The restaurant offers a terrific all–Pacific Northwest wine list.

Beaches & Cream ★★½

AMERICAN **INEXPENSIVE** **QUALITY** ★★½ **VALUE** ★★½
READER-SURVEY RESPONSES 96% 👍 4% 👎 **DISNEY DINING PLAN** YES

Beach Club Resort; ☎ 407-934-8000

Reservations Not accepted. **Dining Plan credits** 1 per person, per meal. **When to go** Anytime. **Cost range** $8–$11.50. **Service** ★★★. **Friendliness** ★★★★. **Parking** Lot. **Bar** Beer only. **Wine selection** None. **Dress** Casual. **Disabled access** Yes. **Customers** Resort guests. **Lunch and dinner** Daily, 11 a.m.–11 p.m.

SETTING AND ATMOSPHERE Casual eats with a retro soda-fountain decor. There's often a line as guests in bathing suits and flip-flops queue up for the hearty burgers and piles of hot fries.

HOUSE SPECIALTIES Burgers (singles and doubles) and fries; giant hot dogs; hand-scooped ice cream including the gargantuan $22 Kitchen Sink dessert, with five flavors of ice cream smothered in topping.

OTHER RECOMMENDATIONS Roast-beef sub, deli turkey sandwich.

SUMMARY AND COMMENTS Grab your burger and sit at a nearby poolside table.

Benihana ★★★

JAPANESE **MODERATE** **QUALITY** ★★★½ **VALUE** ★★★
READER-SURVEY RESPONSES 89% 👍 11% 👎 **DISNEY DINING PLAN** NO

Hilton Walt Disney World, Downtown Disney Resort Area; ☎ 407-827-4865

Reservations Recommended. **When to go** Anytime. **Cost range** $17–$43. **Service** ★★★★★. **Friendliness** ★★★★★. **Parking** Hotel lot. **Bar** Full service.

Wine selection Good. **Dress** Casual. **Disabled access** Yes. **Customers** Hotel guests, some locals. **Dinner** Monday–Thursday, 4–10 p.m.; Friday–Sunday, 2–10 p.m.

SETTING AND ATMOSPHERE Large tables with built-in grills are crammed into small rooms decorated with rice-paper panels and Japanese lanterns. Lighting is low and focused on the stage—the chef's grill.

HOUSE SPECIALTIES Teppanyaki service at large tables (where the chef cooks dinner in front of you). Specialties include tenderloin, ocean scallops, lobster tail, and hibachi vegetables.

OTHER RECOMMENDATIONS Japanese onion soup.

ENTERTAINMENT AND AMENITIES Dinner is the show at this teppanyaki-service restaurant, where the chef does a lot of noisy chopping and grilling.

SUMMARY AND COMMENTS If you're looking for a nice, quiet dinner, be aware that diners sit at tables of eight, making private conversation almost impossible.

Biergarten ★★★½

GERMAN EXPENSIVE QUALITY ★★★ VALUE ★★★★
READER-SURVEY RESPONSES 89% 👍 11% 👎 DISNEY DINING PLAN YES

Germany, World Showcase, Epcot; ☎ 407-939-3463

Reservations Recommended. **Dining Plan credits** 1 per person, per meal. **When to go** Lunch or dinner. **Cost range** Lunch $20 (child $11), dinner $29 (child $14). **Service** ★★★★. **Friendliness** ★★★★. **Parking** Epcot lot. **Bar** Full service. **Wine selection** German. **Dress** Casual. **Disabled access** Yes. **Customers** Theme-park guests. **Lunch** Daily, noon–3:45 p.m. **Dinner** Daily, 4 p.m.–park closing.

SETTING AND ATMOSPHERE Hungry? This is the place to make Advance Reservations if you want to graze at a hefty German buffet that includes schnitzel, a variety of wursts, spaetzle, roast chicken, and sauerbraten (dinner only). Salads, breads, and desserts round out the offerings. The light level is low, and decor is inspired by a German village town square, with seating at long tables in a tiered dining room that surrounds a stage and dance floor. It's Oktoberfest every day, with a lederhosen-clad oompah band (including a singing saw) playing on the stage and encouraging diners to sing along and dance.

HOUSE SPECIALTIES Warm German potato salad, beet salad, various sausages and wieners, homemade spaetzle with gravy, and sauerbraten. There is also pork roast with German mustard and breaded pork schnitzel. The buffet is set up on wooden barrels.

OTHER RECOMMENDATIONS Pork-shank gratin with fried onions, braised red cabbage, potato dumplings (dinner only), beer.

ENTERTAINMENT AND AMENITIES Oompah band and German dancers perform after 1:15 p.m.

SUMMARY AND COMMENTS Unless you have a very big party, you'll be seated with other guests. But the lively 25-minute dinner show (one every hour) and noisy dining room are part of the fun, especially for families.

Big River Grille & Brewing Works ★★

AMERICAN MODERATE QUALITY ★★ VALUE ★★
READER-SURVEY RESPONSES 64% 👍 36% 👎 DISNEY DINING PLAN YES

Disney's BoardWalk; ☎ 407-560-0253

Reservations Not accepted. **Dining Plan credits** 1 per person, per meal. **When to go** Anytime. **Cost range** $15–$29 (child $5). **Service** ★★★. **Friendliness** ★★★★. **Parking** BoardWalk lot. **Bar** Full service. **Wine selection** Minimal. **Dress** Casual. **Disabled access** Good. **Customers** Tourists. **Lunch and dinner** Daily, 11:30 a.m.–11 p.m.

SETTING AND ATMOSPHERE Industrial cubist murals of factories, machinist-metal and wood chairs and tables, and a midnight-blue neon river that flows along the ceiling of the restaurant set a working-class atmosphere. The place is small—it seems like the huge copper brewing tanks take up more room than that allotted to the diners. Outside seating and service, weather permitting.

HOUSE SPECIALTIES Hazelnut-crusted mahimahi; flame-grilled meat loaf topped with rich brown gravy.

SUMMARY AND COMMENTS Run by a Tennessee company, Big River seems like an afterthought along Disney's BoardWalk and competes with nearby ESPN Club for the burger-and-brew crowd. But if you're looking for handcrafted beers, this is the place—they serve five beers, including a light lager, a robust ale, and seasonal choices. While the food is nothing special, this another good late-night choice.

Bistro de Paris ★★★

FRENCH EXPENSIVE QUALITY ★★★½ VALUE ★★
READER-SURVEY RESPONSES 77% 👍 23% 👎 DISNEY DINING PLAN NO

France, World Showcase, Epcot; ☎ 407-939-3463

Reservations Recommended. **When to go** Late dinner. **Cost range** $32–$43. **Service** ★★★★. **Friendliness** ★★★★★. **Parking** Epcot or BoardWalk lot; enter through back gate. **Bar** Full service. **Wine selection** Good but pricey. **Dress** Casual. **Disabled access** Elevator to second level. **Customers** Theme-park guests. **Dinner** Daily, 5:30–8:30 p.m.

SETTING AND ATMOSPHERE This is the more upscale of the two restaurants at Epcot's France Pavilion, up a flight of stairs with its own kitchen. Open only for dinner; request a table at the windows to view World Showcase Lagoon. The quiet dining room, painted yellow with dark-red banquettes, seats just 120, so service is attentive and personal.

HOUSE SPECIALTIES Maine lobster, beef tenderloin, rack of lamb.

SUMMARY AND COMMENTS Most diners enjoy the hustle and bustle of the noisy bistro downstairs, but for a quiet dinner and conversation, this is the spot. Chef Bruno Vrignon, who trained with the famed Paul Bocuse in France, has been with the restaurant since it opened and continues to turn out authentic, indulgent fare. Start with a mussel-and-saffron soup with aioli toast and end with the crème brûlée—you'll think you've been transported to Paris or Lyon.

bluezoo ★★★

SEAFOOD EXPENSIVE QUALITY ★★★ VALUE ★★
READER-SURVEY RESPONSES 50% 👍 50% 👎 DISNEY DINING PLAN NO

Walt Disney World Dolphin; ☎ 407-934-1111

Reservations Required. **When to go** Anytime. **Cost range** $28–$60 (child $10–$16). **Service** ★★★★. **Friendliness** ★★★. **Parking** Valet or self-park.

Bar Full service. **Wine selection** Excellent. **Dress** Dressy casual. **Disabled access** Good. **Customers** Hotel guests, locals. **Dinner** Daily, 5–11 p.m.

SETTING AND ATMOSPHERE In a dreamy setting designed by noted architect Jeffrey Beers, the dining room is swathed in blues with iridescent bubbles suspended from the lights. The name is courtesy of chef Todd English's young son, who saw an under-the-sea movie and said it looked like a "blue zoo." Open kitchen, raw bar, and "dancing fish" on a circular rotisserie.

HOUSE SPECIALTIES Clam chowder, grilled fish, Cantonese lobster.

OTHER RECOMMENDATIONS King salmon, grilled beef tenderloin, shake-and-bake fries.

SUMMARY AND COMMENTS Celebrity chef Todd English opened this stylish Florida outpost, frequented by conventioneers who don't mind the high prices ($2.75 for a single oyster) or the expensive wine list. Food is sophisticated, from the sashimi-grade tuna steak to the tenderloin of beef filet, but you can make a meal of the simple bowl of clam chowder with salt-cured bacon and the roasted-beet salad with greens, goat cheese, and candied walnuts.

Boatwrights Dining Hall ★★½

AMERICAN/CAJUN MODERATE QUALITY ★★★ VALUE ★★
READER-SURVEY RESPONSES 74% 👍 26% 👎 DISNEY DINING PLAN YES

Port Orleans Resort Riverside; ☎ 407-939-3463

Reservations Recommended for dinner. **Dining Plan credits** 1 per person, per meal. **When to go** Early evening. **Cost range** Dinner $16.50–$27 (child $7.50). **Service** ★★★. **Friendliness** ★★★★★. **Parking** Hotel lot. **Bar** Full service. **Wine selection** Fair. **Dress** Casual. **Disabled access** Good. **Customers** Hotel guests. **Dinner** Daily, 5–10 p.m.

SETTING AND ATMOSPHERE Diners sit in a large, noisy room under the skeleton of a riverboat under construction that looks sort of like the carcass of a mastodon. Tables are set with a boatwright's tool kit that contains condiments instead of tools.

HOUSE SPECIALTIES Jambalaya with chicken and andouille sausage.

OTHER RECOMMENDATIONS Prime rib, buttermilk fried chicken.

SUMMARY AND COMMENTS With 200 seats, Boatwrights serves the masses, and the cuisine (basic fare with a Cajun flair) is pretty homogenized. It's the only table-service restaurant in the Port Orleans Resort, so it gets busy and there can be waits. Order a Southern Belle (Southern Comfort and peach schnapps with cranberry juice)—and relax.

Boma ★★★★

AFRICAN EXPENSIVE QUALITY ★★★★ VALUE ★★★★½
READER-SURVEY RESPONSES 91% 👍 9% 👎 DISNEY DINING PLAN YES

Animal Kingdom Lodge; ☎ 407-938-3000

Reservations Mandatory. **Dining Plan credits** 1 per person, per meal. **When to go** Anytime. **Cost range** Breakfast $17 (child $10), dinner $31 (child $15). **Service** ★★★★. **Friendliness** ★★★★. **Parking** Valet or self-park in hotel lot. **Bar** Full service. **Wine selection** All South African. **Dress** Casual. **Disabled access** Good. **Customers** Hotel guests. **Breakfast** Daily, 7:30–11 a.m. **Dinner** Daily, 4:30–10 p.m.

SETTING AND ATMOSPHERE An open area with a number of food stations that encourage diners to roam about and graze, just like the animals that wander about outside the lodge.

HOUSE SPECIALTIES Watermelon-rind salad, Moroccan seafood salad, roasted meats, Durban spiced roasted chicken, vegetable skewers.

OTHER RECOMMENDATIONS Sweet-potato pancakes, Zebra Dome dessert, soups and stews.

SUMMARY AND COMMENTS A local favorite, Boma rarely changes its menu, but the formula—basic cuisine with a flourish of African flavors—is one that works. While Disney calls this a buffet, it's very different from what you'd typically expect (there are no steam tables, for starters). For those who like a major bang for their buck, this is the place to go.

Bongos Cuban Cafe ★★

CUBAN **MODERATE** **QUALITY** ★★ **VALUE** ★★
READER-SURVEY RESPONSES 50% 👍 50% 👎 **DISNEY DINING PLAN** NO

Downtown Disney West Side; ☎ 407-828-0999

Reservations Accepted. **When to go** Anytime. **Cost range** $13–$33 (child $6–$7). **Service** ★★★★. **Friendliness** ★★★★. **Parking** Downtown Disney lot. **Bar** Full service. **Wine selection** Moderate. **Dress** Casual. **Disabled access** Elevator to second level. **Customers** Gloria Estefan fans and Disney guests. **Lunch and dinner** Sunday–Thursday, 11 a.m.–10:30 p.m., Friday and Saturday until 11:30 p.m.

SETTING AND ATMOSPHERE This multilevel restaurant features an airy environment with a tropical theme built around a three-story pineapple. Other touches include a banana-leaf roof, banana-leaf ceiling fans, and palm-tree-shaped columns. Hand-painted murals and mosaics lend an artistic air, and an open wraparound porch provides pleasant outdoor dining.

HOUSE SPECIALTIES *Arroz con pollo* (chicken with rice), *camarones al ajillo* (shrimp in garlic sauce), *ropa vieja* (shredded beef in tomato sauce), *churrasco* (grilled skirt steak).

ENTERTAINMENT AND AMENITIES Latin music.

SUMMARY AND COMMENTS Gloria Estefan and her husband-producer, Emilio, created this large restaurant that marries salsa music with Cuban cuisine. Any number of mom-and-pop Cuban restaurants in the area do a better and more consistent job with this wonderful cuisine, so if you've never had Cuban food, try it somewhere else. Come here to have a drink with an umbrella in it and listen to music. It's upbeat but noisy.

California Grill ★★★★½

AMERICAN **EXPENSIVE** **QUALITY** ★★★★½ **VALUE** ★★★
READER-SURVEY RESPONSES 92% 👍 8% 👎 **DISNEY DINING PLAN** YES

Contemporary Resort; ☎ 407-939-3463

Reservations Recommended. **Dining Plan credits** 2 per person, per meal. **When to go** During evening fireworks. **Cost range** $22–$44 (child $7–$11). **Service** ★★★★★. **Friendliness** ★★★★★. **Parking** Valet on request. **Bar** Full service. **Wine selection** Californian. **Dress** Dressy casual. **Disabled access** Yes. **Customers** Hotel guests and locals. **Dinner** Daily, 5:30–10 p.m. **Lounge** Daily, 5 p.m.–10 p.m.

SETTING AND ATMOSPHERE High atop the Contemporary Resort, the award-winning California Grill sets the standard for Disney dining. The view from the 15th floor is stellar, one of the best spots for watching the Magic Kingdom fireworks. It's so popular that the Grill no longer allows just anyone on the elevator for a ride to the top—you must have a dinner reservation (the restaurant now has a reservation podium on the hotel's second floor). A show kitchen is the centerpiece of the airy dining room.

HOUSE SPECIALTIES Chef Brian Piasecki takes advantage of seasonal produce, fish, and meats. Sushi chef Yoshie has been there for more than ten years, creating sublime, artful sushi that's a meal in itself. Oven-fired flatbreads are always on the menu, as well as grilled pork tenderloin with creamy polenta and Zinfandel glaze, a favorite since day one.

OTHER RECOMMENDATIONS Oak-fired beef filet and any fresh fish on the menu.

ENTERTAINMENT AND AMENITIES The lights are dimmed during the Magic Kingdom fireworks, and the accompanying music is piped in. You can also step outside onto the 15th-floor deck for a closer look. Other entertainment includes watching the chefs; instead of begging for a window seat, sit at the counter—a chef might just slip you a sample.

SUMMARY AND COMMENTS The California Grill still is one of Disney's top dining experiences, but noise levels make conversation nearly impossible, especially if you're seated in "Siberia," to the right of the main dining room. We like the seats at the bar in front of the kitchen, or a coveted window seat. Though it's a sophisticated dining experience, you'll see plenty of kids in the dining room.

Cape May Cafe ★★★½

AMERICAN/BUFFET MODERATE QUALITY ★★★½ VALUE ★★★★
READER-SURVEY RESPONSES 88% 👍 12% 👎 DISNEY DINING PLAN YES

Beach Club Resort; ☎ 407-934-3358

Reservations Recommended. **Dining Plan credits** 1 per person, per meal. **When to go** Anytime. **Cost range** Breakfast $19 (child $11), dinner $27 (child $13). **Service** ★★★★★. **Friendliness** ★★★★★. **Parking** Hotel lot. **Bar** Full service. **Wine selection** Limited. **Dress** Casual. **Disabled access** Yes. **Customers** Theme-park and hotel guests. **Breakfast** Daily, 7:30–11 a.m. **Dinner** Daily, 5:30–9:30 p.m.

SETTING AND ATMOSPHERE The natural-finish wood furniture and padded booths are executed in a clean, nautical New England style.

HOUSE SPECIALTIES The buffet features peel-and-eat shrimp, tasty (albeit chewy) clams, mussels, fish of the day, hand-carved prime rib, barbecued ribs, corn on the cob, Caesar salad, and a good dessert bar. The kids' bar includes chicken fingers, hot dogs, fried fish, and mac and cheese.

OTHER RECOMMENDATIONS The tart Key lime pie from the dessert bar.

ENTERTAINMENT AND AMENITIES Character breakfast with Goofy, Minnie, and Chip 'n' Dale.

SUMMARY AND COMMENTS This buffet serves consistently good food. While the restaurant is large and tables turn over rapidly, Advance Reservations are recommended. Because the Cape May is within easy walking distance of the World Showcase entrance to Epcot, it's a convenient and affordable place to dine before *IllumiNations.*

Cap'n Jack's Restaurant ★★½

SEAFOOD MODERATE QUALITY ★★ VALUE ★★
READER-SURVEY RESPONSES 51% 👍 49% 👎 DISNEY DINING PLAN NO

Downtown Disney Marketplace; ☎ 407-828-3971

Reservations Not required. **When to go** Anytime. **Cost range** Lunch $10–$19 (child $7.60), dinner $15–$24 (child $7.60). **Service** ★★★★★. **Friendliness** ★★★★★. **Parking** Marketplace lot. **Bar** Full service. **Wine selection** Wine not a specialty. **Dress** Casual. **Disabled access** Yes. **Customers** Tourists. **Lunch and dinner** Daily, 11:30 a.m.–10:30 p.m.

SETTING AND ATMOSPHERE A pierhouse on the edge of Buena Vista Lagoon.

HOUSE SPECIALTIES Clam chowder, crab cakes, baked salmon, and shrimp pasta. For landlubbers, there's roast chicken and beef pot roast.

ENTERTAINMENT AND AMENITIES The lagoon-side setting offers views of amateur boaters, and the sunsets are pretty here.

SUMMARY AND COMMENTS Back in the 1970s, this was *the* place for sipping drinks and noshing on seafood. Today it's obvious no one's paying much attention to the menu and decor, but it is convenient for shoppers at Downtown Disney Marketplace. And there's never a wait for a table—sip a cold beer or margarita (or a smoothie if you're a kid) and relax.

Captain's Grille ★★★

AMERICAN MODERATE QUALITY ★★★½ VALUE ★★★
READER-SURVEY RESPONSES 89% 👍 11% 👎 DISNEY DINING PLAN YES

Yacht Club Resort; ☎ 407-939-3463

Reservations Not necessary. **Dining Plan credits** 1 per person, per meal. **When to go** Breakfast or lunch. **Cost range** Breakfast buffet $16 (child $9), lunch $10–$18 (child $7.50), dinner $15–$28. **Service** ★★★★★. **Friendliness** ★★★★★. **Parking** Hotel lot. **Bar** Full service. **Wine selection** Good. **Dress** Casual. **Disabled access** Yes. **Customers** Hotel guests. **Breakfast** Daily, 7–11 a.m. **Lunch** Daily, 11:30 a.m.–2 p.m. **Dinner** Daily, 5:30–9:30 p.m.

SETTING AND ATMOSPHERE This large, somewhat noisy dining room features a bright nautical theme with colorful pastels.

HOUSE SPECIALTIES Breakfast features a buffet or an à la carte menu, with such selections as crab-cake Benedict. Lunch is coffee-shop fare like grilled-chicken and roast-turkey sandwiches. Dinner features standard dishes like prime rib, fish of the day, and roast chicken.

SUMMARY AND COMMENTS Not a dining destination, but it is a favorite of Disney cast members, who like it because it's quiet and the service is quick.

Le Cellier Steakhouse ★★★½

STEAK EXPENSIVE QUALITY ★★★½ VALUE ★★★
READER-SURVEY RESPONSES 88% 👍 12% 👎 DISNEY DINING PLAN YES

Canada, World Showcase, Epcot; ☎ 407-939-3463

Reservations Recommended. **Dining Plan credits** 1 per person, per meal. **When to go** Before 6 p.m. **Cost range** Lunch $12.50–$30, dinner $22–$35 (child $7.50). **Service** ★★★★. **Friendliness** ★★★★★. **Parking** Epcot lot. **Bar** Full bar. **Wine selection** Canadian wines are featured. **Dress** Casual. **Disabled access** Yes. **Customers** Theme-park guests. **Lunch** Daily, 11:30 a.m.–3 p.m. **Dinner** Daily, 4–8:50 p.m.

SETTING AND ATMOSPHERE Designed to look like a wine cellar, Le Cellier is a pleasant respite from World Showcase once you adjust to the dim dining room. Decor is ordinary, but visible wine racks and wall sconces with fat candle-lamps add to the ambience. Most of the servers are Canadian and enjoy sharing stories of their home country.

HOUSE SPECIALTIES Canadian Cheddar cheese soup, steaks, seared King salmon.

OTHER RECOMMENDATIONS Prince Edward Island mussels, salt-crusted prime rib, maple crème brûlée.

SUMMARY AND COMMENTS Though the steaks take center stage here, you can make a meal of the rich Canadian Cheddar cheese soup and a salad, or one of the substantial sandwiches. Pair the mushroom filet mignon with a Moosehead Pale Ale for a Canadian-style treat.

Chef Mickey's ★★½

AMERICAN/BUFFET EXPENSIVE QUALITY ★★★ VALUE ★★★
READER-SURVEY RESPONSES 87% 👍 13% 👎 DISNEY DINING PLAN YES

Contemporary Resort; ☎ 407-939-3463

Reservations Required. **Dining Plan credits** 1 per person, per meal. **When to go** Early evening. **Cost range** Breakfast $23 (child $13), dinner $30 (child $15). **Service** ★★★★. **Friendliness** ★★★★★. **Parking** Resort valet or lot. **Bar** Full service. **Wine selection** Fair. **Dress** Casual. **Disabled access** Yes. **Customers** Theme-park guests. **Breakfast** Daily, 7–11:30 a.m. **Dinner** Daily, 5–9:30 p.m.

SETTING AND ATMOSPHERE A colorful, open dining room with the monorail running overhead, this is one of the most popular Disney character restaurants—mostly because you're guaranteed an audience with Mickey Mouse, who dons a chef's toque and visits every single table for photos. (Goofy, Minnie, Donald, and Pluto are on hand, too.) The buffet circles the center of the room. It's noisy, busy, and fun for families—controlled chaos, but most parents are used to that.

HOUSE SPECIALTIES Breakfast: French toast, biscuits and gravy. Dinner: oven-roasted prime rib and ham.

OTHER RECOMMENDATIONS Fresh greens and mixed salads, pasta selections, Parmesan mashed potatoes and gravy.

ENTERTAINMENT AND AMENITIES Character visits.

SUMMARY AND COMMENTS The all-you-can-eat buffet is a terrific value for families; there's plenty for picky eaters, and you can start or end the day with a full tummy and photos of the top Disney characters already checked off your to-do list. Selections at both breakfast and dinner are freshly prepared and served in casseroles and platters on special heated countertops—a small step up from chafing dishes.

Les Chefs de France ★★★

FRENCH EXPENSIVE QUALITY ★★★ VALUE ★★★
READER-SURVEY RESPONSES 79% 👍 21% 👎 DISNEY DINING PLAN YES

France, World Showcase, Epcot; ☎ 407-939-3463

Reservations Recommended. **Dining Plan credits** 1 per person, per meal. **When to go** Anytime. **Cost range** Lunch $12–$20 (child $7–$8), dinner $18–$33 (child $7–$8). **Service** ★★★★★. **Friendliness** ★★★★★. **Parking** Epcot lot. **Bar** Beer. **Wine selection** Very good. **Dress** Casual. **Disabled access** Yes. **Customers** Theme-park guests. Lunch Daily, noon–3 p.m. **Dinner** Daily, 5–9 p.m.

SETTING AND ATMOSPHERE The smell of buttery croissants is as much a part of the decor here as the carefully placed copies of *Le Monde* and the huge mottled mirrors. White tablecloths and padded banquettes accentuate the classic bistro decor of the main dining room. Another room sits off to the side, this one a more casual sunroom with a better view of what's going on outside. An animatronic version of Remy, the rodent star of Disney/Pixar's *Ratatouille,* visits a few times each day, stopping at tables for brief visits. (He stands just six inches tall and fits on a cheese tray.)

HOUSE SPECIALTIES Les Chefs de France features some of the dishes served at the real restaurants of the three chefs for whom this restaurant is named: Paul Bocuse, the late Gaston LeNotre, and Roger Vergé. You may sample seared tuna, sliced and served with olives and caper sauce, fresh greens, and *frites;* grilled beef tenderloin with a black-pepper sauce; or a silky crème brûlée.

OTHER RECOMMENDATIONS Onion soup topped with Gruyère, chicken crêpes (lunch only), tomato-and-goat-cheese flatbread.

SUMMARY AND COMMENTS Here's your chance to eat in a restaurant created by three of France's best chefs. Paul Bocuse visits from time to time, so you just might get a chance to meet a culinary legend. Executive chef Bruno Vrignon, who trained in Lyon with Bocuse, heads up the kitchen team, and the French servers make it an immersion experience. If you're on a budget, go at lunch: many dinner entrees are available midday at reduced prices. The best deal is the three-course lunch ($20) that starts with French onion soup with Gruyère or lobster bisque and continues with the classic *croque monsieur* (toasted ham-and-cheese sandwich) or quiche, followed by crème brûlée for dessert.

Cinderella's Royal Table ★★★

AMERICAN EXPENSIVE QUALITY ★★★ VALUE ★★
READER-SURVEY RESPONSES 85% 👍 15% 👎 DISNEY DINING PLAN YES

Cinderella Castle, Fantasyland, Magic Kingdom; ☎ 407-939-3463

Reservations Mandatory; credit card required to reserve; must prepay in full. **Dining Plan credits** 2 per person, per meal. **When to go** Early. **Cost range** Character breakfast, $35 adults, $24 children; character lunch, $38 adults, $25 children; character dinner, $43 adults, $27 children. **Service** ★★★★. **Friendliness** ★★★★. **Parking** Magic Kingdom lot. **Bar** None. **Wine selection** None. **Dress** Casual. **Disabled access** Limited. **Customers** Theme-park guests. **Character breakfast** Daily, 8–10:20 a.m. **Character lunch** Daily, noon–3 p.m. **Dinner** Daily, 4–8:30 p.m.

SETTING AND ATMOSPHERE A medieval banquet hall, appointed with the requisite banners and Round Table–like regalia, located on the second floor of Cinderella Castle. Stained-glass windows overlook Fantasyland, but the view is limited.

HOUSE SPECIALTIES All meals are fixed-price character affairs, with the menus changing periodically. Breakfast is standard-issue. Lunch favorites include pasta, salmon, and the signature Major Domo's Favorite Pie (beef in Cabernet sauce, mashed potatoes, and puff pastry). Dinner fare includes roast lamb chops, pan-seared salmon, or prime rib; kids can choose from chicken strips, baked pasta, and a junior-sized Major Domo's Pie.

ENTERTAINMENT AND AMENITIES Assorted princesses attend at breakfast and lunch; the Fairy Godmother, along with Suzy and Perla (two of Cinderella's mice), is present at dinner. The meals are pricey, not so much because the food is good but because Disney forces you to purchase photos of your group that are bundled into the cost of the meal. For more on reserving a spot here (and the travails thereof), see page 354.

Cítricos ★★★½

MEDITERRANEAN **EXPENSIVE** **QUALITY** ★★★★½ **VALUE** ★★★
READER-SURVEY RESPONSES 91% 👍 9% 👎 **DISNEY DINING PLAN** YES

Grand Floridian Resort & Spa; ☎ 407-824-4379

Reservations Recommended; credit card required to reserve Chef's Domain. **Dining Plan credits** 2 per person, per meal. **When to go** Anytime. **Cost range** $22–$46 (child $6–$13). **Service** ★★★★★. **Friendliness** ★★★★★. **Parking** Valet; self-parking is deceptively far away. **Bar** Full service. **Wine selection** Very good. **Dress** Dressy casual. **Disabled access** Good. **Customers** Hotel guests and locals. **Dinner** Daily, 5:30–10 p.m.

SETTING AND ATMOSPHERE The golds and yellows of the Mediterranean color this stylish dining room. A show kitchen in full view of diners is where chef Phillip Ponticelli works his culinary magic.

HOUSE SPECIALTIES Sautéed shrimp with lemon, feta cheese, pasta, tomatoes, and white wine; bone-in rib eye; braised veal shank.

OTHER RECOMMENDATIONS Grilled swordfish Provençal; truffled potato soup; pan-roasted wild striped bass.

SUMMARY AND COMMENTS Chef Ponticelli is very hands-on, and his TLC shows. This is one of the best-kept dining secrets at Disney World—it's generally easy to get Advance Reservations here. For an extra-special night, reserve the Chef's Domain, a private room for up to 12 guests where the chef creates a special menu.

Coral Reef ★★½

SEAFOOD **EXPENSIVE** **QUALITY** ★★ **VALUE** ★★
READER-SURVEY RESPONSES 79% 👍 21% 👎 **DISNEY DINING PLAN** YES

The Seas, Future World, Epcot; ☎ 407-939-3463

Reservations Recommended. **Dining Plan credits** 1 per person, per meal. **When to go** Lunch. **Cost range** Lunch $13–$28 (child $7.59), dinner $17–$31 (child $7.59). **Service** ★★★★. **Friendliness** ★★★★. **Parking** Epcot lot. **Bar** Full service. **Wine selection** Good. **Dress** Casual. **Disabled access** Good. **Customers** Theme-park guests. **Lunch** Daily, 11:30 a.m.–3:20 p.m. **Dinner** Daily, 4 p.m.–park closing.

SETTING AND ATMOSPHERE Coral Reef offers one of the best theme-park views anywhere: below the water level of the humongous saltwater tank in the Seas Pavilion. Sharks, rays, and even humans swim by, and every table has a great view. Tiered seating affords perfect views; special lighting fixtures throw ripple patterns on the ceiling, creating an underwater feel.

HOUSE SPECIALTIES Creamy lobster soup, blackened catfish with pepper Jack cheese grits, grilled New York strip steak, Chocolate Wave dessert.

SUMMARY AND COMMENTS Often overlooked at Epcot for dining rooms in World Showcase, Coral Reef is the only table-service restaurant in Future World where you can sip a glass of wine and enjoy good food in a quiet, informal setting. It's a fun spot for marriage proposals—divers in the tank are willing to hold up a WILL YOU MARRY ME? sign for romantic diners.

The Crystal Palace ★★★

AMERICAN/BUFFET **MODERATE** **QUALITY** ★★★½ **VALUE** ★★★
READER-SURVEY RESPONSES 91% 👍 9% 👎 **DISNEY DINING PLAN** YES

Main Street, U.S.A., Magic Kingdom; ☎ 407-939-3463

Reservations Recommended. **Dining Plan credits** 1 per person, per meal. **When to go** Anytime. **Cost range** Breakfast $19 (child $11), lunch $21 (child $12), dinner $29 (child $14). **Service** ★★★. **Friendliness** ★★★★. **Parking** Magic Kingdom lot. **Bar** None. **Wine selection** None. **Dress** Casual. **Disabled access** Yes. **Customers** Magic Kingdom guests. **Breakfast** Daily, 8–10:30 a.m. **Lunch** Daily, 11:30 a.m.–2:45 p.m. **Dinner** Daily, 3:15 p.m.–park closing.

SETTING AND ATMOSPHERE A turn-of-the-20th-century glass pavilion awash with sunlight and decorated with plenty of summer greenery. Seating is comfortable (a pleasant respite), and buffet lines are open and accessible. There is a low buffet area where kids can help themselves.

HOUSE SPECIALTIES Menu items change often but have included waffles and pancakes layered with fresh fruit, prime rib, slow-roasted pork, Thai curry mussels, grilled vegetables with balsamic glaze, pasta with wild mushrooms and chicken, shrimp, and an ice-cream-sundae bar.

ENTERTAINMENT AND AMENITIES Winnie the Pooh and friends dance about and pose with the kids.

SUMMARY AND COMMENTS The best dining value in the Magic Kingdom—go hungry and fill up. The food here continues to get better and better on the state-of-the-art buffet, which instead of steam tables has casserole dishes and pans that sit on special heated countertops. Kids get their own buffet with mac and cheese and chicken fingers.

ESPN Club ★★½

AMERICAN/SANDWICHES **MODERATE** **QUALITY** ★★★ **VALUE** ★★★
READER-SURVEY RESPONSES 78% 👍 22% 👎 **DISNEY DINING PLAN** YES

Disney's BoardWalk; ☎ 407-939-1177

Reservations Not accepted. **Dining Plan credits** 1 per person, per meal. **When to go** Anytime. **Cost range** $10–$15 (child $8). **Service** ★★★. **Friendliness** ★★★★. **Parking** BoardWalk lot; valet parking, $10. **Bar** Full service. **Wine selection** Minimal. **Dress** Casual. **Disabled access** Good. **Customers** Tourists. **Hours** Daily, 11:30 a.m.–1 a.m.

SETTING AND ATMOSPHERE A sports bar to the *n*th degree, with basketball-court flooring, sports memorabilia, and more television monitors than a network affiliate. The bar area features satellite sports-trivia video games. A large octagonal space with a wall of TVs serves as the main dining room.

HOUSE SPECIALTIES Red wings (Buffalo-style wings), fresh grilled mahimahi on a whole-grain roll, pulled pork with fries, extreme Reuben, marinated grilled chicken breast on a rosemary focaccia roll.

SUMMARY AND COMMENTS Family-friendly and one of the cheapest dining spots on the BoardWalk. Service is a little more brusque than at other Disney restaurants. Portions are large, and the quality is in line with the price. A good choice for late-night dining or when you have to choose between going out for a bite and staying in the room to catch the big game.

ESPN Wide World of Sports Cafe ★★½

AMERICAN MODERATE QUALITY ★★★ VALUE ★★★
READER-SURVEY RESPONSES 79% 👍 21% 👎 DISNEY DINING PLAN YES

ESPN Wide World of Sports Complex; ☎ 407-939-2196

Reservations Not necessary. **Dining Plan credits** 1 per person, per meal. **When to go** Anytime. **Cost range** $8.50–$10 (child $6). **Service** ★★★. **Friendliness** ★★½. **Parking** ESPN Wide World of Sports lot. **Bar** Full service. **Wine selection** Minimal. **Dress** Jerseys if you've got 'em. **Disabled access** Yes. **Customers** Sports fans. **Lunch and dinner** Daily, 11 a.m.–7 p.m. (fall and winter, Thursday–Sunday).

SETTING AND ATMOSPHERE Think Hard Rock Cafe with sports memorabilia instead of musical instruments. More than 20 big-screen TVs play whatever game is on.

HOUSE SPECIALTIES Burgers and sandwiches.

ENTERTAINMENT AND AMENITIES Televised sporting events.

SUMMARY AND COMMENTS Food is unpretentious American cuisine—giant burgers, piles of chicken wings. The menu works for hungry fans at the ESPN Wide World of Sports Complex.

50's Prime Time Cafe ★★★

AMERICAN MODERATE QUALITY ★★★ VALUE ★★★
READER-SURVEY RESPONSES 83% 👍 17% 👎 DISNEY DINING PLAN YES

Hollywood Boulevard, Disney's Hollywood Studios; ☎ 407-939-3463

Reservations Suggested. **Dining Plan credits** 1 per person, per meal. **When to go** Anytime. **Cost range** Lunch $11.50–$17 (child $8), dinner $12.50–$21 (child $8). **Service** ★★★★★. **Friendliness** ★★★★★. **Parking** DHS lot. **Bar** Full service. **Wine selection** Limited. **Dress** Casual. **Disabled access** Yes. **Customers** Theme-park guests. **Lunch** Daily, 11 a.m.–3:55 p.m.; opens at 10:30 a.m. on Sunday and Wednesday. **Dinner** Daily, 4 p.m.–park closing.

SETTING AND ATMOSPHERE Like eating a meal in your own kitchen, 1950s-style: pastel laminate, gooseneck lamps, and black-and-white televisions that play vintage sitcoms are the rule.

HOUSE SPECIALTIES Meat loaf, pot roast, chicken, and other homey fare. We get a lot of mail from readers who like the 50's Prime Time Cafe; most say that the food is good and that it's easy to find something that kids will like. The peanut-butter-and-jelly milk shake is worth every calorie.

ENTERTAINMENT AND AMENITIES Fifties sitcom clips on television.

SUMMARY AND COMMENTS Diners really get a kick out of the classic comedies playing on black-and-white TVs, as well as the servers who nag you to "take your elbows off the table" or "finish every last bite." Skip the appetizers, stick with filling fare like the pot roast or golden fried chicken.

Flying Fish Cafe ★★★★

SEAFOOD EXPENSIVE QUALITY ★★★★ VALUE ★★★
READER-SURVEY RESPONSES 96% 👍 4% 👎 DISNEY DINING PLAN YES

Disney's BoardWalk; ☎ 407-939-3463

Reservations Recommended. **Dining Plan credits** 2 per person, per meal. **When to go** Anytime. **Cost range** $26–$42 (child $6–$12). **Service** ★★★★★. **Friendliness**

★★★★★. **Parking** Valet $12; BoardWalk lot. **Bar** Full service. **Wine selection** Excellent but pricey. **Dress** Casual dressy. **Disabled access** Good. **Customers** Tourists and locals. **Dinner** Sunday–Thursday, 5:30–10 p.m.; Friday and Saturday, 5:30–10:30 p.m.

SETTING AND ATMOSPHERE A whimsical remembrance of a 1930s Coney Island roller coaster served as the inspiration for the decor and the name. (The coaster was actually called the Flying Turns, and one of the cars on the ride was dubbed the Flying Fish.) Booth backs resemble the climbs and swoops of a coaster. On the far wall is a Ferris wheel, and fish fly overhead on a parachute ride. Diners may choose to sit at the counter that overlooks the open kitchen.

HOUSE SPECIALTIES Chef Tim Keating, a repeat James Beard Foundation finalist, adds his touches to the menu with such creations as citrus-zest-and-Szechuan-peppercorn–crusted yellowfin tuna loin in a carrot-and-coconut infusion. The fare here changes frequently, but you'll always find the potato-wrapped snapper, the restaurant's signature dish, served with creamy leek fondue and a red wine–butter sauce; char-crusted New York strip steak; and the Jonah lump crab cakes. Desserts are seasonal, but the house-made sorbets and Valrhona-chocolate galette are divine.

SUMMARY AND COMMENTS Locals love the Flying Fish, and for good reason. Though this is food for grown-ups, you'll often see children in the noisy dining room because of the BoardWalk location (their menu includes fish of the day and a grilled steak). If you can't get a table, check on seating availability at the counter—the food is just as good, and the show in the kitchen is entertaining.

The Fountain ★★

AMERICAN MODERATE QUALITY ★★ VALUE ★★
READER-SURVEY RESPONSES 90% 👍 10% 👎 DISNEY DINING PLAN NO

Walt Disney World Dolphin; ☎ 407-934-4000

Reservations Not taken. **When to go** Anytime. **Cost range** $7.25–$15 (child $8). **Service** ★★★★. **Friendliness** ★★★★. **Bar** Beer and wine only. **Wine selection** Limited. **Parking** Lot. **Dress** Casual. **Disabled access** Yes. **Customers** Hotel guests. **Lunch and dinner** Daily, 11 a.m.–11 p.m.

SETTING AND ATMOSPHERE Informal soda-shop ambience.

HOUSE SPECIALTIES Build-your-own burgers and hot dogs, BLTs, shakes, and ice-cream cones.

OTHER RECOMMENDATIONS Seared-salmon salad, tuna-and-cheddar melt on flatbread.

SUMMARY AND COMMENTS This is the place for Dolphin guests to get a quick bite. Create your own sundae at The Fountain Sweet Treats.

Fresh Mediterranean Market ★★½

MEDITERRANEAN/AMERICAN MODERATE QUALITY ★★½ VALUE ★★
READER-SURVEY RESPONSES 75% 👍 25% 👎 DISNEY DINING PLAN NO

Walt Disney World Dolphin; ☎ 407-934-1609

Reservations Available but not necessary. **When to go** Anytime. **Cost range** Breakfast $18 (child $11); lunch $12–$24 (child $12). **Service** ★★★★. **Friendliness** ★★★★. **Parking** Hotel lot. **Bar** Beer, wine, limited cocktails. **Wine selection** Limited. **Dress** Casual. **Disabled access** Yes. **Customers** Hotel guests.

Breakfast Daily, 6:30–11 a.m. **Lunch** Monday–Friday, 1 a.m.–1 p.m.; Saturday and Sunday, noon–2 p.m.

SETTING AND ATMOSPHERE Brightly colored tiles, light woods, and big windows set the scene. Ask for a veranda table if you want to have a quiet conversation away from the action in the open kitchen.

HOUSE SPECIALTIES For breakfast: fresh-pressed fruit and vegetable juices, made-to-order omelets; for lunch: chicken Marsala, seared black bass, generous salads.

OTHER RECOMMENDATIONS Pasta with porcini mushrooms; Italian panini; beef sliders.

SUMMARY AND COMMENTS A pleasant, quiet spot for breakfast or lunch, with a menu that's more healthful than many.

Fulton's Crab House ★★½

SEAFOOD EXPENSIVE QUALITY ★★★½ VALUE ★★
READER-SURVEY RESPONSES 83% 👍 17% 👎 DISNEY DINING PLAN NO

Downtown Disney Marketplace; ☎ 407-939-3463

Reservations Accepted. **When to go** Early evening. **Cost range** Lunch $10–$18 (child $6–$20), dinner $21–$52 (child $7–$20). **Service** ★★★★. **Friendliness** ★★★★. **Parking** Lot near the former Pleasure Island complex. **Bar** Full service. **Wine selection** Good; mostly American. **Dress** Casual. **Disabled access** Yes. **Customers** Locals and Disney guests. **Lunch** Daily, 11:30 a.m.–3:30 p.m. **Dinner** Daily, 4–11 p.m.

SETTING AND ATMOSPHERE A large lounge on the first deck is where you'll spend a good deal of time waiting for your table. Separate dining areas include the Market Room, a tribute to New York City's Fulton Fish Market (for which the restaurant is named); the Constellation Room, a semicircular room with a starlit night sky; and the Industry Room, which is a tribute to the commercial-fishing industry.

HOUSE SPECIALTIES Stone crab; fresh fish flown in daily; fresh oysters; Fulton's crab-and-lobster bisque; cioppino with crab, shrimp, scallops, clams, mussels, and fish in a tomato broth; Alaskan king and Dungeness crab.

OTHER RECOMMENDATIONS Prince Edward Island mussels and Florida littleneck clams, crab and lobster for two, filet mignon, grilled shrimp.

SUMMARY AND COMMENTS Fulton's once had some of the best seafood in central Florida, but nowadays the selections are rather mundane, although prices remain high. Waits can be long—more than an hour even on weeknights. But if you don't get fresh seafood back home, go early, request a table on the deck, order a Seafood Tower ($20 per person) and while away a few hours.

The Garden Grill Restaurant ★★★

AMERICAN EXPENSIVE QUALITY ★★★ VALUE ★★★
READER-SURVEY RESPONSES 90% 👍 10% 👎 DISNEY DINING PLAN YES

The Land, Future World, Epcot; ☎ 407-939-3463

Reservations Recommended. **Dining Plan credits** 1 per person, per meal. **When to go** Anytime. **Cost range** $29 (child $14). **Service** ★★★★. **Friendliness** ★★★★★. **Parking** Epcot lot. **Bar** Wine, beer, some mixed drinks. **Wine selection** Fair. **Dress** Casual. **Disabled access** Yes. **Customers** Theme-park guests. **Dinner** 4:30–8 p.m.

SETTING AND ATMOSPHERE With the popular Soarin' attraction nearby, The Garden Grill stays busy. You step on a slowly revolving floor to make your way to tables that revolve above scenes from Living with the Land, the pavilion's ride-through attraction (see page 571). If service is prompt, about the time you finish a meal you've revolved around once, past scenes of a desert, a rain forest, and a farm, along with a few mural-painted walls in between. Mickey, Chip 'n' Dale, and various other Disney characters make stops at tables for photo ops and greetings.

HOUSE SPECIALTIES Marinated flank steak, turkey with cranberry-orange relish, fish of the day. Dessert is fruit cobbler. The kids' menu includes mac and cheese, chicken tenders, potatoes, and vegetables.

ENTERTAINMENT AND AMENITIES The view. Character dining. Complimentary nonalcoholic beverages included with meals.

SUMMARY AND COMMENTS Salads are made with produce grown right in The Land's garden downstairs. This is one of the quietest dining spots for getting photos with Disney characters.

Garden Grove ★★

AMERICAN MODERATE QUALITY ★★★ VALUE ★★
READER-SURVEY RESPONSES 40% 👍 60% 👎 DISNEY DINING PLAN NO

Walt Disney World Swan; ☎407-934-1609

Reservations Required. **When to go** Anytime. **Entree range** Breakfast $10–$22 (child $3.25–$5.50), weekday buffet $16.99 (child $10.99), weekend Disney-character buffet $18.99 (child $11.99), lunch $4–$22 (child $6–$7), Disney-character dinner buffet $28.99–$31.99 (child $12.99) **Service** ★★★. **Friendliness** ★★★. **Parking** Valet or lot. **Bar** Full service. **Wine selection** good. **Dress** Casual. **Disabled access** Yes. **Customers** Hotel guests, some locals, tourists. **Breakfast, lunch, and dinner** Daily, 6:30 a.m.–9:30 p.m.

SETTING AND ATMOSPHERE The spacious dining room has a 25-foot faux tree as its centerpiece, and sunlight streams in from the tall windows. At night, the lights are dimmed, the oak tree is full of lanterns and twinkling lights, and street lamps create the pleasant ambience of a nighttime garden.

HOUSE SPECIALTIES Japanese breakfast with fish and miso soup. For lunch, beef sliders, Reuben panini, and signature fries with lime, cayenne, and garlic salt. For dinner, Saturday, Tuesday, and Thursday are Mediterranean-themed (pastas, lamb); Wednesday and Sunday are barbecue night (including prime rib); and Monday and Friday are fish night (seafood risotto, paella, fresh catch).

OTHER RECOMMENDATIONS Superfoods breakfast menu.

SUMMARY AND COMMENTS Garden Grove's dependable fare isn't worth a special trip, but it is a nice departure when your kids are clamoring for time with the Disney characters.

Grand Floridian Cafe ★★½

AMERICAN MODERATE QUALITY ★★★ VALUE ★★
READER-SURVEY RESPONSES 84% 👍 16% 👎 DISNEY DINING PLAN YES

Grand Floridian Resort & Spa; ☎ 407-824-2496

Reservations Recommended. **Dining Plan credits** 1 per person, per meal. **When to go** Anytime. **Cost range** Breakfast $10–$18 (child $5), lunch $10.50–$25 (child $8), dinner $17–$28 (child $8). **Service** ★★★. **Friendliness** ★★★★. **Parking** Valet; self-parking is far away. **Bar** Full service. **Wine selection** Good. **Dress** Casual. **Disabled access** Yes. **Customers** Hotel guests. **Breakfast** Daily, 7–11:30 a.m. **Lunch** Daily, 11:30 a.m.–2 p.m. **Dinner** Daily, 5–9 p.m.

SETTING AND ATMOSPHERE The large dining room, with high ceilings and decorative windows, looks out on the Grand Floridian's pool and center courtyard.

HOUSE SPECIALTIES Breakfast includes eggs prepared just about every way known to mankind, waffles, and French toast. For lunch, there's Cobb salad and the Grand sandwich with hot ham, turkey, and Boursin-cheese sauce. For dinner, choose from salmon, shrimp-and-prosciutto penne pasta, or grilled pork chop.

OTHER RECOMMENDATIONS A hefty Reuben for lunch and a simple New York strip with Red Bliss mashed potatoes for dinner.

SUMMARY AND COMMENTS Not a likely dining choice with so many other options, but hotel guests can get a good meal and scrumptious desserts.

Hollywood & Vine ★★½

AMERICAN | MODERATE | QUALITY ★★★ | VALUE ★★★
READER-SURVEY RESPONSES 67% 👍 33% 👎 | DISNEY DINING PLAN YES

Hollywood Boulevard, Disney's Hollywood Studios; ☎ 407-939-3463

Reservations Recommended; credit card required to reserve *Fantasmic!* dinner package (see page 644). **Dining Plan credits** 1 per person, per meal. **When to go** Anytime. **Cost range** Breakfast buffet $23 (child $13), lunch buffet $25 (child $14), dinner buffet $25 (child $13). **Service** ★★★★. **Friendliness** ★★★★★. **Parking** DHS lot. **Bar** Full service. **Wine selection** Limited. **Dress** Casual. **Disabled access** Yes. **Customers** Theme-park guests. **Breakfast and lunch** Character meals; breakfast daily, 8–11:20 a.m.; lunch daily, 11:40 a.m.–2:25 p.m. **Dinner** Daily, 5–9 p.m.

SETTING AND ATMOSPHERE Large Art Deco–style cafeteria with tile floors and lots of chrome. Huge wall murals resembling old postcards depict vintage scenes of old Hollywood and other California landmarks.

HOUSE SPECIALTIES Chilled salads, fish of the day, carved and grilled meats, vegetables and pasta, fresh fruits and breads. (Menu changes daily.)

SUMMARY AND COMMENTS "Play 'n Dine at Hollywood & Vine" features *Playhouse Disney* characters at breakfast and lunch. If you feel the need to stuff yourself, try this all-you-can-eat buffet. Be warned, though—with all the glass, tile, and chrome, the noise echoes for days.

The Hollywood Brown Derby ★★★★

AMERICAN | EXPENSIVE | QUALITY ★★★★ | VALUE ★★★
READER-SURVEY RESPONSES 78% 👍 22% 👎 | DISNEY DINING PLAN YES

Hollywood Boulevard, Disney's Hollywood Studios; ☎ 407-939-3463

Reservations Recommended; credit card required to reserve *Fantasmic!* dinner package (see page 644). **Dining Plan credits** 2 per person, per meal. **When to go** Early evening. **Cost range** Lunch $15–$29 (child $6–$11), dinner $22–$36 (child $6–$11). **Service** ★★★★★. **Friendliness** ★★★★★. **Parking** DHS lot. **Bar** Full service. **Wine selection** Very good. **Dress** Casual. **Disabled access** Yes. **Customers** Theme-park guests. **Lunch** Daily, 11:30 a.m.–3 p.m. **Dinner** Daily, 3:30 p.m.–park closing.

SETTING AND ATMOSPHERE A replica of the original Brown Derby restaurant (not the one shaped like a derby) in California, the elegant sunken dining room has curved booths, tables draped with yards of white linen, and romantic shaded candles. Tall palm trees in huge pots stand in the center of the room and reach for the high ceiling. The white-jacketed waiters are better dressed than most of the park guests.

HOUSE SPECIALTIES Cobb salad (named for Bob Cobb, the original restaurant's owner), spice-rubbed black grouper, grapefruit cake.

OTHER RECOMMENDATIONS Thai noodle bowl with coconut-crusted tofu, blue-crab-cake appetizer.

SUMMARY AND COMMENTS The decor is so perfect you'll feel as if you're in 1930s Hollywood; everyone really should dress in white ties and long chiffon gowns and do their best Fred Astaire and Ginger Rogers impersonations here. This is the Studios' top dining experience—service is outstanding, and the kitchen turns out above-average creations. *And* the dining room is quiet enough for conversation.

House of Blues ★★★

REGIONAL AMERICAN MODERATE QUALITY ★★★½ VALUE ★★★
READER-SURVEY RESPONSES 93% 👍 7% 👎 DISNEY DINING PLAN NO

Downtown Disney West Side; ☎ 407-934-2623

Reservations Accepted. **When to go** Early evening; Sunday gospel brunch. **Cost range** $11–$28; brunch $33.50 (child $17.25). **Service** ★★★★. **Friendliness** ★★★. **Parking** Downtown Disney lot. **Bar** Full service. **Wine selection** Modest. **Dress** Casual. **Disabled access** Good. **Customers** Blues lovers. **Brunch** 2 seatings on Sunday, 10:30 a.m. and 1 p.m. **Lunch and dinner** Sun.–Tues., 11:30 a.m.–11 p.m.; Wed. and Thurs. 11:30 a.m.–midnight; Fri. and Sat., 11:30 a.m.–1 a.m.

SETTING AND ATMOSPHERE You'd think it was a ramshackle hut in the bayou if the place weren't bigger than all of Louisiana. Nearly every available inch of wall space displays some type of voodoo-tinged folk art. The restaurant area is separated from the performance hall, where blues and rock groups perform. There is often a live band in the restaurant on weekends as well.

HOUSE SPECIALTIES New Orleans–inspired cuisine such as jambalaya and shrimp po'boy sandwiches.

OTHER RECOMMENDATIONS Tennessee-style baby-back ribs, blackened-chicken sandwich with chili-garlic mayonnaise; white chocolate–banana bread pudding.

SUMMARY AND COMMENTS For a themed restaurant, House of Blues does a good job with its food. If you're planning on taking in one of the acts at the performance space next door, you're better off going there first so you can get a good seat, then eating afterward.

Il Mulino ★★★

ITALIAN EXPENSIVE QUALITY ★★★ VALUE ★★
READER-SURVEY RESPONSES 67% 👍 33% 👎 DISNEY DINING PLAN NO

Walt Disney World Swan; ☎ 407-934-1609

Reservations Accepted. **When to go** Anytime. **Cost range** $16–$45 (child $12–$16). **Service** ★★. **Friendliness** ★★. **Parking** Swan lot; valet available. **Bar**

Full service. **Wine selection** Good. **Dress** Dressy casual. **Disabled access** Good. **Customers** Mostly hotel guests and conventioneers. **Dinner** 5–11 p.m. nightly.

SETTING AND ATMOSPHERE Il Mulino takes an upscale-casual approach to Italian cuisine, with family-style platters for sharing in the noisy dining room. Tables are dark wood. An open kitchen creates a bustle. You can request private dining in one of the smaller rooms.

HOUSE SPECIALTIES The cuisine focuses on Italy's Abruzzi region, with hearty pastas and big cuts of meat. Try the bucatini Amatriciana or the 12-ounce filet of beef with spicy caper-tomato sauce.

OTHER RECOMMENDATIONS Fried calamari, gnocchi Bolognese, egg-battered jumbo shrimp sautéed in lemon and white wine.

SUMMARY AND COMMENTS Dinner starts with a complimentary taste of eggplant Parmesan with ciabatta and foccacia breads and ends with a complimentary sip of limoncello, the lemon-flavored Italian liqueur. The dining room's hardwood floors and faux-exposed-brick walls create a contemporary space but don't buffer the noise.

Jiko—The Cooking Place ★★★★½

AFRICAN/FUSION EXPENSIVE QUALITY ★★★★½ VALUE ★★★½
READER-SURVEY RESPONSES 96% 👍 4% 👎 DISNEY DINING PLAN YES

Animal Kingdom Lodge and Villas; ☎ 407-938-3000

Reservations Mandatory. **Dining Plan credits** 2 per person, per meal. **When to go** Anytime. **Cost range** $19–$39 (child $6–$11). **Service** ★★★★★. **Friendliness** ★★★★★. **Parking** Valet or self-park in hotel lot. **Bar** Full bar. **Wine selection** All South African. **Dress** Dressy casual. **Disabled access** Good. **Customers** Hotel guests and locals. **Dinner** Daily, 5:30–10 p.m.

SETTING AND ATMOSPHERE Young students from Africa, part of a yearlong cultural-exchange program, greet guests as they enter Jiko's spacious dining room, created by noted designer Jeffrey Beers and inspired by the opening scenes of *The Lion King*. A pair of large wood-burning ovens dominate the center of the room.

HOUSE SPECIALTIES Kalamata-olive flatbread; cucumber, tomato, and red-onion salad; maize-crusted Pacific halibut.

OTHER RECOMMENDATIONS Fire-roasted mussels, roasted lamb loin, pan-seared jumbo scallops, oak-grilled filet mignon with macaroni and cheese.

SUMMARY AND COMMENTS Jiko has been winning awards and accolades (including AAA's Four Diamond Award) for its interesting fare and stellar wine list—one of the largest collections of South African wines in any North American restaurant, with more than 1,800 bottles. If you're an adventurous diner, give chef John Clark's cuisine a try—his dishes are beautifully spiced and full of flavor. Start with the three African dips and breads, and try the Tanzanian chocolate cheesecake or the wonderful cheese plate.

Kimonos ★★★★

JAPANESE MODERATE QUALITY ★★★★½ VALUE ★★★
READER-SURVEY RESPONSES 90% 👍 10% 👎 DISNEY DINING PLAN NO

Walt Disney World Swan; ☎ 407-934-1609

Reservations Accepted for parties of 6 or more. **When to go** Anytime. **Cost range** Sushi and rolls à la carte, $4.75–$16. **Service** ★★★★★. **Friendliness**

★★★★★. **Parking** Hotel lot; valet, $13. **Bar** Full service. **Wine selection** Very good. **Dress** Casual. **Disabled access** Yes. **Customers** Hotel guests and locals. **Dinner** Daily, 5:30 p.m.–midnight; bar opens at 5 p.m.

SETTING AND ATMOSPHERE The decor consists of black-lacquered tabletops and counters, tall pillars rising to bamboo rafters with rice-paper lanterns, and elegant kimonos that hang outstretched on the walls and between the dining sections. The chefs will greet you with a friendly welcome, and you'll be offered a hot towel to clean your hands.

HOUSE SPECIALTIES Although sushi and sashimi are the focus, Kimonos also serves hot appetizers, including tempura-battered shrimp and vegetables; Kobe beef and duck satays; spicy Thai egg-drop soup; and miso soup.

SUMMARY AND COMMENTS More and more diners are discovering this little out-of-the-way spot for pristine sushi.The skill of the sushi artists is as much a joy to watch as is eating the wonderfully fresh creations. There are no full entrees here, just good sushi and appetizers. The Swan resort hosts many Japanese tourists, and you'll find many of them here on any given night.

Kona Cafe ★★★

NEW AMERICAN/PAN-ASIAN MODERATE QUALITY ★★★ VALUE ★★★★
READER-SURVEY RESPONSES 90% 👍 10% 👎 DISNEY DINING PLAN YES

Polynesian Resort; ☎ 407-939-3463

Reservations Accepted. **Dining Plan credits** 1 per person, per meal. **When to go** Anytime. **Cost range** Breakfast $9–$14.50 (child $5), lunch $11.50–$19 (child $8), dinner $17–$28 (child $8). **Service** ★★★★. **Friendliness** ★★★★★. **Parking** Polynesian lot; valet available. **Bar** Full service. **Wine selection** Moderate. **Dress** Casual. **Disabled access** Good. **Customers** Mostly hotel guests; some locals. **Breakfast** Daily, 7:30–11:45 a.m. **Lunch** Daily, noon–2:45 p.m. **Dinner** Monday–Saturday, 5–9:45 p.m.

SETTING AND ATMOSPHERE Kona Cafe has a postmodern decor, with arched railings and grillwork on the ceiling—a step up from its former coffee-shop ambience. If you want to escape the Magic Kingdom for a quiet lunch, hop on the monorail or take the resort launch to the Polynesian.

HOUSE SPECIALTIES Breakfast: Tonga toast (a decadent French toast layered with bananas). Lunch: Asian noodle bowl, fish tacos, pot stickers, sticky wings. Dinner: macadamia mahimahi, shrimp and scallops with sushi rice, pan-Asian noodles.

OTHER RECOMMENDATIONS Crab cakes, Kilauea torte (chocolate cake with a warm chocolate center), Kona coffee served in a press pot.

SUMMARY AND COMMENTS This isn't a fancy dining room, but the food is on a higher plane than your average java joint's.

LakeView Restaurant ★★

AMERICAN MODERATE QUALITY ★ VALUE ★★★
READER-SURVEY RESPONSES 21% 👍 79% 👎 DISNEY DINING PLAN NO

Regal Sun Resort, Downtown Disney Resort Area; ☎ 407-828-4444

Reservations Accepted. **When to go** Anytime. **Cost range** Character breakfast $22 ($11 ages 3–11), dinner $16–$34. **Service** ★★★. **Friendliness** ★★★. **Parking** Hotel lot. **Bar** Limited service. **Wine selection** Good. **Dress** Casual.

Disabled access Yes. **Customers** Hotel guests. **Breakfast** Daily, 7–11 a.m.; character breakfast Tuesday, Thursday, and Saturday, 7:30–10:30 a.m. **Dinner** Monday–Saturday, 6–10 p.m.

SETTING AND ATMOSPHERE Lakefront views.

ENTERTAINMENT AND AMENITIES Disney-character breakfast (usually Goofy and Pluto) three days a week.

SUMMARY AND COMMENTS There's nothing special about the cuisine, but the best reason to dine here is the Disney-character breakfast, with an all-you-can-eat buffet and a kid-sized buffet just for little ones. Dinner is standard hotel fare—burgers, steaks, salads.

Liberty Tree Tavern ★★★

AMERICAN MODERATE QUALITY ★★★ VALUE ★★★
READER-SURVEY RESPONSES 86% 👍 14% 👎 DISNEY DINING PLAN YES

Liberty Square, Magic Kingdom; ☎ 407-939-3463

Reservations Suggested. **Dining Plan credits** 1 per person, per meal. **When to go** Anytime. **Cost range** Lunch $6–$19 (child $8), dinner $29 (child $14). **Service** ★★★★★. **Friendliness** ★★★★★. **Parking** Magic Kingdom lot. **Bar** None. **Wine selection** None. **Dress** Casual. **Disabled access** Yes. **Customers** Theme-park guests. **Lunch** Daily, 11:30 a.m.–3 p.m. **Dinner** Daily, 4–9 p.m.

SETTING AND ATMOSPHERE Low, exposed-beam ceilings crown rooms framed by pastel-gray chair rails. Colonial-period wall art, much with a nautical theme, accents simple dark-wood tables and chairs with woven seats.

HOUSE SPECIALTIES For lunch, New England–style pot roast, roast turkey, and sandwiches. Family-style character dining at dinner, with all-you-can-eat turkey, carved beef, and smoked pork loin.

OTHER RECOMMENDATIONS Sandwiches and salads are good here, too.

SUMMARY AND COMMENTS Though the Liberty Tree is the best of the Magic Kingdom's full-service restaurants, it's often overlooked at lunch. Make Advance Reservations here for about an hour or so before parade time—after you eat, you can walk right out and watch the parade.

Mama Melrose's Ristorante Italiano ★★½

ITALIAN MODERATE QUALITY ★★★ VALUE ★★
READER-SURVEY RESPONSES 79% 👍 21% 👎 DISNEY DINING PLAN YES

Backlot, Disney's Hollywood Studios; ☎ 407-939-3463

Reservations Suggested; credit card required to reserve *Fantasmic!* dinner package (see page 644). **Dining Plan credits** 1 per person, per meal. **When to go** Anytime. **Cost range** Lunch $12–$20 (child $8), dinner $12–$22 (child $8). **Service** ★★★. **Friendliness** ★★★★★. **Parking** DHS lot. **Bar** Full service. **Wine selection** Limited. **Dress** Casual. **Disabled access** Yes. **Customers** Theme-park guests. **Lunch** Daily, noon–3:30 p.m. **Dinner** Daily, 3:30 p.m.–park closing.

SETTING AND ATMOSPHERE Mama Melrose's looks like a big-city neighborhood restaurant of the 1930s, with red-and-white checkered tablecloths, red vinyl booths, and grapevines hanging from the rafters. By far the most relaxing restaurant at Disney's Hollywood Studios, Mama Melrose's sports a look as comfortable as an old sweatshirt.

HOUSE SPECIALTIES Bruschetta; crispy calamari; toasted Italian bread salad; penne alla vodka; spicy Italian sausage.

OTHER RECOMMENDATIONS Grilled chicken or four-cheese flatbread.

SUMMARY AND COMMENTS Because of Mama Melrose's out-of-the-way location, you can sometimes just walk in, especially in the evening. Portions here are fairly large—it's possible to dine cheaply on just an appetizer or two.

Maya Grill ★

AMERICAN EXPENSIVE QUALITY ★ VALUE ★
READER-SURVEY RESPONSES 76% 👍 24% 👎 DISNEY DINING PLAN YES

Coronado Springs Resort; ☎ 407-939-3463

Reservations Recommended. **Dining Plan credits** 1 per person, per meal. **When to go** Anytime. **Cost range** Breakfast buffet $17 (child $10), dinner $15–$36 (child $9). **Service** ★★★. **Friendliness** ★★★. **Parking** Hotel lot; no valet. **Bar** Full service. **Wine selection** Fair. **Dress** Casual. **Disabled access** Good. **Customers** Hotel guests. **Breakfast** Daily, 7–11 a.m. **Dinner** Daily, 5–10 p.m.

SETTING AND ATMOSPHERE The dining room was designed to evoke the ancient world of the Maya, achieving "a harmony of fire, sun, and water." But the idea falls short, with the fire taking the form of "flames" made of fan-blown fabric at the top of two large columns. The kitchen is open to view, but so is the barren and starkly lit walkway outside.

HOUSE SPECIALTIES The kitchen has backed off from the original Nuevo Latino concept and offers a mainstream menu of steak, ribs, and seafood to suit the resort's convention crowd. There are still a few hints of Latin America, such as a pulled-pork empanada and beef tips with roasted peppers and ancho-chile sauce.

SUMMARY AND COMMENTS The food is ordinary, as is the setting. You're better off eating somewhere else.

Narcoossee's ★★★½

SEAFOOD EXPENSIVE QUALITY ★★★½ VALUE ★★
READER-SURVEY RESPONSES 95% 👍 5% 👎 DISNEY DINING PLAN YES

Grand Floridian Resort & Spa; ☎ 407-939-3463

Reservations Recommended. **Dining Plan credits** 2 per person, per meal. **When to go** Early evening. **Cost range** $20–$59 (child $6–$13). **Service** ★★★★★. **Friendliness** ★★★★★. **Parking** Valet; self-parking is deceptively far away. **Bar** Full service. **Wine selection** Good. **Dress** Dressy casual. **Disabled access** Yes. **Customers** Hotel guests and locals. **Dinner** Daily, 5:30–10 p.m.

SETTING AND ATMOSPHERE Part of the Grand Floridian resort complex, Narcoossee's is a freestanding octagonal building at the edge of Seven Seas Lagoon. It offers a great view of the Magic Kingdom and the boats that dock nearby to pick up and drop off guests after a day at the park.

HOUSE SPECIALTIES Maine lobster, grilled salmon, crab cakes, grilled filet mignon.

OTHER RECOMMENDATIONS Prince Edward Island mussels, Narcoossee's seafood bisque, buttermilk-fried-shrimp appetizer.

SUMMARY AND COMMENTS Prices are steep for such a casual atmosphere, but Narcoossee's is one of the few places at Disney where you can get fresh steamed lobster. The seafood is fresh and the wine list decent, but the dining room is noisy and small.

Nine Dragons Restaurant ★★★

CHINESE | MODERATE | QUALITY ★★★ | VALUE ★★
READER-SURVEY RESPONSES 71% 👍 29% 👎 DISNEY DINING PLAN YES

China, World Showcase, Epcot; ☎ 407-939-3463

Reservations Recommended. **Dining Plan credits** 1 per person, per meal. **When to go** Lunch or dinner. **Cost range** Lunch $15–$22 (child $8), dinner $16–$26 (child $8). **Service** ★★★. **Friendliness** ★★★★. **Parking** Epcot lot. **Bar** Full service. **Wine selection** Minimal. **Dress** Casual. **Disabled access** Yes. **Customers** Theme-park guests. **Lunch** Daily, 11:30 a.m.–4 p.m. **Dinner** Daily, 4:30 p.m.–park closing.

SETTING AND ATMOSPHERE Completely remodeled in 2008, Nine Dragons traded its dated black-lacquer-and-red-highlights color scheme for subdued wood tones; colorful lanterns in pale greens, blues, and red; and beautiful backlit glass sculptures from China. The waiting area features etched glass and gold artwork.

HOUSE SPECIALTIES Honey-sesame chicken; pepper shrimp with spinach noodles; five-spiced fish.

OTHER RECOMMENDATIONS Vegetarian stir-fry; noodle sampler with fresh vegetables and pork and chicken dipping sauces.

SUMMARY AND COMMENTS Cuisine has a lighter, more contemporary touch with the new menu and the service is friendlier than before.

1900 Park Fare ★★½

AMERICAN/BUFFET | MODERATE | QUALITY ★★★ | VALUE ★★★
READER-SURVEY RESPONSES 87% 👍 13% 👎 DISNEY DINING PLAN YES

Grand Floridian Resort & Spa; ☎ 407-824-3000

Reservations Strongly recommended but not required. **Dining Plan credits** 1 per person, per meal. **When to go** Breakfast or dinner. **Cost range** Breakfast $21 (child $12), dinner $30 (child $15). **Service** ★★★★. **Friendliness** ★★★★. **Parking** Valet; self-parking is deceptively far away. **Bar** Full service. **Wine selection** Limited. **Dress** Casual. **Disabled access** Yes. **Customers** Hotel and resort guests. **Breakfast** Daily, 8–11 a.m. **Dinner** Daily, 4:30–8:30 p.m.

SETTING AND ATMOSPHERE This bright, cavernous, high-ceilinged room is warmly appointed in pastels. Tables are set with linen. An antique band organ periodically provides musical accompaniment to dining.

HOUSE SPECIALTIES Buffet includes prime rib, salmon, and chicken Marsala.

OTHER RECOMMENDATIONS Separate buffet for kids includes pasta marinara, mini–corn dogs, chicken nuggets, and macaroni and cheese.

ENTERTAINMENT AND AMENITIES Character dining.

SUMMARY AND COMMENTS A good choice for character dining, but too bright and loud for adults without children. The prime rib is 1900 Park Fare's major draw at dinner, but go someplace else if you prefer your beef on the rare side of medium.

'Ohana ★★★

POLYNESIAN | MODERATE | QUALITY ★★★½ | VALUE ★★★
READER-SURVEY RESPONSES 87% 👍 13% 👎 DISNEY DINING PLAN YES

Polynesian Resort; ☎ 407-939-3463

Reservations Recommended. **Dining Plan credits** 1 per person, per meal. **When to go** Anytime. **Cost range** Character breakfast $23 (child $13), dinner $31 (child $15). **Service** ★★★★. **Friendliness** ★★★★★. **Parking** Hotel lot. **Bar** Full service. **Wine selection** Limited. **Dress** Casual. **Disabled access** Yes. **Customers** Resort guests. **Breakfast** Daily, 7:30–11 a.m. **Dinner** Daily, 5–10 p.m.

SETTING AND ATMOSPHERE A large open pit is the centerpiece of the room. Here the grilled foods are prepared with flair, as well as a flare: from time to time the chef will pour some liquid on the fire, causing huge flames to shoot up. This is usually in response to something one of the strolling entertainers has said, evoking a sign from the fire gods. At any given moment, there may be a hula-hoop contest or a coconut race, where kids are invited to push coconuts around the dining room with broomsticks.

HOUSE SPECIALTIES Skewer service is the specialty here—there is no menu. As soon as you're seated, your server will begin to deliver food. First comes bread and a green salad, followed by shrimp skewers, honey-glazed chicken wings, and wonton chips. The main course is steak, pork loin, turkey, and sausage, accompanied by stir-fried vegetables placed on a lazy Susan in the center of the table.

ENTERTAINMENT AND AMENITIES Strolling singers, games, characters at breakfast.

SUMMARY AND COMMENTS 'Ohana, which means "family," is a fun place. The food is good but not superior. The method of service and the fact that it just keeps coming make it all taste a little better. Insist on being seated in the main dining room, where the fire pit is located.

Olivia's Cafe ★★

AMERICAN MODERATE QUALITY ★★½ VALUE ★★
READER-SURVEY RESPONSES 63% 👍 37% 👎 DISNEY DINING PLAN YES

Old Key West Resort; ☎ 407-939-3463

Reservations Recommended. **Dining Plan credits** 1 per person, per meal. **When to go** Lunch. **Cost range** Breakfast $9–$12 (child $5), lunch $10.50–$17 (child $8), dinner $15–$28 (child $7.50). **Service** ★★★★. **Friendliness** ★★★★. **Parking** Hotel lot. **Bar** Full service. **Wine selection** Limited. **Dress** Casual. **Disabled access** Yes. **Customers** Resort guests. **Breakfast** Daily, 7:30–10:30 a.m. **Lunch** Daily, 11:30 a.m.–5 p.m. **Dinner** Daily, 5–10 p.m.

SETTING AND ATMOSPHERE This is Disney's idea of Key West: lots of pastels, rough wood siding on the walls, mosaic-tile floors, potted palms, tropical trees in the center of the room, and plentiful nautical gewgaws. There is some outside seating, which looks out over the waterway. Tile, wood siding, and no tablecloths add up to a very noisy dining room that's getting a little worn around the edges.

HOUSE SPECIALTIES Appetizers include crab cakes, chicken wings, and conch chowder. Entrees include prime rib, fennel-dusted grouper, and plantain-wrapped mahimahi.

OTHER RECOMMENDATIONS Pork chop with chipotle barbecue sauce and cheese grits, Key lime tart.

SUMMARY AND COMMENTS Olivia's is not a dining destination, but for resort guests it's a nice place for a nice meal.

The Outback ★★

STEAK EXPENSIVE QUALITY ★★★ VALUE ★★
READER-SURVEY RESPONSES 75% 👍 25% 👎 DISNEY DINING PLAN NO

Buena Vista Palace, Downtown Disney Resort Area; ☎ 407-827-2727

Reservations Recommended. **When to go** Very early dinner. **Cost range** $18–$49. **Service** ★★★. **Friendliness** ★★★. **Parking** Free valet at the rear of the hotel. **Bar** Full service. **Wine selection** Excellent. **Dress** Casual. **Disabled access** Yes. **Customers** Tourists. **Dinner** Daily, 5:30–11 p.m.

SETTING AND ATMOSPHERE A large open room with a two-story ceiling and a cascading waterfall. Servers wear khaki garb that resembles bush outfits.

HOUSE SPECIALTIES The Florida lobster tails or any of the steaks are a good bet, as are the king prawns.

OTHER RECOMMENDATIONS Fried-gator bites (just so you can say you've tried them), fish of the day, prime rib, Australian rack of lamb.

SUMMARY AND COMMENTS Not a dining destination (and not to be confused with the steak-house chain), but if you're in the mood for pricey Maine lobster or a decent steak, give The Outback a try.

Paradiso 37 ★★★

GLOBAL INEXPENSIVE QUALITY ★★★ VALUE ★★★
READER-SURVEY RESPONSES TOO NEW TO RATE DISNEY DINING PLAN YES

Downtown Disney; ☎ 407-934-3700

Reservations Only after 9:30 p.m. **Dining Plan credits** To be determined. **When to go** Lunch, dinner. **Cost range** $11.99–$25. **Service** ★★★. **Friendliness** ★★★★. **Parking** Downtown Disney lot. **Bar** Full service. **Wine selection** Limited. **Dress** Casual. **Disabled access** Yes. **Customers** Theme-park guests, locals. **Hours** Sunday–Wednesday, 11:30 a.m.–midnight; Thursday–Saturday, 11:30 a.m.–1 a.m.

SETTING AND ATMOSPHERE Prime location on the waterfront at Downtown Disney. The bar is the centerpiece of a dining room that's deceptively large, with seating (200-plus) on two levels and the best seats outside. Booths, tables, and tall tables. Ambience is festive and casual, with an open kitchen and young servers in bright cotton T-shirts and khakis. Food is inspired by street foods of Central, South and North America, from mac-and-cheese bites to enchiladas and barbecued pork.

HOUSE SPECIALTIES Central American "crazy corn" (roasted on the cob with pepper sauce and cheese); Argentinean skirt steak with chimichurri sauce; bottomless homemade salsa and chips; Paradiso 37 cheeseburger; the "mangled margarita," a combo of a margarita and sangria. (The "37" in the name refers to the number of varieties of tequila.)

OTHER RECOMMENDATIONS Macaroni-and-cheese bites, shrimp ceviche, sausage-and-pepper hoagie.

SUMMARY AND COMMENTS A fresh new spot for casual alfresco dining at Downtown Disney. A diverse menu offers lots of dishes that are ideal for sharing—ask for plenty of napkins. This is one of the few Disney spots that will cook a burger medium-rare. And the joint boasts "the coldest beer in the world," served at a crisp 29°F to 32°F.

Planet Hollywood ★★★

AMERICAN MODERATE QUALITY ★★ VALUE ★★
READER-SURVEY RESPONSES 54% 👍 46% 👎 DISNEY DINING PLAN NO

Downtown Disney West Side; ☎ 407-827-7827

Reservations Accepted. **When to go** Late lunch. **Cost range** $11–$27 (child $8). **Service** ★★. **Friendliness** ★★. **Parking** Lot near the former Pleasure Island complex. **Bar** Full service. **Wine selection** Limited. **Dress** Casual. **Disabled access** Yes. **Customers** Tourists, locals. **Lunch and dinner** Daily, 11–1 a.m.

SETTING AND ATMOSPHERE A large planet-shaped structure "floating" in the lagoon next to the redeveloping Pleasure Island. Planet Hollywood's decor is something of a movie museum, with memorabilia from famous films. Check out artifacts like the bus from the movie *Speed,* Marilyn Monroe's gloves, and the life-size likeness of Robin Williams.

HOUSE SPECIALTIES Pasta, fajitas, huge burgers, dinner salads, and pizzas; for dessert, try the old-fashioned chocolate cake with vanilla ice cream.

OTHER RECOMMENDATIONS Barbecue ribs, "World Famous" Chicken Crunch; mushroom, onion, and Swiss burger; shrimp Alfredo.

SUMMARY AND COMMENTS With more than a dozen Planet Hollywoods around the globe and more on the way, in India and Kuwait, this home base for the chain is resting on its laurels—nothing exciting (including the food).

Plaza Restaurant ★★

AMERICAN MODERATE QUALITY ★★ VALUE ★★
READER-SURVEY RESPONSES 88% 👍 12% 👎 DISNEY DINING PLAN YES

Main Street, U.S.A., Magic Kingdom; ☎ 407-939-3463

Reservations Suggested. **Dining Plan credits** 1 per person, per meal. **When to go** Anytime. **Cost range** $10.50–$12 (child $8). **Service** ★★★★. **Friendliness** ★★★★. **Parking** Magic Kingdom lot. **Bar** None. **Wine selection** None. **Dress** Casual. **Disabled access** Yes. **Customers** Theme-park guests. **Hours** 11 a.m.–15 minutes before park closing.

SETTING AND ATMOSPHERE Tucked away on a side street at the end of Main Street, U.S.A., as you head to Tomorrowland, the Plaza evokes small-town diners across America. You pay top dollar for a tuna-salad sandwich or a burger, but on a hot Florida day it's an air-conditioned respite.

HOUSE SPECIALTIES Vegetarian sandwich, club sandwich, chicken-strawberry salad, ice-cream desserts such as the Plaza banana split or sundae.

OTHER RECOMMENDATIONS Grilled Reuben sandwich, burgers.

SUMMARY AND COMMENTS You wouldn't head here for a gourmet meal, but the pricey sandwiches are just fine. Or just skip the protein and go straight for a sweet ending with a giant sundae or triple-scoop banana split.

Portobello ★★★

ITALIAN EXPENSIVE QUALITY ★★★ VALUE ★★
READER-SURVEY RESPONSES 63% 👍 37% 👎 DISNEY DINING PLAN NO

Downtown Disney; ☎ 407-934-8888

Reservations Recommended. **When to go** Anytime. **Cost range** Lunch $10–$24 (child $5–$13), dinner $20–$80 (child $5–$13). **Service** ★★★★. **Friendliness**

★★★★. **Parking** Lot near the former Pleasure Island complex. **Bar** Full service. **Wine selection** Very good; heavily Italian. **Dress** Casual. **Disabled access** Yes. **Customers** Tourists, locals. **Lunch** Daily, 11:30 a.m.–4 p.m. **Dinner** Daily, 4–11 p.m.

SETTING AND ATMOSPHERE Portobello ("Yacht Club" has been dropped from the name) has a new look—a faux-Tuscan–inspired interior—and a new identity: a "country Italian trattoria."

HOUSE SPECIALTIES Wood-burning-oven pizzas; farfalle pasta with roasted chicken, snow peas, asparagus, and Parmesan cream sauce.

OTHER RECOMMENDATIONS Hand-crafted Luganella sausage, filet mignon, grilled fresh lobster, Florida snapper.

SUMMARY AND COMMENTS Portobello gets a makeover as part of the upcoming Pleasure Island redo. We love the location, but the food could be better.

Raglan Road Irish Pub & Restaurant ★★★★

IRISH **MODERATE** **QUALITY** ★★★½ **VALUE** ★★★
READER-SURVEY RESPONSES 79% 👍 21% 👎 **DISNEY DINING PLAN** NO

Downtown Disney; ☎ 407-938-0300

Reservations Recommended. **When to go** Monday–Saturday after 8 p.m. **Cost range** Lunch $11.50–$16 (child $6.50–$9), dinner $13.50–$24 (child $6.50–$9). **Service** ★★★½. **Friendliness** ★★★★★. **Parking** Marketplace lot or lot near former Pleasure Island complex. **Bar** Full service specializing in Irish whiskeys and beers. **Wine selection** Better than a pub's but not extensive. **Dress** Casual. **Disabled access** Good. **Customers** Tourists and locals. **Hours** 11 a.m.–1 or 1:30 a.m. **Dinner** Served until 11 p.m., with pub food available until closing.

SETTING AND ATMOSPHERE Many elements of this pub, including the bar, were hand-crafted from hardwoods in Ireland and sent to the United States for reassembly. The venue is huge by Irish-pub standards, but the dark polished-wood paneling, as well as the snugs (small, private cubbyholes), preserves the feel of the traditional pub. The pentagonal main room sits beneath an impressive but very unpublike dome. In the middle of the room is a tall, tablelike platform accessible to Celtic dancers via a permanently attached short staircase. A modest bandstand is situated along the wall in front of a large pseudo-hearth. Branching from the cavernous domed center room are cozy dining areas and snugs.

HOUSE SPECIALTIES Oven-roasted loin of ham with cabbage and mashed potatoes, beer-battered fish-and-chips, a very froufrou but yummy Shepherd's Pie, chicken-and-wild-mushroom pie. The must-have appetizer is the Dalkey Duo: batter-fried cocktail sausages with a mustard dipping sauce.

ENTERTAINMENT AND AMENITIES Though you could consider a great selection of Irish lagers and stouts an amenity, the real draw here is the knockout Celtic music. A talented band plays Monday through Saturday. Starting in the early evening with a couple of superb acoustic sets, the band plugs in as the diners filter out and the pub crawlers settle in. In addition to the band, there's a Celtic dancer who wanders in and dances on the aforementioned table to some of the numbers. (The dancing is tasteful—think *Riverdance,* not rap video.)

SUMMARY AND COMMENTS The great thing about Irish pubs is that folks of all ages can have a wonderful time together. The traditional feel-good drinking songs, reels, and sentimental ballads transcend age. A night in a good Irish pub, Raglan Road included, is a joyous and uplifting experience, and as the Brits say, it will set you right up. Irish food generally gets a bad rap, and we've never had ethnic Irish fare of comparable quality on the Emerald Isle, but Raglan Road demolishes the stereotype.

Rainforest Cafe ★★½

AMERICAN **MODERATE** **QUALITY** ★★ **VALUE** ★★
READER-SURVEY RESPONSES 72% 👍 28% 👎 **DISNEY DINING PLAN** NO

Downtown Disney Marketplace; ☎ 407-827-8500
Animal Kingdom; ☎ 407-938-9100

Reservations Accepted. **When to go** After lunch crunch, in late afternoon, and before dinner hour. **Cost range** $11–$40 (child $8). **Service** ★★★. **Friendliness** ★★★★. **Parking** Marketplace lot. **Bar** Full bar. **Wine selection** Limited. **Dress.** Casual. **Disabled access** Good. **Customers** Tourists, locals. **Hours** *Downtown Disney Marketplace:* Sunday–Thursday, 11 a.m.–11 p.m.; Friday and Saturday, 11 a.m.–midnight; *Animal Kingdom:* Daily, 8:30 a.m.–park closing.

SETTING AND ATMOSPHERE The Downtown Disney version of the national chain sits beneath a giant volcano that can be seen (and heard) erupting all over the Marketplace. The smoke coming from the volcano is nonpolluting, in accordance with the restaurant's conservation theme. Inside is a huge dining room designed to look like a jungle (imagine all the silk plants in the world tacked to the ceiling), complete with audio-animatronic elephants, bats, and monkeys—not the most realistic we've seen. There is occasional thunder and even some rainfall. Large aquariums connected with glass "swimways" serve as one of several waiting areas. The Animal Kingdom version, featuring a huge waterfall, is easier on the eyes externally.

HOUSE SPECIALTIES Rasta Pasta with grilled chicken and walnut pesto; turkey wrap; crab-cake sandwich; coconut shrimp; slow-roasted pork ribs; brownie cake with ice cream, caramel, and chocolate sauce.

ENTERTAINMENT AND AMENITIES After the wait you endure, a chair and some sustenance are all the entertainment you'll need. If you're willing to pay to avoid the long wait, stop by the day before and purchase a Safari Club membership for $15. By presenting your card on the day you want to dine, you'll be seated much faster (and get 10% off entrees).

SUMMARY AND COMMENTS Let us say up front that while we are not impressed by the Rainforest Cafes, a lot of our readers rave about them. The shopping experience must be the attraction, because it certainly isn't the food: preparations are spotty, and waits can be horrendous. Of course, you're expected to shop in the adjacent 5,000-square-foot retail area while you wait. By all means visit the gift shop, but eat somewhere else.

Restaurant Marrakesh ★★

MOROCCAN **MODERATE** **QUALITY** ★★½ **VALUE** ★★
READER-SURVEY RESPONSES 81% 👍 19% 👎 **DISNEY DINING PLAN** YES

Morocco, World Showcase, Epcot; ☎ 407-939-3463

Reservations Required. **Dining Plan credits** 1 per person, per meal. **When to go** Anytime. **Cost range** Lunch $17–$28 (child $7), dinner $21–$43 (child $7). **Service** ★★★★. **Friendliness** ★★★★. **Parking** Epcot lot. **Bar** Full service.

Wine selection Limited. **Dress** Casual. **Disabled access** Yes. **Customers** Theme-park guests. **Lunch** Daily, noon–3:15 p.m. **Dinner** Daily, 3:30 p.m.–park closing.

SETTING AND ATMOSPHERE Marrakesh re-creates a Moroccan palace with tile mosaics, inlaid-wood ceilings, brass chandeliers, and red Bukhara carpets.

HOUSE SPECIALTIES Start with *bastilla* (a minced-chicken pie sprinkled with cinnamon sugar), followed by roast lamb. Split an order of couscous.

OTHER RECOMMENDATIONS If you're hungry, curious, or both, try an appetizer combo for two or a combo entrée platter for one.

ENTERTAINMENT AND AMENITIES Moroccan band and belly dancing.

SUMMARY AND COMMENTS This is one of the least busy World Showcase restaurants, so it's usually easy to get a table. Unlike diners at most Moroccan restaurants, those at Marrakesh sit at tables instead of on the floor, and eat with utensils rather than with their hands. Picky kids can choose from chicken tenders, pasta, and burgers.

Rose & Crown Dining Room ★★★

ENGLISH MODERATE QUALITY ★★★½ VALUE ★★
READER-SURVEY RESPONSES 82% 👍 18% 👎 DISNEY DINING PLAN YES

United Kingdom, World Showcase, Epcot; ☎ 407-939-3463

Reservations Recommended. **Dining Plan credits** 1 per person, per meal. **When to go** Anytime. **Cost range** Lunch $11–$16 (child $8), dinner $13–$25 (child $8). **Service** ★★★★★. **Friendliness** ★★★★★. **Parking** Epcot lot. **Bar** Full bar with Bass, Guinness, and Harp beers on tap. **Wine selection** Limited. **Dress** Casual. **Disabled access** Yes. **Customers** Theme-park guests. **Lunch** Daily, noon–3:20 p.m. **Dinner** Daily, 4:30 p.m.–park closing.

SETTING AND ATMOSPHERE The Rose & Crown is both a pub and a dining establishment. The traditional English pub has a large, cozy bar with rich wood appointments, beamed ceilings, and a hardwood floor. The adjoining dining room is rustic and simple.

HOUSE SPECIALTIES Fish-and-chips, bangers and mash (sausage and mashed potatoes), and tamarind-glazed pork loin washed down with Bass ale.

OTHER RECOMMENDATIONS Potato-and-leek soup, shepherd's pie (lunch only), sticky toffee pudding.

SUMMARY AND COMMENTS This is a prime spot for viewing *IllumiNations,* so see if you can get a table on the patio for late evening, order fish-and-chips, and then sit back in your front-row seat for the fireworks-and-laser show.

Sanaa ★★★★

INDIAN/AFRICAN EXPENSIVE QUALITY ★★★★ VALUE ★★★★
READER-SURVEY RESPONSES TOO NEW TO RATE DISNEY DINING PLAN YES

Animal Kingdom Lodge–Kidani Village; ☎ 407-939-3463

Reservations Recommended. **Dining Plan credits** 1 per person, per meal. **When to go** Lunch or dinner. **Cost range** Lunch $14–$19, dinner $18–$28. **Service** ★★★★. **Friendliness** ★★★★. **Parking** Valet or garage. **Bar** Full service. **Wine selection** Good. **Dress** Casual. **Disabled access** Yes. **Customers** Theme-park guests, locals, Disney Vacation Club guests. **Lunch** Daily, 11:30 a.m.–4 p.m. **Dinner** Daily, 4:30 p.m.–park closing.

SETTING AND ATMOSPHERE One floor down from the new Kidani Village lobby, Sanaa's dining room is inspired by Africa's outdoor markets, with baskets, beads, and art on the walls. It's a cozy space, with nine-foot-tall windows that look out on the resort's savanna—giraffes, water buffalo, and other animals wander within yards of you as you dine.

HOUSE SPECIALTIES Indian-style breads (*naan, roti, paratha,* and *paneer paratha*) with mango-lime pickle, coriander chutney, and mint-and-onion *raita;* lamb *kefta;* tandoori chicken; duck confit with red-curry sauce.

OTHER RECOMMENDATIONS Beef short ribs; sustainable fish wrapped in banana leaf; lunchtime burger on naan with minted greens, tomato, and cucumber-yogurt raita; chai cream.

SUMMARY AND COMMENTS Opened in May 2009, Sanaa (sah-NAH) is not as upscale as Jiko, the resort's African restaurant (page 492), but the kitchen offers diners a chance to sample and share a variety of Indian-African creations. Diverse Old and New World wines match the cuisine.

San Angel Inn ★★★

MEXICAN **EXPENSIVE** **QUALITY** ★★ **VALUE** ★★
READER-SURVEY RESPONSES 72% 👍 28% 👎 **DISNEY DINING PLAN** YES

Mexico, World Showcase, Epcot; ☎ 407-939-3463

Reservations Recommended. **Dining Plan credits** 1 per person, per meal. **When to go** Anytime. **Cost range** Lunch $15–$24 (child $8), dinner $24–$34 (child $8). **Service** ★★★. **Friendliness** ★★★. **Parking** Epcot lot. **Bar** Full service. **Wine selection** Limited. **Dress** Casual. **Disabled access** Yes. **Customers** Theme-park guests. **Lunch** Daily, 11:30 a.m.–4 p.m. **Dinner** Daily, 4:30 p.m.–park closing.

SETTING AND ATMOSPHERE The San Angel Inn is inside the great Aztec pyramid of the Mexico Pavilion. A romantically crafted open-air cantina, the restaurant overlooks both the Gran Fiesta Tour attraction and the bustling plaza of a small Mexican village.

HOUSE SPECIALTIES *Tacos de pato,* with duck meat, tamarind sauce, and a garnish of avocado, pineapple, and chives; *mole poblano,* chicken with an exotic sauce made from several kinds of peppers and unsweetened Mexican chocolate; and some interesting regional fish preparations.

OTHER RECOMMENDATIONS Margaritas; grilled mahimahi or grilled beef tenderloin.

ENTERTAINMENT AND AMENITIES Mariachi or marimba bands in the courtyard.

SUMMARY AND COMMENTS The San Angel Inn's prices are much higher than you would find at most Mexican restaurants at home. But the menu goes beyond typical Mexican selections, offering special and regional dishes that are difficult to find in the United States. Even the tacos are corn tortillas with marinated pork, grilled pineapple, onions, and cilantro.

Sand Trap Bar & Grill ★★½

AMERICAN **MODERATE** **QUALITY** ★★½ **VALUE** ★★½
READER-SURVEY RESPONSES 83% 👍 17% 👎 **DISNEY DINING PLAN** YES

Adjacent to Osprey Ridge Golf Course; ☎ 407-824-2602

Reservations Not needed. **Dining Plan credits** 1 per person, per meal. **When to go** Anytime. **Cost range** Breakfast $8–$10, lunch $9–$17 (child $8). **Service** ★★★. **Friendliness** ★★★. **Parking** Lot. **Bar** Full service. **Wine selection** Limited. **Dress** Casual. **Disabled access** Yes. **Customers** Golfers, guests who want a break from the crowds. **Breakfast** Daily, 6:30–10:30 a.m. **Lunch** Daily, 10:30 a.m.–5:30 p.m.

SETTING AND ATMOSPHERE Generally a kid-free zone, Sand Trap is an ideal getaway from the hustle and bustle of the theme parks. Casual atmosphere, with a pretty view of the golf course.

HOUSE SPECIALTIES Fish-of-the-day sandwich, onion rings, Reuben, barbecued-pork sandwich.

OTHER RECOMMENDATIONS Cobb salad; burgers; club wrap with turkey, ham, and bacon.

SUMMARY AND COMMENTS You need a car to get to the Sand Trap, but there's a shady parking lot. Pleasant, unhurried service—an undiscovered gem of a dining spot.

Sci-Fi Dine-In Theater Restaurant ★★

AMERICAN MODERATE QUALITY ★★½ VALUE ★★
READER-SURVEY RESPONSES 72% 👍 28% 👎 DISNEY DINING PLAN YES

Backlot, Disney's Hollywood Studios; ☎ 407-939-3463

Reservations Recommended. **Dining Plan credits** 1 per person, per meal. **When to go** Anytime. **Cost range** Lunch $12–$22 (child $7.50), dinner $12–$23 (child $7.50). **Service** ★★★★★. **Friendliness** ★★★★★. **Parking** DHS lot. **Bar** Full service. **Wine selection** Limited. **Dress** Casual. **Disabled access** Yes. **Customers** Theme-park guests. **Lunch** Sunday and Wednesday, 10:30 a.m.–4 p.m.; Monday and Tuesday and Thursday–Saturday, 11 a.m.–4 p.m. **Dinner** Daily, 4 p.m.–park closing.

SETTING AND ATMOSPHERE Everyone gets a kick out of this unusual dining room—a facsimile of a drive-in from the 1950s, with faux classic cars instead of tables. You hop in, order, and watch campy black-and-white clips. Servers, some on roller skates, take your order from the driver's seat.

HOUSE SPECIALTIES The lunch fare consists of sandwiches, burgers, salads, and shakes. Dinner offerings include pasta, ribs, and steak. While we think the food quality is way out of line with the cost, you can have an adequate meal at the Sci-Fi if you stick with simple fare.

ENTERTAINMENT AND AMENITIES Cartoons and clips of vintage horror and sci-fi movies are shown, such as *Attack of the 50 Ft. Woman, Robot Monster,* and *Son of the Blob.*

SUMMARY AND COMMENTS We recommend making late-afternoon or late-evening Advance Reservations and ordering only dessert—the Sci-Fi is an attraction, not a good dining opportunity. If you don't have Advance Reservations, try walking in at 11 a.m. or around 3 p.m.

Shula's Steak House ★★★★

STEAK EXPENSIVE QUALITY ★★★★ VALUE ★★
READER-SURVEY RESPONSES 60% 👍 40% 👎 DISNEY DINING PLAN NO

Walt Disney World Dolphin; ☎ 407-934-1362

Reservations Recommended. **When to go** Anytime. **Cost range** $24–$85. **Service** ★★★★. **Friendliness** ★★★★. **Parking** Hotel lot; valet $16. **Bar** Full service. **Wine selection** Good; expensive. **Dress** Dressy. **Disabled access** Yes. **Customers** Hotel guests and locals. **Dinner** Daily, 5–11 p.m.

SETTING AND ATMOSPHERE Clubby and masculine, with dark woods and even darker lighting. Large, gilt-framed black-and-white photographs of football players in action offer the only decoration.

HOUSE SPECIALTIES In a word, meat—really expensive but very high-quality meat. Only certified Angus beef is served: filet mignon, porterhouse (including a 48-ounce cut), and prime rib.

OTHER RECOMMENDATIONS The steak-tartare appetizer is special, and the split-lobster cocktail appetizer is excellent.

SUMMARY AND COMMENTS This is part of a chain owned by former Miami Dolphins football coach Don Shula. It's classier than it is kitschy, though printing the menu on the side of a football and placing it on a kickoff tee in the center of the table is a bit much. They could also do without the rehearsed spiel from the waiters, who present raw examples of the beef selections (not to mention a live lobster) at each table. Once you get past that, however, you're in for some wonderful steaks.

Shutters at Old Port Royale ★★

STEAK AND SEAFOOD | MODERATE | QUALITY ★★½ | VALUE ★★
READER-SURVEY RESPONSES 59% 👍 41% 👎 | DISNEY DINING PLAN YES

Caribbean Beach Resort; ☎ 407-939-3463

Reservations Recommended. **Dining Plan credits** 1 per person, per meal. **When to go** Anytime. **Cost range** $16–$28 (child $5–$9). **Service** ★★★. **Friendliness** ★★★★★. **Parking** Hotel lot. **Bar** Full service. **Wine selection** Moderate. **Dress** Casual. **Disabled access** Yes. **Customers** Hotel guests. **Dinner** Daily, 5–10 p.m.

SETTING AND ATMOSPHERE The small dining areas are claustrophobia-inducing. Nothing about the decor will make you wish you'd brought a camera.

HOUSE SPECIALTIES New York strip steak, plantain-crusted red snapper, chicken wings with habanero sauce, tamarind-glazed roasted chicken.

OTHER RECOMMENDATIONS Jerk-style pork ribs, Caribbean pasta with shrimp.

SUMMARY AND COMMENTS The Caribbean Beach Resort is huge—more than 2,000 rooms—but for years it didn't have a full-service restaurant. Shutters exists for that reason; you wouldn't drive here for dinner, but if you need to sit down and be waited on, this will meet your needs. Stick with simple dishes.

Teppan Edo ★★★½

JAPANESE | EXPENSIVE | QUALITY ★★★★ | VALUE ★★★
READER-SURVEY RESPONSES 95% 👍 5% 👎 | DISNEY DINING PLAN YES

Japan, World Showcase, Epcot; ☎ 407-939-3463

Reservations Recommended. **Dining Plan credits** 1 per person, per meal. **When to go** Anytime. **Cost range** $19–$30 (child $9.50–$12.50). **Service** ★★★★★. **Friendliness** ★★★★★. **Parking** Epcot lot. **Bar** Full service. **Wine selection** Limited. **Dress** Casual. **Disabled access** Via elevator. **Customers** Theme-park guests. **Lunch** Daily, noon–3:45 p.m. **Dinner** Daily, 4 p.m.–park closing.

SETTING AND ATMOSPHERE Upscale Japanese, compliments of a beautiful renovation.

HOUSE SPECIALTIES Chicken, shrimp, beef, scallops, and Asian vegetables stir-fried on a teppan grill by a knife-juggling chef. Imagine Benihana, only fancier.

ENTERTAINMENT AND AMENITIES Watching the teppan chefs.

SUMMARY AND COMMENTS The menu includes sushi and appetizers such as edamame and seaweed salad, but most guests stick to the basic teppan offerings. Be aware that diners at the teppan tables (large tables with a grill in the middle) are seated with other parties.

Tokyo Dining ★★★

JAPANESE **MODERATE** **QUALITY** ★★★★ **VALUE** ★★★
READER-SURVEY RESPONSES 83% 👍 17% 👎 **DISNEY DINING PLAN** YES

Japan, World Showcase, Epcot; ☎ 407-939-3463

Reservations Recommended. **Dining Plan credits** 1 per person, per meal. **When to go** Lunch. **Cost range** $18–$25 (child $9.50). **Service** ★★★★. **Friendliness** ★★★. **Parking** Epcot lot. **Bar** Full service. **Wine selection** Limited. **Dress** Casual. **Disabled access** Yes. **Customers** Theme-park guests. **Lunch** Daily, noon–3:45 p.m. **Dinner** Daily, 4 p.m.–park close.

SETTING AND ATMOSPHERE Modern Asian decor, a beautifully lighted sushi bar, and well-orchestrated service distinguish this restaurant.

HOUSE SPECIALTIES Grilled meats and seafood; tempura-battered deep-fried foods, featuring chicken, shrimp, scallops, and vegetables; sushi and sashimi; six kinds of sake.

SUMMARY AND COMMENTS Tokyo Dining is a relatively quiet space on the second floor of the Japan Pavilion. The dining room is sleek, the overfriendly servers wear stylish costumes, and the overall experience is relaxing and congenial. Most of the crowd heads to the teppan tables, but you can't beat a window seat here at fireworks time.

Tony's Town Square Restaurant ★★½

ITALIAN **MODERATE** **QUALITY** ★★★ **VALUE** ★★
READER-SURVEY RESPONSES 70% 👍 30% 👎 **DISNEY DINING PLAN** YES

Main Street, U.S.A., Magic Kingdom; ☎ 407-939-3463

Reservations Recommended. **Dining Plan credits** 1 per person, per meal. **When to go** Late lunch or early dinner. **Cost range** Lunch $11.50–$17 (child $7.50), dinner $17–$28 (child $7.50). **Service** ★★★★. **Friendliness** ★★★★★. **Parking** Magic Kingdom lot. **Bar** None. **Wine selection** None. **Dress** Casual. **Disabled access** Yes. **Customers** Theme-park guests. **Lunch** Daily, 11:30 a.m.–2:45 p.m. **Dinner** Daily, 5 p.m.–park closing.

SETTING AND ATMOSPHERE Tony's is a bit worn on the edges, with tile floors, dark woods, and memorabilia from the Disney classic *Lady and the Tramp* on the walls. The nicest seats are on the glass-windowed porch.

HOUSE SPECIALTIES For lunch, flatbreads, paninis, and spaghetti; for dinner, shrimp scampi and New York strip.

SUMMARY AND COMMENTS Tony's does a decent job with pasta. And the chef keeps gluten-free pasta on hand for diners on special diets. Go at lunch, when the prices aren't so steep.

Trail's End Restaurant ★★★

AMERICAN/BUFFET **MODERATE** **QUALITY** ★★★ **VALUE** ★★★
READER-SURVEY RESPONSES 90% 👍 10% 👎 **DISNEY DINING PLAN** YES

Fort Wilderness Resort; ☎ 407-939-3463

Reservations Recommended. **Dining Plan credits** 1 per person, per meal.**When to go** Breakfast or dinner. **Cost range** Breakfast $14, (child $9), lunch $15 (child

$10), dinner $21 (child $12). **Service** ★★★. Friendliness ★★★. **Parking** Fort Wilderness lot. **Bar** Full-service bar next door. **Wine selection** Limited. **Dress** Casual. **Disabled access** Good. **Customers** Fort Wilderness campers, theme park guests. **Breakfast** 7:30–11:30 a.m. **Lunch** 11:30 a.m.–2 p.m. **Dinner** 4:30–9:30 p.m. Sunday–Thursday, 4:30–10 p.m. Friday and Saturday.

SETTING AND ATMOSPHERE At Fort Wilderness, next to the *Hoop-Dee-Doo Musical Revue,* Trail's End is what a pioneer buffet would have looked like had America's settlers built one out of a log cabin. The interior features exposed log beams, oak tabletops, and walls hung with enough antique kitchen equipment to start a flea market.

HOUSE SPECIALTIES All three meals are served buffet-style. Breakfast features eggs, sausage, bacon, waffles, pancakes, and biscuits, along with fruit and pastries. Lunch includes soup, fried chicken, chili, pulled pork, mac and cheese, and a salad bar. The dinner lineup is fried chicken, ribs, pasta, fish, peel-and-eat shrimp, carved meats, pizza, and fruit cobbler.

OTHER RECOMMENDATIONS At breakfast there's occasionally a doughnut buffet, which is proof enough that Western civilization continues to advance.

SUMMARY AND COMMENTS Trail's End has been a favorite of in-the-know Disney World foodies for years. The menu isn't all that different from anything you'd get elsewhere around the parks, but the food is prepared in smaller batches, so it's fresher and tastier than average. It's an early-morning hike to get to Fort Wilderness for breakfast, but Trail's End makes a great midday break from the Magic Kingdom; take the boat from the park.

T-REX ★★★

AMERICAN MODERATE QUALITY ★★ VALUE ★★
READER-SURVEY RESPONSES 82% 👍 18% 👎 DISNEY DINING PLAN NO

Downtown Disney Marketplace; ☎ 407-828-8739

Reservations Accepted. **When to go** Anytime. **Cost range** $12–$30 (child $7–$8). **Service** ★★★. **Friendliness** ★★★. **Parking** Lot. **Bar** Full service. **Wine selection** Minimal. **Dress** Casual. **Disabled access** Good. **Customers** Families. **Lunch and dinner** Daily, 11 a.m.–11 p.m.; open until midnight Friday and Saturday.

SETTING AND ATMOSPHERE Sensory overload in a cavernous dining room with life-size robotic dinosaurs, giant fish tanks, bubbling geysers, waterfalls, fossils in the bathrooms, and crystals in the walls. Volume: loud and louder, with meteor showers, growling dinos, and overstimulated kids.

HOUSE SPECIALTIES Colosso Nachos, Ice Age Salmon Salad, Bronto Burger.

OTHER RECOMMENDATIONS Prehistoric Panini, Chocolate Extinction fudge cake.

SUMMARY AND COMMENTS Expect a wait unless there's an empty seat at the bar. But nobody's here just for the ordinary, overpriced food—it's nonstop "eatertainment." The coolest spot for dining is the Ice Cave at the back of the restaurant, with glowing blue walls.

Turf Club Bar & Grill ★★

AMERICAN MODERATE QUALITY ★★ VALUE ★★
READER-SURVEY RESPONSES 82% 👍 18% 👎 DISNEY DINING PLAN YES

Saratoga Springs Resort; ☎ 407-824-1100

Reservations Recommended. **Dining Plan credits** 1 per person, per meal. **When to go** Lunch or dinner. **Cost range** Lunch $10.50–$19 (child $7.50), dinner $12–$28 (child $7.50). **Service** ★★★. **Friendliness** ★★★★. **Parking** Lot. **Bar** Full service. **Wine selection** Good. **Dress** Casual. **Disabled access** Good. **Customers** Disney Vacation Club guests. **Lunch** Daily, noon–4 p.m. **Dinner** Daily, 5–9 p.m.

SETTING AND ATMOSPHERE When the weather's nice, ask for an outdoor table; you can spot golfers on the adjacent Lake Buena Vista Golf Course. Tucked away off the lobby of the Saratoga Springs Resort, the dining room is themed with equestrian memorabilia.

HOUSE SPECIALTIES Steamed mussels; penne with shrimp, artichokes, and sun-dried tomatoes; grilled Caesar salad.

OTHER RECOMMENDATIONS Angus cheeseburger or New York strip, or a classic Reuben for lunch; specialty drinks.

SUMMARY AND COMMENTS Not many Disney dining spots have outdoor tables, and Turf Club is worth the trip on a sunny day for a drink and appetizers on the shady terrace. The best Caesar salad in Disney World.

Tusker House Restaurant ★½

AMERICAN/AFRICAN/BUFFET MODERATE QUALITY ★ VALUE ★★
READER-SURVEY RESPONSES 90% 👍 10% 👎 DISNEY DINING PLAN YES

Africa, Animal Kingdom; ☎ 407-939-3463

Reservations Required for character breakfast. **Dining Plan credits** 1 per person, per meal. **When to go** Anytime. **Cost range** Breakfast $20 (child $11), lunch $21 (child $11), dinner $28 (child $13). **Service** ★★★. **Friendliness** ★★★. **Parking** Animal Kingdom lot. **Bar** Full-service bar next door. **Dress** Casual. **Disabled access** Yes. **Customers** Theme-park guests. **Breakfast** Daily, 8–10:30 a.m. **Lunch** Daily, 11:30 a.m.–3:30 p.m. **Dinner** Daily, 4 p.m.–park closing.

SETTING AND ATMOSPHERE In Harambe Village. Donald's Safari Breakfast features Donald, Daisy, Mickey, and Goofy. The setting is a bit austere and the food unexciting, but it's fine for filling up families and a visit with the Disney characters.

HOUSE SPECIALTIES Roasted meats, rotisserie chicken, salmon.

OTHER RECOMMENDATIONS African-Indian influenced dishes such as chutney, couscous, and curry.

SUMMARY AND COMMENTS The menu of this former counter-service restaurant mixes comfort food with more-exotic selections for lunch and dinner. The usual bacon, eggs, fruit, and pastries are served for breakfast.

Tutto Italia ★★½

ITALIAN EXPENSIVE QUALITY ★★½ VALUE ★★½
READER-SURVEY RESPONSES 78% 👍 22% 👎 DISNEY DINING PLAN YES

Italy, World Showcase, Epcot; ☎ 407-939-3463

Reservations Accepted. **Dining Plan credits** 1 per person, per meal. **When to go** Midafternoon. **Cost range** Lunch $15–$28 (child $9), dinner $24–$36 (child $9). **Service** ★★★★. **Friendliness** ★★★★. **Parking** Epcot lot. **Bar** Beer and wine only. **Wine selection** All Italian. **Dress** Casual. **Disabled access** Yes. **Customers** Theme-park guests. **Lunch** Daily, 11:30 a.m.–3:30 p.m. **Dinner** Daily, 4:30–park closing.

SETTING AND ATMOSPHERE The Roman decor features huge murals of an Italian piazza along the wall behind the upholstered banquettes. The atmosphere is elegant, but the dining room is noisy—nearly always full. If the weather is pleasant, request a table on the piazza.

HOUSE SPECIALTIES Spaghetti with veal meatballs and pomodoro sauce; *paccheri* (pasta tubes) with calamari, peas, and a light tomato sauce; pressed chicken with lemon; *copetta sotto bosco,* a creamy gelato with berries and chocolate sauce.

OTHER RECOMMENDATIONS *Antipasto misto,* even though it's $29.

SUMMARY AND COMMENTS Tutto Italia is pricey, but the service is professional and friendly, the cuisine is authentic, and the servings are ample.

Victoria & Albert's ★★★★★

GOURMET EXPENSIVE QUALITY ★★★★★ VALUE ★★★★
READER-SURVEY RESPONSES 86% 👍 14% 👎 DISNEY DINING PLAN YES (PLATINUM)

Grand Floridian Resort & Spa; ☎ 407-939-3463

Reservations Mandatory; must confirm by noon the day of your seating; credit card required to reserve; call at least 180 days in advance to reserve. **Dining Plan credits** 2 per person, per meal (Platinum Plan only). **When to go** Anytime. **Cost range** Fixed price, $125 per person or $185 with wine pairings; Chef's Table, $175 or $245 with wine pairings. **Service** ★★★★★. **Friendliness** ★★★★. **Parking** Valet, $10; self-parking is deceptively far away. **Wine selection** 700 on the menu, 4,200 more in the cellar. **Dress** Jacket required for men, evening attire for women. **Disabled access** Yes. **Customers** Hotel guests, locals. **Dinner** 2 seatings nightly at 5:45–6:30 p.m. and 9–9:45 p.m., plus 1 seating at 6 p.m. for the Chef's Table. Children below age 10 admitted only at Chef's Table.

SETTING AND ATMOSPHERE Frette linens, Riedel crystal, Christofle silver—with only 18 tables in the main dining room and the private Fireplace Room with 5 tables, this is the top dining experience at Disney World. A winner of AAA's Five Diamond Award (the only restaurant in central Florida so honored), Victoria & Albert's is civilized, lavish, and expensive.

HOUSE SPECIALTIES The menu changes daily, but chef Scott Hunnel's favorites include Jamison Farm lamb, Florida seafood, and Australian Kobe beef. The Stilton "cheesecake" with Bosc pears is divine.

ENTERTAINMENT AND AMENITIES A harpist or violinist entertains from the foyer. But the best show is in the kitchen when you book the Chef's Table, where Chef Hunnel starts the evening with a Champagne toast and crafts a personal menu.

SUMMARY AND COMMENTS Hunnel and his team prepare modern American cuisine with the best of the best from around the world. While the main dining room is whisper-quiet, the convivial Chef's Table is a whole other experience. For foodies, it's a bargain.

The Wave ★★★

NEW AMERICAN MODERATE QUALITY ★★ VALUE ★★
READER-SURVEY RESPONSES 80% 👍 20% 👎 DISNEY DINING PLAN YES

Contemporary Resort; ☎ 407-939-3463

Reservations Accepted. **Dining Plan credits** 1 per person, per meal. **When to go** Anytime. **Cost range** Breakfast $8.50–$18, lunch $12–$21, dinner $18–$29. **Service** ★★★. **Friendliness** ★★★. **Parking** Valet, lot. **Bar** Full service. **Wine**

selection All New World screw-caps. **Dress** Casual. **Disabled access** Good. **Customers** Hotel guests, locals. **Breakfast** Daily, 7:30–11 a.m. **Lunch** Daily, noon–2 p.m. **Dinner** Daily, 5:30–10 p.m.

SETTING AND ATMOSPHERE On the first floor of the Contemporary just past the front desk, The Wave has one of the coolest lounges at Disney World, adjoining a dining room with the feel of an upscale coffee shop—wooden tables, white-linen napkins.

HOUSE SPECIALTIES Unusual drinks like the Antioxidant Cocktail and the strawberry-lychee margarita; for breakfast, Supercharged Tropical Smoothie, multigrain pancakes, make-your-own muesli; for lunch, avocado-and-citrus salad, Italian chef salad, Reuben; for dinner, sustainable fish, braised lamb shank.

OTHER RECOMMENDATIONS Grilled pork tenderloin; linguine with Florida littleneck clams; fresh sorbets.

SUMMARY AND COMMENTS Organic beers, organic coffees, hip cocktails, and all-screw-cap wines focusing on New World wines from Argentina, Australia, Chile, New Zealand, and South Africa. The creations coming out of the kitchen aren't executed nearly as well as the drinks, but The Wave is trying to be all things to all guests with the opening of the Contemporary's new Bay Lake Tower.

Whispering Canyon Cafe ★★★

AMERICAN MODERATE QUALITY ★★★½ VALUE ★★★★
READER-SURVEY RESPONSES 81% 👍 19% 👎 DISNEY DINING PLAN YES

Wilderness Lodge and Villas; ☎ 407-939-3463

Reservations Accepted. **Dining Plan credits** 1 per person, per meal. **When to go** Anytime. **Cost range** Breakfast $10–$15 (child $5–$6.50), lunch $11.50–$18 (child $7.50–$9.50), dinner $17–$27 (child $7.50–$9.50). **Service** ★★★★. **Friendliness** ★★★★. **Parking** Hotel lot. **Bar** Full service. **Wine selection** Limited. **Dress** Casual. **Disabled access** Yes. **Customers** Hotel guests. **Breakfast** Daily, 7:30–11:30 a.m. **Lunch** Daily, 11:30 a.m.–2:30 p.m. **Dinner** Daily, 5–10 p.m.

SETTING AND ATMOSPHERE Just off the hotel's atrium lobby, the restaurant looks out on the lobby on one side and a mountain prairie, created by Disney landscapers, on the other. Tables have a barrel-top lazy Susan where food is placed.

HOUSE SPECIALTIES All-you-can-eat skillets with cornbread, ribs, pulled pork, smoked brisket, roast chicken, mashed potatoes, baked beans, cole slaw, salad, and seasonal vegetables.

OTHER RECOMMENDATIONS Grilled ribeye, vegetable enchilada.

SUMMARY AND COMMENTS The real value here is in the family-style service, with all-you-can-eat servings brought to you on platters and in crocks to pass around to your family. You can always order off the regular menu if you don't feel like sharing, but be aware that you may end up paying more for the privilege.

Wolfgang Puck Cafe ★★

CREATIVE CALIFORNIAN EXPENSIVE QUALITY ★½ VALUE ★½
READER-SURVEY RESPONSES 84% 👍 16% 👎 DISNEY DINING PLAN NO

Downtown Disney West Side; ☎ 407-938-9653

Reservations Accepted. **When to go** Early evening. **Cost range** Cafe $12–$29 (child $5–$9), upstairs $25–$43 for 4 courses (child $10–$17). **Service** ★★★. **Friendliness** ★★★. **Parking** Downtown Disney lot. **Bar** Full service. **Wine selection** Very good. **Dress** Casual in the cafe; collared and sleeved shirts for men and no jeans upstairs. **Disabled access** Good. **Customers** Tourists, locals. **Hours** *Cafe:* Daily, 11:30 a.m.–11 p.m. *Upstairs:* Sunday–Wednesday, 6–9 p.m.; Thursday–Saturday, 6–10 p.m.

SETTING AND ATMOSPHERE This is actually two restaurants in one—four if you count the attached Wolfgang Puck Express and the sushi bar that flows into the restaurant's lounge area. Downstairs is the actual cafe, with several open kitchen areas, colorful tile, and plenty of pictures of Wolfgang Puck hanging around (though you won't find him in the kitchen). The upstairs is a more formal dining room, but in name only. Both spaces are inordinately loud, making conversation difficult.

HOUSE SPECIALTIES Puck's wood-fired pizzas, including barbecue chicken and his signature smoked-salmon pie. Sushi is also a good bet. Upstairs, the menu features fresh fish, chicken, and beef.

SUMMARY AND COMMENTS In spite of less-than-stellar food, there's usually a crowd. We can always recommend dining at the sushi bar. Or you can skip the entree and go straight for desserts.

Yachtsman Steakhouse ★★★

STEAK EXPENSIVE QUALITY ★★★½ VALUE ★★
READER-SURVEY RESPONSES 80% 👍 20% 👎 DISNEY DINING PLAN YES

Yacht Club Resort; ☎ 407-939-3463

Reservations Required. **Dining Plan credits** 2 per person, per meal. **When to go** Anytime. **Cost range** $24–$47 (child $6–$12). **Service** ★★★★. **Friendliness** ★★★★★. **Parking** Hotel lot. **Bar** Full service. **Wine selection** Very good. **Dress** Dressy casual. **Disabled access** Yes. **Customers** Hotel guests and locals. **Dinner** Daily, 5:30–10:30 p.m.

SETTING AND ATMOSPHERE Wood beams, white linens, and a view of the sandy lagoon at the resort make this steak house appealing. The menu features seafood, lamb, fowl, and vegetarian creations. The adjacent Crew's Cup Lounge, with 40 types of beer and fine wine by the glass, is a fun place to start the evening.

HOUSE SPECIALTIES Start with seared scallops or Caesar salad. All steaks are cut and trimmed on the premises. The filet mignon, New York strip, and prime rib are just some of the cuts.

OTHER RECOMMENDATIONS Sea bass, boneless lamb loin, trio of Valrhona chocolate. Side dishes are enough to share.

SUMMARY AND COMMENTS Yachtsman has a loyal following of locals—die-hard meat lovers who don't mind paying for a good steak. Vintages from every major wine-producing region of the world complement the menu.

Yak & Yeti ★★★

PAN-ASIAN EXPENSIVE QUALITY ★★★½ VALUE ★★★
READER-SURVEY RESPONSES 85% 👍 15% 👎 DISNEY DINING PLAN YES

Asia, Animal Kingdom; ☎ 407-939-3463

Reservations Recommended. **Dining Plan credits** 1 per person, per meal. **When to go** Dinner. **Cost range** $17–$25 (child $8). **Service** ★★★★.

Friendliness ★★★★. **Parking** Animal Kingdom lot. **Bar** Full service. **Wine selection** Limited. **Dress** Casual. **Disabled access** Yes. **Customers** Theme-park guests. **Lunch** Daily, 11 a.m.–3:30 p.m. **Dinner** Daily, 4 p.m.–park closing.

SETTING AND ATMOSPHERE A rustic two-story Nepalese inn . . . with seating for hundreds. Windows on the second floor overlook the Asia section of the park.

HOUSE SPECIALTIES Seared miso salmon; crispy mahimahi; glazed duck; fried wontons with pineapple for dessert.

SUMMARY AND COMMENTS Though this is not fine dining, much of the food, including the seafood and duck, is a cut above the usual theme-park fare. The steak-and-shrimp combo is also quite good, but the chicken dishes are just average.

PART ELEVEN

The MAGIC KINGDOM

ARRIVING

IF YOU DRIVE, THE MAGIC KINGDOM Transportation and Ticket Center (TTC) parking lot opens about two hours before the park's official opening. After paying a fee, you are directed to a parking space, then transported by tram to the TTC, where you catch either a monorail or ferry to the park's entrance.

A Ridgewood, New Jersey, family recommends the ferry if you bring your own stroller:

> *The ferry from the TTC to the Magic Kingdom dock is a must if you're using a stroller. You can drive the stroller right onto the ferry and then just head to the back of the ferry to be the first ones off when it docks.*

If you're staying at the Contemporary–Bay Lake Tower, Polynesian, or Grand Floridian resorts, you can commute to the Magic Kingdom by monorail (guests at the Contemporary–Bay Lake Tower can walk there more quickly). If you stay at Wilderness Lodge and Villas or Fort Wilderness Campground, you can take a boat or bus. Guests at other Disney resorts can reach the park by bus. All Disney lodging guests, whether they arrive by bus, monorail, or boat, are deposited at the park's entrance, bypassing the TTC.

Not to Be Missed at the Magic Kingdom

Adventureland	Pirates of the Caribbean
Fantasyland	The Many Adventures of Winnie the Pooh
	Mickey's PhilharMagic
	Peter Pan's Flight
Frontierland	Big Thunder Mountain Railroad
	Splash Mountain
Liberty Square	The Haunted Mansion
Special Events	Evening Parade
Tomorrowland	Space Mountain

GETTING ORIENTED

AT THE MAGIC KINGDOM, stroller and wheelchair rentals are in the train station, and lockers are on the right, just inside the park entrance. On your left as you enter **Main Street** is **City Hall,** the center for information, lost and found, guided tours, and entertainment schedules.

unofficial **TIP**
If you don't already have a handout guide map of the park, get one at City Hall or entrance turnstiles.

The guide map found here lists all attractions, shops, and eating places; provides information about first aid, baby care, and assistance for the disabled; and gives tips for good photos. It lists times for the day's special events, live entertainment, Disney character parades, and concerts, and it also tells when and where to find Disney characters. Often the guide map is supplemented by a daily entertainment schedule known as the *Times Guide*. In addition to listing performance times, the *Times Guide* provides info on Disney character appearances and what Disney calls Special Hours. This term usually refers to attractions that open late or close early and to the operating hours of park restaurants.

unofficial **TIP**
Because Cinderella Castle is large, designate a very specific meeting spot, like the entrance to Cinderella's Royal Table restaurant at the rear of

Main Street ends at a central hub from which branch the entrances to five other sections of the Magic Kingdom: **Adventureland, Frontierland, Liberty Square, Fantasyland,** and **Tomorrowland. Mickey's Toontown Fair** is squeezed like a pimple between the cheeks of Fantasyland and Tomorrowland and doesn't connect to the central hub.

Cinderella Castle, at the entrance to Fantasyland, is the Magic Kingdom's architectural icon and visual center. If you start in Adventureland and go clockwise around the Magic Kingdom, the castle spires will always be roughly on your right; if you start in Tomorrowland and go counterclockwise through the park, the spires will always be roughly on your left. The castle is an excellent meeting place if your group decides to split up during the day or is separated accidentally.

STARTING *the* TOUR

VISITORS SOON FIND THEIR FAVORITE and not-so-favorite attractions in the Magic Kingdom. Our personal experience and research indicate that each visitor differs on which attraction is most enjoyable. Don't dismiss a ride or show until *after* you have tried it.

Take advantage of what Disney does best: the fantasy adventures of Splash Mountain and The Haunted Mansion and the various audio-animatronic (talking-robot) attractions, including *The Hall of Presidents* and Pirates of the Caribbean. Don't burn daylight browsing the shops unless you plan to spend at least two and a half days at the Magic Kingdom, and even then wait until midday or later. Minimize the time you spend on midway-type rides; you probably have something similar back home. (Don't, however, mistake Space Mountain and Big Thunder

Mountain Railroad for amusement-park rides. They may be roller coasters, but they're pure Disney genius.) Eat a good breakfast early, and avoid lines at eateries by snacking during the day on food from vendors, or better yet, from your fanny pack. Fare at most Magic Kingdom eateries is on a par with Subway or McDonald's.

FASTPASS *at the* MAGIC KINGDOM

THE MAGIC KINGDOM OFFERS eight FASTPASS attractions, the most in any Disney park. Strategies for using FASTPASS at the Magic Kingdom have been integrated into our touring plans.

Magic Kingdom FASTPASS Attractions	
Adventureland	Jungle Cruise
Fantasyland	The Many Adventures of Winnie the Pooh
	Mickey's PhilharMagic
	Peter Pan's Flight
Frontierland	Big Thunder Mountain Railroad
	Splash Mountain
Tomorrowland	Buzz Lightyear's Space Ranger Spin
	Space Mountain

MAIN STREET, U.S.A.

BEGIN AND END YOUR VISIT ON MAIN STREET, which may open a half hour before, and closes a half hour to an hour after, the rest of the park. The Walt Disney World Railroad stops at Main Street Station; get on to tour the park or ride to Frontierland or Mickey's Toontown Fair.

Main Street is a Disneyfied turn-of-the-19th-century small-town American street. Its buildings are real, not elaborate props. Attention to detail is exceptional: furnishings and fixtures are true to the period. Along the street are shops, eating places, City Hall, and a fire station. Occasionally, horse-drawn trolleys, fire engines, and horseless carriages transport visitors along Main Street to the central hub.

Walt Disney World Railroad ★★½

APPEAL BY AGE PRESCHOOL ★★★★ GRADE SCHOOL ★★½ TEENS ★★★
YOUNG ADULTS ★★★ OVER 30 ★★ SENIORS ★★★

What it is Scenic railroad ride around the perimeter of the Magic Kingdom, and transportation to Frontierland and Mickey's Toontown Fair. **Scope and scale** Minor attraction. **When to go** Anytime. **Special comments** Main Street is usually the least congested station. **Authors' rating** Plenty to see; ★★½. **Duration of ride** About 20 minutes for a complete circuit. **Average wait in line per 100 people ahead of you** 8 minutes; assumes 2 or more trains operating. **Loading speed** Moderate.

Magic Kingdom

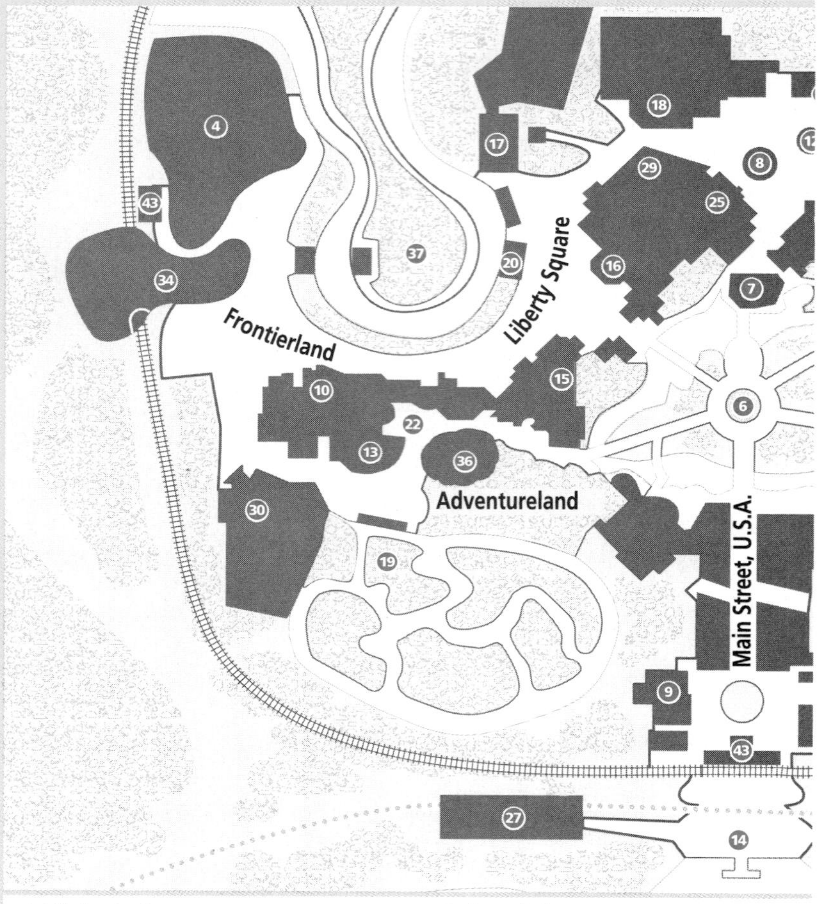

Ariel's Grotto **1**
Astro Orbiter **2**
Barnstormer **3**
Big Thunder Mountain Railroad **4**
Buzz Lightyear's Space Ranger Spin **5**
Central Hub **6**
Cinderella Castle **7**
Cinderella's Golden Carousel **8**
City Hall **9**
Country Bear Jamboree **10**
Donald's Boat **11**
Dumbo the Flying Elephant **12**
Enchanted Tiki Room **13**
Ferry Dock **14**
Frontierland Shootin' Arcade **15**
The Hall of Presidents **16**
The Haunted Mansion **17**
It's a Small World **18**
Jungle Cruise **19**
Liberty Belle Riverboat **20**
Mad Tea Party **21**
The Magic Carpets of Aladdin **22**
The Many Adventures of Winnie the Pooh **23**
Mickey's Country House and Judge's Tent **24**

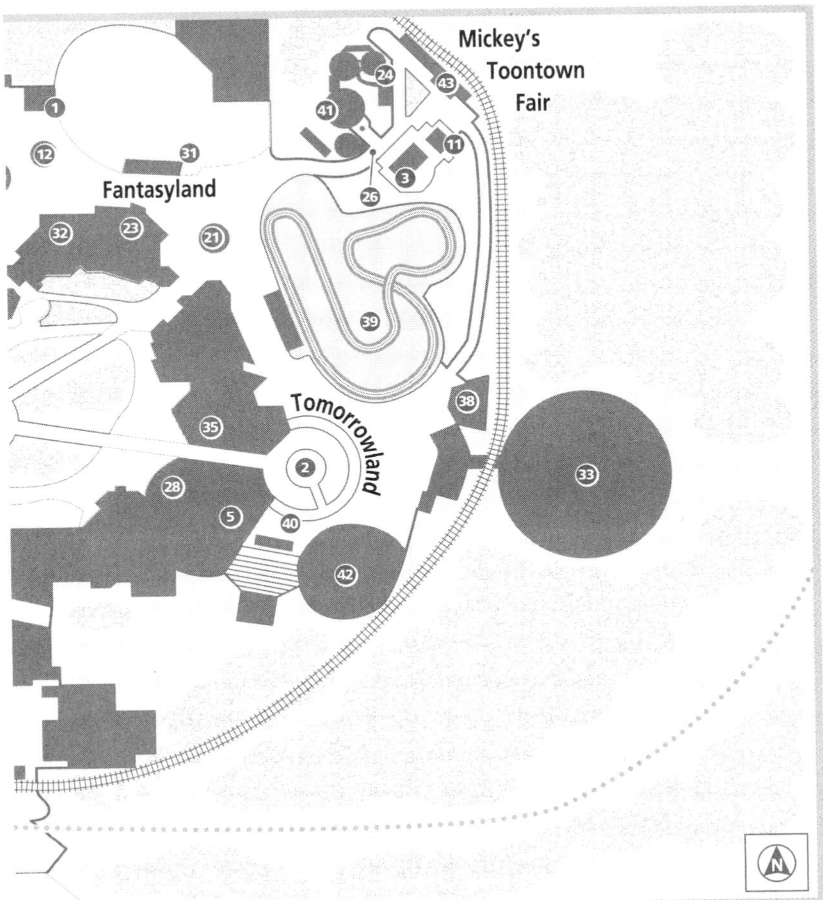

Mickey's *PhilharMagic* **25**
Minnie's Country House **26**
Monorail Station **27**
Monsters, Inc. Laugh Floor **28**
Peter Pan's Flight **29**
Pirates of the Caribbean **30**
Pooh's Playfull Spot **31**
Snow White's Scary Adventures **32**
Space Mountain* **33**
Splash Mountain **34**
Stitch's Great Escape! **35**
Swiss Family Treehouse **36**
Tom Sawyer Island **37**
Tomorrowland Arcade **38**
Tomorrowland Speedway **39**
Tomorrowland Transit Authority **40**
Toontown Hall of Fame **41**
Walt Disney's Carousel of Progress **42**
WDW Railroad Station (multiple stops) **43**

**Under renovation for most of 2009*

Main Street Services

Most park services are centered on Main Street, including:

Baby Center/Baby Care Needs Next to The Crystal Palace, left around the central hub (toward Adventureland)

Banking Services ATMs underneath the Main Street railroad station

First Aid Next to The Crystal Palace, left around the central hub (toward Adventureland)

Live Entertainment and Parade Information City Hall at the railroad-station end of Main Street

Lost and Found City Hall at the railroad-station end of Main Street

Lost Persons City Hall

Storage Lockers Underneath the Main Street railroad station; all lockers cleaned out each night

Walt Disney World and Local Attraction Information City Hall

Wheelchair and Stroller Rentals Ground floor of the railroad station at the end of Main Street

DESCRIPTION AND COMMENTS A transportation ride blending an unusual variety of sights and experiences with an energy-saving way to get around the park. The train provides a glimpse of all lands except Adventureland, with most of the interesting stuff (Native American village, animatronic animals, frontier structures) on the leg between Frontierland and Mickey's Toontown Fair.

A Princeton, New Jersey, dad disputes our comment that there's "plenty to see" on the Walt Disney World Railroad:

We got a great view of lots of trees, a brief glimpse of the queue for Splash Mountain, an even briefer glimpse of Fantasyland, and a view of Toontown Fair, and that's about it. Yeah, it's kind of fun to ride an old steam engine, and our 2-year-old sure likes trains, but I found the sights kind of boring.

TOURING TIPS Save the train ride until after you've seen the featured attractions, or use it when you need transportation. On busy days, lines form at the Frontierland Station but rarely at the Main Street Station. Strollers aren't allowed on the train. Wheelchair access is available only at the Frontierland and Mickey's Toontown Fair stations.

You cannot take your rental stroller on the train, but you can obtain a replacement stroller at your destination. Just take your personal belongings, your stroller name card, and your rental receipt with you on the train.

DISNEY DISH WITH JIM HILL

GIVING "SCALPING" A WHOLE NEW MEANING **Protecting the hairdos of the robotic Native Americans you see while on the train has proved to be quite a challenge for Disney's wigmakers. The birds in the surrounding forest have taken to pulling individual hairs off of these animatronics, which the birds then use to make their nests. That's why the wigmaker's pet name for the Indian chief that you see in this section of the ride is "Sitting Bald."**

Finally, be advised that the railroad shuts down immediately preceding and during parades. Check your park guide map or *Times Guide* for parade times. Needless to say, this is not the time to queue up for the train.

Transportation Rides

DESCRIPTION AND COMMENTS Trolleys, buses, and the like that add color to Main Street.

TOURING TIPS Will save you a walk to the central hub. Not worth a wait.

ADVENTURELAND

ADVENTURELAND IS THE FIRST LAND to the left of Main Street. It combines an African-safari theme with a Caribbean atmosphere.

The Enchanted Tiki Room—Under New Management! ★★★½

APPEAL BY AGE	PRESCHOOL ★★★	GRADE SCHOOL ★★★	TEENS ★★★
YOUNG ADULTS ★★½	OVER 30 ★★★	SENIORS ★★★	

What it is Audio-animatronic Pacific-island musical-theater show. **Scope and scale** Minor attraction. **When to go** Before 11 a.m. or after 3:30 p.m. **Special comments** Frightens some preschoolers. **Authors' rating** Very, very unusual; ★★★½. **Duration of presentation** 15½ minutes. **Preshow entertainment** Talking birds. **Probable waiting time** 15 minutes.

DISNEY DISH WITH JIM HILL

"NO, I SAID 'MOTHER *HUBBARD*' " **Insult comic *par excellence* Don Rickles—who provides the voice of William, the pushy parrot agent in the *Tiki Room*'s preshow—acquired a brand-new and far younger set of fans once he began working on Pixar's *Toy Story* films. Now Rickles finds that he has to be extremely careful about what he says when he's out in public, given the number of times that this acid-tongued comedian has been approached at the airport by youngsters who ask him, "Are you really Mr. Potato Head?"**

DESCRIPTION AND COMMENTS This theater presentation features two of Disney's most beloved bird characters: Iago from *Aladdin* and Zazu from *The Lion King*. The song "Friend Like Me" and a revamped plotline add some much-needed zip, but the production remains (pardon the pun) a featherweight in the Disney galaxy of attractions. Even so, the *Tiki Room* is a great favorite of the 8-and-under set and guests on drugs. It's also reported that the show has been known to induce labor. Although readers like the show, they caution that it may be more frightening to younger children than it used to be. Concerning the scary parts, a mother of three from Coleman, Michigan, was outspoken:

> *The* Tiki Room *show was very scary, with a thunder-and-lightning storm and a loud volcano goddess with glowing red eyes. Can't Disney do anything without scaring young children? It's a* bird show!

A New Jersey dad concurred, commenting:

> The Enchanted Tiki Room *is now REALLY intense—far more intense than I remember fondly from previous visits. Tiki gods storming and smoking, the whole room plunged into utter darkness, and thunder and lightning that*

quite literally shakes the benches you're sitting on—our child (age 2½ years) was terrified. Definitely not recommended for very young children; it seems the attraction is aimed at older children now.

TOURING TIPS Usually not too crowded. We go in the late afternoon, when we appreciate sitting in an air-conditioned theater with our brains in park.

Jungle Cruise (FASTPASS) ★★★

APPEAL BY AGE PRESCHOOL ★★★★ GRADE SCHOOL ★★★★ TEENS ★★★½
YOUNG ADULTS ★★★½ OVER 30 ★★★★ SENIORS ★★★★

What it is Outdoor safari-themed boat-ride adventure. **Scope and scale** Major attraction. **When to go** Before 10 a.m. or 2 hours before closing. **Special comments** A lot of fun to ride at night! **Authors' rating** A long-enduring Disney classic; ★★★. **Duration of ride** 8–9 minutes. **Average wait in line per 100 people ahead of you** 3½ minutes; assumes 10 boats operating. **Loading speed** Moderate.

DESCRIPTION AND COMMENTS An outdoor cruise through jungle waterways. Passengers encounter animatronic elephants, lions, hostile natives, and a menacing hippo. Boatman's spiel adds to the fun. Once one of the most grand and elaborate attractions at the Magic Kingdom, the Jungle Cruise now seems dated and worn technologically speaking. Since the advent of Animal Kingdom, the attraction's appeal has diminished, but in its defense, you can always depend on the Jungle Cruise's robotic critters being present as you motor past.

An Albany, NY, woman agrees that the Jungle Cruise is past its prime:

Jungle Cruise needs updating! My husband gave it a five on the "cheese factor" scale.

TOURING TIPS A convoluted queuing area makes it very difficult to estimate the length of the wait for the Jungle Cruise. A mother from the Bronx complains:

The line for this ride is extremely deceiving. We got in line toward early evening; it was long but we really wanted to take this ride. Every time the winding line brought us near the loading dock and we thought we were going to get on, we'd discover a whole new section of winding lanes to go through. It was extremely frustrating. We must have waited 20 to 30 minutes before we finally gave up and got out.

Fortunately, the Jungle Cruise is a FASTPASS attraction. Before you obtain a FASTPASS, however, ask a cast member what the estimated wait in the standby line is.

The Magic Carpets of Aladdin ★★★

APPEAL BY AGE PRESCHOOL ★★★★½ GRADE SCHOOL ★★★★ TEENS ★★★
YOUNG ADULTS ★★ OVER 30 ★★★ SENIORS ★★

What it is Elaborate midway ride. **Scope and scale** Minor attraction. **When to go** Before 10 a.m. or in the hour before park closing. **Authors' rating** A visually appealing children's ride; ★★★. **Duration of ride** 1½ minutes. **Average wait in line per 100 people ahead of you** 16 minutes. **Loading speed** Slow.

DESCRIPTION AND COMMENTS The Magic Carpets of Aladdin is a midway ride like Dumbo, except with magic carpets instead of elephants. Copying the water innovation of the One Fish, Two Fish, Red Fish, Blue Fish attraction

DISNEY DISH WITH JIM HILL

RECYCLING, DISNEY-STYLE The spitting camels that spritz riders on The Magic Carpets of Aladdin actually started life as parts of parade floats at Disney's Hollywood Studios. There, the dromedaries unashamedly heaped spit on guests watching Aladdin's Royal Caravan, a parade that ran daily from December 1992 through August 1995.

at Universal's Islands of Adventure, Disney's Aladdin ride has a spitting camel positioned to spray jets of water on carpet riders. Riders can maneuver their carpets up and down and side to side to avoid the water. The front seat controls vehicle height, while the backseat controls tilt—if you let the kids sit up front, prepare to get wet!

TOURING TIPS Like Dumbo, this ride has great eye appeal but extremely limited capacity (that is, it loads slowly). Try to get younger kids on during the first 30 minutes the park is open, or try just before park closing.

Pirates of the Caribbean ★★★★★

APPEAL BY AGE PRESCHOOL ★★★½ GRADE SCHOOL ★★★★ TEENS ★★★★ YOUNG ADULTS ★★★★½ OVER 30 ★★★★½ SENIORS ★★★★

What it is Indoor pirate-themed boat ride. **Scope and scale** Headliner. **When to go** Before noon or after 5 p.m. **Special comments** Frightens some children. **Authors' rating** Disney audio-animatronics at their best; not to be missed; ★★★★★. **Duration of ride** About 7½ minutes. **Average wait in line per 100 people ahead of you** 1½ minutes; assumes both waiting lines operating. **Loading speed** Fast.

DISNEY DISH WITH JIM HILL

SO WHAT NOW, JACK SPARROW? With *Pirates of the Caribbean 4* now officially scheduled for release during the summer of 2012, Johnny Depp fans are desperate for info about whom Captain Jack will be tangling with this time around. Given that Disney has just created a face-character version of Captain Barbossa, it's a pretty safe bet that Geoffrey Rush will be reprising his role as Sparrow's apple-loving nemesis in *Pirates 4*.

DESCRIPTION AND COMMENTS An indoor cruise through a series of sets that depict a pirate raid on an island settlement, from bombardment of the fortress to debauchery after the victory. Arguably one of the most influential theme-park attractions ever created, the Magic Kingdom's version retains the elaborate queuing area, grand scale, and detailed scenes that have awed audiences since its debut in Disneyland in 1967. The wildly successful *Pirates of the Caribbean* movies have boosted the ride's popularity, and guests' demands led to the addition in 2006 of animatronic figures of the movie's Captain Jack Sparrow and Captain Barbossa in key scenes.

Regarding debauchery, Pirates of the Caribbean has been administered a strong dose of political correctness. Even so, a Rockville, Maryland, mother was not prepared for what she saw:

I had not understood that it would be as visually violent and historically accurate as it was. I really didn't look forward to explaining to my son why those women had ropes around their necks and such. I wish I'd been better warned that this isn't the Captain Hook view of piracy, but a much more realistic one.

TOURING TIPS Undoubtedly one of the park's most timeless attractions. Engineered to move large crowds in a hurry, Pirates is a good attraction to see in the late afternoon. It has two covered waiting lines.

Swiss Family Treehouse ★★★

APPEAL BY AGE PRESCHOOL ★★★ GRADE SCHOOL ★★★ TEENS ★★½
YOUNG ADULTS ★★½ OVER 30 ★★★ SENIORS ★★½

What it is Outdoor walk-through treehouse. **Scope and scale** Minor attraction. **When to go** Anytime. **Special comments** Requires climbing a lot of stairs. **Authors' rating** Incredible detail and execution; ★★★. **Duration of tour** 10–15 minutes. **Average wait in line per 100 people ahead of you** 7 minutes. **Loading speed** N/A.

DISNEY DISH WITH JIM HILL

GONE WITH THE SWANS **Is that body of water surrounding the Treehouse the Imagineers' attempt to re-create the island on which this 1960 Walt Disney production was set? Nope. It's where, back in the 1970s, the Plaza Swan Boats used to make a brief detour into Adventureland. The elegant (but slow-moving and extremely-low-capacity) Swan Boats flew the coop in 1983.**

DESCRIPTION AND COMMENTS An immense replica of the shipwrecked family's treehouse home will turn your children into arboreal architects. It's the king of all treehouses, with its multiple stories and mechanical wizardry. Children enjoy the climbing and exercise. Adults marvel at the ingenuity.

TOURING TIPS A self-guided walk-through tour involves a lot of stairs up and down, but no ropes, ladders, or anything fancy. People who stop for extra-long looks or to rest sometimes create bottlenecks that slow the crowd flow. Visit in late afternoon or early evening if you're on a one-day tour, or in the morning of your second day.

FRONTIERLAND

FRONTIERLAND ADJOINS ADVENTURELAND as you move clockwise around the Magic Kingdom. The focus is on the Old West, with stockade-type structures and pioneer trappings.

Big Thunder Mountain Railroad (FASTPASS) ★★★★

APPEAL BY AGE PRESCHOOL ★★★★ GRADE SCHOOL ★★★★½ TEENS ★★★★½
YOUNG ADULTS ★★★★ OVER 30 ★★★★½ SENIORS ★★★½

What it is Tame western mining–themed roller coaster. **Scope and scale** Headliner. **When to go** Before 10 a.m., in the hour before closing, or use FASTPASS. **Special comments** Must be 40" tall to ride; children younger than age 7 must ride with an adult. Switching-off option provided (see page 339). **Authors' rating** Great effects; relatively tame ride; not to be missed; ★★★★. **Duration of ride** About 3½ minutes. **Average wait in line per 100 people ahead of you** 2½ minutes; assumes 5 trains operating. **Loading speed** Moderate–fast.

DISNEY DISH WITH JIM HILL

BIG THUNDER MAY GO QUIET **It's been quite a while since "The Wildest Ride in the Wilderness" received some TLC. So don't be surprised if the next time you visit, this Frontierland favorite is down for a lengthy rehab. The upside is that this runaway-train attraction may eventually feature some exciting new elements, perhaps tying in to Jerry Bruckheimer's big-budget *Lone Ranger* redo, which Walt Disney Pictures now plans on releasing during the summer of 2013.**

DESCRIPTION AND COMMENTS Roller coaster through and around a Disney "mountain." The idea is that you're on a runaway mine train during the Gold Rush. This coaster is about a 5 on a "scary scale" of 10. First-rate examples of Disney creativity are showcased: a realistic mining town, falling rocks, and an earthquake, all humorously animated with swinging possums, petulant buzzards, and the like. Ride it after dark if you can.

TOURING TIPS A superb Disney experience, but not too wild a roller coaster. Emphasis is much more on the sights than on the thrill of the ride.

Nearby Splash Mountain affects the traffic flow to Big Thunder Mountain Railroad. Adventuresome guests ride Splash Mountain first, then go next door to ride Big Thunder. This means large crowds in Frontierland all day and long waits for Big Thunder Mountain. The best way to experience the Magic Kingdom's "mountains" is to ride Space Mountain one morning as soon as the park opens, and Splash Mountain and Big Thunder the next morning. If you only have one day, the order should be (1) Space Mountain, (2) Buzz Lightyear (optional), (3) Splash Mountain, and (4) Big Thunder Mountain. If the wait exceeds 30 minutes when you arrive, use FASTPASS.

A Midwestern mom offers this tip to families with children who are too short to ride:

If you're switching off on Thunder Mountain or Splash Mountain and have young kids to entertain, there's a fantastic little playground nearby where you can pass the time (and it's a great meeting place when the others get off the ride). It is completely covered and near the restrooms too! It's located next to Splash Mountain, under the train tracks.

Guests experience Disney attractions differently. Consider this letter from a lady in Brookline, Massachusetts:

Being senior citizens and having limited time, my friend and I confined our activities to attractions rated as four or five stars for seniors. Because of your recommendation, we waited an hour to board the Big Thunder Mountain Railroad, [which you] *rated a 5 on a scary scale of 10. After living through three and a half minutes of pure terror, I will rate it a 15. We were so busy holding on and screaming and even praying for our safety that we did not see any falling rocks, a mining town, or an earthquake. The Big Thunder Mountain Railroad should not be recommended for seniors or preschool children.*

Another woman from New England writes:

My husband, who is 41, found Big Thunder Mountain too intense and feels that anyone who does not like roller coasters would not enjoy this ride.

A woman from Vermont discovered that there's more to consider about Big Thunder than being scared:

Big Thunder Mountain Railroad was rated a 5 on the scary scale. I won't say it warranted a higher scare rating, but it was much higher on the lose-your-lunch meter. One more sharp turn and the kids in front of me would have needed a dip in Splash Mountain!

However, a reader from West Newton, Massachusetts, dubbed the ride "a roller coaster for people who don't like roller coasters."

Country Bear Jamboree ★★★

APPEAL BY AGE PRESCHOOL ★★★½ GRADE SCHOOL ★★★ TEENS ★★½
YOUNG ADULTS ★★½ OVER 30 ★★★ SENIORS ★★★½

What it is Audio-animatronic country-hoedown theater show. **Scope and scale** Major attraction. **When to go** Before 11:30 a.m., before a parade, or during the 2 hours before closing. **Special comments** Shows change at Christmas. **Authors' rating** Old and worn but pure Disney; ★★★. **Duration of presentation** 15 minutes. **Preshow entertainment** None. **Probable waiting time** This attraction is moderately popular but has a comparatively small capacity. Waiting time between noon and 5:30 p.m. on a busy day will average 15–45 minutes.

DESCRIPTION AND COMMENTS A charming cast of audio-animatronic bears sings and stomps in a western-style hoedown. Although one of the Magic Kingdom's most humorous and upbeat shows, *Country Bear Jamboree* has run for so long that the geriatric bears are a step away from assisted living and the fleas all walk with canes.

Readers continue to debate the merits of *Country Bear Jamboree.* The following comments are representative.

First, from a Sandy Hook, Connecticut, mom:

I know they consider it a classic, and kids always seem to love it, but could they PLEASE update it after half a century?

A woman from Carmel, Indiana, put her experience in perspective:

Here is another half hour of my life that I cannot get back.

But a Mississippi dad defends the show:

I find it interesting how my reactions and those of my family change to certain attractions. Take Country Bear Jamboree, *for instance: In my 30s I enjoyed it mildly but considered it somewhat hokey and lame, yet I thoroughly enjoyed my daughter's intense love of it at ages 3 and 8 on two previous trips. This time, at age 54, I sat up fairly close with my wife and loved it—we even sang along! Of course, this was partly to embarrass my now-16-year-old daughter, who sat hunched down in the very last row. She says we have creeping senility, but I told her, "Just wait till you bring YOUR kids!"*

TOURING TIPS The *Jamboree* remains popular and draws large crowds from midmorning on.

Frontierland Shootin' Arcade ★½

APPEAL BY AGE PRESCHOOL ★★½ GRADE SCHOOL ★★★★ TEENS ★★★
YOUNG ADULTS ★★½ OVER 30 ★★ SENIORS ★★

What it is Electronic shooting gallery. **Scope and scale** Diversion. **When to go** Whenever convenient. **Special comments** Costs $1 per play. **Authors' rating** Very nifty shooting gallery; ★½.

DESCRIPTION AND COMMENTS Very elaborate. One of a few attractions not included in Magic Kingdom admission.

TOURING TIPS Not a place to blow your time if you're on a tight schedule. The fun is entirely in the target practice—no prizes can be won.

Splash Mountain (FASTPASS) ★★★★★

APPEAL BY AGE PRESCHOOL ★★★★† GRADE SCHOOL ★★★★½ TEENS ★★★★★ YOUNG ADULTS ★★★★★ OVER 30 ★★★★½ SENIORS ★★★★

†Many preschoolers are too short to ride, and others are intimidated when they see the attraction from the waiting line. Among preschoolers who actually ride, most give it high marks.

What it is Indoor/outdoor water-flume adventure ride. **Scope and scale** Super-headliner. **When to go** As soon as the park opens, during afternoon or evening parades, just before closing, or use FASTPASS. **Special comments** Must be 40" tall to ride; children younger than age 7 must ride with an adult. Switching-off option provided (see page 339). **Authors' rating** A soggy delight, and not to be missed; ★★★★★. **Duration of ride** About 10 minutes. **Average wait in line per 100 people ahead of you** 3½ minutes; assumes ride is operating at full capacity. **Loading speed** Moderate.

DISNEY DISH WITH JIM HILL

A PRETTY TUSHY JOB **Before a new audio-animatronic figure gets installed at a Disney theme park, it must first undergo rigorous testing back at Walt Disney Imagineering—remaining in continuous operation for 100 hours straight to ensure that it won't break down in the field. (Just be glad you weren't the Imagineer in charge of testing the animatronic version of Brer Bear's butt that wiggles at you just before you exit Splash Mountain.)**

DESCRIPTION AND COMMENTS Splash Mountain combines steep chutes and animatronics with at least one special effect for each of the senses. The ride covers more than half a mile, splashing through swamps, caves, and backwoods bayous before climaxing in a five-story plunge and Br'er Rabbit's triumphant return home. More than 100 audio-animatronic characters, including Br'er Rabbit (aka Br'er Hare), Br'er Bear, and Br'er Fox, regale riders with songs, including "Zip-a-Dee-Doo-Dah."

TOURING TIPS This happy, exciting, adventuresome ride vies with Space Mountain in Tomorrowland as the park's most popular attraction. Crowds build fast in the morning, and waits of more than two hours can be expected once the park fills. Get in line first thing, certainly no later than 45 minutes after the park opens. Long lines will persist all day.

If you have only one day to see the Magic Kingdom, ride Space Mountain first, then Buzz Lightyear (also in Tomorrowland), then hotfoot it to Splash Mountain. If the wait is less than 30 minutes, go ahead and ride. Otherwise, get a FASTPASS and return later to enjoy Splash Mountain. FASTPASS strategies have been incorporated into the Magic Kingdom One-day Touring Plans (see pages 815–816 and 819–820). If you have two mornings to devote to the Magic Kingdom, experience Space Mountain and Buzz Lightyear one morning, Splash Mountain and Big Thunder Mountain the next. Spreading your visit over two mornings will eliminate much crisscrossing of the park as well as the backtracking that is inevitable when you use FASTPASS.

As with Space Mountain, hundreds are poised to dash to Splash Mountain when the park opens. The best strategy is to go to the end of Main Street and turn left at The Crystal Palace restaurant. In front of the restaurant is a bridge that provides a shortcut to Adventureland.

Stake out a position at the barrier rope. When the park opens, move as fast as you comfortably can and cross the bridge to Adventureland.

Another shortcut: just past the first group of buildings on your right, roughly across from the Swiss Family Treehouse, is a small passageway containing restrooms and phones. Easy to overlook, it connects Adventureland to Frontierland. Go through here into Frontierland, and take a hard left. As you emerge along the waterfront, Splash Mountain is straight ahead. If you miss the passageway, don't fool around looking for it. Continue straight through Adventureland to Splash Mountain.

Less exhausting in the morning is commuting to Splash Mountain via the Walt Disney World Railroad. Board at Main Street Station and wait for the park to open. The train will pull out of the station a few minutes after the rope drops at the central hub end of Main Street. Ride to Frontierland Station and disembark. As you come down the stairs at the station, the entrance to Splash Mountain will be on your left. Because of the time required to unload at the station, train passengers will arrive at Splash Mountain about the same time as the lead element from the central hub.

A Suffolk, Virginia, mom contends that there are more important considerations than beating the crowds:

> *The only recommendation I have is to definitely wait to do Splash Mountain at the end of the day. We were seated in the front of the ride, and needless to say, we were soaked to the bone. If we had ridden* [first thing in the morning] *according to your plan, I personally would have been miserable for the rest of the day. Parents, beware! It says you will get wet, not drowned.*

At Splash Mountain, if you ride in the front seat, you almost certainly will get wet. Riders elsewhere get splashed but usually not doused. Since you don't know which seat you'll be assigned, go prepared. On a cool day, carry a plastic garbage bag. Tear holes in the bottom and sides to make a water-resistant (not waterproof) sack dress. Be sure to tuck the bag under your bottom. Or store a change of clothes, including footwear, in one of the park's rental lockers. Leave your camera with a nonriding member of your group or wrap it in plastic. For any attraction where there's a distinct possibility of getting soaked, wear Tevas or some other type of waterproof sandal, and change back to regular shoes after the ride.

The scariest part of this adventure ride is the steep chute you see when standing in line, but the drop looks worse than it is. Despite reassurances, however, many children wig out after watching it. A mom from Grand Rapids, Michigan, recalls her kids' rather unique reaction:

> *We discovered after the fact that our children thought they would go under water after the five-story drop and tried to hold their breath throughout the ride in preparation. They were really too preoccupied to enjoy the clever Br'er Rabbit story.*

Tom Sawyer Island and Fort Langhorn ★★★

APPEAL BY AGE PRESCHOOL ★★★★ GRADE SCHOOL ★★★★
TEENS ★★★ YOUNG ADULTS ★★½ OVER 30 ★★★ SENIORS ★★★

What it is Outdoor walk-through exhibit/rustic playground. **Scope and scale** Minor attraction. **When to go** Midmorning–late afternoon. **Special comments** Closes at dusk. **Authors' rating** The place for rambunctious kids; ★★★.

DESCRIPTION AND COMMENTS Tom Sawyer Island is a getaway within the park.

DISNEY DISH WITH JIM HILL

SO *THAT'S* WHY AUNT POLLY IS NEVER AROUND **Not all of the wildlife that you spy along the Rivers of America is animatronic. WDW management continually deals with nuisance gators who make their way into the Magic Kingdom in hopes of dining on the ducks that follow the *Liberty Belle* and food that tourists typically drop in the water. So who does Disney call when it has to have these wayward reptiles removed? The folks at Orlando's original attraction, Gatorland, of course.**

It has hills to climb; a cave, windmill, and pioneer stockade (Fort Langhorn) to explore; a tipsy barrel bridge to cross; and paths to follow. You can watch riverboats chug past. It's a delight for adults and a godsend for children who have been in tow and closely supervised all day.

TOURING TIPS Tom Sawyer Island isn't one of the Magic Kingdom's more celebrated attractions, but it's one of the park's better-conceived ones. Attention to detail is excellent, and kids revel in its frontier atmosphere. It's a must for families with children ages 5 to 15. If your group is made up of adults, visit on your second day or on your first day after you've seen the attractions you most wanted to see.

Although children could spend a whole day on the island, plan on at least 20 minutes. Access is by raft from Frontierland; two operate simultaneously and the trip is pretty efficient, though you may have to stand in line to board both ways.

For a mother from Duncan, South Carolina, Tom Sawyer Island is as much a refuge as an attraction:

In the afternoon when the crowds were at their peak, the weather [at] *its hottest, our organization began to suffer. We retreated over to Tom Sawyer Island, which proved to be a true haven. My husband and I found a secluded bench and regrouped while sipping iced tea and eating delicious soft ice cream. Meanwhile, the kids were able to run freely in the shade.*

Each morning, Disney cast members hide about half a dozen colored paintbrushes around the island for guests to find. Look for colored handles with white paint on the bristles, on display shelves and buildings; they'll all be within arm's reach. Notify a cast member if you find one—you'll be rewarded with a small prize ranging from a front-of-line pass on any Magic Kingdom attraction to free sodas for your entire group. One of each prize is available each day on a first-come basis, so this is a great activity early on the second day in the park.

Walt Disney World Railroad

DESCRIPTION AND COMMENTS Stops in Frontierland on its circle tour of the park. See the description under Main Street, U.S.A. (page 515), for additional details.

TOURING TIPS Pleasant, feet-saving link to Main Street and Mickey's Toontown Fair, but the Frontierland Station is more congested than those stations. You cannot take your rental stroller on the train. If you don't want to make a round-trip to pick up your stroller, take your personal belongings, your stroller name card, and your rental receipt with you on the train. You'll be issued a replacement stroller at your destination.

LIBERTY SQUARE

LIBERTY SQUARE RE-CREATES AMERICA at the time of the Revolutionary War. The architecture is Federal or Colonial. A real 130-year-old live oak, the Liberty Tree, lends dignity and grace to the setting.

The Hall of Presidents ★★★

APPEAL BY AGE PRESCHOOL ★½ GRADE SCHOOL ★★½ TEENS ★★★
YOUNG ADULTS ★★★ OVER 30 ★★★½ SENIORS ★★★★

What it is Audio-animatronic historical theater presentation. **Scope and scale** Major attraction. **When to go** Anytime. **Authors' rating** Impressive and moving; ★★★. **Duration of presentation** Almost 23 minutes. **Preshow entertainment** None. **Probable waiting time** The lines for this attraction look intimidating, but they're usually swallowed up as the theater exchanges audiences. Even during the busiest times, waits rarely exceed 40 minutes.

DISNEY DISH WITH JIM HILL

DIVINE INTERVENTION **By now we all know that Barack Obama is now one of three robotic presidents who get to stand and speak in this Liberty Square attraction. But what most excites the Imagineers in charge of the most recent *Hall of Presidents* redo is the actor they hired to narrate the show: Academy Award winner Morgan Freeman. With the voice of God in Universal's *Bruce Almighty* and *Evan Almighty* now aboard, WDI is thrilled to be adding a most authoritative tone to this electronic patriotic pageant.**

DESCRIPTION AND COMMENTS In 2009 Barack Obama was added and the entire show revamped, including a new narration by Morgan Freeman and a new speech by George Washington. The Father of Our Country joins Presidents Lincoln and Obama as the only chief executives with speaking parts. Although the show is revamped roughly every decade, the presentation remains strongly inspirational and patriotic, highlighting milestones in American history. A very moving show for Americans, coupled with one of Disney's best and most ambitious audio-animatronic efforts.

Through its periodic refurbishments, we've had a high opinion of *The Hall of Presidents.* That said, we receive a lot of mail from readers who get more than entertainment from it. A woman in St. Louis writes:

We always go to The Hall of Presidents *when my husband gets cranky so he can take a nice nap.*

A young mother in Marion, Ohio, adds:

The Hall of Presidents *is a great place to breast-feed.*

But for a Texas family, *The Hall of Presidents* was an unexpected hit:

We were sure our young children would not like The Hall of Presidents, *and so we avoided it for several years. This trip we tried it. What a pleasant surprise; both our 8- and 10-year-olds recognized George W., and the roll call was very moving without being the least sappy. We all loved it.*

TOURING TIPS Detail and costumes are masterful. This attraction is one of the park's most popular among older visitors. Don't be put off by long lines.

The theater holds more than 700 people, thus swallowing large lines at a single gulp when visitors are admitted.

The Haunted Mansion ★★★★

APPEAL BY AGE PRESCHOOL ★★★ GRADE SCHOOL ★★★★ TEENS ★★★★
YOUNG ADULTS ★★★★½ OVER 30 ★★★★½ SENIORS ★★★★½

What it is Haunted-house dark ride. **Scope and scale** Major attraction. **When to go** Before 11:30 a.m. or after 8 p.m. **Special comments** Frightens some very young children. **Authors' rating** Some of Walt Disney World's best special effects; not to be missed; ★★★★. **Duration of ride** 7-minute ride plus a 1½-minute preshow. **Average wait in line per 100 people ahead of you** 2½ minutes; assumes both "stretch rooms" operating. **Loading speed** Fast.

DISNEY DISH WITH JIM HILL

"AND A PRICEY SOUVENIR WILL FOLLOW YOU HOME. . . ." Know how you can buy photos of yourself on virtually every Disney headliner attraction these days? Well, the folks in charge of The Haunted Mansion have been exploring the idea of installing a video camera in the graveyard sequence. This would let them sell a version of Madame Leota's crystal ball that plays footage of guests riding their Doom Buggies through this cheerfully spooky attraction. If Magic Kingdom management can be persuaded to cover the cost of installation, this nifty knickknack could actually be available for sale in a year or so.

DESCRIPTION AND COMMENTS Only slightly scarier than a whoopee cushion, The Haunted Mansion serves up some of the Magic Kingdom's best visual effects. The attraction is a masterpiece of detail. "Doom Buggies" on a conveyor belt transport you through the house from parlor to attic, then through a graveyard. Two new scenes were added in the substantial 2007 refurbishment: an M. C. Escher–like room full of stairs heading in all directions and a montage explaining the fate of the attic bride's many husbands. However, the story line remains thin and unemphasized.

A reader from Australia suggests that knowing the story line in advance really enhances the attraction:

During our behind-the-scenes tour, we were told the story line for [The Haunted Mansion]. *A lady was about to be married when her groom discovered her with the tailor's arms around her (probably just getting a dress fitting, but we'll never know!). The groom killed the tailor in a rage, and she jumped out the window in distress. This is very cleverly shown throughout the attraction: the carriages rise to the attic to see her in her wedding dress, and while descending, the broken window can be seen. At this point, the "guests" assume the role of her ghost, and the gravedigger and faithful dog shiver as the "ghost" passes. The story line really added another dimension to the attraction.*

Some children become overly anxious about what they think they'll see. Almost nobody is scared by the actual sights.

The Haunted Mansion is one of veteran *Unofficial Guide* writer Eve Zibart's favorite attractions. She says:

This is one of the best attractions in the Magic Kingdom. It's jam-packed with visual puns, special effects, hidden Mickeys, and really lovely Victorian-spooky sets. It's not scary, except in the sweetest of ways, but it will remind you of the days before ghost stories gave way to slasher flicks.

TOURING TIPS This attraction would be more at home in Fantasyland, but no matter. It's Disney at its best. Lines here ebb and flow more than those at most other Magic Kingdom hot spots because the Mansion is near *The Hall of Presidents* and the *Liberty Belle* riverboat. These two attractions disgorge 700 and 450 people, respectively, when each show or ride ends, and many of these folks head straight for the Mansion. If you can't go before 11:30 a.m. or after 8 p.m., try to slip in between crowds.

Liberty Belle Riverboat ★★½

APPEAL BY AGE	PRESCHOOL ★★★	GRADE SCHOOL ★★★	TEENS ★★
YOUNG ADULTS ★★★	OVER 30 ★★★	SENIORS ★★★½	

What it is Outdoor scenic boat ride. **Scope and scale** Major attraction. **When to go** Anytime. **Authors' rating** Slow, relaxing, and scenic; ★★½. **Duration of ride** About 16 minutes. **Average wait to board** 10–14 minutes.

DESCRIPTION AND COMMENTS Large-capacity paddle-wheel riverboat navigates the waters around Tom Sawyer Island and Fort Langhorn, passing settler cabins, old mining paraphernalia, a Plains Indian village, and a small menagerie of animatronic wildlife. A beautiful craft, the *Liberty Belle* provides a lofty perspective of Frontierland and Liberty Square.

TOURING TIPS The riverboat is a good attraction for the busy middle of the day. If you encounter huge crowds, chances are that the attraction has been inundated by a wave of guests coming from a just-concluded performance of *The Hall of Presidents.*

FANTASYLAND

FANTASYLAND IS THE HEART OF THE MAGIC KINGDOM, a truly enchanting place spread gracefully like a miniature Alpine village beneath the steepled towers of Cinderella Castle.

Ariel's Grotto ★★★

APPEAL BY AGE	PRESCHOOL ★★★★½	GRADE SCHOOL ★★★½	TEENS ★★
YOUNG ADULTS ★	OVER 30 ★★	SENIORS ★½	

What it is Interactive fountain and character-greeting area. **Scope and scale** Minor attraction. **When to go** Before 11 a.m. or after 9 p.m. **Authors' rating** One of the most elaborate of the character-greeting venues; ★★★. **Average wait in line per 100 people ahead of you** 50 minutes.

DISNEY DISH WITH JIM HILL

WHY DOES THE LITTLE MERMAID NEED SUCH A GREAT BIG BUILDING? Because Ariel's Undersea Adventure—the first new dark ride added to Fantasyland since The Many Adventures of Winnie the Pooh in 1999—is going to be truly epic in scale. Stretching all the way from Ariel's Grotto to Pooh's Playful Spot, this enormous attraction will feature elaborate restagings of the "Under the Sea" and "Kiss the Girl" numbers from Disney's Academy Award–winning animated feature. Look for Ariel's Undersea Adventure to set sail in early 2012.

DESCRIPTION AND COMMENTS On the lagoon side of Dumbo, Ariel's Grotto consists of a small children's play area with an interactive fountain and a rock grotto where Ariel, the Little Mermaid, poses for photos and signs autographs. If "interactive fountain" is new to you, it means an opportunity for your children to get as wet as a trout. Can you say "hypothermia"?

TOURING TIPS The Grotto is small, and the wait to meet Ariel is usually long. Because kids in line are fresh from the fountain, it's very difficult for adults to remain dry.

In the estimation of a mother from Hagerstown, Maryland, the experience was not unlike "being packed in a pen with wet cocker spaniels."

If your children spot the Grotto before you do, there's no turning back. Count on a long queue and a 20- to 50-minute wait to see Ariel, except during the first 15 minutes she's open for business (usually beginning at 10 in the morning). Then there's the fountain. Allow your children to disrobe to the legal limit. (Don't bother with umbrellas or ponchos, because water squirts up from below.) When you're finished meeting Ariel, you will have to navigate an armada of males of varying ages who are plowing upstream through the exit to admire the Little Mermaid's cleavage.

Cinderella's Golden Carousel ★★★

APPEAL BY AGE **PRESCHOOL** ★★★★ **GRADE SCHOOL** ★★★½ **TEENS** ★★½
YOUNG ADULTS ★★★ **OVER 30** ★★★ **SENIORS** ★★★

What it is Merry-go-round. **Scope and scale** Minor attraction. **When to go** Before 11 a.m. or after 8 p.m. **Special comments** Adults enjoy the beauty and nostalgia of this ride. **Authors' rating** A beautiful ride for children; ★★★. **Duration of ride** About 2 minutes. **Average wait in line per 100 people ahead of you** 5 minutes. **Loading speed** Slow.

DESCRIPTION AND COMMENTS One of the most elaborate and beautiful merry-go-rounds you'll ever have the pleasure of seeing, especially when its lights are on.

A shy and retiring 9-year-old girl from Rockaway, New Jersey, thinks our rating of the carousel for grade schoolers should be higher:

I want to complain. I went on Cinderella's Golden Carousel four times and I loved it! Raise those stars right now! Also, kids who don't like things jumping out at them should not go to Honey, I Shrunk the Audience [at Epcot].

TOURING TIPS Unless young children in your party insist on riding, appreciate this attraction from the sidelines. While lovely to look at, the carousel loads and unloads very slowly.

Dumbo the Flying Elephant ★★★

APPEAL BY AGE **PRESCHOOL** ★★★★★ **GRADE SCHOOL** ★★★★ **TEENS** ★★½
YOUNG ADULTS ★★ **OVER 30** ★★★ **SENIORS** ★★

What it is Disneyfied midway ride. **Scope and scale** Minor attraction. **When to go** Before 10 a.m. or after 9 p.m. **Authors' rating** Disney's signature ride for children; ★★★. **Duration of ride** 1½ minutes. **Average wait in line per 100 people ahead of you** 20 minutes. **Loading speed** Slow.

DESCRIPTION AND COMMENTS A tame, happy children's ride based on the lovable flying elephant, Dumbo. Despite being little different from rides at state fairs and amusement parks, Dumbo is the favorite Magic Kingdom attraction of many younger children.

A lot of readers take us to task for lumping Dumbo with carnival rides. A reader from Armdale, Nova Scotia, writes:

I think you have acquired a jaded attitude. I know [Dumbo] *is not for everybody, but when we took our oldest child (then just 4), the sign at the end of the line said there would be a 90-minute wait. He knew and he didn't care, and he and I stood in the hot afternoon sun for 90 blissful minutes waiting for his 90-second flight. Anything that a 4-year-old would wait for that long and that patiently must be pretty special.*

TOURING TIPS If Dumbo is essential to your child's happiness, make it your first stop, preferably within 15 minutes of the park's opening. Also, consider this advice from an Arlington, Virginia, mom:

My kids threw me out of their Dumbo and I had to sit in a Dumbo all by myself! Pretty embarrassing, and my husband got lots of pictures.

A mother of two preschoolers from Carmel, Indiana, suggests escaping the Dumbo crowds on a magic carpet:

For the Magic Kingdom Touring Plan for Families with Young Children, how about giving the alternative of The Magic Carpets of Aladdin instead of Dumbo as the first ride? My kids didn't really know Dumbo but wanted a ride like that, so we went to Magic Carpets first, rode twice (there was hardly anyone else there), then went to Fantasyland for Peter Pan and the rest of the touring plan—worked really well.

It's a Small World ★★★

APPEAL BY AGE PRESCHOOL ★★★★½ GRADE SCHOOL ★★★★ TEENS ★★★
YOUNG ADULTS ★★★ OVER 30 ★★★½ SENIORS ★★★★

What it is World-brotherhood-themed indoor boat ride. **Scope and scale** Major attraction. **When to go** Anytime. **Authors' rating** Exponentially "cute"; ★★★. **Duration of ride** Approximately 11 minutes. **Average wait in line per 100 people ahead of you** 11 minutes; assumes busy conditions with 30 or more boats operating. **Loading speed** Fast.

DESCRIPTION AND COMMENTS Small World is a happy, upbeat indoor attraction with a mind-numbing tune that only a backhoe can remove from your brain. Small boats carry visitors on a tour around the world, with singing and dancing dolls showcasing the dress and culture of each nation. One of Disney's oldest entertainment offerings, It's a Small World first unleashed its brainwashing song and lethally cute ethnic dolls on the real world at the 1964 New York World's Fair. Though it bludgeons you with its sappy redundancy, almost everyone enjoys It's a Small World (at least the first time). It stands, however, along with the *Enchanted Tiki Room* in the "What were they smokin'?" category.

A woman from Holbrook, New York, apparently underwhelmed, suggests that Small World would be much better "if each person got three to four softballs on the way in!"

And a mother from Castleton, Vermont, added this:

It's a Small World at Fantasyland was like a pit stop in the Twilight Zone. They were very slow in unloading the boats, and we were stuck in a line of about six boats waiting to get out while the endless chanting of that song grated on my nerves. I told my husband I was going to swim for it just to escape one more chorus.

And finally, from a Vancouver, British Columbia, teen:

The HAPPIEST CRUISE THAT EVER SAILED *sign at the entrance to the ride should be replaced with one that says* THIS IS YOUR BRAIN ON DRUGS!

TOURING TIPS Cool off here during the heat of the day. With two waiting lines, It's a Small World loads fast and usually is a good bet between 11 a.m. and 5 p.m. If you wear a hearing aid, turn it off.

Mad Tea Party ★★

APPEAL BY AGE PRESCHOOL ★★★★ GRADE SCHOOL ★★★★ TEENS ★★★★ YOUNG ADULTS ★★★ OVER 30 ★★★ SENIORS ★★

What it is Midway-type spinning ride. **Scope and scale** Minor attraction. **When to go** Before 11 a.m. or after 5 p.m. **Special comments** You can make the teacups spin faster by turning the wheel in the center of the cup. **Authors' rating** Fun, but not worth the wait; ★★. **Duration of ride** 1½ minutes. **Average wait in line per 100 people ahead of you** 7½ minutes. **Loading speed** Slow.

Motion Sickness

DESCRIPTION AND COMMENTS Riders whirl feverishly in big teacups. *Alice in Wonderland*'s Mad Hatter provides the theme. Teenagers like to lure adults onto the teacups, then turn the wheel in the middle (making the cup spin faster), until the adults are plastered against the sides and on the verge of throwing up. Unless your life's ambition is to be the test subject in a human centrifuge, don't even consider getting on this ride with anyone younger than age 21.

DISNEY DISH WITH JIM HILL

A LASTING TRIBUTE As you walk past the Mad Tea Party, keep an eye out for a light-blue leaf with some writing on it. This recent Fantasyland addition honors the late Randy Pausch, the Carnegie Mellon University computer scientist and former Imagineer best known for his life-affirming "Last Lecture." In addition to placing this leaf with a quote by Randy ("Be good at something. It makes you valuable. . . .") in the park, The Walt Disney Company has also established a fellowship in Pausch's name at CMU.

A reader we've dubbed Melba the Human Centrifuge advises:

If you want to spin your teacup, DO NOT try to put more than three people in one cup.

TOURING TIPS This ride, well done but not unique, is notoriously slow-loading. Ride the morning of your second day if your schedule is more relaxed.

The Many Adventures of Winnie the Pooh (FASTPASS) ★★★½

APPEAL BY AGE PRESCHOOL ★★★★½ GRADE SCHOOL ★★★★ TEENS ★★★ YOUNG ADULTS ★★★ OVER 30 ★★★½ SENIORS ★★★½

What it is Indoor track ride. **Scope and scale** Minor attraction. **When to go** Before 10 a.m., in the 2 hours before closing, or use FASTPASS. **Authors' rating** As cute as the Pooh Bear himself; ★★★½. **Duration of ride** About 4 minutes. **Average wait in line per 100 people ahead of you** 4 minutes. **Loading speed** Moderate.

DESCRIPTION AND COMMENTS Pooh is sunny, upbeat, and fun—more in the image of Peter Pan's Flight or Splash Mountain. You ride a "Hunny Pot" through the pages of a huge picture book into the Hundred Acre Wood, where you encounter Pooh, Piglet, Eeyore, Owl, Rabbit, Tigger, Kanga, and Roo as they contend with a blustery day. There's even a dream sequence with Heffalumps and Woozles. A 30-something couple from Lexington, Massachusetts, thinks that Pooh has plenty to offer adults:

The attention to detail and special effects on this ride make it worth seeing even if you don't have children in your party. The Pooh dream sequence was great!

TOURING TIPS Because of its relatively small capacity, the daily allocation of FASTPASSes for The Many Adventures of Winnie the Pooh is often distributed by early afternoon. For this same reason, your scheduled return time to enjoy the ride might be hours away. It's not unusual to pick up a FASTPASS for Winnie the Pooh at 12:30 p.m. with a scheduled return time of 5 p.m. or later.

Mickey's PhilharMagic (FASTPASS) ★★★★

APPEAL BY AGE PRESCHOOL ★★★★ GRADE SCHOOL ★★★★½ TEENS ★★★★½
YOUNG ADULTS ★★★★½ OVER 30 ★★★★½ SENIORS ★★★★★

What it is 3-D movie. **Scope and scale** Major attraction. **When to go** Before 11 a.m., during parades. **Special comments** Not to be missed. **Authors' rating** A zany masterpiece; ★★★★. **Duration of presentation** About 20 minutes. **Probable waiting time** 12–30 minutes.

DISNEY DISH WITH JIM HILL

INCOMPREHENSIBLE IN EVERY LANGUAGE *Mickey's PhilharMagic* was kind of a departure for Disney in that it was the first theme-park film deliberately designed for the international market. In order to avoid any translation issues, the film's dialogue was kept to an absolute minimum. This is why Donald Duck was chosen to be the movie's central character: no matter what country you're from or what language you speak, you still can't understand what he's saying.

DESCRIPTION AND COMMENTS With *Mickey's PhilharMagic,* there is a 3-D movie attraction at each of the four Disney theme parks. The *PhilharMagic* features an odd collection of Disney characters, mixing Mickey and Donald with Simba and Ariel as well as Jasmine and Aladdin. Presented in a theater large enough to accommodate a 150-foot-wide screen—huge by 3-D movie standards, the 3-D movie is augmented by an arsenal of special effects built into the theater. The plot involves Mickey, as the conductor of the *PhilharMagic,* leaving the theater to solve a mystery. In his absence Donald appears and attempts to take charge, with disastrous results.

The attraction is one of Disney's best 3-D efforts. Brilliantly conceived, furiously paced, and laugh-out-loud funny, *PhilharMagic* incorporates a hit parade of Disney's most beloved characters in a production that will leave you grinning. A North Carolina mother of a 3-year-old, however, accuses us of pulling our punches regarding the show's appropriateness for young children:

I seem to recall you describing PhilharMagic *as funny and cute, and the best of the 3-D movies for kids. It was one of the attractions to which we were most looking forward. Our family, however, found it way too violent (what seemed like minutes on end of Donald getting the crap kicked out of him by various musical instruments). I had to haul my screaming child out of the theater and submit to a therapeutic carousel ride afterwards.*

A Cincinnati couple, on the other hand, survived the show nicely:

Mickey's PhilharMagic *was the surprise sleeper for us. It was truly a wonderful and delightful experience!*

TOURING TIPS Though the other 3-D movies are intense, loud, in-your-face productions, *Mickey's PhilharMagic* is much softer and cuddlier. Things still pop out of the screen in keeping with the time-tested 3-D model, but they're not scary things. Children for once are enthusiastic and astonished instead of quaking in their Nikes. You should still proceed cautiously if you have kids under age 5 in your group, but it's the rare child who is frightened. The show is very popular, but on the other hand, the theater is very large. Except on the busiest of days you shouldn't wait more than 35 minutes (usually less) in the standby line.

Peter Pan's Flight (FASTPASS) ★★★★

APPEAL BY AGE PRESCHOOL ★★★★½ GRADE SCHOOL ★★★★ TEENS ★★★½ YOUNG ADULTS ★★★★ OVER 30 ★★★★ SENIORS ★★★★

What it is Indoor track ride. **Scope and scale** Minor attraction. **When to go** Before 10 a.m., or use FASTPASS after 6 p.m. **Authors' rating** Nostalgic, mellow, and well done; ★★★★. **Duration of ride** A little over 3 minutes. **Average wait in line per 100 people ahead of you** 5½ minutes. **Loading speed** Moderate–slow.

DISNEY DISH WITH JIM HILL

MAKING ROOM FOR MORE PIRATE BOOTY There's a redo in the works for this Fantasyland attraction that the Imagineers aren't eager to talk about. It involves increasing the size of the passenger sections on each of the pirate ships. Why? To put this as politely as possible, people who visit the Magic Kingdom these days have a lot more junk in their trunks than they did back when the park first opened in October 1971.

DESCRIPTION AND COMMENTS Though not considered a major attraction, Peter Pan's Flight is superbly designed and absolutely delightful, with a happy theme uniting some favorite Disney characters, beautiful effects, and charming music. An indoor attraction, Peter Pan's Flight offers a relaxing ride in a "flying pirate ship" over old London and thence to Never-Never Land, where Peter saves Wendy from walking the plank and Captain Hook rehearses for *Dancing with the Stars* on the snout of the ubiquitous crocodile. Unlike Snow White's Scary Adventures, there's nothing here that will jump out at you or frighten young children.

TOURING TIPS Because Peter Pan's Flight is very popular, count on long lines all day. Ride before 10 a.m., during a parade, just before the park closes, or use FASTPASS.

If you use FASTPASS, pick up your pass as early in the day as possible. Sometimes Peter Pan exhausts its whole day's supply of FASTPASSes by 2 p.m.

Pooh's Playful Spot ★★½

APPEAL BY AGE PRESCHOOL ★★★★ GRADE SCHOOL ★★★ TEENS ½ YOUNG ADULTS ★½ OVER 30 ★★ SENIORS ★

What it is Playground for children. **Scope and scale** Minor attraction. **When to go** Anytime. **Special comments** Good resting place for adults. **Authors' rating** A favorite of the 7-and-under crowd; ★★½.

DESCRIPTION AND COMMENTS Located directly across from The Many Adventures of Winnie the Pooh, Pooh's Playful Spot is a playground imaginatively landscaped as a mini-version of the 100-Acre Wood. An oasis from the bustle of Fantasyland, the playground is small enough and sufficiently enclosed for tired parents to easily keep an eye on their kids. You can plop yourself down on one of the thoughtfully placed rustic benches. Fun features for the kids include water fountains, honey pots, crawl-through logs, a treehouse for climbing, and a slide.

TOURING TIPS When you're ready to collapse and your children are still going strong, stake out a bench here and chill until the kids have had their fill.

Snow White's Scary Adventures ★★½

APPEAL BY AGE PRESCHOOL ★★★ GRADE SCHOOL ★★★ TEENS ★★★ YOUNG ADULTS ★★★ OVER 30 ★★★ SENIORS ★★★

What it is Indoor track ride. **Scope and scale** Minor attraction. **When to go** Before 11 a.m. or after 6 p.m. **Special comments** Terrifying to many young children. **Authors' rating** Worth seeing if the wait isn't long; ★★½. **Duration of ride** Almost 2½ minutes. **Average wait in line per 100 people ahead of you** 6¼ minutes. **Loading speed** Moderate–slow.

DISNEY DISH WITH JIM HILL

THERE'S ALWAYS REALITY TV . . . Life isn't always fair, even when you're The Fairest One of All, which is why Snow White fans are sure to be upset when they learn that the Imagineers are considering tearing out this popular dark ride as part of the upcoming Fantasyland redo. Right now, the top two candidates to replace Snow White are a *Beauty and the Beast* attraction or a Disney Princess–themed ride-through.

DESCRIPTION AND COMMENTS Mine cars travel through a spook house showing Snow White as she narrowly escapes harm at the hands of the wicked witch. Action and effects are not as good as Peter Pan's Flight or Winnie the Pooh.

In 2005 we had the good fortune to experience Snow White with Ben, an autistic tyke who, with his family, has seen the attraction more than 2,000 times. His parents—far better people than we—stay sane by thinking of ways to redesign the attraction each time through.

TOURING TIPS Parents, take note: this attraction scares the pants off many children age 6 and younger. Though a 1994 upgrade gave Snow White a larger role, the witch (who is relentless and ubiquitous) continues to be the focal character. Many readers tell us their children have refused to ride any attraction that operates in the dark after having experienced Snow White's Scary Adventures.

A mother from Knoxville, Tennessee, writes:

The outside looks cute and fluffy, but inside, the evil witch just keeps coming at you. My 5-year-old, who rode Space Mountain three times and took The Great Movie Ride's monster from Alien *right in stride, was near panic when our car stopped unexpectedly twice during Snow White.* [After Snow White,] *my 6-year-old niece spent a lot of time asking "if a witch will jump out at you" before other rides. So I suggest that you explain a little more what this ride is about. It's tough on preschoolers who are expecting forest animals and dwarfs.*

A mom from Long Island, New York, adds:

My daughter screamed the whole time and was shot for the day.

Ride Snow White if lines aren't too long or on a second day at the park.

MICKEY'S TOONTOWN FAIR

MICKEY'S TOONTOWN FAIR is the only new "land" to be added to the Magic Kingdom since its opening and the only land that doesn't connect to the central hub. Attractions include an opportunity to meet Mickey Mouse, tour Mickey's and Minnie's houses, and ride a child-sized roller coaster.

Mickey's Toontown Fair is sandwiched between Fantasyland and Tomorrowland, like an afterthought, on about three acres that were formerly part of the Tomorrowland Speedway. It's the smallest of the lands and more like an attraction than a separate section of the park. Though you can wander in on a somewhat obscure path from Fantasyland or on a totally obscure path from Tomorrowland, Mickey's Toontown Fair generally receives guests arriving by the Walt Disney World Railroad.

Opened in 1988 and reworked in 1996 with a county-fair theme, Mickey's Toontown Fair now serves as the Magic Kingdom's character-greeting headquarters. The fair provides a place where Disney characters are available to guests on a continuing and reliable schedule. Mickey, in the role of the fair's chief judge, meets guests for photos and autographs in the Judge's Tent. Other characters appear in the Toontown Hall of Fame. Characters are available throughout the day except during parades.

unofficial **TIP**
If your children are into collecting character autographs and want to enjoy the Toontown attractions without extraordinary waits, we recommend touring the area as soon as Toontown opens.

In general, Mickey's Toontown Fair doesn't handle crowds very well.

If you have only one day to visit the Magic Kingdom and the children-oriented attractions are a priority, head first to Fantasyland and ride Dumbo, Pooh, and Peter Pan, then split for Toontown. In Toontown, first visit the Hall of Fame for character pics and autographs. Ride the Barnstormer at Goofy's Wiseacres Farm next, and then tour Mickey's and Minnie's houses. Be advised that Mickey's Toontown Fair usually opens an hour later than the rest of the park. Consult your *Times Guide* (available at City Hall) for opening times on the day of your visit.

A South Euclid, Ohio, family took our advice and reported these results:

We followed your advice and hit Fantasyland first (9 a.m. to 10 a.m.). I would strongly urge parents with young children to head next to Mickey's Toontown! It opened at 10 a.m. and we went directly to meet Mickey in his house. Then we went to Toontown Hall of Fame. Due to the lack of lines our daughter got to meet all nine characters—in a row—with no line! Another MK guest told us the line had been an hour just the day before. Do Toontown when it opens!

If you plan to remain in the park until closing, follow the example of this family of four from Lewiston, Maine:

A great time to visit [Toontown] *is the final hour the Magic Kingdom is open. We rode the small roller coaster several times in a row without ever leaving our seats (a great thrill for a toddler who spent much of his day in lines). Also, no queues for a visit with Mickey. A great, fun, relaxing end to a busy day.*

For adults without children, Toontown is visually interesting but otherwise expendable.

DISNEY DISH WITH JIM HILL

BUILDING A BIGGER *PLAYHOUSE* **Given the popularity of *Playhouse Disney* among preschoolers, the Imagineers have something big in the works for Mickey's Toontown Fair. It involves flattening everything in this Magic Kingdom "land" (with the possible exception of The Barnstormer at Goofy's Wiseacres Farm) and rebuilding it so that it better reflects the look and the style of the Disney Channel hit. Should Disney Parks and Resorts give its thumbs-up, expect this Meeska-Mooska-makeover to get under way in 2013.**

The Barnstormer at Goofy's Wiseacres Farm ★★

APPEAL BY AGE PRESCHOOL ★★★★ GRADE SCHOOL ★★★★ TEENS ★★★
YOUNG ADULTS ★★ OVER 30 ★★★ SENIORS ★★

What it is Small roller coaster. **Scope and scale** Minor attraction. **When to go** Before 10:30 a.m., during parades, or in the evening just before the park closes. **Special comments** Must be 35" or taller to ride. **Authors' rating** Great for little ones, but not worth the wait for adults; ★★. **Duration of ride** About 53 seconds. **Average wait in line per 100 people ahead of you** 7 minutes. **Loading speed** Slow.

DESCRIPTION AND COMMENTS The Barnstormer is a very small roller coaster. The ride is zippy but supershort. In fact, of the 53 seconds the ride is in motion, 32 seconds are consumed in leaving the loading area, being ratcheted up the first hill, and braking into the off-loading area. The actual time you spend careering around the track is 21 seconds.

A 42-year-old woman from Westport, Connecticut, warns adults that the Barnstormer may not be as tame as it looks:

Goofy's Barnstormer was a nightmare that should have gone in your "Eats Adults" section. It looked so innocent—nothing hidden in the dark, over quickly. . . . It took hours to stop feeling nauseated, my 8-year-old son and I were terrified.

Though the reader's point is well taken, the Barnstormer is a fairly benign introduction to the roller-coaster genre and a predictably positive way to help your children step up to more adventuresome rides. Simply put, a few circuits on the Barnstormer will increase your little one's confidence and improve his or her chances for enjoying Disney's more-adult attractions. As always, be sensitive and encouraging, but respect your child's decision whether or not to ride. Regarding that decision, a Rochester, New York, mom holds out a glimmer of hope:

Our girls, ages 3 and 5, loved Goofy's Barnstormer. It was short but perfect for Mom and Dad, who are prone to motion sickness. There wasn't enough time for us to feel queasy.

TOURING TIPS The cars of this dinky coaster are too small for most adults and tend to whiplash taller people. This, plus the limited capacity, equals an engineering marvel along the lines of Dumbo. Parties without children should skip the Barnstormer. If you're touring with children, you have a problem. Like Dumbo, the ride is visually appealing. All kids want to ride, subjecting the whole family to slow-moving lines. If the Barnstormer is high on your children's hit parade, try to ride as soon as Mickey's Toontown Fair opens.

Donald's Boat ★★½

APPEAL BY AGE	PRESCHOOL ★★★½	GRADE SCHOOL ★★★	TEENS ★½
YOUNG ADULTS ★		OVER 30 ★	SENIORS ★

What it is Playground and (when the water is running) interactive fountain. **Scope and scale** Diversion. **When to go** Anytime. **Authors' rating** A favorite of the 5-and-under set; ★★½.

DESCRIPTION AND COMMENTS Donald's Boat is an interactive playground themed as a fat, cartoon-style tugboat.

TOURING TIPS A great opportunity for easing regimentation and allowing small children to expend pent-up energy.

Mickey's Country House and Judge's Tent ★★★

APPEAL BY AGE	PRESCHOOL ★★★★★	GRADE SCHOOL ★★★★½	TEENS ★★★
YOUNG ADULTS ★★★		OVER 30 ★★★★	SENIORS ★★★★

What it is Walk-through tour of Mickey's house, and meeting with Mickey. **Scope and scale** Minor attraction. **When to go** Before 11:30 a.m. or after 4:30 p.m. **Authors' rating** A glimpse at Mickey's private life; ★★★. **Duration of tour** 15–30 minutes (depending on the crowd). **Average wait in line per 100 people ahead of you** 20 minutes. **Touring speed** Slow.

DESCRIPTION AND COMMENTS Mickey's Country House is the starting point of a self-guided tour through the famous Mouse's house, into his backyard, and past Pluto's doghouse. If you want to tour Mickey's house but skip meeting Mickey, you'll find an exit just before entering his tent.

TOURING TIPS Discerning observers will see immediately that Mickey's Country House is a cleverly devised queuing area for delivering guests to Mickey's Judge's Tent for the Mouse Encounter. It also heightens anticipation by revealing the corporate symbol on a more personal level. Mickey's Country House is well conceived and contains a lot of Disney memorabilia. Children touch *everything* as they proceed through the house, hoping to find some artifact not welded to the set. (An especially tenacious child actually ripped a couple books from a bookcase.)

Meeting Mickey and touring his house are best done during the first hour Mickey's Toontown Fair is open, or in the evening. If meeting the great Mouse is your child's priority, you can be certain of finding Mickey here. Some children are so obsessed with seeing Mickey that they can't enjoy anything else until they have him in the rearview mirror.

Minnie's Country House ★★

APPEAL BY AGE **PRESCHOOL** ★★★★ **GRADE SCHOOL** ★★★★ **TEENS** ★★½
YOUNG ADULTS ★★½ **OVER 30** ★★★ **SENIORS** ★★★

What it is Walk-through exhibit. **Scope and scale** Minor attraction. **When to go** Before 11:30 a.m. or after 4:30 p.m. **Authors' rating** Getting personal with Minnie; ★★. **Duration of tour** About 10 minutes. **Average wait in line per 100 people ahead of you** 12 minutes. **Touring speed** Slow.

DESCRIPTION AND COMMENTS Minnie's Country House offers a self-guided tour through the rooms and backyard of Mickey's main squeeze. Similar to Mickey's Country House, only predictably more feminine, Minnie's house also showcases fun Disney memorabilia. Among highlights of the short tour are the fanciful appliances in Minnie's kitchen.

TOURING TIPS The main difference between Mickey's and Minnie's houses is that Mickey is home to receive guests. Minnie was never home during our visits. We did, however, bump into her on the street and in the Toontown Hall of Fame. Minnie's Country House is one of the more accessible attractions in the Fair, but we nonetheless recommend touring early or late in the day.

Toontown Hall of Fame ★★

APPEAL BY AGE **PRESCHOOL** ★★★★½ **GRADE SCHOOL** ★★★★ **TEENS** ★★★
YOUNG ADULTS ★★ **OVER 30** ★★★ **SENIORS** ★★

What it is Character-greeting venue. **Scope and scale** Minor attraction. **When to go** Before 10:30 a.m. or after 5:30 p.m. **Authors' rating** You want characters? We got 'em! ★★. **Duration of greeting** About 7–10 minutes. **Average wait in line per 100 people ahead of you** 35 minutes. **Touring speed** Slow.

DESCRIPTION AND COMMENTS The Toontown Hall of Fame is at the end of a small plaza between Mickey's and Minnie's houses. It offers one of the largest and most dependably available collections of characters in Walt Disney World. Just inside to the right are entrances to two or three queuing areas; signs over each suggest which characters you will meet. Two queuing areas are almost always dedicated to Disney's princesses (Sleeping Beauty, Snow White, Cinderella, and others) and fairies (Tinker Bell and her posse). If a third greeting area is running, character assortments may change when characters need a break. Besides princesses and fairies, other character groups available include Mickey's Pals, Disney Villains, Characters on Weight Watchers, Corporate Symbols, and so on.

Each category of characters occupies a greeting room where 15 to 20 guests are admitted at a time. They're allowed to stay 7 to 10 minutes, long enough for a photo, autograph, and hug with each character.

TOURING TIPS If your children want to visit each of the three categories, you'll have to queue up three times. Each line is long and slow-moving, and during busier hours you can spend a lot of time here. The longest waits—more than an hour in many cases—are for the princess and fairy "face characters," who wear no head-covering costumes. They are allowed to speak and engage children in conversation, thus prolonging the visit. All characters work in 25-minute shifts, with breaks on the hour and half hour. Because characters change frequently during the day, it's possible to see quite an assortment if you keep recirculating.

If the cast member can't tell you, walk over to the exit and ask departing guests which characters are on duty. Remember that there is some switching of characters on the hour and half hour.

A mother from Winchester, Virginia, reported her solution to seeing characters without waiting in lines:

Some of the things that surprised us, both good and bad, were the crowding and lines to see the characters. We stopped to visit a few, especially when we got lucky with a shorter line, but mostly we couldn't justify stopping at many because we would have missed so many attractions. The best thing we did with regard to the characters was to have the Winnie the Pooh character dinner at The Crystal Palace. Tigger and Pooh are my kids' favorites, and the characters were VERY attentive; my just-turned 3-year-old was in heaven, and we did not have to fight crowds.

On many days, during the first hour the park is open, a multitude of characters roam the Magic Kingdom's streets. It's just like the old days: spontaneous contact and no lines.

TOMORROWLAND

TOMORROWLAND IS A MIX OF rides and experiences relating to the technological development of man and what life will be like in the future. If this sounds like Epcot's theme, it's because Tomorrowland was a breeding ground for ideas that spawned Epcot. Yet, Tomorrowland and Epcot are very different in more than scale. Epcot is more educational. Tomorrowland is more for fun, depicting the future as envisioned in science fiction.

Exhaustive renovation of Tomorrowland was completed in 1995. Before refurbishing, Tomorrowland's 24-year-old buildings resembled 1970s motels more than anyone's vision of the future. The current design is ageless, revealing the future as imagined by dreamers and scientists in the 1920s and 1930s. Today's Tomorrowland conjures visions of Buck Rogers, fanciful mechanical rockets, and metallic cities spread beneath towering obelisks. Disney calls the renovated Tomorrowland the "Future That Never Was," while *Newsweek* dubbed it "retro-future."

Astro Orbiter ★★

APPEAL BY AGE **PRESCHOOL** ★★★★ **GRADE SCHOOL** ★★★½ **TEENS** ★★½
YOUNG ADULTS ★★ **OVER 30** ★★½ **SENIORS** ★

What it is Buck Rogers–style rockets revolving around a central axis. **Scope and scale** Minor attraction. **When to go** Before 11 a.m. or after 5 p.m. **Special comments** This attraction is not as innocuous as it appears. **Authors' rating** Not worth the wait; ★★. **Duration of ride** 1½ minutes. **Average wait in line per 100 people ahead of you** 13½ minutes. **Loading speed** Slow.

Motion Sickness

DESCRIPTION AND COMMENTS Though visually appealing, the Astro Orbiter is still a slow-loading carnival ride. The fat little rocket ships simply fly in circles. The best thing about the Astro Orbiter is the nice view when you're aloft.

TOURING TIPS Expendable on any schedule. If you ride with preschoolers, seat them first, then board. The Astro Orbiter flies higher and faster than Dumbo and frightens some young children. It also apparently messes with some adults. A mother from Lev Hashomnon, Israel, attests:

I think your assessment of [Astro Orbiter] *as "very mild" is way off. I was able to sit through all the "Mountains," the "Tours," and the "Wars" without my stomach reacting even a little, but after* [Astro Orbiter] *I thought I would be finished for the rest of the day. Very quickly I realized that my only chance for survival was to pick a point on the toe of my shoe and stare at it (and certainly not lift my eyes out of the "jet") until the ride was over. My 4-year-old was my copilot; she loved the ride (go figure), and she had us up high the whole time. It was a nightmare—people should be forewarned.*

Buzz Lightyear's Space Ranger Spin (FASTPASS) ★★★★

APPEAL BY AGE PRESCHOOL ★★★★½ GRADE SCHOOL ★★★★½ TEENS ★★★★½
YOUNG ADULTS ★★★★ OVER 30 ★★★★½ SENIORS ★★★★★

What it is Whimsical space travel–themed indoor ride. **Scope and scale** Minor attraction. **When to go** Before 10:30 a.m., after 6 p.m., or use FASTPASS. **Authors' rating** Surreal shooting gallery; ★★★★. **Duration of ride** About 4½ minutes. **Average wait in line per 100 people ahead of you** 3 minutes. **Loading speed** Fast.

DESCRIPTION AND COMMENTS This attraction is based on the space-commando character Buzz Lightyear from the film *Toy Story.* The marginal story line has you and Buzz Lightyear trying to save the universe from the evil Emperor Zurg. The indoor ride is interactive to the extent that you can spin your car and shoot simulated laser cannons at Zurg and his minions.

TOURING TIPS Each car is equipped with two laser cannons and a scorekeeping display. Each scorekeeping display is independent, so you can compete with your riding partner. A joystick allows you to spin the car to line up the various targets. Each time you pull the trigger you'll release a red laser beam that you can see hitting or missing the target. Most folks' first ride is occupied with learning how to use the equipment (fire off individual shots as opposed to keeping the trigger depressed) and figuring out how the targets work. On the next ride (like certain potato chips, one is not enough), you'll surprise yourself by how much better you do. *Unofficial* readers are unanimous in their praise of Buzz Lightyear. Some, in fact, spend several hours on it, riding again and again. The following comments are representative.

From a Yorktown, Virginia, mom:

I am a 44-year-old woman who has never been fond of shoot-'em-up arcade games, but I decided I'd better check out Buzz Lightyear's Space Ranger Spin after the monorail driver told us that it, along with Space Mountain, were her favorite rides at the Magic Kingdom. What a blast! My husband and I enjoyed it every bit as much as our 10-year-old daughter. After riding it the first time, we couldn't wait to ride it again (and again) in an effort to improve our scores. Alas, I was never able to advance beyond Ranger 1st Class although my husband made it all the way to Space Ace. Warning—Buzz Lightyear is addictive!

And from a Snow Hill, Maryland, dad:

Buzz Lightyear was so much fun it can't be legal! We hit it first on early-entry day and rode it ten times without stopping. The kids had fun, but it was Dad who spun himself silly trying to shoot the Zs. This is the most unique, creative ride ever devised.

See Buzz Lightyear after riding Space Mountain first thing in the morning, or use FASTPASS.

Monsters, Inc. Laugh Floor ★★★½

APPEAL BY AGE **PRESCHOOL** ★★★½ **GRADE SCHOOL** ★★★★½ **TEENS** ★★★★
YOUNG ADULTS ★★★★ **OVER 30** ★★★★ **SENIORS** ★★★★

What it is Interactive animated comedy routines. **Scope and scale** Major attraction. **When to go** Before 11 a.m. or after 4 p.m. **Special comments** Audience members may be asked to participate in skits. **Authors' rating** Good concept, although the jokes are hit-and-miss; ★★★½. **Duration of presentation** About 15 minutes.

DESCRIPTION AND COMMENTS We learned in Disney/Pixar's *Monsters, Inc.* that children's screams could be converted into electricity, which was used to power a town inhabited by monsters. During the film, the monsters discovered that children's laughter was an even better source of energy. In this attraction, the monsters have set up a comedy club to capture as many laughs as possible. Mike Wazowski, the one-eyed character from the film, emcees the club's three comedy acts. Each consists of an animated monster (most not seen in the film) trying out various bad puns, knock-knock jokes, and Abbott and Costello–like routines. Using the same cutting-edge technology as Epcot's popular *Turtle Talk with Crush,* behind-the-scenes Disney employees voice the characters and often interact with audience members during the skits. As with any comedy club, some performers are funny and some are not. A good thing about this attraction is that Disney's shown a willingness to try new routines and jokes, so the show should remain fresh to repeat visitors.

A Sioux Falls, South Dakota, mom is a big fan:

> *The* Laugh Floor *was great. It's amazing how the onscreen characters interact with the audience—I got picked on twice without trying. This should definitely be seen; plus, kids are able to text jokes to Roz.*

TOURING TIPS The theater holds several hundred people, so there's no need to rush here first thing in the morning. Try to arrive late in the morning after you've visited other Tomorrowland attractions, or after the afternoon parade when guests start leaving the park.

Space Mountain (FASTPASS) ★★★★

APPEAL BY AGE **PRESCHOOL** ★★½† **GRADE SCHOOL** ★★★★½ **TEENS** ★★★★★
YOUNG ADULTS ★★★★½ **OVER 30** ★★★★½ **SENIORS** ★★★

†Some preschoolers love Space Mountain; others are frightened by it.

What it is Roller coaster in the dark. **Scope and scale** Super-headliner. **When to go** When the park opens, between 6 and 7 p.m., during the hour before closing, or use FASTPASS. **Special comments** Great fun and action; much wilder than Big Thunder Mountain Railroad. Must be 44" tall to ride; children younger than age 7 must be accompanied by an adult. Switching-off option provided (see page 339). **Authors' rating** An unusual roller coaster with excellent special effects; not to be missed; ★★★★. **Duration of ride** Almost 3 minutes. **Average wait in line per 100 people ahead of you** 3 minutes; assumes 2 tracks, 1 dedicated to FASTPASS riders, dispatching at 21-second intervals. **Loading speed** Moderate–fast.

DESCRIPTION AND COMMENTS Totally enclosed in a mammoth futuristic structure, Space Mountain has always been the Magic Kingdom's most popular attraction. The theme is a space flight through dark recesses of the galaxy. Effects are superb, and the ride is the fastest and wildest in the Magic Kingdom. As a roller coaster, Space Mountain is much zippier than Big Thunder Mountain Railroad, but much tamer than the Rock 'n' Roller Coaster at Disney's Hollywood Studios or Expedition Everest at Animal Kingdom.

Roller-coaster aficionados will tell you (correctly) that Space Mountain is a designer version of the Wild Mouse, a midway ride that's been around for at least 50 years. An extensive refurbishment, completed in late 2009, added new lighting and effects, an improved sound system, and a completely redesigned queuing area with interactive games to help pass the time in line. The track was replaced as well but retains the same paths as the old. There are no long drops or swooping hills as there are on a traditional roller coaster—only quick, unexpected turns and small drops. Disney's contribution essentially was to add a space theme to the Wild Mouse and put it in the dark. And this does indeed make the Mouse seem wilder.

A teen from Colchester, Connecticut, wrote us about her bad-hair day:

WARN Space Mountain riders to take off hair scrunchies. I lost my best one on it and couldn't get it back. This ride was fast, curvy, and very hairdo-messing.

Maybe we're getting old, but when we rode Space Mountain this year we found ourselves agreeing with this Raleigh, North Carolina, reader:

If I were in charge, the name would be "Space for Rent Mountain." I found this jerky and worn-out coaster to be quite painful to ride—I had to clasp my hands around my neck to minimize the pain. And I rode Rock 'n' Roller Coaster and Expedition Everest three times each.

A Texas mother of two advises working up to Space Mountain:

You might want to start all children off on Goofy's Barnstormer, then work up to Thunder Mountain and Space Mountain. We tried Space Mountain first because there was no line, and it ruined the boys for the rest of the trip. It was certainly not the Space Mountain I rode in 1984.

TOURING TIPS People who can handle a fairly wild roller-coaster ride will take Space Mountain in stride. What sets Space Mountain apart is that cars plummet through darkness, with only occasional lighting. Half the fun of Space Mountain is not knowing where the car will go next.

Space Mountain is the favorite attraction of many Magic Kingdom visitors ages 7 to 60. Each morning before opening, particularly during summer and holiday periods, several hundred SM "junkies" crowd the rope barriers at the central hub, awaiting the signal to head to the ride's entrance. To get ahead of the competition, be one of the first in the park. Proceed to the end of Main Street and wait at the entrance to Tomorrowland.

Couples touring with children too small to ride Space Mountain can both ride without waiting twice in line by taking advantage of "switching off." Here's how it works: when you enter the Space Mountain line, tell the first Disney attendant (Greeter One) that you want to switch off. The attendant will allow you, your spouse, and your small child (or children) to continue together, phoning ahead to tell Greeter Two to expect you. When you reach Greeter Two (at the turnstile near the boarding area), you'll be given specific directions. One of you will proceed to ride, while the other stays with the kids. Whoever rides will be admitted by the unloading attendant to stairs leading back up to the boarding area. Here you switch off. The second parent rides, and the first parent takes the kids down the stairs to the unloading area where everybody is reunited and exits together. Switching off is also available at Big Thunder Mountain Railroad and Splash Mountain, and for FASTPASS users.

Seats are one behind another, as opposed to side by side. Parents whose children meet the height and age requirements for Space Mountain can't sit next to their kids.

If you don't catch Space Mountain first in the morning, use FASTPASS or try again during the hour before closing. Often, would-be riders are held in line outside the entrance until all those previously in line have ridden, thus emptying the attraction. The appearance from the outside is that the line is enormous when, in fact, the only people waiting are those visible. This crowd-control technique, known as "stacking," discourages visitors from getting in line. Stacking is used at several Disney rides and attractions during the hour before closing to ensure that the ride will be able to close on schedule. It is also used to keep the number of people who are waiting inside from overwhelming the air-conditioning. Despite the apparently long line, the wait is usually no longer than if you had been allowed to queue inside.

Stitch's Great Escape! ★★

APPEAL BY AGE PRESCHOOL ★½ GRADE SCHOOL ★★½ TEENS ★★½
YOUNG ADULTS ★★ OVER 30 ★★ SENIORS ★½

What it is Theater-in-the-round sci-fi adventure show. **Scope and scale** Major attraction. **When to go** Before 11 a.m. or after 6 p.m.; try during parades. **Special comments** Frightens children of all ages. 40" minimum height requirement. **Authors' rating** A cheap coat of paint on a broken car; ★★. **Duration of presentation** About 12 minutes. **Preshow entertainment** About 6 minutes. **Probable waiting time** 12–35 minutes.

DESCRIPTION AND COMMENTS *Stitch's Great Escape!* is a virtual clone of the oft-maligned *Alien Encounter* attraction. Same theater, same teleportation theme, but this time starring the havoc-wreaking little alien from the feature film *Lilo & Stitch.* In *Great Escape!,* Stitch is a prisoner of the galactic authorities and is being transferred to a processing facility en route to his final place of incarceration. He manages to escape by employing an efficient though gross trick, knocking out power to the facility in the process. At this juncture Stitch lumbers around in the dark in much the same way as the theater's previous resident alien. One wonders why an alien civilization smart enough to master teleportation hasn't yet invented a backup power source.

Guest response to this attraction is so overwhelmingly negative that Disney has been trying to plus it up. This comment from a New South Wales, Australia, reader is typical:

> *My comments on* Stitch's Great Escape! *are . . . It STUNK* [writer's emphasis]. *It was the worst ride at Walt Disney World.*

The pitch-black darkness in the ride was changed to dim lighting, and several scenes were reworked in an attempt to make it less frightening. Even these measures may not have been enough, because Disney raised the height requirement from 35 inches to 38 inches, and finally to 40 inches (the same as Big Thunder Mountain Railroad) in an attempt to keep out smaller children. The fact that Big Thunder is a roller coaster and that this ride doesn't move should be a warning to parents about its fright potential. In our opinion, tinkering at the margins will be futile when it comes to resuscitating this puppy.

TOURING TIPS Disney's press release touting Stitch as a child-friendly attraction was about as accurate as Enron's bookkeeping. You're held in your seat by overhead restraints and subjected to something weird clambering around you and whispering to you in a theater darker than a stack of black cats. Stitch is more than enough to scare the pants off many kids ages 6 and younger. *Parents, note:* The overhead restraints will prevent you from leaving your seat to comfort your child if the need arises.

Tomorrowland Speedway ★★

APPEAL BY AGE PRESCHOOL ★★★★ GRADE SCHOOL ★★★★ TEENS ★★★ YOUNG ADULTS ★★½ OVER 30 ★★★ SENIORS ★★½

What it is Drive-'em-yourself miniature cars. **Scope and scale** Major attraction. **When to go** Before 11 a.m. or after 5 p.m. **Special comments** Kids must be 54" tall to drive unassisted. **Authors' rating** Boring for adults (★★); great for preschoolers. **Duration of ride** About 4¼ minutes. **Average wait in line per 100 people ahead of you** 4½ minutes; assumes 285-car turnover every 20 minutes. **Loading speed** Slow.

DESCRIPTION AND COMMENTS An elaborate miniature raceway with gasoline-powered cars that travel up to seven miles per hour. The raceway, with sleek cars and racing noises, is quite alluring. Unfortunately, the cars poke along on a guide rail, leaving the driver little to do. Pretty ho-hum for most adults and teenagers.

TOURING TIPS This ride is visually appealing but definitely one adults can skip. The 9-and-under crowd, however, loves it. If your child is too short to drive, ride along and allow the child to steer the car while you work the foot pedal.

A mom from North Billerica, Massachusetts, writes:

> *I was truly amazed by the number of adults in line. Please emphasize to your readers that these cars travel on a guided path and are not a whole lot of fun. The only reason I could think of for adults to be in the line would be an insane desire to go on absolutely every ride at Disney World. The other feature about the cars is that they tend to pile up at the end, so it takes almost as long to get off as it did to get on. Parents riding with their preschoolers should keep the car going as slow as* [possible] *without stalling. This prolongs the preschooler's joy and decreases the time you will have to wait at the end.*

The line for the Tomorrowland Speedway snakes across a pedestrian bridge to the loading areas. For a shorter wait, turn right off the bridge to the first loading area (rather than continuing to the second).

Tomorrowland Transit Authority ★★★

APPEAL BY AGE PRESCHOOL ★★★★ GRADE SCHOOL ★★★½ TEENS ★★★½
YOUNG ADULTS ★★★★ OVER 30 ★★★★ SENIORS ★★★★

What it is Scenic tour of Tomorrowland. **Scope and scale** Minor attraction. **When to go** Anytime, but especially during hot, crowded times of day (11:30 a.m.–4:30 p.m.). **Special comments** A good way to check out the FASTPASS line at Space Mountain. **Authors' rating** Scenic and relaxing; ★★★. **Duration of ride** 10 minutes. **Average wait in line per 100 people ahead of you** 1½ minutes; assumes 39 trains operating. **Loading speed** Fast.

DESCRIPTION AND COMMENTS A once-unique prototype of a linear-induction-powered mass-transit system, the Authority's tramlike cars carry riders on a leisurely tour of Tomorrowland, including a peek inside Space Mountain. In ancient times the attraction was called the WEDway PeopleMover.

TOURING TIPS A relaxing ride where lines move quickly. It's a good choice during busier times of day, and it can double as a nursery.

A Texas mom writes:

The [Transit Authority] is an excellent ride for getting a tired infant to fall asleep. You can stay on for several times around. It is also a moderately private and comfortable place for nursing an infant.

Walt Disney's Carousel of Progress ★★★

APPEAL BY AGE PRESCHOOL ★★★ GRADE SCHOOL ★★★ TEENS ★★★
YOUNG ADULTS ★★★½ OVER 30 ★★★½ SENIORS ★★★★

What it is Audio-animatronic theater production. **Scope and scale** Major attraction. **When to go** Anytime. **Authors' rating** Nostalgic, warm, and happy; ★★★. **Duration of presentation** 18 minutes. **Preshow entertainment** Documentary on the attraction's long history. **Probable waiting time** Less than 10 minutes.

DESCRIPTION AND COMMENTS Updated and improved during the Tomorrowland renovation, *Walt Disney's Carousel of Progress* offers a nostalgic look at how technology and electricity have changed the lives of an audio-animatronic family over several generations. The family is easy to identify with, and a cheerful, sentimental tune bridges the generations.

TOURING TIPS This attraction is a great favorite among repeat visitors and is included on all our one-day touring plans. The *Carousel* handles big crowds effectively and is a good choice during busier times of day.

LIVE ENTERTAINMENT *in the* MAGIC KINGDOM

BANDS, DISNEY CHARACTER APPEARANCES, parades, ceremonies, and singing and dancing further enliven the Magic Kingdom. For specific events the day you visit, check the live-entertainment schedule in your guide map (free as you enter the park or at City Hall), or in the *Times Guide* available along with the guide map. WDW

unofficial **TIP**
Be aware: If you're short on time, it's impossible to see Magic Kingdom feature attractions and the live performances.

live-entertainment guru Steve Soares usually posts the Magic Kingdom's performance schedule about a week in advance at **pages.prodigy.net/stevesoares.**

Our one-day touring plans exclude live performances in favor of seeing as much of the park as time permits—parades and shows siphon crowds away from popular rides, thus shortening lines. Nonetheless, the color and pageantry of live events are integral to the Magic Kingdom, and a persuasive argument for a second day of touring. Here's a list of some regular performances and events that don't require reservations.

BAY LAKE AND SEVEN SEAS LAGOON FLOATING ELECTRICAL PAGEANT Performed at nightfall (about 9 p.m. most of the year) on Seven Seas Lagoon and Bay Lake, this is one of our favorites among the Disney extras, but it's necessary to leave the Magic Kingdom to view it. The pageant is a stunning electric-light show aboard small barges and set to nifty electronic music. Leave the Magic Kingdom and take the monorail to the Polynesian Resort. Get yourself a drink and walk to the end of the pier to watch the show.

CASTLE FORECOURT STAGE A new 20-minute forecourt show called *Dream Along with Mickey* debuted as part of the Year of a Million Dreams campaign. Featuring Mickey, Minnie, Donald, Goofy, a peck of princesses and other secondary characters, plus human backup dancers, the show is built around the premise that—*quelle horreur!*—Donald doesn't believe in the power of dreams. Crisis is averted through a frenetic whirlwind of song and dance.

The show is performed several times a day according to the season, with showtimes listed in the daily entertainment schedule (*Times Guide*). The Castle Forecourt Stage is elevated well above ground level, so good viewing spots are available all around Main Street's central hub.

DISNEY CHARACTER SHOWS AND APPEARANCES Usually, a number of characters are on hand to greet guests when the park opens. Because they snarl pedestrian traffic and stop most children dead in their tracks, this is sort of a mixed blessing. Most days, a character is on duty for photos and autographs from 9 a.m. to 10 p.m. next to City Hall. Mickey and two or three assortments of other characters are available most of the day at Mickey's Toontown Fair. Shows at the Castle Forecourt Stage feature Disney characters several times daily (check the entertainment schedule, known as the *Times Guide*). In Fantasyland, Ariel can be found in her grotto daily, while a host of others can be seen at the Character Festival next to Dumbo. Assorted characters also roam the park.

unofficial **TIP**
For information on character whereabouts on the day you visit, check the Character Greeting Guide printed on the inside of the handout park map or the *Times Guide.*

MOVE IT! SHAKE IT! CELEBRATE IT! PARADE Starting at the train-station end of Main Street, U.S.A., and working toward the central hub, this short walk incorporates around a dozen guests with a handful of floats, Disney characters, and entertainers. Music is provided by one of Disney's latest artists (Miley Cyrus currently), and there's a good amount of interaction between the entertainers and the crowd. Unless you're already on Main Street, however, or too pooped for anything else, we don't recommend making a special trip to view this parade.

unofficial **TIP**
The only shade nearby is on the Adventureland side of Main Street.

FANTASYLAND PAVILION Site of various concerts in Fantasyland.

FLAG RETREAT At 5 p.m. daily at Town Square (railroad-station end of Main Street). Sometimes performed with great fanfare and college marching bands, sometimes with a smaller Disney band.

FRONTIERLAND HOEDOWN Characters join square dancers and guests for a hoedown in front of the *Country Bear Jamboree;* check the daily entertainment schedule (*Times Guide*).

MAGIC KINGDOM BANDS Banjo, Dixieland, steel drum, marching, and fife-and-drum bands play daily throughout the park.

STORYTIME WITH BELLE AT THE FAIRYTALE GARDEN Belle and several helpers select children from the small amphitheater audience and dress them up as characters from *Beauty and the Beast*. As Belle tells the story, the children act out the roles. There is a three- to five-minute meet-and-greet with photo and autograph opportunities afterward. Storytime is staged six to eight times each day according to the daily entertainment schedule (*Times Guide*). To find the Fairytale Garden, follow the path on the Fantasyland side of the castle moat toward Tomorrowland.

TINKER BELL'S FLIGHT This nice special effect in the sky above Cinderella Castle heralds the beginning of the *Wishes* fireworks show (when the park is open late).

TOMORROWLAND FORECOURT STAGE A two-story space near the Astro Orbiter, used primarily for special events. Notable as the (brief) home of *Stitch's SuperSonic Celebration,* a show so poorly received that it ran for only six weeks in the spring and summer of 2009. (We've eaten yogurt older than that.) For the time being, Disney has no immediate plans to rework the show or introduce others at the venue.

***WISHES* FIREWORKS SHOW** Memorable vignettes and music from beloved Disney films combine with a stellar fireworks display while Jiminy Cricket narrates a lump-in-your-throat story about making wishes come true. For an uncluttered view and lighter crowds, watch from the terrace of the Tomorrowland Terrace Noodle Station. Another good fireworks-viewing area is the second story of the Main Street train station.

***WISHES* FIREWORKS CRUISE** For a different view, you can watch the fireworks from the Seven Seas Lagoon aboard a chartered pontoon boat. The charter costs $275 and accommodates up to ten people. Your Disney captain will take you for a little cruise and then position the boat in a perfect place to watch the fireworks. For an additional $80 per four persons, the captain will provide deli sandwiches, snacks, and beverages. (We hear that this cruise may be rethemed to incorporate pirates sometime in the near future, but details are still sketchy.) A major indirect benefit of the charter is that you can enjoy the fireworks without fighting the mob afterward. Because this is a private charter rather than a tour, only your group will be aboard. Life jackets are provided, but wearing them is at your discretion. To reserve a charter, call ☎ 407-WDW-PLAY at exactly 7 a.m. about 90 days before the day you want to cruise. Because the Disney reservations system counts days in a somewhat atypical manner, we recommend phoning about 95 days out to have a Disney agent specify the exact morning to call for reservations.

PARADES

PARADES AT THE MAGIC KINGDOM ARE FULL-FLEDGED spectaculars with dozens of Disney characters and amazing special effects. We rate the afternoon parade as outstanding and the evening parade as not to be missed.

In addition to providing great entertainment, parades lure guests away from the attractions. If getting on rides appeals to you more than watching a parade, you'll find substantially shorter lines just before and during parades. Because the parade route doesn't pass through Adventureland, Tomorrowland, or Fantasyland, attractions in these lands are particularly good bets. Be forewarned: parades disrupt traffic in the Magic Kingdom. It's nearly impossible, for example, to get to Adventureland from Tomorrowland, or vice versa, during one. Also be advised that the Walt Disney World Railroad shuts down during parades, thus making it impossible to access other lands by train.

AFTERNOON PARADE

USUALLY STAGED AT 3 P.M., this parade features bands, floats, and marching Disney characters. A new afternoon parade is introduced every year or two. While some elements, such as Disney characters, remain constant, the theme, music, and float design change. Seasonal parades during major holidays round out the mix.

EVENING PARADE(S)

THE EVENING PARADE IS A HIGH-TECH affair that employs electroluminescent and fiber-optic technologies, light-spreading thermoplastics (don't try this at home!), and clouds of underlit liquid-nitrogen smoke. Don't worry, you won't need a gas mask or lead underwear to watch. For those who flunked chemistry and physics, the parade also offers music, Mickey Mouse, and twinkling lights.

unofficial **TIP**
Call ☎ 407-824-4321 before you go to be sure the evening parade is on.

The evening parade is staged once or twice each evening, depending on the season. During less busy seasons, the parade is presented only on weekends, and sometimes not even then.

PARADE ROUTE AND VANTAGE POINTS

MAGIC KINGDOM PARADES CIRCLE TOWN SQUARE, head down Main Street, go around the central hub, and cross the bridge to Liberty Square. In Liberty Square, they follow the waterfront and end in Frontierland. Sometimes they begin in Frontierland and run the route in the opposite direction. Most guests watch from the central hub, or

Magic Kingdom Parade Route

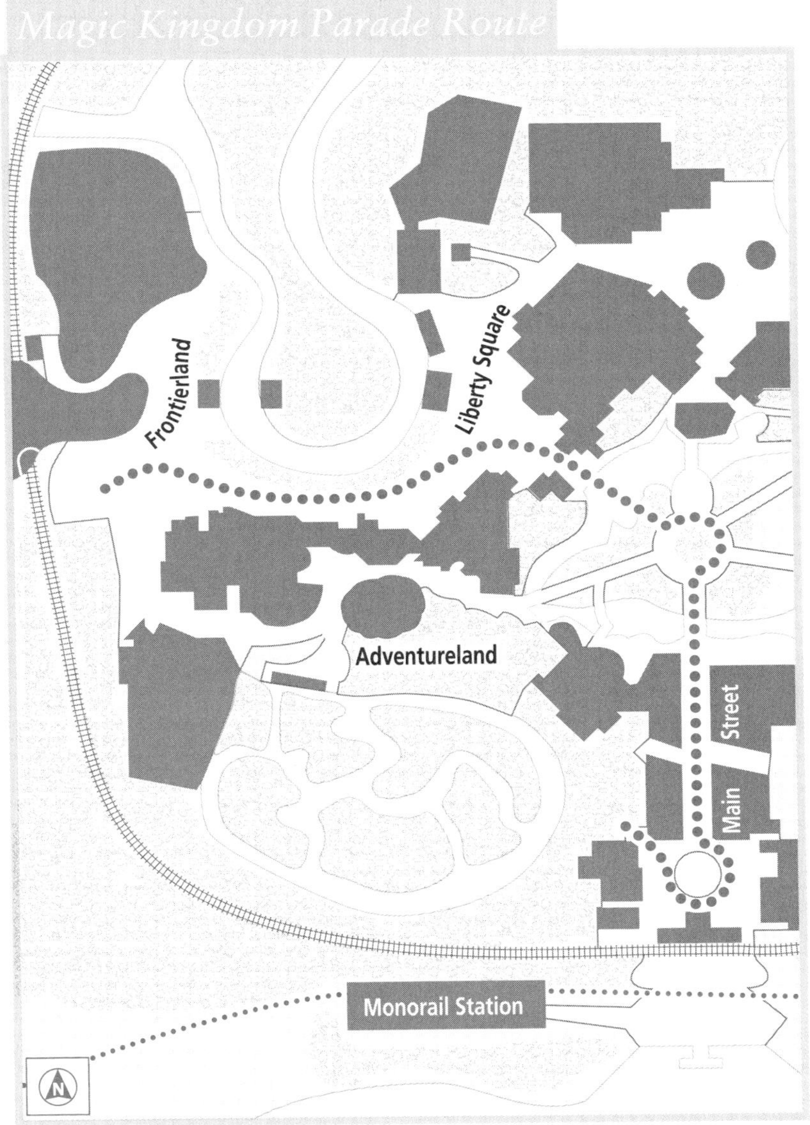

from Main Street. One of the best and most popular vantage points is the upper platform of the Walt Disney World Railroad station at the Town Square end of Main Street. This is also a good place for watching the *Wishes* fireworks show, as well as for ducking out of the park ahead of the crowd when the fireworks end. The problem is, you have to stake out your position 30 to 45 minutes before the events begin.

Because most spectators pack Main Street and the central hub, we recommend watching the parade from Liberty Square or Frontierland. Great vantage points frequently overlooked are as follows:

1. Sleepy Hollow snack-and-beverage shop, immediately to your right as you cross the bridge into Liberty Square. If you arrive early, buy refreshments and claim a table by the rail. You'll have a perfect view of the parade as it crosses Liberty Square Bridge, but only when the parade begins on Main Street.
2. The pathway on the Liberty Square side of the moat from Sleepy Hollow snack-and-beverage shop to Cinderella Castle. Any point along this path offers a clear and unobstructed view as the parade crosses Liberty Square Bridge. Once again, this spot works only for parades coming from Main Street.
3. The covered walkway between Liberty Tree Tavern and The Diamond Horseshoe Saloon. This elevated vantage point is perfect (particularly on rainy days) and usually goes unnoticed until just before the parade starts.
4. Elevated wooden platforms in front of the Frontierland Shootin' Arcade, Frontier Trading Post, and the building with the sign reading FRONTIER MERCANTILE. These spots usually get picked off 10 to 12 minutes before parade time.
5. Benches on the perimeter of the central hub, between the entrances to Liberty Square and Adventureland. Usually unoccupied until after the parade begins, they offer a comfortable resting place and unobstructed (though somewhat distant) view of the parade as it crosses Liberty Square Bridge. What you lose in proximity, you gain in comfort.
6. Liberty Square and Frontierland dockside areas; spots here usually go early.
7. The elevated porch of Tony's Town Square Restaurant on Main Street provides an elevated viewing platform and an easy path to the park exit when the fireworks are over.

Assuming it starts on Main Street (evening parades normally do), the parade takes 16 to 20 minutes to reach Liberty Square or Frontierland.

On evenings when the parade runs twice, the first parade draws a huge crowd, siphoning guests from attractions. Many folks leave the park after the early parade, with many more departing following the fireworks (which are scheduled on the hour between the two parades).

Continue to tour after the fireworks. This is a particularly good time to ride Space Mountain and enjoy attractions in Adventureland. If you are touring Adventureland and the parade begins on Main Street, you won't have to assume your viewing position in Frontierland until 15 minutes after the parade kicks off (the time it takes the parade to reach Frontierland). If you watch from the Splash Mountain side of the street and head for the attraction as the last float passes, you'll be able to ride with only a couple minutes' wait. You might even have time to work in a last-minute ride on Big Thunder Mountain Railroad.

VANTAGE POINTS FOR FIREWORKS

ANYWHERE ALONG MAIN STREET IS FINE for the fireworks. If you plan to leave the park immediately afterward, watch from the train-station end to facilitate a quick departure. Our favorite spot if we intend to remain in the park is the roofless patio of the Plaza Pavilion located in Tomorrowland on the border with Main Street, U.S.A.

unofficial **TIP**
For optimum touring and less congestion, enjoy attractions during the early parade, then break to watch the fireworks.

LEAVING THE PARK AFTER EVENING PARADES AND FIREWORKS

ARMIES OF GUESTS LEAVE THE MAGIC KINGDOM after evening parades and fireworks. The Disney Transportation System (buses, ferries, and monorail) is overwhelmed, causing long waits in boarding areas.

A mother from Kresgeville, Pennsylvania, pleads:

Please stress how terrifying these crowds can be. Our family of five made the mistake of going to the MK the Saturday night before Columbus Day to watch the parade and fireworks. Afterwards, we lingered at The Crystal Palace to wait for the crowds to lessen, but it was no use. We started walking toward the gates and soon became trapped by the throng, not able to go forward or back. There was no way to cross the hordes to get to the dock for our hotel's launch. Our group became separated, and it became a living nightmare. We left the park at 10:30 p.m. and didn't get back to the Polynesian (less than a mile away) until after midnight. How dare they expose children to that nightmare! Even if they were to raise Walt Disney himself from cryogenic sleep and parade him down Main Street, I would never go to the MK on a Saturday night again!

An Oklahoma City dad offers this advice:

Never, never leave the Magic Kingdom just after the 10 p.m. fireworks. I have never seen so many people in one spot before. Go for another ride—no lines because everyone else is trying to get out!

Congestion persists from the end of the early evening parade until closing time. Most folks watch the early parade and then the fireworks a few minutes later. If you're parked at the Transportation and Ticket Center and are intent on beating the crowd, view the early parade from the Town Square end of Main Street, leaving the park as soon as the parade ends.

If you're staying at a Disney hotel not served by the monorail and must depend on Disney transportation, watch the early parade and fireworks at the park and then enjoy the attractions until about 20 to 25 minutes before the late parade is scheduled to begin. At this time, leave the park and catch the Disney bus or boat back to your hotel. Don't cut it too close: Main Street will be so congested that you won't be able to reach the exit.

Here's what happened to a family from Cape Coral, Florida:

We tried to leave the park before the parade began. However, Main Street was already packed and we didn't see any way to get out of the park, so we were stuck. In addition, it was impossible to move across the street, and even the shops were so crowded that it was virtually impossible to maneuver a stroller through them to get close to the entrance.

If you don't have a stroller (or are willing to forgo the $1 return refund for rental strollers), catch the Walt Disney World Railroad in Frontierland or Mickey's Toontown Fair and ride to the park exit at Main Street.

If you plan to escape by train, don't cut it too close.

If you're on the Tomorrowland side of the park, it's actually possible for you to exit during a parade. Leaving Tomorrowland, cut through Tomorrowland Terrace Noodle Station. Before you reach Main Street, bear left into the side door of the corner shop. Once inside, you'll see that Main Street shops have interior doors allowing you to pass from one shop to the next without having to get on Main Street. Work your way from shop to shop until you reach Town Square (easy, because people will be outside, watching the parade). At Town Square, bear left and move to the train station and the park exit.

unofficial **TIP**
Be aware that the railroad shuts down during parades because the floats must cross the tracks when entering or exiting the parade route in Frontierland.

This strategy won't work if you're on the Adventureland side of the park. You can make your way through Casey's Corner restaurant to Main Street and then work your way through the interior of the Main Street shops, but when you pop out of the Emporium at Town Square, you'll be trapped by the parade. As soon as the last float passes, however, you can bolt for the exit.

Another strategy for beating the masses out of the park (if your car is at the TTC lot) is to watch the early parade and then leave before the fireworks begin. Line up for the ferry. One will depart about every eight to ten minutes. Try to catch the ferry that will be crossing Seven Seas Lagoon while the fireworks are in progress. The best vantage point is on the top deck to the right of the pilothouse as you face the Magic Kingdom; the sight of fireworks silhouetting the castle and reflecting off Seven Seas Lagoon is unforgettable. While there's no guarantee that a ferry will load and depart within three or four minutes of the fireworks, your chances are about 50–50 of catching it just right. If you're in the front of the line for the ferry and don't want to board the boat that's loading, stop at the gate and let people pass you. You'll be the first to board the next boat.

TRAFFIC PATTERNS *in the* MAGIC KINGDOM

WHEN WE RESEARCH THE MAGIC KINGDOM, we study its traffic patterns, asking:

1. WHICH SECTIONS OF THE PARK AND WHAT ATTRACTIONS DO GUESTS VISIT FIRST? When visitors are admitted to the lands during summer and holiday periods, traffic to Tomorrowland and Frontierland is heaviest, followed by Fantasyland, Adventureland, Liberty Square, and Mickey's Toontown Fair.

During the school year, when fewer young people are in the park, early-morning traffic is more evenly distributed but remains heaviest in

ATTRACTIONS THAT GET CROWDED EARLY

Tomorrowland	Space Mountain
	Buzz Lightyear's Space Ranger Spin
Frontierland	Splash Mountain
	Big Thunder Mountain Railroad
Fantasyland	Dumbo the Flying Elephant
	The Many Adventures of Winnie the Pooh
	Peter Pan's Flight
Adventureland	Jungle Cruise

Tomorrowland, Frontierland, and Fantasyland. Our researchers tested the frequent claim that most people turn right into Tomorrowland and tour the Magic Kingdom in a counterclockwise sequence. We found the claim to be baseless.

2. HOW LONG DOES IT TAKE FOR THE PARK TO FILL UP? HOW ARE THE VISITORS DISPERSED IN THE PARK? A surge of "early birds" arrives before or around opening time but is quickly dispersed throughout the empty park. After the initial wave is absorbed, there's a lull lasting about an hour after opening. Then the park is inundated for about two hours, peaking between 10 a.m. and noon. Arrivals continue in a steady but diminishing stream until around 2 p.m. The lines we sampled were longest between 1 and 2 p.m., indicating more arrivals than departures into the early afternoon. For touring purposes, most attractions develop long lines between 10 and 11:30 a.m.

unofficial **TIP**
As the park fills up, visitors head for the top attractions before lines get long. This, more than anything else, determines morning traffic patterns.

From late morning until early afternoon, guests are equally distributed through all the lands. However, guests concentrate in Fantasyland, Liberty Square, and Frontierland in late afternoon, with a decrease of visitors in Adventureland and Tomorrowland. Adventureland's Jungle Cruise and Tomorrowland's Buzz Lightyear and Space Mountain continue to be crowded, but most other attractions in those lands are readily accessible.

3. HOW DO MOST VISITORS TOUR THE PARK? Do first-time visitors tour differently from repeat guests? Many first-time visitors are guided by friends or relatives familiar with the Magic Kingdom. These tours may or may not follow an orderly sequence. First-time visitors without personal guides tend to be more orderly in their touring. Many first-time visitors, however, are drawn to Cinderella Castle upon entering the park and thus begin their rotation from Fantasyland. Repeat visitors usually go directly to their favorite attractions.

4. HOW DOES FASTPASS AFFECT CROWD DISTRIBUTIONS? The effect is subtle and depends somewhat on the time interval between when the FASTPASS is obtained and the FASTPASS return period. For example, guests who receive a FASTPASS for Splash Mountain at 10 a.m. with an 11:05 a.m. to 12:05 p.m. return window tend to tour near Splash

Mountain in the interim to minimize the inconvenience of backtracking when it's time to use the pass. However, when the return period is several hours distant, guests don't feel compelled to stay in the immediate area. In general, you won't notice much difference in crowd concentrations because of FASTPASS, but empirically speaking, it increases crowds within proximity of the two anchor attractions, Space Mountain and Splash Mountain, throughout the day.

5. HOW DO SPECIAL EVENTS, SUCH AS PARADES AND LIVE SHOWS, AFFECT TRAFFIC PATTERNS? Parades pull huge numbers of guests away from attractions and provide a window of opportunity for experiencing the more popular attractions with less of a wait. Castle Forecourt Stage shows also attract crowds but only slightly affect lines.

6. WHAT ARE THE TRAFFIC PATTERNS NEAR AND AT CLOSING TIME? On our sample days, in busy times and off-season at the park, departures outnumbered arrivals beginning in midafternoon. Many visitors left in late afternoon as the dinner hour approached. When the park closed early, guests departed steadily during the two hours before closing, with a huge exodus at closing time. When the park closed late, a huge exodus began immediately after the early-evening parade and fireworks, with a second mass departure after the late parade, continuing until closing. Because Main Street and the transportation services remain open after the other six lands close, crowds leaving at closing mainly affect conditions on Main Street and at the monorail-, ferry-, and bus-boarding areas. In the hour before closing, the other six lands are normally uncrowded.

MAGIC KINGDOM TOURING PLANS

STARTING ON PAGE 815, our step-by-step touring plans are field-tested for seeing *as much as possible* in one day with a minimum of time wasted in lines. They're designed to help you avoid crowds and bottlenecks on days of moderate-to-heavy attendance. Understand, however, that there's more to see in the Magic Kingdom than can be experienced in one day. Since we first began covering the Magic Kingdom, four headliner attractions and an entire new land have been added. Today, even if you could experience every attraction without any wait, it would still be virtually impossible to see all of the park in a single day.

unofficial **TIP**
Don't worry that other people will be following the plans and render them useless. Fewer than 1 in every 350 people in the park will have been exposed to this info.

On days of lighter attendance (see "Selecting the Time of Year for Your Visit," page 33), our plans will save you time but won't be as critical to successful touring as on busier days.

CHOOSING THE APPROPRIATE TOURING PLAN

WE PRESENT FIVE MAGIC KINGDOM TOURING PLANS:

- Magic Kingdom One-day Touring Plan for Adults

- Authors' Selective Magic Kingdom One-day Touring Plan for Adults
- Magic Kingdom One-day Touring Plan for Parents with Young Children
- Magic Kingdom Dumbo-or-Die-in-a-Day Touring Plan for Parents with Young Children
- Magic Kingdom Two-day Touring Plan

If you have two days (or two mornings) at the Magic Kingdom, the Two-day Touring Plan is *by far* the most relaxed and efficient. The two-day plan takes advantage of early morning, when lines are short and the park hasn't filled with guests. This plan works well year-round and eliminates much of the extra walking required by the one-day plans. No matter when the park closes, our two-day plan guarantees the most efficient touring and the least time in lines. The plan is perfect for guests who wish to sample both the attractions and the atmosphere of the Magic Kingdom.

unofficial **TIP**
Switching off allows adults to enjoy the more adventuresome attractions while keeping the group together.

If you only have one day but wish to see as much as possible, then use the One-day Touring Plan for Adults. It's exhausting, but it packs in the maximum. If you prefer a more relaxed visit, use the Authors' Selective One-day Touring Plan. It includes the best the park has to offer (in the authors' opinion), eliminating the less-impressive attractions.

If you have children younger than age 8, adopt the One-day Touring Plan for Parents with Young Children. It's a compromise, blending the preferences of younger children with those of older siblings and adults. The plan includes many children's rides in Fantasyland but omits roller-coaster rides and other attractions that frighten young children or are off-limits because of height requirements. Or, use the One-day Touring Plan for Adults or the Authors' Selective One-day Touring Plan and take advantage of switching off, a technique whereby children accompany adults to the loading area of a ride with age and height requirements but don't board (see page 339).

The Dumbo-or-Die-in-a-Day Touring Plan for Parents with Young Children is designed for parents who will withhold no sacrifice for their kids. On the Dumbo-or-Die Plan, adults generally stand around, sweat, wipe noses, pay for stuff, and watch the children enjoy themselves. It's great!

"Not a Touring Plan" Touring Plans

For the type-B reader, these touring plans (see page 811) avoid detailed step-by-step strategies for saving every last minute in line. To paraphrase one of our favorite movies, they're more guidelines than actual rules. Use these to avoid the longest waits in line while having maximum flexibility to see whatever interests you in a particular part of the park.

For the Magic Kingdom, these "not" touring plans include advice for adults and parents with one day in the park, for anyone with two days, and for anyone with an afternoon and a full day to tour.

Two-day Touring Plan for Families with Young Children

If you have young children and are looking for a two-day itinerary, combine the Magic Kingdom One-day Touring Plan for Parents with Young Children with the second day of the Magic Kingdom Two-day Touring Plan.

Two-day Touring Plan for Early-morning Touring on Day One and Afternoon–Evening Touring on Day Two

Many of you enjoy an early start at the Magic Kingdom on one day, followed by a second day with a lazy, sleep-in morning, resuming your touring in the afternoon and/or evening. If this appeals to you, use the Magic Kingdom One-day Touring Plan for Adults or the Magic Kingdom One-day Touring Plan for Parents with Young Children on your early day. Adhere to the touring plan for as long as it feels comfortable (many folks leave after the afternoon parade). On the second day, pick up where you left off. If you intend to use FASTPASS on your second day, try to arrive at the park by 1 p.m. or the FASTPASSes may be gone. Customize the remaining part of the touring plan to incorporate parades, fireworks, and other live performances according to your preferences.

MAGIC KINGDOM TOURING-PLAN COMPANION

WE'VE CONSOLIDATED A GREAT DEAL OF INFORMATION about the Magic Kingdom in the Magic Kingdom Touring-plan Companion, located at the back of the guide just after the various touring plans. Like the plans, the companions are designed to clip out and take with you to the park. The Magic Kingdom Touring-plan Companion includes the best days to go, the best times to visit each attraction, the authors' rating, height requirements, small-child fright potential, and info on dining and cool places to take a break.

THE SINGLE-DAY TOURING CONUNDRUM

TOURING THE MAGIC KINGDOM IN A DAY is complicated by the fact that the premier attractions are at almost opposite ends of the park: Splash Mountain and Big Thunder Mountain Railroad in Frontierland and Space Mountain and Buzz Lightyear in Tomorrowland. It's virtually impossible to ride all four without encountering lines at one or another. If you ride Space Mountain and see Buzz Lightyear immediately after the park opens, you won't have much of a wait, if any. By the time you leave Tomorrowland and hurry to Frontierland, however, the line for Splash Mountain will be substantial. The same situation prevails if you ride the Frontierland duo first: Splash Mountain and Big Thunder Mountain Railroad, no problem; Space Mountain and Buzz Lightyear, fair-sized lines. From ten minutes after opening until just before closing, lines are long at these headliners.

The best way to ride all four without long waits is to tour the Magic Kingdom over two mornings: ride Space Mountain first thing one morning, then ride Buzz Lightyear; then ride Splash Mountain and Big Thunder Mountain first thing on the other. If you have only one day, be present at opening time. Speed immediately to Space Mountain, then take in Buzz Lightyear. After Buzz Lightyear, rush to

Frontierland and scope out the situation at Splash Mountain. If the posted wait time is 30 minutes or less, go ahead and hop in line. If the wait exceeds 30 minutes, get a FASTPASS for Splash Mountain, then ride Big Thunder Mountain Railroad.

PRELIMINARY INSTRUCTIONS FOR ALL MAGIC KINGDOM TOURING PLANS

On days of moderate-to-heavy attendance, follow your chosen touring plan exactly, deviating only:

1. When you aren't interested in an attraction it lists. For example, the plan may tell you to go to Tomorrowland and ride Space Mountain. If you don't enjoy roller coasters, skip this step and proceed to the next.
2. When you encounter a very long line at an attraction the touring plan calls for. Crowds ebb and flow at the park, and an unusually long line may have gathered at an attraction to which you're directed. For example, you arrive at The Haunted Mansion and find extremely long lines. It's possible that this is a temporary situation caused by several hundred people arriving en masse from a recently concluded performance of *The Hall of Presidents* nearby. If this is the case, skip The Haunted Mansion and go to the next step, returning later to retry.

WHAT TO DO IF YOU GET OFF-TRACK

IF AN UNEXPECTED INTERRUPTION OR PROBLEM throws the plan off, see "Magic Kingdom: Recommended Attraction Visitation Times" (pages 813 and 814) for the preferred times of day to visit attractions.

PARK-OPENING PROCEDURES

Your success during your first hour of touring will be affected somewhat by the opening procedure Disney uses that day:

1. All guests are held at the turnstiles until the entire park opens (which may or may not be at the official opening time). If this happens on the day you visit, blow past Main Street and head for the first attraction on the touring plan you're following.
2. Guests are admitted to Main Street a half hour to an hour before the remaining lands open. Access to other lands will be blocked by a rope barrier at the central-hub end of Main Street. Once admitted, stake out a position at the rope barrier as follows:

   If you're going to Frontierland first (Splash Mountain and Big Thunder Mountain Railroad), stand in front of The Crystal Palace restaurant, on the left at the central-hub end of Main Street. Wait next to the rope barrier blocking the walkway to Adventureland. When the rope is dropped, move quickly to Frontierland by way of Adventureland. This is also the place to line up if your first stop is Adventureland.

   If you're going to Buzz Lightyear and Space Mountain first, wait at the entrance of the bridge to Tomorrowland. When the rope drops, walk quickly across into Tomorrowland.

   Between Fantasyland and Tomorrowland is Toontown, which opens at 10 a.m. If you're going to Fantasyland or Liberty Square first, go to the end of Main Street and line up left of center at the rope.

BEFORE YOU GO

1. Call ☎ 407-824-4321 the day before you go to check the official opening time.
2. Purchase admission before you arrive.
3. Get familiar with park-opening procedures (see previous page) and reread the plan you've chosen so you know what you're likely to encounter.

MAGIC KINGDOM ONE-DAY TOURING PLAN FOR ADULTS (see page 815)

FOR Adults without young children.

ASSUMES Willingness to experience all major rides (including roller coasters) and shows.

This plan requires a lot of walking and some backtracking to avoid lines. Extra walking and morning hustling will spare you three or more hours of standing in line. How far you get depends on how quickly you move from ride to ride, how many times you rest or eat, how quickly the park fills, and what time the park closes.

AUTHORS' SELECTIVE MAGIC KINGDOM ONE-DAY TOURING PLAN FOR ADULTS (see page 816)

FOR Adults touring without young children.

ASSUMES Willingness to experience all major rides (including roller coasters) and shows.

This plan includes only the attractions we think are best. It requires a lot of walking and some backtracking to avoid lines. How far you get depends on how quickly you move from ride to ride, how many times you rest or eat, how quickly the park fills, and what time the park closes.

MAGIC KINGDOM ONE-DAY TOURING PLAN FOR PARENTS WITH YOUNG CHILDREN (see page 817)

FOR Parents with children younger than age 8.

ASSUMES Periodic stops for rest, restrooms, and refreshments.

This plan represents a compromise between the observed tastes of adults and those of younger children. Included are many amusement-park rides that children may have the opportunity to experience at fairs and amusement parks back home. Although these rides are included in the plan, omit them if possible. These cycle-loading rides often have long lines, consuming valuable touring time:

Cinderella's Golden Carousel	Mad Tea Party
Dumbo the Flying Elephant	The Magic Carpets of Aladdin

This time could be better spent experiencing the many attractions that better demonstrate the Disney creative genius and are found only in the Magic Kingdom. Instead of this plan, try either of the one-day plans for adults and take advantage of "switching off." This allows parents and young children to enter the ride together. At the boarding area, one parent watches the children while the other rides.

We recommend taking a break and returning to your hotel for a swim and a nap (even if you're not staying in the World). You won't see as much, but everyone will be more relaxed and happy.

This touring plan requires a lot of walking and some backtracking to avoid long lines. A little extra walking and some morning hustle will spare you two to three hours of standing in line. You probably won't complete the tour. How far you get depends on how quickly you move from ride to ride, how many times you rest or eat, how quickly the park fills, and what time the park closes.

unofficial **TIP**
Before entering the park, decide whether you will return to your hotel for a midday rest.

To Convert This One-day Touring Plan into a Two-day Touring Plan

Skip Steps 14 to 23 on the first day. On the second day, arrive 30 minutes prior to opening, take the Walt Disney World Railroad from Main Street to Frontierland, and pick up the plan with Step 15, but do not use FASTPASS unless the wait exceeds 35 minutes.

MAGIC KINGDOM DUMBO-OR-DIE-IN-A-DAY TOURING PLAN FOR PARENTS WITH YOUNG CHILDREN (see page 818)

FOR Adults compelled to devote every waking moment to the pleasure and entertainment of their young children, or rich people who are paying someone else to take their children to the theme park.

PREREQUISITE This plan is designed for days when the Magic Kingdom doesn't close until 9 p.m. or later.

ASSUMES Frequent stops for rest, restrooms, and refreshments.

Note: Name aside, this plan is no joke. Whether you're loving, guilty, masochistic, selfless, or insane, this itinerary will provide a youngster with about as perfect a day as is possible at the Magic Kingdom.

This plan is a concession to adults determined to give their young children the ultimate Magic Kingdom experience. If you left the kids with a sitter yesterday or wouldn't let little Marvin eat barbecue for breakfast, the plan will expiate your guilt.

To Convert This One-day Touring Plan into a Two-day Touring Plan

Skip Steps 16 and 17 on the first day. On the second day, arrive 30 minutes prior to opening and take the Walt Disney World Railroad from Main Street to Mickey's Toontown Fair. See the fair in its entirety.

MAGIC KINGDOM TWO-DAY TOURING PLAN

(see pages 819 and 820)

FOR Those wishing to spread their Magic Kingdom visit over two days.

ASSUMES Willingness to experience all major rides (including roller coasters) and shows.

Timing: This two-day touring plan takes advantage of early-morning touring. Each day, you should complete the structured part of the plan by about 4 p.m. This leaves plenty of time for live entertainment. If the park is open late (after 8 p.m.), consider returning to your hotel at midday for a swim and a nap. Eat an early dinner outside Walt Disney World and return refreshed to enjoy the park's nighttime festivities.

PART TWELVE

EPCOT

OVERVIEW

EDUCATION, INSPIRATION, AND CORPORATE IMAGERY are the focus at Epcot, the most adult of the Disney theme parks. What it gains in taking a futuristic, visionary, and technological look at the world, it loses just a bit in warmth, happiness, and charm.

Some people find the attempts at education to be superficial, while others want more entertainment and less education. Most visitors, however, are in between, finding plenty of entertainment *and* education.

unofficial **TIP**
Visitors must be prepared to do considerable walking between attractions and a comparable amount of standing in line.

Epcot is more than twice as big as the Magic Kingdom or Disney's Hollywood Studios and, though smaller than Animal Kingdom, has more territory to be covered on foot. Epcot rarely sees the congestion so common in the Magic Kingdom, but it has lines every bit as long as those at the Jungle Cruise or Space Mountain.

Epcot's size means you can't see it all in one day without skipping an attraction or two and giving others a cursory glance. A major difference between Epcot and the other parks, however, is that some Epcot attractions can be savored slowly or skimmed, depending on personal interests. For example, the first section of General Motors' Test Track is a thrill ride, the second a collection of walk-through exhibits. Nearly all visitors take the ride, but many people, lacking time or interest, bypass the exhibits.

We've identified several Epcot attractions as not to be missed. But part of the enjoyment of the park is that there's something for everyone.

OPERATING HOURS

EPCOT HAS TWO THEMED AREAS: Future World and World Showcase. Each has its own operating hours. Though schedules change throughout the year, Future World always opens before World Showcase in the morning and usually closes before World Showcase in the evening. Most of the year, World Showcase opens two hours later than Future World. Moreover, some attractions open late or close early. For exact park hours during your visit, call ☎ 407-824-4321.

For the operating schedule of specific attractions, check the park handout map or the supplemental *Times Guide*, available throughout the park at no charge.

unofficial **TIP**
Plan to arrive at the turnstiles 30–40 minutes before official opening time. Give yourself an extra 10 minutes or so to park and make your way to the entrance.

ARRIVING

IF YOU ARE A GUEST AT ONE OF THE EPCOT resorts, it will take you about 20 to 30 minutes to walk from your hotel to the International Gateway (back entrance of Epcot) and from there to the Future World section of the park. Instead of walking, you can catch a boat from your Epcot resort hotel to the International Gateway and then walk about eight minutes to the Future World section. To reach the front (Future World) entrance of Epcot from the Epcot resorts, either take a boat from your hotel to Disney's Hollywood Studios and transfer to an Epcot bus, take a bus to Downtown Disney and transfer to an Epcot bus, or best of all, take a cab.

If you're wondering what all the fuss is about, this reader offers a succinct explanation:

> *Epcot touring plans don't work well if you stay at an Epcot resort. People from the Epcot resorts enter the park at the International Gateway, far away from Test Track* [in Future World]. *We were first in the park from the International Gateway, but when we got to Test Track the line was already 95 minutes long.*

Arriving at the park by private automobile is easy and direct. Epcot has its own parking lot and, unlike at the Magic Kingdom, there's no need to take a monorail or ferry to reach the entrance. Trams serve the parking lot, or you can walk to the front gate. Monorail service connects Epcot with the Transportation and Ticket Center, the Magic Kingdom (transfer required), and Magic Kingdom resorts (transfer required).

GETTING ORIENTED

EPCOT'S THEMED AREAS ARE DISTINCTLY different. Future World examines where mankind has come from and where it's going. World Showcase features the landmarks, cuisine, and culture of almost a dozen nations and is meant to be a sort of permanent World's Fair.

Navigating Epcot is unlike getting around at the Magic Kingdom. The Magic Kingdom is designed so that nearly every location is part

Not to Be Missed at Epcot

World Showcase	*The American Adventure*	*IllumiNations*
Future World	*Honey, I Shrunk the Audience*	Living with the Land
Mission: Space	The Seas	Soarin'
Spaceship Earth	Test Track	

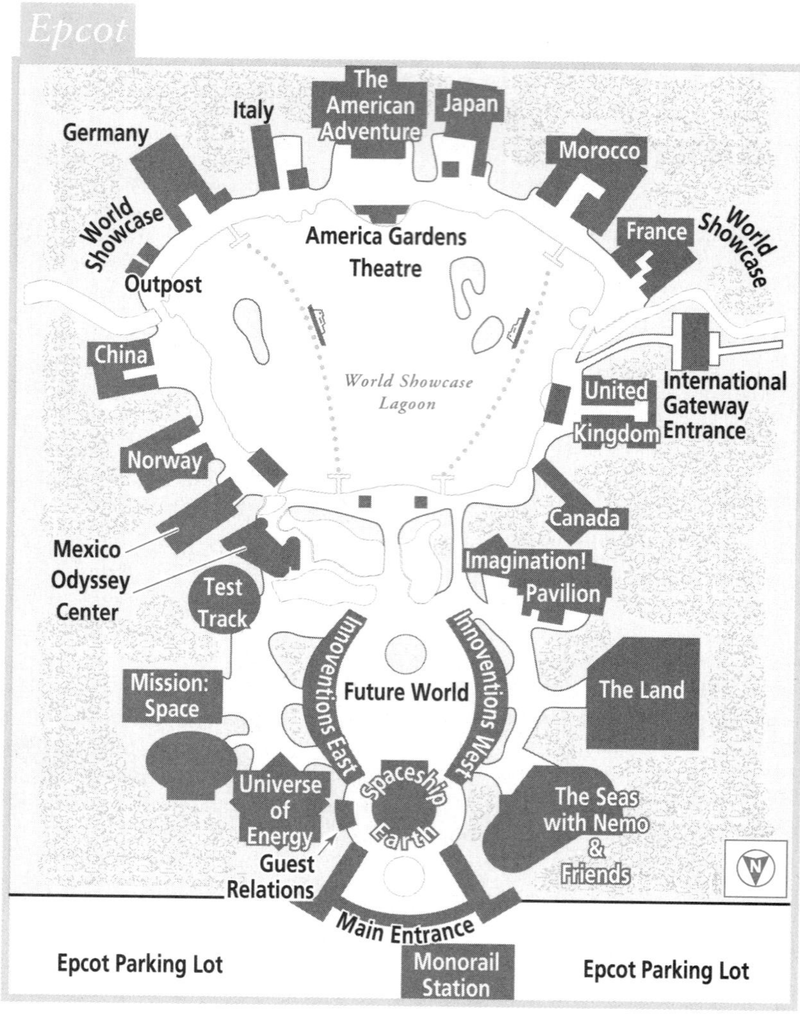

Epcot

of a specific environment—Liberty Square or Main Street, U.S.A., for example. All environments are visually separated to preserve the integrity of the theme.

Epcot, by contrast, is visually open. And while it seems strange to see a Japanese pagoda and the Eiffel Tower on the same horizon, getting around is fairly simple. An exception is Future World, where the enormous Innoventions East and West buildings hide everything on their opposite sides.

At Epcot, the architectural symbol is Spaceship Earth. This shiny, 180-foot geosphere is visible from almost everywhere in the park. Like Cinderella Castle at the Magic Kingdom, Spaceship Earth can help you keep track of where you are in Epcot. But it's in a high-traffic area and isn't centrally located, so it isn't a good meeting place.

Any of the distinctive national pavilions in World Showcase make a good meeting place, but be specific. "Hey, let's meet in Japan!" sounds fun, but each pavilion is a mini-town with buildings, monuments, gardens, and plazas. You could wander quite a while "in Japan" without finding your group. Pick a specific place in Japan—the sidewalk side of the pagoda, for example.

THE EPCOT ACRONYM

ORIGINALLY, Epcot was EPCOT. When envisioned by Walt Disney as a utopian working city of the future, EPCOT was the acronym for Experimental Prototype Community of Tomorrow. Corporate Disney ultimately altered Walt's vision, and the city became a theme park, but the name remained. And because EPCOT was clearly nothing of the sort, the acronym EPCOT became the name "Epcot."

FUTURE WORLD

GLEAMING FUTURISTIC STRUCTURES of immense proportions define the first themed area beyond the main entrance. Broad thoroughfares are punctuated with billowing fountains—all reflected in shiny space-age facades. Everything, including landscaping, is sparkling clean and seems bigger than life. Front and center is **Spaceship Earth,** flanked by **Innoventions East and West,** while pavilions dedicated to mankind's past, present, and future technological accomplishments ring the perimeter of Future World.

Future World Services

Epcot's service facilities in Future World include:

Baby Center/Baby Care Needs On the World Showcase side of the Odyssey Center

Banking Services ATMs outside the main entrance near the kennels, on the Future World bridge, and in World Showcase at the Germany Pavilion

Dining Reservations At Guest Relations

First Aid Next to the Baby Center on the World Showcase side of the Odyssey Center

Live Entertainment Information At Guest Relations, to the left of Spaceship Earth

Lost and Found At the main entrance at the gift shop

Lost Persons At Guest Relations and the Baby Center on the World Showcase side of the Odyssey Center

Storage Lockers Turn right at Spaceship Earth (lockers emptied nightly)

Walt Disney World and Local Attraction Information At Guest Relations

Wheelchair and Stroller Rentals Inside the main entrance and to the left, toward the rear of the Entrance Plaza

Most Epcot services are concentrated in Future World's Entrance Plaza, near the main gate.

GUEST RELATIONS

GUEST RELATIONS, LEFT OF THE GEODESIC SPHERE, is Epcot's equivalent of the Magic Kingdom's City Hall. It serves as park headquarters and as Epcot's primary information center. If you wish to eat in one of Epcot's sit-down restaurants and have not made a reservation by calling ☎ 407-WDW-DINE, you can make a reservation at Guest Relations or at any other sit-down restaurant in any of the parks. If you're near one of these locations, it's often faster than calling.

Innoventions ★★★½

APPEAL BY AGE **PRESCHOOL** ★★★½ **GRADE SCHOOL** ★★★★ **TEENS** ★★★½
YOUNG ADULTS ★★★ **OVER 30** ★★★ **SENIORS** ★★★

What it is Static and hands-on exhibits relating to products and technologies of the near future. **Scope and scale** Major diversion. **When to go** On your second day at Epcot or after you've seen all the major attractions. **Special comments** Most exhibits demand time and participation to be rewarding—there's not much gained here by a quick walk-through. **Authors' rating** Something for everyone; ★★★½.

DISNEY DISH WITH JIM HILL

THERE ARE NO SMALL PARTS, ONLY SMALLER PAYCHECKS **Several longtime entertainers at Pleasure Island's Adventurers Club and Comedy Warehouse eventually found refuge at Epcot when those two venues closed for good in September 2008. These talented actors and actresses now hawk Velcro in the "What's Your Problem?" show while they wait for their next big break.**

DESCRIPTION AND COMMENTS Innoventions, a huge, busy collection of walk-through, hands-on exhibits sponsored by corporations, consists of two huge, crescent-shaped, glass-walled structures separated by a central plaza. Dynamic, interactive, and forward-looking, the area resembles a high-tech trade show. Products preview consumer and industrial goods of the near future. Electronics, communications, and entertainment technology play a prominent role. Exhibits, many of which are changed each year, demonstrate such products as virtual-reality games, high-definition TV, voice-activated appliances, future cars, medical diagnostic equipment, and Internet applications. Each of the major exhibit areas is sponsored by a different manufacturer or research lab, emphasizing the effect of the products or technology on daily living. The most popular Innoventions attraction is an arcade of video and simulator games. One of the coolest exhibits, however, is the demonstration area for the Segway Human Transporter, the much-publicized two-wheeled vehicle that makes riders look as if they're standing on top of a push lawn mower. A limited number of brief test rides are also offered to the general public. Check back at Segway Central (Innoventions West) from early afternoon until Innoventions closes, typically around 7 p.m.

Exhibits change periodically, and there is a definite trend toward larger, more elaborate exhibits, almost mini-attractions. The newer exhibits are certainly more compelling, but they require waiting in line to be admitted. Because the theater at each exhibit is quite small, you often wait as long for an Innoventions infomercial as for a real attraction elsewhere in the park.

A father of three from Tulsa, Oklahoma, liked Innoventions:

The best things at Epcot for my kids were the hands-on exhibits at Innoventions. We bumped into the computer games there as we were passing through en route to something else (I don't remember what, because we never got there).

TOURING TIPS Innoventions East and West provide visitors an opportunity to preview products of tomorrow in a fun, hands-on manner. Some exhibits are intriguing, while others are less compelling. We observed a wide range of reactions by visitors to the exhibits and can suggest only that you form your own opinion. Regarding touring strategy, spend time at Innoventions on your second day at Epcot. If you have only one day, visit later in the day if you have the time and endurance. Many exhibits, however, are technical and may not be compatible with your mood or energy toward the end of a long day.

Also, you can't get much out of a walk-through; you have to invest time to understand what's going on. We've seen a trend at Innoventions toward exhibits that feature shows or activities staged in small theaters. Although many of these productions are quite worthwhile, the guest capacity of each theater is so small that long lines form. A couple of exhibits, such as Where's the Fire?—an interactive program about fire safety—are worth 15 minutes of waiting in line, but they're the exception. We suggest skipping exhibits with waits of more than ten minutes or experiencing them first thing in the morning when there are no lines.

Club Cool

DESCRIPTION AND COMMENTS Attached to the fountain side of Innoventions West is a retail space–soda fountain called Club Cool. It doesn't look like much, but inside, this Coca-Cola–sponsored exhibit provides free unlimited samples of soft drinks from around the world. Some of the selections will taste like medicine to an American, but others will please. Because it's centrally located in Future World, it makes a good meeting or break place, and you can slake your thirst while you wait for the rest of your party.

Spaceship Earth ★★★★

APPEAL BY AGE PRESCHOOL ★★★★ GRADE SCHOOL ★★★★ TEENS ★★★★
YOUNG ADULTS ★★★★ OVER 30 ★★★★ SENIORS ★★★★½

What it is Educational dark ride through past, present, and future. **Scope and scale** Headliner. **When to go** Before 10 a.m. or after 4 p.m. **Special comments** If lines are long when you arrive, try again after 4 p.m. **Authors' rating** One of Epcot's best; not to be missed; ★★★★. **Duration of ride** About 16 minutes. **Average wait in line per 100 people ahead of you** 3 minutes. **Loading speed** Fast.

DESCRIPTION AND COMMENTS This ride spirals through the 18-story interior of Epcot's premier landmark, taking visitors past audio-animatronic scenes depicting mankind's developments in communications, from cave painting to printing to television to space communications and computer networks. The ride is well done and an amazing use of the geosphere's interior.

In 2007, Spaceship Earth completed its most significant renovation since opening. New scenes have been added, including a 1970s-era computer room and a home garage showing what looks suspiciously like the invention of the Apple personal computer (perhaps a homage to Steve Jobs, Disney's largest individual shareholder). New interactive video screens on the ride vehicles allow you to customize the ride's ending animated video. A new narrator (Dame Judi Dench), a new musical score, and improved lighting were also installed. A new postshow area with games and interactive exhibits rounds out the upgrades. We're happy to see this excellent ride get the TLC it deserves.

Apart from going deaf, a family of five from Columbus, Ohio, wrote approvingly of Spaceship Earth's makeover:

We loved the new Spaceship Earth—the kids really thought it was hilarious at the end with the new interactive screen. I did think the volume was too high, however. I felt like the voice was screaming in my ear the whole ride.

TOURING TIPS Because it's near Epcot's main entrance, Spaceship Earth is inundated with arriving guests throughout the morning. If you're interested in riding Test Track, postpone Spaceship Earth until, say, after 4 p.m. Spaceship Earth loads continuously and quickly. If the line runs only along the right side of the sphere, you'll board in less than 15 minutes.

THE SEAS WITH NEMO AND FRIENDS PAVILION

THIS AREA COMPRISES one of America's top marine aquariums, a ride that tunnels through the aquarium, an interactive animated film, and a number of first-class educational walk-through exhibits. Altogether it's a stunning package, one we rate as not to be missed. A comprehensive makeover featuring characters from the animated feature *Finding Nemo* brought some whimsy and much-needed levity to what theretofore was educationally brilliant but somewhat staid.

The Seas Main Tank and Exhibits ★★★½

APPEAL BY AGE **PRESCHOOL** ★★★★ **GRADE SCHOOL** ★★★★ **TEENS** ★★★★
YOUNG ADULTS ★★★★ **OVER 30** ★★★★ **SENIORS** ★★★★

What it is A huge saltwater aquarium, plus exhibits on oceanography, ocean ecology, and sea life. **Scope and scale** Major attraction. **When to go** Before 11:30 a.m. or after 5 p.m. **Authors' rating** An excellent marine exhibit; ★★★½. **Average wait in line per 100 people ahead of you** 3½ minutes. **Loading speed** Fast.

DESCRIPTION AND COMMENTS The Seas is among Future World's most ambitious offerings. Scientists and divers conduct actual marine experiments in a 200-foot-diameter, 27-foot-deep main tank containing fish, mammals, and crustaceans in a simulation of an ocean ecosystem. Visitors can watch the activity through eight-inch-thick windows below the surface (including some in the Coral Reef restaurant). On entering The Seas, you're directed to the loading area for The Seas with Nemo & Friends, an attraction that conveys you via a Plexiglas tunnel through the Seas' main tank. Following the ride, you disembark at Sea Base Alpha, where you can enjoy the attractions mentioned previously. (If the wait for the ride is too long, it's possible to head straight for the exhibits by going through the pavilion's exit, around back, and to the left of the main entrance.)

The Seas' fish population is substantial, but the strength of this attraction lies in the dozen or so exhibits offered after the ride. Visitors can view fish-breeding experiments, watch short films about sea life, and more. A delightful exhibit showcases clownfish (Nemo), regal blue tang (Dory), and other species featured in Disney/Pixar's *Finding Nemo*. Other highlights include a haunting, hypnotic jellyfish tank; a sea horse aquarium; a stingray exhibit; and a manatee tank.

About two-thirds of the main aquarium is home to reef species, including sharks, rays, and a number of fish that you've seen in quiet repose on your dinner plate. The other third, separated by an inconspicuous divider, houses bottle-nosed dolphins and sea turtles. As you face the main aquarium, the most glare-free viewing windows for the dolphins are on the ground floor to the left by the escalators. For the reef species, it's the same floor on the right by the escalators. Stay as long as you wish.

TOURING TIPS With the addition of *Turtle Talk with Crush* and The Seas with Nemo & Friends, The Seas has been transformed from a Future World backwater into one of Epcot's most popular venues. We recommend experiencing the ride and *Turtle Talk* in the morning before the park gets crowded, saving the excellent exhibits for later.

The Seas with Nemo & Friends ★★★

APPEAL BY AGE PRESCHOOL ★★★★½ GRADE SCHOOL ★★★★ TEENS ★★★
YOUNG ADULTS ★★★½ OVER 30 ★★★½ SENIORS ★★★★

What it is Ride through a tunnel in The Seas' main tank. **Scope and scale** Major attraction. **When to go** Before 11 a.m. or after 5 p.m. **Authors' rating** ★★★. **Duration of ride** 4 minutes. **Average wait in line per 100 people ahead of you** 3½ minutes. **Loading speed** Fast.

DISNEY DISH WITH JIM HILL

PEACH SINGS THE BLUES **When you exit your clam-mobile, keep an eye and an ear out for Peach the starfish, who has some of the funniest lines in this entire attraction. Among her best moments is when she pleads with WDW visitors to take her with them. Poor Peach is literally stuck inside The Seas with Nemo & Friends, which means that she's also stuck listening to an infinite loop of the attraction's anthem, "Big Blue World." "I mean, it's a nice song," she grouses. "But it just never stops. I mean, *never.* Never ever ever . . ."**

DESCRIPTION AND COMMENTS The Seas with Nemo & Friends is a high-tech ride featuring characters from the animated hit *Finding Nemo.* The ride likewise deposits you at the heart of The Seas, where the exhibits, *Turtle Talk with Crush,* and viewing platforms for the main aquarium are located.

Upon entering The Seas, you're given the option of experiencing the ride or proceeding directly to the exhibit area. If you choose the ride, you'll be ushered to its loading area, where you'll be made comfortable in a "clam-mobile" for your journey through the aquarium. The attraction features technology that makes it seem as if the animated characters are swimming with live fish. Very cool. Almost immediately you meet Mr. Ray and his class and learn that Nemo is missing. The remainder of the odyssey consists of finding Nemo with the help of Dory, Bruce, Marlin, Squirt, and Crush, all characters from the animated feature. Unlike the film, however, the ride ends with a musical finale.

A reader from Fishers, Indiana, offers this critique:

The Seas with Nemo & Friends attraction was great with effects and theming. There were several blunders in it, though: (1) you didn't have much time to see or comprehend what was being displayed in each scene, and (2) it wasn't designed very well—you could hear scenes being repeated from behind, and sometimes you couldn't hear or see all of one scene.

And a mom from Asheville, North Carolina, warns about underestimating the scare factor:

You need to change the fear rating for The Seas with Nemo & Friends! It IS scary—sharks, jellyfish, and anglerfish, along with growling, etc. My 8-year-old hated it!

TOURING TIPS The ride is new, and anything starring Nemo is an instant draw, so expect good-sized crowds throughout the day. The earlier you experience the ride the better; ditto for *Turtle Talk with Crush.* If waits are intolerable, come back after 5 p.m. or so.

Turtle Talk with Crush ★★★★

APPEAL BY AGE PRESCHOOL ★★★★½ GRADE SCHOOL ★★★★½ TEENS ★★★★
YOUNG ADULTS ★★★★ OVER 30 ★★★★ SENIORS ★★★★

What it is An interactive animated film. **Scope and scale** Minor attraction. **When to go** Before 11 a.m. or after 5 p.m. **Authors' rating** A real spirit lifter; ★★★★. **Duration of presentation** 17 minutes. **Preshow entertainment** None. **Probable waiting time** 10–20 minutes before 11 a.m. and after 5 p.m.; as much as 40–60 minutes during the more crowded part of the day.

DESCRIPTION AND COMMENTS *Turtle Talk with Crush* is an interactive theater show starring the 153-year-old surfer-dude turtle from the Disney/Pixar film *Finding Nemo*. Although it starts like a typical Disney theme-park movie, *Turtle Talk* quickly turns into a surprise interactive encounter as the on-screen Crush begins to have actual conversations with guests in the audience. Real-time computer graphics are used to accurately move Crush's mouth when forming words, and he's voiced by a guy who went to the *Fast Times at Ridgemont High* school of diction.

A mom from Henderson, Colorado, has a crush on Crush:

Turtle Talk with Crush *is a must-see. Our 4-year-old was picked out of the crowd by Crush, and we were just amazed by the technology that allowed one-on-one conversation. It was adorable and enjoyed by everyone from Grammy and Papa to the 4-year-old!*

TOURING TIPS The interactive technology behind *Turtle Talk* proved so successful in drawing crowds that a follow-up attraction, *Monsters, Inc. Laugh Floor*, debuted in the Magic Kingdom's Tomorrowland in 2007. *Turtle Talk* has also moved to a new, larger theater in an attempt to shorten waits, which sometimes exceeded an hour. Still, the attraction's capacity is relatively small, so you'll want to get here as early as you can to avoid long lines.

THE LAND PAVILION

DESCRIPTION AND COMMENTS The Land is a huge themed area containing three attractions and several restaurants. When the pavilion was originally built, its emphasis was on farming, but it now focuses on the environment.

TOURING TIPS This is a good place to grab a fast-food lunch. If you're coming here to see the attractions, however, stay away during mealtimes.

The Circle of Life ★★★½

APPEAL BY AGE PRESCHOOL ★★★ GRADE SCHOOL ★★★ TEENS ★★★
YOUNG ADULTS ★★★ OVER 30 ★★★ SENIORS ★★★½

DISNEY DISH WITH JIM HILL

RECYCLING ON A CINEMATIC SCALE If you missed out on seeing *Earth,* the new documentary that Disneynature released in April 2009, not to worry. The Imagineers are reportedly repurposing that footage as a new 15-minute-long version to replace *The Circle of Life,* which has been playing in The Land's Harvest Theater since January 1995. Look for this recycled version of *Earth* to make its Future World premiere in 2011, just in time for WDW's 40th-anniversary celebration.

What it is Film exploring man's relationship with his environment. **Scope and scale** Minor attraction. **When to go** Before 11 a.m. or after 2 p.m. **Authors' rating** Highly interesting and enlightening; ★★★½. **Duration of presentation** About 12½ minutes. **Preshow entertainment** Ecological slide show and trivia. **Probable waiting time** 10–15 minutes.

DESCRIPTION AND COMMENTS This playful yet educational film, starring Simba, Timon, and Pumbaa from Disney's animated feature *The Lion King,* spotlights the environmental interdependency of all creatures, demonstrating how easily the ecological balance can be upset. The message is sobering, but one that enlightens.

A reader e-mailed us this comment:

> The Circle of Life *is somewhat hypocritical. Simba berates Timon and Pumbaa because they don't understand the ecological impact of putting up a resort. Hello—am I missing something, or didn't Disney do just that?*

TOURING TIPS Every visitor should see this film. To stay ahead of the crowd, see it in late afternoon. Long lines usually occur at mealtimes.

Living with the Land (FASTPASS) ★★★★

APPEAL BY AGE PRESCHOOL ★★★½ GRADE SCHOOL ★★★½ TEENS ★★★★
YOUNG ADULTS ★★★★ OVER 30 ★★★★ SENIORS ★★★★

What it is Indoor boat-ride adventure chronicling the past, present, and future of farming and agriculture in the United States. **Scope and scale** Major attraction. **When to go** Before 10:30 a.m. or after 5 p.m, or use FASTPASS. **Special comments** Go early in the morning and save other Land attractions (except for Soarin') for later in the day. The ride is located on the pavilion's lower level. **Authors' rating** Interesting, fun, and not to be missed; ★★★★. **Duration of ride** About 12 minutes. **Average wait in line per 100 people ahead of you** 3 minutes; assumes 15 boats operating. **Loading speed** Moderate.

DESCRIPTION AND COMMENTS The boat ride takes visitors through swamps, past inhospitable farm environments, and through a futuristic, innovative greenhouse where real crops are grown using the latest agricultural technologies. It's inspiring and educational, with excellent effects and good narrative. Stars of the greenhouse include giant pumpkins and a "tomato tree" that has produced a world-record harvest of more than 20,000 tomatoes with a total weight in excess of 850 pounds.

Many Epcot guests who read about Living with the Land in guidebooks decide it sounds too dry and educational for their tastes. A woman from Houston writes:

> *I had a bad attitude about Living with the Land, as I heard it was an agricultural exhibit. I just didn't think I was up for a movie about wheat farming.*

Wow, was I surprised. I really wished I had not had a preconceived idea about an exhibit. Living with the Land was truly wonderful.

TOURING TIPS See this attraction before the lunch crowd hits The Land's restaurants, or use FASTPASS. If you have a special interest in the agricultural techniques being demonstrated, take the Behind the Seeds tour (see page 629).

Soarin' (FASTPASS) ★★★★½

APPEAL BY AGE **PRESCHOOL** ★★★★ **GRADE SCHOOL** ★★★★★ **TEENS** ★★★★★
YOUNG ADULTS ★★★★★ **OVER 30** ★★★★★ **SENIORS** ★★★★★

What it is Flight-simulation ride. **Scope and scale** Super-headliner. **When to go** First 30 minutes the park is open, or use FASTPASS. **Special comments** Entrance on the lower level of the Land Pavilion. May induce motion sickness; 40" minimum height requirement; switching off available (see page 339). **Authors' rating** Exciting and mellow at the same time; ★★★★½. Not to be missed. **Duration of ride** 5½ minutes. **Average wait in line per 100 people ahead of you** 4 minutes; assumes 2 concourses operating. **Loading speed** Moderate.

DESCRIPTION AND COMMENTS Soarin' is a thrill ride for all ages, exhilarating as a hawk on the wing and as mellow as swinging in a hammock. If you are fortunate enough to have experienced flying dreams in your sleep, you'll have a sense of how Soarin' feels.

Once you enter the main theater, you are secured in a seat not unlike those on inverted roller coasters (where the coaster is suspended from above). When everyone is in place, the rows of seats swing into position, making you feel as if the floor has dropped away, and you are suspended with your legs dangling. Thus hung out to dry, you embark on a simulated hang-glider tour with IMAX-quality images projected all around you, and with the flight simulator moving in sync with the movie. The IMAX images are well chosen and drop-dead beautiful. Special effects include wind, sound, and even olfactory stimulation. The ride itself is thrilling but perfectly smooth. We think Soarin' is a must-experience for guests of any age who meet the height requirement. And yes, we interviewed senior citizens who tried the ride and were crazy about it.

TOURING TIPS Soarin' joins Test Track and Mission: Space as an Epcot super-headliner attraction. Its addition to the lineup takes some of the pressure off the park's other two big attractions. Keep in mind, however, that Test Track and Mission: Space serve up a little too much thrill for some guests. Soarin', conversely, is an almost platonic ride for any age. For that reason, it has climbed to the top of the hit parade. See it before 10:30 a.m., or use FASTPASS. If you opt for the latter, don't expect there to be any passes left after 12:30 p.m. or so.

IMAGINATION! PAVILION

DESCRIPTION AND COMMENTS Multiattraction pavilion on the west side of Innoventions West and down the walk from The Land. Outside is an "upside-down waterfall" and one of our favorite Future World landmarks, the "jumping water," a fountain that hops over the heads of unsuspecting passersby.

TOURING TIPS We recommend late-morning touring. See individual attractions for specifics.

Honey, I Shrunk the Audience ★★★★½

APPEAL BY AGE PRESCHOOL ★★★★½ GRADE SCHOOL ★★★★ TEENS ★★½
YOUNG ADULTS ★★ OVER 30 ★★½ SENIORS ★★

What it is 3-D film with special effects. **Scope and scale** Headliner. **When to go** Before noon or after 4 p.m. **Special comments** Adults should not be put off by the sci-fi theme. The loud, intense show with tactile effects frightens some young children. **Authors' rating** An absolute hoot! Not to be missed; ★★★★½. **Duration of presentation** About 17 minutes. **Preshow entertainment** 8 minutes. **Probable waiting time** 15 minutes (at suggested times).

DESCRIPTION AND COMMENTS *Honey, I Shrunk the Audience* is a 3-D offshoot of Disney's feature film *Honey, I Shrunk the Kids. Honey, I Shrunk the Audience* features an array of special effects, including simulated explosions, smoke, fiber optics, lights, water spray, and moving seats. This attraction is played strictly for laughs, a commodity that's in short supply when it comes to Epcot entertainment.

TOURING TIPS Shows usually begin on the hour and half hour. The sound level is earsplitting, frightening some young children. Many adults report that the loud soundtrack is distracting, even uncomfortable. While *Honey, I Shrunk the Audience* is a huge hit, it overwhelms some preschoolers. A dad from Lexington, South Carolina, writes:

> Honey, I Shrunk the Audience *is too intense for kids. Our 4-year-old took off his* [3-D] *glasses five minutes into the movie. Because of this experience, he would not wear glasses in the Muppet movie at* [Disney's Hollywood Studios].

A Tucson, Arizona, mom tells of a similar reaction:

> *Our 3- and 4-year-olds loved all the rides. They giggled through Thunder Mountain three times, squealed with delight on Splash Mountain, thought Space Mountain was the coolest, and begged to ride Star Tours over and over. They even "fought ghosts" at The Haunted Mansion. But* Honey, I Shrunk the Audience *dissolved them into sobbing, sniveling, shaking, terrified preschoolers.*

Try to work the film into your touring before 10:30 a.m. The show is to the left of Journey into Imagination (see below); you don't have to ride in order to enter the theater. Avoid seats in the first several rows; if you sit too close to the screen, the 3-D images don't focus properly.

Journey into Imagination with Figment ★★½

APPEAL BY AGE PRESCHOOL ★★★★ GRADE SCHOOL ★★★½ TEENS ★★★
YOUNG ADULTS ★★★ OVER 30 ★★★ SENIORS ★★★

What it is Dark fantasy-adventure ride. **Scope and scale** Major-attraction wannabe. **When to go** Anytime. **Authors' rating** ★★½. **Duration of ride** About 6 minutes. **Average wait in line per 100 people ahead of you** 2 minutes. **Loading speed** Fast.

DESCRIPTION AND COMMENTS This attraction replaced its dull and vacuous predecessor in the fall of 1999 and was retooled again in 2002 to add the ever-popular purple dragon, Figment. Drawing on the Imagination Institute theme from *Honey, I Shrunk the Audience* (in the same pavilion), the attraction takes you on a tour of the zany Institute. Sometimes you're a passive observer and sometimes you're a test subject as the ride provides a glimpse of the fictitious lab's inner workings. Stimulating all your senses and then some, you are hit with optical illusions, an experiment in which noise generates colors, a room that defies gravity, and other brain teasers.

DISNEY DISH WITH JIM HILL

IMAGEWORKS TO GET WORKING AGAIN? Folks who visited EPCOT Center back in the 1980s have fond memories of the interactive play area that used to occupy the second floor of this Future World Pavilion. Since ImageWorks closed back in 1998, the space has been used mostly for storage and corporate events. But now the Imagineers are considering reopening this long-unused portion of Imagination! and installing a new generation of interactive exhibits.

All along the way, Figment makes surprise appearances. After the ride, you can adjourn to an interactive exhibit area offering the latest in unique, hands-on imagery technology. One of the coolest interactive exhibits is a photo-morphing computer. First the machine takes your picture, then you select an image from several categories into which your photo is integrated. The final result can be e-mailed on the spot to family and friends. Best of all, there's no charge. We sent a number of photos in which our faces were morphed into pandas, lions, lizards, even a great owl!

Although Journey into Imagination with Figment has certainly improved, it pales in comparison with *Honey, I Shrunk the Audience,* the hilarious 3-D film that occupies the other half of the Imagination! Pavilion. Pleasant rather than stimulating, the ride falls short of the promise suggested by its name. Will you go to sleep? No. Will you find it amusing? Probably. Will you remember it tomorrow? Only Figment.

TOURING TIPS The standby wait for this attraction rarely exceeds 15 minutes. You can enjoy the interactive exhibit without taking the ride, so save it for later in the day.

TEST TRACK PAVILION

DESCRIPTION AND COMMENTS Test Track, presented by General Motors, contains the Test Track ride and Inside Track, a collection of transportation-themed stationary exhibits and multimedia presentations. The pavilion is the last on the left before crossing into the World Showcase. Many readers tell us that Test Track "is one big commercial" for General Motors. We agree that promotional hype is more heavy-handed here than in most other business-sponsored attractions. But Test Track is one of the most creatively conceived and executed attractions in Walt Disney World.

Test Track (FASTPASS) ★★★½

APPEAL BY AGE PRESCHOOL ★★★★ GRADE SCHOOL ★★★★½ TEENS ★★★★★ YOUNG ADULTS ★★★★½ OVER 30 ★★★★½ SENIORS ★★★★

What it is Automobile test-track simulator ride. **Scope and scale** Super-headliner. **When to go** The first 30 minutes the park is open, just before closing, or use FASTPASS. **Special comments** 40" height minimum. **Authors' rating** Not to be missed; ★★★½. **Duration of ride** About 4 minutes. **Average wait in line per 100 people ahead of you** 4½ minutes. **Loading speed** Moderate–fast.

DESCRIPTION AND COMMENTS Visitors test a future-model car at high speeds through hairpin turns, up and down steep hills, and over rough terrain. The six-guest vehicle is a motion simulator that rocks and pitches. Unlike the Star Tours simulator, however, the Test Track model is affixed to a track and actually travels.

DISNEY DISH WITH JIM HILL <JH5>

"START YOUR ENGINES" = "PRESS 'PLAY' " All that tire squealing and motor revving can get pretty loud at the Test Track pavilion—but the ride vehicles themselves are actually very quiet. Because the cars run on a 250-hp electric motor, they hum as they zoom overhead at 65 mph. So where is all that realistic-sounding racetrack noise coming from? It's just sound effects that the Imagineers pipe in to make this experience seem that much more authentic.

Though reader comments on Test Track have been mixed, most like it. From a Shippensburg, Pennsylvania, couple:

We did wait about 30 minutes for Test Track and it was worth it! At first we thought it was a bit of a bust, as the beginning of the ride is not very exciting (though it was interesting), but the last minute or so made up for it!

A Westford, Massachusetts, family agrees:

Test Track was the favorite ride at WDW of all five members of our party. Even my mom ([age] 56), who has always refused to go on roller coasters, was coaxed onto Test Track and loved it. Five stars from one preschooler, three over-30s, and a senior citizen!

But a Monona, Wisconsin, couple were somewhat underwhelmed:

In regard to Test Track, while it was a good ride, it was overrated. Based on the loud whoosh coming from the ride, the build-up in the preshow area, and your comments, I expected a much more intense experience. Compared to the Tower of Terror, Test Track is a Sunday drive in the park.

TOURING TIPS Some great technology is at work here. Test Track is so complex, in fact, that keeping it running is a constant challenge. When it's working properly, it's one of the park's better attractions. But as a Bluemont, Virginia, man wryly reports, it has more than its share of downtime:

GM's and Disney's inability to keep this ride running consistently is no great advertisement for GM products.

If you use FASTPASS, be aware that the daily allocation of passes is often distributed by 12:30 or 1 p.m. If all the FASTPASSes are gone, another time-saving technique is to join the singles line, a separate line for individuals who do not object to riding alone. The objective is to fill the odd spaces left by groups that don't fill up the ride vehicle. Because there are not many singles, and because most groups are unwilling to split up, singles lines are usually much shorter than the regular line.

Mission: Space (FASTPASS) ★★★★

APPEAL BY AGE PRESCHOOL ★★½ GRADE SCHOOL ★★★★ TEENS ★★★★½
YOUNG ADULTS ★★★★ OVER 30 ★★★★ SENIORS ★★★

What it is Space-flight-simulation ride. **Scope and scale** Super-headliner. **When to go** First hour the park is open, or use FASTPASS. **Special comments** Not recommended for pregnant women or people prone to motion sickness or claustrophobia; 44" minimum height requirement; a gentler nonspinning version is also available. **Authors' rating** Impressive; ★★★★. **Duration of ride** About 5 minutes plus preshow. **Average wait in line per 100 people ahead of you** 4 minutes.

DESCRIPTION AND COMMENTS Mission: Space, among other things, is Disney's reply to all the cutting-edge attractions introduced over the past few years by crosstown rival Universal. The first truly groundbreaking Disney attraction since *The Twilight Zone* Tower of Terror, Mission: Space was one of the hottest tickets at Walt Disney World until two guests died after riding it in 2005 and 2006. While neither death was linked directly to the attraction, the negative publicity caused many guests to skip it entirely. In response, Disney added a tamer nonspinning version of Mission: Space in 2006.

Disney's lawyers probably clocked as much time as the ride engineers in designing the "lite" version. Even before you walk into the building, you're asked whether you want your ride with or without spin. Choose the spinning version and you're on the "orange" team; the "green" team trains on the no-spin side. Either way, you're immediately handed the appropriate "launch ticket" containing the first of myriad warnings about the attraction, as this *Unofficial Guide* reader discovered:

Since I hadn't done Mission: Space before, I chose the more intense version and was handed the orange launch ticket to read. Basically, it explained that if I had ever had a tonsillectomy, or even a mild case of pattern baldness, I should take the less intense ride.

We've had a good deal of reader mail about the no-spin version. The following comment is typical. A couple from Chicago had this to say:

For Mission: Space in Epcot, I tried convincing my husband to take the less intense version of the ride but he didn't think it was going to be that bad. Oh, but it was! I felt sick to my stomach after that ride.

Guests for both versions of the attraction enter the NASA Mission: Space Training Center, where they are introduced to the deep-space exploration program and then divided into groups for flight training. After orientation, they are strapped into space capsules for a simulated flight, where, of course, the unexpected happens. Each capsule accommodates a crew consisting of a group commander, pilot, navigator, and engineer, with a guest functioning in each role. The crew's skill and finesse (or, more often, lack thereof) in handling their respective responsibilities have no effect on the outcome of the flight. The capsules are small, and both ride versions are amazingly realistic. The nonspinning version does not subject your body to g-forces, but it does bounce and toss you around in a manner roughly comparable to other Disney motion simulators.

The queuing area and preshow are pretty dazzling. En route to the main event, guests pass space hardware, astronaut tributes and memorials, a cutaway of a huge space wheel showing crew working and living compartments, and a manned mission control where cast members actually operate the attraction. The postshow area features an electronic game called Mission: Space Race that almost three dozen guests, divided into two teams, can play at once. The winning team beats the other team's spaceship back from Mars to the home base. Individuals on each team are responsible for certain tasks essential to the mission and make their ship fly faster by hitting the correct keyboard buttons.

TOURING TIPS In minutes, Disney can reconfigure the ride's four centrifuges to either version of the attraction based on guest demand. Reports indicate that crowds are evenly split between ride options and that wait times, having previously fallen off significantly, are slowly inching upward again. In general, the kinder, gentler version has a wait time of about half that of its more harrowing counterpart.

Having experienced the industrial-strength version of Mission: Space under a variety of circumstances, we've always felt icky when riding it on an empty stomach, especially first thing in the morning. We came up with a number of potential explanations for this phenomenon, involving everything from low blood sugar and inner-ear disorders to some of us just not being astronaut material. Understandably disturbed by the latter possibility, we looked around for an expert opinion to explain what we were feeling. The number of organizations with experience studying the effects of high-g (high-gravity) forces on humans is limited to a select few: NASA, the Air Force, and Mad Tea Party cast members were the first to come to mind. As NASA is a codeveloper of Mission: Space, we called them. Amazingly, a spokesman told us that NASA no longer does much high-g training these days. And the agency was reluctant to pass along anything resembling medical advice to the general public.

Fortunately, a longtime friend put us in touch with a real NASA astronaut who was willing to share (anonymously) some ideas on what causes the nausea, as well as tips astronauts use to prevent it. Our astronaut guesses, as we do, that low blood sugar is the culprit behind the queasiness and suggests eating a normal meal one to two hours prior to experiencing the ride. Try to avoid milk and tomatoes beforehand; they're difficult to keep down and, as our contact noted with the voice of experience, particularly unpleasant if they make a return trip. A banana, we hear, is a good choice for your preflight meal. Also, we were told, one trick astronauts use to avoid nausea while in these simulators is to keep a piece of hard candy or a mint in their mouths; it's not clear, though, whether the candy helps keep blood-sugar levels high or is just a placebo. If all else fails, there are airsickness bags in each simulator.

Make a restroom stop before you get in line; you'll think your bladder has been to Mars and back for real before you get out of this attraction. If you intend to use FASTPASS, assume that all the passes for the day will be distributed by about 4 p.m.

There's nothing our readers enjoy more than kibitzing about rides that can make you puke, and Mission: Space has vaulted to the top of this particular heap. First from a Yakima, Washington, reader:

Mission: Space is awesome, the best attraction yet. It did not have nearly the wait Test Track had. We spoke to a number of people who did not ride as they were intimidated by the number of Disney warning announcements regarding motion sickness.

From Wilton, Connecticut, this 12-year-old's mom had a somewhat different experience:

It was the worst motion sickness my mom ever had at a theme park—airsick bags are available on the ride, and Mom had to use one 20 minutes after leaving the ride, then had to return to the hotel to lie down. Warn future readers!!!

On a lighter note, a woman from Lisbon, Connecticut, used Mission: Space as her own personal relationship lab:

My "senior" (age 71) guy's new favorite is Mission: Space. We rode it four times. All the warnings about motion sickness, spinning, and health concerns almost scared us off, but after the first ride we were hooked. However, we now understand why husbands and wives will probably never go to space together after I (the "navigator") pushed his (the "pilot's") button during the flight. I couldn't help being a backseat driver. He wasn't pushing the button—we could have crashed!

The "Mom, I Can't Believe It's Disney!" Fountain ★★★★

APPEAL BY AGE PRESCHOOL ★★★★★ GRADE SCHOOL ★★★★★ TEENS ★★★★ YOUNG ADULTS ★★★★ OVER 30 ★★★★ SENIORS ★★★★★

What it is Combination fountain and shower. **Scope and scale** Diversion. **When to go** When it's hot. **Special comments** Secretly installed by Martians during *IllumiNations*. **Authors' rating** Yes! ★★★★. **Duration of experience** Indefinite. **Probable waiting time** None.

DESCRIPTION AND COMMENTS This simple fountain on the walkway linking Future World to World Showcase isn't much to look at, but it offers a truly spontaneous experience—rare in Walt Disney World, where everything is controlled, from the snow peas in your stir-fry to how frequently the crocodile yawns in the Jungle Cruise.

Spouts of water erupt randomly from the sidewalk. You can frolic in the water or let it cascade down on you or blow up your britches. On a broiling Florida day, when you think you might spontaneously combust, fling yourself into the fountain and do decidedly un-Disney things. Dance, skip, sing, jump, splash, cavort, roll around, stick your toes down the spouts, or catch the water in your mouth as it descends. You can do all of this with your clothes on or, depending on your age, with your clothes off.

TOURING TIPS We don't know if the fountain's creator has been drummed out of the corps by the Disney Tribunal of People Who Sit on Sticks [probably], but we're grateful for his courage in introducing one thing that's not super-controlled. We do know your kids will be right in the middle of this thing before your brain sounds the alert. Our advice: pack a pair of dry shorts and turn the kids loose. You might even want to bring a spare pair for yourself. Or maybe not—so much advance planning would stifle the spontaneity.

Universe of Energy: *Ellen's Energy Adventure* ★★★★

APPEAL BY AGE PRESCHOOL ★★★ GRADE SCHOOL ★★★ TEENS ★★★ YOUNG ADULTS ★★★ OVER 30 ★★★½ SENIORS ★★★½

What it is Combination ride–theater presentation about energy. **Scope and scale** Major attraction. **When to go** Before 11:15 a.m. or after 4:30 p.m. **Special comments** Don't be dismayed by long lines; 580 people enter the pavilion each time the theater changes audiences. **Authors' rating** The most unique theater in Walt Disney World; ★★★★. **Duration of presentation** About 26½ minutes. **Preshow entertainment** 8 minutes. **Probable waiting time** 20–40 minutes.

DESCRIPTION AND COMMENTS Audio-animatronic dinosaurs and the unique traveling theater make this pavilion one of Future World's most popular. Because this is a theater with a ride component, the line doesn't move while the show is in progress. When the theater empties, however, a large chunk of the line will disappear as people are admitted for the next show. Visitors are seated in what appears to be an ordinary theater while they watch a film about energy sources. Then the theater seats divide into six 97-passenger traveling cars that glide among the swamps and reptiles of a prehistoric forest. Special effects include the feel of warm, moist air from the swamp, and the smell of sulphur from an erupting volcano.

The accompanying film is a humorous and upbeat flick starring Ellen DeGeneres and Bill Nye that sugarcoats the somewhat ponderous discussion of energy. For kids, Universe of Energy remains a toss-up. The dinosaurs frighten some preschoolers, and kids of all ages lose the thread during the educational segments.

TOURING TIPS This attraction draws large crowds beginning early in the morning. Because Universe of Energy can operate more than one show at a time, lines are generally tolerable.

WORLD SHOWCASE

WORLD SHOWCASE, EPCOT'S SECOND THEMED AREA, is an ongoing World's Fair encircling a picturesque 40-acre lagoon. The cuisine, culture, history, and architecture of almost a dozen countries are permanently displayed in individual national pavilions spaced along a 1.2-mile promenade. Pavilions replicate familiar landmarks and present representative street scenes from the host countries.

World Showcase features some of the loveliest gardens in the United States. Located in Germany, France, United Kingdom, Canada, and to a lesser extent, China, they are sometimes tucked away and out of sight of pedestrian traffic on the World Showcase promenade. They are best appreciated during daylight hours, as a Clio, Michigan, woman explains:

> *Make sure to visit the World Showcase in the daylight in order to view the beautiful gardens. We were sorry that we did not do this because we were following the guide and riding the rides that we could have done later in the dark.*

unofficial **TIP**
If you do not want to spring for the Passport Kit, the Disney folks will be happy to stamp an autograph book or just about anything else, even your forehead.

Most adults enjoy World Showcase, but many children find it boring. To make it more interesting to children, most Epcot retail shops sell Passport Kits for about $10. Each kit contains a blank passport and stamps for every World Showcase country. As kids accompany their folks to each country, they tear out the appropriate stamp and stick it in

DISNEY DISH WITH JIM HILL

THE UNDISCOVERED COUNTRY It's been more than 20 years since a new nation was added to the World Showcase, and The Walt Disney Company still hopes it will be able announce an addition to Epcot's international lineup sometime soon. But given what's happened with the world economy—in spite of WDI's very productive talks with Russian, Australian, and Spanish officials—there's been little real progress in getting a new World Showcase pavilion off the drawing board. Now the talk within Walt Disney Imagineering has shifted from "What we hope to do for WDW's 40th anniversary" to "What we hope to have up and running by Disney World's 45th and 50th anniversaries."

the passport. The kit also contains basic information on the nations and a Mickey Mouse button. Disney has built a lot of profit into this little product, but we guess that isn't the issue. More importantly, parents, including this dad from Birmingham, Alabama, tell us the Passport Kit helps get the kids through World Showcase with a minimum of impatience, whining, and tantrums:

> *Adding stamps from the Epcot countries was the only way I was able to see all the displays with cheerful children.*

Children also enjoy Kidcot Fun Stops, a program designed to make World Showcase more interesting for the 5-to-12-year-old crowd. The stops are usually nothing more than a large table on the sidewalk at each pavilion. Each table is staffed by a Disney cast member who stamps passports and supervises children in modest craft projects relating to the host country.

A mom from Billerica, Massachusetts, is a big fan of the Fun Stops:

> *The Kidcot project at Epcot was amazing! Our 2- and 5-year-olds loved making masks and collecting stamps.*

The World Showcase offers some of the most diverse and interesting shopping at Walt Disney World. Unique shops and merchandise are covered in detail in Part Eighteen, Shopping in and out of Walt Disney World.

Kim Possible World Showcase Adventure ★★★★

APPEAL BY AGE TOO NEW TO RATE

What it is Interactive scavenger hunt in select World Showcase pavilions. **Scope and scale** Minor attraction. **When to go** Anytime. **Authors' rating** One of our favorite additions to the parks; ★★★★. **Duration of presentation** Allow 30 minutes per adventure. **Preshow entertainment** None. **Probable waiting time** None.

DESCRIPTION AND COMMENTS Disney Channel's *Kim Possible* show follows a teen heroine as she battles the forces of evil in exotic locations while trying to navigate typical teen challenges like proms, parents, and homework. In the *Kim Possible* World Showcase Adventure, you play the part of Kim and are given a cell-phone-like "Kimmunicator" before being dispatched on a mission to your choice of seven World Showcase pavilions. Once you arrive at the pavilion, the Kimmunicator's video screen and audio provide various clues about the adventure. As you discover each clue, you'll find special effects such as talking statues and flaming lanterns, plus live "secret agents" stationed in the pavilions just for this game.

Kim Possible is Disney's attempt at making static World Showcase pavilions more interactive and kid-friendly. It succeeds wildly, even as Disney is still ironing out all the technological kinks. The adventures have relatively simple clues, fast pacing, and neat rewards for solving the puzzles. Disney clearly put a lot of thought into game play and substantial investment into the effects. Since the experience debuted in early 2009, reader reviews have been uniformly positive.

TOURING TIPS Playing the game is free, and no deposit is required for the Kimmunicator. You'll need a valid theme-park ticket to sign up before you play, and you can choose both the time and location of your adventure.

Register at either Future World's Innovations East or Innoventions West buildings, or along the main walkway from Future World to World Showcase. You'll report to the Italy, Norway, or United Kingdom Pavilion to pick up your Kimmunicator before heading off to your chosen country.

Each group can have up to three Kimmunicators for the same adventure. Because you're working with a device about the size of a cell phone, it's best to have one Kimmunicator for every two people in your group.

NOW, MOVING CLOCKWISE around the World Showcase promenade, here are the nations represented and their attractions.

MEXICO PAVILION

DESCRIPTION AND COMMENTS Pre-Columbian pyramids dominate the architecture of this exhibit. One forms the pavilion's facade, and the other overlooks the restaurant and plaza alongside the boat ride, Gran Fiesta Tour, inside the pavilion.

TOURING TIPS Romantic and exciting testimony to Mexico's charms, the pyramids contain a large number of authentic and valuable artifacts. Many people zip past these treasures without stopping to look. The village scene inside the pavilion is beautiful and exquisitely detailed. The retail shop that formerly occupied most of the left half of the inner pavilion has been replaced with an open, cheerful two-floor space housing Mexico's Kidcot stop, plus hands-on exhibits of Mexico's food, culture, and geography. Be sure to send a video postcard of yourself cliff-diving in Acapulco to your friends back home.

Gran Fiesta Tour Starring The Three Caballeros ★★½

APPEAL BY AGE	PRESCHOOL ★★★★	GRADE SCHOOL ★★★½	TEENS ★★★
YOUNG ADULTS ★★★	OVER 30 ★★★	SENIORS ★★★	

What it is Indoor scenic boat ride. **Scope and scale** Minor attraction. **When to go** Before noon or after 5 p.m. **Authors' rating** Visually appealing, light, and relaxing; ★★½. **Duration of ride** About 7 minutes (plus 1½-minute wait to disembark). **Average wait in line per 100 people ahead of you** 4½ minutes; assumes 16 boats in operation. **Loading speed** Moderate.

DESCRIPTION AND COMMENTS The Gran Fiesta Tour replaces this pavilion's first boat ride, El Río del Tiempo. The new incarnation adds animated versions of Donald Duck, José Carioca, and Panchito—an avian singing group called The Three Caballeros, from Disney's 1944 film of the same name—to spice up what was often characterized as a slower-paced Mexican-style It's a Small World.

The new ride's premise is that the Caballeros are scheduled to perform at a fiesta later that day, but Donald has gone missing. Large video screens show Donald off enjoying Mexico's pyramids, monuments, and water sports while José and Panchito search other Mexican points of interest. Everyone is reunited in time for a rousing concert near the end of the ride. Along the way, guests are treated to newly refurbished scenes in eye-catching colors, and an upgraded music system. At the risk of sounding like the Disney geeks we are, we must point out that Panchito is technically the only Mexican Caballero; José Carioca is from Brazil, and Donald is from Burbank. Either way, more of the ride's visuals seem to be situated on the left side of the boat. Have small children sit nearer to that side to keep their attention, and listen for Donald's humorous dialogue as you wait to disembark at the end of the ride.

A family of three from Fanwood, New Jersey, thinks Disney blew it with the Gran Fiesta Tour:

The Gran Fiesta Tour was dreadful. If the idea was to rid the ride of derogatory Mexican stereotypes, the designers woefully missed the mark. It was much worse than the original—and the original was pretty poor to begin with.

TOURING TIPS The ride tends to get busier during early afternoon.

NORWAY PAVILION

DESCRIPTION AND COMMENTS The Norway Pavilion is complex, beautiful, and architecturally diverse. Surrounding a courtyard is An assortment of traditional Scandinavian buildings, including a replica of the 14th-century Akershus Castle, a wooden stave church, red-tiled cottages, and replicas of historic buildings representing the traditional designs of Bergen, Alesund, and Oslo. Attractions include an adventure boat ride in the mold of Pirates of the Caribbean, a movie about Norway, and a gallery of art and artifacts. The pavilion houses Akershus Royal Banquet Hall, a sit-down eatery that hosts princess character meals for breakfast, lunch, and dinner; breakfast here is one of the most popular character meals in the World. An open-air cafe and a bakery cater to those on the run. Shoppers find abundant native handicrafts.

Maelstrom (FASTPASS) ★★★

APPEAL BY AGE PRESCHOOL ★★★ GRADE SCHOOL ★★★½ TEENS ★★★½
YOUNG ADULTS ★★★½ OVER 30 ★★★½ SENIORS ★★★½

What it is Indoor-adventure boat ride. **Scope and scale** Major attraction. **When to go** Before noon, after 4:30 p.m., or use FASTPASS. **Authors' rating** Too short but has its moments; ★★★. **Duration of ride** 4½ minutes, followed by a 5-minute film with a short wait in between; about 14 minutes for the whole show. **Average wait in line per 100 people ahead of you** 4 minutes; assumes 12 or 13 boats operating. **Loading speed** Fast.

DISNEY DISH WITH JIM HILL

ELVES OR ELSE Fun fact: Walt Disney Studios recently created a department whose sole purpose is to find new ways to fold Disney characters into the parks and resorts. Toward that end, the Imagineers are already trying to find a logical way to add the characters from Walt Disney Animation Studios' big release for 2012—*King of the Elves*—to Epcot's Norway Pavilion. It sounds like a stretch, but when you realize that there are already trolls inside the Maelstrom ride (and that Disney Princesses took over the Akershus restaurant years ago), does adding a few elves to this part of World Showcase really seem all that odd?

DESCRIPTION AND COMMENTS In one of Disney World's shorter water rides, guests board dragon-headed ships for a voyage through the fabled rivers and seas of Viking history and legend. They brave trolls, rocky gorges, waterfalls, and a storm at sea. A second-generation Disney water ride, the Viking voyage assembles an impressive array of special effects, combining visual, tactile, and auditory stimuli in a fast-paced and often humorous odyssey. Afterward, guests see a five-minute film on Norway. We don't have any major problems with Maelstrom, but a vocal minority of our readers consider the ride too brief and resent having to sit through what they characterize as a travelogue.

TOURING TIPS Sometimes, several hundred guests from a recently concluded screening of *Reflections of China* arrive at Maelstrom en masse. Should you encounter this horde, postpone Maelstrom. If you don't want to see the Norway film, not to worry. You will be given the opportunity to exit before the film begins.

CHINA PAVILION

DESCRIPTION AND COMMENTS A half-sized replica of the Temple of Heaven in Beijing identifies this pavilion. Gardens and reflecting ponds simulate those found in Suzhou, and an art gallery features a lotus-blossom gate and formal saddle roof line. The China Pavilion offers two restaurants: a fast-food eatery and a full-service establishment (Advance Reservations recommended) that serves lamentably lackluster Chinese food in a lovely setting. The Joy of Tea, a new tea stand and specialty-drink vendor, feeds your caffeine addiction until you can get to Morocco's espresso bar.

The pavilion also hosts regularly updated exhibits on Chinese history, culture, or trend-setting developments. Past exhibits have covered everything from China's indigenous peoples to the layout of Hong Kong Disneyland. The current exhibit features a look at Chinese funeral sculptures, including miniature clay warriors who protect the tombs' occupants.

Reflections of China ★★★½

APPEAL BY AGE PRESCHOOL ★★½ GRADE SCHOOL ★★★ TEENS ★★★
YOUNG ADULTS ★★★ OVER 30 ★★★½ SENIORS ★★★½

What it is Film about the Chinese people and culture. **Scope and scale** Major attraction. **When to go** Anytime. **Special comments** Audience stands throughout performance. This beautifully produced film was introduced in 2003. **Authors' rating** ★★★½. **Duration of presentation** About 14 minutes. **Preshow entertainment** None. **Probable waiting time** 10 minutes.

DESCRIPTION AND COMMENTS Pass through the Hall of Prayer for Good Harvest to view the Circle-Vision 360 film *Reflections of China.* Warm and appealing, it's a brilliant (albeit politically sanitized) introduction to the people and natural beauty of China.

TOURING TIPS The pavilion is truly beautiful—serene yet exciting. *Reflections of China* plays in a theater where guests must stand, but the film can usually be enjoyed anytime without much waiting. If you're touring World Showcase in a counterclockwise rotation and plan next to go to Norway and ride Maelstrom, position yourself on the far left of the theater (as you face the attendant's podium). After the show, be one of the first to exit. Hurry to Maelstrom as fast as you can to arrive ahead of the several hundred other *Reflections of China* patrons who will be right behind you.

GERMANY PAVILION

DESCRIPTION AND COMMENTS A clock tower, adorned with boy and girl figures, rises above the *platz* (plaza) marking the Germany Pavilion. Dominated by a fountain depicting St. George's victory over the dragon, the platz is encircled by buildings in the style of traditional German architecture. The

DISNEY DISH WITH JIM HILL

INSPIRED BY *THE LOVE BOAT,* PERHAPS? Many WDW history buffs already know about the boat-ride-past-miniature-versions-of-historic-German-landmarks attraction that was supposed to have been part of this World Showcase pavilion back in the early 1980s. But what many people don't realize is that this German canal tour was just one of a quartet of internationally themed boat rides that the Imagineers planned for this theme park. Epcot's U.K. Pavilion was also supposed to have had a canal-boat cruise past British landmarks, while the Italy Pavilion was to have featured a romantic gondola cruise. Of the four boat-based rides planned for World Showcase, only Mexico's now-defunct El Rio del Tiempo ever made it off the drawing board.

main attraction is the Biergarten, a buffet restaurant that serves traditional German food and beer (Advance Reservations are required; see full profile on page 476 of Part Ten). Yodeling, folk dancing, and oompah-band music are part of the mealtime festivities.

Be sure to check out the large and elaborate model railroad located just beyond the restrooms as you walk from Germany toward Italy.

TOURING TIPS The pavilion is pleasant and festive. Tour anytime.

ITALY PAVILION

DESCRIPTION AND COMMENTS The entrance to Italy is marked by a 105-foot-tall campanile (bell tower) said to mirror the tower in St. Mark's Square in Venice. Left of the campanile is a replica of the 14th-century Doge's Palace, also in the famous square. The pavilion has a waterfront on the lagoon where gondolas are tied to striped moorings.

DISNEY DISH WITH JIM HILL

AT DISNEY, A GOOD IDEA NEVER REALLY DIES When Julie Taymor, the director of the Tony Award–winning hit *The Lion King,* tried and failed to get a new stage musical version of *Pinocchio* off the ground, the Parks and Resorts people picked over the wreckage and found a few ideas that they liked. Among these is a theater wagon that would entertain guests in the Italy Pavilion with a stage show where you couldn't really tell where the people leave off and the puppets begin. Provided that WDW brass doesn't string Epcot's entertainment staff along, this new stage show could be running by the fall of 2011.

TOURING TIPS Streets and courtyards in the Italy Pavilion are among the most realistic in World Showcase. You really feel as if you're in Italy. Because there's no film or ride, tour at any hour.

UNITED STATES PAVILION

The American Adventure ★★★★

APPEAL BY AGE PRESCHOOL ★★½ GRADE SCHOOL ★★★ TEENS ★★★
YOUNG ADULTS ★★★★ OVER 30 ★★★★ SENIORS ★★★½

What it is Patriotic mixed-media and audio-animatronic theater presentation on U.S. history. **Scope and scale** Headliner. **When to go** Anytime. **Authors' rating** Disney's best historic/patriotic attraction; not to be missed; ★★★★. **Duration**

of presentation About 29 minutes. **Preshow entertainment** Voices of Liberty choral singing. **Probable waiting time** 25 minutes.

DESCRIPTION AND COMMENTS The United States Pavilion, generally referred to as The American Adventure, consists (not surprisingly) of a fast-food restaurant and a patriotic show.

The American Adventure production is a composite of everything Disney does best. Located in an imposing brick structure reminiscent of colonial Philadelphia, the 29-minute show is a stirring, but sanitized, rendition of American history narrated by an audio-animatronic Mark Twain (who carries a smoking cigar) and Ben Franklin (who climbs a set of stairs to visit Thomas Jefferson). Behind a stage (almost half the size of a football field) is a 28- by 55-foot rear-projection screen (the largest ever used) on which motion-picture images are interwoven with action on stage.

Though the production elicits patriotic emotion in some viewers, others find it overstated and boring. A man from Fort Lauderdale, Florida, writes:

I've always disagreed with you about The American Adventure. *I saw it about ten years ago and snoozed through it. We tried it again since you said it was updated. It was still ponderous. Casey used the time for a nap, and I was checking my watch, waiting for it to be over. I'll try it again in ten years.*

An Erie, Pennsylvania, couple resented Disney's squeaky-clean version of American history:

Our biggest gripe was with The American Adventure. *What was that supposed to be? My husband and I were actually embarrassed by that show. They glossed over the dark points of American history and neatly cut out the audio about who bombed Pearl Harbor (after all, Japan is right next door and everyone is happy at WDW). Why do they not focus on the natural beauty of America, the ethnic diversity, immigration, contributions to the world society? No, it's a condensed and Disneyfied history lesson that made us want to pretend to be Canadians after seeing it.*

But an Iowa City, Iowa, father of three thinks a lot of people are missing the point:

Cramming all of American history into a 20-minute flick is no easy task, and face it, a theme park is hardly the place for a wholly objective, serious critique of the United States. I think that it's perfectly appropriate for the film, as an attraction in Epcot, to emphasize what's good about the United States.

Finally, a father of two from Wellesley, Massachusetts, liked the preshow better than the main attraction:

One surprise: the Voices of Liberty singing group. I wasn't expecting much and was knocked out by the professionalism and talent in their all-too-brief show prior to going into The American Adventure *(which was a real snooze).*

TOURING TIPS Architecturally, the U.S. Pavilion isn't as interesting as most others in World Showcase. But the presentation, our researchers believe, is the very best patriotic attraction in the Disney repertoire. It usually plays to capacity audiences from around 1:30 to 3:30 p.m., but it isn't hard to get into. Because of the theater's large capacity, the wait during busy times of day seldom approaches an hour, and averages 25 to 40 minutes. Because of its theme, the presentation is decidedly less compelling to non-Americans.

The adjacent Liberty Inn serves a quick, nonethnic fast-food meal.

JAPAN PAVILION

DESCRIPTION AND COMMENTS The five-story, blue-roofed pagoda, inspired by a 17th-century shrine in Nara, sets this pavilion apart. A hill garden behind it features waterfalls, rocks, flowers, lanterns, paths, and rustic bridges. The building on the right (as one faces the entrance) was inspired by the ceremonial and coronation hall at the Imperial Palace at Kyoto. It contains restaurants and a large retail store. Through the center entrance and to the left is the Bijutsu-kan Gallery, exhibiting some exquisite Japanese artifacts.

TOURING TIPS Tasteful and elaborate, the pavilion creatively blends simplicity, architectural grandeur, and natural beauty. Tour anytime.

DISNEY DISH WITH JIM HILL

BULLET TRAIN DERAILED Blame the lousy economy for World Showcase once again losing out on a great new attraction. For almost 20 years, plans have been in the works for an indoor roller coaster with the look and feel of bullet train; the ride would be housed in a miniature version of Mount Fuji behind the Japan Pavilion. Unfortunately, all the potential sponsors of this proposed Epcot addition got caught in the economic downturn. Now it's back to square one as the Imagineers seek out a Japanese corporation willing to put up the estimated $150 to $200 million that the attraction would cost.

MOROCCO PAVILION

DESCRIPTION AND COMMENTS The bustling market, winding streets, lofty minarets, and stuccoed archways re-create the romance and intrigue of Marrakesh and Casablanca. Attention to detail makes Morocco one of the most exciting World Showcase pavilions. It also has a museum of Moorish art and the Restaurant Marrakesh, which serves some unusual and difficult-to-find North African specialties.

Another interesting item in Morocco is the water wheel in World Showcase Lagoon that provides irrigation to the flowerbeds opposite the pavilion. Unlike the "scoop and dump" mechanisms most people are familiar with, the water here is actually carried inside the wheel. Through a complex combination of baffles, chambers, and gravity, the water emerges at the highest point of the circle through a spout perpendicular to the wheel's motion. One can only imagine the number of late, espresso-filled nights it took to come up with this design.

TOURING TIPS Morocco has neither a ride nor theater; tour anytime.

FRANCE PAVILION

DESCRIPTION AND COMMENTS Naturally, a replica of the Eiffel Tower (a big one) is this pavilion's centerpiece. In the foreground, streets recall *la belle époque,* France's "beautiful time" between 1870 and 1910. The sidewalk cafe and restaurant are very popular, as is the pastry shop. You won't be the first visitor to buy a croissant to tide you over until your next real meal. And this probably explains why readers rank the France Pavilion as the best in World Showcase.

A group from Chicago found that the pavilion's realism exceeds what was intended:

There were no public restrooms in the France part of Epcot—just like Paris. We had to go to Morocco to find facilities.

DISNEY DISH WITH JIM HILL

FROM RAT TO ROCK STAR Les Chefs de France has always done great dinner business. But this casual brasserie had trouble luring in the lunchtime crowd—at a least until the Living Character Initiative version of Remy the Rat came along, entertaining guests at their tables. With the *Ratatouille* star's dining debut in the spring of 2009, demand for afternoon reservations became so strong that this France Pavilion eatery was actually turning guests away. Now the animatronic rodent is off on a world tour (Hong Kong, Tokyo, and Anaheim) and isn't expected back in Orlando until late 2010, when he'll once again be entertaining the lunchtime crowds at Les Chefs de France.

Impressions de France ★★★½

APPEAL BY AGE PRESCHOOL ★★★ GRADE SCHOOL ★★½ TEENS ★★★
YOUNG ADULTS ★★★½ OVER 30 ★★★½ SENIORS ★★★★

What it is Film essay on the French people and country. **Scope and scale** Major attraction. **When to go** Anytime. **Authors' rating** Exceedingly beautiful film; not to be missed; ★★★½. **Duration of presentation** About 18 minutes. **Preshow entertainment** None. **Probable waiting time** 15 minutes (at suggested times).

DESCRIPTION AND COMMENTS *Impressions de France* is an 18-minute movie projected over 200 degrees onto five screens. Unlike at China and Canada, the audience sits to view this well-made film introducing France's people, cities, and natural wonders.

TOURING TIPS The film usually begins on the hour and half hour. Detail and the evocation of a bygone era enrich the atmosphere of this pavilion. Streets are small and become quite congested when visitors queue for the film.

UNITED KINGDOM PAVILION

DESCRIPTION AND COMMENTS A variety of period architecture attempts to capture Britain's city, town, and rural atmospheres. One street alone has a thatched-roof cottage, a four-story timber-and-plaster building, a pre-Georgian plaster building, a formal Palladian exterior of dressed stone, and a city square with a Hyde Park bandstand (whew!).

The pavilion is composed mostly of shops. The Rose & Crown Pub and Dining Room is the only World Showcase full-service restaurant with dining on the water side of the promenade. For fast food try Yorkshire County Fish Shop.

TOURING TIPS There are no attractions here, hence minimal congestion, so tour anytime. Mary Poppins and/or Pooh can occasionally be found in the character-greeting area; check the *Times Guide* for a schedule. Advance Reservations aren't required to enjoy the pub section of the Rose & Crown, making it a nice place to stop for a midafternoon beer.

CANADA PAVILION

DESCRIPTION AND COMMENTS Canada's cultural, natural, and architectural diversity is reflected in this large and impressive pavilion. Thirty-foot-tall totem poles embellish a Native American village at the foot of a magnificent château-style hotel. Nearby is a rugged stone building said to be modeled after a famous landmark near Niagara Falls and reflecting

Britain's influence on Canada. Le Cellier, a steak house on the pavilion's lower level, is one of Disney World's highest-rated restaurants. It almost always requires reservations; you'd have to be incredibly lucky to get a walk-in spot, but it doesn't hurt to ask.

O Canada! ★★★½

APPEAL BY AGE	PRESCHOOL ★★	GRADE SCHOOL ★★★	TEENS ★★★
YOUNG ADULTS ★★★	OVER 30 ★★★½	SENIORS ★★★★	

What it is Film essay on the Canadian people and their country. **Scope and scale** Major attraction. **When to go** Anytime. **Special comments** Audience stands during performance. **Authors' rating** Makes you want to catch the first plane to Canada! ★★★½. **Duration of presentation** About 18 minutes. **Preshow entertainment** None. **Probable waiting time** 10 minutes.

DESCRIPTION AND COMMENTS *O Canada!* showcases Canada's natural beauty and population diversity and demonstrates the immense pride Canadians have in their country. A new film replaced the decades-old original in 2007. Starring Martin Short, it features new clips and dialogue interspersed with some of the original film's scenes. Visitors leave the theater through Victoria Gardens, which was inspired by the famed Butchart Gardens of British Columbia.

Readers are reacting positively to the new film. This comment from a Texas mom is typical:

> *The updated* O Canada! *movie is a great improvement. The narration was entertaining enough to keep our 8-year-old from being bored, and the scenery was amazing.*

Speaking of Canada's immense pride, cast members often run a preshow quiz on Canadian trivia outside the theater before the show. Helpful tips for Americans: Canada's capital is Ottawa; its $1 coin is nicknamed the Loonie, after the bird engraved on it; and the $2 coin is the Toonie—not, unfortunately, the Doubloonie.

TOURING TIPS This large-capacity attraction (guests must stand) gets fairly heavy late-morning attendance, as Canada is the first pavilion encountered as one travels counterclockwise around World Showcase Lagoon.

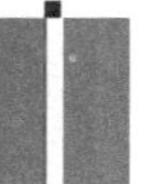

LIVE ENTERTAINMENT *in* EPCOT

LIVE ENTERTAINMENT IN EPCOT is more diverse than in the Magic Kingdom. In World Showcase, it reflects the nations represented. Future World provides a perfect setting for new and experimental offerings. Information about live entertainment on the day you visit is contained in the Epcot guide map, often supplemented by a *Times Guide*. WDW live-entertainment guru Steve Soares usually posts the Epcot performance schedule about a week in advance at **pages.prodigy.net/stevesoares.**

Here are some performers and performances you'll encounter:

AMERICA GARDENS THEATRE This large amphitheater, near The American Adventure, faces World Showcase Lagoon. International talent plays limited engagements there. Many shows spotlight the music, dance, and costumes of the performer's home country. Other programs feature Disney characters.

AROUND THE WORLD SHOWCASE Impromptu performances take place in and around the World Showcase pavilions. They include a strolling mariachi group in Mexico; street actors in Italy; a fife-and-drum corps or singing group (The Voices of Liberty) at The American Adventure; traditional songs, drums, and dances in Japan; street comedy and a Beatles-impersonation band in the United Kingdom; white-faced mimes in France; and bagpipes in Canada, among other offerings. Street entertainment occurs about every half hour.

Live entertainment in World Showcase exceeded the expectations of a mother from Rhode Island and led her son to develop a new talent:

> *You should stress in the new edition that Epcot's World Showcase is really quite lively now. Street performances are scheduled throughout the day in the different pavilions. The schedules were printed on the daily map we picked up at the ticket booth.*
>
> *My 2-year-old was taken with the Chinese acrobats and the Chinese variety performers. We must have watched their shows four times each! As I write this, he's balancing an empty trash can on his feet.*

And an Ayden, North Carolina, woman offers this:

> *I don't feel that you emphasize the street shows at Epcot enough. My husband and I loved the Japanese drumming, the Chinese and Moroccan acrobats, and the street players in Great Britain. These activities were much more indicative of foreign cultures than the rides.*

We think the reader's right on target.

DINNER AND LUNCH SHOWS Restaurants in World Showcase serve healthy portions of live entertainment to accompany the victuals. Find folk dancing and an oompah band in Germany, singing waiters in Italy, and belly dancers in Morocco. Shows are performed only at dinner in Italy, but at both lunch and dinner in Germany and Morocco. Advance Reservations are required.

DISNEY CHARACTERS Once believed to be inconsistent with Epcot's educational focus, Disney characters have now been imported in significant numbers. Characters appear throughout Epcot (see page 346) and in live shows at the America Gardens Theatre and the Showcase Plaza between Mexico and Canada. Times are listed in the *Times Guide* available upon entry and at Guest Relations. Finally, The Garden Grill Restaurant in the Land Pavilion and Akershus Royal Banquet Hall in Norway offer character meals.

IN FUTURE WORLD A musical crew of drumming janitors work near the front entrance and at Innoventions Plaza (between the two Innoventions buildings and by the fountain) according to the daily entertainment schedule. They're occasionally complemented by an electric-keyboard band playing what today's wouldn't-know-good-music-if-it-bit-them-on-the-keister kids would call "oldies."

INNOVENTIONS FOUNTAIN SHOW Numerous times each day, the fountain situated between the two Innoventions buildings comes alive with pulsating, arching plumes of water synchronized to a musical score. Because there is no posted schedule of performances, the fountain show comes as a surprise to many readers, such as this man from Berwickshire, England:

> *You don't mention one of the newer joys of Epcot, so the musical fountain came as a real surprise and treat. I sat down and listened to it from start to finish on two different occasions. The music is catchy, and played through the stereo speakers, the soaring effects of both music and water are really beautiful.*

KIDCOT FUN STOPS Both Future World and World Showcase have areas called Kidcot Fun Stops, where younger children can hear a story or make some small craft representative of the host nation or pavilion theme. The Fun Stops are informal, usually set up right on the walkway. During busy times of the year, you'll find Fun Stops at each country in World Showcase as well as at Test Track, The Seas with Nemo & Friends, Innoventions East and West, and occasionally at the Land Pavilion. At slower times, only a couple of zones operate. Parents from Nanticoke, Pennsylvania, who thought Epcot would be a drag for their kids, were surprised by their experience:

> *Unfortunately we saved Epcot for the last day, thinking the children (ages 5 and 6) would be bored. This was a mistake. They wanted to sit for every storyteller. And the best part was the Kidcot Fun Stops in each pavilion. Imagine, something free at Disney World. It's only a stick, but it has a little something from each country added by the child at his whim. They had a ball.*

ILLUMINATIONS

ILLUMINATIONS IS EPCOT'S GREAT OUTDOOR SPECTACLE, integrating fireworks, laser lights, neon, and music in a stirring tribute to the nations of the world. It's the climax of every Epcot day.

Unlike earlier incarnations of *IllumiNations,* this version has a plot as well as a theme and is loaded with symbolism. We'll provide the *CliffsNotes* version here, because it all sort of runs together in the show itself. The show kicks off with colliding stars that suggest the Big Bang, following which "chaos reigns in the universe." This display is soon replaced by twittering songbirds and various other manifestations signaling the nativity of the Earth. Next comes a brief history of time, from the dinosaurs to ancient Rome, all projected in images on a huge, floating globe. Man's art and inspiration then flash across the globe "in a collage of creativity." All this stimulates the globe to unfold "like a massive flower," bringing on the fireworks crescendo heralding the dawn of a new age. Although only the artistically sensitive will be able to differentiate all this from, say, the last five minutes of any Bruce Willis movie, we thought you'd like to know what Disney says is happening.

Getting Out of Epcot after *IllumiNations* (Read This before Selecting a Viewing Spot)

Decide how quickly you want to leave the park after the show, then pick your vantage point. *IllumiNations* ends the day at Epcot. When

Where to View IllumiNations

it's over, only a couple of gift shops remain open. Because there's nothing to do, everyone leaves at once. This creates a great snarl at Package Pick-Up, the Epcot monorail station, and the Disney bus stop. It also pushes to the limit the tram system hauling guests to their cars in the parking lot. Stroller return, however, is extraordinarily efficient and doesn't cause any delay.

If you're staying at an Epcot resort (Swan, Dolphin, Yacht and Beach Club Resorts, and BoardWalk Inn and Villas), watch the show from somewhere on the southern half (The American Adventure) of World Showcase Lagoon and then leave through the International Gateway between France and the United Kingdom. You can walk or take a boat back to your hotel from the International Gateway. If you have a car and you're visiting Epcot in the evening for dinner and *IllumiNations,* park at the Yacht or Beach Club. After the show, duck out the International Gateway and be on the road to your hotel in 15 minutes. We should warn you that there is a manned security gate at the entrances to most of the Epcot resorts, including the Yacht and Beach clubs. You will, of course, be admitted if you have legitimate business, such as dining at one of the hotel restaurants, or, if you park at the BoardWalk Hotel and Villas (requiring a slightly longer walk to Epcot), going to the clubs and restaurants at Disney's BoardWalk. If you're staying at any other Disney hotel and you don't have a car, the fastest way home is to join the mass exodus through the main gate after *IllumiNations* and catch a bus or the monorail.

Those who have a car in the Epcot lot have a more problematic situation. To beat the crowd, find a viewing spot at the end of World Showcase Lagoon nearest Future World (and the exits). Leave as soon as *IllumiNations* concludes, trying to exit ahead of the crowd (note that thousands of people will be doing exactly the same thing). To get a good vantage point between Mexico and Canada on the northern end of the lagoon, stake out your spot 60 to 100 minutes before the show (45 to 90 minutes during less-busy periods). Conceivably, you may squander more time holding your spot before *IllumiNations* than you would if you watched from the less-congested southern end of the lagoon and took your chances with the crowd upon departure.

More groups get separated and more children get lost following *IllumiNations* than at any other time. In summer, you will be walking in a throng of up to 30,000 people. If you're heading for the parking lot, anticipate this congestion and preselect a point in the Epcot entrance area where you can meet in the event that someone gets separated from the group. We recommend the fountain just inside the main entrance. Everyone in your party should be told not to exit through the turnstiles until all noses have been counted. It can be a nightmare if the group gets split up and you don't know whether the others are inside or outside the park.

For those with a car, the main problem is reaching the parking lot. Once you're there, traffic leaves the parking lot pretty well. If you paid close attention to where you parked, consider skipping the tram and walking. If you walk, watch your children closely and hang on to them for all you're worth. The parking lot is pretty wild at this time of night, with hundreds of moving cars.

Good Locations for Viewing *IllumiNations* and Other World Showcase Lagoon Performances

The best place to be for any presentation on World Showcase Lagoon is in a seat on the lakeside veranda of the Cantina de San Angel in Mexico. Come early (at least 90 minutes before *IllumiNations*) and relax with a cold drink or snack while you wait for the show.

A woman from Pasadena, California, nailed down the seat but missed the relaxation. She writes:

> *Stake out a prime site for* IllumiNations *at least two hours ahead, and be prepared to defend it. We got a lakeside table at the Cantina de San Angel at 6:30 p.m. and had a great view of* IllumiNations. *Unfortunately, we had to put up with troops of people asking us to share our table and trying to wedge themselves between our table and the fence.*

The Rose & Crown Pub in the United Kingdom also has lagoonside seating. Because of a small wall, however, the view isn't quite as good as from the Cantina. If you want to combine dinner on the Rose & Crown's veranda with *IllumiNations,* make a dinner reservation for about 1 hour and 15 minutes before showtime. Report a few minutes early for your seating and tell the Rose & Crown host that you want a table outside where you can view *IllumiNations* during or after dinner. Our experience is that the Rose & Crown staff will bend over backward to accommodate you. If you aren't able to obtain a table outside, eat inside, then hang out until showtime. When the lights dim, indicating the start of *IllumiNations,* you will be allowed to join the diners on the terrace to watch the show.

Because most guests run for the exits after a presentation, and because islands in the southern half (The American Adventure) of the lagoon block the view from some places, the most popular spectator positions are along the northern waterfront from Norway and Mexico on around to Canada and the United Kingdom. Although the northern half of the lagoon unquestionably offers excellent viewing, it's usually necessary to claim a spot 60 to 100 minutes before *IllumiNations* begins. For those who are late finishing dinner or don't want to spend an hour or more standing by a rail, here are some good viewing spots along the southern perimeter (moving counterclockwise from the United Kingdom to Germany) that often go unnoticed until 10 to 30 minutes before showtime:

1. **International Gateway Island** The pedestrian bridge across the canal near International Gateway spans an island that offers great viewing. This island normally fills 30 minutes or more before showtime.
2. **Second-floor (Restaurant-level) Deck of the Mitsukoshi Building in Japan** An Asian arch slightly blocks your sight line, but this covered deck offers a great vantage point, especially if the weather is iffy. Only the Cantina de San Angel in Mexico is more protected. If you take up a position on the Mitsukoshi deck and find the wind blowing directly at you, you can be reasonably sure that the smoke from the fireworks won't be far behind.
3. **Gondola Landing at Italy** An elaborate waterfront promenade offers excellent viewing. Claim a spot at least 30 minutes before showtime.
4. **The Boat Dock Opposite Germany** Another good vantage point, the dock generally fills 30 minutes before *IllumiNations*. Note, however, that this area may be exposed to more smoke from the fireworks because of Epcot's prevailing winds.
5. **Waterfront Promenade by Germany** Views are good from the 90-foot-long lagoon-side walkway between Germany and China.

Do these suggestions work every time? No. A dad from San Ramon, California, writes:

> *Your recommendations for* IllumiNations *didn't work out in the time frame you mentioned. People had the area staked out two hours ahead.*

unofficial **TIP**
Because most of *IllumiNations'* action is significantly above ground level, you don't need to be right on the rail or have an unobstructed view of the water to enjoy it.

None of the previous viewing locations are reservable, and on busier nights, good spots go early. But speaking personally, we refuse to hold down a slab of concrete for two hours before *IllumiNations* as some people do. Most nights, you can find an acceptable vantage point 15 to 30 minutes before the show.

It's important not to position yourself under a tree, awning, or anything that blocks your overhead view. If *IllumiNations* is a top priority for you and you want to be certain of getting a good viewing position, claim your place an hour or more before showtime.

A New Yorker who staked out his turf well in advance made this suggestion for staying comfortable until showtime:

> *Your excellent guidebook also served as* [a] *seat cushion while waiting seated on the ground. Make future editions thicker for greater comfort.*

ILLUMINATIONS CRUISE

FOR A REALLY GOOD VIEW, YOU CAN CHARTER a pontoon boat for $275. Captained by a Disney cast member, the boat holds up to ten guests. Your captain will take you for a little cruise and then position the boat in a perfect place to watch *IllumiNations*. Optional food and beverage items are available through Yacht Club Private Dining at ☎ 407-934-3160. Cruises depart from the BoardWalk and Yacht and Beach Club docks. A major indirect benefit of the charter is that you can enjoy *IllumiNations* without fighting the mob afterward. Because this is a private charter rather than a tour, only your group will be aboard. Life jackets are provided, but you can wear them at your discretion. Because there are few boats, charters sell out fast. To reserve, call ☎ 407-WDW-PLAY at exactly 7 a.m. 90 days before the day you want to charter. Because the Disney reservations system counts days in a somewhat atypical manner, we recommend phoning about 95 days out to have a Disney agent specify the exact morning to call for reservations. Similar charters are available on the Seven Seas Lagoon to watch the Magic Kingdom fireworks.

TRAFFIC PATTERNS *in* EPCOT

IN THE MAGIC KINGDOM, Main Street, U.S.A., with its shops and eateries, serves as a huge gathering place when the park opens and funnels visitors to the central hub, where entrances branch off to the lands. Thus, crowds are first welcomed and entertained (on Main Street), then distributed almost equally to the lands.

At Epcot, by contrast, Spaceship Earth, the park's premier landmark and one of its headliner attractions, is just inside the main entrance. When visitors enter the park, they almost irresistibly head for it. Hence, a bottleneck forms less than 75 yards from the turnstiles as soon as the park opens.

Early-morning crowds form in Future World because most of the park's rides and shows are there. Except at Mission: Space, Test Track, and Soarin', visitors are fairly equally distributed among Future World attractions. Soarin', Mission: Space, and Test Track are the major early-morning magnets.

unofficial **TIP**
Visitors aware of the congestion at Spaceship Earth can take advantage of the excellent opportunities it provides for escaping waits at other Future World attractions.

The three biggies will draw so many guests that the other attractions in Future World do not develop long waits until 11 a.m. or later.

Between 9 and 11 a.m., crowds build in Future World. Even when World Showcase opens (usually 11 a.m., but sometimes noon), more people are entering Future World than are leaving for the Showcase. Attendance continues building in Future World between noon and 2 p.m. World Showcase attendance builds rapidly as lunchtime approaches. Exhibits at the far end of World Showcase Lagoon report capacity audiences from about noon through 6:30 or 7:30 p.m.

The Magic Kingdom's premier attractions are situated on the far perimeters of its lands to distribute crowds evenly. Epcot's cluster of attractions in Future World holds the greater part of the throng in the smaller part of the park. World Showcase has only two major draws (Maelstrom in Norway and *The American Adventure*), but these are not in the same league as the three super-headliners in Future World, and consequently there is no compelling reason to rush to see them. The bottom line: crowds build all morning and into early afternoon in Future World. Not until the evening meal approaches do crowds equalize in Future World and World Showcase. Evening crowds in World Showcase, however, don't compare in size to morning and midday crowds in Future World. Attendance throughout Epcot is normally lighter in the evening.

Some guests leave Epcot in the early evening, but most of them exit en masse after *IllumiNations*. Upward of 30,000 people head for the parking lot and monorail station at once. Still, this congestion doesn't compare with the post-fireworks gridlock at the Magic Kingdom. One primary reason for the easier departure from Epcot is that its parking lot is adjacent to the park, not separated from it by a lake as at the Magic Kingdom. At the Magic Kingdom, departing visitors form bottlenecks at the monorail to the Transportation and Ticket Center and main parking lot. At Epcot, they proceed directly to their cars.

EPCOT TOURING PLANS

OUR EPCOT TOURING PLANS ARE FIELD-TESTED, step-by-step itineraries for seeing all major attractions with a minimum of waiting in line. They're designed to keep you ahead of the crowds while the park is filling in the morning, and to place you at the less-crowded attractions during Epcot's busier hours. They assume you'd be happier doing a little extra walking rather than a lot of extra standing in line.

Touring Epcot is much more strenuous and demanding than touring the other theme parks. Epcot requires about twice as much walking. And, unlike the Magic Kingdom, Epcot has no effective in-park transportation; wherever you want to go, it's always quicker to walk. Our plans will help you avoid crowds and bottlenecks on days of moderate to heavy attendance, but they can't shorten the distance you have to walk. (Wear comfortable shoes.) On days of lighter attendance, when crowd conditions aren't a critical factor, the plans will help you organize your tour. We offer five touring plans:

EPCOT ONE-DAY TOURING PLAN This plan packs as much as possible into one long day and requires a lot of hustle and stamina.

AUTHORS' SELECTIVE EPCOT ONE-DAY TOURING PLAN This plan eliminates some lesser attractions (in the authors' opinion) and offers a somewhat more relaxed tour if you have only one day.

EPCOT TWO-DAY SUNRISE–STARLIGHT TOURING PLAN This plan combines the easy touring of early morning on one day with Epcot's festivity and live pageantry at night on the second day. The first day requires some backtracking and hustle but is much more laid-back than either one-day plan.

EPCOT TWO-DAY EARLY-RISER TOURING PLAN This is the most efficient plan, eliminating 90% of the backtracking and extra walking required by the other plans while still providing a comprehensive tour.

EPCOT "NOT A TOURING PLAN" TOURING PLANS We present for the type-B reader touring plans that avoid detailed step-by-step strategies for saving every last minute in line. For Epcot, these "not" touring plans include advice for adults and parents with one day in the park, for anyone with two days, and for anyone with an afternoon and a full day to tour.

PRELIMINARY INSTRUCTIONS FOR ALL EPCOT TOURING PLANS

1. Call ☎ 407-824-4321 in advance for the hours of operation on the day of your visit.
2. Make reservations at the Epcot full-service restaurant(s) of your choice in advance of your visit.

EPCOT ONE-DAY TOURING PLAN (see page 822)

FOR Adults and children age 8 or older.
ASSUMES Willingness to experience all major rides and shows.

This plan requires a lot of walking and some backtracking in order to avoid long waits in line. A little extra walking and some early-morning hustle will spare you two to three hours of standing in line. You might not complete the tour. How far you get depends on how quickly you move from attraction to attraction, how many times you rest and eat, how quickly the park fills, and what time it closes.

This plan is not recommended for families with very young children. If you're touring with young children and have only one day, use the Authors' Selective Epcot One-day Touring Plan. Break after lunch and relax at your hotel, returning to the park in late afternoon. If you can allocate two days to Epcot, use one of the Epcot two-day touring plans.

AUTHORS' SELECTIVE EPCOT ONE-DAY TOURING PLAN (see page 823)

FOR All parties.

ASSUMES Willingness to experience major rides and shows.

This touring plan includes only what the author believes is the best Epcot has to offer. However, exclusion of an attraction doesn't mean it isn't worthwhile.

Families with children younger than age 8 using this touring plan should review Epcot attractions in our Small-child Fright-potential Chart in Part Six (see pages 330–333). Rent a stroller for any child small enough to fit in one, and take your young children back to the hotel for a nap after lunch. If you can allocate two days to see Epcot, try one of the Epcot two-day touring plans.

EPCOT TWO-DAY SUNRISE–STARLIGHT TOURING PLAN (see pages 824 and 825)

FOR All parties.

This touring plan is for visitors who want to tour Epcot comprehensively over two days. Day One takes advantage of early-morning touring opportunities. Day Two begins in late afternoon and continues until closing.

Many readers spend part of their Disney World arrival day traveling, checking into their hotel, and unpacking. The second day of the Epcot Two-Day Sunrise–Starlight Touring Plan is ideal for people who want to commence their Epcot visit later in the day.

Families with children younger than age 8 using this plan should review Epcot attractions in our Small-child Fright-potential Chart in Part Six (see pages 330–333). Rent a stroller for any child small enough to fit into one. Break off Day One no later than 2:30 p.m. and return to your hotel for rest. If you missed attractions called for in Day One, add them to your itinerary on Day Two.

EPCOT TWO-DAY EARLY-RISER TOURING PLAN (see pages 826 and 827)

FOR All parties.

This is the most efficient of the Epcot touring plans. It takes advantage of easy touring made possible by morning's light crowds. Most folks will complete each day of the plan by midafternoon. While the plan doesn't include *IllumiNations* or other evening festivities, these activities, along with dinner at an Epcot restaurant, can be added at your discretion.

Families with children younger than age 8 using this plan should review Epcot attractions in the Small-child Fright-potential Chart in Part Six (see pages 330–333). Rent a stroller for any child small enough to fit in one.

PART THIRTEEN

ANIMAL KINGDOM

WITH ITS LUSH FLORA, WINDING STREAMS, meandering paths, and exotic setting, Animal Kingdom is a stunningly beautiful theme park. The landscaping alone conjures images of rain forest, veldt, and formal gardens. Soothing, mysterious, and exciting, every vista is a feast for the eye. Add to this loveliness a population of more than 1,000 animals, replicas of Africa's and Asia's most intriguing architecture, and a diverse array of singularly original attractions, and you have the most distinctive of all the Disney theme parks. In Animal Kingdom, Disney has created an environment to savor.

unofficial **TIP**
Three attractions—**Dinosaur, Expedition Everest,** and **Kilimanjaro Safaris**—are among the best in the Disney repertoire.

At 500 acres, Disney's Animal Kingdom is five times the size of the Magic Kingdom and more than twice the size of Epcot. But as is the case with Disney's Hollywood Studios, most of Animal Kingdom's vast geography is accessible only on guided tours or as part of attractions. Animal Kingdom features six sections, or "lands": **The Oasis, Discovery Island, DinoLand U.S.A., Camp Minnie-Mickey, Africa,** and **Asia.**

Its size notwithstanding, Animal Kingdom features a limited number of attractions. To be exact, there are seven rides, several walk-through exhibits, an indoor theater, four amphitheaters, a conservation exhibit, and a children's playground.

The evolution of Animal Kingdom has been interesting. With regard to the Florida theme-park market, it is seen to be taking dead aim at the recently resurgent Busch Gardens in Tampa, a theme park known for its exceptional zoological exhibits and numerous thrill rides. Disney always preferred the neatly controlled movements of audio-animatronic animals to the unpredictable behaviors of real critters. Disney's only previous foray into zoological exhibits landed the Walt Disney Company in court for exterminating a bunch of indigenous birds that tried to take up residence on Disney property. When it comes to rides, Disney won't even dignify the term. In Disney parks, there are no rides, you see—only adventures. Attractions such as modern roller coasters, where the thrill of motion dominates visual, audio, and story-line elements, are antithetical to the Imagineering notion of attraction design.

Not to Be Missed at Animal Kingdom

Africa	Kilimanjaro Safaris
Asia	Expedition Everest
Camp Minnie-Mickey	*Festival of the Lion King*
DinoLand U.S.A.	Dinosaur, *Finding Nemo–The Musical*
Discovery Island	*It's Tough to Be a Bug!*

Unfortunately for Disney, however, the creative natural-habitat zoological exhibits and state-of-the-art thrill rides developed by Busch Gardens are immensely popular, and as any student of the Walt Disney Company can attest, there is nothing like a successful competitor to make the Disney folks change their tune. So, all the smoke, mirrors, and press releases aside, here's what you get at Animal Kingdom: natural-habitat zoological exhibits and state-of-the-art thrill rides. Big surprise!

Even if the recipe is tried-and-true, the Disney version serves up more than its share of innovations, particularly when it comes to the wildlife habitats. In fact, zoologists worldwide practically salivate at the thought of Disney Imagineers applying their talent to zoo design. Living up to expectations, the wildlife exhibits at Animal Kingdom do break some new ground. For starters, there's lots of space, thus allowing for the sweeping vistas that Discovery Channel viewers would expect in, say, an African veldt setting. Then there are the enclosures, natural in appearance, with few or no apparent barriers between you and the animals. The operative word, of course, is *apparent*. That flimsy stand of bamboo separating you from a gorilla is actually a neatly disguised set of steel rods imbedded in concrete. The Imagineers even take a crack at certain animals' stubborn unwillingness to be on display. A lion that would rather sleep out of sight under a bush, for example, is lured to center stage with nice, cool, climate-controlled artificial rocks.

With more than a decade under its belt, Animal Kingdom has received mixed reviews. Guests complain loudly about the park layout and the necessity of backtracking through Discovery Island in order to access the various themed areas. Congested walkways, lack of shade, and insufficient air-conditioning also rank high on the gripe list. However, most of the attractions (with one or two notable exceptions) have been well received. Also praised are the natural-habitat animal exhibits as well as the park architecture and landscaping. We marvel at the fact that demographically similar readers come away with such vastly differing opinions. A 36-year-old mother of three, for example, exclaims:

> *Animal Kingdom is a monstrous disappointment! Disney should be ashamed to have their name on it!*

Meanwhile, a 34-year-old mom with two children reports:

> *Animal Kingdom was our favorite theme park at Disney World. We spent four evenings out of our seven-day vacation there.*

And from an Indiana reader:

> *The architecture, landscaping, and design were INCREDIBLE.*

Animal Kingdom

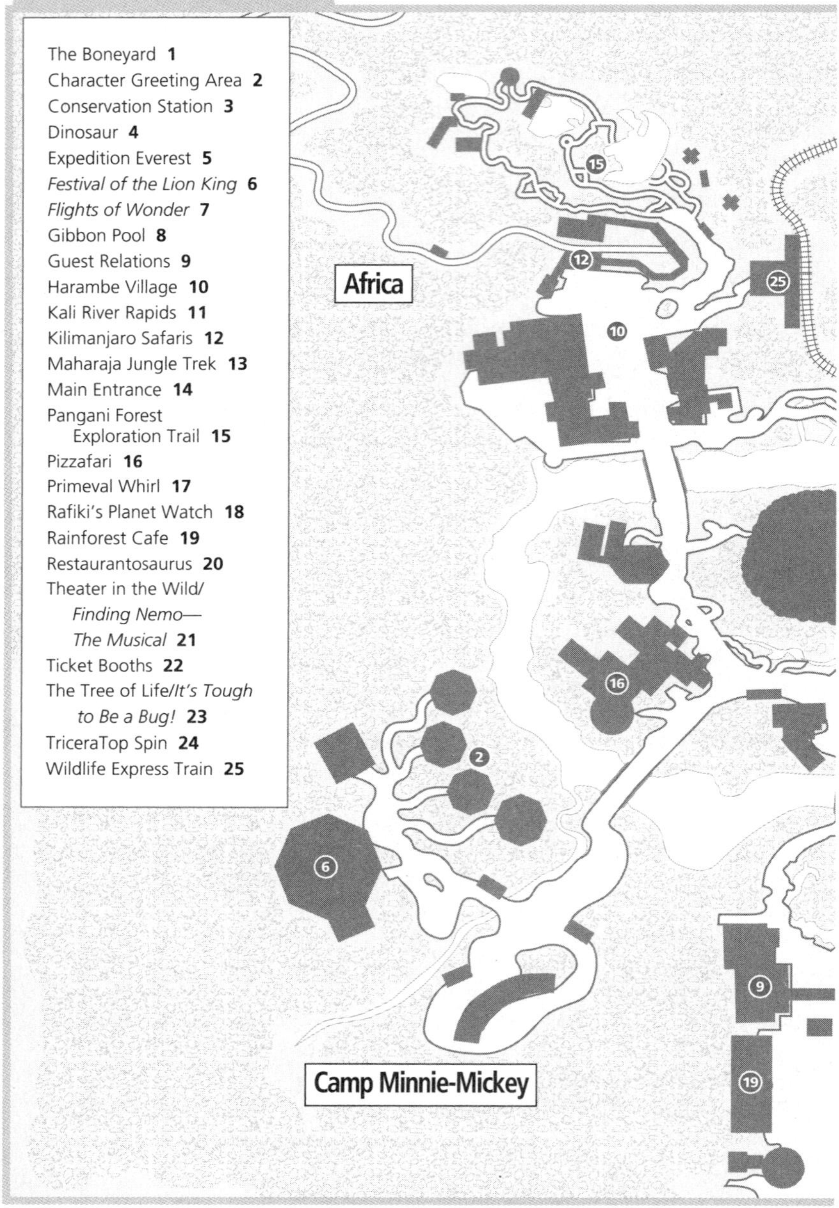

The Boneyard **1**
Character Greeting Area **2**
Conservation Station **3**
Dinosaur **4**
Expedition Everest **5**
Festival of the Lion King **6**
Flights of Wonder **7**
Gibbon Pool **8**
Guest Relations **9**
Harambe Village **10**
Kali River Rapids **11**
Kilimanjaro Safaris **12**
Maharaja Jungle Trek **13**
Main Entrance **14**
Pangani Forest Exploration Trail **15**
Pizzafari **16**
Primeval Whirl **17**
Rafiki's Planet Watch **18**
Rainforest Cafe **19**
Restaurantosaurus **20**
Theater in the Wild/ *Finding Nemo—The Musical* **21**
Ticket Booths **22**
The Tree of Life/*It's Tough to Be a Bug!* **23**
TriceraTop Spin **24**
Wildlife Express Train **25**

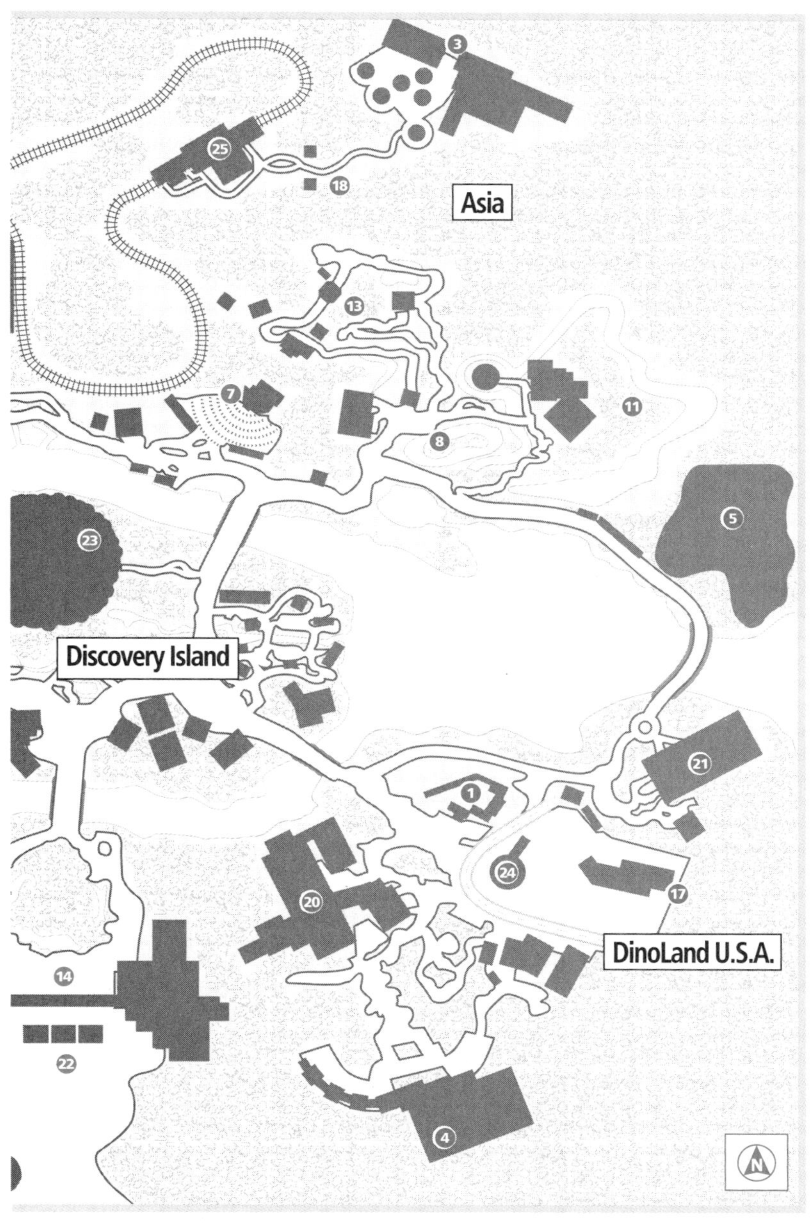

Asia
Discovery Island
DinoLand U.S.A.

In truth, Animal Kingdom is a park to linger over and savor—two things that Disney, with its crowds, lines, and regimentation, has conditioned us not to do. But many people intuit that Animal Kingdom must be approached in a different way, including this mother of three (ages 5, 7, and 9) from Hampton Bay, New York:

Despite the crowds, we really enjoyed Animal Kingdom. In order to enjoy it, you really must have the right attitude. It is an educational experience, not a thrill park. Talk to the employees and you won't regret it. We spoke to an employee who played games with the kids—my daughter found a drawer full of butterflies, and the boys located a hidden ostrich egg and lion skull. If we had not stopped to talk to this guide, we would have joined the hordes running down the trail in search of "something exciting to do."

A southwestern family agrees, writing:

Animal Kingdom with kids should be approached as you would birdwatching, fossil hunting, or nature walks. To enjoy it, you need to slow down, stop and look, and, especially, engage the cast members. Most have years of experience with animals and are very capable of interacting and sharing their knowledge on any level. Encourage your children to ask questions; the answers are educational, enlightening, and a wonderful alternative to standing in a hot queue.

Finally, a suggestion from a Frisco, Texas, reader:

We used your Animal Kingdom touring plan with some very few alterations, and it worked really well. We split our visit to Animal Kingdom into two days, which made it really nice. In the past, we had attempted to spend the whole day there—we were always wiped out by 3:30 and still hadn't seen everything we wanted. This worked much better. I highly recommend it.

And so do we if you have the luxury of spending two days at Animal Kingdom. That goes for the other three parks, too. Spreading your visit over two days makes for a more comprehensive and relaxed tour.

ARRIVING

ANIMAL KINGDOM IS OFF OSCEOLA PARKWAY in the southwest corner of Walt Disney World and is not too far from Blizzard Beach, the Coronado Springs Resort, and the All-Star Resorts. Animal Kingdom Lodge is about a mile away from the park on its west side. From Interstate 4, take Exit 64B, US 192, to the so-called Walt Disney World main entrance (World Drive) and follow the signs to Animal Kingdom. Animal Kingdom has its own 6,000-car pay parking lot with close-in parking for the disabled. Once parked, you can walk to the entrance or catch a ride on one of Disney's trademark trams.

unofficial **TIP**
Mark the location of your car on your parking receipt and tuck it in a safe place (preferably on your person as opposed to in your car).

The park is connected to other Walt Disney World destinations by the Disney bus system.

Animal Kingdom Services

Most of the park's service facilities are located inside the main entrance and on Discovery Island as follows:

Baby Center/Baby Care Needs On Discovery Island, next to the Creature Comforts Shop

Banking Services ATMs located at the main entrance and on Discovery Island

Film and Cameras Just inside the main entrance at Garden Gate Gifts and in Africa at Duka La Filimu

First Aid On Discovery Island, next to the Creature Comforts Shop

Guest Relations/Information Inside the main entrance to the left

Live Entertainment and Parade Information Included in the park guide map, available free at Guest Relations

Lost and Found Inside the main entrance to the left

Lost Persons Can be reported at Guest Relations and at the Baby Center on Discovery Island

Storage Lockers Inside the main entrance to the left

Wheelchair and Stroller Rentals Inside the main entrance to the right

If you're staying at a Disney resort and plan to arrive at Animal Kingdom entrance before park opening, use Disney transportation rather than taking your own car. The Animal Kingdom parking lot often opens only 15 minutes before the park, causing long lines and frustration for drivers.

OPERATING HOURS

ANIMAL KINGDOM, NOT UNEXPECTEDLY, hosted tremendous crowds during its early years. Consequently, Disney management has done a fair amount of fiddling and experimenting with operating hours and opening procedures. Animal Kingdom's opening time now roughly corresponds to that of the other parks. Thus, you can expect a 9 a.m. opening during less busy times of the year and an 8 a.m. opening during holidays and high season. Animal Kingdom usually closes well before the other parks—as early as 5 p.m., in fact, during off-season. More common is a 6 or 7 p.m. closing.

Park-opening procedures at Animal Kingdom vary. Sometimes guests arriving prior to the official opening time are admitted to The Oasis and Discovery Island. The remainder of the park is roped off until official opening time. The rest of the time, those arriving early are held at the entrance turnstiles.

unofficial **TIP**
Arrive, admission in hand, 40 minutes before official opening during the summer and holiday periods, and 30 minutes before official opening the rest of the year.

During the financial turmoil of the last few years, Disney has laid off a number of cast members and trotted out several cost-cutting initiatives. One of these is to delay the daily opening of Kali River Rapids in Asia, as well as the Boneyard playground, the Wildlife Express Train, and Conservation Station until 30 minutes or so after the rest of Animal Kingdom opens. It's not clear whether these delayed openings are temporary or permanent, seasonal or year-round.

On holidays and other days of projected heavy attendance, Disney will open the park 30 to 60 minutes early.

Many guests wrap up their tour and leave by 3:30 or 4 p.m. Lines for the major rides and the 3-D movie in The Tree of Life will usually thin appreciably between 4 p.m. and closing time. If you arrive at 2 p.m. and take in a couple of stage shows (described later), waits should be tolerable by the time you hit The Tree of Life and the rides. As an added bonus for late-afternoon touring, the animals tend to be more active.

Animal Kingdom has joined the other three major theme parks in the Extra Magic Hours early-entry program. Even with Expedition Everest open, getting up early to participate in the program doesn't really save you any time standing in line. Our testing has shown that the additional attendance on early-entry days totally nullifies any advantage associated with being admitted an hour early—the time required to see the same set of attractions is almost exactly equal to the time required on a non-early-entry day. Our advice is to get an extra hour of sleep and visit when early entry is not in effect.

Likewise, Animal Kingdom takes part in the evening Extra Magic Hours rotation when a designated park remains open three hours beyond the official closing time for Disney-resort guests. Because most of the park's animals go to bed early, however, you're pretty much relegated to rides and shows.

Most animal exhibits and all of Rafiki's Planet Watch, including the Wildlife Express Train and Conservation Station, close at the same time that is posted for day guests. Exceptions to this will be Kilimanjaro Safaris and Pangani Forest Exploration Trail. These vary by sunset and stay open during Extra Magic Hours until 7:30 p.m. on days when regular closing hours are 5, 6, 7, or 8 p.m. As days get shorter with the change of seasons, the attractions close earlier. In the fall when the clocks are rolled back, Disney closes all animal exhibits as early as 4:45 p.m.

Extra Magic Hours do, however, space Animal Kingdom theater productions over a longer time period, making it possible to see them all at a more leisurely pace.

GETTING ORIENTED

AT THE ENTRANCE PLAZA ARE TICKET KIOSKS fronting the main entrance. To your right before the turnstiles are the kennel and an ATM. After you pass through the turnstiles, wheelchair and stroller rentals are to your right. Guest Relations, the park headquarters for information, handout park maps, entertainment schedules (*Times Guide*), missing persons, and lost and found, is to the left. Nearby are restrooms, public phones, and rental lockers. Beyond the entrance plaza, you enter The Oasis, a lushly vegetated network of converging pathways winding through a landscape punctuated with streams, waterfalls, and misty glades, and inhabited by what Disney calls "colorful and unusual animals."

The park is arranged somewhat like the Magic Kingdom, in a hub-and-spoke configuration. The lush, tropical Oasis serves as Main Street, funneling visitors to Discovery Island at the center of the park. Dominated by the park's central icon, the 14-story hand-carved Tree of Life, Discovery Island is the park's retail and dining center. From Discovery Island, guests can access the respective themed areas, known as Africa, Camp Minnie-Mickey, Asia, and DinoLand U.S.A. Discovery Island additionally hosts a theater attraction in The Tree of Life, and a number of short nature trails.

unofficial **TIP**
We suggest that you be open-minded and try everything. Disney rides and shows are rarely what you would anticipate.

To help you plan your day, we have profiled all of Animal Kingdom's major attractions.

For the time being, even if you dawdle in the shops and linger over the wildlife exhibits, you should easily be able to take in Animal Kingdom in one day.

The OASIS

THOUGH THE FUNCTIONAL PURPOSE OF THE OASIS is the same as that of Main Street in the Magic Kingdom (that is, to funnel guests to the center of the park), it also serves as what Disney calls a "transitional experience." In plain English, this means that it sets the stage and gets you into the right mood to enjoy Animal Kingdom. You will know the minute you pass through the turnstiles that this is not just another Main Street. Where Main Street, Hollywood Boulevard, and the Epcot entrance plaza direct you like an arrow straight into the heart of the respective parks, The Oasis immediately envelops you in an environment that is replete with choices. There is not one broad thoroughfare, but rather multiple paths. Each will deliver you to Discovery Island at the center of the park, but which path you choose and what you see along the way is up to you. There is nothing obvious about where you are going, no Cinderella Castle or giant golf ball to beckon you. There is instead a lush, green, canopied landscape with streams, grottos, and waterfalls, an environment that promises adventure without revealing its nature.

The natural-habitat zoological exhibits in The Oasis are representative of those throughout the park. Although extraordinarily lush and

DISNEY DISH WITH JIM HILL

NOT AN EASY IDEA TO GET BEHIND Walt Disney Imagineering genuinely struggled to come up with a concept for Animal Kingdom's entrance area that would set the proper style and tone for the theme park beyond. One possibility was a series of animal statues that would be seen marching, two by two, into an enormous re-creation of Noah's Ark. That led Joe Rohde, the creative lead on this project, to say, "Let me get this straight: the very first thing that the guests are going to see as they enter our theme park is this big parade of animal butts?" That was the, um, end of that idea.

unofficial **TIP**
You must be patient and look closely if you want to see the animals.

beautiful, the exhibits are primarily designed for the comfort and well-being of the animals.

A sign will identify the animal(s) in each exhibit, but there's no guarantee the animals will be immediately visible. Because most habitats are large and provide ample terrain for the occupants to hide, you must linger and concentrate, looking for small movements in the vegetation. When you do spot the animal, you may make out only a shadowy figure, or perhaps only a leg or a tail will be visible. In any event, don't expect the animals to stand out like a lump of coal in the snow. Animal-watching Disney-style requires a sharp eye and a bit of effort.

TOURING TIPS The Oasis is a place to linger and appreciate, and although this is exactly what the designers intended, it will be largely lost on Disney-conditioned guests who blitz through at warp speed to queue up for the big attractions. If you are a blitzer in the morning, plan to spend some time in The Oasis on your way out of the park. The Oasis usually closes 30 to 60 minutes after the rest of the park.

A WORD ABOUT ANIMAL KINGDOM LIVE SHOWS

WHILE WE WERE COLLECTING DATA for our touring-plan software, we discovered that the live performances are scheduled in such a way that it's exceedingly difficult to see all of them in one visit, especially if you want to see all the other stuff too. You will, at least once, need to dart out at the conclusion of one show and run halfway across the park to arrive at another show seconds before it begins (and hope that there's enough room at the last minute for you to get a seat). The only solution to the show-schedule conundrum is to take advantage of evening Extra Magic Hours. The Extra Magic Hours add three hours to your touring day, more than enough extra time to see all the shows at a relaxed pace. Showtimes, as well as scheduled character appearances and parades, are listed in the *Times Guide,* available free along with the park guide map.

DISCOVERY ISLAND

DISCOVERY ISLAND IS AN ISLAND OF tropical greenery and whimsical equatorial African architecture, executed in vibrant hues of teal, yellow, red, and blue. Connected to the other lands by bridges, the island is the hub from which guests can access the park's various themed areas. A village is arrayed in a crescent around the base of Animal Kingdom's signature landmark, **The Tree of Life.** Towering 14 stories above the village, The Tree of Life is this park's version of Cinderella Castle or Spaceship Earth. Flanked by pools, meadows, and exotic gardens populated by a diversity of birds and animals, The Tree of Life houses a theater attraction inspired by the Disney/Pixar film *A Bug's Life.*

As you enter Discovery Island via the bridge from The Oasis and the park entrance, you will see The Tree of Life directly ahead at the 12 o'clock position. The bridge to Asia is to the right of the tree at the 2 o'clock position, with the bridge to DinoLand U.S.A. at roughly 4 o'clock. The bridge connecting The Oasis to Discovery Island is at the 6 o'clock position; the bridge to Camp Minnie-Mickey is at 8 o'clock; and the bridge to Africa is at 11 o'clock.

Discovery Island is the park's central shopping, dining, and services headquarters. It is here that you will find the **First Aid** and **Baby Care** centers. For the best selection of Disney trademark merchandise, try the **Island Mercantile** shop. Counter-service food and snacks are available, but there are no full-service restaurants on Discovery Island (the three full-service restaurants in the park are the **Rainforest Cafe,** to the left of the main entrance; **Tusker House,** in Africa; and **Yak & Yeti,** in Asia).

The Tree of Life/*It's Tough to Be a Bug!* ★★★★

APPEAL BY AGE PRESCHOOL ★★★½ GRADE SCHOOL ★★★★ TEENS ★★★★ YOUNG ADULTS ★★★★ OVER 30 ★★★★ SENIORS ★★★★

What it is 3-D theater show. **Scope and scale** Major attraction. **When to go** Before 10:30 a.m., after 4 p.m. **Special comments** The theater is inside the tree. **Authors' rating** Zany and frenetic; ★★★★. **Duration of presentation** About 7½ minutes. **Probable waiting time** 12–30 minutes.

DISNEY DISH WITH JIM HILL

TIME TO BUG OFF? **Never mind how tough it is to be a bug. WDW officials have discovered that it's well-nigh impossible to get guests to make a return trip to The Tree of Life. (People don't enjoy a show where giant black-widow spiders bungee on them from above? Who'da thunk it?) Now the Imagineers are looking into replacing this *Bug's Life*–inspired film with a new Disneynature-sponsored 3-D movie that would clearly explain what Animal Kingdom is all about . . . without scaring the heck out of people.**

DESCRIPTION AND COMMENTS The Tree of Life, apart from its size, is quite a work of art. Although from afar it is certainly magnificent and imposing, it is not until you examine the tree at close range that you truly appreciate its rich detail. What appears to be ancient gnarled bark is, in fact, hundreds of carvings depicting all manner of wildlife, each integrated seamlessly into the trunk, roots, and limbs of the tree. A stunning symbol of the interdependence of all living things, The Tree of Life is the most visually compelling structure to be found in any Disney park.

In sharp contrast to the grandeur of the tree is the subject of the attraction housed within its trunk. Called *It's Tough to Be a Bug!,* this humorous 3-D presentation is about the difficulties of being a very small creature. Contrasting with the relatively serious tone of Animal Kingdom in general, *It's Tough to Be a Bug!* stands virtually alone in providing some much needed levity and whimsy. The show is similar to *Honey, I Shrunk the Audience* at Epcot in that it combines a 3-D film with an arsenal of tactile and visual special effects. We rate the *Bug* as not to be missed.

TOURING TIPS Because it's situated in the most eye-popping structure in the park, and also because there aren't that many attractions anyway, you can expect *It's Tough to Be a Bug!* to be mobbed most of the day. We recommend going in the morning after Kilimanjaro Safaris, Kali River Rapids, Expedition Everest, and Dinosaur. If you miss the *Bug* in the morning, try again in the late afternoon.

Be advised that *It's Tough to Be a Bug!* is very intense and that the special effects will do a number on young children as well as anyone who is squeamish about insects. A mother of two from Williamsville, New York, shared this experience:

> *We went* [to Animal Kingdom] *our very first day and almost lost the girls to any further Disney magic due to the 3-D movie* It's Tough to Be a Bug! *It was their first Disney experience, and almost their last. The story line was nebulous and difficult to follow—all they were aware of was the torture of sitting in a darkened theater being overrun with bugs. Total chaos, the likes of which I've never experienced, was breaking out around us. A constant stream of parents headed to the exits with terrorized children. Those that were left behind were screaming and crying as well. The 11-year-old refused to talk for 20 minutes after the fiasco, and the 3½-year-old wanted to go home—not back to the hotel, but home.*

Most readers, however, loved the bugs, including this mom from Brentwood, Tennessee:

> *Comments from your readers make* It's Tough to Be a Bug! *sound worse than Alien Encounter* [now closed]. *It's not. It's intense like* Honey, I Shrunk the Audience *but mostly funny. The bugs are cartoonlike instead of realistic and icky, so I can't understand what all the fuss is about. Disney has conditioned us to think of rodents as cute, so kids think nothing of walking up to a mouse the size of a porta-john but go nuts over some cartoon bugs.* Get a grip!

CAMP MINNIE-MICKEY

THIS LAND IS DESIGNED to be the Disney characters' Animal Kingdom headquarters. A small land, Camp Minnie-Mickey is about the size of Mickey's Toontown Fair but has a rustic and woodsy theme like a summer camp. In addition to a character meeting-and-greeting area, Camp Minnie-Mickey is home to a live stage production featuring Disney characters.

Situated in a cul-de-sac, Camp Minnie-Mickey is a pedestrian nightmare. Lines for the stage show and from the character-greeting areas spill out into the congested walkways, making movement almost impossible. To compound the problem, hundreds of parked strollers clog the paths, squeezing the flow of traffic to a trickle. Meanwhile, hordes of guests trying to enter Camp Minnie-Mickey collide with guests trying to exit on

DISNEY DISH WITH JIM HILL

BEASTLY BREAKTHROUGH? Could Pixar's first fairy tale hold the key to Disney's Animal Kingdom finally getting an area that will celebrate mythical beasts? The Imagineers certainly hope so, which is why they're keeping a very close eye on *The Bear and the Bow,* due to hit theaters in December of 2011. This Brenda Chapman film is set in Scotland, where a headstrong princess must combine the forces of nature and magic to battle an ancient curse. It's just that mix of nature and magic that WDI hopes will make *The Bear and the Bow* the springboard to finally getting Beastly Kingdom—the long-designed-but-never-built "land" that showcases creatures like unicorns, gryphons, and dragons—off the drawing board.

the bridge connecting the camp to Discovery Island. It's a planning error of the first order, one that seems totally avoidable in a theme park with as much usable acreage as Animal Kingdom.

Character Trails

DESCRIPTION AND COMMENTS Characters can be found at the end of each of several "character trails." Each trail has its own private reception area and, of course, its own queue. A sign in front of each queue tells you to which character the path leads. The most typical lineup has Mickey, Minnie, Goofy, and Donald at one queue each, but Daisy often subs for Donald during his lunch break. Goofy and the ducks often get replaced with characters from Disney's latest film, if the movie has anything to do with nature, animals, or the environment. Mickey and Minnie are constants.

TOURING TIPS Characters usually appear an hour after the rest of the park opens. Waiting in line to see them can be very time-consuming. We recommend visiting early in the morning or late in the afternoon. Because there are fewer attractions at Animal Kingdom than at the other parks, expect to find a disproportionate number of guests in Camp Minnie-Mickey. If the place is really mobbed, you may want to consider meeting the characters in one of the other parks. Ditto for the stage show.

Festival of the Lion King ★★★★

APPEAL BY AGE PRESCHOOL ★★★★½ GRADE SCHOOL ★★★★½ TEENS ★★★★½
YOUNG ADULTS ★★★★½ OVER 30 ★★★★½ SENIORS ★★★★★

What it is Theater-in-the-round stage show. **Scope and scale** Major attraction. **When to go** Before 11 a.m. or after 4 p.m. **Special comments** Performance times are listed in the handout park map or *Times Guide*. **Authors' rating** Upbeat and spectacular, not to be missed; ★★★★. **Duration of presentation** 25 minutes. **Preshow entertainment** None. **When to arrive** 20–30 minutes before showtime.

DESCRIPTION AND COMMENTS This energetic production, inspired by Disney's *Lion King* feature, is part stage show, part parade, part circus. Guests are seated in four sets of bleachers surrounding the stage and organized into separate cheering sections, which are called on to make elephant, warthog, giraffe, and lion noises (you won't be alone if you don't know how to make a giraffe or warthog noise). There is a great deal of parading around, some acrobatics, and a lot of singing and dancing. By our count, every tune from *The Lion King* is belted out and reprised several times. No joke—if you don't know the words to all the songs by the end of the show, you must have been asleep.

Unofficial Guide readers have been almost unanimous in their praise of *Festival of the Lion King*. This letter from a Naples, Florida, mom is typical:

> Festival of the Lion King *is a spectacular show with singers, dancers, fire twirlers, acrobats, robotics, and great set design. My whole family agreed this was the best thing we experienced at Animal Kingdom.*

TOURING TIPS This show is both popular and difficult to see. Your best bet is to go to the first show in the morning or to one of the last two performances in the evening. To see the show during the more crowded midday, you'll need to queue up at least 35 to 45 minutes before showtime. To minimize standing in the hot sun, refrain from hopping in line until the Disney people begin directing guests to the far-right queue. If you have small children or short adults in your party, sit higher up in the bleachers. The first five rows in particular have very little rise, making it difficult for those in rows two through five to see.

AFRICA

AFRICA IS THE LARGEST of Animal Kingdom's lands, and guests enter through Harambe, Disney's immensely sanitized version of a modern rural African town. There is a market (with modern cash registers); dining options consist of a sit-down buffet, limited counter service, and snack stands. What distinguishes Harambe is its understatement. Far from the stereotypical great-white-hunter image of an African town, Harambe is definitely (and realistically) not exotic. The buildings, while interesting, are quite plain and architecturally simple. Though it's better maintained and more idealized than the real McCoy, Disney's Harambe would be a lot more at home in Kenya than the Magic Kingdom's Main Street would be in Missouri.

Harambe serves as the gateway to the African veldt habitat, Animal Kingdom's largest and most ambitious zoological exhibit. Access to the veldt is via the **Kilimanjaro Safaris** attraction, located at the end of Harambe's main drag near the fat-trunked baobab tree. Harambe is also the departure point for the train to **Rafiki's Planet Watch** and **Conservation Station,** the park's veterinary headquarters.

Kilimanjaro Safaris (FASTPASS) ★★★★★

APPEAL BY AGE PRESCHOOL ★★★★½ GRADE SCHOOL ★★★★½ TEENS ★★★★½
YOUNG ADULTS ★★★★★ OVER 30 ★★★★½ SENIORS ★★★★★

What it is Truck ride through an African wildlife reservation. **Scope and scale** Super-headliner. **When to go** As soon as the park opens, in the 2 hours before closing, or use FASTPASS. **Authors' rating** Truly exceptional, not to be missed; ★★★★★. **Duration of ride** About 20 minutes. **Average wait in line per 100 people ahead of you** 4 minutes; assumes full-capacity operation with 18-second dispatch interval. **Loading speed** Fast.

DISNEY DISH WITH JIM HILL

ALL THEY NEED ARE PUNCH CARDS You'd think that catching the very last safari of the day would be a smart move—rather than racing through this 100-acre re-creation of the African savanna, your driver would be able to slow down so you could see more animals. Fact is, these creatures have learned over time that as soon as that last vehicle rolls through, the gates leading to their backstage barns open. So what you tend to see on that last safari is a lot of animals heading offstage, ready to grab a snack and a snooze.

DESCRIPTION AND COMMENTS The park's premier zoological attraction, Kilimanjaro Safaris offers an exceptionally realistic, albeit brief, imitation of an actual African photo safari. Thirty-two guests at a time board tall, open safari vehicles and are dispatched into a simulated African veldt habitat. Animals such as zebras, wildebeests, impalas, Thomson's gazelles, giraffes, and even rhinos roam apparently free, while predators such as lions, as well as potentially dangerous large animals like hippos, are separated from both prey and guests by all-but-invisible, natural-appearing barriers. Although the animals have more than 100 acres of savanna, woodland, streams, and rocky hills to call home, careful placement of water holes, forage, and salt licks ensures that the critters are hanging out by the road when safari vehicles roll by.

A scripted narration provides a story line about finding Big Red and Little Red, a mother elephant and her baby, while an onboard guide points out and identifies the various animals encountered. Toward the end of the ride, the safari chases poachers who are after the elephants.

Having traveled in Kenya and Tanzania, I (Bob) will tell you that Disney has done an amazing job of replicating the sub-Saharan east-African landscape. The main difference that an east African would notice is that Disney's version is greener and, generally speaking, less barren. As on a real African safari, what animals you see, and how many, is pretty much a matter of luck. We've experienced Kilimanjaro Safaris upwards of 50 times and had a different experience on each trip.

If the attraction has a shortcoming, it is the rather strident story about the poachers and Big Red, which, while thought-provoking, is somewhat distracting when you're trying to spot and enjoy the wildlife. Since it's repeated on every trip, it can really get on your nerves after the first couple of times.

TOURING TIPS With Expedition Everest open, Kilimanjaro Safaris is Animal Kingdom's number-two draw. This is good news: by distributing guests more evenly throughout the park, Expedition Everest makes it unnecessary to run to the Kilimanjaro Safaris first thing in the morning. Our Animal Kingdom touring plan has you obtain FASTPASSes for the safaris just before lunch. While your FASTPASS return window approaches, you'll have plenty of time to eat and tour the rest of Africa. Before Everest, seeing the Safaris early meant backtracking to Africa later in the day to see exhibits and attractions that were not open first thing in the morning; our new touring plan eliminates all of that extra walking, too.

Waits for the Kilimanjaro Safaris diminish in late afternoon, sometimes as early as 3:30 p.m. but more commonly somewhat later. As noted previously, Kilimanjaro Safaris is a FASTPASS attraction. If the wait exceeds 30 minutes when you arrive, by all means use FASTPASS. The downside to FASTPASS, and the reason we prefer that you ride around lunchtime, is that there aren't many other attractions in Africa to occupy your attention while you wait for your FASTPASS return time. This means you will probably be touring somewhere far removed when it's time to backtrack to Safaris.

If you want to take photos on your safari, be advised that the vehicle doesn't stop very often, so be prepared to snap while under way. Also, don't worry about the ride itself: it really isn't very rough. Finally, the only thing that a young child might find intimidating is crossing an "old bridge" that pretends to collapse under your truck.

Pangani Forest Exploration Trail ★★★★

APPEAL BY AGE PRESCHOOL ★★★★ GRADE SCHOOL ★★★★ TEENS ★★★★
YOUNG ADULTS ★★★★ OVER 30 ★★★★ SENIORS ★★★★

What it is Walk-through zoological exhibit. **Scope and scale** Major attraction. **When to go** Before 10 a.m. and after 2:30 p.m. **Authors' rating** ★★★. **Duration of tour** About 20–25 minutes.

DESCRIPTION AND COMMENTS Because guests disembark from the safari at the entrance to the Pangani Forest Exploration Trail, many guests try the trail immediately after the safari. Winding between the domain of two troops of lowland gorillas, it's hard to see what, if anything, separates you from the primates. Also on the trail are a hippo pool with an underwater viewing area, and a naked-mole-rat exhibit. A highlight of the trail is an exotic-bird aviary so craftily designed that you can barely tell you're in an enclosure.

TOURING TIPS The Pangani Forest Exploration Trail is lush, beautiful, and jammed to the gills with people much of the time. Guests exiting the safari can choose between returning to Harambe or walking the Pangani Forest Exploration Trail. Many opt for the trail. Thus, when the safari is operating at full tilt, it spews hundreds of guests every couple of minutes onto the Exploration Trail. The one-way trail in turn becomes so clogged that nobody can move or see much of anything. After a minute or two, however, you catch the feel of the mob moving forward in small lurches. From then on you shift, elbow, grunt, and wriggle your way along, every so often coming to an animal exhibit. Here you endeavor to work your way close to the rail but are opposed by people trapped against the rail who are trying to rejoin the surging crowd. The animals, as well as their natural-habitat enclosures, are pretty nifty if you can fight your way close enough to see them.

Clearly this attraction is either badly designed, misplaced, or both. Your only real chance for enjoying it is to walk through before 10 a.m. (that is, before the safari hits full stride) or after 2:30 p.m.

Another strategy, especially if you're more into the wildlife than the thrill rides, is to head for Kilimanjaro Safaris as soon as the park opens and get a FASTPASS instead of riding. Early in the morning, the return window will be short—just long enough, in fact, for an uncrowded, leisurely tour of the Pangani Forest Exploration Trail before you go on safari.

RAFIKI'S PLANET WATCH

THIS AREA SHOWED UP ON PARK MAPS in 2001. It's not a "land" and not really an attraction either. Our best guess is that Disney is using the name as an umbrella for Conservation Station, the petting zoo, and the environmental exhibits accessible from Harambe via the Wildlife Express Train. Presumably, Disney hopes that invoking Rafiki (a beloved character from *The Lion King*) will stimulate guests to make the effort to check out things in this far-flung outpost of the park.

Conservation Station and Affection Section ★★★

APPEAL BY AGE PRESCHOOL ★★★½ GRADE SCHOOL ★★★½ TEENS ★★½
YOUNG ADULTS ★★½ OVER 30 ★★★ SENIORS ★★★

What it is Behind-the-scenes walk-through educational exhibit and petting zoo. **Scope and scale** Minor attraction. **When to go** Anytime. **Special comments**

DISNEY DISH WITH JIM HILL

WATCHING RAFIKI'S PLANET WATCH **As The Walt Disney Company continues to explore different ways to get people excited about their theme parks, among the ideas currently being floated to boost attendance at Animal Kingdom is a new YouTube channel that would be based out of Conservation Station. This proposed series of online programs would showcase the vets who work in this facility and the many creatures that they interact with over the course of a typical workday. Disney hopes that the people who regularly tune in to watch these shows on their laptop might then be compelled to come see the real place the next time they visit WDW.**

Opens 30 minutes after the rest of the park. **Authors' rating** Evolving; ★★★. **Probable waiting time** None.

DESCRIPTION AND COMMENTS Conservation Station is Animal Kingdom's veterinary and conservation headquarters. Located on the perimeter of the African section of the park, Conservation Station is, strictly speaking, a backstage, working facility. Here guests can meet wildlife experts, observe some of the Station's ongoing projects, and learn about the behind-the-scenes operations of the park. The Station includes a rehabilitation area for injured animals and a nursery for recently born (or hatched) critters. Vets and other experts are on hand to answer questions.

While there are several permanent exhibits, including Affection Section (an animal-petting area), what you see at Conservation Station will largely depend on what's going on when you arrive. On the days we visited, there wasn't enough happening to warrant waiting in line twice (coming and going) for the train. Most of our readers comment that Conservation Station is not worth the hassle. A Tinley Park, Illinois, mom writes:

Skip Conservation Station at Animal Kingdom. Between the train ride to get to it and being there, we wasted a precious 1½ hours!

A mother of one from Austin, Texas, had a better experience:

Best thing at Conservation Station was the wildlife experts presenting one animal at a time—live, with info—very interesting.

Ditto for a Denver family:

We really enjoyed Conservation Station at Animal Kingdom. We saw a 13-foot python eating a rat!

And a reader from Kent in the United Kingdom was amused by both the goings-on and the other guests:

The most memorable part of Animal Kingdom for me was watching a veterinary surgeon and his team [at Conservation Station] *perform an operation on a rat snake that had inadvertently swallowed a golf ball, presumably believing it to be an egg! This operation took about an hour and caused at least one onlooker to pass out.*

You can access Conservation Station by taking the Wildlife Express Train directly from Harambe. To return to the center of the park, continue the loop from Conservation Station back to Harambe.

TOURING TIPS Conservation Station is interesting, but you have to invest a little effort, and it helps to be inquisitive. Because it's so removed from the rest of the park, you'll never bump into Conservation Station unless you take the train.

Habitat Habit!

DESCRIPTION AND COMMENTS Listed on the park maps as an attraction is Habitat Habit!, located on the pedestrian path between the train station and Conservation Station. It consists of a tiny collection of signs (about coexistence with wildlife) and a few cotton-top tamarins. To call it an attraction is absurd.

Wildlife Express Train ★★

APPEAL BY AGE PRESCHOOL ★★★★ GRADE SCHOOL ★★★ TEENS ★★★
YOUNG ADULTS ★★½ OVER 30 ★★★ SENIORS ★★★

What it is Scenic railroad ride to Rafiki's Planet Watch and Conservation Station. **Scope and scale** Minor attraction. **When to go** Anytime. **Special comments** Opens 30 minutes after the rest of the park. **Authors' rating** Ho-hum; ★★. **Duration of ride** About 5–7 minutes one-way. **Average wait in line per 100 people ahead of you** 9 minutes. **Loading speed** Moderate.

DESCRIPTION AND COMMENTS This transportation ride snakes behind the African wildlife reserve as it makes its loop connecting Harambe to Rafiki's Planet Watch and Conservation Station. En route, you see the nighttime enclosures for the animals that populate the Kilimanjaro Safaris. Similarly, returning to Harambe, you see the backstage areas of Asia. Regardless of which direction you're heading, the sights are not especially interesting.

TOURING TIPS Most guests will embark for Rafiki's Planet Watch and Conservation Station after experiencing the Kilimanjaro Safaris and the Pangani Forest Exploration Trail. Thus, the train begins to get crowded between 10 and 11 a.m. Though you may catch a glimpse of several species from the train, it can't compare to Kilimanjaro Safaris for seeing the animals.

ASIA

CROSSING THE ASIA BRIDGE FROM DISCOVERY ISLAND, you enter Asia through the village of Anandapur, a veritable collage of Asian themes inspired by the architecture and ruins of India, Thailand, Indonesia, and Nepal. Situated near the bank of the Chakranadi River (translation: "the river that runs in circles") and surrounded by lush vegetation, Anandapur provides access to a gibbon exhibit and to Asia's two feature attractions, the **Kali River Rapids** whitewater raft ride and **Expedition Everest.** Also in Asia is *Flights of Wonder,* an educational production about birds.

Expedition Everest—yep, another mountain, and at 200 feet, the tallest in Florida—is a super-headliner roller coaster. You board an old mountain railway destined for the foot of Mount Everest that ends up racing both forward and backward through caverns and frigid canyons en route to paying a social call on the Abominable Snowman. Expedition Everest is billed as a "family thrill ride," which means simply that it's more like Big Thunder Mountain Railroad than like the Rock 'n' Roller Coaster.

Expedition Everest (FASTPASS) ★★★★½

APPEAL BY AGE **PRESCHOOL** ★★½ **GRADE SCHOOL** ★★★★½ **TEENS** ★★★★★
YOUNG ADULTS ★★★★★ **OVER 30** ★★★★★ **SENIORS** ★★★½

What it is High-speed,outdoor roller coaster through Nepalese mountain village. **Scope and scale** Super-headliner. **When to go** Before 9:30 a.m. or after 3 p.m., or use FASTPASS. **Special comments** 44" height requirement. **Authors' rating** Contains some of the park's most stunning visual elements; ★★★★½. **Average wait in line per 100 people ahead of you** Just under 4 minutes; assumes 2 tracks operating. **Loading speed** Moderate–fast.

DISNEY DISH WITH JIM HILL

MAYBE HE COULD TRY JENNY CRAIG? So why is the 22-foot-tall, 20,000-pound Yeti no longer moving? Because he's so heavy and has moved so fast since his tenure at Expedition Everest began that his metal support is now bent beyond repair. The Imagineers are now working to get the Yeti moving again that won't involve dismantling most of the ride. Given the level of technology involved, this won't be a quick fix, so expect the snowman to give merely a polite (but fierce!) wave for the foreseeable future.

DESCRIPTION AND COMMENTS The first true roller coaster in Animal Kingdom, Expedition Everest earned the park's longest waits in line from the moment it opened—and for good reason. Your journey begins with an elaborate waiting area modeled after a Nepalese village; then you board an old train headed for the top of Mount Everest. Throughout the waiting area you'll find posted notes from previous expeditions, some with cryptic observations regarding a mysterious creature that supposedly guards the mountain. These ominous signs are ignored (as if you have a choice!), resulting in a high-speed encounter with the Abominable Snowman himself.

The ride consists of tight turns (some while traveling backward), hills, and dips, but no loops or inversions. From your departure at the loading station through your first high-speed descent, you'll see some of the most spectacular panoramas available in Walt Disney World. On a clear day, you'll be able to view the arrangement of the buildings at Coronado Springs, Epcot's Spaceship Earth, and possibly downtown Orlando. But look quickly, because you'll immediately be propelled, projectile-like, through the inner and outer reaches of the mountain. The final drop and last few turns are among the best-designed coaster effects Disney has ever made. A few minor criticisms: At a couple of points, your vehicle is stopped while the ride's track is reconfigured, affecting the attraction's continuity. And while the Yeti audio-animatronic is undoubtedly impressive, he's as elusive as his real-life counterpart. But don't let these small shortcomings stop you from riding.

The coaster reaches a top speed of around 50 miles per hour, just about twice that of Space Mountain, so expect to see the usual warnings for health and safety. The first few seats of these vehicles offer the best front-seat experience of any Disney coaster, indoor or out. If at all possible, ask to sit up front. Also, look for the animal poop on display in the FASTPASS return line—a deliberate attempt at verisimilitude, or did Disney run out of money for ride props and use whatever they could find? You decide.

As you might expect for a super-headliner attraction, Expedition Everest was the subject of much reader mail. A Seattle family rated Expedition Everest four thumbs up:

The Expedition Everest ride is tremendous. It has enough surprises and runaway speed to make it one of the more enjoyable in the whole Orlando area. The little details leading up to the ride are unbelievable.

From a Somerset, Kentucky, woman:

This ride is full of surprises! Every time you think you know what's going to happen next, you don't!

For a Kettering, Ohio, mom, the ride was a multigenerational happening:

Expedition Everest alone is worth the cost of park admission—we had three generations on the ride, and everybody loved it!

A Macon, Georgia, teen did some recruiting for the yeti:

Expedition Everest was so smoooooth! I went right out and brought my granny back to ride it. She didn't throw up or anything!

Beating the morning crowds to Expedition Everest is also a hot topic. From a Yonkers, New York, man:

At Animal Kingdom the first ride we rode was Expedition Everest. When the park opened the Disney people walked the crowd through Asia to the ride. We went right toward DinoLand and followed the path around the lake to Everest. We arrived about 90 seconds ahead of the crowd being walked in and were the first to ride. Upon exiting the ride we noticed the line was already enormous and to our delight the wait at the other major rides was negligible.

TOURING TIPS Get FASTPASSes for Everest first thing in the morning. Alternatively, ride immediately after the park opens or during evening Extra Magic Hours. If using FASTPASS in the morning, try to tour DinoLand U.S.A. before you return; Kali River Rapids and *Flights of Wonder* don't usually open with the rest of Asia, so you'll backtrack less if you can get the must-see attractions in DinoLand covered early.

Flights of Wonder ★★★★

APPEAL BY AGE PRESCHOOL ★★★★ GRADE SCHOOL ★★★★ TEENS ★★★★
YOUNG ADULTS ★★★★ OVER 30 ★★★★ SENIORS ★★★★

What it is Stadium show about birds. **Scope and scale** Major attraction. **When to go** Anytime. **Special comments** Performance times listed in handout park map or *Times Guide*. **Authors' rating** Unique; ★★★★. **Duration of presentation** 30 minutes. **Preshow entertainment** None. **When to arrive** 20–30 minutes before showtime.

DESCRIPTION AND COMMENTS Both interesting and fun, *Flights of Wonder* is well paced and showcases a surprising number of bird species. The show has been rescripted, abandoning an improbable plot for a more straightforward educational presentation. The focus of *Flights of Wonder* is on the natural talents and characteristics of the various species, so don't expect to see any parrots riding bicycles. The natural behaviors, however, far surpass any tricks learned from humans. Overall, the presentation is fascinating and exceeds most guests' expectations. A Brattleboro, Vermont, reader found *Flights of Wonder* especially compelling, writing:

DISNEY DISH WITH JIM HILL

UP AND AWAY **Given that the strictly educational slant of *Flights of Wonder* tends to make it something that guests don't repeat during a second trip to Animal Kingdom, WDW Entertainment is looking for ways to freshen up this bird show. Among the ideas currently under consideration is folding in some characters from Pixar's *Up:* Russell, the young Wilderness Explorer, and Kevin, the giant prehistoric bird that famed adventurer Charles Muntz is after.**

In our opinion the highlight of Animal Kingdom is Flights of Wonder. *The ornithologist guide is not only a wealth of information but a talented, comedic entertainer. The birds are thrilling, and we especially appreciated the fact that their antics, although fascinating to behold, were not the results of training against the grain but actual survival techniques the birds use in the wild.*

Flights of Wonder exceeded the expectations of a Colorado Springs family with two elementary-school-age kids:

A coworker with kids the same age as ours said her kids loved Flights of Wonder. *I made a point to take our family and I think it was the highlight of our trip. Midway through the show I stopped taking pictures of the birds and began taking pictures of the expressions of amazement and joy on the faces of my kids and husband.*

TOURING TIPS *Flights of Wonder* plays at the stadium located near the Asia Bridge on the walkway into Asia. Though the stadium is covered, it's not air-conditioned, thus, early-morning and late-afternoon performances are more comfortable. To play it safe, arrive about 10 to 15 minutes before showtime.

Kali River Rapids (FASTPASS) ★★★½

APPEAL BY AGE **PRESCHOOL** ★★★★ **GRADE SCHOOL** ★★★★½ **TEENS** ★★★★½
YOUNG ADULTS ★★★★ **OVER 30** ★★★★ **SENIORS** ★★★★

What it is Whitewater raft ride. **Scope and scale** Headliner. **When to go** Before 10:30 a.m. or after 4:30 p.m., or use FASTPASS. **Special comments** You are guaranteed to get wet. Opens 30 minutes after the rest of the park. 38" height requirement. Switching-off option available (see page 339). **Authors' rating** Short but scenic; ★★★½. **Duration of ride** About 5 minutes. **Average wait in line per 100 people ahead of you** 5 minutes. **Loading speed** Moderate.

DESCRIPTION AND COMMENTS Whitewater raft rides have been a hot-weather favorite of theme-park patrons for more than 20 years. The ride itself consists

DISNEY DISH WITH JIM HILL

LOUD CROWDS AND BIG CATS DON'T MIX **The Imagineers' original plan for Kali River Rapids called for rafts to float through the tiger enclosure so that guests would be able to catch a glimpse of the cats in the wild, so to speak. But when animal behaviorists pointed out that all the screaming from wet guests would likely drive the tigers toward the very back of their enclosure—keeping them well out of sight—Imagineering abandoned its plans for "Tiger River Rapids" and opted for a walk-through tiger exhibit instead.**

of an unguided trip down a man-made river in a circular rubber raft with a top-mounted platform seating 12 people. The raft essentially floats free in the current and is washed downstream through rapids and waves. Because the river is fairly wide, with numerous currents, eddies, and obstacles, there is no telling exactly where the raft will drift. Thus, each trip is different and exciting. At the end of the ride, a conveyor belt hauls the raft up to be unloaded and prepared for the next group of guests.

What distinguishes Kali River Rapids from other theme-park raft rides is Disney's trademark attention to visual detail. Where many raft rides essentially plunge down a concrete ditch, Kali River Rapids flows through a dense rain forest and past waterfalls, temple ruins, and bamboo thickets, emerging into a cleared area where greedy loggers have ravaged the forest, and finally drifting back under the tropical canopy as the river cycles back to Anandapur. Along the way, your raft runs a gauntlet of raging cataracts, logjams, and other dangers.

Disney has done a great job with the visuals on this attraction. The queuing area, which winds through an ancient Southeast Asian temple, is one of the most striking and visually interesting settings of any Disney attraction. And though the sights on the raft trip itself are also first-class, the attraction is marginal in two important respects. First, it's only about three and a half minutes on the water, and second, well . . . it's a weenie ride. Sure, you get wet, but otherwise the drops and rapids are not all that exciting, as this Kansas family points out:

It was boiling hot, [so] *we were happy about the prospect of being drenched. We couldn't believe how short and dull the ride was, even with the lush landscaping. At the end, we all looked at each other and said, "Is that IT?!" We couldn't believe we had stood in line, sweating half to death, for 75 minutes just for that.*

And how wet do you get? A reader from Plymouth, Michigan, has the answer:

The whitewater-rafting ride is great fun but beware! Rather than just getting a little wet, like Splash Mountain, we were soaked to the skin after this ride. It was beyond "fun getting wet," literally drenching you with buckets of water. Poncho sales were brisk the day we were there.

Lastly, from a Worthington, Ohio, 30-something who hadn't intended to enter a wet-T-shirt contest:

I highly recommend the book, and I also recommend not wearing a white T-shirt to Animal Kingdom if you're planning on riding Kali River Rapids.

You can use FASTPASS to ride later in the day when it's a little warmer. A family from Humble, Texas, who rode early in the morning on a cool day, shares this:

Our plan hit a definite wall upon experiencing Kali River Rapids as number two on the schedule. We did not read about the precautions for this ride in your book until after riding. The 6-year-old and mom were COMPLETELY drenched—so much so that we actually had to leave the park and go back to our room at [Port Orleans] *to change clothes. Since the temperature was around 60 degrees that morning, we were pretty miserable by the time we got back to our room. Needless to say, our schedule was shot by that time. We would not recommend Kali River Rapids so early in the morning when the weather is chilly.*

TOURING TIPS This attraction is hugely popular on hot summer days. Ride Kali River Rapids before 11 a.m., after 4:30 p.m., or use FASTPASS. You can expect to get wet and probably drenched on this ride. Our recommendation is to wear shorts to the park and bring along a jumbo-sized trash bag as well as a smaller plastic bag. Before boarding the raft, take off your socks and punch a hole in your jumbo bag for your head. Though you can also cut holes for your arms, you will probably stay drier with your arms inside the bag. Use the smaller plastic bag to wrap around your shoes. If you are worried about mussing your hairdo, bring a third bag for your head.

A Shaker Heights, Ohio, family who adopted our garbage-bag attire discovered that staying dry on the Kali River Rapids is not without social consequences:

I must tell you that the Disney cast members and the other people in our raft looked at us like we had just beamed down from Mars. Plus, we didn't cut arm holes in our trash bags because we thought we'd stay drier. Only problem was once we sat down we couldn't fasten our seat belts. The Disney person was quite put out and asked sarcastically whether we needed wet suits and snorkels. After a lot of wiggling and adjusting and helping each other we finally got belted in and off we went looking like sacks of fertilizer with little heads perched on top. It was very embarrassing, but I must admit that we stayed nice and dry.

Other tips for staying dry (make that drier) include wearing as little as the law and Disney allow and storing a change of clothes in a park rental locker. Sandals are the perfect footwear for water rides. As a last-ditch effort to keep your shoes moderately dry (if you don't have sandals), try to prop your feet up above the bottom of the raft.

Maharaja Jungle Trek ★★★★

APPEAL BY AGE PRESCHOOL ★★★½ GRADE SCHOOL ★★★★ TEENS ★★★★
YOUNG ADULTS ★★★★ OVER 30 ★★★★ SENIORS ★★★★

What it is Walk-through zoological exhibit. **Scope and scale** Headliner. **When to go** Anytime. **Special comments** Opens 30 minutes after the rest of the park. **Authors' rating** A standard-setter for natural habitat design; ★★★★. **Duration of tour** About 20–30 minutes.

DESCRIPTION AND COMMENTS The Maharaja Jungle Trek is a zoological nature walk similar to the Pangani Forest Exploration Trail, but with an Asian setting and Asian animals. You start with Komodo dragons and then work up to Malayan tapirs. Next is a cave with fruit bats. Ruins of the maharaja's palace provide the setting for Bengal tigers. From the top of a parapet in the palace you can view a herd of blackbuck antelope and Asian deer. The trek concludes with an aviary.

Labyrinthine, overgrown, and elaborately detailed, the temple ruin would be a compelling attraction even without the animals. Throw in a few bats, bucks, and Bengals and you're in for a treat.

Most readers agree. A Washington, D.C., couple chimed in with this:

We went on the Maharaja Jungle Trek, which was absolutely amazing. We were able to see all the animals, which were awake by that time (9:30 a.m.), including the elusive tigers. The part of the jungle trek with the birds was fabulous. If you looked, you could spot hundreds of birds, some of which were eating on the ground a mere three feet away from me. Recommend to future visitors to take their time walking through the jungle, since most of the animals are not obvious to the breezing eye and you must look for them. It is worth the extra time to see such an unusual exhibit.

TOURING TIPS The Jungle Trek does not get as jammed up as the Pangani Forest Exploration Trail and is a good choice for midday touring when most other attractions are crowded. The downside, of course, is that the exhibit showcases tigers, tapirs, and other creatures that might not be as active in the heat of the day as mad dogs and Englishmen.

DINOLAND U.S.A.

THIS MOST TYPICALLY DISNEY OF ANIMAL KINGDOM'S lands is a cross between an anthropological dig and a quirky roadside attraction. Accessible via the bridge from Discovery Island, DinoLand U.S.A. is home to a children's play area, a nature trail, a 1,500-seat amphitheater, and **Dinosaur,** one of Animal Kingdom's two thrill rides.

Also in DinoLand are a couple of natural-history exhibits, including **Dino-Sue,** an exact replica of the largest, most complete *Tyrannosaurus rex* discovered to date. Named after the fossil hunter Sue Hendrickson, the replica (like the original) is 40 feet long and 13 feet tall. And no, it doesn't dance, sing, or whistle, but it will get your attention nonetheless.

The Boneyard ★★★½

APPEAL BY AGE PRESCHOOL ★★★★½ GRADE SCHOOL ★★★★ TEENS ★★½
YOUNG ADULTS ★★ OVER 30 ★★½ SENIORS ★★

What it is Elaborate playground. **Scope and scale** Diversion. **When to go** Anytime. **Special comments** Opens 30 minutes after the rest of the park. **Authors' rating** Stimulating fun for children; ★★★½. **Duration of visit** Varies. **Probable waiting time** None.

DESCRIPTION AND COMMENTS This attraction is an elaborate playground, particularly appealing to kids age 10 and younger, but visually appealing to all ages. Arranged in the form of a rambling open-air dig site, The Boneyard offers plenty of opportunity for exploration and letting off steam. Playground equipment consists of the skeletons of *Triceratops, Tyrannosaurus rex, Brachiosaurus,* and the like, on which children can swing, slide, and climb. In addition, there are sandpits where little ones can scrounge around for bones and fossils.

TOURING TIPS Not the cleanest Disney attraction, but certainly one where younger children will want to spend some time. And aside from being dirty, or at least sandy, The Boneyard gets mighty hot in the Florida sun. Keep your kids well hydrated, and drag them into the shade from time to time. If your children will let you, save the playground until after you have experienced the main attractions. Because The Boneyard is situated so close to the center of the park, it's easy to stop in whenever your kids get antsy. While the little ones clamber around on giant femurs and ribs, you can sip a tall cool one in the shade (still keeping an eye on them, of course).

As a Michigan family attests, kids love The Boneyard:

The highlight for our kids was The Boneyard, especially the dig site. They just kept digging and digging to uncover the bones of the wooly mammoth. It was also in the shade, and there were places for parents to sit, making it a wonderful resting place.

And so do parents. This from the father of a 4-year-old:

You should give playgrounds like The Boneyard higher ratings. After having our 4-year-old wait in lines for two days straight, she was thrilled to run around for two hours in The Boneyard without waiting for anything. Perhaps calling it a diversion is accurate, but it was a priceless diversion for us.

Be aware that The Boneyard rambles over about a half acre and is multistoried. It's pretty easy to lose sight of a small child in the playground. Fortunately, there's only one entrance and exit. A mother of two from Stillwater, Minnesota, found the playground too large for her liking:

If you are a parent who likes to have your eyes on your kids at all times, The Boneyard is very scary for adults. Kids climb to the top [of the slides], and you can't see them at the top and you don't know what chute they will be exiting from. It made me VERY nervous because I could not see them at all times.

Dinosaur (FASTPASS) ★★★★½

APPEAL BY AGE PRESCHOOL ★★ GRADE SCHOOL ★★★½ TEENS ★★★★ YOUNG ADULTS ★★★★ OVER 30 ★★★★ SENIORS ★★★½

What it is Motion-simulator dark ride. **Scope and scale** Super-headliner. **When to go** Before 10:30 a.m., in the hour before closing, or use FASTPASS. **Special comments** Must be 40" tall to ride. Switching-off option provided (see page 339). **Authors' rating** Really improved; ★★★★½. **Duration of ride** 3½ minutes. **Average wait in line per 100 people ahead of you** 3 minutes; assumes full-capacity operation with 18-second dispatch interval. **Loading speed** Fast.

DESCRIPTION AND COMMENTS Dinosaur, formerly known as Countdown to Extinction, is a combination track ride and motion simulator. In addition to moving along a cleverly hidden track, the ride vehicle also bucks and pitches (the simulator part) in sync with the visuals and special effects encountered. The plot has you traveling back in time on a mission of rescue and conservation. Your objective, believe it or not, is to haul back a living dinosaur before the species becomes extinct. Whoever is operating the clock, however, cuts it a little close, and you arrive on the prehistoric scene just as a giant asteroid is hurling toward Earth. General mayhem ensues as you evade carnivorous predators, catch Barney, and make your escape before the asteroid hits.

Dinosaur is a technological clone of the *Indiana Jones* ride at Disneyland in California. A good effort, although not quite as visually interesting as *Indiana Jones,* Dinosaur serves up nonstop action from beginning to end with brilliant visual effects. Elaborate even by Disney standards, the attraction provides a tense, frenetic ride that's embellished by the entire Imagineering arsenal of high-tech gimmickry. Although the ride is jerky, it's not too rough for seniors. The menacing dinosaurs, however, along with the intensity of the experience, make Dinosaur a no-go for younger children.

Dinosaur, to our surprise and joy, has been refined and cranked up a couple notches on the intensity scale. The latest version is darker, more interesting, and much zippier. A mother from Kansasville, Wisconsin, liked it a lot, commenting:

Dinosaur is the best ride at WDW. Our group of ten, ranging in age from 65 (grandma) to 8 (grandson), immediately—and unanimously!—got back in line immediately after finishing.

A 20-something guy from Muncie, Indiana, however, wasn't so sure:

The Dinosaur attraction was the scariest ride I have ever been on. I'm 24 and love thrill rides, but I didn't open my eyes for half of the ride. I can't believe younger children are permitted to ride.

And speaking of younger children, we got plenty of feedback about their reactions. First, from a Michigan family:

Beware Dinosaur. My 7-year-old son withstood every ride Disney threw at him, from Space Mountain to Tower of Terror. Dinosaur, however, did him in. By the end of the ride, he was riding with his head down, scared to look around. It is intense, combining scary visual dinosaur effects with some demanding roller coaster–like simulation.

TOURING TIPS Disney situated Dinosaur in such a remote corner of the park that guests have to poke around to find it. This, in conjunction with the overwhelming popularity of Kilimanjaro Safaris and Expedition Everest, makes Dinosaur the easiest super-headliner attraction at Disney World to get on. We recommend, nonetheless, that you ride early after obtaining FASTPASSes for Expedition Everest.

Primeval Whirl (FASTPASS) ★★★

APPEAL BY AGE	PRESCHOOL ★★½	GRADE SCHOOL ★★★★	TEENS ★★★★
YOUNG ADULTS ★★★	OVER 30 ★★★	SENIORS ★★½	

What it is Small coaster. **Scope and scale** Minor attraction. **When to go** During the first 2 hours the park is open, in the hour before park closing, or use FASTPASS. **Special comments** 48" minimum height requirement. Switching-off option provided (see page 339). **Authors' rating** "Wild mouse" on steroids; ★★★. **Duration of ride** Almost 2½ minutes. **Average wait in line per 100 people ahead of you** 4½ minutes. **Loading speed** Slow.

DESCRIPTION AND COMMENTS Primeval Whirl is a small coaster with short drops and curves, and it runs through the jaws of a dinosaur, among other things. What makes this coaster different is that the cars also spin. Because guests cannot control the spinning, the cars spin and stop spinning according to how the ride is programmed. Sometimes the spin is braked to a jarring halt after half a revolution, and sometimes it's allowed to make one or two complete turns. The complete spins are fun, but the screeching-stop half spins are almost painful. If you subtract the time it takes to ratchet up the first hill, the actual ride time is about 90 seconds.

TOURING TIPS Like Space Mountain, the ride is duplicated side by side, but with only one queue. When it runs smoothly, about 700 people per side can whirl in an hour—a goodly number for this type of attraction, but not enough to preclude long waits on busy-to-moderate days. If you want to ride, try to get on before 11 a.m. or use FASTPASS.

Theater in the Wild/*Finding Nemo—The Musical* ★★★★

APPEAL BY AGE **PRESCHOOL** ★★★★½ **GRADE SCHOOL** ★★★★ **TEENS** ★★★★
YOUNG ADULTS ★★★★ **OVER 30** ★★★★ **SENIORS** ★★★★

What it is Enclosed venue for live stage shows. **Scope and scale** Major attraction. **When to go** Anytime. **Special comments** Performance times are listed in the handout park map or *Times Guide*. **Authors' rating** Not to be missed; ★★★★. **When to arrive** 30 minutes before showtime.

DESCRIPTION AND COMMENTS Another chapter in the Pixar-ization of Disney theme parks, *Finding Nemo* is arguably the most elaborate live show in any Disney World theme park. Incorporating dancing, special effects (including trapezes), and sophisticated digital backdrops of the undersea world, it features on-stage human performers retelling Nemo's story with colorful, larger-than-life puppets. To be fair, *puppets* doesn't adequately convey the size or detail of these props, many of which are as big as a car and require two people to manipulate. An original musical score was written for the show, which is a must-see for most Animal Kingdom guests. A few scenes, such as one in which Nemo's mom is eaten, may be too intense for some very small children. Some of the midshow musical numbers slow the pace, so the main concern for parents is whether the kids can sit still for an entire show. With that in mind, we advise parents to catch an afternoon performance—around 3 p.m. would be great—after seeing the rest of Animal Kingdom. If the kids get restless, you can either leave the show and catch the afternoon parade, or end your day at the park.

New Jersey drama critics have their own way with words, as this family of five demonstrates:

> The Finding Nemo *musical is DA BOMB! The musical was amazing! It's a flawless package of puppetry, effects, music, and lots of Disney magic! Even if you don't have kids in your party, go see it!*

TOURING TIPS To get a seat, show up 20 to 25 minutes in advance for morning and late-afternoon shows, and 30 to 35 minutes in advance for shows scheduled between noon and 4:30 p.m. Access to the theater is via a relatively narrow pedestrian path—if you arrive as the previous show is letting out, you will feel like a salmon swimming upstream.

TriceraTop Spin ★★

APPEAL BY AGE **PRESCHOOL** ★★★★½ **GRADE SCHOOL** ★★★★ **TEENS** ★★★
YOUNG ADULTS ★★ **OVER 30** ★★★ **SENIORS** ★★

What it is Hub-and-spoke midway ride. **Scope and scale** Minor attraction. **When to go** First 90 minutes the park is open and the hour before park closing. **Authors' rating** Dumbo's prehistoric forebear; ★★. **Duration of ride** 1½ minutes. **Average wait in line per 100 people ahead of you** 10 minutes. **Loading speed** Slow.

DESCRIPTION AND COMMENTS Another Dumbo-like ride. Here you spin around a central hub until a dinosaur pops out of the top of the hub. You'd think with the collective imagination of the Walt Disney Company, they'd come up with something a little more creative.

TOURING TIPS An attraction for the children, except they won't appreciate the long wait for this slow-loading ride.

LIVE ENTERTAINMENT *in* ANIMAL KINGDOM

WDW LIVE-ENTERTAINMENT GURU Steve Soares usually posts the Animal Kingdon performance schedule about a week in advance at **pages.prodigy.net/stevesoares.**

AFTERNOON PARADE Mickey's Jammin' Jungle Parade is comparable to the parades at the other parks, complete with floats, Disney characters (especially those from *The Lion King, The Jungle Book, Tarzan,* and *Pocahontas*), skaters, acrobats, and stilt walkers.

Though subject to change, the parade starts in Africa, crosses the bridge to Discovery Island, proceeds counterclockwise around the island, and then crosses the bridge to Asia. In Asia, the parade turns left and follows the walkway paralleling the river back to Africa. The walking path between Africa and Asia has several small cutouts that offer good views of the parade and excellent sun protection. As it's used mainly as a walkway, the path is also relatively uncrowded. (*Note:* The paths on Discovery Island get very crowded, making it easy to lose members of your party.)

Here's our advice for watching the festivities:

The parade both begins and ends in Africa. At the beginning of the parade there's a legion of guests vying for a viewing spot in the village of Harambe. As soon as the parade crosses the bridge to Discovery Island, however, the crowd breaks up and leaves Harambe relatively deserted. Because most guests don't realize that the parade cycles back through the village, there's never much of a crowd on hand when the parade rumbles through the second time en route to going offstage. Therefore, if you make your way to Harambe about 20 minutes after the parade time listed in the handout *Times Guide,* you should be able to score yourself an excellent vantage point at the last minute.

ANIMAL ENCOUNTERS Throughout the day, Disney staff conduct impromptu short lectures on specific animals at the park. Look for a cast member in safari garb holding a bird, reptile, or small mammal.

GOODWILL AMBASSADORS A number of Asian and African natives are on hand throughout the park. Both gracious and knowledgeable, they are delighted to discuss their country and its wildlife. Look for them in Harambe and along the Pangani Forest Exploration Trail in Africa, and in Anandapur and along the Maharaja Jungle Trek in Asia. They can also be found near the main entrance and at The Oasis.

KIDS' DISCOVERY CLUB Activity stations offer kids ages 4 to 8 a structured learning experience as they tour Animal Kingdom. Set up along walkways in six themed areas, Discovery Club stations are manned by cast members who supervise a different activity at each station. A souvenir logbook, available free, is stamped at each station when the child completes a craft or exercise. Kids enjoy collecting the stamps and noodling puzzles in the logbook while in attraction lines.

STAGE SHOWS These are performed daily at the Lion King Theater in Camp Minnie-Mickey, at the Theater in the Wild in DinoLand U.S.A., and at the stadium in Asia. Shows at Camp Minnie-Mickey and DinoLand U.S.A. feature the Disney/Pixar characters.

STREET PERFORMERS Street performers can be found most of the time at Discovery Island, at Harambe in Africa, at Anandapur in Asia, and in DinoLand U.S.A.

Far and away the most intriguing street performer is the one you can't see—at least not at first. Totally bedecked in foliage and luxuriant vines is a stilt walker named **DeVine,** who blends so completely with Animal Kingdom's dense flora that you never notice her until she moves. We've seen guests standing less than a foot away gasp in amazement as DeVine brushes them with a leafy tendril. Usually found at The Oasis or Discovery Island, DeVine is a must-see. If you don't encounter her, ask a cast member when and where she can be found. At press time, a video of DeVine was available at YouTube (go to **www.youtube.com** and search for "DeVine Disney's Animal Kingdom"), and excellent photographs of her are featured at **www.arondaparks.com/devine.htm.**

TRAFFIC PATTERNS *in* ANIMAL KINGDOM

THE FIVE CROWD MAGNETS ARE *It's Tough to Be a Bug!* in The Tree of Life, Kilimanjaro Safaris in Africa, Dinosaur in DinoLand U.S.A., and Kali River Rapids and Expedition Everest in Asia.

Because the park hosts large crowds with only a relative handful of attractions, expect for all attractions to be extremely busy, and for Expedition Everest and Kilimanjaro Safaris to be mobbed. Most guests arrive in the morning, with a sizable number on hand before opening and a larger wave arriving before 10 a.m. Guests continue to stream in through the late morning and into the early afternoon, with crowds peaking at around 2 p.m. From about 2:30 p.m. on, departing guests outnumber arriving guests by a wide margin, as guests who arrived early complete their tour and leave. Crowds thin appreciably by late afternoon and continue to decline into the early evening.

unofficial **TIP**
If you visit during late afternoon, you'll almost certainly have to return another afternoon to finish seeing everything.

Because the number of attractions, including theater presentations, is limited, most guests complete a fairly comprehensive tour in two-thirds of a day if they arrive early. Thus, generally speaking, your best bet for easy touring is either to be on hand when the park opens or to arrive at about 3 p.m. (if the park stays open until 7 or 8 p.m.), when the early birds are heading for the exits.

How guests tour Animal Kingdom depends on their prior knowledge of the park and its attractions. Guests arriving without much prior knowledge make their way to Discovery Island and depend on their handout park map to decide what to do next. Those guests who have boned up on Animal Kingdom make straight for Kilimanjaro Safaris in Africa and Expedition Everest in Asia. Kali River Rapids in Asia and *It's Tough to Be a Bug!* in The Tree of Life are also early-morning favorites.

With so many guests heading first thing for either Kilimanjaro Safaris in Africa or Expedition Everest in Asia, the remaining lands and attractions are lightly trafficked backwaters until late morning. As the day wears on, the masses who have experienced Kilimanjaro Safaris and Expedition Everest turn their attention to other shows and attractions, and the crowds become more equally distributed. Attractions that did not draw large crowds until 10:30 a.m. or so before Expedition Everest now do not experience high traffic until 11:30. In a park-to-park comparison, Expedition Everest has increased Animal Kingdom's attendance figures. But the super-headliner attraction comes with a heavy price: the further jamming of the park's already severely clogged pedestrian walkways.

ANIMAL KINGDOM TOURING PLANS

TOURING ANIMAL KINGDOM IS NOT AS COMPLICATED as touring the other parks because it has fewer attractions. Also, most rides, shows, and exhibits are oriented to the entire family, eliminating differences of opinion regarding how to spend the day. Here, the whole family can pretty much see and enjoy everything together.

unofficial **TIP**
For the time being, the limited number of attractions in Animal Kingdom can work to your advantage.

Because there are fewer attractions than at the other parks, expect the crowds at Animal Kingdom to be more concentrated. If a line seems unusually long, ask a cast member what the estimated wait is. If the wait exceeds your tolerance, try the same attraction again after 3 p.m., while a show is in progress at the Theater in the Wild in DinoLand U.S.A., or while some special event is going on.

BEFORE YOU GO

1. Call ☎ 407-824-4321 before you go for the park's operating hours.
2. Purchase your admission prior to arrival.

ANIMAL KINGDOM "NOT A TOURING PLAN" TOURING PLANS (see page 812)

WE PRESENT FOR THE TYPE-B READER touring plans that avoid detailed step-by-step strategies for saving every last minute in line. For Animal Kingdom, these "not" touring plans include advice for adults and parents with one day in the park, for anyone with two days, and for anyone with an afternoon and a full day to tour.

ANIMAL KINGDOM ONE-DAY TOURING PLAN (see page 829)

THIS TOURING PLAN assumes a willingness to experience all major rides and shows. Be forewarned that Expedition Everest, Dinosaur,

Kali River Rapids, and Primeval Whirl are sometimes frightening to children under age 8. Similarly, the theater attractions at The Tree of Life might be too intense for some preschoolers. When you're following the touring plan, simply skip any attraction you do not wish to experience.

Many readers have asked us whether fewer animals are visible from Kilimanjaro Safaris around lunchtime than at park opening, out of concern that the animals might be less active in the midday heat. To help answer that question, we sent a team of researchers to ride continuously during one week in the summer and had them count the number of animals visible at different times of day. We subdivided our counting into large animals (elephants, hippos, and lions, for example), small (deer and other ungulates), and birds. Our results indicate that you'll probably see the same number of animals regardless of when you visit. As we mention in the Kilimanjaro Safaris review, this finding is almost certainly due to Disney's deliberate placement of water, food, and shade near the safari vehicles.

PART FOURTEEN

BEHIND *the* SCENES *at* WALT DISNEY WORLD

IF YOU'RE INTERESTED in the Mouse's innards—um, make that inner workings—a number of guided tours offer a glimpse of what goes on behind the scenes. Although a few tours include park admission, most require you to buy your admission pass separately. Tours range from learning how the Magic Kingdom's steam locomotives operate to swimming with the fish at The Seas with Nemo & Friends in Epcot. Reservations must be guaranteed with a credit card, and there is a 48-hour cancellation policy for a full refund.

unofficial **TIP**
The walking tours involve a considerable amount of walking, standing, and time spent outdoors (depending on the tour), so make sure you're up to the challenge before you book.

We recommend making reservations as early as possible. Although there's a high demand for behind-the-scenes tours, booking one of these is nowhere as difficult as, say, reserving a table for the *Hoop-Dee-Doo Musical Revue* or Cinderella's Royal Table. The **Epcot DiveQuest, Dolphins in Depth,** and **Seas Aqua Tour** in particular are especially popular and fill up fast. Ask about discounts available for AAA Diamond Card holders, Disney Visa Card holders, Disney Vacation Club members, Annual Pass holders, and military personnel. Certain tours are available only certain days of the week (see chart on pages 630 and 631 for details). For reservations and more information, call ☎ 407-WDW-TOUR.

BEHIND *the* SCENES *at the* MAGIC KINGDOM

AS ITS NAME MAKES CLEAR, **Keys to the Kingdom** takes guests behind the scenes at the Magic Kingdom. This fascinating guided tour provides an informative and detailed look at the park's logistical, technical, and operational sides. Included are the parade-assembly area, the waste-treatment plant, and tunnels (utilidors) under the theme park. The program ($62 per person) includes lunch and runs about four and a half to five hours; children must be at least 16 years old to participate. Park admission is not included.

For those interested in the tour, a reader from Ludington, Michigan, offers the following advice:

People thinking of taking the Keys to the Kingdom tour should know that it is not for the faint of heart. This is a four-hour walking tour with only one 15-minute break, plus a few minutes to sit a while on Pirates of the Caribbean, The Haunted Mansion, and the Tomorrowland Transit Authority. It wore me out, and I am on my feet most of any given working day. If you do this, make it the last day of your visit—it took me three days to recover.

Backstage Magic, a seven-hour, $219 tour, goes behind the scenes at all the parks except Animal Kingdom and includes lunch (guests must be at least 16 years old to participate). Theme-park admission is included. **Disney's Magic Behind Our Steam Trains,** a three-hour tour for children age 10 and up, takes a backstage look at the steam locomotives of the Walt Disney World Railroad. Cost is $45 per person. A less costly tour is the **Family Magic Tour,** an interactive romp through the park following clues in a sort of treasure hunt. The two-and-a-half-hour tour is offered daily for $30. Another bargain tour, at $25 per person, is **Mickey's Magical Milestones.** Available Monday, Wednesday, and Friday, the two-hour tour visits attractions and places throughout the Magic Kingdom that retrace Mickey Mouse's long-running career.

BEHIND *the* SCENES *at* EPCOT

A TOUR CALLED **Undiscovered Future World** traces the history of Epcot, including Walt Disney's original concept. The tour takes guests to behind-the-scenes areas and lasts a bit over four hours. The cost is $55; children must be at least 16 years old to participate.

Behind the Seeds is shorter and takes guests behind the scenes to vegetable gardens and aquaculture farms in the Land Pavilion. The quality of the experience—a cross between science lecture and Willy Wonka factory tour—depends heavily on the tour guide's presentation and enthusiasm. Because those vary considerably, we don't recommend the tour for children under age 8. You're not permitted to touch or sample the plants shown on the tour, but it's hard to resist the urge. We found the lemongrass surprisingly tasty, and we didn't have to be rescued by Oompa Loompas.

Behind the Seeds requires same-day reservations; make them on the lower level of The Land (to the far right of the fast-food windows). The cost of the hour-long tour, including tax, is $16 for adults and $12 for children ages 3 to 9.

The **Around the World at Epcot** tour is a change of pace from the average walking tour. On this two-hour tour, guests can take a Segway Human Transporter for a spin around the World Showcase after mastering the machine during an hour-long indoor riding lesson. The cost is $95 per person. A shorter and less costly version is the **Simply Segway Experience.** The one-hour class includes training and some indoor riding and costs $35 per person. Debuting in 2008 was **Disney's Wilderness**

Behind-the-scenes Tours at Walt Disney World

	TOUR LENGTH	COST	MINIMUM AGE
MAGIC KINGDOM			
Backstage Magic	7 hours	$219	16
Disney's Magic Behind Our Steam Trains	3 hours	$45	10
Family Magic Tour	2½ hours	$30	None
Keys to the Kingdom	4½–5 hours	$62	16
Mickey's Magical Milestones	2 hours	$25	None
EPCOT			
Around the World at Epcot	2 hours	$95	16
Behind the Seeds	1 hour	$16 adults, $12 kids ages 3–9	None
Dolphins in Depth	3 hours	$175	13
Epcot DiveQuest	3 hours	$175	10
Seas Aqua Tour	2½ hours	$140	8
Simply Segway Experience	1 hour	$35	16
Undiscovered Future World	4 hours	$55	16
ANIMAL KINGDOM			
Backstage Safari	3 hours	$70	16
Wild by Design	3 hours	$60	14
FORT WILDERNESS CAMPGROUND			
Disney's Wilderness Back Trail Adventure	2 hours	$85	16

Back Trail Adventure ($85), a two-hour Segway romp on the trails and walking paths of Fort Wilderness Campground. For all three programs, guests must be at least 16 years old and weigh less than 250 pounds.

EPCOT DIVEQUEST

THE SOGGIEST BEHIND-THE-SCENES experience available anywhere is **Epcot DiveQuest,** in which open-water-scuba–certified divers (age 10 and up; kids age 12 and younger must be accompanied by an adult) can swim around with the fish at The Seas with Nemo & Friends. Offered twice daily, at 4:30 and 5:30 p.m., each tour lasts about three hours, including a 40-minute dive. The cost is about $175 per diver and includes all gear, a souvenir T-shirt, a dive-log stamp, and refreshments. A video recording of your dive will be made; you can buy the tape for

FOCUS	DAYS AVAILABLE
MAGIC KINGDOM	
All parks except Animal Kingdom	Monday–Friday
Steam locomotives of the Walt Disney World Railroad	Monday, Tuesday, Thursday, Saturday
Following clues in a sort of treasure hunt	Daily
Park's logistical, technical, and operational sides	Daily
Review of Mickey Mouse's long-running career	Monday, Wednesday, Friday
EPCOT	
Taking a spin around the World Showcase on Segways	Daily
Vegetable gardens in the Land Pavilion	Daily
Visiting the dolphin-research facility at The Seas	Monday–Friday
Swimming with the fish at The Seas	Daily
Swimming in the main tank at The Seas	Daily
Instruction in using a Segway	Daily
The history of Epcot	Monday, Wednesday, Friday
ANIMAL KINGDOM	
Observing how the animals are housed and cared for	Monday, Wednesday, Thursday, Friday
Inside look at the creation of the Animal Kingdom	Thursday, Friday
FORT WILDERNESS CAMPGROUND	
Segway romp on campground trails and paths	Tuesday–Saturday

$35. For recorded information, call ☎ 407-560-5590. Theme-park admission is not required, but a dive-certification card is.

DOLPHINS IN DEPTH

THIS TOUR (FOR GUESTS AGE 13 AND OLDER) visits the dolphin-research facility at The Seas with Nemo & Friends. There you'll witness a training session and then wade into the water for a photo (but not a swim) with the two dolphins. Cost for the three-hour experience is $175; children under age 18 must be accompanied by an adult. Theme-park admission is not required. Wet suits are provided. Only eight guests per day can participate, so call ☎ 407-WDW-TOUR as soon as you're sure you want to book (either the booking will be accepted or Disney will tell you exactly when to call back).

If you really dig dolphins, keep in mind that for $269 to $289, you can visit SeaWorld's **Discovery Cove,** and actually swim with the dolphins. Though the dolphin-swim experience is only about an hour long, the ticket entitles visitors to an entire day at Discovery Cove (where, among other activities, you can snorkel in a man-made coral reef). Admission includes a decent lunch, gear, all-day parking, and a seven-consecutive-day pass to SeaWorld. For more information, see page 709.

SEAS AQUA TOUR

THIS TOUR IS SORT OF a watered-down (chuckle) version of Epcot DiveQuest. The two-and-a-half-hour tour lets you swim with goggles, a mini–air tank, and a flotation vest in the main tank for 30 minutes and explore backstage areas at The Seas with Nemo & Friends. It costs $140, accepts guests as young as 8 years old, and does not require separate park admission. Children under age 18 must be accompanied by an adult. Gear, refreshments, a T-shirt, and a group photo are included.

BEHIND *the* SCENES *at* ANIMAL KINGDOM

THE ANIMAL KINGDOM OFFERS TWO behind-the-scenes tours. The three-hour **Backstage Safari** tour offers a glimpse of how the animals are housed and cared for. Animal keepers and vets discuss conservation, animal nutrition, behavioral studies, and medicine, among other topics. Limited to guests age 16 and older, the Backstage Safari costs $70 in addition to your paid park admission. This is a behind-the-scenes tour in the truest sense: you'll see animal enclosures, feed bins, medical facilities, and labs, but not many animals.

The second tour, **Wild by Design,** offers an inside look at the creation of the Animal Kingdom, explaining how architecture, functionality, habitats, themes, and storytelling are combined to provide a complete theme-park experience. This tour also runs three hours and costs $60 per person plus park admission. Open to guests age 14 and older; call ☎ 407-WDW-TOUR for reservations.

PART FIFTEEN

DISNEY'S HOLLYWOOD STUDIOS, UNIVERSAL ORLANDO, *and* SEAWORLD

DISNEY'S HOLLYWOOD STUDIOS *versus* UNIVERSAL STUDIOS FLORIDA

DISNEY'S HOLLYWOOD STUDIOS (DHS) and Universal Studios Florida are direct competitors. Because both are large and expensive and require at least one day to see, some guests must choose one park over the other. To help you decide, we present a head-to-head comparison of the two parks, followed by a description of each in detail. In the summer of 1999, Universal launched its second major theme park, **Universal's Islands of Adventure,** which competes directly with Disney's Magic Kingdom. (**Universal Studios Florida** theme park, Islands of Adventure, the three Universal hotels, and the **CityWalk** complex are collectively known as **Universal Orlando.**) A summary profile of **SeaWorld** concludes this chapter.

Both DHS and Universal Studios Florida draw their theme and inspiration from film and television. Both offer movie- and TV-themed rides and shows, some of which are just for fun, while others provide an educational, behind-the-scenes introduction to the cinematic arts.

Unlike DHS's open area, Universal Studios Florida's includes the entire back lot, where guests can walk at leisure among movie sets. Universal Studios Florida is about twice as large as DHS, and because almost all of it is open to the public, the crowding and congestion so familiar at DHS are eliminated.

Both parks include working film and TV-production studios. Guests are more likely, however, to see a movie, commercial, or television production in progress at Universal Studios than at DHS. On any day, production crews will be shooting on the Universal back lot in full view of guests who care to watch.

> *unofficial* **TIP**
> Half of Disney's Hollywood Studios is off-limits to guests—except by guided tour—while most of Universal Studios Florida is open to exploration.

Attractions at both parks are excellent, though DHS's are on average engineered to move people more efficiently. Each park offers stellar attractions that break new ground, transcending in power, originality, and technology any prior standard for theme-park entertainment. Though Universal Studios must be credited with pioneering a number of innovative and technologically advanced rides, we must also point out that Universal's attractions break down more often than DHS's.

Amazingly, and to the visitor's advantage, each park offers a completely different product mix, so there is little or no redundancy for those who visit both. DHS and Universal Studios Florida each provide good exposure to the cinematic arts. DHS over the years has turned several of its better tours into infomercials for Disney films. At Universal, you can still learn about postproduction, soundstages, set creation, and special effects without being bludgeoned by promotional hype.

We recommend you try one of the studios. If you enjoy one, you probably will enjoy the other. If you have to choose, consider:

1. TOURING TIME If you tour efficiently, it takes about 8 to 10 hours to see DHS (including a lunch break). Because Universal Studios Florida is larger and contains more rides and shows, touring, including one meal, takes about 9 to 11 hours. One reader laments:

> *There is a lot more "standing" at Universal Studios, and it isn't as organized as* [DHS]. *Many of the attractions don't open until 10 a.m., and many shows seem to be going at the same time. We were not able to see nearly as many attractions at Universal as we were at* [DHS] *during the same amount of time. The one plus* [at Universal Studios] *is that there seems to be more property, and things are spaced out better so you have more elbowroom.*

As the reader observes, many Universal Studios attractions do not open until 10 a.m. or later. During one research visit, only a third of the major attractions were up and running when the park opened, and most theater attractions didn't schedule performances until 11 a.m. or after. This means that early in the day all park guests are concentrated among the relatively few attractions in operation. DHS also has attractions that open late and shows that schedule no performances until late morning. The number of attractions operating at opening time varies according to season, at both parks. As a postscript, you will not have to worry about any of this if you tour either park using our touring plans. We'll keep you one jump ahead of the crowd and make sure that any given attraction is running by the time you get there.

2. CONVENIENCE If you're lodging along International Drive, Interstate 4's northeast corridor, or the Orange Blossom Trail (US 441), or in Orlando, Universal Studios Florida is closer. If you're lodging along US 27 or US 192 or in Kissimmee or Walt Disney World, DHS is more convenient.

3. ENDURANCE Universal Studios Florida is larger and requires more walking than DHS, but it is also much less congested, so the walking is easier. Both parks offer wheelchairs and disabled access.

4. COST Universal's standard one-day, one-park admissions are less expensive than similar ones at Disney parks. In fact, for the price of a one-day, one-park pass to a Disney park, you can buy a Universal admission that includes park-hopping privileges and no expiration date. When Disney instituted the multiday Magic Your Way admission system, in which you pay extra for park-hopping and No Expiration options, Universal was quick to move in the opposite direction. With Universal passes, all these extras are included at no additional charge. What's more, unlike Disney, Universal offers modest discounts when you purchase passes online and is always running specials on admissions. Not long ago, Universal offered a free two-day, two-park park-hopping ticket for kids (ages 3 to 9) for every adult two-day, two-park ticket purchased online at **www.universalorlando.com.** Total cost was $212 for the whole family, tax included. For the same family to spend two days with park-hopping privileges at Walt Disney World, the cost was a whopping $656.

5. BEST DAYS TO GO In order, Tuesdays, Fridays, and Saturdays are best to visit Universal Studios Florida. Tuesdays, Mondays, and Saturdays are best for Islands of Adventure. For DHS, see the Crowd Calendar at **TouringPlans.com.**

6. WHEN TO ARRIVE For DHS, arrive with your ticket in hand 30 to 40 minutes before official opening time. For Universal Studios, arrive with your admission already purchased about 25 to 35 minutes before official opening time.

7. YOUNG CHILDREN Both DHS and Universal Studios Florida are relatively adult entertainment offerings. By our reckoning, half the rides and shows at DHS and about two-thirds at Universal Studios have a significant potential for frightening young children.

8. FOOD For counter-service food, Universal Studios has a decided edge. DHS full-service restaurants are marginally better.

9. FASTPASS VERSUS UNIVERSAL EXPRESS Until recently, Disney's FASTPASS and Universal Express were roughly comparable. They both offered a system whereby any guest could schedule an appointment to experience an attraction later in the day with little or no waiting. Universal was the first to monkey with the status quo by making unlimited Universal Express passes available to guests in Universal-owned resorts. This meant that resort guests could go to the front of the line anytime. Next, Universal cooked up an enhanced Express pass, called Universal Express Plus, available to anyone—for an extra charge. Then they got really greedy. In the last installment, Universal terminated Express privileges for all day guests unless they were willing to cough up the extra bucks for Universal Express Plus. This relegates day guests (guests not staying at Universal-owned resorts) without Express Plus to long lines all day.

FASTPASS and the old Universal Express system worked because setting appointment times to experience attractions helped to more equally distribute crowds throughout the day. Without appointments, Universal will return to the same recurring bottlenecks as before Universal Express was introduced. Disney, by way of contrast, has maintained an egalitarian philosophy with regard to FASTPASS. Though they're considering some FASTPASS perks for resort guests, the basic program will continue to be available for every Bubba, Bob, and Betty who passes through the turnstiles.

For the moment at least, here is how the current Universal Express program works. Guests at Universal hotels can access the Universal Express lines all day long simply by flashing their hotel keys. This can be especially valuable during peak season. With Universal Express Plus, for an extra $20 to $56 (depending on the season) you can buy a pass that provides line-cutting privileges at each Universal Express attraction at a given park. The Plus feature is good for only one day at one park (in other words, no park hopping), and for one ride only on each participating attraction. Speaking of participating attractions, more than 90% of rides and shows are included in the Universal Express program, a much higher percentage than are included in the FASTPASS program at the Disney parks.

When we tested Express Plus one recent summer, we discovered that Universal employees very rarely scrutinize the Express Plus card, and that we could use the card several times on most attractions as long as we waited 15 minutes or so between attempts. Although there's a bar code on the pass, it was never scanned, nor did we see any scanning devices at the entrances of the attractions.

DISNEY'S HOLLYWOOD STUDIOS

FORMERLY KNOWN AS DISNEY-MGM STUDIOS, Disney's Hollywood Studios was hatched from a corporate rivalry and a wild, twisted plot. At a time when the Disney Company was weak and fighting off greenmail—hostile-takeover bids—Universal's parent company at the time, MCA, announced it was going to build an Orlando clone of its wildly successful Universal Studios Hollywood theme park. Behind the scenes, MCA was courting the real-estate-rich Bass brothers of Texas, hoping to secure the brothers' investment in the project. The Basses, however, defected to the Disney camp, helped Disney squelch the hostile takeovers, and were front and center when Michael Eisner suddenly announced that Disney would also build a movie theme park in Florida. A construction race ensued, with Universal and Disney each intent on opening first. Universal, however, was in the middle of developing a host of new attraction technologies and was no match for Disney, which could import proven concepts and attractions from its other parks. In the end, Disney's Hollywood Studios opened more than a year before Universal Studios Florida.

THE END OF THE MGM CONNECTION

SO WHAT HAPPENED TO "DISNEY-MGM STUDIOS"? Disney purchased Pixar Animation Studios after partnering with the company on a series of highly successful films, including *Toy Story; A Bug's Life; Monsters, Inc.; Finding Nemo;* and *The Incredibles.* The cost of continuing an association with MGM, coupled with Pixar's arguably greater popularity, probably convinced Disney to rename the theme park. But rather than replace "MGM" with "Pixar," Disney decided that "Hollywood" represented a more generic reference to moviemaking. In practice,

Not to Be Missed at DHS

DHS Backlot Tour	*Fantasmic!*
Jim Henson's Muppet-Vision 3-D	*Lights! Motors! Action! Extreme Stunt Show*
Rock 'n' Roller Coaster	*Toy Story* Mania!
Voyage of the Little Mermaid	*The Twilight Zone* Tower of Terror

however, many folks drop the "Hollywood" entirely, referring to the park simply as "Disney Studios" or "The Studios."

SELF-PROMOTION RUN AMOK

WHILE IT'S TRUE THAT DHS educates and entertains, what it does best is promote. Whereas self-promotion of Disney films and products was once subtle and in context, it is now blatant, inescapable, and detracting. Although most visitors are willing to forgive Disney its excesses, Studios veterans will lament the changes and remember how good it was when education was the goal instead of the medium.

HOW MUCH TIME TO ALLOCATE

IT'S IMPOSSIBLE TO SEE ALL OF EPCOT or the Magic Kingdom in one day. However, DHS is more manageable. There's much less ground to cover by foot. Trams carry guests through much of the back lot and working areas, and attractions in the open-access parts are concentrated in an area about the size of Main Street, Tomorrowland, and Frontierland combined. Someday, no doubt, as DHS develops and grows, you'll need more than a day to see everything. For now, though, the Studios is a nice one-day outing.

Because DHS is smaller, however, it's more affected by large crowds. Our touring plans will help you stay a step ahead of the mob and minimize waiting in line. But even when the park is crowded, you can see almost everything in a day.

DISNEY'S HOLLYWOOD STUDIOS IN THE EVENING

BECAUSE DHS CAN BE SEEN in three-fourths of a day, many guests who arrive early in the morning run out of things to do by 5 p.m. or so and leave the park. Their departure greatly thins the crowd and makes the Studios ideal for evening touring. Lines for most attractions are manageable, and the park is cooler and more comfortable. The *Indiana Jones Epic Stunt Spectacular* and productions at other outdoor theaters are infinitely more enjoyable during the evening than in the sweltering heat of the day.

unofficial **TIP**
A drawback to touring DHS at night is that there won't be much activity on the production soundstages.

In 1998 the Studios launched *Fantasmic!* (see page 642), which is arguably the most spectacular nighttime-entertainment event in the Disney repertoire. Staged twice weekly (weather permitting) in its own theater behind *The Twilight Zone* Tower of

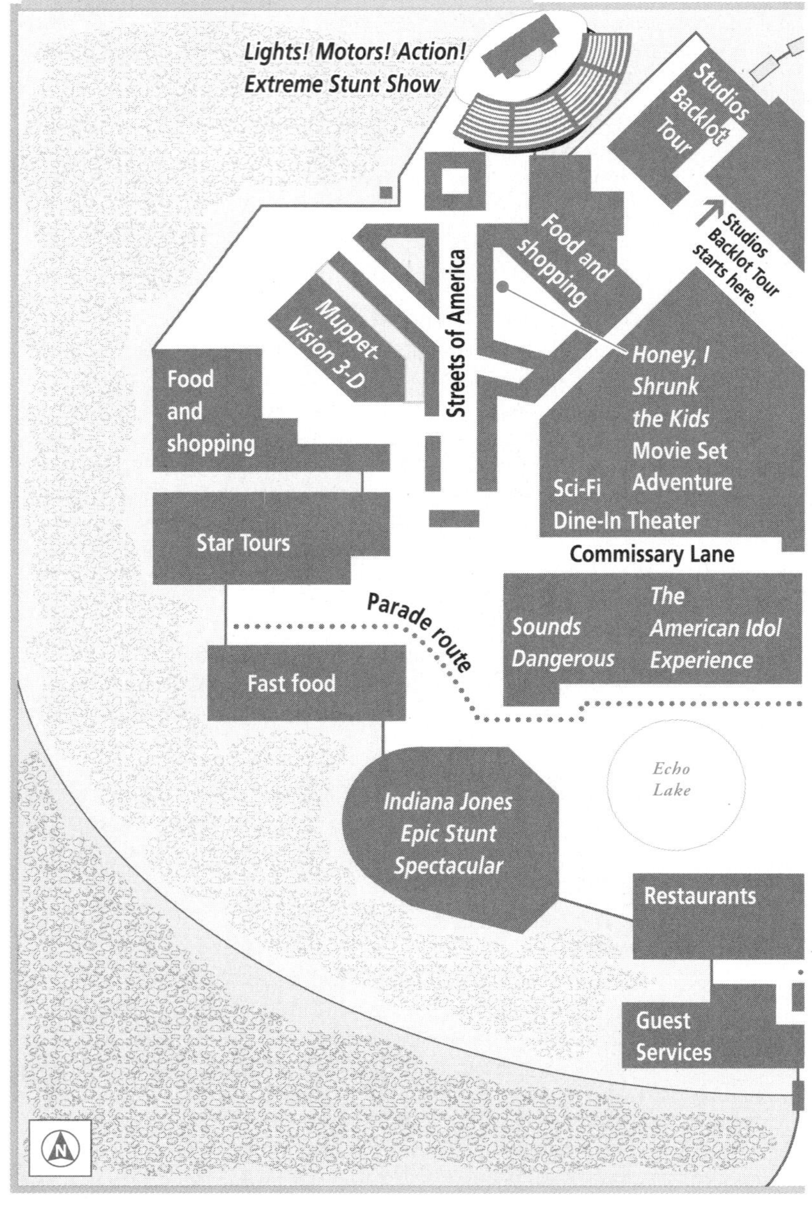
Disney's Hollywood Studios
Lights! Motors! Action!
Extreme Stunt Show
Studios Backlot Tour
Food and shopping
Studios Backlot Tour starts here.
Muppet-Vision 3-D
Streets of America
Honey, I Shrunk the Kids Movie Set Adventure
Food and shopping
Sci-Fi Dine-In Theater
Star Tours
Commissary Lane
Parade route
The American Idol Experience
Sounds Dangerous
Fast food
Echo Lake
Indiana Jones Epic Stunt Spectacular
Restaurants
Guest Services
N

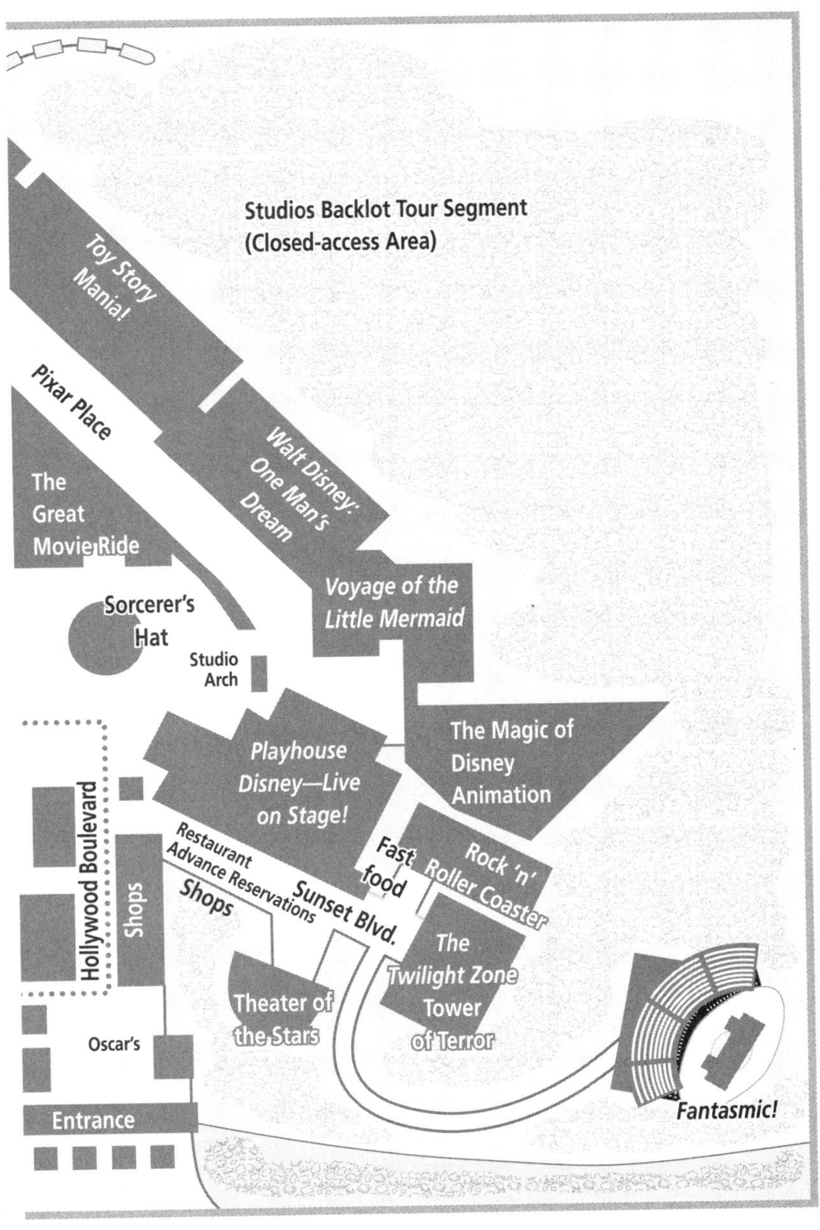
Studios Backlot Tour Segment
(Closed-access Area)
Toy Story Mania!
Pixar Place
Walt Disney: One Man's Dream
The Great Movie Ride
Voyage of the Little Mermaid
Sorcerer's Hat
Studio Arch
The Magic of Disney Animation
Playhouse Disney—Live on Stage!
Hollywood Boulevard
Shops
Restaurant Advance Reservations
Shops
Sunset Blvd.
Fast food
Rock 'n' Roller Coaster
The Twilight Zone Tower of Terror
Theater of the Stars
Oscar's
Fantasmic!
Entrance

Hollywood Boulevard Services

Most of the park's service facilities are on Hollywood Boulevard, including:

Baby Center/Baby Care Needs At Guest Relations; baby food and other necessities available at Oscar's Super Service

Banking Services ATM outside the park to the right of the turnstiles

Film At The Darkroom on the right side of Hollywood Boulevard as you enter the park, just past Oscar's Super Service

First Aid At Guest Relations

Live Entertainment, Parade, and Character Information Available free at Guest Relations and elsewhere in the park

Lost and Found At Package Pick-Up, to the right of the entrance

Lost Persons Report lost persons at Guest Relations

Storage Lockers Rental lockers to the right of the main entrance, on the left of Oscar's Super Service

Walt Disney World and Local Attraction Information At Guest Relations

Wheelchair and Stroller Rentals To the right of the entrance, at Oscar's Super Service

Terror, *Fantasmic!* is rated as not to be missed. Unfortunately, evening crowds have increased substantially because of *Fantasmic!*. Some guests stay longer at DHS, and others arrive after dinner from other parks expressly to see the show. Although the crowds thin in the late afternoon, they build again as performance time approaches, making *Fantasmic!* a challenge to get into. Also adversely affected are *The Twilight Zone* Tower of Terror and the Rock 'n' Roller Coaster, both situated near the entrance to *Fantasmic!* The crowd levels throughout the remainder of the park, however, are generally light.

ARRIVING AT DISNEY'S HOLLYWOOD STUDIOS

DHS HAS ITS OWN parking lot and is served by the Disney Transportation System. If you drive, Disney's ubiquitous trams will convey you to the ticketing area and entrance gate.

GETTING ORIENTED AT DISNEY'S HOLLYWOOD STUDIOS

GUEST SERVICES, on your left as you enter, serves as the park headquarters and information center, similar to City Hall in the Magic Kingdom and Guest Relations at Epcot and Animal Kingdom. Go there for a schedule of live performances/*Times Guide*, lost persons, Package Pick-Up, lost and found (on the right side of the entrance), and general information, or in an emergency. If you haven't received a map of the Studios or a *Times Guide*, get one here. To the right of the entrance are locker, stroller, and wheelchair rentals.

About half of the complex is set up as a theme park. As at the Magic Kingdom, you enter the park and pass down a main street. Only, this time it's **Hollywood Boulevard** of the 1930s and 1940s. At the end of Hollywood Boulevard is a replica of Hollywood's famous Chinese Theater. Lording over the plaza in front of the theater is a 122-foot-tall replica of the sorcerer hat Mickey Mouse wore in the animated classic *Fantasia*. Besides providing photo ops, the hat is the park's most central landmark, making it a good meeting place if your group becomes separated. (In case you're wondering, Mickey would have to be 350 feet tall to wear the hat.)

Though modest in size, the open-access areas of the Studios are confusingly arranged (a product of the park's hurried expansion in the early 1990s). As you face the hat, two guest areas—**Sunset Boulevard** and the **Animation Courtyard**—branch off Hollywood Boulevard to the right. Branching left off Hollywood Boulevard is the **Echo Lake** area. The open-access back lot wraps around the back of Echo Lake, the **Chinese Theater,** and the Animation Courtyard. You can experience all attractions here and in the other open-access sections of the park according to your tastes and time. Still farther to the rear is the limited-access back lot, consisting of the working soundstages, technical facilities, wardrobe shops, administrative offices, and back-lot sets. These are accessible to visitors on a guided tour by tram and foot.

DISNEY'S HOLLYWOOD STUDIOS ATTRACTIONS

HOLLYWOOD BOULEVARD

HOLLYWOOD BOULEVARD IS A PALM-LINED re-creation of Hollywood's main drag during Los Angeles's Golden Age. Architecture is streamlined moderne with Art Deco embellishments. Most service facilities are here, interspersed with eateries and shops. Merchandise includes Disney trademark items, Hollywood and movie-related souvenirs, and one-of-a-kind collectibles obtained from studio auctions and estate sales.

Hollywood characters and roving performers entertain on the boulevard, and daily parades and other happenings pass this way.

SUNSET BOULEVARD

SUNSET BOULEVARD, EVOKING THE 1940S, is a major component of DHS. The first right off Hollywood Boulevard, **Sunset Boulevard,** provides another venue for dining, shopping, and street entertainment.

The American Idol Experience ★★★★

APPEAL BY AGE PRESCHOOL ★★★ GRADE SCHOOL ★★★★ TEENS ★★★★
YOUNG ADULTS ★★★½ OVER 30 ★★★★ SENIORS ★★★

What it is Theme-park version of the TV show. **Scope and scale** Major attraction. **When to go** Anytime. **Special comments** Guests must be at least age 14 to perform. **Author's rating** Even if you don't watch the show, you'll find someone to cheer for; ★★★★. **Duration of presentation** 20 minutes for daytime preliminary shows, 40 minutes for the nighttime finale. **When to arrive** 20–30 minutes before showtime.

DESCRIPTION AND COMMENTS Based on the wildly popular TV talent search, *The American Idol Experience* is your chance to unleash your song stylings on the world. Your path to superstardom goes like this: Guests audition a cappella in front of a judge, just as in *American Idol*'s first shows of the season. Those who make the cut move on to a second audition and sing, karaoke-style, to a prerecorded track. The judges' picks from this round get to perform in one of the attraction's preliminary shows, held several times a day.

During the preliminaries, each contestant repeats his or her song from the second audition in front of a live audience of theme-park guests. As with *Idol,* three judges—in this case, Disney cast members—provide feedback. Don't fret that your operatic rendition of "Boot Scootin' Boogie" will be raked over the coals: for the most part, the Disney panel uses gentle humor to tell you not to quit your day job, although the judge who stands in for Simon Cowell does let fly the occasional zinger ("I can picture you on the cover of *Rolling Stone* . . . standing next to someone who can sing on key").

Audience members decide the preliminary winners, who meet for one last showdown at night. The winner of the finale receives a "Dream Ticket"—a front-of-the-line pass to try out for *American Idol* in his or her hometown.

TOURING TIPS The last show of the day offers (ostensibly) the best talent but runs twice as long as the daytime shows. If you have dinner reservations or are lining up early for *Fantasmic!* (see below), see one of the daytime shows. For complete details on auditioning and eligibility, go to **www.tinyurl.com/americanidolexperience.**

Fantasmic! ★★★★★

APPEAL BY AGE PRESCHOOL ★★★★ GRADE SCHOOL ★★★★½ TEENS ★★★★½ YOUNG ADULTS ★★★★★ OVER 30 ★★★★½ SENIORS ★★★★½

What it is Mixed-media nighttime spectacular. **Scope and scale** Super-headliner. **When to go** Staged only at night, generally Monday and Thursday. **Special comments** Disney's best nighttime event. **Authors' rating** Not to be missed; ★★★★★. **Duration of presentation** 25 minutes. **Probable waiting time** 50–90 minutes for a seat; 35–40 minutes for standing room.

DISNEY DISH WITH JIM HILL

SEE EVERYTHING YOU'VE BEEN MISTING **Are you tired of looking at blurry animation when you watch *Fantasmic!*'s water screens? So is DHS management, which is why they're proposing a significant upgrade of the equipment currently used to present this popular nighttime show. As we hear it, the biggest expense will be in replacing the three 70-millimeter projectors. For the new models, Mickey's looking to go high-def digital, bringing a clarity and color saturation to this show that WDW guests have never seen before.**

DESCRIPTION AND COMMENTS *Fantasmic!* is a mixed-media show presented twice weekly when the park is open late. Located off Sunset Boulevard behind the Tower of Terror, *Fantasmic!* is staged on an island opposite a 6,900-seat amphitheater. By far the largest theater facility ever created by Disney, the amphitheater can accommodate an additional 3,000 standing guests for an audience of nearly 10,000.

Until recently, *Fantasmic!* was staged nightly and always played to a full house. Presumably as a cost-containment measure, Disney has cut performances to two evenings a week. As you might imagine, trying to cram seven nights of capacity crowds into two nights is not working very well, as a reader from Sandwich, Illinois, reports:

The reduction in Fantasmic! *shows per week is ridiculous to me. The Studios is an absolute ghost town on nights it doesn't show and packed to capacity on nights when it does! There has to be a happy medium.*

Nonetheless, *Fantasmic!* is far and away the most innovative outdoor spectacle ever attempted at any theme park. Starring Mickey Mouse in his role as the Sorcerer's Apprentice from *Fantasia,* the production uses lasers, images projected on a shroud of mist, fireworks, lighting effects, and music in combinations so stunning you can scarcely believe what you are seeing. The plot is simple: good versus evil. The story gets lost in all the special effects at times, but no matter; it's the spectacle, not the story line, that is so overpowering. While *beautiful, stunning,* and *powerful* are words that immediately come to mind, they fail to convey the uniqueness of this presentation.

A Queensbury, New York, dad loved it and offers some advice to boot:

Fantasmic! *is the most entertaining show we've ever seen, and the technology is beyond belief. It really takes the shine off the other shows, which were truly wonderful. Don't see it before you see the laser and fireworks show at Epcot* [IllumiNations, *page 590*].

A reader from Australia found *Fantasmic!* a bit too sentimental:

We were disappointed by this show. While it features boats, characters, water, and light, it was a bit too nostalgic about Disney films. If this is what Mickey thinks about when he dreams, Minnie must be a little disappointed!

A mom from Pearland, Texas, found *Fantasmic!* too intense for her young child:

Fantasmic! *should come with a warning label. The show features a multitude of characters in various vignettes interspersed with water and laser-light interludes as Mickey Mouse begins his lighthearted and fanciful dream. Unfortunately for the impressionable and tender of mind, the dream becomes a nightmare as the evil villains take over Mickey's imagination. The combination of actual characters, their larger-than-life laser visages, ominous, unbearably loud music, and thundering explosions with blinding flashes of light, fire, and sparks (which went on for a seemingly interminable length of time) sent hordes of parents with screaming children fleeing for the exits. Naturally, good does eventually prevail over evil, and the finale returns to the beautiful, magical Disney style, but not soon enough. Please, please warn parents not to take young children to this show. (For adults and teenagers, it is truly spectacular.)*

Though we do not receive many reports of young children being terrified by *Fantasmic!*, the reader's point is well taken. We suggest you spend a little time preparing your younger children for what they will see. Also, make sure to hang on to your children after *Fantasmic!* and to give them explicit instructions for regrouping in the event you are separated. Also, you can mitigate the fright factor somewhat by sitting back a bit.

TOURING TIPS *Fantasmic!* provides a whole new dimension to nighttime at DHS. As a day-capping event, it is to the Studios what *IllumiNations* is to Epcot. While it's hard to imagine running out of space in a 10,000-person stadium, it happens almost every time the show is staged. On evenings when there are two performances, the second show will always be less crowded. If you attend the first (or only) scheduled performance, then show up at least an hour in advance. If you opt for the second show, then arrive 50 minutes early.

From a Yorktown, Virginia, mom:

I think you seriously underestimated the time when people should arrive to see Fantasmic! *if they want to get a seat. The stadium was already full when we arrived 45 minutes before the show was scheduled to start, and the remaining seats filled up quickly. Keep in mind this was during the off-season on one of the slower days of the week at* [DHS].

A mother of two from Narragansett, Rhode Island, provides a tip on avoiding *Fantasmic*'s "bouncers"—a skill we're sure she picked up from the Junior League, not trying to get closer to Bon Jovi in concert:

The park and its cast members will announce standing room only promptly at 8:50 p.m. Don't believe them! Twice my family and I enjoyed the show front and center, arriving just before the overture. Simply find an aisle without a cast member standing guard (they rarely do!) and slip into empty seats down in front—there's plenty! Also most families are willing to make room in these LONG bleachers!

A father of three from Clarksburg, West Virginia, found that staying for the late performance worked best (note that late shows are offered only during busier times of the year):

Fantasmic! *was fantastic. The 9:15 p.m. show was jammed all the time. We chose the 11 p.m. show (three times). The 11 p.m. show was never full. The second and third times we saw the show, we waited until 10:45 and walked right in and sat down. It's a must-see!*

A Cross Junction, Virginia, woman offers this tip:

If you're planning to go to Fantasmic!, *it's a good idea to buy deli sandwiches outside the park, pack them with snacks and water in your backpack, and get a seat early. Then you can sit and eat your dinner as you wait for a great show.*

A mom from Virginia warns about sitting too close to the action:

Avoid sitting near the front. We were stuck in the fourth row, and despite no detectable wind, we were constantly sprayed by the fountains during the show. That might feel good after a hot summer day, but it was very unpleasant on a cool fall evening.

Rain and wind conditions sometimes cause *Fantasmic!* to be cancelled. Unfortunately, Disney officials usually do not make a final decision about whether to proceed or cancel until just before showtime. We have seen guests wait stoically for over an hour with no assurance that their patience and sacrifice would be rewarded. We do not recommend arriving more than a few minutes before showtime on rainy or especially windy nights. On nights like these, pursue your own agenda until ten minutes or so before showtime and then head to the stadium to see what happens.

Finally, exiting *Fantasmic!* via the show's single exit can be hair-raising, as this retired elementary-school teacher attests:

It was like a cattle stampede, but at a snail's pace! You felt as if you were suffocating. Twice I almost ran over toddlers whose mothers did not have the sense or energy to pick up their children and carry them.

FANTASMIC! DINNER PACKAGE If you dine at the **Hollywood & Vine** buffet or at **Mama Melrose's Ristorante Italiano** or **The Hollywood Brown**

Derby full-service restaurants, you can obtain a voucher for the members of your dining party to enter *Fantasmic!* via a special entrance and sit in a reserved section of seats. In return for your patronage of the restaurant, you can avoid 30 to 90 minutes waiting in the regular line to be admitted.

You must call ☎ 407-WDW-DINE 180 days in advance and request the *Fantasmic!* Dinner Package for the night you want to see the show. This is a real reservation rather than an Advance Reservation and must be guaranteed with a credit card at the time of booking. There is no additional charge for the package itself, but there is a $10 charge for canceling a reservation with less than 48 hours' notice.

To keep people from ordering the cheapest thing on the menu just to get *Fantasmic!* vouchers, Disney used to include a fixed-price menu in the package for all three restaurants; as of June 2009, however, you may order à la carte at the Brown Derby and Mama Melrose's.

Dinner at Hollywood & Vine ($26.99 adults, $13.99 kids) is an all-you-can-eat buffet with dishes such as prime rib and baked chicken. Nonalcoholic drinks are included; park admission, tax, and gratuity are not. If you've made ordinary Advance Reservations for Hollywood & Vine, they will not include reserved seats for *Fantasmic!*—you have to buy the package to get the seats.

You will receive your vouchers at the restaurant. After dinner, report to the Highlands Gate on Sunset Boulevard—between Theater of the Stars and the Once Upon a Time store—30 to 45 minutes before showtime. A cast member will collect your vouchers and direct or escort you to the reserved seating section of the amphitheater. Though you're required to arrive early, you can be seated immediately and won't have to stand in any lines. Be advised that the reserved seats are off to the far right, though they afford a good line of sight. You will not have specific assigned seats in the reserved section. It's first come, first served, so arrive early for the best choice; try to sit in the middle three or four sections, preferably a bit off-center. Finally, understand that you're out of luck if *Fantasmic!* is canceled due to weather or other circumstances; you will not receive a refund or even a voucher for another performance.

The Great Movie Ride ★★★½

APPEAL BY AGE PRESCHOOL ★★★ GRADE SCHOOL ★★★½ TEENS ★★★½ YOUNG ADULTS ★★★½ OVER 30 ★★★★ SENIORS ★★★★

What it is Movie-history indoor adventure ride. **Scope and scale** Headliner. **When to go** Before 11 a.m. or after 4:30 p.m. **Special comments** Elaborate, with several surprises. **Authors' rating** Unique; ★★★½. **Duration of ride** About 19 minutes. **Average wait in line per 100 people ahead of you** 2 minutes; assumes all trains operating. **Loading speed** Fast.

DESCRIPTION AND COMMENTS Entering through a re-creation of Hollywood's Chinese Theater, guests board vehicles for a fast-paced tour through soundstage sets from classic films, including *Casablanca, Tarzan, The Wizard of Oz, Alien,* and *Raiders of the Lost Ark.* Each set is populated with new-generation Disney audio-animatronic (robot) characters, as well as an occasional human, all augmented by sound and lighting effects. One of

DISNEY DISH WITH JIM HILL

HOLLYWOOD FACE-LIFT **In the 20-plus years that Disney's Hollywood Studios has been open, the Imagineers have changed The Great Movie Ride's ending movie montage a few times, but they've never touched the attraction's interior. That's all going to change in late 2011 or early 2012, when this ride-through history of the movies receives its first significant redo. Among the scenes that may end up on the cutting room floor are the mummy's tomb and Ripley's encounter with the Alien.**

Disney's larger and more ambitious dark rides, The Great Movie Ride encompasses 95,000 square feet and showcases some of the most famous scenes in filmmaking. Life-size audio-animatronic sculptures of stars, including Gene Kelly, John Wayne, James Cagney, and Julie Andrews, inhabit some of the largest sets ever constructed for a Disney ride.

A Tennessee family thinks the attraction needs some freshening up:

As someone who attended the grand opening of [DHS] *in 1989, I think some of the park's attractions are badly in need of updating, especially The Great Movie Ride, which seems stuck in the 1980s.*

TOURING TIPS The Great Movie Ride draws large crowds (and lines) from midmorning on. As it's an interval-loading, high-capacity ride, lines disappear quickly. Even so, waits can exceed an hour, after midmorning. (Actual wait times usually run about one-third shorter than the time posted.)

Honey, I Shrunk the Kids Movie Set Adventure ★★½

APPEAL BY AGE PRESCHOOL ★★★★½ GRADE SCHOOL ★★★★ TEENS ★★½ YOUNG ADULTS ★★ OVER 30 ★★½ SENIORS ★★★

What it is Small but elaborate playground. **Scope and scale** Diversion. **When to go** Before 11 a.m. or after dark. **Special comments** Opens an hour later than the rest of the park. **Authors' rating** Great for young children, more of a curiosity for adults; ★★½. **Duration of presentation** Varies. **Average wait in line per 100 people ahead of you** 20 minutes.

DISNEY DISH WITH JIM HILL

DON'T FORGET YOUR EAR PLUGS **Keep a close eye on Soundstage One at Disney's Hollywood Studios—construction of a monstrous new attraction is just about to get under way. This time around, it's a family-friendly inverted coaster with a *Monsters, Inc.* theme. Warning: this coaster will supposedly be powered by screams, so the louder you scream, the faster each vehicle will go.**

DESCRIPTION AND COMMENTS This elaborate playground appeals particularly to kids age 11 and younger. The story is that you have been "miniaturized" and have to make your way through a yard full of 20-foot-tall blades of grass, giant ants, dog poop (just kidding), lawn sprinklers, and other oversize features.

TOURING TIPS This imaginative playground has tunnels, slides, rope ladders, and a variety of oversize props. All areas are padded, and Disney personnel are on hand to help keep children in some semblance of control.

While this attraction undoubtedly looked good on paper, it has problems that are hard to "miniaturize" in practice. First, it's nowhere near large enough to accommodate all the children who would like to play. Only 240 people are allowed "on the set" at a time, and many of these are supervising parents or curious adults who hopped in line without knowing what they were waiting for. Frequently by 10:30 or 11 a.m., the playground is full, with dozens waiting outside (some impatiently).

Also, kids get to play as long as parents allow. This creates uneven traffic flow and unpredictable waits. If it weren't for the third flaw, that the attraction is poorly ventilated (as hot and sticky as an Everglades swamp), there's no telling when anyone would leave.

A mom from Shawnee Mission, Kansas, however, disagrees:

Some of the things your book said to skip were our favorites (at least for the kids). We thought the playground from Honey, I Shrunk the Kids *was great—definitely worth seeing.*

A mom from Tolland, Connecticut, however, found the playground exasperating:

We let the kids hang out at [Honey, I Shrunk the Kids] *because we thought it would be relaxing. NOT! You have three choices here: (1) Let your kids go anywhere and hope if they try to get out without your permission someone will stop them. Also hope that someone else will help your kids if they get caught up in the exhibit. (2) Go everywhere with your kids—this takes a lot of stamina and some athleticism. If you care about appearances, this could be a problem because you look pretty stupid coming down those slides. (3) Try to visually keep track of your kids. This is impossible, so you will be either on the edge of or in the middle of an anxiety attack the whole time you are there.*

If you visit during warmer months and want your children to experience the playground, get them in and out before 11 a.m. By late morning, this attraction is way too hot and crowded for anyone to enjoy. Access the playground via the Streets of America or Pixar Place.

Indiana Jones Epic Stunt Spectacular (FASTPASS) ★★★★

APPEAL BY AGE PRESCHOOL ★★★ GRADE SCHOOL ★★★★ TEENS ★★★★ YOUNG ADULTS ★★★★ OVER 30 ★★★★ SENIORS ★★★★

What it is Movie-stunt demonstration and action show. **Scope and scale** Headliner. **When to go** First 3 morning shows or last evening show. **Special comments** Performance times posted on a sign at the entrance to the theatre; FASTPASSes available seasonally. **Authors' rating** Done on a grand scale; ★★★★. **Duration of presentation** 30 minutes. **Preshow entertainment** Selection of "extras" from audience. **When to arrive** 20–30 minutes before showtime.

DISNEY DISH WITH JIM HILL

"THIS IS JUST OFF THE TOP OF MY HEAD. . . ." **Given that the *Epic Stunt Spectacular* has been entertaining WDW visitors for more than 20 years now, it's kind of startling to hear how quickly this popular DHS attraction actually came together: from the moment that the rough idea for its 2,000-seat arena was first sketched on a napkin to the day that the first guest took a seat in the theater was just 11 months.**

DESCRIPTION AND COMMENTS Coherent and educational, though somewhat unevenly paced, the popular production showcases professional stunt men and women who demonstrate dangerous stunts with a behind-the-scenes look at how they're done. Sets, props, and special effects are very elaborate.

While most live shows at Walt Disney World are revised from time to time, the *Epic Stunt Spectacular,* as a Hamden, Connecticut, man laments, has not changed for years:

Another bust was the Indy Jones *show. The show is the same as it has been since it opened, but the acting grows tired.*

TOURING TIPS The Stunt Theater holds 2,000 people; capacity audiences are common. The first performance is always the easiest to see. If the first show is at 9:30 a.m. or earlier, you can usually walk in, even if you arrive five minutes late. If the first show is scheduled for 9:45 a.m. or later, arrive 20 or so minutes early. For the second performance, show up about 20 to 35 minutes ahead of time. For the third and subsequent shows, arrive 30 to 45 minutes early or use FASTPASS. If you plan to tour during late afternoon and evening, attend the last scheduled performance. If you want to beat the crowd out of the stadium, sit on the far right (as you face the staging area) and near the top.

To be chosen from the audience to be an "extra" in the stunt show, arrive early, sit down front, and display unmitigated enthusiasm. A woman from Richmond, Virginia, explains:

Indiana Jones *was far and away the best show—we saw it twice on two different days. After the first performance, I realized the best way to get picked was to stand up, wave my arms, and shout when the "casting director" called for volunteers—sheer enthusiasm wins every time, and sitting toward the front helps too.*

Jim Henson's Muppet-Vision 3-D ★★★★½

APPEAL BY AGE PRESCHOOL ★★★★ GRADE SCHOOL ★★★★ TEENS ★★★★
YOUNG ADULTS ★★★★ OVER 30 ★★★★ SENIORS ★★★★

What it is 3-D movie starring the Muppets. **Scope and scale** Major attraction. **When to go** Before 11 a.m. or after 3 p.m. **Authors' rating** Uproarious; not to be missed; ★★★★½. **Duration of presentation** 17 minutes. **Preshow entertainment** Muppets on television. **Probable waiting time** 12 minutes.

DISNEY DISH WITH JIM HILL

THE KERMIT OF CHRISTMAS FUTURE? The Mouse is reportedly considering a special edition of *The Muppet Christmas Carol* as a Christmastime replacement for the standard (and dated) movie shown here. This time around, the originally-86-minute-long motion picture would be cut back to just shy of 20 minutes, so that the abridged—and 3-D!—version could be shown twice hourly both here and at Disney's California Adventure.

DESCRIPTION AND COMMENTS *Muppet-Vision 3-D* provides a total sensory experience, with wild 3-D action augmented by auditory, visual, and tactile special effects. If you're tired and hot, this zany presentation will make you feel brand new. Arrive early and enjoy the hilarious video preshow.

TOURING TIPS This production is very popular. Before noon, waits are about 20 minutes. Watch for throngs arriving from performances of the *Indiana Jones Epic Stunt Spectacular.* If you encounter a long line, try again later.

Lights! Motors! Action! Extreme Stunt Show ★★★½ (FASTPASS)

APPEAL BY AGE PRESCHOOL ★★★½ GRADE SCHOOL ★★★★ TEENS ★★★★½ YOUNG ADULTS ★★★★ OVER 30 ★★★★ SENIORS ★★★★

What it is Auto stunt show. **Scope and scale** Headliner. **When to go** First show of the day or after 4 p.m. **Special comments** FASTPASSes available seasonally. **Authors' rating** Good stunt work, slow pace; ★★★½. **Duration of presentation** 25–30 minutes. **Preshow entertainment** Selection of audience volunteers. **When to arrive** 25–30 minutes before showtime.

DISNEY DISH WITH JIM HILL

CARS 2 TO THE RESCUE Expect 2011's *Cars 2* to have a huge impact on Disney's Hollywood Studios. Not only will Lightning McQueen and Mater begin making appearances in the *Lights! Motors! Action! Extreme Stunt Show,* but the Imagineers are thinking of ripping out the Backlot Tour's Catastrophe Canyon. This would open up room for a huge new expansion of this theme park's Pixar Place "land," which would draw its inspiration from the *Cars*-themed area that will open at Disney's California Adventure in the summer of 2012.

DESCRIPTION AND COMMENTS This show, which originated at Disneyland Paris, features cars and motorcycles in a blur of chases, crashes, jumps, and explosions. The secrets behind the special effects are explained after each stunt sequence, with replays and different camera views shown on an enormous movie screen; the replays also serve to pass the time needed to place the next stunt's props into position. While the stunt driving is excellent, the show plods along between tricks, and you will probably have had your fill by the time the last stunt ends. Expect about 6 to 8 minutes of real action in a show that runs 25 to 30 minutes. Because of this, small children may become restless during the show.

TOURING TIPS The auto stunt show, located at the end of the Streets of America, presents three to five shows daily. As a new attraction, it is popular, but its remote location (the most distant attraction from the park entrance) helps distribute and moderate the crowds. Seating is in a 3,000-person stadium, so it's not difficult to find a seat except on the busiest days. Note that FASTPASS for this attraction is not linked to the rest of the Studios' FASTPASS rides, so you can obtain FASTPASSes for this show immediately after you get them for any other FASTPASS attraction.

A family of four from Mount Pleasant, South Carolina, notes that it's easier to get into the stadium than out:

When we exited the 3,000-seat Lights! Motors! Action! *arena (which was full the day we visited), it was horrible! The cast members directed us all to the same exit, and it was a HUGE bottleneck that took us 20 minutes to break free from—seriously dented our touring plan!*

The Magic of Disney Animation ★★½

APPEAL BY AGE **PRESCHOOL** ★★★ **GRADE SCHOOL** ★★★½ **TEENS** ★★★½ **YOUNG ADULTS** ★★★½ **OVER 30** ★★★½ **SENIORS** ★★★★

What it is Overview of Disney Animation process, with limited hands-on demonstrations. **Scope and scale** Minor attraction. **When to go** Before 11 a.m. or after 5 p.m. **Special comments** Opens an hour later than the rest of the park. **Authors' rating** Not as good as previous renditions; ★★½. **Duration of presentation** 30 minutes. **Preshow entertainment** Gallery of animation art in waiting area. **Average wait in line per 100 people ahead of you** 7 minutes.

DESCRIPTION AND COMMENTS The consolidation of Disney Animation at the Burbank, California, studio has left this attraction without a story to tell. Park guests can still get a general overview of the Disney animation process but will not see the detailed work of actual artists, as was possible in previous versions.

The revamped attraction starts in a small theater, where the audience is introduced to a cast-member host and Mushu, the dragon from *Mulan.* Between the host's speech, Mushu's constant interruptions, and a very brief taped segment with real Disney animators, guests are hard pressed to learn anything about actual animation. The audience is shown a plug for current Disney animated releases, which falls flat.

The audience then moves to another room, this one with floor seating, where another cast member gives guests a verbal description of what used to be the walking tour of the actual animation studio. The cast member supplies bits of Disney character trivia (for example, Buzz Lightyear's original name was Lunar Larry) and fields questions from the audience, but nothing truly enlightening is presented.

Afterward, guests have the option of exiting the attraction or attending the Animation Academy (the limited space is on a first-come, first-served basis). This is by far the most interesting part of the attraction, but not designed for all guests. The animator works quickly, which seems to frustrate younger guests who need more time or assistance to get their drawing right. For those who keep up with the animator, this part gives a good idea of how difficult hand-drawn animation really is.

Judging by the low wait times, the Animation tour may be in need of yet another overhaul. A mother of two from Oak Ridge, North Carolina, writes:

> *The new* [Animation] *tour is missing the essence of Disney animation, with little to no mention of the modern classics that helped revitalize Disney. The new version is a shell of its former self. It's hard to avoid the word* lame.

TOURING TIPS Some days, the animation tour doesn't open until 10 or 11 a.m., by which time the park is pretty full. The tour is a relatively small-volume attraction, and lines can build on busy days by mid- to late morning. Character greetings take place at the end of most tours. If you want to meet characters without taking the tour, go through the Animation Gallery gift shop and head to the back of the store. A path leads directly from the shop to the characters.

Movie Promo Soundstage

DESCRIPTION AND COMMENTS Disney has been using the soundstage between *Walt Disney: One Man's Dream* and *Toy Story* Mania! to promote the

Chronicles of Narnia films, but to call this sparse offering an attraction is a stretch. Disney's biggest effort went into building the set's doors in the shape of the wardrobe described in the *Narnia* books. If you're a C. S. Lewis fan, see the attraction—it has some behind-the-scenes footage and concept art from the films, new props and costumes, and a Prince Caspian greeting area. Otherwise, skip it.

A middle-aged Disney veteran recalls:

We went to the Prince Caspian *attraction at DHS and stood in the preshow. When the doors opened, they led outside—there was no show. I thought the actual attraction was the preshow. Totally not worth it.*

Playhouse Disney—Live on Stage! ★★★★

APPEAL BY AGE **PRESCHOOL** ★★★★½ **GRADE SCHOOL** ★★★★ **TEENS** ★★½ **YOUNG ADULTS** ★★ **OVER 30** ★★★ **SENIORS** ★★½

What it is Live show for children. **Scope and scale** Minor attraction. **When to go** Per the daily entertainment schedule. **Special comments** Audience sits on the floor. **Authors' rating** A must for families with preschoolers; ★★★★. **Duration of presentation** 20 minutes. **When to arrive** 20–30 minutes before showtime.

DESCRIPTION AND COMMENTS The show features characters from the Disney Channel's *Little Einsteins, The Book of Pooh,* and *Handy Manny,* as well as Mickey, Minnie, Donald, Daisy, and Goofy. Reengineered in 2007, *Playhouse Disney* replaced live Disney characters with elaborate puppets. A simple plot serves as the platform for singing, dancing, some great puppetry, and a great deal of audience participation. The characters, who ooze love and goodness, rally throngs of tots and preschoolers to sing and dance along with them. All the jumping, squirming, and high-stepping is facilitated by having the audience sit on the floor so that kids can spontaneously erupt into motion when the mood strikes. Even for adults without children, it's a treat to watch the tykes rev up. If you have a younger child in your party, all the better: just stand back and let the video roll.

For preschoolers, *Playhouse Disney* will be the highlight of their day, as a Thomasville, North Carolina, mom attests:

Playhouse Disney *at [DHS] was fantastic! My 3-year-old loved it. The children danced, sang, and had a great time.*

Many readers are less than enthralled with the new version of *Playhouse Disney—Live on Stage!* These comments from a Virginia Beach, Virginia, couple are typical:

We were disappointed with the newly updated Playhouse Disney. *This did not consist of "live" characters, and I think the level of excitement from the kids was lower because of this. I mean, the kids enjoyed it, but you would think they would be more excited when it's a show with some of their favorite characters.*

TOURING TIPS The show is headquartered in what was formerly the Soundstage Restaurant, located to the right of the Animation Tour. Because the tykes just can't get enough, it has become the toughest ticket at the Studios. Show up at least 30 minutes before showtime. Once inside, pick a spot on the floor and take a breather until the performance begins.

Rock 'n' Roller Coaster (FASTPASS) ★★★★

APPEAL BY AGE **PRESCHOOL** ★ **GRADE SCHOOL** ★★★★½ **TEENS** ★★★★★
YOUNG ADULTS ★★★★★ **OVER 30** ★★★★★ **SENIORS** ★★★

What it is Rock-music-themed roller coaster. **Scope and scale** Headliner. **When to go** Before 10 a.m., in the hour before closing, or use FASTPASS. **Special comments** Must be 48" tall to ride; children younger than age 7 must ride with an adult. Switching-off option provided (see page 339). Note that there is a single-rider line for this attraction. **Authors' rating** Disney's wildest American coaster; not to be missed; ★★★★. **Duration of ride** Almost 1½ minutes. **Average wait in line per 100 people ahead of you** 2½ minutes. **Assumes** All trains operating. **Loading speed** Moderate–fast.

DISNEY DISH WITH JIM HILL

TAKE THE FIRST CORKSCREW OFF THE 5. . . . According to several Imagineers I've spoken with over the years, the route that your "stretch limo" takes from G-Force Records to the Forum actually would take a driver to this venerable Los Angeles performance venue. Of course, duplicating this trip in the real world would have to be pretty tricky, given that you'd have to copy the directions off those highway signs while zipping along at 60 mph—upside down.

Motion Sickness

DESCRIPTION AND COMMENTS This is Disney's answer to the roller-coaster proliferation at Universal's Islands of Adventure and Busch Gardens theme parks. Exponentially wilder than Space Mountain or Big Thunder Mountain in the Magic Kingdom, Rock 'n' Roller Coaster is an attraction for fans of cutting-edge thrill rides. Although the rock icons and synchronized music add measurably to the experience, the ride itself, as opposed to sights and sounds along the way, is the focus. Rock 'n' Roller Coaster offers loops, corkscrews, and drops that make Space Mountain seem like the Jungle Cruise. What really makes this metal coaster unusual, however, is that first, it's in the dark (like Space Mountain, only with Southern California nighttime scenes instead of space), and second, you're launched up the first hill like a jet off a carrier deck. By the time you crest the hill, you'll have gone from 0 to 57 miles per hour in less than three seconds. When you enter the first loop, you'll be pulling five g's. By comparison, that's two more g's than astronauts experience at liftoff on a space shuttle.

Reader opinions of Rock 'n' Roller Coaster have been predictably mixed, colored invariably by how the reader feels about roller coasters. The comments that follow are typical.

First, from a mother of two from High Mills, New York:

You can't warn people enough about Rock 'n' Roller Coaster. My daughter and I refused to go on it at all. My 9-year-old son, who had no problems with any ride, including Tower of Terror, went on with my husband first thing in the morning. My son came off so shaken he was "done for" the rest of the day and never fully recuperated. My husband just closed his eyes and hoped for the best.

And from a Longmont, Colorado, dad:

Rock 'n' Roller Coaster: the first 15 seconds of this ride are spectacular. I've never experienced anything like the initial take-off.

From an Australian couple who traveled a long way to ride a coaster:

My wife and I are definitely not roller-coaster people. However, we found Rock 'n' Roller Coaster quite exhilarating—and because it's dark, we didn't always realize that we were being thrown upside down. We rode it twice!

TOURING TIPS This ride is not for everyone. If Space Mountain or Big Thunder pushes your limits, stay away from Rock 'n' Roller Coaster.

It's eye-catching, and it's definitely a zippy, albeit deafening, ride. Expect long lines except in the first 30 minutes after opening and during the late-evening performance of *Fantasmic!*. Ride as soon as possible in the morning, or use FASTPASS.

If you're on hand when the park opens, position yourself on the far left side of Sunset Boulevard as close to the rope barrier as possible. If there's already a crowd at the rope, you can usually work yourself forward by snaking along the wall of the Beverly Sunset Shop. Once in position, wait for the rope drop. When the park opens, cast members will walk the rope up the street toward Rock 'n' Roller Coaster and Tower of Terror. Stay on the far left sidewalk and you'll be among the first to make the left turn to the entrance of the coaster. Usually the Disney people get out of the way and allow you to run the last 100 feet or so.

A good strategy for riding both Tower of Terror and Rock 'n' Roller Coaster with minimum waits is to rush first thing after opening to Rock 'n' Roller Coaster and obtain FASTPASSes, then line up for the Tower of Terror. Most days, by the time you finish experiencing the Tower of Terror, it will be time to use your FASTPASS for Rock 'n' Roller Coaster. If the Tower of Terror, the Rock 'n' Roller Coaster, and the new and popular *Toy Story* Mania! are all must-sees for you, check out our recommendations for how to experience all three in our *Toy Story* Mania! touring tips on page 657.

Sounds Dangerous ★★★

APPEAL BY AGE PRESCHOOL ★ GRADE SCHOOL ★★ TEENS ★★★
YOUNG ADULTS ★★ OVER 30 ★★ SENIORS ★★½

What it is Show demonstrating sound effects. **Scope and scale** Minor attraction. **When to go** Before 11 a.m. or after 4 p.m. **Authors' rating** Funny and informative; ★★★. **Duration of presentation** 12 minutes. **Preshow entertainment** Video introduction to sound effects. **Probable waiting time** 15–30 minutes.

DESCRIPTION AND COMMENTS *Sounds Dangerous,* a film presentation starring Drew Carey as a blundering detective, is the vehicle for a crash course on movie and TV sound effects. While the film itself is funny and well paced and (for once) doesn't hawk some Disney flick or product, time has not been kind to the attraction. Earphones, worn throughout the show, often do not work properly, and the theater itself seems run-down. Readers rank *Sounds Dangerous* the lowest of any attraction at Disney's Hollywood Studios, and it sits with the Magic Kingdom's *Stitch's Great Escape!* as one of the least popular attractions in Walt Disney World.

Most young guests have no idea who Drew Carey is. If your group needs a break from the heat, however, the air-conditioning still works well. Note that part of the show is presented in the dark so guests can focus on the sound effects, and the darkness disturbs some small children. Beware this warning from a Pasadena, Texas, reader:

I would recommend a stronger child warning for Sounds Dangerous. *Of all the attractions* [at DHS], *this had the most screaming children. Since we were plunged in complete darkness, mothers couldn't leave with their screaming children.*

TOURING TIPS *Sounds Dangerous* is periodically inundated by guests coming from a just-concluded performance of the *Indiana Jones Epic Stunt Spectacular.* This is not the time to get in line. Wait at 30 minutes and try again.

A reader from Israel suggests that a good time to catch *Sounds Dangerous* is just before the afternoon parade. If the parade starts on Hollywood Boulevard, it takes about 15 minutes to wind over to the theater—just long enough to catch the show and pop out right in time for the parade.

Star Tours (FASTPASS) ★★★★

APPEAL BY AGE	PRESCHOOL ★★★½	GRADE SCHOOL ★★★★	TEENS ★★★★
YOUNG ADULTS ★★★★	OVER 30 ★★★★	SENIORS ★★★½	

What it is Indoor space flight–simulation ride. **Scope and scale** Headliner. **When to go** First 90 minutes after opening. **Special comments** Expectant mothers and anyone prone to motion sickness are advised against riding. Too intense for many children younger than age 8. Must be 40" tall to ride. **Authors' rating** A classic adventure; ★★★★. **Duration of ride** About 7 minutes. **Average wait in line per 100 people ahead of you** 5 minutes; assumes all simulators operating. **Loading speed** Moderate–fast.

Motion Sickness

DESCRIPTION AND COMMENTS Based on the *Star Wars* movie series, this attraction was Disney's first modern simulator ride. Guests ride in a flight simulator modeled after those used for training pilots and astronauts. You're supposedly on a vacation outing in space, piloted by a "droid" (android, aka robot) on his first flight with real passengers. Mayhem ensues almost immediately. Scenery flashes by, and the simulator bucks and pitches. You could swear you were moving at the speed of light. After several minutes of this, the droid somehow lands the spacecraft.

An interactive show, *Jedi Training Academy,* is staged several times daily to the left of the Star Tours building entrance, opposite Backlot Express. Young Skywalkers-in-training are selected from the audience to train in the ways of The Force and do battle against Darth Vader. If all this sounds too intense, it's not—Storm Troopers provide comic relief, and just as in the movies, the Jedi always wins. Check the daily entertainment schedule for showtimes.

TOURING TIPS Except on unusually busy days, waits for Star Tours rarely exceed 35 to 45 minutes. For the first couple of hours the park is open, expect a wait of 25 minutes or less. Even so, ride before 11 a.m. or use FASTPASS. If you have young children (or anyone) who are apprehensive about this attraction, ask the attendant about switching off (see page 339). Watch for throngs arriving from performances of the *Indiana Jones Epic Stunt Spectacular.* If you encounter a long line, try again later.

Streets of America ★★★

APPEAL BY AGE	PRESCHOOL ★★½	GRADE SCHOOL ★★★	TEENS ★★★
YOUNG ADULTS ★★★	OVER 30 ★★★	SENIORS ★★★½	

What it is Walk-through back-lot movie set. **Scope and scale** Diversion. **When to go** Anytime. **Authors' rating** Interesting, with lots of detail; ★★★. **Duration**

of presentation Varies. **Average wait in line per 100 people ahead of you** No waiting.

DESCRIPTION AND COMMENTS Guests can stroll an elaborate urban street set and appreciate its rich detail.

TOURING TIPS There's never a wait to enjoy the Streets of America; save it until you've seen the attractions that develop long lines. Characters such as Kim Possible and the Power Rangers often make appearances here.

Studios Backlot Tour ★★★★

APPEAL BY AGE	PRESCHOOL ★★★	GRADE SCHOOL ★★★½	TEENS ★★★½
YOUNG ADULTS ★★★½	OVER 30 ★★★½	SENIORS ★★★½	

What it is Combination tram and walking tour of modern film and video production. **Scope and scale** Headliner. **When to go** Anytime. **Special comments** Use the restroom before getting in line. **Authors' rating** Educational and fun; not to be missed; ★★★★. **Duration of presentation** About 30 minutes. **Preshow entertainment** A video before the special-effects segment and another video in the tram boarding area.

DESCRIPTION AND COMMENTS A substantial part of the Studios is a working film and television facility, where actors, artists, and technicians occasionally work on actual productions. Everything from television commercials, specials, and game shows to feature motion pictures is produced. Visitors to DHS can take a backstage studio tour to learn production methods and technologies.

Disney periodically changes the name of this tour. At press time, it was called the Studios Backlot Tour.

The tour begins on the edge of the back lot with the special-effects walking segment, then continues with the tram segment. To reach the DHS Backlot Tour, turn right off Hollywood Boulevard through the Studio Arch into the Animation Courtyard. Bear left at the corner where *Voyage of the Little Mermaid* is situated. Follow the street until you see a red brick warehouse on your right. Go through the door and up the ramp.

The first stop is a special-effects water tank where technicians explain the mechanical and optical tricks that "turn the seemingly impossible into on-screen reality." Included are rain effects and a naval battle. The waiting area for this part of the tour displays miniature naval vessels used in filming famous war movies.

A prop room separates the special-effects tank and the tram tour. Trams depart about once every four minutes on busy days, winding among production and shop buildings before stopping at the wardrobe and crafts shops. Here, costumes, sets, and props are designed, created, and stored. Still seated on the tram, you look through large windows to see craftsmen at work.

The tour continues through the back lot, where western desert canyons exist side by side with New York City brownstones. The tour's highlight is Catastrophe Canyon, an elaborate special-effects movie set where a thunderstorm, earthquake, oil-field fire, and flash flood are simulated.

TOURING TIPS Because the Backlot Tour is one of Disney's most efficient attractions, you will rarely wait more than 15 minutes (usually less than 10). Take the tour at your convenience, but preferably before 5 p.m., when the workday ends for the various workshops.

Theater of the Stars/ *Beauty and the Beast—Live on Stage* ★★★★

APPEAL BY AGE PRESCHOOL ★★★★½ GRADE SCHOOL ★★★★ TEENS ★★★★
YOUNG ADULTS ★★★★ OVER 30 ★★★★ SENIORS ★★★★½

What it is Live Hollywood-style musical, usually featuring Disney characters; performed in an open-air theater. **Scope and scale** Major attraction. **When to go** Anytime; evenings are cooler. **Special comments** Performances are listed in the daily *Times Guide.* **Authors' rating** Excellent; ★★★★. **Duration of presentation** 25 minutes. **Preshow entertainment** None. **When to arrive** 20–30 minutes before showtime.

DESCRIPTION AND COMMENTS Theater of the Stars combines Disney characters with singers and dancers in upbeat and humorous Hollywood musicals. The *Beauty and the Beast* show, in particular, is outstanding. The theater offers a clear field of vision from almost every seat. Best, a canopy protects the audience from the Florida sun (or rain). The theater still gets mighty hot in the summer, but you should make it through a performance without suffering a heatstroke.

TOURING TIPS Unless you visit during the cooler months, see this show in the late afternoon or the evening. The production is so popular that you should show up 25 to 35 minutes early to get a seat.

Toy Story Mania! (FASTPASS) ★★★★½

APPEAL BY AGE PRESCHOOL ★★★★★ GRADE SCHOOL ★★★★★ TEENS ★★★★★
YOUNG ADULTS ★★★★★ OVER 30 ★★★★★ SENIORS ★★★★½

What it is 3-D ride through indoor shooting gallery. **Scope and scale** Headliner. **When to go** Before 10:30 a.m., after 6 p.m., or use FASTPASS (if available). **Authors' rating** ★★★★½. **Duration of ride** About 6½ minutes. **Average wait in line per 100 people ahead of you** 4½ minutes. **Loading speed** Fast.

DISNEY DISH WITH JIM HILL

FINDING NEMO: IT AIN'T ROCKET SCIENCE Nemo seems to be *everywhere* at Walt Disney World these days. The little clownfish stars in his very own stage musical at Animal Kingdom, he's mentioned in the title of Epcot's The Seas with Nemo and Friends, and he even figures in the design motif for an entire wing of rooms at Disney's Caribbean Beach Resort. In his latest bid for total Disney World domination, the Orange One also makes an appearance in *Toy Story* Mania! Check out the drawing that's posted in this attraction's queue area, right next to the Linkin' Log 3-D glasses dispensary: there, along with a not-so–Hidden Mickey, is a not-all-that-hard-to-find Nemo.

DESCRIPTION AND COMMENTS *Toy Story* Mania! ushers in a whole new generation of Disney attractions: "virtual dark rides." Since Disneyland opened in 1955, ride vehicles have moved past two- and three-dimensional sets often populated by audio-animatronic (AA) figures. These amazingly detailed sets and robotic figures defined the Disney Imagineering genius in attractions such as Pirates of the Caribbean, The Haunted Mansion, and Peter Pan's Flight. Now for *Toy Story* Mania!, the elaborate sets and endearing AA characters are gone. Imagine long corridors, totally empty, covered with reflective material. There's almost nothing there . . . until you put on your 3-D glasses. Instantly, the corridor is full and brimming with color, action, and activity, thanks to projected computer-graphic (CG) images.

Conceptually, this is an interactive shooting gallery much like Buzz Lightyear's Space Ranger Spin (see page 542), but in *Toy Story* Mania!, your ride vehicle passes through a totally virtual midway, with booths offering such games as ring tossing and ball throwing. You use a cannon on your ride vehicle to play as you move along from booth to booth. Unlike the laser guns in Buzz Lightyear, however, the pull-string cannons in *Toy Story* Mania! take advantage of CG image technology to toss rings, shoot balls, even throw eggs and pies. Each game booth is manned by a *Toy Story* character who is right beside you in 3-D glory, cheering you on. In addition to 3-D imagery, you experience various smells, vehicle motion, wind, and water spray. The ride begins with a training round to familiarize you with the nature of the games, then continues through a number of "real" games in which you compete against your riding mate. The technology has the ability to self-adjust the level of difficulty, and there are plenty of easy targets for small children to reach. *Tip:* Let the pull-string retract all the way back into the cannon before pulling it again.

Finally, and also of note, a new generation of "living character" audio-animatronic figures has been introduced in the preshow queuing area of *Toy Story* Mania! A six-foot-tall Mr. Potato Head breaks new ground for an audio-animatronic character by interacting with and talking to guests in real time (similar to *Turtle Talk with Crush*).

Reader reviews of *Toy Story* Mania! have been over-the-top enthusiastic. This praise from a Fanwood, New Jersey, reader is typical:

> Toy Story *Mania! is the best ride at Disney. The combo of a midway competition and the 3-D is an experience worth the 70-minute wait. Five stars from one teen and two over-30s!*

TOURING TIPS Because it's new, it's a ton of fun, and it has a relatively low rider-per-hour capacity, *Toy Story* Mania! has become the biggest bottleneck in Walt Disney World, surpassing even Test Track at Epcot. The only way to get aboard without a horrendous wait is to be one of the first through the turnstiles when the park opens and zoom to the attraction. Another alternative is to obtain FASTPASSes for *Toy Story* Mania! as soon as the park opens and then backtrack to ride the Rock 'n' Roller Coaster and Tower of Terror (*Toy Story* Mania! actually draws some of the crowds from these attractions). Don't think you'll have all day to procure FASTPASSes, though: even on days of moderate attendance, all FASTPASSes for the day are gone by 11 a.m. Also, expect long queues at the FASTPASS kiosks.

Following are reports from readers. First from a Cold Spring, NY, mom:

> *There was a 20-minute wait just for FASTPASSes as soon as the park opened, and by 11 o'clock all 3 FASTPASSes were gone for the day. Thanks to the DIS forums [***www.disboards.com***], though, I was aware of how popular the ride was, so I got FASTPASSes for it first, then followed the touring plan, and everything fell into place nicely.*

A Nashville, Tennessee, mom shares this:

Toy Story Mania! was swamped by the time we got to it, still fairly early in the day. We had to resort to getting some of the last FASTPASSes, and it elongated our day to wait until our [return] time came up. But oh my gosh, what fun! It was worth the wait!

From an Evansville, Indiana, mom:

We immediately went to Toy Story Mania! and found a HUGE line for the ride. We figured we'd be smart and get a FASTPASS. Turns out the huge line WAS the FASTPASS line! Unfortunately, we had to skip this ride due to the long wait.

The Twilight Zone Tower of Terror (FASTPASS) ★★★★★

APPEAL BY AGE PRESCHOOL ★★½ GRADE SCHOOL ★★★★ TEENS ★★★★½
YOUNG ADULTS ★★★★★ OVER 30 ★★★★★ SENIORS ★★★★

What it is Sci-fi–themed indoor thrill ride. **Scope and scale** Super-headliner. **When to go** Before 9:30 a.m., after 6 p.m., or use FASTPASS. **Special comments** Must be 40" tall to ride; switching-off option offered (see page 339). **Authors' rating** Walt Disney World's best attraction; not to be missed; ★★★★★. **Duration of ride** About 4 minutes plus preshow. **Average wait in line per 100 people ahead of you** 4 minutes; assumes all elevators operating. **Loading speed** Moderate.

DESCRIPTION AND COMMENTS The Tower of Terror is a different species of Disney thrill ride, though it borrows elements of The Haunted Mansion at the Magic Kingdom. The story is that you're touring a once-famous Hollywood hotel gone to ruin. As at Star Tours, the queuing area immerses guests in the adventure as they pass through the hotel's once-opulent public rooms. From the lobby, guests are escorted into the hotel's library, where Rod Serling, speaking from an old black-and-white television, greets the guests and introduces the plot.

The Tower of Terror is a whopper at 13-plus-stories tall. Breaking tradition in terms of visually isolating themed areas, it lets you see the entire Studios from atop the tower . . . but you have to look quick.

The ride vehicle, one of the hotel's service elevators, takes guests to see the haunted hostelry. The tour begins innocuously, but at about the fifth floor things get pretty weird. Guests are subjected to a full range of eerie effects as they cross into the Twilight Zone. The climax of the adventure occurs when the elevator reaches the top floor (the 13th, of course) and the cable snaps.

The Tower of Terror is an experience to savor. Though the final plunges (yep, make that plural) are calculated to thrill, the meat of the attraction is its extraordinary visual and audio effects. There's richness and subtlety here, enough to keep the ride fresh and stimulating after many repetitions. Disney tinkers with the Tower of Terror incessantly. Recently, random ride and drop sequences were introduced that make the attraction faster and keep you guessing about when, how far, and how many times the elevator will drop. We interviewed a family from Toronto who claimed that as they were preparing to disembark at the unloading area, the doors suddenly closed and the elevator shot back up for yet another drop! In addition to random sequencing, new visual, auditory, and olfactory effects were added.

A senior from the United Kingdom tried the Tower of Terror and liked it very much, writing:

I was thankful I had read your review of the Tower of Terror, or I would certainly have avoided it. As you say, it is so full of magnificent detail that it is worth riding, even if you don't fancy the drops involved.

The Tower has great potential for terrifying young children and rattling more-mature visitors. If you have teenagers in your party, use them as experimental probes. If they report back that they really, really liked the Tower of Terror, run as fast as you can in the opposite direction.

TOURING TIPS The Tower is a veritable beacon, visible from outside the park and luring curious guests as soon as they enter. Because of its popularity with schoolkids, teens, and young adults, you can count on a foot race to the attraction, as well as to the nearby Rock 'n' Roller Coaster and *Toy Story* Mania!, when the park opens. Expect the Tower to be mobbed most of the day. Experience it as early as possible in the morning, in the evening before the park closes, or use FASTPASS.

If you're on hand when the park opens and want to ride Tower of Terror first, position yourself on the middle right side of Sunset Boulevard as close to the rope barrier as possible. Once in position, wait for the rope drop. When the park opens, cast members will walk the rope up the street toward Rock 'n' Roller Coaster and Tower of Terror. Just stay on the outside of the far-right sidewalk, and you'll be among the first to make the right turn to the entrance of the tower. Usually the Disney people get out of the way and allow you to run the last 100 feet or so. Also, be aware that about 65% of the folks waiting for the rope walk will head for Rock 'n' Roller Coaster. If you are not positioned on the far right, it will be hard to move through the throng of coaster enthusiasts to make a right turn into Tower of Terror.

To save time, when you enter the library waiting area, stand in the far back corner across from the door where you entered and at the opposite end of the room from the TV. When the doors to the loading area open, you'll be one of the first admitted.

If you have young children (or anyone) who are apprehensive about this attraction, ask the attendant about switching off (see page 339).

A good strategy for riding both Tower of Terror and Rock 'n' Roller Coaster with minimum waits is to rush first thing after opening to Rock 'n' Roller Coaster and obtain FASTPASSes, then line up for the Tower of Terror. Most days, by the time you finish experiencing the Tower of Terror, it will be time to use your FASTPASS for Rock 'n' Roller Coaster. Factoring a ride on the new and overwhelmingly popular *Toy Story* Mania! into the equation requires a different strategy. See our touring tips on page 542.

Voyage of the Little Mermaid (FASTPASS) ★★★★

APPEAL BY AGE PRESCHOOL ★★★★ GRADE SCHOOL ★★★★ TEENS ★★★½
YOUNG ADULTS ★★★½ OVER 30 ★★★★ SENIORS ★★★★

What it is Musical stage show featuring characters from the Disney movie *The Little Mermaid*. **Scope and scale** Major attraction. **When to go** Before 9:45 a.m., just before closing, or use FASTPASS. **Authors' rating** Romantic, lovable, and humorous in the best Disney tradition; not to be missed; ★★★★. **Duration of presentation** 15 minutes. **Preshow entertainment** Taped ramblings about the decor in the preshow holding area. **Probable waiting time** Before 9:30 a.m., 10–30 minutes; after 9:30 a.m., 35–70 minutes.

DESCRIPTION AND COMMENTS *Voyage of the Little Mermaid* is a winner, appealing to every age. Cute without being silly or saccharine, and infinitely lovable,

The Little Mermaid show is the most tender and romantic entertainment offered anywhere in Walt Disney World. The story is simple and engaging, the special effects impressive, and the Disney characters memorable.

We receive a lot of mail from Europeans who complain about the "soppy sentimentality" of Americans in general and of Disney attractions in particular. These comments of a man from Bristol, England, are typical:

Americans have an ability to think as a child and so enjoy the soppiness of The Little Mermaid. *English cynicism made it hard for us at times to see Disney stories as anything other than gushing, namby-pamby, and full of stereotypes. Other Brits might also find the sentimentality cloying. Maybe you should prepare them for the need to rethink their wry outlook on life temporarily.*

TOURING TIPS Because it's well done and located at a busy pedestrian intersection, *Voyage of the Little Mermaid* plays to capacity crowds all day. FASTPASS has helped redistribute crowds at *Voyage of the Little Mermaid.* Half of each audience is drawn from the standby line. As a rough approximation, guests in the front third of the queuing area will usually make it into the next performance, and quite often folks in the front half of the queuing area will be admitted. Those in the back half of the queuing area will probably have to wait through two showings before being admitted.

When you enter the preshow lobby, stand near the doors to the theater. When they open, go inside, pick a row of seats, and let six to ten people enter the row ahead of you. The strategy is twofold: to obtain a good seat and be near the exit.

Finally, a Charlotte, North Carolina, mom took exception to our fright-potential assessment of *Voyage of the Little Mermaid:*

The Guide *let me down on the* Little Mermaid *show at* [DHS]*—the huge sea witch portrayed in laser lights, cartoon, and live action TERRIFIED my 3-year-old. The description of the show led me to believe it was all sweetness and romance with no scariness.*

Walt Disney: One Man's Dream ★★★

APPEAL BY AGE PRESCHOOL ★★ GRADE SCHOOL ★★★ TEENS ★★★½
YOUNG ADULTS ★★★★ OVER 30 ★★★★ SENIORS ★★★★

What it is Tribute to Walt Disney. **Scope and scale** Minor attraction. **When to go** Anytime. **Authors' rating** Excellent! And about time; ★★★. **Duration of presentation** 25 minutes. **Preshow entertainment** Disney memorabilia. **Probable waiting time** For film, 10 minutes.

DESCRIPTION AND COMMENTS *One Man's Dream* is a long-overdue tribute to Walt Disney. Launched in 2001 to celebrate the 100th anniversary of Disney's birth, the attraction consists of an exhibit area showcasing Disney memorabilia and recordings, followed by a film documenting Disney's life. The exhibits chronicle Walt Disney's life and business. On display are a replica of Walt's California office, various innovations in animation developed by Disney, and early models and working plans for Walt Disney World, as well as various Disney theme parks around the world. The film provides a personal glimpse of Disney and offers insights regarding both Disney's successes and failures.

TOURING TIPS Give yourself some time here. Every minute spent among these extraordinary artifacts will enhance your visit, taking you back to

DISNEY DISH WITH JIM HILL

DREAM ON, WALT This walk-through exhibit was slated for closure just last year, with all of the exhibits to be packed away and sent back to the Disney Studios' archives. But then along came D23—The Official Community for Disney Fans—and *One Man's Dream* suddenly got a reprieve. As of now, this collection of Walt-centric displays is expected to hang on at DHS through 2012, when it will move to Disney's California Adventure for an all-new history exhibit, expected to be housed inside a recreation of the Carthay Circle Theater.

a time when the creativity and vision that created Walt Disney World were personified by one struggling entrepreneur. Located at Pixar Place, between *Toy Story* Mania! and *Voyage of the Little Mermaid, Walt Disney: One Man's Dream* will not be difficult to see. Try it during the hot, crowded middle part of the day.

LIVE ENTERTAINMENT *at* DISNEY'S HOLLYWOOD STUDIOS

WHEN THE STUDIOS OPENED, live entertainment, parades, and special events weren't as fully developed or elaborate as those at the Magic Kingdom or Epcot. With the introduction of an afternoon parade and elaborate shows at **Theater of the Stars,** the Studios joined the big leagues. In 1998, DHS launched a new edition of *Fantasmic!* (see page 642), a water, fireworks, and laser show that draws rave reviews. Staged in its own specially designed 10,000-person amphitheater, *Fantasmic!* makes the Studios the park of choice for spectacular nighttime entertainment. WDW live-entertainment guru Steve Soares posts the DHS performance schedule about a week in advance at **pages.prodigy.net/stevesoares.**

unofficial **TIP**
If you're anywhere on the parade route when the parade begins, your best bet is to stay put and enjoy it. Our favorite vantage point is the steps of the theater next to *Sounds Dangerous.*

AFTERNOON PARADE Staged once a day, the parade begins near the park's entrance, continues down Hollywood Boulevard, and circles in front of the giant hat. From there, it passes in front of *Sounds Dangerous* and ends by Star Tours. An alternate route

DISNEY DISH WITH JIM HILL

HEY, IT'S NEW TO SOMEBODY. . . . WDW fans were somewhat distressed when they learned that Disney's Hollywood Studios would be getting a recycled parade. Block Party Bash, which premiered at the World in March of 2008, was actually the same parade that had rolled daily through Disney's California Adventure from May of 2005 through January 2008. Well, get ready for déjà vu all over again. In the fall of 2011, DCA's Pixar Play Parade is expected to be heading east, where it will then begin daily performances as part of Walt Disney World's 40th-anniversary celebration.

begins at the far end of Sunset Boulevard and turns right, onto Hollywood Boulevard.

The Studios' latest parade, **Block Party Bash,** features floats and characters based on Disney's animated features, including *Toy Story; Monsters, Inc.;* and *A Bug's Life*. It's a colorful, high-energy affair with plenty of acrobatics, singing, and dancing. It's also loud beyond belief. *Unofficial Guide* coauthor Len Testa, who considers most Disney afternoon parades to be cliché-ridden mobile musicals affording a high chance of heat stroke, grudgingly concedes that this may be the best of the lot.

HIGH SCHOOL MUSICAL PEP RALLY We can't fault Disney for trying to cash in on the phenomenal success of the *High School Musical* movie franchise, and the kids who sing and dance their way through this 20-minute recap of several major musical numbers do an admirable job. With little dialogue and stage scenery that consists of nothing more than a few blow-up basketball-shaped balloons and cheesy "Go Wildcats!" banners, Disney's not giving them much to work with. Children will be disappointed at not seeing the actual stars from the movie. Adults will spend more time wondering what the school's feeding these kids to eliminate all traces of teen angst and raging hormones.

DISNEY CHARACTERS Find characters at the Theater of the Stars, in parades, at Al's Toy Barn (near Mama Melrose's on Streets of America), in the Animation Courtyard, on the Backstage Plaza, and along Pixar Place. Mickey sometimes appears for autographs and photos on Sunset Boulevard. Times and locations for character appearances are listed in the complimentary *Times Guide*.

STREET ENTERTAINMENT With the possible exception of Epcot's World Showcase Players, the Studios has the best collection of roving street performers in all of Walt Disney World. Appearing primarily on Hollywood and Sunset boulevards, the cast of characters includes Hollywood stars and wannabes, their agents, film directors, and gossip columnists, as well as various police officers and Hollywood public-works crews.

The performers are not shy about asking you to join in their skits, and you may be asked anything from explaining why you came to "Hollywood" all the way to reciting a couple of lines in one of the directors' new films. If you're looking for a spot to rest and a bit of entertainment, grab a drink and seek out these performers.

THEATER OF THE STARS This covered amphitheater on Sunset Boulevard is the stage for production revues, usually featuring music from Disney movies and starring Disney characters. Performances are posted in front of the theater and are listed in the daily entertainment schedule in the handout *Times Guide*.

DISNEY'S HOLLYWOOD STUDIOS TOURING PLAN

BECAUSE THE STUDIOS ATTRACTIONS INCLUDE many live performances, more backtracking had been necessary at this park to avoid long waits in line. Since the removal of the old *Who Wants to Be a Millionaire* show in favor of the more traditional *Toy Story* Mania! attraction, a fair amount of backtracking has been obviated. To keep waits low, the plan now begins in the back of the park with *Toy Story* Mania!, then brings you toward the front of the park for Rock 'n' Roller Coaster and Tower of Terror. After those two, however, you'll begin a roughly counterclockwise tour of the park starting in the area around The Great Movie Ride. We've tested this tour during peak and off-peak seasons and found that when we specify a show or live performance, you're rarely more than a step away from it on the plan (and often right on time). The tour ends on Sunset Boulevard, where you'll be able to get a bite to before you find seats for *Fantasmic!*

BEFORE YOU GO

1. Call ☎ 407-824-4321 to verify the park's hours.
2. Buy your admission before arriving.
3. Make lunch and dinner Advance Reservations or reserve the *Fantasmic!* dinner package (if desired) before you arrive, by calling ☎ 407-WDW-DINE.
4. The schedule of live entertainment changes from month to month and even from day to day. Review the handout daily *Times Guide,* available free throughout Disney's Hollywood Studios.

DISNEY'S HOLLYWOOD STUDIOS "NOT A TOURING PLAN" TOURING PLANS (see page 812)

WE PRESENT FOR THE TYPE-B READER touring plans that avoid detailed step-by-step strategies for saving every last minute in line. For DHS, these "not" touring plans include advice for adults and parents with one day in the park, for anyone with two days, and for anyone with an afternoon and a full day to tour.

DISNEY'S HOLLYWOOD STUDIOS ONE-DAY TOURING PLAN (see page 831)

BY WAY OF INTRODUCTION, we didn't believe it when our software (see page 75) spit out this touring plan. It postpones several big attractions until later in the day. Field testing, however, confirmed that it saves about 40 minutes over all other plans.

The one-day plan assumes a willingness to experience all major rides and shows. Be aware that Rock 'n' Roller Coaster, Star Tours, The Great Movie Ride, *The Twilight Zone* Tower of Terror, and the Catastrophe Canyon segment of the tram tour sometimes frighten children younger than age 8. Further, Star Tours and the Rock 'n' Roller Coaster can upset anyone prone to motion sickness. When following the plan, skip any attraction you don't wish to experience.

UNIVERSAL ORLANDO

UNIVERSAL ORLANDO HAS TRANSFORMED into a complete destination resort, with two theme parks, three hotels, and a shopping,

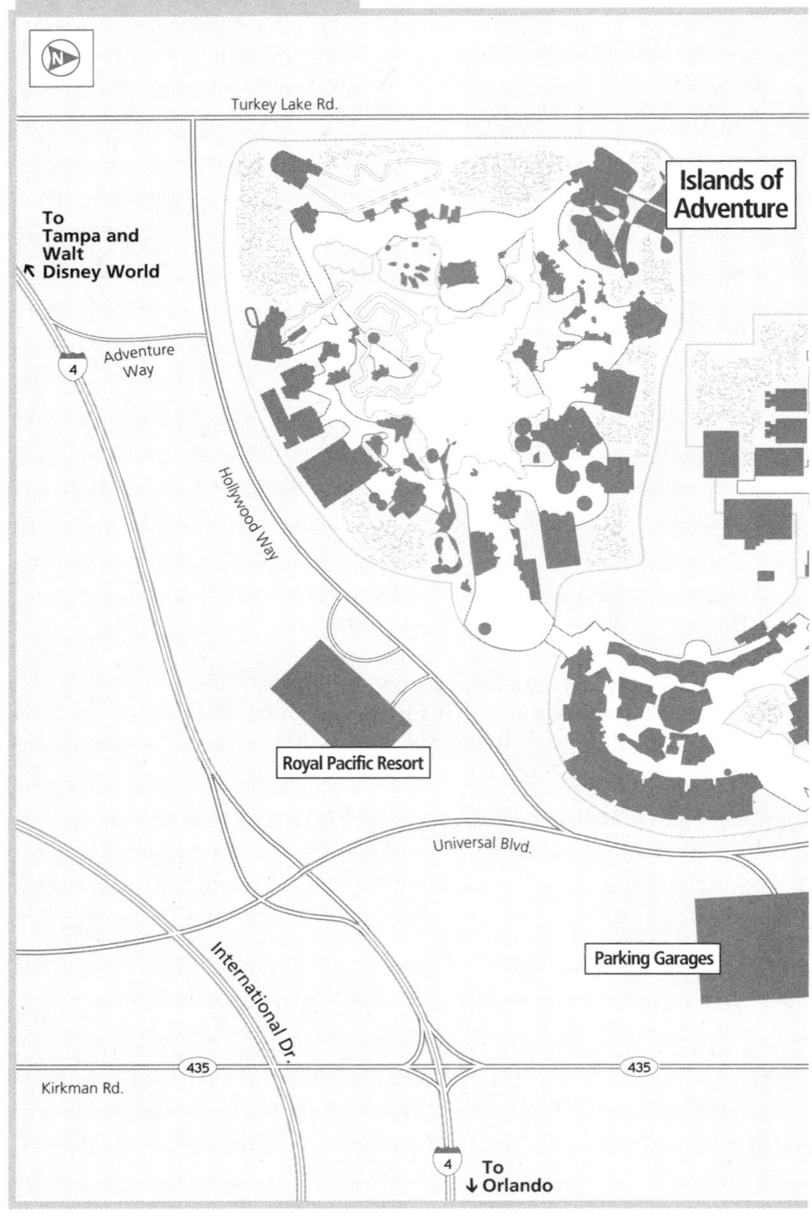
Universal Orlando
N
Turkey Lake Rd.
Islands of Adventure
To Tampa and Walt Disney World
Adventure Way
4
Hollywood Way
Royal Pacific Resort
Universal Blvd.
International Dr.
Parking Garages
435
435
Kirkman Rd.
4
To Orlando

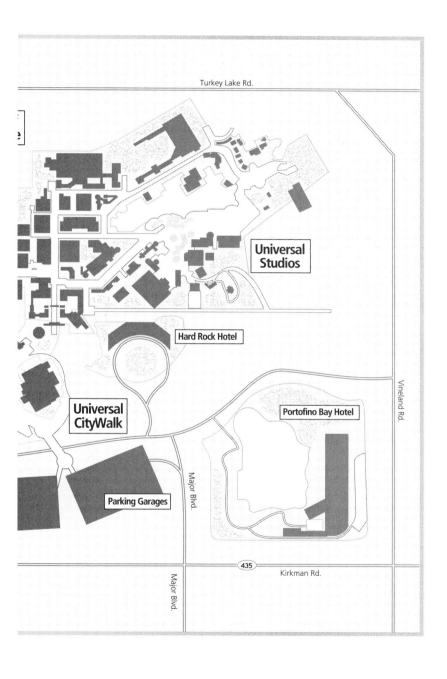

Turkey Lake Rd.

Universal Studios

Hard Rock Hotel

Universal CityWalk

Portofino Bay Hotel

Vineland Rd.

Parking Garages

Major Blvd.

435

Kirkman Rd.

Major Blvd.

dining, and entertainment complex. The second theme park, **Islands of Adventure,** opened in 1999 with five themed areas.

A system of roads and two multistory parking facilities are connected by moving sidewalks to **CityWalk,** a shopping, dining, and nighttime-entertainment complex that also serves as a gateway to the **Universal Studios Florida** and Islands of Adventure parks. (For more on CityWalk dining, see page 423; for CityWalk entertainment, see page 773.)

LODGING AT UNIVERSAL ORLANDO

UNIVERSAL CURRENTLY HAS THREE OPERATING resort hotels. The 750-room **Loews Portofino Bay Hotel** is a gorgeous property set on an artificial bay and themed like an Italian coastal town. The 650-room **Hard Rock Hotel** is an ultracool "Hotel California" replica, with slick contemporary design and a hip, friendly attitude. The 1,000-room, Polynesian-themed **Loews Royal Pacific Resort** is sumptuously decorated and richly appointed. All three are excellent hotels; the Portofino and the Hard Rock are on the pricey side, and the Royal Pacific ain't exactly cheap.

Like Disney, Universal offers a number of incentives for visitors to stay at its hotels. Perks available that mirror those offered by the Mouse include free parking, delivery to your room of purchases made in the parks, tickets and reservation information from hotel concierges, priority dining reservations at Universal restaurants, and the ability to charge purchases to your room account.

In addition, Universal offers complimentary transportation by bus or water taxi to Universal Studios, Islands of Adventure, CityWalk, SeaWorld, Aquatica (SeaWorld's new water park; see page 721), and Wet 'n Wild. Hotel guests may use the Universal Express program without limitation all day long (see following pages). Universal lodging guests are also eligible for "next available" table privileges at CityWalk restaurants and similar priority admission to Universal Orlando theme-park shows.

ARRIVING AT UNIVERSAL ORLANDO

THE UNIVERSAL ORLANDO COMPLEX can be accessed directly from I-4. Once on-site, you will be directed to park in one of two multitiered parking garages. Parking runs $12 for cars and $15 for RVs ($8 after 6 p.m.). Be sure to write down the location of your car before heading for the parks. From the garages, moving sidewalks deliver you to the Universal CityWalk dining, shopping, and entertainment venue described previously. From CityWalk, you can access the main entrances of both Universal Studios Florida and Islands of Adventure theme parks. Even with the moving walkways, it takes about 10 to 12 minutes to commute from the garages to the entrances of the theme parks. If you are staying at Walt Disney World and don't have a car, Mears Transportation will shuttle you from your hotel to Universal and back for $16. Pickup and return times are at your convenience. To schedule a shuttle call ☎ 407-423-5566 or 800-407-4275.

Universal offers One-day, Two-day, Seven-day (Unlimited Admission), and Annual Passes. All can be obtained in advance on the phone at ☎ 800-711-0080 or at Universal's Web site (**www.universalorlando.com**). Prices shown on the next page for One-day Passes are for buying those passes at the gate; you will receive a small discount on One-day Passes if you buy them online. The Two-park Unlimited Admission Pass is available only online; you'll save $10 if you purchase this pass in advance. Be sure to check Universal's Web site for seasonal deals and specials.

	ADULTS	CHILDREN (AGES 3–9)
One-day, One-park Pass	$75	$63
One-day, Two-park Pass	$90	$80
Two-park Unlimited Admission Pass	$130	$120*
Two-park Annual Preferred Pass	$200	$200*
Two-park Annual Power Pass	$140	$140*
Two-park Premier Annual Pass	$280	$280*
		*No discount

If you want to visit more than one park on a given day, have your park pass and hand stamped when exiting your first park. At your second park, use the readmission turnstile, showing your stamped pass and hand.

unofficial **TIP**
The Two-park Unlimited Admission Pass allows you to visit both Universal theme parks on the same day; it's good for seven consecutive days of admission.

Combination passes are available: a five-park, 14-day pass allows unlimited entry to Universal Studios, Universal's Islands of Adventure, SeaWorld, Aquatica, and Wet 'n Wild and costs about $235 for adults and $215 for children (ages 3 to 9). A six-park, 14-day pass provides unlimited entry to Universal Studios, Universal's Islands of Adventure, SeaWorld, Wet 'n Wild, and Busch Gardens and costs about $280 for adults and $260 for children.

The main Universal Orlando information number is ☎ 407-363-8000. Reach Guest Services at ☎ 407-224-4233, and order tickets by mail at ☎ 877-247-5561. The numbers for Lost and Found are ☎ 407-224-4244 (Universal Studios) and 407-224-4245 (Islands of Adventure).

EARLY ENTRY AND UNIVERSAL EXPRESS

UNIVERSAL NO LONGER OPERATES an early-entry program. The Universal Express program is actually two programs, one for Universal hotel guests, called Universal Express, and one available to everyone for an additional fee, called Universal Express Plus. There is no longer a basic program similar to Disney's FASTPASS.

This discontinuation of the old Universal Express has enraged many readers. This comment from a Manchester, England, dad is typical:

> *Imagine my shock when I arrived this year to find Universal and IOA have done away with their free version of FASTPASS. I have written to them to explain that although I can afford to pay for their Express Plus, I will not. Why pay for something Disney gives you for free?*

A countryman from Basingstoke agrees:

> *The Disney FASTPASS is great but the Universal Express Plus concept stinks! The Disney FASTPASS is free for all and represents a fair opportunity for limited queue-jumping for anyone prepared to plan*

ahead. Universal Express Plus on the other hand allows richer patrons to pay quite a lot extra to jump every queue, thus creating first-class and second-class customers. Since [Universal Express Plus] results in much longer waits for those without [it], the second-class customers who haven't paid extra in are truly second-class!

UNIVERSAL EXPRESS PLUS If you're willing to drop the extra cash, you can upgrade your regular ticket to Universal Express Plus, which allows you to use the Express entrance one time only at each designated Universal Express attraction (although we have found that one-time use policy is loose and is enforced only for major attractions on crowded days). Universal Express Plus is good only for the date of purchase *at one park* (though there's also a more expensive two-park option) and can be used only by one person.

Universal Express Plus prices vary from $20 to $56, cheaper in the off-seasons and more expensive during peak seasons and holidays. You can purchase Universal Express Plus at the theme park's ticket windows, just outside the front gates. Once in the Universal Studios theme park, Universal Express Plus is available at Nickstuff. Inside Islands of Adventure, you can buy Universal Express Plus at Jurassic Outfitters, Toon Extra, and the Marvel Alterniverse Store. Universal Express Plus is available on the Internet for up to eight months in advance. You must also know what date you plan on using Universal Express Plus, because different dates have different prices.

A father of four from Watford, England, reports on his experience using Universal Express:

The Universal parks' attractions were better than I expected; however, crowd management is poorer than at Disney, and it gets very busy around the middle of the day. I bought Universal Express add-ons to our tickets in advance. They were expensive ($40 per person extra per day) but, I think, worth it—we never waited more than ten minutes for anything, as not many people have these passes. As we also arrived early at the parks, we could get on the main attractions without waiting or using the Express passes. Then later we went back a second or third time to our favorites using the passes and completely avoided the queues, which were up to two hours long at that point. My son went on the Hulk coaster four times without any wait as a result of using my Express pass.

A New York mom had a similarly trouble-free experience but questions the value of the investment:

We bought Universal's Express Plus, but it was both less necessary and less consistently effective. Arriving at park opening, we were able to see many attractions right away without needing the passes at all. They helped on about three attractions between the two parks—a poor return for an investment of $156, but it was like life insurance: a good thing to have "just in case." On Dudley Do-Right, we still had to wait 30 minutes even with Universal Express Plus, whereas with Disney's free FASTPASS we never waited more than 5 minutes for an attraction. The only aspect of UEP that was better than FP is that *touring order was unaffected: UEP could be used whenever you first approached an attraction instead of your having to come back later.*

UNIVERSAL EXPRESS PROGRAM AVAILABLE TO UNIVERSAL RESORT GUESTS The Universal Express program for Universal resort guests allows guests to bypass the regular line anytime and as often as desired by simply showing their room key. This perk far surpasses any perk accorded to guests of Disney resorts.

How Universal Express Affects Crowd Conditions at the Attractions

This system dramatically affects crowd movement (and touring plans) in the Universal parks. A woman from Yorktown, Virginia, writes:

People in the [Express] *line were let in at a rate of about ten to one over the regular-line folks. This created bottlenecks and long waits for people who didn't have the Express privilege at the very times when it is supposed to be easier to get around!*

SINGLES LINES

AND THERE'S YET ANOTHER OPTION: the singles line. Several attractions have this special line for guests riding alone. As Universal employees will tell you, this line is often even faster than the Express line. We strongly recommend you use the singles line whenever possible, as it will decrease your overall wait and leave more time for repeat rides or just bumming around the parks.

LOCKERS

UNIVERSAL HAS INSTITUTED a mandatory locker system at its big thrill rides. Bags and other items must be placed in lockers outside the attractions. Lockers are free for the first 45 minutes. Then, you can either pay $8 for the entire day or $2 per hour with a $10 maximum.

The locker banks are easy to find; each bank has a small computer in the center. When the sun is bright, the screen is almost impossible to read, so have someone block the sun or use a different computer. After selecting your language, you press your thumb onto the keypad and have your fingerprint scanned. We've seen people walk off cursing at this step, having repeated it over and over with no success. Most patrons press their thumb down too hard. The computer cannot read your thumbprint if it's squished together, so take a deep breath and just place your thumb on the scanner.

After your thumb scans, you will receive a locker number. Write it down! When you return from your ride, go to the same kiosk machine, enter your locker number, and scan your thumb again. At Guest Services, family-sized lockers are available for $10 for the entire day, but remember that only the person who used his or her thumb to get the locker can retrieve anything from it.

UNIVERSAL, KIDS, AND SCARY STUFF

ALTHOUGH THERE'S PLENTY FOR YOUNGER CHILDREN to enjoy at the Universal parks, the majority of the major attractions have the potential for wigging out kids under 8 years of age. At Universal Studios Florida, forget Revenge of the Mummy, *Twister, Disaster!, Jaws, Men in Black,* The Simpsons Ride, and *Terminator 2: 3-D.* The first part of the *E.T.* ride is a little intense for a few preschoolers, but the end is all happiness and harmony. Interestingly, very few families report problems with *Beetlejuice's Rock 'n' Roll Graveyard Revue* or the *Universal Horror Make-Up Show.* Anything not listed is pretty benign.

At Universal's Islands of Adventure, watch out for The Incredible Hulk Coaster, Doctor Doom's Fearfall, The Amazing Adventures of Spider-Man, the *Jurassic Park* River Adventure, Dueling Dragons, and *Poseidon's Fury!* Popeye & Bluto's Bilge-Rat Barges is wet and wild, but most younger children handle it well. Dudley Do-Right's Ripsaw Falls is a toss-up, to be considered only if your kids like water-flume rides. The *Sindbad* stunt show includes some explosions and startling special effects, but once again, children tolerate it well. Nothing else should pose a problem.

unofficial **TIP**
If you have tots age 7 or younger, consider that many of Universal's attractions can be frightening for little ones.

QUITTING TIME

BECAUSE THE PARKING FOR BOTH UNIVERSAL theme parks and the CityWalk shopping, dining, and entertainment complex is consolidated in the same parking structure, chaos ensues when the parks close. An Orlando woman, obviously very perturbed, comments thusly:

> *Universal needs to change the hours when each park closes! Both Universal Studios and Islands of Adventure share the same parking lot. IT MAKES NO SENSE for the two theme parks to close at the same time (especially since Islands has no night finale). I cannot even explain the amount of people. It was insane at closing (and other people were coming IN to go to CityWalk so it was SUCH a big mess)! There was less of a crowd coming out of Epcot on July 4! I think they really need to rethink their hours, especially on the weekend in the summer!*

TNA WRESTLING AND BLUE MAN GROUP

UNIVERSAL ORLANDO OFFERS TWO theater productions. At Soundstage 21, guests can sit in on the taping of Spike TV's ***TNA iMPACT!*** professional-wrestling program, while Universal Studios' Sharp Aquos Theatre, near CityWalk, is home to **Blue Man Group.** Tickets for the latter can be purchased online or at the Universal Box Office. There is no admission fee for the rasslin'.

TNA iMPACT!

About five TNA (Total Nonstop Action) shows are filmed each month, usually with audience seating at 6 p.m. and taping starting at 6:30 p.m. For the uninitiated, TNA, like any good pro-wrestling show, is more brawl than sporting event; whether you consider it good theater is a matter of taste. Abandoning the usual square ring for a six-sided rumpus room, TNA features "concept matches" like "Ultimate X," "King of the Mountain," and "Six Sides of Steel," accompanied by the usual out-of-ring histrionics you see on TV.

Wrestlers include Kurt Angle, Christopher Daniels, Jeff Jarrett, Samoa Joe, Sting, AJ Styles, and Team 3D, among others. If you go, you can pretty much depend on witnessing great athleticism, terrible acting, horrifying staged brutality, and a down-to-earth introduction to chaos theory. It's as American as bluegrass banjo, and a perfect show to see on a first date. The taping calendar and directions to Soundstage 21 (from both inside and outside of Universal Studios) can be found at **www.universalorlando.com/shows/tna-wrestling.html.** Arrive an hour early to score the best seats. Minimum age is 14.

Blue Man Group

Blue Man Group gives Orlando its first large-scale introduction to that nebulous genre called "performance art." If the designation "performance art" confuses you, relax—it won't hurt a bit. Blue Man Group serves up a stunning show that can be appreciated by folks of all ages.

The three blue men are just that—blue—and bald and mute. Wearing black clothing and skull caps slathered with bright-blue grease paint, they deliver a fast-paced show that uses music (mostly percussion) and multimedia effects to make light of contemporary art and life in the information age. The Universal act is just one expression of a franchise that started with three friends in New York's East Village. Now you can catch their zany, wacky, smart stuff in New York, Las Vegas, Boston, Chicago, and Berlin, among other places.

Funny, sometimes poignant, and always compelling, Blue Man Group pounds out vital, visceral tribal rhythms on complex instruments (made of PVC pipes) that could pass for industrial intestines, and makes seemingly spontaneous eruptions of visual art rendered with marshmallows and a mysterious goo. The weekly supplies include 25.5 pounds of Cap'n Crunch, 60 Twinkies, 75 gallons of Jell-O, 996 marshmallows, 9.5 gallons of paint, and 185 miles—yes, miles—of rolled recycled paper. If all this sounds silly, it is, but it's also strangely thought-provoking and deals with topics such as the value of modern art, DNA, the persistence of vision, the way rock music moves you, and how we are all connected. (*Hint:* It's not the Internet.)

A live percussion band backs the Blue Man Group with a relentless and totally engrossing industrial dance riff. The band resides in long, dark alcoves above the stage. At just the right moments, the lofts are lit to reveal a group of pulsating neon-colored skeletons.

Audience participation completes the Blue Man experience. The blue men often move into the audience to bring audience members on stage. At the end of the show, the entire audience is involved in an effort to move a sea of paper across the theater. And a lot of folks can't help standing up to dance—and laugh. Magicians for the creative spirit that resides in us all, Blue Man Group makes everyone a co-conspirator in a joyous explosion of showmanship.

This show is decidedly different and requires an open mind to be appreciated. It also helps to be a little loose, because, like it or not, everybody gets sucked into the production and leaves the theater a little bit lighter in spirit. If you don't want to be pulled onstage to become a part of the improvisation, don't sit in the first half-dozen or so rows.

The Universal Box Office (☎ 888-340-5476 or 407-224-3200) is open 9 a.m. to 7 p.m. EST, or you can purchase tickets online at **www.universalorlando.com.** Advance tickets at the Universal Orlando Web site run $64 to $74, $25 for children; tickets purchased at the box office are $10 higher. The current ticket price for kids is a time-limited special and may revert to the old $49-to-$64 range at any time. The show is staged in the former Nick Studios Live theater, which can be accessed from inside or outside Universal Studios theme park. We recommend seats at least 15 rows back from the stage.

UNIVERSAL STUDIOS FLORIDA

UNIVERSAL CITY STUDIOS INC. HAS RUN a studios tour and movie-themed tourist attraction for more than 30 years, predating all Disney parks except Disneyland. In the early 1980s, Universal announced plans to build a new theme-park complex in Florida. But while Universal labored over its new project, Disney jumped into high gear and rushed its own studios and theme park into the market, beating Universal by more than a year.

Universal Studios Florida opened in June 1990. At the time, it was almost four times the size of Disney's Hollywood Studios (which has since expanded), with much more of the facility accessible to visitors. Like its sister facility in Hollywood, Universal Studios Florida is spacious, beautifully landscaped, meticulously clean, and delightfully varied in its entertainment. Rides are exciting and innovative and, as with many Disney rides, focus on familiar and/or beloved movie characters or situations.

While these rides incorporate state-of-the-art technology and live up to their billing in terms of excitement, creativity, uniqueness, and special effects, some lack the capacity to handle the number of guests who frequent major Florida tourist destinations. If a ride has great appeal but can accommodate only a small number of guests per ride or per hour, long lines form. It isn't unusual for the wait to exceed an hour and a quarter for the *E.T.* ride.

Like the Disney parks, Universal posts expected wait times at most attractions. However, as this reader from Oxford, United Kingdom, comments, the estimates are often far from accurate:

> *The day we visited Islands of Adventure, the queues were awful. Universal is not as accurate as Disney at predicting queue times. A 45-minute wait for Dudley Do-Right's Ripsaw Falls (which we felt was reasonable) was actually 90 minutes—we would not have even considered this ride had we known. This meant that when we saw*

Not to Be Missed at Universal Studios Florida

Disaster!	*Hollywood Rip Ride Rockit*
Jaws	*Men in Black* Alien Attack
Revenge of the Mummy	*Shrek 4-D*
Terminator 2: 3-D	The Simpsons Ride

the queues for Spider-Man at no less than two hours during the day—we daren't risk it! Presumably with people paying a fortune for express passes they have to keep those lines short!

Universal is not as organized with their queue systems, either. The top of Dueling Dragons was completely disorganized, with no one sorting out seating. This meant that despite a 40-minute queue, there were empty seats and even empty rows!

Happily, most shows and theater performances at Universal Studios Florida are in theaters that accommodate large numbers of people. Since many shows run continuously, waits usually don't exceed twice the show's performance time (15 to 30 minutes).

Universal Studios Florida is laid out in an upside-down-L configuration. Beyond the main entrance, a wide boulevard stretches past several shows and rides to the park's New York section. Branching off this pedestrian thoroughfare to the right are four streets that access other areas of the park and intersect a promenade circling a large lake.

The park is divided into six sections: Production Central, New York, Hollywood, San Francisco–Amity, Woody Woodpecker's KidZone, and World Expo. Where one section begins and another ends is blurry, but no matter. Guests orient themselves by the major rides, sets, and landmarks and refer, for instance, to "New York," "the waterfront," "over by *E.T.*," or "by Mel's Diner." The area of Universal Studios Florida open to visitors is about the size of Epcot.

Dining at Universal Studios is on par with Disney's Hollywood Studios. Our favorites include **Finnegan's Bar & Grill,** with a fun setting and good burgers and fish-and-chips; **Lombard's Seafood Grille,** the park's premier restaurant (but not in the same league as DHS's Hollywood Brown Derby); and **Universal Studios' Classic Monsters Cafe,** a pizza-and-chicken place that shows promotional trailers for 1950s and '60s horror movies. For something quick and satisfying, there's usually a **Nathan's Famous Hot Dogs** stand at Central Park in the New York section of the studios.

The park offers all standard services and amenities, including stroller and wheelchair rental, lockers, diaper-changing and infant-nursing facilities, car assistance, and foreign-language assistance. Most of the park is accessible to disabled guests, and TDDs are available for the hearing impaired. Almost all services are in the Front Lot, just inside the main entrance.

UNIVERSAL STUDIOS FLORIDA ATTRACTIONS

Animal Actors on Location (Universal Express) ★★★

APPEAL BY AGE PRESCHOOL ★★★★ GRADE SCHOOL ★★★★ TEENS ★★★
YOUNG ADULTS ★★★ OVER 30 ★★★ SENIORS ★★★★

What it is Animal-tricks and comedy show. **Scope and scale** Major attraction. **When to go** After you have experienced all rides. **Authors' rating** Cute li'l critters; ★★★. **Duration of presentation** 20 minutes. **Probable waiting time** 25 minutes.

Universal Studios Florida

1. *Animal Actors on Location*
2. *Beetlejuice's Rock 'n' Roll Graveyard Revue*
3. *A Day in the Park with Barney*
4. *Disaster!*
5. *E.T.* Adventure
6. *Fear Factor Live* (open seasonally)
7. Fievel's Playland
8. Hollywood Rip Ride Rockit
9. *Jaws*
10. Jimmy Neutron's Nicktoon Blast
11. *Lucy—A Tribute*
12. *Men in Black* Alien Attack
13. Revenge of the Mummy
14. *Shrek 4-D*
15. The Simpsons Ride
16. *Terminator 2: 3-D*
17. *Twister*
18. *Universal 360: A Cinesphere Spectacular*
19. *Universal Horror Make-Up Show*
20. Woody Woodpecker's Nuthouse Coaster, Curious George Goes to Town

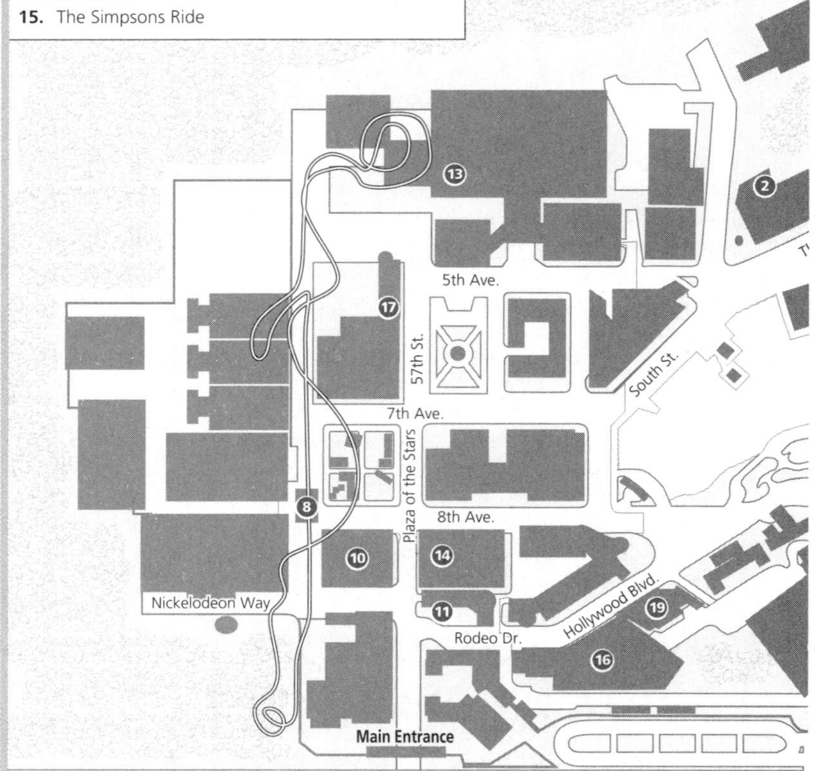

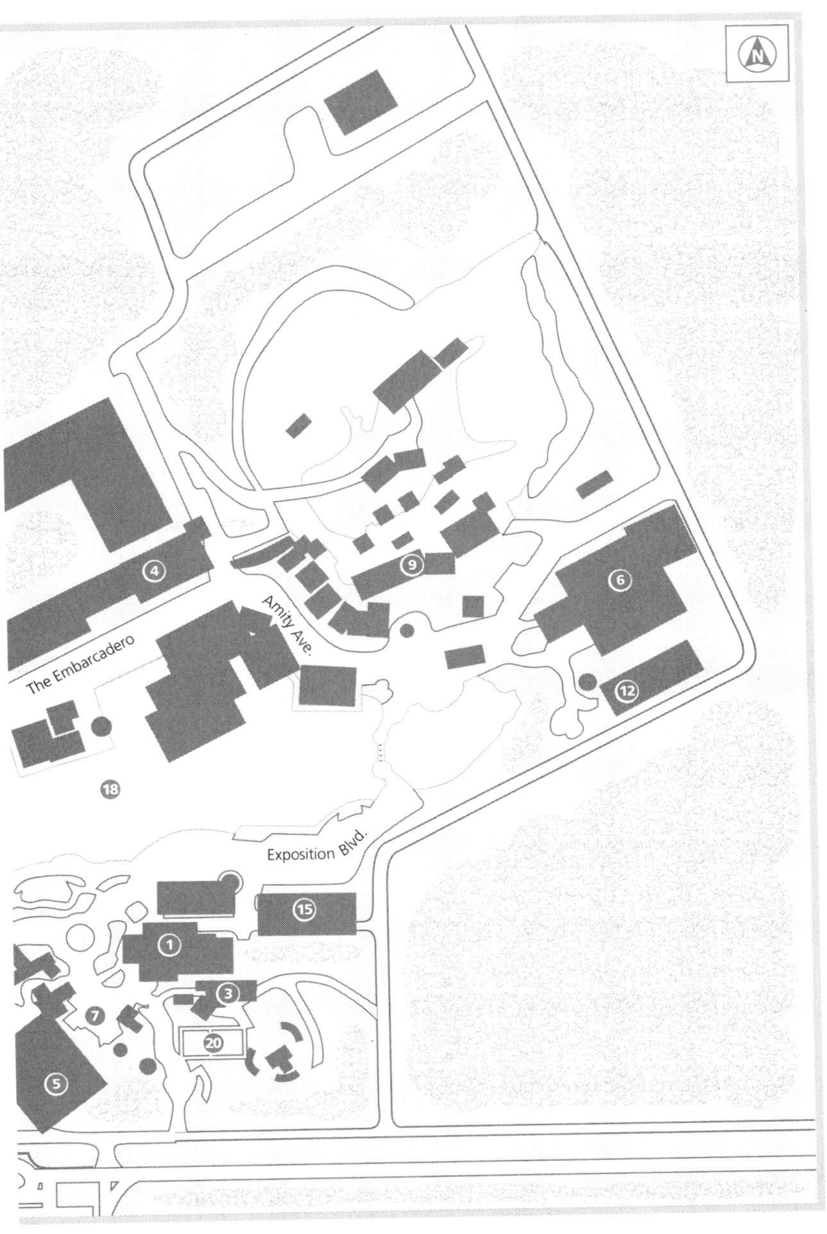
N
The Embarcadero
Amity Ave.
Exposition Blvd.
1
3
4
5
6
7
9
12
15
18
20

DESCRIPTION AND COMMENTS This show integrates video segments with live sketches, jokes, and animal tricks performed onstage. The idea is to create eco-friendly family entertainment. Several of the animal thespians are veterans of television and movies; many were rescued from shelters. Audience members can participate as well—where else will you get the chance to hold an eight-foot albino reticulated python in your lap?

TOURING TIPS Check the daily entertainment schedule for showtimes. You shouldn't have any trouble getting in to this show.

Beetlejuice's Rock 'n' Roll Graveyard Revue (Universal Express) ★★★½

APPEAL BY AGE	PRESCHOOL ★★★★	GRADE SCHOOL ★★★★	TEENS ★★★★
YOUNG ADULTS ★★★★		OVER 30 ★★★★	SENIORS ★★★★

What it is Rock-and-roll stage show. **Scope and scale** Almost major attraction. **When to go** At your convenience. **Authors' rating** Capable of waking the dead; ★★★½. **Duration of presentation** 18 minutes.

DESCRIPTION AND COMMENTS Revamped in 2006, this high-powered rock-and-roll stage show stars Beetlejuice, Frankenstein, the Bride of Frankenstein, Wolfman, Dracula, and a pair of fly girls called Hip and Hop. The show features contemporary dance and pop songs rather than classic rock. High-energy, silly, bawdy, and generally funnier than it has any right to be, the new version brings this long-running *Revue* back to life (pun intended).

TOURING TIPS Mercifully, this attraction is under cover.

The Blues Brothers ★★★½

APPEAL BY AGE	PRESCHOOL ★★★	GRADE SCHOOL ★★★½	TEENS ★★★½
YOUNG ADULTS ★★★½		OVER 30 ★★★★	SENIORS ★★★★

What it is Blues concert. **Scope and scale** Diversion. **When to go** Scheduled showtimes. **Special comments** A party in the street. **Authors' rating** High energy; ★★★½. **Duration of presentation** 15 minutes.

DESCRIPTION AND COMMENTS An impromptu concert featuring live singing and saxophone playing with a background track. The show takes place on a stoop in the street scene, across from Revenge of the Mummy. The show is one of the more unconventional diversions we've found. Jake and Elwood pull up in the infamous police cruiser from the *Blues Brothers* movie and hop on stage. Interacting with the audience, they begin conga lines in the audience, turning the city set into a scene from a musical—people are literally dancing together in the streets.

TOURING TIPS The concert is a great pick-me-up, and the short running time keeps the energy high. Don't miss this little bit of magic. If you arrive early, you might be able to find a seat on a stoop across the street, but why would you want to sit?

A Day in the Park with Barney (Universal Express) ★★★★

APPEAL BY AGE	PRESCHOOL ★★★★★	GRADE SCHOOL ★★★	TEENS ★★
YOUNG ADULTS ★★★		OVER 30 ★★★	SENIORS ★★★

What it is Live character stage show. **Scope and scale** Major children's attraction. **When to go** Anytime. **Authors' rating** A great hit with preschoolers; ★★★★. **Duration of presentation** 12 minutes plus character greeting. **Probable waiting time** 15 minutes.

DESCRIPTION AND COMMENTS Barney, the purple dinosaur of public-television fame, leads a sing-along with the help of the audience and sidekicks Baby Bop and BJ. A short preshow gets the kids lathered up before they enter Barney's Park (the theater). Interesting theatrical effects include wind, falling leaves, clouds and stars in the simulated sky, and snow. After the show, Barney exits momentarily to allow parents and children to gather along the stage. He then returns and moves from child to child, hugging each and posing for photos.

TOURING TIPS If your child likes Barney, this show is a must. It's happy and upbeat, and the character greeting that follows is the best organized we've seen in any theme park. There's no line and no fighting for Barney's attention. Just relax by the rail and await your hug. There's also a great indoor play area nearby, designed especially for wee tykes.

Disaster! (Universal Express) ★★★★

APPEAL BY AGE PRESCHOOL ★★★ GRADE SCHOOL ★★★★ TEENS ★★★★
YOUNG ADULTS ★★★★ OVER 30 ★★★★ SENIORS ★★★★

What it is Combination theater presentation and adventure ride. **Scope and scale** Major attraction. **When to go** In the morning or late afternoon. **Special comments** May frighten young children. **Authors' rating** Shaken, not stirred; ★★★★. **Duration of presentation** 20 minutes. **Loading speed** Moderate.

DESCRIPTION AND COMMENTS *Disaster!* is a retooled and modernized version of *Earthquake*—The Big One, one of Universal Studios' charter attractions. In the new version, guests are recruited for roles in a film called *Mutha Nature,* directed by the overbearing and conceited Frank Kincaid (Christopher Walken) and starring an unnamed actor you'll recognize as Dwayne "The Rock" Johnson. After the recruiting, the audience enters a sound stage where a number of seemingly random scenes are filmed starring the guests-cum-volunteers. The filming demonstrates various techniques for integrating sets, blue screens, and matte painting with live-action stunts. Next, guests board a faux subway where they experience a simulated earthquake. Following the quake, while the subway returns to the station, guests view a finished cut of *Mutha Nature* that incorporates all the sound-stage shots.

TOURING TIPS Experience *Disaster!* after tackling the park's other rides.

E.T. Adventure (Universal Express) ★★★½

APPEAL BY AGE PRESCHOOL ★★★★ GRADE SCHOOL ★★★★ TEENS ★★★
YOUNG ADULTS ★★★ OVER 30 ★★★★ SENIORS ★★★★

What it is Indoor adventure ride based on the *E.T.* movie. **Scope and scale** Major attraction. **When to go** During the first 90 minutes the park is open. **Authors' rating** A happy reunion; ★★★½. **Duration of ride** 4½ minutes. **Loading speed** Moderate.

DESCRIPTION AND COMMENTS Guests aboard a bicycle-like conveyance escape with E.T. from earthly law enforcement officials and journey to E.T.'s home planet. The attraction is similar to Peter Pan's Flight at the Magic Kingdom but longer with more elaborate special effects and a wilder ride.

TOURING TIPS Most preschoolers and grade-school children love *E.T.* We think it worth a 20- to 30-minute wait, but nothing longer. Lines build quickly after 10:30 a.m., and waits can be more than two hours on busy days. Ride in the morning or late afternoon. Guests who balk at sitting on the bicycle can ride in a comfortable gondola.

A mother from Columbus, Ohio, writes about horrendous lines at *E.T.*:

The line for E.T. *took two hours! The rest of the family waiting outside thought that we had gone to E.T.'s planet for real.*

A woman from Richmond, Virginia, objects to how Universal represents the waiting time:

We got into E.T. *without much wait, but the line is very deceptive. When you see a lot of people waiting outside and the sign says "ten-minute wait from this point," it means ten minutes until you are inside the building. But there's a very long wait inside* [before] *you get to the moving vehicles.*

Fear Factor Live* (Universal Express) ★★★★ *(Open seasonally)

APPEAL BY AGE	PRESCHOOL ½	GRADE SCHOOL ★★	TEENS ★★★★
YOUNG ADULTS ★★★		OVER 30 ★★★	SENIORS ★½

What it is Live version of the gross-out-stunt television show on NBC. **Scope and scale** Headliner. **When to go** 6–8 shows daily; crowds are smallest at the first and second-to-last shows. **Authors' rating** Engrossing; ★★★★. **Duration of presentation** 30 minutes. **Probable waiting time** 25 minutes.

DESCRIPTION AND COMMENTS *Fear Factor* is a live stage show in which up to six volunteers compete for one prize; this varies but is always a package that contains at least $400 worth of Universal goodies ranging from park tickets to T-shirts. Contestants must be 18 years or older (with a photo ID to prove it) and weigh at least 110 pounds. Those demented enough to volunteer should arrive at least 75 minutes before showtime to sign papers and complete some obligatory training for the specific competitive events. Anyone who does not wish to compete in the stage show itself can sign up for the Critter Challenge or the Food Challenge (described later). With an adult's permission, volunteers as young as age 16 can compete in the latter.

The stage show is performed in a covered theater and consists of three different challenges. In the first, all six contestants are suspended two and a half stories in the air and try to hang on to a bar as long as possible. The difficulty is compounded by heavy-duty fans blasting the contestants' faces while they hold on for dear life (are we having fun yet?). Only four people go on to the next round, and the person who hangs on to the bar the longest gets to choose his or her partner for the next event.

Once the first two contestants are eliminated, it's time for a brief intermission called the Desert Hat Ordeal. This involves a brave audience member–lunatic who has signed up for the Critter Challenge. Prepared with eye goggles and a mouthpiece, the volunteer is put in a chair with a glass case over his or her head. A wheel is spun to determine what will be crawling over the volunteer's head; the creepy-crawly choices include spiders, snakes, roaches, and scorpions. The only incentive to participate is a free photo of the ordeal for contestants to take to their therapists.

Back at the main competition, the four remaining contestants are split into two teams to compete in the Eel Tank Relay. This consists of one team member grabbing beanbags out of a tank full of eels and throwing them to his or her partner to catch in a bucket. Audience members drench the contestants with high-powered water guns, further spicing up the event. The team that buckets the most beanbags wins, with the winning team members going on to compete against each other in the final round for the $400 prize package.

As the stage is prepared for the finale, the folks who volunteered for the Food Challenge steel themselves for the Guess What's Crawling to Dinner event. Here four contestants are split into two teams and invited to drink a mixture of sour milk, mystery meat, and various live bugs that are all blended together on stage. The team that drinks the most of the mixture within the time limit wins a glamorous plastic mug that says, "I Ate a Bug," a convenient euphemism for "I have the brain of a nematode." The winners (?) are asked to refrain from upchucking all over the audience as they return to their seats to watch the final challenge.

The last event has the two remaining contestants scramble up a wall to retrieve flags, jump into a car that is lifted in the air, then jump out of the car to retrieve more flags. When the required climbing, jumping, and flag grabbing are accomplished, the first contestant to remove a rocket launcher from the backseat of the car and hit a target on the stage wall wins.

Whether you participate or simply watch, this show will keep your innards in an uproar. But look at the bright side: eating the insect goop in the Food Challenge is the only free lunch available at any Orlando-area theme park.

TOURING TIPS *Fear Factor Live* is a seasonal attraction, meaning that it operates only during the busiest times of the year. Frequently when Universal or Disney relegates an attraction to seasonal status, that foreshadows a permanent closing. If it's open, however, and if you've ever wanted a chance to test your mettle (sanity?), this theme-park show may be your big chance. Participants for the physical stunts are chosen early in the morning and between performances outside the theater, so be sure to head there first thing if you want to be a contestant. Although there are usually female contestants in every show, the game is weighted against women. The first challenge, hanging from the bar, requires exceptional upper-body strength. In the several performances we observed, the first two contestants eliminated were almost always women. In fact, the only way women usually make it to the second round is when there are three or four (very rare) female contestants to start with. The victims—er, contestants—for the ick-factor stunts, like the bug-smoothie drinking, are chosen directly from the audience. Sit close to the front and wave your hands like crazy when it comes time for selection. Finally (and seriously), this show is too intense and too gross for children age 8 and under.

Fievel's Playland ★★★★

APPEAL BY AGE	PRESCHOOL ★★★★	GRADE SCHOOL ★★★★	TEENS –
YOUNG ADULTS –	OVER 30 –	SENIORS –	

What it is Children's play area with waterslide. **Scope and scale** Minor attraction. **When to go** Anytime. **Authors' rating** A much-needed attraction for preschoolers; ★★★★. **Probable waiting time** 20–30 minutes for the waterslide; otherwise, no waiting.

DESCRIPTION AND COMMENTS Imaginative playground features ordinary household items reproduced on a giant scale, as a mouse would experience them. Preschoolers and grade-schoolers can climb nets, walk through a huge boot, splash in a sardine-can fountain, seesaw on huge spoons, and climb onto a cow skull. Most of the playground is reserved for preschoolers, but a waterslide–raft ride is open to all ages.

TOURING TIPS Walk into Fievel's Playland without waiting, and stay as long as you want. Younger children love the oversize items, and there's enough to keep teens and adults busy while little ones let off steam. The waterslide–raft ride is open to everyone but is extremely slow-loading and carries only 300 riders per hour. With an average wait of 20 to 30 minutes, we don't think the 16-second ride is worth the trouble. Also, you're highly likely to get soaked.

Lack of shade is a major shortcoming of the entire attraction—the playground is scorching during the heat of the day.

Hollywood Rip Ride Rockit (Universal Express) ★★★★½

APPEAL BY AGE TOO NEW TO RATE

What it is Super-high-tech roller coaster. **Scope and scale** Headliner. **When to go** Immediately after park opening. **Special comments** Expect *long* waits in line. **Authors' rating** *Woo-hoo!* Not to be missed; ★★★★½. **Duration of ride** 2½ minutes. **Probable waiting time** 4 minutes.

DESCRIPTION AND COMMENTS Opened in the summer of 2009, Hollywood Rip Ride Rockit is Universal Studios' candidate for the most technologically advanced coaster in the world. Well, we know how long that distinction will last, but for sure this ride has some features we've never seen before. Let's start with the basics: Rip Ride Rockit is a sit-down X-Car coaster that runs on a 3,800-foot steel track, with a maximum height of 167 feet and a top speed of 65 miles an hour. Manufactured by German coaster maker Maurer Söhne, X-Car vehicles are more maneuverable than most other kinds and use less restrictive restraints, making for an exhilarating ride.

You ascend—vertically—at 11 feet per second to crest the 17-story-tall first hill, the highest point reached by any roller coaster in Orlando. The drop is almost vertical, too, and launches you into Double Take, a loop inversion in which you begin on the inside of the loop, twist to the outside at the top (so you're upright), and then twist back inside the loop for the descent. Double Take stands 136 feet tall, and its loop is 103 feet in diameter at its widest point. You next hurl (not *that* hurl—it comes later) into a stretch of track shaped like a musical treble clef. As on Double Take, the track configuration on Treble Clef is a first. Another innovation is Jump Cut, a spiraling negative-gravity maneuver. Usually on coasters, you experience negative gravity on long, steep vertical drops; with Jump Cut you feel like you're in a corkscrew inversion, but you never actually go upside down. Other high points include a 95-degree turn, a downhill into an "underground chasm" (gotta love those Universal PR wordsmiths!), and a final incline loop banked at 150 degrees.

The ride starts in the Production Central area; weaves into the New York area near *Twister,* popping out over the heads of guests in the square below; and then storms out and over the lagoon separating Universal Studios from Islands of Adventure. Another first: the coaster has an entrance outside the theme park where you can buy individual rides after the rest of Universal Studios has closed for the day.

Each train consists of two cars, with riders arranged two across in three rows per car. Each row is outfitted with color-changing LEDs and high-end audio and video technology for each seat. Like the Rock 'n' Roller Coaster at Disney's Hollywood Studios, this coaster features a musical soundtrack. With Rip Ride Rockit, however, you can choose the genre of music you want to hear as you ride: classic rock, country, disco, pop, or rap. After the ride, Universal flogs a digital-video "rip" of your ride, complete with the soundtrack you chose, that you can upload to Web sites such as YouTube.

TOURING TIPS Hollywood Rip Ride Rockit can put more trains on the tracks simultaneously than any other coaster in Florida, which means on paper that the ride should be able to handle about 1,850 riders per hour. In practice, you'll wait about five minutes for every 100 people in the queue ahead of you, indicating an hourly capacity of 1,500 riders. Because the ride is so close to the Universal Studios entrance, it will be a crowd magnet and create bottlenecks from park opening on. Unless you intend to spring for the Universal Express admission add-on (see page 668), your only chance to ride without a long wait is to be one of the first to enter the park when it opens.

Jaws (Universal Express) ★★★★

APPEAL BY AGE PRESCHOOL ★★★ GRADE SCHOOL ★★★★ TEENS ★★★★
YOUNG ADULTS ★★★★ OVER 30 ★★★★ SENIORS ★★★★

What it is Adventure boat ride. **Scope and scale** Headliner. **When to go** Before 11 a.m. or after 5 p.m. **Special comments** Will frighten young children. **Authors' rating** World's largest bathtub toy—not to be missed; ★★★★. **Duration of ride** 5 minutes. **Loading speed** Fast. **Probable waiting time per 100 people ahead of you** 3 minutes. **Assumes** All 8 boats are running.

DESCRIPTION AND COMMENTS *Jaws* delivers five minutes of nonstop action, with the huge shark repeatedly attacking. A West Virginia woman, fresh from the Magic Kingdom, told us the shark is "about as pesky as that witch in Snow White." While the story is entirely predictable, the shark is fairly realistic and as big as a boxcar; but what makes the ride unique is its sense of journey. *Jaws* builds an amazing degree of suspense. It isn't just a cruise into the middle of a pond where a rubber fish assaults the boat interminably. Add inventive sets and powerful special effects, and you have a first-rate attraction.

A variable at *Jaws* is the enthusiasm and acting ability of your boat guide. Throughout the ride, the guide must set the tone, elaborate the plot, drive the boat, and fight the shark. Most guides are quite good. They may overact, but you can't fault them for lack of enthusiasm. Consider also that each guide repeats this wrenching ordeal every eight minutes.

TOURING TIPS *Jaws* is well designed to handle crowds. People on the boat's left side tend to get splashed more. If you have young children, consider switching off (see page 339).

A mother of two from Williamsville, New York, who believes our warning about getting wet should be more strongly emphasized, has this to say:

Your warning about the Jaws attraction . . . is woefully understated. Please warn your readers—we were seated on the first row of the boat. My 9-year-old sat at the end of the boat (first person on the far left), and I was seated next to him. We were wary of these seats as I had read your warning, but I felt prepared. NOT! At "that" moment the water came flooding over the left front side of the boat, thoroughly drenching the two of us and filling our sneakers with water.

A dad from Seattle suggests that getting wet takes a backseat to being terrified:

Our 8-year-old was so frightened by Jaws *that we scrapped the rest of the Universal tour and went back to* E.T. *An employee said she wouldn't recommend it to anyone under age 10. Maybe you should change "may frighten small children" to "definitely will scare the pants off most children."*

Jimmy Neutron's Nicktoon Blast ★★★ (Universal Express)

APPEAL BY AGE PRESCHOOL ★★★ GRADE SCHOOL ★★★★ TEENS ★★★
YOUNG ADULTS ★★★ OVER 30 ★★★ SENIORS ★★

What it is Cartoon science demonstration and simulation ride. **Scope and scale** Major attraction. **When to go** The first hour after park opening or after 5 p.m. **Authors' rating** Incomprehensible but fun; ★★★. **Duration of ride** A little over 4 minutes. **Loading speed** Moderate to slow. **Probable waiting time per 100 people ahead of you** 5 minutes. **Assumes** All 8 simulators in use.

DESCRIPTION AND COMMENTS This ride features motion simulators that move and react in sync with a cartoon projected onto a huge screen. Based on the Nickelodeon movie *Jimmy Neutron: Boy Genius,* this attraction replaced The Funtastic World of Hanna-Barbera. In addition to Jimmy, the attraction features a mob of other characters from Nickelodeon, including SpongeBob SquarePants, the Rugrats, the Fairly OddParents, and the Wild Thornberrys. The story, inasmuch as Universal explains it, takes place in two parts. First, guests are invited to participate in a demonstration of Jimmy's newest invention, which is stolen before the demonstration can proceed. After that, an alien plot is revealed, and guests are strapped into motion-simulator vehicles in order to help Jimmy rescue his invention and defend the Earth. In practice, the plot is incomprehensible (at least to an adult). All we can report after riding about a dozen times is that there is a frenetic high-speed chase punctuated by an abundance of screaming in piercing, very high-pitched, cartoony voices.

TOURING TIPS This attraction draws sizable crowds primarily because it's just inside the entrance and is next door to the *Shrek 4-D* attraction. We think Jimmy Neutron is at best a so-so effort, and not much of an improvement over its predecessor. Except for avid *Jimmy Neutron* cartoon fans, in other words, it's expendable. If you can't live without it, ride during the first hour the park is open or after 5 p.m. Be aware that a very small percentage of riders suffer motion sickness. Stationary seating is available and is mandated for persons less than 40 inches tall.

Lucy—A Tribute ★★★

APPEAL BY AGE PRESCHOOL ★ GRADE SCHOOL ★★ TEENS ★★
YOUNG ADULTS ★★★ OVER 30 ★★★ SENIORS ★★★

What it is Walk-through tribute to Lucille Ball. **Scope and scale** Diversion. **When to go** Anytime. **Authors' rating** A touching remembrance; ★★★. **Probable waiting time** None.

DESCRIPTION AND COMMENTS The life and career of comedienne Lucille Ball are spotlighted, with emphasis on her role as Lucy Ricardo in the long-running television series *I Love Lucy.* Well designed and informative, the exhibit succeeds admirably in recalling the talent and temperament of the beloved redhead.

TOURING TIPS See Lucy during the hot, crowded midafternoon, or on your way out of the park. Adults could easily stay 15 to 30 minutes. Children, however, get restless after a couple of minutes.

Men in Black Alien Attack (Universal Express) ★★★★½

APPEAL BY AGE PRESCHOOL† GRADE SCHOOL ★★★★★ TEENS ★★★★★
YOUNG ADULTS ★★★★★ OVER 30 ★★★★★ SENIORS ★★★★

†Due to height requirement, sample size is too small for an accurate rating.

What it is Interactive dark thrill ride. **Scope and scale** Super-headliner. **When to go** During the first 90 minutes the park is open. **Special comments** May induce motion sickness. Must be 42" tall to ride. Switching off available (see page 339). **Authors' rating** Buzz Lightyear on steroids; not to be missed; ★★★★½. **Duration of ride** 2½ minutes. **Loading speed** Moderate–fast.

DESCRIPTION AND COMMENTS Based on the movie of the same name, *Men in Black* brings together actors Will Smith and Rip Torn (as Agent J and MIB director Zed) for an interactive sequel to the hit film. The story line has you volunteering as a Men in Black (MIB) trainee. After an introduction warning that aliens "live among us" and articulating MIB's mission to round them up, Zed expands on the finer points of alien spotting and familiarizes you with your training vehicle and your weapon, an alien "zapper." Following this, you load up and are dispatched on an innocuous training mission that immediately deteriorates into a situation where only you are in a position to prevent aliens from taking over the universe. Now, if you saw the movie, you understand that the aliens are mostly giant exotic bugs and cockroaches and that zapping the aliens involves exploding them into myriad gooey body parts. Thus, the meat of the ride (no pun intended) consists of careening around Manhattan in your MIB vehicle and shooting aliens. The technology at work is similar to that used in the Spider-Man attraction at Universal's Islands of Adventure, which is to say that it's both a wild ride and one where movies, sets, robotics, and your vehicle are all integrated into a fairly seamless package.

Men in Black is interactive in that your marksmanship and ability to blast yourself out of some tricky situations will determine how the story ends. Also, you are awarded a personal score (as at the Magic Kingdom's Buzz Lightyear's Space Ranger Spin) and a score for your car. There are about three dozen possible outcomes and literally thousands of different ride experiences determined by your pluck, performance, and, in the final challenge, your intestinal fortitude.

TOURING TIPS Each of the 120 or so alien figures has sensors that activate special effects and respond to your zapper. Aim for the eyes and keep shooting until the aliens' eyes turn red. Also, many of the aliens shoot back, causing your vehicle to veer or spin. In the mayhem, you might fail to notice that another vehicle of guests runs along beside you on a dual track. This was included to instill a spirit of competition for anyone who finds blowing up bugs and saving the universe less than stimulating. Note that at a certain point, you can shoot the flashing "vent" on top of this other car and make its occupants spin around. Of course, they can do the same to you.

Although there are many possible endings, the long lines at this headliner attraction will probably dissuade you from experiencing all but one or two. To avoid a long wait, ride during the first 90 minutes the park is open.

Revenge of the Mummy (Universal Express) ★★★★½

APPEAL BY AGE PRESCHOOL ★★ GRADE SCHOOL ★★★★ TEENS ★★★★★
YOUNG ADULTS ★★★★½ OVER 30 ★★★★ SENIORS ★★★½

What it is Combination dark ride and roller coaster. **Scope and scale** Super-headliner. **When to go** The first hour the park is open or after 6 p.m. **Special comments** 48" minimum height requirement. **Authors' rating** Killer! ★★★★½. **Duration of ride** 4 minutes. **Probable waiting time per 100 people ahead of you** 7 minutes. **Loading speed** Moderate.

DESCRIPTION AND COMMENTS It's hard to wrap your mind around the attraction, but trust us when we say you're in for a very strange experience. Here, quoting Universal, are some of the things you can look forward to:

- Authentic Egyptian catacombs
- High-velocity show-immersion system (something to do with fast baptism?)
- Magnet-propulsion launch wave system
- A "Brain Fire" (!) that hovers [over guests] with temperatures soaring to 2,000°F
- Canoptic jars containing grisly remains

When you read between the lines, Revenge of the Mummy is an indoor dark ride based on the *Mummy* flicks, where guests fight off "deadly curses and vengeful creatures" while flying through Egyptian tombs and other spooky places on a high-tech roller coaster. The special effects are cutting edge, integrating the best technology from such attractions as *Terminator 2: 3-D,* Spider-Man (the ride), and *Back to the Future,* with groundbreaking visuals. It's way cool.

The queuing area serves to establish the story line: you're in a group touring a set from the *Mummy* films when you enter a tomb where the fantasy world of film gives way to the real thing. Along the way, you are warned about a possible curse. The visuals are rich and compelling as the queue makes its way to the loading area where you board a clunky, Jeep-like vehicle. The ride begins as a slow, very elaborate dark ride, passing through various chambers, including one where flesh-eating scarab beetles descend on you. Suddenly your vehicle stops, then drops backward and rotates. Here's where the "magnet-propulsion launch wave system" comes in. In more ordinary language, this means you're shot at high speed up the first hill of the roller coaster part of the ride. We don't want to ruin your experience by divulging too much, but the coaster part of the ride offers its own panoply of surprises. We will tell you this, however: there are no barrel rolls or upside-down stuff. And though it's a wild ride by anyone's definition, the emphasis remains as much on the visuals, robotics, and special effects as on the ride itself.

TOURING TIPS The newer Hollywood Rip Ride Rockit and The Simpsons Ride have diminished the early-morning crowds. Nevertheless, try to ride during the first hour the park is open. One fallback is to use the singles line. This is often more expedient than Universal Express. Concerning motion sickness, if you can ride Space Mountain without ill effect, you should be fine on Revenge of the Mummy. Switching off is available (see page 339).

Shrek 4-D (Universal Express) ★★★★½

APPEAL BY AGE PRESCHOOL ★★★★ GRADE SCHOOL ★★★★★ TEENS ★★★★★ YOUNG ADULTS ★★★★★ OVER 30 ★★★★★ SENIORS ★★★★★

What it is 3-D movie. **Scope and scale** Headliner. **When to go** The first hour the park is open or after 4 p.m. **Authors' rating** Warm, fuzzy, sometimes smelly mayhem; ★★★★½. **Duration of presentation** 20 minutes.

DESCRIPTION AND COMMENTS Based on characters from the hit movie *Shrek,* the preshow presents the villain from the movie, Lord Farquaad, as he appears on various screens to describe his posthumous plan to reclaim his lost bride, Princess Fiona, who married *Shrek.* The plan is posthumous since Lord Farquaad ostensibly died in the movie, and it's his ghost making the plans, but never mind. Guests then move into the main theater, don their 3-D glasses, and recline in seats equipped with "tactile transducers" and "pneumatic air propulsion and water spray nodules capable of both vertical and horizontal motion." As the 3-D film plays, guests are also subjected to smells relevant to the on-screen action (oh boy).

Technicalities aside, *Shrek 4-D* is a real winner. It's irreverent, frantic, laugh-out-loud funny, and iconoclastic. Concerning the latter, the film takes a good poke at Disney with Pinocchio, the Three Little Pigs, and Tinker Bell (among others) all sucked into the mayhem. The film quality and 3-D effects are great, and like the feature film, it's sweet without being sappy. Plus, in contrast to Disney's *Honey, I Shrunk the Audience* or *It's Tough to Be a Bug!, Shrek 4-D* doesn't generally frighten children under age 7.

TOURING TIPS Universal claims it can move 2,400 guests an hour through *Shrek 4-D.* However, the show's popularity means that waits in line may exceed an hour. Bear that in mind when scheduling your day.

The Simpsons Ride (Universal Express) ★★★★

APPEAL BY AGE PRESCHOOL – GRADE SCHOOL ★★★★ TEENS ★★★★ YOUNG ADULTS ★★★★ OVER 30 ★★★★ SENIORS ★★★½

What it is Mega–simulator ride. **Scope and scale** Super-headliner. **When to go** During the first hour the park is open. **Special comments** Must be 40" tall to ride; not recommended for pregnant women or people prone to motion sickness. Switching off available (see page 339). **Authors' rating** Jimmy Neutron with attitude; not to be missed; ★★★★. **Duration of ride** 4 minutes and 20 seconds, plus preshow. **Probable waiting time per 100 people ahead of you** 5 minutes. **Loading speed** Moderate.

Motion Sickness

DESCRIPTION AND COMMENTS *Back to the Future*—The Ride was closed in spring 2007 to make way for a new ride based on the Fox animated series that is now TV's longest-running sitcom. Featuring the voices of Dan Castellaneta (Homer), Julie Kavner (Marge), Nancy Cartwright (Bart), Yeardley Smith (Lisa), and other cast members, the new attraction takes a wild and humorous poke at thrill rides, dark rides, and live shows "that make up a fantasy amusement park dreamed up by the show's cantankerous Krusty the Clown."

Two preshows involve *Simpsons* characters speaking sequentially on different video screens around the line area. Their comments help define the characters for guests who are unfamiliar with the TV show. The attraction is a simulator ride similar to Star Tours at DHS and Jimmy Neutron's Nicktoon Blast at Universal, but with a larger screen more like that of Soarin' at Epcot. The visuals aren't as sharp as Soarin's, but they're sharp enough.

The story line has the conniving Sideshow Bob secretly arriving at Krustyland, the aforementioned amusement park, and plotting his revenge on Krusty and Bart, who, in a past *Simpsons* episode, revealed that Sideshow Bob had committed a crime for which he'd framed Krusty. Sideshow Bob gets even by making things go wrong with the attractions that the Simpsons (and you) are riding.

Like the show on which it's based, The Simpsons Ride definitely has an edge, and more than a few wild hairs. Like *Shrek 4-D,* it operates on several levels. There will be jokes and visuals that you'll get but will fly over your children's heads—and most assuredly vice versa.

A mom from Huntington, New York, had this to say:

> *The ride is lots of fun and suitable for all guests. I'm not a fan of wild motion* [simulators], *but I was fine on this ride. The field of vision makes it very engrossing, like Soarin'. However, our family still rates Star Tours higher than The Simpsons Ride or Jimmy Neutron, as participating in the Star Tours simulation was most like actually being a character in the original* [Star Wars] *movie!*

TOURING TIPS Because The Simpsons Ride is new, you can expect large crowds all day. We recommend arriving at the park before opening and making the ride your third stop after riding Hollywood Rip Ride Rockit and Revenge of the Mummy. Though not as rough and jerky as its predecessor, *Back to the Future*—The Ride, it's a long way from being tame. Skip it if you're an expectant mom or prone to motion sickness. Several families we interviewed found the humor a little too adult for their younger children.

Street Scenes ★★★★★

APPEAL BY AGE PRESCHOOL ★★★ GRADE SCHOOL ★★★★★ TEENS ★★★★★
YOUNG ADULTS ★★★★★ OVER 30 ★★★★★ SENIORS ★★★★★

What it is Elaborate outdoor sets for making films. **Scope and scale** Diversion. **When to go** Anytime. **Special comments** You'll see most sets without special effort as you tour the park. **Authors' rating** One of the park's great assets; ★★★★★. **Probable waiting time** No waiting.

DESCRIPTION AND COMMENTS Unlike at DHS, all Universal Studios Florida's back-lot sets are accessible for guest inspection. They include a New York City street, San Francisco's waterfront, a New England coastal town, Rodeo Drive, and Hollywood Boulevard.

TOURING TIPS You'll see most as you walk through the park.

Terminator 2: 3-D (Universal Express) ★★★★

APPEAL BY AGE PRESCHOOL ★★★ GRADE SCHOOL ★★★★ TEENS ★★★★
YOUNG ADULTS ★★★★★ OVER 30 ★★★★★ SENIORS ★★★★

What it is 3-D thriller mixed-media presentation. **Scope and scale** Superheadliner. **When to go** After 3:30 p.m. **Special comments** The nation's best theme-park theater attraction; very intense for some preschoolers and grade-schoolers. **Authors' rating** Furiously paced high-tech experience; not to be missed; ★★★★. **Duration of presentation** 20 minutes, including an 8-minute preshow. **Probable waiting time** 20–40 minutes.

DESCRIPTION AND COMMENTS The evil "cop" from *Terminator 2* morphs to life and battles Arnold Schwarzenegger's T-100 cyborg character. In case you missed the *Terminator* flicks, here's the plot: A bad robot arrives from the future to kill a nice boy. Another bad robot (who has been reprogrammed to be good) pops up at the same time to save the boy. The bad robot chases the boy and the rehabilitated robot, menacing the audience in the process.

The attraction, like the films, is all action, and you really don't need to understand much. What's interesting is that it uses 3-D film and a theater full of sophisticated technology to integrate the real with the imaginary. Images seem to move in and out of the film, not only in the manner of traditional 3-D, but also in actuality. Remove your 3-D glasses momentarily and you'll see that the guy on the motorcycle is actually onstage.

We've watched this type of presentation evolve, pioneered by Disney's *Captain EO; Honey, I Shrunk the Audience;* and *Muppet-Vision 3-D. Terminator 2: 3-D,* however, goes way beyond lasers, with moving theater seats, blasts of hot air, and spraying mist. It creates a multidimensional space that blurs the boundary between entertainment and reality. Is it seamless? Not quite, but it's close. We rank *Terminator 2: 3-D* as not to be missed.

TOURING TIPS The 700-seat theater changes audiences about every 19 minutes. Even so, because the show is popular, expect to wait about 30 minutes. *Terminator 2: 3-D* has been eclipsed somewhat by newer attractions like Hollywood Rip Ride Rockit, The Simpsons Ride, and Revenge of the Mummy. We suggest that you save *Terminator* and other theater presentations until you've experienced all the rides. If you can't stay until late afternoon, see the show first thing in the morning. Families with young children should know that the violence characteristic of the *Terminator* movies is largely absent from the attraction. There's suspense and action but not much blood and guts.

Twister (Universal Express) ★★★½

APPEAL BY AGE	PRESCHOOL ★★	GRADE SCHOOL ★★★★	TEENS ★★★★
YOUNG ADULTS ★★★★	OVER 30 ★★★★	SENIORS ★★★	

What it is Theater presentation featuring special effects from the movie *Twister*. **Scope and scale** Major attraction. **When to go** Should be your first show after experiencing all rides. **Special comments** High potential for frightening young children. **Authors' rating** Gusty; ★★★½. **Duration of presentation** 15 minutes. **Probable waiting time** 26 minutes.

DESCRIPTION AND COMMENTS *Twister* combines an elaborate set and special effects, climaxing with a five-story-tall simulated tornado created by circulating more than 2 million cubic feet of air per minute.

TOURING TIPS The wind, pounding rain, and freight-train sound of the tornado are deafening, and the entire presentation is exceptionally intense. Schoolchildren are mightily impressed, while younger children are terrified and overwhelmed. Unless you want the kids hopping in your bed whenever they hear thunder, try this attraction yourself before taking your kids.

Universal Horror Make-Up Show ★★★½ (Universal Express)

APPEAL BY AGE	PRESCHOOL ★★★	GRADE SCHOOL ★★★★	TEENS ★★★★
YOUNG ADULTS ★★★★		OVER 30 ★★★★	SENIORS ★★★★

What it is Theater presentation on the art of makeup. **Scope and scale** Major attraction. **When to go** After you've experienced all rides. **Special comments** May frighten young children. **Authors' rating** A gory knee-slapper; ★★★½. **Duration of presentation** 25 minutes. **Probable waiting time** 20 minutes.

DESCRIPTION AND COMMENTS Lively, well-paced look at how makeup artists create film monsters, realistic wounds, severed limbs, and other unmentionables. Funnier and more upbeat than many other Universal Studios presentations, the show also presents a wealth of fascinating information. It's excellent and enlightening, if somewhat gory.

TOURING TIPS Exceeding most guests' expectations, the *Horror Make-Up Show* is the sleeper attraction at Universal. Its humor and tongue-in-cheek style transcend the gruesome effects, and most folks (including preschoolers) take the blood and guts in stride.

It's the exception that proves the rule, as this reader relates:

My 7- and 9-year-olds had no problem with Jurassic, Terminator, Spider-Man, *or the like but were scared by the* Horror Make-Up Show *(despite my telling them the guy really was not cutting anyone's arm off!). We ended up leaving before the show was over.*

Universal 360: A Cinesphere Spectacular ★★★½ *(Open seasonally)*

APPEAL BY AGE	PRESCHOOL ★★★	GRADE SCHOOL ★★★★	TEENS ★★★½
YOUNG ADULTS ★★★★		OVER 30 ★★★★	SENIORS ★★★★

What it is Fireworks, lasers, and movies. **Scope and scale** Major attraction. **When to go** 1 show a day, usually 10 minutes before park closes. **Authors' rating** Good effort; ★★★½. **Special comments** Movie trailers galore. **Duration of presentation** 10 minutes.

DESCRIPTION AND COMMENTS *Universal 360* is a nighttime spectacular presented at the Universal Studios lagoon in the middle of the park. The presentation, a celebration of hit movies, is built around four 360-degree projection cinespheres, each 36 feet tall and 30 feet wide. The cinespheres project images relating to the chosen films, augmented by lasers and fireworks; three hundred speakers positioned around the lagoon broadcast the shows' original scores. You'll be surprised to see the number of films the studio has released over its 95-year existence. *Universal 360* is presented during the summer and holiday periods.

A local Universal season-pass holder was a bit disappointed with *Universal 360:*

Universal's nighttime fireworks were a bit of a letdown. The whole 360 thing would work great if you could actually see the movies on these balls in the water. I stood directly in front of one of the balls, and I could only see half of the projection—guests have to be at an angle to see the whole movie screen. The show really did not flow at all. All around me people would jump and scream when the fireworks went off because no one was expecting them. The only theme seemed to be showing a bunch of movies and putting fireworks in the air every now and then. I had to laugh when they showed scenes from The 40-Year-Old Virgin *where Steve Carell gets his chest waxed: he screams in pain and then fireworks go off!*

TOURING TIPS The 360-degree projections are split rather awkwardly, since the movies weren't shot to be projected on a sphere. The ends of the lagoon are not recommended for viewing. The best spot is directly across the lagoon from Richter's Burger Co., where the sidewalk makes a small protrusion into the water. This side of the lagoon also offers the best view of the projections on the buildings. Acquiring a place here can be very difficult. We recommend arriving at least 45 minutes ahead of time and taking turns holding the spot while the rest of your crew rides *Jaws* at night.

Before the show begins, realize that not all of the movie clips may be suitable for young viewers. During the horror-movie montage, which includes scenes from *An American Werewolf in London,* parents may want to cover some eyes. The action movie montage is also stuffed with gunplay and gore. When the same studio that made movies as diverse as *Psycho* and *Shrek,* or *Hannibal* and *SpongeBob,* wants to make an all-inclusive montage, it's bound to run into some difficulties.

Woody Woodpecker's Nuthouse Coaster and Curious George Goes to Town ★★★

APPEAL BY AGE PRESCHOOL ★★★★ GRADE SCHOOL – TEENS – YOUNG ADULTS – OVER 30 – SENIORS –

What it is Interactive playground and kids' roller coaster. **Scope and scale** Minor attraction. **When to go** Anytime. **Authors' rating** *The* place for rambunctious kids; ★★★.

DESCRIPTION AND COMMENTS Rounding out the selection of other nearby child-friendly attractions, this Woody Woodpecker's KidZone offering (lovingly dubbed "Peckerland" by Universal employees) includes Woody Woodpecker's Nuthouse Coaster, Fievel's Playland, and an interactive playground called Curious George Goes to Town. The child-sized roller coaster is small enough for kids to enjoy but sturdy enough for adults, though its moderate speed might unnerve some smaller children (the minimum height to ride is 36 inches). The Curious George playground exemplifies the Universal obsession with wet stuff; in addition to innumerable spigots, pipes, and spray guns, two giant roof-mounted buckets periodically dump a thousand gallons of water on unsuspecting visitors below. Kids who want to stay dry can mess around in the foam-ball playground, also equipped with chutes, tubes, and ball-blasters.

TOURING TIPS Visit after you've experienced all the major attractions.

LIVE ENTERTAINMENT *at* UNIVERSAL STUDIOS

IN ADDITION TO THE SHOWS PROFILED PREVIOUSLY, Universal offers a wide range of street entertainment. Costumed comic-book and cartoon characters (Shrek, Donkey, SpongeBob SquarePants, Woody

Woodpecker) roam the park for photo ops supplemented by look-alikes of movie stars, both living and deceased, plus the Frankenstein monster, who can be said to be neither. Musical acts also pop up.

UNIVERSAL STUDIOS FLORIDA TOURING PLAN

BUYING ADMISSION TO UNIVERSAL STUDIOS FLORIDA

ONE OF OUR BIG GRIPES ABOUT UNIVERSAL STUDIOS is that there are never enough ticket windows open in the morning to accommodate the crowds. You can arrive 30 minutes before official opening time and still be in line to buy your admission when the park opens. Therefore, we strongly recommend that you buy your admission in advance. Passes are available by mail from Universal Studios at ☎ 800-711-0080. They are also sold at the concierge desk or attractions box office of many Orlando-area hotels. If your hotel doesn't offer tickets, try Guest Services at the Doubletree Universal Hotel (☎ 407-351-1000), at the intersection of Major Boulevard and Kirkman Avenue.

Many hotels that sell Universal admissions don't issue actual passes. Instead, the purchaser gets a voucher that can be redeemed for a pass at the theme park. Fortunately, the voucher-redemption window is separate from the park's ticket-sales operation.

UNIVERSAL STUDIOS FLORIDA ONE-DAY TOURING PLAN (see page 833)

THIS PLAN IS FOR ALL VISITORS. If a ride or show is listed that you don't want to experience, skip that step and proceed to the next. Move quickly from attraction to attraction and, if possible, don't stop for lunch until after Step 9. Minor street shows occur at various times and places throughout the day; check the daily schedule for details.

UNIVERSAL'S ISLANDS *of* ADVENTURE

WHEN UNIVERSAL'S ISLANDS OF ADVENTURE theme park opened in 1999, it provided Universal with enough critical mass to actually compete with Disney. Universal finally has on-site hotels, a shopping and entertainment complex, and two major theme parks. Doubly interesting is that the new Universal park is pretty much just for fun—in other words, a direct competitor to Disney's Magic Kingdom, the most-visited theme park in the world. How direct a competitor is it? Check out the box on the next page for a comparison.

unofficial **TIP**
Roller coasters at Islands of Adventure are the real deal—not for the faint of heart or for little ones.

And though it may take central Florida tourists a while to make the connection, here's what will dawn on them when they finally do:

ISLANDS OF ADVENTURE VERSUS THE MAGIC KINGDOM

ISLANDS OF ADVENTURE	MAGIC KINGDOM
Six Islands (includes Port of Entry)	Seven Lands (includes Main Street)
Two adult roller-coaster attractions	Two adult roller-coaster attractions
A Dumbo-type ride	Dumbo
One flume ride	One flume ride
Toon Lagoon character area	Mickey's Toontown Fair character area

Universal's Islands of Adventure is a state-of-the-art park competing with a Disney park that is more than 35 years old and has not added a new super-headliner attraction for many years.

Of course, that's only how it looks on paper. The Magic Kingdom, after all, is graceful in its maturity and much loved. And then there was the question on everyone's mind: could Universal really pull it off? Recalling the disastrous first year that the Universal Studios Florida park experienced, we held our breath to see if Islands of Adventure's innovative high-tech attractions would work. Well, not only did they work, they were up and running almost two months ahead of schedule. Thus, the clash of the titans is still hot. Universal is coming on strong with the potential of sucking up three days of a tourist's week (more, if you include Universal's strategic relationship with SeaWorld and Busch Gardens). And that's more time than anyone has spent off the Disney campus for a long, long time.

Disney and Universal officially downplay their fierce competition, pointing out that any new theme park or attraction makes central Florida a more marketable destination. Behind closed doors, however, the two companies share a Pepsi versus Coke–type rivalry that will keep both working hard to gain a competitive edge. The good news, of course, is that all this translates into better and better attractions for you to enjoy.

BEWARE OF THE WET AND WILD

ALTHOUGH WE HAVE DESCRIBED Universal's Islands of Adventure as a direct competitor to the Magic Kingdom, there is one major qualification you should be aware of. Whereas most Magic Kingdom attractions are designed to be enjoyed by guests of any age, attractions at Islands of Adventure are largely created for an under-40 population. The roller coasters at Universal are serious with a capital *S*, making Space Mountain and Big Thunder Mountain look about as frightening as Dumbo. In

Not to Be Missed at Islands of Adventure

- The Adventures of Spider-Man
- The Incredible Hulk Coaster
- *Poseidon's Fury!*
- Dueling Dragons
- *Jurassic Park* River Adventure
- The Wizarding World of Harry Potter (opens late 2009)

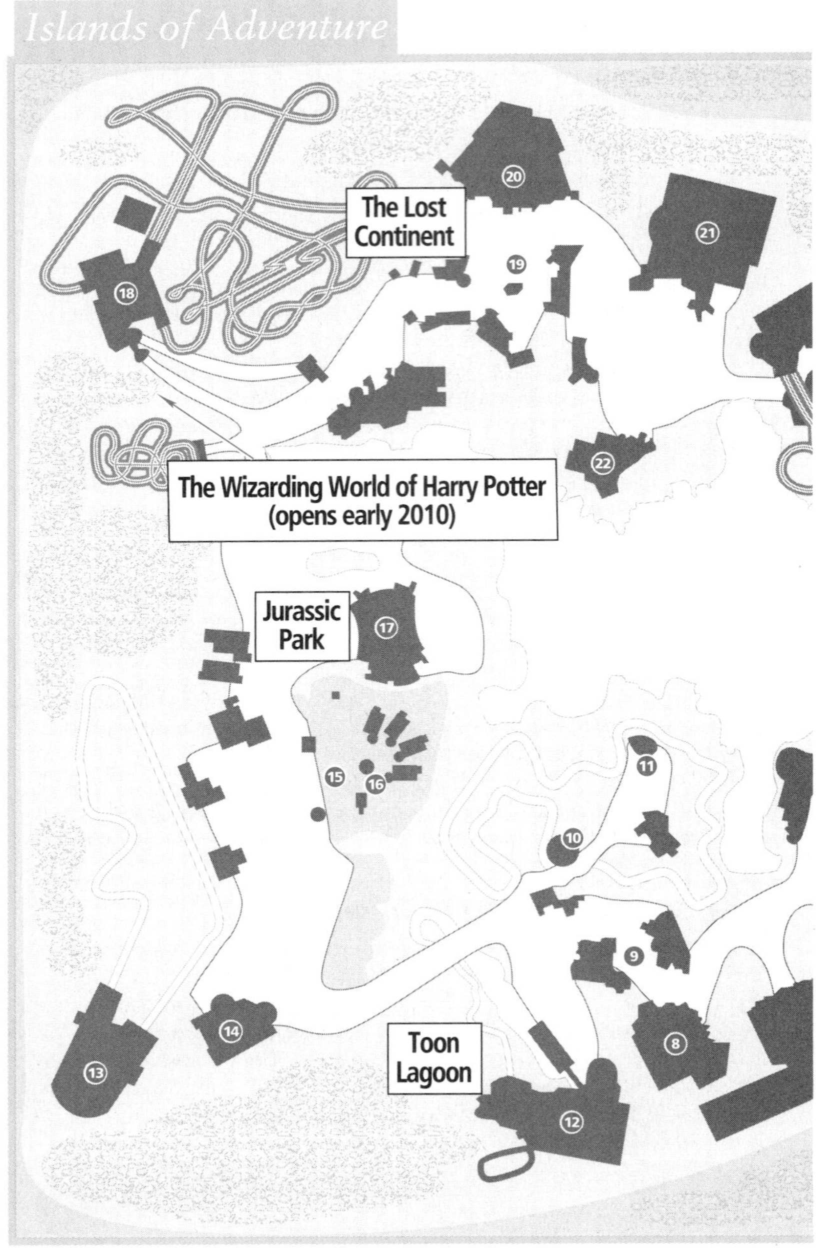
Islands of Adventure
The Lost Continent
The Wizarding World of Harry Potter (opens early 2010)
Jurassic Park
Toon Lagoon
20
21
19
18
22
17
11
15
16
10
9
14
13
8
12

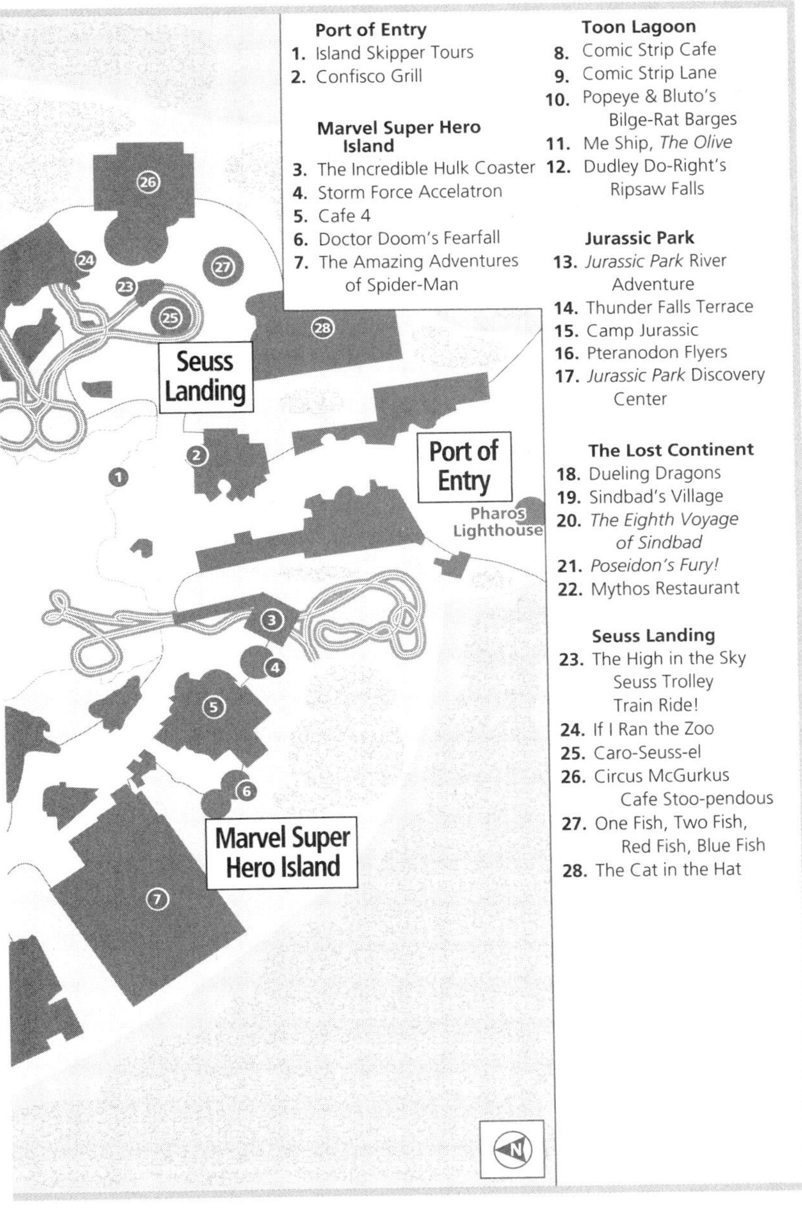
Seuss Landing
Port of Entry
Pharos Lighthouse
Marvel Super Hero Island
N

Port of Entry
1. Island Skipper Tours
2. Confisco Grill

Marvel Super Hero Island
3. The Incredible Hulk Coaster
4. Storm Force Accelatron
5. Cafe 4
6. Doctor Doom's Fearfall
7. The Amazing Adventures of Spider-Man

Toon Lagoon
8. Comic Strip Cafe
9. Comic Strip Lane
10. Popeye & Bluto's Bilge-Rat Barges
11. Me Ship, The Olive
12. Dudley Do-Right's Ripsaw Falls

Jurassic Park
13. Jurassic Park River Adventure
14. Thunder Falls Terrace
15. Camp Jurassic
16. Pteranodon Flyers
17. Jurassic Park Discovery Center

The Lost Continent
18. Dueling Dragons
19. Sindbad's Village
20. The Eighth Voyage of Sindbad
21. Poseidon's Fury!
22. Mythos Restaurant

Seuss Landing
23. The High in the Sky Seuss Trolley Train Ride!
24. If I Ran the Zoo
25. Caro-Seuss-el
26. Circus McGurkus Cafe Stoo-pendous
27. One Fish, Two Fish, Red Fish, Blue Fish
28. The Cat in the Hat

unofficial **TIP**
Consider yourself warned: several attractions at Islands of Adventure will drench you to the bone.

fact, seven out of the nine top attractions at Islands are thrill rides, and of these, there are three that not only scare the bejeepers out of you but also drench you with water.

For families, there are three interactive playgrounds as well as six rides that young children will enjoy. Of the thrill rides, only the two in Toon Lagoon (described later) are marginally appropriate for young children, and even on these rides your child needs to be fairly stalwart.

GETTING ORIENTED *at* ISLANDS *of* ADVENTURE

BOTH UNIVERSAL THEME PARKS are accessed via the Universal CityWalk entertainment complex. Crossing CityWalk from the parking garages, you can bear right to Universal Studios Florida or left to Universal's Islands of Adventure.

Islands of Adventure is arranged much like Epcot's World Showcase, in a large circle surrounding a lake. Unlike Epcot, however, the Islands of Adventure themed areas evidence the sort of thematic continuity pioneered by Disneyland and the Magic Kingdom. Each land, or island in this case, is self-contained and visually consistent in its theme, though you can see parts of the other islands across the lake.

You first encounter the Moroccan-style Port of Entry, where you'll find Guest Services, lockers, stroller and wheelchair rentals, ATM banking, lost and found, and shopping. From the Port of Entry, moving clockwise around the lake, you can access Marvel Super Hero Island, Toon Lagoon, Jurassic Park, the Lost Continent, and Seuss Landing. You can crisscross the lake on small boats, but there is no in-park transportation.

A WORD ABOUT THE WIZARDING WORLD OF HARRY POTTER

THE FIRST PHASE of the Wizarding World of Harry Potter is scheduled to open in early 2010. Many of the elements and attractions to be featured in this new section of the park were unknown at press time. What is known is that the Wizarding World, especially if done well, will dominate Islands of Adventure for some time to come. In practical terms, this means that crowds will rush to the Wizarding World as soon as the park opens. If the Wizarding World is open during your visit, arrive at the turnstiles, admission in hand, 30 minutes before park opening, and zip over to Harry's on your Nimbus 3000 as soon as you clear the turnstiles. Experience any attractions there that appeal to you, and leave the rest to explore later in the day. Backtrack to Marvel Super Hero Island and begin hitting the rides that are on your must-do list. In the profile of each attraction, we list the best time to go. After the Wizarding World comes online, these times will change in a way that isn't knowable now. Our best estimation is that lines for the most popular non-Potter attractions will form long queues somewhat later in the day than they do now—probably around 90 minutes after the park opens.

ISLANDS *of* ADVENTURE ATTRACTIONS

MARVEL SUPER HERO ISLAND

THIS ISLAND, WITH ITS FUTURISTIC AND RETRO-FUTURE design and comic-book signage, offers shopping and attractions based on Marvel Comics characters.

The Amazing Adventures of Spider-Man (Universal Express) ★★★★★

APPEAL BY AGE PRESCHOOL ★★★ GRADE SCHOOL ★★★★★ TEENS ★★★★★
YOUNG ADULTS ★★★★★ OVER 30 ★★★★★ SENIORS ★★★★

What it is Indoor adventure simulator ride based on Spider-Man. **Scope and scale** Super-headliner. **When to go** During the first 40 minutes the park is open. **Special comments** Must be 40" tall to ride. **Authors' rating** Our choice for the best attraction in the park; ★★★★★. **Duration of ride** 4½ minutes. **Loading speed** Fast.

DESCRIPTION AND COMMENTS Covering one and a half acres and combining moving ride vehicles, 3-D film, and live action, Spider-Man is frenetic, fluid, and astounding. The visuals are rich, and the ride is wild but not jerky. Although the attractions are not directly comparable, Spider-Man is technologically on a par with DHS's Tower of Terror, which is to say that it will leave you in awe.

The story line is that you are a reporter for the *Daily Bugle* newspaper (where Peter Parker, aka Spider-Man, works as a mild-mannered photographer), when it's discovered that evil villains have stolen (we promise we're not making this up) the Statue of Liberty. You are drafted on the spot by your cantankerous editor to go get the story. After speeding around and being thrust into "a battle between good and evil," you experience a 400-foot "sensory drop" from a skyscraper roof all the way to the pavement. Because the ride is so wild and the action so continuous, it's hard to understand the plot, but you're so thoroughly entertained that you don't really care. Plus, you'll want to ride again and again. Eventually, with repetition, the story line will begin to make sense.

TOURING TIPS Ride first thing in the morning after The Incredible Hulk Coaster or in the hour before closing.

Doctor Doom's Fearfall (Universal Express) ★★★

APPEAL BY AGE PRESCHOOL – GRADE SCHOOL ★★★ TEENS ★★★★
YOUNG ADULTS ★★★★ OVER 30 ★★★ SENIORS –

What it is Lunch liberator. **Scope and scale** Headliner. **When to go** During the first 40 minutes the park is open. **Special comments** Must be 52" tall to ride. **Authors' rating** More bark than bite; ★★★. **Duration of ride** 40 seconds. **Loading speed** Slow.

DESCRIPTION AND COMMENTS Here you are (again) strapped into a seat with your feet dangling and blasted 200 feet up in the air and then allowed to partially free-fall back down. If you're having trouble forming a mental image of this attraction, picture the midway game wherein a macho guy swings a sledgehammer, propelling a metal sphere up a vertical shaft. At the top of the shaft is a bell. If the macho man drives the sphere high enough to ring the bell, he wins a prize. Got the idea? OK, on this ride you're the metal sphere.

The good news is this ride looks much worse than it actually is. The scariest part by far is the apprehension that builds as you sit, strapped in, waiting for the thing to launch. The blasting up and free-falling down parts are really very pleasant.

TOURING TIPS We've seen glaciers that move faster than the line for Doctor Doom. If you want to ride without investing half a day, be one of the first in the park to ride. Fortunately, if you're on hand at opening time, being among the first isn't too difficult (mainly because the nearby Hulk and Spider-Man attractions are bigger draws).

The Incredible Hulk Coaster (Universal Express) ★★★★½

APPEAL BY AGE	PRESCHOOL ★	GRADE SCHOOL ★★★★★	TEENS ★★★★★
YOUNG ADULTS ★★★★		OVER 30 ★★★★	SENIORS ★★★

What it is Roller coaster. **Scope and scale** Super-headliner. **When to go** During the first 40 minutes the park is open. **Special comments** Must be 54" tall to ride. **Authors' rating** A coaster-lover's coaster; ★★★★½. **Duration of ride** 2¼ minutes. **Loading speed** Moderate.

Motion Sickness

DESCRIPTION AND COMMENTS There is, as always, a story line, but for this attraction it's of no importance whatsoever. What you need to know about this attraction is simple. You will be shot like a cannonball from 0 to 40 miles per hour in two seconds, and then you will be flung upside down 100 feet off the ground, which will, of course, induce weightlessness. From there it's a mere six rollovers punctuated by two plunges into holes in the ground before you're allowed to get out and throw up.

Seriously, the Hulk is a great roller coaster, perhaps the best in Florida, providing a ride comparable to that of Montu (Busch Gardens) with the added thrill of an accelerated launch (instead of the more typical uphill crank). Plus, like Montu, this coaster has a smooth ride.

TOURING TIPS The Hulk gives Spider-Man a run as the park's most popular attraction. Ride first thing in the morning. Universal provides electronic lockers near the entrance of the Hulk to deposit any items that might depart your person during the Hulk's seven inversions. The locker is free if you use it only for a short time. If you leave things in the locker for a couple of hours, however, you'll have to pay a rental charge. When you reach the boarding area, note that there is a separate line for those who want to ride in the first row.

Storm Force Accelatron (Universal Express) ★★★

APPEAL BY AGE	PRESCHOOL ★★★★	GRADE SCHOOL ★★★	TEENS ★★★
YOUNG ADULTS ★★★		OVER 30 ★★★	SENIORS ★★★

What it is Indoor spinning ride. **Scope and scale** Minor attraction. **Special comments** May induce motion sickness. **When to go** During the first hour the park is open. **Authors' rating** Teacups in the dark; ★★★. **Duration of ride** 1½ minutes. **Loading speed** Slow.

Motion Sickness

DESCRIPTION AND COMMENTS Storm Force is a spiffed-up indoor version of Disney's nausea-inducing Mad Tea Party. Here you spin to the accompaniment of a simulated thunderstorm and swirling sound and light. There's a story line that loosely ties this midway-type ride to the Marvel Super Hero Island area, but it's largely irrelevant and offers no advice on keeping your lunch down.

TOURING TIPS Ride early or late to avoid long lines. If you're prone to motion sickness, keep your distance.

TOON LAGOON

TOON LAGOON IS CARTOON ART TRANSLATED into real buildings and settings. Whimsical and gaily colored, with rounded and exaggerated lines, Toon Lagoon is Universal's answer to Mickey's Toontown Fair in the Magic Kingdom. The main difference between the two toon lands is that (as you will see) you have about a 60% chance of drowning at Universal's version.

Comic Strip Lane

What it is Walk-through exhibit and shopping and dining venue. **Scope and scale** Diversion. **When to go** Anytime.

DESCRIPTION AND COMMENTS This is the main street of Toon Lagoon. Here you can visit the domains of Beetle Bailey, Hagar the Horrible, Krazy Kat, the Family Circus, and Blondie and Dagwood, among others. Shops and eateries tie into the funny-papers theme.

TOURING TIPS This is a great place for photo ops with cartoon characters in their own environment. It's also a great place to drop a few bucks in the diners and shops, but you probably already figured that out.

Dudley Do-Right's Ripsaw Falls (Universal Express) ★★★½

APPEAL BY AGE PRESCHOOL ★★★ GRADE SCHOOL ★★★★ TEENS ★★★★
YOUNG ADULTS ★★★ OVER 30 ★★★★ SENIORS ★★★

What it is Flume ride. **Scope and scale** Major attraction. **When to go** Before 11 a.m. **Special comments** Must be 44" tall to ride. **Authors' rating** A minimalist Splash Mountain; ★★★½. **Duration of ride** 5 minutes. **Loading speed** Moderate.

DESCRIPTION AND COMMENTS Inspired by the *Rocky and Bullwinkle* cartoons, this ride features Canadian Mountie Dudley Do-Right as he attempts to save Nell from evil Snidely Whiplash. Story line aside, it's a flume ride, with the inevitable big drop at the end. Universal claims this is the first flume ride to "send riders plummeting 15 feet below the surface of the water." In reality, though, you're just plummeting into a tunnel.

The only problem with this attraction is that everyone inevitably compares it to Splash Mountain at the Magic Kingdom. The flume is as good as Splash Mountain's, and the final drop is a whopper, but the theming and the visuals aren't even in the same league. The art, sets, audio, and jokes at Dudley Do-Right are minimalist at best; it's Dudley Do-Right's two-dimensional approach versus Splash Mountain's three-dimensional presentation. Taken on its own terms, however, Dudley Do-Right is a darn good flume ride.

TOURING TIPS This ride will get you wet, but on average not as wet as you might expect (it looks worse than it is). If you want to stay dry, however, arrive prepared with a poncho or at least a big garbage bag with holes cut out for your head and arms. After riding, take a moment to gauge the timing of the water cannons that go off along the exit walk. This is where you can really get drenched. While younger children are often intimidated by the big drop, those who ride generally enjoy themselves. Ride after experiencing the Marvel Super Hero rides.

Me Ship, *The Olive* ★★★

APPEAL BY AGE PRESCHOOL ★★★★ GRADE SCHOOL ★★★★ TEENS ½ YOUNG ADULTS ½ OVER 30 ½ SENIORS –

What it is Interactive playground. **Scope and scale** Minor attraction. **When to go** Anytime. **Authors' rating** Colorful and appealing for kids; ★★★.

DESCRIPTION AND COMMENTS *The Olive* is Popeye's three-story boat come to life as an interactive playground. Younger children can scramble around in Swee'Pea's Playpen, while older sibs shoot water cannons at riders trying to survive the adjacent Bilge-Rat raft ride.

TOURING TIPS If you're into the big rides, save this for later in the day.

Popeye & Bluto's Bilge-Rat Barges (Universal Express) ★★★★

APPEAL BY AGE PRESCHOOL ★★★ GRADE SCHOOL ★★★★★ TEENS ★★★★ YOUNG ADULTS ★★★★ OVER 30 ★★★★ SENIORS ★★★

What it is Whitewater raft ride. **Scope and scale** Major attraction. **When to go** Before 11 a.m. **Special comments** Must be 42" tall to ride. **Authors' rating** Bring your own soap; ★★★★. **Duration of ride** 4½ minutes. **Loading speed** Moderate.

DESCRIPTION AND COMMENTS This sweetly named attraction is a whitewater raft ride that includes an encounter with an 18-foot-tall octopus. Engineered to ensure that everyone gets drenched, the ride even provides water cannons for highly intelligent nonparticipants ashore to fire at those aboard. The rapids are rougher and more interesting, and the ride longer, than Animal Kingdom's Kali River Rapids. But nobody surpasses Disney for visuals and theming, though the settings of these two attractions (cartoon set and Asian jungle river, respectively) are hardly comparable.

TOURING TIPS If you didn't drown on Dudley Do-Right, here's a second chance. You'll get a lot wetter from the knees down on this ride, so use your poncho or garbage bag and ride barefoot with your britches rolled up. In terms of beating the crowds, ride the barges in the morning after experiencing the Marvel Super Hero attractions and Dudley Do-Right. If you are lacking foul-weather gear or forgot your trash bag, you might want to put off riding until last thing before leaving the park. Most preschoolers enjoy the raft ride. Those who are frightened react more to the way the rapids look as opposed to the roughness of the ride.

JURASSIC PARK

JURASSIC PARK (FOR ANYONE WHO'S BEEN ASLEEP for 20 years) is a Steven Spielberg film franchise about a theme park with real dinosaurs. Jurassic Park at Universal's Islands of Adventure is a real theme park (or at least a section of one) with fictitious dinosaurs.

Camp Jurassic ★★★

APPEAL BY AGE PRESCHOOL ★★★ GRADE SCHOOL ★★★ TEENS –
YOUNG ADULTS – OVER 30 – SENIORS –

What it is Interactive play area. **Scope and scale** Minor attraction. **When to go** Anytime. **Authors' rating** Creative playground, confusing layout; ★★★.

DESCRIPTION AND COMMENTS Camp Jurassic is a great place for children to cut loose. Sort of a Jurassic version of Tom Sawyer Island, it allows kids to explore lava pits, caves, mines, and a rain forest.

TOURING TIPS Camp Jurassic will fire the imaginations of the under-13 set. If you don't impose a time limit on the exploration, you could be here a while. The layout of the play area is confusing and intersects the queuing area for Pteranodon Flyers. If your child accidentally lines up for the Pteranodons, he'll be college age before you see him again.

Jurassic Park Discovery Center ★★★

APPEAL BY AGE PRESCHOOL ★★★ GRADE SCHOOL ★★★★ TEENS ★★★
YOUNG ADULTS ★★★ OVER 30 ★★★ SENIORS ★★★

What it is Interactive natural history exhibit. **Scope and scale** Minor attraction. **When to go** Anytime. **Authors' rating** Definitely worth checking out; ★★★.

DESCRIPTION AND COMMENTS The Discovery Center is an interactive educational exhibit that mixes fiction from the movie *Jurassic Park,* such as using fossil DNA to bring dinosaurs to life, with various skeletal remains and other paleontological displays. One exhibit allows guests to watch an animatronic raptor being hatched. Another allows you to digitally "fuse" your DNA with a dinosaur's to see what the resultant creature would look like. Other exhibits include dinosaur-egg scanning and identification and a quiz called "You Bet Jurassic."

TOURING TIPS Cycle back after experiencing all the rides or on a second day. Most folks can digest this exhibit in 10 to 15 minutes.

Jurassic Park River Adventure (Universal Express) ★★★★

APPEAL BY AGE PRESCHOOL ★★★ GRADE SCHOOL ★★★★★ TEENS ★★★★★
YOUNG ADULTS ★★★★ OVER 30 ★★★★ SENIORS ★★★★

What it is Indoor-outdoor adventure river-raft ride based on the *Jurassic Park* movies. **Scope and scale** Super-headliner. **When to go** Before 11 a.m. **Special comments** Must be 42" tall to ride. **Authors' rating** Better than its Hollywood cousin; ★★★★. **Duration of ride** 6½ minutes. **Loading speed** Fast.

DESCRIPTION AND COMMENTS Guests board boats for a water tour of Jurassic Park. Everything is tranquil as the tour begins, and the boat floats among large herbivorous dinosaurs such as brontosauruses and stegosauruses. Then, as word is received that some of the carnivores have escaped their enclosure, the tour boat is accidentally diverted into Jurassic Park's maintenance facilities. Here, the boat and its riders are menaced by an assortment of hungry meat-eaters led by the ubiquitous T-Rex. At the climactic moment, the boat and its passengers escape by plummeting over an 85-foot drop billed as the "longest, fastest, steepest water descent ever built."

TOURING TIPS Though the boats make a huge splash at the bottom of the 85-foot drop, you don't get all that wet. Once you're under way, there's a little splashing but nothing major until the big drop at the end of the ride. Fortunately, not all that much water lands in the boat.

Young children must endure a double whammy on this ride. First, they are stalked by giant, salivating (sometimes spitting) reptiles, and then they're sent catapulting over the falls. Unless your children are fairly stalwart, wait a year or two before you spring the River Adventure on them.

Because the Jurassic Park section of IOA is situated next to the Wizarding World of Harry Potter, the boat will experience heavy crowds earlier in the day. Try to ride before 11 a.m.

Pteranodon Flyers ½

APPEAL BY AGE	PRESCHOOL ★★★	GRADE SCHOOL ★★★	TEENS ★
YOUNG ADULTS ★★	OVER 30 ★	SENIORS ★★	

What it is Slow as Christmas. **Scope and scale** Minor attraction. **When to go** When there's no line. **Authors' rating** All sizzle, no steak. ½. **Duration of ride** 1¼ minutes. **Loading speed** Slower than a hog in quicksand.

DESCRIPTION AND COMMENTS This is Islands of Adventure's biggest blunder. Engineered to accommodate only 170 persons per hour—about half the hourly capacity of Dumbo!—the ride dangles you on a swing below a track that passes over a small part of Jurassic Park. We recommend skipping this one. Why? Because the Jurassic period will probably end before you reach the front of the line! And your reward for all that waiting? A 1-minute-and-15-second ride. Plus, the attraction has a name that nobody over 12 years old can pronounce.

TOURING TIPS Photograph the pteranodon as it flies overhead. You're probably looking at something that will someday be extinct.

Triceratops Encounter

DESCRIPTION AND COMMENTS This attraction is strongly rumored to be returning to IOA in mid-2009 after an absence of several years. We don't know yet what exactly it'll entail, but in the old version guests were ushered into a "feed and control station," where they could view and pet a 24-foot-long animatronic *Triceratops.* While the trainer lectured about the creature's behaviors, habits, and lifestyle, the "trike" breathed, chewed, and flinched at the touch of guests.

TOURING TIPS Though not a major attraction, Triceratops Encounter historically has been popular and has tended to develop long lines. If the reincarnated version turns out to be anything like the original, we recommend making it your first show/exhibit after experiencing the rides.

THE LOST CONTINENT

THIS AREA IS AN EXOTIC MIX of Silk Road bazaar and ancient ruins, with Greco-Moroccan accents. (And you thought your decorator was nuts.) This is the land of mythical gods, fabled beasts, and expensive souvenirs.

The Wizarding World of Harry Potter, based on the novels of J. K. Rowling, will be partially carved out of The Lost Continent. We expect the current attractions to survive with the probable exceptions of the Dueling Dragons roller coasters and the *Eighth Voyage of Sindbad* show, both of which will convert to a Harry Potter theme. A third attraction, the Flying Unicorn children's roller coaster, has already been shut down. The Wizarding World of Harry Potter is scheduled to open in early 2010.

Dueling Dragons (Universal Express) ★★★★½

APPEAL BY AGE	PRESCHOOL –	GRADE SCHOOL ★★★★	TEENS ★★★★
YOUNG ADULTS ★★★★		OVER 30 ★★★★	SENIORS ★★

What it is Roller coaster. **Scope and scale** Headliner. **When to go** Before 10:30 a.m. **Special comments** Must be 54" tall to ride. **Authors' rating** As good as the Hulk coaster; ★★★★½. **Duration of ride** 2¼ minutes. **Loading speed** Moderate.

Motion Sickness

DESCRIPTION AND COMMENTS This high-tech coaster launches two trains (Fire and Ice) at the same time on tracks that are closely intertwined. Each track is differently configured so that you get a different experience on each. Several times, a collision with the other train seems imminent, a catastrophe that seems all the more real because the coasters are inverted (that is, suspended from above so that you sit with your feet dangling). At times, the two trains and their passengers are separated by a mere 12 inches.

Because this is an inverted coaster, your view of the action is limited unless you are sitting in the front row. This means that most passengers miss seeing all these near collisions. But don't worry; regardless of where you sit, there's plenty to keep you busy. Dueling Dragons is the highest coaster in the park and also claims the longest drop at 115 feet, not to mention five inversions. And like the Hulk, it's a smooth ride all the way.

Coaster cadets argue about which seat on which train provides the wildest ride. We prefer the front row on either train, but coaster loonies hype the front row of Fire and the last row of Ice.

It's highly likely that Dueling Dragons will be renamed and incorporated into the new Wizarding World of Harry Potter themed area, due to open in late 2009 or early 2010.

TOURING TIPS The good news about this ride is that you won't get wet unless you wet yourself. The bad news is that wetting yourself comes pretty naturally. The other bad news is that the queuing area for Dueling Dragons is the longest, most convoluted affair we've ever seen, winding endlessly through a maze of subterranean passages. After what feels like a comprehensive tour of Mammoth Cave, you finally emerge at the loading area where you must choose between riding Fire or Ice. Of course, at this critical juncture, you're as blind as a mole rat from being in the dark for so long. Our advice is to follow the person in front of you until your eyes adjust to the light. Try to ride during the first 90 minutes the park is open. Warn anyone waiting for you that you might be a while. Even if there is no line to speak of, it takes 10 to 12 minutes just to navigate the caverns and not much less time to exit the attraction after riding. However, if lines are low, park employees will open special doors marked "Reentry to Fire" or "Reentry to Ice" (depending on what coaster you just rode) that allow you to get right back to the head of the queue and ride again. Finally, if you don't have time to ride both Fire and Ice, the *Unofficial* crew unanimously prefers Fire to Ice.

The Eighth Voyage of Sindbad (Universal Express) ★★

APPEAL BY AGE	PRESCHOOL ★★★	GRADE SCHOOL ★★★★	TEENS ★★★
YOUNG ADULTS ★★★	OVER 30 ★★★	SENIORS ★★★	

What it is Theater stunt show. **Scope and scale** Major attraction. **When to go** Any time on the daily entertainment schedule. **Authors' rating** Vapid; ★★. **Duration of presentation** 17 minutes. **Probable waiting time** 15 minutes.

DESCRIPTION AND COMMENTS A story about Sindbad the Sailor is the glue that (loosely) binds this stunt show featuring water explosions, ten-foot-tall circles of flame, and various other daunting eruptions and perturbations. The show reminds us of those action movies that substitute a mind-numbing succession of explosions, crashes, and special effects for plot and character development. Concerning *Sindbad,* even if you bear in mind that it's billed as a stunt show, the production is so vacuous and redundant that it's hard to get into the action.

TOURING TIPS See *Sindbad* after you've experienced the rides and the better-rated shows.

Poseidon's Fury! (Universal Express) ★★★★

APPEAL BY AGE	PRESCHOOL ★★	GRADE SCHOOL ★★★★	TEENS ★★★★
YOUNG ADULTS ★★★★	OVER 30 ★★★★	SENIORS ★★★★	

What it is High-tech theater attraction. **Scope and scale** Headliner. **When to go** After experiencing all the rides. **Special comments** Audience stands throughout. **Authors' rating** Much improved; ★★★★. **Duration of presentation** 17 minutes, including preshow. **Probable waiting time** 25 minutes.

DESCRIPTION AND COMMENTS In the first incarnation of this story, the Greek gods Poseidon and Zeus duked it out, with Poseidon as the heavy. Poseidon fought with water, and Zeus fought with fire, though both sometimes resorted to laser beams and smoke machines. In the new version, the rehabilitated Poseidon now tussles with an evil wizardish guy, and everybody uses fire, water, lasers, smoke machines, and angry lemurs (*Note:* Lemurs are not actually used—just seeing if you're paying attention). As you might have inferred, the new story is somewhat incoherent, but the special effects are still amazing, and the theming of the preshow area is quite imposing. The plot unfolds in installments as you pass through a couple of these areas and finally into the main theater. Though the production is a little slow and plodding at first, it wraps up with quite an impressive flourish. There's some great technology at work here. *Poseidon* is far and away the best of the Islands of Adventure theater attractions.

TOURING TIPS If you're still wet from Dudley Do-Right, the Bilge-Rat Barges, and the *Jurassic Park* River Adventure, you might be tempted to cheer the evil wizard's flame jets in hopes of finally drying out. Our money, however, is on Poseidon. It's legal in Florida for theme parks to get you wet, but setting you on fire is frowned on.

Frequent explosions and noise may frighten younger children, so exercise caution with preschoolers. Shows run continuously if the technology isn't on the blink. We recommend catching *Poseidon* after experiencing your fill of the rides.

The Wizarding World of Harry Potter

(Opens early 2010)

DESCRIPTION AND COMMENTS In what may prove to be the competitive coup of all time between archrivals Disney and Universal, the latter has scored a deal with Warner Brothers Entertainment to create a "fully immersive" Harry Potter–themed environment based on the best-selling children's books by J. K. Rowling and the companion blockbuster movies from Warner Brothers. The project was blessed by Rowling, who is known for tenaciously protecting the integrity of her work. In the case of the films, she demanded that Warner Brothers be true, almost to an unprecedented degree, to the books on which the films were based. She has had many suitors vie over the years for the right to translate her novels into a theme park, but she's never consented until now. When it comes to exercising control over her work, Rowling is every bit as adamant as Disney—which probably explains why The Wizarding World of Harry Potter ended up at Universal.

Universal, not unexpectedly, has been tight-lipped about the details of The Wizarding World. What follows is what we know for sure, augmented by some well-educated assumptions.

Envisioned as a "theme park within a theme park," the new 20-acre area is carved out of the Lost Continent section of Islands of Adventure, stretching on a northeast–southwest axis down the side of the Dueling Dragons roller coasters before angling south onto some undeveloped land bordered by Turkey Lake Road. It's probable that Dueling Dragons will be rethemed and incorporated into The Wizarding World. Likewise, it's expected that the theater currently housing *The Eighth Voyage of Sindbad* will be annexed.

The themed area draws its inspiration from all the Harry Potter movies and books, creating an amalgamation of landmarks, sights, creatures, and themes that are faithful to the films. Guests will access The Wizarding World through an imposing gate that opens onto Hogsmeade Village, depicted in winter and covered in snow. This section will be the themed area's primary shopping and dining venue. Exiting Hogsmeade Village, you'll first glimpse towering Hogwarts Castle, flanked by the Forbidden Forest and Hagrid's Hut, and anchoring the far end of the themed area. Guests will be able to explore both the grounds and interior of the castle, which will house a headliner attraction. Universal is reportedly going all-out on the castle, with the intention of developing an icon even more beloved and powerful than Cinderella Castle at Disney's Magic Kingdom.

The Wizarding World will encompass multiple attractions, including one that Universal promises will be "state of the art." Many speculators are putting their money on a ride derived from the Knights' Tournament "robocoaster" at Legoland California. Each ride vehicle (holding two persons in the Legoland version) is perched at the end of a huge robotic arm that can essentially fling the ride vehicle pitching and yawing upside down and in any direction. The arms can be programmed for various degrees of intensity and can operate independently of one another, giving riders anything from a gentle swing to a gut-wrenching ordeal. Without tracks or hills, Knights' Tournament can replicate all the sensations of a roller coaster, including broad swoops, inversions, and flips. When you view all the arms at work, the effect is of a very precisely choreographed yet chaotic ballet.

Though we *Unofficials* think the technology is way cool, and certainly groundbreaking, the Legoland robocoaster loads notoriously slowly and would be instantly overwhelmed by the size of crowds at Disney World and Universal Orlando. As of press time, you can see a video of this monster in action at the Internet Archive (go to **www.archive.org** and search for "Knights' Tournament at Legoland California" at the top of the home page).

A good Web site for monitoring the progress of The Wizarding World is **www.wizardingworldharrypotter.com.** This unofficial site has construction photos, attraction updates and speculation, and concept art depicting various scenes in the new themed area.

TOURING TIPS When The Wizarding World opens—and if Universal pulls it off in style—it will be the hottest ticket in theme park–dom. Overall attendance at Islands of Adventure will increase dramatically, and we expect most guests to make a beeline to Potterland. Your only chance of avoiding long queues for the attractions is to arrive at the turnstiles 30 minutes before park opening and make The Wizarding World your first stop. Once you arrive, hit the new rides first and then the roller coaster, followed by any other rides. Save shows and general exploration of the themed area for last. If the lines are as long as we expect, this might be the occasion to spring for the pricey Universal Express admission add-on, which lets you go to the front of the line.

If you're having trouble sizing up how big a deal The Wizarding World is, you need only check the discussion boards of any Web site associated with Orlando, theme parks, Harry Potter, Daniel Radcliffe, J. K. Rowling, or dozens of other tenuously related topics. What you're likely to see is a billion or so postings like this:

OMG!!!!!!!!!!!!! I CAN'T WAIT!!!!!!!!! I LOVE Harry Potter SOOOOOOOO much you wouldn't BELIEVE!!!!!!!!!!!!!!!!!! I was just looking for Harry Potter stuff and I saw a link to this!! I am so EXCITED!!!!

One final note: The Wizarding World will suck up guests like a vacuum on steroids. This means that crowds will be considerably lighter in other sections of Islands of Adventure, especially in the morning.

SEUSS LANDING

A TEN-ACRE THEMED AREA BASED ON Dr. Seuss's famous children's books. As at Mickey's Toontown in the Magic Kingdom, all the buildings and attractions replicate a whimsical, brightly colored cartoon style with exaggerated features and rounded lines. Seuss Landing has four rides (described below and on the following pages) and an interactive play area, **If I Ran the Zoo,** populated by Seuss creatures.

Caro-Seuss-el (Universal Express) ★★★½

APPEAL BY AGE PRESCHOOL ★★★★ GRADE SCHOOL ★★★★ TEENS — YOUNG ADULTS — OVER 30 — SENIORS —

What it is Merry-go-round. **Scope and scale** Minor attraction. **When to go** Before 11 a.m. **Authors' rating** Wonderfully unique; ★★★½. **Duration of ride** 2 minutes. **Loading speed** Slow.

DESCRIPTION AND COMMENTS Totally outrageous, the Caro-Seuss-el is a full-scale, 56-mount merry-go-round made up exclusively of Dr. Seuss characters.

TOURING TIPS Even if you are too old or don't want to ride, this attraction is worth an inspection. Whatever your age, chances are good you'll see some old friends.

The Cat in the Hat (Universal Express) ★★★½

APPEAL BY AGE	PRESCHOOL ★★★★	GRADE SCHOOL ★★★★	TEENS ★★★
YOUNG ADULTS ★★★★	OVER 30 ★★★★	SENIORS ★★★★	

What it is Indoor adventure ride. **Scope and scale** Major attraction. **When to go** Before 11:30 a.m. **Authors' rating** Seuss would be proud; ★★★½. **Duration of ride** 3½ minutes. **Loading speed** Moderate.

DESCRIPTION AND COMMENTS Guests ride on "couches" through 18 different sets inhabited by animatronic Seuss characters, including The Cat in the Hat, Thing 1, Thing 2, and the beleaguered goldfish who tries to maintain order in the midst of bedlam. Well done overall, with nothing that should frighten younger children.

TOURING TIPS This is fun for all ages. Try to ride early.

A father of three from Natick, Massachusetts, thinks we're off-base when we say that nothing should frighten younger children:

I think you need to revise the Cat in the Hat ride review by saying that it has quite the fright potential. My fairly advanced 3½-year-old was terrified on the ride. Besides all the things popping out at you, it whips you around very wildly. My wife took her on the ride, and she was screaming her head off. I did a switch-off and rode it just to see; it was pretty intense, and I nearly got whiplash! Nearly two years later, she still reminds me of the scary Cat in the Hat ride (it hasn't affected her love for the books, though!). Please reconsider your opinion.

One Fish, Two Fish, Red Fish, Blue Fish (Universal Express) ★★★½

APPEAL BY AGE	PRESCHOOL ★★★★	GRADE SCHOOL ★★★★	TEENS ★★★
YOUNG ADULTS ★★★	OVER 30 ★★★	SENIORS ★★★	

What it is Wet version of Dumbo the Flying Elephant. **Scope and scale** Minor attraction. **When to go** Before 10 a.m. **Authors' rating** Who says you can't teach an old ride new tricks?; ★★★½. **Duration of ride** 2 minutes. **Loading speed** Slow.

DESCRIPTION AND COMMENTS Imagine Dumbo with Seuss-style fish instead of elephants and you've got half the story. The other half of the story involves yet another opportunity to drown. Guests steer their fish up or down 15 feet in the air while traveling in circles. At the same time, they try to avoid streams of water projected from "squirt posts." A catchy song provides clues for avoiding the squirting.

Though the ride is ostensibly for kids, the song and the challenge of steering your fish away from the water make this attraction fun for all ages.

TOURING TIPS We don't know what it is about this theme park and water, but you'll get wetter than at a full-immersion baptism.

The High in the Sky Seuss Trolley Train Ride! (Universal Express) ★★★½

APPEAL BY AGE	PRESCHOOL ★★★★	GRADE SCHOOL ★★★½	TEENS ★
YOUNG ADULTS ★★½	OVER 30 ★★½	SENIORS ★★★	

What it is Elevated train. **Scope and scale** Major attraction. **When to go** Before 11:30 a.m. **Special comments** A relaxed look at the park. **Authors' rating** ★★★½. **Duration of ride** 3½ minutes. **Loading speed** Molasses.

DESCRIPTION AND COMMENTS Trains putter along elevated tracks while a voice reads a Dr. Seuss story over the train's speakers. As each train makes its way through Seuss Landing, it passes a series of animatronic characters in scenes that are part of the story being told. Little tunnels and a few mild turns make this a charming ride.

There are two tracks at the station. As you face the platform, to your left is the Beech track, which is aquamarine; to your right is the Star track, which is purple. Each track offers a different story.

TOURING TIPS The line for this ride is much less charming than the attraction. The trains are small, fitting about 20 people, and the loading speed is glacial. Save High in the Sky for the end of the day or ride first thing in the morning.

ISLANDS *of* ADVENTURE TOURING PLAN

ISLANDS OF ADVENTURE ONE-DAY TOURING PLAN

(see page 835)

BE AWARE THAT IN THIS PARK there are an inordinate number of attractions that will get you wet. If you want to experience them, come armed with ponchos, large plastic garbage bags, or some other protective covering. Failure to follow this prescription will make for a squishy, sodden day.

When it comes to dining, the best restaurant in Islands of Adventure is the exotic **Mythos** in The Lost Continent, serving pizza, pasta, burgers, sandwiches, and Asian specialties.

The IOA touring plan is for groups of all sizes and ages and includes thrill rides that may induce motion sickness or get you wet. If the plan calls for you to experience an attraction that does not interest you, simply skip that attraction and proceed to the next step. Be aware that the plan calls for some backtracking. If you have young children in your party, customize the plan to fit their needs and take advantage of switching off at thrill rides.

SEAWORLD

MANY DOZENS OF READERS HAVE WRITTEN to extol the virtues of SeaWorld. The following are representative. An English family writes:

> *The best-organized park* [is] *SeaWorld. The computer printout we got on arrival had a very useful show schedule, told us which areas were temporarily closed due to construction, and had a readily understandable map. Best of all, there was almost no queuing. Overall, we rated this day so highly that it is the park we would most like to visit again.*

A woman in Alberta, Canada, gives her opinion:

We chose SeaWorld as our fifth day at "The World." What a pleasant surprise! It was every bit as good (and in some ways better) than WDW itself. Well worth the admission, an excellent entertainment value, educational, well run, and better value for the dollar in food services. Perhaps expand your coverage to give them their due!

unofficial **TIP**
Discount coupons for SeaWorld admission are available in the free visitor magazine found in most (but not Disney) hotel lobbies.

OK, here's what you need to know (for additional information, call ☎ 800-327-2424 or 407-351-3600, or visit **www.seaworld.com**). SeaWorld is a world-class marine-life theme park near the intersection of I-4 and the Beachline Expressway. It's about eight miles east of Walt Disney World. Open daily at 9 a.m. and closing between 6 and 11 p.m. depending on the season, SeaWorld charges about $75 admission for adults and $65 for children ages 3 to 9. Six-park Combination Orlando FlexTickets, which include admission to SeaWorld, Aquatica, Universal Studios, Islands of Adventure, Wet 'n Wild, and Busch Gardens, are available as well. SeaWorld offers some super advance-purchase discounts on its Web site. Not long ago, for example, you could purchase an adult one-day admission for the price of a child's admission. Parking is $12 per car, $15 per RV or camper.

Figure on eight to nine hours to see everything, six or so if you stick to the big deals. Discovery Cove is directly across the Central Florida Parkway from SeaWorld. Parking at Discovery Cove is free.

unofficial **TIP**
If you don't purchase your admission in advance, take advantage of the automatic admission machines located to the right of the main entrance. The machines are a pain in the rear, asking for your name, age, home zip code, and billing zip code. But if you have a credit card, the machines are faster than standing in line at the ticket windows.

SeaWorld is about the size of the Magic Kingdom and requires about the same amount of walking. In terms of size, quality, and creativity, it's unequivocally on par with Disney's major theme parks. Unlike Walt Disney World, SeaWorld primarily features stadium shows and walk-through exhibits. This means you'll spend about 80% less time waiting in line during eight hours at SeaWorld than you would for the same-length visit at a Disney park.

Because lines, except those for Journey to Atlantis, Kraken, and Manta (see next page), aren't much of a problem at SeaWorld, you can tour at almost any time of day. If you visit in the morning, arrive early. Morning arrivals tend to create long waits at the ticket windows, so consider buying your admission in advance. Like those at other area parks, SeaWorld's turnstiles often open at either 8:30 a.m. or 8:45 a.m., depending on the season, which means you can enter the park before the scheduled 9 a.m. opening.

A mother of two correctly points out that crowds at SeaWorld on some days can be as daunting as those at the Disney parks:

Your reference to [crowds at] *SeaWorld should be changed. We were there on a Sunday and it was extremely crowded, so crowded that we were not able to see everything, even the major attractions. Waits were way too long for us to consider the rides.*

A daily entertainment schedule is printed conveniently on a place-mat-sized map of the park. The five featured shows are:

- *A'lure: The Call of the Ocean* (Cirque du Soleil–type revue)
- *Believe* (Shamu and killer-whale show)
- *Blue Horizons* (whale, dolphin, and bird show)
- *Clyde and Seamore Take Pirate Island* (sea-lion, walrus, and otter show)
- *Pets Ahoy!* (show with performing domestic animals)

You'll notice immediately as you check the performance times that the shows are scheduled so that it's almost impossible to see them back to back. *Believe,* for example, might run from 5 to 5:25 p.m. Ideally, you'd like to bop over to *Clyde and Seamore,* which begins at 5:30 p.m. Unfortunately, five minutes isn't enough time to exit Shamu Stadium and cross the park to the Sea Lion and Otter Stadium. SeaWorld, of course, planned it this way so you would stay longer. A Cherry Hill, New Jersey, visitor confirms this rather major problem, complaining:

> *The shows were timed so we could not catch all the major ones in a seven-hour visit.*

Trying to sort out a game plan for seeing the shows while you're on the run is somewhat exasperating. A better alternative is to visit **www.seaworld.com/orlando** and, under "Park Information," click on "Park Hours and Show Schedules." Here you can see the show schedule for the day of your visit and can plan your touring itinerary in advance.

Much of the year, you can get a seat for the stadium shows by showing up ten or so minutes in advance. When the park is crowded, however, you need to be at the stadiums at least 20 minutes in advance (30 minutes in advance for a good seat). All of the stadiums have "splash zones," specified areas where you're likely to be drenched with ice-cold salt water by whales, dolphins, and sea lions. Trust us when we say you should take these seriously. You don't have to be in the tank for Shamu to drown you.

Journey to Atlantis, Kraken, and **Manta** are SeaWorld's entries into the theme-park super-attraction competition. Occupying the equivalent of six football fields, Journey to Atlantis is the world's first attraction to combine elements of a high-speed water ride and a roller coaster. (By the way, you'll get soaked.) Kraken is currently the second-longest roller coaster in Orlando.

Opened in the spring of 2009, Manta is a steel coaster that arranges riders four across, lying facedown and parallel to the track, beneath the expanse of a giant manta ray–shaped carriage. The coaster is said to emulate the movements of a manta ray, but if that's the case, it's a mighty frisky ray. The coaster soars and swoops through a pretzel loop, a 360-degree inline roll, and two corkscrews—not to mention a first drop of 113 feet. Manta reaches a height of 140 feet and speeds of more than 55 miles per hour. But don't worry: lying facedown puts you in the perfect position to throw up. Actually, the ride is very smooth. If you get sick, it'll be from the bugs you pick out of your teeth (keep you mouth closed at all times—you're supposed to be a ray, not a bat). The queuing area is a stunning underwater exhibit featuring 300 rays from five different species; several fish keep the rays company.

Catch all three rides just after the park opens, or be prepared to wait.

STAR RATINGS FOR SEAWORLD ATTRACTIONS

★★★★½	*Believe* (high-tech Shamu and killer-whale show)
★★★★	Manta (roller coaster)
★★★★	*Clyde and Seamore Take Pirate Island* (sea-lion, walrus, and otter show)
★★★★	Shark Encounter
★★★★	Kraken (roller coaster)
★★★★	Wild Arctic (simulation ride and Arctic wildlife viewing)
★★★★	*A'lure: The Call of the Ocean* (Cirque du Soleil–type presentation)
★★★★	Shamu's Happy Harbor (children's play area)
★★★½	*Blue Horizons* (whale, dolphin, and bird show)
★★★½	*Pets Ahoy!* (show with performing birds, cats, dogs, and a pig)
★★★½	Pacific Point Preserve (sea lions and seals)
★★★½	Penguin Encounter
★★★½	Key West at SeaWorld (dolphin, stingray, and turtle viewing)
★★★	Manatee Rescue (manatee viewing)
★★★	Journey to Atlantis (combination roller coaster–flume ride)
★★½	Clydesdale Hamlet (Budweiser Clydesdale horses)
★★	Sky Tower (400-foot-tall observation tower)

SeaWorld offers quite a few guided tours. Most include the major shows, a glimpse behind the scenes, rides (without waiting) on Journey to Atlantis and Kraken, and some seal, ray, and dolphin feeding. Some tours also include lunch in the backstage area of the killer-whale facility. The tour guides, both personable and well informed, are a font of interesting and useful information. We learned on a recent tour, for example, that in the United States, more people are killed each year by vending machines than by sharks. Think about that next time you buy a Coke.

DISCOVERY COVE

SEAWORLD'S INTIMATE NEW PARK, Discovery Cove, is a welcome departure from the hustle and bustle of other Orlando parks; its slower pace could be the overstimulated family's ticket back to mental health.

The main draw at Discovery Cove is the chance to swim with its troupe of 25 Atlantic bottlenose dolphins. The 90-minute experience (30 minutes in the water) is open to visitors age 6 and up who are comfortable in the water. The experience begins with an orientation led by trainers and an opportunity for participants to ask questions.

unofficial **TIP**
With a focus on personal guest service and one-on-one animal encounters, Discovery Cove admits only 1,000 guests per day.

Next, small groups wade into shallow water to get an introduction to the dolphins in their habitat. The experience culminates with two to three guests and a trainer swimming into deeper water for closer interaction with the dolphins.

Other exhibits at Discovery Cove include the Coral Reef and the Aviary. Snorkel or swim in the Coral Reef, which houses thousands of exotic fish as well as an underwater shipwreck and hidden grottoes. In the Aviary, you can touch and feed gorgeous tropical birds. The park is threaded by a "tropical river" in which you can float or swim and is dotted with beaches that serve as pathways to the attractions. You can also wade in the Ray Lagoon.

All guests are required to wear flotation vests when swimming, and lifeguards are omnipresent. You'll need your swimsuit, pool shoes, and a cover-up. On rare days when it's too cold to swim in Orlando, guests are provided with free wet suits. Discovery Cove also provides fish-friendly sunscreen samples; guests may not use their own sunscreen.

Discovery Cove is open 9 a.m. until 5:30 p.m. daily. Admission is limited, so purchase tickets well in advance; call ☎ 877-4-DISCOVERY or visit **www.discoverycove.com.** Prices vary seasonally from $269 per person to $289, excluding tax (no children's discount). Admission includes the dolphin swim, self-parking, Continental breakfast, a substantial lunch, snacks and drinks, and use of beach umbrellas, lounge chairs, towels, lockers, and swim and snorkel gear. Discovery Cove admission also includes a seven-day pass to SeaWorld, Busch Gardens, or Aquatica. If you're not interested in the dolphin swim, you can visit Discovery Cove for the day for $169 to $189 per person, depending on the season.

PART SIXTEEN

The WATER PARKS

YOU'RE SOAKING *in* IT!

DISNEY HAS TWO WATER PARKS, and there are two competitive water parks in the area. At Disney World, **Typhoon Lagoon** is the more diverse splash pad, while **Blizzard Beach** takes the prize for the greater number of slides and the more bizarre theme. Outside the World are **Wet 'n Wild** on International Drive and **Aquatica by SeaWorld.**

At all Disney water parks, the following rules and prices apply: one cooler per family or group is allowed, but no glass and no alcoholic beverages; towels are $2; lockers are $8 small, $10 large (includes $5 refundable deposit); life jackets are available at no cost.

Guests can use automated ticket-vending machines to purchase admission tickets at Blizzard Beach and Typhoon Lagoon. These machines use touch-screen technology and are intended to reduce the amount of time spent standing in line at ticket windows. Admission, including tax, runs $48 for adults and $42 for children ages 3 to 9.

WATCH THE WEATHER

IF YOU BUY YOUR WALT DISNEY WORLD admission tickets before leaving home and are considering the Water Park Fun and More (WPFAM) add-on (see page 52), you might want to wait until you arrive and have some degree of certainty about the weather during your stay. You can add the WPFAM option at any Disney resort or Guest Services window at the theme parks. This is true regardless whether you purchased your Base Tickets separately or as part of a package.

EXTRA MAGIC HOURS

LIKE THE FOUR MAJOR DISNEY PARKS, the swimming parks participate in the Extra Magic Hours program. Each day, Disney-resort guests can enter either of the water parks one hour before the park is open to the public. During the summer and some spring holiday periods, evening Extra Magic Hours are offered at Typhoon Lagoon only on two to five designated evenings a month; on these days, Typhoon Lagoon stays open until 10 p.m., three hours beyond the normal closing time. For our money, Typhoon Lagoon is the best possible place to be on a hot Florida summer evening. As a postscript, Disney is cutting costs left and right. Don't be surprised if Extra Magic Hours goes the way of the dodo.

BLIZZARD BEACH

BLIZZARD BEACH IS DISNEY'S MORE EXOTIC water-adventure park and, like Typhoon Lagoon, it arrived with its own legend. This time, the story goes, an entrepreneur tried to open a ski resort in Florida during a particularly savage winter. Alas, the snow melted; the palm trees grew back; and all that remained of the ski resort was its Alpine lodge, the ski lifts, and, of course, the mountain. Plunging off the mountain are ski slopes and bobsled runs transformed into waterslides. Visitors to Blizzard Beach catch the thaw—icicles drip and patches of snow remain. The melting snow has formed a lagoon (the wave pool), fed by gushing mountain streams.

Like Typhoon Lagoon, Blizzard Beach is distinguished by its landscaping and the attention paid to executing its theme. As you enter Blizzard Beach, you face the mountain. Coming off the highest peak and bisecting the area at the mountain's base are two long slides. To the left of the slides is the wave pool. To the right are the children's swimming area and the ski lift. Surrounding the layout like a moat is a tranquil stream for floating in tubes.

unofficial **TIP**
Picnic areas are scattered around the park, as are pleasant places for sunbathing.

On either side of the highest peak are tube, raft, and body slides. Including the two slides coming off the peak, Blizzard Beach has 17 slides. Among them is **Summit Plummet,** Disney World's longest speed slide, which begins with a 120-foot free fall, and the **Teamboat Springs** water-bobsled run, 1,200 feet long.

One reader reports that the Blizzard Beach slides picked her husband's pocket:

> *You mentioned lots of ladies losing their tops on Summit Plummet, but didn't mention the atomic wedgies it bestows upon its riders! Still, it is a thrill slide not to be missed and all four of us in our family absolutely loved it! It did, however, claim all four of our park pass/room key cards as its victims. My husband had the four cards in an exterior pocket of his swimsuit, secured closed by Velcro AND a snap. We both thought it was a safe, secure spot for the cards. After doing Summit Plummet and Slush Gusher twice apiece and Teamboat Springs once, he looked down, noticed the pocket flapping open and found all four cards missing! So we had to cancel all the cards (they had charging privileges) and couldn't purchase any food or drink while we were there (*[we]* didn't bring any cash because we planned to charge with our cards)!*

For our money, the most exciting and interesting slides are the **Slush Gusher** and Teamboat Springs on the front right of the mountain, and **Runoff Rapids** on the back side of the mountain. Slush Gusher is an undulating speed slide that we consider as exciting as

Blizzard Beach Attractions

ATTRACTION | HEIGHT REQUIREMENT | WHAT TO EXPECT

SUMMIT PLUMMET | 48 inches | A 120-foot free fall, at 60 mph. Needless to say, this ride is very intense. Make sure your child knows what to expect. Being over 48 inches tall does not guarantee an enjoyable experience. If you think you'd enjoy washing out of a 12th-floor window during a heavy rain, then this slide is for you.

SLUSH GUSHER | 48 inches | A 90-foot double-humped slide. Ladies, cling to those tops—all others, hang on to live.

DOWNHILL DOUBLE DIPPER | 48 inches | Side-by-side tube-racing slides. At 25 mph, the tube zooms through water curtains and free falls. It's a lot of fun, but rough.

CHAIR LIFT UP MT. GUSHMORE | 32 inches | Great ride even if you only go up for the view. When the park is packed, use the singles line.

TEAMBOAT SPRINGS | None | 1,200-foot whitewater group raft flume. Wonderful ride for the whole family.

RUNOFF RAPIDS | None | Three corkscrew tube slides to choose from. The center slide is for solo raft rides; the other two slides offer one- or two-person tubes. The dark, enclosed tube makes you feel as if you've been flushed down a toilet.

SNOW STORMERS | None | Three mat-slide flumes; down you go on your belly.

TOBOGGAN RACERS | None | Eight-lane race course. You go down the flume on a mat. Less intense than Snow Stormers.

MELT-AWAY BAY | None | Wave pool with gentle, bobbing waves. Great for younger swimmers.

CROSS COUNTRY CREEK | None | Lazy river circling the park; grab a tube.

TIKE'S PEAK | 4 feet and under only | Kid-sized version of Blizzard Beach. This is *the* place for little ones.

SKI PATROL TRAINING CAMP | Ages 5–11 | A place for preteens to train for the big rides.

the more vertical Summit Plummet without being as bone-jarring. On Teamboat Springs, you ride in a raft that looks like a children's round blow-up wading pool.

Runoff Rapids is accessible from a path that winds around the far left bottom of the mountain. The rapids consist of three corkscrew tube slides, one of which is enclosed and dark. As at Teamboat Springs, you'll go much faster on a two- or three-person tube than on a one-person tube. If you lean so that you enter curves high and come out low, you'll really fly. Because we like to steer the tube and go fast, we much prefer the open slides (where we can see) to the dark, enclosed tube. We thought crashing through the pitch-dark tube felt disturbingly like being flushed down a toilet.

unofficial **TIP**
The more people you load into the raft, the faster it goes. If you have only a couple in it, the slide is kind of a snore.

The **Snow Stormer**'s mat slides on the front of the mountain are fun but not as fast or as interesting as Runoff Rapids or **Downhill Double Dipper** on the far left front. The **Toboggan Racers** at front and center on the mountain consists of eight parallel slides where riders are dispatched in heats to race to the bottom. The ride itself is no big deal, and the time needed to get everybody lined up ensures that you'll wait extra-long to ride. On one visit, as an added annoyance, we had to line up once to get a mat and again to actually ride. A faster, more exciting race venue can be found on the side-by-side slides of the undulating Downhill Double Dipper. Competitors here can reach speeds of up to 25 miles an hour.

A ski lift carries guests to the mountaintop (you can also walk up), where they can choose from Summit Plummet, Slush Gusher, or Teamboat Springs. For all other slides at Blizzard Beach, the only way to reach the top is on foot. If you're among the first in the park and don't have to wait to ride, the ski lift is fun and provides a bird's-eye view of the park. After riding once to satisfy your curiosity, however, you're better off taking the stairs to the top. There is a minimum-height restriction of 48 inches on Slush Gusher, Summit Plummet, and Downhill Double Dipper.

unofficial **TIP**
If you're going primarily for the slides, you'll have about two hours in the early morning to enjoy them before the wait becomes intolerable.

The wave pool, called **Melt-Away Bay,** has gentle, bobbing waves. The float creek, **Cross Country Creek,** circles the park, passing through the mountain. The children's areas, **Tike's Peak** and **Ski Patrol Training Camp,** are creatively designed, nicely isolated, and, like the rest of the park, visually interesting.

Like Typhoon Lagoon, Blizzard Beach is a bit convoluted in its layout. With slides on both the front and back of the mountain, it isn't always easy to find a path leading to where you want to go.

At the ski resort's now-converted base area are shops; counter-service food; restrooms; and tube, towel, and locker rentals. Blizzard Beach has its own parking lot but no lodging, though Disney's All-Star and Coronado Springs resorts are almost within walking distance. Disney resort and campground guests can commute to the park aboard Disney buses.

Because it's novel and has popular slides, Blizzard Beach fills early during hotter months. To stake out a nice sunning spot and to enjoy the slides without long waits, arrive at least 35 minutes before the official opening time.

TYPHOON LAGOON

TYPHOON LAGOON IS COMPARABLE in size to Blizzard Beach. Eleven waterslides and streams, some as long as 420 feet, drop from the top of a 100-foot-tall man-made mountain. Landscaping and an aftermath-of-a-typhoon theme add interest and a sense of adventure to the wet rides.

Guests enter Typhoon Lagoon through a misty rain forest, then emerge in a ramshackle tropical town where concessions and services are situated. Special sets make every ride an odyssey as swimmers encounter bat caves, lagoons and pools, spinning rocks, formations of dinosaur bones, and many other imponderables.

Typhoon Lagoon has its own parking lot but no lodging. Disney-resort and -campground guests can commute to the water park on Disney buses.

Typhoon Lagoon Attractions

ATTRACTION | HEIGHT REQUIREMENT | WHAT TO EXPECT

CRUSH 'N' GUSHER | 48 inches | Water roller coaster where you can choose from among three slides: Banana Blaster, Coconut Crusher, and Pineapple Plunger, ranging from 410 to 420 feet long. This thriller leaves you wondering what exactly happened—if you make it down in one piece, that is: not for the faint of heart. If your kids are new to water-park rides, this is not the place to break them in, even if they're tall enough to ride.

HUMUNGA KOWABUNGA | 48 inches | Speed slides that hit 30 mph. A five-story drop in the dark rattles the most courageous rider. Women should ride this one in a one-piece swimsuit.

KEELHAUL FALLS | None | Fast whitewater ride in a single-person tube.

GANG PLANK FALLS | None | White-water-raft flume in a multiperson tube.

MAYDAY FALLS | None | The name says it all: wild single-person tube ride. *Hang on!*

STORM SLIDES | None | Three body-slides down and through Mount Mayday.

SHARK REEF | None | After you're equipped with fins, mask, snorkel, and a life vest, you get a brief lesson in snorkeling. Then off you go for about 60 feet to the other side of the saltwater pool, where you swim with small, colorful fish; rays; and very small leopard and hammerhead sharks. If you don't want to swim with the fish, visit the underwater-viewing chamber anytime during the day. Surface Air Snorkeling, a scubalike pursuit involving a "pony" tank, small regulator, and buoyancy vest, is also offered. The fee is $20 per half hour for the first person, $15 for the second person. Participants must be at least 5 years old. To sign up and get more information, visit the kiosk near the entrance to Shark Reef.

SURF POOL | None | World's largest inland surf facility, with waves up to 6 feet high. Adult supervision is required. Three mornings a week at 6:30 a.m. (before the park opens), half-hour surfing lessons are offered (surfboard provided). Cost is $150 for 2½ hours; minimum age is 8; class size is 12. Call ☎ 407-WDW-PLAY. The price does *not* include park admission.

CASTAWAY CREEK | None | Half-mile lazy river in a tropical setting. Wonderful!

KETCHAKIDDEE CREEK | 48 inches and under only | Toddlers and preschoolers love this area reserved only for them. Say "splish-splash" and have lots of fun.

If you indulge in all features of Typhoon Lagoon, admission is a fair value. If you go primarily for the slides, you will have only two early-morning hours to enjoy them before the wait becomes prohibitive. Speaking of crowds, a Maryland family tried a little experiment and reports the following:

> *We did Typhoon Lagoon one morning and it was fun. So we theorized that since it was crowded midday, that maybe it clears out late afternoon. My wife took our oldest there at 3* [p.m.] *on Friday and said it was wide open—they rode waterslides without any wait at all for two hours and loved it.*

Typhoon Lagoon provides water adventure for all ages. Activity pools for young children and families feature geysers, tame slides, bubble jets, and fountains. For the older and more adventurous are the enclosed **Humunga Kowabunga** speed slides, corkscrew **Storm Slides,** and three whitewater-raft rides (plus one children's rapids ride) plopping off **Mount Mayday.** Billed as a "water roller coaster," **Crush 'n' Gusher** consists of a series of flumes and spillways that course through an abandoned tropical-fruit-processing plant. It features tubes that hold one or two people, and you can choose from three different routes: Banana Blaster, Coconut Crusher, and Pineapple Plunger, ranging between 410 and 420 feet long. There is a minimum height requirement of 48 inches. Of all the Typhoon Lagoon slides, only Crush 'n' Gusher and the Humunga Kowabunga speed slides, where you can hit 30 miles an hour, have a minimum height requirement of 48 inches. Slower metabolisms will enjoy the scenic, meandering, 2,100-foot-long stream that floats tubers through a hidden grotto and rain forest. And, of course, the sedentary will usually find plenty of sun to sleep in. Typhoon Lagoon's surf pool and **Shark Reef** are unique, and the wave pool is the world's largest inland surf facility, with waves up to six feet high (enough, so Disney says, to "encompass an ocean liner"). Shark Reef is a saltwater snorkeling pool where guests can swim among real fish.

SHARK REEF

FINS, MASK, SNORKEL, AND WET-SUIT VEST ARE PROVIDED free in the wooden building beside the diving pool. After you obtain the proper equipment (no forms or money involved), you shower and then report to a snorkeling instructor. After a brief lesson, you swim about 60 feet to the other side of the pool. You aren't allowed to paddle aimlessly but must traverse the pool more or less directly.

The reef is fun in early morning. Equipment collection, shower, instruction, and the quick swim can be accomplished without much hassle. Also, because few guests are present, attendants are more flexible about your lingering in the pool or making minor departures from the charted course.

Later, as crowds build, it becomes increasingly difficult and time-consuming to provide the necessary instruction. The result is platoons of would-be frogmen restlessly awaiting their snorkeling lesson. Guests are grouped in impromptu classes with the entire class briefed and then launched together. What takes four or five minutes shortly after opening can take more than an hour by 11 a.m.

By far the most prevalent species in the pool is the dual-finned *Homo sapiens.* Other denizens include small, colorful tropical fish; some diminutive rays; and a few very small leopard and hammerhead sharks. In terms of numbers, it would be unusual to cross the pool and not see some fish. On the other hand, you aren't exactly bumping into them.

unofficial **TIP**
Try Shark Reef in the morning—afternoons can get crowded, and you may be ushered out of the pool more quickly than in the early hours.

It's very important to fit your diving mask on your face so that it seals around the edges. Brush your hair from your forehead and sniff a couple of times once the mask is in place, to create a vacuum. Mustaches often prevent the mask from sealing properly. The first indication that your mask isn't correctly fitted will be salt water in your nose.

If you don't want to swim with fish early in the morning or fight crowds later in the day, visit the underwater viewing chamber, accessible anytime without waiting, special equipment, showers, instruction, or water in your nose.

SURF POOL

WHILE BLIZZARD BEACH and Wet 'n Wild have wave pools, Typhoon Lagoon has a *surf pool*. Most people will encounter larger waves here than they have in the ocean. The surf machine puts out a wave about every 90 seconds (just about how long it takes to get back in position if you caught the previous wave). Perfectly formed and ideal for riding, each wave is about five to six feet from trough to crest. Before you join the fray, watch two or three waves from shore. Since each wave breaks in almost the same spot, you can get a feel for position and timing. Observing other surfers is also helpful.

unofficial **TIP**
A final warning: The surf pool has a knack for loosening watchbands, stripping jewelry, and sucking stuff out of your pockets. Don't take anything out there except your swimsuit (and on to that).

The best way to ride the waves is to swim about three-fourths of the way to the wall at the wave-machine end of the surf pool. When the wave comes (you will both feel and hear it), swim vigorously toward the beach, attempting to position yourself one-half to three-fourths of a body length below the breaking crest. The waves are so perfectly engineered that they will either carry you forward or bypass you. Unlike an ocean wave, they won't slam you down.

A teenage girl from Urbana, Illinois, notes that the primary hazard in the surf pool is colliding with other surfers and swimmers:

> *The surf pool was nice except that I kept landing on really hairy fat guys whenever the big waves came.*

A reader from Somerset, New Jersey, alerted us to yet another problem:

> *Typhoon Lagoon is a great family water park. Our unexpected favorite. However, please tell your readers not to sit on the bottom of the wave pool—I got a horrible scratch/raspberry and saw about five others with similar injuries. The waves are stronger than they look.*

Sitting on the bottom also disturbs the hippos.

The best way to avoid collisions while surfing is to paddle out far enough that you will be at the top of the wave as it breaks. This tactic eliminates the possibility of anyone landing on you from above and assures maximum forward visibility. A corollary to this: the worst place to swim is where the wave actually breaks. You will look up to see a six-foot wall of water carrying eight dozen screaming surfers bearing down on you. This is the time to remember every submarine movie you've ever seen. . . . Dive! Dive! Dive!

Four summer mornings each week from 6:45 to 10 a.m. (before the park opens), you can take surfing lessons (with a surfboard) from Craig Carroll's **Ron Jon Surf School.** Practice waves range from three to six feet tall. Most of the school's students are first-timers. Cost is $150 per person, and equipment is provided. For reservations and information, call ☎ 407-WDW-PLAY.

WET *'n* WILD

WET 'N WILD (on International Drive in Orlando, one block east of I-4 at exit 75A; ☎ 800-992-WILD or 407-351-1800; **www.wetnwildorlando.com**) is a non-Disney water-park option. Unlike Typhoon Lagoon and Blizzard Beach, in which scenic man-made mountains and integrated themes create a colorful atmosphere, Wet 'n Wild's only themes appear to be concrete, plastic, and water. Fortunately, the thrill, scope, and diversity of its rides make Wet 'n Wild an excellent alternative to the Disney swimming parks. Besides, contrary to what some Disney execs might believe, their water isn't any wetter.

unofficial **TIP**
Wet 'n Wild, though attractive and clean, is cluttered and not very appealing to the eye.

Mears Transportation operates a shuttle to Wet 'n Wild that stops three times a day at Disney hotels. It's the same shuttle that commutes between Walt Disney World and Universal Orlando. Cost is $16 for guests age 3 and older. There is no transportation to Wet 'n Wild from Disney property. If you are staying in Walt Disney World, in Lake Buena Vista, or along US 192, you will need a car. If you're staying on International Drive, you can take the **International Drive trolley** (visit **www.iridetrolley.com** for schedules and fees). If you drive, there is a large Wet 'n Wild parking lot that charges $10 per day for cars and $11 for vans and RVs. Parking is ample; just be sure to hold the kids' hands when crossing the street.

You can buy your Wet 'n Wild tickets at the main gate. Prices are about $45 for adults and $39 for children, and weekday season passes are $50, but call beforehand for special deals and discounts for those in the military, AAA members, Florida residents, and groups. For the same price as a single-day ticket, Wet 'n Wild offers a Length of Stay pass on its Web site that is good for 14 consecutive days. Ticket prices are similar to those of the Disney parks, but if you attend during the summer, the park is open late (hours vary, from 9 a.m. until 11 p.m. at the latest; call or visit the Web site for details), allowing visitors to hit the slides in the morning, go back to their hotels for lunch and a nap, and then return for a dip at night. Disney water parks typically close by 6 or 7 p.m.

When you get hungry, the main food pavilions are the centrally located **Bubba's BBQ, Manny's Pizza,** and **Surf Grill,** together offering such staples as burgers, pizza, and barbecued-pork sandwiches as well as more-nutritious (and nontraditional) items such as veggie burgers and tabbouleh. Wait times are long, and prices are high but not outrageous. For guests whose budgets and impatience thresholds are less flexible, feel free to bring in a cooler of lunch fixings (remember, glass containers and alcoholic beverages are prohibited, but you can purchase beer inside).

All the slides outside the **Kids' Park** have a 48-inch height requirement except for multipassenger slides, for which the minimum height is 36 inches if an adult accompanies the short rider; the only exceptions to this are the rides at the **WakeZone,** with a height requirement of 51 inches (The Wild One) and 56 inches (KneeSki and Wake Skating).

BODY AND MAT SLIDES

SLIDES AT WET 'N WILD INCLUDE **Mach 5, Bomb Bay, Der Stuka,** and **The Storm.** The Mach 5 tower, located to the left of the park entrance, consists of three mat slides. The mats increase your speed and eliminate the chafing often experienced on body slides. To go even faster, try to get a newer mat with a smoother bottom. They are easily distinguishable: the new mats have white handles, while the old mats have blue ones.

Among the body slides (those without mats or rafts) are Bomb Bay and Der Stuka, twin speed flumes with pitches up to 79 degrees that descend from the top of a six-story tower. On Bomb Bay you stand on a pair of doors that open, dropping you into the chute. You have to work up the nerve to launch yourself on Der Stuka. The lack of a fully enclosed tube (such as the one on the Humunga Kowabunga speed slide at Typhoon Lagoon) adds the (perhaps justifiable) fear of falling off the 250-foot slides, but their ability to float your stomach somewhere near your teeth is a pretty unforgettable thrill.

> *unofficial* **TIP**
> Although ride attendants say that all three of the Mach 5 slides are equal, the center slide appears to be the zippiest route to the bottom.

The Storm body slide, located near Bomb Bay and Der Stuka, is a hybrid ride: half slide, half toilet bowl. The steep slide creates enough momentum to launch riders into a few laps around the bowl below before they begin slipping toward the hole in the center, eventually falling into a six-foot-deep pool. The ride is exhilarating and disorienting; when the lifeguard at the ending pool begins hollering, just stumble toward his voice and give him a thumbs-up.

RAFT AND TUBE RIDES

THE HEADLINERS AT WET 'N WILD are the raft and tube rides, including **Brain Wash, Disco H2O, The Surge, Black Hole,** the **Bubba Tub, The Flyer,** and **The Blast.** Brain Wash is an extreme six-story tube ride with a 53-foot vertical drop into a 65-foot funnel; tubes hold two or four riders. Disco H2O holds up to four people in one raft, ushering them down a long tube into a 1970s-era nightclub complete with lights, music, and a disco ball. The basic design of the ride is similar to that of The Storm (a long tube into a bowl), only not as frantic and disorienting; the disco theme, coupled with the fluidity of the ride, makes it a main draw.

The Surge launches from the same tower as Disco H2O and uses the same four-person rafts. Riders spin down the open-air course, drifting high onto the walls on each banked corner. To reach the top of the walls, try to go with a full raft—as with all raft rides, the more riders squeezed in, the faster you'll all go. Directly across from The Surge's splashdown pool is the entrance for Black Hole. Bring a partner for this one; Black Hole requires two riders on each raft, and honestly, who wants to embark into endless murk without some company? As impressive as the ride seems from afar, the anxiety created by the gaping entrance is the most exciting part of the ride. Yes, it's dark—there is a green piece of track lighting down the entire course—but besides the darkness, the ride lacks the dips and turns found on the other slides. If you're claustrophobic and scared of the dark, this isn't the ride for you; if tight spaces and inky blackness don't give you a rush, then this isn't the ride for you either.

The three gentler raft rides are The Flyer, The Blast, and the Bubba Tub. The first two launch from the same tower as the Mach 5, but their entrance is accessible through the Kids' Park. At the base of the entrance are one- and two-person rafts; these are only for The Blast, so don't carry them up to the tower to the Flyer entrance. The Flyer is a calmer, toboggan-style ride in which riders sit one behind the other; it's suitable for families with smaller children. The Blast is a themed ride, like Disco H20, and is the wettest you can get without swimming. The theme of The Blast appears to be a broken waterworks, complete with spinning dials and broken pipes, all painted in comic-book red and yellow. From mist to falling water to spraying pipes, this is the best way to cool off at Wet 'n Wild. The Bubba Tub, located across the park from The Flyer and The Blast, is a long, straight track with three hummocks to impede momentum, but with a full tube of four people, you hit the "tub" at a pretty good clip.

OTHER ATTRACTIONS

THE CENTRAL FIXTURE AT WET 'N WILD, the **Surf Lagoon** wave pool, is on par with Blizzard Beach's. Unlike at Typhoon Lagoon, there's no surfing in this wave pool, but you can rent tubes at the main rental stand or go bobbing with your body. The wave-making machine takes long breaks every day, so when you walk by and see waves, be sure to wade in.

Another any-time-of-day option is the **Lazy River.** Unlike the Lazy River at Typhoon Lagoon, the Lazy River at Wet 'n Wild is misnamed: the circuit is short, the current fast. Don't even bother trying to walk upstream to catch a tube—it's better to swim down the river or wait patiently until one passes within reach.

Wet 'n Wild's 3,200-square-foot **Kids' Park** is a smaller-scale version of the adult menu. It's located to the left of the main gate; look for the oversize sand castle capped off with a big blue bucket. The bucket actually fills with water and tips over, soaking the people in front of the castle, while the castle has two slides that leave from its porticos and one small wet ramp for toddlers located on the castle's left side. There are three longer slides in back of the castle: two body slides and one tube slide. The kids' area also contains a mini–wave pool, a kid-sized climbing net, a junior river ride, and two very short zip lines. If keeping your towels in a rented locker is too much of a hassle, the kids' area is a good safe place to keep your towels (but double-check them for boogers before drying off).

WAKEZONE

THE MOST DISTINCTIVE OFFERING AT WET 'N WILD is the WakeZone, situated on a lake that's roughly the same size as the rest of the park and offering three different activities: wakeboarding, kneeboarding, and tubing. The lines can be considerable, especially since the attraction only runs from noon to dusk and is open on weekends only from mid-March to June, daily during the summer, and weekends only from September to mid-October. Be sure to call before going to Wet 'n Wild to see if the area is open that day. To avoid lines, wander over to the WakeZone at least 20 minutes before noon.

At the boarding area, you can choose either a wakeboard or a kneeboard. Helmets and life jackets, provided free at the entrance, are required; there is also a height requirement of 56 inches. The ride is basically a cable with hanging towlines that, like a T-bar at a ski resort, pull riders along the half-mile loop. You board from a slightly submerged dock where you grab the towline as it passes overhead. Brace yourself—towlines have a tendency to jerk. Keep your arms rigid and the nose of the board up. There are no instructors, so watch the other riders and chat up the good ones for tips while you're in line. If you fall down while riding, get out of the cable's path and swim to shore. If you fall where there is no nearby dock, a Jet Ski will come and pick you up.

The name of the tubing ride is **The Wild One.** For an extra fee ($6 per person), a Jet Ski will pull you around the lake while you sit in an inner tube. The ride lasts five minutes, but it's worth the money if you've never been tubing before.

AQUATICA *by* SEAWORLD

ORLANDO'S FIRST NEW SWIMMING PARK to open in more than a decade, Aquatica is across International Drive from the back side of SeaWorld. From Kissimmee, Walt Disney World, and Lake Buena Vista, take I-4 east, exiting onto the Central Florida Parkway and then bearing left on International Drive. From Universal Studios, take I-4 west to FL 528 and from there exit onto International Drive. Admission costs about the same as at the Disney water parks: $45 for adults and $39 for kids. If you don't want to wait in a queue to purchase tickets, buy them in advance at **www.aquaticabyseaworld.com,** or use the credit-card ticket machines to the left of Aquatica's main entrance.

Aquatica is comparable in size to the other water theme parks in the area. Attractively landscaped with palm, ferns, and tropical flowers, it's far less themed than Disney's Typhoon Lagoon and Blizzard Beach but much greener and more aesthetically appealing than Wet 'n Wild. Promotional material suggests that Aquatica is unique by virtue of combining SeaWorld's signature marine-animal exhibits with the expected water-park assortment of wave pools, slides, and creek floats. Marine exhibits, however, stop and end with a float-through tank of tropical fish and a pool of black-and-white Commerson's dolphins. Print, Web, and television ads for the park show guests viewing the dolphins while descending through a see-through tube on the **Dolphin Plunge** body slide—a corkscrewing romp through a totally dark tube until you blast through the clear tube at the end. The reality, however, is that you are flushed through the clear tube so fast, and with so much water splashing around your face, that it's pretty much impossible to see anything. At Aquatica, the best option by far is to view the dolphins from the walkway surrounding the exhibit or from the subsurface viewing windows.

A Yorkshire, England, woman reacted to the Dolphin Plunge:

> *The slide had the longest queue in the park. We queued for the best part of an hour and all agreed that it was a waste of time! You can barely see through the* [transparent] *part of the tube where the dolphins are (if you are lucky!), the slide is short, and the see-through bit lasts about two seconds!*

SeaWorld's promotion hype, coupled with the location of the Plunge just inside the park entrance and the slide's low carrying capacity (approximately 280 persons per hour), ensures that the slide stays mobbed all day. To experience the slide without a long wait, be on hand at park opening and ride first thing.

Other slides include **Tassie's Twisters,** in which an enclosed tube slide spits you into an open bowl where you careen around the bowl's edge much in the manner of the ball in a roulette wheel. Located close to the Dolphin Plunge, Tassie's Twisters should be your second early-morning stop. Next, head over to **Walhalla Wave** and **HooRoo Run,** both on the park's far right side. Both slides use circular rafts that can accommodate up to three people. Walhalla Wave splashes down an enclosed twisting tube, while HooRoo Run is an open-air run down a steep, straight, undulating slide. The same entrance serves both slides. Line up for Walhalla (vastly more popular) on the right, for HooRoo on the left. Make Walhalla your third slide of the day, followed by HooRoo.

Then pass along the right side of the children's adventure area, **Walkabout Waters,** to **Taumata Racer,** the park's highest-capacity slide with eight enclosed corkscrewing tubes. The remaining slide is **Whanau Way,** all the way across the park to the left of the entrance. Sporting one corkscrew and a few twists, Whanau Way employs tubes that can carry one or two people. Because it's hard to see from the park entrance, Whanau Way doesn't attract long lines until midmorning.

Taken as a whole, the slides at Aquatica are not nearly as interesting, thrilling, or imaginative as those of its competitors, and aside from whisking you through a dolphin tank, they don't break any new ground. Also, all the slides except HooRoo Run have you launching yourself down a black hole, making every ride seem like the one before it. Dark slides are an essential part of every water-park lineup, but to have all slides dark save one makes for a very homogenized experience.

In addition to the slides, Aquatica offers side-by-side wave pools, **Cutback Cove** and **Big Surf Shores.** This arrangement allows one cove to serve up body-surfing waves while the other puts out gently bobbing floating waves. A spacious beach arrayed around the coves is the park's primary sunning venue. Shady spots, courtesy of beach umbrellas, ring the perimeter of the area for the sun-sensitive.

Loggerhead Lane and **Roa's Rapids** are the two floating streams. The former is a slow and gentle tube journey that circumnavigates the Tassie's Twisters slide. Its claim to fame is a section of the float where a Plexiglas tunnel passes through the Fish Grotto, a tank populated by hundreds of exotic tropical fish. Unique to Aquatica, Roa's Rapids is a much longer course with a very swift current. (The other water parks have floating creeks, but they're leisurely affairs where you can fall asleep in your tube.) Buoyancy vests are available, but most adults float or swim the stream. The name notwithstanding, there are no rapids, but the flow is constricted from time to time, considerably increasing the already fast speed of the current. There's only one place to get in and out, so if you miss the takeout, you're in for another lap.

When it comes to children's water attractions, Aquatica more than equals the other area parks. In the back of the park, to the left of the wave pools, is **Kata's Kookaburra Cove,** featuring a wading pool and slides for the preschool crowd. But the real pièce de résistance is Walkabout Waters. If you have children under age 10, this alone may be worth the price of admission. Located in a calf-deep 15,000-square-foot pool, it's an immense three-story interactive playground set with slides, stairs, rope bridges, landings, and more. Water sprays, spritzes, pulsates, and plops at you from every conceivable angle. Randomly placed plastic squirting devices allow kids to take aim at unsuspecting adults, but the kids disperse quickly when either of two huge buckets dumps hundreds of gallons of water down on the entire structure. It's impossible not to get wet. It's also impossible not to have fun.

As at the other water parks, there are lockers, towels, wheelchairs, and strollers to rent, gift shops to browse, and places to eat. The three restaurants are **WaterStone Grill,** offering specialty sandwiches, fried fish, wraps, and salads; **Banana Beach Cookout,** an all-you-can-eat venue dishing up burgers, hot dogs, and chicken; and **Mango Market,** a diminutive eatery serving pizza, wraps, and salads. WaterStone Grill and Mango Market serve beer.

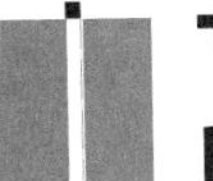

TYPHOON LAGOON *versus* BLIZZARD BEACH

MANY WALT DISNEY WORLD GUESTS aren't interested in leaving the World. For them, the question is: which is better, Typhoon Lagoon or Blizzard Beach? Our readers answer.

A mother of four from Winchester, Virginia, gives her opinion:

> *At Blizzard Beach, the family raft ride is great,* [but] *the kids' area is poorly designed. As a parent, when you walk your child to the top of a slide or the tube ride, they are lost to your vision as they go down because of the fake snowdrifts. There are no direct ways down to the end of the slides, so little ones are left standing unsupervised*

[while] *parents scramble down from the top. The Typhoon Lagoon kids' area is far superior in design.*

A couple from Woodridge, Illinois, writes:

We liked Blizzard Beach much more. It seems like they took everything from Typhoon Lagoon and made it better and faster. Summit Plummet was awesome—a total rush. Worth the half-hour wait. Toboggan and bobsled rides were really exciting—bobsled really throws you around. Family tube ride was really good—much better and much longer than at Typhoon Lagoon. Tube rides were great, especially in enclosed tube. If you have time to go to only one water park, go to Blizzard Beach.

unofficial **TIP**
If you're into slides, Blizzard Beach is tops among the Disney water parks.

A hungry reader from Aberdeen, New Jersey, complains:

At Blizzard Beach, there is only one main place to get food (most of the other spots are more for snacks). At lunchtime, it took almost 45 minutes to get some sandwiches and drinks.

A couple from Bowie, Maryland, didn't enjoy Summit Plummet:

The tallest and fastest slide at Blizzard Beach gave me a bunch of bruises. Even my husband hurt for a few days. It wasn't a fun ride, and we both agree that it wasn't worth waiting in line for. Basically, you drop until you hit the slide and that is why everyone comes off rubbing their butts. They say you go 60 mph on a 120-foot drop. I'll never do it again.

WHEN *to* GO

THE BEST WAY TO AVOID STANDING IN LINES is to visit the Disney water parks when they're less crowded. Our research, conducted over many weeks in the parks, indicates that tourists, not locals, make up the majority of visitors on any given day. And because weekends are popular travel days, the water parks tend to be less crowded then. In fact, of the weekend days we evaluated, the parks never reached full capacity; during the week, conversely, one or both parks closed every Thursday we monitored, and both closed at least once every other weekday. If you're a Disney resort guest, by all means use your morning Extra Magic Hours privileges; otherwise, we recommend going on a Monday or Friday.

unofficial **TIP**
During summer and holiday periods, Typhoon Lagoon and Blizzard Beach sometimes fill to capacity and close their gates before 11 a.m.

From a mom from Manlius, New York, here's what *crowded* means:

Because we had the [all-inclusive] *pass, we also visited Typhoon Lagoon, arriving before opening so we could stake out a shady spot. The kids loved it until the lines got long (11 a.m. to noon), but I hated it. It made Coney Island seem like a deserted island in the Bahamas. Floating on Castaway Creek was really unpleasant. Whirling around in a chlorinated, concrete ditch with some stranger's feet in my face, periodically getting squirted by waterguns, passing under cascades of cold water, and getting hung up by the crowd is not at all relaxing for me. My husband and I then decided to "bob" in the surf pool. After about ten minutes of being tossed around like corks in boiling water, he turned a little green around the gills, and we sought the peace of our shady little territory which, in our absence, had become much, much smaller. The kids, however, loved the body slides and the surf waves.*

A visitor from Middletown, New York, had a somewhat better experience at Typhoon Lagoon:

On our second trip [to Typhoon Lagoon], *we dispensed with the locker rental (having planned to stay for only the morning when it was least crowded), and at park's opening just took right off for the Storm Slides before the masses arrived—it was perfect! We must have ridden the slides at least five times before any kind of line built up, and then we were also able to ride the tube and raft rides (Keelhaul and Mayday Falls) in a similar uncrowded, quick fashion because everyone else was busy getting their lockers! We also experienced the Shark Reef, snorkeling three times with minimal crowds that day, because, I think, most people overlook this attraction. Shark Reef is fun and a great way to cool off since their water temp is well below the wave pool's.*

If your schedule is flexible, a good time to visit the swimming parks is midafternoon to late in the day when the weather has cleared after a storm. The parks usually close during bad weather. If the storm is prolonged, most guests leave for their hotels. When Typhoon Lagoon or Blizzard Beach reopens after inclement weather has passed, you almost have a whole park to yourself.

PLANNING YOUR DAY *at* DISNEY WATER PARKS

DISNEY WATER PARKS ARE ALMOST AS LARGE and elaborate as the major theme parks. You must be prepared for a lot of walking, exercise, sun, and jostling crowds. If your group really loves the water, schedule your visit early in your vacation. If you go at the beginning of your stay, you'll have more flexibility if you want to return.

To have a great day and beat the crowds, consider:

1. GETTING INFORMATION Call ☎ 407-828-3058 the night before you go to ask when your chosen park opens.

2. TO PICNIC OR NOT TO PICNIC Decide whether you want to carry a picnic lunch. Guests are permitted to take lunches and beverage coolers into the parks. However, alcoholic beverages and glass containers of any kind are forbidden.

3. GETTING STARTED If you are going to Blizzard Beach or Typhoon Lagoon, get up early, have breakfast, and arrive at the park 40 minutes before opening. If you have a car, drive instead of taking a Disney bus.

4. ATTIRE Wear your bathing suit under shorts and a T-shirt so you don't need to use lockers or dressing rooms. Regarding women's bathing suits, be advised that it is extremely common for women of all ages to part company with the top of their two-piece suit on the slides. Wear shoes. Paths are relatively easy on bare feet, but there's a lot of ground to cover. If you have tender feet, wear your shoes as you move around the park, removing them when you raft, slide, or go into the water. Shops in the parks sell sandals, Reef Runners, and other protective footwear that can be worn in and out of the water.

5. WHAT TO BRING You will need a towel, suntan lotion, and money. Since wallets and purses get in the way, lock them in your car's trunk or leave them at your hotel. Carry enough money for the day and your Disney resort ID (if you have one) in a plastic bag or Tupperware container. Though nowhere is completely safe, we felt very comfortable hiding our plastic money bags in our cooler. Nobody disturbed our stuff, and our cash was much easier to reach than if we'd stashed it in a locker across the park. If you're carrying a wad or you worry about money anyway, rent the locker.

A Canadian reader offers another option if you don't feel comfortable stashing your valuables:

> *As our admission was from* [an all-inclusive] *ticket, I was concerned about our multiday passes being stolen or lost, yet I didn't want the hassle of a locker. Once inside, I noticed several guests wearing small plastic boxes on strings around their necks, and was pleased to find these for sale in the gift shop. They are waterproof and available in two sizes for around $5, with the smallest being just big enough for passes, credit cards, and a bit of money. I would have spent nearly as much on a locker rental, so I was able to enjoy the rest of the day with peace of mind.*

6. WHAT NOT TO BRING Personal swim gear (fins, masks, rafts, and the like) isn't allowed. Everything you need is provided or available to rent. If you forget your towel, you can rent one (cheap!). If you forget your swimsuit or lotion, they're for sale. Personal flotation devices (life jackets) are available at no cost.

7. ADMISSIONS Buy your admission in advance or about 45 minutes before official opening time. If you're staying at a Disney property, you may be entitled to a discount; bring your hotel or campground ID. Guests staying five or more days should consider the Plus Pack add-on, which provides admission to both Disney swimming parks.

8. LOCKERS Rental lockers are $8 per day for a small one and $10 per day for a large, $5 of which is refunded when you return your key. Small lockers are roomy enough for one person or a couple, but a family will generally need a large locker. Though you can access your locker freely all day, not all lockers are conveniently located.

Getting a locker at Blizzard Beach or Typhoon Lagoon is truly competitive. When the gates open, guests race to the locker rental desk. Once there, the rental procedure is somewhat slow. If you aren't among the first in line, you can waste a lot of time waiting to be served. We recommend you skip the locker. Carry only as much cash as you will need for the day in a watertight container you can stash in your cooler. Ditto for personal items including watches and eyeglasses. With planning, you can manage nicely without the locker and save time and hassle in the bargain.

9. TUBES Tubes for bobbing on the waves, floating in the creeks, and riding the tube slides are available for free.

10. GETTING SETTLED Establish your base for the day. There are many beautiful sunning and lounging spots scattered throughout both Disney swimming parks. Arrive early, and you can almost have your pick. The breeze is best along the beaches of the surf pools at Blizzard Beach and Typhoon Lagoon. At Typhoon Lagoon, if there are children younger than age 6 in your party, choose an area to the left of Mount Mayday (ship on top) near the children's swimming area.

Also available are flat lounges (nonadjustable) and chairs (better for reading), shelters for guests who prefer shade, picnic tables, and a few hammocks.

The best spectator sport at Typhoon Lagoon is the bodysurfing in the surf pool. It's second only to being out there yourself. With this in mind, position yourself to have an unobstructed view of the waves.

If you've got money to burn, a handful of private covered seating areas are available at both Disney water parks for up to six guests at $250 per day. That includes your own lounge chairs, tables, towels, private lockers, a refillable drink mug, and a cabana boy who'll be at your beck and call. These seating areas are first-come, first-served.

unofficial **TIP**
When lines for the slides become intolerable, head for the surf or wave pool or the tube-floating streams.

11. A WORD ABOUT THE SLIDES Waterslides come in many shapes and sizes. Some are steep and vertical, some long and undulating. Some resemble corkscrews; others imitate the pool-and-drop nature of whitewater streams. Depending on the slide, swimmers ride mats, inner tubes, or rafts. On body slides, swimmers slosh to the bottom on the seat of their pants.

Modern traffic engineering bows to old-fashioned queuing. At the waterslides, it's just one person, one raft (or tube) at a time, and the swimmer on deck can't go until the person preceding him or her is safely out of the way. Thus, the slide's hourly capacity is limited compared with the continuously loading rides in the major theme parks. Because a certain interval between swimmers is required for safety, the only way to increase capacity is to increase the number of slides and rapids rides.

Though Typhoon Lagoon and Blizzard Beach are huge parks with many slides, they're overwhelmed almost daily by armies of guests. If your main reason for going to Typhoon Lagoon or Blizzard Beach is the slides, and you hate long lines, be among the first guests to enter the park. Go directly to the slides and ride as many times as you can before the park fills.

For maximum speed on a body slide, cross your legs at the ankles and cross your arms over your chest. When you take off, arch your back so almost all of your weight is on your shoulder blades and heels (the less contact with the surface, the less resistance). Steer by shifting most of your upper-body weight onto one shoulder blade. For top speed on turns, weight the shoulder blade on the outside of each curve. If you want to go slow, distribute your weight equally as if you were lying on your back in bed. For curving slides, maximize speed by hitting the entrance to each curve high and exiting the curve low.

Some slides and rapids have a minimum height requirement. Riders for Humunga Kowabunga at Typhoon Lagoon and for Slush Gusher and Summit Plummet at Blizzard Beach, for example, must be four feet tall. Pregnant women and persons with back problems or other health difficulties shouldn't ride.

12. FLOATING STREAMS Disney's Blizzard Beach and Typhoon Lagoon and the independent Wet 'n Wild offer mellow floating streams. A great idea, the floating streams are long, tranquil inner-tube rides that give you the illusion that you're doing something while you're being sedentary. For wimps, wussies, and exhausted people of all ages, floating streams are an answered prayer.

Disney's streams flow ever so slowly around the entire park, through caves, beneath waterfalls, past gardens, and under bridges. They offer a relaxing alternative to touring a park on foot.

Floating streams can be reached from several put-in and take-out points. There are never lines; just wade into the creek and plop into one of the inner tubes floating by. Ride the current all the way around, or get out at any exit. It takes 30 to 35 minutes to float the full circuit.

Predictably, there will be guests on whom the subtlety of floating streams is lost. They'll be screaming and splashing. Let them pass, stopping a few moments, if needed, to distance yourself from them.

13. LUNCH If you didn't bring a picnic, you can buy food. Quality is comparable to fast food; prices (as you might expect) are a bit high.

14. MORE OPTIONS If you really are a water puppy, consider returning to your hotel for a heat-of-the-day nap and coming back to the water park for some early-evening swimming. Special lighting after dusk makes Typhoon Lagoon and Blizzard Beach enchanting; crowds tend to be lighter, too. If you leave the park and want to return, keep your admission ticket and have your hand stamped. If you're staying in a hotel served by Disney buses, older children can return on their own to the water parks, giving Mom and Dad a little private quiet time.

unofficial **TIP**
Because Florida is so flat, approaching weather can be seen from atop the slide platforms at the swimming parks. Especially if you're dependent on Disney buses, leave the park earlier, rather than later, when you see a storm moving in.

15. BAD WEATHER Thunderstorms are common in Florida. On summer afternoons, storms can be a daily occurrence. Water parks close during a storm. Most storms, however, are short-lived, allowing the water park to resume normal operations. If a storm is severe and prolonged, it can cause a great deal of inconvenience. In addition to the park's closing, guests compete aggressively for shelter, and Disney-resort guests may have to joust for seats on a bus back to the hotel.

We recommend you monitor the local weather forecast the day before you go, checking again in the morning before leaving for the water park. Scattered thundershowers are to be expected, but moving storm fronts are to be avoided.

16. ENDURANCE The water parks are large and require almost as much walking as one of the theme parks. Add to this wave surfing, swimming, and all the climbing required to reach the slides, and you'll be pooped by day's end. Unless you spend your hours like a lizard on a rock, don't expect to return to the hotel with much energy. Consider something low-key for the evening. You'll probably want to hit the hay early.

17. LOST CHILDREN AND LOST ADULTS It's easier to lose a child or become separated from your party at one of the water parks than it is at a major theme park. Upon arrival, pick a very specific place to meet in the event you are separated. If you split up on purpose, set times for checking in. Lost-children stations at the water parks are so out of the way that neither you nor your lost child will find them without help from a Disney cast member. Explain to your children how to recognize cast members (by their distinctive name tags) and how to ask for help.

PART SEVENTEEN

BEYOND *the* PARKS

DOWNTOWN DISNEY

DOWNTOWN DISNEY IS A SHOPPING, DINING, AND entertainment development strung out along the banks of Lake Buena Vista. On the far right is the **Downtown Disney Marketplace;** on the far left is **Disney's West Side.** See pages 748 and 749 for a map of the area.

DOWNTOWN DISNEY MARKETPLACE

ALTHOUGH THE MARKETPLACE OFFERS interactive fountains, a couple of playgrounds, a lakeside amphitheater, and watercraft rentals, it is primarily a shopping and dining venue. The centerpiece of shopping is the 50,000-square-foot **World of Disney,** the largest store in the world selling Disney-trademark merchandise.

World of Disney Kids stocks a wide variety of clothing, plush toys, and collectibles, and **Disney Tails** offers an assortment of pet products as well as baked treats. Another noteworthy retailer is the **LEGO Imagination Center,** showcasing a number of huge and unbelievable sculptures made entirely of LEGO "bricks." Spaceships, sea serpents, sleeping tourists, and dinosaurs are just a few of the sculptures on display. **Once Upon a Toy** is a toys, games, and collectibles superstore. Rounding out the selection are stores specializing in resort wear, athletic attire and gear, Christmas decorations, Disney art and collectibles, and handmade craft items. Most retail establishments are open from 9:30 a.m. until 11:30 p.m. Detailed coverage of shopping opportunities can be found in Part Eighteen, Shopping in and out of Walt Disney World.

Rainforest Cafe is the headliner restaurant at the Marketplace. There is also **Cap'n Jack's Restaurant, Wolfgang Puck Express,** a soda fountain, a gourmet-sandwich shop, and a **McDonald's.** Full-service restaurants are profiled in Part Ten, Dining in and around Walt Disney World.

WHITHER PLEASURE ISLAND?

FORMERLY DISNEY'S NIGHTTIME-ENTERTAINMENT COMPLEX, Pleasure Island effectively shut down in September 2008 when its six admission-charging nightclubs closed. Disney plans to replace these with a more family-oriented mix of shops and restaurants. Remaining open during the transition are **Fulton's Crab House** and **Portobello** restaurants, along with **Raglan Road,** an Irish pub and restaurant featuring live Celtic music; **Fuego by Sosa Cigars,** a posh cigar bar; **Curl by Sammy Duval,** a surf shop; a **Harley-Davidson** apparel store; and all outdoor food-and-beverage locations.

DISNEY'S WEST SIDE

THE WEST SIDE IS THE NEWEST ADDITION to Downtown Disney and offers a broad range of entertainment, dining, and shopping. Restaurants include the **House of Blues,** which serves Cajun specialties; **Planet Hollywood,** offering movie memorabilia and basic American fare; **Bongos Cuban Cafe,** serving Cuban favorites; and **Wolfgang Puck Cafe,** featuring California cuisine. All four West Side restaurants are profiled in Part Ten, Dining in and around Walt Disney World.

West Side shopping is some of the most interesting in Disney World. For starters, there's **Pop Gallery,** selling high-end paintings and sculpture. Other shops include a cigar shop, a magic shop, and a designer-sunglasses studio.

In the entertainment department, there is **DisneyQuest,** an interactive theme park contained in a building; the **House of Blues,** a concert and dining venue; and a 24-screen **AMC** movie theater. The West Side is also home to **Cirque du Soleil**'s *La Nouba,* an amazing production show with a cast of more than 70 performers and musicians. The House of Blues concert hall and *La Nouba* are described in Part Nineteen, Nightlife in and out of Walt Disney World. DisneyQuest is described in detail below.

DISNEYQUEST

FOR MORE THAN A DECADE, major theme parks have experimented with attractions based on motion-simulation and virtual-reality technologies. Among other things, these technologies have allowed thrill rides with the punch of a roller coaster to be engineered and operated in spaces as small as a one-car garage. Analogous to the computer industry, where the power of a room-filling mainframe is now available in an iPhone, Disney is pioneering the concept of a theme park in a box, or in the case of DisneyQuest, a modest five-story building.

Opened in 1998, DisneyQuest contains all the elements of the larger Disney theme parks. An entrance area facilitates your transition into the park environment and leads to the gateways of four distinct themed lands, here referred to as zones. As at other Disney parks, almost everything is included in the price of your admission.

It takes about two to five hours to experience DisneyQuest once you get in, depending on the crowd. Disney claims to limit the number of guests admitted to ensure that each person has a positive experience. Well, so does the Super Bowl, and that's how big the crowd feels at DisneyQuest. Once the complex hits capacity, newly arriving guests are lined up outside to wait until departing guests make some room.

unofficial **TIP**
Weekday mornings are the least crowded times to visit DisneyQuest.

DisneyQuest is aimed at a youthful audience, say, 8 to 35 years of age, though younger and older patrons will enjoy much of what it offers. Those who haunt the video arcades at shopping malls will be most at home here. And similar to what occurs at most malls, when late afternoon turns to evening, the median age at DisneyQuest also rises toward adolescents and teens who have been released from parental supervision for a while.

You begin your experience in the **Departure Lobby,** adjacent to admission sales. From the Departure Lobby you enter a "Cyberlator," a "transitional attraction" (read: elevator) hosted by the Genie from *Aladdin,* that delivers you to an entrance plaza called **Ventureport.** From here you can enter the four zones. As in the larger parks, each zone is distinctively themed. Some zones cover more than one floor, so, looking around, you can see things going on both above and below you. The four zones, in no particular order, are **Explore Zone, Score Zone, Create Zone,** and **Replay Zone.**

Though most kids and adolescents aren't going to care, the zone layout at DisneyQuest may confuse adults trying to orient themselves. Don't count on trapping certain kids in certain zones either, or planning a rendezvous inside one without designating a specific location. Each zone spreads out over multiple levels, with stairways, elevators, slides, and walkways linking them in a variety of ways. Still, as we said, the labyrinthine design of the place won't bother most youngsters, who are usually happy just to wander (or dash madly) between games and rides.

Admission to DisneyQuest is $43 for adults and $36 for children ages 3 to 9, including tax. The facility is open Sunday through Thursday from 11:30 a.m. to 10 p.m.; Friday and Saturday from 11:30 a.m. to 11 p.m. For more information, call ☎ 407-828-4600.

Explore Zone

The gateway to Explore Zone is the tiger's-head cave from *Aladdin.* You can descend to the attractions area on a 150-foot corkscrew slide or use more traditional means like elevators or ramps. The headline attraction in Explore Zone is the **Virtual Jungle Cruise,** in which you paddle a six-person raft. The raft is a motion simulator perched on top of blue air bags that replicate the motion of water. Responding to the film of the river projected before you, you can choose among several routes through the rapids. The motion simulator responds to sensors on your paddle, so the ride you experience simulates the course you choose. As if navigating the river isn't enough, man-eating dinosaurs and a cataclysmic comet are tossed in for good measure. Another Explore Zone attraction, **Aladdin's Magic Carpet Ride,** is a virtual-reality trip through the streets of Agrabah. On **Pirates of the Caribbean,** you fight pirates attacking your ship. The entire battle takes place in 3-D on a motion-base platform, which shudders with every hit by the pirates' cannonballs.

Score Zone

Here you pass through a slash in a giant comic book to enter a themed area based on comic-book characters and competition. The big deals here are enlarged, high-tech versions of electronic and video games where you pit your skill and reflexes against other players. The headliner is **Mighty Ducks Pinball Slam,** where you stand atop a mammoth hockey puck. By manipulating a joystick, you control the motion of your puck as it bounces around a virtual-reality pinball machine. In **Ride the Comix,** you don virtual-reality headgear to ride off into comic-book scenes and do battle with archvillains. In **Invasion! An Alien ExtraTERRORestrial Encounter,** you and your friends team up to steer a spaceship over an alien planet, rescue the human colonists there, and destroy the enemy.

Create Zone

A digital artist's palette serves as the entrance to Create Zone. Featured here is **CyberSpace Mountain,** an attraction where you can design your own roller coaster—including 360-degree loops—and then go for a virtual-reality motion-simulator ride on your creation. Also in the Create Zone are **Animation Academy,** a sort of crash tutorial on Disney animation, and **Magic Mirror,** where you can perform virtual plastic surgery on yourself.

Replay Zone

Replay Zone draws its theme from a 1950s view of the future. Basically, it's three levels of classic midway games with a few futuristic twists. The balls on the **Skeeball** games, for example, glow in the dark. Winners of the various games earn redemption tickets, which can be redeemed for midway-type prizes. The pièce de résistance of Replay Zone is **Buzz Lightyear's AstroBlasters,** a fancy version of bumper cars. Here, guests pilot two-person bumper bubbles that suck up grapefruit-sized balls from the floor and fire them from an air cannon at other vehicles. Direct hits cause the other vehicles to spin momentarily out of control.

Reader response to DisneyQuest is very mixed, as evidenced by the following comments.

From a Pennsylvania family with kids ages 11 and 13:

Our only really big disappointment was DisneyQuest. My husband and daughters paid $32 to get in because the guy at the window told us that fee covered nearly all the experiences. Once inside, they found that at least half the stuff they wanted to do cost mega-extra-bucks. It's truly an offensive deal for people who have already spent scads in their darned parks.

But for a Cleveland family of five, DisneyQuest was a slam dunk:

Your description and reader feedback had us a little skeptical. But with another cold day on hand, we gave it a shot. If you have right-brained (creative) *kids, you can't miss. Your book said two to three hours for DQ. We had dinner reservations that forced a cutoff at seven hours, otherwise we could have pulled an all-nighter with them! The interactive stuff was fascinating. I think DQ provides parents the best chance to see their kids' brains and personalities in action.*

A family from Columbia, Maryland, offers this advice to parents with babies and toddlers:

Alert your readers to bring a baby carrier–backpack to DisneyQuest. You're there for several hours, and absolutely no strollers are allowed in the entire building.

ESPN WIDE WORLD *of* SPORTS COMPLEX

THIS 220-ACRE, STATE-OF-THE-ART competition and training center consists of a 9,500-seat ballpark, a fieldhouse, and dedicated venues for baseball, softball, tennis, track and field, beach volleyball, and 27 other sports. From Little League Baseball to rugby to beach volleyball, the complex hosts a mind-boggling calendar of professional and amateur competitions.

In late winter and early spring, the complex is the spring-training home of the Atlanta Braves. While Disney guests are welcome at the ESPN Wide World of Sports as paid spectators (prices vary according to event), none of the facilities are available for guests unless they are participants in a scheduled, organized competition. To learn which sporting events, including Major League Baseball exhibition games, are scheduled during your visit, call ☎ 407-939-GAME (4263) or check the online calendar at **www.disneyworldsports.com.**

Admission is $13 adults, $10 children ages 3 to 9. Some events carry an extra charge. Counter-service and full-service dining are available, but there's no lodging on-site.

Located off Osceola Parkway, on Victory Way, ESPN Wide World of Sports Complex has its own parking lot and is accessible via the Disney Transportation System.

WALT DISNEY WORLD SPEEDWAY

ADJACENT TO THE TRANSPORTATION and ticket center parking lot sits the Walt Disney World Speedway, a one-mile tri-oval course. If you're a NASCAR fan, check out the **Richard Petty Driving Experience,** where you can ride in a two-seater stock car for $109 (3 laps) or learn to drive one for $449 (8 laps), $849 (18 laps), or $1,299 (30 laps). For information call ☎ 800-BE-PETTY or check out **www.1800bepetty.com.**

Also at the speedway is the **Indy Racing Experience.** Usually starting in the afternoon when the Richard Petty folks have finished, this experience features sleeker, faster open-wheeled cars like those seen in the Indianapolis 500. You can ride in a modified two-seat Indy car or drive one of the single-seat cars. Cost is $109 to ride (3 laps) or $399 to drive (8 laps). For information call ☎ 317-243-7171, ext. 106, or visit **www.indyracingexperience.com.**

For either driving course, you'll be paired with an experienced instructor who'll show you how the car handles, how the various gauges and pedals work, and most importantly, where to change into the flame-retardant driving suit you'll be wearing. If you choose to drive, the instructor will drive a pace car ahead of you and (we're told) will happily go as fast as you can demonstrate you're comfortable with—up to 180 mph in the Indy cars.

Both the Richard Petty and Indy experiences are by reservation only. Plan on arriving an hour before your appointment to fill out paperwork and go through an orientation session. To drive any of these cars, you must be age 18 or older, have a valid driver's license, and be able to operate a stick shift; for the Indy course, you must also be less than 6 feet 5 inches tall and weigh less than 250 pounds. Richard Petty riders must be at least age 16; Indy riders must meet the same age, height, and weight requirements as drivers. The Indy Racing Experience is closed around some major holidays and when Disney hosts PGA golf events, so check the Web site for schedules before you go.

WALT DISNEY WORLD GOLF

RECENT YEARS HAVE BROUGHT big changes to Walt Disney World golf. Disney is one of the longest-running venues for the PGA Tour, at nearly four decades, and in 2007 the tournament here, the Children's Miracle Network Classic, was bumped to the coveted final week of the tour calendar, where it closes out the golf season in mid-November. Until 2007, the resort had six golf courses, all expertly designed and meticulously maintained. Now there are five, since the closing of the Bonnet Creek Golf Club's **Eagle Pines** course in 2007, and while this total will remain, one new course is coming and one more is closing. The **Magnolia,** the **Palm,** and the **Oak Trail,** across Floridian Way from the Polynesian Resort, will be unaffected. They envelop the Shades of Green recreational complex, and the pro shops and support facilities adjoin the Shades of Green hotel (for active and retired military personnel only). Also to remain is the **Lake Buena Vista Golf Course** at Saratoga Springs, near the Downtown Disney Marketplace and across the lake from the redeveloping Pleasure Island.

At **Bonnet Creek Golf Club,** near the Fort Wilderness Campground, golf is being displaced by a 900-acre luxury resort, anchored by a Four Seasons hotel and a 450-acre retail, dining, and lodging district. The **Osprey Ridge** course is slated to be replaced by a new course that will anchor a golf community of private homes. Osprey Ridge was originally scheduled to close in mid-2010, but with the economy having put a damper on the Four Seasons project, the course is now expected to remain open until 2012 at the earliest.

The Magnolia and Palm have completed substantial renovations and upgrades over the past few years. These two 36-hole courses host the Children's Miracle Network Classic. Oak Trail is a nine-hole course for beginners. The other four courses are designed for the midhandicap player and, while interesting, are quite forgiving. All courses are popular, with morning tee times at a premium, especially from January through April. In addition to the golf courses, there are driving ranges and putting greens at each location.

Peak season for all courses is January to May, and off-season is May through October; however, summer is peak season for the nongolf

unofficial **TIP**
To avoid the crowds, play on a Monday, Tuesday, or Wednesday, and sign up for a late-afternoon tee time.

parts of Walt Disney World, including the hotels. Off-season and afternoon twilight rates are available. Carts are required (except at Oak Trail) and are included in the greens fee. Tee times may be reserved 90 days in advance by Disney-resort guests and 60 days in advance by day guests with a credit card. Proper golf attire, including spikeless shoes, is required. A collared shirt and Bermuda-length shorts or slacks meet the requirements.

Besides the ability to book tee times further in advance, guests of Walt Disney World–owned resorts get other benefits that may sway a golfer's lodging decision. These include discounted greens fees, free club rental, and charge privileges. The single most important, and least known, benefit is the provision of free round-trip taxi transportation between the golf courses and your hotel, which lets you avoid moving your car or dragging your clubs on Disney buses. The cabs, which make access to the courses much simpler, are paid by vouchers happily supplied to hotel guests.

Note: In the following Disney golf profiles (except for Oak Trail), we've listed two sets of fees for resort guests, day visitors, and twilight play. Lower fees reflect weekdays for the 2009–2010 off-season (May 11, 2009, through January 14, 2010); higher fees reflect weekends. Fees for replaying the same course on the same day (if space is available) are half the full rate.

Palm Golf Course ★★★★

ESTABLISHED 1970 DESIGNER Joe Lee STATUS Resort

1950 West Magnolia/Palm Drive, Lake Buena Vista, FL 32830;
☎ 407-WDW-GOLF

Tees • **Blue: 7,010 yards, par 72, USGA 73.9, slope 138**
• **White: 6,461 yards, par 72, USGA 71.6, slope 130**
• **Gold: 6,029 yards, par 72, USGA 69.5, slope 126**
• **Red: 5,311 yards, par 72, USGA 71.2, slope 123**

Fees Resort guest, \$89/\$99; day visitor, \$104/\$114; twilight special: \$59/\$69.

Facilities Pro shop, GPS, driving range, practice green, locker rooms, food and beverage cart, and club and shoe rentals.

Comments Designed by Joe Lee, this is Disney's best course. Home to a PGA Tour event, the Palm has numerous lakes coming into play on nine holes, and sand everywhere, with 94 hazards. The highlight, however, is a set of excellent greens—a real surprise given the heavy volume of play. The defining characteristic is a set of holes where water separates tees from landing areas and landing areas from greens, a wet take on desert-style target golf. The signature 18th, with its island green, caps a fine set of finishing holes and has been ranked as high as fourth in difficulty among all holes on the PGA Tour's many venues. But four sets of well-spaced tees make the course playable for all abilities.

Magnolia Golf Course ★★★½

ESTABLISHED 1970 **DESIGNER** Joe Lee **STATUS** Resort

1950 West Magnolia/Palm Drive, Lake Buena Vista, FL 32830; ☎ 407-WDW-GOLF

Tees
- **Black: 7,516 yards, par 72, USGA 76.5, slope 140**
- **Blue: 7,182 yards, par 72, USGA 74.6, slope 136**
- **White: 6,642 yards, par 72, USGA 72.1, slope 134**
- **Gold: 6,091 yards, par 72, USGA 69.1, slope 127**
- **Red: 5,232 yards, par 72, USGA 70.1, slope 127**

Fees Resort guest, $89/$99; day visitor, $104/$114; twilight special: $59/$69.

Facilities Pro shop, GPS, driving range, practice green, locker rooms, food and beverage cart, and club and shoe rentals.

Comments Another fine Joe Lee creation, Magnolia is Disney's longest course and features a whopping 97 bunkers, including the famous one in the shape of Mickey Mouse's head. But the layout is slightly less challenging than the Palm's. Ten holes were lengthened and all greens resurfaced with TifEagle turf in 2005 as part of an "extreme makeover." This refurbishment added 300 yards to the already long course, and at more than 7,500 yards, it will be the longest most guests ever have the opportunity to play. Like the Palm, this course hosts the PGA Tour.

Osprey Ridge Golf Course ★★★½

ESTABLISHED 1992 **DESIGNER** Tom Fazio **STATUS** Resort

3451 Golf View Drive, Lake Buena Vista, FL 32830; ☎ 407-WDW-GOLF

Tees
- **Talon: 7,101 yards, par 72, USGA 74.4, slope 131**
- **Crest: 6,680 yards, par 72, USGA 72.3, slope 129**
- **Wings: 6,103 yards, par 72, USGA 69.5, slope 127**
- **Feathers: 5,402 yards, par 72, USGA 71.3, slope 127**

Fees Resort guest, $89/$99; day visitor, $104/$114; twilight special: $59/$69.

Facilities Pro shop, GPS, driving range, practice green, locker rooms, Sand Trap Bar & Grill, food and beverage cart, and club and shoe rentals.

Comments This Tom Fazio layout is a thoroughly modern course that involved a large amount of earth-moving in its construction. Its main characteristics are large, rolling mounds and elevated tees and greens. The greens are huge, almost to the point of being bizarre, making them easy to hit but leaving approaches at four-putt distances where you almost cannot hit the ball hard enough to get it to the hole. *Note:* Osprey Ridge is projected to close in 2012 to make way for a new luxury resort–golf course project.

Lake Buena Vista Golf Course ★★★

ESTABLISHED 1971 **DESIGNER** Joe Lee **STATUS** Resort

2200 Club Lake Drive, Lake Buena Vista, FL 32830; ☎ 407-WDW-GOLF

Tees
- **Blue: 6,749 yards, par 72, USGA 73, slope 133**
- **White: 6,264 yards, par 72, USGA 70.1, slope 129**
- **Gold: 5,919 yards, par 72, USGA 68.6, slope 123**
- **Red: 5,194 yards, par 73, USGA 69.9, slope 122**

Fees Resort guest, $89/$99; day visitor, $104/$114; twilight special: $59/$69.

Facilities Pro shop, GPS, driving range, practice green, locker rooms, snack bar, food and beverage cart, and club and shoe rentals.

Comments There are several memorable holes here, but this layout is the only one at Disney with housing on it—a lot of housing—which detracts from the golf experience. The course is geographically unique among the other layouts, tucked behind Saratoga Springs, and has a swampy feel reminiscent of the area's pre-Disney wetlands, with trees dripping Spanish moss. Narrow fairways and small greens emphasize accuracy over length.

Oak Trail Golf Course ★★½

ESTABLISHED 1980 DESIGNER Ron Garl STATUS Resort

1950 West Magnolia/Palm Drive, Lake Buena Vista, FL 32830;
☎ 407-WDW-GOLF

Tees • **White: 2,913 yards, par 36**
• **Red: 2,532 yards, par 36**

Fees Adult, $38; junior (age 17 and under), $20. Pull carts, $6 (course is walking only). Replaying the course costs an additional $19 for adults and $10 for junior players.

Facilities Pro shop, driving range, practice green, locker rooms, food and beverage cart, and club and shoe rentals.

Comments This Ron Garl nine-holer is a "real" course, not an executive par-3 like many nine-hole designs. Geared toward introducing children to the game, it also makes a good quick-fix or warm-up before a round, and the walking-only layout is the only such routing at Walt Disney World.

GOLF *beyond* WALT DISNEY WORLD

THE GREATER ORLANDO AREA has enough high-quality courses to rival better-known golfing Meccas such as Scottsdale, Arizona, and Palm Springs, California. But unlike these destinations, with their endless private country clubs, Orlando is unique because almost all its courses are open for some sort of public play. Of the many courses and resorts in the area, one stands head and shoulders above the rest, especially because it actually abuts Walt Disney World. Not only is the location of this course excellent, but the sprawling 1,500-acre **Grand Cypress Resort** is also superb in every way, with top-notch lodging, dining, and grounds, and an enormous fantasy-pool complex. But the standout feature is the golf, which would be worth a trip regardless of where the resort was located. The facilities are first-rate, from the luxurious clubhouse with its free shoe shines to the computerized GPS systems on the carts. The golf club is also home to an excellent instructional facility, the **Grand Cypress Academy of Golf.** Because of its many amenities and wonderful location, the Grand Cypress is one of the priciest resorts in Orlando—but because only guests can play the courses, you should consider making the investment.

Grand Cypress Golf Club ★★★★½ North/East/South Courses

ESTABLISHED 1984 **DESIGNER** Jack Nicklaus **STATUS** Resort (Guests Only)

1 North Jacaranda, Orlando, FL 32836; ☎ 877-330-7377 or 407-239-4700; www.grandcypress.com

Tees NORTH/SOUTH TEES

- **Gold: 6,993 yards, par 72, USGA 74.4, slope 136**
- **Blue: 6,454 yards, par 72, USGA 72, slope 131**
- **White: 5,943 yards, par 72, USGA 69.3, slope 123**
- **Red: 5,328 yards, par 72, USGA 71.2, slope 120**

NORTH/EAST TEES

- **Gold: 6,955 yards, par 72, USGA 74.2, slope 135**
- **Blue: 6,374 yards, par 72, USGA 70.9, slope 131**
- **White: 5,878 yards, par 72, USGA 68.7, slope 125**
- **Red: 5,056 yards, par 72, USGA 69.4, slope 117**

SOUTH/EAST TEES

- **Gold: 6,906 yards, par 72, USGA 73.8, slope 135**
- **Blue: 6,382 yards, par 72, USGA 71.1, slope 129**
- **White: 5,821 yards, par 72, USGA 68.4, slope 122**
- **Red: 5,126 yards, par 72, USGA 69.8, slope 117**

Fees $175–$190 ($120 in summer).

Facilities Pro shop, driving range, practice greens, locker rooms, restaurant, food and beverage cart, carts equipped with GPS, and club rentals ($65) and shoe rentals ($20).

Comments This course can be played in three different 18-hole combinations, but the South (renovated by Jack Nicklaus in the summer of 2007) is the very best nine at the resort, so try to book either North/South or South/East. The North/South combination hosted the LPGA Tournament of Champions from 1994 to 1996, as well as the PGA Tour Skills Challenge and the Shark Shootout. The course is one of the most beautiful in Orlando, and water is found on 13 of the holes, creating additional peril. There are many unique and interesting holes, several with true risk–reward choices such as shortcuts over lakes. The undulating greens are guarded by pot bunkers and grass depressions and are kept in superb shape. Unlike the New Course, this group of courses provides very few opportunities to bump and run the ball onto the green.

Grand Cypress Golf Club, New Course ★★★★

ESTABLISHED 1988 **DESIGNER** Jack Nicklaus **STATUS** Resort (Guests Only)

1 North Jacaranda, Orlando, FL 32836; ☎ 877-330-7377 or 407-239-4700; www.grandcypress.com

Tees

- **Blue: 6,773 yards, par 72, USGA 71.5, slope 122**
- **White: 6,181 yards, par 72, USGA 69.1, slope 119**
- **Red: 5,314 yards, par 72, USGA 69.7, slope 113**

Fees $175–$190 ($120 in summer).

Facilities Pro shop, driving range, practice greens, locker rooms, restaurant, food and beverage cart, carts equipped with GPS, and club and shoe rentals.

Comments The New Course is Jack Nicklaus's homage to the famous Old Course at St. Andrews, Scotland, the birthplace of golf. The first and last two holes are near-replicas of those at the Old Course; other features, such as the famous Swilcan Bridge and some of the huge bunkers, are re-created here. In between are Nicklaus's original holes, done in a links style, with double greens; pot bunkers; tall rough; and wide, hard fairways. As on most Scottish links courses, there are no trees, and the wind will play havoc with your shots when it is blowing. If you've never had a chance to play Scottish courses, the New is a reasonable facsimile that captures the spirit and history of the sport's earliest form.

OTHER STANDOUT COURSES IN ORLANDO

AMONG THE MANY PUBLIC COURSES throughout the area, a handful stand out and are worth leaving Walt Disney World to play. Good-quality golf resorts such as **Grenelefe** and **Mission Inn** are well outside Orlando, but the following are quite convenient to the theme parks.

CHAMPIONSGATE GOLF CLUB

THREE MILES FROM WALT DISNEY WORLD and close to Celebration lies one of the city's more recent additions. The complex includes an Omni hotel, but the centerpieces of the $800 million, 1,500-acre facility are the two Greg Norman–designed courses. For more information, visit **www.championsgategolf.com.**

ChampionsGate International Course ★★★★

ESTABLISHED 2000 DESIGNER Greg Norman STATUS Public

1400 Masters Boulevard, ChampionsGate, FL 33896; ☎ 888-558-9301 or 407-787-4653

Tees
- **Black: 7,363 yards, par 72, USGA 76.8, slope 143**
- **Blue: 6,792 yards, par 72, USGA 74.1, slope 137**
- **White: 6,239 yards, par 72, USGA 71.5, slope 132**
- **Gold: 5,618 yards, par 72, USGA 68, slope 117**

Fees $78 weekdays, $99 weekends. Discounts available for Omni hotel guests and Florida residents, changing throughout the year.

Facilities Pro shop, driving range, practice greens, locker rooms, restaurant, GPS-equipped carts, beverage cart, and club and shoe rentals.

Comments The tougher and more highly ranked of ChampionsGate's two layouts, the International lives up to its name by re-creating the feel of the championship courses of the British Isles. Laid out in a links style, the course has carpetlike fairways framed by the stark, unfinished look of brown dunes, mounds, and severe pot bunkers. From the tips, it is one of the state's most challenging courses, with a USGA rating of 76.8.

ChampionsGate National Course ★★★½

ESTABLISHED 2000 DESIGNER Greg Norman STATUS Public

1400 Masters Boulevard, ChampionsGate, FL 33896; ☎ 888-558-9301 or 407-787-4653

Tees
- **Black: 7,128 yards, par 72, USGA 75.2, slope 138**
- **Blue: 6,427 yards, par 72, USGA 71.9, slope 133**
- **White: 5,937 yards, par 72, USGA 69.1, slope 124**
- **Gold: 5,150 yards, par 72, USGA 65.3, slope 117**

Fees $68 weekdays, $88 weekends. Discounts available for Omni hotel guests and Florida residents, changing throughout the year.

Facilities Pro shop, driving range, practice greens, locker rooms, restaurant, GPS-equipped carts, beverage cart, and club and shoe rentals.

Comments The kinder, gentler course at ChampionsGate, the National is a resort-style layout, which ambles through 200 acres of citrus groves in a traditional parkland routing with far less water than the International. Deep greens welcome bump-and-run shots, and the length is manageable from every set of tees.

ORANGE COUNTY NATIONAL GOLF CENTER

FIVE MILES NORTH OF DISNEY, in Winter Garden, lies Orlando's premier daily-fee public facility, winner of numerous industry awards and consistently named among the nation's top public clubs by most golf publications. Forty-five holes (including a nine-hole short course) and one of the country's best practice facilities occupy 922 verdant acres, without homes or other distractions—just pure golf. It is also easily the region's best value, with inexpensive on-site lodging and two-night, three-round packages that run from $164 to a high-season maximum of $360 (prices include daily breakfasts and free play on the nine-hole course). For more information, visit **www.ocngolf.com.**

Panther Lake ★★★★½

ESTABLISHED 1997 **DESIGNERS** Isao Aoki, David Harman, and Phil Ritson **STATUS** Public

16301 Phil Ritson Way, Winter Garden, FL 34787; ☎ 888-727-3672 or 407-656-2626

Tees
- **Q-School: 7,350 yards, par 72, USGA 76, slope 139**
- **Championship: 6,849 yards, par 72, USGA 73.2, slope 132**
- **Back: 6,394 yards, par 72, USGA 71.2, slope 127**
- **Middle: 6,011 yards, par 72, USGA 69.2, slope 120**
- **Forward: 5,319 yards, par 72, USGA 70.8, slope 123**

Fees $39–$85, varying by time of day, day of week. and time of year.

Facilities Lodging, GPS, pro shop, driving range, practice greens, locker rooms, restaurant, beverage cart, and club and shoe rentals.

Comments Panther Lake was the nation's first course designed to showcase 18 signature holes, and no expense was spared to make the course beautiful, just as none is spared to keep it in excellent condition. The front nine is carved from Florida wetlands with water at every turn, while the much-different back has a Carolinas-like style with surprising elevation changes, stands of pines and oaks, and hard-to-hold greens emphasizing accuracy.

Crooked Cat ★★★★

ESTABLISHED 1997 **DESIGNERS** Isao Aoki, David Harman, and Phil Ritson **STATUS** Public

16301 Phil Ritson Way, Winter Garden, FL 34787; ☎ 888-727-3672 or 407-656-2626

Tees
- **Q-School: 7,493 yards, par 72, USGA 76.6, slope 139**
- **Championship: 6,927 yards, par 72, USGA 73.7, slope 132**
- **Back: 6,432 yards, par 72, USGA 71.4, slope 126**
- **Middle: 6,020 yards, par 72, USGA 66.8, slope 122**
- **Forward: 5,112 yards, par 72, USGA 69.6 slope 120**

Fees $39–$79, varying by time of day, day of week, and time of year.

Facilities Lodging, GPS, pro shop, driving range, practice greens, locker rooms, restaurant, beverage cart, and club and shoe rentals.

Comments Variety is the spice of life, and this partner to the very modern Panther Lake is a throwback to Scottish-style links courses, with few trees, wide fairways, and heather mixed in the rough. Large, sloped greens welcome bump-and-run shots but are protected by deep bunkers of both grass and sand. Crooked Cat is as well maintained as its sibling.

GINN REUNION RESORT

THIS 2,300-ACRE RESORT and residential golf community has three courses, designed by Arnold Palmer, Tom Watson, and Jack Nicklaus. In 2007, the resort saw the addition of Annika Sorenstam's Annika Academy. (Sorenstam, now retired after the greatest career in women's golf, lives here part-time, shows up occasionally, and focuses on this single location.) Reunion is now the region's largest golf destination outside of Walt Disney World itself. For more information, visit **www.reunionresort.com.**

The Independence ★★★★

ESTABLISHED 2004 **DESIGNER** Tom Watson **STATUS** Resort (Guests Only)

1000 Reunion Way, Reunion, FL 34747; ☎ 888-418-9611 or 407-662-1100

Tees
- **Black: 7,154 yards, par 72, USGA 74.7, slope 140**
- **Gold: 6,697 yards, par 72, USGA 72.2, slope 131**
- **Blue: 6,319 yards, par 72, USGA 70.6, slope 124**
- **White: 5,990 yards, par 72, USGA 69.4, slope 120**
- **Red: 5,395 yards, par 72, USGA 66.3, slope 114**

Fees Golf available only as part of inclusive lodging packages, starting at $119 per day in off-peak season. All-inclusive packages ($750 per person, per night), available year-round, include unlimited golf, spa treatments, meals, and more.

Facilities Lodging, pro shop, driving range, practice greens, locker rooms, restaurant, beverage cart, and club and shoe rentals.

Comments Tom Watson is said to have made more than 40 site visits during construction to ensure that his British Isles–inspired masterpiece here was built correctly. Greens are huge but undulating, so getting on is no insurance against three- (or four-) putting. Bunkers are everywhere, from fairways hazards to greenside pot bunkers; from the back, where all the hazards come into play, this is one of Orlando's stiffest tests, yet the course gets appreciably easier as you move to shorter tees.

The Legacy ★★★★

ESTABLISHED 2004 **DESIGNER** Arnold Palmer **STATUS** Resort (Guests Only)

1000 Reunion Way, Reunion, FL 34747; ☎ 888-418-9611 or 407-662-1100

Tees
- **Black: 6,916 yards, par 72, USGA 73.4, slope 137**
- **Gold: 6,419 yards, par 72, USGA 70.9, slope 132**
- **Blue: 6,058 yards, par 72, USGA 69.2, slope 128**
- **White: 5,529 yards, par 72, USGA 67.0, slope 116**
- **Red: 4,802 yards, par 72, USGA 63.3, slope 106**

Fees Golf available only as part of inclusive lodging packages, starting at $119 per day in off-peak season. All-inclusive packages ($750 per person, per night), available year-round, include unlimited golf, spa treatments, meals, and more.

Facilities Lodging, pro shop, driving range, practice greens, locker rooms, restaurant, beverage cart, and club and shoe rentals.

Comments Palmer frames vast green fairways with numerous shapely white bunkers, and there is plenty of water, so much so that the course needs elaborate boardwalk-style cart bridges to whisk guests around. Still, the possibility for lost balls is offset by very generous fairways, with lots of room for errant drives, and this is the easiest of the three layouts here.

The Tradition ★★★★

ESTABLISHED 2006 **DESIGNER** Jack Nicklaus **STATUS** Resort (Guests Only)

1000 Reunion Way, Reunion, FL 34747; ☎ 888-418-9611 or 407-662-1100

Tees
- **Gold: 7,244 yards, par 72, USGA 76.7, slope 147**
- **Blue: 6,537 yards, par 72, USGA 72.6, slope 142**
- **White: 6,260 yards, par 72, USGA 71.3, slope 140**
- **Red: 5,055 yards, par 72, USGA 65.4, slope 116**

Fees Golf available only as part of inclusive lodging packages, starting at $119 per day in off-peak season. All-inclusive packages ($750 per person, per night), available year-round, include unlimited golf, spa treatments, meals, and more.

Facilities Lodging, pro shop, driving range, practice greens, locker rooms, restaurant, beverage cart, and club and shoe rentals.

Comments Nicklaus went for a flat parkland design here. This does not mean the course is easy, however, as he used a target-style layout, with forced carries of the tees to small landing areas in the fairways; small greens; and the constant temptation to go for it with risk–reward gambles over a variety of hazards, including water and sand. Water is in play on fully half the holes, and since the course is built through a bird sanctuary, it is quiet and pristine and a world apart from the city's hustle and bustle.

THE BEST OF THE REST

Arnold Palmer's Bay Hill Club & Lodge ★★★★

ESTABLISHED 1961 **DESIGNER** Dick Wilson **STATUS** Resort

9000 Bay Hill Boulevard, Orlando, FL 32819; ☎ 888-422-9445 or 407-876-2429; www.bayhill.com

Tees
- **Palmer: 7,267 yards, par 72, USGA 75.3, slope 140**
- **Shootout: 6,920 yards, par 72, USGA 73.6, slope 135**
- **Championship: 6,647 yards, par 72, USGA 72.3, slope 131**
- **Men's: 6,220 yards, par 72, USGA 70.5, slope 129**
- **Ladies': 5,235 yards, par 72, USGA 76.6, slope 140**

Fees Golf packages with lodging (for two) from $474 per night in summer to $726 in peak season.

Facilities Lodging, pro shop, driving range, practice greens, locker rooms, restaurant, beverage cart, and shoe rentals.

Comments Bay Hill is famous in the golf world as the home club of The King, Arnold Palmer, and is the site of his invitational tournament each year. You have to stay to play, and the luxury resort features a spa, fine dining, and a comprehensive golf academy. When he is in town, which is most of the time, Palmer makes a point of stopping by the clubhouse daily, and half the attraction of staying and playing here is to see him. The other half is the course. It is composed of three nines, but it is the Challenger–Champion combination that is the most popular, and the one on which the PGA Tour event is played. This combo starts off with a roar, featuring the toughest opening hole on the PGA Tour, an uphill, 441-yard, dogleg left that is heavily bunkered, both in the fairway and around the green. The course ends in similar fashion with one of the toughest closers around, but in between are lots of gentler birdie opportunities. Variety, class, and tradition are the mainstays of Bay Hill.

Rosen Shingle Creek Resort ★★★★

ESTABLISHED 2003 **DESIGNER** David Harman **STATUS** Public

9939 Universal Boulevard, Orlando, FL 32819; ☎ 866-996-9933 or 407-996-9933; www.shinglecreekgolf.com

Tees
- **Black: 7,228 yards, par 72, USGA 75.1, slope 139**
- **Gold: 6,758 yards, par 72, USGA 71.7, slope 134**
- **Blue: 6,393 yards, par 72, USGA 69.8, slope 130**
- **Silver: 5,835 yards, par 72, USGA 67.8, slope 118**
- **Ivory: 5,131 yards, par 72, USGA 70.5 slope 132**

Fees $79–$119; twilight, $49–$65. Further discounts for resort guests; golf and lodging packages also available.

Facilities Lodging, pro shop, driving range, practice greens, locker rooms, restaurant, GPS-equipped carts, beverage cart, and club and shoe rentals.

Comments Hotelier Harris Rosen runs the state's largest privately owned hotel company, and Shingle Creek is his newest resort, opened in 2006. The $300 million, 1,500-room property includes a new golf course by David Harman of nearby Orange County National fame, and the layout quickly won a place among *Golfweek*'s Top 40 Best New Courses in the United States after it opened in late 2003. The main feature is the namesake creek, originating some 10 miles north as part of the headwaters of the Everglades and meandering through the design, surrounded by native oaks and pines. Even in peak season, Shingle Creek has quickly become one of the very best golf values in the Orlando region, even more so for resort guests.

Waldorf-Astoria Golf Club ★★★★

ESTABLISHED 2009 **DESIGNER** Rees Jones **STATUS** Resort

14224 Bonnet Creek Resort Lane, Orlando, FL 32821; ☎ 888-924-6531 or 407-597-3300; www.waldorfastoriaorlando.com

Tees
- **Professional: 7,113 yards, par 72, USGA 72.5, slope 130**
- **Championship: 6,666 yards, par 72, USGA TBD, slope TBD**
- **Standard: 6,297 yards, par 72, USGA TBD, slope TBD**
- **Forward: 5,820 yards, par 72, USGA TBD, slope TBD**
- **Junior: 5,092 yards, par 72, USGA TBD, slope TBD**

Fees TBD (golf and lodging packages will also be available).

Facilities Lodging, pro shop, driving range, practice greens, locker rooms, restaurant, GPS-equipped carts, beverage cart, and club and shoe rentals.

Comments As Disney prepares to usher in its new luxury golf resort (see page 735), another has opened just outside the park, between the Caribbean Beach Resort and Interstate 4. This 482-acre resort features two hotels: a 497-room Waldorf-Astoria and a 1,000-room Hilton, both opening in October 2009. The Rees Jones–designed course, finished in spring 2009 but wisely kept closed until the hotels were ready, combines a classic parkland routing where holes are separated by stands of towering pines with the omnipresent lakes for which Florida golf is known. Several holes wrap dramatically along the shore or feature greens set against the water—in fact, only one hole from the 12th to 18th holes (17) is dry. The complex also features a large spa and golf academy.

MINIATURE GOLF

YEARS AGO, THE DISNEY INTELLIGENCE PATROL (DIP) noticed that as many as 113 guests a day were sneaking out of Walt Disney World to play Goofy Golf. Applying the logic of the boy who jammed his finger in the dike, Disney feared a hemorrhage of patrons from the theme parks. The thought of those truant guests making instant millionaires of miniature-golf entrepreneurs on International Drive was enough to give a fat mouse ulcers.

The response to this assault on Disney's market share was **Fantasia Gardens Miniature Golf,** an 11-acre complex with two 18-hole dink-and-putt golf courses. One is an "adventure" course, themed after Disney's animated film *Fantasia*. The other, geared more toward older children and adults, is an innovative approach-and-putt course with sand traps and water hazards.

Fantasia Gardens is beautifully landscaped and creatively executed. It features fountains, animated statues, topiaries, flower beds, and a multitude of other imponderables that you're unlikely to find at most mini-golf courses.

Fantasia Gardens is on Epcot Resorts Boulevard, across the street from the Walt Disney World Swan; it's open daily, from 10 a.m. to 11 p.m. To reach the course via Disney transportation, take a bus or boat to the Swan resort. The cost to putt is $11.75 for adults and $9.75 for children. If you arrive hungry or naked, Fantasia Gardens has a snack bar and gift shop. For more information, call ☎ 407-WDW-PLAY.

In 1999, Disney opened **Winter Summerland,** a second miniature-golf facility located next to the Blizzard Beach water park. Winter Summerland offers two 18-hole courses—one has a "blizzard in Florida" theme, while the other sports a tropical-holiday theme. The Winter Summerland courses are much easier than the Fantasia courses, which makes them a better choice for families with preteen children. Operating hours and cost are the same as for Fantasia Gardens.

PART EIGHTEEN

SHOPPING *in and out of* WALT DISNEY WORLD

HEY, BIG SPENDER

THE *UNOFFICIAL GUIDE* aims to help you see as much as possible, not buy as much as possible. But we acknowledge that for many people, a vacation is an extended shopping spree. If you're among these shoppers, you'll love exploring the stores at and around Walt Disney World. You'll notice that our touring plans keep you on track to see attractions, dissuading you somewhat from shopping. However, to give you a notion of what shopping means to an enthusiast, we share this letter from a Los Angeles couple:

> *Although your book discourages it, the shopping is a divine experience at WDW for those who like to shop. One does not shop in WDW for bargains (that's what flea markets, garage sales, and Target are for), but Disney buyers obtain a large selection of above-average to excellent-quality merchandise, much of it not available anywhere else (not even a Disney Store or catalog). They are marketing geniuses! Not even the largest shops have all the merchandise they have to offer, hence, a shopper can make little discoveries in almost every shop. That, coupled with congenial, helpful Disney staff, and services like complimentary hotel delivery, makes shopping an attraction of its own at WDW.*

And a woman from Suffolk, Virginia, offers this:

> *Let readers know if they are into shopping to allot at least six hours for Downtown Disney Marketplace and West Side.*

Central Florida is a shopper's Mecca. With more than 52 million square feet of retail space, Orlando now has nine first-rate malls and three top shopping outlets, and millions of visitors from around the globe have retailers scrambling to keep up with demand.

Beyond the ubiquitous mouse ears and T-shirts, avid shoppers can find a wide array of items, from hard-to-find imports at Epcot's World Showcase to designer bargains from hundreds of off-price outlets. We figure you haven't come to Orlando *just* for the shopping, so we'll whittle down our lists to the best of the best. We'll take a look at all four

Disney Pinformation

Since pin trading is such a serious business, here's a primer on Disney's pin-trading etiquette, courtesy of **www.disneypins.com:**

1. Pins should be in good, undamaged condition.
2. You can only trade pins one at a time. The back of the pin must be attached.
3. Guests may trade a maximum of two pins per cast member.
4. Do not touch a cast member's, or another individual's, pins or lanyard. If you want to view a pin up close, just ask the person you're trading with for a closer look.
5. Pins must represent a Disney event, location, character, or icon.
6. "Name pins" cannot be traded with cast members.
7. If the cast member already has the same pin that you want to trade, don't even bother trying.
8. You may trade only one pin of the same style with a particular cast member.
9. Don't try to buy a pin from a cast member–that is unacceptable.
10. Some cast members have what's called a "showcase" pin on their lanyard. These pins are just for show, and cast members are not allowed to trade them. Sorry!

Disney theme parks and Downtown Disney, then head for the other shopping hot spots around central Florida.

There are too many shops to mention every single one, but we'll tell you what's special and point out the smart buys—along with the overpriced merchandise. We'll also tell you where to locate hard-to-find goods. If a shop has a special, not-to-be-missed quality, we've marked it with a ★ .

PIN MANIA

CALL IT A HOBBY OR AN OBSESSION—serious pin traders show up at the theme parks decked out in vests, hats, and sashes decorated with collectible Disney pins, always on the lookout for the one that got away. The mania started in October 1999 with the launch of Disney's Millennium Celebration, and today Disney churns out thousands of pins annually at its resorts around the world. The pins generally sell for around $8 to $20, with one for every occasion, from new attractions to special events.

The spot for the largest collection of pins is **Disney's Pin Traders** at Downtown Disney Marketplace. The store has tables for trading and two Internet stations where you can visit the official Disney pin-trading Web site (**www.disneypins.com**) to catch up on the latest pin releases and special events in the theme parks.

There's a real camaraderie in the chase. Most agree there's no great monetary gain in the trade, just lots of fun. But there is "pin etiquette" (see "Disney Pinformation," above). For instance, pins must be cloisonné, semicloisonné, or hard-enamel metal and must be traded one at a time, hand to hand.

Downtown Disney
N
Disney's West Side
Lake Buena Vista
Cirque du Soleil
House of Blues
Disney Quest
Wolfgang Puck Cafe
Bongos Cuban Cafe
Specialty Shopping
Parking
AMC Movie Theaters
Planet Hollywood
Parking
Buena Vista Drive

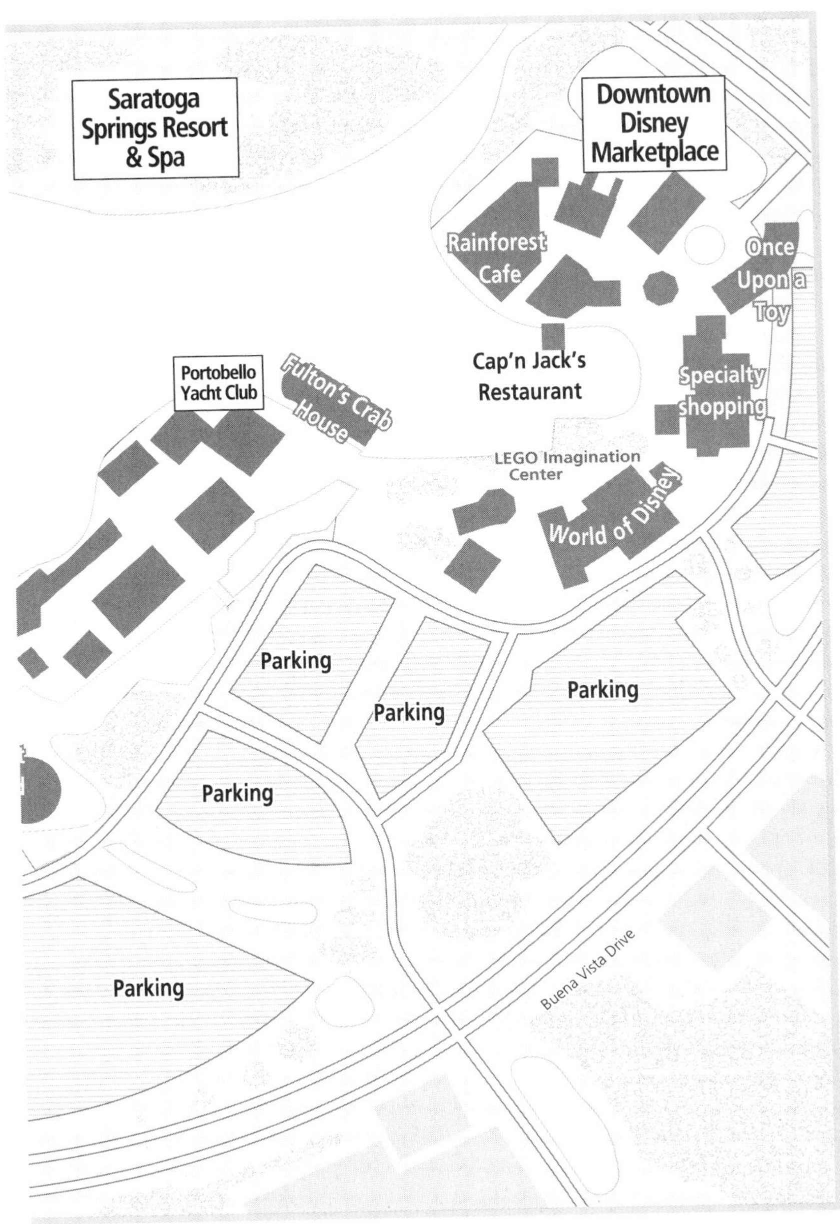
Saratoga Springs Resort & Spa
Downtown Disney Marketplace
Rainforest Cafe
Once Upon a Toy
Cap'n Jack's Restaurant
Portobello Yacht Club
Fulton's Crab House
Specialty shopping
LEGO Imagination Center
World of Disney
Parking
Parking
Parking
Parking
Parking
Buena Vista Drive

Many Disney cast members wear lanyards festooned with the ubiquitous pins and happily trade with park visitors. Cast members wearing pin-trading lanyards can be found at all four theme parks, Downtown Disney, and some resorts.

SHOPPING *in* WALT DISNEY WORLD

TIPS FOR DISNEY SHOPPING

AFTER EXHAUSTIVE RESEARCH in all four Disney theme parks, water parks, and resorts, we can assure you that Disney-brand merchandise is pretty much the same wherever you go. The only big differences are items with logos for specific resorts or theme parks. So if you're short on time, save your shopping spree for one favorite theme park or for the **World of Disney** shop in Downtown Disney Marketplace, the largest Disney-character shop in the world.

Merchandise costs do not differ across Disney property. A beach towel, for instance, was the same price at every location we checked. Ditto for sale merchandise: if it's on sale at one store, it's on sale in all stores (though you may not be able to find it at all locations).

unofficial **TIP**
Beyond Epcot, shopping is hit-and-miss in the other three theme parks. You'll find the same basic Disney merchandise everywhere, with specialty items for each park tossed in. Nevertheless, amid all the Disney goods are some unusual shops.

If you're staying at a Disney hotel, you can have all of your packages delivered to your resort from any of the four Disney parks. If you make a purchase before 1 p.m., packages will be delivered to your hotel's gift shop by 10 p.m. that same day; purchases made after 1 p.m. will be delivered by noon of the following day, so this service is unavailable if you are checking out of your room the same day. Same-day pickup inside the theme parks is also available. For a nominal charge, you can ship items to your home.

If you remember on your flight home that you forgot to buy mouse ears for your nephew, call Walt Disney World Mail Order Merchandise on weekdays at ☎ 407-363-6200, or visit the Disney Catalog online at **www.disneyparks.com/store.** Most trademark merchandise sold at Walt Disney World is available.

I NEED . . .

WHERE AT WALT DISNEY WORLD IS THE BEST SELECTION of a particular item? Here are a few recommendations:

BATHING SUITS

Beach Club Marketplace, Disney's Beach Club Resort
Calypso Trading Post, Disney's Caribbean Beach Resort
Curl by Sammy Duval, former Pleasure Island site
Tren-D, Downtown Disney Marketplace

Theme-park Shops with the Best Disney Stuff

ANIMAL KINGDOM
Serka Zong Bazaar | **Asia**
Island Mercantile and Disney Outfitters | **Discovery Island**

DISNEY'S HOLLYWOOD STUDIOS
Animation Gallery | **Animation Courtyard**
Mickey's of Hollywood | **Hollywood Boulevard**

EPCOT
MouseGear **(largest selection at Epcot) Future World**

MAGIC KINGDOM
Emporium **(largest selection at Magic Kingdom) Main Street**

MEN'S CLOTHING

Team Mickey, Downtown Disney Marketplace
ESPN Club, Disney's BoardWalk
Mickey's of Hollywood, Disney's Hollywood Studios

WOMEN'S CLOTHING

BouTiki, Disney's Polynesian Resort
Tren-D, Downtown Disney Marketplace

SPORTSWEAR

ESPN Club, Disney's BoardWalk
Team Mickey's Athletic Club, Downtown Disney Marketplace

JEWELRY

Mitsukoshi Department Store (pearls and watches), Japan Pavilion, Epcot World Showcase
Uptown Jewelers, Magic Kingdom
World of Disney (Disney-themed jewelry), Downtown Disney Marketplace

DOWNTOWN DISNEY

IF SHOPPING IS AN ESSENTIAL PART of your Disney vacation, we recommend that your first stop be Downtown Disney, which comprises two shopping areas, each with its own special feel: the **Marketplace** and **West Side.** (**Pleasure Island,** the onetime nightlife district, has largely closed but still has a few shops. Disney plans to remake the area with a mix of dining and shopping.) If you have time constraints and need to limit your shopping spree to a single stop, this is it.

Downtown Disney stretches along the shore of Lake Buena Vista at the intersection of Buena Vista Drive and Hotel Plaza Boulevard. It's a pleasant walk from the Marketplace on the east end to the West Side. The West Side has smaller shops with trendy merchandise; the Marketplace is loaded with Disney merchandise and a smattering of non-Disney products. So what you're shopping for determines the best place to park—free parking on a surface lot spreads from one end to the other.

unofficial **TIP**
Except for specialty items, like silk rugs from the Japan Pavilion at Epcot, you can find a little bit of everything at Downtown Disney.

The Marketplace

Hours at the Marketplace vary among shops, but stores are generally open by 9:30 a.m. There are more than 30 shops and 10 places to eat, including Rainforest Cafe and T-REX. Wheelchair and stroller rentals are available at Guest Relations. It's a comfortable place to stroll and people-watch. Near the central area is a carousel that runs daily; it's decorated with hand-painted renderings of the Marketplace shops. Cost is $2 per ride (there's also a kiddie train ride for $2). If you don't mind the kids getting wet, check out the free "Fun Fountains" throughout the Marketplace. These streams of water squirt out of the spongy sidewalk, soaking energetic youngsters on hot summer days.

The Marketplace is accessible by Disney bus or boat. A few lockers are available on the dock near Guest Relations close to Arribas Bros.

Longtime Marketplace shoppers have complained that the merchandise is "too Disney" and that all the unusual shops have disappeared and been replaced with Disney shops. You'll still find non-Disney merchandise (like clothes and swimwear), just not in the abundance of the old Marketplace.

TOP SHOPS AT THE MARKETPLACE

THE ART OF DISNEY Sells limited-edition animation cels and pricey Disney creations, from pottery to crystal. Most of the merchandise is high-quality and therefore expensive, but you'll find a few affordable souvenirs in the mix.

BASIN Browse among wooden tubs filled with soaps and lotions, then scoop your own bath salts or build your own gift basket. All the store's products are chemical-free and made with natural ingredients.

★ **DISNEY'S DAYS OF CHRISTMAS** This shop is just plain fun, with hundreds of holiday decorations from ornaments to stockings to stuffed animals wearing their Christmas Day best. We especially like the back room, with stations for engraving, embroidery, and ornament personalization. A hot seller in all the Christmas shops is the Disney monorail train with tracks to put around the Christmas tree like an old-fashioned train (also carried at some toy stores).

DISNEY'S DESIGN A TEE A new store where guests can create custom T-shirts and personalized merchandise. (It took over the space formerly occupied by Disney's Wonderful World of Memories.)

DISNEY'S PIN TRADERS The spot for the largest collection of pins, with tables for trading and two Internet stations for visiting the official pin-trading Web site (**www.disneypins.com**).

GOOFY'S CANDY CO. An interactive show kitchen with sweets . . . *lots* of sweets!

★ **WORLD OF DISNEY** It's a Disney superstore with 12 rooms—50,000 square feet—stacked with Disney merchandise, from underwear to clocks to princess dresses. Pick up a basket as you walk in, shop throughout, and check out at any cash register in the store. It's decidedly less crowded and frenetic than theme-park shops, except on evenings when the parks close early.

The World of Disney is also home to one of Disney World's two **Bibbidi Bobbidi Boutiques,** sort-of salons that can turn your snot-nosed tomboy into a little princess (the second location is inside Cinderella Castle in the Magic Kingdom). At the boutique, girls can try on various princess costumes before repairing to the beauty parlor for hairstyling, makeup, and/or a manicure, depending on which of the three packages you choose. The Downtown Disney location also offers an enormously popular (and exclusive) Hannah Montana–themed makeover called the Secret Star, complete with Hannah wig, guitar purse, and headset microphone. Call the boutique at ☎ 407-WDW-STYLE for more details.

Bibbidi Bobbidi costs a bundle, but this Northport, Alabama, mother of a 4-year-old thought it was worth it:

> *One thing that was great was the Bibbidi Bobbidi Boutique! Yes, we spent $200, but the look on my 4-year-old's face was priceless as she walked to the castle to eat. Everyone spoke to her, calling her 'Princess.' There hasn't been a day in three months since we've been home that she has not asked to go back.*

To appease the boys while sister is being transfigured, send them to the front of the shop, where they can build their own pirate hat or fill a skull with trinkets and treasures. If all else fails, there are video games.

★ **LEGO IMAGINATION CENTER** This is an ideal rest stop for parents, and you don't even have to go inside the store. A 3,000-square-foot hands-on outdoor play area has bins of LEGOs that the kids can go crazy with while Mom and Dad take a break. Inside is all the latest LEGO paraphernalia. Check out the larger-than-life dragon made entirely of LEGOs or the "sea monster" across from the store "swimming" in Lake Buena Vista.

ARRIBAS BROTHERS Not the place to take rambunctious kids—there is beautiful glassware and crystal at every turn. Watch artisans at work blowing glass or carving monograms on crystal. Nearly all the merchandise is expensive.

GHIRARDELLI SODA FOUNTAIN AND CHOCOLATE SHOP You can smell the chocolate when you walk in, and most of the time a cast member is on hand to dole out free samples. Chocolate souvenirs abound, but treat yourself to a "world famous" sundae topped with the decadent hot fudge made daily at the shop. The line for ice cream often winds out the door—it's that good.

MICKEY'S MART A small outdoor breezeway with all souvenirs priced at $10 or less.

MICKEY'S PANTRY A small shop with Disney home products, kitchen gadgets, and appliances.

ONCE UPON A TOY Five rooms of toys, from build-your-own Mr. Potato Heads and light sabers to popular board games. Several favorites, including Tonka, Play-Doh, and Tinkertoys, are on the shelves. Also for sale are

miniature play sets of Cinderella Castle, Hannah Montana and *High School Musical* dolls, and plenty of pirate, princess, and fairy items.

TEAM MICKEY'S ATHLETIC CLUB From soccer to basketball to golf, this shop features sports apparel. Not much of it has Mickey Mouse or Goofy logos—instead, there's a decent selection of Nike and Adidas sportswear and tennis shoes. You'll also find plenty of sports memorabilia such as jerseys and sports balls. Baseball fans should check out the new **Rawlings Making the Game** kiosk at the front of the store—there you can get an engraved baseball bat or the authentic helmet of a Major League Baseball all-star.

TREN-D A hot new urban-inspired boutique with hip fashion apparel. Also one of the best selections of women's bathing suits at Disney.

Pleasure Island, or What's Left of It

This nighttime-entertainment complex largely shut down in September 2008. Restaurants and stores are slated to replace the clubs, but in the meantime a few shops remain that are worth a look. The **Harley-Davidson** shop sells primarily Harley outerwear, including men's and women's T-shirts and (of course) leather jackets. The small shop adjacent to **Raglan Road Irish Pub & Restaurant** stocks a nice selection of Irish goods (surprise, surprise) ranging from kitschy to cute. **Curl by Sammy Duval** offers men's, women's, and children's summer clothing, along with watches, sunglasses, and lots of bathing suits. **Fuego by Sosa Cigars** is an upscale cigar bar.

Disney's West Side

The West Side opens daily at 10:30 a.m. This is the hip extension of the Marketplace, with shops that are full of fun tchotchkes for compulsive buyers.

TOP SHOPS ON DISNEY'S WEST SIDE

DISNEY'S CANDY CAULDRON Watch as gooey treats are made in the open kitchen. You can buy everything from jelly beans to caramel apples and cotton candy—more than 200 sweets are on the shelves.

★ **HOYPOLOI** Not a set of mouse ears in sight, but one of our favorite shops, with one-of-a-kind pieces of art from various regions of the United States—Zen water fountains, contemporary art, blown glass, wooden boxes, and Judaica including mezuzahs and menorahs. One of Hoypoloi's signature items is the Zen Board—a canvas whose ink magically disappears—intended to encourage you to "live in the present."

MAGIC MASTERS An elegant little shop with decor inspired by Harry Houdini's personal library. Magic tricks, from simple to elaborate, are for sale, with a resident magician to demonstrate and entertain.

MAGNETRON MAGNETZ You've got to see this place to believe the funky collection of 20,000 magnets lining the steel walls—magnets that talk, sing, ring, beep, light up, and glow in the dark. Kids love it, and souvenirs are pretty cheap.

MICKEY'S GROOVE An eclectic collection of merchandise that changes often but mostly features general Mickey-and-friends stuff.

POP GALLERY The sister store to Hoypoloi, this gallery-like shop features a wide variety of contemporary art, including limited-edition sculptures and paintings, high-end gift items, and even a small collection of inexpensive souvenirs such as art-instruction kits and brightly painted ceramic piggy banks.

SOSA FAMILY CIGARS They hand-roll 'em here and feature premium imports, including Arturo Fuente, Cuesta-Rey, Diamond Crown, La Gloria Cubana, Macanudo, Puros Indios, Padrón, Partagas, and Sosa. A walk-in humidor stores the top brands.

SUNGLASS ICON Designer sunglasses and eyewear.

THE MAGIC KINGDOM

BECAUSE THE MAGIC KINGDOM is usually the most crowded theme park, you're best off browsing the shops in the early afternoon, when attractions are crowded. Much of the non-Disney merchandise that was once available here has disappeared from the shelves. For instance, longtime visitors may remember Liberty Square's Olde World Antiques, which sold unique brass, silver, and pewter, but today it's a shop full of Disney Christmas ornaments. Or remember when the Yankee Trader stocked soufflé dishes and escargot holders? Now it's mostly kitchenware.

MAIN STREET, U.S.A. Because this area stays open an hour after official park closing, you could save your shopping time until the end of the day; just be prepared for crowds. Two shops here are of note: if you want a monogrammed mouse-ears hat, ★ **The Chapeau on Main Street** has scores of them, along with a nice selection of other Disney-themed hats. It's also home to the **Build Your Own Ears** stand,

unofficial **TIP**
Store your purchases in lockers at the Main Street rail station while you tour, or have them forwarded from shops to Package Pick-Up and retrieve them when you leave the park.

where guests can personalize their Mickey ears by choosing custom bases, ears, and patches. At **The Emporium,** a Disney superstore, you can browse among four huge rooms categorized by kids' apparel, adult apparel, toys and costumes, and souvenirs. It's one-stop shopping if time is of the essence.

Fun for browsing is **Crystal Arts.** Two glassblowers entertain, and the merchandise includes jewelry, swords, Disney figurines, and traditional glass and crystal. Occupying prime real estate on the corner of Town Square, **Main Street Confectionery** is the biggest candy shop in all four theme parks, with every sweet imaginable. Watch as cast members make fudge and candy apples. For expensive jewelry, lots of Disney pins, and Lenox and Armani figurines, check out **Uptown Jewelers.** Next to Town Hall, the **Firehouse Gift Station** sells firefighter-themed clothing, hats, and patches, with a small selection of accessories for furry friends, including bows, leashes, and dog clothes. Lots of parents bring babies and toddlers to the **Harmony Barber Shop** (open daily from 9 a.m. to 5 p.m., no reservations necessary) for their first haircut, but anyone can stop in for a trim. For interactive spending, let the artists at **Silhouettes,** a tiny kiosk in the alcove between Crystal Arts and Uptown Jewelers, snip your silhouette out of black paper (similar kiosks can be found in Liberty Square). Inside the Main Street Cinema you'll find yet another **Art of Disney** locale (VMK Central is no more) that replicates the merchandise found in the other Art of Disney stores around the parks. **Exposition Hall,** adjacent to Tony's Town Square restaurant as you enter the park, sells film and photo supplies, including picture frames and scrapbooks.

ADVENTURELAND Across from The Magic Carpets of Aladdin, **Agrabah Bazaar** and the adjacent **Zanzibar Trading Co.** specialize in safari-themed clothing and toys, *Aladdin* merchandise, and moderately priced imports from Africa. The shops are worth a look solely for their wide selection of beautifully handcrafted African sculptures, masks, and pottery. Near Pirates of the Caribbean, the **Plaza Del Sol Caribe Bazaar** carries an ample selection of *Pirates* merchandise, including costumes, play sets, men's and women's T-shirts, swords, eye patches, and Jack Sparrow dreadlocks. Young pirate wannabes can join Captain Jack's crew at **The Pirates League** in the same plaza, where three packages offer buccaneer makeovers and souvenir portraits. **Island Supply Company,** across from the Swiss Family Treehouse, carries men's and women's clothing from such designers as O'Neill, Roxy, and Quiksilver.

FRONTIERLAND The **Frontier Trading Post** has been converted into a Disney pin-trading shop; **Big Al's,** a small kiosk across the way, sells a very limited selection of frontier-themed items. Those who forget to try the fudge at the Main Street Confectionery have another chance at the **Prairie Outpost,** a small bakery and candy shop. **Briar Patch** is a small store that sells primarily Splash Mountain merchandise.

LIBERTY SQUARE **Heritage House** has American souvenirs and T-shirts. **Ye Old Christmas Shoppe** is a repeat of the holiday shops in all the other Disney parks. **Yankee Trader,** near The Haunted Mansion, stocks primarily kitchenware such as character aprons, plates, and cute salt-and-pepper-shaker sets.

FANTASYLAND Shops are themed to the attractions, like **Pooh's Thotful Shop** at The Many Adventures of Winnie the Pooh and **Seven Dwarfs Mining Co.** near Snow White's Scary Adventures. A favorite of little girls is ★ **Tinker Bell's Treasures,** with a large selection of princess costumes—Belle, Snow White, Cinderella, and others—plus an impressive assortment of Disney fairy and Tinker Bell merchandise. A second **Bibbidi Bobbidi Boutique** occupies the former King's Gallery space in the breezeway of Cinderella Castle.

MICKEY'S TOONTOWN FAIR **County Bounty** is a good place to load up on souvenirs. It's mostly kid stuff, but there's still an assortment of goods for the older set, with photo albums, mugs, and DVDs. It's also the only store of note in Mickey's Toontown Fair. Kids can kill time by playing for free at the ceiling-high kiosk in the center of the store, which invites little ones to create their own Mr. Potato Head or My Little Pony. Merchandise is similar to that at Once Upon a Toy in Downtown Disney.

TOMORROWLAND The sci-fi stock in **Merchant of Venus** is limited to items with a Disney tie-in. The predominating character is Stitch, but you'll also find a sampling of *Star Wars,* Power Rangers, and *Pirates of the Caribbean* products. A corner of the store is occupied by a photo station, where guests can have their faces transplanted onto a character from a favorite *Star Wars* or Disney scene. The adjacent **Mickey's Star Traders** is a general Walt Disney World souvenir shop. While the decor has a Tomorrowland theme, there is no space- or future-themed merchandise here. Neither shop is a must-see unless you're killing time.

EPCOT

WE ENJOY WANDERING IN AND OUT of the shops in the 11 World Showcase pavilions, looking for unusual finds and bargains. Often you'll see sale items, especially in the shops in France and Italy, but most of the imported merchandise is relatively expensive. However, the Epcot shops may be among the few places in the United States that carry some of the merchandise found here.

Aside from World Showcase, two stores in Future World are worth a mention: **MouseGear,** on the east side of Future World, is the biggest Disney shop in any of the four theme parks. You can find almost any Disney merchandise here, and there's an enormous selection of adult and children's clothing. Prices and selection are about the same as at other Disney merchandise shops. On the other side of Future World is **The Art of Disney,** featuring framed artwork, Giuseppe Armani and Lenox figurines, and character models.

Walking clockwise around World Showcase, you'll find:

★ **MEXICO** The foyer of this pavilion is home to the **Animales Fantásticos: Spirits in Wood** kiosk, which sells hand-carved and hand-painted animal sculptures in brilliant fluorescent colors. You can watch an artist paint and sand individual creations as you browse—and browsing is what we suggest: even the smallest items (we're talking a two-inch-long turtle) are in the $15-and-up neighborhood. From there, let your eyes adjust to the dim light in the **Plaza de los Amigos,** a lovely re-creation of a charming Mexican city at dusk; here, a live mariachi band often entertains passersby. Carts and kiosks are piled with blankets, sombreros, paper flowers, and tambourines. Sure, the merchandise may be cheaper south of the border, but these prices aren't bad: piñatas are wildly popular, starting at about $10, while blankets start at $20. (Rumor has it that a tequila bar may take the place of many of these small kiosks in the near future; at press time, however, no renovations had begun.) Two shops along the perimeter are **La Princesa Cristal** (a small crystal shop) and an unnamed store that sells leather handbags, wallets, and jewelry.

★ **NORWAY** **The Puffin's Roost** is a series of small shopping galleries with popular imports such as trolls (from $15) and wooden Christmas ornaments ($4 and up). Other hard-to-find imports include Laila perfume and body lotion as well as Helly Hansen and Dale of Norway clothing, including thick woolen sweaters. You'll also find sterling-silver jewelry, butterfly pins, and classic Viking hats (with or without blond braids).

★ **CHINA** This pavilion features one of our favorite shops, piled with imports from real silk kimonos to cloisonné and thick silk rugs. **Yong Feng Shangdian** is more like a rambling department store than a shop. You'll find everything here from silk fans to $4,000 jade sculptures to antique furniture. The silk dresses and robes are competitively priced in the $100 range. Darling handbags are $10 and up, and silk ties are $19. We always admire the handwoven pure-silk carpets, starting around $320 for a two-by-four-foot rug and topping out around $2,500 for a four-by-eight-foot rug. The prices are comparable to what you would pay in a retail shop—if you could find one that imports carpets like these.

Village Traders, a shop between China and Germany, sells African woodcarvings as unusual as they come. Every day, an artist carves new creations using a special tool called a *ngomo*. Guests can even commission individual sculptures if they're willing to pay the price.

★ **GERMANY** Shops interconnect on both sides of the cobblestoned central plaza and purvey an impressive collection of imports. Tiny **Das Kaufhaus** stocks a nice selection of Adidas sportswear. Next door is **Volkskunst,** where the walls are covered with Schneider cuckoo clocks and the shelves are stocked with limited-edition steins and glassware. Next is **Der Teddybär,** featuring Engel-Puppen dolls and Steiff plush toys, among other delights for kids. Across the plaza, **Kunstarbeit in Kristall** carries a fabulous collection of Swarovski crystal, including pins, glassware, and Arribas Brothers collectibles (check out the limited-edition $37,500 replica of Cinderella Castle, blinged out with more than 20,000 Swarovski crystals). Next is the **Weinkeller,** with nearly 300 varieties of German wine. Adjoining the Weinkeller is **Süssigkeiten,** full of imported sweets and fresh baked goods such as fudge and cookies. Step through the door to **Die Weihnachts Ecke,** where Christmas ornaments and handmade nutcrackers are on display year-round. The beautiful nutcrackers go all the way to $400. Last stop is **Glas und Porzellan,** showcasing Goebel and Hummel glass and porcelain objects. You'll often find a German artist painting the delicate M. I. Hummel figurines here.

★ **ITALY** **Il Bel Cristallo** showcases Puma sportswear, Bulgari and Ferragamo fragrances, Giuseppe Armani figurines from Florence, and a small selection of Christmas decorations in the back room. Across the walkway, **Enoteca Castello** offers a small wine room with tastings, Perugina candies, elaborate Venetian masks, and Murano glass.

THE AMERICAN ADVENTURE **Heritage Manor Gifts** carries hand-crafted souvenirs, such as those by Jim Shore, and lots of American-flag-inspired apparel.

★ **JAPAN** A U.S. branch of Japan's 300-year-old **Mitsukoshi Department Store** stretches along one entire side of the pavilion. Kid-friendly merchandise—Hello Kitty, Naruto, and Yu-Gi-Oh!—fills the front, with kimonos, slippers, handbags, and lots more at the back of the store. Mitsukoshi's expanded culinary display includes a sake-tasting bar, along with chopsticks, pretty rice bowls, and imported snacks. Pricey Mikimoto pearls (rings, necklaces, earrings, and bracelets) are showcased in a separate room. No bargains here, but cool stuff all the same. And tourists line up for an oyster guaranteed to have a pearl in its shell (pearls are polished for you by the salesperson).

★ **MOROCCO** Several shops wend through this pavilion: **Tangier Traders** sells traditional Moroccan clothing, shoes, and fezzes; **Marketplace in the Medina** peddles straw bags, ceramic-tile furniture, and belly-dancing kits; **The Brass Bazaar** features brass, of course, and ceramic and wooden kitchenware (not dishwasher safe); **Casablanca Carpets** offers a wider variety of Moroccan rugs, as well as decorative pieces such as abstract-shaped lamps, sequined pillows, and incense holders; and **Medina Arts,** which as of late appears to be an extension of the merchandise sold at the Brass Bazaar, stocks larger pottery and ceramic pieces.

★ **FRANCE** We always find a few moments to browse in **Plume et Palette,** a perfume shop with more than 100 imports. You'll find scents by Dior, Chanel, Givenchy, and other top names. Across the shaded walkway is **Guerlain Paris,** with a wide selection of Guerlain makeup and perfumes that range from the enduring Shalimar to newer fragrances like Insolence. Cross over to **Les Vins de France** and **L'Esprit de la Provence,** two stores in one, with a wine room and a small selection of Provençal goods. At the back of the pavilion, **Souvenirs de France** offers T-shirts, traditional berets, *Aristocats* merchandise, and Eiffel Tower collectibles.

★ **UNITED KINGDOM** A handful of interesting imports are scattered throughout a half-dozen small shops. **The Toy Soldier** stocks costumes, books, and plush toys featuring English characters from favorite films. You'll find plenty of Alice in Wonderland, Peter Pan, and Winnie the Pooh merchandise here. Stop in **The Crown & Crest** to look up your family name in the coat-of-arms book, and the shop will create your family's insignia in a beautiful frame of choice. Also found here are Beatles merchandise and memorabilia, including T-shirts, calendars, mugs, CDs, and more. At the adjacent **Sportsman's Shoppe,** you'll find plenty of football (soccer) apparel, balls, and books.

Across the street, **The Queen's Table,** a perfume-and-toiletries shop, opens into **The Magic of Wales,** a quaint store selling lambswool scarves, a selection of British and Irish souvenirs, and Rose and Crown–branded items. **The Tea Caddy** stocks Twinings tea, biscuits, and candies.

★ **CANADA** There's not much shopping here, but the popular Hatley boutique in **Northwest Mercantile** has a wide selection of merchandise, including T-shirts, sweatshirts, aprons, and pajamas. Teens may want to pick up a CD by **Off Kilter,** the rockin' kilt-clad band that plays on Canada's outdoor stage, and we like the pure maple syrup for an edible souvenir (about $15 for a large bottle).

ANIMAL KINGDOM

THOUGH DISNEY MERCHANDISE DOMINATES, Animal Kingdom has a fair selection of animal-themed items. The largest cluster of shops is in the centrally located Discovery Island: **Disney Outfitters** carries men's, women's, and children's clothing, jewelry, and fine artwork, and recently added an area dedicated to "going green," with recycled candy-wrapper handbags and T-shirts made from recycled water bottles. **Island Mercantile** offers more (yawn) Disney character merchandise; and **Creature Comforts** is the best stop for children's clothing and toys.

In Africa, ★ **Mombasa Marketplace** and the adjoining **Ziwani Traders** showcases reasonably priced African-themed pottery, musical instruments, South African wines, and housewares, plus plenty of plush animal toys and a large selection of Animal Kingdom–themed merchandise. Asia has several open-air kiosks, but the main attraction in shopping is the ★ **Bhaktapur Market,** next to Yak & Yeti restaurant. The venue is small but packed with extraordinary themed merchandise, including cast-iron teapots and tea sets; sushi kits and Asian cookbooks; bonsai kits; origami; and some beautiful Southeast Asian–inspired clothing, PJs, and shoes for women and children. At Expedition Everest's exit is **Serka Zong Bazaar,** where the merchandise is more interesting than that of most post-attraction shops. Although mostly Disney branded, the goods don't scream Mickey Mouse. The selection is mostly Everest- and Yeti-themed, with T-shirts, apparel, collectibles, and historical books and videos for those interested in the legend of the Yeti.

Chester & Hester's Dinosaur Treasures in DinoLand U.S.A. is worth a look simply to check out the amusing architecture. The atmosphere inside is reminiscent of a dollar store (although the prices can't compare)—we found a ton of knickknacks and toys cluttering the walls and in countless bins—but most of it is junk.

DISNEY'S HOLLYWOOD STUDIOS

ON HOLLYWOOD BOULEVARD, just to the left of the park entrance, is a California Mission–style house called ★ **Sid Cahuenga's One-of-a-Kind,** which is loosely inspired by junk shops in southern California, the land of movie stars. You'll find plenty of autographed photos of film and TV stars, old movie posters, even costumes worn by celebrities on daytime soaps and in recent and vintage films.

Other shops on the right side of the street include **The Darkroom,** for Kodak cameras, film, and accessories; **Celebrity 5 & 10,** with men's, women's, and children's T-shirts and other small souvenirs; and **L.A. Prop Cinema Storage,** full of kids' clothing (mostly for girls), PJs, and lots of toys and plushes (there is also a substantial infant area). **Adrian & Edith's Head to Toe** has an embroidery station where you can get any Disney item embroidered with a name, phrase, or character of your choice. (One caveat: the item needs to have been purchased on Disney property and be unworn.) On the left side of the street, **Mickey's of Hollywood** carries plush toys, watches, T-shirts, hats, sunglasses, and more—virtually none without a Disney logo—while **Keystone Clothiers** offers an array of Disney wear for grown-ups. There's plenty to look at but not much to recommend.

On Sunset Boulevard, you'll find **Villains in Vogue,** featuring merchandise themed to the bad guys and gals of Disney films, with substantial *Nightmare before Christmas* and *Pirates of the Caribbean* selections. Other Sunset Boulevard shops, such as **Sunset Club Couture** and **Mouse About Town,** carry a sizable stock of Disney jewelry and scads of watches, as well as clothing and Disney collectibles.

Elsewhere in the park: ★ **Animation Gallery** in the Animation Courtyard carries an impressive collection of paintings, sculptures, and other artwork. You'll pay the same price here as in all the other Disney art galleries. You can pick up a hat or trench coat just like Harrison Ford's, or an Indy-style T-shirt, action figure, or Mickey plush at the **Indiana Jones Adventure Outpost** outside the amphitheater. **Stage 1 Company Store** carries a wide variety of Muppet-themed merchandise, and *Star Wars* fans will eat their hearts out at ★ **Tatooine Traders,** where everything from light-saber key chains to $200 glass light-saber collectibles is for sale. **In Character,** next to *Voyage of the Little Mermaid,* is the best spot in the Studios for Disney-princess dress-up clothes and accessories for little ones.

DISNEY OUTLET STORES

ORLANDO IS HOME TO TWO **Disney's Character** outlets—one at **Prime Outlets International,** at the north end of International Drive (☎ 407-354-3255; **www.primeoutlets.com/orlando**), and another at **Orlando Premium Outlets,** off FL 535 (☎ 407-477-0222; **www.premiumoutlets.com/orlando**). The Prime Outlets store, **Disney's Character Warehouse,** in the complex's Mall 1, gets liquidation merchandise directly from Walt Disney World stores, so you never know what you'll find. **Disney's Character Premiere** outlet, in Orlando Premium Outlets, has even more sale-price souvenirs of similar selection and vintage.

A Kentucky family had a hard time getting to Prime Outlets International, warning:

> *Avoid International Drive between the Beachline Expressway and Oak Ridge Road. After crawling for what seemed like an hour, we reached Prime Outlets International. We were grinding our teeth at the congestion. Take Interstate 4 directly to the Oak Ridge Road exit. It's much faster. P.S.: Prime Outlets had some great buys on Disney stuff. Worth the trip.*

SHOPPING *beyond* WALT DISNEY WORLD

CELEBRATION

"THE TOWN THAT DISNEY BUILT," near Walt Disney World off US 192 (**www.celebrationfl.com**), gets its fair share of tourists who like to stroll the sidewalks. No one shop is worth going out of the way for, but you'll find good restaurants here (including Italian, Spanish, and American), as well as a two-screen theater and a handful of shops. Because Celebration is an upscale community, the shops are all high-end.

You can purchase fresh coffee beans at **Starbucks,** where Celebration residents often gather on the patio for a freshly brewed cup. Specialty stores include **Market Street Gallery,** with greeting cards, candles, and gifts for the home; **Soft as a Grape,** offering casual clothing for the whole family; **Village Mercantile,** which stocks men's and women's clothing; **Day Dreams,** featuring collectible dolls and bears; **Hopskotch,** a women's clothier; **Jewel Box,** featuring fine jewelry, diamonds, and watches; **Kilwin's Chocolates & Ice Cream,** an extraordinary confectionery; and **Sherlock's of Celebration,** a wineshop and tearoom.

UNIVERSAL CITYWALK

WHILE DOWNTOWN DISNEY is 120 acres (with a strolling area equivalent to about ten city blocks), CityWalk (**www.citywalk.com**) comprises 30 acres in a relatively compact area between the two Universal theme parks. It features 9 shops to Downtown Disney's 32.

unofficial **TIP**
CityWalk is open 11 a.m.–2 a.m. (although some stores may close earlier). Parking, though plentiful in the Universal garage, costs a steep $12 before 6 p.m. but only $3 in the evening.

At both destinations, the shopping complements the restaurants and clubs. Without question, Disneyphiles will prefer Downtown Disney, where at least a third of the shops are Disney themed. CityWalk is most comparable to the West Side at Downtown Disney—fun for browsing and impulse buys. Our favorites include **The Endangered Species Store,** with merchandise from T-shirts to jewelry to housewares designed to "raise awareness of the plight of endangered species, ecosystems, and cultures worldwide"; **Fresh Produce,** featuring colorfully designed clothes for men, women, and children; **Cigarz at CityWalk,** with hand-rolled cigars, cordials, single-malt Scotches, and coffees; and **Quiet Flight Surf Shop** for cool customized surfboards and beachwear.

For jewelry, **Fossil** has a notable collection of watches, as well as sunglasses and leather goods.

The Universal Studios Store offers one-stop shopping for all theme-park merchandise.

INTERNATIONAL DRIVE

"I-DRIVE" IS THE HEART of central Florida's tourist district, jammed with hotels, motels, discount stores, and restaurants. Locals generally avoid the area except for the outlet malls (which we'll discuss separately).

On the more refined south end of International Drive is **Pointe Orlando** (9101 International Drive; ☎ 407-248-2838; **www.pointe orlando.com**), with about 25 stores. This complex gets a lot of its business from the convention center, less than a mile away, rather than from locals. Hours are Monday through Saturday, 11 a.m. to 8 p.m; Sunday, noon to 8 p.m. (Bars and restaurants stay open later.)

Clothing stores at Pointe Orlando include **Boardwalk Surf & Sport,** carrying Billabong, No Fear, O'Neill, Rip Curl, and Quiksilver; **Everything But Water,** with an excellent selection of bathing suits; **Chico's; Hollister; Millennium,** which carries casual wear, nightclub attire, shoes, and accessories; **Tommy Bahama; Synergy;** and **Victoria's Secret.**

Among the specialty shops are **Artsy Abode,** with Vera Bradley merchandise and Pandora jewelry; **Kiehl's** for hair- and body- care products; **Brighton Collectibles** for small leather goods and watches; **Tharoo & Co.** jewelry boutique, **Sunglass Hut,** featuring shades from Ray-Ban and Prada; and **Bath & Body Works.** Pointe Orlando prices are full retail, but there are always sales.

OUTLETS

LIKE EVERY MAJOR TOURIST DESTINATION in the United States, central Florida has hundreds of factory-outlet stores, most of them near major attractions. Having spent many hours checking prices and merchandise, we generally conclude that at most stores you will save about 20% on desirable merchandise and up to 75% on last-season (or older) stock. Some stores in the outlet malls are full retail or sell a few brands at a 20% discount and the rest at full price.

unofficial **TIP**
If you're picky, a major department store's end-of-season sales often yield deals as good as or better than an outlet store's.

Prime Outlets International (☎ 407-352-9600; **www.primeoutlets .com/orlando**), on the north end of International Drive, is the largest outlet shopping center in the South and the second largest in the United States. The shops feature 175 of the world's hottest designers and brand names, among them **BCBG Max Azria Factory Store, Hugo Boss Factory Store, Coach Factory Store, Ed Hardy Outlet, Kenneth Cole, Juicy Couture, Michael Kors, Saks Fifth**

Avenue OFF 5TH, Sean John Factory Store, Kate Spade, Tommy Hilfiger, Victoria's Secret Outlet, and the only **Neiman Marcus Last Call Clearance Center** in central Florida.

Festival Bay Mall (☎ 407-351-7718; **www.shopfestivalbaymall.com**), nearby on International Drive, includes **Bass Pro Shops Outdoor World, BCBG Max Azria, Hot Topic, PacSun, Ron Jon Surf Shop, Sheplers Western Wear,** and a handful of small shops. Other big draws are a 20-screen movie theater and a **Vans Skatepark.**

Another popular outlet center is **Lake Buena Vista Factory Stores** (☎ 407-238-9301; **www.lbvfs.com**), on FL 535 near Walt Disney World (take Exit 68 off I-4, then go two miles south on FL 535). Hours are Monday through Saturday, 10 a.m. to 9 p.m.; Sunday, 10 a.m. to 7 p.m. We were a little disappointed in the inventory, and the discounts were mostly in the 10%-to-20% range, though we did find a few deeper price cuts. Key tenants include **Eddie Bauer, Gap Outlet, Nike Factory Store, Old Navy, Liz Claiborne Outlet, Oshkosh B'Gosh, Tommy Hilfiger, VF Outlet,** and **Reebok.**

Setting new standards for outlet shopping is ★ **Orlando Premium Outlets** (☎ 407-238-7787; **www.premiumoutlets.com/orlando**), off I-4 (Exit 68) at Vineland Avenue, near Lake Buena Vista (open Monday through Saturday, 10 a.m. to 11 p.m.; Sunday, 10 a.m. to 9 p.m.). An impressive array of 150 stores includes **Giorgio Armani, Banana Republic Factory Store, Barneys New York Outlet, Brooks Brothers, Salvatore Ferragamo, Nautica, Nike Factory Store,** and **Polo Ralph Lauren Factory Store.** You'll also find **Disney's Character Premiere,** featuring plenty of Disney merchandise, plus a food court and a convenient parking garage.

TRADITIONAL SHOPPING

THE PREMIERE SHOPPING EXPERIENCE in central Florida is **The Mall at Millenia** (☎ 407-363-3555; **www.mallatmillenia.com**), anchored by **Bloomingdale's, Macy's,** and **Neiman Marcus.** Of about 150 stores, nearly half are new to the Orlando market, including **Cartier, Burberry, Crate & Barrel, Tiffany & Co., Gucci,** and **Louis Vuitton.** The mall also has eight restaurants, a full-service concierge, and a U.S. Post Office. Hours are Monday through Saturday, 10 a.m. to 9 p.m.; Sunday, 12 p.m. to 7 p.m.

We're told that next to Walt Disney World, more tourists visit ★ **The Florida Mall** (☎ 407-851-6255; **www.simon.com**)—that's one of the reasons it offers currency exchange and foreign-language assistance. This is the biggest mall in the area, with about 200 shops, including **Saks Fifth Avenue, Macy's, Nordstrom,** and **Pottery Barn.** Go early and park near one of the major stores you want to explore. The mall is located at 8001 South Orange Blossom Trail, at the corner of Sand Lake Road (FL 482) and South Orange Blossom Trail (US 441); hours are Monday through Saturday, 10 a.m. to 9 p.m.; Sunday, noon to 6 p.m.

Another not-to-be-missed shopping destination in central Florida is ★ **Park Avenue** in **Winter Park,** a small town just north of Orlando. Anchored by Rollins College at the south end, the street is lovely for strolling, window-shopping, and dining. Popular shops include **Restoration Hardware, Pottery Barn, Tuni's** (stylish women's apparel), **Bebe's** (trendy children's wear), **Williams-Sonoma, Gap, Talbots, Caswell-Massey,** and **Timothy's Gallery** (exquisite one-of-a-kind jewelry). Prices are high, but you can find terrific sidewalk sales a few times a year.

Park Avenue store hours vary but are generally Monday through Friday, 10 a.m. to 6 p.m.; Saturday, 10 a.m. to 5 p.m.; and Sunday, 12 p.m. to 5 p.m. Traffic on the two-lane brick street can be a bear, so avoid driving down Park; instead, take a side street and search for on-street parking a block or two off the main drag. We also recommend using the new parking garage on the south end of the street.

unofficial **TIP**
If time permits, visit the **Charles Hosmer Morse Museum of American Art** (445 North Park Avenue; ☎ 407-645-5311; **www.morsemuseum.org**), at the north end of the Park Avenue shopping district in Winter Park. It's home to the world's largest collection of Tiffany glass and a wonderful little gift shop featuring jewelry, stained-glass, textiles, and fine art.

To get to Park Avenue from the International Drive–WDW/Universal area, take I-4 east, exit at Fairbanks Avenue (Exit 87), and head east. Park Avenue is a little more than a mile away on the left-hand side.

PART NINETEEN

NIGHTLIFE *in and out of* WALT DISNEY WORLD

WALT DISNEY WORLD *at* NIGHT

DISNEY SO CLEVERLY CONTRIVES to exhaust you during the day that the thought of night activity sends most visitors into shock. Walt Disney World, however, offers much for the hearty and the nocturnal to do in the evenings.

IN THE THEME PARKS

EPCOT'S MAJOR EVENING EVENT is *IllumiNations,* a laser and fireworks show at World Showcase Lagoon. Showtime is listed in the daily entertainment schedule (*Times Guide*).

In the Magic Kingdom are the popular evening parade(s) and *Wishes* fireworks. Consult the *Times Guide* for performances.

On selected nights when the park is open late, Disney's Hollywood Studios features *Fantasmic!,* a laser, special-effects, and water spectacular. The *Times Guide* lists showtimes.

Presently there is no nighttime entertainment at Animal Kingdom.

AT THE HOTELS

THE FLOATING ELECTRICAL PAGEANT is a sort of Main Street Electrical Parade on barges. Starring creatures of the sea, the nightly pageant (with background music played on a doozy of a synthesizer) is one of our favorite Disney productions. The first performance of the short but captivating show is at 9 p.m. off the Polynesian Resort docks. From there, it circles around and repeats at the Grand Floridian at 9:15 p.m., heading afterward to Fort Wilderness Campground, Wilderness Lodge and Villas, and the Contemporary Resort–Bay Lake Tower.

For something more elaborate, consider a dinner theater. If you want to go honky-tonkin', the Buena Vista Palace, Hilton, and Royal Plaza hotels at the Downtown Disney Resort Area have lively (OK, OK, relatively lively) bars.

AT FORT WILDERNESS CAMPGROUND

THE FREE NIGHTLY campfire program at Fort Wilderness Campground begins with a sing-along led by Chip 'n' Dale and progresses to cartoons and a Disney movie. For Disney lodging guests only.

AT DISNEY'S BOARDWALK

THE BOARDWALK'S **Jellyrolls** features dueling pianos and sing-alongs. The BoardWalk also has Disney's first and only brewpub. An ESPN sports bar; the **Atlantic Dance Hall,** an upscale and largely deserted dance club; and several restaurants complete the BoardWalk's entertainment mix. Access is by foot from Epcot, by launch from Disney's Hollywood Studios, and by bus from other Disney World locations. The *Unofficial Guide* research team rates Jellyrolls as its second favorite of all Disney nightspots (Raglan Road at the old Pleasure Island is our top pick). It's raucous, frequently hilarious, and positively rejuvenating. The piano players are outstanding. Best of all, it's strictly for adults.

AT CORONADO SPRINGS RESORT

PERHAPS DISNEY'S MOST HIP NIGHTSPOT is the 5,000-square-foot **Rix Lounge,** a Vegas-ultralounge clone. DJs spin Top 40 tracks from 9 p.m. to 2 a.m.; a percussion band performs on select evenings. Few locals or resort guests have discovered Rix, so the place is frequently dead unless there's a big meeting or trade show at Coronado Springs. Also at this resort is the **Laguna Bar,** a romantic outdoor-terrace affair arrayed alongside the lake.

DOWNTOWN DISNEY

PLEASURE ISLAND Walt Disney World's nighttime-entertainment complex cashed in its chips in the fall of 2008. Gone, we think forever, are the BET Soundstage Club, Mannequins Dance Palace, Motion, 8 TRAX, the Comedy Warehouse, and the much-loved Adventurers Club. This last so exemplified Disney whimsy that everyone thought it would surely escape the ax. No such luck. All the Pleasure Island restaurants survived, though, as did a few shops. For now, the only live-music venue is **Raglan Road,** an Irish pub (see page 500).

DOWNTOWN DISNEY MARKETPLACE It's flog your wallet each night at the Marketplace with shops open until 11:30 p.m.

DISNEY'S WEST SIDE Disney's West Side is a 70-acre shopping, restaurant, and nightlife complex situated to the left of the old Pleasure Island. This area features a 24-screen **AMC** movie complex; **DisneyQuest,** a pay-for-play indoor theme park (see page 731); a permanent showplace for **Cirque du Soleil**'s extraordinary ***La Nouba;*** and a **House of Blues** concert hall with a seating capacity of 2,000. Dining options include **Planet Hollywood;** a 450-seat Cajun restaurant at **House of Blues; Wolfgang Puck** (serving California fare); and **Bongos Cuban Cafe,** owned by Gloria and Emilio Estefan. The complex can be accessed via Disney buses from most Disney World locations.

Cirque du Soleil's *La Nouba* ★★★★★

APPEAL BY AGE Under 21 ★★★★ 21–37 ★★★★★ 38–50 ★★★★ 51 and up ★★★★½

Type of show Circus as theater. **Tickets and information** ☎ 407-939-7600; www.cirquedusoleil.com/lanouba. **Admission cost** *Category Front & Center:* $117 adults, $94 children (ages 3–9); *Category 1:* $102 adults, $82 children; *Category 2:* $83 adults, $67 children; *Category 3:* $67 adults, $54 children. *Category 4:* $53 adults, $43 children. **Cast size** 72. **Night of lowest attendance** Thursday. **Usual showtimes** Tuesday–Saturday, 6 p.m. and 9 p.m. **Authors' rating** ★★★★★. **Duration of presentation** 1½ hours (no intermission) plus preshow.

DESCRIPTION AND COMMENTS Cirque du Soleil's *La Nouba* is a far cry from a traditional circus but retains all the fun and excitement of it. It is whimsical, mystical, and sophisticated, yet pleasing to all ages. The action takes place on an elaborate stage that incorporates almost every part of the theater. The original musical score is exotic, like the show.

Note: In the following paragraphs, we get into how the show *feels* and why it's special. If you don't care how it feels, or if you are not up to slogging through a boxcar of adjectives, the bottom line is simple: *La Nouba* is great. See it.

La Nouba is a most difficult show to describe. To categorize it as a circus does not begin to cover its depth, though its performers could perform with distinction in any circus on earth. *La Nouba* is more, much more, than a circus. It combines elements of classical Greek theater, mime, the English morality play, Dalí surrealism, Fellini characterization, and Chaplin comedy. *La Nouba* is at once an odyssey, a symphony, and an exploration of human emotions.

The show pivots on its humor, which is sometimes black, and engages the audience with its unforgettable characters. Though light and uplifting, it is also poignant and dark. Simple in presentation, it is at the same time extraordinarily intricate, always operating on multiple levels of meaning. As you laugh and watch the amazingly talented cast, your mind enters a dimension seldom encountered in a waking state. The presentation begins to register in your consciousness more as a seamless dream than as a stage production. You are moved, lulled, and soothed as well as excited and entertained. The sensitive, the imaginative, the literate, and those who love good theater and art will find nothing in all of Disney World that compares with *La Nouba.*

Thus far, as the following comments suggest, we have not received one negative comment about *La Nouba.*

From an Iowa City, Iowa, couple:

> *In terms of shows and attractions, Cirque du Soleil was absolutely wonderful and anyone with the time should make an attempt to go. I could go on and on about it, but I think just "GO!" is enough.*

The comments of a mom from Kansasville, Wisconsin, whose teens reluctantly consented to attend the show:

> *Even my hard-to-impress MTV-generation teens were awestruck.*

From a 40-something mom from Chester, New Hampshire:

> *Cirque du Soleil was spectacular—plan to arrive a half hour early for the preshow.*

From a mother of three from Stafford, Washington:

Cirque du Soleil is fantastic. If you go to Disney World and your kids are older than ten, you should definitely do this. If it means giving up a day at the park due to the expense, Cirque du Soleil is worth it.

Finally, from an Andover, Massachusetts, mother:

One of the true highlights of the trip was seeing Cirque du Soleil. The ticket prices were a bit steep and I debated doing it. But I thought it might be enjoyable for my non-Disney-loving husband and decided it was no more expensive than the rest of the trip. In fact, we all loved it, and it was the best money we spent.

TOURING TIPS Be forewarned that the audience is an integral part of *La Nouba* and that at almost any time you might be plucked from your seat to participate. Our advice is to loosen up and roll with it. If you don't want to get involved, politely but firmly decline to be conscripted. Then fix a death grip on the arms of your chair. Tickets for reserved seats can be purchased in advance at the Cirque box office or over the phone, using your credit card. Don't wait until the last minute; book well in advance from home.

House of Blues

Type of show Live concerts with an emphasis on rock and blues. **Tickets and information** ☎ 407-934-2222; **www.hob.com. Admission cost with taxes** $8–$95, depending on who's performing. **Nights of lowest attendance** Monday and Tuesday. **Usual showtimes** Varies between 7 p.m. and 9:30 p.m. depending on who's performing.

DESCRIPTION AND COMMENTS The House of Blues, developed by original Blues Brother Dan Aykroyd, features a restaurant and blues bar, as well as the concert hall. The restaurant serves Thursday through Saturday from 11 a.m. until 1:30 a.m., which makes it one of the few late-night-dining options in Walt Disney World. Live music cranks up every night at 10:30 p.m. in the restaurant–blues bar, but even before then, the joint is way beyond 110 decibels. The music hall next door features concerts by an eclectic array of musicians and groups. During one visit, the show bill listed gospel, blues, funk, ska, dance, salsa, rap, zydeco, hard rock, groove rock, and reggae groups over a two-week period.

TOURING TIPS Prices vary from night to night according to the fame and drawing power of the featured band. Tickets ranged from $8 to $62 during our visits but go higher when a really big name is scheduled.

The music hall is set up like a nightclub, with tables and bar stools for only about 150 people and standing room for a whopping 1,850 people. Folks dance when there's room and sometimes when there isn't. The tables and stools are first-come, first-served, with doors opening an hour before showtime on weekdays and 90 minutes before showtime on weekends. Acoustics are good, and the showroom is small enough to provide a relatively intimate concert experience. All shows are all ages unless otherwise indicated.

Sunday night at the House of Blues is Service Industry Night (aka SIN), when hospitality-industry employees (read: cast members) get in free; other folks are welcome but pay a cover of $8 (age 21 and older). A Florida Gen Y reader describes it:

Ahh, SIN night . . . there is always a DJ who will play club music, and all the times I went it was packed. It's more of a club atmosphere, and both floors are open for people to dance and mingle, but it's still a great time for tourists if they want to stay on-property and dance all night. Basically, each Sunday night is a huge party there.

WALT DISNEY WORLD DINNER THEATERS

SEVERAL DINNER-THEATER SHOWS play each night at Walt Disney World, and unlike other Disney dining venues, they make hard reservations instead of Advance Reservations, meaning you must guarantee your reservation ahead of time with a credit card. You will receive a confirmation number and be told to pick up your tickets at a Disney hotel Guest Services desk. Unless you cancel your tickets at least 48 hours before your reservation time, your credit card will still be charged the full amount. Dinner-show reservations can be made 180 days in advance; call ☎ 407-939-3463. While getting reservations for the *Spirit of Aloha Dinner Show* isn't terribly tough, booking the *Hoop-Dee-Doo Musical Revue* is a trick of the first order.

A couple from Bismarck, North Dakota, explains:

I'm glad we made our reservations so early (a year in advance). I was able to reserve space for us at Spirit of Aloha *at the Polynesian and the* Hoop-Dee-Doo Musical Revue. *At both of these, they seat you according to when you made your reservation. At the* Hoop-Dee-Doo Musical Revue, *we had a front center table. We were so close to the stage, we could see how many cavities the performers had!*

If you can't get reservations and want to see one of the shows:

1. Call ☎ 407-939-3463 at 9 a.m. each morning while you're at Disney World to make a same-day reservation. There are three performances each night, and for all three combined, only 3 to 24 people total will be admitted with same-day reservations.
2. Arrive at the show of your choice 45 minutes before showtime (early and late shows are your best bets) and put your name on the standby list. If someone with reservations fails to show, you may be admitted.

unofficial **TIP**
To make reservations for the *Hoop-Dee-Doo Musical Revue*, call as soon as you're certain of the dates of your visit. The earlier you call, the better your seats will be.

Borrowing a page from Las Vegas strip joints where nearsighted old coots are charged extra to sit way up front, Disney now offers tiered pricing for the *Hoop-Dee-Doo Musical Revue* and the *Spirit of Aloha Dinner Show*. The best seats are Category 1 at $60 for adults and $31 for kids 3 to 9. Category 2, with seats off to the side or behind Category 1, goes for $55 and $27, respectively. Category 3 seats are at the Orlando Greyhound Station, where you watch the show on a video feed. (OK, OK, you caught us.) They're farther still to the side or back, or on another level from the stage, and cost $51 for adults and $26 for children. For both the *Spirit of Aloha Dinner Show* and the *Hoop-Dee-Doo Musical Revue,* there's a good view from almost all seats, so you can decide if sitting closer to the action is worth the extra bucks.

Hoop-Dee-Doo Musical Revue

Pioneer Hall, Fort Wilderness Campground ☎ 407-939-3463. **Showtimes** 5, 7:15, and 9:30 p.m. nightly. **Cost** $51–$60 adults, $26–$31 children ages 3–9. **Discounts** Seasonal. **Type of seating** Tables of various sizes to fit the number in each party, set in an Old West–style dance hall. **Menu** All-you-can-eat barbecue ribs, fried chicken, corn, and strawberry shortcake. **Vegetarian alternative** On request (at least 24 hours in advance). **Beverages** Unlimited beer, wine, sangria, and soft drinks.

DESCRIPTION AND COMMENTS Six Wild West performers arrive by stagecoach (sound effects only) to entertain the crowd inside Pioneer Hall. There isn't much plot, just corny jokes interspersed with song or dance. The humor is of the *Hee Haw* ilk but is presented enthusiastically.

Audience participation includes sing-alongs, hand clapping, and a finale that uses volunteers to play parts onstage. Performers are accompanied by a banjo player and pianist who also play quietly while the food is being served. The fried chicken and corn on the cob are good, the ribs a bit tough though tasty. With the all-you-can-eat policy, at least you can get your money's worth by stuffing yourself silly.

Traveling to Fort Wilderness and absorbing the rustic atmosphere of Pioneer Hall augments the adventure. For repeat Disney World visitors, an annual visit to the revue is a tradition of sorts. Plus, warts and all, the revue is all Disney, and for some folks that's enough. The fact that performances sell out far in advance gives the experience a special aura.

Most of our readers enjoy the *Hoop-Dee-Doo Musical Revue,* but not all, as this letter from a Texas family attests:

> *What is all the hoop-dee-doo with the* Hoop-Dee-Doo Musical Revue*? The food was OK, if "gut-busting" fare is your idea of a fine night out, and the entertainment was pleasant. As a dinner theater, however, our family of three found it unexceptional in every respect but its cost. Had your review of the Revue tempered its enthusiasm (much as you present its Polynesian counterpart), we probably would have canceled our reservation, pocketed the $100, and spent the evening joyously stunned by another glorious light-and-fireworks spectacle.*

More typical are the remarks of a Cambridge, Massachusetts, mom:

> *The kids in our group (ages 3 to 8) thought the* Hoop-Dee-Doo Musical Revue *was just terrific. They watched intently the whole time, laughing hysterically. With them having such a good time, how could the adults not enjoy themselves? But I would not recommend the show for adults on their own. One thing we adults appreciated was the lack of commercialism: no movie tie-in, no merchandise sales. The entire experience, including its setting in the rustic Fort Wilderness campground, brought us back to simpler days and gave the kids exposure to entertainment before there were special effects.*

If you go to the *Hoop-Dee-Doo Musical Revue,* allow plenty of driving time (about an hour) to get there. Or do as this California dad suggests:

> *To go to the* Hoop-Dee-Doo Musical Revue *at Fort Wilderness, take the boat from the Magic Kingdom rather than any bus. This* [is] *contrary to the "official" directions. The boat dock is a short walk from Pioneer Hall* [in Fort Wilderness], *while the bus goes to the* [main] *Fort Wilderness parking lot where one has to transfer to another bus to Pioneer Hall.*

Mickey's Backyard BBQ

Fort Wilderness Campground ☎ 407-939-3463. **Showtimes** March–December, Thursday and Saturday, 6:30 p.m. **Cost** $45 adults, $27 children ages 3–9. **Special comments** Operates seasonally. **Type of seating** Picnic tables. **Menu** Baked chicken, barbecued pork ribs, burgers, hot dogs, corn, beans, mac and cheese, salads and slaw, bread, and watermelon and ice-cream bars for dessert. **Vegetarian alternatives** On request. **Beverages** Unlimited beer, wine, lemonade, and iced tea.

DESCRIPTION AND COMMENTS Situated along Bay Lake and held in a covered pavilion next to the now-closed River Country swimming park, *Mickey's Backyard BBQ* features Mickey, Minnie, Chip 'n' Dale, and Goofy, along with a live country band and line dancing. Though the pavilion gets some breeze off Bay Lake, we recommend going during the spring or fall, if possible. The food is pretty good, as is, fortunately, the insect control.

Because the barbecue is seasonal, dates are usually not entered into the WDW-DINE reservations system until late February or early March. Once the dates are in the system, you can make an advance reservation for anytime during the dinner show's ten-month season.

The easiest way to get to the barbecue is to take a boat from the Magic Kingdom or from one of the resorts on the Magic Kingdom monorail. Though getting to the barbecue is not nearly as difficult as commuting to the *Hoop-Dee-Doo Musical Revue,* give yourself at least 45 minutes if you plan to arrive by boat.

Spirit of Aloha Dinner Show

Disney's Polynesian Resort ☎ 407-939-3463. **Showtimes** Tuesday–Saturday, 5:15 and 8 p.m. **Cost** $51–$60 adults, $26–$31 children ages 3–9. **Discounts** Seasonal. **Type of seating** Long rows of tables, with some separation between individual parties. The show is performed on an outdoor stage, but all seating is covered. Ceiling fans provide some air movement, but it can get warm, especially at the early show. **Menu** Tropical fruit, roasted chicken, island pork ribs, mixed vegetables, rice, and pineapple bread; chicken tenders, PB&J sandwich, mac and cheese, and hot dogs are also available for children. **Vegetarian alternative** On request. **Beverages** Beer, wine, and soft drinks.

DESCRIPTION AND COMMENTS Formerly the *Polynesian Luau,* this show features South Seas–island native dancing followed by an all-you-can-eat "Polynesian-style" meal. The dancing is interesting and largely authentic, and the dancers are attractive though definitely PG-rated in the Disney tradition. We think the show has its moments and the meal is adequate, but neither is particularly special.

Despite the name change, not much else differentiates this show from the old *Polynesian Luau.* The revised show follows (tenuously) the common "girl leaves home for the big city, forgets her roots, and must rediscover them" theme. The performers are uniformly attractive ("Stud muffins!" said an *Unofficial* femme when asked about the men), and the dancing is very good. The story, however, never really makes sense as anything other than a slender thread between musical numbers. Our show lasted for more than 2 hours and 15 minutes.

The food does little more than illustrate how difficult it must be to prepare the same meal for hundreds of people simultaneously. The roasted chicken is better than the ribs, but neither is anything special. We conditionally recommend *Spirit of Aloha* for special occasions, when the people celebrating get to go on stage. But go to the early show and get dessert somewhere else in the World.

A well-traveled couple from Fond du Lac, Wisconsin, comments:

> Spirit of Aloha *was a beautiful presentation, better than some shows we have seen in Hawaii! The food, however, lacked in all areas. Better food has come out of Disney kitchens. During our visit, the fruit platter was chintzy, the honey-roasted chicken was a bit fatty, and the pineapple cake was dry.*

OTHER AREA DINNER THEATERS

CENTRAL FLORIDA PROBABLY HAS MORE DINNER attractions than anywhere else on earth. The name "dinner attraction" is something of a misnomer, because dinner is rarely the attraction. These are audience-participation shows or events with food served along the way. They range from extravagant productions where guests sit in arenas at long tables, to intimate settings at individual tables. Don't expect terrific food, but if you're looking for something entertaining outside Walt Disney World, consider one of these.

If you decide to try a non-Disney dinner show, scavenge local tourist magazines from brochure racks and hotel desks outside the World. These free publications usually have discount coupons for area shows.

UNIVERSAL CITYWALK

CITYWALK WAS UNIVERSAL' ORLANDO'S ANSWER to Pleasure Island. Now, with Pleasure Island defunct, CityWalk takes its place as the preeminent nightlife venue. In addition to a number of restaurants, you'll find **CityWalk's Rising Star,** a karaoke club where singers are backed by a live band; reggae at **Bob Marley—A Tribute to Freedom;** a **Pat O'Brien's** dueling-pianos club; a **Hard Rock Cafe** and **Hard Rock Live** concert venue; **Jimmy Buffett's Margaritaville;** the **Latin Quarter,** for Nuevo Latino music, food, and dancing; the **Red Coconut Club,** a two-story upscale cocktail lounge with live music and dancing; and a dance club called **The Groove,** with high-tech lighting and visual effects. If you do decide to dine at CityWalk, your options include **Jimmy Buffett's Margaritaville, Emeril's Restaurant, the Latin Quarter, Pat O'Brien's, Hard Rock Cafe, NBA City, NASCAR Sports Grille,** the **Bubba Gump Shrimp Co., CityWalk's Rising Star, Bob Marley—A Tribute to Freedom,** and **Pastamoré** (for more on CityWalk restaurants, see page 423). For dancing, try The Groove, the Latin Quarter, the Red Coconut Club, or Bob Marley—A Tribute to Freedom. And if you're in the mood for live music, check out Pat O'Brien's, Bob Marley—A Tribute to Freedom, the Red Coconut Club, or Jimmy Buffett's Margaritaville.

There's no admission charge to enjoy the shops, restaurants, and street entertainment. As for the clubs, you can buy a pass for about $12 that admits you to all of them, or if you prefer, you can pay a cover charge (usually about $7) at each club you visit. In addition to the clubs, shops, and restaurants, there's a 20-screen **AMC Universal Cineplex** movie theater. Add a movie to your CityWalk pass for a total cost of $15, or spring for a meal-and-movie deal for a grand total of $22.

APPENDIX

READERS' QUESTIONS *to the* AUTHORS

FOLLOWING ARE QUESTIONS AND COMMENTS from *Unofficial Guide* readers. Some frequently asked questions are addressed in every edition of the *Guide*.

QUESTION:

> *When you do your research, are you admitted to the parks free? Do the Disney people know you're there?*

ANSWER:

We pay the regular admission, and usually the Disney people don't know we're on-site. Similarly, both in and out of Walt Disney World, we pay for our own meals and lodging.

QUESTION:

> *How often is the* Unofficial Guide *revised?*

ANSWER:

We publish a new edition once a year, but we revise every time we go to press, usually twice a year.

QUESTION:

> *Where can I find information about what has changed at Walt Disney World in between published editions of the* Unofficial Guide*?*

ANSWER:

We post important changes, especially those that affect our touring plans, at **TouringPlans.com.**

QUESTION:

> *Do you write each new edition from scratch?*

ANSWER:

Nope. With a destination the size of Walt Disney World, it's hard enough to keep up with what's new. Moreover, we put great effort into communicating the most salient, useful information in the clearest possible language. If an attraction or hotel has not changed, we are very reluctant to tinker with its coverage for the sake of freshening the writing.

QUESTION:

> *I've never read any other* Unofficial Guides. *Are they all as critical as* The Unofficial Guide to Walt Disney World?

ANSWER:

What some readers perceive as critical we see as objective and constructive. Our job is to prepare you for both the best and worst of Walt Disney World. As it happens, some folks are very passionate about what one reader calls "the inherent goodness of Disney." These readers might be more comfortable with press releases or the *Official Guide* than with the strong consumer viewpoint represented in our guide. That said, some readers take us to task for being overly positive.

QUESTION:

> *I have an old edition of the* Unofficial Guide. *How much of the information* [in it] *is still correct?*

ANSWER:

Veteran travel writers will acknowledge that 5% to 8% of the information in a guidebook is out of date by the time it comes off the press. Walt Disney World is always changing. If you're using an old edition of the *Unofficial Guide,* descriptions of attractions still existing should be generally accurate. However, many other things change with every edition, particularly the touring plans and the hotel and restaurant reviews. Finally, and obviously, older editions of the *Unofficial Guide* don't cover new attractions or developments. Corrections and updates for the current edition can also be found at **TouringPlans.com.**

QUESTION:

> *How many people have you surveyed for your age-group ratings regarding the attractions?*

ANSWER:

Since the first *Unofficial Guide* was published in 1985, we have interviewed or surveyed slightly more than 34,000 Walt Disney World patrons. Even with such a large survey population, however, we continue to find certain age groups under-represented. Specifically, we'd love to hear more from seniors about their experiences with Splash Mountain, Big Thunder Mountain Railroad, Space Mountain, Star Tours, the Tower of Terror, the Rock 'n' Roller Coaster, Test Track, Mission: Space, Soarin', Kali River Rapids, Expedition Everest, and Dinosaur.

QUESTION:

Do you stay in Walt Disney World? If not, where?

ANSWER:

We stay at Walt Disney World lodging properties quite often. Since we began writing about Walt Disney World in 1982, we've stayed at more than 75 different properties in various locations around Orlando, Lake Buena Vista, and Kissimmee.

QUESTION:

Bob, what's your favorite Florida attraction?

ANSWER:

What attracts me (as opposed to my favorite attraction) is **Juniper Springs,** a stunningly beautiful stream about one and a half hours north of Orlando in the Ocala National Forest. Originating in a limestone aquifer, the crystal-clear water erupts from the ground and begins a ten-mile journey to the creek's mouth at Lake George. Winding through palm, cypress, and live oak, the stream is more exotic than the Jungle Cruise, and alive with birds, turtles, and alligators. Put in at the Juniper Springs Recreation Area on FL 40, 36 miles east of Ocala. The seven-mile trip to the FL 19 bridge takes about four and a half hours. Canoe rentals and shuttle service are available at the recreation area. Call ☎ 352-625-3147 for more information.

READERS' COMMENTS

READERS LOVE TO SHARE TIPS. Here's one from a St. Louis mom:

> *When dining at Downtown Disney, it's best to arrive before 7 p.m. We ate there twice and had no problem getting seated immediately, but after 7 p.m. everywhere was packed.*

And from an Ann Arbor, Michigan, mother of three:

> *Even though we stayed on Disney property, we stopped off on [US] 192 and loaded up on the local freebie visitor magazines and coupon books. We estimate they saved us over $200, mostly on food.*

From an Annapolis, Maryland, reader:

> *Have your hotel fax you a confirmation of your reservation. If we hadn't done this, we would have found ourselves without a room over the Easter holiday.*

An Iowa City, Iowa, couple offers this observation about being in touch with your feelings:

> *We didn't build rest breaks into our plans but were willing to say, "OK, I'm just not having fun right now; we should leave the park," and go on to something else (like a water park, hotel pool, or shopping trip to Downtown Disney). This is a skill I would like to see more people develop. I can't count the number of people or families I saw who were obviously not having fun.*

A woman from Suwanee, Georgia, offers a suggestion for the perfect Disney vacation:

Your book made our trip a much more successful one. It also frustrated our male adults, who erroneously believed this was a trip for their enjoyment. We followed your advice to get up early and see as much as possible before an early lunch. But the men refused to go back to the hotel for a nap and a meal outside the park, so we fought the crowds until 3 or 4 p.m., by which time everyone was exhausted and cranky. My mother and I decided our next trip will include your guidebook and the children—but no men!

An Athens, Georgia, reader thinks Disney World could do with a little less cheer:

On the last day, there was a cheerleading competition. This resulted in tons of loud, annoying cheerleaders running around the park. The worst part was, they kept practicing their cheers while waiting in line.

A Norwalk, Ohio, mom searches for happy feet:

On the subject of footwear, support is just as important as comfort. On one trip I wore Keds—big mistake. My shins ached unbelievably before the end of the second day. From then on I was a die-hard tennis-shoe girl, until I discovered FitFlops from Bath & Body Works. You get the support of a tennis shoe with the comfort of a flip-flop. They're grrrreat! *(A little Thurl Ravenscroft reference for you there.)*

From a Greenville, Kentucky, mom who wasn't able to take advantage of the free-admission promotion on her daughter's birthday:

We were disappointed that a birth certificate was the only acceptable ID for my daughter. We had certified shot records and they still wouldn't accept them.

A reader from Crofton, Maryland, discovered that the best bargains on Disney merchandise sometimes turned up in unexpected places:

People who want to save $$$ on Disney trinkets and aren't fussy about selection really should go to the Disney shop at Orlando Premium Outlets. It was great for finding items to bring back for family and friends. I would note that I bought a talking Goofy doll for my nephew and was very pleased with the $19.99 price, which was significantly lower than the list price. However, the VERY SAME doll was only $9.99 at (of all places!) Publix grocery store! In fact, Publix has loads of cute dolls, T-shirts, keychains, and other gifts at great prices! . . . We went there for coffee and found the Disney section!

A Midwestern mom loved getting in the game, writing:

It was a thrill for me to stand behind the ropes and wait till the park officially opened—to hear the music and announcements, then hurry with the throngs to the first ride. It was so exciting! I loved being so punctual and ahead of the mob. I felt so prepared and on top of things. I knew that the other early birds were in the know, too. It felt like family. OK, I'm probably weird, but it was one of the highlights of the trip for me. My husband wasn't so thrilled. He teased me for days about running over old ladies and little children—I DID NOT RUN! I was speed-walking!

Henry Ford famously said, "You can have any color car you want, as long as it's black." A hungry (and persistent) Fairfax, Vermont, reader found that mind-set alive and well at his Disney resort's food court:

The real difficulty of our stay began when I made the ill-advised decision to request a hamburger at the food court. I was first given a cheeseburger. I then informed the cast member that I requested a hamburger. She placed the burger back under the heat lamp, and I proceeded to watch the person at the grill place cheese on all 14 burgers that had just been put on the grill. Sensing my unease, another cast member asked me what I had ordered. I informed him that I was waiting for a hamburger. He then reached under the heat lamp and proceeded to give me the original cheeseburger. Had I realized that, at that very moment, fate had determined that I was not to enjoy a hamburger on this night, then I would have given up. Sadly, I did not come to this realization at that time. Instead, I chose to "spit into the wind" and insist on getting my hamburger. Thus, I watched as another 14 burgers were placed on the grill. I could almost taste the reward for my patience . . . until I saw the cast member delicately place cheese on each and every one of the new burgers. Alas, my quest for a burger ended, and my call to Pizza Hut delivery was made.

A Fenton, Missouri, woman evidently took her banker with her:

Love your book! Our last trip was in 2006 with eight people total: Grandma, Grandpa, my sister and her husband and two sons (ages 4 and 12), and my finance and me.

A Lafayette, Louisiana, dad overheard this comment:

The "out of the mouths of babes" award goes to a very cute little blonde girl, about 3 years old. We were racing past her and the rest of the goats standing in the regular line for the Kilimanjaro Safaris. She asked her mother, "Why do they get to go?" and Mom said, "They have FASTPASSes." The girl immediately replied, "Well, why did we get Slow Passes?" Good question, kid.

A father of two from Widnes, England, knows who butters his bread:

While we did not make the early starts, the guide still managed to advise of enough short-cuts that enabled us to keep everyone happy. (Let's face it, I'm talking about my wife.)

A Yardley, Pennsylvania, woman of few words sums up the Walt Disney World experience thus:

Expect to wait for everything—except the bathroom!

A Cleveland dad complains about fellow citizens from New Jersey:

We would not go again during "Jersey Week." I was sick of tank-top-wearing fathers yelling "ANTHONY, git ova here!"

A Nashville, Tennessee, family of three report a tough reentry:

My wife and I were so depressed when we had to adjust to reality after a week of being in Disney's alternate universe. We think Disney needs to offer some sort of debriefing or transition program to ease its visitors back into the real world. Perhaps they could send Mickey and Minnie over to make blueberry pancakes the morning after you return.

A woman from Concord, North Carolina, has all the bases covered, writing:

Thank you for continuing the irreverent style that makes me laugh while giving me excellent advice about what to pursue with pleasure (or avoid with condescension and mild disgust).

An Atlanta reader relates the story of a dirty bird and a solicitous cast member:

While riding Splash Mountain, a mother and teenage son in our boat had brought ponchos (smart move), and the son took his off before we got out of the boat, just in time for a bird to poop on him. He went to buy a clean shirt in the gift shop, and when the cast member found out what happened, he gave the kid a free shirt. I thought that was very nice!

From a husband and wife, also from Atlanta:

My brother-in-law, Pat, and his wife were planning a trip to Disney for the first time with their 4-year-old daughter. My other brother-in-law, Robert, who has three kids and has taken them to Disney twice, asked Pat if he had taken the "Disney test": take a $100 bill, throw it in the toilet, and flush. If you can do this without flinching, you're ready for Disney.

A dad from Geneva, New York, is a man in motion, writing:

One thing that I seem to forget every time I prepare for a trip to the World is this: from the moment I get on the airplane here at home, my body is constantly in motion in some sort of unfamiliar manner—from the airplane to the bus to the rides to the waterslides . . . on and on. After about three days, my equilibrium is just SHOT! Rest and a good dose of Dramamine might just prove your most important allies!

And so it goes. . . . .

ACCOMMODATIONS INDEX

Note: Page numbers of profiles are in **boldface** type.

RESTAURANT INDEX

Note: Page numbers of restaurant profiles are in **boldface** type.

SUBJECT INDEX

Note: Attractions at non-Disney parks are labeled; those at Disney parks are unlabeled.

TOURING PLANS

"Not a Touring Plan" TOURING PLANS

IT'S EASIER TO DEVISE A GOOD TOURING PLAN than an optimal one. Or maybe we've been doing this so long we've finally achieved Zen enlightenment. Either way, below are the simple rules we use when friends ask us for touring plans that don't sound like a space shuttle launch checklist. Use these when you don't want the regimentation of a step-by-step plan but do want to avoid long waits in line. Skip attractions that don't suit you. Use FASTPASS if waits seem too long.

MAGIC KINGDOM

FOR PARENTS OF SMALL CHILDREN WITH ONE DAY TO TOUR, ARRIVING AT PARK OPENING See Fantasyland first. If characters are important, see Mickey's Toontown Fair next; otherwise, save it for later. See Frontierland and some of Adventureland, then take a midday break. Return to the park and complete your tour of Adventureland. Next see Liberty Square, Mickey's Toontown Fair (if missed earlier), and Tomorrowland. End on Main Street for parades and fireworks.

FOR ADULTS WITH ONE DAY TO TOUR, ARRIVING AT PARK OPENING First see Space Mountain and Buzz Lightyear in Tomorrowland, then Fantasyland, Frontierland, Adventureland, Liberty Square, Mickey's Toontown Fair, and the rest of Tomorrowland. End on Main Street for parades and fireworks.

FOR PARENTS AND ADULTS WITH TWO DAYS TO TOUR *Note:* Day One works great for Disney-resort guests on Extra Magic Hour mornings. Start Day One in Fantasyland, then tour Frontierland and Pirates of the Caribbean in Adventureland. Take a midday break and return to Adventureland. Next see Liberty Square and the evening parade. See fireworks from Main Street. Begin Day Two in Tomorrowland, then head to Mickey's Toontown Fair. See any missed Adventureland or Frontierland attractions before leaving the park around midday.

FOR PARENTS AND ADULTS WITH AN AFTERNOON AND A FULL DAY For the afternoon, get FASTPASSes, if possible, for any Frontierland and Adventureland headliners you can; save other headliners for later in the evening. Tour Liberty Square, Adventureland, and Frontierland, then see the evening parade and fireworks. On your full day of touring, see Fantasyland, Tomorrowland (use FASTPASS for Space Mountain), and Mickey's Toontown Fair, then catch any missed attractions from the previous afternoon.

EPCOT

FOR PARENTS AND ADULTS WITH ONE DAY TO TOUR, ARRIVING AT PARK OPENING Obtain FASTPASSes for Soarin' first, then see Test Track and Mission: Space. See remaining Future World West attractions, then tour Future World East. Tour World Showcase clockwise, starting in Mexico.

FOR PARENTS AND ADULTS WITH ONE DAY TO TOUR, ARRIVING LATE MORNING Try to obtain FASTPASSes for Soarin', Test Track, or Mission: Space (in that order). See Future World East attractions, then Future World West. Tour World Showcase counterclockwise, starting in Canada.

FOR PARENTS AND ADULTS WITH TWO DAYS TO TOUR On Day One, see Future World East attractions and Mexico through the United States in World Showcase. On Day Two, tour Future World West and Canada through Japan.

ANIMAL KINGDOM

FOR PARENTS AND ADULTS ARRIVING AT PARK OPENING Obtain FASTPASSes for Expedition Everest in Asia, then begin a land-by-land counterclockwise tour of park starting in DinoLand U.S.A. Work in shows as you near them, but leave *Finding Nemo—The Musical* for last.

FOR PARENTS AND ADULTS ARRIVING LATE MORNING Obtain FASTPASSes for Kilimanjaro Safaris, then begin counterclockwise tour of park starting in Africa, saving Kali River Rapids and Expedition Everest for last.

DISNEY'S HOLLYWOOD STUDIOS

FOR PARENTS ARRIVING AT PARK OPENING Ride *Toy Story* Mania!, then head to Animation Courtyard to begin a counterclockwise tour of the park starting with *Voyage of the Little Mermaid*. Work in other shows as you near them. End day on Sunset Boulevard for *Fantasmic!*

FOR ADULTS ARRIVING AT PARK OPENING See Rock 'n' Roller Coaster, Tower of Terror, and then begin a counterclockwise tour of the park with *Toy Story* Mania! and The Great Movie Ride. End in Animation Courtyard for *Voyage of the Little Mermaid* and The Magic of Disney Animation. Work in other shows as you near them. End day on Sunset Boulevard for *Fantasmic!*

unofficial **TIP**
In the parks? Help other *Unofficial Guide* readers plan their next move by sending any wait times you notice to **m.TouringPlans.com** from your smart phone. You can also view current and future wait times here.

FOR PARENTS AND ADULTS ARRIVING LATE MORNING Try to get FASTPASSes for Rock 'n' Roller Coaster, *Voyage of the Little Mermaid,* or Tower of Terror (in that order). Start clockwise tour of park with Backlot Tour, working in shows as you near them. Save *Toy Story* Mania! for last, grab a bite to eat, and see *Fantasmic!*

Please see the following pages for our detailed clip-out touring plans.

Magic Kingdom

Magic Kingdom
Recommended Attraction Visitation Times

It is best to see attractions with visitation times listed as "anytime" during the more crowded middle part of the day (noon–4 p.m.).

1. Ariel's Grotto: Before 11 a.m./after 9 p.m.
2. Astro Orbiter: Before 11 a.m./after 5 p.m.
3. The Barnstormer at Goofy's Wiseacres Farm: Before 10:30 a.m., during events, or just before closing.
4. Big Thunder Mountain Railroad: Before 10 a.m., hour before closing, or use FASTPASS.
5. Buzz Lightyear's Space Ranger Spin: Before 10:30 a.m./after 6 p.m.
6. Cinderella's Golden Carousel: Before 11 a.m./after 8 p.m.
7. *Country Bear Jamboree:* Before 11:30 a.m., during parades, or 2 hours before closing.
8. Donald's Boat: Anytime.
9. Dumbo The Flying Elephant: Before 10 a.m./after 9 p.m.
10. *Enchanted Tiki Room:* Before 11 a.m./after 3:30 p.m.
11. Frontierland Shootin' Arcade: Whenever convenient.
12. *The Hall of Presidents:* Anytime.
13. The Haunted Mansion: Before 11:30 a.m./after 8 p.m.
14. It's a Small World: Anytime.
15. Jungle Cruise: Before 10 a.m., 2 hours before closing, or use FASTPASS.
16. *Liberty Belle* Riverboat: Anytime.
17. Mad Tea Party: Before 11 a.m./after 5 p.m.
18. The Magic Carpets of Aladdin: Before 10 a.m./1 hour before closing.
19. The Many Adventures of Winnie the Pooh: Before 10 a.m./2 hours before closing.

—continued on other side—

If you have a Web-enabled cell phone, you can view current and future wait times for every attraction—and add the ones you see in the parks—at **m.TouringPlans.com.**

Magic Kingdom
Recommended Attraction Visitation Times

It is best to see attractions with visitation times listed as "anytime" during the more crowded middle part of the day (noon–4 p.m.).

—continued from other side—

20. Mickey's and Minnie's Country Houses: Before 11:30 a.m./after 4:30 p.m.
21. *Mickey's PhilharMagic:* Before 11 a.m./during parades.
22. *Monsters, Inc. Laugh Floor:* Before 11 a.m./after 4 p.m.
23. Peter Pan's Flight: Before 10 a.m., after 6 p.m., or use FASTPASS.
24. Pirates of the Caribbean: Before noon/after 5 p.m.
25. Pooh's Playfull Spot: Anytime.
26. Snow White's Scary Adventures: Before 11 a.m./after 6 p.m.
27. Space Mountain: Opening, 6–7 p.m., 1 hour before closing, or use FASTPASS.
28. Splash Mountain: Opening, during parades, just before closing, or use FASTPASS.
29. *Stitch's Great Escape!:* Before 11 a.m., during parades, or after 6 p.m.
30. Swiss Family Treehouse: Anytime.
31. Tom Sawyer Island: Midmorning–late afternoon (closes at dusk).
32. Tomorrowland Speedway: Before 11 a.m./after 5 p.m.
33. Tomorrowland Transit Authority: Anytime.
34. Toontown Hall of Fame: Before 10:30 a.m./after 5:30 p.m.
35. *Walt Disney's Carousel of Progress:* Anytime.
36. Walt Disney World Railroad: Anytime.

If you have a Web-enabled cell phone, you can view current and future wait times for every attraction—and add the ones you see in the parks—at **m.TouringPlans.com.**

Magic Kingdom

Magic Kingdom
One-day Touring Plan for Adults

1. Arrive at the entrance to the Magic Kingdom 50 minutes (Disney-resort guests) to 70 minutes (non-Disney-resort guests) prior to opening. Get guide maps and the daily entertainment schedule.
2. In Tomorrowland, ride Space Mountain.
3. Ride Buzz Lightyear.
4. In Fantasyland, ride Winnie the Pooh.
5. Ride Snow White's Scary Adventures.
6. Ride Peter Pan's Flight.
7. Ride It's a Small World.
8. In Liberty Square, see The Haunted Mansion.
9. In Frontierland, ride Splash Mountain if wait is 20 minutes or less. If not, obtain FASTPASS.
10. Ride Big Thunder Mountain Railroad.
11. In Adventureland, ride Pirates of the Caribbean.
12. If you missed it earlier, ride Splash Mountain using FASTPASS.
13. Eat lunch.
14. Take the train from Frontierland to Mickey's Toontown Fair.
15. Tour Mickey's Toontown Fair.
16. Take the train back to Frontierland.
17. In Adventureland, ride the Jungle Cruise if wait is 20 minutes or less. If not, obtain FASTPASS.
18. See *Enchanted Tiki Room.*
19. In Frontierland, see *Country Bear Jamboree.*
20. If you missed it earlier, take the Jungle Cruise in Adventureland using FASTPASS.
21. Explore the Swiss Family Treehouse.
22. In Liberty Square, ride the *Liberty Belle* Riverboat.
23. Experience *The Hall of Presidents.*
24. In Fantasyland, see *Mickey's PhilharMagic.*
25. Eat dinner.
26. In Tomorrowland, see *Monsters, Inc. Laugh Floor.*
27. Experience *Stitch's Great Escape!* Or don't, if you're running late or you just don't feel up to it.
28. Ride the Tomorrowland Transit Authority.
29. See *Walt Disney's Carousel of Progress.*
30. See the evening parade on Main Street.
31. See the evening fireworks on Main Street. A good viewing spot is to the right of the central hub, on the walkway toward Tomorrowland.

If you have a Web-enabled cell phone, you can view currer and future wait times for every attraction—and add the or you see in the parks—at **m.TouringPlans.com.**

Magic Kingdom

Magic Kingdom
Author's Selective One-day Touring Plan for Adults

1. Arrive at the entrance to the Magic Kingdom 50 minutes (Disney-resort guests) to 70 minutes (non-Disney-resort guests) prior to opening. Get guide maps and the daily entertainment schedule.
2. In Tomorrowland, ride Space Mountain.
3. Ride Buzz Lightyear.
4. In Fantasyland, ride Winnie the Pooh.
5. Ride Peter Pan's Flight.
6. Ride It's a Small World. Next, schedule therapy to get song out of head.
7. In Liberty Square, see The Haunted Mansion.
8. In Frontierland, ride Splash Mountain if wait is 20 minutes or less. If not, obtain FASTPASS.
9. Ride Big Thunder Mountain Railroad.
10. In Adventureland, ride Pirates of the Caribbean.
11. If you missed it earlier, ride Splash Mountain using FASTPASS.
12. Eat lunch.
13. Take the train from Frontierland to Mickey's Toontown Fair.
14. Tour Mickey's Toontown Fair.
15. Take the train back to Frontierland.
16. In Adventureland, ride the Jungle Cruise if wait is 20 minutes or less. If not, obtain FASTPASS.
17. See *Enchanted Tiki Room.*
18. In Frontierland, see *Country Bear Jamboree.*
19. If you missed it earlier, take the Jungle Cruise in Adventureland using FASTPASS.
20. Explore the Swiss Family Treehouse.
21. In Liberty Square, ride the *Liberty Belle* Riverboat.
22. Experience *The Hall of Presidents.*
23. In Fantasyland, see *Mickey's PhilharMagic.*
24. Eat dinner.
25. In Tomorrowland, ride the Tomorrowland Transit Authority.
26. See *Monsters, Inc. Laugh Floor.*
27. See the evening parade on Main Street.
28. See the evening fireworks on Main Street. A good viewing spot is to the right of the central hub, on the walkway toward Tomorrowland.

If you have a Web-enabled cell phone, you can view current and future wait times for every attraction—and add the ones you see in the parks—at **m.TouringPlans.com.**

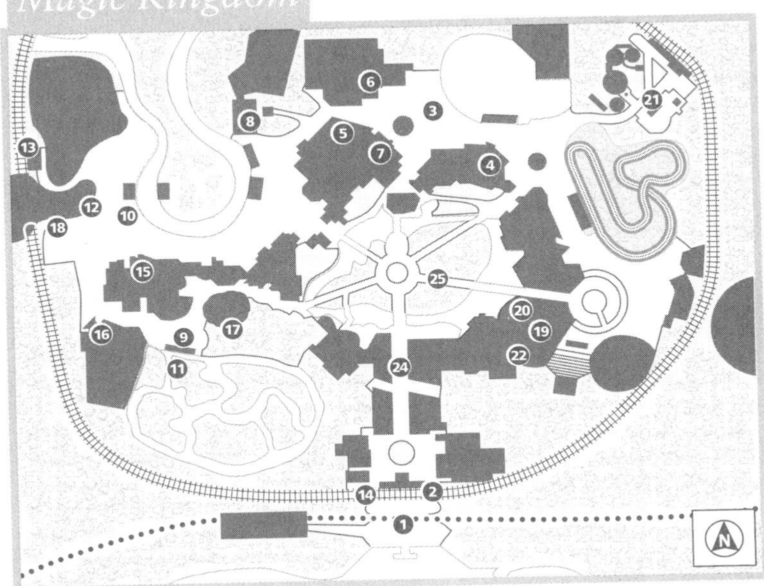

Magic Kingdom
One-day Touring Plan for Parents with Young Children

(Review the Small-child Fright-potential Chart on pages 330–333.)

1. Arrive at the entrance to the Magic Kingdom 50 minutes (Disney-resort guests) to 70 minutes (non-Disney-resort guests) prior to opening. Get guide maps and the daily entertainment schedule.
2. Rent strollers (if necessary).
3. In Fantasyland, ride Dumbo.
4. Ride Winnie the Pooh. Unless the wait exceeds 30 minutes, do not use FASTPASS.
5. Ride Peter Pan's Flight. Unless the wait exceeds 30 minutes, do not use FASTPASS.
6. Ride It's a Small World.
7. See *Mickey's PhilharMagic.*
8. In Liberty Square, see The Haunted Mansion.
9. In Adventureland, take the Jungle Cruise (use FASTPASS if wait exceeds 30 minutes).
10. In Frontierland, take the raft over to Tom Sawyer Island.
11. Ride Jungle Cruise if you have a FASTPASS. If not, skip to the next step.
12. Obtain FASTPASSes for Splash Mountain. If wait is 20 minutes or less, ride now instead of using FASTPASS.
13. Ride train to Main Street. Leave the park for lunch and a nap.
14. Return to the park and take the train to Frontierland.
15. See *Country Bear Jamboree.*
16. In Adventureland, ride Pirates of the Caribbean.
17. Explore the Swiss Family Treehouse.
18. Ride Splash Mountain using FASTPASS.
19. In Tomorrowland, get FASTPASS for Buzz Lightyear.
20. See *Monsters, Inc. Laugh Floor.*
21. Tour Mickey's Toontown Fair.
22. Ride Buzz Lightyear using FASTPASS.
23. Eat dinner.
24. See the evening parade on Main Street.
25. See the evening fireworks on Main Street. A good viewing spot is to the right of the central hub, on the walkway toward Tomorrowland.

If you have a Web-enabled cell phone, you can view current and future wait times for every attraction—and add the ones you see in the parks—at **m.TouringPlans.com.**

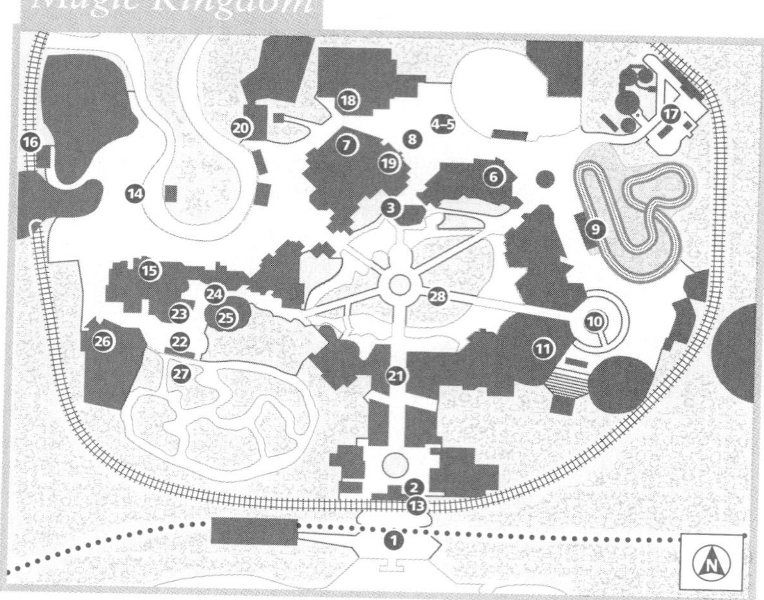

Magic Kingdom Dumbo-or-Die-in-a-Day Touring Plan for Parents with Young Children

(Review the Small-child Fright-potential Chart on pages 330–333. Interrupt the touring plan for lunch, rest, and dinner.)

1. Arrive at the entrance to the Magic Kingdom 50 minutes prior to opening. Get guide maps and the daily entertainment schedule.
2. Rent strollers (if needed).
3. Go to Fantasyland via Cinderella Castle. Make dinner reservations at the castle on the way. To save time, call ☎ 407-WDW-DINE to make dinner reservations up to 180 days in advance.
4. Ride Dumbo.
5. Ride Dumbo again. *Tip:* Have one parent stand in line 24 people behind the other parent and child. When first parent is done riding, hand child to second parent in line.
6. Ride Winnie the Pooh. Unless wait exceeds 30 minutes, do not use FASTPASS.
7. Ride Peter Pan's Flight. Unless wait exceeds 30 minutes, do not use FASTPASS.
8. Ride Cinderella's Golden Carousel.
9. In Tomorrowland, ride the Speedway.
10. Ride the Astro Orbiter.
11. Ride Buzz Lightyear.
12. Leave the park for lunch and a nap.
13. Return and take the train to Frontierland.
14. In Frontierland, take the raft to Tom Sawyer Island.
15. See *Country Bear Jamboree.*
16. Take the train from Frontierland to Mickey's Toontown Fair.
17. See Mickey's Country House, Minnie's Country House, Donald's Boat. Meet Disney characters and take pictures at the Toontown Hall of Fame.
18. In Fantasyland, ride It's a Small World.
19. See *Mickey's PhilharMagic.*
20. In Liberty Square, see The Haunted Mansion.
21. See the evening parade on Main Street.
22. In Adventureland, obtain FASTPASS for the Jungle Cruise if still available.
23. See *Enchanted Tiki Room.*
24. Ride The Magic Carpets of Aladdin.
25. Explore the Swiss Family Treehouse.
26. Ride Pirates of the Caribbean.
27. If you have a FASTPASS for Jungle Cruise, ride now. If not, skip to the next step.
28. See the evening fireworks on Main Street. A good viewing spot is to the right of the central hub, on the walkway toward Tomorrowland.

If you have a Web-enabled cell phone, you can view current and future wait times for every attraction—and add the ones you see in the parks—at **m.TouringPlans.com.**

Magic Kingdom

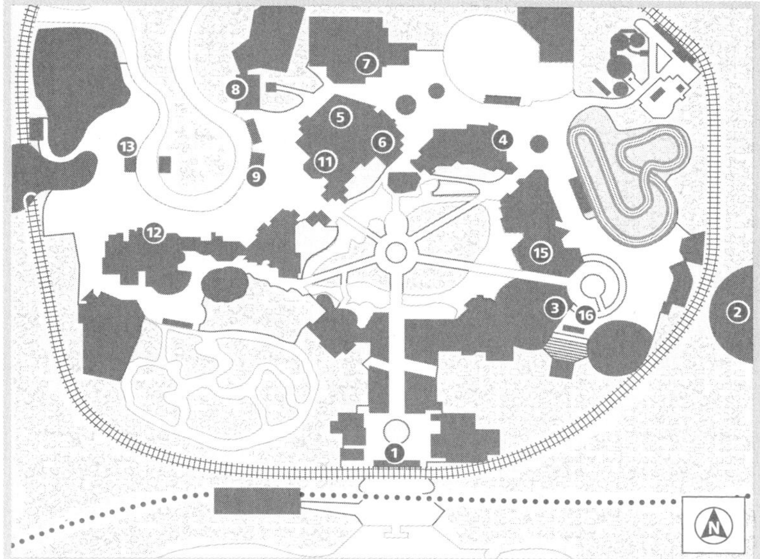

Magic Kingdom Two-day Touring Plan Pocket Outline Version Day One

1. Arrive at the entrance to the Magic Kingdom 50 minutes (Disney-resort guests) to 70 minutes (non-Disney-resort guests) prior to opening. Get guide maps and the daily entertainment schedule.
2. In Tomorrowland, ride Space Mountain.
3. Ride Buzz Lightyear.
4. In Fantasyland, ride Winnie the Pooh.
5. Ride Peter Pan's Flight.
6. See *Mickey's PhilharMagic.*
7. Ride It's a Small World.
8. In Liberty Square, see The Haunted Mansion.
9. Experience the *Liberty Belle* Riverboat.
10. Eat lunch.
11. See *The Hall of Presidents.*
12. In Frontierland, see *Country Bear Jamboree.*
13. Explore Tom Sawyer Island.
14. Go to Tomorrowland via the central hub.
15. See *Stitch's Great Escape!*
16. Ride the Tomorrowland Transit Authority.
17. Shop, see live entertainment, or revisit favorite attractions.

If you have a Web-enabled cell phone, you can view current and future wait times for every attraction—and add the ones you see in the parks—at **m.TouringPlans.com.**

Magic Kingdom
Two-day Touring Plan
Pocket Outline Version
Day Two

1. Arrive at the entrance to the Magic Kingdom 50 minutes (Disney-resort guests) to 70 minutes (non-Disney-resort guests) prior to opening. Get guide maps and the daily entertainment schedule.
2. In Frontierland, ride Splash Mountain. Do not use FASTPASS.
3. Ride Big Thunder Mountain Railroad.
4. In Adventureland, Ride Pirates of the Caribbean.
5. Take the Jungle Cruise (use FASTPASS if needed).
6. See *Enchanted Tiki Room.*
7. Explore the Swiss Family Treehouse.
8. Eat lunch.
9. Take the train from Frontierland to Mickey's Toontown Fair.
10. Tour Mickey's Toontown Fair and meet the characters.
11. Go to Tomorrowland.
12. If you haven't eaten, try Cosmic Ray's or the Tomorrowland Terrace Noodle Station.
13. See *Monsters, Inc. Laugh Floor.*
14. See *Walt Disney's Carousel of Progress.*
15. See the evening parade on Main Street.
16. See the evening fireworks on Main Street. A good viewing spot is to the right of the central hub, on the walkway toward Tomorrowland.

If you have a Web-enabled cell phone, you can view current and future wait times for every attraction—and add the ones you see in the parks—at **m.TouringPlans.com.**

Epcot
Recommended Attraction Visitation Times

It is best to see attractions with visitation times listed as "anytime" during the more crowded middle part of the day (noon–4 p.m.).

1. *The American Adventure:* Anytime.
2. *The Circle of Life* (The Land): Before 11 a.m./after 2 p.m. if open
3. Gran Fiesta Tour (Mexico): Before noon/after 5 p.m.
4. *Honey, I Shrunk the Audience:* Before noon/after 4 p.m.
5. *Impressions de France* (France): Anytime.
6. Innoventions: Second day or after major attractions.
7. Journey into Imagination: Anytime.
8. *Kim Possible* World Showcase Adventure (not mapped, various World Showcase pavilions): Anytime.
9. Living with the Land (The Land): Before 10:30 a.m., after 5 p.m., or use FASTPASS.
10. Maelstrom (Norway): Before noon, after 4:30 p.m., or use FASTPASS.
11. Mission: Space: First hour the park is open, or use FASTPASS.
12. *O Canada!* (Canada): Anytime.
13. *Reflections of China* (China): Anytime.
14. The Seas with Nemo & Friends (ride and main tank–exhibits), *Turtle Talk with Crush:* Before 11 a.m./after 5 p.m.
15. Soarin': First 30 minutes the park is open, or use FASTPASS.
16. Spaceship Earth: Before 10 a.m./after 4 p.m.
17. Test Track: First 30 minutes the park is open, just before closing, or use FASTPASS.
18. Universe of Energy: Before 11:15 a.m./after 4:30 p.m.

If you have a Web-enabled cell phone, you can view current and future wait times for every attraction—and add the ones you see in the parks—at **m.TouringPlans.com.**

Epcot

Epcot
One-day Touring Plan
(Interrupt the touring plan for lunch, dinner, and *IllumiNations*.)

1. Arrive 40 minutes before official opening time. Pick up a park map and daily entertainment schedule when entering the park.
2. Obtain FASTPASSes for Soarin'.
3. In Future World East, ride Test Track.
4. Ride Mission: Space. Do not use FASTPASS.
5. Ride Living with the Land in the Land Pavilion.
6. Now might be a good time to pick up a second FASTPASS for Soarin', if available.
7. See The Seas with Nemo & Friends and *Turtle Talk with Crush*.
8. Ride Journey into Imagination.
9. See *Honey, I Shrunk the Audience*.
10. Return to the Land Pavilion and see *The Circle of Life*.
11. Ride Soarin' using the FASTPASSes obtained in Step 2.
12. Eat lunch.
13. Ride Spaceship Earth.
14. Ride Universe of Energy in Future World East.
15. Tour the exhibits in Innoventions East.
16. Take the Gran Fiesta Tour boat ride at Mexico.
17. Ride Maelstrom and tour the stave church in Norway.
18. See *Reflections of China*.
19. Tour Germany.
20. Visit Italy.
21. See *The American Adventure*.
22. Explore Japan. If you have kids and time permits, try the *Kim Possible* World Showcase Adventure.
23. Visit Morocco.
24. See *Impressions de France*.
25. Eat dinner.
26. Visit the United Kingdom.
27. Tour Canada and see *O Canada!*
28. See *IllumiNations*. Prime viewing spots are along the lagoon between Canada and France.

If you have a Web-enabled cell phone, you can view current and future wait times for every attraction—and add the ones you see in the parks—at **m.TouringPlans.com.**

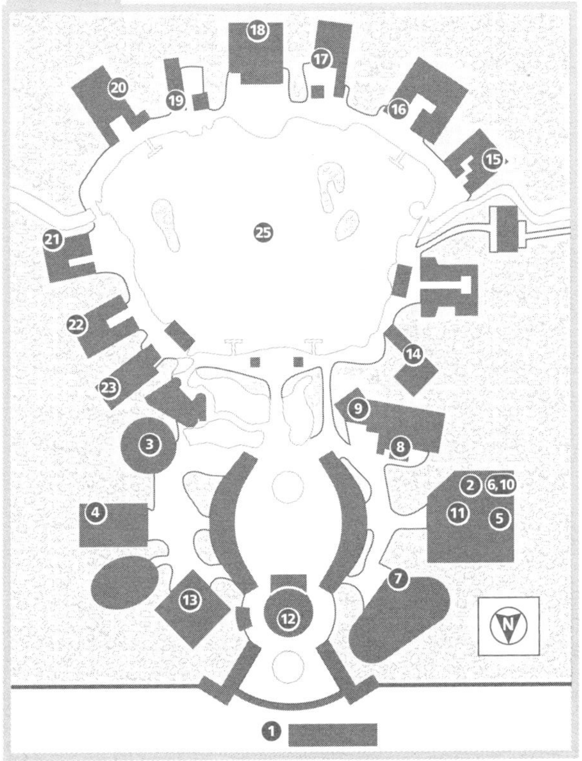

Epcot

Epcot

Author's Selective One-day Touring Plan

(Interrupt the touring plan for lunch, dinner, and *IllumiNations.*)

1. Arrive 40 minutes before official opening time. Pick up a park map and daily entertainment schedule when entering the park.
2. Obtain FASTPASSes for Soarin'.
3. In Future World East, ride Test Track.
4. Ride Mission: Space. Do not use FASTPASS.
5. Ride Living with the Land in the Land Pavilion.
6. If you want a second FASTPASS for Soarin', get it now.
7. See The Seas with Nemo & Friends and *Turtle Talk with Crush.*
8. Ride Journey into Imagination.
9. See *Honey, I Shrunk the Audience.*
10. Return to the Land and ride Soarin' using the FASTPASSes obtained in Step 2.
11. Eat lunch.
12. Ride Spaceship Earth.
13. Visit the Universe of Energy.
14. Tour Canada and see *O Canada!*
15. See *Impressions de France.*
16. Visit Morocco.
17. Explore Japan.
18. See *The American Adventure.*
19. Visit Italy.
20. Tour Germany.
21. See *Reflections of China.*
22. Ride Maelstrom and tour the stave church in Norway.
23. Take the Gran Fiesta Tour boat ride in Mexico.
24. Eat dinner.
25. See *IllumiNations.* Prime viewing spots are at Mexico and at the front of World Showcase lagoon.

If you have a Web-enabled cell phone, you can view current and future wait times for every attraction—and add the ones you see in the parks—at **m.TouringPlans.com.**

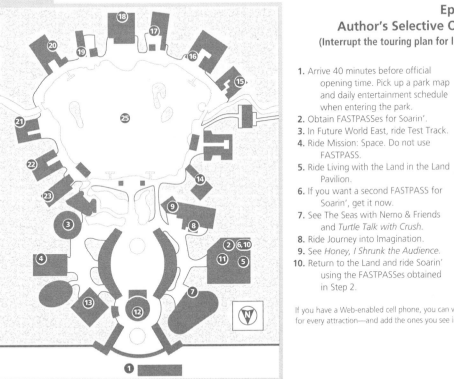

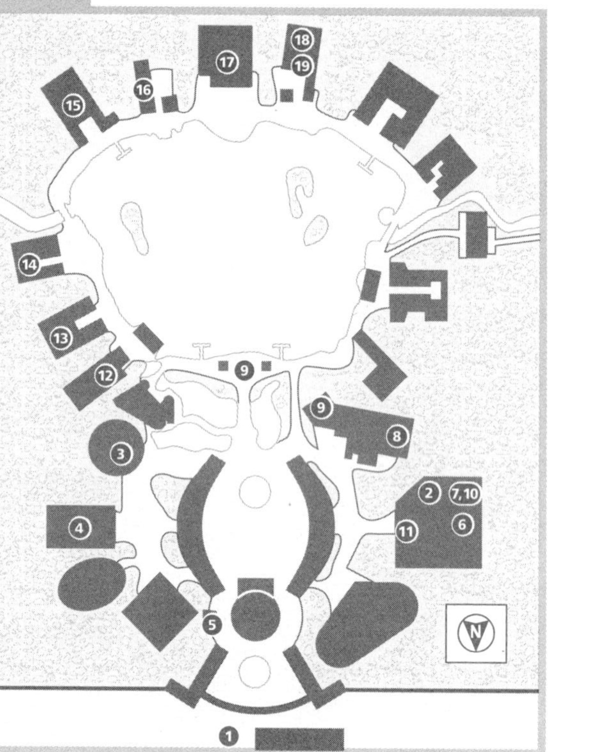

Epcot
Two-day Sunrise–Starlight Touring Plan
(Interrupt the touring plan for lunch.)
Day One

1. Arrive 40 minutes before official opening time. Pick up a park map and daily entertainment schedule when entering the park.
2. Obtain FASTPASSes for Soarin'.
3. In Future World East, ride Test Track.
4. Ride Mission: Space.
5. Make dinner reservations at Guest Relations or by calling ☎ 407-WDW-DINE.
6. In the Land Pavilion, ride Living with the Land.
7. If you want a second FASTPASS for Soarin', get it now.
8. Ride Journey into Imagination.
9. See *Honey, I Shrunk the Audience.*
10. Ride Soarin' using the FASTPASSes obtained in Step 2.
11. Eat lunch.
12. Take the Gran Fiesta Tour boat ride at the Mexico Pavilion in World Showcase.
13. Ride Maelstrom at Norway. Use FASTPASS if wait exceeds 20 minutes.
14. See *Reflections of China.*
15. Visit Germany.
16. Tour Italy.
17. See *The American Adventure.*
18. Visit Japan.
19. If you have kids, try the *Kim Possible* World Showcase Adventure in Japan.

If you have a Web-enabled cell phone, you can view current and future wait times for every attraction—and add the ones you see in the parks—at **m.TouringPlans.com.**

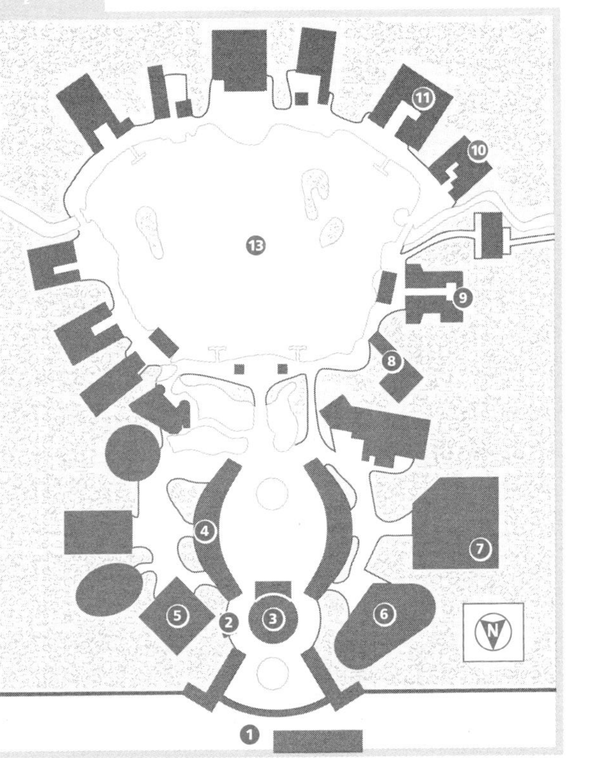

Epcot
Two-day Sunrise–Starlight Touring Plan
(Interrupt the touring plan for dinner and *IllumiNations.*)
Day Two

1. Arrive at Epcot at 1 p.m. Get a park map and daily entertainment schedule.
2. Make dinner reservations at Guest Relations or by calling ☎ 407-WDW-DINE.
3. Ride Spaceship Earth.
4. Tour Innoventions East.
5. See the Universe of Energy.
6. See The Seas with Nemo & Friends and *Turtle Talk with Crush.*
7. At the Land Pavilion, see *The Circle of Life.*
8. See *O Canada!*
9. Visit the United Kingdom.
10. See *Impressions de France.*
11. Visit Morocco.
12. Eat dinner.
13. See *IllumiNations.* Good viewing spots are along the waterway between France and Canada.

If you have a Web-enabled cell phone, you can view current and future wait times for every attraction—and add the ones you see in the parks—at **m.TouringPlans.com.**

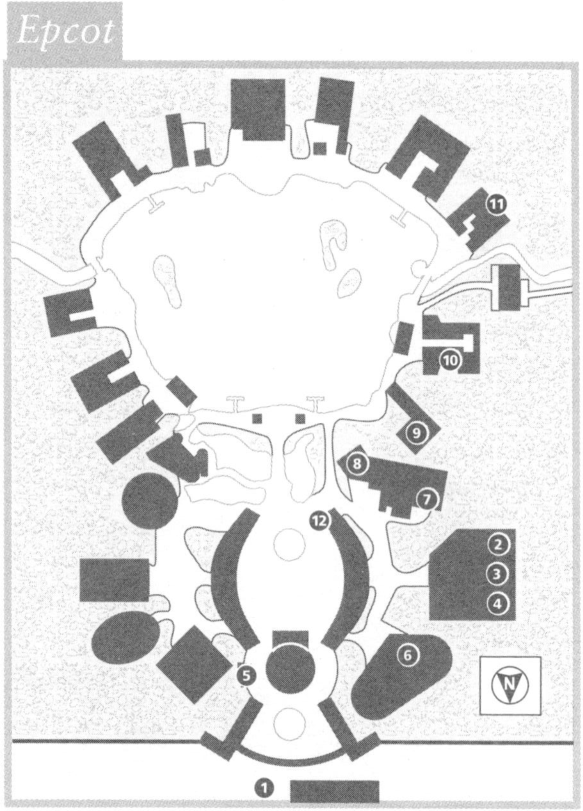

Epcot

Epcot
Two-day Early-riser Touring Plan
(Parents with young children should review the Small-child Fright-potential Chart on pages 330–333.)
Day One

1. Arrive 40 minutes before official opening time. Pick up a park map and daily entertainment schedule when entering the park.
2. At the Land Pavilion, ride Soarin'.
3. Ride Living with the Land. If you want to ride Soarin' again, get FASTPASSes now.
4. See *The Circle of Life.*
5. Make dinner reservations at Guest Relations or by calling ☎ 407-WDW-DINE.
6. See The Seas with Nemo & Friends and *Turtle Talk with Crush.*
7. Ride Journey into Imagination.
8. See *Honey, I Shrunk the Audience.*
9. Start a counterclockwise tour of World Showcase with the film *O Canada!* at Canada.
10. Explore the United Kingdom.
11. See *Impressions de France.*
12. Continue around the lagoon, or visit the exhibits in Innoventions West.

If you have a Web-enabled cell phone, you can view current and future wait times for every attraction—and add the ones you see in the parks—at **m.TouringPlans.com.**

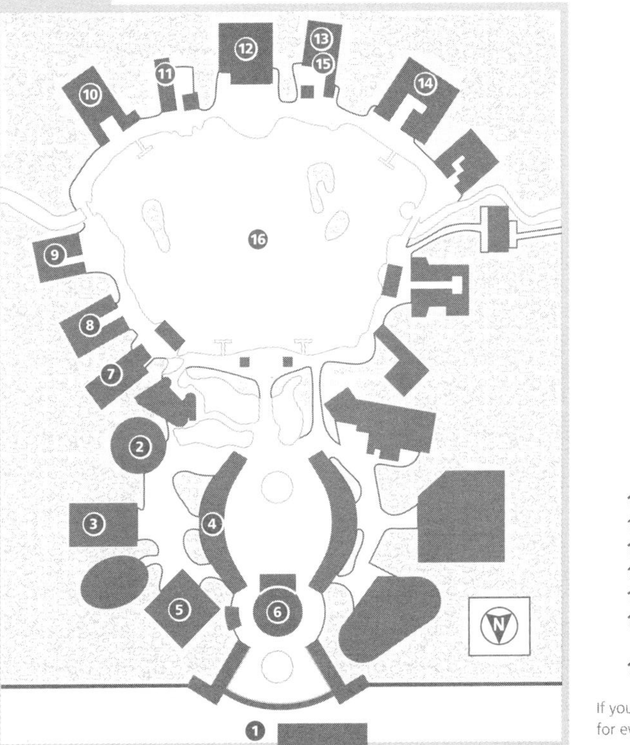

Epcot
Two-day Early-riser Touring Plan
(Parents with young children should review the Small-child Fright-potential Chart on pages 330–333.)
Day Two

1. Arrive 40 minutes before official opening time. Pick up a park map and daily entertainment schedule on your way in.
2. Ride Test Track. Use FASTPASS if wait exceeds 30 minutes.
3. Ride Mission: Space.
4. Tour Innoventions East.
5. See the Universe of Energy.
6. Ride Spaceship Earth.
7. Take the Gran Fiesta Tour boat ride at the Mexico Pavilion in World Showcase. This begins a clockwise tour of World Showcase.
8. Ride Maelstrom at Norway. Use FASTPASS if wait exceeds 20 minutes.
9. See *Reflections of China.*
10. Visit Germany.
11. Visit Italy.
12. See *The American Adventure.*
13. Visit Japan.
14. Visit Morocco.
15. If you have kids, try the *Kim Possible* World Showcase Adventure in Japan.
16. Eat dinner and enjoy *IllumiNations.*

If you have a Web-enabled cell phone, you can view current and future wait times for every attraction—and add the ones you see in the parks—at **m.TouringPlans.com.**

Animal Kingdom

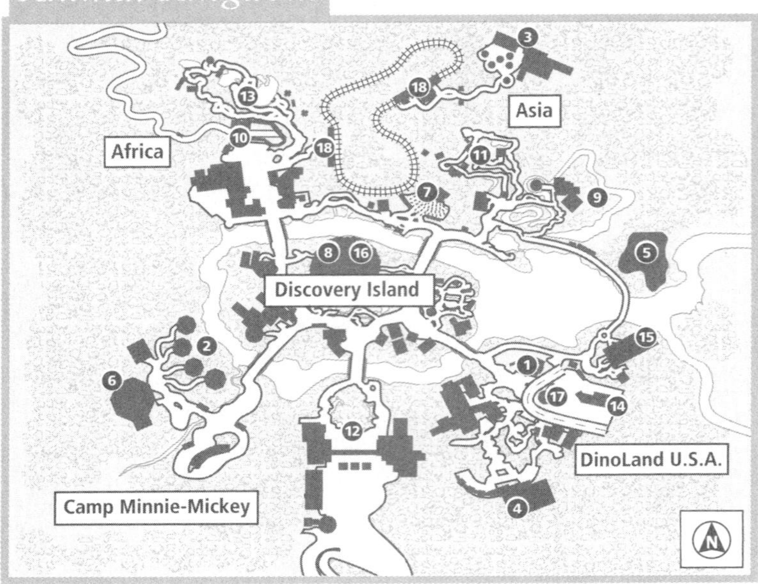

Animal Kingdom Recommended Attraction Visitation Times

It is best to see attractions with visitation times listed as "anytime" during the more crowded middle part of the day (11 a.m.–3:30 p.m.).

1. The Boneyard: Anytime.
2. Character Greeting Area: Early morning/late afternoon.
3. Conservation Station: Anytime.
4. Dinosaur: Before 10:30 a.m., 1 hour before closing, or use FASTPASS.
5. Expedition Everest: Before 9:30 a.m./after 3 p.m., or use FASTPASS.
6. *Festival of the Lion King:* Before 11 a.m./after 4 p.m.
7. *Flights of Wonder:* Anytime.
8. *It's Tough to Be a Bug!:* Before 10:30 a.m./after 4 p.m.
9. Kali River Rapids: Before 10:30 a.m./after 4:30 p.m., or use FASTPASS.
10. Kilimanjaro Safaris: Park opening, 2 hours before closing, or use FASTPASS.
11. Maharaja Jungle Trek: Anytime.
12. The Oasis: Anytime.
13. Pangani Forest Exploration Trail: Anytime.
14. Primeval Whirl: First 2 hours park is open, 1 hour before closing, or use FASTPASS.
15. Theater in the Wild/*Finding Nemo—The Musical:* Anytime.
16. Tree of Life Animal Exhibits: Anytime.
17. TriceraTop Spin: First 90 minutes park is open/1 hour before closing.
18. Wildlife Express Train: Anytime.

If you have a Web-enabled cell phone, you can view current and future wait times for every attraction—and add the ones you see in the parks—at **m.TouringPlans.com.**

Animal Kingdom

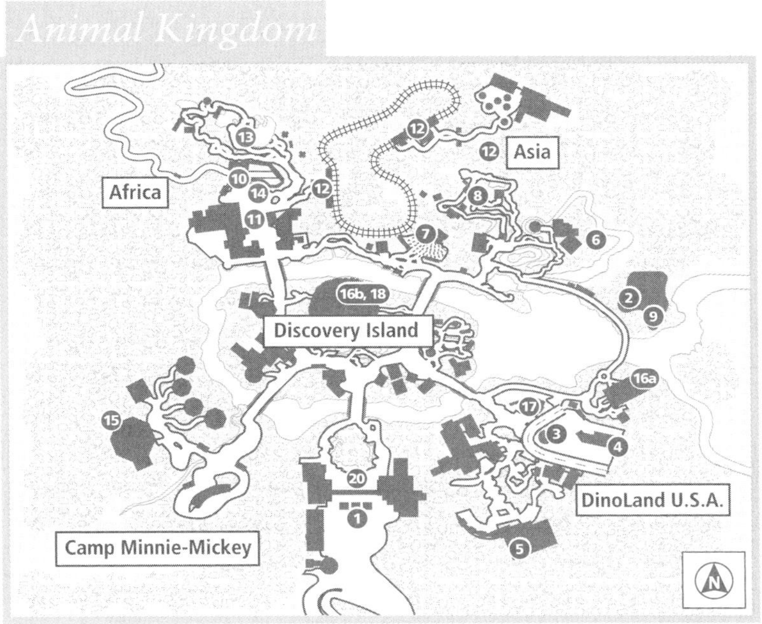

Animal Kingdom
One-day Touring Plan

1. Arrive 30–40 minutes prior to opening.
2. Send one member of your party to obtain FASTPASSes for Expedition Everest. The group should meet up at TriceraTop Spin.
3. Ride TriceraTop Spin if you have young children in your group.
4. Ride Primeval Whirl.
5. Follow the signs to Dinosaur, and ride.
6. Ride Kali River Rapids.
7. See *Flights of Wonder*. If wait exceeds 20 minutes, walk the Maharaja Jungle Trek first, then see the show.
8. Walk the Maharaja Jungle Trek if you have not already done so.
9. Return to Expedition Everest and ride.
10. Visit Africa, and send one member of your party to obtain FASTPASSes for Kilimanjaro Safaris.
11. Eat lunch.
12. Take the Wildlife Express train from Africa to Conservation Station/Rafiki's Planet Watch. Tour the exhibits, and take the train back to Africa.
13. Walk the Pangani Forest Exploration Trail in Africa.
14. Experience Kilimanjaro Safaris using the FASTPASSes that were obtained in Step 10.
15. See *Festival of the Lion King* at Camp Minnie-Mickey.
16. See *Finding Nemo—The Musical* at Theater in the Wild in DinoLand U.S.A. (**16a**) if next show is within 25 minutes. Otherwise, see *It's Tough to Be a Bug!* on Discovery Island (**16b**). Also check out exhibits at The Tree of Life.
17. If you have the time and interest, check out The Boneyard in DinoLand U.S.A.
18. If you've not already done so, see *It's Tough to Be a Bug!* and the exhibits at The Tree of Life on Discovery Island.
19. Shop, snack, or repeat any attractions you especially enjoyed.
20. Visit the zoological exhibits at The Oasis.

If you have a Web-enabled cell phone, you can view current and future wait times for every attraction—and add the ones you see in the parks—at **m.TouringPlans.com.**

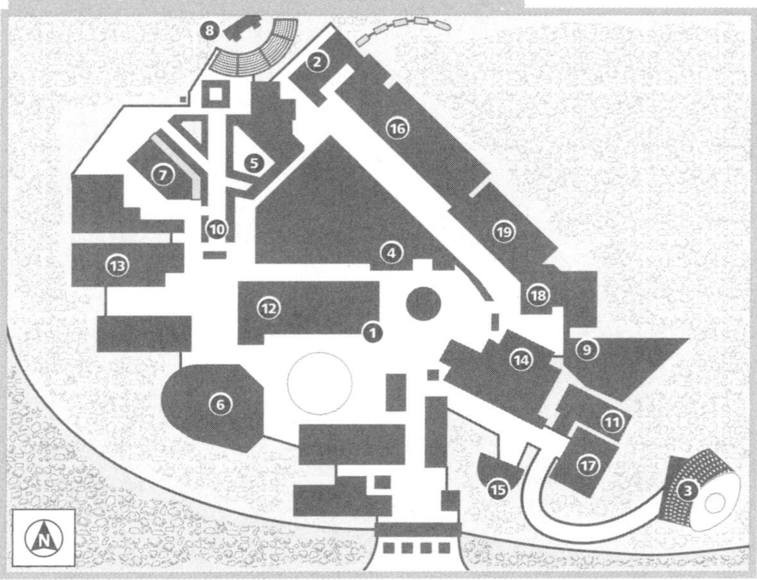

Disney's Hollywood Studios
Recommended Attraction Visitation Times

It is best to see attractions with visitation times listed as "anytime" during the more crowded middle part of the day (noon–4 p.m.).

1. *The American Idol Experience:* Anytime.
2. Backlot Tour: Anytime.
3. *Fantasmic!:* Evening, twice a week (generally Monday and Thursday). Late show is less crowded.
4. The Great Movie Ride: Before 11 a.m./after 4:30 p.m.
5. *Honey, I Shrunk the Kids* Movie Adventure: Before 11 a.m./after dark.
6. *Indiana Jones Epic Stunt Spectacular:* First three morning shows or last evening show.
7. *Jim Henson's Muppet-Vision 3-D:* Before 11 a.m./after 3 p.m.
8. *Lights! Motors! Action! Extreme Stunt Show:* Anytime.
9. The Magic of Disney Animation: Before 11 a.m./after 5 p.m.
10. *Playhouse Disney—Live on Stage!:* Per entertainment schedule.
11. Rock 'n' Roller Coaster: Before 10 a.m.,1 hour before closing, or use FASTPASS.
12. *Sounds Dangerous* (open seasonally): Before 11 a.m./after 4 p.m.
13. Star Tours: First hour and a half after opening, or use FASTPASS.
14. Streets of America: Anytime.
15. Theater of the Stars: Anytime, but arrive 25 minutes early.
16. *Toy Story* Mania!: Before 10:30 a.m., after 6 p.m., or use FASTPASS (if available).
17. *The Twilight Zone* Tower of Terror: Before 9:30 a.m., after 6 p.m., or use FASTPASS.
18. *Voyage of the Little Mermaid:* Before 9:45 a.m., just before closing, or use FASTPASS.
19. *Walt Disney: One Man's Dream:* Anytime.

If you have a Web-enabled cell phone, you can view current and future wait times for every attraction—and add the ones you see in the parks—at **m.TouringPlans.com.**

Disney's Hollywood Studios

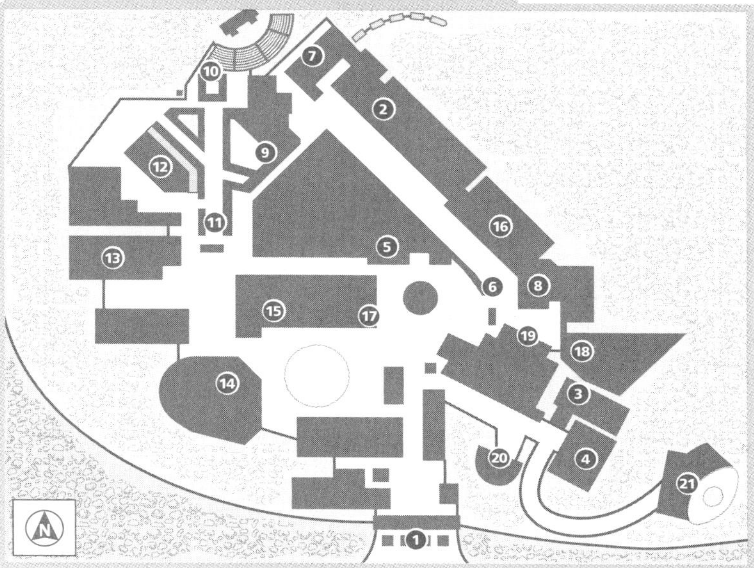

Disney's Hollywood Studios One-day Touring Plan

1. Arrive at the park 30–40 minutes before official opening time. Obtain a park map and daily entertainment schedule.
2. As soon as the park opens, ride *Toy Story* Mania! on Pixar Place.
3. Ride Rock 'n' Roller Coaster.
4. Ride the Tower of Terror. Use FASTPASS if wait exceeds 30 minutes.
5. Ride The Great Movie Ride.
6. Obtain FASTPASSes for *Voyage of the Little Mermaid.*
7. Take the Backlot Tour.
8. If your FASTPASS showtimes for *Voyage of the Little Mermaid* are soon, return for your performance. Disney rarely enforces the return times on FASTPASSes, so you could also skip to Step 9 and return to *Mermaid* after seeing *One Man's Dream* in Step 16.
9. Check your entertainment schedule for the next performance of the *Lights! Motors! Action!* show. Either see the show or eat lunch.
10. See the *Lights! Motors! Action!* show if you haven't already.
11. Explore the Streets of America on the way to *Muppet-Vision 3-D.*
12. See *Muppet-Vision 3-D.*
13. Head toward Echo Lake and ride Star Tours. Use FASTPASS if wait exceeds 20 minutes.
14. Check your entertainment schedule for the next performance of the *Indiana Jones* show. if the next show is within 25 minutes, get in line now. Otherwise, see *Sounds Dangerous* first, then *Indiana Jones.*
15. See *Sounds Dangerous* (open seasonally).
16. See *Walt Disney: One Man's Dream.*
17. Check your entertainment schedule for the next performance of *The American Idol Experience.* If time is short, choose between this and The Magic of Disney Animation tour.
18. Tour The Magic of Disney Animation.
19. Work in *Playhouse Disney—Live on Stage!* if you have small children.
20. See *Beauty and the Beast.*
21. Tour Hollywood and Sunset boulevards. Enjoy *Fantasmic!* if it's playing.

If you have a Web-enabled cell phone, you can view current and future wait times for every attraction—and add the ones you see in the parks—at **m.TouringPlans.com.**

Universal Studios

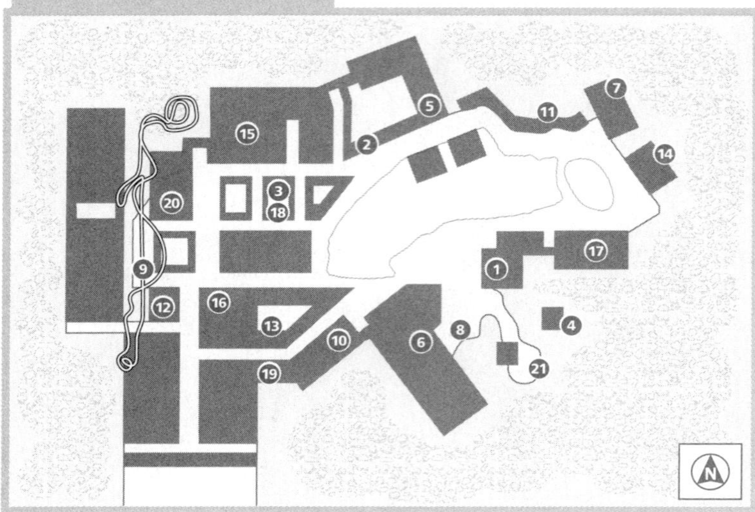

Universal Studios Florida Recommended Attraction Visitation Times

It is best to see attractions with visitation times listed as "anytime" during the more crowded middle part of the day (noon–4 p.m.).

1. *Animal Actors on Location:* After experiencing all rides.
2. *Beetlejuice's Rock 'n' Roll Graveyard Revue:* At your convenience.
3. *The Blues Brothers:* During scheduled showtimes.
4. *A Day in the Park with Barney:* Anytime.
5. *Disaster!*: In morning or late afternoon.
6. *E.T.* Adventure: During the first 90 minutes the park is open.
7. *Fear Factor Live* (open seasonally): First and second-to-last shows.
8. Fievel's Playland: Anytime.
9. Hollywood Rip Ride Rockit: Immediately after park opening.
10. *Universal Horror Make-Up Show:* After experiencing all rides.
11. *Jaws:* Before 11 a.m. or after 5 p.m.
12. Jimmy Neutron's Nicktoon Blast: First hour after park opening or after 5 p.m.
13. *Lucy—A Tribute:* Anytime.
14. *Men in Black* Alien Attack: During the first 90 minutes the park is open.
15. Revenge of the Mummy: First hour in the morning or after 6 p.m.
16. *Shrek 4-D:* First hour in the morning or after 4 p.m.
17. The Simpsons Ride: First hour in the morning.
18. Street Scenes: Anytime.
19. *Terminator 2: 3-D:* After 3:30 p.m.
20. *Twister:* First show after experiencing all rides.
21. Woody Woodpecker's KidZone: Anytime.

If you have a Web-enabled cell phone, you can view current and future wait times for every attraction—and add the ones you see in the parks—at **m.TouringPlans.com.**

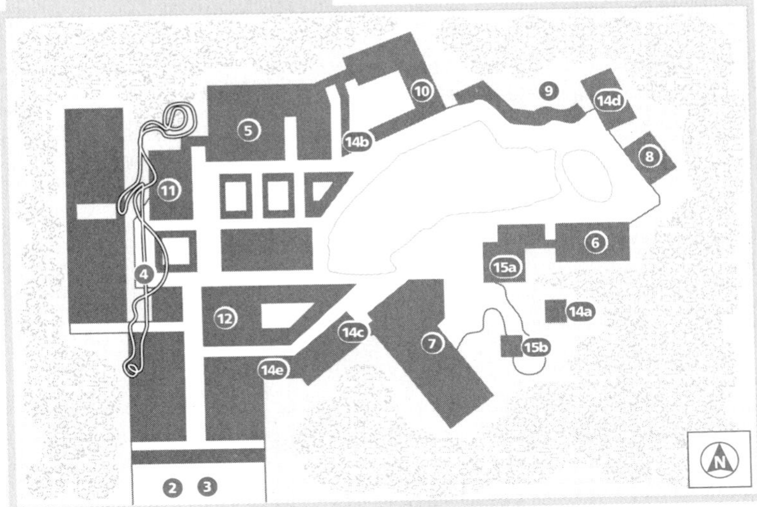

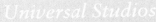

Universal Studios Florida One-day Touring Plan

1. Call ☎ 407-363-8000 the day before your visit for the official opening time.
2. Arrive 50 minutes before opening and pick up a map and entertainment schedule.
3. Line up at the turnstile. Ask if any rides or shows are closed, and adjust touring plan.
4. Ride Hollywood Rip Ride Rockit.
5. Ride Revenge of the Mummy.
6. Ride The Simpsons Ride.
7. Ride *E.T.* Adventure (expendable if there are no young kids in your group).
8. Ride *Men in Black* Alien Attack.
9. Ride *Jaws*.
10. Experience *Disaster!*
11. See *Twister*.
12. See *Shrek 4-D*.
13. Take a break for lunch.
14. See *Animal Actors on Location* **(14a)**, *Beetlejuice's Rock 'n' Roll Graveyard Revue* **(14b)**, the *Universal Horror Make-Up Show* **(14c)**, and *Fear Factor Live* **(14d)** as convenient according to the daily entertainment schedule. See *Terminator 2: 3-D* **(14e)** after 3:30 p.m.
15. Take preschoolers to see Barney **(15a)** after riding *E.T.*, and then head for Woody Woodpecker's KidZone **(15b)**.
16. Revisit favorite rides and shows. See any live performances you may have missed.

If you have a Web-enabled cell phone, you can view current and future wait times for every attraction—and add the ones you see in the parks—at **m.TouringPlans.com.**

Islands of Adventure

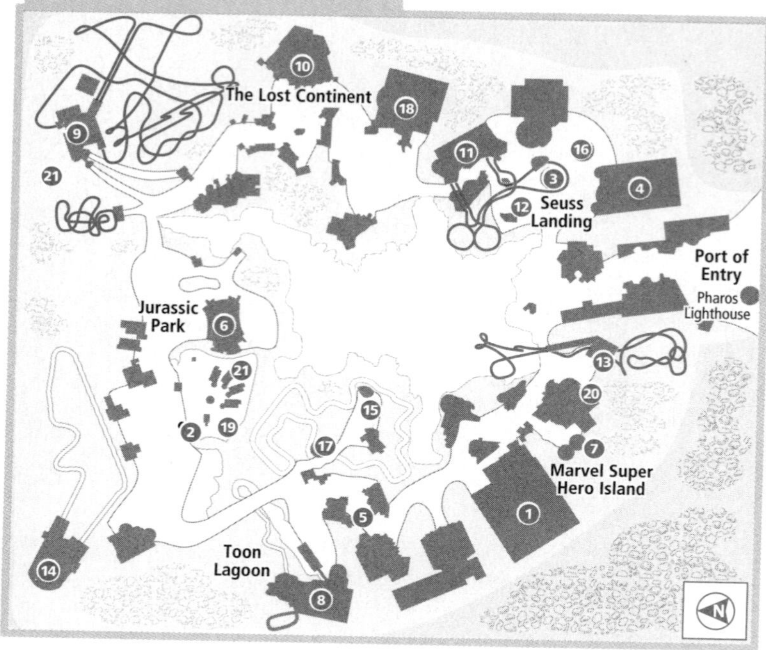

Universal's Islands of Adventure Recommended Attraction Visitation Times

It is best to see attractions with visitation times listed as "anytime" during the more crowded middle part of the day (noon–4 p.m.).

1. The Adventures of Spider-Man: During first 40 minutes park is open or after 6 p.m.*
2. Camp Jurassic: Anytime.
3. Caro-Seuss-el: Before 11 a.m.*
4. The Cat in the Hat: Before 11:30 a.m.*
5. Comic Strip Lane: Anytime.
6. Discovery Center: Anytime.
7. Doctor Doom's Fearfall: During the first 40 minutes the park is open.*
8. Dudley Do-Right's Ripsaw Falls: Before 11 a.m.*
9. Dueling Dragons: Before 10:30 a.m.*
10. *The Eighth Voyage of Sindbad:* Anytime per the entertainment schedule.
11. The High in the Sky Seuss Trolley Train Ride!: Before 11:30 a.m.
12. If I Ran the Zoo: Anytime.
13. The Incredible Hulk Coaster: During first 40 minutes park is open.*
14. *Jurassic Park* River Adventure: Before 11 a.m.*
15. Me Ship, *The Olive:* Anytime.
16. One Fish, Two Fish, Red Fish, Blue Fish: Before 10 a.m.*
17. Popeye & Bluto's Bilge-Rat Barges: Before 11 a.m.*
18. *Poseidon's Fury!:* After experiencing all the rides.*
19. Pteranodon Flyers: When there's no line.
20. Storm Force Accelatron: During the first hour the park is open.*
21. The Wizarding World of Harry Potter: Immediately after park opening.**

**Offers Universal Express.* ***Opens early 2010.*

If you have a Web-enabled cell phone, you can view current and future wait times for every attraction—and add the ones you see in the parks—at **m.TouringPlans.com.**

Islands of Adventure

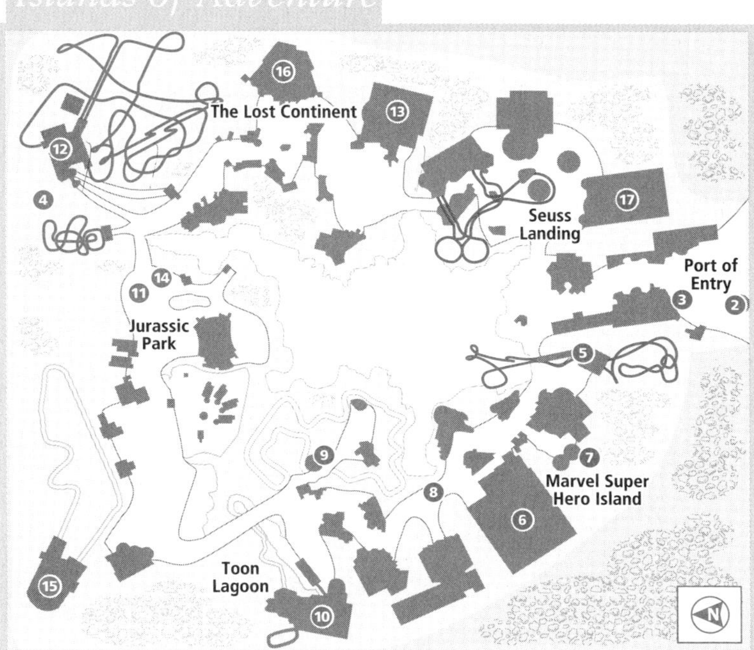

Universal's Islands of Adventure One-day Touring Plan

1. Call ☎ 407-363-8000 the day before your visit for the official opening time.
2. Arrive 50 minutes before opening time, and pick up a map and daily entertainment schedule.
3. Line up at the turnstile. Ask if any rides or shows are closed, and adjust touring plan accordingly.
4. If the Wizarding World of Harry Potter is open (scheduled to open early 2010), hurry there as soon as you clear the turnstiles. Experience all the rides that interest you, but save shows and general exploration for the afternoon. If the Wizarding World isn't open yet, skip to Step 5.
5. At Marvel Super Hero Island, ride The Incredible Hulk Coaster.
6. Exit left and experience The Adventures of Spider-Man.
7. On exiting Spider-Man, backtrack right and ride Doctor Doom's Fearfall.
8. Depart Super Hero Island and cross into Toon Lagoon.
9. On your right ride Popeye & Bluto's Bilge-Rat Barges.
10. Continue yor clockwise circuit of the park. Ride Dudley Do-Right's Ripsaw Falls.
11. Continue around the lake and pass through Jurassic Park. Head to The Lost Continent.
12. Ride both tracks of Dueling Dragons.*
13. Continue clockwise and experience *Poseidon's Fury!**
14. Depart The Lost Continent and backtrack to Jurassic Park.
15. Ride the *Jurassic Park* River Adventure.
16. See *The Eighth Voyage of Sindbad* stunt show in The Lost Continent.*
17. Continue clockwise to Seuss Landing and ride The Cat in the Hat.
18. Revisit favorite rides and check out attractions you may have missed.

**May be closed due to construction of The Wizarding World of Harry Potter.*

If you have a Web-enabled cell phone, you can view current and future wait times for every attraction—and add the ones you see in the parks—at **m.TouringPlans.com.**

MAGIC KINGDOM
Touring-plan Companion

ATTRACTION | RECOMMENDED VISITATION TIMES | AUTHOR'S RATING

Ariel's Grotto | **Before 11 a.m., after 9 p.m** | ★★★

Astro Orbiter | **Before 11 a.m., after 5 p.m.** | ★★

The Barnstormer | **Before 10:30 a.m., during events, just before closing** | ★★

Big Thunder Mountain Railroad (FASTPASS) | **Before 10 a.m., hour before closing** | ★★★★
Special comments **40" minimum height; expectant mothers should not ride.**

Buzz Lightyear's Space Ranger Spin (FASTPASS) | **Before 10:30 a.m., after 6 p.m.** | ★★★★

Cinderella's Golden Carousel | **Before 11 a.m., after 8 p.m.** | ★★★

Country Bear Jamboree | **Before 11:30 a.m., before parades, 2 hours before closing** | ★★★

Donald's Boat | **Anytime** | ★★½

Dumbo | **Before 10 a.m., after 9 p.m.** | ★★★

Enchanted Tiki Room—Under New Management! | **Before 11 a.m., after 3:30 p.m.** | ★★★½

Frontierland Shootin' Arcade | **Anytime** | ★½

The Hall of Presidents | **Anytime** | ★★★

The Haunted Mansion | **Before 11:30 a.m., after 8 p.m.** | ★★★★
Special comments **Fright potential**

It's a Small World | **Anytime** | ★★★

Jungle Cruise (FASTPASS) | **Before 10 a.m., 2 hours before closing** | ★★★

Liberty Belle Riverboat | **Anytime** | ★★½

Mad Tea Party | **Before 11 a.m., after 5 p.m.** | ★★
Special comments **Expectant mothers should not ride.**

The Magic Carpets of Aladdin | **Before 10 a.m., hour before closing** | ★★★

The Many Adventures of Winnie the Pooh (FASTPASS) |
Before 10 a.m., 2 hours before closing | ★★★½

Mickey's and Minnie's Country Houses | **Before 11:30 a.m., after 4:30 p.m.** | ★★★/★★

Mickey's PhilharMagic (FASTPASS) | **Before 11 a.m., during parades** | ★★★★

Monsters, Inc. Laugh Floor | **Before 11 a.m., after 4 p.m.** | ★★★½

Peter Pan's Flight (FASTPASS) | **Before 10 a.m., after 6 p.m.** | ★★★★

Pirates of the Caribbean | **Before noon, after 5 p.m.** | ★★★★★

Pooh's Playful Spot | **Anytime** | ★★½

Snow White's Scary Adventures | **Before 11 a.m., after 6 p.m.** | ★★½
Special comments **Fright potential**

Space Mountain (FASTPASS) | **At opening, 6–7 p.m., hour before closing** | ★★★★
Special comments **44" minimum height; expectant mothers should not ride.**

Splash Mountain (FASTPASS) | **At opening, during parades, just before closing** | ★★★★★
Special comments **40" minimum height; expectant mothers should not ride.**

Stitch's Great Escape! | **Before 11 a.m. during parades, after 6 p.m.** | ★★
Special comments **Fright potential; 40" minimum height**

Swiss Family Treehouse | **Anytime** | ★★★ | ***Special comments*** **Lots of stairs; fright potential due to height**

Tom Sawyer Island | **Midmorning–late afternoon** | ★★★ | ***Special comments*** **Closes at dusk**

Tomorrowland Speedway | **Before 11 a.m., after 5 p.m.** | ★★ | ***Special comments*** **54" to drive; expectant mothers should not ride.**

Tomorrowland Transit Authority | **Anytime** | ★★★

Toontown Hall of Fame | **Before 10:30 a.m., after 5:30 p.m.** | ★★

Walt Disney's Carousel of Progress | **Anytime** | ★★★ | ***Special comment*** **Good during busy times**

WDW Railroad | **Anytime** | ★★½

DINING INFORMATION—Counter Service

RESTAURANT | LOCATION | QUALITY | VALUE

Casey's Corner | Main Street, U.S.A. | Good | B
Selections Hot dogs, fries

Columbia Harbour House | Liberty Square | Fair | C+
Selections Fried fish, chicken strips, sandwiches, soups, chili, garden salad

Cosmic Ray's Starlight Cafe | Tomorrowland | Good | B
Selections Burgers (veggie available), rotisserie chicken, sandwiches, some kosher

El Pirata y el Perico *(seasonal)* | Adventureland | Fair | B
Selections Tacos, taco salad, chili

Golden Oak Outpost | Frontierland | Good | B+
Selections Chicken nuggets, fried-chicken-breast sandwiches, vegetarian flatbread wraps

The Lunching Pad | Tomorrowland | Good | B–
Selections Smoked turkey legs, pretzels, frozen sodas

Mrs. Potts' Cupboard | Fantasyland | Good | B
Selections Ice cream and other sweets

Pecos Bill Tall Tale Inn and Cafe | Frontierland | Good | B
Selections Burgers, chicken wraps, chicken salad, chili, kids' meals

The Pinocchio Village Haus | Fantasyland | Fair | C
Selections Personal pizzas, chicken nugggets, salads, kids' meals

Scuttle's Landing | Fantasyland | Good | B
Selections Frozen Cokes, soft pretzels, chips

Tomorrowland Terrace Noodle Station | Tomorrowland | Good | B
Selections Noodle bowls; Caesar salad, beef and broccoli; kids' meals

DINING INFORMATION—Full Service

RESTAURANT | MEALS SERVED | LOCATION | PRICE | QUALITY | VALUE

Cinderella's Royal Table | B, L, D | Fantasyland | Expensive | ★★★ | ★★
Selections Pasta, prime rib, seafood, kids' menu

The Crystal Palace | B, L, D | Main Street | Moderate | ★★★½ | ★★★
Selections Buffet; varies

Liberty Tree Tavern | L, D | Liberty Square | Moderate | ★★★ | ★★★
Selections Pot roast, roast turkey, pork loin, sandwiches, salads

Plaza Restaurant | L, D | Main Street, U.S.A. | Moderate | ★★ | ★★
Selections Sandwiches, burgers, ice cream

Tony's Town Square Restaurant | L, D | Main Street, U.S.A. | Moderate | ★★★ | ★★
Selections Paninis, pasta, New York strip

Advance dining reservations recommended for Magic Kingdom full-service restaurants; call ☎ 407-939-3463.

GOOD REST AREAS IN THE MAGIC KINGDOM

PLACE | LOCATION | NOTES

Covered tables | Adventureland | Across from Swiss Family Treehouse; has padded seats, nearby refreshments

Covered porch with rocking chairs on Tom Sawyer's Island | Frontierland | Across the water from the *Liberty Belle* Riverboat dock; bring refreshments from Frontierland

Shaded benches | Liberty Square | Between central hub and entrance to Liberty Square, on left

Cul-de-sac | Main Street | Between the china shop and Main Street Market House on right-hand side of street as you face the castle; nearby refreshments

Quiet seating area | Tomorrowland | Near restrooms on the right as you approach Space Mountain—look for pay phones, and there's a covered seating area farther back of that corridor; refreshments nearby

EPCOT *Touring-plan Companion*

ATTRACTION | RECOMMENDED VISITATION TIMES | AUTHOR'S RATING

The American Adventure | **Anytime** | ★★★★
The Circle of Life (The Land) | **Before 11 a.m., after 2 p.m.** | ★★★½
Gran Fiesta Tour (Mexico) | **Before noon, after 5 p.m.** | ★★½
Honey, I Shrunk the Audience | **Before noon, after 4 p.m.** | ★★★★½
Special comments **Fright potential.**
Impressions de France | **Anytime** | ★★★½
Innoventions | **Second day or after major attractions** | ★★★½
Journey into Imagination with Figment | **Anytime** | ★★½
Kim Possible World Showcase Adventure | **Anytime** | ★★★★
Living with the Land (The Land) (FASTPASS) | **Before 10:30 a.m., after 5 p.m.** | ★★★★
The Seas Main Tank and Exhibits | **Before 11:30 a.m., after 5 p.m.** | ★★★½
The Seas with Nemo & Friends | **Before 11 a.m., after 5 p.m.** | ★★★
Maelstrom (Norway) (FASTPASS) | **Before noon, after 4:30 p.m.** | ★★★
Mission: Space (FASTPASS) | **First hour the park is open** | ★★★★
Special comments **44" minimum height; expectant mothers should not ride; motion-sickness potential.**
O Canada! (Canada) | **Anytime** | ★★★½
Reflections of China (China) | **Anytime** | ★★★½
Special comments **Audience stands throughout performance.**
Soarin' (The Land) (FASTPASS) | **First 30 minutes the park is open** | ★★★★½
Special comments **Expectant mothers and people prone to motion sickness should not ride.**
Spaceship Earth | **Before 10 a.m., after 4 p.m.** | ★★★★
Test Track (FASTPASS) | **First 30 minutes the park is open, just before closing** | ★★★½
Special comments **40" minimum height**
Turtle Talk with Crush | **Before 11 a.m., after 5 p.m.** | ★★★★
Universe of Energy: *Ellen's Energy Adventure* | **Before 11:15 a.m., after 4:30 p.m.** | ★★★★

DINING INFORMATION—Counter Service

RESTAURANT | LOCATION | QUALITY | VALUE | SELECTIONS

Africa Coolpost | **Between Germany and China** | **Good** | **B–**
Selections **Hot dogs, ice cream, fresh fruit, frozen slushes, coffee and tea, beer**
Boulangerie Pâtisserie | **World Showcase, France** | **Good** | **B**
Selections **Croissants, pastries, cheese plate, quiche, coffee, wine, beer**
Cantina de San Angel | **World Showcase, Mexico** | **Fair–Good** | **C+**
Selections **Tacos, burritos, nachos, beer, frozen margaritas**
Crêpes des Chefs de France | **World Showcase, France** | **Good** | **B+**
Selections **Dessert crêpes, ice cream, beer, espresso**
Electric Umbrella Restaurant | **Future World, Innoventions Plaza East** | **Fair–Good** | **B–**
Selections **Burgers, veggie wraps, kids' meals, island chicken salad**
Fife and Drum Tavern | **World Showcase, United States** | **Fair** | **C**
Selections **Turkey legs, pretzels, ice cream, smoothies**
Kringla Bakeri og Kafé | **World Showcase, Norway** | **Good–Excellent** | **B**
Selections **Pastries, open-faced sandwiches, green salad, fruit cup, beer**
Liberty Inn | **World Showcase, United States** | **Fair** | **C**
Selections **Burgers, hot dogs, chicken nuggets, salads, kids' meals**
Lotus Blossom Cafe | **World Showcase, China** | **Fair** | **C**
Selections **Egg rolls, pot stickers, stir-fries**
Promenade Refreshments | **Between World Showcase and Future World** | **Fair** | **C**
Selections **Turkey legs, hot dogs, pretzels, chips, ice cream, smoothies**
Refreshment Port | **Between World Showcase and Future World** | **Good** | **B**
Selections **Chicken nuggets, fries, ice cream**
Rose & Crown Pub | **World Showcase, United Kingdom** | **Good** | **C**
Selections **Fish-and-chips, turkey sandwich, British beers**
Sommerfest | **World Showcase, Germany** | **Good** | **B–**
Selections **Bratwurst and frankfurter sandwiches with kraut, pastries, beer**

DINING INFORMATION—Counter Service (cont'd)

Sunshine Seasons Food Fair | Future World, The Land | Excellent | A
Selections Rotisserie meats, salads, sandwiches, Asian noodles and stir-fries

Tangierine Cafe | World Showcase, Morocco | Good | B
Selections Chicken and lamb *shawarma,* hummus, chicken and tabbouleh wraps, wine and beer

Yakitori House | World Showcase, Japan | Excellent | B
Selections Beef and chicken teriyaki, tempura, sushi, miso soup, beer and sake

Yorkshire County Fish Shop | World Showcase, United Kingdom | Good | B+
Selections Fish-and-chips, shortbread, draft ale

DINING INFORMATION—Full Service

RESTAURANT | MEALS SERVED | LOCATION | PRICE | QUALITY | VALUE

Akershus Royal Banquet Hall | B, L, D | Norway | Expensive | ★★★ | ★★★★
Selections *Koldtbord* (Norwegian buffet), braised pork, mustard-glazed salmon

Biergarten | L, D | Germany | Expensive | ★★★ | ★★★★
Selections Buffet with schnitzel, sausages, spaetzle, pork roast

Bistro de Paris | D | France | Expensive | ★★★½ | ★★
Selections Lobster, beef tenderloin, rack of lamb

Le Cellier Steakhouse | L, D | Canada | Expensive | ★★★½ | ★★★
Selections Canadian Cheddar cheese soup, steaks, seafood, sandwiches and salads

Les Chefs de France | L, D | France | Expensive | ★★★ | ★★★
Selections Seared tuna, beef tenderloin, French onion soup, crêpes

Coral Reef | L, D | The Seas | Expensive | ★★ | ★★
Selections Creamy lobster soup, blackened catfish, steaks

The Garden Grill Restaurant | D | The Land | Expensive | ★★★ | ★★★
Selections Steak, fish of the day, kids' menu with chicken tenders, potatoes, and fresh veggies

Nine Dragons Restaurant | L, D | China | Moderate | ★★★ | ★★
Selections Honey-sesame chicken, pepper shrimp with spinach noodles, five-spiced fish

Restaurant Marrakesh | L, D | Morocco | Moderate | ★★½ | ★★
Selections *Bastilla* (minced-chicken pie), roast lamb, couscous

Rose & Crown Dining Room | L, D | United Kingdom | Moderate | ★★★½ | ★★
Selections Fish-and-chips, bangers and mash (sausage and mashed potatoes), pork loin

San Angel Inn | L, D Mexico | Expensive | ★★ | ★★
Selections *Tacos de pato* (duck tacos), *mole poblano* (chicken in chile-chocolate sauce), fish dishes

Teppan Edo | L, D | Japan | Expensive | ★★★★ | ★★★
Selections Chicken, shrimp, beef, scallops, and Asian vegetables stir-fried on teppan grill

Tokyo Dining | L, D | Japan | Moderate | ★★★★ | ★★★
Selections Tempura, sushi, and sashimi

Tutto Italia | L, D | Italy | Expensive | ★★½ | ★★½
Selections Pastas, *antipasto misto* (appetizer plate), *copetta sotto bosco* (gelato)

Advance dining reservations recommended for Epcot full-service restaurants; call ☎ 407-939-3463.

GOOD REST AREAS IN EPCOT

PLACE | LOCATION | NOTES

Benches | The Seas | Ample room throughout Pavilion; air-conditioned

Benches | Innoventions | Air-conditioned; usually not crowded

Covered gazebo | In garden behind shops on left side of United Kingdom | Often empty; refreshments nearby

Rotunda and lobby | United States Pavilion | Ample room; air-conditioned; refreshments nearby; usually quiet unless singers are performing

ANIMAL KINGDOM

Touring-plan Companion

ATTRACTION | RECOMMENDED VISITATION TIMES | AUTHOR'S RATING

The Boneyard | Anytime | ★★★½

Character Greeting Area | Early morning, late afternoon | N/A

Conservation Station/Rafiki's Planet Watch | Anytime | ★★★

Dinosaur (FASTPASS) | Before 10:30 a.m., 1 hour before closing | ★★★★½
Special comments Fright potential; expectant mothers should not ride.

Expedition Everest (FASTPASS) | Before 9:30 a.m., after 3 p.m. | ★★★★½

Festival of the Lion King | Before 11 a.m., after 4 p.m. | ★★★★

Flights of Wonder | Anytime | ★★★★

It's Tough to Be a Bug! | Before 10:30 a.m., after 4 p.m. | ★★★★
Special comments Fright potential

Kali River Rapids (FASTPASS) | Before 10:30 a.m., after 4:30 p.m. | ★★★½
Special comments You will get wet; expectant mothers should note that ride is bouncy.

Kilimanjaro Safaris (FASTPASS) | Park opening, 2 hours before closing | ★★★★★

Maharaja Jungle Trek | Anytime | ★★★★

The Oasis | Anytime

Pangani Forest Exploration Trail | Anytime | ★★★★

Primeval Whirl (FASTPASS) | First 2 hours park is open, 1 hour before closing | ★★★
Special comments Expectant mothers should not ride.

Theater in the Wild/*Finding Nemo—The Musical* | Anytime | ★★★★

Tree of Life Animal Exhibits | Anytime | N/A

TriceraTop Spin | First 90 minutes park is open, 1 hour before closing | ★★

Wildlife Express Train | Anytime | ★★

DINING INFORMATION—Counter Service

RESTAURANT | LOCATION | QUALITY | VALUE

Flame Tree Barbecue | Discovery Island | Good | B–
Selections Pork and chicken sandwiches, ribs, crisp green salad with barbecued chicken, child's plate of baked chicken drumsticks or hot dog

Kusafiri Coffee Shop | Africa | Good | B
Selections Pastries, yogurt, coffee, cocoa, juice

Picnic in the Park | Various | Fair | C
Selections Premade picnic meals: ham or turkey sandwiches, grilled-chicken wraps, rotisserie chicken or sliced ham, various sides

Pizzafari | Discovery Island | Fair | B
Selections Cheese and pepperoni pizzas, grilled-chicken Caesar salad, Italian deli sandwiches

Restaurantosaurus | DinoLand U.S.A. | Good | B+
Selections Cheeseburgers, hot dogs, chicken nuggets, veggie burgers, baked goods, beer and soft drinks

Royal Anandapur Tea Company | Asia | Good | B
Selections Hot and iced teas, coffee, lattes, baked goods

Tamu Tamu | Africa | Good | C
Selections Milk shakes, sandwiches and burgers in season

Yak & Yeti Local Food Cafe | Asia | Fair | C
Selections Crispy honey chicken with steamed rice, kung pao beef, lo mein, Asian salads

DINING INFORMATION—Full Service

RESTAURANT | MEALS SERVED | LOCATION | PRICE | QUALITY | VALUE

Rainforest Cafe | L, D | AK Park Entrance | Moderate | ★★ | ★★
Selections Pasta with grilled chicken, turkey wraps, coconut shrimp, ribs, brownie cake

Tusker House Restaurant | B, L, D | Africa | Moderate | ★ | ★★

Selections Rotisserie chicken, couscous, curry, carved roast and pork loin, fruit cobbler, pastries

Yak & Yeti | L, D | Asia | Expensive | ★★★½ | ★★★
Selections Seared miso salmon, crispy mahimahi, glazed duck

Advance dining reservations recommended for Animal Kingdom full-service restaurants; call ☎ 407-939-3463.

GOOD REST AREAS IN ANIMAL KINGDOM

PLACE | LOCATION | NOTES

Walkway between Africa and Asia | Between Africa and Asia | Plenty of shaded rest spots, some overlooking running streams; refreshments nearby; a favorite of *Unofficial Guide* researchers

Gazebo behind Flame Tree Barbecue | Discovery Island | Follow the path towards the water along the left side of Flame Tree Barbecue; gazebo has ceiling fans.

Outdoor covered benches near exit from Dinosaur | DinoLand U.S.A. | Gazebo-like structure with nearby water fountain

Tusker House Restaurant | Africa | Note how the panoramic photos are made.

DHS *Touring-plan Companion*

ATTRACTION | RECOMMENDED VISITATION TIMES | AUTHOR'S RATING

The American Idol Experience | Anytime | ★★★★ |

Backlot Tour | Anytime | ★★★★ |

Fantasmic! | Evening, twice a week (generally Monday and Thursday) | ★★★★★ |

The Great Movie Ride | Before 11 a.m., after 4:30 p.m. | ★★★½ |

Honey, I Shrunk the Kids Movie Set Adventure | Before 11 a.m., after dark | ★★½ |

Indiana Jones Epic Stunt Spectacular (FASTPASS) | First 3 morning shows or last evening show | ★★★★

Special comments FASTPASSes available seasonally.

Jim Henson's Muppet-Vision 3-D | Before 11 a.m., after 3 p.m. | ★★★★½ |

Lights! Motors! Action! Extreme Stunt Show (FASTPASS) | First show, after 4 p.m. | ★★★½

Special comments FASTPASSes available seasonally.

The Magic of Disney Animation | Before 11 a.m., after 5 p.m. | ★★½

Playhouse Disney—Live on Stage! | Per entertainment schedule | ★★★★ |

Rock 'n' Roller Coaster (FASTPASS) | Before 10 a.m., 1 hour before closing | ★★★★

Special comments 48" minimum height; expectant mothers should not ride.

Sounds Dangerous | Before 11 a.m., after 4 p.m. | ★★★ |

Star Tours (FASTPASS) | First 90 minutes after opening | ★★★★

Special comments 40" minimum height; expectant mothers should not ride; motion-sickness potential.

Streets of America Backlot | Anytime | ★★★ |

Theater of the Stars | Anytime | ★★★★ |

The Twilight Zone Tower of Terror (FASTPASS) | Before 9:30 a.m., after 6 p.m. | ★★★★★

Special comments 40" minimum height; expectant mothers should not ride.

Toy Story Mania! (FASTPASS) | Before 10:30 a.m., after 6 p.m. | ★★★★½ |

Voyage of the Little Mermaid (FASTPASS) | Before 9:45 a.m., just before closing | ★★★★

Walt Disney: One Man's Dream | Anytime | ★★★ |

DINING INFORMATION—Counter Service

RESTAURANT | LOCATION | QUALITY | VALUE

ABC Commissary | Backlot | Fair | B–

Selections Asian salad, chicken curry, burgers, kids' meals, some kosher

Backlot Express | Backlot | Fair | C

Selections Burgers, fries, chicken nuggets, hot dogs, child's plate with chicken nuggets or sloppy joe with vegetables

Catalina Eddie's | Sunset Boulevard | Fair | B

Selections Pizzas, sandwiches, salads, apple pie, chocolate cake

Min and Bill's Dockside Diner | Echo Lake | Fair | C

Selections Shakes, beer and soft drinks, chips, cookies, pretzels

Pizza Planet | Backlot | Good | B+

Selections Pizza, salads, cookies

Rosie's All American Cafe | Sunset Boulevard | Fair | C

Selections Burgers, chicken strips, soups, side salads, child's cheeseburger or chicken nuggets

Starring Rolls Cafe | Sunset Boulevard | Good | B

Selections Sandwiches, salads, pastries, baked goods, coffee

Studios Catering Co. | Backlot | Good | B

Selections Barbecued pork, grilled chicken, hot dogs, wraps, salads

Toluca Legs Turkey Co. | Sunset Boulevard | Good | B

Selections Smoked turkey legs, hot dogs, coffee and soft drinks

DINING INFORMATION—Full Service

RESTAURANT | MEALS SERVED | LOCATION | PRICE | QUALITY | VALUE

50's Prime Time Cafe | L, D | Echo Lake | Moderate | ★★★ | ★★★

Selections Meat loaf, pot roast, chicken, other homey fare

Hollywood & Vine | B, L, D | Echo Lake | Moderate | ★★★ | ★★★
Selections Fresh fish of the day, carved and grilled meats, vegetables and pasta, fresh fruits and breads

The Hollywood Brown Derby | L, D | Hollywood Boulevard | Expensive | ★★★★ | ★★★
Selections Cobb salad, spice-rubbed grouper, Thai noodle bowl

Mama Melrose's Ristorante Italiano | L, D | New York Street | Moderate | ★★★ | ★★
Selections Bruschetta, crispy calamari, four-cheese flatbread, spicy Italian sausage

Sci-Fi Dine-In Theater Restaurant | L, D | Commissary Lane | Moderate | ★★½ | ★★
Selections Sandwiches, burgers, salads, shakes; pasta, ribs, steak

Advance dining reservations recommended for DHS full-service restaurants; call ☎ 407-939-3463.

GOOD REST AREAS IN DHS

PLACE | LOCATION | NOTES

Covered seating behind Toluca Legs Turkey Co. | Sunset Boulevard | Refreshments nearby; ample seating

Studios Catering Co. | Backlot | Ample covered seating; refreshments nearby

Benches along Echo Lake | Echo Lake | Some are shaded; refreshments nearby.

Inside *Sounds Dangerous* | Echo Lake | Quiet if you don't wear the headphones; air-conditioned. (Thanks to Matt Hochberg of **www.studioscentral.com** for this tip.)

2010 *Unofficial Guide* Reader Survey

If you would like to express your opinion in writing about Walt Disney World or this guidebook, complete the following survey and mail it to:

Unofficial Guide Reader Survey
P.O. Box 43673
Birmingham, AL 35243

Or fill out the survey online at **TouringPlans.com.**
Inclusive dates of your visit:
Your hometown:
Your e-mail address:

Members of your party:	Person 1	Person 2	Person 3	Person 4	Person 5
Gender:	M F	M F	M F	M F	M F
Age:	_____	_____	_____	_____	_____

How many times have you been to Walt Disney World? _________

CAR RENTALS Did you rent a car?____ From what company? ______________
Concerning your rental car, on a scale with 5 being best and 1 worst, how would you rate: Pickup-processing efficiency? ____ Return-processing efficiency? ____ Condition of the car? ____ Cleanliness of the car? ____ Airport-shuttle efficiency? ____

LODGING On your most recent trip, where did you stay?

____

Have you stayed at any other hotels in the past 12 months? Yes ___ No ___

Please indicate the hotels you have stayed at in the past year, or write in others.
☐ Ritz-Carlton ☐ Marriott Hyatt ☐ Super 8 ☐ Holiday Inn ☐ Fairfield Inn ☐ Embassy Suites ☐ Omni ☐ Ramada Inn ☐ Days Inn ☐ Hilton ☐ Drury Inn ☐ Hampton Inn ☐ Millennium ☐ Four Seasons ☐ Quality ☐ Radisson ☐ Best Western
Write in ____

Please tell us how important the following amenities were in your selection of a Walt Disney World–area resort/hotel. Select up to five amenities, and rank them in order of importance using 1 for the most important and 5 for the least. Feel free to add others in the margins.

Cost ___ Bar ___ Distance to parks ___ In-room dining/room service ___ Food court ___ Shuttle service to parks ___ Sit-down restaurant ___ Room size ___ Fine dining ___ Multiple bedroom suites ___ Spa/fitness center ___ In-room kitchen ___ Pool ___ Shuttle service to/from airport ___ Architecture/theme ___ Kids' activity center ___ Location inside WDW ___

On a scale with 5 being best and 1 being worst, please indicate how satisfied you were with your accommodations. Feel free to add other items you feel are important. *When rating food services, please rate only meals eaten at your resort.*

Cleanliness of room ___ Size and layout of pool ___ Comfort of beds and pillows ___ Crowd level at the pool ___ Room size and layout ___ Cleanliness of pool area ___ Quietness of room ___ Shuttle to/from airport ___ Check-in/out process ___ Shuttle to/from parks ___ Resort staff accessibility, friendliness, and knowledge ___ Recreational amenities (marina, bikes, fitness center, etc.) ___ Overall food-court experience ___

Continued on next page

Ability to easily find your way around ____ Overall food-court value ____ Child-care services and facilities ____ Overall experience with the full-service restaurant ____ Overall layout of the resort ____ Overall value of full-service restaurant ______________________________

Please check the number that best describes how satisfied you were with your total resort experience during this trip.

1 Very dissatisfied 2 Somewhat dissatisfied 3 Neither satisfied or dissatisfied
4 Somewhat satisfied 5 Very satisfied

Would you stay at this resort again? Yes ☐ No ☐

How likely are you to recommend this resort to a friend?

☐ Will definitely recommend ☐ May recommend ☐ Neutral
☐ Probably won't recommend ☐ Definitely will not recommend

DINING **Concerning your dining experiences:**

How many restaurant meals (including fast food) did you average per day? ______

How much (approximately) did your party spend on meals per day? ____________

Favorite restaurant outside Walt Disney World? ____________

PARK TOURING On a scale with 5 being best and 1 being worst, please rate how the touring plans worked:

PARK	NAME OF PLAN	RATING
Magic Kingdom		
Epcot		
Animal Kingdom		
Disney's Hollywood Studios		
Universal Studios		
Islands of Adventure		

OTHER How did you hear about this guide? ______________________

What other guidebooks or Web sites did you use on this trip? On the 5-as-best, 1-as-worst scale, how would you rate them?

	NAME	RATING
Guidebooks		
Web sites		

Using the same scale, how would you rate the *Unofficial Guide*? ________________

Have you used other *Unofficial Guides*? Which ones? ______________________

____

Additional comments you would like to share with us about your Walt Disney World vacation or about the *Unofficial Guide:*

____

____

____

____

____

____

____

WALT DISNEY WORLD RESTAURANT SURVEY

TELL US ABOUT YOUR WALT DISNEY WORLD dining experiences. Listed below are all counter-service and full-service restaurants. Beside each restaurant is a thumbs-up and thumbs-down symbol. If you enjoyed the restaurant enough that you would like to eat there again, circle the thumbs-up symbol. If not, circle the thumbs-down symbol.

WALT DISNEY WORLD COUNTER-SERVICE RESTAURANTS (IN ALPHABETICAL ORDER):

Africa Coolpost Epcot

ABC Commissary Disney's Hollywood Studios

Backlot Express Disney's Hollywood Studios

Boulangerie Pâtisserie France Pavilion, Epcot

Cantina de San Angel Mexico Pavilion, Epcot

Casey's Corner Magic Kingdom

Catalina Eddie's Disney's Hollywood Studios

Columbia Harbour House Magic Kingdom

Cosmic Ray's Starlight Cafe Magic Kingdom

Crêpes des Chefs de France France Pavilion, Epcot

El Pirata y El Perico Magic Kingdom

Electric Umbrella Restaurant Innoventions East, Epcot

Fife and Drum Tavern United States Pavilion, Epcot

Flame Tree Barbecue Animal Kingdom

Golden Oak Outpost Magic Kingdom

Kringla Bakeri og Kafé Norway Pavilion, Epcot

Kusafiri Coffee Shop Animal Kingdom

Liberty Inn United States Pavilion, Epcot

Lotus Blossom Cafe China Pavilion, Epcot

The Lunching Pad Magic Kingdom

Min and Bill's Dockside Diner Disney's Hollywood Studios

Mrs. Potts' Cupboard Magic Kingdom

Pecos Bill Cafe Magic Kingdom

Picnic in the Park Animal Kingdom

The Pinocchio Village Haus Magic Kingdom

Pizzafari Animal Kingdom

Pizza Planet Disney's Hollywood Studios

Promenade Refreshments Epcot

Refreshment Port Epcot

Restaurantosaurus Animal Kingdom

Rose & Crown Pub United Kingdom Pavilion, Epcot

Rosie's All American Cafe Disney's Hollywood Studios

Royal Anandapur Tea Company Animal Kingdom
Scuttle's Landing Magic Kingdom
Sommerfest Germany Pavilion, Epcot
Starring Rolls Cafe Disney's Hollywood Studios
Studio Catering Co. Flatbread Grill Disney's Hollywood Studios
Sunshine Seasons Food Fair The Land Pavilion, Epcot
Tamu Tamu Animal Kingdom
Tangierine Cafe Morocco Pavilion, Epcot
Toluca Legs Turkey Co. Disney's Hollywood Studios
Tomorrowland Terrace Noodle Station Magic Kingdom
Yak & Yeti Market Animal Kingdom
Yakitori House Japan Pavilion, Epcot
Yorkshire County Fish Shop United Kingdom Pavilion, Epcot

WALT DISNEY WORLD FULL-SERVICE RESTAURANTS (IN ALPHABETICAL ORDER):

Akershus Royal Banquet Hall Norway Pavilion, Epcot
Andiamo Italian Bistro & Grille Hilton, Downtown Disney
Artist Point Wilderness Lodge Resort
Beaches & Cream Beach Club Resort
Benihana—Steakhouse & Sushi Hilton, Downtown Disney
Biergarten Germany Pavilion, Epcot
Big River Grille & Brewing Works Disney's BoardWalk
Bistro de Paris France Pavilion, Epcot
bluezoo WDW Dolphin
Boatwright's Dining Hall Port Orleans Resort
Boma Animal Kingdom Lodge
Bongos Cuban Cafe Downtown Disney West Side
California Grill Contemporary Resort
Cape May Cafe Beach Club Resort
Cap'n Jack's Restaurant Downtown Disney Marketplace
Captain's Grille Yacht Club Resort
Le Cellier Steakhouse Canada Pavilion, Epcot
Chef Mickey's Contemporary Resort
Les Chefs de France France Pavilion, Epcot
Cinderella's Royal Table Magic Kingdom
Cítricos Grand Floridian Resort & Spa
Coral Reef The Seas Pavilion, Epcot
The Crystal Palace Magic Kingdom
ESPN Club Disney's BoardWalk
ESPN Wide World of Sports Cafe ESPN Wide World of Sports
50's Prime Time Cafe Disney's Hollywood Studios

Flying Fish Cafe Disney's BoardWalk
The Fountain WDW Dolphin
Fresh Mediterranean Market WDW Dolphin
Fulton's Crab House Former Pleasure Island site
The Garden Grill Restaurant The Land Pavilion, Epcot
Garden Grove WDW Swan
Grand Floridian Cafe Grand Floridian Resort & Spa
Hollywood & Vine Disney's Hollywood Studios
The Hollywood Brown Derby Disney's Hollywood Studios
House of Blues Downtown Disney West Side
Il Mulino WDW Swan
Jiko—The Cooking Place Animal Kingdom Lodge
Kimonos WDW Swan
Kona Cafe Polynesian Resort
LakeView Restaurant Regal Sun Resort
Liberty Tree Tavern Magic Kingdom
Mama Melrose's Ristorante Disney's Hollywood Studios
Maya Grill Coronado Springs Resort
Narcoossee's Grand Floridian Resort & Spa
Nine Dragons Restaurant China Pavilion, Epcot
1900 Park Fare Grand Floridian Resort & Spa
'Ohana Polynesian Resort
Olivia's Cafe Old Key West Resort
The Outback Buena Vista Palace, Downtown Disney
Paradiso 37 Downtown Disney
Planet Hollywood Downtown Disney West Side
Plaza Restaurant Magic Kingdom
Portobello Downtown Disney
Raglan Road Former Pleasure Island site
Rainforest Cafe Animal Kingdom and Downtown Disney
Restaurant Marrakesh Morocco Pavilion, Epcot
Rose & Crown Dining Room United Kingdom Pavilion, Epcot
San Angel Inn Mexico Pavilion, Epcot
Sanaa Animal Kingdom Lodge
Sand Trap Bar & Grill Osprey Ridge/Eagle Pines Golf Courses
Sci-Fi Dine-In Theater Restaurant Disney's Hollywood Studios
Shula's Steak House WDW Dolphin
Shutters at Old Port Royale Caribbean Beach Resort
Teppan Edo Japan Pavilion, Epcot
Tokyo Dining Japan Pavilion, Epcot
Tony's Town Square Restaurant Magic Kingdom

T-REX Downtown Disney Marketplace
Trail's End Restaurant Fort Wilderness Resort
Turf Club Bar & Grill Saratoga Springs Resort
Tusker House Restaurant Animal Kingdom
Tutto Italia Italy Pavilion, Epcot
Victoria & Albert's Grand Floridian Resort & Spa
The Wave Contemporary Resort
Whispering Canyon Cafe Wilderness Lodge Resort
Wolfgang Puck Cafe Downtown Disney West Side
Yachtsman Steakhouse Yacht Club Resort
Yak & Yeti Animal Kingdom